GW00994438

DAVID PERRY ON GAME DESIGN: A BRAINSTORMING TOOLBOX

DAVID PERRY AND RUSEL DEMARIA

Charles River Media
A part of Course Technology, Cengage Learning

COURSE TECHNOLOGY
CENGAGE Learning™

Australia, Brazil, Japan, Korea, Mexico, Singapore, Spain, United Kingdom, United States

COURSE TECHNOLOGY
CENGAGE Learning™

David Perry on Game Design: A Brainstorming Toolbox

David Perry and Rusel DeMaria

Publisher and General Manager, Course Technology PTR: Stacy L. Hiquet

Associate Director of Marketing: Sarah Panella

Content Project Manager: Jessica McNavich

Marketing Manager: Jordan Casey

Acquisitions Editor: Heather Hurley

Development Editor: Cathleen D. Small

Project Editor/Copy Editor: Cathleen D. Small

Editorial Services Coordinator: Jen Blaney

Interior Layout: Jill Flores

Cover Designer: Mike Tanamachi

Indexer: Valerie Haynes Perry

Proofreader: Kim V. Benbow

Library of Congress Control Number: 2008932483

ISBN-13: 978-1-58450-668-3

ISBN-10: 1-58450-668-7

Course Technology, a part of Cengage Learning
20 Channel Center Street
Boston, MA 02210
USA

Printed in Canada
1 2 3 4 5 6 7 11 10 09

Preface

Hi,

I'm David Perry. I've been making professional games (getting paid for it) for more than 25 years. It's the best job ever! I've had multiple #1 chart hits and lots of "Game of the Year" awards, and the games I've worked on have generated more than a billion dollars in revenues at retail stores around the world. I've been really lucky to work with some of the best talent in the industry, and I've also been lucky because I've become friends with some of the most respected game development luminaries in the world.

Who is this book for?

If you're a game design student, someone burning with new video game ideas, or you're working your way up through the design ranks to become a game director, this book is written specifically for you!

Why make a game design book? There are plenty of others.

There are plenty of great game design books that tell you all about the subject and the job. Instead of explaining to you what's important, such as, "It's important to make characters interesting," my goal is to give you hundreds of ways to *do exactly that.* If I say, "Make it funny," I also want to give you endless examples of *how* to make it funny. That's the difference.

You're saying I can create new ideas *never* seen before in video games?

Yes, that's the whole idea. This book is designed to help trigger your own creative ideas—original ideas that have never been seen before, ever! I have absolutely no doubt this will happen many times as you use the materials I provide here.

Are you sure it works?

Absolutely. As an example, I tested a chapter on a large group of IGDA *(International Game Developer's Association*) members. I asked them to come up with an original weapon never seen before in a video game; I wanted one from everyone in the room, and they had just two minutes.

As you can imagine, that's a tough challenge! But after showing them the section on "Ways to Die" (Chapter 32 of this book), I was hit by a deluge of ideas none of us had ever seen before.

Who is Rusel DeMaria?

Rusel is a good friend of mine and one of the most published writers in the video game industry. It was frankly impossible for me to write this entire book (I'm always running game companies and projects), so I hired Rusel to be my ghostwriter. I don't know if he anticipated the hundreds of phone calls every time I was driving anywhere, but it became a labor of love for him also. In the end, he devoted so much time and effort on it that I had to admit he was more of a coauthor than a ghost writer.

To be clear, when we are old and gray (already happening), we are hoping to hand over the manuscript to new up-and-coming designers who enjoy the art of creation.

What about new ideas that come up?

This is the first edition of the book. I consider it the stake in the sand and invite the readers to team up with us for the second edition. We've created a website at www.gamedesignbook.org to help that discussion happen. (Come and say hi!)

We hope this body of work will continue to be refined—by our readers and by professional designers—and will evolve into the key "reference and inspiration book" for the future generations of game designers.

This book is dedicated to my wife, Elaine, and my little daughter, Emmy.

Big thanks go to Rusel (you rock) and all the people who have contributed in one way or another along the way.

For those reading this, I can't wait to play your games!

David Perry

www.dperry.com

A Word from Rusel DeMaria

When DP first approached me about this project, he said, "I've got this idea I've been wanting to do. I know I won't have time to do it if I don't get help." Then he said, "I have been making lists of things to do with games—like the items you might find along a freeway. Let me send you my notes and see what you can do with them." I really didn't have any idea what I was getting into and what a fantastic romp it would be, but four years and more than a thousand pages of manuscript later, here we are.

There's no way we could ever complete this book. Period. At some point we had to say, "It's done for now." The many days I spent with my head in my hands, just trying to come up with one more example or one more idea, were a futile attempt to finish something—anything—but what's exciting is that both DP and I know that *you* will find things we didn't think of.

We hope we made it just a little difficult for you to think of what we missed, but we are counting on you to take the material in this book and run with it. If you do—if you create games with ideas that were inspired from this book—then we will have done our job.

Obviously, I never would have had this opportunity without David Perry, a man of infinite creativity, drive, and ideas. It has been massively fun—and that's the name of the game, isn't it? Thanks, DP.

Acknowledgments

We want to thank several people for their contributions to this project:

- Stephane Bura
- David Freeman
- David Bergeaud
- Mike Doran
- Michelle Montierth
- Yana Malysheva
- Steven Egan
- James Baldwin
- David Slauenwhite
- Michael Vaj
- Max Ehrman

Thanks to Heather Hurley, for her constant support and flexibility in seeing this project to completion, and to Cathleen Small, for having the fortitude to copyedit even the most grisly portions of the manuscript.

Thanks to Jill Flores, for doing a fantastic job with the challenge of making this book readable and keeping it to just over 1,000 pages! And to all the people at Cengage Learning who work behind the scenes to make great books.

Special thanks, also, to Viola Brumbaugh, for unrelenting support.

Also, a big, big thank you to all the people and friends who contributed ideas and feedback on our various websites and wikis.

About the Authors

David Perry is a 26-year veteran of the video game business—and he's also probably the tallest in the business! Atari bought his development studio, Shiny Entertainment, which was known for titles such as *Earthworm Jim*, *MDK*, and *The Matrix*. These days he's a co-founder and chief creative officer of Acclaim Games, the number-one American Free-to-Play MMO Publisher (www.acclaim.com). Perry's games have generated more than a billion dollars in revenue, and he has had numerous number-one hits and "Game of the Year" awards. In his spare time, he helps students into the industry and writes articles for BusinessWeek.com. In the last couple of years, he has been awarded a master's, a doctorate, and a fellowship for his achievements. He has spoken at almost every major video game conference as well as at major universities, such as MIT, USC, and UCLA, and at the prestigious TED conference. To help the industry grow, Perry is personally funding an initiative to bring together investors, publishers, and developers worldwide (www.GameInvestors.com) and a new Flash gaming site (www.TheFanHub.com). For more information, visit www.dperry.com.

Rusel DeMaria began playing video games in 1967 and has been writing about them since 1981, so although he isn't as tall as David Perry, he has been around video games since their inception. He has been a senior editor on three magazines, a columnist nationally and internationally, and the founding editor and creative director of Prima Publishing's strategy guide division, which he started in 1990. He has written more than 60 game-related books, including *High Score: The Illustrated History of Electronic Games*, *Reset: Changing the Way We Look at Video Games*, *Spore: Evolution*, and many others, with sales in excess of 2.5 million copies. DeMaria has appeared on TV and radio and was one of the primary commentators and consultants for PBS' *Videogame Revolution*. He has been a speaker at several industry events, including GDC, and has also been a game designer and a consultant for companies such as Sega, Maxis, LucasArts, Oddworld, and Acclaim. Currently, he is assistant director of David Perry's Game Consultants, Inc.

Contents

Introduction

What Is a Game and Why Do We Play?

It may seem obvious that a game is a game. You know one when you play it. But why do you play it? What are the essential elements that make this particular game *fun*? Is it a secret recipe? Do you need to take special classes to understand? Is there a way for the professionals who make games to actually share their knowledge with *you*? Maybe there is...

I got tired of reading books that said, "Hey, just make it fun!" or, "It's important that your game is fun!" and then didn't help you get there. The chapters that follow are a sincere effort to actually deliver time-tested methods of creating fresh, new, innovative game designs. And to do that, our book's goal is not to tell you to do it, but to provide practical information to actually help and inspire you to make better games.

Why Play Games?

So why do we play games? Or a better question is: What rewards do we receive from the experience? Perhaps the simple answer is *entertainment.* We are entertained by books, movies, plays, TV, paintings, mud wrestling, and a wide variety of other creative human endeavors. In that sense, games are no different. However, games do offer some unique ways to be entertained by virtue of their interactive nature.

I used to laugh and say that the opposite of entertainment is boredom, so if you move *anywhere* beyond boredom, it's already a game! Meaning if you were locked in a jail with nothing to do, then throwing an object at a target in your cell could immediately be more fun than boredom...and so a game is born.

Natural game designers tend to be the ones who have multiple ideas on how to improve even such a basic game:

- How many hits in a period of time?
- How might you track scores?
- Who gets the most hits in 20 throws...or 50...or 100?
- "Eyes closed" hits are worth three times the points.
- An "eyes closed" hit earns a bonus chance to ricochet off a wall for 10 times the points.
- Maybe the target has regions worth more or fewer points.
- And so on...

Game designers of this type tend to go through life looking for fun ways to improve situations by improving the entertainment value. They are the ones who come out of movies annoyed that the writer didn't think of a certain plot twist or who get off a rollercoaster thinking, "I wish the final loop was faster, so riders would finish at the peak of excitement."

With such a model in mind, our goal here is to inspire increased entertainment value...but that's where things get complicated, and that's why this book is so thick! And yet, whatever the challenges, we must work out how to increase entertainment value if we are to keep boredom at bay.

Evolutionary Factors

There are those who make a compelling argument that much of what we do in games relates directly to key human drivers, such as the hunter/gatherer instinct. Certainly there's reason to consider this seriously when you think how much fun games are when you are hunting and fighting or gathering items ranging from magic potions to powerful treasures. The fun of the hunt—whether it involves hunting something to fight or kill or finding some items that you value highly—is integral to a significant majority of games. In fact, in many Real-Time Strategy games, players must literally hunt and gather for hours on end.

A second possible link to our evolutionary past is the human activity of taming and nurturing creatures to work for us and supply our food or even protect us. We have domesticated and trained dogs, cats, cattle, pigs, horses, falcons, and even elephants, dolphins, and seals. In some games, we raise, train, and breed creatures—and such activities can be fun in themselves. Nintendogs (released in the summer of 2005) is a great example. But to stretch the point a little further, consider role-playing characters. Granted, a part of what compels us is identification with the player character—he/she is you in the fictional world of the game. But, in addition, perhaps something of that instinct to raise and nurture creatures comes into play as we raise a character's stats (attributes) and watch him grow stronger and more powerful. Perhaps we are also following some instinct when we do that, however obscure the connection may seem. No matter what, it's an investment of your time and resources, and, ultimately, the more time and resources you spend, the more protective you may get.

Another instinct or human trait that is somewhat connected to hunter/gatherer instincts is the concept of collecting. This goes far beyond collecting all of U2's albums or all *Harry Potter* books or Disney videos. When there's clearly a collection available, people are often inspired to buy something just to complete the collection. Does this same urge work in the video game world? Absolutely! *Pokemon* (as one of its many features) has lived off this concept for years.

The collecting urge can also become a completing urge, meaning if you hear there were 11 possible quests available and you only did 10, you might go out of your way to find and complete that last quest...all that work just to complete the set. Maybe we're just talking about the more anal gamers there, but maybe not. But one thing this does suggest is that it's a good idea to let players know how they're progressing and what there still is to do. When you provide this kind of progress indicator—however you choose to do it (see also Chapter 30, "Ways to Communicate with the Player")—many players will use that information to inspire them to explore further, and many won't be happy until the game is truly 100-percent defeated.

Preparation for life is a natural aspect of the development of most mammals. There are many theories of why we play, but one that is often mentioned can be seen in the animal world. Almost all young mammals rehearse their adult roles in playful activities. Historically, young boys and girls have also played games that specifically prepared them for the activities of adulthood. Today, it is often more difficult to see the connection between the real-world games young people play and the survival skills they are learning. However, in games we play to explore new ideas and new locations, to learn things, and to face new challenges. We play to pit ourselves against some sort of opposition, which may come in the form of the game's designer, other players, or a set of rules that limits and governs our options. And while the connection between modern play and real life may seem tenuous at best, many people have postulated that video game play is, in fact, true preparation for a future that will involve digital media and input methods far beyond joysticks and keyboards. The future may also involve working with tools that feature a considerable abstraction from flesh-and-blood reality (where we might someday work and play together virtually).

I used to think this kind of stuff was only for the movies and science-fiction writers, but not too long ago, I saw a demonstration of a technology that watches your brain activity and can reverse-engineer tracked signals, knowing what command you are thinking. It can tell when you blink and, amazingly, how your body is moving. Let's call that version 1.0 in 2006. When version 5 of that technology mixes with a next-generation high-definition stereo VR helmet with 10.2 surround sound, I immediately become jealous of the people who are just getting into game development! When I started, everything was just black-and-white blobs. Designers of the future will be challenged far beyond what we can imagine today, but I predict that many of the elements that drive us to play games today will still work in your virtual future.

Challenge and Mastery

Games provide challenges, and successfully completing these challenges provides a sense of mastery. This is a highly satisfying experience, and the way that games repeatedly present challenges and opportunities for mastery makes them particularly rewarding. (The basics of how games do this can be found in Chapter 23, "Goals," and Chapter 24, "Rewards, Bonuses, and Penalties.") Commonly, we use the "evolve or die" technique, where as the game continues, you are expected to continue to evolve if you have any hope of survival. For those who are able to dominate a game more effectively than others, there are ranking systems and multiplayer games built specifically to enable them to compete with and to learn from each other. The concept of challenge and mastery is key because it can turn a game from a normal 10-hour experience into hundreds of hours when people set their intentions toward being great at the game instead of just playing it. Valve's *Counter-Strike* is a good example of this phenomenon.

Fantasy

I used to say that washing the dishes is boring, so nobody would ever want to buy a "washing the dishes" game. I felt really safe stating this. Imagine a really great ironing-board game! (I don't think that could sell either!) I then normally went on to say that games are fantasies for sale. People love to be able to experience things they'll have little chance of ever doing, such as flying a stealth fighter, winning four consecutive NASCAR championships, or riding into battle leading 10,000 warriors willing to die for them. That's not a normal day for most people, and that's when fulfilling certain fantasies can lead to hit games. So it's easy, right? Just make games that make good fantasies! I would have said yes to this, but we are now seeing casual games that experiment with many unsafe concepts—some insanely boring, such as mastering the times tables (Nintendo has managed to make this fun in *Brain Age*) or waiting tables in *Diner Dash.* So now I have to admit that perhaps no subject is really off the table; it's just up to you to make it fun by applying certain systems or techniques (many of which appear later in this book).

Secondary Rewards

Along with challenge and mastery comes secondary rewards, such as learning and improving new skills (even virtual ones) and experiencing positive feedback loops (in which performing something correctly rewards us and also empowers us to continue performing well). Game scores used to be a good example of a secondary reward, meaning they're just numbers, but they really matter. However, if you don't take the calculation of the score number seriously, you can end up with irate gamers—for example, if they find out that the values don't equate properly to difficulty.

Praise and encouragement used to be a major factor we tested in the past, too. People love a pat on the back, and games are well equipped to provide that feedback. Surprisingly, over the years, this concept of really timely feedback has diminished, but don't underestimate its power. Some games (from the old days) would literally end with a brass band and fireworks celebrating your victory. Wouldn't you prefer that than just a lame end video and a bunch of credits?

If anything, I see this as one of the major areas for which designers in the coming years will evolve new techniques—to really deliver emotional bang for the buck. Rewards will take a lot of interesting information into consideration before deciding how (or how not) to reward the player—for instance, situational information, such as what you just did, who else is present, what their relationship or past history is with you, what they've heard about you, what they think you did versus what you really did, and so on. They might cheer when you win a battle, even when you know the guy fell on his own sword and died, and when they cheer, overtly praising you, you have an entirely different experience. But what if they start attacking you, complaining, or catcalling? It's a different experience, a different message, and a different gameplay opportunity.

Emotional complexity and emotion in games is something we will cover in this book (especially in Chapter 9, "Storytelling Techniques," Chapter 12, "Character Design," and to some extent Chapter 20, "Music and Sound"), but know that there's much room for development around emotion in games, including what rewards are, what they are not, what they are perceived to be, and what others perceive them to be. (See also Chapter 24, "Rewards, Bonuses, and Penalties.")

Optimal Arousal Level

Some theorists have suggested that mammals require a certain level of stimulation in their lives, which they call the *optimal arousal level*, and when that stimulation is missing (which we might call a state of boredom), then we start seeking other activities. These activities do not necessarily have to be directly related to survival, and they may include an element of the unknown. And some of these activities might be thought of as play.

I like to think of experimentation as being a key part of this theory. In a world of complete boredom, even just having a bunch of keys in your hand can offer momentary escape as you play around with them. If you are in a game and it seems boring—for example, you're in a room where everything is drawn in, meaning there's nothing real to interact with—it can quickly become very boring. Any element of control, experimentation, and flexibility that you can offer will immediately attract the gamer like a moth to a flame.

Boredom quickly leads to frustration (the designer's nightmare), and frustration leads to the game being turned off (and possibly some swearing, too). Frustration can easily be tracked by "watching" what players do. We see them repeat cycles, such as trying to open a locked door, not finding a key, then trying to open the same locked door over and over, or endlessly pacing around a certain area. Managing frustration immediately therefore becomes one of the designer's key roles.

Choices and options are the solution to killing off your worst enemies (boredom and frustration). The trick is for you (the designer) to look at the room and imagine that you are stuck in there. What would you try? Forget what you can and can't do—focus on what you would try if this was a game you had just bought. Some of the best gaming experiences I've had have come when it's clear that the things I'm experimenting with are actually working, when the designer has remained one step ahead of me, and especially when I think I'm being clever at figuring something out, only to realize that the designer had anticipated my cleverness.

That rarely happens by accident!

Subjective Time Shifting

Games also allow us to focus intensely on an activity. When presented well, this activity and focus combination becomes highly immersive, which generally makes time seem to go by very quickly and allows us to be absorbed in our experience to an extent that is often missing in daily life. This experience is common among creative artists and craftspeople who become very absorbed in what they are doing creatively, and the same holds true for musicians and gamblers. You know this is happening when you find yourself starting a game at 8:00 P.M., then glancing down at your watch and realizing that it's 2:00 A.M. What the heck?! Six hours in what seemed like 90 minutes!

Time shifting is generally caused by the game keeping interruptions to an *absolute minimum*, because when the game is interrupted you are forced back into reality, noticing clocks and so on. Stacking goals is also a good way to keep people immersed. Think of *Civilization*, which is famous for the "just one more move" phenomenon. You simply have to play just one more move to see what happens.

Time-shifting focus is further enhanced by providing players with mechanisms for tracking their progress (no matter how small). When they see they are getting to where they want to be, they'll find it harder to get up and walk away. If they lose track or don't know where the heck they are in relation to their goal, they stop being able to convince themselves to press on; instead, they tend to think, "I'll get back to this later."

I think the art of sustained immersion is one of the most incredible game design techniques to understand, and I'm sure you can think of games where this has happened to you. Sadly, it's not the norm, so really take this topic seriously as you consider interruptions in your game and how you will provide momentary feedback that urges the gamer that his goal is his for the taking. When the gamer achieves that goal (or before), immediately reveal a higher goal or something that's even more attractive. In short, make the goals attractive, provide progress indicators, and stack or effectively sequence compelling goals.

Personality Projection

Like good literature or films, games can involve us in stories with characters and plots that keep us interested. They also excel at creating identification between the player and the character the player is controlling. This identification with the player character helps to trigger some very genuine emotions and a deep immersion in the game's fantasy world. The problem is allowing players to express themselves through the actions of the character they are playing. That's where the disconnect can happen—when players experience that the game character is not up to par with their aspirations, when they need more and want to do more. They can quickly disassociate and simply lose interest.

Games are about entertainment, so characters need to entertain the gamer. Don't just focus on the gameplay or goals; focus on what this character is doing, who he is, what he can do, how he reacts, what his attitude is, how his attitude changes, and so on.

Good homework for this is watching movies. Note that the characters in movies don't have a small set of moves (running, jumping, falling, landing, and so on). They and their actions evolve based on the emotional elements of the situation. This situational response requires new perspectives and "moves" from your animations—instead of "firing gun," we now need "firing aggressively," "firing with concern," "firing confidently," and so on. The more the character emotes what you (the player) are feeling or at least a greater range of probable character responses, the more you will connect—and to some extent, the more the game can lead your feelings.

Some of the hunting games actually used to do this quite well. In the game, someone nearby would whisper, "I think I hear something." Your character would immediately stop and listen. Perhaps you'd hear something, too—you'd certainly be straining your ears. And often (completing the loop) there would actually be something there, so the whisper was correct. So the long-term dream is that the character is not just a robotic projection of you—it's a living, breathing, emotionally complex, intelligent character that is actually kind of cool to be! (For more along these lines, see Chapter 9, "Storytelling Techniques," and Chapter 12, "Character Design.")

Empowerment

In a world where we may feel unempowered, games can give us a sense of control over our environment. After all, games are created for us to win, so it is in the nature of a game to offer players a measure of control over what happens. In real life, it is not always so clear that we can control what is happening. Games can give us a sense of power and satisfaction, however temporary and illusory.

Therefore, adding an element of certainty can actually be very attractive to gamers. When I fire *this* gun, *this* happens, and *this* kind of person will be terminated without question. That feels good. If you fire and have no idea whether that bullet or the next five bullets will kill the enemy, it's much less empowering. Perhaps even more importantly, when you fire *this* gun and use the *skills* you have developed by practicing your shooting ability, you will *succeed* because you have improved, and the game *rewards* your efforts.

People love to understand and use their knowledge to grow and dominate, so help them do that. Teach them, reward them, penalize them for mistakes (they understand that), but give them confidence that by doing it the right way, they will succeed. If "right" is not a clear concept, you may leave them feeling weak and possibly out of control of their destiny. Even if there is more than one "right" way, it should be clear to the player (by the way the game is laid out or by positive feedback loops or explicit rules) that there is an effective way to succeed. Without that kind of clarity, frustration can quickly overcome the player's interest.

Probably the worst game design mistake dealing with empowerment is when a game has some rules that just make no sense to the gamer. When I started making games, I once made a game where the boss was impossible to beat. It made sense to me because I didn't have time to add anything after the boss. Now, *I* knew why I left it that way, but the gamers didn't. They had never faced a problem like this before, so they kept fighting and fighting and fighting, trying all the tricks they had learned. All they had learned before suddenly didn't make sense; all their skills were useless. I soon understood that I had hit upon a great way to guarantee frustration—a pissed-off gamer and a turned-off game!

Bottom line: Empowerment is a powerful tool if used well. Extended periods of uncertainty are a nightmare.

Social Contact

Games are often played with other human players. In this way, games allow for some level of contact with other people, although the depth and type of contact varies from game to game and from player to player. Games are also a form of popular media that is shared by gamers from modern generations. As such, they offer a common experience and language. In other words, there's a "meta game" in which we talk about the games and share our experiences, offer our opinions, and derive satisfaction from that sharing.

I think the designers on steroids are the ones actually imagining the two gamers sitting side by side on a sofa (playing a game, probably trash-talking or collaborating), thinking how to stir that conversation up: "Did you see that?!" "What the hell was that?!" Ideally, these designers succeed in making sure that the players experience fun events/challenges together and that the shared experience will remain with them even after the game is turned off.

Pride

A designer I really respect is Will Wright (designer of *The Sims* and many other games). In an MTV E3 2006 interview, he noted that *pride* is something games can offer over and above movies and books. Do you remember the last time you felt proud as you sat in a movie theater or as you read a book? Games have the ability to make you feel *very* proud. Recently I've been consulting with some different companies, and in looking at their games, I'm amazed by how much this concept is ignored.

In some cases the player does something really amazing (such as knowing he had a five-percent chance of winning a battle, but risking it all and going for it...and winning an epic battle!), and the game just continues.

The history of games has taught us to pat gamers on the head, with the music lifting, showing us the scores, showing reactions to the player's success, special effects, and so on. Somehow that's not so trendy now—scores don't matter as much, and the pat on the back happens less often. In some games, it's just a loading screen as you go to the next level. So listen to Will—the man is *dead on*! We have an advantage over books and Hollywood, so go out of your way to use it! Pride is an extremely strong human emotion, and it's there for the taking. Make sure to add it to your games!

So what is a game? Many things. There are many reasons to play, but it's ultimately about fun! There are a lot of theories about why we play, and we can even analyze the subject scientifically, but the bottom line is that we play because it's fun. And let's face it: Fun is fun. Ask yourself this: How long do you continue to play a game that isn't fun?

What Is a Game?

Legendary designer Sid Meier is often quoted as saying that a game is a "series of meaningful choices." In other words, choices are not empty and without relevance to the player's experience—they are meaningful in the game context, which is part of what makes them interesting. It may also imply that the choices are not always black and white—you do this and you win; you do that and you lose—but they offer diverse options that lead the player to the achievement of a goal, preferably with more than one "right" decision path. Of course, if the arcade game *Dragon's Lair* is considered a game, then the choices offered really were sometimes black and white...right or wrong. One misstep in the branching structure of the game, and it was "game over" and time to put in another quarter. But few games have been as linear as *Dragon's Lair*, and certainly modern game designs look for a greater variety of options. Overall, good games offer a series of choices—or decisions, if you will—and those exist on a scale ranging from relatively trivial to life-and-death decisions with regard to your character or other characters.

As projects become delayed and publishers push to ship the game anyway, one of the most hard-hit pieces of a game involves the choices that were going to be made available but were dropped. The loss of those choices commonly kills the spirit of the game. So the publisher gets a game, but not the experience that was originally intended. Blame is irrelevant, but it's the gamer who ultimately is left unsatisfied.

Required Elements

Let's start with what a game is. A game design should have the following six elements:

- Challenge (mental and/or physical)
- Goal(s)
- Rewards
- Rules (implied or obvious)
- Interactivity (do > observe > respond > repeat)
- Decision making (which is required to meet the "challenge" criterion)

NOTE

Goals can be stated within the game—capture the flag, save the princess, and so on—or created on the fly by the player, as in games such as SimCity, Chess, *or* The Sims. *Goals can also be incremental and ongoing—as in old arcade games,* Tetris, *or online multiplayer games such as* EverQuest *or* Dark Age of Camelot.

More Game Elements

The previous list focused on core elements of what games require. Obviously, there are many other elements you can find in games, but pretty much everything else is optional. Here are just a few examples of design elements that a game can have:

- Graphics. (Not just dressing—I mean graphics actually leading the gameplay.)
- Sound. (This is not just background audio—the audio cues actually help or mean something to the player. This can include voice acting and in the future will likely contain quality speech generation.)
- Story. (This is not just preamble or back story, but where the story leads or responds to gameplay.)
- Plot twists or splits. (These usually mean the path is not completely predictable and linear.)
- Cut-scene movies. (These are commonly used as an introduction, then to fill gaps in the story, then as an ending. The best ones use the game engine, and you can actually interact within them.)
- Tutorial. (This can get people going without reading a manual first.)
- Credits. (These are usually at the end, but sometimes they are delivered as the game starts playing, like in a movie.)
- Game characters. (This sometimes requires actors or sports stars to deliver credible performances, but also include all the various enemies, allies, and neutral characters in the game.)
- Dialog. (This is usually written by the writer, so the characters ooze the personality that's been set up by the story.)
- Interactive dialog. (Sometimes this allows you to converse with the characters. In the long term, we expect voice recognition to make this somewhat free-flowing.)
- Back story. (This is important to help guide your decisions—if you know that you were a thief, it might lead the game design.)
- A manual. (This is good for revealing the potential depth of the game, so the gamer will want to dive in deeper.)
- In-game help. (This is good for keeping the gamer from getting frustrated—one of the most requested items of in-game help is a map.)
- Levels. (These should be laid out so that the gamer will want to see what's next.)
- Missions. (Give your player big goals so they keep focused.)
- Sub-missions. (Give your player small, rewarding goals that they don't have to complete.)
- An ending. (If the ending of a movie is weak, no matter how great the movie was, you are left unsatisfied—and games are the same way.)
- Puzzles to make the gamer think. (This works in almost every game—even sports games or First-Person Shooters. The days of mindless shooting are pretty much over.)
- Character statistics. (In movies, the hero tends to improve in some way, and games are the same—even if you don't reveal it to the gamer as statistics, there should be growth going on.)
- Time pressure. (This can be a good way to get people focused on missions; however, it can also make them start ignoring sub-missions if they are in too much a hurry, so be careful with this.)

- Status feedback system. (This is some kind of feature in the design where it's clear that it's the player's fault for failing—it should *never* be a surprise. A health bar is a simple example of this.)
- A scoring system. (This is usually for comparing progress with others, but it can be used to motivate gamers to take more risk or as an indicator to challenge themselves to improve on previous performances. It can even be used as a qualification test for further advancement in the game.)
- Levels of difficulty. (In the future there will be a lot of automatic difficulty systems and pre-test systems so you won't be able to pick "difficult" if you're not ready for difficult.)
- Villains. (It's always good to have enemies or challengers.)
- Violence. (This works best when it has a reason to exist, such as to make you hate someone or to win in a fight against seemingly impossible odds. I think the days of blood spray selling your game are pretty much over.)
- Death. (It's important to take death seriously. Some games just immediately restart, so death has little meaning. I like when you feel the impact of death and become much more cautious. Paintball versus laser tag is a great example: If the shots don't hurt, you don't care. After being shot in paintball, you take getting shot again much more seriously.)
- Visual effects. (These are most commonly used for explosions and so on. What we care about here is whether you can use visual effects to lead or affect gameplay. The answer is absolutely! Think about fog, a building on fire, being caught in a blizzard...these can all affect the experience. Of course, great effects also make the gameplay more fun for their sheer visual impact, but they can go much further than that.)
- Sexual content. (Sex is supposed to sell, but in games it's pretty lame. It can, however, be good for humor and can also be fun for flirting and so on.)
- Humor. (Probably the most underused element of game design is humor, yet we all love funny movies, TV shows, and so on. Humor can be dark, too, so you don't need to have a comedy game to have a funny moment.)

Still more game design elements might include:

- Pathos
- Romance
- Inventory
- Power-ups
- Easter Eggs
- Cheat codes
- Weapons
- Controls
- Vehicles
- Sequels
- Multiple players
- A language parser
- Artificial intelligence
- Artificial life
- Buildings
- Towns and/or cities
- Professions
- Animals
- Aliens
- Avatars (graphically represented player characters)
- Clothing
- Armor
- Magic
- Music
- Geography
- Exploration
- A Z axis

Design Challenge

1. Think of at least five items you can add to the lists in the preceding "More Game Elements" section.
2. What is the minimum requirement for something to be a game? Using the lists in this introduction, come up with some game ideas that use the fewest number of options.
3. Now create some game ideas that use as many of the optional elements of games that you can.
4. Can you create something that fulfills the requirements of a game and still isn't a game? Try it.
5. Can you create something that is a game but does not meet the requirements listed in this introduction? Try it.
6. Create a very simple game concept—perhaps the one you created in Step 1. Now add some of the options from the lists in the "More Game Elements" section. How does each element you add change the game? Does it inspire new ideas and directions? Experiment with different optional elements and see where they take you and your design concept.

Part I How to Use This Book

1 Using This Book as a Reference

This book is the result of several years of research and mental exercise, as well as the product of years of game playing and designing. The goal was always to provide a tool to encourage designers and to assist *anyone* connected with a game project. My vision was that this book would accompany you to design meetings and brainstorming sessions, and that everyone on the team would have access to a fund of ideas and possibilities.

Of course, my initial goal was to think of absolutely everything possible, but, of course, I knew that would never happen. This book is a work in progress, and I fully intend on seeing it improve over time. I welcome suggestions and ideas, which you can offer by posting at davidperry.ning.com.

As the book evolved, it became clear that it could serve both as a reference and as a brainstorming tool. I envision people sitting with the book at hand, considering different approaches to their design and referring to different sections of the book for ideas and inspirations. Throughout the book, my coauthor and I have added suggestions about other sections to consider. By checking different lists and descriptions throughout the book, you may discover ideas or possibilities you hadn't previously considered, or you may simply find it easier to refer to the lists in this book to help you with different areas of design.

For instance, Chapter 12, "Character Design," includes a step-by-step method for filling out the personality and background details of any character in your game, referring constantly to more fully fleshed-out sections of the chapter for further detail. If you're looking to consider items you might place along a road or highway, we have a list of possible items. Another list describes the different roles characters may play or the jobs they may perform, and one of our favorites is a categorized list of ways to die (or kill, for that matter).

You want weapons? We have tons of them, including historical, ethnic, and modern weapons, with a bit of history and technology thrown in for good measure.

Simply put, we encourage you to open the pages of this book in any way that serves your needs. You can read it as a textbook, use it as a reference, or simply refer to it for ideas from time to time. You can take the challenge to discover something we've missed and let us know what it is, or you can take it to meetings and use it to discuss different design decisions. It's completely up to you how you use this book, but we sincerely hope you find it useful.

Delving Deeper

None of the lists in this book is complete, and no discussion covers every angle. For instance, in the lists of weapons and armor that occur at the end of the book, there is no way we could include complete details for each item listed. Therefore, if you are interested, say, in modeling the early tanks of World War I, find some tanks and look them up in other references to find pictures and more specifics about armament, horsepower, and firepower. If you find yourself intrigued by our chapter on puzzles, use it to inspire further thinking and ponder the depths of puzzle design. Wherever you find a discussion or list in this book, use it to expand your design options, and always realize that the material in this book is only the suggestion of ideas—the rest is up to you.

In the next chapter, you'll find some suggestions on how to brainstorm new ideas. You can brainstorm with a group of your fellow developers or in your own mind. We hope you'll find this book helpful and inspiring, not only with its specific information, but with its suggestion of new ideas and its constant challenge to you to discard the ordinary and seek the remarkable, innovative, and unique solutions that will make your game not only massively fun to play, but a trendsetter, a pioneer, and a fresh experience for your players.

2 Brainstorming and Research

This book is meant to be a page-turner—literally. I want you to turn the pages often, using different sections of the book as you produce original ideas and concepts for your games. I see this as the equivalent of your own built-in brainstorming process. By using the many sections of this book, the lists, and the concepts, you can produce your own ideas, test and expand them, and challenge yourself to go beyond what I've presented here.

I call this a *brainstorming book* because brainstorming is one of the most effective ways to discover new ideas. In a group of creative individuals, brainstorming can uncover options and directions that one individual would rarely discover. Using this book, you can expand your ideas—and ours—to create the most original concepts possible, while staying within the context of effective game design.

In this chapter:

- Using Brainstorming in Groups
- Kaleidoscope Brainstorming Process
- Brainstorming Solo
- Brainstorming Exercise
- Brainstorming Examples
- Games and Research
- What to Look For
- Research Sources

Using Brainstorming in Groups

One of the best ways to get great ideas for your games is to hold brainstorming sessions with your whole staff—designers, artists, programmers, producers, marketing and PR people, and so on. Not only does this produce some really great and original ideas, but it reinforces and builds teams and gets the whole group invested in the result. For those without a design background, this book can be especially helpful, because they can instantly look up different solutions to design challenges.

Hold on, whoa, did I really say "PR and marketing people?" In a game design brainstorming meeting? Absolutely, the more minds in the room (that are willing to speak up), the better. Even if they don't play games and they have bad ideas, sometimes really bad ideas spark thoughts that lead to really good ideas, so don't filter the room to just people who like what you like—that's really going to tone down the potential breakthroughs.

Brainstorming is a very specific process. It essentially consists of freeform thinking out loud. Here are some suggestions for conducting effective brainstorming sessions:

- Have a whiteboard, chalkboard, or flipchart to write ideas on. Expect a lot of ideas, so plan ahead. (Ideally, the person leading is focused on the group, not on drawing.)

- Provide some pizza and beer. Seriously—depending on the company and its personality, have some snacks and drinks. For marathon sessions at some companies, that might be pizza and beer, or for shorter sessions, possibly chips and sodas. Coffee and tea can be useful, too. Caffeine actually lowers inhibitions and makes people talk more freely. (That's why cops are happy to offer you coffee or cola during interrogation.) The particular fare is entirely optional and based on the company culture. In more formal meeting structures, snacks may not be appropriate, but eating sometimes makes the session seem less formal and therefore encourages a freer expressive atmosphere.
- Agree as a group on the objective of the specific session. Concentrate on specific areas of the game instead of trying to design everything at once.
- Agree to a time limit. When people get too tired, they may start dropping out of the process. Limit sessions to a time that works for your group, which could be anywhere from half an hour to several hours.
- Set ground rules for the meeting.
- Make it clear to the group that there are no bad ideas or stupid suggestions. You want to encourage complete freedom.
- The facilitator of the session should make an effort to get everyone to participate.
- Encourage people to be brief and concise. Discourage long, drawn-out stories and descriptions. Find ways to condense an idea into its essential elements. One- or two-word descriptions often do the job.
- Ask the group initially not to comment on, and certainly not to disparage, anybody's remarks. Some people are very sensitive to criticism and will withhold their ideas if they feel attacked. Yet those people may sometimes come up with ideas that are original and can lead to innovation and great new design elements.
- Establish a respectful process for people speaking, one that encourages blurting and spontaneity but that also recognizes other people when they are speaking. One way to look at this is that the session should be ordered and structured, but with considerable leeway for spontaneous outbursts, humor, and off-the-wall ideas.
- Write all the ideas down as they are expressed. If ideas link, draw connecting lines. Limit discussion to clarification only. Designate someone to be the writer and/or facilitator of the session, or just record it if nobody can back you up. Note that you can sometimes recognize that an idea is a variant on something already expressed, and, if so, you can combine or refine the original idea.
- If you get stuck with nowhere to turn for new ideas, backtrack and clearly state (aloud) all the reasons why you are following this path and what restrictions are trapping you. This commonly leads to new paths.
- Once all the ideas have been expressed—or at some point based on time or energy—determine that it is time to examine the options listed on the board.
- Have the group look at each item on the list and discuss its merits and weaknesses. Some will simply not work, and that will be clear from the beginning. Eliminate any obviously inappropriate or unusable options.
- Document the ideas that have been found acceptable, possibly ranking them by their usability and popularity with the group.
- Determine what action steps need to be taken following the session. Perhaps some ideas can be implemented and tested or further refined and fleshed out. Be sure those responsible for the follow-up know who they are, what they are to do, and when it is to be completed.
- Determine a procedure for evaluating the results of the action steps and, optionally, schedule another brainstorming session.

KALEIDOSCOPE BRAINSTORMING PROCESS

Some brainstorming techniques suggest that participants periodically engage in silent times of reflection, notating their ideas without speaking—even to the point of writing down their best guess about the ideas other participants might be having. Though this may seem odd, it actually opens up the creative process even more by having the participants get outside their own concepts and ideas and attribute an idea to someone else. In reality, the ideas they attribute to others are their own ideas, but the process of attributing them to someone else opens a different creative channel.

This concept can even go further, to the point where each participant not only guesses what other participants are thinking, but what other participants are thinking about each other's ideas. Confused? Participant A not only writes down his own ideas, but also the ideas he thinks B is thinking and the ideas he thinks B thinks C is thinking, and so on. This is called the *Kaleidoscope Brainstorming Process* and was developed by Dr. KRS Murthy.

As convoluted as this sounds, it can exponentially expand the creative process if people are focused enough to engage in it. However, this may be too formal a process for most game design teams, and the basic steps may be sufficient.

BRAINSTORMING SOLO

Brainstorming is often thought of as a group exercise, but in reality a designer often brainstorms alone. The way to brainstorm alone is to examine all your ideas from as many angles as possible. Ask yourself questions about your ideas and concepts, such as:

- What are you trying to accomplish with this idea? What is the specific result?
- Is your current solution a cliché? (Want to know more about clichés in games? Check out Chapter 22, "Game Conventions and Clichés.")
- If it is a cliché, is there a more innovative way to accomplish the same result, or is the cliché a necessary one? If so, why?
- Assuming you are past the cliché issue, is there any more interesting way to accomplish the result? How many alternative ways can you think of? List them and consider whether any are useful in the current situation or elsewhere. Here's where the lists throughout this book can come in handy. Check your ideas against the ones suggested. Use my lists to expand your thinking as you ask yourself these questions and list your answers.
- Might you change other elements of the situation? For instance, what if the environment was different? What if the characters involved or the properties of the objects radically changed? Could that make the idea more interesting? Again, there's plenty of information in this book to help you find alternatives to issues of environment, characters, and objects, as well as plots, puzzles, obstacles, and even types of scenarios.
- How much freedom of choice does the player have? Check out Chapter 17, "Game Worlds," Chapter 19, "Objects and Locations," Chapter 25, "Barriers, Obstacles, and Detectors," Chapter 26, "Traps and Counter Traps," and even Chapter 28, "Controlling Pacing," and Chapter 29, "Time Limits and Time Manipulation."
- Thinking from the player's perspective, is there a way to make the player's experience more interesting, more powerful, more fun, or more emotionally intense? Check Chapter 12, "Character Design" and Chapter 30, "Ways to Communicate with the Player."

Brainstorming Exercise

Let's do an exercise. Suppose you take an object...say a nuclear bomb. Now consider altering its properties in the following ways. For each alteration, imagine how that change might affect how the bomb can be used in a game and what result it might have on the bomb's effect, portability, versatility, power, and so on. For instance, how strong would a microscopic nuclear bomb be? And where would it be most useful? Could it be used in medicine? Could it be used as a tiny assassination weapon? We once designed one for our *MDK* game, to open door locks. For each of the following ideas, consider the effect of each individual change and then consider combinations of changes and how they would affect the object and its uses:

- Make it smaller (a nuclear bomb that fits in a car's glove box).
- Make it really tiny (a nuclear bomb you hide in a hearing aid).
- Make it microscopic (a nuclear bomb in a syringe).
- Distort, disfigure, or contort it. (You can separate the flash/cloud/explosion.)
- Make it bigger. (You can blow up the universe.)
- Make it heavier. (The cloud crushes everything.)
- Make it lighter. (The radioactive material heads off into space.)
- Make it weightless. (The radioactive material floats in the air.)
- Change its shape. What shapes could it take? (It's stored in a cigarette, a baseball bat, or a football.)
- Change its dimensions. (Its blast is extremely wide, but only one inch from the ground.)
- Change its strength/power. (It's so weak it can't blow over a deck chair.)
- Change its frictional properties. (Its blast gets hotter the farther it goes, becoming plasma in the outer rim.)
- Change its temperature. (It sucks all the heat out of anything in the vicinity.)
- Change how it looks or appears. (It's pretty, like fireworks.)
- Change its translucence. (It's invisible; you can't see anything until it's too late.)
- Change its appeal. (It's a cure to a plague.)
- Change its speed or motion. (You can walk away from the explosion.)
- Change its value. (Every nation on the planet now has them, so they are worthless.)
- Change its colors. (It sucks the photons out of the space it explodes.)
- Change the rules that control it. (It goes off when you sneeze.)
- Consider its side effect(s)—good or bad. (It could turn people into ticking time bombs or it could boost their abilities for a finite amount of time.)
- Consider its byproduct(s)—good or bad. (If triggered in the right place, such as in the heart of a volcano, it could create a new material never seen before.)
- Consider what it would be useful for in a fantasy world. (It's a way to summon a demon.)
- Consider what happens if it captures something. (That flying beast chokes to death in the plumes of toxic smoke and ash.)

I typed those in real time, meaning over 10 minutes or so. As you can see, something pretty clichéd, such as a nuclear bomb, can have tons of new directions in just minutes. If you want more ideas, just restart the list and come up with a bunch more. We could have been talking about cars, weapons, buildings—pretty much anything—and really getting creative with them.

In the end, the goal is to question the normal assumptions and go beyond the ordinary conception of things into the extraordinary and the original. If you find yourself stuck following the obvious, don't give up. Use flexible lists (heck, make your own questions if you need to) to *force* yourself to think outside the box.

Remember, you can also change the situation at any time. That might help you then play with the physical properties even more. For instance:

- Change the weather. (For example, it's raining bodies.)
- Change the environment or location. (For example, you crash-landed on the ear of a dog.)
- Change the altitude. (For example, you're at the bottom of the deepest trench of a crack in an ice cube.)
- Change the temperature. (For example, don't face north.)
- Change the footing—make it uneven, with more or less friction, wet/dry, and so on. (For example, you're knee-deep in dust; it's all that remains from the bones of 1,000,000 warriors who were wiped out in a single day.)
- Make it underwater or in the air instead of on the ground, or vice versa. (For example, it's a space probe that splashes down underwater on a newly discovered planet to scan for life.)
- Change the time period in which the event takes place. (For example, is it before civilization? After civilization? One day before man becomes extinct?)
- Change the weapons available. (For example, the hero has something living in his body, and when it takes control he becomes the weapon.)
- Change the items in the environment. How could they be used? (For example, you are the guy who actually invents the weapons that Q presents in James Bond movies.)

Brainstorming Examples

In the following examples, imagine that the lists included were proposed by members of a brainstorming session. The first step is to identify the purpose of the session—in this case, to create one or more very cool weapons. The next step is to identify as many qualities of the weapon(s) as possible. No idea is too outlandish at this point. Finally, you try to put together the most useful qualities into something everybody is excited about. Then you work on creating and testing it, once you have come up with a viable design.

Basic Qualities of Weapons

Weapons come in all shapes and sizes, but they share some properties. By looking at the range of options available, you might come up with some interesting weapons. Let's start with basic weapon design.

Design a Weapon

Imagine you are brainstorming a weapon. You want to create something more or less from scratch. One way to approach the task is to model your weapon on something you've seen before or something you can find by research. Another way to create a weapon is to start from scratch and consider all the properties that go into a weapon. With an understanding of those properties, you can make adjustments and even create improbable (but cool) new weapons. So first, imagine you are brainstorming all the qualities a weapon might have, and you come up with a list like the ones in Chapter 33, "Historical and Cultural Weapons," and Chapter 34, "Standard Modern Weaponry and Armor." Imagine the weapon taking shape, and imagine how it would be used. Then, once you have designed the basic weapon, move on to the next section and consider magical properties you might also assign to this weapon.

Using the lists from Chapter 33, you could come up with nearly endless weapon concepts, but even those lists are only the beginning. In a simple example, for instance, you might have come up with an unusual weapon with a heavy hook inside a daggered bludgeon, and this weapon could remove a heart from a body in one single move. But you can go even further. When selecting the qualities of your weapon, for each element, such as length, weight, balance, materials, and so on, think of unusual ways to define these qualities. For instance, with weight, perhaps it is lighter than air. Maybe it's alive or maybe it's made from an exotic corrosive gel. For materials, think about nonstandard materials, such as fiber optics or maybe even alien material that is endlessly reconfigurable. There's no limit.

Next, let's imagine a different kind of weapon with a slightly more specific initial description.

A Magical Sword

How might you create a sword with magical properties? What might make it interesting, fun, and unique? Let's explore some of what you might do with a sword to give it unique qualities. Remember, in a brainstorming session, not all the ideas are necessarily good. But even bad ideas sometimes lead to great inspirations and unique concepts or implementations. So what magical properties could a sword possess?

- It can sense the presence of fear. When it does so, it:
  - Makes a sound, such as a low hum, or it vibrates, rings, or sings.
  - Glows a beautiful radioactive glow, meaning enemies can't resist coming to take a closer look, but they die on the way there.
  - Powers up, and you can leave it there to guard an area. Like a sentry, it leaps into action as enemies approach.
  - Creates a force field around you to protect you.
  - As a result of a certain move, creates a magical shadow warrior to fight along with you.
  - Opens its mouth and takes a bite out of an enemy it is swung into.
  - Turns invisible when an enemy picks it up.
  - Flies through the air (under its own power), taking you with it as it's thrown.
  - Can be thrown through the heart of an enemy from a mile away if it is aimed in the right direction.
- It can change shape. It can:
  - Elongate instantly, piercing the heads of your enemy and the enemy behind him.
  - Divide into two blades, so you can charge an enemy and remove his torso section in one piece.
  - Turn into any other weapon when a special move is performed. It might turn into an axe, a quarterstaff, a pike, or even a sharp-bladed boomerang.
- It can shoot a projectile of some kind or emit something. For instance, things you might have seen in the past are:
  - Flames
  - Fireballs
  - Ice
  - Electricity/lightning
  - Bullets or other projectiles
  - Serpents
  - Frogs (death by angry frog!)
  - Slippery substances, such as oil
  - Smaller blades
  - Sonic waves
  - Blinding light
  - Traps, such as nets
  - Plasma balls
  - Graviton fields
  - Poisons or diseases
  - Sticky goo or webs, such as a spider web
  - Spinning blades
  - Skeletal warriors
  - Bombs/grenades
  - Alien creatures that suck out the enemy's brains
  - Energy beams
  - Strong winds, hurricanes, tornados, and so on

- Typical effects a sword might have include:
  - Fire
  - Ice
  - Gravity
  - Sound/sonic effects
  - Electricity/lightning
  - Poison
  - Paralysis
  - Disease
  - Confusion
  - Fear
  - Bright light
  - Blinding
  - Bleeding wounds
  - Slowing the enemy
  - Lower enemy protection
  - Increasing protection
  - Hypnotizing the enemy
  - Summoning a storm
  - Summoning a genie or elemental
  - Knowledge
  - Added strength, speed, agility, dexterity, wisdom, and so on
  - Unerring accuracy
  - Enhanced damage
  - Calmness
  - Happiness
  - Ability to quell anger
  - Ability to convert an enemy
  - Ability to force an enemy to dance
  - Ability to force an enemy to start sneezing
  - Ability to give the enemy a nasty headache
  - Ability to call for help
  - Ability to clone itself

Ultimately, you will come up with ideas for very unusual and original weapons using a combination of basic weapon qualities and, optionally, special abilities. The ideas presented here are only the beginning of the process, and I challenge you to go beyond these ideas and create a magic sword unlike any you've ever seen or imagined.

Games and Research

Although many games are based on completely original ideas and set in completely fictional worlds, many are based on historical subjects, real-world subjects, literature or movies, or even current events. To name just a notable few:

- *Civilization* (all versions)
- *Pirates!*
- *SimCity* (and other *Sim* products)
- *Age of Empires*
- *God of War*
- *Medal of Honor* (series)
- *Rainbow Six*
- Every flight simulator and most racing games
- Almost all sports games
- Numerous movie-based games

Even games that don't appear on the surface to be based on any specific subject often are inspired by or influenced by other stories. For instance, many of the Japanese RPGs borrow liberally (even if loose on accuracy) from various world mythologies.

The value of research cannot be overstated. The more you know about a subject, the more you can add to your game and (with really good research) the more convincing it will be. Even if your game is completely fictional, research into a variety of subjects can add depth, value, and new ideas to your game. In fact, it often happens that an idea you come across while researching can provide you with some game ideas you had not previously thought of. For example, suppose you are doing some patrol sequence. It's good to study what patrol guards do, what they say, and how they interact to make them real. They don't just walk in a straight line from one corner of a building to another and ping-pong back and forth 24 hours a day, yet you see that kind of thing all too often in games. When they talk on their radios, do they say really clichéd stuff? "All clear on the west perimeter," or does it sound fake? In Hollywood, the writers who get a million dollars a script research this kind of thing constantly so they can cover the details and make things feel tangible and real.

What to Look For

One of the main benefits of good research is that you have a lot of good data at hand, and that data can lend authenticity to your project. But perhaps even more important is the often unexpected inspiration that can come from studying a subject more deeply. Often, you will gain an insight or have an inspiration based on the real facts or the true story you have read—something you simply would not have considered on your own. Even a small fact or comment by a character or a minor bit of information can give you important game structures, hooks, or even whole concepts.

When you are doing research on nontechnical subjects, look for the following:

- The main characters. (Who matters most?)
- The secondary characters. (Who else fills in the social network?)
- The relationships. (How do they interact?)
- The main settings (the actual locations and so on).
- The main objects/activities. (What do they do hour to hour?)
- Their beliefs. (What are they?)
- Whether they have a façade. (Do they need to appear a certain way?)
- How money enters into it.
- How love, affection, or lust enters into it.
- What they do (technically speaking).
- What they are really good at.
- What they let slide.
- What dangers there are.
- And so on!

Among the most useful elements is the information you can get from themes and cultural aspects of the subject you are researching. These can lead you directly to many gameplay options. For instance, look at a game such as *Grand Theft Auto.* The activities and missions you receive are pretty much inspired by the specific culture depicted in the game.

Of course, some games will be based (in whole or in part) on very technical subjects, such as flying aircraft (in a flight simulator or air combat game, for instance). Games based on modern battle scenarios will need information about modern weaponry, and the research you conduct on those subjects is more straightforward. Even so, when you start investigating technical subjects, you may be surprised to find that there are very cool innovations, technologies, or products that you can incorporate in your design. For instance, you may not have known that there was a gun that could see around corners, using optical fibers. How cool is that? So now, perhaps you can give a gun like that to your main character or even to his enemies! Or maybe instead of looking around a corner, it watches your back.

But suppose you are creating a battle game based in a specific era, such as ancient Rome, World War I, World War II, or World War III? Clearly, each of these eras will have different equipment, military knowledge and tactics, settings, and even command structures. In Rome, you wouldn't have guns and lasers, though you might find some interesting and little-known weapons and formations if you do some research. And between WWI and WWII there were many changes and advancements. As a simple example, tanks in WWI were rudimentary and not terribly effective or widely used. By WWII, tanks had become highly sophisticated and played significant roles in some theaters of operation. By WWIII, who knows what may happen. Here, research can help you extrapolate from the latest research to the possible future of warfare. For instance, the military is experimenting with special exoskeleton suits that will turn their fighters into super soldiers who can run faster and carry much heavier loads, more ammo, bigger (more powerful) weapons, and at the same time have greatly increased stamina. Nanotechnology allows us to look at naturally made things, such as red-blood cells, and redesign them to work even better, so now this soldier can hold his breath under water for 35 minutes. Maybe he can comfortably breathe thick, black, sooty smoke. Basically, take an idea and run with it. Ask yourself, "What if?"

For technical research, you want statistics—lots of statistics. What is the rate of fire, the top speed, or the kinds of bullets the gun takes? There are lots of very factual statistics for different machines and devices you might use. And there are many resources that list those specifics.

Why? Well, because these days gamers commonly look for character/player growth and leveling up (sometimes over a hundred levels), and we can help that process with weapon improvements. So you want a range of constantly improving weapons for the player to look forward to.

You also may want to look into how things are used, and this aspect of the research can be more interesting. For instance, suppose you have all the flight and mechanical statistics for a specific supersonic jet. That's great for doing the computer model of the jet, but how is that particular aircraft used? Is it an air-to-air combat jet? Protection? A reconnaissance craft or a strafing weapon? Maybe it is used in several contexts. At any rate, knowing how something is used as well as what makes it tick is all part of the research. That doesn't mean you have to stick to the uses you find, unless you are going for absolute accuracy and authenticity. It may be that you can extrapolate some information and create new (improved) uses or new situations that allow its weaknesses to be exposed.

In any case, with a few keywords, you can generally come up with books, videos, and websites full of useful information on just about any topic. This is often the first step in designing a game—knowing the subject and using that knowledge (with the aid of Google) to help inspire the creative thinking that ultimately will yield new hooks, concepts, characters, objects, situations, stories, and game flow.

Research Sources

Of course, there's no secret to research. It's pretty straightforward, and with the Internet it is much easier; however, at the same time, it's a bit more perilous. Your main sources of information when doing research are:

- Books on applicable subjects.
- Internet sites.
- Experts on the subject.
- The actual sources (firsthand experience).
- Eyewitnesses (when possible).
- Movies/documentaries.
- Myths and fables.
- People who have access to information. (Yes, you can call a library!)
- Other games.

One concern is the lack of standards of accuracy on the Internet. Although there is a lot of very good information available on various websites, there is also a lot of inaccurate material. People can write anything they want on a website, and often the information found by Internet searches can be inaccurate, incomplete, poorly prepared and written, and/or misleading. What makes the situation worse is that, often, other websites will gain their material from an incorrect source, so even checking multiple sites doesn't always guarantee that you'll discover errors. Some sites are better than others, and some sources are far more credible. So use the Internet, definitely, but use it with caution, check your sources, and check multiple sources if in doubt, especially those with more credible authors and those that document where they obtained their information (especially if you are going to hinge your entire game on a certain fact you read somewhere).

Another way to get some ideas is simply to ask gamers: "Tell me some of your favorite video game moments of all time." Then just listen (carefully) to what they say. What are they really saying? What really became such a great memory? How could that be enhanced for a different game? When you watch a movie, read a book, watch TV, or even read a newspaper, always have that filter going: "Hmmm...that's a really neat idea. I wonder how I could springboard from that idea into something never seen before in the video game industry."

Done right, it won't be long before you have more ideas than time.

Part II Which Game Will You Make?

3 Hooks

What is a hook?

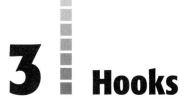

Ideally, a hook should be something that makes the game unique and that you can show on a TV commercial to make gamers everywhere salivate. What hooks them is something amazingly cool about your game—something they probably haven't done before in a game (or seen before anywhere else—not even in a movie) or something that makes the game very intriguing/alluring. A great hook is that element of the game that the players, the press, and the retailers can all recognize instantly, without much explanation. (You just *know* the press will be itching to talk about it!)

Remember, games are fantasies for sale; there are plenty of hooks out there, so don't give up quickly. This is the DNA that can take you from being a good designer to being a *great* designer, when you can approach familiar subject matter with really fresh ideas.

If you really want to get a game published, you will nearly always need a hook. Games are going to get more and more difficult to pitch for funding in the long term, and you need a way to differentiate your designs from all others. However, I must caution that *hook* does not have to mean *risk* in the eyes of a publisher, but certain hooks will mean just that. So always consider who you are going to be pitching this to.

"It will have the most amazing artificial intelligence ever" sounds like a hook, but in reality there's more risk than hook on offer there. It's not specific, but just a promise of some technology and not how it's implemented or what makes it a hook. The risk is in placing your reliance on "the most amazing" anything, where it may not be relevant to players or it may be superseded by some better technology.

Recently, Electronic Arts has started calling this *Feature IP.* (By the way, IP stands for *intellectual property.*) It sounds better, but it's just a hook. They've also announced that if you want to pitch a game to them, it had *better* have some new Feature IP. (For the industry this is a good thing, as it will help pull us away from copycat games.)

In this chapter:

- ➤ Benefits of a Hook
- ➤ Hook Evaluator v3: DP's Forty Questions

Benefits of a Hook

So what are some benefits of a hook?

- It's an easier pitch to the publisher. (It's something to focus on.)
- You can test it with your audience. (Did they like it or didn't they?)
- It gives you something to focus your advertising on.
- It gives your team a goal upon which to base daily decisions—meaning, "Will this new idea help or hinder our main goal of delivering our hook?" (Remember that the hook is the crown jewel.)

- It gives the press something to write about and sets your game apart from other products.
- Gamers will buy your game to experience it for the first time.

Picking a giant seller, let's talk about *Grand Theft Auto*. What was the hook? Killing people? No, that's old news. Stealing cars? Maybe—it did add to the experience, but any driving game could add that feature, and I still don't think it would be *GTA*. In my personal opinion, the hook was freedom, something we are always begging for when trapped in a world of linear games (especially linear driving games!). The unparalleled freedom offered in *GTA* was fantastic—even the giant maps let us roam around without loading every two minutes. Do what you want, when you want, the way you want to do it. The game just had to handle it and simulate a somewhat credible response.

Another driving game I enjoyed was the original *Driver*, from Atari. That game made it really fun to be chased by police around a city. It was a great way to get you to push yourself to drive more crazily than ever before, by putting numerous police cars right on your rear. In *GTA IV*, the driver is real, meaning it's not just a car you're driving—there's a person in it, and when you crash you literally end up out on the street. That idea of real people (when we generally accept the convention that there's nobody "really" in the car) is the beginning of a new hook.

In evaluating the strength of your proposal, look for the hook. You'll rarely get anybody really excited by going in and pitching a game that's "just like *X* or *Y*" (where *X* or *Y* is some existing game). If your hook is that *X* was a hit game and your game is better, it should be 10 times better, not just one tiny little idea better. (I know that sounds obvious, but trust me, I get those pitches all the time.) "You know *StarCraft*? Well, my idea is just like that, but there's a certain weapon with a hit ratio of 45 percent, and my game will be much more fun at a 75-percent hit ratio on that kind of weapon." (Yes, I do get these pitches.) But you'll notice people's eyes light up when you suggest something unique—something they haven't heard of before.

For example, which would you invest in?

- "Hi, my new game is called *Super Car Racer*. It's as close to *Gran Turismo* as we can make it. We've got all the cool features in there, and the graphics are at least as good! Our hook is that our cars on average go 15 miles per hour *faster* than their cars! They have 700 cars from 80 manufacturers, but we have 732 from 82 manufacturers."
- "Hi, my new game is called *Beast Racer*. A community of several thousand people got together to discuss the topic of their dream racing game. Within weeks they had come up with a hook that your vehicle is actually a living, breathing beast that you can raise and train. Yes, you literally feed your 'car' and grow it into a monster. You can cross-breed it, upgrade it with battle armor, and race in different styles of circuits where the 'cars' can even fight, and you can actually rip apart a competitor's 'car.' Would you like to see it?"

How do you identify a hook? One way is to examine your concept and look for what makes it unique. Then ask the following questions:

- Is it unique? Has anybody done it before?
- Is it really fun and will it remain fun for the full game experience?
- Does it tap into something universally felt by your target audience?
- Can you show it in a TV commercial?
- Is the target audience large enough to make this a worthwhile project?
- Can you pull it off technically? Legally? Financially?

Hook Evaluator v3: DP's Forty Questions

If you really want to evaluate your hook concepts, try filling in the following information. These are the questions you should ask yourself to see how strong your game proposal is.

NOTE *If you are pitching a game, you should by all means try to be ready for these questions.*

Grade each one "Yes" or "Heck yeah!" and write it down. (A "Yes" is worth 1 point, and a "Heck yeah!" is worth 2 points, so if you score more than 30 points, you are on to something good.)

1. Does the target audience already respect the **developer** of this game?
2. Does any aspect of this game design bring back fond memories or **nostalgia** for the target audience?
3. Are the **graphics** generally likely to be better than rival/competitive products?
4. Are your artists going to be able to make this subject matter look **breathtaking**?
5. Based on the story scenes, do you expect people to want to watch every minute of the **cinematics**? (Get a point if there are no cinematics in your game.)
6. Will the game feel **new/original/fresh**?
7. Will it be **easier to play** (easier to get into by design) than competitive games?
8. Is the **functionality/depth/range of features** planned for the game more impressive when compared to other games in the same genre?
9. Do you think a player would be perceived as **"cool" by his friends** if he introduced them to this game?
10. Would **most people (not just hardcore gamers)** be able to play your game and get into the most fun parts relatively quickly?
11. Does the game have a cool-sounding, **easy to remember/easy to say/easy to spell name** that suggests or reveals what the game is about?
12. Is there an exciting feature that can be saved for the **Limited Edition version**?
13. Does the game potentially have any **collectable value**? (Is it part of a series, for example?)
14. Can the owner play the game **with his friends sitting on the sofa next to him**?
15. Can the owner play the game **with his friends through the Internet**?
16. If playing through the Internet, can the player **chat with his friends** easily while playing?
17. Can the player **share or trade his success (his spoils of war)** with his friends?
18. Can the game be **customized or personalized**?
19. Is the game going to be presented by a **respected game designer/programmer or producer**?
20. Will the game star a really **well-known celebrity** character, actor, or actress?
21. Will the soundtrack be crafted by a very (globally) popular or **famous composer or band**?
22. Is the story written by a famous or **respected writer**?
23. Is the focus on a **subject matter** that the target audience is really excited about these days? (One that hasn't already been done many times before?)
24. Will people be amazed by the **visual effects**?
25. Does the global gaming audience **really *love* this game genre**?
26. Is there any **controversy** regarding this game that the target audience will hear about?
27. Is there a way to make the **price** lower than that of your direct competitors?
28. Do you have any **clever plans** for marketing the game?
29. Will the game engine have a way to avoid **long boring periods, long load times**, or other elements that try a gamer's patience?

30. Are you sure people won't think this game is **weird or strange**?
31. Will gamers playing this game **laugh out loud** at any time while playing?
32. Would it be possible to reveal the unique hook in this game in a **television commercial** of 30 seconds?
33. Can you play this game without ever **reading a manual** (by design)?
34. Will you have movie-quality **sound effects/ambiance/speech** in the game?
35. Will the game offer immediate **replayability**?
36. If a player gets stuck, will the game detect this and **help him out of this problem**?
37. Will the game have **interesting "very memorable moments" (high points)**, as opposed to repetitive gameplay?
38. Will the story have an **exciting start**?
39. Will the story have a **surprising ending** that will compel people to talk about it?
40. Will the game have a fun and interesting learn-as-you-play in-game **tutorial**?

Why do this?

Say you have four ideas, and you just can't decide which to really flesh out and start working on. Run them through this test and then go with the winner. Or, run the test, get the score, then try to add 10 more points to that score. Go back and read the questions for inspiration on how you could add those 10 more points.

4 What Publishers Want

Part II

How do you get your game published? What's your best chance of getting a publisher to take your project seriously? In short, what do publishers want?

This chapter can help you if you are pitching a product, whatever its current stage. The sections in this chapter are:

- Why Do We Need Publishers?
- Getting Your Game Published
- Preparing for the Pitch
- Artistic License
- Pitching Games to Publishers
- The 45-Second Elevator Pitch
- A Good Pitch
- Good Pitches versus Bad Pitches
- Elements of a Game Design Submission
- Getting Work in the Game Industry

Why Do We Need Publishers?

Few games succeed in reaching their full markets without the help of publishers. Even successful companies that started with shareware (such as id and Epic) ultimately moved to the publishing model. Publishers take much of the risk, but they also fund, market, distribute, and handle manufacturing for most games. Some successful companies have been their own publishers, marketers, and distributors, but it is difficult at best to fulfill all these roles. The chances are you will be working with publishers on your next game.

Getting Your Game Published

Getting your game published is ultimately your goal, and one all-important aspect of getting the green light from a publisher is the game pitch. Most publishers want answers to a number of questions. Also, they are busy and have concerns you may or may not be aware of. Here are a few facts to consider when you decide it's time to pitch your project:

- Many publishers receive dozens to hundreds of new game proposals every month. There are simply too many for each to get the full attention of the decision makers.
- More than 95 percent of game submissions from external developers get rejected, and quite a few internal submissions are rejected, too.

- Product acquisition and development people are always swamped, and their time is limited and very valuable. The amount of focus they will give any particular submission is generally equivalent to how memorable, unique and, understandable the submission is.
- Game production and distribution is a high-risk business.
- Most games do not make money, and most publishers have had games that cost a lot to make and didn't turn a profit.
- Most publishers have been burned by developers who miss milestones, go way over budget, miss ship dates, or overestimate their capabilities.
- Adding to publisher's risk aversion, many games, even those that get funding and support, end up being cancelled before they are ever released. There are a variety of reasons for this, including that the game failed to live up to expectations, the game concept or technology is no longer marketable because of changes in the industry, something better came along and required the company's resources, the development team was too difficult to work with, and so on. The bottom line is that the company always loses money on cancelled games.
- Publishers prefer to work with people they know and trust. The game business is about relationships.

Preparation for the Pitch

Having a great idea is only the beginning. To get a publisher to develop your idea, you have to bring a lot to the table. All publishers are working with companies and teams they know well. You have to convince them not only that your idea stands out from the crowd, but that you have done your homework and you can bring a strong team to the table. This section looks at what you can do to help ensure that you will be taken seriously.

1. Clear, realistic, honest, and well-thought-out milestones for completion.
2. Sufficient projected staff to accomplish the project.
3. Sufficient projected budget allocated for each phase of development.
4. Sufficient time and manpower allocated to testing and tuning.

The team should have:

1. A strong team track record
2. Team experience in the genre

Design Elements

Your game doesn't need to have every one of these elements, but this list can help you identify what elements it does have and what elements you might be able to add to make the game better and more likely to be produced.

For many of these suggested elements, I have noted relevant chapters and/or sections in this book that can provide you with more information.

- Know the genre of your game. (See also Chapter 5, "Game POV and Game Genres.") Be familiar with the best games in that genre, and then make your game even better. For instance:
  - Shooter: *Halo/Halo 2*
  - Racing: *Gran Turismo*
  - Stealth action: *Metal Gear Solid*
  - FPS: *Medal of Honor*
  - Football: *Madden*
  - Platformer: *Ratchet & Clank, Jak II*
  - RPG: *Final Fantasy XII*

- If you are mixing genres, be familiar with other games that have mixed genres and be clear why your game will work and what the elements of each genre add to the gameplay.
- Know your hooks! (See also the Hook Evaluator in Chapter 3, "Hooks.")
- Suggest a recognizable and/or memorable name/title. This can include a good, strong name for the main characters.
- Have fast or minimal load times. The less time spent loading assets the better, and definitely do not interrupt the game flow by loading at critical moments!
- Have fully realized worlds.
- Ensure considerable interaction with the environment (both objects and characters).
- Use secondary animations, such as clothes and hair, realistic cloaks, flags and trees bending in the wind, and so on—more than simple textures.
- Make sure you have replay value. Your game should be more than just a rehash of models and bigger weapons...you need to provide real reasons to play again.
- Use plenty of visual effects and details.
- Include online play options and solutions—head-to-head, small multiplayer, or massive multiplayer.
- Ensure customizability. Can the player make an impact on the game world? Can players create their own missions/levels?
- Include multiplayer modes for console games.
- Use real and compelling original content—strong gameplay elements.
- Ensure innovative and effective use of control devices.
- Provide responsive controls.
- Provide in-game help and/or tutorials.
- Create ways to help players deal with difficult sections. Include dynamic music.
- Have an exclusive license (if applicable).
- Have a strong, well-identified demographic and demonstrate understanding of the kinds of games that are popular with that audience.
- Ensure cultural relevance to the intended audience.
- Include a strong feature set.
- Have a unique and recognizable character design.
- Include good character animation.
- Describe possible environmental design options.
- Describe sample environmental animations.
- Use color effectively.
- Use voice and/or acting effectively.
- Use sound effects effectively.
- Provide good overall responsiveness.
- Use effective level design.
- Include artificial intelligence.
- Use the camera effectively.
- Provide different modes of play.
- Have a well-tuned difficulty progression.
- Include interesting and fun character abilities.
- Include good use of rewards.
- Make sure it's possible to complete all elements of the game.
- Make sure the goal of the game is attainable.
- Provide an actual "ending" to the game as a solid reward to the user for completing it. The genre of the game and other variables will determine whether this is applicable. A few simple screens and then the credits rolling is not always an appropriate ending that users want to see in their games.

- Include interactive and believable characters. NPCs (non-playing characters) shouldn't be so easy to pick out in an RPG (Role-Playing Game), for instance.
- Create a believable, unique, and well-written story.
- This book is full of game elements, so feel free to explore any of the other chapters to help you prepare your design. That's what it's all about, after all.

Technical Elements

While there are many creative elements that go into your game and that you will need to identify when designing and presenting your design, don't forget the technical elements. You will need to show publishers that you fully understand the technical side. Here are a few suggestions:

- Demonstrate or propose a high consistent frame rate (for example, 60 FPS).
- Have fast or minimal load times. The less time spent loading assets the better. This is both a technical and a design factor to consider.
- Use clear, readable fonts.
- Include surround sound capability.
- Clearly define your interface design concepts and ergonomics.
- Use analog controls.
- Use pressure-sensitive controls.
- Use vibration controls.
- Include high-quality textures.
- Use effective lighting.
- Use "real-world" physics.
- Include good professional audio—preferably Dolby Pro Logic or equivalent.
- Include progressive scan support.
- Include support for appropriate peripherals.
- Use anti-aliasing.
- Include exceptional collision detection.
- Use efficient draw distance.
- Include an easy-to-understand user interface (UI). It should be easy for the user to start the game and get into playing it however they desire in the shortest amount of time. The user should also be able to navigate through the UI without getting "lost." Getting a user lost with the UI is a quick way to get them to stop playing the game permanently.
- Include easy-to-use controls. The majority of the populace is not hardcore gamers. If your game has "so many buttons to keep up with," it can be very intimidating for a user to ever want to play the game.

What Adds Real Value to Your Design?

Even the best design can use some extra help. Does yours benefit from any of the following?

- **Hooks.** A need for it—like shampoo.
- **A Strong Respect for the Brand/Reputation.** An example is the Ford Expedition—Eddie Bauer Edition. It's got a famous name brand standing for a passion for outdoors that has been around since 1920. Eddie Bauer is a good license. They could have gone with a guy called William Clark. He was another explorer, but the retail recognition is really low. So the brand counts.
- **A History of Using the Products.** People like to play safe and buy what they know. Sometimes it can also bring back strong nostalgic memories.

- **The Way It Looks or Feels.** Basically, the game's aesthetics.
- **Word of Mouth.** This sells objects, too—by perceived popularity.
- **Price.** The price matters a lot—or at least the perceived price.
- **Newness.** Some people are attracted to originality and a fresh approach to a problem.
- **Features and Functionality.** An impressive range of features can sell objects by improved functionality.
- **Guarantees.** They effectively give peace of mind to a sale.
- **Recognized Quality.** Having read reviews/ratings or seeing a game's awards gives an aura of quality, effectively lifting it above its competitors.
- **Clear, Sensible Advertising That Gets the Message Across.** If done well, advertising can help sell objects. However, in the past some of the .com Super Bowl ads were so obscure that they left people wondering what they were actually trying to sell. Clear, sensible advertising is important.
- **Status.** Can the object improve a person's perceived worth? Or does it make the person look cool by having it, like a platinum card?
- **Comfort.** Is the object very comfortable to use? Does it feel good?
- **Ease of Use.** Can someone with an average IQ use the object? As VCR programming has taught us, don't rely on people reading the manual.
- **Name.** Does the object have a cool or catchy name?
- **Packaging.** Does the object have slick/high-quality packaging? Does it catch your attention in a store?
- **Special Edition.** Is the object rare? Is it a special edition? Or does it have a story attached that makes it feel rare to you?
- **Collectability.** Is the object collectable? Will people feel they need to keep a collection going with this object?
- **Customizability.** Can a person customize or personalize the object? (Nokia cell phones and TiVo are great examples of this.)
- **Availability.** Is the object easy to purchase? Can impulse buyers get their hands on it quickly?
- **Innovation.** Does it ooze innovation?

Other Factors to Consider

I asked myself, what other things attract people to see or buy movies, music, or even comics?

- Boredom is a good reason—it's a great motivator.
- Was it made by a director you respect?
- Does it star an actor/actress you respect?
- Is the soundtrack or music by a composer or band you like?
- Was the story written by a writer you respect?
- Is it based on subject matter that interests you?
- What is the usage situation? Is this a great movie to see with your friends?
- Does it have breathtaking visuals or special effects?
- Is it based on a genre that you generally enjoy, such as horror/comedy/action/kids?
- Does it sound fresh and full of creativity?
- Does the title interest you?
- Is there controversy, touching on a nerve? *Grand Theft Auto III* obviously oozes controversy, but when I first heard about *The Sims*, it sounded like a "You get to wash the dishes and put out the trash" simulator. But I found out later that it has nudity and lesbian kissing, among other potentially controversial elements.

Artistic License

Often you may base a game on some specific idea from a book, movie, or other existing source. On rare occasions you'll expect to stay pretty true to the source material, but most often doing so will result in a game that is far less fun than it could be. So what do you do? You embellish. You exaggerate. You change the story, the characters, and their abilities to make the game more fun. In short, you exercise artistic license. For instance, if your main character was a really strong guy who carried a big sword, make the sword huge. Give it a magical glow and maybe even let it fire energy beams or burn red-hot. Or suppose you read a newspaper story about a drug cartel and you were inspired by the story to create a game set in a drug culture. You can create something close to the truth, which might concern a local small-time operation, or you could create *Scarface* and make it a really big international adventure complete with the seamy underworld bottom dwellers and the glitzy crime bosses, plenty of victims, and plenty of opportunities to go overboard in gameplay.

Or suppose you are creating a gunfight. Even though the guns your characters are using probably wouldn't have much muzzle flash, you add lots of muzzle flash anyway. Why? Because it looks cool and it makes the scene more dramatic. Because it's about better entertainment. Truthfulness is important in setting up a world, but the one thing that overrides truthfulness is fun. Fun comes first.

Artistic license gives you the ability to explore alternatives and new directions and to make a good concept much better, or even to take a boring concept and make it great. However, there's no way to guarantee good taste or success when you attempt to change a property or concept. Using artistic license offers possibilities, but only a good understanding of what is fun and what is feasible can lead to consistently good results.

Pitching Games to Publishers

How do you present a game design that will generate interest, and who do you present it to? What are they looking for? What will kill it stone dead? How can you get it onto the desk of the people who can make decisions?

To answer who:

- Producers? In some cases—depends on the company.
- CEO? Probably not, but he/she might send you to the right person.
- Acquisitions specialists (the most appropriate way to go).
- Someone you know well (who might be able to grease the wheels and at least get you the attention you need).
- And so on...

To answer where/when:

- Industry shows, such as GDC and the Austin Game Conference
- Other shows
- Agents and recruiters
- Cold calls
- Site visits with an appointment (your site or theirs)
- Creativity you find a way

The 45-Second Elevator Pitch

Imagine you happened to be on the elevator with just the person you want to talk to about your game. You're on the way to the 10th floor. You have just 45 seconds (maybe only 30) to get him interested. What will you say? How can you sum up your game so that he'll say, "I really want to know more?"

The fact is, you often have very little time to get someone's attention. When you are pitching a new game, you are competing with possibly hundreds of other game designers who passionately want their games to be produced. The publishing executives in charge of new acquisitions are often busy and have little time for a lengthy discussion. However, they are always looking for the next "killer app" or mega-hit game project. Therefore, one of the most important aspects of pitching your game can be your ability to condense the key elements of your game—the elements that make it unique and marketable—into a very short statement. This is your chance to make your game sound irresistible. At the same time, it's a challenge to boil down possibly months of work and hundreds of pages of documentation full of fantastic details you would die to see in your game to something truly succinct and exciting. This is how you express the "nugget" of your game. In Hollywood terms, it is known as the *45-second elevator pitch.*

- Give a brief high-level description, such as, "It's a game set in the rap culture, featuring Eminem and Diddy in an action musical inner-city gangland adventure that combines elements of *Tomb Raider* and *Grand Theft Auto III.*"
- Offer some reasons why your game is especially cool—especially if your game is the first to do something. For instance, "My game, *The Rapland Killings,* is the first to allow players to compose their own rap songs and have them reach number one on the charts. It is also the first to star major rap stars. It is designed to play equally well in single-player mode or in competitive or cooperative multiplayer modes."
- Mention who is on your team and what they have worked on before. The better their overall track record, the more seriously someone will take your project.
- Where are you at? It's best if you have playable levels (or even a complete alpha version), but in any case, you want to mention the current status of the game and your projection for completion.

A Good Pitch

There are different ways to present a game concept to publishers. Here's a list of elements your pitch must contain if it is to compete in the current world of 3D games.

NOTE

Please note that exceptions may exist, such as arcade and puzzle games, which may not require all these criteria to be met.

- A good in-person presentation (a pitch) can make or break a project right from the start. Although a good pitch probably won't guarantee a contract, a bad pitch can practically guarantee that the publisher will lose interest, and it's very difficult to get their attention a second time.
- When you have arranged a meeting with a publisher, be prepared. Try to have all the answers ready, because there will always be questions. Be confident and enthusiastic, but not stubborn, inflexible, or cocky. Remember, most publishers see dozens, if not hundreds, of new game proposals each month. You may think you have the best thing since sliced bread, but overconfidence can turn off a publisher. They are looking for talented people, but also people they can work with successfully. Nobody wants

a prima donna, and you had better be awfully damned good to get away with having a 'tude with a publisher. (Of course, if you already have offers from one or more publishers, you have leverage.)

- In general, most mortals must do their best to convince the publisher to hand over a contract. Here are some additional guidelines:
  - Be prepared with a convincing oral presentation, something to show (preferably working assets), and something you can leave with the publisher after the meeting.
  - Mix graphics and demos with your oral presentation. Have something to show or illustrate what you're talking about. (See the "Animate!" sidebar a bit later in this chapter.)
  - The oral section should begin with a succinct description of the game, giving the big picture and essential information, such as the game genre, what platform(s) it's for, number of players, and so on. When identifying the genre, you may want to mention other games in that genre, but that leads to the next part of the oral presentation....
  - Talk about why the game is unique:
    - What are the hooks?
    - What's the cool factor?
    - What do you do that nobody else has done, or how do you do it better than previous games?
    - Do you have the coolest technology?
    - Do you have a license?
    - Does the game lend itself to sequels, branding, franchises, ancillary rights (such as comic books, novels, action figures, lunch boxes, and so on)?
  - Project analysis: Up to this point, there's hopefully a lot of excitement, but now it's time to talk nuts and bolts—er, budgets and timelines. This is where the dollar meets the donut. Have this charted out and be prepared to whip out a really nice-looking milestone chart and a carefully prepared budget.
  - Talk about the team and provide a personnel list with specific information about the members' backgrounds and experience and their roles in the project. Be sure to talk up your team's qualifications. It helps if some or all of them have worked on previously published products. Publishers like to know that you can complete what you start.
  - Be prepared to answer questions and also to discuss possible adjustments to the timeline and budget. Be honest and forthcoming with answers, and always be prepared. But, if you really don't have an answer for a question, don't make something up. Tell the publisher you don't know at this moment, but you can find out quickly enough.
  - If you have put everything but the kitchen sink into your game, you may have to be realistic about the possibility that not all your ideas can be implemented, and some publishers might start questioning parts of your design even at this early date. Be prepared to defend your ideas, but also to be flexible. Know what is expendable and what is essential, and be ready to compromise where you can or must.
  - Be prepared to talk terms. You may be surprised; a publisher might start talking deal points right then and there. You need to have a good idea of what kind of deal you want. If you have an agent representing you or your team, this is the time to bring the agent into the discussion. If you have no agent, then you need to consider what contract terms you would want. See the "Contracts" section in Chapter 8, "Protecting Your Intellectual Property."

Animate!

I pitched a game once (*MDK*) with just storyboard images, and it was turned down. My team took the exact same images and made a simple 3D video version of the storyboards. The game publisher loved it (the same people!), and they funded it.

So I did a test. I took a 3D war scene video from a Hollywood friend and showed it to the president of Atari. He said, "We want it!" Now hold on. There's *no* game design at all present, not even any documents. The point is to understand the power and the value of an artist's impression of your idea. Many people think they need to make a game demo to get interest, but that's not necessarily true! Face it, it's *much* cheaper to make a video than it is to make a game demo–and it's quicker, too!

Think of it this way: Have you ever seen a movie trailer that made you go, "Whoa, I want to be there opening night!" or one that made you say, "I think I'll pass?" We are trained by movie trailers to make media decisions in just a couple of minutes. So make your trailer.

To quote my friend Tommy Tallarico, the math is quite simple. Take the famous saying, "A picture is worth a thousand words," and then remember that video is generally 30 frames (pictures) per second, so that's 30,000 words a second. If you think about it that way, a three-minute trailer video is the equivalent of 5.4 million words!

So there you go! Now, Tommy is a musician, but he's not far off the truth here. I'd rather watch the trailer for your game and see your vision than read a 500-page document about it.

So how do you do it? Find the best artists you can–artists who would love to be a part of a game that gets green-lit–and try them out. The talent is out there, as I've been able to prove again and again. So get creative, go find them, and make it happen.

Part II

Good Pitches versus Bad Pitches

My number-one warning sign when people pitch me is when they don't have one idea—they have a whole boatload of ideas, and they don't have a clue which is the best one.

It's a bit like me saying, "Here taste this," and you going, "Yuck!" Then I say, "Yeah, I thought so, but maybe you'll like this." After we go through this five times, would you call me a good chef? If I'm any good, I should know what tastes good, and if I don't, why would you want to buy food from me?

The point is that you want rejection to come as a real shock, meaning you've put forward your best idea ever, honed it to perfection, and now you get a "yuck!" It should completely shock you because you really believed in what you were pitching.

I've been in professional pitches where Hollywood executives have pitched me a game idea. When I've said it won't make a good game, they've said, "Yeah, we thought so." Then they just reach farther into their drawer for another idea. "How about a mummy game?" "A young boy goes to his first wedding?" "A used-car salesman becomes president?" It's random, it's painful to sit through, and I have to give professional responses (gag!).

I call this the *buckshot technique*. They hope that something will strike the target—anything—and they don't really care what.

So that's what *not* to do. Instead, come in with something you care *passionately* about, that you know inside out would make a great game. Also, make sure you know who you are pitching to, and that they are interested in that kind of game. You might not pitch a 2D arcade game to John Carmack, and you probably wouldn't pitch a First-Person Shooter to Will Wright—although, who knows? You wouldn't pitch me a game about a used-car salesman becoming president—or if you do, it had better blow my socks off!

There are tools in this book, such as the Hook Evaluator, to make sure you are on to something that will be interesting. My advice is to be your own filter, taste your own food...test your ideas on people who are *not* your friends and family. Get clear about where your focus needs to go and really pour your effort into it. Be realistic, too. Don't assume your idea is great; be sure other people do, too—people who understand games, presumably not the waitress at the local bar and grill. Reread this chapter and be sure you've got everything you need, then go and present your idea.

And if the first person you pitch it to rejects it, don't give up. Ask why he rejected it and learn from the response. Perhaps the idea is great but doesn't fit his plan. Perhaps there's something you're missing but it can be fixed, and he might be nice enough to set you straight. Don't be angry or dejected by rejection—be curious.

Elements of a Game Design Submission

A good game design submission should come with enough material to give the potential publisher a chance to say yes. You want to give them enough material to impress them and make them want more. But how much is enough, and how much is too much? It's best to have a very strong but easily digested initial pitch with supporting materials, but have something in reserve. If you can get them hooked and they want to see more, then it's good to have more to offer. However, what you bring initially should be well presented and organized, easy to read and view, and a very good representation of what makes your game special and unique. If you have any part of the game in a playable or demo stage, it will help immensely.

Every submission, particularly one that is not part of an in-person pitch, should ideally have:

- A pitch sheet—essentially a one-page executive summary of the project, detailing the main points.
- A design document or treatment, preferably with:
  - Summary page(s)
  - A full treatment of the game and its elements
  - Multiplayer and online strategies
  - Supporting graphics
  - Market/demographic and comparative analysis
  - Plans for sequels
  - Technical design
  - Team/personnel list
  - Well-thought-out milestones
  - Budget
- Something that shows your progress—preferably a CD ROM or cartridge of the game at some stage of completion, whether it is only one level or a technology demo, a full alpha, or even the complete game.
- If necessary, a clear instruction sheet to be sure they can get the demo up and running. Possibly also include some notes to help them discover those features of your game that you most want them to see.

Design Challenge

1. Take one or more games you like and consider how you would pitch each of them.
   a. Write a 45-second elevator speech and a brief summary for each one, emphasizing those qualities that make the games you like successful. For instance, imagine you were pitching *Diablo II*, or *The Sims*, or *Grand Theft Auto III*, or *EverQuest*.... You get the point.
   b. Write a summary page. How could you summarize the games you like? Be succinct. Remember, you need to grab the publisher's attention and keep it. The longer your pitch goes, the more risk you'll lose them, unless they are the ones prolonging it.
   c. If you want, pick one game and actually develop a complete pitch for it.

2. Now pick a game you would like to pitch. Check your concept/design against the lists in this chapter. If you want, go through the other chapters in this book for more ideas and ways to expand, refine, or improve your game. Depending on the type of game you want to create, almost any of the chapters in this book might have useful information.
   a. Create a summary of your game. Be sure to make the summary very succinct, focusing on the most compelling and original aspects of your game. Be sure to include at least one hook, and be sure to identify the game well enough so that someone reading the summary a) can identify what you're proposing to do, and b) will want to know more.
   b. Create a 45-second elevator speech for the game. The summary can help.
   c. Create a whole game submission, including the summary, a full treatment of the game, and so on.
   d. After you have created a submission for your game, look it over. Is there anything else you can do to improve it? Can you shorten it? Does it cover all the elements of the game and the project that it needs to?
   e. Imagine a publisher asking you tough, realistic questions about the game. Be prepared with answers about the following subjects:
      - The market/demographic for the game
      - The budget
      - The team
      - The schedule and milestones
      - The technology
      - Sequels
      - Online and multiplayer aspects
      - Why this game will stand out from the crowd
      - What kind of deal you're looking for
   f. Have someone pretend to be the publisher and go through the pitch with them. Practice your presentation so that it is clear, concise, and informative. It should be confident without being too cocky, though this may depend on who you pitch to. Not every style of presentation will work the same for every publisher.

3. If you can, obtain some game submissions from other designers and look at how other people have approached their game pitches. And if you can, look at some that have resulted in successful games.

Getting Work in the Game Industry

As some of you know, I've spent a lot of time helping people get jobs in the game industry. I even created a massive project—Project: Top Secret—that allowed a community of game players to design their own game. This book is about game design, so I'm not going to go into detail on how to get a job in the industry, but I can offer a little advice.

First, check out the DP Challenge and other articles on www.dpfiles.com. Also (and here's my little tip), did you realize that it's a lot harder to get to a Hollywood executive producer, such as Joel Silver, than it is to get to just about any executive in the game industry? So far, most of them don't have executive assistants to run interference, so you can just pick up the phone and call them, find them on a social network, or get their email from the company website.

So feel free to send your job application to HR. But if you want to jump the line, choose the executive producer, game director, or creative director who is working on the team you want to work on. Don't send him a job application, send him a flattering letter and casually mention what you do, then have a website (which should be slick and professional) and have your resume right there. If it's a cool letter, then he is likely to go check out your site and see who you are. So you are streets ahead of being in the HR pile, which, of course, you can be anyway.

Also, when you apply these days, tidy up your MySpace, Facebook, Twitter, and blog. If someone goes looking for you and you look like a freak or obviously party like a freak, they're likely to just close their browser and go back to work.

Here's a simple example of a letter that might get someone's attention:

> Hi Rob,
>
> I'm a major fan of your games, and I hope you don't mind that I'm writing to you directly. I'm personally heavily into game design research (what the hit games have in common), especially game design deconstruction (what the actual elements are that made the difference), so it's my goal to really study all the game mechanics that have had a long-term impact on the game industry. Several, like the Sniper Rifle idea we first saw in your game *MDK*, ended up getting used in hundreds of games. So I just wanted to say I respect your work and the impact you are having on the industry; I hope to have the same kind of impact on design someday. In the meantime, if you ever need someone to do some research for you, I'd be more than happy to for free. I'm also very interested in game balancing and have started writing a book on the subject. If you ever need someone fresh to give you direct feedback, I'd be happy to help. Anyway, my name is Bob Smith (www.xxxxxBobSmithxxxx.com).
>
> Thanks for taking the time to read this and I look forward to *MDK 3* to see what your team comes up with next! Also, I've studied some design ideas from Asian titles that I've not seen done here in the West. If you would like me to forward those, I'd be happy to.
>
> Warmest regards,
> Bob Smith

5 Game POV and Game Genres

Categorizing games is complex because they are often seen both by the type of game and by the way we view it. Before we look at the many ways that games are categorized by genre, let's look at the different visual perspectives—points of view—that are commonly used in games.

This chapter covers:

- POV: How to View the Game
- Basic View Options
- Types of Graphical Views
- Making 2D Games
- Future Game Views
- Visual Styles
- Game Genres

POV: How to View the Game

When you are brainstorming your own games, try changing the point of view of your game and see how that might affect the way it plays. For instance, how different were the original *Prince of Persia* games from the original *Tomb Raider* games? In some ways they were remarkably similar, yet one was a side-scrolling 2D game and the other was a full 3D environment.

Basic View Options

As in written literature, where you have first-person, second-person, and different sorts of third-person perspectives, games also use a viewer perspective. Some games in the early days were text only and were generally set in a second-person "voice," but with graphical games, the perspectives most commonly used are first- and third-person.

- First-person perspective is the direct view as seen from the eyes of your player character.
- Second-person perspective is the view of a character through someone else's eyes.
- Third-person perspective is the view from outside your player character. This is generally a view that follows the character from somewhere behind, above, or above and behind the character.

Types of Graphical Views

There are three major categories of games graphically:

- Text only (no graphics)
- 2D graphics
- 3D graphics

In addition to pure text games, there also used to be games that were essentially text games but with a few still images thrown in, like an illustrated book. This is not a viable format for today's mainstream market; however, for some web-based game experiences, it may still be used on occasion. In addition, technically games can also be in color, black and white, or even some special format, such as solarized or sepia tinted. But variants are also extremely rare, and to use an alternate to color would require a specific stylistic rationale. (For more style options, see the "Visual Styles" section later in this chapter.)

So, within this context, there are several possibilities for each graphical style, as discussed in the following subsections.

2D Graphics

The views with 2D graphics include:

- **Side View.** This is common in platform arcade games, such as many early games including *Defender*, *Load Runner*, *Pitfall*, *Donkey Kong*, and so on. It is also used in puzzle games, such as *Tetris* or *Bubble Bobble*. There are some variations on the side-view perspective, such as the two-player side-view game (early *Street Fighter*, *Pong*, and so on) or the spectator view (*Jordan vs. Bird: One on One*). In addition, some side-view games showed static screens, but later ones added scrolling (becoming known as *side-scrolling* games). Examples include *Double Dragon*, *Final Fight*, *Prince of Persia*, *Earthworm Jim*, and other popular game series, such as *Mega Man* and *Mario*.
- **Top-Down View.** This view has the player looking directly down on the action. It is common in games such as the original versions of *Pac-Man*, *Gauntlet*, *Ultima*, and *The Legend of Zelda: Link's Awakening*. Many board games, such as *Monopoly*, and card games were (and still are) displayed from the top-down perspective.
- **Isometric.** This is a slightly tilted top-down view, which gives an illusion of depth. The most common example is the original *Zaxxon*. Many Role-Playing Games, such as the Game Boy *Pokemon* series, *Diablo*, and *Baldur's Gate* also use isometric graphics.
- **First-Person Fake Perspective.** This views the world from the first-person perspective and uses vanishing-point graphics to create an illusion of depth in a purely 2D environment. It was common in early maze games, such as *Wizardry*. Sometimes these games used color-filled graphics; other times they used wireframe graphics to further the illusion of 3D.
- **Third-Person Fake Perspective.** This is like first-person fake perspective, but you also see your character. One example is the arcade shooter *Tempest*.
- **Cockpit View.** This uses the perspective as seen from within a vehicle, which could be a car, plane, tank, boat, sub, spaceship, and so on. Early examples included *Battlezone*, *Formula One*, *Chuck Yeager's Advanced Flight Trainer*, and early entries in the Microsoft *Flight Simulator* series.

Advanced 2D graphics that try to create the illusion of three dimensions, such as the fake perspective, isometric, and cockpit views, are sometimes referred to as *2.5D*. Games such as *OutRun* (an arcade driving game) and the 1993 game *Stronghold*—a D&D themed city-building game—can be considered 2.5D.

3D Graphics

The views with 3D graphics include:

- **First Person.** This is the view from the player character's perspective, but in a fully realized 3D world. Examples range from *Castle Wolfenstein 3D* to *Doom, Quake, Unreal, Metal Gear Solid, Half-Life/Counter-Strike*, and *Ridge Racer.*
- **Third Person.** Including:
  - **Isometric (Three-Quarter) View.** A view from slightly above the action, such as in *X-COM* and *Diablo.*
  - **Follow Camera.** The camera follows the player character (including vehicles). This is very common in games such as *Tomb Raider, Mario 64, Enter the Matrix*, and so on.
  - **Overhead View.** The player views the action from directly above.
  - **Side View.** The action is seen from the side, as in *Oddworld: Abe's Oddysee* or *Paper Mario.*
- **Variable Camera.** The angle and distance from the player's character is adjustable. Thus, the view can vary between the different types of third-person view or change to first-person view and back. Some games, such as *Grand Theft Auto IV*, even allow for switching between follow camera, isometric, first person, cockpit view, and so on. The variations can be either user-controlled camera or algorithmically controlled.
  - **Player Controlled.** The player can set the angle and distance of the view, relative to the player's character in the game. *Mario 64* and *Dark Age of Camelot* are examples of this technique.
  - **Algorithmic.** The game has programming that can determine the best view based on the environment, presence of enemies, and so on. Examples include *Madden NFL '08, Enter the Matrix*, and so on.
  - **Mixed.** Often in 3D games, the variability of the camera is a mix of algorithmic and player controlled: There is an algorithm for camera position, but there is also a way for the player to override that algorithm and control the camera himself.

Making 2D Games

Most commercial games today are made using 3D technology, even if they use a 2D point of view. The reason is that it's just easier and quicker to model objects and environments using today's 3D tools. In essence, then, a 2D game created with 3D tools is like having a 3D game with a fixed dolly camera. It is entirely possible to create good games with 2D perspectives, but they will probably be created with 3D tools.

Future Game Views

Nobody knows what the future will bring, but we've seen inklings of future points of view. Here are a few ideas to spark your creativity, but don't stop with these suggestions. Think to the future. What is possible? What do you imagine could happen?

- **Virtual Reality.** Total immersion games will tend to use a first-person POV or possibly a variant of third-person. The main difference will be what kind of control the player will have and what kinds of feedback. For instance, turning your head may turn your view. You may be wearing devices that convey physical sensations based on gameplay. In the future, you may even be able to "touch" and "smell" the environment you're in. The ultimate virtual reality, the Star Trek "Holodeck," is probably somewhere far in an imaginary future, but we can dream.

- **In the Real World.** Already people are starting to employ cell phones, personal HUD devices, GPS, video, and other technologies to take games out of arcades and homes and into the streets and office buildings. Games can generate agents who make phone calls and send faxes and otherwise involve themselves in players' non-game lives. Games can also take input from the real world, such as the player's global location, his proximity to a Wi-Fi spot, or the current weather conditions, and incorporate them into the game. Thus, the game is no longer contained in the device that is used to play it; the lines blur as games and reality seem to blend into one continuum.
- **Multi-Screen Viewing.** Games have had split-screen views for multiplayer action for years. Some games have multiple screen views of the same action, even within a single-player game. This kind of viewing could incorporate all viewpoints—first-, second-, and third-person—each in its own window. Or, alternatively, it could display the viewpoints of different characters, as in *Mario Kart* and other multiplayer, multi-screen games.
- **Theater-Screen Viewing.** With TVs getting to wall size these days, playing games in theater environments might become more affordable and common in the average household.
- **Small-Screen Viewing.** With more and more games being played on handheld devices with small screens and resolutions, we're seeing a lot of games that go back to earlier types of views—in particular, the 2D games of the '80s and early '90s. Fitting good games onto small screens is a new challenge, and new ideas may appear to take advantage of these devices—their strengths and their weaknesses. However, the main differences will probably be in design, as opposed to POV. This is changing rapidly, of course, as full 3D technologies are fitted to the small screen, so that many future handheld and telephone mobile games will feature full 3D.
- **HUD Display.** This incorporates viewing the game through some wearable device that allows you to see it without a separate screen, possibly combining reality with the game graphics.

Visual Styles

There are many ways to tell a story, and there are also many ways to present an image. Here are some of the main visual styles that you can use in creating games. Using different styles can convey a specific atmosphere to your game, and using something unique can set a game apart. However, keep in mind that unique visual style with bad gameplay still results in a bad game.

- Cinematic
- Photorealistic
- 2D cartoon graphics
- 3D cel shaded
- Rotoscoped
- Watercolor
- Oil/acrylic paint
- Pen/pencil sketch
- Stylized
- Comic illustration
- Anime
- Black and white with spot colors
- Silhouette/shadow puppet
- Motion blur/tracers
- Solarized
- Primary colors
- Impressionistic
- Mezzotint

Design Challenge

1. Take any of your favorite games and imagine changing the perspective or visual style of them. How would they change? Would it affect gameplay and overall game design?
2. Take one of your own concepts and play with different sorts of views and visual styles. How might these changes affect the game and design? Do you prefer one over another?
3. Look over the lists in this chapter and consider how you might make novel use of different points of view and visual styles. What would happen if you used different styles at different points in your game? What would happen if you changed point of view at different points?

Game Genres

When designing a game, it's often useful to think in terms of game genres, not necessarily to create a game that purely fits a particular genre, but to think in terms of the existing archetypes of computer and video games. Being aware of archetypes is often useful in considering the features and characteristics of a game design. It is clear that over time, game genres begin to borrow from each other, such that RTS games often incorporate RPG-like features, for instance, and RPGs often incorporate features from all kinds of other game genres, ranging from FPS to platform action to puzzle games. Where once the lines were drawn clearly, now they are often blurred as new hybrid genres develop. Still, in essence, there are only a few basic types of games from which all others are developed.

Additionally, much of our taste in entertainment is influenced by the movies, so we might find inspiration for games in the kinds of movies we watch.

This section lists the known universe of game genres. When you break it down, there are a lot of variations. (For some insight into movie genres, check Chapter 10, "Movie Genres."

The earliest games were text adventures, text Role-Playing Games, or arcade action games of one kind of another. As time passed and technology improved, new kinds of games quickly emerged so that, by the mid-'80s, almost every kind of game had appeared in one form or another. Throughout the '90s, many of these genres, such as First-Person Shooters, Real-Time Strategy games, and multiplayer games, were further refined and popularized. Here is a list of every game genre we've seen so far:

Text Games

- Adventure: *Zork*
- RPG: *First Age*
- Sports (stat-based): *Footy Fanatic*
- Online
  - Play-by-email: *Lords of the Earth*
  - MUD: *Scepter of Goth*
  - Wordplay: *Boggle*
  - Social: *Clandestine*
- Text-based graphic adventure (2D or 3D): *NewAge*

Action

- Beat-em-up
    - Traditional: *Kung-Fu Master*
    - Hack 'n slash: *Devil May Cry*
    - Fighting (including head-to-head, platform, exploration, side-scrolling, and story-based)
        - 2D: *Mortal Kombat*
        - 3D: *Tekken*
- Wrestling: *WWF WrestleMania 2000*
- General: *Super Smash Bros. Brawl*
    - 2D: *Karateka*
    - 3D: *Mortal Kombat: Shaolin Monks*

Shooter

- First-person
    - Fantasy: *Turok*
    - Historic: *Battlefield: 1942*
    - Modern: *Call of Duty 4: Modern Warfare*
    - Sci-fi: *Halo: Combat Evolved*
    - Horror: *Doom*
    - Tactical: *Tom Clancy's Rainbow Six: Vegas*
- Light gun: *Super Mario Bros., Duck Hunt*
- Rail: *Star Fox 64*
- Scrolling: *Gradius*
- Third person
    - Fantasy: *Tomb Raider*
    - Historic: *Medal of Honor*
    - Modern: *Gears of War*
    - Sci-fi: *Star Wars: Battlefront*
    - Tactical: *SOCOM: U.S. Navy SEALs*
    - Arcade (follow cam, overhead, or isometric views): *Ikari Warriors*

Action Adventure

- Fantasy: *Prince of Persia: The Sands of Time*
- Horror: *The House of the Dead*
- Modern: *Grand Theft Auto III*
- Sci-fi: *Tom Clancy's Splinter Cell*

Adventure

- First-person: *Fahrenheit*
- General: *Blade Runner*
- Horror: *Resident Evil*
- Text: *Zork: Grand Inquisitor*
- Third-person: *Indiana Jones and the Emperor's Tomb*

Driving

- Car combat: *Twisted Metal: Black*
- Demolition derby: *Ultimate Demolition Derby*
- General: *Juiced*
- Mission-based: *Cars*
- Racing
    - Gran Turismo: *Gran Turismo 3: A-Spec*
    - Arcade: *OutRun*
    - Drag: *Hot Rod: American Street Drag*
    - Formula One: *Grand Prix Legends*
    - Futuristic: *F-Zero*
    - GT/street: *GT Legends*
    - Kart: *Mario Kart 64*
    - Motorcycle: *MotoGP 2*
        - Motocross: *Motocross Madness*
        - Street: *Midnight Club: Los Angeles*
        - Combat racing: *Road Rash*
    - On foot: *Hyper Sports*
    - Other: *The Simpsons: Hit & Run*
    - Space: *Wipeout Pure*
    - Rally/off-road: *Colin McRae Rally 2005*
    - Snow/water: *Splashdown*
    - Stock car: *NASCAR 07*
    - Truck: *Monster Truck Madness*

Role-Playing

- Action RPG: *Diablo, The Legend of Zelda, Secret of Mana*
- Console-style RPG: *Final Fantasy* series
- First-person: *The Elder Scrolls III: Morrowind*
- Turn-based: *Final Fantasy Tactics, Shining Force: The Legacy of Great Intention, X-COM*
- Massively multiplayer online: *EverQuest*
- Fantasy: *World of Warcraft*
- Modern: *Hellgate: London*
- Sci-fi: *RF Online*

Multiplayer Games (small scale or massive multiplayer)

- RPG: *Baldur's Gate*
- RTS: *StarCraft*
- Shooter: *Counter-Strike: Source*
- Board games: *Monopoly*
- Card games: *Bridge*
- Social: *Second Life* (arguably not a game)

Simulation

- Civilian plane: *Microsoft Flight Simulator 2002* (Standard)
- Helicopter: *RC Helicopter*
- Modern jet: *X-Plane*
- WWI: *Medal of Honor: Allied Assault*
- WWII: *IL-2 Sturmovik*
- Sci-fi
  - Futuristic jet: *Wing Commander*
  - Futuristic sub: *Submarine Titans*
  - Mech: *MechWarrior 2: 31st Century Combat*
  - Spaceships (large and small): *Microsoft Space Simulator*
- Ship: *Ship Simulator 2008*
- Submarine: *Silent Hunter III*
- Tank: *M1 Tank Platoon*
- Train: *Microsoft Train Simulator*
- Pinball: *Pinball Hall of Fame: The Williams Collection*
- Social and artificial life: *Spore*
- Commerce: *Big Biz Tycoon!*
- Spaceflight: *Microsoft Space Simulator*
- Boat racing: *Extreme River Boat Racing*
- War
  - Infantry: *Brothers in Arms: Road to Hill 30*
  - Tank: *Panzer General*
  - Helicopter: *Comanche 3*
  - Modern jet: *Ace Combat 5: The Unsung War*
  - WWI: *Red Baron*
  - WWII: *Microsoft Combat Flight Simulator 2: WW II Pacific Theater*
  - Future: *FreeSpace 2*
  - Naval: *Ship Simulator 2008*
  - Submarine: *Battlestations Midway*
  - Battlefield: *Battlefield: 1942*

God Games

- *Populous* (the original)

Sports (including text/stat-based, simulation, and arcade sports games)

- Biking: *Dave Mirra Freestyle BMX 3*
- Bowling: *Super Bowling* (for Nintendo 64)
- Cricket: *Cricket 2005*
- Futuristic: *PSX Pitball*
- Rugby: *Rugby 08*
- Skateboarding: *Tony Hawk's Pro Skater*
- Ice skating: *Michelle Kwan Figure Skating*
- Snowboarding: *Amped: Freestyle Snowboarding*
- Surfing: *Transworld Surf*
- Wakeboarding: *Wakeboarding Unleashed*
- Fishing: *Sega Bass Fishing*

- Hunting: *Ultimate Duck Hunting*
- Table tennis: *Rockstar Games Presents Table Tennis*
- Baseball
  - Arcade: *Baseball Stars*
  - Management: *Baseball Mogul 2009*
  - Sim: *MLB 08: The Show*
  - Stats: *Out of the Park Baseball 9*
- Basketball
  - Arcade: *NBA Jam*
  - Management: *World Basketball Manager*
  - Sim: *NBA 2K2*
- Boxing: *Knockout Kings*
- American football
  - Arcade: *Madden NFL Season 2* arcade machine from Global VR
  - Management: *Fantasy Football Draft Edge*
  - Sim: *Madden NFL 08*
  - Stats: *Action! PC Football*
- Wrestling: *WWE WrestleMania 21*
- Golf
  - Arcade: *Golden Tee*
  - Sim: *Tiger Woods PGA Tour 08*
- Ice hockey
  - Arcade: *Wayne Gretzky's 3D Hockey '98*
  - Management: *NHL Eastside Hockey Manager 2007*
  - Sim: *NHL 08*
- Soccer
  - Arcade: *World Cup 90: Arcade Soccer*
  - Management: *Worldwide Soccer Manager 2008*
  - Sim: *FIFA Soccer 08*
- Tennis: *Top Spin*
- Volleyball: *Outlaw Volleyball: Spike or Die*

Strategy

- Breeding/constructing: *Theme Park*
- City building
  - Historic: *Glory of the Roman Empire*
  - Modern: *Tycoon City: New York*
  - Futuristic: *SimCity 3000 Unlimited*
- Real-time
  - Fantasy: *Warcraft: Orcs & Humans*
  - Historic: *Age of Empires II: The Age of Kings*
  - Military: *Command & Conquer*
  - Modern: *Age of Empires III*
  - Sci-fi: *Earth 2140*
- Turn-based
  - Fantasy: *Disciples: Sacred Lands*
  - Historic: *Civilization*

- Modern: *Axis & Allies*
- Sci-fi: *X-COM*
- Mission-based: *WarCraft III*
- Online: *Mankind*

War Game

- Real-time: *Metal Gear Solid 4: Guns of the Patriots*
- Turn-based: *Advance Wars: Days of Ruin*
- Board (statistical): *Risk*
- Online multiplayer: *Call of Duty 4: Modern Warfare*
- Modern warfare: *Call of Duty 4: Modern Warfare*
- Historical: *Medal of Honor: Airborne*
- Horror: *F.E.A.R.: First Encounter Assault Recon*
- Fantasy: *Half-Life*
- Space: *Star Wars: Empire at War*
- Air combat: *Ace Combat 6: Fires of Liberation*
- Naval combat: *Silent Hunter 4: Wolves of the Pacific*
- Strategic: *Tom Clancy's Rainbow Six: Lockdown*

Other Game Genres

- Tycoon: *SimCity*
- Board games/card games (traditional): *Monopoly*
- Card battle: *Magic: The Gathering*
- Music maker: *Elite Beat Agents*
- Billiards/pool: *Pool Party*
- Gambling: *Texas Hold 'Em*
- Pinball: *Dream Pinball 3D*
- Party: *Mario Party*
- Puzzle: *Tetris*
- Rhythm: *Guitar Hero*
- Dancing: *Dance Dance Revolution Extreme*
- Trivia/game show: *Jeopardy!*
- Virtual life: *The Sims 2*

Design Challenge

1. Using the list of game genres, test out some combinations. For instance, how about a snowboarding soccer game? Or a breeding section in a futuristic crime thriller game?
2. In what ways can you consider these typical genres and create less-than-typical games?
3. Take a normally serious game genre and add humor to it. (See also Chapter 9, "Storytelling Techniques," and the section called "Creating Comedy.")
4. Invent a genre that hasn't been created yet. You can be the first!

For more ideas, see Chapter 2, "Brainstorming and Research."

6 Business Models

Welcome to a new and constantly changing world. No, I'm not talking about the latest persistent world. I'm talking about the world of game monetization—in other words, how we make money from games. You may still be thinking that we make all our money from retail sales, selling box products in brick-and-mortar stores such as GameStop and Virgin Megastore. You may also be aware that online retail outlets, such as Amazon, EBGames, and others are increasing in market share. But change is coming, and you can't rely on the boxes and jewel cases forever. It's time to prepare for the future.

In the long term, digital distribution is going to dominate the game sales landscape. Good examples are the online stores of Microsoft, Nintendo, and Sony. In addition, there are the direct-to-consumer services on PCs, such as Valve Software's SteamPowered.com and IGN's Direct2Drive. These services offer direct downloads, or unlocking codes for games already on their services. Another good example is the application store on the iPhone/iPod Touch from Apple, showing not only how to do it, but how to make it profitable.

Digital distribution is just the beginning, however. What interests me the most is how many different ways we can monetize our products. Personally, I'm trying to learn as much as I can about free-to-play games because by massively increasing the number of players you get (removing the up-front cost), there are many ways to make money later, such as through microtransactions, premium packages, and even from outside sources, such as advertisers and sponsors.

Before addressing different monetization methods, however, let's admit that not all strategies will be popular with all players. Change always faces resistance, so it's not surprising that some players will complain about new ways to make money, but in the end they will play and grow accustomed to the changes—if they work. Some will fall by the wayside as we discover, perhaps, that they don't actually work, but change is happening already, and Sony's decision to incorporate microtransactions into their games is just another indicator that game companies are aware of the new options available to them and anxious to take advantage of those that work.

While writing this, I'm just waiting for Apple and Facebook to announce their microtransaction strategies, so developers that make games or widgets can assess "pay as you go" charges to the users of the applications. I don't know if Apple and Facebook will do this; I just think they'd be crazy not to!

Giving it some thought, it's not too hard to come up with a few ways to monetize games, other than the usual box products and digital distribution methods most common today. This chapter covers some of them:

- In-Game Advertising
- Around-Game Advertising
- Finder's Fee from First Dollar
- Advert-Games/Advergaming/Re-Dressed Games
- Try before You Buy
- Episodic Entertainment/Expansion Packs
- Buy the Win
- Insurance
- Financing
- Velvet Rope or Member's Club
- Subscription
- Support Tiers
- Become a "Brand Member"
- In-Game Stores and Microtransactions

- Selling Consumables
- Skill-Based Progressive Jackpots
- Player-to-Player Wagering and Item Sales/Trades
- Pay Players to Meet a Challenge
- Charityware
- Sponsored Games/Donationware
- Pay per Play/Pay as You Go/Pay for Time
- Player-to-Player Trading/Auctions
- Foreign Distribution Deals
- Sell Player Access/Co-Registration Offers
- Freeware
- Loss Leaders
- Peripheral Enticement
- User-Generated Content
- Pay for Storage Space
- Host a Private Game Server
- Rentals
- Licensing
- Sell Branded Physical Items
- Pre-Sell a Game to Its Players
- Before-Game Advertising
- Virtual Item Sponsorship
- Add Download Insurance
- Feed Me or I Die!
- Methods of Avoiding Buyer's Regret

In-Game Advertising

There are essentially two kinds of in-game advertising: banner ads (of various shapes and sizes) and product placement. Banner ads can be placed strategically in some games, although this works best in free-to-play games, where the players understand that the publisher needs to make money somehow, and it's only a minor distraction. At Acclaim Games, we did an experiment in our *2Moons* game where we included banner ads but gave players the option to turn them off. Keeping the ads on gave them a small experience boost, however, and the vast majority of players (96 percent) left the ad banners on.

Hollywood has used product placement for years. Every time you see a Coke or a Macintosh laptop in a movie, someone's making a little extra dough. Why not in games? Why not, indeed, as it's already happening (for instance, certain clothing, sunglasses, or vehicles you'll see in *Gaia Online*). You can go even further with this idea by putting paid advertising directly into your story. One clear example occurred in the *Lonelygirl15* series on YouTube, in which it just so happened that her "scientist friend" worked for Neutrogena. Nice plug. There's no doubt that the money is flowing for in-game advertising, as there are several in-game advertising companies doing good business already, such as Double Fusion, IGA Worldwide, and Massive. These three field leaders are already supplying the advertising inventory images needed to be streamed into the game world.

Around-Game Advertising

Not all game-related advertising has to fit inside the game. In some cases, it can appear around the game—making money from the banner and skyscraper ads around the gameplay window. Around-game advertising is already common on Flash game aggregator sites, such as Kongregate.com, Armor Games, and Crazy Monkey Games, and many others use services such as Google, Commission Junction, or myriad other banner providers. Revenue from banner-type ads is earned using different methods:

- CPM (cost per thousand views)
- CPC (cost per click)
- CPA (cost per acquisition of a player—who actually plays the game)
- CPP (cost per "paying" player who buys something; people generally only want to pay a few cents for clicks but will pay many dollars to gain paying players)

So don't forget the fringes. These ads don't interfere with the game itself, but they do offer advertisers a way to be seen, players a way to find new products and services, and game publishers new ways to take in some cash.

Finder's Fee from First Dollar

You need people to come and play your game, but if you can't afford CPM (cost per thousand views) advertising (where you essentially bet on the effectiveness of someone else's website), don't despair! Even with no money to pay up front, you can offer video game websites either a percentage of net revenue or a "finder's fee from first dollar." As money comes in from a player who's been directed to you from another site, that finder takes all the money until you hit the agreed fee (say $2.00 per player). In reality the finder takes all the risk and will be more aggressive in advertising your property than any campaign you could have paid for at CPM rates. If you balance the numbers, you can get a lot of websites working for you and sending you traffic this way. To make money from this, send your players to non-competitor games for this kind of arrangement.

Advert-Games/Advergaming/Re-Dressed Games

The idea of a game being one big advertisement is not particularly new. One of the early examples I made was the game *Cool Spot*, created in the 1990s as an advergame for 7-UP. Lots of people bought and played it without being overly concerned by its advertising message. The reason *Cool Spot* was successful as an advergame was because it was successful as a game, and it would have been even if the red 7-UP spot had simply been a red disk with no affiliation. It did get some added publicity because of its product ties, but making a playable game certainly enhances the idea of promoting a product through a game. More recently, the U.S. Army created *America's Army* as a recruiting tool, but once again, the game is actually very well done, so it stands on its own merits.

Not every advergame is going to be particularly original or good, but in some cases, such as the Flash games you find on company websites these days, the quality or originality doesn't matter. If it's just another clone of *Bejeweled*, such as *Bewitched*, made for the Sony Pictures feature of the same name (get.games.yahoo.com/proddesc?gamekey=bewitched) by the Blitz Agency, it's still fun to play and gets its message across for a relatively affordable price. Advergames don't appear only on PCs, either, as evidenced by the *Burger King* games on the Xbox 360. Although the advertiser helps fund the game, your reputation as a developer, publisher, or designer determines how much cash you can ask for.

Finally, it's not always necessary to create a new game. If you have something that can be repurposed for an advertiser, it's often very quick and easy to modify some assets and provide a specific custom version of an existing game to serve an advertiser's purpose and leverage your product catalog, sort of like those companies that put your logo on a pen or a fridge magnet. Okay, maybe it's not quite that simple, but you get the point.

Try before You Buy

It's called *trialware*, *shareware*, *demoware*, or *timedware*, and the point of all these "wares" is to let you play a crippled, truncated, or a time-restricted version of a game free of charge—the goal being to up-sell the full version. Various try-before-you-buy strategies have their challenges. How much of the game do you offer? Too much, and you may kill the future sale of the full version. Too little or the wrong content, and you may give the prospective purchaser the wrong impression of the product and once again lose a sale.

Xbox Live seems to have hit on a pretty good formula: Offer one complete level and end with a cliffhanger. For instance, just as you are getting really into it, you find out there's a major encounter straight ahead, and then you're told, "Buy the full version to continue!" Of course, if you've gotten hooked, you're going to want to "turn the next page," so to speak.

Episodic Entertainment/Expansion Packs

People have been talking about episodic games for years, but only in the past few years has the concept become a viable reality. In part, that's because persistent-world games, such as *EverQuest,* have established the "expansion pack" concept, which keeps the game world expanding and growing and not only sells more box products or per-pay downloads, but also extends subscriptions and generates new ones. A few companies, such as Telltale Games, have adopted episodic games as their primary model, initially with their *Bone* series, followed up by the *Sam & Max* and *Strong Bad* series of episodic games. While episodic content began with literature and was adopted quickly in movie theaters (with serials), then moved on to radio and TV, it has taken some time to become popular in the game industry. However, some companies are finding that "chapter-based" episodic content, in the form of true episodes of an ongoing tale or as expansion packs that add content and gameplay without remaking the entire game, are viable ways to increase cash flow, reuse engine technology, and leverage properties.

Buy the Win

This is the trick used on auction sites such as www.swoopo.com. What happens is that you sell items for a fraction of their value to the winner of an auction process, but (here's the important part) players must pay to bid for the item. So, let's say the purchase price starts at 1 cent. Imagine there's a timer counting down 10 seconds, then you enter your bid, and that bid costs you 25 cents. The purchase price of the item goes up another cent, and because you entered a bid, the clock adds on 15 seconds (or some amount), and the process repeats. Then someone else bids, the clock goes up, the bid goes up 1 cent, they pay 25 cents...and this keeps happening until the time runs out because there are no new bids, and someone is the last bidder. This way you can have 100 people paying you for the same item or experience that only one person will win. If you take the time to do the math, you'll see that you can make a ton of money doing this, and if the winner just joined the auction, maybe they just bought the item for 25 cents (for the bid) plus the final price (commonly a fraction of the real price). Say the item was normally $10. You (the company) ended up selling it for $3. However, to get to $3 one cent at a time is 300 bids. So you made 300 $\times$ 0.25 = $75 for the item. It might sound crazy, but that's how Swoopo works.

Insurance

Think of games like regular items sold in stores. What do stores do to add incremental revenue? One thing they do is offer you on-the-spot warranties. "Sir, what if this hard drive was to fail? We'd replace it free of charge if you pay now." How might this be used in games? As one example, perhaps many online games could offer anti-hacking insurance (so you *never* lose virtual items from hacking). I've never seen this, but the idea of this section is to think about *all* the possible monetization methods. So please don't shoot the messenger (if you hate insurance salespeople). You would also need to be careful with the word "insurance," because if you enter the domain of "real" insurance, that space is highly regulated. So for this one, legal advice is strongly recommended.

Financing

Again, just an idea I've never seen, but in plenty of sales situations, if you can't afford what you want (and you are impatient), there's often some kind of financing plan, where you end up paying interest on the deferred payments. In the game world, this could be a lot less complex, as there could just be an extra cost if the buyer pays later. Fraud will be a major issue (but if the items the person buys are virtual, the loss isn't as significant as in the real world), and it would be prudent to seek legal advice on this one, too. But for now, it's just food for thought. What other retail "tricks" are used to get people to pay more than they were planning to?

Velvet Rope or Member's Club

There is always a free area, but there's also a "members only" or VIP level of access that offers special privileges, access to special areas on your site or in your games, or even special cosmetic items, price discounts, and so on. VIPs may get access to certain products or updates before non-VIPs. The idea is to offer special perks to your "members," who have paid a premium. In a variant of this concept, you may even empower your VIP members with special in-game abilities. For instance, a VIP player might have access to special areas of the game and could "invite" non-VIPs, but for a fee or for a limited time.

Subscription

Of course, the subscription model is the original online gaming model, first established with *Ultima Online* and then followed by most of the major MMOs, up through *World of Warcraft* and, more recently, *Age of Conan* and *Warhammer Online*. When you sign up to play these games, you also agree to pay a monthly charge, usually by credit card or automatic debit payment. You may also be able to purchase game cards in retail outlets or other places that have specific codes to unlock the service for a designated time period. Subscription games are often coupled with retail box products, which offer additional resources, such as maps, CDs or DVDs with all the installation files, a printed manual, and sometimes collectible items or special promotions. Since most subscription models allow players to set up an account that pays automatically from a credit card, companies often get paid by people who have stopped playing but didn't cancel their subscription. From a company's point of view, it's not a bad deal to get paid by people who aren't even playing and using bandwidth or requiring support. Some companies that maintain multiple online games offer special subscriptions that allow players to play some or all of their games, such as with Sony Online Entertainment's Station Pass.

Support Tiers

This is where you offer different levels of support and charge. Basic support is free, but "front of the line" support costs money. It's a bit like my last trip to Universal Studios. They offer "front of the line" passes if you pay a little more. There's a certain percentage of people in society who are incredibly impatient (like me), and they will fork over the cash just to save time. So money can actually be made from your customer support. (Again, don't be mad at me if you hate customer support systems; I'm just talking about monetization methods here!)

Become a "Brand Member"

Just so this doesn't cause confusion, this doesn't mean VIP service, nor does it mean subscribing or anything like that. This is where you join a membership in the publishing company, not any specific game. It's like buying an "EA Sports Backstage Pass"—now you are just super-special to EA, as you've paid money to them that you really didn't need to. So they will get creative to find ways to say thanks! Again, a certain percentage of people just don't want to miss out on anything, and if they were *not* a member, they would actually be missing out on cool stuff.

What could you offer to people who pay just to be in the "inner circle" with your brand? American Express charges $5,000 to get their Black Card, and once you have it, you know you're getting 100 percent of all the credit card services they offer. The mistake American Express makes is that they have made a VIP program, not a *brand* program. So the people who would pay even more for "Brand Member" status would want to know that for *everything* American Express does today *and* in the future, they will be invited to without question. For example, say they make a new "super-duper diamond card." This person wants to be in the front of the line to get one. Say they sponsor a Formula One race; this person wants to be invited as a guest of American Express. The TED.com conference has a special $10,000 contribution you can make, which lets you get into the room before everyone else to get a killer seat. For a certain percentage of people, that's totally worth it, but again, that's a VIP feature. "For the opening night of the conference, want to join us for dinner tonight with the founders of Google?"—that's the invite everyone else doesn't get, so now the brand loyalty kicks in. You get the point. The Brand Members become people you need to think about when anything special is happening.

In-Game Stores and Microtransactions

Recently, especially in free-to-play games and console titles, the in-game store has become more and more common. These virtual stores allow players to make various kinds of purchases (using real money), generally for small, impulse-driven purchases. Items in in-game stores are often vanity items (such as cool ornamental gear), extra levels, time savers, special items for better communication options, special buffs and boosts (such as an item that temporarily boosts the amount of experience you gain), or maybe song packs for music-based games. In games that offer optional advertising, the in-game store may offer a special 30-day item for turning off advertising. Some sort of special points or value system (earned in the game or paid for with real money) is generally the currency used for making such microtransactions.

Selling Consumables

A specific category of microtransactions is the sales of consumable items, such as potions and ammunition, a virtual birthday card for another player, or maybe even the virtual gas you need to drive a car. Just like in the real world, it's okay to offer price levels too, so if you want the "high-octane sports-car gas," it costs more. If you want to really focus on the fact your game is *free*, you can also make the consumable items available in the game through ordinary gameplay (earned by playing). In addition, you might offer some special variants, such as auto-potions that automatically refresh health or energy when it drops below a certain level, special tracer or armor-piercing bullets, or maybe magic paint that you can put on armor that strengthens it for some time. These items might be rare in the game, but, though very useful, they are not required to succeed. Purchasing them might be a quicker/easier way to get them, and the advantage they confer on the player may be worth that small payment. They aren't the most valuable of virtual items, so they don't necessarily upset players in free-to-play games. Of course, to find out if this strategy works, you should check with your players, as different game communities will respond differently to certain monetization strategies. The good news (for the developer that sells consumables) is that because players keep re-buying the same item(s), it stops the developer from having to make a ton of different items to keep the players happy. That said, the basic caveat is that whatever you sell in-game (as a consumable) should never be anything the player *has to buy* to succeed. There must always be another way to get it for free.

Skill-Based Progressive Jackpots

Players buy a ticket to enter a virtual tournament, which generates a virtual jackpot, and the winner is determined by the criteria of the tournament. Of course, the developer keeps a percentage of the jackpot. For this to be legal (according to current international gambling laws), the tournament must be skill based. Two skill-based prize sites are www.king.com and www.prizee.com, although you can also create a skill-based progressive jackpot based around your own game property, either as a mini-game or an additional web game for a larger game property, or as a game in itself. The warning here is that when there are real prizes to be won, you can expect people to try to cheat, so you will need your cheat detection strategy in place when you launch. In my experience (I made a game called *Prize Potato* for Facebook), I've seen people cheat to win, even when it's easier to just play the game! Meaning, they'll work harder to cheat because they enjoy knowing they beat the system. So don't assume that because cheating is tough, people won't bother. We stopped the cheating, but it's important that you know you will have to!

Player-to-Player Wagering and Item Sales/Trades

Again, players can engage in optional wagering before certain events, such as duels or guild battles, or even in certain types of missions and quests. The winner gets the spoils, but the "house" (the game publisher) gets a cut. This option is subject to the same conditions as the skill-based progressive jackpots model in that it also must be skill based. In place of money (or the game equivalent), players may wager with virtual items, as well as buy/sell or trade them. Although the publisher has made their money on these items already, there are ways to make the items ultimately obsolete, so that they no longer occupy a place in the economy, freeing the way for new purchases. This can be accomplished by making the item untradeable or by having it lose its qualities over time, such as a sword that started out as a +3 and gradually becomes an ordinary sword with no enhancements, perhaps losing value as it is used or with each trade. To prevent other items from being used as part of the in-game economy, developers may cause them to be "bound" to the user once they are equipped, preventing them from being sold to any other player.

Pay Players to Meet a Challenge

Some games will now offer you money to accomplish some specific challenge. One game once offered a million dollars to the first person who could verify that they had completed the game. I also saw an offer in a Mafia-style game (www.mafiamob.com) that offered $1,000 (in real money) if players could "Whack a Don" in the game. Of course, you make the task very difficult, but you also build in other revenue sources, such as incremental payments they will make for items, extra turns, or whatever. It may seem as if the game publishers are paying you to play, but in reality, they are extracting money from you in different ways, possibly receiving advertising revenues and collecting on other sources. The game is making enough money to cover those payments, and probably more. Also, the more players the game gets, the bigger the reward can be, which then attracts more hopefuls. With just the right balance, this can be a very successful monetization method.

Charityware

This is when you run your company as a charity or nonprofit. For example, you can form a real video game publishing or development company, but clearly the profits go to charities. Working with major charities can, of course, provide a lot of free and valuable PR. Is this a real business plan? Well, yes. The staff gets paid salaries and bonuses, and down the road (if the business is successful), the owner can sell the nonprofit entity to someone else who wants to merge or take it over.

Sponsored Games/Donationware

Sponsored games literally are games that have been paid for by some entity other than a for-profit game company or investor. Think of something like PBS or National Public Radio. It can literally come down to $5 from here, $5 from there. In practice, this sort of thing is generally applied to what we call "serious games," which are generally games created to teach or to have a specific effect on players and society. Big sources of funding might include individual philanthropists, state or government grants, and so on. If you do get a sponsored game, make sure to include your profit in that development bid!

Pay per Play/Pay as You Go/Pay for Time

This is a pretty tried-and-true model, much like that of the old arcade and pinball machines. Players pay only for a specific experience, which might be defined as a limited time period or a specific number of lives, or just a session that lasts until they fail (such as the old *Missile Command*). This model is also used in some Internet cafes and game parlors where they sell computer time.

Player-to-Player Trading/Auctions

Some games and online worlds now allow players to trade land, property, characters, or items with other players—one on one, through in-game options, or even through external websites, with the publisher taking a cut of all money exchanged. By officially sanctioning and monitoring these exchanges, you also keep players safe from fraud and other pitfalls of the black market. There are even games that allow game money to be converted to real money, which can result in people making a lot of money in the real world, but can also open the door to various kinds of fraud, such as using fake credit cards or stealing personal information (phishing) to use in the transactions. Companies such as Live Gamer (www.livegamer.com) are trying to make this safer for players.

Foreign Distribution Deals

If you are seeking more development money, you can pre-sell foreign distribution rights to your game and use that to fund your project. It might work like this: You take advances from Russia, Asia, and Europe to fund a title you plan to release in the U.S. (where you own the rights). Once the game is successful in your primary market, you'll be able to expand it to other markets. You can save a lot of money, and you own the IP rights to whatever you build, which you'll appreciate if you end up with a hit game.

Sell Player Access/Co-Registration Offers

In effect, you obtain information from your players via a questionnaire or registration form, which you can then sell to an agency that provides the information to external marketing companies. Just Google for "co-registration." In this model, you get paid for each form you provide, and the value of a lead is equal to how exclusive, how revealing, and how fresh the data is. The agency generally provides the questions and the website capture forms.

Freeware

Freeware isn't about making money on the surface, but it's one way to get your game out there, gain a lot of players, and position yourself to field acquisition offers or possibly to get lucrative deals for future games. It works out pretty well if you release something for free, get noticed, put yourself on the map, sell your company, or get hired into a good opportunity—all because you put something out for free.

Loss Leaders

Loss leaders are common in the retail world—in department stores and on car sales lots. Basically, you offer something very cheap to get people to come and shop with you. In the game world, it's often the case that a console system is underpriced because the real money comes from selling the software—the games. For most of us making games, it means that we may sell a game for far less than the market might suggest in order to establish a strong and passionate following. Your loyal players then become resources for other types of monetization, ranging from microtransactions to big-money opportunities, such as toys or TV and movie deals. In reality, you're establishing a brand or recognizable (and trademarkable) characters, which you can then use for other financial purposes. One example is www.KiddieCastle.com, which is doing something like this to get parents and kids to notice their vending machines at airports and theme parks.

Peripheral Enticement

Games can easily monetize through peripheral equipment, such as special guitars for *Guitar Hero* from Activision or *Rock Band* from Electronic Arts, and the Wii Balance Board or other gym equipment (such as virtual bikes or rowing machines) for the Nintendo Wii Fit game. Players will spend money on relatively expensive peripheral equipment if it is a necessary (or extremely desirable) addition to the game experience, which is really just an up-sell.

User-Generated Content

When your users are the content providers, the sky's the limit. This was the genius of *Spore*—that to populate a universe of a million stars, they only had to empower the players to create the content, and there is no end to the creativity. Users can make endless new content, such as buildings, clothing, music, characters, whole planets—whatever you empower them to make. If you also make it possible for players to sell and trade items and you take a small commission from the exchanges, everybody wins.

Pay for Storage Space

In many games, players collect items—generally more than their personal inventory can handle. These items can be weapons and potions in some games, cars (for instance, in *GTA*), or music in a karaoke game, where players might pay to store an instant library of their favorite songs with their customized reverb/volume/lyrics settings. Or, in other types of games, and also referring back to the model for user-generated content, you can sell extra storage space (perhaps in the form of an item from your in-game store—a new backpack, for instance) for players to store all the virtual items they just can't get rid of.

Host a Private Game Server

Think of hardcore players of games such as *Counter-Strike.* They require dedicated servers with very fast response times to get the most out of the experience. So you rent dedicated servers with the gameplay server software preinstalled. This meets the needs of the hardcore players, who can share access with their group of close friends. In such a case, either a guild or an established group may share the expense, or individuals may pony up a share. Of course, anyone can rent a server to enjoy a lag-free game experience with their friends. If your game has such a dedicated following that requires high-quality connections, it can become an up-sell for you.

Rentals

Renting games is another way to make money from your property. When games were first being rented, the idea was to make it so players couldn't complete the game within one rental period, thus increasing the amount of revenue you (and the company renting out the game) received. Now, with such services as Netflix, which don't fix a time limit on the rental, game completion time is not so important, and perhaps the total satisfaction element (money's worth) is more important because you are more likely to get repeat customers if they loved your previous games. Because rental stores often stock the newest titles, they can also drive early sales of your boxed products. You can encourage specific store chains to support your products by making a "special edition" of your game for them to market or by working out special promotions. If you can come up with something special for the rental version of the product that gamers will want, you can encourage more rental revenues and make the rental companies happy at the same time.

Licensing

Licensing a property is a whole different approach, but one that can be very lucrative if you can build a licensable brand or property. For instance, you might be able to ink a deal with a cybercafé chain to unlock your game for their users. I believe https://cafe.steampowered.com offers this service.

Perhaps you can find a way to get your game incorporated in a TV show or let a corporation use your game brand and its "cool factor" to attract their customers. A good example of this is the McDonald's/*Line Rider* ad (www.youtube.com/watch?v=SZw1lCPVbtY).

Sell Branded Physical Items

For instance, use a service such as CafePress to sell T-shirts and branded objects to your fans, or set up a deal with one or more companies that can create ancillary products, such as miniatures or action figures, board games, and collectibles based on your brand.

Pre-Sell a Game to Its Players

In this case, the fans actually pay for the development of the game. For instance, they pay $10 in advance for a $50 game. They get to beta test the game and give feedback before it's launched, and once it is released, they get the game for no additional cost. But you got that $10 per player to help get the game out there. This is only likely to work if you have a fantastic reputation already or an idea or demo that is hot enough to attract people and excite them about the end result. It really helps if you have something to show, to prove that you are legitimately creating the game you are promising. This not only funds your game development, but it also generates good word-of-mouth publicity. This is the kind of game that could have pulled this system off: www.darkfallonline.com.

Before-Game Advertising

Players watch a video ad before playing a free-to-play game. They have to sit through the ad to get to the game, but most players will be a little bit patient if the game is worthwhile. It's a pretty easy way to add to your revenue, and companies such as Game Jacket, Mochi Media, Google, VideoEgg, and Ultramercial can provide lots of advertising inventory. The actual revenue you'll receive is pretty small, however, unless you are driving a lot of traffic, but you can also make a little money by selling players something to turn off the advertising, such as a 30-day item that exempts them from having to sit through the ad. Or, the other way is to make the advertising optional and offer an additional reward for players who opt in to the advertising instead of turning it off. Another relatively new trick is to offer what we call *invisible wrappers.* If the game is played at your website, there's no advertising, but if someone takes the game and puts it on their site (and as of this writing, about 20,000 sites do this), the before-game ad turns on automatically, and, of course, you get revenue for it. Currently, you can find this type of technology at www.inviziads.com.

Virtual Item Sponsorship

Gamers love free stuff, and developers love to make their gamers happy. Why not do so, and at the same time make some bucks? The idea is to get an advertiser to sponsor free items for your players. This can be done in a variety of ways. For instance, a specific item might be won in a contest, and when the player receives it, he also receives a message saying, "This item was provided to you by XYZ Company." Or, perhaps you sell Coca-Cola 500,000 magic potions (that boost a character's energy) at a low cost, and you make the same item very expensive for the gamer to buy on his own. But you hold a special promotion with Coca-Cola, and players receive a pop-up where Coca-Cola offers them the item for free. Really, everybody is happy. The player gets a useful item that would be expensive to buy. Coca-Cola makes the player happy and, at the same time, gets their brand in players' minds, and the publisher of the game gets paid by Coca-Cola to provide the virtual item. It's kind of like making money from nothing, but it's really a matter of achieving a trifecta of mutual benefit.

Add Download Insurance

These days, when you purchase a digital downloaded item, some companies offer you a way to keep that download available past the normal availability period. For a small extra charge—say, $3.95—you can download the file(s) again any time you need to. It's another funky kind of digital insurance policy (mentioned earlier), just in case your drive fails or you lose the data somehow; but it's also a way to make extra money, because you can charge more than the cost of data storage, and you also save customer service time since you won't be getting that phone call: "Uh. My hard drive died. How can I get my product back?"

Feed Me or I Die!

Virtual characters can exert a tremendous, if only partially explicable, hold on players. Once you establish a bond between a player and a pet or other virtual character, you have people who are going to be very reluctant to let that character die or disappear—especially after they've spent uncountable hours nurturing and protecting that creature. There are quite a few ways to monetize this attachment. You can require that players purchase food for the character or items to keep it from becoming despondent. (For instance, in the case of a pet dog, toys and exercise are important, and you can offer special items that increase the dog's happiness.) You could, less creatively, simply charge the player for access to the virtual characters, but this isn't the most desirable method. There are a lot of possible options, other than the few I've just mentioned. You might require virtual visits to virtual doctors to maintain your virtual character's virtual health. You might even introduce virtual diseases into your society (a different kind of computer virus), so that the player must seek out some cure or risk losing the virtual creature. The secret here is not to do these things just to make money, but to realize that it has to be fun, in the sense that nurturing a pet and meeting challenges is fun, and that the cost of upkeep is not extraordinary. So, again, keeping it reasonable, providing free options and "premium" paid options, and making the fun factor first on the list are all good guidelines when considering monetization in the "virtual pet" context. Acclaim has a game called *Ponystars* that does this, and we really are in shock over just how many people seem to want to do this!

Methods of Avoiding Buyer's Regret

Micropayments have become a great way to monetize an online game. Players will purchase items from an online store for use in the game, and though typical purchases are inexpensive, in volume they end up being excellent sources of profit. After all, you're selling virtual objects for real cash, and as long as your players think they're getting real value for their money, everyone is happy.

Okay, what happens when someone buys something they aren't happy with? This can be a problem. You want happy customers. Here are a few suggestions to keep your customers from having buyer's regret.

- **Offer a Cooling-Off Period.** This is similar to gun laws or large-item purchases.
- **Pre-Warning from the Seller.** Let players know before purchasing if it's something they can't use immediately or it requires some preconditions or other items—for example, if they are going to purchase a boat when the lake is dry or a gun when they haven't earned the "shooting" skill.
- **Use Intelligent Pre-Selection.** Make useful suggestions by pre-selecting the "best" options for your virtual customer. This would be similar to the automatic selection of the right golf club in a golf game. For instance, based on the player's level and other stats, perhaps some weapons are out of their current range, so you have the store select something appropriate to their current situation. The player is always free to select something else.
- **Give Free Advice.** Offer some tips on the purchase—something more than the basic stats of the item. For instance, maybe suggest the kinds of situations in which the item might be used.
- **Give Advice for a Price.** Unlike the free advice, this should be more detailed, offering tips that would be hard to discover on your own, such as perhaps special ways to use the item or less-common circumstances in which it might come in handy. For instance, you are buying a shotgun, but all you

know is that it's good for blowing people away. If you find the "gun expert," who offers advice for a small price, he tells you about special walls or items that you can blow away with the shotgun to access extra locations or secret items. Or maybe he even tells you about a specific place where the shotgun can help you accomplish an unusual task.

- **Warning Labels.** If you look closer before buying, the information you need is right there. "Carrying this weapon will make you more attractive to PvP players and will greatly increase the likelihood of you being attacked."
- **By Reputation.** Items get rated by other players, and you can see their reputation before you complete a purchase.
- **Try before You Buy.** You can either get a loan of the item from a friend, or the seller can give you some kind of limited trial. (I saw a cool driving game that did this. You could drive any car just by walking up to it; if you wanted to "own" it, you had to pay.)
- **Demonstrate the Item.** The seller will show you how to use the item.
- **Research Available.** Provide a wealth of research information, including comparisons to similar items, to help players make the right decision.
- **Buy-Back.** Let the player sell back any unused or unwanted items into the game store.

7 Branding

There are two aspects of branding. One occurs when you work with someone else's brand or property. The other occurs when you want to create a brand—such as *Tetris* or *Zelda*—based on your own intellectual property.

In my career I've had quite a few spikes caused by working on licensed properties, such as the Teenage Mutant Ninja Turtles, Disney's Aladdin, Cool Spot (the red dot on 7-Up cans), Global Gladiators for McDonald's, *The Matrix* movie, and so on. What turned out to be really interesting was how the lifecycle of consoles played into the timing of licensing power. When new console hardware ships, so do new franchises, new brands, and commonly new game experiences. Then as the hardware matures, so does the market—we get more sequels, and we get a ton of brands. I gave a speech at GDC once about this and showed the Christmas charts, where *every single* title in the Top 10 was a licensed brand or a sequel of a brand. So just know there's power in branding, as these brands have achieved familiarity with your audience (thanks to massive marketing budgets or being current in society for a long time).

These days, the iPhone market is a great example of the "Wild West," where brands just aren't needed. People are being really creative, and the iPhone platform is so new, popular, and wide open that people will snatch up the creative products that appear on it. That said, later in the lifecycle of the iPhone, when there are 10,000 games available, the products that become brands will start to pop out of the noise. That's the cycle I expect to see.

To test the brand-power theory, I once went to a game store and just stood there and watched the activity of buyers. It was really interesting to see the kids' wandering around the shelves, and, as if little magnets were hidden in the boxes, their hands were attracted to the known brands first.

The worst case I saw was a grandmother offering to buy a game for a kid. The kid said, "I want *Mortal Kombat*" on the Sega Genesis, and the grandmother choked when she saw the price. She said she was really sorry, but she couldn't afford it. She then pulled out *Gunstar Heroes*, a fantastic Sega Genesis game. I smiled, thinking, "Nice job, Grandma!" What happened? The kid refused the game and left the store with the most horrible excuse for a game—a *Mortal Kombat* LCD watch. Okay, I get it. Brands have power.

This chapter covers both types of branding in the following sections:

- Working with Someone Else's Brand
- Picking a Brand
- Creating a Brand
- Qualities of Successfully Branded Properties
- Building Value on a Character Licensed Property

Working with Someone Else's Brand

To begin with, when you negotiate to use someone's brand, you really want to convince them to work with you.

People with brands all want the same things:

- **Safety.** To work with people they perceive as experts.
- **Respect.** To know you'll comply with their rules.
- **Quality.** To know you'll protect the value of their franchise.
- **Confidence.** To know you'll solve any problems they have.
- **Reporting.** To know you'll keep them in the loop on everything.
- **Approvals.** To know they have a final say to keep them legally safe.
- **Help.** To know you'll help when they report to their bosses. (Yes, they have bosses, too.)
- **Understanding.** To know you are patient. *Everything* takes time.
- **Support.** To know you support and love their property.
- **Innovation.** To know that with you, this work is relevant—that you will put your best efforts into making the game fresh and representative of the property.

Picking a Brand

When you decide you want to work with someone's branded property, you will often find it a competitive, demanding, and expensive arena. Table 7.1 provides some guidelines for how these factors will affect your chances.

Table 7.1 Relative Brand Availability

	Cheaper	Expensive
Easier	Popular catchphrases	Bestselling novels
	Games based off another game	Bestselling comic books
	Public-domain properties	Sequels to hit video games
	Parodies of a hit	Games based on a toy
	Expansion packs	Games based on a universe
Difficult	Cult movies	Motion-picture franchises
	Cult TV shows	Hit TV series
	Remakes of classic games	Popular music icons
	Reinventing a property	Big sports franchises

With the previous information in mind, it is also possible to work with licenses in different ways. Here are a few examples of how you might work with a movie license:

- Can't afford a movie license? Use a catchphrase from the movie or spoof it.
- License the logo only, nothing else—not even music! (For example, *Top Gun.*)
- License the movie name/characters, but not story. (The designer writes a new storyline.)
- Build a license. (For example, James Bond: *Everything or Nothing.*)
- Base a game on a key element or event from the movie. (For example, the Hoth battle from *The Empire Strikes Back.*)
- License all the best bits of the movie. (For example, in *The Lord of the Rings*, just the Orcs or the Hobbits.)
- License the whole enchilada plus actors/crew/world.

- Let Hollywood make the game. (To hell with us!)
- Reinvent the license. (For example, *American McGee's Alice.*)
- Make your own game, make your own movie. (For example, *Wing Commander.*)
- Collaborate on a new movie that's being made. (For example, *Gears of War.*)
- Use the game to preview new music for an upcoming CD (a la *Guitar Hero*).
- Have a new movie and a new music album released as a game first.
- License the entire series for one game deal—one seriously potent game (a la *Dirty Harry*).
- Personally acquire the rights to a movie, then do your own deal.
- Have a Hollywood celebrity start a video game team. He or she is your brand.

Creating a Brand

Finding someone else's brand and licensing it can be rewarding, but it carries with it many challenges and risks. In contrast, creating a brand of your own can result in tremendous rewards but requires a combination of factors, including:

- **The Property.** You need a property that can be branded, such as a character (Mario, Mickey Mouse), a series of successful games (*Final Fantasy*), or a killer concept or story (*Diablo*).
- **The Vision.** You need to see clearly what you want to accomplish before you can begin to make it happen. This doesn't mean you know from day one that you are going to create a brand. You might, but you might also be taken by surprise by your success. Being prepared to take advantage of unexpected success is another example of having vision.
- **Partners.** Branding is a multidisciplinary effort, and to successfully establish a brand, you will need marketing, distribution, and possibly ancillary products (such as action figures, collector cards, posters, and so on).

Qualities of Successfully Branded Properties

What makes a property a brand? There's no easy answer to that question, but one way to discover the answer is to take a look at some qualities of successfully branded properties.

- A very entertaining product. (People have lots to talk about.)
- Often a very memorable character (the signature character).
- Superior execution in at least one critical area. (They are known for it!)
- Timing (and flow).
- Cultural relevance. (They are interesting today somehow.)
- Versatility. (They can be used in other ways, such as in games.)
- Uniqueness. (They stand apart from the crowd and are not a clone of something else.)
- Hooks. (See also Chapter 4, "What Publishers Want," and the "Hook Evaluator v3: DP's Forty Questions" section in Chapter 3, "Hooks.")

Some Golden Guidelines from the Toy Industry

Years ago, I discovered this list of guidelines from an executive in the toy industry. I've used its precepts ever since. As with anything, there are different ways to evaluate or understand a complex subject. I encourage you to look at every industry that has branded products. See what you can learn from them, and bring it into your game career.

- The product must be highly differentiated from existing products and must contain unique features.
- It must communicate instantly to the consumer, who should be able to look at it and instantly recognize what it is.
- It must contain important demonstratable features.
- It must be able to make an impact and be newsworthy.
- It must be able to generate incremental sales, independent of existing product sales.
- It must possess significant volume potential with the ability to sell hundreds of thousands of pieces every year.
- It must provide both price and play value to the consumer.
- It should not be a one-shot item, but rather should be extendable into a product line or product extensions.
- It must be compatible with the image of the company.

Examples from video games include:

- ***Doom.*** There is no signature character and no story to speak of, but the game has superior execution, atmospheric setting, lots of action, huge cultural impact, perfect timing (being at the forefront of a new genre), and so on.
- **Mario.** He is the perfect signature character—cute, funny, and versatile. He has far superior execution and staying power.
- ***Star Wars.*** This has everything.
- **Harry Potter.** This is a hot property; repertory characters, magic is fun, it's light-hearted, it has a well-defined fantasy world, there's room for innovation, and it's very adaptable.
- ***South Park.*** This has an inferior animation style, but memorable characters and superior writing/story/cultural relevance—even if it isn't to everyone's taste. Similar is *The Simpsons*, but with better animation and many "guest stars."
- ***Peter Pan.*** This has an engaging and versatile character and memorable supporting characters, an imaginative and timeless storyline, and a wide-open fantasy world.
- ***Charlie's Angels.*** This has a combination of beautiful women, slight absurdity, a campy story/concept, action and potential for multiple storylines, a nostalgia factor, tongue-in-cheek humor—and did I say beautiful women?
- **Dracula/Vampires.** This has recognizable, strong characters, a wealth of literature and lore, and free license/public domain. It's adaptable to just about any setting and even to many genres, from mystery to comedy.

Not so Licensable

SimCity is not as licensable. There are no main characters, no story, and no hook for a story (or at least it's very hard to find one). That said, it's great for conversion to other platforms!

Building Value on a Character Licensed Property

- The licensed property can be expanded from toys to toddlers. Teenage Mutant Ninja Turtles is a good example.
- A property can go from kitchen play sets to food products, such as the Looney Tunes frozen foods and so on.

- Value increases by moving from product licensing to promotional licensing. Think Tom and Jerry promoting Welch's grape juice, Disney's gargoyles on Chef Boyardee meals, Disney's partnering with Burger King, and so on.
- The property can move from frivolous products to helpful products, such as the Flintstones line of vitamin products.
- A licensing property can move from a corporate product line into consumer products. General Motors has been very successful in expanding the use of its trademarks, such as Camaro, Chevrolet, Cadillac, and Corvette, on to consumer products (toy cars, model kits, and so on).
- A fully mature licensing property can move from products to promotions to sponsorships. Disney, the NFL, and Major League Baseball have all moved from products to promotional licensing and now into sponsorship income.
- A property can move from insisting on single-property licensing to joint-venture licensing. (For example, TV teaming up with the NFL, then licensing the combination as if it's a new property.)
- A licensing property can move from the visual or mechanical to the electronic. Carmen Sandiego has moved from software to TV and from TV to electronic games and consumer products. Dora the Explorer is another example.

Design Challenge

1. Think of games that might use some existing property. Think of movies, TV, novels, other games, and popular culture. Evaluate these brands in terms of expense and ease of licensing. A friend of mine did this; he bought the rights to Conan when everyone had forgotten about it, then brought it back from the dead, signing big licensing deals in multiple entertainment media simultaneously.
2. Come up with at least five game concepts that use existing properties that would be cheap and easy to obtain. For example, I wanted to do the Smurfs game because it's incredibly well known but also pretty dead as far as a property goes right now. (The license would not have been expensive.)
3. Come up with a way to use one or more specific movies or TV programs to create a game without having to pay for the whole license. For example, perhaps you just want the rights to the villains in the Disney movies (none of the typical popular characters), or maybe just one villain that they had no plans to promote.
4. Think of some original game concepts that you could turn into a brand—signature characters such as Spider-Man or James Bond, as well as concepts with a lot of depth, such as *The Sims* or *Warcraft*. How would you plan the development of your brand? How would your ideas lead to a branding opportunity?
5. Go back to Chapter 4, "What Publishers Want," and create a hook summary and a 45-second elevator pitch for the best concept you have come up with here.
6. If you like any of your ideas well enough, go ahead and create a full design for it. (We have *plenty* of chapters to help.)

8 Protecting Your Intellectual Property

NOTE

DISCLAIMER: We are not attorneys, and this is not intended to be legal advice. The information in this chapter is simply to give you a basic idea about how to deal with your intellectual properties. After all, if you're going to create the most innovative and original games, you may want to know how to protect your specific creations. However, if you really want to know how to protect yourself, we advise that you find an attorney who specializes in intellectual property and is familiar with the business practices of the games industry, or at least read some books dedicated to the subject. Therefore, we repeat that this chapter is only a bare overview to get you started.

Generally, if you are an independent designer or a small development house, you will be trying to get your projects funded and distributed by a larger publisher. This means making contact and disclosing the details—all the details—of your project to the publisher's agent and possibly to an acquisitions committee. You might also be thinking about releasing your project for free or as shareware, in the hopes of getting other opportunities when people see the quality of your work. In any case, you may want to know what can be protected and how to protect it.

There are various legal means for protecting your work, including trade-secret laws, copyrights, trademarks, and patents. Unless you have created some very specific new technology, you probably won't be dealing with patents, but you could, at various points, be using trade secrets, copyrights, and trademarks.

In this chapter:

- Trade Secrets
- Copyright
- Trademarks

Trade Secrets

Basic protection is available by the very fact that a work is yours and original, and it is unknown to others. A work does not have to be unique or revolutionary to be a trade secret—only a combination that has potential economic value and has not been freely disclosed to others. If it is kept secret, you may have the protection of trade-secret laws. Trade secrets do not expire. As long as the details of your work are kept secret and appropriate steps are taken to limit unrestricted access to, and disclosure of, the information, you may be protected. This means that you cannot allow information about the work to be known by public means, including an overheard conversation, leaking by employees, or a design document carelessly left open or lost, for instance, in an airport or on a train. You must take affirmative steps to maintain the secret nature of your work. Examples of such steps include restricting access to your labs and requiring anyone exposed to your work to sign an adequate NDA. Unless someone has specifically signed a non-disclosure agreement (NDA) agreeing to maintain your information in secret, they have no legal duty to hold information they learn by any means as confidential. So, if you are submitting a document to an outside party, be sure to have them sign an NDA and mark each page of the document "CONFIDENTIAL AND PROPRIETARY" along with the project name and date.

The best protection for trade secrets is to keep them secret, by whatever means you have at your disposal. When it is no longer a secret, it is no longer a trade secret.

An example of a famous trade secret is the formula for Coca-Cola. It is known by only a few people, and it is held in a bank vault. It has never been disclosed since John Pemberton created it in 1886.

COPYRIGHTS

Copyrights can provide powerful protection for your original work, such as a literary, dramatic, musical, or artistic work, but there are limitations. For instance, you cannot copyright an idea, only the expression of the idea. For instance, you could copyright a design document for an auto racing game, but not the idea of an auto racing game. Anyone would be free to develop their own design for an auto racing game, and so long as their design is an original work of authorship, they have rights to their own design. If someone reads your document and writes essentially the same game concept, using elements from your design, their work could be considered a "derivative work" from your design and a copyright infringement. However, even if their design is virtually identical to yours, but they truly had no access to your work, the author of the other design would also be protected as the copyright owner of his or her work. The key concept is that copyright protects the author of an original work of authorship from the moment the work is fixed in a tangible form of expression. Uniqueness is not an element of copyright. Similarly, you can copyright a piece of source code, but someone else could write code to do the same thing, and that would not be an infringement of the copyright unless they had access to your code and their work was based on your work. If they took your code and used it verbatim, or their code was derived from your code, that would be an infringement.

Copyright grants the owner the exclusive right to reproduce the work and distribute it (through sale [transfer of ownership], rent, lease or loan), to make derivative works, and to perform the work or display it.

So long as your work is an original work of authorship fixed in a tangible form of expression, you have an automatic copyright—meaning that you can put a copyright notice next to any original work, such as art assets that accompany your game submission or written source code. One correct form for this notice is:

©(year of creation) (your name)

However, this automatic copyright is not as effective as a registered copyright. It is easy to obtain a copyright. Check at www.copyright.gov for more information. There is a section at copyright.gov for publications and circulars. Check Circular 1, "Copyright Basics," for easy-to–understand, basic information.

If you are an employee and have created something as a "work for hire," then the copyright is owned by your employer unless you have specific terms that grant you copyright to the works you have created under the contract. If you create a work in partnership with others, the copyright naturally becomes co-owned. When working with others, a simple collaboration agreement, laying out ownership of the work product and materials, is always a good idea. When ownership of a copyright is held by more than one person, the rights and responsibilities of each, in connection with the work and each other, are complex.

To qualify for a copyright, your work must be a) original, b) owned by you, and c) at least somewhat creative. Finally, d) it must be something that can be tangibly produced, such as a piece of artwork, a printout of code, or a specific document that can be printed (or recorded).

Not everything can be copyrighted. For instance, you cannot copyright something that has not been made tangible. You can't copyright an improvised speech that wasn't recorded or transcribed. You cannot copyright names, short phrases, slogans, symbols and designs, and so on. You may be able to trademark these items. Also, as mentioned before, you cannot copyright an idea, a method/system/process/concept/principle/discovery, or a device, other than the specific written description of it. For example, you cannot copyright a blank/empty spreadsheet grid. There is no original work of authorship there. Moreover, you cannot copyright something that is entirely assembled from common properties. Some original work must be present, besides merely assembling material from the public domain. An example of this is the copyright notices that appear in reprints of Shakespeare's plays. In nearly every instance, there is an essay from a noted academic explaining the work. It is the essay that is protected by the copyright notice, not the work of Shakespeare. If the play were to be abridged, it is possible the abridgement would represent sufficient original authorship to qualify for a registered copyright—but that would be the call of the copyright office.

Copyrights expire in time. The laws for a work created after January 1, 1978, state that the copyright will last for the lifetime of the author (or the last surviving author) plus 70 years. If a work is anonymous or pseudonymous, and the author's real identity is not associated with the copyright, the term is 95 years from publication or 120 years from the date the work was created—whichever is the shorter period. For copyrights created or published before January 1, 1978, the rules are a bit more complicated, but for the purposes of this book, we'll assume you are working with material created after 1978. More recent laws make the renewal of the original copyright optional, and that copyright automatically extends for works created before the 1978 date.

Note that some items may fall out of copyright but remain trademarked. (See the upcoming "Trademarks" section.)

When you are pitching a concept to a publisher, remember that your ideas are not copyrighted, but your entire design is. If you go in and propose a baseball game, the idea of a baseball game is not copyrighted. However, if you present a full design of a superhero baseball game, that full concept is copyrighted, and you would have a lawsuit if it were stolen, providing you could prove that it was your design that was used. To be clear, the *idea* of a superhero baseball game is not something you can copyright, but your full design is.

Most companies require you to sign a document before pitching a game that, in essence, states that the company *may* have something substantially similar already in production, and therefore they cannot be held liable if a game is released that is similar to what you are pitching. If you think the situation is otherwise, you would probably need to consult a lawyer.

TRADEMARKS

Trademarks are used to denote the origin of goods or services and avoid confusion in the marketplace, and they are typically in the form of names, words and phrases, logos and symbols, designs and images, and various combinations of the aforementioned. Even a specific shape, the scent of an item, or a sound can be trademarked if it distinguishes one company's specific goods from those of another company or provider. For instance, brands such as Coca-Cola or Sony Style are trademarked names. The traditional shape of the Coca-Cola bottle is a trademark. That means that nobody but The Coca-Cola Company can use the name Coca-Cola or the shape of the bottle on an item, whether it is another soft drink or a related item, without permission. The symbols ™ and ® are virtually interchangeable designations of trademark, except that ™ refers to an unregistered trademark and ® refers to one that has been registered. (When referring to a service rather than a product, similar protection is available as a service mark.)

There are lots of laws and restrictions about trademarks. The simplest way to establish a trademark is to use it in the marketplace. For instance, if you created a skateboard brand and called it Blastobean Skateboards, you would be able to trademark the name Blastobean if nobody else had done so. To find out whether something has been trademarked, you can conduct a trademark search in the particular jurisdiction in which you want to establish the trademark. In the United States, you can search at the United States Patent and Trademark Office (www.uspto.gov). I also conduct a Google search for the name I want to trademark, because that can often reveal other people using the same name (or even embarrassing associations and meanings you were unaware of), even though nobody has trademarked it officially. You might also want to engage an attorney who specializes in patents, copyrights, and trademarks, especially if you are looking to ensure protection of something you think is going to be very *big* and something that others might try to copy.

The "official" way to trademark something is to register it in the jurisdiction in which you want to protect it. Each country has different trademark laws, and not all countries recognize trademarks based on use—for instance, China and the European Union.

Remember, the primary reason to trademark something is to identify and to prevent confusion as to the identity or source of goods or services—in other words, to make sure that when someone sees Blastobean on an item, they know it came from your company or was used with permission. If it is used without permission, you can institute a lawsuit against whoever is infringing your trademark. In simplistic terms, the test for trademark infringement is whether something seems to be selected intentionally to confuse consumers or users of a product or service, or whether actual confusion exists, regardless of intent.

As long as the trademark remains in use, it does not expire. However, United States law requires periodic filings in connection with registered trademarks, or else they will be treated by the Trademark Office as abandoned.

There are exceptions to both copyright and trademark laws. For instance, you cannot copyright a title, no matter how original, but you may be able to trademark it, particularly if it gets associated with a recognizable brand, such as *The Matrix.* And, while copyrights do expire in time, because a trademark does not expire as long as it continues to be used, legal protection for specific names or entities, such as Harry Potter, Mickey Mouse, Popeye, or Sherlock Holmes, can remain in force indefinitely, even after the expiration of any copyrights associated with them. Trademarks that are regarded as merely descriptive cannot be registered. For example, the name "brown shoes" cannot be registered if it is intended to be a trademark for brown shoes.

This section is a very cursory look at trademarks. We highly recommend that you get legal advice or further research the subject if you intend to trademark anything and enforce the trademark.

Special thanks to Jim Charne, video game attorney *par excellence* (www.charnelaw.com and igda.org/columns/lastwords), for help with this chapter.

Part III Storytelling

9 Storytelling Techniques

Not all games have a story. Some are abstract and don't require any story at all. *Tetris* is one such example, as is *SimCity*, in which there is no explicit story, but each player makes his or her own story—in which case you could say that the story is *implicit*. Other games have little or no story simply because the designers decided the game didn't need any. But games are generally more powerful when they include the elements of a good story along with the important elements of gameplay. For instance, in the early days of the genre, First-Person Shooters had minimal stories. Games such as *Doom* and *Quake* didn't require much to get you to pull the trigger. But later games, such as the *Half-Life* and *Halo* series and others, have begun to rely on strong story elements to complement the strong gameplay. Even Real-Time Strategy games, which rarely had a lot of storyline, now often include an unfolding fiction to accompany the frenetic building, researching, exploring, and fighting, which you can see in a game such as *Warcraft III*. Still other games—*Deus Ex* comes to mind—contain far deeper stories with more subtlety and range.

This chapter looks at traditional storytelling techniques and concepts. However, it is important to keep in mind that even when electronic games are based around stories, they may not always follow conventional storytelling structures. This is partly because in games, the hero is always the player, and the player is always faced with the challenges of the game interaction. In more passive media, it is necessary to take the audience through a hero's journey in such a way as to entertain and absorb them, to focus the audience on identification with the hero of the story. In games, this focus is automatic.

Moreover, because games are often nonlinear, stories may not unfold in the neat three-act structures used almost universally in the movies or television. Where stories exist, they must have the flexibility to allow for variation in the way they unfold, simultaneously allowing the player to determine the hero's path to as great a degree as is possible. Arguably, the best game stories are *emergent* stories, meaning that they are not fixed storylines, but stories that result from gameplay and player actions.

In fact, in games such as those featuring Massive Multiplayer persistent worlds, the main story of the game is secondary to the individual experiences of each player. In this way, each player creates his own story, while the larger story of the persistent world plays out around him. The individual's part in determining that story is generally minimal, but in each player's mind and experience, it is paramount. However, the underlying story of the world itself and its lore still plays an important role in the success of MMORPGs, such as *EverQuest* and *World of Warcraft*. Considerable time and effort go into creating stories, both fundamental back stories and ongoing stories through quests and character interactions, for many Massive Multiplayer Games.

The purpose of this chapter is, in part, to provide you with some sense of traditional storytelling concepts and ideas. But my greater purpose is to inspire you to take these traditional elements and concepts and use them to explore, invent, and expand upon what has been traditionally done and to inquire into the role of interactive, nonlinear, experiential design in the future of storytelling. I'm not convinced that the three-act structure is necessarily the way to go for computer and video games, and in the section called "Story and the Player's Character" later in this chapter, I explore some models of interactive story structure to further stimulate thought and discussion on this subject. At the same time,

I am equally convinced that a strong grounding in and familiarity with the traditions of literature, myth, and cinema will help us, as game designers, evolve storytelling to its ultimate interactive potential. And that's mostly what this chapter is about.

In this chapter:

- Elements of a Good Story
- The Basic Story Arc: Games and the Three-Act Structure
- Joseph Campbell Meets *Star Wars* and *The Matrix*
- Story and the Player's Character
- Ways to Start a Story
- Ways to End a Story
- Story Techniques
- Plot Twists
- Dilemmas
- Timelines
- Relevance Today (Endless New Ideas)
- Social Pressures (Grow Every Year)
- Sources of Current Information
- Multi-Session Storytelling
- Keeping Secrets
- Wrong-Headedness
- Creating Comedy
- Making Things Scary
- Enhancing the Player's Emotional Response
- Creating Emotional Responses toward Characters
- Story-Builder Activity

Elements of a Good Story

Good stories often contain certain elements, and knowing something about creating a good story can help you make better games. In fact, the combination of great gameplay with great story can create an outstanding experience for players. When executed correctly, players will often forgive games that lack graphical quality as long as they have a rich storyline. You just have to look back to the old text-only adventure games we used to get addicted to.

The section below offers some of the elements that traditionally make up good stories. You don't have to include everything on this list to have a good story, nor do you have to reveal to the player all elements that you have considered. A good example is the back story. It is very important that *you* know what it is so that your characters will develop consistently, but the player does not need to know everything you know. So, you may want to think of the following list as a reference. Apply these principles to your own game design ideas and see how many of them fit or how you might be able to expand and improve your game concept by incorporating more of these elements.

The concept of story is that somebody (the hero or the player's character, if not necessarily a hero) has to fix something about himself (or sometimes discover something about himself). The hero or character commonly also resolves conflicts and, in the end, finds some resolution. This isn't necessarily a blueprint for writing a story. But it is a story boiled down to its most basic form. Beyond that, stories take twists and turns and have moments of up and down from the protagonist's (the player's) point of view.

Think of it this way: Draw a graph to show how interesting the situations/scenes/key moments are from start to finish. If it's flat and predictable, it's boring; if it's hilly and unpredictable, it's interesting. So here are a few elements to consider when creating a story for your games:

- **The Elevator Pitch.** This is the story boiled down to its essence. If you were to pitch this story to a friend in 30 seconds, what would you focus on?
- **The Back Story.** This lets you know what has happened and who the characters are before the story action begins. What is the pattern of the characters' lives, and how might it change as a result of the events of the game? How did the character get into that pattern? What were his motivations or expectations of life up until the game began? What is the *pivot* of each character (see the upcoming Character Pivots bullet point)? What are the location and environment like—use as much detail as you can imagine. (Research similar places for inspiration.)

  How much of this kind of information you develop depends on individual preferences. Some people write volumes of back story; others do almost none. If you're working as part of a team (which you probably will be), having a good back story and character bible can help keep the vision clear. Add to that an art bible, and you have the foundations for the game that will keep everything internally consistent and will allow you to create far richer experiences for your players.
- **Conflict and Change.** No story is interesting if there isn't some conflict or challenge to the characters. A story about a man who sits in his chair every day and smokes his cigar, gets up to feed his dog and eat some canned meat, then goes to sleep would not be very interesting. But now introduce a spunky little girl who, for some reason, is left in the man's care, and now you could have a story. Similarly, a story about a woman who works in an office and goes through the same routine every day would not hold your interest. But bring in a brash, young, new manager who decides to shake up the office and with whom the woman has an adversarial relationship, tinged by a love triangle of sexual tension (they were married before), and you have the makings of a story.

  The essence is that there is conflict introduced by a change in circumstances. And often, one change leads to a snowball effect, where the entire status quo is shaken up and the situation changes dramatically. What happens when you learn that a large comet is heading toward Earth and is expected to hit in three days? The chaos generates conflict, opening up endless threads of ideas and interesting situations. A friend of mine always says, "Make 'em suffer!"—so give your characters real problems and intense situations to deal with.
- **Character Pivots.** Think of characters as people who have internal conflicts—goals and desires along with fears and weaknesses. Every character should have one or two very strong desires—rule the world, get the girl, make the most money, be the best, survive, prove their worth, and so on. Each should also have fears—of ridicule, poverty, pain, obscurity, mortality, and so on. Characters may also have weaknesses—perhaps a character is small and weak, is a woman in a male-dominated world, or has poor impulse control and loses it whenever certain events occur. If you know the story of your characters, you can establish their desires and goals and juxtapose them against their fears and weaknesses. Beware of cardboard-cutout characters, however. Just giving a character some pivot for the sake of justifying your story can be seen as gratuitous by your players. Make it real, not fake. (See also Chapter 12, "Character Design.")
- **Interesting Characters.** Make sure your characters are not clichés; they should possess emotional depth and personal history. Nobody is entirely "normal," so what do your characters possess that sets them apart from simple mindless description? Maybe your high-powered lawyer loves to read comic books in his spare time, instead of legal texts. Your sexy ingénue likes to dress up like a man and go pick fights in bars. Who knows what interesting character traits you might come up with?

- **Character-Driven Plot.** Stories can be driven by the plot or by the character. In a plot-driven story, the characters must adapt to the needs of the plot. In a character-driven story, the actions of the characters are authentic, and the plot derives from who they are and what they do naturally.
- **The Beginning.** A common trick is to drop us into the world by starting us in the middle of a scene. In games, sometimes the beginning is really the training aspect, allowing players to become familiar with how the game works. This training can also be combined with establishment of the player's initial goals in the game, which hooks them into the story, focuses the identification with the character, and immerses the player in the game's reality.
- **Plot Twists.** An easy way to add a twist is to take what the audience (or your character) thought they knew, and make it turn out to be completely wrong. You do need to be careful with plot twists, however, because if they are misused (such as if you have too many), it could ruin a good story because the audience will give up even trying to keep track, and the story will start to feel random. Using plot twists well is like telling a good joke: Timing, audience, and not overdoing it are all key. How big should a plot twist be? How upside down can you make things? It probably depends on the story you are telling and your audience. Try to be sure the twist actually makes some kind of sense in the context. Remember, also, that people need to feel they at least had a chance to "predict" their in-game future. They *love* twists, but they need to know you won't just take 180-degree turns whenever you feel like it. Set the groundwork for your twists, even if the clues are incredibly subtle.
- **Playing with Perspective.** This is when the gamer knows something the people in the story don't know about, or you see the story unfold from different points of view. Playing with perspective can make interesting situations and scenes—for instance, when the audience knows there's a giant monster hiding, waiting to tear someone's head off, and yet we see the NPC obliviously strolling right toward the danger.

  Perspective works best when there has been some setup; we think we know what's going to happen next. Perspective can also come from seeing what other characters in the game are aware of. For example, there's a game called *Fahrenheit* in which you are in the bathroom of a diner. There's a dead body, and you are trying to get rid of it, but at the same time you get to see a small-screen window that lets you watch a cop in the diner. He finally gets up and slowly heads to the bathroom, which exponentially increases your panic as you are trying to get rid of the body and clean up the blood. So, giving you that other perspective or point of view can make gameplay even more exciting.
- **Memorable Moments.** These are the key scenes and events that stand out, challenge you the most, make you laugh hardest, or shock you the most.
- **Talking Points.** Think of any game you've ever told a friend about. What moments did you focus on? Those are the high points. When you're creating a game, it's really easy just to forget about high points, but they are very important. One way to work out whether you have any is to do some product testing (sometimes called *focus testing*) and then just listen to the conversation between the testers after they've played. See what they seem to latch onto. If the game doesn't exist yet, just imagine that this is going to happen 18 months from now, and make sure to load the story/gameplay with moments you think people will be excited to discuss with their friends and online.
- **Humor.** It's okay for the humor to be dark. For more on humor, see the "Creating Comedy" section later in this chapter.
- **Believable Worlds and Situations.** Do your research. Make your world—fictional or based on historical or modern reality—consistent and believable, and do research as needed to ensure that it is so. (See also Chapter 2, "Brainstorming and Research.")

- **Realism and Consistency.** Establish the rules of your world and your characters, and stick to them. Think of cause and effect and make character actions and reactions consistent with events as they occur. If something happens in the early or middle part of the story, how does it affect later events and character responses? Don't forget what your characters have done or how the world has been affected by their actions.
- **Dialogue.** Work hard on your characters' dialogue (if any) and use it to establish who they are and to enhance the plot. Does it sound natural, like real people speaking? More importantly, does it sound like the specific character is speaking? For instance, a court noble, a common merchant, a drill sergeant, a professor, and a scientist all sound different in many ways. Without resorting to stereotypes, how do you establish who they are through what they say and how they say it? (For some more ideas, see Chapter 16, "Speech.")
- **Execution.** Expect the best from every aspect of the story and the game itself—from characters, to plots, to beginning, to end. Let nothing be sloppy, lazy, or half-assed. Give complete attention to detail in all aspects of the game. Pay particular attention to voice acting—bad acting or bad delivery. Timing can ruin any attempt you make to create a good story for your game.

Additional useful information about the characters in your stories can be found in Chapter 12, "Character Design."

The Basic Story Arc: Games and the Three-Act Structure

This section will cover the basics of the story arc and the three-act structure. But first, take a look at Figures 9.1 and 9.2, which depict a rather boring story arc and a more interesting story arc, respectively.

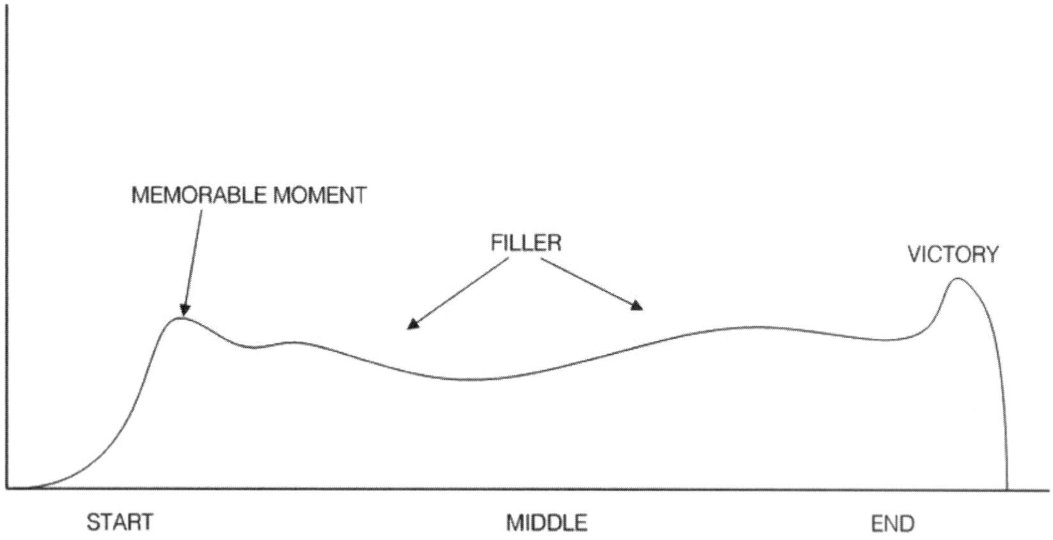

FIGURE 9.1
A boring story arc.

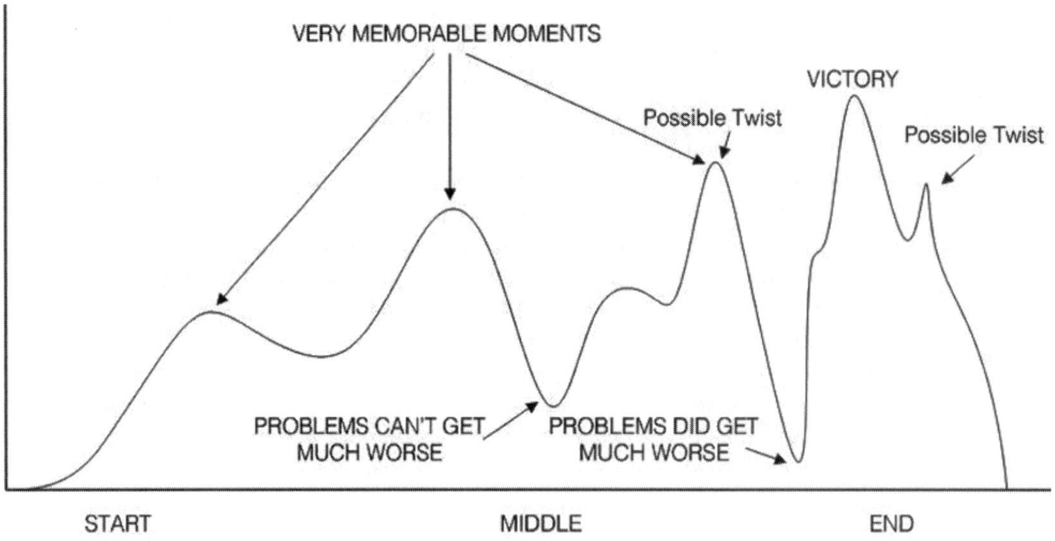

FIGURE 9.2
A more interesting story arc.

Beginning the Story

- **Prelude.** This is optional. Before the real story begins with the main characters, you may sometimes want to set the scene or context through events that precede the introduction of the main characters into the storyline.
- **Characters.** Introduce at least one of the main characters. (Sometimes you only foreshadow them, but rarely is this the case.)
- **Conflict.** Introduce the conflict. What's the problem and why should anyone care?
- **Timeframe.** Know the timespan of the story. In other words, over what period of time does this story take place? Also consider whether you will use flashbacks to reach outside the timeline.
- **Time Period.** What time period is this story in? Will the game feature time travel?
- **Setting.** Know the setting of the story. What is the world and what are its characteristics? A trick here is to draw the map where this all takes place. Doing the map can be really inspiring, too.
- **What's at Stake?** Show what's at stake (or at least give a sense of it).
- **Foreshadowing.** This is optional, but it can sometimes be interesting if you hint at or reveal future events. Sometimes this can involve a flash-forward or even a flashback.
- **Tone or Style.** Set a tone for the game, such as humorous, dark, grand, or gritty, and stick to it.

Mid-Story

- **Purposeful Scenes.** Think in terms of scenes with purpose, obstacles/challenges, and resolution.
- **Character Development.** Develop the characters by letting the player see something new about them as the game progresses. Also, keep in mind how the characters will change as a consequence of their adventures. If your main character is very young, how does he react the first time he kills someone? How might he be changed when he succeeds for the first time at some difficult task?
- **Character Motivation.** Give your characters (including the player character) adequate motivation for what they are doing. They may do exceptional or amazing things, but they do them because they have

sufficient reason to make the effort involved. For instance, you might not lift up a car one-handed to grab a dime that rolled under it, but you would do so to save someone you love from being crushed.

- **Ups and Downs.** Create changes of fortune—times of success, times of challenge, times of anxiety or loss—all leading up to the ending sequence. It's okay for the player to have reversals of fortune and build back up again. Most games have a more or less linear increase in challenge—the game gets consistently harder. Many players come to expect that. But in a good story, there will be times when events go badly and times of greater success. A good story is not necessarily linear in its event structure, but it consists of sequential scenes that test and challenge different aspects of the main characters. Such changes of fortune in a game can dramatically change the level of emotional involvement of the player.
- **Consistency.** Establish logical consistency. Things don't just happen without previous events leading to them. Think about why your characters do what they do, and what they did that led up to these actions.
- **Consequences.** Establish consequences and logical results. Whatever decisions the characters in your game make, they should have consequences that affect other characters and future events. Think things through. If the player decides to let an enemy agent live, how might that affect the game? And how would it be different if he killed the agent? What if the agent was the big boss's brother or sister? How might that affect the actions of the boss and his henchmen?
- **Ambiguity.** Create ambiguity with different possible solutions and different possible explanations.
- **Clichés.** Be aware of the clichés used in the type of game you are creating and find ways to do things differently. Challenge the player's assumptions if you can do so while maintaining gameplay quality.

End Game

- **Foreshadowing the Ending.** Optionally, you can let the player anticipate the final events. This can work well in games with time travel, but it also works in more traditional story contexts.
- **Climax.** Determine that pivotal moment when everything can be gained or lost and when the outcome is uncertain.
- **Doubt or Tension.** Create tension by making the player uncertain of how to succeed or by giving the player difficult choices at the end.
- **Sequel Introduction.** If you have planned for a future game based on this story—and you should always have that in mind—then you can introduce something at the end to suggest that there could be more to come. This was done well in the movie *Batman Begins*, which ended with the Joker's card and led directly into *The Dark Knight.*

Epilogue/Catharsis

Catharsis is a Greek word that represents the feeling of emotional release, specifically at the end of a play or other art form. For instance, watching Luke, Leia, Han, and Chewbacca receive medals at the end of *Star Wars* (Episode IV) was a cathartic moment.

- **Rewards.** Reward the player for succeeding.
- **Effects of player's accomplishments.** If possible, show how the player and other main characters have changed as a result of their adventures. You can do this through visuals (the player character looks much stronger and battle-hardened, for instance), through dialogue, or through scenes that reveal the changes in the character. I personally like it when you feel the hero had to work for the victory. For example, when you see Arnold Schwarzenegger at the end of the movie *Predator*, you really feel he's had a heck of a battle. So instead of dancing around, he's lucky he's even able to walk away.

JOSEPH CAMPBELL MEETS *STAR WARS* AND *THE MATRIX*

If you've ever wondered where good stories come from, one place to start is Joseph Campbell's seminal book, *The Hero with a Thousand Faces.* Campbell examined stories and myths from many cultures and times in history, coming up with a sort of blueprint of what he calls the *Hero's Journey.* Although this is not the only way to look at stories, it has been used by many successful modern storytellers as a guide, so I suggest you consider it.

In its simplest form, the Hero's Journey is summarized as a rite of passage represented in three basic stages: separation, initiation, and return. In Campbell's words:

> "A hero ventures forth from the world of common day into a region of supernatural wonder: fabulous forces are there encountered and a decisive victory is won: the hero comes back from this mysterious adventure with the power to bestow boons on his fellow man."

This simplistic synopsis forms the basis for many stories, fables, and myths. It can be seen recurring through many cultures and is even modeled in the biographies of many famous and accomplished men and women. One simple example that illustrates this story admirably is the well-known series of images taken from Zen Buddhism, sometimes called the *10 Bulls.* The hero of this simple story undergoes an allegorical journey, outwardly seeking a bull (sometimes an ox) in the wilderness, but inwardly finding his own inner truth. These 10 stages are (in my own words):

1. **The Search.** This is the normal wandering search of all people for truth, as represented in this case by the elusive bull. The Seeker is an ordinary man.
2. **Discovering the Footprints.** This is the first sign that leads the Seeker to what he seeks. It is evidence that the bull exists and is nearby.
3. **First Sight.** With all his senses alert, the Seeker catches his first glimpse of the bull. He sees the truth he seeks for the first time, but it is only a glimpse to inspire his going further into the "initiation" that Campbell mentions.
4. **Capture.** The Seeker catches up with the bull, and after some struggle manages to capture it. After his first glimpse, he must stay focused upon the bull in order to catch it.
5. **Taming.** Even captured, the bull is wild and willful. The Seeker must use discipline, intuition, and resolve to bring the wild beast under control. But once he has achieved this task, the bull becomes docile and does the Seeker's bidding. Now he has found truth, and it follows his path.
6. **Riding Upon Its Back.** In this stage, the Seeker no longer walks with the bull behind him, but rides upon its back. He is at home with his truth and easily continues on his life path. In many pictures the Seeker is playing a flute while riding the bull. To me, this is an image of contentment and repose as well as communication with others that the truth has been found.
7. **Transcendence.** The Seeker returns home; the bull is known as a transitory aspect of life. The Seeker is at home, at peace, and no longer attached to the duality of truth or not-truth (bull or no bull).
8. **Emptiness.** At last, free of duality, the Seeker transcends seeking, the bull, home, and even the self. This image is generally depicted as a blank circle.
9. **The Source.** From emptiness, the Seeker now connects with the source of all knowledge and knowing. He perceives truth and existence without illusion, masks, or interpretation. This is depicted as a beautiful garden with plants symbolic of the desirable traits of the enlightened Seeker.
10. **The World.** Having completed his journey, the Seeker returns to the everyday world, but now with a great boon to offer to all who encounter him. He lives as an ordinary man doing ordinary things, but those who encounter him receive enlightenment from his presence.

In the *10 Bulls*, the Seeker goes from the ordinary world of seeking through the initiation and back to the ordinary world. He is changed, however, and brings something back from his journey...a gift for all to share if they will. In this sense, the Seeker is much like a great many mythical heroes; even though this series of images represents a personal allegory and a spiritual journey, on some level so do all heroes' journeys, myths, and fables.

The Hero's Journey

According to Campbell, the basic stages of the Hero's Journey are:

- Separation (Departure)
  1. The Call to Adventure
  2. Refusal of the Call
  3. Supernatural Aid
  4. Crossing the First Threshold
  5. The Belly of the Whale
- Initiation
  1. The Road of Trials
  2. The Meeting with the Goddess
  3. Woman as the Temptress
  4. Atonement with the Father
  5. Apotheosis
  6. The Ultimate Boon
- Return
  1. Refusal of the Return
  2. The Magic Flight
  3. Rescue from Without
  4. Crossing of the Return Threshold
  5. Master of the Two Worlds
  6. Freedom to Live

Joseph Campbell's analysis, originally written in the 1940s and later updated in the late 1960s, is a combination of myth and fable, psychoanalysis and comparative theology. Throughout his writings, he dwells more in the psychological and spiritual meanings of myth than in the aspect of strict storytelling. Many of the stages of his Hero's Journey, however, are easily adapted to modern storytelling in movies and perhaps in games.

A practical example of how Campbell's work fits with modern storytelling can be seen by comparing the stages of the Hero's Journey with the elements of two huge hit movies—*Star Wars* and *The Matrix*.

Table 9.1 provides an interesting extension of Campbell's ideas as they relate to *Star Wars* and *The Matrix*. The chart is the work of Kristen Brennan and is used with permission. More information can be found at www.moongadget.com/origins/myth.html, including a further exploration of people who have studied the cultural archetypes of storytelling.

Table 9.1

Campbell	*Star Wars*	*The Matrix*
I: Departure		
The Call to Adventure	Princess Leia's message	"Follow the white rabbit"
Refusal of the Call	Must help with the harvest	Neo won't climb out window
Supernatural Aid	Obi-Wan rescues Luke from the Sand People	Trinity extracts the "bug" from Neo
Crossing the First Threshold	Escaping Tatooine agents	Capture Neo/he takes the red pill
The Belly of the Whale	Trash compactor	Torture room/awakens in a pod
II: Initiation		
The Road of Trials	Lightsaber practice	Sparring with Morpheus
The Meeting with the Goddess	Princess Leia	Trinity
Temptation Away from the True Path	Luke is tempted by the Dark Side	Cypher (the failed messiah) is tempted by the world of comfortable illusions
Atonement with the Father	Darth and Luke reconcile	Neo rescues and comes to agree (that he's The One) with his father figure, Morpheus
Apotheosis (becoming god-like)	Luke becomes a Jedi	Neo becomes The One
The Ultimate Boon	Death Star destroyed	Humanity's salvation now within reach
III: Return		
Refusal of the Return	"Luke, come on!" Luke wants to stay to avenge Obi-Wan	Neo fights agent instead of running
The Magic Flight	Millennium Falcon	"Jacking in"
Rescue from Without	Han saves Luke from Darth	Trinity saves Neo from agents
Crossing the Return Threshold	Millennium Falcon destroys pursuing TIE fighters	Neo fights agent Smith
Master of the Two Worlds	Victory ceremony	Neo declares victory over machines in final phone call
Freedom to Live	Rebellion is victorious over Empire	Humans are victorious over machines
Common Mythic Elements		
Two worlds (mundane and special)	Planetside vs. the Death Star	Reality vs. the Matrix
The mentor	Obi-Wan Kenobi	Morpheus
The oracle	Yoda	The Oracle
The prophecy	Luke will overthrow the Emperor	Morpheus will find (and Trinity will fall for) "The One"

continued

Campbell	*Star Wars*	*The Matrix*
Failed hero	Biggs	In an early version of the script, Morpheus once believed that Cypher was "The One" [Also, before understanding he was "The One," Neo failed in the battle against the agent]
Wearing enemy's skin	Luke and Han wear stormtrooper outfits	Neo jumps into agent's skin
Shapeshifter (the hero isn't sure if he can trust this character)	Han Solo	Cypher
Animal familiar	R2-D2, Chewbacca	N/A
Chasing a lone animal into the enchanted wood (and the animal gets away)	The Millennium Falcon follows a lone TIE fighter into range of the Death Star	Neo "follows the white rabbit" to the nightclub, where he meets Trinity

According to Campbell, each stage of the Hero's Journey has been told again and again throughout the ages in a multitude of cultures around the world. Some of these stages are quite common in games; others are not often included.

Separation (Departure):

- **The Call to Adventure.** Something happens that takes the hero of the game from ordinary life into a specific adventure. It could be a catastrophic event: a kidnapping, a crash landing, an invasion from without, treachery from within, and so on. It could be a message the hero receives from a herald character. (See also Chapter 12, "Character Design.") Whatever the motivation, the hero's circumstances change in such a way that he must seriously consider a path that leads out of the Ordinary World into an Extraordinary and often Supernatural World, beset by many challenges and dangers...the realm of the unknown.
- **The Refusal of the Call.** Some heroes never question their role and take to their adventure without pause; however, many heroes are reluctant at first and, whether because of fear, conflicting circumstances, loyalty to something or someone who must be left behind, or other reasons, they hesitate and even refuse to take on the mantle of hero. Many game heroes are thrust reluctantly into their roles, but for the most part, game designers do not place much doubt or soul-searching in their main characters. Because the hero is an extension of the player, this kind of storyline is complicated by the blending of imaginary characters with real human motivations. We often play games because we enjoy the surrogate violence of the digital world. However, a reluctant hero—one with conflicts and doubts—can still serve as a vessel for our enjoyment as players and can provide an even more interesting plotline and more diverse gameplay options.
- **Supernatural Aid.** Many games include some mentor or magical agency that empowers the hero in special ways and often convinces those who are reluctant or informs them to help them along the road ahead. This is as common in games as it is in myth and story. In fact, even when there is no specific mentor (see Chapter 12, "Character Design") or other magical agency, the magic is inherent in the hero, who is faster, stronger, more agile and skilled than ordinary people from the get go, or who wields a magic sword or other implement that aids him in the quest. Again, it's a very common theme.
- **Crossing the First Threshold.** There comes a time when the hero must set out, leave the ordinary world behind, and truly enter into unknown territory. Often there are obstacles that appear to prevent or impede the hero's progress, but these threshold guardians, in Campbell's terms, serve only as the

first of many tests the hero will face. Once the first threshold has been passed, the hero is truly on the journey. In many games, this might be the end of the "training" element of the game.

- **The Belly of the Whale.** Symbolic of the total immersion and disappearance of the hero into the unknown, this is a less common stage in games, but it is not unknown. In some games, the player's character, the hero, is plunged into some world or some situation that is very much like the belly of the whale that Jonah inhabited. In psychological terms, Campbell likens this to a return to the womb—apparent death and subsequent rebirth in the world of the mystery or adventure. As a symbol, this is a powerful component of myths and legends. As a story device, it may be useful to consider but not necessarily as ubiquitous as some of the other stages, particularly in modern stories. One way to look at this from a game perspective, however, is as the descent into dungeons, which happens in many games. In a way, the dungeon could be analogous to the belly of the whale. Another way to look at it is when the player has perhaps really entered into the fantasy world from the relatively safe starting point of the game.

Initiation:

- **The Road of Trials.** Nothing could be more game-like than this section, in which the hero, in order to attain his goal, must face various tests, challenges, journeys, tasks, and other trials. This stage is in many ways the essence of game design. In some ways, the other stages serve to create a framework for the Road of Trials. Generally speaking, the vast majority of the time spent in game design and in gameplay will be in this stage of the Hero's Journey. However, Campbell's examples in *The Hero with a Thousand Faces*, taken from myths and fables, are rich with imagination, symbolic tests, and unique perspectives. They might serve as inspiration for a richer variety of game design decisions and directions, helping designers break out of repetitive patterns and jump into more universal symbology combined with archetypical and often surprising events.

  In the next three stages—the Meeting with the Goddess, Woman as Temptress, and Atonement with the Father—Campbell's discussion is highly psychological and refers to many of the roles of man/woman, father/mother, and god/goddess in the human psyche. There are elements in these sections that can definitely be used in games, especially to symbolize those deeper psychological and mythical aspects of our Jungian collective unconscious. In an essential way, these three stages represent the hero's (or individual's) struggle with the father/mother archetypes in his life. These stages are not as common in games but are seen often in other stories where powerful male and female figures exemplify the various aspects and pairs of opposites of the father and the mother. Some examples are:

- Mother Archetypes
  - Beautiful
  - Nurturing
  - Understanding
  - Protector
  - Loving
  - Hideous
  - Threatening
  - Spiteful
  - Persecutor
  - Overprotective
- Father Archetypes
  - Wise
  - Ally
  - Mentor
  - Kindly
  - Vengeful
  - Rival
  - Enemy
  - Wrathful

NOTE

Collective unconscious *is a concept introduced by psychologist Carl Jung that suggests a universal, shared consciousness distinct from the personal consciousness of each individual. In some ways, you could think of it as a psychological principle similar to The Force from* Star Wars.

Keeping in mind these concepts, it may be possible to introduce into games these stronger archetypes of male and female characters, whether they appear as kindly allies, terrible enemies, gods and goddesses, or other types of characters. This doesn't have to be blatant, but an awareness of the power of the mother/father archetypes can cause unconscious resonance with the player. Fairy tales used these archetypes in the stories of wicked queens and stepmothers, fairy godmothers, kindly kings, and helpful or vengeful gods. An surprisingly interesting twist in a lot of animated Disney movies is that there's no nurturing mother figure or sometimes the mother dies in the story. (Think about the classic Disney animated movies that stand the test of time, such as *Snow White*, *Cinderella*, and *Aladdin.*)

- **Apotheosis.** Apotheosis means to deify, and it is at this point that the hero has successfully fulfilled his tasks, met his challenges, and vanquished those who sought to block his way. In games, this may be the point at which the player has attained some goal that dramatically increases his power(s). In a way, certain forms of leveling up are like mini-apotheoses. In spiritual terms, it is the individual's connection with the godhead and ultimate attainment of enlightenment. In story terms, it is the culmination of a search or sequence of important events.
- **The Ultimate Boon.** With the hero's apotheosis comes the great gift promised by the adventure. It could be something the hero brings back to the world, as Prometheus brought back the gift of fire to mankind (for which he was severely punished by the gods from whom he stole the fire), or it could be something closer to home—the hand of the princess or even the peace of mind that comes with having avenged a terrible wrong. Whatever this great gift is, it is something the hero has sought, or it is a great reward for his efforts. It signals the end of the Initiation phase of Campbell's Hero's Journey, but not the end of the journey itself. As in the Apotheosis phase, this stage can also be part of the mini-cycles of leveling or completion of stages, so that in games particularly, the Road of Trials often has recurring moments of apotheosis and ultimate (or at least recurring) boons. At the end game, presumably, the ultimate boon is presented.

Return:

- **Refusal of the Return.** In myths and legends, the hero, having attained the highest gifts, sometimes is unable or unwilling to return to the Ordinary World. In the story of the Buddha, after he has attained enlightenment, he doubted that the wonders he perceived could be communicated to others. In other stories, the hero may be seduced by the Extraordinary or Supernatural World and may want to remain there, never to return to the world of his origins. In other stories, the hero returns without reluctance, so this is not always present. In a game context, this Refusal of the Return would be most relevant if there were compelling reasons for the hero to return and he was resistant to it. Some story point and new herald event might be necessary to prompt the hero to undertake the return to the Ordinary World. However, in most games and stories, the hero's return is more or less assumed and automatic once the goal has been attained. Looking back at the *10 Bulls* example earlier in this section, however, the return is part of the journey, and the sharing of the gift is the ultimate culmination.
- **The Magic Flight.** In myths, the Ultimate Boon is often stolen or taken without permission, and what ensues is a chase scene that—in myths, at any rate—often involves supernatural events and symbols. This involves the hero attempting to return to the safety of the Ordinary World while being pursued by some aspect of the mysterious world where the adventure has taken place. In game terms, this is an opportunity to create additional excitement, challenges, puzzles, and storylines, extending the game from the attainment of the goal to the safe return. This could be a dangerous journey to return the rescued princess to the safety of her father's castle, or it could be the return of a magic elixir that will save a dying village, and so on. Danger pursues the hero until safety has been reached or the pursuer has been vanquished.

- **Rescue from Without.** Whether the hero is simply reluctant to return to the Ordinary World or whether he is engaged in a dangerous Magic Fight, it is often the case that some agency, some outside force, will be needed to assist him back to safety. This is common in myths and stories where the hero must be brought back from the adventure by something outside himself. Not all heroes require this assistance, but some do. For instance, at the end of *The Lord of the Rings*, Sam and Frodo are rescued by the eagles. Without that rescue, they would have died after the fall of Mordor. They accomplished their task of destroying the Ring, but to return to the world, they required something from the outside.

The next three stages of the Hero's Journey may have less to do with games than the others, since they deal with the hero's re-assimilation and ultimate mastery of the two worlds—the one of adventure and the common world of his origins.

- **Crossing of the Return Threshold.** This aspect of the story is the hero's re-assimilation into the world, which comes with its own hazards and challenges. It may be that the ordinary world no longer holds much appeal to the adventurer who has seen greater horizons and the wonders of self-discovery. Or it may be that people cannot accept the hero, changed as he is and no longer seeming to be one of them. In any case, from a game perspective, this is probably not a common stage that will be used. Once the adventure and the action are finished, the return home is generally not dealt with or—if it is, it is only an epilogue to complete the cycle.
- **Master of the Two Worlds.** In this stage, the hero must learn, in essence, to straddle the phenomenal world of his journey and the mundane world of his return. In somehow bringing these divergent aspects into unity, he comes to see that they are indeed aspects of the same world, and he is able to move fluidly between those aspects. His difficulties with returning to the ordinary world are gone, and he is truly the Master of the Two Worlds. Again, this is less likely to be a theme carried out in games, unless it is as an epilogue or perhaps the beginning of a new adventure.
- **Freedom to Live.** The assimilation is complete, and the hero is reborn into a new image with the knowledge of the transcendent truths of his journey fully integrated into his earthly existence. In essence, this is the ultimate happy ending.

How useful this Hero's Journey will be in designing games depends on the kind of game you're producing and how much your hero's story contains a deeper subtext or metaphor of mythical proportions. Most games do not attempt such lofty pursuits, nor should they. And, to the extent that great game stories are more often than not emergent from the gameplay and players' choices, it is interesting to see how closely player-created emergent stories follow Campbell's sequence of the Hero's Journey and to what extent game designers can bridge the gap between story structure and interactive emergent game stories. The question of the relevance of the Hero's Journey to game design depends a lot on the designer, the game structures, and the players themselves. In reality, however, the concepts can be inspiring and therefore useful, so they are definitely worth the time to consider.

Years after Campbell's work was published and widely read, Christopher Vogler created a condensed and somewhat modernized treatment of Campbell's work in his book, *The Writer's Journey.* Vogler's revised version of the Hero's Journey has found a home in Hollywood and elsewhere and is often used by Hollywood writers, producers, and directors. Although similar to Campbell's original sequence, Vogler's version is perhaps more suitable to modern storytelling, and although it contains some of the psychological insight of Campbell's original work, it is in general more practical and story-oriented. Like Campbell's work, this treatment of the writer's journey is only relevant to some extent in game design, depending on the kind of game being produced and whether it is structured toward a specific story arc or toward emergent, more freeform gameplay.

Vogler's steps, which he fits into the more standard three-act structure of modern moviemaking, include the following stages:

- Act One
  - Ordinary World
  - Call to Adventure
  - Refusal of the Call
  - Meeting with the Mentor
  - Crossing the First Threshold
- Act Two
  - Tests, Allies, Enemies
  - Approach to the Inmost Cave
  - Supreme Ordeal
  - Reward
- Act Three
  - The Road Back
  - Resurrection
  - Return with Elixir

In Act One, Vogler's hero experiences more or less the same types of events, situations, and pivotal characters as does Campbell's, though Vogler eliminates the Belly of the Whale stage. In Act Two, Vogler summarizes much of what, in Campbell, was very psychological and theological, condensing the second act into a discussion of the tests and other characters in the story (Tests, Allies, Enemies), then condenses Campbell's discussion of the father/mother principles and the psychosexual elements into the Approach to the Inmost Cave—the area the hero must go in order to complete the quest. The Apotheosis of Campbell is gone, but a Supreme Ordeal is added, which may equate to the ultimate Boss Battle of a videogame—or, at any rate, the ultimate test of the hero. This test, if successfully completed, leads to the reward, followed by the third act, with its Road Back, Resurrection (back into the world), and Return with Elixir—or returning with the gifts the quest has given the hero. Again, in games, these last elements are often minimized, with the Supreme Ordeal and the Reward being the effective ending of the game.

This more simplified form of the Hero's Journey fits well into modern storytelling, and Vogler offers many examples from modern film archives. However, no formula or absolute structure works for all stories, and neither will it work for all games. In fact, games are a unique case, and many of them require no deep story or psychological or spiritual meaning. I've included this section for a few reasons, however. First, because these ideas—Campbell's, and to some degree Vogler's—have infused our consciousness through movies and pop culture. Second, because as games become more sophisticated, game designers will be seeking ways to deepen and enrich the power and influence their stories have on the players of those games.

Today, people often watch other players. There are now game audiences—people who enjoy the unfolding of the game story passively, just as people used to gather around campfires and listen to storytellers or, later, gather around radios, TVs, and in movie theaters to watch stories unfold. As more people find games enjoyable to watch, as well as to play, some aspects of story may become more compelling, and archetypal stories that affect the players and the observers with powerful, if unconscious, symbolism of myths and the human condition can be as effective as great movies.

Story and the Player's Character

Linear stories work in movies and literature, and some elements of good linear stories can certainly be applied to games. However, it wouldn't be fun to play a character—even a great character—from literature if all you could do is exactly what that character did in the original story. If the player has no choice at all, it's not really a game. That is not to say that literature hasn't contributed some great game plots, or that you would have to change the overall story arc to adapt literature to games. But players must be able to make choices and, ideally, even deviate from the story in some ways in order for a game to feel alive. Good games allow players to test all paths to discover the ones that work best for them and also the ones that lead to failure. In games (as in life), failure is often a great opportunity to learn and can even be cool to experience—depending on the game. So, when adapting another source, it's often best to use a more open approach to the story's world, not the strictly linear storyline.

In games, the world the character inhabits should be alive and somewhat unpredictable. Players should have the ability to choose their directions, and the world around them should respond. In place of simple repetitive and predictable scenes, such as characters who always do and say the same thing every time a player's character interacts with them, consider creating game situations in which things might change. People's attitudes could change based on circumstances or based on the player's previous actions. Some characters might have a past history with the player's character, which would affect their behavior and make it less predictable but more consistent with the player's experience.

One other way to create more interesting game worlds is to create a responsive game system in which players may take different approaches and, ultimately, experience different events and outcomes based on those approaches.

Story Visualization and Structure in Games

Although many of the ideas contained in this chapter are applicable to games, they trace their origins to linear storytelling. Although linear methods are helpful and often useful when designing games, they cannot encompass the wide range of possibilities that are available for designers of games with their myriad interactive possibilities. For games, new paradigms are inevitable, and new approaches to the art of the story are almost mandatory. These new approaches will most likely borrow heavily from linear approaches but will expand to make the best and most creative use of nonlinear or interactive entertainment.

Even in more or less linear plots, adding an element of freedom can give players a more rewarding experience. For instance, even if the quests, missions, and tasks the player must perform to succeed in the game are essentially linear, if players can accomplish these tasks in different ways or different orders, or if they can engage in other interesting activities while completing these tasks, the game won't feel linear and limiting. Even in games such as *Halo* and *Halo 2*, in which your objectives are pretty linear, there are many tactical options, multiplayer options, and often different paths to get to your goals. Probably the least inspiring examples of linear game design involve "rail" games and games in which your path is preset and offers no branches or options. You must tread a predefined path toward the goal, and no deviation or variation is offered. (Even if you see a door that goes somewhere else, it will be locked.) Personally, I find these games generally unsatisfying, although some arcade games essentially do this, but with enough nonstop action that all you really care about is surviving the current level, and with enough tactical options and power-up items to keep things interesting.

I should note that just adding more choices, options, or rooms does not necessarily make a better game. It is always a balance that must be struck between playability and accessibility on the one hand and freedom, variety, and interesting choices on the other, but an excessively confining and limiting game is probably going to be poorly received. By contrast, many popular games have a plethora of choices and options, and by setting appropriate limits and structures, they still manage to be fun to play.

In thinking about storytelling in nonlinear media, I've thought in terms of metaphors and systems. I really don't think it's very useful to dwell on theoretical models for too long, but some of these ideas might be useful in brainstorming and in considering new ways to structure games. For instance, working with 3D webs, snowflakes, or cubic spaces might not really mean much in the reality of designing a game, but they might inspire some new approaches, resulting in more original and unusual game designs.

Linear Story

The linear story simply takes a character from Point A to Point B in a straight line. For this to qualify as a game it must be interactive, and the player must have to accomplish some goals, but there are no options but to succeed or fail at each stage of the game and no alternatives to each situation. The original *Karateka* (precursor to *Prince of Persia*) was a clear example of linear game design, as were arcade games such as *Gradius*, *Castlevania*, *Mega Man*, and *Golden Axe* and most racing games. Many games from the 2D era were essentially linear, but such games are quite rare in the 3D era of game design. For instance, the original *Abe's Oddysee* and *Abe's Exoddus* were essentially linear games, but with a great variety of gameplay and puzzles to solve.

Linear Branching

In contrast to the straight linear approach, the branching structure consists of a linear story with choice points. This is like a logic exercise in which you have essentially either/or choices. You pick Path A or Path B. The path you choose determines the direction the gameplay will take, ultimately arriving at an ending point. There can be more than one branch at a decision node, and branches can reconnect with each other, but ultimately the gameplay heads in one direction from the beginning of the game to the end. In this type of game, some branches lead to dead ends (the player dies or gets stuck or has to backtrack to another node). In some cases, only one decision tree—only one sequence of choices—can succeed. This type of structure was typical of the early text adventure games, and one of the best graphical game examples was the arcade game *Dragon's Lair*.

Webs (2D and 3D)

The web structure is similar to the branching game, but it's far less linear. This type of game consists of a series of interconnected paths or branches that can be taken in virtually any order to accomplish a particular phase, mission, level, or other determinable section of the game or story. Players travel along the strands of the web, which branch again and again, but the player's actions are somewhat restricted in that they still have to stay on the paths and take the many branches the game offers. However, if you can imagine walking around on a huge web, you see that you can essentially go in any direction—around, toward the center, or toward the edge—and each decision in this metaphor results in gameplay consequences.

At some point, the player completes enough of the required elements of the game or has experienced enough elements of the story to move forward to the next web structure, which is connected to other web structures via node points. These node points can be specific plot elements of the story, or they can be level bosses and so on. The player is prevented from moving through a node point by some obstacle or game requirement—for instance, the need to have obtained certain information or objects, or to have accomplished certain goals—including perhaps defeating a boss. The idea here is that players have the opportunity for nearly free exploration of a part of the game or story, but they always have to funnel through the node point to move to another part of the story. From a design standpoint, this allows players moments of increased freedom and choice and less restriction, occasionally punctuated by moments when their choices narrow. It also allows designers to control the flow of the story, the ramping up of difficulty, or the pacing of exploration.

This concept could be thought of as widening and narrowing options, and it can be applied to many of the structures of game design. In this case I'm referring to the overall game flow, but the same principle can be applied at the microcosmic level, in which many of the actions and circumstances the player experiences contain expansions of choices, at some point followed by a more restrictive structure. A simple example would be standing before a locked door. At the point where the player encounters the locked door, there are many possible choices, including going another direction, getting someone to open the door, letting someone with security clearance open the door (then following him in), finding another way in and ignoring the door altogether, finding a way to unlock the door (which might entail various means), or even breaking through the door using a variety of possible methods. There are a lot of choices at the moment, but once the door has been successfully removed as an obstacle, the choices narrow down to two main ones: go through the door or don't.

This all seems pretty obvious, and the amount of analysis required depends on how theoretical you want to be. However, you can consider the overall game design as an example of this sort of structure, and you can also consider subsections of the game in a similar way.

Web structures can have both two- and three-dimensional aspects. In the 2D realm, each separate web/story structure can connect along specific nodes to another web. Crossing into another web can expose the player to new story elements and new experiences, but movement through the game still requires movement through the nodes, which act as the funnel points to ensure that the player experiences the important plot points and accomplishes the necessary prerequisites for advancement in the game. A good example would be a point in a story where the player might encounter a boat that could provide transportation to an island. The opportunity to travel by sea might open whole new areas of the game, and in this structural model, it would represent the gateway to a whole new web or set of webs. The boat would be like a node in the web structure. Likewise, the island you could reach by boat would also be a web or system of web structures, each of which contains choices, options, and gameplay experiences that ultimately lead to either a dead end in the story or a new node to even more web structures.

In the 2D model, the game can be visualized on a flat plane comprised of interconnected webs, each of which represents some aspect of the game—an area, a level, a quest or mission, and so on. In this structure, the player's path through the game can branch wherever the designer has decided there is a node or connection between areas of the web, and when the player is approaching these nodes, options will narrow. This concept can be expanded in several ways. One way involves expanding the system of webs and nodes into a 3D space, in which specific web structures of the game can connect not only on a single plane, but across other planes in a three-dimensional space. This structure suggests a very open environment in which the player can virtually enter a wide variety of new "experience spaces" from almost any given situation or location in the game. This might be particularly useful to visualize if the player always has access to some specific dimension, area, or "experiential space" of the game at any time.

In some ways, access to the player's inventory/equipment screens is a modal change from the main game experience that can be accessed at any time while playing. In the 3D web model, it exists as a link off any branch or activity on any part of any web. But other, more gameplay-oriented, examples might be possible. For instance, another way to think of this structure is as a series of planes of activity connected to each other via the nodal gates. Imagine that a particular game allows the player to travel in time whenever they wish, and they can access the same locations at different points in time. Although the fantasy is maintained that this location is the same but only time has shifted, in reality the player is accessing a completely different location in terms of gameplay and game design. Such instant access would not be easy to accomplish with the strictly mono-planar 2D web structure, but would be quite consistent with a 3D multi-planar system.

Snowflake (2D or 3D)

The suggestion of a snowflake model is only to inspire you to think in new ways about structure. To my knowledge, there is no current snowflake model of design. However, that doesn't mean you can't use it to inspire a new sort of structure. That's why it's here in this book—to inspire you.

This purely theoretical concept of a snowflake structure is a more freeform variant of the web structure. Because no two snowflakes are exactly alike, presumably no two snowflake game structures would be exactly the same, either. I visualize this as a series of snowflakes set side to side and laid out in planes, like the web system. The difference is that instead of branching paths, as you have with the web, you have freeform movement within each of the snowflake domains, with the center of each snowflake providing the transition point to another plane of the story/game. The only significant difference between the web and snowflake systems is that the former is based somewhat more on specific story/game/action branching, and the snowflake is based on freeform movement and exploration.

Does the snowflake metaphor work? That's up to you. I only include it as a possible source of inspiration. When I think about webs, snowflakes, and other structural metaphors, my goal is to use these to imagine more interesting and diverse gameplay opportunities, not bind myself to some theoretical model. These ideas should be expansive, not contractive. So, I put it to you: Can you imagine a snowflake model that could make your games more interesting and fun?

Cubes

The cubic system is somewhat difficult to understand, in that it is more or less a big empty box into which you dump the elements of your story and game. There is no implied or underlying structure here—only a three-dimensional space in which to create. However, within each empty "cube" are the elements of game exploration and play, and each cube then connects to other cubes that are equally open-ended in structure. Cubes can be connected at any interface, either by seamless migration from cube to cube or by means of structural connectors.

For instance, consider a series of cubes connected by short, tubular connecting structures. These connectors would, in fact, be story transitions or markers. They would represent specific events or situations that the player would experience once they have satisfied the conditions of entry into the connector. This would then lead to the next cube.

The cube model might also include areas of web or snowflake design, so that your players would migrate between completely open areas and areas restricted by branching paths or some other type of experience. In some ways, *Grand Theft Auto III* and later games might fit into this model, because they provide nearly unlimited freedom within a zone but require the accomplishment of certain prerequisites to gain access to new territories. In a different way, so could products such as *SimCity* or *The Sims*, in which the game is a virtual sandbox for players to explore and create their own goals. However, this might also be better modeled by the empty-sandbox approach. (See the upcoming "Empty Box with Toys/Sandbox" section.)

Although this is purely theoretical, this cubic structure implies that elements of the game are entirely freeform and that the player has no restrictions within one of the cubes. Although this may not be very satisfying as a structural model, since it fails to define choice points for the player other than at the nodes or interfaces between cubes, it might inspire some new way to conceptualize gameplay. By offering players essentially a blank canvas in which to immerse themselves, with transitional pathways to other blank canvases—or even to more traditional game structures—what kind of gameplay experiences might emerge? How do you create the blank canvas of the cubic structure? This is why the *GTA* series has been so successful. In each game, you get more and more freedom and more things you can do. You can date, fly a plane, drive a car, go into buildings, kill people...whatever you like.

Empty Box with Toys/Sandbox

The empty box with toys/sandbox approach is for construction-type games and sim games, such as *SimCity*, in which you give players lots of elements; set properties, rules of interaction, and behaviors for these objects; and let the players go for it. This really doesn't describe a story-based structure, for the most part, but stories could emerge from the interaction of elements within the game, as they do with *The Sims*. The emergent stories are essentially created in the minds of the players themselves. In this sort of environment, each player conceives an individual story based on the experience he has. But, of course, with clever and careful control of the types of tools available, the kinds and qualities of experiences can be, to some extent, predetermined. For instance, it's obvious that many players of *The Sims* will have romantic adventures. What makes it obvious is a combination of knowing human nature and providing the appropriate game elements to allow that kind of story to emerge. Of course, there are other examples of sandbox games. Can you think of a few? What makes them sandbox games?

Emergent Behavior

Many games exhibit the phenomenon of emergent behavior, in which the interaction of various elements can produce unexpected, unplanned, or unanticipated results or behaviors. The previous example of *The Sims* describes this sort of phenomenon to some extent. In essence, most Massively Multiplayer games rely on the emergent behavior of thousands of people to create the essence of the gameplay. The structures, rules, and setting of the game are provided, but the players create much of the emergent story, from ad hoc teaming, organized guilds, and affinity groups and various other human-to-human interactions, to commerce systems, thievery, exploits and cheats, and so on. Each player in a Massive Multiplayer game is the "author" of an individual story that is told only in his own mind but has the added effect of influencing the stories of all the other players with whom he interacts.

Even games that are for single players or for small numbers of players can have emergent stories and behaviors. The more complex the system you create, the more likelihood there will be for emergent behavior. If you create a (virtual) living world with many elements interacting according to determinate rules, you are likely to see emergent behaviors. The question is, are they behaviors you want or are they going to detract from the game? One challenge is to create games in which there is a lot of emergent behavior, and it is those very behaviors that make the game unique. This works because sometimes the things that happen are more interesting (to the gamer who made them happen) than something we might think up for the player at a design meeting.

Players don't even mind if this becomes hard work for them. For example, they might find that if an exploding barrel triggers the ones beside it to explode, they might go and collect every barrel in the game and try to lay out a long fuse of them to go and blow up something else (that the designer had never planned to be blown up). Using the elements of the game world to achieve unlikely results can become a focus in itself, and many players end up getting very skilled at it.

Often emergent behavior can result from very simple systems when they interact with multiple instances of the same system or with other simple systems. One example occurred when Will Wright was designing ocean currents for *SimEarth*. He used a very simple system of vectors—almost too simple to take seriously as a model for something as complex as ocean currents, and certainly not a complex mathematical algorithm based on complex interactions in the ocean—and the simple system resulted in a remarkably realistic result. The emergent behavior of this simple system, when applied in the holistic environment Will had created, resulted in a very complex and satisfyingly realistic simulation.

Ways to Start a Story

The opening line of a story, book, or play is always significant. The opening scene of a movie can set a tone and intrigue the audience. Likewise, the beginning of a game can be used to draw in players, establish the story or current situation, familiarize the player with the game's controls and systems, introduce some of the main actors, and/or set a mood or tone that will establish the pace of the game.

There are various ways to begin a game—some fairly common and some less so—including:

- Opening with a movie scene that sets the history and context of the game to come. This is very common in major games today.
- Opening with a montage, which can depict any number of initial images and story elements (some of which are mentioned in this list).
- Plunging right into the action (such as the middle of a fight, a chase scene, or a crash).
- Starting with an easy, slow, gentle setup (such as two people chatting while drinking tea).
- Starting with a major challenge (for example, a race is about to start).
- Starting in the future.
- Starting in the past.
- Starting very simply in a game that gradually (or suddenly) becomes more complex.
- Starting with a bluff or premonition (which could just be a dream).
- Starting as the consequence of a great or catastrophic event (trying to survive chaos).
- Starting in an idyllic situation that gets disrupted soon after (for example, the spacecraft or plane crashes into where you are).
- Starting with a powerful character who is soon stripped of his power.
- Starting with a mystery (so the gamer has no idea what's going on).
- Starting at the end and playing the entire game as a flashback.
- Starting with the hero under threat of being killed.
- Starting right in a sex (or lust) scene.
- Starting right in a medical emergency, surgery, or the like.
- Following someone who's oblivious and entering hell. (For example, someone walking into a bank that's in the middle of an armed robbery or enjoying a cruise ship that the viewer knows is filled with explosives.)
- Starting with the hero being tortured or humiliated.
- Starting right in an adventure sequence (just like Indiana Jones).
- Opening with a continuous shot connecting lots of people and their conversations that paint a picture of the situation.
- Following something, such as an animal as it heads toward the main action. (Imagine a happy rabbit bounding along and arriving at a bloody war.)
- Starting by showing the working mind of the main nemesis in operation.
- Seeing someone who is on the edge go over the edge, such as with road rage.
- Starting with someone close to the hero being killed, tortured, kidnapped, or otherwise threatened.
- Seeing something evil take place, then shifting to the hero and establishing his connection to it or interest in it.
- Starting with a view from far out in space and then zooming in closer and closer until the hero is at the center of the action. (Or going the opposite way, pulling out into space to something we need to know about.)
- Starting with a briefing (such as a military briefing scene that sets both the story and the mission objectives).
- Having a narrator start the story, but without a movie rolling. As a camera pans over the game, a narrator explains the situation.

Ways to End a Story

Stories in literature can end in a variety of ways, including having the hero die. In games, however, the hero's death, while possibly a common occurrence during the course of the game, is not the most desired ultimate outcome, given that games are about challenges and successes, not story alone. That's not to say that a great game couldn't be designed in which the hero dies at the end—*God of War* being a notable example. Several scenarios come immediately to mind. But, in general, the endings of games (where there is any kind of explicit story and ending) have been limited to the basic cliché of defeating the enemy in a great battle, followed possibly by some feel-good scenes of congratulations. (And that's okay, so don't go with something else unless it's better than the cliché.)

Of course, not all games involve stories and plots, and many games end in different ways. Some do end when you lose (such as certain arcade games in which there is no true ending). Other games end when you succeed, but not in the sense of a story ending—just successful completion of the game events, such as winning a race in a racing simulation or winning/losing a game or season in a sports game.

Here are some possible story game endings, other than the clichéd battle-and-reward sequence:

- The hero solves a great mystery and watches as all the pieces of a game-long puzzle fall into place.
- The "voilà" moment, when the clouds of mystery clear.
- The epic (bring you to tears) heartfelt speech by a key character or someone in authority, such as the president.
- After a rousing adventure, the hero (anti-hero?) realizes that the task he was on is either impossible or unimportant in the long run, and instead chooses what's really important (either the final character growth step, saving someone, or maybe saving a relationship).
- Everything shifts at the end of the game, and the hero must determine who is an enemy and who is a friend, who is right and who is wrong, who is good and who is bad, and so on, and then act accordingly. This was the ultimate challenge of *Myst*, for instance.
- The hero must make a great sacrifice at the end, perhaps letting someone he loves die in order to serve the greater cause.
- The player's character reaches an important and anticipated milestone in his life, such as achieving godly status, reaching his 21st birthday without being killed, or reuniting with a lost family member, lover, or other significant person/creature/thing.
- The player has succeeded in becoming the ruler of the land or conquering all enemies and fulfilling some life goal or prophecy.
- The hero becomes who he always should have been, and he takes that place and accepts it.
- The cure to a disease is discovered.
- Realizing all hope is lost, the nemesis commits suicide (sometimes taking his minions with him).
- The hero returns home, finally.
- The all-or-nothing bet is resolved.
- This will be the last embrace between the hero and the heroine.
- As he dies, the hero sees victory that he made happen.
- The nemesis just won't die or can't be killed, so the hero goes an unexpected route—maybe not to kill him, but to resolve the problem. (For example, Jafar in the final battle scene of *Aladdin*, wishing he was a genie to become even more powerful, but ending up trapped in a lamp. So he's not killed, but he's trapped forever, and the impossible is resolved.)
- The hero realizes the entire story was a dream or a drug-induced coma and wakes up somewhere completely disconnected to where he thought he was.
- The hero realizes home no longer exists, as did Charlton Heston in *Planet of the Apes*.

- A mystery ending (usually the setup to the sequel): Who was that? What the heck just happened? *The Blair Witch Project* is a good example.
- What you had accepted turns out to be completely wrong, forcing you to rethink the entire story. (Think of the movie *The Sixth Sense* with Bruce Willis.)
- A project or challenge the hero has been working on for the entire game is finally completed.

Bad Endings

By "bad endings," I don't mean endings that suck; I mean endings in which everything doesn't come out right from the player's point of view. These so-called bad endings can serve several purposes, however. On one hand, they provide a good look at what happens if the hero fails. On the other hand, clever designers could use an apparently catastrophic ending to set up a sequel. In such a case, the player would have to be rewarded somehow. Game players don't play games to fail. Still, it is possible that an ending could deviate dramatically from the expected "good" result and still be satisfying—and it could set up some great story and gameplay for future productions. Alternatively, it's great for replaying (and generating discussion) if the game can have multiple radically different endings based on how you play it.

Some examples include:

- The hero must die at the end in order to be resurrected as something stronger or different, or in order to enter the land of the dead and continue the story in a sequel. This can also include self-sacrifice for the good of others. The movie *Thelma & Louise* had a suicide ending, for example. (This is generally a bittersweet ending.)
- Somebody important dies (love object, beneficent ruler, and so on).
- Something important is destroyed, despite all efforts to preserve it.
- Civilization as we know it is destroyed.
- The hero "seems" to be dead.
- This victory has turned out small, and the real hope is lost.

Story Techniques

Storytelling, particularly in movies, TV, and games, can engage the viewer/player and make the story more dynamic and effective. Here are a few techniques you can use effectively in telling stories in games:

- **Flashbacks (Interactive or Non-Interactive).** These are good if they are cross-linked directly back to game action. (For example, an alarm goes off in the flashback, and that links to an alarm in the gameplay.)
- **Real-Time Events That Reveal Story or Infer Things While You Play.** For example, people dropping to their knees and praying to you when you walk up their street. Or a helicopter following you, but then being shot down...by whom?
- **Live Moment-to-Moment Character Actions (Not Speech).** For example, hand signals (SWAT signals, pointing, waving, and so on), head nods, ducking to anticipate something, or cowering in fear as you pass.
- **Third-Party One-Way Information.** For example, radio, TV, signs, overheard rumors, graffiti, objects such as books or maps, and so on. Basically, these are things that can convey messages to you. (See also Chapter 30, "Ways to Communicate with the Player.")

- **Third-Party Two-Way Information.** For example, overhearing two people talking (or asking questions or arguing), tapping their telephone line, seeing someone use a computer or ATM and reading over their shoulder, or using one of those laser devices that bounces light off office windows so you can hear the discussion inside.
- **Non-Interactive Cinematics (Preferably Played in the Game Engine So There's No Quality Change in the Graphics).** Seamless integration helps where the gameplay turns into non-interactive cinematics and right back to gameplay without disturbing breaks in the visuals. Interactive cinematics are getting better and better as time goes on; you don't need to listen to the story if you don't want to, or you can focus on a single part—maybe follow the characters you are most interested in and listen to their private conversation.
- **Full-Motion Video.** This refers to traditional movie footage used to tell a story. This footage could be live action or CG. It's clear that the action of switching to full-motion video will generally interrupt gameplay, and if the video cannot be skipped, it usually generates resentment in a certain percentage of gamers. So full-motion video should only be used when needed or when its effect is maximally positive and not disruptive to the game flow. Some games, such as later *Final Fantasy* games, have blended video cut scenes seamlessly with the action, making a less disruptive connection between the non-interactive and the interactive elements.
- **Text.** This can be displayed on a separate screen, scrolled, or page flipped; alternatively, text can overlay the action (providing information on progressing the story), or it can be on billboards and other in-game items and locations.
- **Narration/Voiceover/Live Blow-by-Blow Commentary.** With this technique, the hero himself can talk—for example, "I'm out of bullets!" You can use pop-up heads on the screen with speech or text (as in *Metal Gear Solid*). Or, sports commentators can describe the ongoing action during a sports game.
- **Picture-in-Picture.** This is effective if you want the story to be revealed from two (or more) locations at once. (It's good to make a player worry about another location, even though they're not actually there—it adds complexity and breadth to the game by requiring the player to be aware of more than just the immediate surroundings. The *Fahrenheit* game is an example. So was the original *Maniac Mansion.*)
- **Loading Sequence and Downtime.** Information or the story can be revealed during loading sequences or downtime. (This helps hide delays that the gaming hardware causes.)
- **External Sources.** You can reveal information from external sources (outside the game), such as live online from other players or mentors, on the web, through "real" phone numbers, and so on.

Plot Twists

In many stories, there are times when the hero discovers that whatever he thought was true was not, or the situation dramatically changes. The line, "Luke, I am your father," from *Star Wars* comes to mind.

Often plot twists are major zingers that happen at the end of a story, such as in the movies. *The Usual Suspects* and *The Sixth Sense* are both examples of this. Other times, plot twists can be major events that weren't foreseen, but which dramatically change the events that follow and, presumably, the protagonists' actions. Suppose you didn't know the story of the Titanic. Talk about plot twists. The rich and successful are on the ultimate luxury cruise when it all turns to disaster. There must be a story in there somewhere....

Plot twists can happen at various points in a story. The term "the plot thickens" usually refers to a moment when something new has been added to the story, making the situation more complex. This often involves a revelation or discovery that significantly alters the course the protagonists must take.

A good example is in *The Maltese Falcon*, when the ship's captain delivers the "black bird" to Sam Spade's office, putting him suddenly in possession of the item everybody's after.

In games, plot twists are common. There are many opportunities within a game to provide information or situations that will alter the course of the game and, consequently, the direction the player must go in order to succeed. It's not uncommon to be playing a game and think you are very close to the ending, only to discover that a whole new set of tasks is required before you reach that point. These tasks often come after you discover some new information about the nature of the final threat or the solution to the big puzzle you face.

Note that plot twists, in the game sense, can be major shifts of the story or of the player's circumstances, or they can be minor temporary situations that simply require the player to adjust to circumstances. For instance, you step through a teleporter, and suddenly you find out that your squad members were actually enemies all along—they were just trying to get you through the portal, and now they are revealed. Unexpected? Yes. So what do you do? Assuming you somehow survive this encounter, the twisty part is over. The game has not substantially changed. This was a temporary change of circumstances. However, if you were to discover that the agency for whom you have been working actually represents the evil you thought you were fighting (as in *Deus Ex*), the twist substantially changes the rest of the game. Your goals just completely changed, thanks to the twist.

Some common examples are detailed in the following list. See also Chapter 11, "Scenarios."

- The enemy is really an ally.
- An ally is really an enemy.
- It's all a dream.
- Bad to worse: You think you've solved a situation or overcome an obstacle, only to find that the situation is far worse than before.
- Breakdowns: Everything you need to succeed fails, either by nature or by intent.
- The enemy has discovered your plans (maybe even a long time ago, you now find out).
- The enemy takes a key hostage that changes everything, including your goals.
- Your (secret) identity has been discovered.
- Something happened just as planned, but it's too late.
- An event causes the schedule to change (usually for the worse). For example, there's a runaway train, and everyone is worried about when it will reach the end of the line. Then a bridge is destroyed, leaving only 10 minutes to disaster and increasing the time urgency considerably.
- Your senses, intelligence, perception, or super powers have failed you.
- Somehow the information you counted on did not arrive.
- You have received information and possibly already acted on it, but it turns out to be incorrect or false.
- The wrong characters fall in love; for example, A loves B, who loves C. C hates A, and B doesn't even know A is interested.
- The options change, and some of the new options are very challenging.
- What you were fighting for just changed. (Generally, now it will be much more important.) For example, perhaps you were saving your family, and now you are saving the world as we know it.
- What you were sure of, you are now not at all sure of.
- You told someone what you thought they needed to know, but they interpreted it very differently and took action you hadn't anticipated as a result.
- A new person enters the story and becomes a rival.
- The hero is given no choice but to do what he would *never* do.
- Someone new enters the story and becomes an unanticipated asset—you have new options as a result.
- Your element-of-surprise advantage is suddenly blown.
- Someone key dies in a freak accident.

- A promise on which you were relying was not kept.
- The proof you needed is gone forever—or worse still, it now incriminates you!
- You find out that to get something to work will require a string of things done correctly, or in perfect sync, or you will need to cooperate with your enemy.
- Nobody trusts anyone else, nobody knows who to believe, and nobody knows who to rely on.
- Uncertainty takes control.
- Someone uninvited shows up.
- Your plans start to fail, or maybe all of them fail at the same time.
- A new person has new information, outlook, or perspective.
- Someone leaves, dies, or quits who you were desperately counting on.
- Someone defects at the wrong moment, or you discover that someone is a mole or traitor.
- A character faces his worst nightmare.
- You meet someone unexpectedly who can help you, offer you something you need, or maybe even steal something from you that was crucial.
- There's a set time schedule triggered before disaster, and you are at its mercy.

DILEMMAS

Many games involve a straightforward approach: Anything that moves is bad; shoot it! The story, if there is one, involves no complexity or ambiguity. The hero is in the right, and that's all you need to know. However, some games have attempted to create situations that present players with difficult choices—moral, ethical, or logical dilemmas.

WHAT IS A DILEMMA?

A dilemma is essentially a choice of actions, each of which has undesirable or imperfect consequences. For instance, the choice of whether to get burned from a fire (when escaping a building through a corridor that's on fire) or to burn to death is not really a dilemma, because the first solution is clearly good from the chooser's point of view, and the second choice is clearly bad. There's no ambiguity and no difficulty in making the choice. But suppose the choice were to be almost burned alive, endure horrific pain for months, and live the rest of your life disfigured and grotesque to save five of your friends, or to endure minor burns but only save three of your friends. For some, this might be a somewhat more difficult decision to make, because neither choice is perfectly desirable. A related dilemma would be a situation in which you had to choose who to save from the fire (assuming you could only save one person or thing): your wife, your baby, your father or mother, your dog or cat, or your computer. You would have to consider a rationale for your actions, given that only one could be saved. So, to be a dilemma, a situation must have two or more choices, each of which results in imperfect or undesirable consequences—often the lesser of two (or more) evils.

Dilemmas make great scenes for games and movies because different gamers will have very different responses to such situations. (Some will care about only themselves; some will care about everyone but themselves.)

THE PRISONER'S DILEMMA

In traditional game theory, one of the classic dilemmas is known popularly as the *Prisoner's Dilemma*. I thought it worth mentioning here as a model. Much has been written about the Prisoner's Dilemma, but here's my version: Two accomplices have been arrested and placed in separate cells. The prosecutor visits each one separately and tells him that he has two choices. He can confess and plea bargain or he can remain silent. However, his fate is tied to the choice his accomplice makes as well. If one prisoner confesses and the other remains silent, then the first one will go free, and the one who remains silent will get the maximum sentence based on the testimony of the one who confesses. If they both confess, they will both be found guilty, but they will get lighter sentences. If they both remain silent, they will be convicted on a lesser charge.

Look at it from the prisoners' perspective. If they are both silent, they are taking a cooperative approach, and they each get the minimum sentence. However, if either of them confesses and plea bargains, it can be seen as a betrayal of the other—*a defection.*

Clearly, the best solution from an individual's point of view is to confess (defect), but only if the accomplice remains silent (cooperates). The next best solution (from the individual's point of view) is for both to remain silent and take the lesser rap. If they both confess, they get the middle result. This can be seen numerically by assigning values to each option—in this case, how many years the prison sentences would be.

Results (Prisoner 1, Prisoner 2)

	Prisoner 2	
Prisoner 1	Cooperate	Defect
Cooperate	1,1	10,0
Defect	0,10	5,5

It is clear that the best result Prisoner 1 could get would be if he confesses (defects) and Prisoner 2 remains silent (cooperates) (0,10). If both remain silent (cooperate), they each suffer (1,1). Again, the best overall solution would be for both to remain silent. Both confessing/defecting results in each of them getting a medium result (5,5)—not the best result either of them could have obtained. The question is, does each one trust the other to do the most rational thing?

Assuming that each prisoner is only out for himself and wants to get the minimum sentence, there is considerable reward for betraying the other, but the risk is great as well. Do you go for the big payoff or do you assume the other prisoner will stay silent and each of you will get off lightly? The safest move is to confess—you can win big, and at worst you lose less—but the best outcome comes when both remain silent (cooperate).

What would you do? Obviously, the most likely result is to betray the other by defecting since you have to assume the other guy is going to try to get his best result as well. How can you trust the other guy to stay silent when he can get off all together by betraying you? So, even though the "best" result involves cooperation, in a pure situation where each prisoner is out for himself, it is unlikely that both will choose cooperation.

This model has applications both in real life and in games. Real-life examples of the Prisoner's Dilemma occur in a variety of settings. One example is the arms race that can occur between two rival countries. Do they divert their assets to build a larger military or do they negotiate a disarmament treaty? If one builds up and the other does not, it tips the scales in favor of the one that builds up. If they both build up, they both lose because they have to divert their resources into the military instead of, say, domestic reinvestment. If they both disarm, both come out ahead, which would seem to be the most beneficial choice. In fact, usually the "rational" choice these countries would take is to build up—the price of trusting the other to disarm is too great, so rarely does this situation result in the "best" solution.

Another example occurs during road races, where the leaders may pull ahead of the pack. If two runners or cyclists, for instance, are leading, they can help each other by taking turns in the lead, where the one in front works harder to break the force of the wind, and the one behind gets to "draft" on the frontrunner and therefore not work as hard. In a cooperative strategy, they take turns drafting and leading, allowing both the opportunity to finish at least first and second, barring any unexpected racers overtaking them both. If they don't cooperate and one consistently takes the lead, the other one has a big advantage. If they run side by side and don't help each other, neither gains any advantage—and in fact they may lose ground to the pack and both tire before the end.

Take another example. A boy and a girl are on a date. They both hope the date goes well and that they can deepen their relationship. So they both have a stake in the outcome. If the boy pays for the meal, the girl will invite him up to her apartment after the date. If they go dutch, then she will kiss him goodnight at the door and possibly accept another date. If she pays, then she will say goodnight at the restaurant and there will be no kiss, no next date. In this case, there is mutual benefit if the boy pays—they both get a nice result. If they go dutch, then the benefit is less, but it's still better than if she pays, when nobody gains anything—and in fact they lose an opportunity to find what they are seeking.

Later work on the Prisoner's Dilemma involves iterative situations in which the participants made Prisoner's Dilemma–like decisions sequentially, with an evaluation of the results in between. This tests whether participants in such a situation can learn to adapt and find the "best" strategy in which both win the most points. If both sides cooperate in each of (typically) 10 turns, they mutually get the most points possible. If one defects and the other cooperates, then the defecting group gets the most points, and the cooperating group gets none. If both defect, they get the medium result. So it would look something like this:

Results (Group A, Group B)

	Group B	
Group A	Cooperate	Defect
Cooperate	3,3	5,0
Defect	0,5	1,1

In practice, many people go for the most points their side can get by defecting every time. If they do that, ultimately the other side will defect, too, even if they are tempted to cooperate. It turns out that the best strategies for obtaining the optimal solution involve being cooperative on the first move, then doing a "tit for tat" response to the other side's move. If they cooperate, the first side continues to cooperate. If they defect, then the first side will defect, although improved models suggest occasional "forgiveness" moves, in which the first group will meet a defection with another cooperation, just in case the other side gets the message.

A practical example of this iterative model can be seen with the racers who cooperate. It always takes one of them to cooperate first, but if the other reciprocates on the next "turn," then cooperation can become the standard. But if the second racer resists the other's attempt to give up the lead, then the defection can lead to a breakdown of the cooperative attitude of that first runner, who will then become competitive.

In games, the Prisoner's Dilemma can be used effectively to examine some of the choices available to a player. For instance, suppose when you meet an enemy, you can draw your weapon and try to kill him. Presumably the enemy will do the same. This is the usual encounter with an enemy, and one that is consistent with the likely outcome of a Prisoner's Dilemma. But suppose in the game either party could offer to join up by approaching unarmed. Here's the dilemma: If one of you approaches unarmed and the other does not, you are at a distinct disadvantage. If both approach unarmed, you can join forces and be stronger together than you were individually. However, you can still take the normal approach and fight it out, but there is at least the risk of injury or death in the encounter.

Here's an example of an iterative dilemma in a game: Suppose you and your enemy each hold 10 hostages, and you begin 10 rounds of negotiation with the enemy. At the end of the 10 rounds, the negotiations will be terminated. In each "turn" you can either release a hostage or not release a hostage. Your goal is to get your hostages to safety and to release as few of the hostages you have as possible. Again, as in the Prisoner's Dilemma, there are better and worse outcomes. If you both release a hostage, you have at least saved one of your people and so has your adversary. If neither releases a hostage, nothing changes, but at least one hostage will remain in captivity at the end of the negotiations. If one releases a hostage and the other does not, of course the side that did not gains, in terms of the exchange, by receiving a hostage but not releasing one.

In this example, the best result you can gain (if saving your hostages is most important to you) is a complete one-to-one exchange of hostages. However, by occasional defections (meaning you don't release any hostages, but the enemy does) you can have a net gain.

This example shows the beauty of the Prisoner's Dilemma. It's clear that mutual distrust would result in no prisoners being exchanged. It's also clear that total trust would result in a complete exchange of prisoners, perhaps the best overall result. But putting yourself in the place of one of these sides, you will be tempted to "cheat" and gain an advantage. It isn't really all that satisfactory to lose all your hostages, even if you do gain all of the enemy's hostages. Players in this scenario would attempt to cheat at least some of the time. In this case, each time you release no hostages, you ensure that at least one prisoner remains a prisoner. If you defect and the enemy defects, two prisoners remain in captivity. Under these circumstances, it's possible that no hostages will be released, and if the trust is betrayed once, it's likely that it won't be regained and no more hostages will be released.

One strategy in this scenario would be to establish cooperation until the last move, then defect. The worst that could happen is that you both defect. But suppose the last hostage was the most important. That might change the situation. Perhaps you needed to establish trust with the first nine, because the last one was critical. How does that change your approach? Can you risk betrayal earlier? Would you really release the last hostage, knowing that the other side has nothing to lose by not releasing theirs?

Of course, using the Prisoner's Dilemma as a model is only the start. You can create all kinds of dilemmas in games, and you can modify and alter the parameters—even of the Prisoner's Dilemma, which is, after all, only a model. There are other variants, such as the Chicken model (named after the game of driving cars toward each other and trying to make the other one swerve or back down). In this model, the consequences of both defecting are severe—a head-on collision. So the stakes are far higher in the lose/lose scenario. In this case, there is still a bigger reward if you "defect" and the other does not—meaning he swerves first. But the risk of waiting for the other to swerve first is far greater than the equivalent risk in a Prisoner's Dilemma scenario, in which mutual defection is bad, but not so much worse. In this case, it's a matter of weight and degree.

The Chicken Model

	Group B	
Group A	Cooperate	Defect
Cooperate	5,5	1,10
Defect	10,1	−10,−10

Part III

Another variant is called an Assurance Game, in which cooperation is rewarded far more than defection. In this case, the matrix would look like this:

Assurance Game Model

	Group B	
Group A	Cooperate	Defect
Cooperate	10,10	1,5
Defect	5,1	3,3

In this type of game, cooperation is clearly the best choice, and the motivation to defect is considerably reduced. The best outcome, by far, involves mutual cooperation.

Still another type of dilemma that is quite applicable to games is called the *Tragedy of the Commons*, which involves the shared use of resources with limited renewal rates. For instance, if all loggers can cut wood from the forest equally, then each logger can gain individually by cutting the trees and selling the wood. However, without restraint the forest will be decimated if trees are cut faster than they can renew, and ultimately nobody will be able to log—there will be no more trees. With cooperation, the loggers could work together to ensure that they logged in a sustainable manner, thus maintaining a consistent flow of logs and income. However, without cooperation, each individual logger will cut as much as he can until ultimately there's nothing left.

The dilemma in the Tragedy of the Commons example is similar to that of the Prisoner's Dilemma in that cooperation provides a better result overall, but defection (in the case of cutting trees only for individual gain) results in a good result for the defector (at least at first) and a bad result for the group overall. The difference here is that the bad result ultimately catches up even with the defector, and the Tragedy of the Commons is generally applied to groups of more than two, in contrast to the Prisoner's Dilemma.

There are lots of ways to explore game theory and lots of nuances to explore. However, it isn't my goal to get bogged down in pure theory. Often, when you are designing puzzles and scenarios in games, you will be operating more instinctively. You won't likely stop and say, "I'm going to design a Prisoner's Dilemma or a Chicken model here." You may in fact be doing just that, but only because it's good game design and makes the game more fun. Even so, knowledge of some of the aspects of classical game theory can be helpful and can allow you to recognize patterns and opportunities when you are creating your own masterpieces.

You can also have a *lot* of fun with this when deciding how prizes (or the spoils of war) will be split amongst a group, by letting them decide.

Types of Dilemmas

Types of dilemmas include logical, moral and ethical, and emotional dilemmas, all of which are covered in the following subsections.

Logical Dilemmas

Logical dilemmas are probably the most common in games. The Prisoner's Dilemma is largely a logical one (with possible moral, ethical, and emotional elements, depending on how it's set up—suppose the other prisoner is your brother…), but there are others, some quite simple. For instance, do you take the low road or do you take the high road? Do you cut the green wire or the red one? Do you save the priest, the artist, or the political leader? Do you kill the strongest enemy first or the weakest?

Most game puzzles involve logical choices, but in order to be a dilemma, there must be specific consequences to each choice. And there is a noticeable risk/reward factor in operation. A fairly common example might be the Lady and the Tiger dilemma. Behind one door is a beautiful woman. Behind the other is a vicious man-eating tiger. The consequences of your choice matter considerably. Of course, to be a logical choice and not just a random one, the person deciding must have some way to guess which door is which based on previous elements of the story or game.

Here's another example: Suppose you have a puzzle to open a door by adjusting a series of levers. If nothing happens when you try a wrong choice, it is a still puzzle—to find the right configuration—but it isn't a dilemma. If, on the other hand, certain configurations would result in someone important to you being killed or your party being bombarded by machine-gun fire, then it becomes more of a dilemma. Do you risk the wrong action? Do you find a way to neutralize the threat first? Do you seek out more clues to the proper configuration so you don't risk suffering the unfortunate consequences of choosing incorrectly?

It shouldn't be difficult to think of some logical dilemmas you can use in your games. But think in terms of interesting consequences resulting from different outcomes and different strategies and approaches to the dilemma. Think of every possible choice a player might make.

- You capture an enemy agent. Should you kill him outright and lose any possibility that he has useful information or could be used as a hostage? Or do you keep him alive, hoping to get something useful out of him, but risk his escape—or worse, that he has a way of attacking you or revealing your position to the enemy?
- There's something you want, but the risk of getting it is very high. For instance, there's a dandy sword at the end of a long tunnel. Obtaining the sword will make your character much more powerful in the future, but getting to it you risk death. Or even worse, perhaps you risk losing the weapons you currently have, which would mean even if you tried for the sword again, you would be far weaker than the first time, and the rest of the game would become substantially harder.
- You can embed a sacred stone in your sword to improve it, but there's a 50-percent chance you will destroy the sword during the process (and all previous stones you embedded). Every stone you add (to keep improving it) puts everything before in jeopardy.
- There is a book on a desk that contains the names and locations of all the enemy agents. However, if you take it, the risk is that the enemy will quickly notice its absence and will implement all its security measures. You may not be able to escape with the book, and once it is discovered that the book is missing, all the enemy agents will quickly be alerted. Additionally, if you are caught, some of your allies will be implicated and hunted down by the enemy. In a situation like this, of course, you want to give the player options that allow him to minimize the risk of discovery, such as substituting a false replica of the book, copying the contents without actually taking the book, or somehow disposing of the person who might discover its absence. However, once you successfully minimize the risk, this is no longer a dilemma.

Moral and Ethical Dilemmas

Morality involves our beliefs about right and wrong. In its purest form, morality is a universal belief. For instance, most cultures believe it is wrong to kill (at least one of your own tribe). However, in practice, morality is subjective and based on cultural norms. So morality is to a great extent determined by the individual or the culture to which the individual belongs.

In games, this presents interesting opportunities. For instance, in classic *Dungeons & Dragons*, there are Good and Evil characters, plus characters who are nuanced versions of these. Thus, a Good character is expected to behave according to certain models of morality, while an Evil character would behave differently. And, of course, Good characters and Evil characters are like oil and water; they don't mix well.

But even in games without such formal descriptions and categories, there are implied morals (and ethics, which involve proper behavior based on moral values). So, for instance, playing the character in *Grand Theft Auto* is different from playing a character in *Dark Age of Camelot*. Playing a Jedi Knight in a *Star Wars* game is different from playing a Dark Jedi or the lead character in *Devil May Cry*. Why? Because the implied morality of the characters is different, and therefore the acceptable actions they can take are different.

Knowing the presumed morality of the main character in a game is still somewhat different from knowing the morality of the player. Some players cannot justify doing evil acts. For instance, in *Fable*, many players can only play according to a more or less Good alignment. But some players really enjoy playing the Evil way. Because in *Fable* you have a choice of what kinds of actions you want to take—good or evil—the game is full of moral dilemmas, the consequences of which help determine whether you are on a good path or an evil one. Ultimately, moral dilemmas add to the emotional impact of a game. If a moral dilemma is well established, the player should really have to consider the consequences of each choice, and there should be real consequences!

Often, the question asked is whether you violate your moral code for the greater good or for personal gain? For instance:

- Do you open the door that leads to the treasure, but that also unleashes a terrible demon upon the world?
- Do you travel back in time and kill the kindest person in the world, knowing that if you do not, the person will make a terrible mistake in the future and cause untold multitudes to suffer?
- Do you allow a man's daughter to be taken away to slavery and torture in order to gain the enemy's trust so you can ultimately defeat him?
- From a burning building, do you save a baby, a beautiful woman you desire, or an old man who may hold the key to world peace?
- Do you put a dam on the river to provide power to thousands of homes, even though it will starve out several small communities that depend on the river?
- Do you steal a man's most prized possession, believing that it is an important weapon against the evil that is coming?

All of these are examples of moral/ethical dilemmas, but these are only a few to inspire you to consider how these kinds of dilemmas can create great game situations.

Emotional Dilemmas

Although to some extent all dilemmas involve emotional responses, some dilemmas rely almost entirely on the emotional response of the player to a situation. For instance, if faced with a choice of killing a cute little puppy dog or a grotesque half-worm/half-centipede creature, which would you choose? But what if the grotesque creature was really a highly intelligent being, critical to the survival of the universe, and the puppy was just little Billy's pet? What if the dog were really an evil mastermind bent on the destruction of all you hold dear, and the worm creature was, well, just little Billy's pet? Or, as another example, do you stay behind to save your mother/daughter/sister/brother/father, or do you run because there's a chance you can reach the commander in charge of the army and warn him in time to prevent a disaster? What makes it a hard emotional dilemma is that there is an immediately obtainable and desirable choice and a different, possibly even more desirable, choice—but one that is not at all certain and requires abandoning the immediate and strongly personal option. Emotionally, can you ever compare saving thousands of strangers to saving one loved one?

Similar dilemmas might involve choosing between a beautiful, innocent-looking young woman who acts shy and dependent or a gnarled old crone who speaks her mind and is rude and excessively direct. The first instinct in each case is to protect the one who seems most attractive and most innocent or helpless. Providing clues to the player about the true nature of the situation—perhaps those who appear innocent and helpless are really the most evil and dangerous—the player must go against the emotional response in order to find the best solution.

Other emotional dilemmas may involve sacrificing loved ones, giving up a prized possession, or even betraying a friend. In each of these cases and many more, the decisions that must be made also risk strong emotional responses. For instance, suppose you spent a good part of a game in a courtship with a beautiful companion, someone your character (and also you, as a player) came to see as a potential, albeit virtual, partner and a love interest. Then suppose the companion contracted a deadly and virulent disease. If you leave your companion infected, the disease will ultimately kill not only you, but millions of other victims. You must destroy the disease, and there is no known cure. You can risk seeking a cure, but in the time it takes to find one, the disease might have spread or it might kill your companion anyway. Perhaps the safest solution is to burn the victim and the disease with her. But how hard will that be when you have formed such an attachment with this character, and you have already foreseen a future with her? In real life, this would be tragic. In a game, perhaps it's not so tragic, but certainly it would have some emotion tied to it if the connection between the characters was well established. A great example of this might be found in the game *BioShock*.

Likewise, suppose you completed a series of difficult quests in order to earn a certain item—say an über-weapon. Then, at a certain point in your game, that weapon—yes, that one—suddenly is needed by another character, or it must be sacrificed in order to beat back a powerful enemy. In any case, some noble cause requires you to relinquish your hard-earned, precious weapon. It would be the equivalent of asking Gollum to toss the One Ring into the fires of Mordor—painful. But what if you could, just maybe, save the day by the strength of that weapon, so that instead of sacrificing it, you would wield it for the common good? Risky, perhaps, but worth a try? One way is a sure thing; the other is risky, but you keep your weapon. Another dilemma.

So make sure to put the characters or the player in positions where they have really *tough* decisions. It's a good story trick to make some situations in your game really memorable.

Timelines

In any story or any game, one of the main goals is to keep the player's interest and to keep the experience progressing. One way to examine this is to break the experience into definable timelines. Think of them as the intensity level or amplitude of a particular aspect of the overall experience measured over time. There will be times of lower intensity and times when the intensity spikes. Think of it as a rollercoaster track viewed from the site. You don't want things to lull for long periods of time.

Not all games will have all the timelines mentioned in the following sections. Some will have more exploration/discovery than others, and some will be mostly about the action timeline. However, thinking about timelines can also get you thinking about ways to add more depth and range to a game. If your game has only an action timeline, think about putting some surprise in it. If it has mostly a discovery timeline, perhaps it could use some action.

The following sections cover some possible timelines to track. (See also Chapter 28, "Controlling Pacing.")

Learning and Information Line

Although initially players must learn the mechanics and rules of a game, the learning line is more about how players will discover new information within the game's story or universe. Many games are structured like mysteries in which players must search and uncover clues that ultimately reveal the truth. In such games, the learning line must keep players' attention by steadily rewarding their efforts and occasionally offering an especially significant piece of the puzzle, causing the learning line to spike.

Even in games that are less dependent on mystery and puzzles, players are always learning by meeting new challenges. For instance, even in a shooter where there may be little or no storyline, the introduction of new enemies, new weapons, and new battlefields provides opportunities for players to learn, which invigorates the learning line.

So just start drawing a staircase. Getting three steps up is when you learn something new. Getting one step down is when you don't learn something new. (You can modify that ratio based on how many features are appropriate for your game.) The trick is to be on the lookout for long periods of learning nothing, so you can see whether you can stop that from happening.

Action Line

Games commonly depend on action as their primary component, yet within the action timeline, there is room for peaks and valleys—times of intensity, followed by times of even more intensity, followed by times of rest and recovery. In games where there is a lot of discovery and dialogue, looking at the action line may be important to keep the game exciting.

Games often include a main action line for the game as a whole, but separate action lines for the individual incidences along the way. How do you add action? You just make things go wrong. Flip comfort into chaos. What was predictable is now unpredictable. What was expected failed somewhat or went entirely wrong. Maybe the enemy takes a major stride forward. Just try to put the gamer into a new situation in which his adrenaline will pick back up.

Surprise

In addition to the peaks and valleys of information and action, it is very useful to include surprises—times to really wake up players and provide extra stimulation. This is often done by using twists (see the "Plot Twists" section earlier in this chapter); by introducing new elements or new enemies, or new information from NPCs; or by shifting the rules a little to force players to leave the familiar and readjust their techniques and/or expectations. For example, perhaps they get used to a weapon and then something eats it, or the cave characters have been walking through has many monsters buried beneath their feet, which now decide to pop up and say hi.

Space/Area

One way a game can seem fresh or can turn stale is if players feel free or confined, respectively. So, in many games, the rate at which new territories or new areas are uncovered is an important timeline. You want players to get the most out of any area, but periodically expanding the available game space and/or opening up new aspects of existing ones is important. Frankly, it feels good to keep changing the environment, so you don't just play in tight corridors for hours on end. So try to give the feeling of wide-open spaces and contrast that with really tight spaces—again, it will play with their experience. You can do the same with other perspective changes, such as with height—for example, going from underground (or underwater), to on the ground, to in the air, to very high up.

Emotion

The emotion timeline in games runs the gamut from laughter to fear, from curiosity to anger. In some games, there may also be a buildup of emotional attachment to characters. Depending on how you design and plan a game, you may be able to access a wide range of human emotions. Even in a relatively simple game, you know that players will have emotional responses to certain events within the game. It may simply be increased excitement at the prospect of a huge battle or anticipation as they approach some dangerous intersection. It may also involve cursing the developers for making something too hard or for implementing rules that the player doesn't like, but these reactions are not part of our focus, however valid they may be in many game players' experiences. In any case, emotion plays an important part in games, as we identify with our player character and focus on winning. Considering that emotion and tracking it in a timeline can help you see where your game needs more work or where it is working perfectly.

Frustration Tracking

Frustration tracking is when you think about what negative feelings a gamer is having, and you attempt to track it. For example, if finding a way out of a space is tough, but 60 percent of people find the exit pretty quickly, what about the poor 40 percent who are stuck and frustrated? Should you make the problem really simple, so 100 percent of the people sail through? The goal is to understand where people might get frustrated and only help them when needed.

There's a trick people are now using in game testing to try to work this out. You have someone play a level, then digitally start drawing a graph. If the gamer hits a button, he is signaling that he is frustrated; the more he hits the button, the more frustrated he feels right then. You can track this info with the gamer's exact location and start to get a feeling where your players are suffering. Again, the trick is to look at the graph and put in automatic sensing support to wipe out the high-frustration spikes. Unlike the other timelines, the frustration timeline should be reasonably flat. Some players tolerate and even enjoy a little frustration, while others get quickly discouraged. Your game design should deal with each player as an individual, helping him just when he needs it, in the areas where frustration is likely to happen.

Relevance Today (Endless New Ideas!)

One hook on which you can hang your game is cultural relevance. Start by looking at what's going on in the world at the time you plan to ship. Suppose you notice that the 100-year anniversary of flight is coming up. Can you make a game that commemorates that event and ties into its publicity? Or, if you're making a game of political commentary, does it tie into a certain war? Or maybe the Olympics are coming.... Comedians, advertising companies, and movie writers all study what's going on in the world and also what is happening in homes and on the streets. This is where "fresh" ideas often come from. For instance, I just read about new Israeli defense weapons. They look like high-tech rifles that bend in the middle so their LCD displays can allow you to aim and fire around corners. Simple innovations like these can immediately be carried into the game world. I first saw the weapon described a few years ago, and it was recently used in the movie *Wanted*. I haven't seen it in a video game yet, but what a cool concept!

Social Pressures (Grow Every Year)

One of the biggest surprises to game makers is when they make a game that doesn't have current relevance—for instance, a game about swashbuckling pirates, which has had its moments, but lately has not been very popular—and then they wonder why it's not a giant hit. They need to look at who's buying the games. These young guys, steered heavily by peer pressure, just don't want to be seen with the pirate game in their hands, even if they secretly want it. Be aware of that concern—it's not only very real, but it's getting worse every year. Watching the evolution of the *Prince of Persia* games is a good example, as they have adjusted to player expectations.

Sources of Current Information

So where do you look for relevant information? How do you keep abreast of the trends, the interests of people, and the specific inspirations that would lead to better, more successful, and more culturally relevant games?

You can start with popular culture and go from there:

- **Movies.** What's been hot over the last few years? What generates a lot of press/discussion?
- **Music.** What's hot, what's controversial, what's edgy, and what's not?
- **Videos.** Any new "looks" or rendering styles? (The *Stash* DVD series is great inspiration for new looks.)
- **Television.** What new camera effects, lighting, or angles are people using? How are top-rated shows presented? What's new on VH1 or MTV? What kind of comedy works best these days?
- **Radio.** What is the mix that makes the most popular shows? What do they talk about?
- **Books.** What are some very popular books and novels?
- **Newspapers.** What headlines (mashed up) can lead to entirely new ideas?
- **Major Trend, Technology, or Design Magazines.** What's in *T3*, for example? How about *Popular Science*, *Discover*, or even *Popular Mechanics*?
- **Teen Magazines.** What's being covered in teen magazines?
- **Subject-Specific, Culturally Relevant Magazines and Websites.** What do you find in magazines or on websites about such topics as skateboarding or music?
- **Internet.** What's hot on MySpace, Facebook, blogs, and so on?
- **Politics.** Isn't there always lots of good villain material here?
- **World News.** What's going on in the world around you?
- **Other Edgy Games.** What's hot in other games right now?

If you're really doing your job, you want to get into the trenches. Talk to people from different groups, particularly those who are likely to buy the games you are going to make. Don't take what they say too literally; read between the lines. People will tell you all kinds of stuff. You need to interpret what they say into what will make a game that they will look forward to and will be happy to play with their friends.

Multi-Session Storytelling

Multi-session storytelling is a major concern for game developers today. Unlike movies, which we generally watch in one sitting, or TV, which we watch in discrete segments, game players often play one game over many sessions. Some players even play more than one game during the same period of time, going back and forth between them. These issues are especially true of games that take from 20 to 60 hours to play—or even more! It's pretty unrealistic to devote that much time at one session. Add to that the growing popularity of persistent world games online, and you have people moving back and forth, interrupting gameplay regularly and then randomly returning to the story environments. How can they be expected to remember all that was going on when 95 percent of games make no attempt to help people catch up where they left off?

This problem has been compounded by the use of mobile phones and handhelds for games, when the session times can be as short as waiting in the line at the local coffee shop. So how can players keep track?

The solution is to make smarter games. Here are a few ideas, some perhaps new and others already in use in some games. No doubt you can think of a few more:

- A smart game can look at the save date or track the dates of play sessions and think, "This dude has not played me for 18 weeks!"
- Create reminder systems to help players keep on track, including quest log descriptions and progress indicators, maps, review movies or journals, NPC dialogue, and so on.
- The game can auto-monitor your continuation rate and maybe gently ease back on difficulty as you get the controls down again. (Imagine saving in a really tough area, coming back seven days later, and being rusty—now that area is twice as tough! That's not good.)
- Have the game welcome the player back, fill him in, and remind him what he was up to.
- The in-game characters can add extra feedback based on things you might have forgotten.
- The game could use frustration tracking. (See the "Frustration Tracking" section earlier in this chapter.) For example, maybe the player keeps trying to open a locked door, then walks around and tries the same door yet again. The game might think, "You probably forgot you need the key."
- The game could use easy-to-cancel helper systems to remind the player of the control mechanisms. (For example, if the player keeps trying to fire without reloading, it reminds him how to reload.)
- The game could provide a map to show the player where he is in relation to his goal (just in case he forgot the lay of the land).
- The game could use snapshots of the milestones passed so far, so the player can be reminded of the cool stuff that's happened and can get back into the context of everything.
- The game could use a quick movie to show the story so far. It would work like the little synopsis you get sometimes with TV shows, when they tell you what happened in previous episodes.

Keeping Secrets

This section is about secrets and how they function in game designs. I'm not referring to the meta-game aspect where players may reveal secrets to each other outside the game sessions (or even within a session in a multiplayer game). What I'm referring to is the way a game designer keeps information from the player until it is needed or until it is most effective—or even keeps it entirely from the player if it is something that never needs to be revealed or that must be discovered through intuition instead of by explicit means.

Alternatively, this section might have been titled, "Information: When to Reveal It and When to Withhold It," but I like "Keeping Secrets" more. Why? Because as a game designer, you are for the most part and in most games omniscient. You know the whole story and every variation. You almost always know what will happen when the player does *x* or *y*. And it is through the game structures that you reveal information.

Although the designer tends to know everything, it is not desirable for the player to have equal knowledge. Players want to discover, to explore, and to experiment. They want to engage in a mystery. So in keeping secrets, designers can foster that game experience.

How do you keep secrets? You can reveal information:

- By the use of clues.
- When the person you were keeping the secret for is now dead.
- When the person keeping the secret is threatened.
- When a friend or lover is threatened.
- When the player has met some preordained obligation or challenge.
- When the player has satisfied certain tasks.
- When the player has shown mastery according to certain conditions.
- When the player has discovered certain objects or methods that give him the power to reveal the secret.

- When the player has constructed a specific object, device, or machine that reveals secrets and so on.
- By begging, "Please tell me!"
- By torture.
- By wanting to belong to a group, thus revealing information that might aid in acceptance.
- When the player desperately needs the information.
- When specific elements of the plot have occurred and "the reveal" happens.
- When a specific amount of game time has elapsed.
- When the player gets to a certain location where the answer is waiting.
- When the player learns to decipher a code.
- When a player triggers a specific event.
- Or perhaps the information was always available, but the player must understand the message or notice the source of information.

Simple Mystery and Meta-Mystery

Mystery is getting pretty critical in storytelling these days. You should watch the speech by J.J. Abrams (on the mystery box) at TED.com. He created hit shows such as *Lost*, which always contains a lot of mystery and questions for the audience. Gaming is the same. It's commonly more fun *not* to know the answer, but to discuss it with your friends and think a lot about it. Gamers have *great* imaginations, so let them use those imaginations!

Really study mystery and always try to keep questions in the player's mind; try to anticipate their predictions and play with that knowledge. This also allows you to create meta-mysteries, which are not just simple things players don't understand. They may confuse everyone (including non-linked people in the story). Some meta-mysteries are revealed so slowly that they last years, meaning multiple sequels! They actually tie the sequels together and keep the gamers wanting answers.

More options may be found in Chapter 30, "Ways to Communicate with the Player."

Wrong-Headedness

Often in a story, particularly a mystery, thriller, or comedy, one of the main characters will simply do the wrong thing over and over again. As an audience, you want to scream at the person and tell him what to do. It's often a painful but suspense-building aspect of a story. Although this kind of suspense can occur in games, it's generally somewhat harder to orchestrate. One easy way is to have an NPC take the wrong action while the player knows the NPC is going the wrong way but can't stop him. You can use this method similarly to how it's used in movies and literature.

But there is another kind of wrong-headedness that can work in games, where the player is the main character. As such, he is no longer the outside observer, watching helplessly while the main character makes mistakes or walks heedlessly into danger. In this case, since the main character is under the player's control, such plot-directed wrong-headedness is not an issue—at least with the main (player) character. Clearly, players as individuals may (and often will) do things in games that from the point of view of the game's stated goals are wrong. But this is part of gameplay, experimentation, and to some degree, the natural rebelliousness of game players. Again, this may be wrong-headedness from a particular point of view, but it is perfectly acceptable game-player behavior.

What the game designer must do is anticipate when the player does something that is obviously wrong—or at least that isn't the most sensible response to a situation. Players will often go the wrong way because they legitimately don't know which way to go. Some will do so in order to experiment and test the limits. Still other players will understand perfectly well what the game designer intends and will purposefully do something else to see what happens. You want to reward all these people with some result—the more creative and unexpected, the better.

Although players often enjoy finding ways to outwit the game designers, they also tend to have great admiration for games that account for their most unexpected and off-the-wall actions. Players who try outlandish stunts in a game will be impressed when the game responds in such a way as to confirm that the designers had considered even those actions. "Wow. They even thought of that!" So, what the player will discover when he or she takes a wrong-headed approach can vary from reward to punishment, from opportunity to death, but it should be interesting and entertaining, and it should prove that the designers were prepared for all contingencies.

Types of results, discoveries, penalties, and/or rewards for wrong-headed actions:

- Traps
- Easter eggs (the term for discovering a hidden secret)
- Attacks
- Secret rewards
- Secret places
- Unexpected encounters
- False or misleading clues
- Clues to redirect player on course
- Discovery of new quests, paths, areas, or activities
- Something funny or ironic
- Death, but something amusing or really brutal—a memorable death
- Impassable barriers
- Cool animations
- Long-term consequences (for instance, you kill a shopkeeper, and there is no longer a shop in that location for the rest of the game)
- Nothing at all

Creating Comedy

It's strange that there's an incredible drought of humor in games, but it's kind of hard to do. Yet game reviewers love it when they get some humor...but only if it is done well.

So, if I'm a designer and I want to try to make a funny weapon, how might I do that? In the game *Armed and Dangerous* by Planet Moon, they take something dangerous (such as a shark) and put it somewhere you would never expect it, such as in a gun! So you have a shark-gun you can fire at enemies. Not only is it an amusing idea, it's fun to watch the sharks eat your enemies! Frankly, it's not just a more interesting weapon—when you get one, you can't *wait* to fire it at your enemies!

Something to remember is that humor can be consumed like a meal, one mouthful at a time. Think of the TV show *Friends*, which is respected for being funny to a wide audience. Instead of relying on one big hilarious joke, they pepper you with a mix of humor so that very different people in the audience would all find something funny.

So what's an easy way to add humor to a scene you're making in your game?

Following the mantra of this book, I offer a mix of methods to get you started. To begin with, all professional comedy writers will tell you that writing humor is work. It takes discipline and effort. Most of them write lists and ideas *ad nauseum* to find the associations that spring forth, with the proper amount of massaging, into full-blown humor. These same professionals (or some of them, at least) say that anyone can write comedy if they will do the work and understand some of the basics.

Fundamentally, humor is based on assumptions and surprise. That's one way of seeing it, anyway. Your audience will make assumptions based on what they see or hear. Your job is to lead them to some obvious expectation, provide just the right amount of tension as they anticipate the outcome, then surprise them with a roast turkey sandwich...er, something completely unanticipated. There are, of course, many ways to accomplish this, as you will see.

What follows is my quick-and-dirty method for putting humor into games. But first, let's consider what kinds of humor work best in games. Is it:

A. Puns?
B. Clichés?
C. Sight gags?
D. Funny situations?
E. Long monologues?

If you answered anything but E, you might be correct, but certainly C and D are the most likely correct answers. As you'll see, both puns (mostly visual) and clichés can be used as material for humor. However, most of what has been written about humor is about how to write humor. In other words, it is about the written or spoken word. Games rely far less on spoken or written material than media such as radio, movies, or TV. So, puns and clichés are a bit more difficult to incorporate in a game. However, it is not unheard of to find oral humor in games. *Monkey Island* is a great example of a game that thrived on humorous dialogue mixed with puzzles, but most games are more about visuals and action than they are about words. Therefore, much of the humor you are likely to put into your games is going to be in the form of sight gags or funny situations.

In some ways, this puts games (in terms of comedy) closer to the old days of silent stars, such as Charlie Chaplin and Harold Lloyd, who used sight gags and situations extensively, than to modern comedians, such as Robin Williams or Chris Rock, who rely primarily on wordplay. The physical comedy of a comedian such as Jim Carrey would translate more easily into game humor.

Different Strokes

There are different types of humor that can work in games. As mentioned, there can be humor in dialogue, humor in situations, slapstick visual humor, and even humor in the unfolding story. Some humor is entirely in the moment and doesn't rely all that much on anything but the immediate situation. Someone banging their head doesn't require a lot of setup or character exploration. In the right context, it's funny. However, a lot of humor is derived from the interactions of characters with the situations they find themselves in, and for that type of humor, it helps to understand something about the characters themselves and what can make them funny.

Another aspect of humor unique to games is that the game itself is an interactive experience. So, the shark-gun mentioned previously might be funny in a cartoon, but it's even funnier when you can fire it yourself! The humor in this case is somewhat within the control of the player, and the player can amuse himself with this funny novelty again and again.

Although humor can be enhanced by repetition, it also wears off eventually. Something that was side-splittingly hilarious on the first or second exposure ultimately becomes a "so what?" joke if it sticks around too long. The spoilage rate on humor varies with the joke and with changes in culture over time. So the shark-gun will probably become just another gun after the tenth time you've fired it. It could last longer by varying the way the shark eats its targets or by introducing new enemies that add nuances to the shark's attacks—for instance, metal enemies that cause the shark's teeth to break with humorous animations (for example, it's left holding its mouth, speaking funnily after attacking a robot). Or maybe there are different kinds of animals you can collect to shoot from the gun, each with different humorous effects. "Damn, I'm out of sharks! The enemy has no shirt on, so I'm going to fire the hundred angry kittens."

At any rate, because games are interactive and the player is in control (more or less), there are new opportunities and challenges that have yet to be fully explored. This chapter, however, can provide you with some good tools and ideas for that exploration.

Step 1: Characters

(See also Chapter 12, "Character Design.")

Comedy often boils down to conflict of characters with other characters, with the world around them, or even within themselves. The heroes of games are often offbeat and different. They are perfect comic characters. Even those characters who seem outwardly normal may have the elements required for humor—with a little help. So, in order to create comedic action in a game, first consider your characters:

- How do they see the world?
- Is there a way to turn their view of the world into something comical? This would be a way to distinguish how they view the world from the norm. Perhaps they are very innocent and naive, or maybe neurotic, like Woody Allen in many of his roles. Take this characteristic and exaggerate it. Woody isn't just a little neurotic in *Annie Hall*; he's very neurotic. This is using exaggeration, which is one of the main tools of comedy. To be clear on that, as an example, you can make it funny when someone is scared of spiders, but you can make it even funnier (after exaggeration) if the person is absolutely petrified of spiders, so always push beyond the normal limits. Imagine this person is more scared of spiders than anyone in history. Now what?
- What is the character's greatest strength? What does he do well? What are his best character traits? For instance, maybe the character is really good at cooking and kind to children and animals. You can push those characteristics to their limits as well.
- What are the character's flaws? Perhaps he is overly optimistic or too cynical. Or too gullible. Perhaps he is a vampire and can't be in sunlight, but he is vain, hates being so pale, and wants a nice tan. The character's flaws can take him to places that could generate ideas.
- Can you flip the character's comfort level? If he is a vegetarian, put him in meat situations and vice versa. If the character likes slow, give him fast. Flip the situation in which he feels comfortable.
- Can you turn his characteristics into something comical? For instance, if the character tends to be a little bit loud and bombastic, make him really loud—like Foghorn Leghorn, the chicken in the old cartoons. If the character is naturally shy, make him painfully shy, to the point where he tends to gravitate to the most isolated corner of every location and tries to blend into the walls. Then make him do something that pushes him into the limelight, and have him squirm and suffer through every funny interaction, with his shyness at the center of his reactions to events. If the character is very precise, make him the most anal character you've ever heard of. Think of *The Odd Couple*, where Felix is the ultimate anal retentive and Oscar is the ultimate slob.
- What does the character want? What drives him? Consider that he may want something on the surface—a cushy defense industry contract or a date with a movie star—and something different on the inside—love, for instance, or self-acceptance.

By using the information about your characters—how they tend to see the world and be in it, and what they want from the world—you can create funny situations that are consistent with your characters.

This may seem like a lot of extra work. After all, what does a gun-totin' aardvark really want, other than to mow down everything in his path? And, to be honest, not every game needs full character development. A gun-totin' aardvark is sort of funny in itself. But then, think of ways that an aardvark can be even funnier. What does an aardvark do? Who does an aardvark love or hate? How does this aardvark see the world? If you explore your characters—all of them—more thoroughly, the opportunities for humor will naturally increase.

Almost any character can be funny. For instance, how would you make a trash compactor funny? Maybe that seems like a tall order, but Pixar did it in *WALL·E*. How did they do it? Watch the movie.

Step 2: Story Structures

There's a lot written about story structure for any type of story. That's part of what this chapter is all about. But now let's look at just a few of the basic types of stories that lend themselves to comedy:

- **Which Side of Normal?** In this type of story, the hero is either a very normal guy put in a very abnormal situation (Bob Hoskins in *Who Framed Roger Rabbit?*) or a very strange character put in a normal world (Bill Murray playing Hunter S. Thompson in *Where the Buffalo Roam*, Robin Williams as Mork in *Mork and Mindy*, or Jim Carey in almost any of his comedies).
- **The Incompetent Hero.** The hero is a doofus, but, well, he is the hero. Think of Hong Kong Phooey or Inspector Clouseau.
- **Altered Perspective.** The hero is otherwise normal, but something has happened to change his perspective of the world—something pretty strange and radical. Think of Tom Hanks in *Big* or Bill Murray in *Groundhog Day*.
- **Power and Magic.** This is a story in which the main character is somehow affected by a supernatural or scientific event. This can be comedy or not, but it can definitely be comedy. Examples include Jim Carrey in *The Mask*, Chevy Chase in *Modern Problems*, and so on.
- **Character Clash.** Simply put two characters in opposition, and you have the makings of comedy. In *Adam's Rib*, Katharine Hepburn and Spencer Tracy play two lawyers who are also married to each other. He's prosecuting a case against a woman who shot her husband. She's defending the same case. It's a perfect character clash.

There are other types of story situations that also can lend themselves to comedy. Some are not particularly applicable to games, such as ensemble comedy, which works well on week-to-week TV sitcoms (and might one day work on episodic online game sitcoms, if they ever become a reality). You can also base comedy on parody and satire—for instance, a boxing or wrestling game featuring George Bush against Osama bin Laden. Okay, taste in humor is subjective.... How about Brad Pitt against a team of camera-wielding paparazzi? Or Brad Pitt and Angelina Jolie as a married couple who are also rival assassins, as in *Mr. and Mrs. Smith*?

Elements of Comedic Story Structures

The basic comedy story structure is:

1. Introduce us to the world of the main character(s).
2. Who are the characters? Give the player a taste of their issues.
3. What do they want? The player gets to see something about the characters' ostensible goals.
4. Some change happens in the characters' world that presents an opportunity or a challenge.
5. Good things happen—the characters begin to get a handle on the new world they are in.
6. Bad things happen—they meet opposition or some obstacles that make the situation get much worse.
7. Hitting rock bottom, they reach a critical point. It's sink or swim, live or die, succeed or fail.
8. The hero must make the ultimate risky choice in order to complete the adventure. It may seem to be the wrong choice, or it may seem to be one that will likely end in his ruin or even death, but it is the only right choice for that character.

9. The hero generally gets both his outer desire (to win the lottery and be rich, for example) and his secret inner desire, which has become clear throughout the story (to find love or self-acceptance, and so on).

Actually, this structure could be applied more or less to many stories, whether funny or not. One interesting difference with games is the fact that Steps 3 through 7 occur again and again on a micro scale. Even though there may be a major story arc to which this structure is applicable, in games there are a lot more elements of action, tension, challenge, and reward. So, when designing any story, including comedic ones, in games, it's important to realize that you may have several stories within the main story, and that the story may even have multiple paths and different outcomes. For that reason, creating stories in games is far more complex than creating stories for linear media, and new rules may need to be created. One of several possible story arcs for a game might look like the following list of steps, although sometimes you introduce the character first and let the "situation" develop as the game progresses. Note that, given the interactive nature of games, I'm using a pseudo programming style for this outline. This could also be shown as a flowchart:

1. Introduce the situation. What is the key event that triggers the game?
2. Introduce the hero. How does the hero relate to the world and to the trigger event?
3. Set the hero on the path. Start the quest to resolve the situation caused by the trigger event.
4. Begin loop:
   a. Offer challenge.
   b. Player uses skill.
   c. Player uses strategy.
   d. Offer risk.
   e. Give reward.
5. Until X (where X represents the player reaching a goal or a new milestone). This could be reaching a new location or a new character level, finding a specific item, or meeting a specific character.
6. Add to story (main plot quest or side quest)?
7. Modify plot? In other words, at this point do you add information or changes to the main storyline? Do you increase, decrease, or otherwise change the nature of the challenges the hero faces? Do you increase tension? Do you accelerate the effect of the trigger event?
8. If you're not at a major milestone, then go back to 4.
9. Plot milestone. Here is a major event in the story where something specific must happen before gameplay continues. It could be dealing with a boss, a problem, or a major quest.
10. If not at the end of the game, go back to 4.
11. End. This is the ending of the game and the final scenes leading up to it.
12. Epilogue. This is the reward sequence where the outcome is revealed and the hero's success is celebrated and rewarded.

Step 3: Using the Tools of Comedy

Here's a way to approach writing humorous content in your games: First, write down the *key* elements that matter to you in your scene. Now compress these elements down to just the most essential. For example, suppose you pick *hero* and *dog* and *quest* to be the key parts of your scene. Now, I'm not any good at comedy writing, but I will try to show how each of the systems works. You only need to use one of the methods, but I am going to attempt to use them *all.* (Gulp!)

So the scene is a guy (who is our Hero) with his Dog, getting ready to leave home to go on an epic quest...or at least on a camping trip.

So first I look at my key words (hero, dog, quest) and then I start to brainstorm by systematically applying the following techniques to any of the words, hoping to add humor to the scene.

- **Cause or use a misunderstanding.** For example, the Hero says to his girlfriend on the phone, "It's gonna be a *long* trip!" Overhearing them, Dog starts packing his bone, his blanket, a canister of mace, and so on. Then he overhears, "He's not coming; he just slows me down." Dog drops his bone, shocked. Now pissed, he poops in his owner's suitcase. Later, the owner walks in and says, "Rover, better pack your stuff; we've got a long trip ahead." The Dog is happy, but then looks to the suitcase and freezes. (Now you also have a preloaded joke for later, with the poop in the case that the audience is aware of but the Hero is not.)
- **Use visual comedy by making something slapstick happen.** This usually works best when, due to being clumsy or stupid, someone gets hurt or inconvenienced. For example, Dog bites the guy's sandwich, and the guy jumps to his feet and bangs his head. Reacting to the pain, he drops the remains of the sandwich, and the Dog takes off with it. Basically, you can easily do anything that plays with visual, embarrassing, or painful reactions.
- **Strange as it sounds, you can make use of fear to get humor.** The fear can be of someone/something, or it can be fear of an idea or concept. For example, Dog is going on the quest with the Hero because he's supposed to be a really fierce dog, but it's dark outside, and we find out the Dog is scared of the dark! The Hero finally pushes the Dog out into the street with its knees knocking; the Dog has about 30 flashlights strapped to him. Fear is easy to create if you refer to the list of phobias in Chapter 12, "Character Design," and sometimes it's fun to invert them. So instead of a fear of spiders, perhaps the Dog has a fear of dead spiders—or, ironically, he thinks spiders are cute and adorable. Or instead of a rational fear of height, he's scared of catching his paw nails in the cracks in the pavement, so he prefers to walk on the road (the reactions to that could be funny). You get the idea.
- **Along with fear naturally comes danger.** Humor can be heightened when you raise the stakes for the character(s) involved, and there is no better way to raise the stakes than to increase the danger of the situation. In fact, the more dire the circumstances, the greater the opportunity for humor. In this instance, consider that the Dog is running at full speed and suddenly comes to a chain-link fence. He starts climbing, getting slower and more frightened, sweating; he looks down and is a full 12 inches from the ground. He looks back up and has 50 feet to go. It's funnier because the stakes are higher and the reaction is real.
- **There are other ways to raise the stakes (besides danger, that is).** For instance, there isn't much tension if your Hero is risking 10 bucks on a bet, but suppose he's risking everything he owns, which means everything the Dog owns, too. The fact that the stakes really matter makes it fun to play with the stress, and then you have the reactions and objections of the third party (Dog, in this case) to play with as well.
- **You can insinuate something.** Tease the player that what he thinks he knows is possibly wrong—insinuate something! The Dog hints to the Hero that someone will make moves on the Hero's girlfriend if he disappears again on another long and dangerous quest. (When truthfully, Dog really doesn't want him to leave.) Knowing Dog is willing to go down that path—making up anything, trying to be subtle, trying to plant seeds of doubt—can be a fun way to go.
- **You can also consider adding some innuendo.** This is the classic stuff, such as saying, "Those are nice melons," when talking to a girl.) For innuendo, the trick is that the girl doesn't get the joke, so you can continue down that path, laying it on: "I like to test them with a squeeze" and so on. There's a lot of space for *blue* jokes (adult jokes) when you go down this innuendo path.
- **Use wordplay.** Martha Focker was a favorite name from the movie *Meet the Parents.*

- **Use double entendre.** This is simply when there are two completely different meanings to a statement. The phrase "I'm having an old friend for dinner" isn't special until Hannibal Lecter (the serial killer who eats his victims) says it.
- **Sometimes it can be funny when a plan backfires.** So, having set up a plan (which was to avoid something undesirable, scary, or dangerous), now cause the plan to fail. Now the characters have to face the problem head-on. For instance, Dog wants to make sure Hero takes him on the quest, so he starts telling Hero how dangerous the quest is, thinking he'll for sure take his trusty dog then. But Hero thinks, "He's right. It *will* be dangerous—too dangerous to take my trusty dog and risk his safety." The plan backfires, and now Hero doesn't want to take Dog. Of course, more comedy options are generated because Dog tries to come anyway.
- **Like the previous example, humor can result from having absolutely the worst-case scenario occur.** For instance, the Hero is all packed and ready to go. The only thing he dreads is a visit from his mother. He tells the Dog, "Dog, we're outta here. Just as long as Mom doesn't find out, we're golden." Of course, just as he approaches the car, carrying all his suitcases, backpacks, kayaks, portable boom box, shortwave radio, GPS, skis, bicycle, and tennis racket (see the upcoming discussion of *exaggeration*), his mother walks up the driveway. "Where do you think you're going?" she asks. Whatever the punch line, it's funny because the player (audience) was clued in that only a visit from his mother could screw things up, and that's what happens. I did this once with an old car we had. When I was a kid, my father told me not to drive it, but I decided to. Then I had a head-on crash with my father in his car. Think a slow-motion crash—just enough to damage the car and leave us staring at each other over crumpled metal. (In the worst-case scenario, as long as nobody is hurt, it suddenly turns funny for the audience.)
- **Use the technique in which only the audience knows something.** Or you can call it the *oblivious hero*. In this, the audience/player can see what's going to happen, but the character doesn't. It's like when the hero complains about someone (maybe his boss), and the audience knows that the boss is overhearing every word. As another example, it may be that another character in the scene has a different perspective. For instance, suppose Hero is walking along the street, and some guy ahead of him tosses a banana peel onto the sidewalk. Dog sees it and says, "Uh, boss…" just as Hero steps on the banana peel and does a beautifully executed pratfall. Score it 9 out of a possible 10! What might make this even funnier is to reverse the situation. Hero tries to warn Dog about the banana peel, but he's too late. However, contrary to expectations, Dog doesn't fall over. He's a four-footed creature, after all. He just sort of runs in place for a moment and continues, kicking the banana peel back behind him where, of course, Hero steps on it and does his pratfall!
- **Exaggeration is one of the main comedic tools.** If there's a situation and you want to make it funny, exaggerate it! If you've got the Dog facing a vicious cat, make the cat really vicious, snarling, bug-eyed, and huge. It will be funnier that way. Or, if Hero is talking to the Dog about the dangers of the trip ahead (eight police dogs have perished so far) while Dog packs his things, exaggerate the descriptions, then exaggerate Dog's reaction—he starts shaking and begins to unpack his baseball hats, sunscreen, and sunglasses. Now he starts to pack weapons, such as a pistol, a sword, and a cat costume.
- **Although exaggeration is one of the most commonly used elements in comedy, understatement can have great comic effect, especially when it's applied inappropriately.** In the previous example, where Hero is explaining the upcoming adventure, suppose it involves parachuting into the heart of a live volcano, finding a passage into the Earth, and digging through a rock wall 100 feet thick to get to a treasure chamber guarded by supernatural mummies with bad tempers. Now suppose the player knows all this, but Hero only tells Dog, "Bring your shorts. It'll be hot where we're going." Or they are about to enter a building with about 4,000 enemies waiting to rip them apart. Hero says, "Hey Dog. Sharpen your teeth. You might have to break a sweat in there."

- **There are two kinds of reverses.** One is to reverse a situation, such as Dog talking on the phone and deciding whether he wants to take the owner with him. The other is used in jokes all the time, where you build up anticipation and assumptions and then provide the opposite result. This works in jokes like Jonathan Winters' "I couldn't wait for success, so I went ahead without it." In a game situation, imagine a big buildup—dark music, heartbeat percussion like in *Jaws*, and a big, scary door. There's gotta be a giant scary monster on the other side. Open the door and there's…an earthworm. The lion with no courage in *The Wizard of Oz* is another good example, given that at first he seems to be ferocious, like we think a lion ought to be.
- **Every comedy writer knows the power of threes.** "Life, liberty, and the pursuit of happiness," "of the people, by the people, and for the people," and so on. In a joke or comedy situation, the first instance of an idea establishes the audience's expectation. The second reinforces that expectation. The third completely violates it. One person slaps someone else in the face, they slap back, and now you need to surprise (by not doing another slap—do something crazy instead) to achieve a triple. Suppose Dog is barking, and Hero comes over to investigate. Out of a small hole comes a mouse, followed after an appropriate pause (or beat) by another mouse, and then, squeezing itself improbably through the tiny hole, an elephant! Or a kangaroo… It's incongruous and surprising and, presumably, funny.
- **Use an analogy.** For example, you might compare the upcoming quest to a past event that Hero feels good about, but that strikes fear into the heart of Dog. "Dog, I know you hated losing your hair, but I'll be more careful with the flamethrower this time."
- **Give an unexpected response to a communication or situation.** This does not have to be verbal. Perhaps the Hero says, "Okay, pack your stuff, Rover," but Dog just comes over and bites him in the groin. Or if up to now Dog has been barking his responses, maybe this time he actually speaks his reply: "No way, José."
- **Force instant emotion.** Create a situation that will trigger an immediate and high-level emotional response. Use the characters' responses for comedic effect. For example, the moment Dog realizes his owner is going to take another Dog on the quest instead of him—imagine the variety of reactions (jealousy is always fun) that Dog might have.
- **Use sarcasm.** Hero is talking about how he's going to go in there and kick ass, but Dog is shaking his head while looking to the camera. The more the guy boasts how great he is, the more Dog shakes his head, does that thing where you make it look like your hand is talking, and makes funny expressions.
- **Use dark humor.** The player hears Dog's thoughts. He looks like a pretty little puppy to the owner, but he reveals a twisted, dark, sarcastic side to the viewer. You can fade to hear his thoughts even over the top of his owner talking or superimpose another graphic of the true "inner" dog. Or perhaps the cute, cuddly little dog actually has a grisly appetite for human flesh, and Hero is always trying to find ways to satisfy that hunger because, in reality, Dog has power over him. This kind of humor can be seen in classics such as *Arsenic and Old Lace* and *Little Shop of Horrors.*
- **Use irony.** Every time Dog goes on the quest, something goes wrong and he gets turned into a pig (which he *hates*), but this quest actually needs a pig.
- **Make fun of something commonly known.** For example, you could make fun of Dog thinking he's better than Lassie. Take something the audience is familiar with and feel free to make fun of it. Think about things like reality TV, *Lost, Heroes, Fringe,* Donald Trump saying "You're fired," *American Idol, Survivor, Shrek, Harry Potter,* "You are the weakest link," and so on.

  By the way, there are two kinds of making fun—satire and parody. The basic difference is that satire attacks specific cultural values and phenomena, whereas parody provides a funny, contrasting look at something. So you might create a satire about lawyers and their win-at-all-costs attitudes. Or you might parody Harry Potter by wearing his glasses and acting like him.

- **Make fun of someone's vices.** This would be like Dog knowing the owner is really anal, and him going along with it because he's so used to it. Then Dog catches himself being anal, just like the owner. For example, maybe he's putting his bone in the dishwasher and then making his bed when other dogs are watching through the window. Be sure to show his embarrassment at this point to emphasize and exaggerate the effect.
- **Remind the audience of some comedy moment earlier.** This can be a repercussion—for example, Dog got sick and threw up in the kitchen. It was funny when it happened, but then later, Hero slips in it.
- **Use repetition.** For example, perhaps Dog sneaks up and eats some of Hero's meal, then leaves, then realizes it tastes amazing and comes back for more, over and over, even distracting Hero to make sure he gets just one more mouthful (escalating the effect). But don't repeat repetition too often or you'll get repetitive, and, as you can see, repetitive repetition if repeated repeatedly gets tiring. The trick is timing and making good use of each event.
- **Show clichés or pranks backfiring.** That's the old gag like a guy seeing a dog poop in the street, stepping around it and then walking into a tree in his distracted state. Or the old one of laying a coat over a puddle for a girl, but the puddle is six feet deep. There are tons of cliché situations that we know of (slipping on a banana peel, and so on), and they are good starting points for gags. Your job is to make them fresh. When you use a cliché—either a verbal cliché or a cliché situation—the audience is already sure they know what is going to happen. Set them up and then change the outcome. This is the basic assumption/surprise effect of a good joke. In another example, Dog comes in with his leash in his mouth, looking happy and excited. Hero is going to take him for a walk. Switch to the next scene, and it's the dog walking the guy! (This is also a *reverse.*)
- **Use puns.** Most people think of puns as perhaps the lowest form of humor, and most puns are simply wordplay without any real setup or payoff. However, in games, the most likely puns would be visual puns or puns used in the names of characters and items. For instance, a combination of a helicopter and a motorcycle might be called a rotorcycle. A very shaggy protagonist might be called Harry. Visual puns are more challenging to create. Or, imagine a creature with three spots arranged vertically along the front of its body—one red, one yellow, and one green. Its spots randomly light up one at a time, and when it stands in the road, it causes all kinds of commotion. Or imagine Road Runner spreading pancake syrup over Coyote after he's flattened by some giant weight falling on him.
- **Use metamorphosis.** This is when something changes on your body. For example, maybe you grew a giant zit or a giant butt overnight.
- Use **comments/heckles/insults.** When someone makes a comment out of the blue—"You're going up against a dragon with that stupid-looking poodle? You gotta be kidding!"—it's usually a criticism or sarcasm. This can also be any insult, regardless of whether it's from a main character. Insults generally get better the more over the top they become. For example, "She joined an ugly contest, and they said, 'Sorry, no professionals.'" Or, "She's so ugly, they filmed *Gorillas in the Mist* in her shower." Or, "She's so ugly, people wear costumes of her to Halloween parties." The two old theater-box dudes in the *Muppet Show* were good at this stuff.
- **Use bodily humor or scatological humor.** One surefire way to get a laugh is to do something gross with the human body—farts, burps, and so on. However, this can easily be overdone. A well-placed gross joke, image, or sound, however, can break tension quite well. Suppose Hero is having an intense argument with his girlfriend. Just at the point when they are about to say something they will both regret, Dog farts loudly, then offers a sheepish smile. Hero and his girlfriend fan the air in front of their faces and back out of the room. I wasn't even going to add this section until I had a child, and now I get just how funny all the fart and, "Hello, my name is David Doo-Doo" humor is. Kids just love it,

Part III

and you can have a lot of fun with it. So if you don't have kids yet, don't worry—you'll find out why bodily humor is written into just about every kid's movie.

- **Use sexual humor.** Although you often tread dangerous ground in our culture with sexual jokes and innuendos, it's generally a good way to add humor to a scene. For instance, Dog could be planning a big date with FiFi, but now he has to go on this damn quest. We can keep cutting to his dreams of how his romantic trip would have gone (in his dreams the Dog is super macho—a suave, hot lover) and then he awakens to his owner's leg shaking violently, trying to stop the damn Dog from mounting it. This dream can repeat randomly through the quest until the Dog awakens to find himself accidentally shagging the leg of the dragon they were searching for (which makes use of repetition and exaggeration).
- **Use silly voices.** For example, suppose someone you are really used to hearing suddenly speaks in a very different voice (as if they've been kicked in the groin or breathed helium). Or, perhaps Dog finds an "evil bone" in the museum. He eats it and suddenly he has the booming voice of Satan.
- **Use silly faces.** Reaction comedy is common, and in many of the situations already mentioned, the faces of the actors in the scene will convey the meaning of the scene and often provide much of the comedy. Use exaggeration or understatement as required. Think of Tex Avery's eye-bulging wolf watching the hot female performer in old cartoons, or think about Ren and Stimpy in *The Ren and Stimpy Show*. Or, in contrast, think of Cartman's blank stare in *South Park* when something bad happens and he simply says, "Okay." (In fact, that's homework—watch as much Tex Avery as you can.)
- **Use distortion.** Physically distorting your characters can be very funny. This is done mostly in cartoons, and it works very well in games. Distortion can include sight gags, such as having a 20-ton anvil fall on someone and flattening the person like a crepe, or causing a person's eyes to bug out comically when he sees something he likes or wants (or, alternatively, when he sees something really scary). Or you might have someone's hair stand on end—something like that.
- **Defy logic.** We're making games here, not scientific demonstrations. If it can be logical, fine. But if it will be funnier if it defies logic—logic be damned! Suppose Dog is thirsty, and he pulls from the shelf a box labeled Powdered Water. He pours it into his dish and begins to lap it up, burping happily when he's done. Of course, Hero will be watching with a befuddled look on his face. Another great example of both exaggeration and defying logic is the cartoon gag when one guy pulls a gun and the other guy pulls a gun, but the second guy's gun is a gigantic thing the size of a howitzer! (On the *Spore* team, they often encountered unintended behaviors and bugs in the making of the game, but their credo was, "If it's funny, it stays.")

Making Things Scary

Games often involve scary situations, events, images, and moments. What makes something scary?

> "The essential fact is, to get real suspense you must let the audience have information. Now let's take the old-fashioned 'bomb' theory. You and I are sitting talking...we'll say about baseball. We're talking for five minutes. Suddenly a bomb goes off, and the audience has a 10-second terrible shock. Now let's take the same situation. Tell the audience at the beginning that under the table—and show it to them—there's a bomb, and it's going to go off in five minutes. Now we talk baseball. What is the audience doing? They're saying, 'Don't talk about baseball. There's a bomb under there. Get rid of it.' But they're helpless. They can't jump out of their seats up into the screen and grab hold of the bomb and throw it out."
>
> —Alfred Hitchcock

There are three significant elements to making something scary—danger, suspense, and surprise/shock.

- **Danger** (or risk) is essential. There must be something at stake. In movies and books, the danger is to characters in the story, but in a game, it is often the character being played, making it potentially a more visceral experience. In a game, the danger can be the loss of the character's life, the loss of progress the player has made through hard effort, or the loss of something the player has worked hard for, such as weapons/armor. In addition, there are dangers that can threaten other characters, situations, places, or things the player cares about or wants to (must) protect.
- **Suspense** draws out uncertainty and fear of what might happen. Used correctly, it can dramatically increase how scary a situation or event is. (For example, consider the Hitchcock quote.) I personally believe we have a built-in need to try to predict the future. I'm not even going to begin to justify that statement; I just think we do. The twist is that we give up when we feel we have no chance and then the suspense is broken. Writers who change fundamental rules arbitrarily also destroy all hope of suspense, because the player can't predict anything with a random rule base. When the player feels he has a chance of being right, he gets hooked. The problem is, he actually needs to be wrong sometimes (surprisingly often) to keep it interesting. Therefore, the point here is to provide long-term suspense—you need to let the player be right some of the time, but often enough for him not to just give up.
- **Surprise** is used often to shock or jolt the player (or audience in passive media) into an immediate reaction. Used too often or too predictably, however, it becomes less effective—there's no such thing as a *completely* predictable surprise. Sometimes, however, even when you're expecting something to come jumping out of the shadows, you don't know when or where (using suspense), so when it does inevitably come, you still jump in your seat. And working with predictability, you might have set up a series of surprises, only to completely violate your own setup with something unpredictable. For instance, if you almost always have an enemy waiting behind doors when the player opens them, sometimes don't have the enemy there—but have the enemy appear in a different place, such as crashing through a window or jumping down from the ceiling. The player comes to expect the enemy behind the door, but when there isn't one the tension rises, and then you spring the surprise. The equation of surprise isn't, however, just a case of something being there that wasn't before (see the upcoming Suddenness/Shock point). Imagine you just sat down to a movie and you are distracted, opening up your candy. Then the director throws a black cat at the hero. It will have a fraction of the impact that it could if you combine the surprise with suspense, meaning the movie takes the time to gain your full 110-percent attention—you know the cat is out there somewhere, that it's got some killer disease, and that it's hunting the hero. The hero then finds a dead dog, and boom—a surprise attack from the cat. There are some funny examples of this; just type "Scary Maze Game" into YouTube.com to see what I'm talking about.

There are other ways to make something scary, of course:

- **Music and Sound.** There's no doubt that music and sound affect the emotional content of a scene, and these auditory elements can make a situation very scary, very happy, very sad, and so on. In *Jaws*, the heartbeat music built up the tension and made the shark's presence visceral. In *Psycho*, the insane, strident music intensified the insanity of Norman Bates. Low, almost subsonic sounds sustained in a scene can create an element of expectation and anxiety. Similarly, so can very high sustained sounds. In fact, to some degree, any sustained note implies the need for resolution and therefore creates tension.

  Sound effects can also create fear. The sound of some scary animal or machine getting closer and closer certainly gets your hackles up. Wolves howl in the distance. You hear the sound of an animal's death cry. Snarling. Certain sounds act immediately on the psyche, such as blood-curdling screams, gun and artillery sounds, a bullet ricochet, smashing glass, a crash or explosion in a very quiet scene, and so on. Even the sound of laughter can be disturbing—especially if it is somewhat demented. (For more on music and sound, see Chapter 20, "Music and Sound.")

- **Pacing.** Using the expertise of good movies and good novels, a well-paced story can work to increase the level of suspense, anticipation of danger, and fear. It works well when it builds up your adrenalin and gently lets you relax, then builds you up again. The old movie *An American Werewolf in London* did this well.
- **Foreknowledge.** This goes along with suspense in that when you know there is danger ahead, even knowing what it is, you get anxious or fearful about it.
- **Suddenness/Shock.** There's no doubt that one of the best ways to invoke fear in someone is to startle them. In games, this can be accomplished by creating scenes and situations in which the player feels safe, or even where they may anticipate some danger, but then you have the danger spring on them suddenly. This has been done well in the *Resident Evil* games, where enemies may suddenly appear apparently from nowhere, and you must react instantaneously. Another great example of a game that shows this is *BioShock*. You can be walking through the darkness when all of a sudden bad guys come running at you, and you only have a wrench to kill them with!
- **Fears of the Real World.** There's a lot to be afraid of in any world—historical, futuristic, or modern. In today's world, we have terrorism, disease, environmental fears, cops and robbers, relationship fears, addictions, politics, religion, and so on. All of these fears can play a part in a game and can be used to make the experience scary. (For more on what people fear, see Chapter 12, "Character Design.")
- **Extreme Limits.** Some players may respond with some fear when their world is somehow restricted. For instance, suddenly turning off the lights and having the screen go black can be unnerving. Or, imagine a character who depends on magic to survive or for protection. What happens to the player when the character enters a "no magic" zone, and he must make it through alive or he will lose something of value, such as experience or good items? Suddenly the character is vulnerable, and his familiar options are severely restricted. I also call this *weak to strong*, and it's a great game mechanic. It was the basis of *Earthworm Jim*—going from a weak earthworm to a superhero in seconds and vice versa.
- **Safe Places Become Dangerous.** There's nothing as scary as a place you normally would consider safe suddenly being dangerous. When a bloody hand comes out of the bathroom sink, the bathtub starts pouring blood, or the face in the mirror starts talking to you, it's disturbing. When you hear strange noises in the house at night and suddenly realize that the electricity is not working, look out! This is especially powerful when the location is very familiar or when the player has had a chance to become comfortable in a place. It can also be fun to flip this. Try to make dangerous places safe and try to seek comfort in a spooky place. For example, suppose you are trying to brush your teeth and go to bed while staying at a house that's clearly haunted.
- **Safe People Become Dangerous.** This was the case in *The Shining*. Having someone who seems to be an ally turn into an enemy can be scary if handled correctly, especially if the person is a very real threat. This device is often used in Role-Playing Games, but the threat isn't very significant so it becomes more of a plot device than something to create fear. But if the switch of allegiance can truly threaten all that you have been working for, it will get the blood pumping, especially if the character(s) involved create the proper amount of creepiness, threat, or derangement. Here are some examples:
  - **Clowns and Dolls.** There's something innately sinister about clowns and dolls. Probably because we are supposed to trust them so utterly, they make excellent characters for creating fear.
  - **Children.** Like clowns and dolls, children are supposed to be innocent and harmless, so they can seem especially scary when used correctly. One way this is often done is by using a demonic child with scary powers (Damien in *The Omen*). Another way this can be used is with children

going feral and attacking in groups (*Lord of the Flies*). Or you could use both tactics, as in *Village of the Damned.*
    - **The Reassuring, Suave, or Urbane Villain.** Villains who seem good or who are entertaining and seem quite likeable but are really dangerous can be very scary. One classic example is Count Dracula, who appeared to be a very regal and charming, if mysterious, foreigner to his new English friends, but who, of course, was a blood-sucking fiend with frightening inhuman abilities. Hannibal Lecter is another example—talented, urbane, fascinating, but a serial killer and a cannibal. There are many examples in literature and movies of the suave villain. Likewise, there are the serial-killer types who appear to be just the guy next door. Scary.
- **Safe Things Become Dangerous.** For instance, perhaps the television starts displaying evil messages or tuning into some satanic entity. Or the telephone rings and an evil voice talks to you. (This is used often in horror movies, such as *The Ring* and others.)
- **Camera Tricks.** There are several camera tricks often used in movies that may be useful in games, such as:
    - **Pans.** You can pan the camera to reveal a part of something scary, such as a claw or a silhouette in the window.
    - **Close-Ups.** Getting really up-close and personal with something scary makes its effect stronger, such as an eye peeking through your keyhole.
    - **Killer First-Person View.** You can show the world from the point of view of the stalker.
    - **Victim View.** You can show the world from the point of view of someone being stalked. This is especially effective if you know they are in danger (which somehow you always do know in movies by the way they choose that point of view and the musical clues they use).
- **The Utterly Amoral Character.** Characters who simply have no moral restraints (again, such as Hannibal Lecter) can be very scary. This is especially true if they are very charming and effective at gaining the trust of others or very powerful and ruthless and in a position to wreak havoc on the player's goals. I also call this *dangerous people pretend to be safe*—just a flip of *safe people become dangerous.* In this version, someone you know is a killer and cannot be trusted is now acting way too nice. Or you have to trust them, as in *Silence of the Lambs.* You just can't tell when they will show their true colors. As I write this chapter, this device is being used in the TV show *Heroes* for the lead villain, Sylar. (We've seen him kill so many people, yet now he's baking cookies.)
- **The Slow, but Inescapable.** The prototype of this kind of threat is the mummy from the original Boris Karloff movies. The plodding mummy never moved very quickly, but somehow his victims could never get away from him. Anything that operates like this—and it could be a character, a machine, a collapsing room, and so on—is scary, and it gets scarier the more futile the escape seems to be. *Resistance is futile.* The first two *Alien* movies handled this device well.
- **Creepy Villains.** Some villains are just scary by design, such as the Predator from the *Predator* movies. For more on villain types, see Chapter 14, "Enemies."
- **Darkness/Exposure/Isolation/Vulnerability.** You can use scenes where the character/player is very alone and feels very vulnerable. Darkness or reduced visibility can accentuate this feeling, especially where there is the real threat of danger. For instance, diving in the ocean with complete visibility is fun. Being deep under murky water where there could be sharks and worse is unnerving. Here are a couple other examples:
    - **Lights Going Out/Pulsating Light.** Simple effects of lighting, from the clever use of colors, to strobe effects, to sudden utter darkness, can create an uncomfortable sensation in the player, and if really well done, these effects can signal danger and instill fear.
    - **Light and Shadows.** The use of light and shadows can often enhance the fear already created by other factors. Harsh, soft, or dim lighting changes the emotional impact and the feelings of safety or vulnerability. Shadows can be fleeting glimpses of danger or distorted monsters

of the mind. You might be able to see just fine in a dimly lit room, but not when you step into shadows, meaning a safe space can contain lots of hidden dangers.

- **Truth That Is Scarier Than Fiction.** If you can use a true situation, it is often more bizarre than anything you can imagine. (The *Texas Chainsaw Massacre* and *Hostel* are good examples.)
- **Nightmare Symbols.** A study of human psychological symbols, such as the work of Jung, can reveal some elements to inspire and instill fear in a story. Finding spooky symbols can work very well. The original *Blair Witch Project* comes to mind. If you add mysterious symbols to your game, and people do some research, they might find out that your symbols actually do symbolize something.
- **The Unseen.** You know it's out there, but it doesn't reveal itself. It just leaves a wake of corpses...or something like that. Some of my favorite scenes in the *Alien* movies are where the aliens are in the ship. You don't know where they are, but you know they could be anywhere. It's very scary and unnerving.
- **Diseases.** Some diseases, such as the common cold, lack fear value, but take a truly frightening disease such as Ebola, and you have something to work with. The movies *Outbreak*, *28 Days*, and *I Am Legend* are good examples. Disease fear tends to be based on the idea of transmission being accidental or airborne. The stakes are raised when you already have the disease but didn't know it, or when we all have a disease that's keeping us alive for now. It can become even more sinister if the people with the disease are trying actively to infect others; this is essentially what some vampire and zombie stories involve, but this premise can include other kinds of diseases and conditions. Think of *Invasion of the Body Snatchers*, for instance. I guess the point is there are still plenty of places to take the disease idea.
- **Everyman Fear.** This is something horrible that anyone can relate to. If it makes us all squirm, it's probably good stuff for a scary situation. How about the surgeon banned forever from doing surgery due to his shaky hands? He's now operating on some innocent person in the *Hostel* movie. Or how about the psychotic monkey holding a syringe to the girl's eye in the movie *Monkey Shines*? The trick to finding tons of ideas that worked (for inspiration) is to search "Scariest Movie Scenes" in Google.
- **No Way to Stop It.** This describes something that keeps on happening and you can't stop it. This could be the *Marathon Man* dental torture or it could be something inexorable, such as locusts eating your crop, artillery destroying your fortress, a disease or maggots eating away your body as you watch (while strapped to a table), or an inexorable pursuer who never gives up the chase.
- **Power versus Vulnerability.** The juxtaposition between power and vulnerability can be used effectively to create a scary situation, especially if the player character, or some sympathetic character or group, is the vulnerable one. In particular, imagine that your player is generally quite powerful and can plow through hordes of enemies without breaking a sweat. But then suddenly, you are confronted by creatures that can really kick your ass badly. Suddenly, that feeling of invincibility evaporates. This is why I sometimes refer to this as *survival mode*!
- **Insane but Verbal.** Again, a character such as Hannibal Lecter or Norman Bates can be verbal and even seem charming, but can be completely whacko. Only by listening do you start to work out, "Hold on, this dude is nuts!"
- **Something Comes Back to Life.** It's pretty easy to make almost anything that was dead—or should be dead but now isn't—become scary.
- **Evil Groups.** Evil groups are scary, especially if they have infiltrated the otherwise safe world and they are after you! In movies this is commonly Satanic groups, but there's plenty of room for great secret evil societies.
- **Who Do You Trust?** In any situation where there is great danger and you don't know who to trust, there is fear. When your allies might be plotting against you and those who seem to be enemies may actually be on your side, the ambiguity makes for a scary and uncertain situation.

- **Horror and Comedy.** Sometimes something can be scary and funny at the same time. *Little Shop of Horrors* and even *The Shining* at times seem funny in a macabre way. Horror mixed with comedy is an interesting way to play with horror, to give the audience a break from the horror for a short while, making it okay to have a laugh. Then you remind them of why they're there, plummeting them back into fear.
- **Clichés.** This list contains some horror-movie clichés. There are others, and they can be used to create recognition in the player or even to create humor, since they are often obvious and overused. For instance, think about the big buildup to a dangerous creature right around the corner, which uses visuals and tension-producing music—only to end up with the big, bad monster being a little white bunny rabbit. Another example is the scantily clad young woman alone in a house and the telephone rings. In some movies, that's a dead giveaway—and I do mean dead. How might you turn that around and make it funny?
- **Gore.** Sheer gore usually isn't all that scary, but if used with restraint and well positioned within a scene, it can be quite frightening. There's a difference between campy or cartoony use of gore and carefully planned and selective use. Gore can be shocking, gross, or scary...or even ho-hum boring, depending on the context. Usually gore mixed with surprise works well, such as when someone blows their head off, and a lead character who loves that person gets splattered with blood completely by surprise. It can be shocking.
- **Messing with the Rules.** Uncertainty can cause fear, and placing players in a world where the rules are a little uncertain and the stakes are high can cause anxiety in a majority of players, particularly those who rely on the rules to provide stability and predictability of outcomes. Of course, any time you mess with the game rules, you must do it with very clear intention and delicacy, or it can just seem like cheating or lazy design. But think about the Joker in *The Dark Knight*, and how he made up his own rules and forced people to follow them.
- **Misdirection by a Character.** One of my favorites, misdirection can be used to drive a player somewhat bonkers, particularly if trust is first established, then violated in subtle but increasingly disastrous ways. This method is subtle and must be used with care, but it involves using a character in the game to establish the player's trust and then, when the trust is absolute, violating it. In fact, the character who has befriended the player is in reality the player's enemy and is leading him to his doom, or something of that nature.
- **Misdirection by Trickery.** Designers can use various tricks to unsettle a player. For instance, in the original *Uninvited* game, you came across a lady in a fancy dress, seen from the back. By the time you encountered this lady, the haunted-house atmosphere of the setting was pretty well established. It was quiet, empty, and creepy. Then you saw what seemed to be a sophisticated lady walking down the hall. You approached her, and suddenly she faced you, and her face was a horrible death's head. Similarly, you might fool players into thinking something was very dangerous, but have it turn out to be harmless, while something they ignored really gets them.
- **Reactions of Other Characters.** One way to tell an audience (and/or player) that something is scary is to have the other characters in the scene demonstrate their fear in different ways—turning white, becoming paralyzed, screaming, running, cowering, fainting, and so on.

Enhancing the Player's Emotional Response

Games are full of challenges and rewards. The events, structure, and emotional responses of a game all affect us when we play. But as games become more sophisticated, we will be able to affect players in more and deeper ways. Even in simple games, such elements as emotional response, surprise, twists, comedy, and so forth can be included in the design approach and philosophy.

To judge the depth of experience a player has, I've created a checklist of elements that can deepen the game experience, making it more fun and more memorable. Using your best-guess methods, put a checkmark next to each element your game (or another game you have played) contains. Total the number of checkmarks at the end to see how the game scores. Do the same thing with other games you like and games you don't like. How about games you raved about—how did they score? Can you improve your score by adding some elements to your game?

Emotional responses: When playing the game, what emotions would a player be likely to feel? (Check each emotional response you believe your game will elicit in players and total that number at the end of the list.)

__ Challenged
__ Determined
__ Motivated
__ Fear
__ Inner conflict
__ Humor
__ Joy/elation
__ Pride
__ Hate
__ Love
__ Sense of belonging/acceptance
__ Betrayal
__ Rejection
__ Ostracism (expulsion)
__ Satisfaction
__ Relief
__ Gratitude
__ Magnanimity (ability to encounter danger/ trouble with tranquility and firmness)
__ Anxiety and anticipation
__ Disappointment
__ Guilt
__ Desire
__ Forgiveness
__ Hope
__ Anger/rage
__ Frustration
__ Embarrassment
__ Jealousy
__ Curiosity
__ Suspicion
__ Shame
__ Empathy
__ Sexually titillated in some way
__ Sympathy
__ That uh-oh sinking feeling
__ Confusion
__ Surprise
__ Attraction to someone else
__ Attachment to some person or thing
__ Sense of accomplishment
__ Wow!

Total of Emotional States ___________

How many emotional states did the game you are testing contain? Which ones? Are there ways to invoke other emotions that could be included in this game?

More Ways to Assess Your Games

Place a checkmark wherever you think your game scores a true response. Then total up the number of checkmarks at the end.

__ **The Hero's Journey.** How does your hero's story match with Joseph Campbell's stages of the Hero's Journey? (Not that this is a prerequisite, but it's a great way to come up with new ideas for your story, especially if you've left out stages and could add something to increase the power and flow of your game.) See "The Hero's Journey" section earlier in this chapter for a brief look at the Hero's Journey structure.

__ **Key Events.** Are there events that take place as the story unfolds that significantly move the player's experience forward and increase his motivation to continue, solve puzzles, complete the story arc, or delve further into the game?

__ **Fortunes Change.** Are there significant moments in the story where the player's fortunes are raised or lowered? Draw a graph of the rise and fall of the player's fortunes throughout the story arc. This can even apply to a mission-based game where there is at least an ongoing story component.

__ **Emotional Scenes.** Does the player witness scenes that can cause an emotional reaction? For example:
- The player overhears someone telling a secret or some gossip.
- The player sees somebody being mean to someone else. (This is stronger if it's someone you care about or someone you would want to protect, such as a child or a woman.)
- The player is in a dark alleyway, tunnel, or other scary, isolated place and he sees something move.
- Does the player catch someone in a lie?
- Is the player forced to lie?
- Does the player suddenly encounter a really scary, dangerous creature right in his path?
- Is the player involved in a betrayal—either him betraying someone or him being betrayed?
- Does the player witness a terrible accident?
- Someone the player respected suddenly begins to act irrationally and thoroughly embarrasses himself in front of the player and a lot of other people. What emotions would the player feel?

__ **Interesting Characters.** Does the player encounter interesting characters (with some depth and interesting traits) during the game? (Check Chapter 12, "Character Design" for some ideas.)

__ **Character Interactions.** Are the interactions between characters in the story (player with NPCs, player with other players, NPCs with NPCs) more than superficial? Do character interactions have depth?

__ **Plot Twists.** Are there twists and shifts in the plot that cause the player to respond emotionally? These would be different from key events.

__ **Dramatic Moments.** Are there moments in the story that enhance the player's response by their dramatic intensity?

__ **Sound.** Is the sound used intentionally to intensify the experience and the emotional impact of events?

__ **Music.** Is the music used intentionally to intensify the experience and the emotional impact of events?

__ **Power of New Information.** Do you reveal new information to the player in the course of the game that can have an emotional impact?

__ **Power of New Locations.** Does the player encounter locations that expand his horizons or that elicit an emotional response?

__ **People You Care About.** Does anything happen to other people in the story—people the player cares about?
- Does the story cause the player to care about anyone else?
- Does anyone important die, disappear, or fall into serious trouble?
- Does someone or something threaten people the player cares about?
- Is the player put in a position of protecting someone?
- Is the player put in a position where someone is protecting him?
- Is the player forced to decide between outcomes that could cause harm to someone he cares about?
- Is there a dog in the story?

__ **Communication Systems.** Do you find interesting ways to communicate with the player? (See Chapter 30, "Ways to Communicate with the Player.")

__ **Surprises.** Are there surprising elements, plot twists, events, or characters in the game?

Score ____________________

How many of these elements did your game contain? How could you improve your game by adding more of these elements?

Have ideas or suggestions? Join the discussion at www.gamedesignbook.org.

Creating Emotional Responses toward Characters

The goal of this section is to show ways to further enhance the player's response to characters in the game. This invests the player more deeply into the experience and ultimately makes the gameplay far more satisfying. This kind of technique is common in literature and in movies, and the same techniques can easily apply to games where there's significant story content and more complex characters.

- **Fairness.** Somebody innocent is falsely accused.
- **Victims.** Somebody weak is victimized by somebody strong.
- **Good Deeds.** A character goes out of his way to help somebody else.
- **Bad Deeds.** A character goes out of his way to do something mean.
- **Unnecessary Cruelty.** Someone takes a vanquished foe or prisoner and intentionally inflicts pain, suffering, or maiming out of sheer cruelty.
- **Checked Out.** A character is unaware of how he affects others and does things that cause dissension or anger.
- **Show More about the Character.** A character reveals something about his past.
- **Strong/Weak.** A strong character reveals a weakness.
- **Weak/Strong.** A weak character reveals surprising strength or ability.
- **What the Character Likes.** A character likes dogs or flowers or teddy bears. For instance, perhaps a ruthless gangster is very attentive to his mother or really loves his son/daughter. Or, conversely, perhaps a priest likes to rip the wings off flies…oh my!
- **What the Character Hates.** A character hates injustice, Walmart, people who wear retro clothing, people from other countries, people with different-colored skin, and so on.
- **Beauty.** A character is very beautiful.
- **Ugliness.** A character is very ugly.
- **Humor.** A character is funny and makes you laugh.
- **Annoyance.** A character is annoying and gets on your nerves.
- **Reliance.** You rely on someone and/or he relies on you.
- **Mutual Goals.** You and another character have mutual goals. For example, perhaps you both want to kill the boss, Devastator, or you both have to get to the Big City, though for different reasons.
- **Complementary Goals.** You and another character have complementary goals. For example, perhaps you want to kill the boss, Devastator, but the other character simply wants to get him out of the way to usurp his power. This trait is not as powerful as having mutual goals.
- **Conflicting Goals.** You and another character have conflicting goals. For instance, you want to kill the boss, Devastator, and the other character wants to keep him alive (or in the case of Devastator himself, he wants to stay alive and probably kill you in the bargain).
- **The Gatekeeper.** A character stands in your way. You must satisfy him or get past him in order to progress or accomplish some goal.
- **The Good Fairy.** A character can be relied on to help you in some way. For most emotional responses, it should be possible to call upon this character for help more than once. For even better emotional response, you should not be able to call on this character without imposed limits, and there should be times of stress when you wish you could call on this character, but for various reasons you can't.
- **Accidental Bad Fortune.** Something bad, unexpected, and accidental happens to a character, such as being hit by a bus or being attacked randomly by a wild animal. The emotional response the player will have depends largely on his relationship with this character, although this could be the first encounter, and a relationship is created after the event. Perhaps with his dying breath, the character tells you a horrible secret, entrusts you with a great task, or gives you something of great value that

you must protect with your life. Or he recovers from the accident with your help and becomes your staunchest ally. Or maybe he is an ungrateful scoundrel and steals you blind.

- **The Protector.** A character is strong enough to protect you from danger. This is most likely in the early part of the game or during a segment of the game where you have to go into territory too dangerous for your character's current condition.
- **The Strong Ally.** This character is especially strong and fights side by side with you. You tend to rely on his abilities to balance yours.
- **The Buddy.** This character is like a friend or companion who sticks with you throughout the story (or much of it). He may be funny and make you laugh, or he may be just loyal and a good companion. If something bad happens to the buddy, it can have a greater effect emotionally than if something happens to another character.
- **The Object of Desire.** Another character can be desirable, perhaps in a sexual or romantic way. Or, she might just be very rich, and you want her gold and/or possessions.
- **Too Cool for School.** This is a character who is just very interesting, with an unusual and powerful persona. This may be an intriguing villain (once again, Hannibal Lecter comes to mind) or someone on the good or neutral side who is just very impressive. This kind of character probably relies on a strong and possibly flamboyant personality to stand out from the crowd. Other examples might be people of great presence, such as Jesus walking among the multitudes, or Gandhi.

Story-Builder Activity

This section guides you to create a story of your own, using the elements in this book as a reference. You will do this in two stages. First, as a foundation test, you will create a game story based on another movie or game you like, changing some aspects of it, such as the time and location. Following that, you will create a story using your own ideas and the suggestions found in this book. To begin, consider what elements a story game must have:

- Setting
  - Location(s)
  - Time
- Style
- Main character (player)
- Characters, allied or neutral
- Characters, enemies
- Current situation
- Goals (main, supplemental)

Modifying an Existing Story (Common in the Game Industry)

1. Think of a movie or game (or another source, such as myth or literature) that you absolutely *love* and know inside out—something with a great story and characters.
2. Move it somewhere else in location, situation, and time. Make changes to the names and characters' activities to match the new setting. For instance, suppose you took the myth of Ulysses and set it in modern times. Or, look at how *The Magnificent Seven*, an American western, was based entirely on Akira Kurosawa's *Seven Samurai*. If you are familiar with either of these movies, what other settings and situations might these movies inspire? Perhaps you could set the scene in a remote village in Russia during World War II. Or a human colony on an alien planet that must fend off the local intelligent life form intent on using them for nefarious, or possibly culinary, purposes.

3. Use the main elements of the story to create a new game. Say it's *Star Wars.* Then your creative challenge would have to consider the main locations, characters, and relationships and create some kind of inspired connection between them and places, people, and events in another location and time, such as a samurai movie. (Lightsabers are special samurai swords, and so on.)

This gives you a scene-by-scene framework that you know works, so you can delicately test many of the ideas in this book to add or modify characters, emotions, situations, and so on.

So use the elements you find in this book to develop something you love into an entirely new story and develop a game idea around it. Especially use this chapter, Chapter 17, "Game Worlds," and Chapter 12, "Character Design," but draw from all the other relevant parts of the book as well. For instance, you might find some inspiration in Chapter 11, "Scenarios," Chapter 27, "Puzzles," Chapter 28, "Controlling Pacing," Chapter 29, "Time Limits and Time Manipulation," and so forth.

While you may find it easy to create a game when starting with an established story or setting, since a certain amount of the creative visualization has been established already, what about creating a game without a specific story to inspire you?

Creating a New Story

There is no one "right" way to create a story. In fact, stories can be created from real-life experiences, from news stories, from historical research, from chance encounters, or even from dreams. Anything can be the inspiration for a story. So, what follows is simply a possible way to inspire you to create stories for games.

Note that the story you create can be independent of the type of game you are creating, though it is probably desirable to have some concept of the game genre you want to make. For instance, it may be that you'll spend a little less time developing game story structure in a Real-Time Strategy game or Action-Based Shooter than in a more RPG-like or adventure-oriented game. Still, having a strong story with strong characters and good structure can help almost any game, even if much of the detail is not really included directly in the gameplay. As an example, imagine you were creating a game like *Doom* or *Quake*, but you started with a complex story in which the main character had a history—a background and relationship with the enemies he faces—and in which the character ultimately will learn something about himself. So, given the story structure, you have the opportunity to create more varied and interesting interactions between the character and the world he is blowing up. The action is still there, but a story and character arc are also present. If handled correctly, the end result will be even more emotional release and satisfaction upon defeating the end boss or otherwise completing the game. (Of course, some games do not have explicit story structures. Most puzzle games lack stories, and games like *SimCity* have only the implicit story that the player finds for himself.)

A Note on Emergent Stories and Games

Some designers think explicit storytelling in games is both unnecessary and counterproductive to the goal of the game, which is—in some ways, at least—to empower the player to make choices and deal with consequences. If a story is too linear or predetermined, it may not be the best game vehicle. Often, the best game stories are stories that emerge from the gameplay. However, it is possible to create a story and plot, characters, and all the other elements of a story and let the player discover that story in different ways. Likewise, you can create the characters and the settings—the props and locations—and let the player explore the world and discover what stories emerge from interacting with those characters and settings.

It would be intriguing to have NPCs of such depth and subtlety that they could be like real people, and interacting with them would produce unexpected stories and opportunities—something like *The Sims*, but even more sophisticated. Artificial intelligence is a long way from accurately modeling real human intelligence and responses, but even at a crude level, if artificially intelligent NPCs have simple, definable goals and motivations, then they may respond differently to the player under different circumstances. For instance, a pickpocket would respond differently to a player character who is obviously loaded than to one who looks dirt poor. But then suppose the thief gets caught in the act. And suppose he also has a motivation to stop being a thief. Could some kind of unexpected interaction occur between the player's character and the thief, given multiple goals and motivations on both ends? Perhaps the person recognizes the urge in the thief to reform and, at the same time, needs someone with the thief's skills to accomplish an important deed. Can you think of other ways to use these dynamics?

Or suppose the most beautiful and desirable woman in the world also happens to be the princess, and in order to gain her favor (and her father's, presumably), you have to be wealthy and/or in some way heroic. So, the player is then motivated to do great deeds and earn money, possibly in order to be considered as a suitor for the princess. But perhaps the player doesn't have to do that. There are other paths through the game, and the princess only represents one of them. In this simple way, gameplay and story can be inspired, and yet the actual player's experience could be full of adventure, exploration, and action. Anyway, whether you choose to include explicit, implicit, or emergent stories in your games, some of the following tips should prove useful.

Creating Stories in Games

Assuming an explicit story is appropriate for the kind of game you want to produce, the first step is, optionally, to determine the type/genre of game you will create. After that...

- **What Is Your Story About?** By this, I mean what is the high concept? What kind of story are you going to tell? More inspirations for the high concept can be found in this chapter, in Chapter 5, "Game POV and Game Genres," Chapter 23, "Goals," and in various parts of Chapter 12, "Character Design."
- **Pick a Setting.** Where and when does this story take place? Is it in the past, the present, or the future? Is it in a real place or a fictional place? If the place is fictional, describe it in some detail. If it is historical, research it. If it is modern, consider what kinds of settings you will include. Cities? Suburbia? Rural places? Wild places? Do you know this setting well? If not, how can you get more information about it? Check out Chapter 17, "Game Worlds," for some ideas on settings you can use.
- **Create Characters.** Go to Chapter 12, "Character Design," and use it to help you create the main characters for your story. If your story is based on real or mythical characters, it will still help to know what their characteristics are with regard to the story you're telling. For instance, it might be interesting to research the mythical Achilles and find out that, in addition to his heroic actions and his prowess in battle, he had vices and personal traits that made him more interesting. In fact, most of the greatest mythical heroes also had character-defining flaws. Defining what makes your characters tick will help you create more interesting situations for them and will also create more consistency in their responses to the world around them. Even more importantly, it will help determine how they evolve in the course of the story—something that a lot of game characters don't do, but that is the essence of great storytelling. Look at Chapter 12, "Character Design," and Chapter 14, "Enemies," for more inspiration on designing your characters.
- **Consider the Structure of Your Game.** How will the player interact with it and how will the story unfold? Review the section "Story and the Player's Character" earlier in this chapter for some ideas of game story structure. Look also at Chapter 23, "Goals," for ideas of different long- and short-term goals.

- **Consider the Specifics of the Character's Journey through the Game/Story.** Now that you have the setting and the type of story, the characters, and the structure, put in the specifics of the story arc. Create the beginning, middle sections, and ending of your story using all the tools you have available. Consider the flow of the story and the potential to create ups and downs, challenges and reversals of fortune, and so on. Borrowing from movie and fiction structures, can you create a game in which the story follows a traditional three-act structure? Can you create only the framework—setting and characters with motivations and goals—and set your players loose in that world? Refer back to the "Elements of a Good Story" section earlier in this chapter, as well as "The Basic Story Arc: Games and the Three-Act Structure." Refer again to the "Joseph Campbell Meets *Star Wars* and *The Matrix*" section, as well as any of the other chapters in this book, all of which have useful information that you can use to create a better story.

NOTE

Optionally, check out the "Dilemmas," "Timelines," "Multi-Session Storytelling," "Creating Comedy," "Making Things Scary," and "Enhancing the Player's Emotional Response" sections, all in this chapter.

- **Pay Special Attention to Your Ending.** Check out the "Ways to End a Story" section earlier in this chapter.

10 Movie Genres

Part III

Why do we have a chapter on movie genres in a book about game design? Is it because we love movies? Or is it because movies and games have a lot in common—story, characters, plots, action, mysteries, and puzzles, to name a few things? And, while movies are not interactive—the key difference between them and games—the evolution of movies over the past 100 or so years is a window into our collective entertainment preferences. As such, we can learn a lot from the types of movies that are being made.

Additionally, we can use movie genres as templates from which to develop our game concepts. While I'm not suggesting that you necessarily base your games on movies—though that is also a valid approach—you can use movies for inspiration, drawing ideas from moviemakers' established skills in directing, acting, music and sound composition and engineering, drama, and comedy.

There are so many types of movies that it is difficult to create a definitive and incontrovertible list of the main categories. It's safe to say, however, that just about every movie is either a comedy, a drama, or some combination of both. There are some plotless and absurd themes that might defy those descriptions, and some documentary films may be neither comedy nor drama. But the vast majority of films—and literature, for that matter—can be seen as comedy or drama.

One way to look at this book is to think of movie genres as key words or concepts. There is a wealth of ideas contained in the history of movies, and you can use the many movie styles available as inspiration. As always, these lists are just a beginning, but imagine how useful they'd become if you were to mix the concepts—for example, if you mix "martial arts" with "buddy movie." You come up with something like *Rush Hour*. There's nothing wrong with existing genres, but how wonderful would it be if you could come up with something altogether new, simply by looking at what's already been done? Also reference Chapter 17, "Game Worlds."

Under the categories of comedy and drama, you can find a wide variety of themes, many of which have become recognized as genres in themselves.

In this chapter, we'll discuss:

- Main Genres
- Sub-Genres
- Types of Comedies
- Movie Genres Used in Games

Main Genres

- Action
- Adventure
- Children's/family
- Crime/gangster
- Documentary
- Epic/historical
- Horror
- Musical
- Mystery
- Romance
- Science fiction
- War
- Western

Note that each of these genres can be comedic, serious, or both. In the case of documentaries, they can also be neutral.

Sub-Genres

In addition to what are often considered main genres, there are many further distinctions—sub-genres, if you will. Like other genres and themes, these can also be combined. For instance, you can have a martial arts buddy movie or an aviation chase film. The permutations are pretty much endless. Sub-genres include films with recognizable themes, such as:

- Aviation
- B movies
- Biographical
- Buddy
- Caper
- Chase
- Chick flicks
- Coming of age
- Courtroom
- Cult films
- Detective/mystery
- Disaster
- Episodic
- Espionage
- Fallen woman
- Fantasy
- Film noir
- Guy flicks
- Jungle
- Legal
- Martial arts
- Medical
- Military
- Parody
- Police
- Political
- Political or social satire
- Prison
- Religious
- Road
- Sexual/erotic
- Slasher
- Sports
- Supernatural
- Swashbucklers
- Tear jerkers
- Thrillers/suspense
- Vampire

Types of Comedies

Comedy is one of the roads less traveled in the world. The list of truly funny games is very short, and yet comedy is a mainstay of literature, stage, TV, and cinema. Think about it...

- Screwball
- Romantic
- Musical (song and dance)
- Buddy
- Satirical
- Comedy of manners (social satire)
- Cerebral
- Absurdist
- Ethnic (black, Jewish, Greek, etc.)
- Dumb
- Dumber

Movie Genres Used in Games

So far games do not make use of all the themes that have been used in movies. Some movie themes are not particularly suited to making games, which require lots of interactivity and challenge. However, some of the movie themes that have been used successfully in games include:

- War
- Fantasy
- Epic/historical
- Martial arts
- Sports
- Swashbuckler
- Crime/detective
- Aviation
- Science fiction
- Vampire

Other useful references for this subject include Chapter 9, "Storytelling Techniques," Chapter 12, "Character Design," and Chapter 17, "Game Worlds."

Design Challenge

1. Pick five movie genres and adapt them to a game design.
2. Take a movie genre and a game genre and combine them into an original game concept.
3. Pick a game genre and turn the game into a movie. What kind of movie would it be?

11 Scenarios

Part III

Most games involve some elements of a plot within a story, though not all do. In games where there is a storyline, there is usually a long-range plot—the ultimate goal of the game. (See Chapter 23, "Goals.") And then there are the smaller elements of the story and the gameplay, which I am calling *scenarios.* There are many types of scenarios, and I've attempted to list as many as I could think of. Perhaps you can come up with some new ones....

This chapter lists many common (and some less common) types of scenarios, along with some variations and refinements. Some are just keywords, such as *birth,* that are intended to trigger a scenario in your head. Armed with this list, you should be able to come up with all kinds of ideas for plot elements for your games. For variety, consider combining elements of more than one scenario. Also remember that, while most of this book is designed as a reference, it's also a brainstorming tool in print. So let your mind go wild; *don't get too literal.* For instance, when you see a word like birth, please don't feel that you should skip over that part unless it's a normal situation of a woman having a baby. Let it sit with you for a moment.

What did birth make me think of? It immediately made me think of two things. I once went scuba diving to see a submarine that would hide airplanes inside, so it could "pop one out" and surprise the enemy. So suddenly, an airplane would be in the air and perform completely unexpected attacks on enemy ships in the middle of the ocean. It's a cool idea that went terribly wrong as, I believe, someone got stuck in a hatch, and it sank the whole submarine (hence me diving to it). Birth also made me think of that scene in the first *Alien* movie where the Alien pops out of the guy's chest. I hope you get the point. Use the ideas and words in this chapter as just simple touch points, and really open up your mind to where they can take you.

In this chapter:

- Missing Persons
- Ways to Gain Allies
- Memory Games
- Something's Screwy
- Time Travel
- The Observer
- The Gauntlet
- Imprisonment Scenarios
- Godlike Roles
- Misdirection

Fleeing Something

There's a major problem somewhere, such as a tornado, tsunami, white squall, or tidal wave. For this scenario, you need to get away, to flee or to escape. It could be something like a serial killer, an animal, or a monster that is chasing you, or maybe it's on its way to get you. Maybe you are with the wife (inappropriately occupied, shall we say?) and the husband is about to get home. Maybe you've found a dead body, and people will think you killed this person. If the best option is to bail, then that's the scenario.

Unexpected Danger

Something has been caused by accident, maybe even not by you, but now you're involved. It was unexpected and most likely is compounding your current problems. It could be immediate, such as a volcano erupting, or it could be slow, such as the town running out of water. (See the "Ways to Trigger Events and Flags" section later in this chapter.)

Hot Pursuit/The Chase

Some evil deed has already been done by the bad guys, or maybe it's just about to happen. The bad guys flee, and now they must be chased down and captured before they get away. This can flip both ways, meaning you are chasing but then find yourself being chased, and so on. It can also get interesting when you're chasing the people who are chasing someone else. Or you're chasing a plane or train.

Tit for Tat

Someone did something unpleasant to someone else, and now it's payback time. This was common when I grew up in Northern Ireland. Someone would get executed; the next morning someone on the other side would get executed. It has a tendency to run out of control, and there's a good scenario event—particularly when it's just about to get out of control.

Preemptive Strikes

This is the surprise attack, out of the blue or maybe meticulously preplanned. Usually the goal is to weaken the defenses before the main strike. Sometimes the planning part is the fun part of this scenario, not the actual strike itself. You can, of course, take this concept to the extreme, when you have an asteroid coming to hit Earth and you send up a response before the collision occurs. Or maybe you try to wipe out an alien species before they arrive, after you discover that their visits to other planets are rarely in peace. Maybe you blow up the top of a volcano to implode it before it erupts. Maybe you cut off your leg before the virus or poison spreads. There's a lot of latitude in the concept of preemptive strikes. One of my "old" favorite movies was *War Games*, and it's a fun experimentation with this concept.

Struggle for Resources

Resources are always a part of games in one form or another. Here are some ideas for how to create scenarios based on resources:

- Maybe you need more resources because your society used them all up too fast or because there was never much to begin with. Or perhaps a natural disaster destroyed them all. Or it could be that someone (or something) is taking them.
- Maybe you need something else, a new or better solution, because you've nearly exhausted something you had relied on heavily.
- Maybe your goal is the destruction of your opponents' resources. Maybe there's only one of this resource in existence. It could be controlling the flow or delivery of a resource, such as water into an area that has no other source.
- Or it could be the reverse of that, where you're defending your own resources against attacks.
- It could be the expansion of your own resources—you just want more of something. And yes, money is a resource.
- Sometimes you are just collecting whatever is available (scavenging), such as in the movie *Waterworld.*
- Sometimes you're stealing. Sometimes you're trying to gather the components to manufacture the resource you want or need. Sometimes you are bringing supplies to someone (or people you care about), such as taking food into a dangerous area or doing air drops. Sometimes you are moving the resources, such as a cowboy cattle drive. It's a common theme to squabble or fight over resources, and as you can see, there are many ways to use this concept to your advantage when brainstorming.

Political Motivations

Politics in games can take many forms. It doesn't have to be about governments. It can be about any group where there are leaders and followers and, presumably, tensions and opportunities. Here are just a few ways to think about political motivations in scenarios:

- Someone wants to be a leader of a group.
- Someone wants increased wealth (commonly, *dramatically* more wealth).
- Someone wants influence (manipulation, or a voice in something, the ability to make changes, the power to force changes).
- Someone wants to assassinate competition or to exile someone.
- Someone needs to provide protection for someone else.

Environmental Goals

These are commonly scenarios that involve the restoration or destruction of the environment. Sometimes, they can include destruction or extinction of a certain type of life form (such as specific animals, plants, or organisms).

Another example you see in stories is terraforming to make an environment suitable for another cause or purpose. Please don't automatically assume this is all about global warming or something like that. It could be adding or removing graffiti in a city. It could even be a rampaging Godzilla game, where you are intent on flattening a city and so on. It can be microcosmic, dealing with local environments and ecologies, or it can be macrocosmic, dealing with large events, such as global warming or even some huge intergalactic situation.

Cultural Differentiation

What happens when someone from one culture encounters another? You can create all kinds of settings and scenarios using this kind of cultural differentiation—on a grand scale, where you base your entire game premise on it, or on a smaller scale, where perhaps your hero simply enters a town that operates along very different guidelines and cultural rules than the rest of the world you've created.

There are many examples in TV, movies, and literature. Crocodile Dundee was out of place going from the outback into a city. So many mermaid stories like to play with culture as they experiment with the "fish out of water," trying to understand what drives "real" people. The Disney movie *Enchanted* is another great example of this. Or the aptly titled *Stranger in a Strange Land* and Mark Twain's classic, *A Connecticut Yankee in King Arthur's Court.*

Looking at norms we accept that are actually quite strange from a different perspective is a fun place to go. It's also fun in certain TV shows, such as *Going Tribal,* where you see the host enduring incredibly painful rituals that other human beings just accept as a part of their culture. So imagine you're doing a sci-fi game. You could have a lot of fun designing the initiation of an alien soldier, especially if your character had to go through the experience. (The Navy SEALs think they've got it tough; just wait until they see what alien soldiers go through!)

You can use real-world cultures literally or simply as inspirations, the way the *Harry Potter* books use the culture of the British school system as the model for Hogwarts and its students. What would an alien race be like if they were similar to the ancient Polynesians, the Chinese, or the Mayans? Many *Star Trek* episodes have dealt with these themes, but you can do more in an interactive medium.

Cultural Manipulation

These are scenarios where you play with how people live/work/think/dress/act (either some members of a society or all of them). When you change something in the world, how does it affect society? How does it affect events? Use the idea of changing the way people behave or present themselves to change how a story or event changes. For instance, how would your player's character be treated if he entered a conservative town dressed as a gangsta, as a street person, or as a hippie? Contrast that with how people would respond to the character dressed in a business suit or a religious outfit.

Imagine taking someone from one job and forcing him into another. For instance, consider the nuclear physicist arrested and made to work in the coalmine—or vice versa, the coalminer forced to become a physicist or a chemist or a baker...whatever. Don't limit your imagination. Take a stable situation and make, perhaps, one significant change. How does that affect the culture and reactions of people?

Remember, you can make these kinds of changes as a central theme of your whole game, as a small subsection of the game, or even as the basis for a specific story element. It's fun to brainstorm the many possible parts of our lives that we think of as "normal" and then make changes and imagine what might happen.

Mortal Threats

This could be the mental exercise of dealing with, planning for, or recovering from natural disasters, such as earthquakes, storms, famine, and so on. It could be that a serial killer is talking to you and just hasn't killed you yet. It's also emotionally heightened when it's just a threat that could happen or might not. Uncertainty is the key to really good threats: Maybe it won't be as bad as expected, or maybe it will be 10 times worse. Regardless, fear of death or impending doom is a strong emotion to play with, but it can become a crutch that too many people lean on. So I wouldn't just dive for this scenario right away, because 90 percent of your competitors are probably already leaning on this one, and that leads to a lot of clichéd game scenarios. If anything, I'd probably rebel and actually make fun of the cliché or flip it in some way. For example, maybe you are a serial killer who kills serial killers, and you're actually not under any mortal threat at all.

There are other examples of mortal threats; these are things like genocide (exterminating groups of people), terrorism, and so on. It could even be a slow disease or mutation; drought that threatens a whole population; declining birth rates that threaten to make a species (maybe yours) extinct; impending doom from aliens, asteroids, solar flares, or other extraterrestrial threats, and so on. Anyway, pick your doom and have fun—but be original.

Family and Personal Issues

This is a tough section; I was torn about whether I should even include it. After all, what's it doing in a game design book? In reality it's one area that a lot of game writers would just leave alone. But these are the elements that can strongly resonate with individuals, so why not at least consider them in your story? For instance:

- Becoming the new head of a household, clan, or brotherhood.
- Discovering family secrets. Uncovering genealogy and researching the family tree. DNA testing. Who is really related to whom, and who isn't really the person he's pretending to be?
- Creating or managing family fractures—either individuals or entire families.
- Resolving/fixing broken family ties—either individuals or entire families.
- Weddings/marriage/divorce/cheating/separation.
- Deaths/loss/suicide.
- Births/pregnancy/infertility/breastfeeding/contraception/handling a baby/babysitting/miscarriage/adoption.
- Positive or negative relationships with parents/uncles/aunts/grandparents/siblings/etc.

Family and personal issues are also excellent elements of mysteries and stories that might involve family secrets, murders, unknown parentage, and so on.

Games such as *The Sims* have opened up the door to a sort of "normal life" game, and it's certainly possible that games could explore family dynamics in a very real way, perhaps tackling difficult subjects such as alcoholism, sexism, racism, or child abuse. I know that's a stretch, but when we're talking about scenarios, nothing real should be totally out of bounds for consideration, and these are very real issues. These kinds of sensitive issues should not be the central theme of the game but can be touched upon or become part of the plot points of individual sub-stories or even quests. If you want to take games down new pathways, consider pushing the envelope and redefining how we approach game content. It's risky, but with risk comes opportunity.

The Plot Thickens

I actually like this element (in some way or other) in just about every story. We find out that the situation isn't quite as simple as we had expected. Maybe it's a much bigger conspiracy, movement, or cult than we knew. The stakes get raised considerably. Important details emerge.

We were too close to be able to see the big picture. The truth steps forward. We have to learn who to trust and who not to trust. Maybe someone forgot (or was hiding) something important and now it's revealed....

The idea of this scenario type is that information is revealed to the player that changes, in small or significant ways, his understanding of the situation he is in. It generally makes the situation more complicated, more challenging, and more interesting. So imagine the player in your game going along as if he knows what is happening and can predict, more or less, what is coming. Now throw a monkey wrench into the works, or a monkey, or an alien plumber, or a monkey who is also a plumber… or maybe just reveal that all is not as it seems. Introduce new characters who change the balance of power or who have new information. Or let players discover information about characters they think they know but perhaps did not know so well.

Of course, plot thickening is standard fare in most storytelling, but it's one to keep in mind. Can you think of new ways to thicken your plot—new twists and turns and reversals? One way to do so is to make a list of everything that could possibly happen at specific key points in the game story, then consider what effect those changes would have on your player and the future events of the game. By doing so, you'll first exhaust the obvious ideas, and maybe—just maybe—come up with something brilliant and original next.

Collaborating with the Enemy

Is someone or a group doing the bidding of the bad guys? Here are some possible reasons:

- **Blackmail.** The bad guys have something over the player.
- **Kidnapping.** The bad guys hold an important hostage, and you may have to work with them or bargain with them to get the hostage released.
- **Loyalty.** The bad guys helped the player out, and now the favor is due.
- **No-Choice Threat.** The bad guys "make an offer" to do their bidding. But you know the "offer" is little more than a veiled threat. For example, they may say, "Do this for us," but what they really mean is, "Do this, or we will reveal your secrets!" Or, "Do this, or your family dies!"
- **Trickery.** The bad guys have misinformed the player, so the player cooperates with them, not realizing that it's a setup.
- **Antidote.** The player (or someone else who is important to the player) will die from some slow-acting poison. Only the bad guys have the antidote. (So it's a slightly more specific form of blackmail.)
- **Something You Need.** The bad guys have something the player needs to complete a sub-quest or the main quest of the game. It could be something physical, something magical, or even just something like a password, a tip on how to kill something (that's very tough to kill), or a lead on how to find who or what the player is after.
- **Pay.** The player might help the bad guys if he really needs the money or reward.
- **Justified.** Maybe the bad guys are actually fighting the good fight, like fighting against a corrupt government or regime.

Infiltration

The player or party must infiltrate an enemy base or an enemy-controlled location. This often means fighting through or circumventing the location's defenses.

Here are some possible reasons:

- **Get an Object.** You have to retrieve an important object.
- **Get a Clue.** You have to retrieve important information, either directly from a person, by stealing some evidence, object, or person that has the information, or by spying on the enemy.

- **Get a Life.** You have to rescue someone.
- **Destruction.** You have to destroy something (such as the crystal that is the source of the bad guys' power, false evidence against the good side, or the mad scientist's cloning laboratory).
- **Plant It!** You have to leave something (such as a bomb, a listening device, or a message for an ally) or maybe you plant something that was previously stolen and must be replaced before it's missed.
- **Transit.** You want to gain access to another location that can only be reached through here. (And that transit can be difficult or awkward.)
- **Visit the Wizard.** You need to talk to someone who can help you.
- **Find the Boss.** You enter the place to find a boss protecting what you seek.
- **Trials and Tribulations.** You must infiltrate the place to pass a test given to you by someone who can help you; see also the upcoming "Qualification Tests (Tests of Worthiness)" section.
- **Because It's There.** It's there, and you like to challenge yourself. (Base jumpers do this all the time.)
- **Because You Can.** Meaning you get unique access to somewhere other people could only dream of knowing, such as maybe you're the president's dog.

There are endless methods, reasons, and ways to infiltrate. Usually it gets more interesting when things change on the fly. So don't let it get too fixed. Consider forcing the story to mix methods of infiltration to pull off the goal.

Methods of stealthy entry include:

- **The Front Way.** Walk in the front entrance.
- **The Hidden Way.** Hide in a truck, wagon, Trojan horse, laundry basket, casket, and so on.
- **Up and Over.** Climb a wall.
- **Down and Under.** Go through the basement or tunnel under the fence.
- **Buy Your Way In.** Bribe a guard or bring gifts.
- **It's Not Me...Really!** Go in disguise (such as dressing like a guard).
- **From the Air.** Fly over and parachute, jump, or magically float in.
- **Poof, You're In!** Teleport inside.
- **You Can't See Me.** Use an invisibility potion or ability.
- **Shh...I Know the Secret.** Learn the secret password, incantation, combination, or other secret of entry and use it.
- **Hey, Look Over There!** Create a diversion, then sneak in.
- **Sleep Tight.** Silently assassinate the guards that are blocking your path without anyone noticing.

Neutralize the Base

Take over or neutralize an enemy base, stronghold, or other asset. (The reasons are mostly the same as for infiltration, but sometimes with different goals.)

Methods include:

- **Frontal Assault.** Attack with superior numbers (usually not), firepower (possibly), or intelligence (more likely).
- **Cripple the Defense.** Disable a key element, such as a source of power, leader, or mini-boss defender.
- **Kaboom!** Aerial or long-range assault, heavy bombing, crippling the structure.
- **Sabotage.** Infiltrate the troops, get someone inside to do the dirty work, plant a worm in the computer system, and so on.
- **The Art of Persuasion.** Defection—get the bad guy's minions to realize they are on the wrong side and to join you.

- **Trojan Horse.** Pretend to be an ordinary merchant, then sneak out at nightfall and open the gates, letting your army (or party, friends, or secret weapons) inside.
- **Downsize.** Make it really, really small with a shrink ray or level it with a weapon or spell.
- **Find a Bigger Stick.** Get someone else bigger than you or even stronger mad at your enemy and let them destroy the enemy base (for instance, a rival king, an alien emperor, or a giant).
- **That Sinking Feeling.** Tunnel under it and sink it.
- **A Good Rinse.** Destroy a dam and cause a flood to wash it away.
- **A Poisonous Plan.** Send in poison gas or a plague to wipe out the guardians of the place.
- **Start a Panic.** Watch the defenders flee as they anticipate doom.
- **Impairment.** Get the defenders drunk (or drugged) and distracted or incapacitated.

Special challenges might include:

- **The Guardian.** While neutralizing the base, you must protect innocent citizens.
- **The Liberator.** You must release or save prisoners, perhaps before you do anything else.
- **The Most Important Thing.** You must find, steal, preserve (protect), destroy, or neutralize some important object.
- **Get the Boss.** You must capture the monarch, alien presence, crime lord, or other big boss. You can't let them die with the others (for any number of reasons).
- **The Clock Is Ticking.** You must do it on a timer; for instance, a bomb has been set or another invasion is planned to coincide with your success.
- **The Clock Is Ticking 2.** You must disable something, then escape on a timer, before the whole structure blows up or becomes poisoned, irradiated, or full of zombies
- **There Must Be a Way.** The place is impregnable, and you have to find its special weakness (such as the Death Star).

Making an Area Safe

This often entails finding the source of the problem. For example:

- **Kill Them All!** Clearing all bad guys/enemies/threats.
- **Target the Leader.** Removing or disabling the leader or boss (or at least disabling his control).
- **On Guard.** Bringing in guards or vigilantes (maybe even bounty hunters).
- **The Bad Seed.** Destroying the source of the poison that's killing all the crops or stopping whatever is making the environment toxic.
- **Faux Evil.** Helping the "evil" creatures (who are, in reality, good)—in other words, removing a curse or finding a potion to turn the wolfmen back into normal people again.
- **Cleaning Up.** Removing the nuclear ash or the virus that wiped everyone out or dispersing the gas cloud.
- **Hiding Evidence.** Making everything seem normal so the enemies pass on through. You hide all your weapons, have everyone dressed in civilian clothing, and so on.
- **Neutralizing the Threat.** For example, locating and disabling the system that managed control over everyone (as in *Logan's Run*). Or just disarming a bomb.
- **Nonviolent Solutions.** For example, leading everyone to a new, "safe" location or planting special plants or casting a spell that will neutralize the poison, curse, or whatever.
- **Fixing Something.** For instance, fixing a dam that has broken and flooded the area or that is about to break and cause a catastrophic flood. (Getting it back under control.)

- **Putting Out Fires.** For instance, putting out a forest fire or a fire in a city, but also, more metaphorically speaking, anything that is spreading and causing damage that you must contain—such as a plague, poison gas, or cloning machines that are spewing out minions and so on.

Special challenges might include:

- **Sub-Quests.** Sometimes making an area safe requires a secondary quest or even a whole series of quests; see also the upcoming "Delayed Gratification" section.
- **Not Being Ready.** Sometimes you aren't strong enough yet or you don't have the necessary party members, skills, or objects/weapons to resolve the situation, so you will have to assess what is going on and come back when you are ready; see also the "Delayed Gratification" section.
- **Ally = Enemy.** Sometimes finding the cause of the problem leads you back to someone you thought was an ally, and you will have to either become his enemy or find out why he is doing bad things.
- **Resource Assembly.** The change requires resources you just don't have, so assembling the resources (which can include people) is required.
- **Changing Conditions.** The conditions change, so you are simultaneously cleaning up different problems.

Timed and/or Cyclic Events

Timed events are common in games—so much so that we devoted a couple of chapters to the ideas around time and games: Chapter 28, "Controlling Pacing," and Chapter 29, "Time Limits and Time Manipulation." In this section, we suggest a few common ways that time is used in games.

- **29 Days to Doomsday.** You have so many hours/days/months/years to complete your quest or all hell breaks loose and life as you know it will come to an end...or something even less pleasant will happen.
- **The Big Buildup.** Similar to 29 Days to Doomsday, this occurs when the enemy is working to achieve a goal and you are racing time to complete some quest(s) before he achieves that goal. This could mean building an army, maturing some guardian creature or thing into its final form, discovering the secret formula of invincibility, or constructing the ultimate weapon.
- **Survive Until...** The player is required by circumstances to stay in a dangerous location until some specific event occurs. Or something is broken, and you can't move until it is repaired. Or you must guard an entrance until help arrives. Or the Mothership isn't due for two days, and meanwhile man-eating plants are closing in on your party. Or perhaps you have to keep arguing until the governor grants a stay of execution and stops them from throwing the switch.
- **Every Friday at Nine.** Something happens on a regular schedule, and it causes destruction or otherwise unpleasant results. If you can be there to stop it, you can avoid some of the damage. If you can find its source, you can stop it all together. As an alternative, it could be a good thing that happens—a portal to magic fairyland or a visit from the Wise Wizard, who heals you and grants you special powers.
- **The 30-Second Escape.** The player does something that triggers a catastrophic event or other terrible consequence, but it will happen in x seconds/minutes. Usually, this is a reasonably short period of time; otherwise, it is 29 Days to Doomsday. Also, the timer for this kind of event is usually displayed on the screen to freak out the player as he tries to figure out how to get out or disable the threat before the timer reaches zero.

- **Fake 30-Second Escape.** As with the Fake Emergencies (below), the player receives a message that something terrible is going to happen in x seconds/minutes; however, there is no real timer, and generally there are all kinds of visual and sound effects making it seem as if all hell is breaking loose, but really the situation isn't changing at all. The screen may shake, and big boulders, girders, or other structural elements may be falling all around, but the player has as much time as he needs to escape or neutralize the threat. To be really clear, when it comes to faking I'm not suggesting you do this, but just know that it is done in situations where you just want to raise the stakes. There are times when a real time limit is fun. There are other times when just the impression of a time limit is sufficient, but players may have more to do than the time limit would allow. The trick here is that players may tend to panic and run for the exits, but in doing so, they may miss some cool opportunities (items, side paths, secret characters, and so on). So, in a game where the time limit is real, the player must run like hell, deal with any obstacles, and escape safely. With a fake time limit, they simply have the illusion of immediacy, but they might not know whether it's real.
- **Fake Emergencies.** The player gets a message that he must hurry before something happens. This often sounds like 29 Days to Doomsday or The Big Buildup, but in reality the game does not keep track of time at all. The big event will occur when (and only when) the player triggers a flag by, for instance, opening a specific door, crossing a specific point in the terrain, picking up a specific object, killing a specific enemy, and so on. (See also the upcoming "Ways to Trigger Events and Flags" section.)
- **Time Trials and Races.** These are usually used in mini-games or tests to prove worthiness. For instance, the king will help you only if you prove yourself by breaking 21 barrels in 30 seconds or completing a complex obstacle course within a time limit (or beating his champion). Rewards for time trials and races usually involve special items, gaining favor from someone, or achievement of a specific rank or title that lets you do things in the game that you couldn't do without that rank or title. In other games, such as racing games, that's the whole game, but in RPGs these are never more than sub-events. (See also the upcoming "Qualification Tests" section.)

Ways to Trigger Events and Flags

Events are triggered by setting the value of a flag in the code, and they can have immediate effects (such as stepping on a pressure plate and having a guillotine blade fall) or delayed or even invisible effects (such as talking to an NPC in Middletown and getting a clue that changes the options or dialog available from a different NPC in Highland). Talking to an NPC might also activate a whole new quest, heal the player, or cause the NPC to attack, and so on. Pulling a lever in one place might unlock or open a door somewhere completely different, or it could release a trapdoor and send the player down a dark shaft into a rat-infested sewer. These are some of the ways to trigger events:

- **Cross the Line!** The player crosses an invisible line within a region, causing an event to occur.
- **Enter It!** The player enters an area (which could also mean a vehicle, room, teleporter, and so on), which triggers an event.
- **Open It!** The player opens something (door, chest, cabinet), which triggers an event. This could also include solving a combination lock or hacking a code or password.
- **Step on It!** Similar to Cross the Line, but in this case the player steps on a specific location—a pressure plate, loose rock, loose board, button in the floor or invisible spot—and the event is triggered.
- **Press/Push/Pull/Spin/Shoot/Hack It!** The player messes with a button, lever, wheel, or other mechanical device, which triggers an event.

- **Talk about It!** The player talks to an NPC and receives some vital information, which triggers an event. The event could be immediate or delayed, or it could just be a flag that allows the player access to some new aspect of the game.
- **Kill It!** The player kills some specific monster, which triggers an event.
- **Complete It!** The player completes a task, such as killing the last monster in a room, delivering a message to an NPC, or winning a race, which triggers an event.
- **Observe It!** Just hearing or seeing an event can trigger another event or set a flag for something in the game to change.

DELAYED GRATIFICATION

A lot of what happens in games involves more or less instant gratification. Often you are involved in moment-to-moment events that provide consistent rewards. Other times, you may be working toward a specific reward that cannot be completed immediately—a new level, more skill points to allocate, a special weapon, a new power, the completion of a milestone in the game, and so on. This is one form of delayed gratification. Another type of delayed gratification occurs when you can see something or know it's there, but you can't get to it. In its most basic form you might know (or suspect) that something good (or at least interesting) lies on the other side of a door, but you'll have to wait until later, when you have the key, code, or other means to open the door.

The same sort of situation involves being able to accomplish certain goals, obtain certain items, or reach certain locations only when you have gained enough power, specific skills, or specific objects that allow you to do so. Concepts of gratification, whether immediate or delayed, are also closely aligned with goals (see Chapter 23, "Goals") and rewards (see Chapter 24, "Rewards, Bonuses, and Penalties").

- **You Can't Touch Me...Yet.** You can't kill a certain enemy until you get a better or specific weapon, new skills, higher level, and so on.
- **You Can't Get Me...Yet.** You won't be able to get that tantalizing chest high up on the cliff until you can either fly or find some other way to reach it.
- **You Have to Earn It.** Some NPC has offered you a very cool reward (such as a powerful new weapon) if you can do a few "errands" for him.
- **Completing Levels.** With level-based characters, every level achievement is an example of delayed gratification.
- **Strategic Planning.** In a strategy game, often the results of your strategic movements do not become clear until later. For instance, you have chosen to build a lot of your aerial units, thinking to fly over the enemy's defenses. But you don't know what the enemy is doing, so the strategy might or might not be effective. Or, you decide to concentrate on exploration, resources, and technology, hoping to blow the enemy away with the most advanced troops and defenses. In any case, you won't know if your strategy worked until the game unfolds and you see what the enemy has been doing and how effective your strategy was.
- **It Ain't Over 'Til It's Over.** All long-term goals involve delayed gratification, so in that sense, almost all games have an element of delayed gratification.
- **Setting the Table.** In complex turn-based games, you may make a dozen moves, but you don't know what will happen until you hit the End Turn button (or its equivalent) and see what your opponents will do.
- **What Will It Be When It Grows Up?** You're training a creature, but you don't know if your training choices will result in the kind of creature you want.

- **Dangerous Terrain.** Without the right equipment, it can be nearly impossible to find your way or survive the environment. You remember the area, however, and come back when you have your special item(s) or skills.

Qualification Tests (Tests of Worthiness)

These qualification tests or tests of worthiness are activities that test a payer's abilities and readiness for some other aspect of the game—often in the form of a mini-game, tutorial, or side quest. They can also be a qualification for a race (such as NASCAR) or some sort of round-robin sports tournament. In some cases, the qualification test is a part of the game's storyline—for instance, an NPC demands that you face some trial before you can obtain his cooperation. When a qualification test is a part of the storyline, it often serves as a mini-game—something to provide variety, new challenges, a break from the general gameplay, and, possibly, a good test of the player's abilities. In such cases, there is generally a reasonably desirable reward if the player can pass the test.

Another type of qualification test is really about the developers of the game giving players an opportunity to practice the skills they need—a way to challenge, test, and assess their abilities—before they continue. This can be done in the form of a tutorial with obvious guidance, as qualification rounds or missions that are required before the player can continue to the next aspect of the game, in the form of easy early levels and situations, or in the form of a practice area specifically designated for the purpose.

Qualification tests or tests of worthiness can include:

- **Qualification Races.** These can be in actual racing games but sometimes are used within RPGs as a test and way to give the player more experience with the controls.
- **Qualification Rounds.** These are used primarily in various sports games to train the player and bring him up to the level of the actual game.
- **Guided Tutorials.** These teach and test the player's understanding and abilities.
- **Logic Puzzles.** Sometimes these are used to require a player to solve certain puzzles before continuing the game. These puzzles often demonstrate a certain principle of the game—something the player will see more of in more complicated circumstances.
- **Bosses.** In some ways, mid-bosses are qualification tests. If you can't pass the mid-boss, you clearly aren't going to get far in the game as it increases in difficulty.
- **Obstacle Courses.** These are a great way to provide a variety of challenges and practice for players before they move into the real game. The *Tomb Raider* games included basic obstacle course trainers.
- **Special Challenges.** Designers almost always include certain especially challenging obstacles that the player will have to get past in order to continue. This is similar to the mid-boss, but it may only be a particularly nasty group of thugs or muggers or an especially monster-infested area that must be navigated. This is an aspect of tuning a game and can be mostly transparent to the player who has mastered the necessary skills and difficult for players who are not sufficiently prepared. This also works well in Role-Playing Games, where a section can be tuned to be too difficult for low-level players, without creating any artificial barriers to prevent them from trying it.
- **The John Henry.** John Henry (the "steel drivin' man") was really good at pounding spikes to set railroad tracks. In the legend, he races a mechanical engine to prove the superiority of man over machine. This is typical of a race to prove worthiness, although races can be more simple—just run/drive/ride and get there first—or even more complex—run, jump, ride, drive, swim, destroy, fight, rearrange something, swing, fly...and any combination thereof.

- **Break 10 Barrels.** In this scenario, you must accomplish some physical task within a time limit, such as breaking 10 barrels with your sword in five seconds or killing x monsters before returning. Such trials often require you to complete several progressively more difficult challenges.
- **Practice Makes Perfect.** Often, when characters have learned a new skill or obtained a new weapon, they are given specific quests or game elements designed to help them learn to use what they have just gained. A good example of this would be in the *Zelda* games when Link gets a new weapon; he is presented with a new dungeon in which that new weapon is required. It's not a qualification test so much as a qualification practice.
- **You Da Man.** You must go fight some champion or monster and return with its golden eyeball, silver dagger, or some token of your success. An alternative is that you must fight in an arena, gladiator-style, and beat all comers in waves until finally you beat the champ! Another variant is the one-on-one duel with the NPC in question or their champion. Defeat him, and you get what you want.
- **What's In It for Me?** Some tests of worthiness involve finding some rare item, substance, or object that will cure the king's daughter of a mysterious ailment, stop people from turning into zombies, unlock a treasure chest, grant invisibility to the user, cause the magic tree to grow, and so on—anything that the NPC really wants badly enough to trade for what you want from him. This can be a physical object, accomplishing a specific task, or acquiring information the NPC wants. Sometimes this takes the form of a scavenger hunt, where you must bring back a bunch of stuff. Sometimes you are given the list at the beginning. Sometimes the NPC keeps adding items and sending you back out for more. Generally, however, once the task is complete, you are given what it was you set out to achieve or something of value that makes the test worthwhile.
- **Deliver the Message.** This is just what it sounds like.
- **Find the Criminal.** A crime has been committed, and the NPC will give you what you want if you can solve the crime. (See also the upcoming "Criminal Investigation" section.)

Special circumstances include:

- The NPC giving the task may be lying and planning to double-cross you once you complete the trial. This is rarely a problem. Just kill him. Of course, sometimes the NPC escapes, but you'll get him later. This technique is good for making you hate the bad guy even more. (See also the "How to Make You Hate Them" section in Chapter 14, "Enemies.")

Criminal Investigation

All RPG plots involve solving mysteries and finding clues, but this variant deals directly with solving crimes. Generally, these are small sub-quests and occur within a single community or town, though they also can involve travel to other areas to find clues or track down important people—even the criminal. However, it could be that the RPG has a detective theme, in which case criminal investigation would be a main part of the story. Criminal investigation is not limited to RPGs, however, and various kinds of shooters and third-person games can involve criminal plots, with the player having a reason to find the perpetrator. In any case, here are the basic elements of the criminal investigation plot:

- **What Happened?** One or more crimes have been committed.
- **Whodunit?** You have to find out who the criminal is.
- **Where?** Find out where the crime took place.
- **When?** When was the crime committed?
- **Motive.** It helps to seek out the motive for the crime.

- **Gather Clues.** This phase is where the detective work goes into high gear. Players must look for physical clues in and around the crime scene, and they must also talk to people and figure out who is telling the truth and who is lying.
- **Apprehend the Criminal.** Once you figure out whodunit, go get 'em! There will generally be a reward.

Reversals of Fortune

Reversals of fortune can occur in several ways. Some are permanent (one of your party dies—sometimes permanently, although in some games they might return or can be resurrected. (Think Gandalf the Grey in *The Lord of the Rings*, who "died" and returned as Gandalf the White.) Some are temporary—you enter an area where magic is nullified. Some are cyclic—a party member seems to leave from time to time and then returns. Of course, not all reversals are negative, and some can result in a new advantage or better circumstances for the player. Mostly, positive reversals come as a reward for the player's efforts, whereas negative reversals are often plot elements that occur *despite* the player's efforts.

Reversals of fortune include:

- **Stripped and Demoted.** In the course of the story, you might lose your special items, your rank and some abilities, your powerful weapons, and so on. Sometimes you even start very strong and feel practically invincible, then you suddenly become a wimpy newbie. This was a trick we used in *Earthworm Jim.* When he was in his cybernetic suit, he was a super-worm. Then, once the player was used to that feeling of power, we took the suit away. Suddenly, they were playing as a naked little fleshy earthworm! The reversal suddenly adds pressure and offers new gameplay challenges.
- **You Lose a Friend.** A new party member joins you and is really useful because he is very strong or has some cool abilities. Then, for some reason, you lose that party member just when you've come to rely on him. This variation happens in both RPG parties and with "pets" or sidekicks. They commonly fight for you, so when they're gone you *really* miss them.
- **The Party's Over.** Sometimes the circumstances of the story cause the party to break up. Either a key member leaves to pursue goals of his own (possibly returning to the party later) or the whole party separates, and you are on your own. This latter example is usually temporary, and the party will reform later.
- **Now What?** You try to achieve a goal or complete a quest, but for some reason you fail. The object of the goal or quest may no longer exist or may be destroyed. The reason for completing the goal or quest may no longer apply to your situation, or the reward for completion is no longer useful.
- **Snatching Defeat from the Jaws of Victory.** You think you have the upper hand in a situation, when the enemy reveals a trump card...a secret weapon or ability, or perhaps they take a hostage at the last moment, or enemy reinforcements arrive just as you are about to deliver the final blow.
- **Loose Backing/Sponsorship.** The organization behind the party either stops supporting the party by choice or can no longer support the party. It could be that the company no longer exists, can't afford the costs, legally can't continue to be a benefactor, or one of many other reasons. This is different from the Now What? scenario due to the fact that the group and goals are likely still intact, but the "officialness" is gone, and the difficultly of the tasks increase.
- **Where's Home Base?** The safe location or meeting place is gone or compromised, and now the player/party has lost their safe haven.
- **Really, Really Dead?** The quest seemed complete and the goal accomplished, but it's not really over, such as defeating a boss that keeps getting back up or reappearing. (It's the classic trick in movies, "Is he *really* dead?) So basically you thought you'd won, but don't go celebrating just yet!

Party Members

There are four basic party members in a fantasy-based (*D&D* derivative) RPG and a few basic derivatives. The basic party members are Fighter, Thief, Cleric, and Mage. The derivatives are various combinations of those four, such as the Friar, who can fight and cast Cleric spells, or the Ninja, who can fight really well and has a high sneak factor, like the Thief. Then there are Archers, who are like Thieves with bows and arrows, Sharpshooters, and other ranged classes.

The names don't matter; what is important is the function. There are characters who must be able to dish out and take damage, especially in hand-to-hand combat. Others must be able to heal and support the group. These are probably the two most important classes. Then there are the magic classes, who cast a variety of types of magic spells. Both Clerics and Mages use magic in fantasy RPGs, but Mages are generally more concerned with offense, while Clerics are generally more concerned with defense and healing arts. There is some possible crossover.

In other games, magic can be replaced by technological wonders, pharmaceuticals, robotics, and so on. The Thief character is generally used to do sneaky things, disarm traps, steal, and so forth, dealing out less damage overall but having good agility to avoid damage. Variants of the Thief are the Ninja, Monk, or Assassin, while there are also variants of basic fighters, such as Paladins, Knights, and so on.

Traditional Classes of Party Members

See also the "Player Roles in Multiplayer Games" section in Chapter 13, "Character Roles and Jobs." Traditional classes of party members include:

- Fighter/Tank
- Cleric/Healer
- Thief
- Mage
- Archer/Sniper/Sharpshooter
- Paladin/Knight
- Sorcerer
- Necromancer
- Enchanter
- Ninja
- Samurai

Nontraditional Classes of Party Members

Nontraditional classes of party members include:

- Robot (nonorganic, something "made")
- Alien (not the same species as the other, can be ethereal)
- Child (specifically a child in a group of adults)
- Mysterious member or outsider (someone who "feels" outside the scope of the group)
- Psychic (clairvoyant, telekinetic, hypnotist, etc.)
- Village idiot (savant?)

Party Member Encounters

How do you meet new party members? Here are some of the common ways. Can you think of some new and more interesting ones?

- **Rescued.** You rescue them, and they join you after hearing your story.
- **Rescuer.** They come to your aid and then join you after hearing your story.

- **Chance Meeting.** You come across them on the road, in town, at the tavern, etc. Sometimes you encounter them fighting enemies, and you may help them (or not). In any case, they will generally prevail and offer to join your party.
- **Former Enemy.** They were your enemy or rival, but they have changed sides and become your ally. This may occur after you defeat them in battle or after the real enemy messes with them. It may also occur because they were really good and didn't know the bad guys were bad. Once they find out, they switch sides.
- **The Reformed Criminal.** This is someone who once led a life of crime and arrogance, who has fallen on hard times and realized the error of his ways. He seeks redemption through heroic acts, and you are just the player to give him that opportunity.
- **The Last Survivor.** His town/province/forest/habitat/race/family was wiped out by the bad guys, and he has nowhere else to go. He often seeks revenge, although sometimes Last Survivors are wistful, sad, and fatalistic.
- **The Assignment.** Some NPC, often someone important like the King or a significant Oracle, tells you to take along a daughter, son, captain of the guard, hero, talented dog, strange energy being, dark stranger, mysterious old man, or just about any stray creature he may have hanging around.
- **The Seeker.** You meet someone who is seeking something and decides to join you, thinking that what he seeks may be found in your company. Seekers are among the most likely to leave a party if the player's goals cease to coincide with theirs.
- **The Transformation.** You may liberate a cursed toad or a petrified statue of a creature, only to have it turn into a useful character that joins you.
- **The Ideologue.** You meet someone who simply believes in your cause or in justice in general.
- **The Fugitive.** Someone is running or hiding from something fearsome. He joins you for the safety found with your group. It is possible that what pursues him is also what you are hunting, but not necessarily.
- **The Ne'er Do Well.** Not a very nice person/creature, but useful. He joins you but has an attitude and isn't necessarily on your side. He usually can be trusted in battle; however, sometimes he defects or turns out to be a spy/mole. But generally, his role is to create color and attitude and to conflict with the party dynamics, especially with other NPC party members.
- **Happy Go Lucky.** The motley fool, the shiftless traveler who joins you with a light heart and no responsibilities. Since you, the player, generally have the fate of the world on your shoulders, Happy Go Lucky represents a contrasting character who takes things more lightly throughout the adventure. He may be a clown, a fool, or simply someone who takes things as they come.

Unwanted Sidekicks

Sometimes you find someone attached to your party, even though he is not your first choice and is of limited usefulness. He may even be annoying and a liability to the group. Here are some types of unwanted sidekicks:

- **The Incompetent Cop.** He's assigned to you ostensibly to help you investigate a mystery, but he's all thumbs and annoying to boot.
- **The King's Brother.** He's someone connected to someone else who is important, but he's no help and really doesn't want to be there in the first place. He's probably the most likely to betray you, given the opportunity.
- **The Loyal Idiot.** It could be a dog, an alien being, Tinker Bell, or even a person, but basically, this is some creature that attaches itself to you and can't be gotten rid of. It's not particularly helpful, but

for reasons known only to the game designer, you can't get rid of it. However, often this annoying appendage will turn out to be very important toward the end of the story and may even turn into one of the most powerful characters.

- **Stop Following Me!** Some irritating and useless creature that follows you around and won't go away. Like the Loyal Idiot, but more annoying and less useful, Stop Following Me almost never comes in handy. At best, this creature may, at a critical time in the game, show you where a secret entrance is or remember something useful. (This is the role of Donkey in the *Shrek* movies.)
- **Just Doing My Job.** You must escort or protect an NPC, who temporarily becomes attached to your party. (See the following "Is It Safe?" section.)

Is It Safe?

Protection tasks can involve people/creatures, objects, and places. The task can involve escorting someone or something safely from one place to another, generally protecting a person/creature or thing without a specific destination in mind, or protecting a stationary object or location, such as a castle or a strategic bridge. Generally speaking, while you're in protection mode, you will also be fighting off enemies bent on destroying you and your charge.

- **Person/Creature.** You must protect a person or other living being, keeping it from harm.
- **Vehicle.** Especially in naval- or space-based games, but sometimes in other games, you must escort a particular vehicle safely from one location to another. Of course, there will be plenty of enemies trying to blow it up or hijack it.
- **Object.** You must protect an object of importance, meaning it can't be damaged, destroyed, or stolen while you are responsible for it.
- **Emplacement.** You must protect a location, such as a bridge, castle, crime scene, throne room, cave entrance, or tree. This is a stationary location, where objects you protect would be mobile.

Special conditions include:

- **Point to Point.** You must get the person/creature or object from one place to another safely. Failure can be devastating to the game.
- **Escorting the Fool.** The person/creature you are escorting may be foolhardy and constantly getting in trouble or may be an Unwanted Sidekick who is simply annoying. He may be very weak, very brave, or very cowardly. In any case, he often makes your job very hard.
- **The Curse.** An object you are carrying must be protected, but it's cursed and causes you to slowly bleed to death or something equally unpleasant.
- **It's Not Over 'Til It's Over 2.** You may get a key person/creature to the end location only to find that he can't perform his function for some reason, and you'll have to do it yourself. Or, a safe place where you were supposed to drop him off is no longer safe, and you will have to make it safe.
- **Escorting the Enemy.** The person/creature you are escorting is really a bad guy, but you still can't let anything happen to him. He may even try to get you into more hot water while you are trying to protect him.
- **Escorting a Prisoner.** The person/creature you are escorting could be a prisoner who must be kept from harm but who must not be allowed to escape. He will do whatever he can to get away, although he'll generally welcome your help in protecting him from other enemies.

- **Trade Item.** The person/creature/object you are protecting is a key element in securing something you want—a bargaining chip. It may be a hostage or an item of special value, and it may buy the cooperation of someone, the release of a prisoner, or some other useful and necessary result.
- **Finding a Safe Route.** The danger you are protecting someone from is natural, such as a landslide, flood, erupting volcano, or earthquake, and your job is mostly to find a safe route. This might also be true if the outside danger is from a distant enemy using bombardment tactics, such as artillery, aircraft, catapults, or other long-range projectiles.
- **Stealth Escort.** The escort mission might not involve fighting or avoiding attacks, but it might involve preventing discovery. For instance, you might be attempting to lead someone to safety while avoiding discovery by surveillance equipment—escaping a penal colony or trying to move unseen through an enemy castle or a futuristic Orwellian city.
- **From a Distance.** Instead of being right there between harm and the charge, shooting, redirecting, and other measures may be needed to protect the charge. Cover fire is the obvious example.
- **Bait and Smash.** Lure the enemy into a trap and cut them down as a preemptive measure.

The Call for Help

Players often take on the hero's role, and as heroes they are there to help the less fortunate. How do they find themselves in the hero's role? There are many ways. Luke Skywalker got a message from Princess Leia that started a major saga. In other cases, it may be less dramatic. Here are some common ways to create what we call "the call for help."

- **The Direct Plea.** You meet someone, and he asks you to help him.
- **Obscure Messages.** You receive some cryptic information that leads you to believe someone is in trouble—such as the holographic recording of Princess Leia in *Star Wars.*
- **Moral Choices.** You can see that help is needed, but you have to decide whether it is the right thing to do. Perhaps these are brigands or otherwise disreputable types, or even minions of your enemy. Then again, helping them might result in something good for you in the long run. Or, it might cause further harm to the good folk. What to do???
- **Whether You Like It or Not.** You are forced somehow to help someone, either by physical force, threats to others, or some other form of manipulation or mind control.
- **Get the Message.** You get a message (which can be in any form) revealing the need for help. (It can even be a message in a bottle!)

Unexpected Location Changes

You're going along just fine, exploring your limited world. You know where you are and possibly where you're going. But in games, we have so many ways to snap you out of your complacency and, at the same time, give you whole new worlds to explore and situations to handle, puzzles to solve, people to meet, and deeds to do. We can do it simply by offering new adventures in your current location, but isn't it fun to travel? Here are some ways to change a player character's location and open all sorts of new plot- and location-related doors.

- **Shipwreck.** After the big storm or explosion aboard the ship, you find yourself washed up on a strange and unfamiliar shore.

- **Plane Crash.** The plane crashes in an unfamiliar area—a deep forest, jungle, or desert, perhaps—almost certainly a wild and untamed region filled with dangers.
- **Unexpected Teleportation.** Who knew that pulling that lever, pressing that button, or stepping into that beam of light would suddenly send you somewhere else?
- **NPC Action.** With the wave of a wand or the press of a button, some NPC has sent you to a new world. You might know where you are going, or you might have no clue. You might have gone willingly, or you might have been sent there by an enemy.
- **Chutes and Ladders.** Somehow, you trigger a trapdoor or you step on a slippery slope, release a powerful spring, or step onto a floating platform. In any case, you end up floating, flying, or falling into a new place. It may not be immediately obvious how to get back where you came from, but it will likely be pretty obvious that the new place is full of danger.
- **Missed Jump.** You are jumping from one platform to another, but you misjudge the leap and fall. Do you die? Not this time. This time you end up way down below in an irritating area full of enemies and obstacles. You have to get back up to the top and try the jump(s) again. Sometimes there are minor power objects at the bottom or secondary routes.
- **Guidance System Malfunction.** You're out in space, en route to the Galactic Capitol to visit the Viceroy, when your guidance system malfunctions. You can be sure you'll end up in a new location.
- **The Space Jump.** This is the emergency button on a spacecraft for when you're being attacked. There's no time to plot a course, so you end up somewhere else in space, and you need to work out where.
- **Shanghaied.** The bad guys got you! And they're taking you somewhere (sometimes blindfolded). The next thing you know, you are in the dungeon, the prison, the jungle, tied up in a tent, in a pot of water over a blazing fire, in a rocket ship headed for parts unknown, in a soft canopied bed with servants all around…well, anyway, you're somewhere else.
- **Time Warp.** Suddenly, you find yourself as you were in the past or as you will be in the future. Even if you're technically in the same physical place, things are different now.
- **Character Switch.** You're deep into the story. You just gained a new, much more powerful weapon, and you're feeling ready for anything. Then the scene shifts, and all of a sudden you are playing a cute little creature that's a cross between a Pekingese and a gopher, and its only attack is a weak head butt. Well, now what do you do?
- **La-La Land.** You become unconscious/die and are all of a sudden in a trancelike state. This could be either where you previously were or somewhere you have never seen before. Either way, you are clearly no longer in the "normal" world.
- **The Hospital.** Beaten to a pulp: You have passed out or fallen asleep only to wake up someplace else, where people are tending to your injuries.

The Obscure Object of Desire

There's something that's critical, and one or more rival groups are after it, too.

- **The Race.** The object may be hidden or easy to find. In any case, you must get to it before someone else does. This scenario can be very straightforward. You simply go faster than your rival(s). Or it can be much trickier. For instance, you have to fight your way past some minions, but while you are fighting, your rival runs by and gets ahead of you. Maybe you would have been better off to let him go first and fight the minions?
- **What, That Old Thing?** The precious object is in the possession of another group. They don't think it's all that important. If they knew it was, they would make it far more expensive or they would simply keep it. So you must find a way to get it from them without letting them know its value.

Part III

- **That's Impossible.** There's no way you can figure out how to get the object. However, your rivals may be able to get where you cannot. In this scenario, you let someone else get the object, then you steal it.
- **Too Late!** Someone else got it first. You will have to steal it, purchase or trade, or convince him to give it to you.
- **Prove Yourself.** You aren't the only one who wants something, and the owner decides to set up a test to see who is most worthy of it. (See also the "Qualification Tests" section earlier in this chapter.)
- **Even Trades.** The object you and your rivals want is controlled by someone else. They don't want it, but they won't give it to you unless you do something for them, which could be to trade for another object or do some kind of errand for them. In any case, your rivals have an equal chance to accomplish this task, so you must prevent them from succeeding and accomplish the task yourself.
- **Unknown Object.** You need to obtain an object in order to progress. (See the "Delayed Gratification" section earlier in this chapter.) However, you do not know what the object is or where it is until later in the game. Time is ticking, as you know you are not the only one after this object.
- **Lost and Found.** You had it, now you don't. Time to get it back.

Innocent Bystanders

You are just minding your business when some enemy attacks you. This isn't just a generic monster attack, but an attack by a group with some agenda. This is often the encounter that first introduces you to the game's main theme or to a sub-quest within the game, and there is generally some dialog before, during, or after the battle that indicates why they are attacking you.

- **Mistaken Identity.** They mistake you for someone else.
- **Secret Identity.** You are really someone important (a prince, the savior, the sword bearer, the eyewitness), but you don't realize it. Your enemies do, however.
- **It's Just My Father's Rusty Sword.** Something you are carrying—preferably a family heirloom—is incredibly valuable or important, and the bad guys will stop at nothing to get it. Probably, at this point in the story, you have no idea of the immense power contained within the thing, but this is your first clue.
- **Stolen Goods.** You innocently picked up something interesting, perhaps taking it out of a locked chest in a small retreat in the woods. How were you to know that someone would take offense? Of course, it can all be worked out, and once you explain yourself, your attackers will enlist your aid in going after the real enemy. Alternatively, taking the object has upset the balance of the universe, and now you must repair the damage you have done.
- **Town without Pity.** Commonly, you will enter a town or village that just seems depressed. The people won't attack you directly, but they are hostile, surly, and uncooperative. Of course, all you have to do is clear some monsters, remove a curse, vanquish a boss or monster, or make the sun shine again (see the previous "Is It Safe?" section), and they will all be friendly and happy again.
- **Oops!** You're standing around, and suddenly a big boulder drops on your foot, or something like that. Then some doofus comes along and says, "Sorry." But then it turns out that the doofus tells you some story that sounds like a quest in the making, and away you go. The doofus may or may not join your party.

Missing Persons

In games, people often go missing, and it's the hero's job to find them—or at least to find out what happened to them. If possible, perhaps you can escort them safely home. At any rate, here are a few common "missing persons" scenarios. Try to think of some new ones.

- **The Old Folks.** A sick and deranged old person is missing. Find him and return him safely, perhaps with a cure for his ailments.
- **The Kids Are All Right.** Some little tyke has turned up missing. He was last seen running after a DayGlo orange butterfly that flew into the deep, dark woods. Oh please, go find my little boy/girl/cub/calf/nestling/etc.
- **Where Oh Where Has My Little Dog Gone?** Yes, someone's pet is missing. Perhaps finding it will lead you to something interesting. The reward is probably not too spectacular, but you never know what the dog has dug up or what future rewards a good deed can reap. Of course, this could be any other pet creature, not only a wayward pooch.
- **Kidnapped.** Sure, someone is missing. He has been kidnapped. Perhaps there's a ransom note. Or maybe he is just missing, and you have to find out that he is being held hostage or scheduled for execution, and so on.
- **Personal Quest.** Someone is missing, and you follow the trail. It turns out that the person is on a quest of his own. To get him to come back, you may have to join him in his quest and help him complete it.
- **Still Missing.** Sometimes someone is missing, and you have no clues at all. Or the clues lead you to somewhere far away. In such cases, the one who is missing will probably turn up later in the story, after you've pretty much forgotten that you are searching for him. Finding this kind of missing person seems like a random encounter, but it's generally pretty well scripted into the flow of the story. This is also an example of delayed gratification.
- **Should Have Arrived by Now.** Whether left behind or split up, the persons in question have not arrived when they were expected. Now you have to go find them.

Ways to Gain Allies

Sometimes you have to make friends or get someone on your side. Here are some of the scenarios to consider:

- **Save the Princess.** Well, save someone who needs saving. (As a twisted alternative, devious and not so hero-like, you could arrange for someone to be kidnapped or otherwise threatened, then move in and save the person.)
- **Money Talks.** You can sometimes buy your way in with gold or with something of great value.
- **Be Impressive.** Do something that shows how powerful you are, such as defeating a 100-foot dragon in single combat.
- **Veiled Threats.** This is not the preferred method, but you can subtly suggest that cooperation is preferable to the alternative. Few RPG heroes would resort to this, except under duress and when dealing with really bad guys.
- **Make It Safe.** Resolve some problem that besets the NPC or the area. (See also the previous "Is It Safe?" section.)
- **Enter the Contest.** Enter a local contest and win. (See also the "Qualification Tests" section earlier in this chapter.)

Part III

- **Friends of Friends.** Sometimes the best way to get someone to cooperate with you is to get a recommendation from a friend or an important family member. Go do something nice for one of the NPC's allies or his daughter or brother. When you return, you have the friend/daughter/brother's recommendation; even better, that person may have become one of your party.
- **Flattery Will Get You Anything.** Yes, make a monument to the person you want to impress. Build a statue in his honor or just pump him up with his own self-importance.
- **Look What I Did for You.** Do something helpful for someone, and he will be more likely to trust and like you. This can apply to the good folk or to the bad folk, depending on whose trust you want to gain.
- **Enemy of My Enemy.** Though possibly a complete stranger, he will team up with you to take down a common foe.

Memory Games

All through the history of literature and movies, the events of the past have shaped the events of the present and the future. Games are no exception, and many games deal with how the player's character must deal with what happened once upon a time. Sometimes it's simply dealing with amnesia and the need to recover lost memories. Sometimes it's more sinister or complex or more earthshaking. How many ways can you weave the character's need to deal with the past into the current story?

- **The Mysterious Past.** Your character (or one of your party members) has a mysterious past. You (or the party member) can't remember what it is, but it is important. Often, little vignettes and cut scenes will help you piece together the story over the course of the adventure. Other times, you may actually go back in time to play your former self and uncover the mystery. Usually, you (or the other party member) lost these memories due to some traumatic event—usually, the loss of your family at the hands of the bad guys. Sometimes there's another NPC who you must find. This NPC is the only one who can help you, and you may have to prove yourself before he will.
- **Power Lock.** You may remember your past well enough, but you don't know how to unlock your immense potential power. Learning the keys to your potential is a big part of your quest.
- **Intentional Erasure.** Somewhere in your past, you erased your memories for your own good. Perhaps it was an act of conscience because you had too much power and misused it. But now you need to regain your powers in order to save the world. Fortunately, you've left yourself clues that will lead you to the truth. Hurry!
- **Forgetful Spells.** Someone casts a spell and makes the player (or a party member) forget what he knows. This can affect the character's abilities—for instance, causing him to forget spells he knows or combat skills, and so on. This is usually something temporary and reversible, but you probably have to live with the effect for a while until you find the cure. In extreme cases, party members may be turned into blithering idiots, useless for anything until cured.
- **Forgotten Detail.** Sometimes success depends on the smallest of details. Whether the time has passed or has yet to pass, that one detail can complicate matters. How do you remind the player of those details without being obvious?

Something's Screwy

You enter an area, and all the animals are walking backward, the people are acting like zombies, water is glowing with a purplish tint, everybody is sick, or they all have been turned into pigs. This means something's screwy, and you will have to figure out how to set it right.

Complications might include:

- **Your Fault.** The problem is the direct result of something you have done.
- **Beware the Obvious.** The cause of the problem appears to be simple but is actually something far less obvious. For instance, the problem is that everyone in town is divided over an issue that seems fairly unimportant. The obvious solution is to sit down and talk it over. The actual problem is being caused by a spell cast by a nasty witch, or it's from a saboteur who has been sent in to stir up trouble.
- **This Is Normal?** There is no problem. This is how they always act. Or they really are pigs!
- **Relapse.** You already thought the problem was solved, but apparently it wasn't, because the same thing is happening again.

Time Travel

Previously, I had some ideas around how we deal with people's forgotten or locked past memories. But how do we deal with time in games—especially time travel? Here are some common ideas. Can you think of some new time-travel scenarios or conundrums? Time travel can be one of the most interesting plot points, if done correctly. (I remember reading a book years ago—Robert Heinlein's *The Door into Summer*—which had the main character traveling back and forth in time and unknowingly interacting with himself. It was a fascinating interweaving of events as told from the character's "current" timeline, and yet connecting all his actions to events you had already experienced.)

- **He Did It!** Somebody did something terrible, and the only way to fix it is to go into the past.
- **You Did It!** You did something terrible (obviously without realizing it), and you can only fix it by going to the past.
- **It Happened!** Nobody did anything terrible, but something terrible has happened in the past, so you have to go back and prevent it.
- **Stop Me Before I Do It!** You're about to do something terrible in the past, but your future self can travel back and warn you not to do it.
- **Time Pursuit.** The bad guy escapes to the past or future, and you have to follow him.
- **Its Former Self.** There's an ancient carving that has the key to the whole mystery, but it's worn out and unreadable. Why not travel to the past, before it got worn out, and read it there?
- **Warning from the Past.** You witness a prophecy that shows your future. It isn't good. You use a time machine (or a time-travel spell) to go there and argue with yourself. If you win, your future changes.
- **Gifts from the Past.** You find out something that could alter the future, but you know you can't use it now. You travel to the future, where people will understand its importance and act on it.
- **Bring Back the Future.** The technology doesn't exist to travel in time, so you have to wait until it is developed, travel back in time and give it to yourself, then develop it so you can travel through time.
- **The Riddle.** A shadowing, menacing figure has been stalking you. You keep escaping it, but it is relentless. Finally, years later, you find out it was you from the future trying to catch up with you, but you successfully eluded yourself and got freaked out in the process, completely affecting the rest of your life, up until the time when you got older and traveled to the past to tell yourself it was all right, but failed to do so.
- **Dead Sleep.** You get knocked out and are suddenly in a dreamlike past. The only way to awaken from this dream is to complete some sort of quest and/or kill/defeat someone/something.

The Observer

Not all game action is direct. Sometimes being an observer or playing "stealthy" can be rewarding. Here are some ideas. Can you think of more?

- **The Sneak.** You must sneak into an area, avoiding all contact with the natives and avoiding surveillance devices. You must observe but not get caught.
- **The Infiltrator.** You must enter an area and observe what is going on. You are under cover. You must not act in any way to blow your cover.
- **The Stakeout.** You know something is wrong, but you have to find out what it is. You suspect that someone in town has been tampering with the water supply, so you find a hiding place and wait. Once you see your suspect dropping little green pills into the local well, you have your culprit.
- **The Audience.** You just have to be there for some reason, which will ultimately become clear. For instance, perhaps you will gain a clue or see something happen and later meet the people involved, knowing what they did or did not do.

The Gauntlet

This is from the term "running the gauntlet," which has many historical meanings, but generally is the act of running through a group of people who are raining blows on you. In the case of games, it refers to situations where you have to deal with masses of enemies or challenges while moving from one location to another. The arcade game *Gauntlet* was a great example, but there are situations like this in many games. Here are a few common situations that we think meet our definition.

- **Dangerous Journey.** You have to get an urgent message to someone. To get where you're going, you have to walk/run/fly/hop/skip/jump/ride through a hostile terrain. Generally, you don't have time to stop and fight everything that attacks you, so you have to avoid fighting whenever possible while also avoiding other obstacles, of which there will be many.
- **Testing.** You are being tested by having to complete an obstacle course. See the "Qualification Tests (Tests of Worthiness)" section earlier in this chapter.
- **The Overpopulated Dungeon.** You're in a dungeon. At the bottom is a power crystal that controls the whole Evil Empire. You must fight your way to the crystal through hordes of enemy minions.
- **Battle Runner.** You're in the midst of a great battle and must get to one of the generals. This means running through the entire battle, avoiding enemies and friends alike.
- **Asteroid Belt.** You're in a spaceship, traveling at high speed. Between you and your destination is an asteroid belt filled with spinning, twisting rocks that could pulverize your puny ship with a single blow. To make matters worse, strange forces are affecting your guidance systems, so you'll have to fly on manual controls. Maybe you can shoot some of the smaller asteroids out of the way! Alternatively, there's the cliff walk where you have to jump gaps while dodging falling boulders and dive-bombing birds.
- **Collapse!** Everything is collapsing around you; you must avoid the debris and make it out. (Note: This can also be weather related, such as a tornado.)
- **Sensing Motion.** There are automated systems to keep prisoners in. You'll have to work out how to defeat the systems and get out.
- **Look Up.** Snipers are on the rooftops; helicopters (or drones) are in the air. The eyes are in the sky, and you must make it through a well-protected area.

Imprisonment Scenarios

Captured? It's not always bad. You'll want to escape sooner or later, but if the designers were thinking, they added some interesting opportunities for you to discover. Actually, any situation involving jails, dungeons, locked rooms, or other imprisonment will do.

- **The Evil Dungeon.** The bad guy has captured you and thrown you into his dungeon. Don't worry—you'll escape, but you'll likely find someone down there to join your party, not to mention some cool stuff.
- **The Good Dungeon.** The good guys don't know who you are yet, so they throw you into the dungeon. You'll have to escape, of course, but you might get help from an unexpected ally.
- **Intentional Incarceration.** You get yourself thrown in the dungeon on purpose to spy on someone, to rescue someone, to find something that you believe is there, and so on.
- **The Break-In.** You break into the dungeon to rescue someone or find something.
- **The Locked Room.** You're locked in a room—not a dungeon, but somewhere hard to get out of.
- **Paralysis.** A wizard has cast a paralysis spell on you, and you must watch helplessly as he prepares his master plan for world domination.
- **How Did That Get in Me?** Something has taken up residence in your head or your body (or both). You're trapped while it runs the show.
- **Cut Off.** Due to changes of circumstances, you have no apparent way out of your current location. For instance, you arrived on an island by boat, but the boat sank when you arrived or was stolen.

Godlike Roles

Sometimes you are the god in the game, as in *Populous* or *Black & White*. Other times it's someone else—often your enemies. But godlike powers—and gods themselves—are common in games. Here are some typical ways to use godlike roles:

- **The Friendly God.** All your actions are being watched and guided by a godlike entity. The entity doesn't actually do much for you, but it appears from time to time to say that you are on the right (or wrong) track.
- **The Friendly Voice.** You sometimes hear a voice in your head. It warns you of upcoming dangers. It tells you to do things. If you do what the voice tells you, good things appear to happen.
- **Big Bad Boss.** The main bad guy seems to have godlike powers. He's going to be tough. But he must have a weakness, if only you can discover it and live long enough to exploit it!
- **Oh, the Power!** Somehow you are turned into a veritable god, and you wield enormous powers. This is usually very short lived, toward the end of the game, or countered by an entity even more powerful than you.
- **You Are the God.** In certain games, you are, in effect, the god of that world. This includes so-called "god games," such as *Populous* and its variants, or *SimCity* and other sim games where you truly have a top-down perspective and godlike control of the world. Of course, if you want to accomplish the game's goals (or the goals you set for yourself within the game), you will have to learn to work within even a god's limitations. If you had no limitations at all, it wouldn't be much of a game.
- **Toying with You.** You are the god's entertainment—an unwitting court jester, in a sense. Whatever it does, it does for its own amusement. Annoying wrinkle: If it gets bored with you, it will kill you, so you have to stay amusing or die.

- **The Bystander.** You were not a part of its plans, and it had no intention to harm, hinder, or help you. But you blundered into a situation that is of interest to a godlike entity, and you just have to deal the hand you've been dealt.

MISDIRECTION

Misdirection is often the key to an interesting game. What seems obvious should be suspect. Players should be looking for subtle or unusual explanations. However, there are times when designers intentionally mislead players by carefully selecting the information they provide.

(See also the "Misdirection: Ways to Mislead the Player" section in Chapter 30, "Ways to Communcate with the Player.")

- **False or Incomplete Info.** The player is given information or receives a quest that sets a particular goal. However, some time during the completion of the quest, the player discovers that the real story is quite different and has to change focus. For instance, the player learns that the Wise Man on the Mountain can reverse the weather and return peace to the land. But at the top of the mountain, the player discovers that the Wise Man on the Mountain is dead or is a fraud, or maybe that the weather doesn't need to be fixed at all.
- **The False Friendly Voice.** Some NPC or godlike voice has been guiding the player, offering good advice that, when followed, leads to good results. However, in reality, the NPC or the godlike voice is the enemy and has lulled the player into believing his information. Now the player will blindly follow, and the NPC can lower the boom.
- **Choosing Paths.** The road less traveled? When coming to a junction in a path, one will look much more promising than the other. Sometimes, it's the less-promising path that leads to the most important location.
- **Appearances Can Be Deceiving.** A magnificent weapon is encrusted in barnacles. It looks worthless. If the player takes it to the smithy, he'll discover its true value. A beggar is really a prince. A beautiful woman is treacherous while her surly stepsister has a heart of gold. Usually, the bigger the enemy, the stronger, but sometimes you can get hammered by a tiny creature with a heavy attack. Or you can roll right over some giant clod. And so forth...
- **Containers.** Something really awesome is hidden in a plain-looking chest, cabinet, or desk drawer. Something with little perceived value is hidden in the ornate chest or other container. Don't always assume the most useful item will be the most obvious. You might give the plain items some real value, such as using the peanut butter sandwich to bribe the troll that blocks the bridge. If you took the golden necklace instead, he'll realize where you got it and attack. Teaching the gamer to pause and think before doing the obvious can be fun, but be careful to give him a decent chance to be right.
- **The Smoking Gun.** Just because you caught Uncle Ronald with the murder weapon doesn't necessarily mean "he done it." See also Chapter 22, "Game Conventions and Clichés," because playing with the clichés can be a great way to create misdirection.

Part IV Characters

12 Character Design

Characters in games range from one-dimensional drones to reasonably complex artificial characters and player heroes. However, at least at the time I wrote this, very few games have included characters with complete personalities or complex qualities, yet one fantastic way to make games more interesting is to feature characters who come alive for the player. This includes any NPC character as well as the player's character. In this chapter I provide you with a collection of tools that, when used together, can help you create all kinds of characters with all kinds of realistic qualities.

There is a caveat, however. Combining separate elements from lists and working with specific archetypes, while useful, will not necessarily result in complex and realistic characters. Some of that has to come from you. There are other questions to ask when creating any character or substance:

> "I should hope to approach the problem of characters, of heroes and villains especially, from a little more total perspective. After all, what makes a person? It is some ineffable mix of values and reactions, good intentions and bad, effective behaviors and ineffective behaviors. Even in a short play, a person may show a complexity of motive and confused aims. Macbeth, for example, was a mixture of hero and villain—brave, ambitious, loyal (to a point), but under the pressures of guilt and recognition of the presence of enemies, became cruel, faithless, and fearful.
>
> "One way of understanding people is in terms of life search, although often life search is not single nor simple. Sometimes a dominating theme in the search stands out—power, ambition, givingness, justification. Another way of understanding people is in terms of the value systems which inform their actions. And, of course, the repetition of history in the individual's adaptations and behaviors is impressive—the repetition of mistakes, of successes, of the family history.
>
> "So in creating a hero (or a villain), what motivates him (or her)? What is being proved in his actions? How do his behaviors represent attempts to belong, to garner good will, or to reject those possibilities in an excess of rage and frustration? How has serendipity created opportunities which encourage (or discourage) his struggle to arrive, or his struggle to regain what has been lost?"
>
> —Donald Ehrman, PhD

This chapter is rich with information, ranging from sections about character arcs and specific character roles and motivations to lists of traits, hobbies, moods, and so on, to deeper information about how to build more believable characters. The chapter starts out with one potential method for developing main characters—heroes and villains—for your games.

- ➤ Character Racial/Species Options
- ➤ Strong Character Names
- ➤ Relationships of Characters
- ➤ Jobs
- ➤ Character Goals
- ➤ How a Character Grows...Character Arcs
- ➤ Character Flaws and Strengths
- ➤ Real People's Attributes
- ➤ Contrasting Traits
- ➤ Identities
- ➤ Creating Interesting Characters with
- ➤ the Character Diamondœ©
- ➤ Character Traits
- ➤ Quirks
- ➤ Moods
- ➤ Hobbies
- ➤ Religious and Spiritual Practices
- ➤ Phun with Phobias
- ➤ Catchphrases
- ➤ Attributes of Funny Characters
- ➤ Kinds of Heroes, Villains, and Minions
- ➤ Functional Character Roles
- ➤ Personality Types
- ➤ Mental/Emotional Signals: The Other 93%
- ➤ Other Ways to Show Character Emotions/States
- ➤ Physical Changes
- ➤ Facial Expressions
- ➤ Ways to Customize Avatars
- ➤ Human Universals

Ask the Next Question

One of the best ways to create characters and stories is to question everything. Bestselling author Orson Scott Card suggests that you ask questions—that you interrogate your characters and your ideas. He suggests that you don't accept the first thought, but keep asking questions to get to something deeper than the stereotype or cliché that probably came to mind first. If you question causes and results, motivations and meaning, you will probably find your ideas and your characters improve significantly. Another great author, Theodore Sturgeon, put it very succinctly in his personal motto: "Ask the next question...."

Dave Perry's Build-a-Character System

This chapter contains a lot of information about characters, ranging from their physical characteristics to their emotions, hobbies, and fears. Although you can't just randomly combine elements from these lists and essays like a chemical formula and get a truly satisfying result, you can use the information in this chapter to further inspire your creative process. There are a lot of systems for creating characters in stories. None of them will do it for you, but many can help you inspire your own creative process.

My Build-a-Character system is not necessarily better or worse than any other systems out there. It does, however, have the advantage of giving you reference material at your fingertips. Using the references available in this chapter and elsewhere in this book, you can think more deeply and come up with more possibilities for your characters, which is what I hope you will do.

Some Characters Are Roles

Of course, if you just want to create a mindless drone, give it a gun, and set it loose on the world, there's not too much I can offer to help you (other than Chapter 34, "Standard Modern Weaponry and Armor"). And, to be honest, mindless drones with guns have a place in games, as do shopkeeper characters who are little more than vending machines. Not all characters need to be important, well established, complex, or particularly interesting. It would be boring and unbelievably tedious to tell the life story of every character you might meet in a game. I mean, do you really care about the childhood traumas of the sentient reptilian soldier you blew up along with 50 of its buddies? You don't even care about the reptilian soldier's even more dangerous and intelligent commander. You only care that they'll shoot you if you don't shoot them first. Likewise, you might be slightly interested in the marital woes of Glenda the Good Witch, but I doubt it. You just care that she appears at key moments in the story to offer Dorothy some encouragement, some red shoes, and some information about clicking them together to go home. So, when you consider fleshing out characters in considerable detail, giving them a history, a family, complex motivation, a set of specific traits and individual behaviors, and so on, consider how important the character is and how much the player needs to know.

In some cases, you may go to a lot of trouble to create deeper and more realistic characters but find that most of the detail never appears in the final game. You may also discover that you have been inspired by the process of deepening your characters—that such characters inhabit your game world in unexpected ways, and that their dialog and actions are far more diverse and intriguing than they would have been if you had not taken the time to know them better. Their behavior and dialog may turn out to be far more characteristic of a real being than of a cardboard cutout.

So, while some characters are not much more than the roles they play in the game or story, others are important, and their behaviors and choices can significantly alter the course of the game. These types of characters may not appear in every game. Many "hero" characters are simply cartoons with no personality. If you think of the early comic-book heroes, such as the original Batman, Superman, or Dick Tracy, they had no personal problems (other than in some cases protecting their secret identities and juggling would-be girlfriends). But later comic superheroes, such as Spider-Man, introduced the idea of a complex human character with super powers. With the new Marvel Comics characters, suddenly the superhero became complex, human, and in some ways quite ordinary, with eccentricities, weaknesses, families, financial problems, quirks, and even hobbies outside of their role as superhero.

When creating game characters, you have choices in determining how much detail and depth to include. It may be completely appropriate to treat your heroes and villains as more or less two-dimensional caricatures. It totally depends on the type of game you are creating. But in any game genre, the possibility of story lurks, and if you have a strong story you may also want to consider some stronger, more complex and self-consistent characters. If you really want to go all out, you can consider characters who encounter life-altering experiences and who change significantly as a result of the events of the game. This is not so common in current games.

For instance, Lara Croft really doesn't change from game to sequel. It is technically possible to have her evolve, perhaps fall in love, get married, have babies...and still she could be the adventurer. But somehow it would be a little more difficult to see her in all those significant life roles. It's so much simpler if she doesn't change from game to game—or if she does change, it is something reflected in the gameplay by her abilities or perhaps in the shifting of her character toward slightly different goals or motivations. For instance, you could conceivably do a Lara Croft adventure in which she became enamored of the Dark Side, to mix metaphors. Perhaps that would be interesting, but Lara's home life is of little interest unless she were to do a cameo appearance in *The Sims.*

Nor do we want to see a whole lot of Indiana Jones doing college lectures and settling down to a life of quiet complacency as a college professor. It's all right to establish his "normal" identity, but we want to see him in a pit full of snakes (which, incidentally, give him the creeps), rappelling down some steep cliff, or running for his life, dodging spears chucked at him by angry tribesmen—or bantering with a tough, beautiful woman. Maybe Lara Croft and Indiana Jones should meet....

While some characters are not meant to change as a result of their adventures, others are on a life path that requires them to change or die (spiritually or physically). Some are caught up in events they can't control or have been slowly dying in their ordinary lives and crave something new. Sometimes the whole world must be saved, and the player's character is just the one to do it. Sometimes the character is simply seeking, but doesn't know what he seeks when the story begins, or he may have some half-cocked idea about what he wants or needs. Inevitably, in a good story, the character will discover a lot about himself and possibly about others, and he will change as a result of what he experiences and how he responds to it.

So what follows is simply one way to explore your characters—those characters you really want to know well and who will engage the player and even provide some surprises and individuality. If you are interested in making games with deeper stories and deeper characters, my Build-a-Character system is a decent place to start, along with references to places in this book that can provide you with more information or resources.

Build a Character

My Build-a-Character system begins here. It is not just a questionnaire to fill out. It is an interactive process that uses the material in this book to help you come up with new ideas and more complete characters for your games—whether they are heroes, villains, or NPCs of various kinds. Any character you want to create, you can create here, but be sure to use the cross-references to help expand your possibilities.

Roles

What kind of character are you creating? (Reference this chapter, the "Kinds of Heroes, Villains, and Minions" section. Also see Chapter 13, "Character Roles and Jobs.")

- Player hero
- Main enemy
- Sub-boss
- Enemy minion
- Enemy group leader (lieutenant)
- Ally/party member/companion
- Leader (ally)
- Love interest
- Victim (significant to the story)
- Guide character
- Shopkeeper
- Random NPC
- Gatekeeper

Characters could be other than these, such as:

- Yourself
- A mystery
- An amnesiac
- A disembodied voice
- A shape-shifter or role-player, imposter
- A puppeteer
- A god

Basic Characteristics

What is this character's:

- Age?
- Gender?
- Ethnicity?
- Economic status?
- Social status?
- Marital status?
- Name?

References in this chapter include "Gender/Type of Character," "Character Racial/Species Options," and "Character Traits."

Optionally, describe the character's family—parents, grandparents, and siblings—and what his/her relationship was like with them. Look for influences, traumas, and other profound effects that the character's family might have had on him or her. Examples include a famous and highly successful parent, a jealous brother or sister, being orphaned at an early age, an alcoholic or workaholic parent, a dysfunctional relationship with parents and/or siblings but a close relationship with a grandparent, lost parents at an early age, and so on. Be wary of clichés, however. Use these ideas as guidelines for possible behavioral tendencies, but not as stereotypes.

Professions

Does this character have a job? If so, what is it? (Reference Chapter 13, "Character Roles and Jobs.")

The Situation

Describe the events that bring the character into the story. (Reference Chapter 5, "Game POV and Game Genres," Chapter 9, "Storytelling Techniques," Chapter 11, "Scenarios" and Chapter 21, "Experiential Design.")

Goals

What does this character want or think he wants? These are conscious goals and may not be what the character *needs*, which is often described in the character arc. (See the next section.) (Reference Chapter 23, "Goals" and the "Character Goals" section in this chapter.)

Arc

What does the character need and how does he change inwardly in the story? (Reference the "How a Character Grows...Character Arcs" section in this chapter.)

Flaws and Limitations

Does this character have any significant flaws or limitations? (Reference the "Character Flaws and Strengths" and "Character Traits" sections in this chapter.)

Personal Strengths

Does the character have any particular strengths that help him get what he wants or deal with challenges and adversity? (Reference the "Character Traits" section in this chapter.) This is different from powers and special abilities, which you can determine in a later step of this process.

Basic Emotional States (Moods)

What kinds of emotions or moods are predominant in this character? This is not a single mood, but possibly a range of emotions or a predominant theme. For instance, some people tend to be pessimistic and depressive, while others may be steady and unflappable. Still others could be manic or highly optimistic. (Reference the "Moods" section in this chapter.)

Traits

What are the other general traits of this character? (Reference this chapter the "Character Traits" and "Personality Types" sections in this chapter.)

Quirks

Does this character have any interesting individual quirks? (Reference the "Quirks" section in this chapter.)

Fears

What is this character afraid of? (Reference the "Phun with Phobias" section in this chapter.)

General Activities

Where does this character spend most of his time? In a modern story, where does the character shop and hang out?

Hobbies

Does the character have any hobbies? How can you define the character through his hobbies? Can you combine two or more hobbies to further define the character as unique? (Reference the "Hobbies" section in this chapter.)

Pets

What kinds of pets (if any) does the character have? If the player has pets, what kind of relationship does he have with the pets? How many does he have?

Preferences

What are the character's preferences in food, music, and other entertainment? (Reference the "Character Traits" and "Hobbies" sections in this chapter.)

Sexuality

What kind of sexual preferences or deviations does this character have? What sexual activities and habits? (Note: This information may or may not appear in the character's activities in the game, but it can be interesting to consider in terms of the total character. This could be especially so if the character has something to hide or be ashamed of, or if he is particularly affected by some specific sexual stimulus. (Reference the "Gender/Type of Character" section in this chapter.)

Travel

How does the character ordinarily get around/travel? (Reference Chapter 18, "Travel.")

Abilities

Does the character have special abilities or powers? (Reference the "Character Traits" section in this chapter and Chapter15, "Character Abilities.")

Stress Management

How does the character deal with stressful situations? (Reference the "Personality Types" section in this chapter.)

The Spiritual Side

What religious or spiritual beliefs does the character have? How does he practice them? (Reference the "Religious and Spiritual Practices" section in this chapter.)

Relations to Other Characters

How is this character related to other characters in the story at the beginning? Do you anticipate that the relationship will evolve? If so, what will it become? (Reference the "Relationships of Characters" section in this chapter and Chapter 13, "Character Roles and Jobs.")

Physical Description and Changes

What is the characters' initial physical description? Does the character change physically? If so, how? (Reference the "Physical Changes" and "Ways to Customize Avatars" sections in this chapter.)

Humor

Is the character funny? (Reference the "Attributes of Funny Characters" section in this chapter and "Creating Comedy" in Chapter 9, "Storytelling Techniques.")

Step-by-Step Examples

We'll create a couple of characters using the Build-a-Character system—one relatively simple character and one that's somewhat complex.

A Simple Example

For the first character, we'll create a basic ally character. This character should have some personality, and the more we give it, the more options we'll have with it as we develop the game, dialog, and plot. Because this character is not a major hero or villain, some qualities might not matter too much. For some inspiration, I might start with the "Kinds of Heroes, Villains, and Minions" section in this chapter.

Although this character is not the main hero, he might share some qualities with the hero. We might decide that certain aspects of the character aren't important to design for a minor character, or we might want to create a deeper description, even if much of it is never seen or experienced by the player. The more detail the character has, the more ideas we will have for him when designing the game, and the more consistently we'll treat that character. But for simpler characters, filling in all the details of the Build-a-Character system is certainly optional, and it may be desirable to simplify the process for less important characters.

Step 1: Roles

You can reference Chapter 13, "Character Roles and Jobs," for ideas on character roles. We're going to create an ally to the player's character—perhaps someone who will join the player and be part of his party.

Step 2: Basics

Let's define the basic characteristics of this character, using the "Gender/Type of Character," "Ethnicity/Race," and "Character Traits" sections from this chapter to help with some of this information.

- Age: 25
- Gender: Male
- Ethnicity: Elf
- Economic Status: N/A
- Social Status: None
- Marital Status: Unmarried
- Name: Evar Bowstringer

Step 3: The Family

For a minor character, you normally wouldn't need to go into too much detail, but we will find out that Evar had a family that was lost—that they are all presumed dead—and that he had a close relationship with them. Even though Evar could be a relatively minor character, simply giving him some family history could inspire a larger role for him and possible plot threads for the player to follow.

Step 4: Professions

Here we can get some information from Chapter 13, "Character Roles and Jobs." I've decided that Evar will be an archer.

Step 5: The Situation

Evar will meet the player character in the forest in a seemingly random encounter. It will turn out that his immediate goals coincide well with the player's, so he will offer his help. It might be that the bad guys have murdered his village, he feels responsible for failing to protect them, and he seeks revenge and vindication. Or it might be that he wants to get to the town that's on the way the player is headed. Or he might be looking for his long-lost sister, and he thinks that the player might be able to help him. There are many ways that Evar might become the player's ally. You can get more ideas from Chapter 5, "Game POV and Game Genres,"Chapter 10, "Movie Genres," Chapter 11, "Scenarios," and Chapter 21, "Experiential Design."

Step 6: Goals

Evar's goals are probably simplistic and may match one of the scenarios outlined in Step 5. I'm going to choose "the bad guys have murdered his village, he feels responsible for failing to protect them, and he seeks revenge and vindication" scenario. However, for more ideas, check out Chapter 23, "Goals," the "Character Goals" section in this chapter, and Chapter 11, "Scenarios."

Step 7: Arc

It is entirely optional whether Evar has a true character arc. Does he change in the course of the story? For this example, I'm going to say yes. But probably most NPC characters in your game will not have a true character arc. Their goals will be simplistic, if any, and they will not truly change in the course of the story.

However, in this case, Evar's goal is revenge, and he's an angry and ashamed archer when the player first encounters him. Then, looking at the "How a Character Grows...Character Arcs"section in this chapter, his arc—the true evolution of his character—could be "coming to terms with his own (past or present) actions and taking responsibility," or "forgiveness of self or others."

Notice that simply the fact that Evar has this history and that his progression as a character will lead to a resolution of his emotional damage offers a deeper progression of gameplay and story than we would have had if we had simply decided to add a generic archer to the player's party.

Step 8: Flaws and Limitations

In the "Character Flaws and Strengths" and "Character Traits" sections in this chapter, we can look for interesting elements that further describe Evar's character. I'm going to select, as flaws and limitations, that he:

- Is headstrong (or reckless)
- Is inconsistent (or irresponsible)
- Is melodramatic
- Is provincial (mostly)
- Is promiscuous
- Goes all to pieces when he's faced with magical enemies

These traits will create a pretty interesting character—one who expresses himself in dramatic terms, can't always be relied upon, is somewhat unsophisticated, and definitely has an eye for the women.

Also, check Step 21 for more ideas on how Evar's personality can be further defined.

Step 9: Strengths

Turning back to the "Character Traits" section in this chapter, I want to balance Evar's flaws with some useful traits, such as:

- Skill. (He's damn good with that bow.)
- Sharp senses. (He notices everything and can see a bug on an elephant's ear at 1,000 paces.)
- Kindness and generosity. (For all his faults, he's kind and generous at heart.)
- Loyalty. (He may not be the most reliable guy, but he doesn't change sides or abandon his friends.)

He sounds like someone who could be useful now, but still someone who can make mistakes or cause trouble for the player. Could be fun, eh?

Step 10: Basic Emotional States (Moods)

Checking the "Moods" section in this chapter, we can characterize Evar as basically a cheerful sort of bloke, but with a smoldering anger and inner shame beneath his outward bravado. As one of his flaws is being melodramatic, his darker emotions do surface from time to time, and when they do, you really know about it! You might also find some interesting ideas in the "Personality Types" section. For more on that, see Step 21 of Evar's design.

Step 11: Traits

Here is where we can assign some other interesting traits to our character, again referring to the "Character Traits" section. I see Evar as:

- Being bit careless.
- Being determined.
- Being direct.
- Being musical. (He plays tunes on his bowstring.)
- Having poor impulse control (gambling and women).
- Ultimately being a romantic at heart.

See also Step 21.

Step 12: Quirks

Referring to the "Quirks" section in this chapter, we can come up with some individual behaviors or preferences to further distinguish and identify Evar. In this case, he:

- Walks on the tips of his feet, lightly, and sometimes skips as he walks.
- Often stops and sniffs the air, making faces that reflect what he has smelled.
- Often has an arrow in his hand, smoothing the feathers and feeling the edge of the arrowhead.
- Is never seen without his cap.
- Will eat anything and everything.
- Stops and gawks when he spots a pretty wench.

Step 13: Fears

Looking at the list of phobias in the "Phun with Phobias" section, you can see that people can develop an unholy fear of almost anything—and everything. But if their particular brand of fear is to be at all significant, they should be afraid of something that is likely to occur in the game and make a situation more interesting. In this case, I've decided that Evar has a deathly fear of:

- Going bald (which is why he never takes off his cap)
- Homosexuality
- Witchcraft
- Failure (to protect those he loves)

His fear of homosexuality will affect his behavior toward men and his sometimes overly macho bravado. His fears of witchcraft make him less effective when facing magic users. He will still fight—and fight hard—but he is obviously scared and rattled. He might be a little less accurate unless somehow bolstered by the player character or other NPCs. In a swords-and-sorcery type of game, this could be an interesting development and could ultimately become one of his major limitations.

His fear of the failure to protect those he loves is something that has developed since the loss of his family and his village. It motivates his actions at times and can make him more reckless, but also more determined.

By using the "Personality Types" section, you may ever further refine Evar's character. See Step 21 for an example.

Step 14: General Activities

Evar can probably be found in the local tavern or gambling joint when he's not on duty or off with some wench.

Step 15: Hobbies

How much can you learn from somebody's hobbies? Looking at the available range in the "Hobbies" section of this chapter, it's obvious that there is tremendous variety here. For instance, it wouldn't be too surprising to learn that Evar collects feathers, which he can use to fletch his arrows. But he could be interested in other activities, such as storytelling, poetry, tree climbing, or even weaving. For this game, however, I'm going to assume that Evar has no hobbies other than collecting feathers, unless you consider gambling and wenching hobbies.

Step 16: Pets

I don't think Evar has any pets, though he might have lost one when his village was destroyed. Poor old Fluffy...

I did consider giving him a hawk, which could be used for hunting and fighting, but I decided against it.

Step 17: Preferences

Other than those preferences and traits already mentioned, I see no need to add more to Evar's description. But if I did, I'd probably check the "Character Traits" and "Hobbies" sections again.

Step 18: Sexuality

In this case, Evar is an inveterate womanizer, and he has a strong appetite for sex of just about any kind. I'd categorize him as insatiable and experimental. His aversion to homosexuality does affect his behavior toward men, however, as was noted already. You might look at the "Gender/Type of Character" section for other ideas.

Step 19: Travel

Evar walks a lot, though he can ride a horse if necessary. He doesn't have any special powers that allow him to fly or anything like that, so he's just consigned to basic transportation. Of course, he may find other ways to move around during the course of the story. You can find some suggestions in Chapter 18, "Travel."

Step 20: Abilities

Evar is a pretty skilled archer with very sharp senses, but he doesn't have any supernatural or magical powers. But if he did, I'd look in the "Character Traits" section in this chapter and Chapter 15, "Character Abilities."

Step 21: Stress Management

People behave differently under stress. How can we estimate Evar's behavior when he's in danger or when events are out of control? One way is to check the "Personality Types" section and see whether we can match Evar with some typing system, then determine how he might behave. Another way is just to make it up based on his other qualities, which is easier. I might decide that Evar is the Enneagram Type 4: The Romantic/Individualist. In the Myers-Briggs system, he might be an ESFP, with several of their positive and negative traits. He might also be an ENTP, but I'm leaning more toward the ESFP's qualities. I wouldn't necessarily try to make a character exactly like one of the personality types, but I would look for ways he might behave, given his other traits, and use the personality information to help fill in some of his behaviors under stress. So, from the "Personality Types" section, I'd take the following ideas:

Myer's Briggs: ESFP

- Can be distracted by social interests.
- Can feel hurt if warmth is not reciprocal.
- Often lacks the ability to see logical consequences of his actions.
- Can become bored and restless.
- Looks for immediate gratification.
- Avoids working alone.
- Doesn't always take care of himself.

Enneagram Type 4:

- Can be self-absorbed.
- Expects solutions from outside himself.
- Somewhat moody and temperamental.
- Fears abandonment.
- Womanizing comes from a fear of being ordinary or unlovable.

I would keep these characteristics in mind whenever I designed a scene with Evar in it, and I might even check these traits and design scenes expressly to evoke a specific reaction consistent with who Evar is.

Step 22: The Spiritual Side

It may turn out that Evar's fear of witchcraft is based on some conservative religious beliefs. Whether this is useful to the storyline and plot is debatable and depends on the story itself and the world you are creating. For instance, it would be very appropriate in a world like that of the early American colonies in the late 1600s.

With less well-drawn characters, it may not always be necessary to imbue them with a deeper spiritual life. In Evar's case, he was raised in a strict tradition but has strayed considerably from its tenets. He still retains a few old beliefs, however, such as his fear of magic in general. See also the "Religious and Spiritual Practices" section.

Step 23: Relations to Other Characters

It is necessary to have other characters designed before you can complete this step, but overall, based on what I've already done with Evar, it would be safe to say that he is flirtatious with pretty women, kind with most people, angry or defensive when reminded of his past, and loyal if treated well. He may struggle with emotional commitment because, loyal as he is, he is afraid to fail again and once again lose those closest to him. For more ideas, I'd check the "Relationships of Characters" section.

Step 24: Physical Description and Changes

This step is really about how you visualize the character. Useful references in this chapter are in the "Physical Changes" and "Ways to Customize Avatars" sections. For some observable behavioral traits, see also "Mental/Emotional Signals: The Other 93%."

Step 25: Is the Character Funny?

Evar is not specifically designed to be a comedic character, but he may have some funny characteristics. Looking at "Creating Comedy" in Chapter 9, "Storytelling Techniques," as well as the "Attributes of Funny Characters" section, I can imagine some moments of humor with Evar.

- He could have some funny expressions he uses at key moments, such as when he sees a pretty woman or just before a battle.
- He could be a practical joker and play pranks on another of the player character's allies—or even on the player character.
- He could do funny things when distracted, such as walk into a lamp pole when he's gawking at a woman on the street.
- His favorite cap, which he never takes off, could be funny in some way, or he might be even funnier if he lost it.

Finishing Up

You may want to find a way to summarize your character. One way is with a simple statement, such as:

> **Evar Bowstringer.** Archer who seeks revenge and resolution of his past. Loyal, if a bit unpredictable, companion with a deep fear of magic. Womanizer, gambler, and a bit melodramatic at times. But a good scout, a helluva shot with a bow and arrow, and sometimes makes you laugh!

Another way to summarize your character would be to create a character summary sheet that lists all these traits and characteristics.

I took a lot of time to consider Evar Bowstringer. I might have skipped more parts of the process and still had a good, solid archer ally for my game. It's possible that I will never use or explicitly reveal some of Evar's real traits to the player, but whenever I involve Evar in a situation, I will have this character design to refer to, and I will be able to create a character with some depth, consistency, and unique personality. By using the Build-a-Character system, I have avoided creating a pure cookie-cutter character. Instead, I have one who I can use in a variety of ways in whatever game I create.

Also, although some of the details of Evar's descriptions would need to be adjusted, this profile could be changed to fit a modern soldier in a different sort of game or possibly even a gangster character in an urban setting. The process of examining a character to this extent in some ways becomes its own reward as you begin to think more deeply about characters in general, and—because in many ways characters make and inspire stories and action—about the possibilities in your games.

A More Complex Example

Evar is a relatively simple character, but he is a good example of how a *role* that is common in many games—an archer—can be expanded into a *character*. In most games, the archer is just the archer. In my game, Evar would be Evar *and* an archer, and I would be able to use his unique qualities to develop special situations, events, and storylines that would not be suggested with the pure role of archer.

This next example takes the idea of creating a character quite a bit beyond Evar and into some creative territory. It involves a very complex character—really two characters in one body—and suggests the kind of story that might evolve from the juxtaposition of two completely different characters with adversarial goals, who must share the same body...for now, at least.

Step 1: Roles

This character is a main villain *and* the main heroine at the same time. Let's look at the villainous character first. For some ideas on roles, see Chapter 13, "Character Roles and Jobs," and, since this is going to be a main character villain, also see the "Kinds of Heroes, Villains, and Minions" section in this chapter and Chapter 14, "Enemies." In this case, I'm going to pick The Demon archetype for my main villain and possibly take a few characteristics from other examples in that section.

Because this story will involve possession (take my word for it for now), there will be a second character, a sub-hero if you like, who is the victim of the possession. I'm going to model her on the Reluctant Hero archetype (from the "Kinds of Heroes, Villains, and Minions" section), but probably borrow from other personality types. For that, I might check the "Personality Types" section to round her out a bit. But I'm getting ahead of myself. Let's move on to Step 2.

Step 2: Basics

Entering age, gender, and so on may or may not be important right away. You may choose to wait until later to flesh out these details. Or, if you have a clear idea of the character, you can begin now. The type of character you create might change based on age or if the character is American, Latino, or Middle Eastern, for instance. And, of course, gender often makes a difference.

Sometimes you may know the function of the character, but these specific details may not make much difference. In other cases, these qualities have profound effects on the character's personality and interaction in the story. For our purposes, we'll make a character as follows:

- Age: 3,200 (more or less)
- Gender: Male
- Ethnicity: Egyptian
- Economic Status: None
- Social Status: Dead
- Marital Status: N/A
- Name: Nebtawi (which means Lord of the World in ancient Egyptian)

This character is somewhat unusual because he has inhabited the body of another character, who we describe as follows:

- Age: 36
- Gender: Female
- Ethnicity: Irish/Iranian
- Economic Status: Loaded
- Social Status: High society
- Marital Status: Divorced
- Name: Monica Iwazi

Step 3: The Family

In this story, the family plays a less important role than it might in some stories. Nebtawi's family background is essentially irrelevant, but we could make one up. Because he's practically a personification of evil, he is somewhat two-dimensional, and family history isn't going to make much difference in how we handle him in a story.

Monica, on the other hand, does have a history with the family—in particular, with her grandfather, who was her mentor and who, until he died when she was only eight, showed her the affection she never got from her parents; and with her mega-wealthy father, who disapproves of her lifestyle. Monica, on the other hand, acts out to get her father's attention because while she was growing up, he was rarely there for her. Because he is powerful, influential, and successful, she craves his approval and love, but she has rarely received it. She resorts to actions that she knows will get his attention, however negative, in order to prove to him that she exists. This could be important later on when she comes to grips with her own life, perhaps at the end or close to the end of the story. It could also come into play if her father enters into the story.

Her mother, on the other hand, secretly lives vicariously through Monica, whose wildness is something the mother could never express but always wished she could. Where she has essentially an antagonist in her father, she has a secret ally in her mother, should the plot require it. (Also see the "Relationships of Characters" section in this chapter.)

Step 4: Professions

No job. Monica is a wealthy playgirl. Nebtawi is a discorporate evil entity. He was once a great wizard under Ramses the Great. But you can always check out Chapter 13, "Character Roles and Jobs."

Step 5: The Situation

Looking in the "Basic Game Activities" section in Chapter 21, "Experiential Design," I found:

> Possession (taking over the bodies of other characters, pretending to be them, or forcing them to take pain for you, such as beating out the fire or killing themselves, and so on)
>
> In Chapter 11, "Scenarios," I found in "Imprisonment Scenarios":
>
> How Did That Get In Me? Something has taken up residence in your head or your body (or both). You're trapped while it runs the show.
>
> And also in Chapter 11, in "Godlike Roles," I found:
>
> Big Bad Boss. The main bad guy seems to have godlike powers. He's going to be tough. But he must have a weakness, if only you can discover it and live long enough to exploit it!

So this is the scene I've come up with: Monica's grandfather was a dabbler in the dark arts. While exploring in his long-forgotten basement laboratory, she stumbles on a terrifying secret—a mummified body. She removes some odd stones marked with various hieroglyphs and unwittingly frees the dark soul of Nebtawi, the Lord of the World. Although she is outwardly unchanged, the dark energy of Nebtawi takes control of her and, through her, is bent on unleashing a reign of terror upon humanity. As time passes, Nebtawi's power grows, and Monica's personality begins to lose its grip on her body.

Step 6: Goals

In this chapter, I've added a short list of possible "Character Goals," while more general game goals can be found in Chapter 23, "Goals." While the ostensible character, Monica, wants to marry the hero (find a mate), Nebtawi wants to subjugate first Monica, then the human race under his power (obtaining power and revenge). He is after revenge for what he considers ill treatment in ancient Egypt and, well, because he has been dead for nearly 3,200 years and he has become quite cranky.

Step 7: Arc

For this section, I referred to the "How a Character Grows…Character Arcs" section in this chapter.

Monica does have a character arc. She starts out being flighty and simply wanting to have fun and perhaps marry the hero. She discovers that her true happiness and fulfillment will come from helping others, but that's only after her harrowing adventure is completed. This would be something like the arc called Finding Their Life's Purpose.

On the other hand, Nebtawi's not a character who really changes. He's dead at the beginning of the story and, hopefully, will be really and positively dead at the end. Alternatively, he could have an arc. Since he is infatuated with the ancient Egyptian Serpent Goddess, Menhit, a possible arc for Nebtawi is that he realizes that his hatred of humanity is misguided, that Menhit is a snake, and that he can leave a last gift to the people he has harmed, then die in peace. This would conform to Resolving or Releasing Some Issue of Their Past, or even Discovering Inner Truth.

Or suppose Nebtawi's arc is that he is able to inhabit a brand-new body all his own, and he decides to take up residence in Monica's world (but without using her body this time). This is a different story, but it could conform to Finding a Way to Be Part of a New Culture, World, Environment, Society….

Step 8 and 9: Strengths and Flaws/Limitations

Because we are actually creating two characters here—Monica and Nebtawi—let's look at their traits side by side. That will be helpful when creating the character's behavior to make subtle differences in the way the character behaves when one is more dominant than the other. I found all these traits in the "Character Traits" section.

Strengths

Monica	Nebtawi
Beautiful	Determined
Charming	Persuasive
Honest	Powerful
Resilient	Brilliant intelligence
Simplistic	Crafty

Flaws/Limitations

Monica	Nebtawi
Forgetful	Arrogant
Frivolous	Bodiless/dead
Fragile	Fixated
Temperamental	Humorless
Willful	
Drama queen	

Step 10: Basic Emotional States (Moods)

During the course of events, each character can display a wide variety of emotions. But some emotional states and states of mind are more basic to the character's personality. Looking in the "Moods" section in this chapter, you can find some suggestions for these more basic emotions and mindsets.

Moods

Monica		Nebtawi	
Cheerful	Jealous	Condescending	Proud
Confused	Petulant	Angry	Predatory
Sweet			

Step 11: Traits

This chapter contains a long list of possible character traits in the "Character Traits" section as well as the "Character Flaws and Strengths" section. Looking through these lists, you can get some ideas about the character in addition to strengths, flaws, limitations, and basic emotions/mindsets. The "Character Traits" section is also a good place to seek additional characteristics. For instance, though we have begun to define both Monica and Nebtawi, we might also give them some additional qualities, such as that Monica is also alert, anal about her makeup, and big-hearted about children and puppies. Nebtawi may also be an expert at many things and sentimental about someone he knew in the past. Of course, when you get to Step 21, you can further enhance their characteristics by referring to the "Personality Types" section.

Step 12: Quirks

Again, checking the "Quirks" section, let's see whether we can come up with some interesting quirks for both Monica and Nebtawi, keeping in mind that these quirks will be useful in identifying who is dominant in the body.

Quirks

Monica	Nebtawi
Adjusts her hair	Unblinking stare
Taps her foot when impatient	Mutters under his breath
Files her nails when bored	Rolls his eyes around
Tends to avoid eye contact	Stares intensely into people's eyes

Step 13: Fears

What people fear often affects their behavior and how they make decisions. Let's look at what Monica and Nebtawi fear by referring to the "Phun with Phobias" section. We can pick out a few fears that might help further define their characters. Obviously, each could have many fears:

Fears

Monica	Nebtawi
Snakes	Extinction (permanent death)
Being misunderstood	Vulnerability
Objectification as a sex object	Loss of power
Abandonment	Abandonment

The last of Nebtawi's fears could be the most important. In reality, perhaps all his evil acts stem from this one fear, and this could be the key to dealing with him. This could be the one human side he still has, and it could be manipulated in the plot. And because it is a fear they both share, it might be fun to explore some point when they realize their common fear. On the other hand, since Nebtawi seeks reunion with the Serpent Goddess, this will create more than a little stress for Monica, given her fear of snakes.

Step 14: General Activities

Nebtawi has spent a virtual eternity trapped in a moldering mummy case, so he hasn't really been hanging around anyplace interesting. On the other hand, Monica can often be seen at chic restaurants, parties, clubs, and shopping districts. She is well known about town—at least in the high-society circles. However, her craving for hamburgers (see Step 17) has her sneaking into various hamburger joints from time to time, and she has a few favorites. She's furtive about it, though. Hamburger joints and high society don't seem to go along with each other very well. (As a side note, this could be a great way to build a relationship with the hero, who might also crave hamburgers and could introduce Monica to the absolute best burger she's ever had, or something like that.)

Step 15: Hobbies

The characters of Monica and Nebtawi are starting to take shape, but in an effort to bring them more fully into focus, let's look at what they do for fun—their hobbies. The "Hobbies" list is pretty extensive. Let's say that Monica likes to write in her diary and do ballroom dancing. Nebtawi, coming from a different time, likes to dabble in alchemy and the occasional wench (though occupying Monica's body somewhat limits his enthusiasm for that particular penchant...interesting possibilities, however). He also used to make his own magical weapons, and he may recognize new opportunities to indulge in that hobby with modern technologies...more interesting possibilities there.

Step 16: Pets

What kinds of pets do people have? It's not a big issue, but it can tell you something about who they are. In this case, Monica keeps a large wolfhound dog while Nebtawi, when he was alive, kept a pet monkey and several Nubian slaves.

Step 17: Preferences

Monica really enjoys hamburgers, but she rarely gets them, being that she is far too involved in the high-society set and eats fancy food most of the time. She likes music from the Big Band era as well as some soft rock and classical. She likes movies—especially comedies and tearjerkers. Nebtawi likes a rousing tale told by a good storyteller, eats everything except braised papyrus, and, though he misses the haunting melodies of the ancient lira, soon develops an appreciation of the work of early rap pioneers, which Monica disdains. He does show a certain appreciation for the Big Band music that Monica likes—a possible link between their otherwise opposing personalities.

Step 18: Sexuality

Monica actually likes a dominant man, but although she can be flirtatious, she's sexually innocent...she hasn't fully discovered that yet. Nebtawi is quite turned on by women with snakes and enjoys subjugating women. He secretly likes to be dominated by a woman, but only the Serpent Goddess has ever been psychically strong enough to do that. (See also the "Gender/Type of Character" section.)

Step 19: Travel

Monica gets around in her limo. Nebtawi used to have a palanquin carried by six of his Nubian slaves, but he must make do with Monica's motorized contraptions. For more options, check out Chapter 18, "Travel." As his powers increase, Nebtawi may gain the ability to travel as a bodiless astral projection and/or by teleportation.

Step 20: Abilities and Powers

You might find some abilities in the "Character Traits" section, but for the real juicy powers, check out Chapter 15, "Character Abilities."

While Monica has no real powers—in fact, she's quite ordinary—Nebtawi more than makes up for it by having a full complement of abilities, including Control of People, Possession, Summoning and Sorcery, and apparent Immortality.

Step 21: Stress Management

Most interesting characters in a game will be faced with challenging situations and various difficulties. How do they react when the stress is poured on? One place to go for that kind of information is the "Personality Types" section in this chapter. That section deals with various theories of personalities and includes at least some information about how these types of personalities react when under stress. It isn't necessary to stick to types, however. Just use the section as a reference, along with the "Moods" section for general emotional options.

Monica, for instance, often responds to stress by becoming confused and rattled. She loses command of language and tends to blather. After a time, however, she often finds inner strength and tends to externalize her frustration into a high degree of focus on the cause of the stress. In these times, she can be quite effective.

Nebtwai responds to most stressful situations by lashing out and trying to hurt something. However, his weakness has to do with his fears of abandonment and of love, so in deeper emotional situations he withdraws, becomes sulky, and often shifts his attention to something else, which he then wants to hurt.

Step 22: The Spiritual Side

Monica thinks she is a Christian with some New Age leanings, but in fact she has no deeper moral or spiritual values. She will revert to prayer and invocations of God when scared, but she doesn't really believe any of it.

Nebtawi has direct experience with the old gods—knows them personally, in fact—and consequently believes in the pantheon of ancient Egypt. He also believes that he is a demi-god and that divinity is his true right and calling.

Step 23: Relations to Other Characters

This section is best added after you have created other main characters, but one place to begin is the "Relationships of Characters" section. In this case, we know that Monica is sweet on the hero (or player character). We looked at some family ties in Step 3. She might also have some best friends, male and/or female, that we can add. For instance, her best friend Adelita is the daughter of a wealthy Argentine family who is as spoiled and wild as Monica, and her gay pal, George, simply adores her wardrobe and likes to accompany her to clubs and on shopping expeditions.

Nebtawi generally hates everyone, but he may come to hate the hero most and create some attachment to Monica. At the beginning of the story, at least, he has a desire relationship with the Serpent Goddess.

You might find some clues in the "Personality Types" section for different ways people relate, and you can go further into that subject with some research on the web.

Step 24: Physical Description

This step is required to finally render these characters, but I'll leave it to your imagination what Monica looks like and what Nebtawi would look like if he ever got his own body. In this game, Monica might actually change appearance based on how much control Nebtawi has.

Step 25: Is the Character Funny?

This is a specific step only if you want to identify humorous characteristics of the characters you have created, particularly if they are meant to be funny characters. In this case, although she is the heroine in distress, Monica could also be a funny caricature of a dizzy blonde or a spoiled heiress. If so, check out "Creating Comedy" in Chapter 9, "Storytelling Techniques," as well as the "Attributes of Funny Characters" section. I might choose a) funny voice, b) says funny things, and c) does funny things. She might also have d) the "says or does funny things in times of danger" attribute, since she's going to be in danger a lot.

That's it. All that's left is to summarize these characters' personalities somehow, as we did for Evar, our comparatively simple archer.

One possible summary might go:

> Nebtawi, a sorcerer in ancient Egypt, died 3,200 years ago, and his mummified remains awaited the arrival of Monica, a young, attractive, and flighty socialite who unwittingly freed his evil spirit, which quickly entered her body. Now Nebtawi is bent on seeking power and revenge over the entire human race, but he first has to subdue Monica by taking full control of her body and soul. Monica turns out to be spunkier than one would have guessed, and she doesn't give up control easily. In the battle for control, sometimes Nebtawi achieves dominance, and sometimes Monica does. Can our innocent heroine prevent the ancient sorcerer from achieving his evil plans?

Okay. That's one possible summary of this complex dual character. Can you think of another way to summarize Nebtawi and Monica? Can you alter some of the characteristics and completely change the nature of these characters? Perhaps it is really a comedy or a love story. Treat it as an exercise to take this situation and alter it to fit your own imagination. Who knows? You might come up with an idea for a completely original game.

Character Descriptions and Gameplay

Of course, creating characters such as Monica and Nebtawi might be amusing, and the possibilities for stories range from true horror to some kind of warped buddy comedy. However, games are not purely stories, but interactive experiences, and it is important to consider the gameplay possibilities of the characters you describe. Evar Bowstringer (the first example I presented) is an obvious character for a swords-and-sorcery RPG, and his basic description could be used in any number of games. However, the possession model of Monica/Nebtawi is less common, and using this model in a game might require some thought. While I was designing the character, I imagined that there would be a player character who was the hero and who would ultimately save Monica from Nebtawi's clutches. However, another way to consider this would be that Monica is the player character, and the game evolves around the player attempting to do what Monica wants but sometimes having to do what Nebtawi requires, all the while dealing with the inner dialog of the characters. It's not readily apparent how to make this a fun game experience, but it is something different, so it's worth considering.

In the end, I might end up discarding this character in favor of something simpler, but the process of creating it does present some ideas. As a challenge, take the Monica/Nebtawi character and story descriptions and consider different ways to use them in a game. What kind of games could you create? What would make them fun? What challenges would they present?

As you create games with characters in them, you can use the various parts of this book—with my Build-a-Character system or not—to consider the specific nature of those characters. Where appropriate, you can gain a deeper understanding of what makes them tick and use that knowledge to create more interesting situations and more consistent responses to those situations. Again, depending on the type of games you are creating, you can use this sort of deeper character design as a basis for some artificial intelligence system, thereby creating non-player characters with more complex, consistent, and realistic responses to the world you create for them.

The next few sections of this chapter are devoted to simple lists of characteristics. I've added these lists both as references and as brainstorming challenges. It's easy enough to create characters and imbue them with the most immediately obvious characteristics, but what you end up with are likely to be less imaginative, cookie-cutter characters, and as a consequence, the basis for your game may be less innovative than it could be. I'm not saying that you can't create characters simply from your own knowledge of people or from established character types. There are certainly plenty of examples in literature, movies, and games to draw from, but the goal of this book is to get you thinking of new ideas, so these lists ideally will help you see some of what already exists and perhaps find some characteristics that would inspire more interesting characters—and as a consequence, more interesting games.

I encourage you to use these lists at any time. Take them to meetings and refer to them during design discussions. Keep the book on your desk and refer to it when you're considering the characters in your game or even the situations in which they will find themselves. And also, think of anything we've left out. Can you add to these lists? If so, let us know what you've come up with.

Gender/Type of Character

Known genders:

- Male
- Female
- Androgynous
- Hermaphroditic
- Asexual
- Transsexual
- Eunuch

Other possible genders:

- Vampiric
- Full copy/duplication
- Body snatcher
- Plant (vegetative)
- Multi-species (requires cross-species reproduction)

Sexual orientation:

- Heterosexual
- Homosexual
- Autoerotic
- Bisexual
- Trisexual
- Anything goes
- Nothing doing (asexual)

Character Racial/Species Options

Earthly origin:

- Human (any known race—see the "Ethnicity/Race" category later in this section)
- Humanoid (basically like human, but not a known race—such as most of the races in *Star Trek*, but not necessarily alien):

- Insectoid
- Reptilian
- Aquatic
- Amphibious
- Avian
- Vampiric
- Demonic
- Fungal
- Gaseous
- Viral
- Amorphous
- Prehistoric
- Futuristic
- Robotic
- Ape
- Rock/siliconoid
- Arborial

Alien:

- Humanoid
- Insectoid
- Reptilian
- Aquatic
- Amphibious
- Avian
- Vampiric
- Non-corporeal
- Gaseous
- Fungal
- Viral

Spirit:

- Nature spirits
  - Earth
  - Air
  - Water
  - Fire
  - Metal
  - Stone
  - Tree (plant/wood)
  - Wind
  - Electricity/lightning
  - Ether
- Evil
- Good

Fantasy:

- Elvish
- Dwarven
- Ogre
- Troll
- Barbarian
- Halfling
- Undead
- Gnome
- Orc
- Centaur
- Minotaurs
- Cyclops
- Demons
- Angels
- Gods
- Fairies
- Nymphs
- Sirens
- Cerberus, the Three-Headed Dog
- Leviathan
- Earthworm Jim
- Dryads
- Satyr
- Griffon
- Manticore
- Gargoyle
- Chimera
- Dragon
- Imps
- Naga
- Ents

Ethnicity/race:

- Generic human
- Caucasian
- Black
- Latin
- Asian
  - Chinese
  - Japanese
  - Korean
  - Thai
  - Malaysian
  - Singaporean
  - Tibetan/Nepalese/Bhutanese
  - Vietnamese
  - Mongolian
- Jewish
- WASP
- Scandinavian
- Irish
- Scot
- French
- German
- Italian
- Spanish
- Portuguese
- South American (various)
- Brazilian
- Mexican
- Australian
- New Zealander
- Filipino
- African
- North African
- Gypsy
- Inuit
- Native American
- Indian
- Arab
- European (generally)
- Polynesian
- Basque
- Aborigine
- Pygmy
- Zulu
- Masai
- Nomad
- Faerie
- Elvish
- Dwarvish
- Orcish
- Goblin
- Troll
- Giant/titan
- Hobbit
- Gnomish
- Entish (tree creature)
- Gods and demi-gods
- Mer-people (mermaids/mermen)
- Monster type (varies)
- Sentient plant creature
- Insectoid
- Avian
- Reptilian
- Sentient mineral creature
- Discorporate entity
- Shape-shifter
- Alien (other planetary—varies)

Strong Character Names

What makes a strong character name? In truth, almost any name can be strong if the character and the setting are right. Harry isn't a particularly heroic-sounding name, and neither is Potter. And someone named Harry Potter wouldn't seem to be particularly impressive, from his name alone. But, unless you have just crawled out from under a particularly soundproof rock, you know that Harry Potter is a household name throughout much of the Western world. So, Harry can be a strong name in the right context. What about a name like Lenny or Tony? In some cases, those names might not be particularly interesting, but set them in a Mafia story in Little Italy, and they suddenly increase in potential.

Therefore, the context of a game or story may help determine what names can be strong and effective. And the action and experience of the player will certainly contribute to the power of the name. Without

Tolkien, names such as Gandalf and Frodo would simply seem odd. But to many people, those names are loaded with power.

I started out thinking I could create a list of strong names for male, female, good, and evil characters. What is a good villain name? What is a good hero name? The more I thought about it, the more I realized that creating a name should be not only contextual, but individual, and the power of the name comes from the power of the player's experiences and the designer's depiction of that character. An archvillain named Percy could be a joke, but with the right mixture of evil and ruthlessness, I guarantee you that the name Percy could become pretty frightening—perhaps even more so because it sounds so un-macho, effete, and anything but evil.

I often come up with names simply by finding something that sounds good to me—a name that never existed (as far as I know), but could have been a perfectly good, if unusual, name. Tolkien drew names from mythology. Other people use names allegorically. For instance, a very strong character might be called Rock. A devious character might be Snake or Fox or even a word that means *fox* in some other language. A ferocious character might be named Wolf, Wulf, or Wolfe. Or a wise character could be some exotic word for *owl.* But as we see with characters such as Harry Potter, Frodo, Mario and Luigi, Link, Luke Skywalker, and Mickey Mouse, names can be imbued with power by how we use them. "Call me Ishmael."

Of course, there are many resources for finding names. Any Internet search for names will produce hundreds of name lists—more than you probably have time to deal with. But some are probably more useful for naming game characters than the general name-your-baby sites. You'll probably find many that interest you, but I found the site www.lowchensaustralia.com/names/fantasylinks.htm, which contains lots of links to various fantasy name lists and even a name generator (www.prairieden.com/articles/character_names.php).

(See also the "Nicknames" section in Chapter 16, "Speech," for some examples of nicknames that also can serve as good character names.)

So, you can start with a name such as Flash, Rocky, or Brigitte that you figure has a certain inherent implication of strength or sex appeal (or whatever), or you can make any name a household word by creating a great name out of a great game.

Relationships of Characters

Relationships are not only those of father, mother, sister, brother, son, and daughter; they are what involves people with each other. Some people are related by common interests or the work they do. Some are bound to each other by rivalries, grudges, or prejudicial feelings. The range of relationships of one character to another is actually quite large, but it's a wonderful way to explore characters as you introduce them into a game. In the best of worlds, your more important characters will have multiple relationships. A grandfather is a part of the family but could also be a guide. A best friend could be a rival. A love interest could also be an enemy, a guide, a partner, a victim, or a supernatural helper—or all of those at once, somehow. The point is, relationships help create story, and story can help create gameplay opportunities. So here are some possible relationships you can use in various ways. Feel free to mix and match and to add to the list any relationships you don't see here.

- Father
- Mother
- Brother
- Sister
- Son
- Daughter
- Wife/husband
- Cousin
- Aunt
- Uncle
- Grandfather
- Grandmother

- Great-grandfather
- Great-grandmother
- Ancestor
- Step-relation
- In-law relation
- Bastard
- Lover
- Partner
- Teacher/trainer/guide
- Friend
- Neighbor
- Buddy
- Sidekick
- Someone who needs protection/victim
- Gatekeeper (someone who bars the way)
- Law enforcer
- Hero
- Enemy
- Archenemy
- Heir
- Accomplice
- Ally
- Minion/henchman
- Servant/slave
- Annoyance
- Employee
- Employer/Boss
- Assistant
- Slave
- Servant
- Lieutenant
- Oracle
- Ruler
- Subject
- Pet
- Stranger
- Captive
- Captor
- Authority figure
- Protector
- Alibi (provider of)
- Scapegoat (takes the blame)
- Living deity
- Imaginary friend
- Hallucination
- Conscience (embodied)
- Benefactor
- Sugar daddy
- Mistress

Jobs

For information about jobs, see Chapter 13, "Character Roles and Jobs," specifically the "NPC Jobs" and "Evil Jobs" sections.

Character Goals

(See also Chapter 23, "Goals.")

Every character has some goals, regardless of whether they are shown or implemented. Even random NPCs walking down the street presumably have the goal of getting somewhere (although in reality they will never actually get anywhere unless the programmers gave them a destination). Or the typical shopkeeper in a game presumably has the goal of buying low and selling high. But in reality, most game shopkeepers have no real depth or intelligence. They are basically vending machines. If a shopkeeper were created as a real character with a real life, he might, for instance, lower prices when business was bad or when the tax collector was threatening to foreclose on his house, in the hope of stimulating more sales. He might raise prices when other merchants raise their prices. In short, his behavior would be based on a more complex set of circumstances and emotional responses. He might, for instance, give you a better deal if he likes you—a feature that is present in some games already, though implemented fairly crudely. Or he might offer volume discounts, something I have not seen. For instance, if you buy a sword from a shopkeeper, you pay full price. But suppose you were purchasing a whole set of armor and weapons all at one time. Wouldn't you expect to get some kind of a break on all that? Not with a vending machine, you won't.

Main characters, on the other hand, have specific goals that are often important to the plot or unfolding gameplay. But it is important to realize that a character's ostensible goals in a story (speaking in the literary sense) are sometimes different from whatever it is they need to accomplish for their own growth. For instance, in *Shrek*, the main character has the conscious goal of being left alone, but what he really gets and needs is to feel better about himself and his place in the world.

In every good story, of course, obstacles stand in the way of the character achieving his goals. This is the essence of story, in fact. If the characters had no goals and no obstacles to attaining them, there would be little to no story.

While some goals can be deep-seated and unchanging, others will change from moment to moment—particularly those intermediate goals that are common in stories, in life, and in games. A man driving home from work may have the goal of getting home and watching a ballgame on TV, but when an alien spaceship lands in front of his car, his immediate goals are likely to change.

In many games, the player's character has no important goals at the beginning and is subsequently thrown into a situation that defines his goals. In the typical Japanese Role-Playing Game, the main character is often a kid with no particular direction. Then the village is destroyed, some girl is kidnapped, or something cataclysmic happens in his world. Suddenly, a wise person (the guide or mentor character—see also "Functional Character Roles") tells him that he has to go save the world or the girl or something. Now he has a goal. In a typical FPS, the player's character has a goal, which is generally to kill every enemy, remove the source of the enemy's power, and protect his base and/or take over or destroy the enemy's base, whatever that is.

In such games, there is really very little character growth. The character may get better stats and abilities, weapons, armor, and items, but really, there's no character arc. (See the "How a Character Grows...Character Arcs" section later in this chapter.) The character doesn't grow inwardly.

So what is the importance of goals? Simply this: Goals motivate the actions of the character, and stories are about action. Characters may grow in all kinds of ways. They may realize their dreams or may fail miserably. They may come to realize that what they wanted was in reality not good for them, or they may find their perfect Shangri-La. But something drove them in the first place, and that's what goals are all about.

Also, the very fact that a character has a particular goal means he doesn't have that thing (or at least he doesn't know he has it). For instance, if a character's goal is to find peace of mind, then it's a safe assumption that he isn't at peace. So that suggests the question: What state *is* he in, if he isn't at peace? And what does he do to achieve his goal of peace of mind, assuming this is his conscious goal at the beginning of the story? He might think some time in the country would provide the relief he needs, only to find out that the experience in the country is challenging in different ways. But, perhaps through the experiences he has in the country, he will truly find what he is seeking in a way he hadn't anticipated, as in the movie *City Slickers*.

I do want to point out that this section does not deal with the player's goals, which are inherent elements of any game design. The whole purpose of games is to motivate the player to take action, but that action takes place through the player's in-game character and with the other characters in the games—allies, enemies, and neutral NPCs—or with other players in multiplayer games. The point is that a player's goals may differ entirely from those of the character he plays in the game, or they may coincide. This section deals primarily with goals of in-game characters, including the non-player characters.

The following list contains some goals that would apply to non-player characters in a game. (For a list of short- and long-term goals applicable primarily to player characters, see Chapter 23, "Goals.") Note that sometimes these goals can be the same as what the character needs to find—the character arc, as shown in the next section. But the character's conscious goals are not necessarily the character's arc, which often involves his inner and unconscious needs. A character's goal could be to find a girlfriend, but his arc is to achieve self-acceptance or to become compassionate. This deserves repetition: It's important to recognize the distinction between goals and the character's arc.

Character goals:

- Make money/get rich
- Get out of debt
- Find a mate
- Rescue someone
- Save the world
- Get revenge
- Get justification
- Obtain power
- Retain power
- Gain fame
- Look good
- Be sexually attractive
- Get a job
- Express anger
- Express love
- Be normal
- Fit in
- Be creative
- Be smart
- Succeed (at anything)
- Accomplish something big or personally significant (such as skiing down K-2 or running a mile in less than four minutes)
- Prove something to someone (themselves or another)
- Convert others to their way of thinking (missionary)
- Follow a spiritual or religious path
- Lose weight
- Become stronger or more fit
- Get big muscles and a six-pack
- Fool people
- Repair something
- Prevent a disaster
- Find happiness
- Find love
- Kick a bad habit
  - Drugs/alcohol
  - Overeating
  - Laziness
  - Compulsive gambling
  - Compulsive lying
- Master a trade or art
- Get through school/graduate
- Get through one day at a time
- Get divorced
- Commit suicide (think of the beginning of *It's a Wonderful Life*)
- Run for office
- Get something tangible (a new car, a fancy TV, a home, etc.)
- Hide
- Escape danger
- Be noticed
- Be left alone
- Climb the corporate ladder (or equivalent)
- Keep things the same (stability)
- Find adventure/excitement
- Find spiritual fulfillment/faith
- Find peace of mind
- Be brave
- Cure cancer (or other societal woes)

How a Character Grows...Character Arcs

It is generally held that in any good story, one or more of the characters changes. Usually it is the main character, but it can be other characters who change, while the main character stays more or less the same. In essence, each character is on his own journey through the events of the story, and each of them encounters individual challenges and has individual goals. Whenever you are creating a major character in a game (or any type of story, for that matter), consider what he is seeking through his involvement in the events that occur. Note that what he outwardly seeks may be different from what he actually accomplishes. This is the essence of the character arc.

NOTE

Character arc *is the term used to describe how a character changes in the course of a story. This is particularly true of the main character(s). There are a lot of ways to think of a character arc, and many sort of canned or categorized approaches exist. But some old-school writers say that the term* character arc *is a buzzword, and that, quite simply, what you want to do is tell a story about people—what happens to them, what they do in response, and how they change as a result.*

In the preceding section, I discussed character goals—the outward goals of the character. But the character's inner goal may be different, and this is where the character's true opportunity for growth, evolution, or other sorts of change comes in. For instance, a character may be outwardly seeking a love interest, but really comes to find his independence and self-reliance. Or he may be seeking a cure for the common cold, but he finds true love. The character goals in this list are what the character actually finds, but not always what he thinks he wants.

There are many ways to describe character arcs, some more specific and some more general. Here are a few to fire up your imagination. Think how your main characters—even the player character—might follow these paths:

- Acceptance/love/appreciation of themselves and/or others
- Balancing conflicting elements in their lives
- Becoming a leader
- Becoming self-confident
- Becoming the master/mistress of their own fate
- Being honest with themselves and/or with others
- Coming of age
- Coming to terms with their own (past or present) actions and taking responsibility
- Creating a new self-image or direction
- Dealing with disaster (overcoming hardship)
- Discovering inner truth
- Eliminating self-destructive behavior
- Examining, understanding, and maybe changing their inner beliefs and/or resolving conflicting beliefs
- Finding a way to be part of a new culture, world, environment, or society
- Finding a way to fit into the world they live in
- Finding happiness or peace of mind
- Finding love, romance, or a mate (generally as a consequence of some other inner understanding or growth)
- Finding something to believe in
- Finding their life's purpose
- Forgiving self or others
- Learning self-reliance or assertiveness; no longer being a victim
- Learning to be compassionate or empathetic
- Learning to trust (themselves, others, or life generally)
- Letting go of fear
- Making a difference in the world
- Resolving or releasing some issue of their past
- Revitalizing their lives
- Trusting their intuition or inner guidance

A typical plot might be "rags to riches," in which a poor man or woman somehow gains great wealth. But what is the character's arc? Did he or she start out greedy and selfish, only to become a great philanthropist, valuing relationships more than the money he or she has acquired? Or does he or she start out humble and kind, only to end up miserly, lonely, and miserable because of his or her accumulated wealth and its impact? These two examples describe possible character arcs based on a "rags to riches" plot. Of course, the character might start out poor but honest and end up rich but honest. He or she might start out poor and unhappy and end up rich and unhappy. Just about any combination of poor to rich is possible, some being more interesting than others. The goal is to examine what happens as this poor person seeks and finds riches: What does he or she experience along the way, and what effect does it have on his or her life? There must be some impact from being poor and then being rich. In the case of the character in this story, what is that impact? How does the character grow or change because of it? Does he or she change inwardly? Do his or her values change? Does his or her behavior change? Is he or she better off in the long run?

What is interesting from a game design perspective is that, although other characters can have character arcs, the main character is inevitably the player's character, and it is up to the player to guide that character and make the decisions. The story, too, is often nonlinear and can take different directions. There may be no fixed storyline, and the story emerges as a result of the gameplay. How, then, do you use character arcs with a character who is an actor in an unfolding story and is simultaneously an extension of a living person—a persistent *deus* in *machina*, if you will? The question arises: Can you, in fact, move the player character through the necessary changes to see him or her develop and evolve in order to complete the arc? What happens with the player? How does the player's experience parallel that of the character? Or does it?

The answers to these questions depend on the type of game you are creating. Generally speaking, however, you can create a story in which both the player's character and the player have a significant experience, though that experience might be different in each case. For instance, the player's experience is usually of satisfaction for having completed the game, combined, perhaps, with the audience's traditional response to the resolution of a good story—whether that is sadness, elation, thoughtfulness, a warm and fuzzy moment, a good laugh, or whatever. To the extent that you can get the player to identify with the character, you will be successful. Meanwhile, the character's arc could be the happiness that comes with a successful romantic outcome, the sense of empowerment that comes with having overcome the odds, or the peace at the end of a long struggle. The hero character could even have a darker ending, becoming embittered and disillusioned at the end, but if the game is good and the story is successful, the player will still feel satisfaction and an emotional connection to the character.

What is important here is to remember that the character's experience and the player's experience are different, but that both can be served by a good story.

Here are a few more examples of character arcs in some common plots:

Revenge

Revenge plots revolve around past events and a character's driving need to punish those responsible.

- The hero ultimately hunts down and kills/arrests/destroys those responsible and feels vindicated. Now his life can go forward—but where? Is there a love interest?
- The hero learns new information in the course of the story that reveals his quest for revenge is misguided or aimed at the wrong person or group. The hero then comes to realize that his life has been a lie and has an awakening—either continuing to go after those truly responsible or perhaps moving off in a new direction and walking away from the whole revenge motive.
- At some point, probably at the very end of the story, the hero realizes that revenge is self-defeating and walks away from the quest without completing it—now at peace with himself.

- The hero becomes an avenging angel and destroys the guilty. But perhaps he later discovers that the people he destroyed were actually innocent. Perhaps nobody was consciously guilty. Perhaps the player was most at fault. Perhaps now the player's character must find a way to atone for his mistake.

Self-Discovery

Self-discovery plots involve a character who is basically going through the motions of life and, because of some pivotal event in the story, comes to question who he is. The story is about finding the answer.

- The hero faces impossible odds and, in meeting all the challenges, grows from someone with little to no self-esteem into someone with confidence. This may allow him to return to a former situation where he was ineffectual and succeed there—for instance, getting the girl he lost at the beginning of the story because he was a nerd or beating up the bad men who victimized him at the beginning. In a game setting, imagine that something is terribly wrong at home, and the player's character is not powerful enough or skilled enough to deal with the situation. However, by taking on a great quest or adventure, the player's character becomes stronger and more skilled so that, by the time he returns to the original location, the tables have turned and the enemy is easily (or not so easily) vanquished.
- The hero has everything—or so it seems. But when the situation changes, he comes to realize that what he didn't have was love. In the end, the character's priorities change, and he comes to value his relationships and, as a consequence, he becomes happier and more loved by those around him. Although successful before, he becomes even more successful—or, he abandons all material success for a simple, happy life. Although this kind of storyline wouldn't work in all games, it could be effective in some game situations, if there were a substantial payoff for the player in taking the character in that direction.
- The hero is stuck in a dead-end situation in life, but circumstances change, and he embarks on an adventure—at the end of which he knows what he really wants out of life. He goes from essentially living dead to fully alive. Again, this may be difficult to implement exactly in a game, but the concept of going from the ordinary to the extraordinary works quite well. What the character (and the player) learns from the experience depends on the game and how it's designed.

Identity

The hero has some issue about his identity. It could be something as broad as the quest of an amnesiac to find out who he really is or an adoptee who seeks his birth parents. These are examples of the "unknown identity" plot. Or, it could have to do with someone who is seeking his place in the world—the current one or a new one. This sort of story is similar to the self-discovery genre, but it can be more subtle.

- The amnesiac must search for clues to his identity. To make things worse, there is probably someone who doesn't want him to find out, or there is something dark and dangerous associated with who the hero is or was. In the end, the hero will always discover the truth and deal with the dangers. However, although he may then return to a former life, the greater change and the more interesting arc is that he has learned something about himself from his amnesiac persona, and it is those unique lessons that determine who he will be at the end. Or perhaps his wife finds he was nicer or a better person without his memories and connections to the present world than he becomes when his memories return.
- The adoptee searches for his parents and family identity. Along the way he confronts many obstacles—some bureaucratic, perhaps, or even real dangers. Or he travels and has adventures in the course of the search. Perhaps the travel and associated adventures are the real lessons of the story. Or it could be a comedy of errors, as in *Meet the Parents.* In the end, the character grows to greater self-knowledge throughout the search, regardless of the results. For instance, the ending could

involve a warm and tearful reunion where everyone feels happy and fulfilled and the character feels love and a true sense of belonging for the first time. Or, the parents could turn out to be crooks or rotten people, and the character has to confront his own rottenness or revulsion toward such parents. Or the parents could be dead, and the character has to piece together their lives, in the course of which he grows to understand the meaning of his own life, and so on.

- The main character is somehow a stranger in the story's environment. For instance, perhaps he's a California surfer who somehow gets drafted into the Intergalactic Army or a robot who must find where it fits in the world of humans, such as Data in *Star Trek: The Next Generation.* In the course of the story, the robot becomes more aware of what humans are all about and how it differs from them. It learns where it fits in the world and learns to understand its human masters on one hand and its own robot nature on the other. Or perhaps it becomes the leader of a robot underground rebellion and goes to war against the human oppressors. But then, in the end, it must have some realization of who it really is or what its place in the world is. Another example of identity might be an aging athlete who must find where he fits into the world, no longer young and skilled, but now older and wiser....

Stranger in a Strange Land

Put the protagonist in a completely unfamiliar and alien environment, and you have instant conflict and opportunity for myriad stories. Often called the "fish out of water," this sort of theme offers the hero the opportunity to learn about an unfamiliar society and environment, and generally in the process, learn a lot more about himself.

Some aspects of self-discovery and identity exist in these stories, but they can also be about learning lessons of diversity and tolerance, learning new skills, or overcoming bigotry or preconceptions. Other examples include "country bumpkin in the big city" or "city slicker in the country," time-travel stories—to the past or future—and adventure stories of various kinds in which the protagonist is lost, shipwrecked, crash landed, and so on and has to find his way back to civilization or adapt to a wild environment. This can also include stories among aliens, native tribes and societies, animal communities, and so on. Classic examples are Hank in Mark Twain's *A Connecticut Yankee in King Arthur's Court*, Billy Crystal's character in *City Slickers*, Robinson Crusoe (of course), or Tom Hanks' character in *Castaway.*

Romance

Boys and girls, men and women—it's a perfect chemistry set for stories and character arcs. This is about as basic as it gets, and, not surprisingly, every kind of story and character development option you can think of fits neatly into the romantic drama, comedy, or adventure. Romance can be of the love-at-first-sight variety, or it can grow from shared experience or even evolve from animosity. In the end, characters learn about themselves. The guy or gal who fears commitment goes through the adversity of really loving someone enough to fight those fears and ultimately (probably) overcome them. The man or woman who has been wounded in the past learns to feel safe. The shy kid finds love. The dull, boring office drone finds adventure and excitement with a vibrant love interest. The sky's the limit. So how do you put this in a game?

War Time

As with romance, war stories abound throughout history and mythology. Sometimes they are combined. War and romance, it seems, often coincide. But war stories often involve heroism and cowardice, adventure, danger, objectives, mistakes and catastrophes, wild triumphs, and lots of fighting and/or intrigue. No game player is a stranger to war as a theme, but how can you take stories that ring true and turn those into great game experiences? Can you create a great game set in a war scenario and add strong story elements to it? It's done in movies all the time. Why not in games? Why not a *Band of Brothers*, *Saving Private Ryan*, *Platoon*, *Basic*, or *The Guns of Navarone*, or even a *Schindler's List*? These movies had action, but they also had strong characters and character interactions, and, at least in some cases, changes the characters experienced as a consequence of the actions and situations that occurred.

Social Drama or Comedy

Social stories involve people in very specific social environments and generally also contain an outsider (sometimes the hero) who doesn't fit in and therefore exposes the society's foibles, weaknesses, and flaws. Where the hero is the outsider, he may attempt to fit into the society, or he may actually change the people around him by force of his personality. There are many examples, such as the old movie *Mr. Smith Goes to Washington*, in which an idealistic man becomes a U.S. Senator and ultimately has a profound effect on people around him; or *Meet Joe Black*, in which a mysterious man shakes up the lives of a family; or *Six Degrees of Separation*, in which a brash black man completely overturns the lives of a set of wealthy white society people. The examples are numerous. How might such a scenario work in a game? What kind of game might it be?

Character Flaws and Strengths

Characters are defined by a complex combination of qualities. Among the most important qualities of any complex character are his flaws. Character flaws contrast with the character's strengths, generally giving him depth and challenges in his life. Both flaws and strengths are basically traits of the character, and many examples can be found in the upcoming sections "Real People's Attributes" and "Character Traits." When creating a character, be sure to include strengths and flaws. These can be physical, psychological, or emotional strengths and weaknesses. The movie *Crash* was a great example of showing people with flaws who, nevertheless, could show great heroism, empathy, or grace, proving that a character can have both flaws and strengths, and sometimes it is simply circumstance that causes one or the other to be revealed.

Real People's Attributes

People are diverse and quirky and have traits that make them individuals. All people have unique qualities that make them different and similar qualities that they share with others. When you create characters in a story or game, you want to give them unique qualities that make them seem real. Some of this is done by how the characters are modeled, what they wear, and how they move. Some of it is done by their speech patterns and language or by tricks, such as giving them a facial tic or giving them something they do repetitively (for example, excessive blinking or adjusting their glasses). These little tricks are easy ways to distinguish characters and set them apart from others. But these tricks are merely surface effects.

To make deeper and more realistic characters, consider that real people are not static and one-dimensional. They have past histories. They display different identities and even act in contradictory ways. For instance, a murderous villain might be very kind to animals. A judge who upholds the law may go home, running stop signs along the way, and later steal music off the Internet. People also have hopes and dreams balanced against their fears, limitations, and past histories that affect their decisions. By thinking about the characters in a story or game, giving them traits, past histories, interests, special abilities, and skills, you can create situations in which they respond to events like real people, not like cardboard cutouts. Their beliefs and past experiences will determine how they respond to situations, what they say and how they say it, and how their outward actions may differ from their inner selves.

Some of this information will never appear directly. The game player may not actually know all the details you have created for your characters, but when you are creating the game's plot or even when you are creating a realistic response system for your characters, all this information will go into who they are, what they do, and why they do it.

In addition to the deeper level of character development, which is often revealed in how scenes play out and the choices your characters make, there are some less subtle tricks you can use to distinguish your characters and make them seem more believable and unique. These "tricks" are quick and easy ways to make a character unique, but they do not really create deep and believable characters on their own. Here are some examples:

Speech traits:

- They stutter.
- They speak very fast or very slow.
- They put words together in unusual ways: "A right dicey little mess, to be sure it is."
- They have a common word or expression: "Dang," "To be sure," or "Make it so."
- They have an accent or speak in a dialect: "Methinks yon laddie kin provide ye wi' fodder for yer mounts."

Behavioral traits:

- They ask a lot of questions, as if they can't trust what you tell them.
- They don't react well to change.
- They can't face the truth, and they live in denial or in a fantasy world.
- They get angry whenever their brother/sister/mother/father/best friend/ex/past love/ex-business partner/etc. is mentioned.
- They yell and curse whenever they don't get what they want.
- They are an upstanding citizen—for instance, a judge in the courts—who steals music off the Internet.
- They are the life of the party, and they yell at their wife and kids when they are at home.
- Their behavior changes dramatically around certain people or in certain situations.
- They constantly lie about themselves and their accomplishments to impress people or to get something from people.

Action traits:

- They light up a pipe or cigarette when nervous.
- They drink a lot.
- They sweat profusely.
- They pound the table when they get excited, or they stamp their foot.
- They tap their fingers.
- They scratch a lot.
- They turn to watch pretty girls whenever one walks by.
- They walk with a limp.
- They brush hair out of their face often or toss their head.
- They chew tobacco and spit.
- They smoke.
- They stand in a distinctive posture.
- The wring their hands.

Contrasting Traits

Contrasting traits are best revealed by actions that show the contrasting nature of a character. As such, they are a bit more complex than the simpler examples mentioned earlier. Some examples of contrasting traits are:

- They are tough and mean, but terrified of snakes, spiders, or rats.
- They are brutal and evil but have a soft spot for women and won't allow them to be harmed.
- They are meek and mild ordinarily but will fight like a tiger when cornered.
- They are a magnificent performer but shy and awkward when not performing.
- They are powerful and successful, but in private they are a mass of worries, anxieties, and low self-esteem.
- They are awkward and socially inept but have an intellect the size of the Pacific Ocean. (And they are great lovers.)
- They seem to have no emotional response to life, except when they are alone and they weep copiously. Or they write eloquent and scathing letters to the newspaper, signing them, "Anonymous."

Identities

People create identities as layers of personality they reveal to the world, often to cover or hide their real feelings. Some identities are adopted intentionally and serve as useful vehicles for being effective in life, especially in professional roles. For instance, a judge on the bench may be stern and formal, but he may have a bawdy sense of humor at a party.

However, often identities are like costumes people wear based on their fears, self-perceived or real limitations, needs, or life traumas. In many cases, the character is not even aware that he is presenting a false or cover identity to the world because it is so much ingrained in who he is and intertwined with what he wants to hide. Examples of such identities characters might adopt are:

- Someone with low self-esteem acting like a snob or presenting a superior air around others.
- Spending much of their energy seeking some idealized state of personality, when the activities they engage in are only used to create the image of a "seeker," and not really to effect change.
- Being critical of others when, in actuality, they are unhappy with their own performance.
- Habitually acting sad or morose in order to get sympathy and attention.
- Habitually acting brave when they are terrified.
- Acting as if they are very poor when they are rich but insecure about money.
- Basing their behavior on an attitude or belief that is really at odds with who they are, such as a licentious person condemning sin based on moral principles when they really want to behave sinfully.
- Blaming their misfortunes incorrectly on some trait of their own, such as that their nose is too big or they are too stupid, too ugly, or not sexy enough.
- Playing a habitual part or role in a relationship with others, such as the successful executive who becomes passive around his mother.
- The braggart who makes all kinds of claims about his prowess, but is in reality terribly insecure.
- The quiet character who appears shy and insecure but is really a devious genius studying the rest of humanity. Or maybe he is an alien sent to scout out an invasion or a serial killer watching for his next victim.

Creating Interesting Characters with the Character Diamond©

By David Freeman (www.freemangames.com)

NOTE

I've taken multiple Hollywood screenwriting classes. One I particularly enjoyed was by a guy named David Freeman. He's a classic deconstructionist and reminded me just how much I enjoy taking concepts apart. He focuses on adding emotion and depth to writing and making interesting characters, and his classes are highly inspiring. (I suggest you go!)

I was once invited to meet Michael Jackson at his Neverland home. He wanted to discuss some game/story ideas. I decided to test out Dave Freeman, so one time when I returned, I brought him with me. Watching him sit with Michael Jackson and deconstruct what his visions were was really something you had to see to believe. So this idea of laying out a map of idea components and then using them as springboards to make new ideas never seen before really works.

I asked David if he would share some of his ideas, so he has written this section of the chapter, which is his take on character creation. It's just a taste of what he teaches, but you can find out more at: http://www.freemangames.com or http://www.beyondstructure.com.

Character Diamonds

A key to making a major NPC interesting, or to making the character played by the gamer interesting, is to give that character a "Character Diamond."

Picture a diamond. Each corner of the Character Diamond represents a different major facet of the character's personality. These major facets determine the character's dialogue and actions.

Search the Internet for the script for *The Matrix* and locate the first scene, where Neo meets the Oracle. The Oracle has an interesting Diamond. Analyzing her actions and dialogue, we see her traits are:

- **An Easy Power.** She's so powerful that the agents either can't find her or avoid her out of fear. And she's quite secure and relaxed about this fact. Of course, in *The Matrix Reloaded*, we learn why the agents don't destroy her. However, someone who has only viewed the first film, *The Matrix*—whether they think the Oracle is human or whether they think she's a sentient computer creation—will assume that she's too powerful for the agents to find or too powerful to control.
- **Psychic and Intuitive.** She knows a lot about what Neo is thinking and that he's going to break a vase even before he does.
- **Motherly.** She bakes cookies and has kids in her living room bending spoons and whatnot. She speaks in a motherly way.
- **Revolutionary.** She says she's on Morpheus' side and supports his cause.
- **Wry Humor.** She makes a number of jokes that Neo doesn't get. For instance, after telling him that no one can tell him whether he's the One, she then proceeds to completely contradict this by looking in his mouth and ears and proclaiming that what she sees reveals that he isn't the One.

A Five-Cornered Diamond?

But wait—her Character Diamond has five corners! It's a Character Pentagon.

Thus, you see that, according to my private, offbeat geometry, a Character Diamond can have three, four, or five corners.

For a major NPC or a character played by a gamer, three traits is the minimum you need to make a character interesting; five is the maximum. If you have more than five major traits, then your character will turn to mush. No one will be able to get a sense of who the character is.

Whether a character has three, four, or five traits, for simplicity's sake, we can still call that combination a Character Diamond.

Clichés Suck

The way to make a character interesting is to make sure you don't have a grouping of traits on the Character Diamond that we've seen frequently before. For instance, I'm not aware of any movie with a character who has the same Diamond as the Oracle.

Let's say you have a Greek warrior, but you don't want him to be a cliché. He could be:

- **Sly.** He steals some food off of a merchant's cart.
- **Heroic.** He'll always jump into a fight for a just cause, no matter the odds against him.
- **Absentminded.** He forgets all sorts of minor details.
- **Aesthetic.** He likes to pause and enjoy a scenic vista or a striking sunrise. And he fights with incredible grace and style—it's wonderful to watch him.

Character Types

If you want to quickly have the player identify your character as a type (such as a Mafia type), you can still give your character one or two atypical traits so that the character isn't a total cliché.

To be honest, quite often when game designers create types, it's not because a type is required by the game, but just because they're thinking in terms of clichés, and they don't know how to create characters with interesting Diamonds.

What about Minor Characters?

They just need one or two traits, not three or more.

And That's All There Is?

Well, not quite—there are other aspects to characters besides Diamonds, such as techniques to make us like or hate them, ways to make us bond with them, or ways to give them depth. And some characters have fake personalities that cover up who they really are inside. But all of these are above and beyond the Character Diamond, which is the foundation of character creation.

A Trait Can Be Manifested in Action or Dialog

Remember, a trait can be manifested in action and/or dialog. But why did I have to restate that—didn't you read the header for this section?

An Example of a Character Diamond in a Sample Game Script

Let's say you're playing an action-adventure game with a swashbuckling *Three Musketeers* type of feeling.

Luther (an NPC) is a swashbuckler who is your rival—sort of. Sometimes you two are enemies; sometimes you get along…somewhat.

His Diamond is that he's:

- Cocky, ironic
- Incredibly athletic and a superb swordsman, beautiful to watch in action
- Touched by a deep sadness, which might be fueled by guilt
- Keenly insightful into and empathetic with people
- Sneaky/stealthy

The way Luther speaks, the choices he makes, even the way he fights—all these will be determined by his Diamond.

Some notes about the following example:

- There is no standard format for game scripts. The format for one game might be as different from the next as a porpoise is from pickled ham.

(continued)

Part IV

- In this example, I adapted a screenplay format. However, this format doesn't allow for all of the "if X happens, then Y happens" types of events that are often written into games, although one such example is included.
- The format must be further changed when the following scenarios are present: "If X happens, then either Y or Z happens." In this case, Y or Z might be randomly chosen by the computer—or, alternatively, selected due to whether events A, B, or C happened earlier in the game.
- And, of course, if the script branched in any way, even for a short time, the format would have to change again.

So what's below is a simplified game script, but not a particularly representative one. It does, however, offer an easy way to study an NPC Character Diamond.

I've worked on game scripts that were written with hot-linked documents, written using Excel, and created using formats you'd have to see to believe—all in an effort to try to assist programmers in programming all possible variations of "If X then Y" scenarios.

IN GAMEPLAY:

You're driving a stagecoach at night, on a muddy dirt road lined by dense trees. You're moving at top speed, since you heard Helena is in danger. You need to steer the stagecoach to avoid fallen logs, pits in the road, etc., which could overturn the coach.

CINEMATIC

NOTE *A cinematic is a section of the game where the player has no control and instead watches action unfold as if watching a short movie. Cinematics can either be pre-rendered or constructed in real time using the game engine.*

FOUR HIGHWAYMEN step out from the trees. They block your path. The horses stop and rear up. The highwaymen pull out pistols.

HIGHWAYMAN #1 (to you; coolly threatening) Sweet night for a ride.

Suddenly the end of a WHIP wraps around a branch, and Luther SWINGS OUT onto the road, holding onto the handle of the whip. In his swing, he KNOCKS OVER Highwayman #1.

HIGHWAYMAN #2 (to LUTHER) You!

LUTHER (to you) They all know me. But they never get the name right. (To Highwayman #2) It's not "you"; it's Luther.

RESUME GAMEPLAY

You and Luther together fight the four Highwaymen. He's extremely fast and fluid in his movements.

SCRIPTED SEQUENCE

NOTE *A scripted sequence is like a cinematic in that something is triggered to happen at a certain point—but you don't lose control of your character.*

When your sword is knocked from your hand by one of the Highwaymen, Luther TOSSES you his and pulls out a dagger.

RESUME GAMEPLAY

The two of you eventually defeat the Highwaymen.

CINEMATIC

You climb up on the carriage seat. Luther, like a cat, jumps up next to you, his dagger still drawn. Will he kill you?

RESUME GAMEPLAY

IF YOU DRAW YOUR SWORD [CHOICE 4a-1]:

–Then you two fight on the stagecoach for 45 seconds.

CINEMATIC

He then jumps off the stagecoach.

LUTHER (disappointed) Betrayal–it doesn't suit you. And it's far too familiar to me.

He SLAPS the rump of the lead horse, and the carriage VAULTS FORWARD.

[NOTE: CHOICE 4a-1 mandates Cinematic 13c-2 in Mission 13]

IF YOU DON'T DRAW YOUR SWORD [CHOICE4a-2]:

Luther waits for a moment.

CINEMATIC

LUTHER (small smile) My sword?

You hand him back the sword he had tossed you earlier.

LUTHER (serious) Helena is too pure. She'll crack under his torture. Godspeed.

He LEAPS off the carriage.

LUTHER I have my burden. Helena is yours.

He SLAPS the rump of the lead horse, and the carriage VAULTS FORWARD.

[NOTE: CHOICE 4a-2 mandates Cinematic 13c-3 in Mission 13]

NO MATTER WHICH OF THE ABOVE CHOICES IS MADE BY PLAYER:

RESUME GAMEPLAY

You must continue to steer the carriage around various obstacles without tipping it over. This time, your task is made more difficult because other HIGHWAYMEN occasionally shoot at you from between the trees. If you're hit, or if you don't kill at least one of them with your pistol, then you won't make it to Helena in time.

Clearing Up Some Possible Misunderstandings

The idea of creating Character Diamonds seems easy. Yet, in one of my most recent screenwriting classes, most of the students struggled to create interesting Diamonds. Here are few guidelines:

- Remember that we're only talking about major NPCs here, not minor ones. Minor NPCs don't need Diamonds–just one or two traits.
- In giving an NPC different traits, we're not trying to make a character well rounded by somehow balancing the traits. For instance, you don't give the character a strong trait–for example, being a leader–and then balance that with a soft trait–for example, loves furry little animals. Of course, there's no law against this if it serves your game.
- Nor is the idea to confuse the player as to who his friends are and who the bad guys are by making NPCs both friendly and hostile–unless you specifically want this effect.
- Nor is the idea to balance out likeable (or virtuous) and unlikable (or evil) traits–unless you want this effect.

(continued)

Part IV

A Game Script Is Not a Dartboard

One game designer told me that, if all you need is a colorful grouping of traits to make an interesting major NPC, then it sounds like you could put a list of traits up on the wall and throw darts at it and then create a Character Diamond by using whichever three, four, or five traits the darts hit.

He might be right—this method could potentially create an interesting character. I doubt, though, that it would create a character who would be useful in your game.

Picking the traits is where the art comes in. There are many factors that might weigh in on the selection, but ultimately it's up to the person who creates the character to make the difficult choices.

This is exactly why I and so many other professional writers study the work of writers we admire: to examine what choices they made and to try to discern the thinking behind those choices.

Personally, I give very serious consideration to the traits I pick when creating a major NPC's Diamond. I deliberate on the choices, since I, the other designers, and ultimately the players will have to live with these characters for a long time.

Dialogue Is Sometimes Not Your Friend

But it's not necessarily your enemy—more like an annoying uncle.

Because games are more about action than dialogue, it's usually a good idea to pick traits that can be shown without dialogue, but instead through the character's choices, actions, animations, taunts, clothing, signature gestures, and the way he fights. In general, the more traits that can be revealed without dialogue, the better.

Character Traits

Characters in life and in stories always have specific traits that tend to define their personalities. Character traits do not live in a vacuum, but are interrelated with the other elements of the whole person. Some seem to be inherent to the person. Others may have been affected by his history and life experiences. Some traits are physical, and some are emotional or personality based. Here is a list of many different character traits. Can you think of more?

- Able
- Absentminded
- Abstract thinker
- Abusive
- Academic
- Accepting
- Accommodating
- Accomplishing
- Accountable
- Accurate
- Activist
- Adaptable
- Addictive/addicted
- Adventurous
- Aesthetic
- Affectionate
- Aggressive
- Airhead
- Alcoholic
- Alert
- Alien
- Aloof
- Ambitious
- Amiable
- Amputee
- Anal
- Analytical
- Angry
- Annoying
- Antisocial
- Anxious
- Apathetic
- Appreciative
- Appropriate
- Argumentative
- Aristocratic

- Arrogant
- Articulate
- Artistic
- Ashamed
- Aspiring
- Assertive
- Athletic
- Authoritarian
- Available
- Avenger
- Average
- Avoids attention
- Avoids conflict
- Aware
- Awkward
- Axe grinder
- Backs away from commitment
- Bad
    - Attitude
    - Behavior
    - Body odor
    - Breath
    - Digestion
    - Memory
    - Sense of style
    - Teeth
- Balanced
- Beatnik
- Beautiful
- Belligerent
- Big-hearted
- Bigoted
- Biker
- Bitchy
- Black sense of humor
- Blaming
- Bland
- Boastful
- Boisterous
- Bold
- Bombastic
- Bookish
- Boring
- Bossy
- Boyish
- Brave
- Bright
- Broken
- Brotherly
- Bullsh*tter
- Bully
- Buoyant
- Burned out
- Busy
- By-the-book thinker
- Callous
- Calm
- Cantankerous
- Capable
- Capacity
- Careless
- Casual
- Causal/initiating
- Caustic
- Cautious
- Charismatic
- Charitable
- Chaste
- Cheap
- Cheerful
- Childish
- Chiseler
- Clairvoyant
- Class conscious
- Clean
- Clean-cut
- Clear communicator
- Clear thinker
- Clever
- Clumsy
- Cold fish
- Collegiate
- Comedian
- Comfortable with ambiguity
- Commanding presence
- Commanding voice
- Committed
- Compassionate
- Competitive
- Composed
- Compulsive
- Con artist
- Conceited
- Concerned
- Concerned with trivia
- Conciliatory

- Concise
- Condescending
- Confident
- Conformist
- Confused
- Congratulatory
- Conservative
- Considerate
- Consistent
- Conspiratorial
- Constructive
- Content
- Conventional
- Convict
- Cool
- Cooperative
- Corporate
- Corrupt
- Cosmopolitan
- Courageous
- Courteous
- Cowboy
- Craftsman
- Crazy
- Creative
- Cries easily or a lot
- Crippled/injured
- Crude
- Cruel
- Crusader
- Cultist
- Cultured/cultivated
- Cunning
- Curious
- Cynical
- Dainty
- Daring
- Dark
- Deceitful
- Decisive
- Defensive
- Defiant
- Delicate
- Deluded
- Demanding
- Democratic
- Dependable
- Dependent
- Depressed
- Destructive
- Detached
- Determined
- Devious
- Diligent
- Diplomatic
- Direct
- Disagreeable
- Discerning
- Discouraged
- Discreet
- Disfigured
- Dishonest
- Disinterested
- Disorganized
- Dissatisfied
- Distrustful
- Ditto head
- Docile
- Dogmatic
- Dominating/domineering
- Dorky
- Dramatic
- Dreamer
- Drifter
- Drug user
- Dry
- Dynamic
- Earthy
- Easily
  - Bored
  - Distracted
  - Embarrassed
  - Frustrated
  - Offended
- Easygoing
- Eccentric
- Effective
- Effeminate
- Effete
- Egotistical
- Emotional
- Empathetic
- Emphatic
- Empirical thinker
- Encouraging
- Encyclopedic or eidetic memory

- Energetic
- Enlightened
- Enthusiastic
- Epileptic
- Eruptive
- Ethical
- Evasive
- Evil
- Excited
- Exhibitionistic
- Expert
- Expressive
- Extravagant
- Extroverted
- Fair
- Fair-minded
- Fake
- Fanatic
- Fancy
- Fascinated
- Fascist
- Fast learner
- Fatherly
- Fearful
- Fearless
- Feels sorry for self
- Feminine
- Fickle
- Fighter
- Flake
- Flamboyant
- Flappable
- Flexible
- Flippant
- Focused
- Foggy thinker
- Follower
- Foolish
- Forgetful
- Formal
- Freaky
- Freeloader
- Friendly
- Frivolous
- Frugal
- Frustrated
- Fugitive
- Fun-loving
- Funny
- Fussy
- Gallant
- Gambler
- Gangster
- Generalist
- Generous
- Genius
- Genteel
- Gentle
- Gentleman
- Giggly
- Girlish
- Given to fantasy
- Glamorous
- Goal-oriented
- Gold digger
- Good at detail
- Good at sex
- Good judge of character
- Good listener
- Good self-understanding
- Good sense of humor
- Good-natured
- Gossip
- Graceful
- Gracious
- Grandiose
- Grandstander
- Grateful
- Greedy
- Gregarious
- Grief
- Grotesque
- Grouchy
- Grubby
- Grudge holder
- Grumbler
- Guilt-ridden
- Gullible
- Gypsy
- Handsome
- Happy
- Hard
- Hard-boiled
- Hard-headed
- Hardworking
- Has deadly disease or condition

- Has poor self-image
- Has seizures
- Has skin condition
- Headstrong
- Healthy
- Hears voices
- Heartbroken
- Heavy drinker
- Helpful
- Helpless
- Hesitant
- Hick
- High frustration tolerance
- High standards
- Highly controlled
- High-strung
- Hippy
- Holy
- Homeless
- Honest
- Honorable
- Hospitable
- Hostile
- Hot-tempered
- Humanitarian
- Humble
- Humorless
- Humorous
- Hypochondriac
- Iconoclastic
- Idealistic
- Ignorant
- Illiterate
- Ill-mannered
- Ill-tempered
- Imaginary companions
- Imaginative
- Immature
- Impassive
- Impatient
- Impeccable
- Impertinent
- Impractical
- Impudent
- Impulsive
- Inconsistent
- Indecisive
- Independent
- Indifferent
- Indirect
- Individualistic
- Industrious
- Inferiority complex
- Inflexible
- Influence peddler
- Inhibited
- Innovative
- Insane
- Insecure
- Insensitive
- Insincere
- Insubordinate
- Integrated
- Intellectual
- Intelligent
- Intense
- Interested
- Introverted
- Intuitive
- Inventive
- Investing
- Irrational
- Irresponsible
- Irritable
- Isolated
- Jealous/envious
- Jerk
- Job hopper
- Jock
- Joyful
- Judicious
- Jumps to conclusions
- Juvenile
- Keen
- Kind
- Knowledgeable
- Lackadaisical
- Lacks integrity
- Ladylike
- Laughs inappropriately
- Lazy
- Leader
- Lethargic
- Level-headed
- Liar
- Liberal

- Light
- Lighthearted
- Listless
- Literal thinker
- Logical
- Lonely
- Loner
- Losing
  - Fortune
  - Hearing
  - Keys
  - Memory
  - Mind
  - Sense of humor
  - Sight
- Loud
- Lovable
- Loving
- Loyal (to family, friends, country, employers)
- Lucky
- Macho
- Malicious
- Maniac
- Manic
- Manic depressive
- Manipulative
- Masculine
- Masochistic
- Masterful
- Materialistic
- Mature
- Mean
- Mediocre
- Melodramatic
- Mentally healthy
- Messy
- Middle class
- Mild-mannered
- Militaristic
- Mindful
- Mischievous
- Miserly
- Missionary
- Modernistic
- Modest
- Money-oriented
- Monotonous voice
- Moody
- Moral
- Morbid
- Motherly
- Motivated
- Mundane
- Musical
- Mysterious
- Naïve
- Name dropper
- Narcissistic
- Narcoleptic
- Narrow-minded
- Nationalistic
- Natural leader
- Neat
- Needs job satisfaction
- Negative
- Nerdy
- Nervous
- Neurotic
- Nice
- No style
- Nonconformist
- Obedient to authority
- Objective
- Obnoxious
- Obscene
- Observant
- Obsessive
- Obsessive-compulsive
- Obstinate
- One-track mind
- Open-minded
- Opinionated
- Opportunist
- Optimistic
- Orderly
- Organizer
- Outlaw
- Overachiever
- Overactive
- Overly serious
- Overweight/obese/fat
- Pagan
- Paranoid
- Party animal
- Passionate
- Passive

- Patient
- Patrician
- Patriotic
- Peaceful
- Peevish
- People pleaser
- People-oriented
- Perceptive
- Perfectionist
- Perky
- Persevering
- Persistent
- Personable
- Persuasive
- Pessimistic
- Philosophical
- Phony
- Photographic memory
- Pious
- Pitiful
- Plain
- Playboy
- Pleasant
- Pleasing
- Poised
- Polished
- Political
- Poor
- Poor impulse control
  - Anger
  - Drugs
  - Food
  - Gambling
  - Sex
  - Shopping
  - Video games
- Popular
- Positive
- Possessive
- Practical
- Practical joker
- Pragmatic
- Precise
- Preoccupied
- Present-oriented
- Prestige-oriented
- Presumptuous
- Pretentious
- Pretty
- Prim
- Procrastinator
- Prodigy
- Productive
- Professional
- Promiscuous
- Proper
- Proud
- Provincial
- Prudent
- Prudish
- Psychic
- Psychotic
- Punctual
- Pushy
- Quick
- Quick-tempered
- Quick-witted
- Quiet
- Rabble rouser
- Racist
- Radical
- Rash
- Rational
- Realistic
- Reasonable
- Rebellious
- Reckless
- Redundant
- Reflective
- Reformer
- Relativistic
- Relentless
- Reliable
- Religious
- Resentful
- Reserved
- Resilient
- Resourceful
- Respectful
- Responsible
- Rich
- Rich inner life
- Rigid
- Robust
- Role player
- Romantic

- Rude
- Rule follower
- Ruler/leader/king/queen/etc.
- Ruthless
- Sad
- Sadistic
- Sagacious
- Saintly
- Sarcastic
- Savvy
- Scapegoater
- Scarred
- Schemer
- Schizoid
- Schizophrenic
- Secretive
- Secure
- Seductive
- Seedy
- Seeks approval
- Seeks attention
- Seeks conflict
- Self-absorbed/narcissistic
- Self-blaming
- Self-caring
- Self-centered
- Self-confident
- Self-conscious
- Self-debasing
- Self-deluded
- Self-denying
- Self-destructive
- Self-educated
- Selfish
- Self-motivated
- Self-reliant
- Self-righteous
- Self-satisfied
- Self-seeking
- Self-starter
- Sense of mission
- Sensible
- Sensitive
- Sentimental
- Serene
- Serious
- Sexually obsessed
- Sexy
- Shallow
- Sharing
- Sharp senses (sight, hearing, smell, and so on)
- Short
- Short attention span
- Showman
- Shrewd
- Shy
- Simple
- Simple-minded
- Simplistic
- Sincere
- Sisterly
- Skeptical
- Skillful
- Slothful
- Small-town
- Smart
- Smug
- Snob
- Social climber
- Socially militant
- Soft
- Soft-spoken
- Sophisticated
- Sour
- Speculative
- Spiritual
- Spiteful
- Stable
- Stereotype thinker
- Stern
- Stingy
- Storyteller
- Straight-forward
- Straight-laced
- Street smart
- Stressed
- Strong
- Strong achievement drive
- Stubborn
- Studious
- Stupid
- Stylish
- Suave
- Subservient
- Successful
- Suicidal

- Sulky
- Super intelligent
- Superficial
- Superstitious
- Suppressed anger
- Survivor
- Sympathetic
- Sympathy seeker
- Synthesizer
- Tactful
- Takes initiative
- Talented
- Talkative
- Talks to self
- Talks with hands
- Tall
- Team player
- Tease
- Temperamental
- Tender
- Tense
- Theatrical
- Theorist
- Thief
- Thin-skinned
- Thorough
- Thoughtful
- Threatening
- Thrifty
- Thrill seeker
- Thrilling
- Throws tantrums
- Tight
- Time conscious
- Timid
- Tireless
- Tolerant
- Tough
- Traditionalist
- Trashy
- Trusting
- Trustworthy
- Ugly
- Uncomfortable (situational)
- Uncomfortable with ambiguity
- Uncooperative
- Underachiever
- Unflappable
- Unhappy
- Unhealthy
- Uninhibited
- Unselfish
- Unstable
- Uptight
- Vain
- Vampish
- Verbally adept
- Vibrant
- Violent
- Visionary
- Visual
- Volatile
- Volunteers
- Wacky
- Weak
- Wealthy
- Well-dressed
- Well-groomed
- Well-prepared
- Wild
- Willing
- Wise
- Withdrawn
- Witty
- Workaholic
- Worldly
- Worrier
- Worthless
- Youthful
- Zealot
  - Ideological
  - Political
  - Racial
  - Religious/spiritual
- Zombie

Quirks

Quirks are odd individual traits that fall outside the norm in some way. They are highly individualized and unique to a particular character. Not that other characters might not have similar quirks, but the nature of a quirk is that it is not a common behavior and is probably based on some habit, behavior, or past history of the character that is specific to that character alone. For instance, a ballet dancer might stand in one of the ballet positions even at casual moments. A cowboy might walk with a bowlegged swagger. An electrical engineer might be always fiddling with a notepad or calculator. A young woman might always watch everything intently because she grew up in an alcoholic household and learned to be hypervigilant, and so on. The following list suggests just a few quirks a person might have, but not why they would have those quirks. If you are doing a thorough job of character development, you can also come up with a reason why a character has these quirks:

- Adjusts neck
- Adjusts sleeves, collar, belt, tie, etc.
- Always adds a bit of powder to her beverages (and claims it is a health tonic)
- Always agrees with everything
- Always asks people to repeat themselves—is either deaf or not very attentive
- Always carries a big wad of money in pockets/purse
- Always carries a hidden weapon
- Always has a dark suntan, even in the deep of winter
- Always has a drink—soda or coffee, etc.
- Always has a glass or a beer in hand
- Always has a mild sunburn
- Always plugs her favorite politician (or guild, royal family member, etc.)
- Always seen with certain items—such as certain jewelry or Laverne's L on her sweaters from *Laverne and Shirley*, Michael Jackson's single glove, and Indiana Jones' hat and leather jacket.
- Always snacking on something (peanuts, raisins, candies, etc.)
- Always starts sentences with some catch phrase: "Ummm," "Here's the thing," or "Don't get me wrong…"
- Always wears shades
- Apologizes a lot
- Asks a PC for a lock of his or her hair
- Avoids eye contact
- Believes firmly that the culture is degenerating and always talks about the "old days"
- Bites nails
- Blinks obsessively
- Blows his nose into his hand and then shakes it clean
- Boasts about his sexual exploits (real or imagined)
- Breaks into dance moves in the middle of doing something normal
- Can add a column of figures in his head
- Carries lots of bags, parcels, and packages
- Changes the subject
- Checks in mirrors and windows for people who might be tailing him
- Chews fingernails (or toenails)
- Chokes or swallows something wrong in the middle of conversation
- Cleans/trims/files fingernails in public
- Collects something strange, such as a hit man who collects dolls
- Constantly has to brush hair out of face
- Constantly refers to her (always present) "friend" (who only she can see)
- Constantly refers to herself in the third person
- Does various stretches, such as yoga stretches, at random times
- Doesn't finish thoughts
- Doodles when talking with someone or on the phone
- Drums fingers
- Eats other people's leftovers (without asking)
- Eternal pessimist/optimist
- Farts or belches a lot
- Flips coins or rolls them across knuckles
- Freaks out and runs away in the middle of a conversation (maybe she remembers an important appointment or maybe it is more sinister)

- Grins constantly
- Groans, grunts, and emits other monosyllabic utterances
- Has a bad cold or a chronic sinus condition
- Has a distinctive laugh (Woody Woodpecker, Horshack, etc.)
- Has a nasty rash
- Has a noticeable accent
- Has a one-track mind
- Has a peculiar walking style
- Has a pouch of candied giblets
- Has a very hairy neck
- Has bird droppings on his turban
- Has fleas
- Has Parkinson's disease and shakes
- Has shifty eyes
- Has strong body odor
- Has Tourette's syndrome and makes random statements, possibly obscenities
- Has trouble hearing
- Hates going to new restaurants
- Hocks loogies and spits
- Hypervigilant
- Impresses all with the ability to play music through her nose
- Injures himself while talking to the PCs
- Interrupts people
- Is a serious flirt
- Is excessively cheap/miserly
- Is extremely clumsy
- Is injured (broken bone, recent burn, etc.)
- Is never without her pet mouse (or rodent of choice)
- Is really awkward around the opposite gender
- Is rude to waiters and waitresses
- Juts out lower lip
- Laughs nervously
- Likes a particular currency better than others and insists that people change their money first
- Looks at watch frequently
- Looks people intently in the eyes
- Loves to dance
- Makes funny or odd faces
- Makes specific hand gestures, such as the "finger gun" or fingers to represent "air quotes"
- Makes strange movements with mouth
- Mangles people's names (calls Jane Julie, Bob Bill, etc.)
- Mumbles to others
- Mumbles to self
- Odd juxtapositions—a boxer afraid of spiders
- Often disappears into a bathroom, claiming a weak bladder
- Paces back and forth
- Pats pockets to be sure something is still there (wallet, gun in shoulder holster, etc.)
- Picks nose
- Picks teeth a lot (with a knife?)
- Plays with ear
- Plays with hair
- Plays with some talisman, such as a pet rock
- Purses lips when nervous or when thinking about something
- Remembers one of the PCs from school (or a similar chapter in the character's life)
- Repeats a specific phrase often: "Capiche?" "Am I right or am I right?" "I'm all over that!" "Gollum," "Okie dokie," "Groovy," "No way," "Like," etc.
- Rocks back and forth or side to side while standing
- Rocks in chair
- Scratches a lot
- Scratches butt or crotch
- Sits or stands oddly slouched
- Sits or stands very erect
- Sits with back to corner in restaurants and other public places
- Smells really good (subtle perfume, very clean, whatever)
- Some unusual aspect of apparel—one glove, fur-lined jacket, mismatched socks, or a bedraggled old hat on an otherwise spiffy outfit
- Spaces out
- Spins ring on finger
- Spins the cylinder of a revolver
- Stops in front of mirrors (and reflective windows) to look at herself
- Stumbles into one of the characters while walking (maybe a pickpocket, maybe not)
- Stutters, especially when under duress
- Talks obsessively

- Talks very loudly
- Talks very softly
- Taps foot
- Tells a lot of jokes, perhaps at inappropriate times
- Thinks the world is far too loud
- Throws things—trash into trashcan, for instance, or rocks at passersby, etc.
- Tosses an item into the air repeatedly—a coin, knife, rock, etc.
- Twitches (eyes, mouth, hands, fingers, knee, leg)
- Uses clichés a lot
- Uses words in odd ways
- Wears a turban and nothing else to bed every night
- Wears a turban and nothing else until noon each day
- Wears gaudy jewelry
- Wears hair in an unusual and distinctive style
- Whistles (tuneless or tuneful)
- Yawns under very specific circumstances

Moods

People display a wide range of emotional states, which can change rapidly in any given circumstances. People's moods and emotional responses can be surprising, especially when their responses are based on misconceptions and miscommunications. This is very common, and a person can become angry, sad, or scared instantly, depending on how they interpret a situation, action, or statement.

This list contains a wide range of mood descriptors. Use them as a reference and consider the range of available moods any given character might have. For instance, some people are predominantly positive and tend to stay on the happy side of life. Others are morose and tend to be bitter, cynical, and angry. Most people are in between, and almost all people have a wide range, except for some clinically disturbed people with flattened emotional responses. On the other hand, some clinically crazy folks can jump from extreme highs to extreme lows in a heartbeat. But the way to use this list is simply as a guide for the kinds of emotions and associated behaviors your characters may display. Note that these descriptors are neither scientific nor a specific emotional state (in every case). However, they do indicate an attitude or emotion that could be useful in developing a character's responses to situations:

- Accepting
- Admiring
- Adventurous
- Afraid/fearful
- Aggressive
- Agitated
- Alienated
- Aloof
- Altruistic
- Amazed
- Ambitious
- Amorous
- Angry
- Anxious
- Apathetic
- Apologetic
- Appreciative
- Approving
- Arrogant
- Ashamed
- Assertive
- Assuming
- Aware
- Awestruck
- Balanced
- Bigoted
- Blissful
- Bored
- Burned out
- Caring
- Charitable
- Cheerful
- Civil
- Committed
- Compassionate
- Competitive

Part IV

- Complacent
- Condescending
- Confident
- Confused
- Contemptuous
- Content
- Cooperative
- Courageous
- Courteous
- Creative
- Credible
- Critical
- Cruel
- Curious
- Cynical
- Decisive
- Delighted
- Depressed
- Desirous
- Despairing
- Detached
- Determined
- Devoted
- Disappointed
- Disillusioned
- Distracted
- Distressed
- Doubtful
- Dysfunctional
- Eager
- Ecstatic
- Embarrassed
- Empathetic
- Envious
- Excited/Enthusiastic
- Expansive
- Extravagant
- Fair
- Forgiving
- Frightened
- Frugal
- Frustrated
- Generous
- Glad
- Glamorous
- Gloating/self-satisfied
- Gluttonous
- Grateful
- Gratified
- Greedy
- Grief-stricken
- Grumpy
- Guilty
- Happy
- Hateful
- Homesick
- Hopeful
- Horny
- Hostile
- Humble
- Hysterical
- Impatient
- Indecisive
- Indifferent
- Inhibited
- Ironic
- Irritable
- Irritated
- Jealous
- Joyful
- Kind
- Lonely
- Longing
- Loving
- Lustful
- Mad
- Manic
- Mischievous
- Morose
- Motherly
- Nostalgic
- Obedient
- Obsessed
- Open-minded
- Optimistic
- Panicky
- Paralyzed with fear
- Passionate
- Patient
- Pitying
- Predatory
- Prideful
- Relieved
- Reluctant
- Remorseful
- Reproachful

- Resentful
- Resigned
- Resistant
- Resourceful
- Restless
- Righteous
- Sad
- Satisfied
- Self-loathing
- Shamed
- Shy
- Surprised
- Suspicious
- Sweet
- Sympathetic
- Tender
- Vengeful
- Wistful
- Worried

HOBBIES

Sometimes characters can be further differentiated by the things they do for fun. Imagine a stockbroker who likes mountaineering versus one who likes stamp collecting. Just the difference in hobbies gives you a very strong impression of how these two stockbrokers would differ from each other. What about a stockbroker who likes mountaineering *and* stamp collecting? Or the general of an army who plays chess versus one who likes to go out drinking and whoring?

With this list, you can easily give your characters more depth, even if you don't *show* the hobby in the game. Just knowing that the character has this hobby tells you a lot about him or her and can help you create more realistic actions and dialog for the character. Just pick a couple at random and imagine how your character would be if that were his hobby.

- Acrobatics
- Acting
- Air hockey
- Alchemy
- Amateur radio
- Animal breeding
- Anthropology
- Archeology
- Archery
- Architecture
- Armory
- Astrology
- Astronomy
- Auctioneering
- Auto mechanics
- Auto restoration
- Aviation
- Babysitting
- Backpacking
- Badminton
- Baking
- Ballet
- Balloonography
- Barbecuing
- Baseball
- Basketball
- Basketry
- Baton twirling
- Beadwork
- Beekeeping
- Begging
- Berry picking
- Bicycling
- Billiards
- Bingo
- Bird watching
- Black powder shooting
- Blacksmithing
- Board games
- Bobsledding
- Bocce
- Body painting
- Bodybuilding
- Bonsai
- Bookbinding
- Boomeranging
- Bowling
- Boxcar hitching

Part IV

- Break dancing
- Breeding
  - Dogs/cats/birds/horses, etc.
  - Plants (including orchids)
- Bungee jumping
- Butchering
- Butter churning
- Cake decorating
- Calisthenics
- Calligraphy
- Camping
- Candy striping
- Canning
- Canoeing
- Card playing
- Carpentry
- Cars
- Cartography
- Cartooning
- Caving
- Ceramics
- Chemistry
- Cinema
- Cinematography
- Clamming and crabbing
- Clowning
- Coaching (sports)
- Collecting
  - 1965 Volkswagen Beetles
  - Acoustical record players
  - Americana
  - Antiques
  - Art
  - Autographs
  - Balls
  - Bed Pans
  - Beer Cans
  - Bells
  - Belt buckles
  - Bolo ties
  - Bookmarks
  - Books
  - Bottle Caps
  - Bottles
  - Business cards
  - Campaign buttons
  - Celebrity handshakes
  - Christmas decorations
  - Cigarette lighters
  - Clocks
  - Coins
  - College paraphernalia
  - Computers
  - Coupons
  - Crayons
  - Credit cards
  - Dolls
  - Elements
  - Feathers
  - Figurines
  - Flags
  - Fonts and clip art
  - Fossils
  - Guns
  - Hair ornaments
  - Handkerchiefs
  - Hat pins
  - Hats
  - Hobbies
  - Hotel artifacts
  - Insects
  - Jell-O molds
  - Jewelry
  - Key chains
  - Keys
  - Kitchen utensils
  - Knickknacks
  - Knives
  - Lapel pins or brooches
  - Lawn ornaments
  - Leaves
  - License plates
  - Maps
  - Matchbooks
  - Memorabilia
  - Military paraphernalia
  - Miniature spoons
  - Mouse pads
  - Mugs
  - Music
  - Neckerchief slides
  - Neckerchiefs
  - Oddities
  - Other

- Outhouse artifacts
- Outhouse graffiti
- Papal paraphernalia
- Periodicals
- Photographs
- Plates
- Pop cans
- Postcards
- Postmarks
- Refrigerator magnets
- Rental properties
- Rocks
- Salt and pepper shakers
- Shells
- Soap scraps
- Software
- Soil
- Sports memorabilia
- Stamps
- Statistics
- Stocks and bonds
- Stuffed animals
- Thimbles
- Ties
- Tools
- Toys
- Trivia
- T-shirts
- Uniforms
- Videos
- Wines
- Winter camp artifacts
- Wire samples
- Wood samples
- Writing implements

- Comedy (standup)
- Comedy writing
- Community service
- Competitive mathematics
- Computer programming
- Conservation and ecology
- Continuing education
- Cooking
- Cosmetology
- Cosmology
- Cricket
- Crocheting
- Croquet
- Cross-country skiing
- Crossword puzzles
- Cruising for the opposite sex
- Curling
- Dancing
  - Ballet
  - Ballroom
  - Country Line
  - Ethnic
    - African
    - Afro/Cuban
    - Balinese
    - Belly dance/Middle Eastern
    - Chinese
    - Flamenco
    - Indian
    - Japanese
  - Folk
  - Modern
  - Polka
  - Salsa
  - Square
  - Tap
  - Trance
- Darts
- Dating
- Debate
- Decoupage
- Diapering
- Diving
- Dodgeball
- Dog grooming
- Dog training
- Dominoes
- Downhill skiing
- Drawing
- Drinking
- Dry walling
- Eating human flesh
- Egg decorating
- Electricity
- Electronics
- Electroplating
- Embroidery
- Engraving
- Exercise
- Falconry

Part IV

- Fantasy role playing
- Farming
- Fashion design
- Fencing
- Field hockey
- Fife and drum
- Figure skating
- Fine dining
- Fire eating
- Firemanship
- First aiding
- Fishing
- Flea marketing
- Flower arranging
- Football
- Foursquare
- Frisbee
- Furniture refinishing
- Futurism
- Gaelic Football
- Gambling
- Game designing
- Gaming
- Gardening
    - Flowers
    - Vegetable
- Genealogy
- Genetic engineering
- Geography
- Geology
- Glass blowing
- Grain milling
- Graphic arts
- Gymnastics
- Hackey sack
- Handball
- Hang gliding
- Heraldry
- Hiking
- Historical reenactment
- History
- Hog calling
- Home decorating
- Hopscotch
- Horsemanship
- Horseshoe pitching and quoits
- Hot-air ballooning
- House painting
- Hunting
- Hurling (Irish sport)
- Hydrology
- Hypnosis
- Ice climbing
- Ice hockey
- Ice sculpting
- Ice skating
- Indian lore
- Internet surfing and chatting
- Inventing
- Investing
- Jai alai
- Journalism
- Jousting
- Juggling
- Karate
- Kayaking
- Kickball
- Kite flying
- Knitting
- Lacrosse
- Landscaping
- Language (foreign)
- Language (signing)
- Lapidary
- Lawn darts
- Leatherwork
- Lexicography
- Lexicology
- Lithography
- Lumberjacking
- Machine restoration
- Macramé
- Magic and prestidigitation
- Making
    - Barrels
    - Candles
    - Candy
    - Cider
    - Clocks
    - Costumes
    - Dioramas
    - Furniture
    - Gum
    - Jerky
    - Jewelry
    - Light bulbs

    - Musical instruments
    - Paper
    - Progeny
    - Puzzles
    - Radios
    - Rope
    - Rugs
    - Sand castles
    - Sausage
    - Soap
    - Soft drinks
    - Time capsules
- Marbles
- Martial arts
    - Jujitsu
        - Brazilian
        - Gracie system
        - Japanese
    - Karate, many styles including:
        - Goju Ryu
        - Kenpo
        - Kyokushinkai
        - Shorin-Ryu
        - Shotokan
    - Aikido
    - Bagua
    - Boxing (Western style)
    - Capoeira
    - Escrima
    - Fencing
    - Haganah
    - Hapkido
    - Hsing Yi (Xing Yi)
    - Jeet Kune Do
    - Judo
    - Kapu Kuialua (Hawaiian "bone-breaking" style)
    - Kendo
    - Krav Maga
    - Kuk Sool Wan (modern Korean fighting style)
    - Kung Fu (many styles)
    - Lan Shou
    - Modern pragmatic hybrid martial arts, such as those inspired by the Ultimate Fighting Championships (UFC):
        - ASAX
        - Jo Son Do
        - Moo Yea Do
        - Pitfighting
        - Ruas Vale Tudo
        - SAFTA
        - Shootfighting
        - Tung Kung Kalan
    - Muay Thai (Thai boxing)
    - Ninjutsu (Ninja training)
    - Pencak Silat (Indonesian style)
    - Russian Sambo
    - Savate
    - Street fighting
    - Sumo
    - Tae Kwon Do
    - Taebo
    - Tai Chi (taiji) Chuan (different forms)
    - Testa (African "big knuckle" head fighting)
    - Wing Chun
    - Wrestling (Greco-Roman or others)
- Masonry
- Metal casting
- Metal detecting
- Metalwork
- Meteorology
- Miniature golf
- Mining
- Model railroading
- Modeling
    - Cars
    - Clay
    - Planes
    - Rockets
    - Ships
    - Ships in a bottle
    - Yourself
- Motorboating
- Motorcycling
- Mountain biking
- Mountaineering
- Mushroom picking
- Music (creating)
- Music (DJ)
- Music (listening)
- Mythology
- Needlepoint
- Off-road vehicle driving

Part IV

- Old-time radio
- One-armed paper hanging
- Orienteering
- Origami
- Pageantry
- Paintball
- Painting pictures
- Pantomiming
- Paperclip sorting
- Papier-mâché
- Parade marching
- Parasailing
- Partying
- Personal recordkeeping
- Pet raising
- Pet showing
- Philosophy
- Photograph developing
- Photography
- Picnicking
- Picture framing
- Pigeon raising
- Pinball
- Ping pong
- Pioneering
- Play grounding
- Playing a musical instrument
- Plumbing
- Poetry
- Pogo sticking
- Policing
- Politics
- Pottery
- Public speaking and lecturing
- Puzzle solving
- Quilting
- Racing
  - Automobiles
  - Bicycles
  - BMX
  - Greyhounds
  - Horses
  - Radio-controlled cars
  - Running
  - Sled dogs
  - Speed skating
  - Yacht
- Racquetball
- Radio-controlled airplanes
- Rafting
- Rappelling
- Rapping
- Reading
- Refereeing or judging sports contests
- Religious study
- Riflery
- Rock climbing
- Rock polishing
- Roller hockey
- Roller skating
- Rollerblading
- Roofing
- Rowing
- Running and jogging
- Sailing
- Scatology
- Scatterball
- Scouting
- Scuba diving
- Sculpture
- Search and rescue
- Sewing
- Shopping
- Short-wave listening
- Signaling
- Silk-screening
- Silversmithing
- Singing
- Skateboarding
- Skittles
- Skydiving
- Snorkeling
- Snowboarding
- Snowmobiling
- Snowshoeing
- Soccer
- Social activism
- Softball
- Spectator sports
- Spinning yarn
- Spying
- Squash
- Stained-glass art
- Stilt walking

- Stone tooling
- Storytelling
- Sunbathing
- Surfing
- Sweepstakes entering
- Swimming
- Taxidermy
- Taxidermy with humans
- Tennis
- Tetherball
- Theater
- Tiling
- Tobogganing and sledding
- Topiary
- Track and field
- Tracking and stalking
- Trading
  - Magic cards
  - Patches
  - Sports cards
- Tie-dying
- Trap and skeet
- Trapping
- Travel gaming
- Traveling
- Treasure hunting
- Tree climbing
- Tree tapping
- Unicycling
- Ventriloquism
- Video gaming
- Visiting
  - Amusement parks
  - Canadian provinces
  - Canals
  - Castles
  - College campuses
  - Continents
  - Counties
  - Countries
  - County courthouses
  - Covered bridges
  - Cruise ships
  - Friends and relatives
  - Frontiers
  - Hard Rock Cafes
  - Highpoints
  - Historical sites
  - Interstate highways
  - Lighthouses
  - McDonald's restaurants
  - Museums
  - National park operations
  - Outhouses
  - Peak bagging
  - Sports stadiums
  - State capitols
  - State tri-points
  - States
  - Tourist traps
  - U.S. highways
  - White Castle restaurants
- Volleyball
- Walking
- Wally-ball
- Water polo
- Weaving
- Weightlifting
- Welding
- Whoring
- Wilderness survival
- Windsurfing
- Wood burning
- Wood carving
- Woodworking
- Wrestling
- Writing
  - Diary
  - Letters
  - Novels
  - Stories
- Xylography
- Yo-yoing
- Yodeling
- Zymurgy

Religious and Spiritual Practices

People's religious and spiritual beliefs can have a profound effect on how they behave, so it's worth considering the various types of beliefs that are possible. Some of them are fairly obscure, but perhaps looking into them more deeply can suggest some interesting character traits. At any rate, here's a sample of world religions and spiritual practices.

- Abacua
- Agnostic
- Ancient Egyptian Pantheon
- Ancient Greek Pantheon
- Ancient Roman Pantheon
- Animism
- Astrology
- Atheistic
- Babylonian (Hammurabi)
- Bacchanalian
- Buddhist (many branches)
- Candomble
- Christianity (many branches)
- Confucianism
- Divination (various methods)
- Freemasons
- Hinduism (many branches)
- Hoodoo
- Islam (many branches)
- Jainism
- Judaism (several branches)
- Macumba
- Mormon
- Native American traditions
- New Age spirituality
- Norse Pantheon
- Paganism
- Palo Mayombe
- Parsis (Zoroastrianism)
- Rosicrucian
- Santeria
- Satan worship
- Shinto
- Sikhism
- Sun worship
- Taoism
- Tarot
- Theosophist
- Umbanda
- Voodoo
- Wicca

Phun with Phobias

This list of things we fear is derived from a list of scientific phobias. As phobias, they represent extreme cases, and it may be that you want to give your characters a phobia if you can use it in plot development or as an element of the gameplay. But this list may also serve simply as a source of inspiration for developing characters who are afraid of something, even if it doesn't manifest as a full-blown phobia. Many of these phobias seem quite silly, and I've left them on the list just to give you a chuckle. If you can find a way to use them, be my guest. Others are very common, and even if someone doesn't have a phobia about, say, spiders, he or she may have more than a little uneasiness around them.

The degree to which someone has fear may determine how he'll behave when faced with what he fears. If he has a phobia, it can be quite paralyzing. If he is merely uneasy, it may have little impact. Just about anyone would have a fear of sexual abuse, but some people may change their habits and behaviors specifically to avoid the possibility of being sexually abused. So, you can use fears to modify the behavior of your characters. At any rate, this list gives you a good glimpse into the range of human fears. I'm sure you'll find some you can relate to. In fact, looking at this list for any length of time tells you that, as a whole, the human race is afraid of just about everything!

Note that each of these phobias has a nice fancy Latin scientific name, but I left them out to spare you.

Fear of:

- Accidents
- Air drafts
- Alcohol
- Amnesia
- Amphibians (frogs, toads, newts, salamanders, etc.)
- Amputees
- Anger
- Angina
- Animal skins
- Animatronics
- Ants
- Asymmetrical things
- Ataxia
- Atomic explosions
- Aurora Borealis
- Automobiles
- Bacteria
- Bald people
- Bathing
- Beards
- Bearing a deformed child
- Beautiful women
- Becoming angry
- Becoming homosexual
- Becoming ill
- Bees
- Beggars
- Being accidentally poisoned
- Being alone
- Being beaten severely
- Being beaten with a rod
- Being buried alive
- Being close to high buildings
- Being contagious
- Being dirty
- Being eaten
- Being enclosed
- Being forgotten
- Being hypnotized
- Being ignored
- Being in a house
- Being in love
- Being infested with worms
- Being locked in enclosed places
- Being rained on
- Being ridiculed
- Being robbed
- Being scratched
- Being seen
- Being smothered
- Being stared at
- Being tickled by feathers
- Being tied up
- Being touched
- Being unable to stand
- Bicycles
- Birds
- Biting insects
- Blindness
- Blood
- Blushing
- Body odor
- Bogeymen
- Bolsheviks
- Books
- Brain disease
- Bullets
- Bulls
- Bums
- Burglars
- Cancer
- Cats
- Celestial space
- Cemeteries
- Certain fabrics
- Changes
- Chemicals
- Chickens
- Childbirth
- Children
- Chinese
- Chinese culture
- Chins
- Choking
- Cholera
- Church
- Clocks
- Clothing
- Clouds
- Clowns
- Coitus

Part IV

- Cold
- Colors
- Comets
- Computers
- Confined spaces
- Constipation
- Cooking
- Cosmic phenomena
- Crawly things
- Creepy things
- Criticism
- Crosses
- Crossing bridges
- Crossing streets
- Crowded, public places
- Crowds
- Crystals
- Dampness
- Dancing
- Darkness
- Dawn
- Daylight
- Dead things
- Death
- Decaying matter
- Defeat
- Defecation
- Definite plans
- Deformity
- Demons
- Dental surgery
- Dentists
- Dependence on others
- Depth
- Diabetes
- Dining
- Dinner conversation
- Disease
- Disorder
- Dizziness
- Doctors
- Dogs
- Dolls
- Double vision
- Drafts
- Dreams
- Drinking
- Drugs
- Dryness
- Dust
- Eating
- Electricity
- Empty spaces
- England or English culture
- Epilepsy
- Erect penis
- Everything
- Expressing opinions
- Extinction
- Extreme cold
- Eyes
- Failure
- Fainting
- Falling
- Falling in love
- False statements
- Fatigue
- Fecal matter/feces
- Feeling pleasure
- Female genitalia
- Fever
- Fire
- Firearms
- Fish
- Floods
- Flowers
- Flutes
- Flying
- Fog
- Food
- Foreign languages
- Foreigners
- Foreplay
- Forests
- Forests at night
- Forgetting
- France
- Freedom
- French culture
- Friday the 13th
- Frogs
- Frost
- Fur
- Gaiety
- Gaining weight
- Garlic (one of Dracula's favorites)

- Genitals
- German culture
- Germany
- Germs
- Getting polio
- Getting wrinkles
- Ghosts
- Glaring lights
- Glass
- God/gods
- Going bald
- Going mad
- Going to bed
- Going to school
- Going to the doctor
- Gold
- Gravity
- Greek terms
- Growing old
- Hair
- Halloween
- Hands
- Handwriting
- Having an erect penis
- Hearing certain words or names
- Hearing good news
- Heat
- Heaven
- Heights
- Hell
- Heredity
- Holy/sacred things
- Home
- Homosexuality
- Horses
- Hospitals
- Houses
- Ice
- Ideas
- Imaginary crimes
- Imperfection
- Infinity
- Injections
- Injury
- In-laws
- Insanity
- Japanese
- Jealousy
- Jews
- Jumping (from high or low places)
- Justice
- Kissing
- Knees
- Knowledge
- Lakes
- Large things
- Laughter
- Lawsuits
- Learning
- Leaving a safe place
- Left-handedness
- Leprosy
- Lice
- Light
- Liquids
- Loneliness
- Long waits
- Long words (*Hippopotomonstrosesquippedaliophobia*)
- Looking up
- Losing an erection
- Loud noises
- Machines
- Magic
- Magic wands
- Making decisions
- Making mistakes
- Marriage
- Materialism (the same word describes fear of epilepsy)
- Meat
- Memories
- Men
- Menstruation
- Metal
- Meteors
- Mice
- Microbes
- Mind
- Mirrors
- Missiles
- Mobs
- Moisture
- Money
- Monotony
- Monsters

- Moths
- Movement or motion
- Mushrooms
- Music
- Myths
- Names
- Narrow places or things
- Needles
- Negative evaluations
- Neglecting duty or responsibility
- New drugs
- Night
- Noise
- Nosebleeds
- Novelty (newness)
- Noxious substances
- Nuclear weapons
- Nudity
- Numbers
- Objects on the right side of the body
- Old people
- One's own voice
- Oneself
- Open high places
- Open spaces
- Opening eyes
- Operating (surgeon)
- Opinions
- Otters
- Outer space
- Pain
- Painful bowel movements
- Paper
- Parasites
- Parents-in-law
- Peanut butter sticking to the roof of the mouth
- Pellagra
- People or society
- People who smell bad
- Performing (stage fright)
- Philosophy
- Phobias
- Phobic's preference for fearful situations (some people like to scare themselves)
- Pins
- Plants
- Poetry
- Pointed objects
- Poison
- Politicians
- Poverty
- Precipices
- Pregnancy
- Priests
- Progress
- Property
- Prostitutes
- Punishment
- Puppets
- Rabies
- Radiation
- Radical deviation
- Railroads
- Rain
- Rape
- Rats
- Razors
- Receiving praise
- Rectal diseases
- Rectums
- Red lights
- Relatives
- Religion
- Religious ceremonies
- Remaining single
- Reptiles
- Responsibility
- Returning home
- Riding in a car
- Rivers
- Road travel
- Rodents
- Rooms
- Ruin
- Ruins
- Running water
- Russians
- Saints
- Satan
- Scabies
- School
- Scientific terminology
- Scratches
- Seeing an erect penis
- Seeing oneself in a mirror

- Sermons
- Sex
- Sexual abuse
- Sexual love
- Sexual perversion
- Sexual topics
- Shadows
- Sharks
- Shellfish
- Shock
- Sinning
- Sitting
- Skin disease
- Skin lesions
- Sleep
- Slime
- Small things
- Snakes
- Snow
- Sourness
- Speaking in public
- Speed
- Spiders
- Spirits
- Stairs
- Stars
- Stealing
- Steep slopes
- Stepparents
- Stings
- Stooping
- Stories
- Strangers
- Streets
- String
- Stuttering
- Suffering
- Sunshine
- Surgical operations
- Swallowing
- Symbolism
- Symmetry
- Syphilis
- Taking medicine
- Taking tests
- Tapeworms
- Taste
- Technology
- Teenagers
- Teeth
- Telephones
- Termites and other wood-eating insects
- Tetanus
- The color black
- The color purple
- The color red
- The color white
- The color yellow
- The crucifix
- The Dutch
- The figure 8
- The great mole rat
- The heart
- The moon
- The number 13
- The opposite sex
- The Pope
- The sea
- The sun
- The word yellow
- Theaters
- Theology
- Things on the left side of the body
- Thinking
- Thinking about an erect penis
- Thunder
- Thunder and lightning
- Time
- Toads
- Tombstones
- Tornadoes and hurricanes
- Train travel
- Trains
- Trees
- Trembling
- Trichinosis
- Tuberculosis
- Tyrants
- Ugliness
- Undressing in front of someone
- Untidiness
- Urinating
- Urine
- Vaccinations
- Vegetables
- Vehicles

- Venereal disease
- Ventriloquist's dummies
- Vertigo (yes, you can be afraid of a fear)
- Virgins
- Voices
- Voids
- Vomiting
- Walking
- Walloons (certain Belgian people)
- Wasps
- Waves
- Wax statues
- Weakness
- Wealth
- Wet dreams
- Whirlpools
- Wild animals
- Wind
- Witchcraft
- Witches
- Women
- Wooden objects
- Work
- Working on computers
- Working with chemicals
- Worms
- Writing
- Writing in public
- X-rays
- Young girls

CATCHPHRASES

A catchphrase is something a character says that becomes a signature for that character. In ideal circumstances, the phrase "catches on" and starts being used by people outside the game/movie/TV show/book where it originated. Catchphrases such as Dirty Harry's "Make my day," the Terminator's "I'll be back," and Duke Nukem's "Come get some" become popular for a variety of reasons. A catchphrase can be used as shorthand for a more complex thought, or it can be a simple utterance used at an unusual time. Each of the previous examples illustrates that concept.

While based in common experience, the combination of style of delivery, timing, and simple phrasing can turn an expression into a catchphrase. In movies they are used a lot to identify a character. In Elmore Leonard's *Get Shorty*, the Chili Palmer character keeps saying, "Look at me" in a commanding but surprisingly gentle voice. After hearing it a few times, you identify the character with the phrase, which means a lot more than just "look at me." In *Things to Do in Denver When You're Dead*, the characters say, "Give it a name…" as a shorthand catchall expression. The phrase sticks with you after you've seen the movie because it is used in an unusual way.

Here are some elements that can produce a catchphrase:

- **Repetition.** Use it several times during the story.
- **Distinctive Delivery.** Tie the phrase with some accent, cadence of voice, tonal quality, or other distinctive quality.
- **Timing.** When do you use it? Use the catchphrase at meaningful moments, often to break tension or to create it. Saying, "Make my day" when the waitress brings a hamburger has a very different impact than when the wounded crook is reaching for his gun and Dirty Harry has his monster .357 Magnum pointed at him.
- **Simplicity.** Keep it simple.
- **Base the Phrase on Common Experience.** Base it on what people think about all the time—greetings, eating, sleeping, taking a dump, money (such as, "Show me the money" from *Jerry Maguire*), and so on.
- **Unusual Use of Usual Phrase.** Consider that the catchphrase has a deeper meaning than the words themselves and may even have more than one meaning, depending on the context. For instance, imagine a guy who says "Oh baby" whenever he does something well or something good happens. But then imagine he is making love and says, "Oh baby." It will be the same phrase in a different context, and it could be humorous if properly set up.

Attributes of Funny Characters

The following list contains some of the attributes that can make a character funny in a game (or even in movies and literature). No one character has to have all these traits, but many can have more than one.

Creating funny characters is tricky, however. Many people set out to make a funny character and end up with an extremely annoying one, a stupid one, or an overly cute one. We're not going for annoying, stupid, or cute here. We're going for funny.

For further help with the concept of funny, check out the "Creating Comedy" section in Chapter 9, "Storytelling Techniques." And remember, much of what strikes us as funny comes from some combination of surprise and timing. Some of the qualities you might find in a funny character are:

- Funny physical features, particularly hair, nose, eyes, way of walking, etc.
- Funny voice.
- Funny name.
- Funny and unusual turn of phrase—not so much what they say, but how they say it.
- Funny style of dress.
- Says funny things—particularly one-liners and humorous statements at odd times. This depends on timing.
- A good time for a funny character to be funny is during great danger. A well-timed joke or a quirky observation can do wonders to endear the character to you. Bruce Willis often plays this kind of character in movies such as *Die Hard.* The more dire the circumstances, the more offhand his comments.
- Does funny things, such as falling down holes or suddenly doing the tango with other characters.
- Makes funny faces at the right times—reacts humorously to what the boring, evil, or annoying characters say and do.
- Practical joker—likes to play little tricks on people. This is especially humorous if the victim is someone with little or no sense of humor—someone all too serious. (For those who remember that far back, Groucho Marx and Margaret Dumont come to mind.)
- Oddball—someone who tends to see the world differently from most people and whose observations are weird or offbeat enough to be funny. A classic example would be the humorist Steven Wright.
- Simpleton—someone so dense and slow that his very inability to "get it" is funny.

Kinds of Heroes, Villains, and Minions

This section attempts to lay out a few conceptual sketches of different heroes, villains, and minions based on experience with games as well as with movies, literature, and myths. As sketches, these are nothing more than suggestions or hints at some characteristics you might have encountered before. The real trick is to use these "archetypes" as inspirations to go further. As with the majority of this chapter, there's nothing carved in stone here, and I hope you'll take these ideas and mold them to your own uses.

Heroes

It may seem obvious to you what a hero is, but in fact there are different archetypes for heroes and heroines, and much literature has been written about them. Although the player character in games is generally the ultimate hero, there are different sorts of heroic types that players will meet (and embody) during the course of their gameplay experience. We've all seen these heroic types in other entertainment media, such as literature and movies, and you will probably recognize these archetypes when you read about them. In this section, I've put some characteristics of a few hero/heroine archetypes to help you create your own versions. Note that just about any hero archetype can apply to a female character, though some traits and characteristics might differ.

The Heroic Path

Before the archetypes, look at some of the elements of the hero's world. See also the "Joseph Campbell Meets *Star Wars* and *The Matrix*" section in Chapter 9, "Storytelling Techniques."

- The hero usually suffers a great loss or some significant danger exists to start him on a quest.
- There is generally someone with enough wisdom—an oracle or guide—who helps the hero understand how to start and what to do, at least at the beginning.
- The path is beset with dangers and trials, which must be overcome.
- The possibility of death (physical, psychological, or symbolic) is often present, and narrow escapes are common.
- The hero often must penetrate the realm of the evil enemy to prevail over that evil.
- When the quest is completed, the hero generally returns to society with new accolades and status rewards.
- In most modern heroic epics, there is a happy ending, but that is not required.

Hero Archetypes

Heroes are a basic part of our human life. We have probably always had heroes, or we have at least as far back as recorded history goes. With all that history to draw from, we've also come up with some basic templates for heroes—the hero archetypes.

In some cases, the player's character, while the protagonist of the story, has no real characteristics, being more of a tool in the control of the player. The player character has abilities that the player uses to accomplish the goals and to meet the challenges of the game, but there is no indication that the character has any depth or characteristics beyond those abilities. For instance, what did we know of the personalities of Mega Man, Donkey Kong, or the Prince of Persia?

So, it's up to you whether you create a player character or NPC as a tool or a role, and not a personality, or whether you decide to attempt the creation of a fuller character. I think hero archetypes are very useful, however, and for each archetype, I've added some possible characteristics, with an emphasis on *possible*. Pick the characteristics that work for you. Not all of them are necessary, and in some cases, they may even be contradictory.

A note about comedic heroes: Comedic heroes can often be parodies of these archetypes. For instance, Inspector Clouseau and Maxwell Smart are parodies of various types of heroes, such as the Smooth Hero and the Super Spy, but in their own way they are also Impetuous Heroes or Reluctant Heroes. They best fit the description of the Inept Hero, but they may be related to any of the other hero archetypes through parody. Among the best examples of comedic heroes in games were *ToeJam & Earl*, *Sam & Max Hit the Road*, and *Earthworm Jim*. Of course, comedic heroes might only be wise-talkers, such as Bugs Bunny, Duke Nukem, or the main characters in *The Neverhood* and *Secrets of Monkey Island*.

Strong Leader Heroes

The Strong Leader is a hard-as-nails fighter who probably won his position as leader the hard way—with fists or with a domineering personality. Strong Leaders are very effective and can win tremendous loyalty from their followers, despite their gruffness and sometimes unapproachable demeanor. But this kind of Strong Leader doesn't tolerate failure well and is also feared.

Possible characteristics:

- Leadership
- Focused on goal
- Confident
- Decisive
- Forceful
- Serious, not very playful
- Ultra responsible
- Possessive
- Stubborn
- Unsympathetic/insensitive to human frailty
- Domineering
- Not a big talker (generally) unless it is important
- Likes to be in control

Anti-Hero Heroes

The Anti-Hero is someone who comes from, or exists outside of, normal society, but who fights for something good. Often misunderstood, the Anti-Hero often works outside the law and in the fringes of society. The Anti-Hero may actually be at home among those he fights, and although outwardly he may seem angry or apathetic about the issues that affect ordinary people, deep inside Anti-Heroes are idealists, humanists, and true believers in what is right and good. Although we, the audience, may see Batman as a pure hero in *The Dark Knight*, one theme of the movie was that society needed to view him as an Anti-Hero.

Possible characteristics:

- Charismatic
- Disillusioned idealist
- Street smart
- Outwardly casual and uncommitted (but only outwardly)
- Romantic at heart
- Operates from intuition
- Pessimistic
- Bitter
- Volatile
- Troubled past
- Conflicted
- Victim of conventional society
- Emotionally defended
- Keeps his secrets

Smooth Heroes

Smooth Heroes are guys like James Bond—self-confident, smooth-talking, and highly competent operators who can take over a situation or charm everyone in a room. They often accomplish their missions with a clean and simple result, but when things get nuts, things often start to blow up—literally. Smooth Heroes are often several steps ahead of their adversaries.

Possible characteristics:

- Very charismatic
- Smooth talker
- Snappy dresser
- Quick wit
- One step ahead
- Easygoing
- Hard to nail down
- Manipulative
- Takes things as they come
- Irresponsible
- Can seem self-centered, but may have unseen loyalty

Super Spies

When you mention a Super Spy, you probably think of James Bond. And that would be accurate. But there are other types of Super Spies who may be less debonair and not really like the Smooth Hero. In fact, the Super Spy can incorporate elements of several other hero archetypes, including the Smooth Hero, the Thinker, and even the Anti-Hero. He can even have aspects of the Impetuous Hero or the Fighting Machine. What makes him a Super Spy is that he specializes in infiltration, uncovering mysteries within political worlds, and he is generally working for an organization with some kind of political (and sometimes financial) agenda. The villain archetype that has the most in common with the Super Spy is the Professional Killer/Assassin.

Possible characteristics:

- Master of infiltration
- Versatile—can improvise
- Can be like a Smooth Hero (James Bond)
- Can be a more or less ordinary character (George Smiley in *The Spy Who Came in from the Cold* or Dashiell Hammett's Pinkerton detective, the Continental Op)
- Also can have aspects of the Thinker Hero, the Fighting Machine, or the Impetuous Hero
- Generally proficient with a variety of weapons, including hand-to-hand, but that is not always a prerequisite
- Knows how to blend in, to tail a suspect, to set up surveillance, and to infiltrate the enemy's location

Outsider Heroes

Outsider Heroes are similar to Anti-Heroes, but even more on the fringes of society. They are even more angry and disillusioned, and they may be somewhat single-minded. Where an Anti-Hero is basically a "bad boy on the side of good," Outsider Heroes are sometimes somewhat psychopathic, violent, and dark. For instance, think about the hero of *Sin City.* Because they are so far outside of society, Anti-Heroes have little love for the "ordinary" people, at least on the surface, but because they are heroes, they fight against injustice, are kind to children and small dogs, and have a few redeeming qualities. You might not want to invite them over for dinner, but you are glad they are on your side. In some ways, the Sociopath villain is similar to the Outsider Hero, but more deranged and less in touch with human empathy. However, both the Outsider Hero and the Sociopath desire to be included at some level, but they act out their separation in different ways. In simplistic terms, the Outsider Hero still retains a connection with humanity as a whole, while the Sociopath is intent on victimizing humanity.

Possible characteristics:

- Live outside society
- Generally tortured—sad, angry, or both
- Hyper-aware, missing nothing
- Focused on some principle or belief
- Sensitive, easily affected emotionally if his guard is down
- Dark
- Fatalistic
- Unforgiving
- Hates injustice
- Implacable enemy

Thinker Heroes

Thinker Heroes are often more intellectual types who do not have great physical powers. However, they can plan, outthink enemies, and sometimes unleash awesome mental powers. The X-Men's Professor X is a good example, but not the only kind. Sometimes Thinker Heroes have absolutely no special abilities but somehow manage to outwit the criminals; for instance, the character of Nick Charles in the *Thin Man* movies or another of Dashiell Hammett's creations—Sam Spade from *The Maltese Falcon.* Sherlock Holmes was the ultimate Thinker Hero. Some Thinker Heroes can throw a good punch or fire a weapon, but they rely on wits over force whenever possible. The natural enemy for the Thinker Hero is the Mad/Evil Genius, but of course a good Thinker Hero should be able to beat any villain by use of superior intellect.

Possible characteristics:

- Possible genius
- Intuitive
- Plans and analyzes
- Accomplished
- Sincere
- Sometimes cryptic
- Set in his ways
- Egotistical
- Impatient
- Always confident in his abilities
- No problem too hard
- May be social or anti-social
- May be absentminded or exceptionally present and organized

Impetuous Heroes

Impetuous Heroes tend to charge right into a situation. In some ways, they are the opposite of the Thinker Hero. They rely on a combination of power or skills and lots of luck. They tend to ignore danger and focus on accomplishing goals to the exclusion of other situations. Although they can be quite dramatic, Impetuous Heroes can be hard on their followers, who may become victims of their leader's lack of planning. But on the positive side, Impetuous Heroes waste no time thinking. They are all action.

Possible characteristics:

- Dives right in
- Doesn't calculate the odds
- Takes unnecessary risks
- Keeps things moving
- Knows no fear
- Highly skilled (or he wouldn't still be alive)
- Honorable
- Unreliable
- Self-centered
- Can be charming and charismatic
- Can be lighthearted in the face of danger
- Ignores rules
- Individualistic
- Can charge ahead and do the wrong thing, creating trouble for his friends—but that's half the fun, isn't it?

Part IV

Inept Heroes

The Inept Hero is generally a comedic figure but is still the protagonist of the story. Inspector Clouseau and Maxwell Smart are prime examples, as is the Tick. In games, my favorites were ToeJam & Earl and Sam & Max. The Inept Hero blunders through the story, making mistakes, toppling buildings and regimes, somehow making love to women despite his ineptitude, and solving crimes, mostly by dumb luck. Making an inept hero in a game is not easy. Players like to be in control, so a character who is always punching himself in the arm with a letter opener or falling down a flight of stairs might not be easy to sell to players. However, it would be fun to see whether anyone could solve the problems of the Inept Hero as a player character. The resulting game could be a lot of fun and different from almost all other games we've seen.

Possible characteristics:

- Nerdy
- Friendly
- Innocent/naïve
- Shall we say, "dumb as a post?"
- Lucky!
- Nervous
- Self-deluded
- Mimics others
- Resourceful in crisis
- Boundless energy
- Fast runner

Fighting Machines

The Fighting Machine is similar to the Impetuous Hero, but far more serious and intent. It's an attitude thing.... And the Fighting Machine is also far less emotional—nearly a robot that doesn't so much charge ahead, but moves implacably to defeat the enemy. Fighting Machine heroes are very strong and capable, dedicated to their beliefs and not very social or jovial. They are not necessarily great leaders, but they are terrible enemies to have. They may have studied the arts of war, hand-to-hand and weapons combat, and strategy and tactics, or they may just be naturally strong and dangerous. They don't take pity on the weak. If you are deemed an enemy, you are in the way.

Possible characteristics:

- Deadly serious
- High sense of honor
- On a mission
- Totally reliable
- A formidable warrior
- Highly skilled (often in many different fighting methods)
- Strong and self-disciplined
- Absolute sense of righteousness
- No mercy
- Can be cruel
- Impatient with weakness
- Loyal to his cause
- Rule-oriented
- Never gives up
- Protects the weak but doesn't respect them

Reluctant Heroes

Reluctant Heroes are ordinary people thrust into the role of hero by circumstances. They rarely choose to be heroes and often resist the idea with considerable effort. However, something about them always comes to the surface—a great intelligence, strong intuition, dogged determination, hidden and previously unknown powers, or old-fashioned luck. Whatever it is, Reluctant Heroes are common in literature, movies, and games. Reluctant Heroes also have more to learn from their heroism than other types of heroes. Whatever quest they find themselves engaged in, the experience changes them in certain ways. Many other types of heroes, because they are already heroes, may not learn much about themselves or life in general. Anti-Heroes also can learn about themselves, as can Outsider Heroes sometimes, but most other hero types don't really change much in the course of a story. Classic examples of Reluctant Heroes are Frodo and Harry Potter.

Possible characteristics:

- Often small, weak, or bookish—a dreamer (Frodo, Harry Potter)
- Relies on wits and relationships
- Humble
- Discovers courage and self-confidence
- May have hidden, untapped abilities
- Fights against fate
- Very noble at heart
- Strong moral values
- Romantic by nature
- Sense of duty
- Acute fear
- Strong loyalty
- A survivor
- Lucky (often very lucky)

Sidekicks

What kind of character makes a great sidekick? Sidekicks are not nearly as interesting as, say, the villain's henchmen. Generally speaking, sidekicks are very much less powerful than the hero, loyal to a fault, and helpful in an emergency. Sidekicks always have a positive view of the future, based on their unfailing admiration for the hero. They also can have some skills that the hero finds useful, but they are generally less glamorous skills. For instance, the hero might be handsome/beautiful, tall, smart, powerful, and clever. The sidekick might be good at looking up stuff on Google. The sidekick is always shorter, younger (generally), and generally quite unimpressive overall. Batman's sidekick, Robin, is the prototypical sidekick, especially in the earlier days, when he was completely overshadowed by his hero partner. In the animated series *The Tick*, the satire of the sidekick (Arthur) was a perfect parody. He was sycophantic, almost useless, unfailingly positive (despite any kind of abuse), and had the most ridiculous power.

But sidekicks do serve a purpose. They act as a contrast to the hero. They also can do things that are useful when the hero is otherwise tied up (sometimes literally). They allow the hero to talk out loud while revealing elements of the plot and displaying how clever they are. There's a special bond between hero and sidekick, and if you can create that chemistry, more power to you.

Sidekick qualities:

- Unfailing loyalty
- Occasionally useful
- Slightly skilled
- Not the hero
- Somebody to work things out with
- Sometimes funny
- Positive attitude
- An extra set of arms and legs
- Cute
- Someone to rescue (from time to time)
- Someone to save the hero or come to his aid in dire circumstances
- Someone to get the coffee

Villains

See also Chapter 14, "Enemies."

What would a hero do if there weren't villains? It would be a much duller world for the average hero type. What is interesting is that villains are often very similar to heroes. They both share certain characteristics, and often it is simply which side you pick that determines who is the hero and who is the villain. And, in general, villains are heroes in their own minds. In games, however, the distinctions are pretty clear: Villains are in opposition to the player and the player's character. (Of course, in some games, that can change.)

There are some characteristics shared by most villains. They are:

- Driven
- Arrogant/egotistical
- Rule breakers
- Unconventional
- Self-righteous
- Able to rationalize their actions
- Likely to feel victimized
- Likely to feel entitled (to something—the world owes it to him)
- Self-centered
- In denial (to a greater or lesser extent)

It might seem fair to say that all villains are greedy or ruthless; however, some villains can be fair minded and even altruistic (in their own minds, anyway). Some villains take up a cause in the belief that they represent some greater good. They may have all kinds of fine qualities. Other villains are heartless fiends who seem to enjoy the suffering of others. Some are reluctant villains, much the way that some are reluctant heroes. But what is always true of good villains is that they will do whatever they think they have to do to get what they want. Whether villains are torn by doubt and guilt or completely amoral and mean, they would not be good villains if they ever could be dissuaded from their villainy. (One exception would be if the hero was able to convince the villain of his mistakes and get him to change. In that case, there would be an even worse villain—an über-villain—who would have to turn up and be revealed as the true enemy and the one who had manipulated or controlled the reformed villain.)

Just as there are comedic versions of heroes, so there are comedic villains, and they often go hand in hand. A comedic hero does well battling a comedic villain. Austin Powers and Dr. Evil (and Mini-Me, of course) are perfect examples. Of course, villains may have comedic qualities or quirks but not be complete comedy characters. Even though they may sit around petting a plush Persian cat, that does not mean they can't take over the world and threaten the lives of millions. At any rate, many of the archetypes in this section could be created as comedic parodies.

Villain Archetypes

At the same time that we've had heroes throughout history, those heroes would have little to do if there weren't villains—or generally, enemies. And just as we have been able to identify some hero archetypes, so we have archetypes for our villains.

Just as I did with the hero archetypes, I've added a short list of possible characteristics for each entry, with an emphasis on *possible.* Remember, not all of these characteristics need to exist in every villain of any particular type, and in some cases, they may even be contradictory traits. The point of these archetypes is to help you develop the most interesting villains you can.

The Great Tyrant

The history of the world is littered with the stories of Tyrants of one kind or another. The quote (below) from Joseph Campbell does a good job of presenting one view of a Tyrant. Essentially, Tyrants wield power, and they wield it absolutely. They may have different reasons for being Tyrants, but ultimately they serve their own ends first and those of the people they rule second, if at all. If they were good to their people, they probably would be a) not villains and b) benevolent dictators instead of Tyrants.

Possible characteristics:

- Shares much with the Leader hero type
- In control
- Absolute
- Decisive
- Rules with an iron hand
- Is responsible for some great injustice
- May have a weak spot for son, daughter, or spouse…or pet or something surprising
- Greedy
- Often very cruel, even sadistic
- Sometimes convinced of divine right or demigod status
- Can believe he is best for his "people"
- Sometimes insane
- Sometimes a brilliant strategist or warrior
- Sometimes a great leader turned into a doddering old fool
- Sometimes a noble leader whose actions are poisoned by advisors

> The inflated ego of the tyrant is a curse to himself and his world—no matter how his affairs may seem to prosper. Self-terrorized, fear-haunted, alert at every hand to meet and battle back the anticipated aggressions of his environment, which are primarily the reflections of the uncontrollable impulses to acquisition within himself, the giant of self-achieved independence is the world's messenger of disaster, even though, in his mind, he may entertain himself with humane intentions.
> —Joseph Campbell, *The Hero with a Thousand Faces*

The Conqueror

Conquerors are villains who are determined to conquer other countries for some reason. Conquerors are often Tyrants as well. But the Conqueror has some drive to expand territory and defeat enemies. Alexander the Great comes to mind, as do Napoleon and Hitler. Each may have had different reasons for conquest, but they were Conquerors nonetheless. The classic case of a Conqueror from legends suggests a warrior leader. However, modern Conquerors often wear suits and direct others to do all their fighting. Either way...

- Ambitious
- Visionary
- Ruthless
- Charismatic
- Shares qualities of the Leader and the Fighting Machine heroes
- Greedy
- Certain
- Absolute
- Brave
- Military and/or political strategist
- May or may not be noble
- Driven by some idea, concept, dream, vision, or outside influence
- May see self as liberator
- May be guided by religious ideal
- May be cruel or sadistic
- May be merciless or can sometimes be merciful
- So focused on conquest that he does not have many other interests
- Very egotistical

Part IV

The Patriarch/Matriarch

Patriarch/Matriarchs are generally seen as benevolent, ruthless older leaders of a group. They have a certain accumulated wisdom and maturity that helps their younger followers stay in line, but they also have an iron hand with discipline and never forget an insult or betrayal. Their enemies don't usually live long. They often seem very calm and in control, despite the fact that they may be leading an all-out war among factions. Because they are older, they tend to have younger lieutenants and sub-leaders (see also "Minions").

Possible characteristics:

- The Godfather
- Fatherly/motherly demeanor
- In control
- Absolute authority
- Delegates
- Reads people
- Cunning
- Ruthless
- Thoughtful
- Protective of his/her own
- May be extremely loyal to the "family"
- Can be brutal and cruel
- Can be balanced or unbalanced (sane or crazy)
- Interested in keeping order
- Sometimes interested in conquest/expansion

The Smooth Villain

The Smooth Villain is much like the Smooth Hero, but working more for self-interest than some noble cause. But Smooth Villains are every bit as urbane and charming as Smooth Heroes—the anti-007, if you will. Smooth Villains vary somewhat in their approach. Some are dabblers who like to be criminals for the excitement and the challenge. They tend to take things a bit lightly. Others are psychopaths who hide their mania behind a false smile and a ready quip. But when the chips are down, they can turn quite nasty...or craven when standing in front of the barrel of a gun. They can also be quite mad, sharing some of the characteristics of the Mad/Evil Genius. In fact, many other villain archetypes can also be Smooth Villain types.

Possible characteristics:

- Very charismatic
- Smooth talker
- Snappy dresser
- Quick wit
- One step ahead
- Easygoing
- Hard to nail down
- Manipulative
- Quite self-centered
- Egotistical

The Mad/Evil Genius

Everyone knows the Mad/Evil Genius villain. Usually he's male, but that doesn't have to be so. He always has some mad plan to turn himself into a cyborg, subjugate the human race through chemistry, or build the ultimate weapon and blackmail the world. Or he may simply be an evil genius who is pulling the strings behind a lot of mysterious events, such as a rash of perfectly executed bank robberies or the disappearance of key politicians. So the Mad/Evil Genius can be a scientific type or a genius of the Moriarty type from the *Sherlock Holmes* stories. Often he is a legitimate scientist whose passion for a particularly unsavory direction of experiments is met with typically shortsighted responses from his superiors or fellow scientists, so he is determined to "prove them wrong." Of course, he's mad as a hatter. Likewise, he may be simply a mastermind who finds a life of crime far preferable to a life of mediocre accomplishments in the legitimate world. It's both the ill-gotten gains and the thrill of breaking the rules that attracts this kind of genius. The Mad/Evil Genius is somewhat similar to the Thinker Hero, but obviously either insane or intent on using his powers for criminal purposes.

Possible characteristics:

- Brilliant but warped
- May be scientific genius
- May be intellectual genius (strategist)
- Has a definite goal in mind (wealth, revenge, glory, get the girl, etc.)
- Often the victim of his own creation
- Arrogant
- Generally wants recognition for his genius
- Often has a grudge against society
- May believe he is doing something for the greater good
- Madness may come from experimenting on self
- Likes to tell the hero how clever he is—explains everything
- Often a recluse with few or no close associates
- May have one or more lab-type minions
- Almost always thinks everyone else is inferior (superiority complex)
- Lonely, longing to meet an equal
- Often enjoys matching wits with the hero—a somewhat worthy opponent

The Sociopath

Sociopaths are people who have problems relating to society in various ways. The Sociopath villain is one who often feels excluded from society, possibly since he was very young, and has a deep-rooted bitterness about people within a society that can never accept him. The Sociopath may commit evil acts for revenge or for recognition. Secretly, the Sociopath is suffering, but that suffering may not be apparent. Or the Sociopath may have discovered people on the fringes of society who will accept him, and therefore he finds a place among the criminal element, where his ruthlessness and abilities often make him rise to the leadership position within that society. Sociopaths often can do anything without remorse—even the most heinous acts—and that makes them among the most dangerous villains, especially when they are also cunning and clever or endowed with superhuman abilities. In some ways, the Sociopath is similar to the Outsider Hero, but rather than being impelled to protect the innocent and right the wrongs, the Sociopath has become amoral and sees others as enemies. The Sociopath may also derive pleasure and satisfaction from harming others and can be quite sadistic.

Possible characteristics:

- Clever or just sick
- Amoral
- Warped
- May be working out childhood trauma
- No empathy for others
- Manipulates others
- Can appear completely normal
- Can be charming
- Can be a serial killer
- Generally a loner
- May be a planner or may commit acts impulsively
- Can join with others—has a secret wish to be included
- Hides inner pain
- May have some specific nervous or reflexive habit—can be very subtle or very blatant
- Often takes feeling of victimization to an extreme
- May be extremely sadistic and may derive intense pleasure from harming others

The Professional Killer/Assassin

The Professional Killer/Assassin is just doing a job. He may be quite skilled, like the Super Spy, and may work for a specific organization. Professional Killer/Assassins might also be freelance killers or part of a mob. The Professional Killer/Assassin can be like the Smooth Hero in some ways, working more or less out in the open, or he may work from the shadows and never be seen or identified. However, Professional Killer/Assassins are rarely very emotionally connected with what they are doing. They kill for money or because they are told to by their organization. They may have political reasons for killing, but still it is very rarely personal. They are usually stealthy, careful, and hard to catch. Another type of Killer/Assassin is more of an ordinary enforcer type—like the guys in *Pulp Fiction*, who were neither smooth nor clever, but did their job with a sort of offhand efficiency. The Professional Killer/Assassin can seem quite ordinary outside his job and may even live an ordinary life with a family and a house in the suburbs.

Possible characteristics:

- Careful
- Unemotional
- Not empathetic to others
- Matter of fact
- Probably working for someone else—just a job
- Highly skillful
- Clever and cunning
- Might be a family man/woman
- Generally has a favorite method, but may be quite versatile
- Can blend in with the crowd
- Shrewd
- Can be quite flexible and adaptive, though some may be very fixed and will not proceed if conditions are not perfect
- Takes care of Number One
- Compartmentalizes feelings

The Demon

Demon villains are enemies from demonic dimensions, and as such they aren't human. They may vary in appearance from caricatures of devils to very human in appearance, but it is generally a mistake to assume that they respond to situations in the same way a human enemy would. Demon villains in fiction are often implacable enemies of humanity and want only to wreak havoc on the human world. However, more subtle Demons also exist, who may want to use humanity for some specific purpose, such as a breeding ground for demonic offspring or as a source of food. Some Demons are based in the Judeo-Christian tradition and may want to "steal men's souls," while others may come from other traditions with other agendas. Demon villains can also be vampires and undead of one kind or another—or even destructive deities from Eastern traditions. Demon villains almost always have supernatural powers of one sort or another. There is a lot of range in how to depict a Demon villain. Interestingly, there isn't much fictional tradition for a Demon hero, although it may be possible to consider a demon in the role of Anti-Hero or even Outsider Hero.

Possible characteristics:

- Supernatural origin
- Has powers
- Is generally evil for evil's sake—pure evil
- Has a weakness, if you can find it
- Often shows up when you least expect it
- May be sadistic
- May be implacable
- May be fixated on one victim or indiscriminate
- Often grotesque, but can also be charming, handsome or beautiful, etc.
- Can be misunderstood (not really evil)
- Can be a good person twisted into a demon in some way
- Can be a good being whose appearance causes people to treat it like a demon and it is only protecting itself
- May think of itself as good and think the hero is evil

The Defector

The Defector is a dangerous villain because he knows the hero's strengths and weaknesses. He probably has some agenda against the hero or what the hero represents. He may have been "turned" by the enemy and can be redeemed, but most likely the Defector has become an implacable enemy of whatever the hero represents. There can be any number of reasons why the Defector defected, and these can be revealed in the story, but what is important is that the Defector is a special sort of enemy with ties to the hero's own world and possibly even ties to the hero as well.

Possible characteristics:

- Was once part of the hero's affiliation/group
- Has special knowledge of the hero or hero's group
- Is especially dangerous because of special knowledge
- Has a grudge or a plan not shared by the group
- May have special animosity toward the hero
- May perceive that the group is wrong—has a higher purpose
- May have fallen under the control of a rival or opposing group or leader
- May turn out to be a double mole, actually only pretending to be a Defector
- May have the characteristics of a hero, but has some flaw or weakness that prevents him from realizing his heroic nature
- Or, may be basically weak and craven, selling to the highest bidder
- Needless to say, has issues with loyalty

The Unscrupulous Bastard/Nasty Bitch

The Unscrupulous Bastard/Nasty Bitch is just a person who is really not nice at all. He may not be as amoral as the Sociopath, but he is pretty ruthless and often greedy. What Unscrupulous Bastards/Nasty Bitches do, they do for themselves, and they care little for anyone else—including their own followers and henchmen. They can be devious and deceitful, often putting on a mask of civility and graciousness, but it is only a mask and is utterly false. They look out for Number One and nobody else—although sometimes exceptions can be made for family members. They are impatient with others and insistent on having what they want. They probably aren't in touch with their true self-hatred, and they spend a lot of time justifying their actions to themselves, though rarely to anyone else—the exception being when the hero has them cornered, at which point they are quick to justify their actions or put on a show of false penitence. In an odd and less noble way, the Unscrupulous Bastard/Nasty Bitch villain has some elements in common with Strong Leader Heroes, especially in their single-pointed approach to their goals, their impatience with others, and their ruthlessness.

Possible characteristics:

- Often someone with power already, or someone who manipulates from within a closed group (family, workplace, community, etc.)
- Wants something and stops at nothing to get it
- Amoral
- May have a grudge or rage against someone or some group
- Completely selfish
- Probably greedy
- Probably self-justified and rationalized
- Can be sadistic and take pleasure from the suffering or failure of others
- Probably secretly wants to be loved
- Has extreme but well-hidden self-hatred
- May play rôles, pretending to be subservient, obedient, or cooperative in order to gain advantage over others
- Everything is about getting what they want
- Ultimately a loner, though they need people to manipulate—able to be alone amidst a group

Part IV

The False Ally

The False Ally is a subtle enemy pretending to be a friend. False Allies can be in a position of authority over the hero—such as the head of the security agency who is, in reality, an agent for the enemy. Or the False Ally might simply be a friend or member of the hero's organization, an informant, or anyone pretending to be on the hero's side—maybe even a boyfriend or girlfriend. Ultimately, the False Ally attempts to lead the hero into trouble or onto a false trail.

Possible characteristics:

- Friendly (on the surface)
- Helpful (where it suits them)
- Wears a constant disguise
- May occasionally slip and reveal hidden animosity, but covers it up quickly
- Works behind the scenes to the hero's detriment
- Probably has a grudge or secret reason for wanting to see the hero's downfall
- May be associated with a hero's nemesis (or may be the nemesis)
- Has contempt for the hero and all like him
- Wants to think he is superior
- May have self-esteem problems
- May not take direct action against hero, but only engage in various betrayals
- Must at some point be revealed for what he is

The Avenger

Avenger villains are dedicated to some cause that, to them, is noble or important. The cause was initiated by something horrible that happened to the Avenger or to people who mattered to the Avenger. For instance, a subway accident might have killed the Avenger's little sister, causing the villain to vow vengeance on the negligent subway company, or something like that. Sometimes, if the hero is involved, the Avenger can also become a Personal Enemy of the hero. Avengers are often a bit unbalanced and become very single-minded in the pursuit of their revenge. They also have a great capacity for justifying even the most horrible actions in the name of their cause. They are very similar to the Fanatic villain, but in the case of the Avenger, the issue is revenge, where in the case of the Fanatic, at issue is a cause or an ideal.

Possible characteristics:

- Driven by a self-justified purpose.
- The purpose may, in fact, have come from a justifiable cause.
- Even where the cause is justifiable, the methods are not acceptable from the hero's point of view.
- Believes that he is righting a wrong.
- Tries to get the hero to see his side.
- Ruthless against what he perceives to be great evil.
- To be a good villain, this character probably has to be driven somewhat mad by his anger/hatred or lust for revenge.
- Definitely sees self as the hero.
- Sometimes a loner, though not always.
- Can be charismatic, or can be antisocial and unskilled with people.
- Has a one-track mind.
- Shares some qualities with the Fighting Machine hero.

The Fanatic

The Fanatic is a lot like the Avenger. In fact, they are practically the same, but the difference is that the Avenger is set on righting a wrong—seeking vengeance—and it is generally something personal. The Fanatic is not necessarily engaged in a war initiated by a personal experience, but by a war of ideas and convictions. The Fanatic is full of righteous zeal and an equal disdain for those who do not share his fanaticism. Fanatics can engage in all kinds of nasty actions, justifying them in the name of their cause. Sometimes whether someone is a hero or a villain is a matter of point of view. The Fanatic does believe in his cause, and he believes it is right. But from the hero's point of view, it is not right—or, even if it is a righteous cause, the villain's method of solving it is not right. For instance, the Fanatic villain may have a righteous anger about chemical plants that poison soil or pollute rivers, but from the hero's point of view, blowing up the plant or assassinating the owner of the plant is probably not an appropriate solution. At any rate, the Fanatic has something in common with many heroes, and Fanatics aren't necessarily evil. But, being Fanatics, they are unbalanced and generally a bit wacky. And though some of the causes Fanatic villains may stand for are justified, sometimes they simply stand for something completely out to lunch, such as taking a militant stand on dental hygiene or human rights violations against postage stamps.

Possible characteristics:

- Is focused on a cause.
- Is convinced the cause is right.
- Probably isn't looking for a successful conclusion, but uses the cause as a way to express hatred, rage, frustration, and feelings of victimization.
- Is inflexible.

- Sees issues as black and white.
- Probably has some deep-rooted rage from childhood.
- Shuts out feelings and contradictory thoughts.
- Has a low tolerance for ambiguity.
- Has no tolerance for other ideas.
- May display traits of a spoiled child (who reverts to violence when he doesn't get what he wants).
- Would rather see wholesale destruction than lose.
- Some Fanatic villains will consider suicide preferable to losing.

The Rival/Personal Enemy

The Rival/Personal Enemy can be almost any kind of villain from this list, but he is distinguished in that he has an intensely personal relationship with the hero, and everything he does is in competition with, or actively aimed at harming, the hero. Unlike the False Ally, who pretends to be a friend, the Rival/Personal Enemy villain pretends nothing and openly admits enmity toward the hero. Even when performing evil actions not directly related to the hero, there is an element of rivalry in what this villain does, and the conflict between the hero and the Rival/Personal Enemy takes on a much more emotional character. There are many possible reasons for this situation, all related to some past relationship. The hero may have gotten the girl. Or the villain may blame the hero for the girl's death. Or they may have been friendly rivals, but the villain was slighted, became angry, and blamed the hero for his failures. Generally, it boils down to the villain blaming the hero for some offense and essentially declaring a vendetta against him. And, of course, once the hero is seen as the source of all wrongs, then so is the society the hero represents—thus justifying the villain to start a life of crime and/or criminal activities.

Possible characteristics:

- Has past history with the hero.
- Wants to cause the hero's downfall or hurt the hero.
- Different from the False Ally. This is out in the open.
- To be a villain, he must want more than a friendly rivalry, but he sometimes makes it look as if he is no more than a friendly adversary, instead of a mortal enemy.
- Can be a man/woman scorned.
- Can be someone who thinks he or she deserves the accolades/rewards the hero got.
- Often a loner.
- Tends to see things in black and white.
- Generally inflexible.
- Can be subtle (working behind the scenes) or blatant (tries to blow up the hero with a half ton of dynamite wired to his car).
- Generally unbalanced by the relationship with hero.
- Generally this villain's attempts to hurt the hero cause collateral suffering and destruction.
- May choose to victimize someone close to the hero—a girlfriend, for instance—by using her as bait or threatening her to get the hero to capitulate.
- May rationalize hatred for the hero and use it to excuse other crimes.

The Complete Lunatic

The Complete Lunatic is simply crazy. Many other villains (and a few heroes, probably) are crazy, too, but whereas other crazy villains have some kind of justification for their craziness and their evil deeds, the Complete Lunatic is totally irrational and unpredictable and may do things for no obvious or logical reason. Although he may or may not appear to be insane on the surface, mentally the Complete Lunatic lives in a fantasy world of his own creation. Despite being a total fruitcake, Complete Lunatics can also be cunning and clever, unpredictable, and very dangerous. For instance, they might drop you from 1,000 feet, not because they mean you harm, but because they think you can fly or because they want to see what happens when you hit the ground. To be an interesting villain, the Complete Lunatic probably has some fantasy about reality that causes him to take antisocial actions requiring the services of a hero.

Possible characteristics:

- Unpredictable.
- May display wild mood swings.
- Individuals can vary from very urbane and normal in behavior to completely wacko.
- May seem to be merely eccentric.
- Can also be a Mad Genius.
- Has a completely distorted but self-referential view of reality.
- Actions may seem illogical (for instance, blows up a building at night to watch the pretty flames).
- Often cunning and elusive.
- If able to seem sane, may have power and even an organization.
- May have lost mind after attaining power, knowledge, abilities, etc.
- May have moments of clarity or may even have normal emotional responses to some things—for instance, family members or a pet cat.
- Lacks empathy, but may parrot it.
- May have moments of clarity and even remorse.

The Unseen

The Unseen is an enemy that cannot be seen or easily identified. The Unseen could be a deadly disease from outer space or an invisible killer, a presence that takes over the minds and bodies of its victims, or any of a number of insidious but unseen enemies. As such, the Unseen may or may not be a villain in the human sense, but it is generally distinct from other types of enemies. In the sense that a "villain" is a personified enemy, defining the Unseen as a villain is a judgment call.

Possible characteristics:

- Something that threatens the hero or the hero's world, but cannot be easily identified.
- May be of alien origin.
- May be a disease.
- Is deadly.
- Generally does not have human feelings.
- May not be intentionally malicious.
- Can be implacable.
- Knowing the identity of the Unseen is part of defeating it.
- It has a weakness, or there is a solution.
- Sometimes the solution is simple.
- The Unseen can attack the body, the mind, or even the whole person (body snatchers).

The Meek

The Meek are villains who really seem quite timid or harmless. Little kids can be Meek villains, as can be computer nerds, seemingly innocent young women, or even cute, cuddly puppies. Whatever fools us into thinking it is harmless when it is, in reality, a terrible threat to all we hold dear—that is the Meek villain. Meek villains may have powerful hidden abilities, or they may be more like the Mad Genius type, who can manipulate others and outwit their enemies, all the while appearing to be innocent and ineffectual. Meek villains may also be Sociopaths, Avengers, or Fanatics.

Possible characteristics:

- The meekest and mildest person.
- Deep, hidden anger, or trauma.
- Though he appears meek, mild, and agreeable, he is the real villain. May even be very powerful.
- Has similarities to the Sociopath and may share many traits. Typified by the meek, unthreatening demeanor. Nobody would suspect this was a villain.
- When revealed, he likes to boast and/or tell his story, justify actions, and so on.

Giant Monsters

Giant Monsters are generally beasts, such as King Kong or Godzilla, ill-tempered dragons from mythology, or any giant creature that the hero must face. Giant Monsters are usually just beasts, and therefore aren't really villains in the sense that they have much conscious volition to be evil or to commit evil acts. In fact, most Giant Monsters aren't really evil at all—they are often victims of Man's meddling. However, occasionally a Giant Monster is also a sentient creature who opposes the hero, and in such cases, Giant Monsters are also villains.

Possible Characteristics:

- Huge
- Dangerous
- May be non-sentient
- Rarely sentient
- Sometimes a victim of Man's meddling
- Sometimes a tragic creature that must be sacrificed for the safety of people
- Sometimes (rarely) a giant mastermind who is the ultimate enemy of the hero

What if the giant monster were really an incredibly intelligent superbeing instead of the rampaging behemoth that is usually depicted?

Minions

Many villains work alone, but others attract a gang (or even a small army) of willing allies. We like to call these allies *minions.* Now, minions don't tend to be as interesting as the villains or the heroes they fight. In fact, many of them are sort of one-dimensional caricatures. But that doesn't mean there aren't several minion archetypes, and minions often play an important role in a story or game. Some, such as the lieutenant sort, can even have somewhat developed personalities and play larger roles within a game—as mini-bosses and as threshold guardians. (See the upcoming "Functional Character Roles" section.)

What I've put in the following list are stereotypical minions. However, that isn't to say that even within these archetypes, there isn't plenty of room for creativity and new ideas. Although minions are generally disposable characters lacking in depth, you can provide some of them with more depth and personality and find a way for that to be used in the game. Suppose the hero meets a random minion who turns out to be a scholar and loves playing chess. Engaging the minion in a game of chess might be a way to get out of trouble or gain useful information. There are many possibilities.

Also, although many of these minion types are associated with the "bad" side, many of them could also be a hero's allies just by shifting perspective. Perhaps if they are on the hero's side, they would be called *allies* instead of *minions.*

Minion Archetypes

Heroes often have sidekicks and allies, but villains, many of whom seek power over others, have a natural tendency to accumulate followers—what we often call *minions.* Minions are important in game settings, as they give you enemies who pose different levels of challenges and present different possible situations, leading up to the ultimate challenge—the main boss. Here are several types of minions, listed with their possible characteristics.

The Number 2:

- May be very loyal to the boss.
- May be jealous of the boss.
- Sometimes more competent than the boss.
- May be highly ambitious, but not bold enough to take power.
- May be content with role as second banana.
- May see the boss as a father/mother figure.
- Can be a more intelligent form of muscle, but more likely a sub-boss with power and many characteristics of one of the villain archetypes.
- Could be promoted to boss in a power struggle or in the case of some misfortune to the boss. In this case, the Number 2 should turn out to be worse than the original villain, or the story loses power.

The Lieutenant:

- A little stronger and more capable than other minions.
- May have special abilities.
- May have some ambition. Could be promoted to Number 2 or even to boss in a power struggle.

The Random Grunt:

- This is a simple character with no personality, but he is used in a variety of places and is easily expendable.
- Different from the Red Shirt, who may or may not have some personality.

The Red Shirt:

- Borrowed from *Star Trek*, Red Shirts are characters with only a little more personality than Random Grunts, but they are expendable, and you can expect them to get killed. Sometimes they are given a small role and a little personality, but still you know they are ultimately doomed. (Note: Red Shirts can be on either side—good or evil.)

The Guard:

- Generic character assigned to guard a doorway, entrance, area, or object.
- Basically a Random Grunt or Red Shirt with a specific task.
- Differentiated from the Jailer in that Guards are not complex enough to guard people.
- May be stronger than ordinary Random Grunts.

The Jailer:

- Can have personality.
- Can interact with the player's character.
- Can be the Muscle or the Sadist if they have some personality, or a Random Grunt or Red Shirt.
- Can also be kindly.
- Can be corruptible or gullible.
- Basically used to guard prisoners.
- Can be taken from the existing minion pool—the boss assigns them to the job of guarding some prisoners.

- Different from normal guards, who have no interaction with other characters other than to challenge and/or fight.

The Muscle:

- Stereotypically intellectually substandard.
- Very strong.
- A follower.
- Lacks subtlety.
- Can do a lot of damage and sustain a lot, too.
- Undeterred by sentiment.
- Will do the dirty jobs.
- Can be outwitted but rarely out-muscled.
- May have a cute hobby.
- May have an attachment to something surprising.
- Can form attachments to innocent characters in some scenarios.
- Can occasionally have loyalty shifted.

The Sadist:

- Basically, a brutal follower of the boss, who gets pleasure out of hurting and/or humiliating people.
- Can also be a Number 2 or a Lieutenant.
- As a minion, probably isn't drawn as a very complex character, so no psychological conflicts or redeeming factors. Could be far more complex as a Sociopathic boss.

The Lab Minion:

- Generally a mindless drone who can operate the Mad Genius' equipment.
- Sometimes can be a higher-caliber drone with special abilities used to protect the Mad Genius.
- Almost always wears a white lab coat, unless a specialized type with specific gear, such as a radiation suit or a surgical outfit.

The Sneak:

- Has special abilities to sneak or hide.
- Makes a good thief or assassin.
- Likes his role as a stealthy character.
- Doesn't have ambition to be boss.
- Can have a more complex character description and personal story.
- Can have complex psychology.

The Crazy Joker:

- Loose cannon.
- Prankster (commonly backfires.)
- Fun to be around.
- A wildcard/almost suicidal.
- A gossip.
- A loudmouth.

The Family Member:

- Will fight to the death for his family.
- Will fight to the death for the *name* of his family.
- Feels his family is in some way better.
- Respects his elders (Mafia style).
- Even if he disagrees with ideals, the family tie will make him do whatever it takes.
- Responds to kidnapping (over the top).
- Probably reliant on the villain's money for his own lifestyle.
- Another type of family member might be secretly resentful and rebellious toward the family, which would offer different possibilities.

The Worshipping Fan:

- In *love* with the villain (even if it's only one way).
- Would take a bullet for the villain.
- Will treat the villain's enemies as his own.
- Feels as if he can speak for the villain because he knows him so well.
- Feels close to the villain, even if he is not really.

The Mole:

- A special type of minion who has infiltrated some part of the "good" world.
- More complex than most minions, in that he must fill dual roles.
- Loyal to the villain or evil cause.
- Not the main villain.
- Can be found out.
- Will be discovered or reveal himself at some point.
- May have a complex history and psychology.
- May have been co-opted by the villain or may have been placed in role.

Functional Character Roles

In addition to their descriptive archetypes, characters may fulfill certain functional requirements of the story, particularly with reference to their relationship to the hero or, in the case of games, the player's character. In Christopher Vogler's book, *The Writer's Journey* (Michael Wiese Productions, 1998), he mentions six character functions—essentially distillations of functional character roles mentioned or alluded to by Joseph Campbell in *The Hero with a Thousand Faces.* (More on Joseph Campbell's work can be found in the "Joseph Campbell Meets *Star Wars* and *The Matrix*" section in Chapter 9, "Storytelling Techniques.") Some of these character roles should seem quite familiar to game players, particularly the threshold guardians, mentors, and shapeshifters, though perhaps we in game design do not necessarily consider them in a literary light.

The following sections describe functional roles that characters can play within a story, and those same characters may take on one or more of these roles at different times. These are not hard-and-fast archetypes, but simply functional parts of a story as exemplified often by characters, but also by events and even subtler means.

Vogler identifies six functional archetypes: Mentor, Herald, Threshold Guardian, Shapeshifter, Shadow, and Trickster. Although I highly recommend reading both *The Hero with a Thousand Faces* and *The Writer's Journey*, following are my brief summaries of these six functional roles, particularly as they might appear in games.

Mentor

The Mentor, which Joseph Campbell called the Wise Old Man or the Wise Old Woman, is the guide, often the one who sets the hero on his path of adventure and who protects and helps him learn what he needs—up to a point. At some point, however, the hero must go it alone. This is seen in many stories, such as Gandalf in *The Lord of the Rings*, Obi Wan and Yoda in *Star Wars*, Morpheus in *The Matrix*, and other equally obvious examples. But Mentors need not always be so clearly drawn, nor do they need to be old. Young children ("out of the mouths of babes...") and even the village idiot can be Mentors. Mentors can also be any character who comes with a bit of guidance for the hero in need, and they can appear at any point in the story. Characters can fulfill the function of Mentor even when they have other roles in the story. In fact, even a villain can be a Mentor at some stage of the story, offering some tidbit of advice to the hero in a confrontation that might turn out to be useful. In games—particularly in Role-Playing Games—the Mentor character is almost essential. In other games, such as a Real-Time Strategy game or a First-Person Shooter, the Mentor may be absent all together. Whether there is a Mentor character depends to some degree on how story-based the game is. Games with minimal story are less likely to include a Mentor role. Note that the Mentor character can often shift roles, becoming at different times a Threshold Guardian, a Herald, a Shapeshifter, or even the Shadow.

Herald

The Herald role calls the hero to action. The Herald is not necessarily a character in the story, though it can be. It can also be a force of nature, such as the looming storm in *The Day After Tomorrow* or the holographic message from Princess Leia that propels Luke Skywalker into the story. Something has to signal a change to take the hero out of the ordinary world and into the world of adventure, be it a character, an event, or possibly a revelation or truth previously untold. In essence, the Herald provides motivation for the hero, and as such it can be anything that fulfills that function. In some stories, the Mentor is also the Herald, as in *The Lord of the Rings* where it is Gandalf who impels Frodo into the adventure (and who previously had done the same with Bilbo in *The Hobbit*). Although some games more or less drop the player into the unfamiliar world of adventure without any "ordinary world" experience, many games do, in fact, begin with the player's character in a familiar world, only to propel him into adventure by means of some event—for example, the princess has been kidnapped—or some new information, such as "you are the Chosen One, and if you don't take up this magic sword and defeat the great evil, the world as we know it will come to a fiery end."

Threshold Guardian

Every gamer is familiar with the role of the Threshold Guardian, which occurs in many forms in games. Level bosses are among the most obvious examples, but NPCs who hold some necessary item or information often appear as Threshold Guardians as well. In some ways, any barrier to the hero's advancement is a Threshold Guardian, even a river or mountain range. Even a character who is otherwise an ally could, under the right circumstances, become a Threshold Guardian. Remember, these archetypes are roles and functions within a game, not fixed and inflexible character descriptions. They act in fluid ways within the story.

In games, the response to a Threshold Guardian is dependent on circumstances, but likely as not, if it can be shot or otherwise destroyed, that's the answer. But in stories, the Threshold Guardian functions to test the hero and to facilitate his growth as a character. And getting past the Threshold Guardian is often a matter not only of brawn, but also of brains. In some cases, it might even be possible to convert a Guardian character into an ally or fool him into doing what you want him to do. So when you recognize the functional relationship of a character in a game as that of a Threshold Guardian, consider options beyond the simplistic approach of always fighting and destroying and consider alternative approaches that test the player's character in other ways.

Shapeshifter

The Shapeshifter role is often (though not always) someone of the opposite sex to the hero who may shift in various ways—in allegiance, in attraction, in appearance, and so on. The Shapeshifter may literally change forms, something that happens reasonably often in games. But that is only one aspect of the Shapeshifter role. A more interesting aspect is the role of a character who is difficult to define and whose motivations are confusing or suspect or whose future actions cannot be predicted. Characters in

Alfred Hitchcock's movies are often Shapeshifters. And, of course, the player's character (the hero) can also take on the role of Shapeshifter as required. Functionally, the Shapeshifter creates suspense, intrigue, and uncertainty in the story. For instance, Aragorn in *The Lord of the Rings* begins the story as a shadowy and mysterious, even somewhat frightening figure the Hobbits call Strider. But in the course of the story he becomes the noble Aragorn, heir to the throne of Gondor, and by the end of the story he is the King returned. This is an example of a Shapeshifter who goes from foul to fair, so to speak. But then there are characters who seem fair but are truly evil—such as Saruman in *The Lord of the Rings*, who appears to be a great and good wizard, but who is corrupted and ultimately evil. The infamous *femme fatale* of many stories is a Shapeshifter who appears desirable and accessible to the hero, but is devious, dangerous, or even psychotic. Nor do Shapeshifters have to be on the poles of good and evil. They can also exist in the gray areas where they may be neither all good nor all evil, but shifting around the light and shadows of the hero's journey.

Shadow

In its simplest form, the Shadow is the function of the villains of the story, but that's overly simplistic. The Shadow is every element of the darker side of the story, including the hero's own dark side. Every character—every person—has a dark side to his nature, just as every person also has something of the good in him. Villains can have redeeming qualities and even admirable traits. Heroes can carry storms within them. In a good story, the outer Shadows, as represented by the villains and antagonists of the story, may often have their counterparts within the psyche of the hero himself and/or some of his closest and most trusted allies. Exploring the inner darkness is a good way to deepen a story and can add complexity and interesting game design opportunities. Especially interesting is the repressed Shadow that lurks within every character. How could you unleash the Shadow in an otherwise upstanding, moral, and ethical hero? How then would the hero react? Or, what if you unleash the repressed darkness within one of the hero's allies? How might that change the game? How might that aid or hinder the efforts of the hero?

Trickster

The Trickster is often the comic relief in a story, but it can be much more. Depending on circumstances, the Trickster can also be a mentor or a dangerous enemy. There are several mythological Tricksters, such as the Native American Coyote and the Norse Loki, who were far more than simple jokers. In Christopher Moore's humorous novel, *Coyote Blue* (Simon & Schuster, 2008), the Trickster Coyote wreaks havoc on the life of the main character, but in the end functions as a mentor by forcing him to face the truth of his life and the lies he has been telling himself. Of course, Batman's Joker was also a trickster…and an archenemy. One of the primary roles of the Trickster character is to shake things up. At times you could see Han Solo as a Trickster, though that wasn't his only role in *Star Wars*. But he did provide some humor and an unpredictability that tended to shake things up. Some game heroes, particularly those who are derived from cartoonlike characters, have a lot in common with the Trickster type of character, being funny and mischievous in nature. In other games, the Trickster would have to be someone other than the hero. Many games seem to have no Trickster character at all, which leaves me wondering if this archetype couldn't be more widely incorporated into game stories with good results.

The application of these six functional character roles is a matter of story structure more than personality development. And these six functional roles are only basic archetypes. As there can be many types of hero and villain, there can be many functional roles within stories and games. For instance, in games there are often allies who serve functional roles within a group—such as mages, archers, tanks/fighters, healers, and so on. These are less story-oriented roles than roles of functional action, but they are common game-related roles, nonetheless. And of course, this list doesn't include the victim role. There are often victims in games who, similar to Heralds, serve to motivate the hero to rescue or avenge them or as proof of the necessity of taking action against the persecutors. Seeing characters in terms of the functions they fulfill within the story context and seeing those functions as fluid and flexible roles the characters may play can further clarify the way you might use characters within a game, particularly one where story is used significantly.

Personality Types

People are always studying people, which results in lots of theories about people, their behaviors, and their personality types. As a consequence, people have come up with many personality typing systems to try to describe and categorize people in some meaningful and predictable way. There are clearly too many such systems to examine them all here. Some are old and some are new. Some are well-established, such as the Myers-Briggs Type Indicator (MBTI) tests, and some have become increasingly popular, such as the Enneagram.

I hope you'll recognize that this section is nothing more than a reference of qualities that some people believe describe whole personalities. You can use it to help you round out your characters. For instance, if you have someone you want to create who is a deep thinker, introspective, and perhaps a bit antisocial, you might find some additional traits that go well with that type of character by looking at both the Myers-Briggs and the Enneagram systems. Or you might simply find some interesting types of character traits by browsing this section.

Be aware that these lists of qualities often deal with both the positive and the negative, with the abnormal and the stressed, the healthy and the unhealthy versions of these personalities. No one person would necessarily exhibit all the traits attributed to one of these personality designations. However, under stress, people are more likely to reveal their more negative traits. At the same time, stressful situations may incline healthy characters to respond with their most admirable and positive qualities. Villains may be seen as characters who have turned the traits of their characters toward antisocial activities, perhaps because they have accentuated the negative qualities of their personalities or perhaps because they have misinterpreted events or misapplied their positive qualities.

Also, some of the personality types listed in this section may seem less interesting or less likely to produce interesting and dynamic character types, but those may be the very ones you can use to create characters who defy stereotypes and who are more original.

Finally, I don't necessarily think any of this information is true. I just think you can learn from all kinds of sources—the more varied and off the beaten path, the better.

The Myers-Briggs Type Indicator (MBTI) System

The Myers-Briggs tests are based originally on work by Carl Jung, which divides people into sets of paired opposite qualities. These are organized by function as follows:

Relating	Information	Decisions	Ordering
Extravert	Sensing	Thinking	Judging
Introvert	Intuitive	Feeling	Perceiving

The following tables show the basic characteristics and qualities for each function.

Relating **Extraverted (E)**	**Introverted (I)**
Outwardly focused	Inwardly focused
Interaction with others	Reflective thinkers
Easily shares thoughts	May appear reserved, quiet, thoughtful
Likes company	Needs solitude
Many friends, makes friends easily	Few friends, cautious about new relationships
Uninhibited	Inhibited
Action, people, things	Ideas, feelings, impressions
Manager, salesperson	Librarian, legal secretary

Information Gathering **Sensing (S)**	**Intuitive (N)**
Factual, data from environment	Perceives patterns and relationships, hunches
Joe Friday (*Dragnet*)	Albert Einstein
Here and now	Past and future
Practical	Imaginative
Realist	Idealist
Literal	Figurative, metaphorical
Simple	Complex
Traditional	Innovative
Banker, surgeon, pilot, police	Artist, scientist, poet, reformer, philosopher

Decision Making **Thinking (T)**	**Feeling (F)**
Objectivity and logic	Harmony, relationships
Can be close-minded	Persuasive
Serious	Loose
Requires order	Can thrive in disorder
Hardworking	Flexible about work
Very responsible	Can be irresponsible

Ordering Life	
Judging (J)	**Perceiving (P)**
Quick to action	Takes time
Decisive	Adaptable
Task-oriented	Flexible, curious
Completion of tasks	May start many, but not finish all

By creating a dominant and secondary characteristic for each personality, the system comes up with 16 different personality types, each with a specific four-letter abbreviation, as follows:

Dominant and Secondary	**Abbreviated As...**
Extraverted Sensing and Introverted Thinking	ESTP
Extraverted Sensing and Introverted Feeling	ESFP
Introverted Sensing and Extraverted Thinking	ISTJ
Introverted Sensing and Extraverted Feeling	ISFJ
Extraverted Intuitive and Introverted Thinking	ENTP
Extraverted Intuitive and Introverted Feeling	ENFP
Introverted Intuitive and Extraverted Thinking	INTJ
Introverted Intuitive with Extraverted Feeling	INFJ
Extraverted Thinking with Introverted Sensing	ESTJ
Extraverted Thinking with Introverted Intuitive	ENTJ
Introverted Thinking with Extraverted Sensing	ISTP
Introverted Thinking with Extraverted Intuitive	INTP
Extraverted Feeling with Introverted Sensing	ESFJ
Extraverted Feeling with Introverted Intuitive	ENFJ
Introverted Feeling with Extraverted Sensing	ISFP
Introverted Feeling with Extraverted Intuitive	INFP

The interpretation of these 16 personality types covers some range, and not all sources have the exact same interpretations, but here's a brief overview:

ESTP (Extraverted Sensing Thinking Perceiving): Adventurer, artisan, idealist, guardian, thrill, risk

Downside:

- May avoid planning ahead, can be disorganized and frantic
- Can rely too much on humor and seem insincere in doing so
- May neglect commitments
- Fail to understand how their behaviors may affect others
- Feel dead inside if there's not enough excitement
- Under stress, they can create scenes and trouble with others
- May be very competitive
- Speaking before thinking
- Not looking at a situation deeply enough
- Flitting from one project to another without coming to completion

ESFP (Extraverted Sensing Feeling Perceiving): Performer, the joker, life of the party, storyteller, fun, generous, independent, fesourceful

Downside:

- Failure to plan ahead
- Can be distracted by social interests
- Can feel hurt if their warmth isn't reciprocated
- Can become overcommitted
- Often lack the ability to see logical consequences
- Often lack objectivity and see life in personal and subjective terms
- Can disrupt others by socializing too much
- Resistant to rules and restrictions
- Can become bored, restless
- Can become self-destructive
- Can be highly judgmental against others
- Value immediate gratification over long-term results
- Avoid conflict or direct confrontation
- Avoid working alone
- Doesn't always take care of self
- Takes things at face value

ISTJ (Introverted Sensing Thinking Judging): Duty, punctuality, loyalty, honesty/integrity, the inspector, simple, dependable

Downside:

- Keep things to themselves
- Can seem cold
- Can be self-absorbed when solving problems, to the exclusion of those around them

ISFJ (Introverted Sensing Feeling Judging): Nurturer, service to others, conventional, personal loyalty, hardworking, conscientious, shy about self-aggrandizement, reluctant to express anything that would disturb someone else

Downside:

- Can be overwhelmed while caring for others
- Not always capable of making their needs known or putting them at the forefront
- Can become resentful or hypercritical
- Can be pessimistic

ENTP (Extraverted Intuitive Thinking Perceiving): Energetic, interested in anything new, see patterns, problem solvers, great talkers, imaginative, sees possibilities, improvisers, sometimes artists and performers

Downside:

- Can overwhelm quieter people
- Can get involved with too many projects
- Can move too fast from one thing to another
- Can be defensive
- Can use natural expressiveness and energy against others when stressed

Doesn't do well with routine tasks

ENFP (Extraverted Intuitive Feeling Perceiving): Love of anything new, people-oriented, energetic, enthusiastic, spontaneous, flexible, adaptable, good with words, innovative metaphorical, see patterns, may be artists/performers, the strategist, "Variety is the spice of life"

Downside:

- More interested in what's new than in completion
- Needs a lot of freedom
- Can become overcommitted
- Sometimes lacks organization—seat of the pants
- Can become critical
- Can become a bully in stressful situations

INTJ (Introverted Intuitive Thinking Judging): Insightful and logical, visionary, systematic, task-oriented, creative, future-oriented, perseverant, sees patterns, original, works hard to realize dreams, highly independent, ignores rules that don't agree, loner

Downside:

- Can be overly critical of others
- Can be too truthful
- Not good at delegating
- Not good at reinforcing others
- Can be highly rejecting
- Can be stubborn in defense of his ideas
- May not listen to criticism

INFJ (Introverted Intuitive Feeling Judging): People-oriented, intuitive (inner world of ideas and possibilities), creative, compassionate, visionary, loyal, idealistic, seeks harmony, persuasive, open-minded, independent, leaders

Downside:

- Can be too independent
- Can present ideas as if they were complete and not open to discussion
- Hypersensitive to criticism
- Perfectionist
- May not criticize others, even when justified
- Can turn others off with their idealism
- Can become hypercritical when stressed
- Can fail to understand that others may have differing opinions or beliefs

ESTJ (Extraverted Sensing Thinking Judging): Pragmatic, ordered, logical, systematic, responsible, serious, takes charge, analytical, direct, fair, hardworking, impersonal (on tasks), rule-driven

Downside:

- Narrow focus (not interested in anything that doesn't seem relevant to the task at hand)
- Can expect others to conform to the rules
- Can be inflexible and close-minded
- Can be withdrawn under stress—or the opposite
- Must make decisions, even when lacking data or the timing isn't right
- Not interested in the conceptual side of things
- Sees things often in terms of black and white values

ENTJ (Extraverted Intuitive Thinking Judging): Analytical, logical, future-oriented, abstract, leader, prefer structure and organization, hardworking, persistent, good executive

Downside:

- Can be blunt
- Can be insensitive
- Can be impatient
- Can bottle up feelings until they explode
- May seem detached from close personal relationships
- Can withdraw if hurt
- Can forge ahead too quickly under stress
- Can show intolerance for those who don't share their high standards

Part IV

ISTP (Introverted Sensing Thinking Perceiving): The thinker, logical, analytical, critical, realistic, troubleshooter, observant, pragmatic, cautious, independent, curious, precise, principled, adaptable, impulsive, adventurous

Downside:

- Can appear aloof
- Cautious around people
- Can be too oriented to current situations, ignoring the long term
- Can go overboard with efficiency
- Can have difficulty communicating what's important to them
- Can be hypersensitive
- Can become reckless
- Can be pessimistic
- Can be resentful of others and can become blaming

INTP (Introverted Intuitive Thinking Perceiving): Creative, original, conceptual, logical, analytical, theoretical, detached, curious, flexible and adaptable lifestyle, objective, involved, good explainer, reflective

Downside:

- Does not communicate thoughts or feelings well
- Does not always express justifiable criticism
- Does better with impersonal situations
- Self-absorbed
- Complex ideas sometimes defy explanation
- Stubborn about being right and about doing things the "right" way
- Intolerant of others' failures or lack of high standards (from the INTP's point of view)
- Can become hypersensitive and blaming
- Can turn blame on self
- Not good with anything ordinary or routine

ESFJ (Extraverted Sensing Feeling Judging): Harmony, caring, service to others, expressive, empathetic, humanitarian, guided by values, duty, loyalty, conscientious, relationship-oriented, helper, good communicators, gracious, adaptive to environment, cheerleader

Downside:

- Can over-idealize others they admire
- Needy for approval
- Takes on the values of those around them, not necessarily creating an individual approach
- Can try too hard to please
- Can subvert own feelings and needs in order to accommodate those of others
- Can become bossy
- Can become demanding
- Can be depressed
- Can make snap decisions when too stressed
- Can become rigid and stubborn

ENFJ (Extraverted Intuitive Feeling Judging): Caring, harmony, empathetic, humanitarian, social, active, gets things done, team player, good communicator, takes on values of those around them, natural leader (in media and politics, for example), deals with possibilities, promotes wellbeing of others

Downside:

- Can be pushy
- Can ignore reality in favor of goals based on personal values
- Can be hypercritical
- Can shy away from conflict
- Doesn't like criticism
- Can ignore the feelings of others

ISFP (Introverted Sensing Feeling Perceiving): Caring, adventurous, playful, adaptable, insightful, patient, here and now, free spirit, good listener, realistic, idealistic, empathetic, individualistic, not rule-oriented, high standards, can be activist, can be artistic, demands integrity, tolerant, open-minded, likes to read, aesthetic, good in groups (good followers)

Downside:

- Sometimes fail to express appreciation for others (though they may feel it)
- Can work too hard for the benefit of others, to their own detriment
- Can be overly trusting of others
- Can fail to communicate their thoughts and feelings
- Can become overly critical
- Can be pessimistic
- Can be bossy
- Can become paranoid

INFP (Introverted Intuitive Feeling Perceiving): Caring, idealistic, good communicator, adaptable, visionary, sensitive, discreet, personal and individual values, moral, demand integrity, good listener, likes to read, tolerant, open-minded, can be activist, seeks unity, good listener, mediator, can work well alone

Downside:

- Can seem aloof; sometimes fails to demonstrate warmth that is felt
- Can be overly perfectionistic
- Can spend too much time preparing before actually acting
- Can become too emotionally involved, vulnerable
- Can seem out of touch with reality
- Can be hypercritical
- Can become picky (about unimportant issues)

The Enneagram

Another personality type method is called the *Enneagram*, a modern system that claims to be based on a synthesis of ancient traditions. Whereas the Myers-Briggs system is primarily about how people function in the world, the Enneagram is more focused on people's motivations in their lives, and for that reason, there aren't any easy and surefire one-to-one equivalents from one system to another.

The Enneagram divides people into nine types:

1. Perfectionist/Reformer
2. The Giver/The Helper
3. The Performer/The Motivator/The Achiever
4. The Romantic
5. The Observer/The Thinker
6. The Skeptic (a.k.a. The Loyal Skeptic)
7. The Epicure/The Enthusiast
8. The Boss/The Leader
9. The Mediator/The Peacemaker

The naming of these nine types varies from one source to another, but often they are referred to by number. For instance, the first type, which is sometimes called the Reformer or the Perfectionist, is always referred to as *Type 1* or a *One.* (And no, this isn't *The Matrix*, and we're not necessarily talking about "The One," though an Enneagram One might like to be "The One.") The second type is generally referred to as *Type 2* or a *Two*, and so forth.

Some people further subdivide these nine types into three categories:

- Heart/emotional types: 2, 3, 4
- Head/thinking types: 5, 6, 7
- Gut/instinctual types: 1, 8, 9

You might be able to use these nine personality types to further refine a character you are creating or to give him qualities that are consistent with this system. For instance, it is easy to see the Eight (The Leader) in the role of hero or villain. In fact, many of the traits attributed to the Eight are recognizable as common traits in megalomaniacal villains. However, it is a more interesting challenge to take some of the other Enneagram types and consider how they might fill the roles of characters in your games. Think, particularly, in terms of their extreme responses to conditions and changes in life. Are they protective? Are they self-absorbed? What can make their actions change in extreme ways? How might they act?

Here are a few characteristics often associated with each of the nine Enneagram types:

1. The Perfectionist/Reformer
   - Is action-oriented
   - Is a perfectionist
   - Is a reformer
   - Judges
   - Is a crusader
   - Is a critic
   - Seeks perfection and tries to fix what's wrong
   - Feels disappointment when his high standards are not met (by self or others)
   - Works very hard and expects others to work as hard
   - Takes things too seriously
   - Compares self to others
   - Avoids making mistakes
   - Has integrity
   - Can become obsessed with the pursuit of self-worth through accomplishments and being right
   - Can be driven and ambitious
   - Can be tense
   - Can have a hard time relaxing
   - Avoids emotional responses, can be emotionally repressed
   - Is intelligent
   - Is independent
2. The Helper/Giver
   - Wants to be needed
   - Avoids disappointing people
   - Makes friends easily
   - Is generous and caring
   - Is selfless, but proud of it
   - Is afraid to seem selfish
   - Thinks love is the highest ideal
   - Is perceptive about others and their needs
   - Can have a good sense of humor and enthusiasm
   - Fears rejection and obtains self-worth by helping and being acknowledged
   - Does not always take care of self
   - Finds it hard to say no
   - Believes you must give to receive and you must be needed to be loved
   - Is practical
   - Is emotional
   - Can think something is owed to them for what they give
   - Can become dark, hysterical, irrational, or abusive under extreme cases of disappointment or despair
   - Can fail to take care of themselves while overly caring for others

3. The Achiever
   - Requires external validation
   - Is optimistic
   - Is a good provider
   - Adjusts well to misfortune—forges ahead
   - Is competitive
   - Is hardworking
   - Can be charismatic
   - Knows what's up
   - Gets things done
   - Is a good motivator
   - Is impatient with incompetence
   - Fears failure
   - Thinks second best isn't good enough
   - Is image-conscious—it's important what others think of him/her
   - Must be "on" all the time
   - Ignores feelings
   - Can have problems with intimacy
   - Can be narcissistic
   - Can become ruthless
   - Can confuse appearances of success with real happiness

4. The Romantic/The Individualist
   - Identifies with self as different or unique
   - Deeply feels emotions
   - Easily communicates emotions
   - Finds meaning through connections with people
   - Often feels disconnected when alone
   - Aspires to nobility, truth, and beauty
   - Is creative
   - Is passionate
   - Is intuitive
   - Has a good sense of humor
   - Creates a personal and unique approach to life
   - Needs self-expression
   - Is often artistic and creative
   - Can feel superior to others because they perceive themselves as unique
   - Can feel personally flawed because they perceive themselves as unique
   - Is aware of the feelings of others
   - Is susceptible to depression, despair, and emptiness
   - Has low self-esteem
   - Is generally self-absorbed
   - Can become highly self-indulgent
   - Often thinks a solution to their problems will come from outside, not inside
   - Capable of feeling guilty if he/she disappoints someone
   - Tends to feel hurt in conflict with others
   - Can be moody and temperamental
   - Has high expectations overall
   - Fears abandonment
   - Seeks some ideal of love or life situation
   - Fears being ordinary or unlovable

5. The Thinker/The Investigator
   - Is sage
   - Is objective
   - Is voyeuristic
   - Has high integrity
   - Often lacks social skills
   - Can act defensively
   - Can seem like a know-it-all
   - Becomes distant when uncomfortable
   - Fears they can't be competent enough
   - Most comfortable in their own world of thoughts
   - Can be artistic
   - Is individualistic
   - Is sometimes eccentric
   - Is shy
   - Is not comfortable in the world of emotions
   - Is reluctant to seek help
   - Due to feelings of inadequacy, can adopt compensating attitudes (unrealistic nonchalance or intellectual arrogance) that drive people away
   - Can become irritated when forced to repeat things
   - Likes seclusion and privacy
   - Doesn't like big, loud groups

- Can be devoted to long-term friends, if intimacy is achieved
- Is perceptive
- Feels "different"
- Sees cause and effect

6. The Skeptic/The Loyalist
   - Is motivated by deep-rooted fear
   - Is rebellious
   - Is cooperative
   - Is loyal to family and friends
   - Is responsible
   - Works hard
   - Is a good troubleshooter
   - Is compassionate
   - Is intellectual
   - Is a nonconformist
   - Is witty
   - Is direct
   - Is assertive
   - Has difficulty with decisions
   - Procrastinates
   - Has a fear of failure
   - Has anxiety
   - Has low self-esteem
   - Worries
   - Is on the lookout for danger (hypervigilant)
   - Seeks something or someone to believe in
   - Is slow to trust
   - Once trust is given, is hyper-loyal, even when inappropriate
   - Has fear of fear itself
   - Is self-critical
   - Seeks security and faith
   - Avoids uncertainty
   - Lacks spontaneity
   - Can be highly phobic or equally counter-phobic, depending on the strategies that they adopt to deal with fear

7. The Enthusiast/Adventurer
   - Is energetic
   - Is optimistic
   - Likes companionship
   - Is individualistic
   - Is spontaneous
   - Is a free spirit
   - Is outspoken
   - Is skilled in multiple areas
   - Is generous
   - Is altruistic
   - Seeks a path
   - Is playful
   - Is self-promoting
   - Is self-centered
   - Is a risk-taker
   - Is future-oriented
   - Keeps options open
   - Is a quick thinker
   - Is extraverted
   - Is creative
   - Is open-minded
   - Has a sometimes obsessive pursuit of pleasure
   - Is prone to addictive behaviors
   - Has a high self-image
   - Suffers from feelings of entitlement
   - Avoids difficult emotional states
   - Dislikes boredom
   - Fears incompleteness
   - Wants to do everything
   - Can be unreliable
   - Doesn't always finish things
   - Has trouble with commitment
   - Feels trapped in relationships that are too close
   - Can suffer from anxiety disorders
   - Can suffer from depression

8. The Leader/Challenger
   - Is independent
   - Is the master of his/her own fate
   - Is highly focused
   - Has courage
   - Is honest
   - Is defiant
   - Is a maverick
   - Is a protector
   - Is a boss
   - Is self-reliant
   - Is strong-willed
   - Is decisive
   - Feels invincible
   - Has strength
   - Is practical
   - Has powerful physical appetites
   - Is self-indulgent without shame or guilt
   - Is supportive of others
   - Prefers financial independence
   - Protects others
   - Works for causes
   - Seeks a higher truth
   - Pressures self
   - Can be overly blunt
   - Fears humiliation
   - Fears vulnerability and weakness
   - Has difficulty with intimacy
   - Has significant trust issues
   - Can inspire close allies
   - Is highly reactive to betrayal
   - Disdains the mediocre
   - Focuses on power and influence
   - Gets impatient with incompetence
   - Is inclined toward anger, which can become rage under extreme conditions
   - Can find enjoyment from intimidating others
   - Will bulldoze weaker people who stand in their way
   - Can be brutal
   - Can be dangerous
   - Wants appreciation from others
   - Tends to remember slights, injuries, and injustice
   - Expects people to live up to high standards
   - Can be histrionic
   - Demands loyalty
   - Can be "bigger than life"
   - May have a sentimental side, but rarely lets it show

9. The Peacemaker
   - Needs peace and harmony
   - Avoids or fixes conflict
   - Is conciliatory
   - Is introverted
   - Tends to withdraw somewhat
   - Tends to be accepting of others
   - Likes to be cared for
   - Hates to be overlooked or unappreciated, but suppresses feelings
   - When feelings overflow, may explode in quick bursts of temper or become temporarily uncooperative
   - Can feel great but unexpressed sadness
   - Shows concern for others
   - Is relaxed
   - Is easy to be around
   - Is reliable
   - Is self-effacing
   - Can tend to blend in with the people around them, diffusing their own personalities
   - Is likeable
   - Is optimistic
   - Seeks unconditional love
   - Seeks union with others
   - Can see many sides of an issue
   - Is very aware of what's going on
   - Is adaptable
   - Loves nature
   - Has a sense of belonging
   - Can seem indecisive or too laidback
   - Sometimes resists change, but ultimately is adaptable
   - Is unassuming
   - Can be self-critical, especially around issues of self-discipline and taking initiative

- Can be hypersensitive to criticism
- Sometimes doesn't know own needs/desires
- Thinks image is important—what do others think of them?
- Can be ignored or not taken seriously
- Dislikes outside pressure
- Seeks harmony, avoids discord
- Prefers simplicity

MENTAL/EMOTIONAL SIGNALS: THE OTHER 93%

NOTE

The information in this section is not intended to be complete. It could be useful, but it is by no means exhaustive. Consider this a summary of the (primarily nonverbal) emotional and mental signs that can be observed and that can, in theory, be applied to digital actors in games.

Years of study have shown that only 7 percent of all communication is verbal. Thirty-eight percent is conveyed through tonal qualities of voice, such as how loud or soft, how fast, and other subtleties. Fifty-five percent is from body position, posture, gestures, and facial expression. For that reason, the development of artificial characters can be substantially improved by paying attention to the 93 percent of the information we receive that is nonverbal.

The information in this section is not necessarily true in all individual instances. These are generalities based on observation and drawing from techniques such as NLP (neuro-linguistic programming). Even though something on this list can often turn out to be true, specific individuals may behave quite differently, and these guidelines may be completely unreliable in those specific cases. This information can be useful in creating more realistic characters, however—particularly contrasting characters under duress—and giving them realistic nonverbal behaviors, but in no way would this be applicable to real-world use without training.

ABOUT RAPPORT

One phenomenon that can occur when people interact is called *rapport*. Rapport is an indication that people are in some kind of conscious or unconscious harmony with each other. Rapport can manifest when people are positively connecting, leading to more effective communications, or when people are in conflict. For instance, people can be in rapport when angry with each other, which doesn't lead to more effective outcomes, but does mean that they are connecting in unconscious disharmony. In games, the signs of rapport—or the lack of those signs—can be used to more realistically depict the interactions between NPCs or even between the player's character and other NPCs. It would be more difficult to implement these indications in player-to-player interactions in multiplayer games, though probably not impossible.

The following list includes some of the more obvious and observable manifestations of rapport:

- Breathing in synch
- Head/shoulder tilt matching
- Overall body posture matching (such as leaning toward or away from each other, crossed limbs, and so forth)
- Gestures matching
- Rates of movement matching
- Rates of speech matching
- Paraverbal patterns—non-word sounds, such as "um" or "uh"; also overall tone, timbre, intensity, volume
- Shared word or phrase uses—same language patterns

NLP Perspectives: How People Process Information

People receive information from the sensory systems, such as sight, sound, touch, taste, and smell. The ways that the brain sorts and codes this information are known as *modalities* or *representational systems*, which means our five senses. The modalities most commonly observed with regard to people's behavior are visual, auditory, and kinesthetic. Within each of these modalities, there can be many submodalities; for example, in the visual modality some submodality examples are distance, size, shape, color, light, foreground/background. In auditory modalities, some submodalities include volume, rate of speech, timbre, pitch, tempo, and so on. In the kinesthetic modality, submodalities include pressure, duration, temperature, density, and so on.

We are using all five senses all the time, but we are only conscious of one or two in any given circumstance. And even then, people will almost always have one that is favored—one that is more dominant in their experience, in their awareness, and in their processing. This is normal and natural, and it is also a good news/bad news situation. As an example, it's good news that visual artists have great sensibilities for light when they work, but it's bad news when they are in a situation where they need to hear clearly. They may be looking when it might be more effective to listen. People are creatures of habit, and they default to one modality over another. Nevertheless, all the data is there all of the time.

The methods described in NLP are:

- **Visual.** Using the visual senses to gather and process information.
- **Auditory.** Using sound at any and all levels to process information.
- **Kinesthetic.** Gathering information through the physical—the body—and through feelings.
- **Auditory Digital.** This is a specific type of auditory processing that is characterized by a very flat, emotionless attention to detail—in this sense, something like Mr. Spock from *Star Trek*. But Spock is not a complete example because, in addition, there is an extremely specific connection of meaning to words, such that a person processing in this modality simply does not relate to any other word. They literally do not experience a situation without the specific word or words to describe it. If you ask them, "Are you angry?" and the word they think describes their experience is "frustrated," they will simply say they are not angry. They are not attempting to lie or misrepresent. It is simply that only the word "frustrated" will do. So if you ask them, "Are you feeling frustrated?" they will say, "That's it!" Literally, in the absence of the correct word, their experience is on hold.

Barring physical impairment, people use all of the representational systems simultaneously. What is most useful and significant in terms of character design in games is that the predominant modality a person is using is observable through their unconscious body language and through the specific speech patterns (words, expressions, and paraverbals) they are using at the time.

It bears repeating that these are *not exclusive* methods. Someone can obviously be watching (using visual) while listening (using auditory) and sensing/feeling (using kinesthetic) simultaneously. However, it is often true that someone is using one of these *predominantly*, and it is this fact that can be used in character design to further distinguish one character from another.

For the purpose of character design, these modality habits, or preferences, can be used to further distinguish one character from another—creating more variety and individuality among the characters you create. Here are some very general aspects of someone who is using visual, auditory, or kinesthetic.

Visual

- **Expressions.** "We saw eye to eye." "She has a sunny disposition." "I'm feeling a little blue today."
- **Voice Tone/Speed/Volume.** High and clear, rapid and loud, sometimes staccato.
- **Tempo changes.** Quick bursts of words.
- **Breathing Level and Rate.** High in chest; rapid, with cessation between breaths.

Part IV

- **Postures.** Neck extended, straight, erect; head and shoulders up; hands behind head, very still; watching with little or no movement.
- **Movements.** Tight, jerky.
- **Gestures.** Points while talking, gestures tend to be upward in direction, arms extend, often observes with chin down and eyes high in sockets.
- **Eye Accessing Cues.** Eyes up left, eyes up, eyes straight ahead (defocused).
- **Eye Elevation.** Above others' eyes.
- **Looking While Listening?** Has to look in order to listen.
- **Lower Lip Size.** Thin, tight.
- **Muscle Tension.** Tight shoulders and abdomen.
- **Facial Color.** Pale or waning.
- **Memory.** Quick, fast forward/fast reverse/freeze frame in slide or movie form.

Auditory

- **Expressions.** "That rings a bell." "I hear you." "That rings true."
- **Voice Tone/Speed/Volume.** Clear, melodic, expressive, resonant.
- **Tempo Changes.** Even, rhythmic.
- **Breathing Level and Rate.** Even breathing over whole chest area; cessation and long exhale.
- **Postures.** Body slightly leaning forward (external orientation) or back (internal orientation); head well balanced or slightly at an angle; hands in pockets, head tilted down.
- **Movements.** Rhythmic; some part of the body moving like a metronome.
- **Gestures.** Touches face, hands toward mouth, cups ear.
- **Eye Accessing Cues.** Laterally left or right.
- **Eye Elevation.** Often diverted, down to listen.
- **Looking While Listening?** Often looks away, avoiding visual stimulus—does not have to look to listen.
- **Lower Lip Size.** Variable.
- **Muscle Tension.** Even, with rhythmic movement.
- **Facial Color.** Varies between visual and kinesthetic.
- **Memory.** Sequential/whole chunks—rhythmic access.

Kinesthetic

- **Expressions.** "I'm finally on an even keel." "He just can't seem to get a handle on it." "This just feels perfect."
- **Voice Tone/Speed/Volume.** Low, airy, slow, soft, deep.
- **Tempo Changes.** Slow, long pauses.
- **Breathing Level and Rate.** Low in stomach, slow.
- **Postures.** Neck extended, curved, centered, and bowed head; shoulders down, slouching, blocky.
- **Movements.** Loose, flowing, a lot of movement, wants to stand or sit close to others.
- **Gestures.** Behavioral representation of what is being said, or palms turned up, arms bent; touches others while talking or listening (within cultural norms).
- **Eye Accessing Cues.** Eyes down to non-dominant side.
- **Eye Elevation.** Below others' eyes.
- **Looking While Listening?** Rather touch than look.
- **Lower Lip Size.** Full, soft.
- **Muscle Tension.** Not too much tension.
- **Facial Color.** Increased, fuller color.
- **Memory.** Slower; muscle memory; knows answer immediately, but takes time to articulate it.

Auditory Digital. (This is a specific case of the auditory processing submodality, but when people are using this as a representational system, they exhibit unique and observable characteristics.)

- **Expressions.** "That doesn't add up." "I understand." "Yes, we complemented each other well."
- **Voice Tone/Speed/Volume.** Consistently clipped, monotones.
- **Tempo Changes.** Generally none.
- **Breathing Level and Rate.** High in chest, barely breathing.
- **Postures.** Arms crossed, hands together; erect/rigid body, controlled, head up; often leaning to one side; resting head on hands or hands near mouth/chin.
- **Movements.** Rigid, stiff.
- **Gestures.** Controlled, minimal, counts off fingers.
- **Eye Accessing Cues.** Laterally right or left, or down on the non-dominant side.
- **Eye Elevation.** Gazes over others' heads.
- **Looking While Listening?** Rarely makes eye contact.
- **Lower Lip Size.** Thin, tight.
- **Muscle Tension.** Tense.
- **Facial Color.** Minimal, gray.
- **Memory.** Sequential, whole chunks.

More Observable and Representable Data

In addition to rapport and the various representational systems, there are many ways to "read" people and therefore many ways to represent them in digital characters. Here are some additional elements you can consider when animating realistic characters. Some of this information is quite subtle, but to the extent that you can accurately incorporate these elements into a digital character, they will further the sense of realism in the game and the characters involved. Even untrained people recognize many of these observable behaviors, at least on an unconscious level, and they will respond to the same signs in a game—to some extent—that they respond to in real life. Keep in mind, however, that this response is necessarily limited because digital avatars are still not conveying all the information that real people are—such as smell, physical presence, and possibly some intangible qualities we may or may not have as human beings that digital actors can never have—an electrical field or some spiritual presence.

Eye Movements

This refers to eye movements from the observer's (or player's) point of view. Note that this can be reversed for some people, including but not limited to, those who are left-handed.

NOTE

Disclaimer: Many people believe that a person's eye movements can reveal whether they are lying. However, experts with decades of experience will tell you that this is not true. *It is quite often possible to tell whether someone is lying, but this requires far more information than just the way their eyes move.* You cannot tell whether someone is lying from eye accessing information alone. *Just wanted to be sure that was clear.*

- **Top Left.** Visual construction. They are creating images that they have not seen before—remembering a context into which they insert your statement or question.
- **Top Right.** Visual recall/remembering. This generally means they are remembering past events by visualizing them.

- **Straight Up or Straight Ahead Defocused.** Simply looking at images. This can be either constructed or remembered, usually visual, but not always. There is always a visual image they are seeing, regardless of whether they are conscious of it.
- **Horizontal Left.** Auditory construction. This could be creating new sounds, words, sentences, or sequencing of words. A character *might* use this accessing if he was making it all up or lying. He might also simply be remembering poorly and having to fill in by making up parts—for instance, he remembers a situation pretty well, but not the exact words that were spoken.
- **Horizontal Right.** Auditory remembering. This probably means he is remembering auditory information, such as a song or melody, the sounds of a traumatic event or a conversation, or even tone of voice from some event.
- **Down Left.** Kinesthetic—experiencing feelings in the body. Many people respond to events and people in their lives with a deeper physical response, as if their feelings were located somewhere in their bodies.
- **Down Right. Self-Talk.** Most likely, the person is holding some kind of inner dialog—he may be somewhat "checked out."

Head Movements

People often cock their head to one side or another. This can mean that they are thinking or engaging in an inner auditory process.

Other Body Language

This refers to observable effects during interactions. Changes may occur immediately or very soon after a character has an internal response to some event or information.

- **Limbs Crossed or Open.** Many people believe that when someone's arms or legs are crossed, it means he is uncomfortable or even angry. This may be true, but from an NLP perspective, what is happening is that the person is engaged in an auditory process. It is what he is telling himself internally and how he is "saying" it to himself that is the key here. If he is uncomfortable, he is probably saying something like, "This is really boring," or "My butt hurts in this uncomfortable seat." If he is angry, he might be thinking, "He's so full of it. I wish he would just shut up." Or, he might not be uncomfortable or angry, but simply talking to himself about something unrelated to the current circumstances.

  Whatever the character is experiencing, crossed limbs facilitate auditory process. So, when creating a character with this sort of behavior, you can go further than just to say he is uncomfortable, angry, or thinking about other matters. You can actually look at that character in terms of what he is saying to himself at that moment and how he is saying it.
- **Erect Body Position.** Erect posture is most often associated with someone who is processing information visually.
- **Slouched Body Position.** If hands are clasped behind the head, this is still a visual process, but disassociated from what is happening, as if just viewing it but not involved in it. If arms or hands are not above the head, this may indicate that the person is feeling the situation internally rather than processing it visually.
- **Stiff or Bent Knees.** Some people think that beliefs are stored in the knees and that rigidity in the knees could indicate rigid belief systems. Often people who are primarily auditory will lean forward with slightly more rigidity in the knees; however, when more relaxed, they may stand more erect, and the knees may relax. Leaning forward may also have to do with balancing the person's energy to the front instead of all around him.

- **Hands at Side.** This is not necessarily a definitive sign of anything. It depends on the context.
- **Hands Clasped.** There are different ways that someone's hands can clasp together. For instance, if the hands are forced between the legs, it tends to help people with some internal awareness or process. In contrast, if their legs are crossed and their hands are on the arms of a chair, there is somewhat less facilitation of internal process, and they are probably less aware that it is going on.
- **Counting Off on Fingers.** Hands can be moving for a variety of reasons. If a person is counting off on his fingers, it's likely that he is using the auditory digital process (auditory with words, but without connected emotions).
- **Hand Movements.** Hands below the waist tend to indicate more kinesthetic process. From waist to shoulders is auditory and some visual. Above the shoulders is all visual. Hand movement in the mid-body range is often associated with representing what the person is talking about—the hand gestures may be an analog of what they are saying. Wringing of hands, especially lower with respect to the body, could be an analog of what is going on inside the person.
- **Hand on Hip.** One or both hands on the hips indicates an auditory process. This is often accompanied by some slight weight imbalance, which indicates a subtle disconnection from himeslf—in some way he is literally "beside himself." This can be used to get a different perspective or because the person doesn't like what it feels like inside, or to keep himself from feeling. He may be thinking about an experience more than actually being in the experience.
- **Hand in Pocket.** This indicates auditory processing.
- **Hand Touching Face.** This is always an indication of auditory processing—the telephone posture, hands around the mouth. This is a catalyst for auditory processing and often also indicates a certain degree of disassociation or internal thought process (also known as *metacomment* or *self-talk*).
- **Hands behind Head.** Disassociated visual processing
- **Arms Clasped behind Body.** Indicates visual processing.
- **Arms in Front of Body.** Indicates auditory processing, particularly when hands are together.
- **Weight.** Rhythmic rocking, shifting the weight, is generally an indication of auditory process. Non-rhythmic weight shifts are more likely a kinesthetic process.
- **Body Shifts.** Sudden shifts in the body can also be unconscious responses to significant thoughts or reactions, such as an "aha" moment or sudden comprehension. These changes can be subtle or obvious, but they are noticeable to trained observers. In many cases, the changes are obvious enough to be observed by any interested party.
- **Tension in Muscles.** Noticeable muscle tension can have many meanings. In people who are predominantly processing visually, there is a certain tension in keeping the body still—to keep the lens of vision still. There are different types of kinesthetic as well—those who are externally oriented and those who are more internal. External kinesthetics tend toward athleticism and may have more muscle tension. This can be healthy muscle tonus or tension related to steeling themselves against vulnerability, depending on their level of personal growth and self-integration. Internal kinesthetics tend to be more emotionally involved and tend to have softer bodies.
- **Body Matching Modality.** What this refers to is how, on average, bodies tend to match the predominant modality (visual, auditory, kinesthetic) a person uses. For instance, visuals tend to have larger eyes and be somewhat slighter in the upper body. Auditory types may have larger chests. Kinesthetics may have bigger muscles if they tend to be tactile/external. These are not hard-and-fast rules, but they could be applied to character design if you have some idea of how the person would tend to process information (which in itself determines some of his behavior and expressions).
- **Rate of Eye Blinking.** The rate of eye blinking can actually be meaningful in some cases. In particular, when someone is looking straight ahead and is unfocused—seeing images in their heads. Some people see movies in their heads, while others see still images. For those who see still images, their eye

blinks actually correspond to a change in the image—like a slide projector changing slides. I don't know how useful this would be in character design, but it's interesting.

- **Color Changes.** There are a lot of obvious color change clues. In general, people who are predominantly visual tend to have less color in the face and neck. Kinesthetics tend to have the most color naturally, and auditory processors are in between, with some variation.

  More common are the color changes associated with anger, embarrassment, fear, and surprise. Interestingly, when someone is surprised, there is a good likelihood that he will respond according to his predominant modality. For instance, visuals may freeze, their eyes get very large, and they stop breathing. Auditory processors may make some kind of noise, while kinesthetics will move in some way—even if it is jumping up and down!
- **Lower Lip Size.** Interestingly, lower lips can indicate a fair amount about a person under some circumstances. It is well known that lips engorge when a person is aroused—sexually or otherwise. This is a subtle cue, but one that people recognize. Why else would all the Hollywood actresses want their lips to be artificially fattened? It simulates sexual arousal and works subconsciously on people who see them.

  Overall, in terms of modalities, visuals tend to have the thinnest lips, with auditorys' lips thicker, and kinesthetics' lips thicker still. All show some variation of lip size, but the visuals vary the least. Auditory processors may also move their lips as an analog of the sounds—not necessarily subvocalizing, but moving in association with internal sounds.
- **Chin Position.** There is a lot of thought about what it means if someone has his chin raised or lowered. How much of it is true is debatable. In NLP, the chin may be raised or lowered by people who are predominantly visual in order to change the angle of the eyes in the sockets. For instance, with the chin lowered, the eyes are looking from high in the sockets, which can actually be an analog of how they are viewing the world. This may have a different and more emotional connotation to some people. The same holds true of the chin tilted up. Some people would interpret that as a sort of challenging, even arrogant body language. In NLP it is not necessarily meaningful. Moving the chin up and down is associated with an inner auditory process.
- **Sidelong Look (Head Turned Slightly Away from Direction of Gaze).** This look can be seen, from an NLP perspective, as a way of positioning the eyes to a corner of the socket—which might stimulate some kind of remembering or creating of images. However, in common responses, people often see this as a coy look—a come-on—or a sidelong glance.
- **Facial Expressions.** There is a lot of study of basic facial expressions. (See the upcoming "Facial Expressions" section.) From an NLP perspective, a person's face tends to be more expressive when he is more "in" his body. When a person is disassociated, he tends to have a less responsive face. Some people, due to their past histories, have trained themselves to have a poker face—for instance, if they were punished for being expressive in some way. This is a habit that inhibits natural expression and can be seen on some people who are highly controlled emotionally.

  The face displays what kind of trance a person is in—is it a laughter trance, or sexual fantasy, fear, considering what to do or what not to do, surprise, curiosity, and so on? The face quickly reveals a person's state or current trance state.
- **Eyes (Irises, Dilation, Etc.).** The iris of the eye responds very quickly to a variety of stimuli, including, but not limited to, changes of light. Generally speaking, the more relaxed someone is, the greater the level of dilation. When someone has a significant realization or thought, the eyes dilate, as they also do when the person sees an internal problem image of some type. Strangely, in fearful situations, it's possible that people tense up, the irises constrict, and they may see only one way out—tunnel vision. In contrast, someone trained in martial arts or other methods of staying calm in crisis may exhibit different behaviors and stay relaxed, seeing more options.

- **Breathing.** Breathing tends to be rapid and shallow when someone is fearful or ill at ease. Visuals tend toward shallow, smooth breathing when they are watching something without really being connected. Breathing in the mid-chest, if ragged and heaving, is likely to be fear or something similar, while even mid-chest breathing is like normal conversational breathing. Deep abdominal breathing also ranges from ragged, heaving, big gasping breaths associated with sorrow, grief, and other deep emotional or physical pain, to deep, even breathing associated with a very relaxed state or even a meditative state.
- **Personal Space.** In general, there is a cultural component to how close is comfortable—meaning that in different cultures the distance people can be to each other (in non-intimate settings) varies. However, there is also a phenomenon recognized in NLP in which people can be more comfortable if someone is on one side of them than another. This may have to do with how those people store imagery internally. If they tend to store the problematic images on their left, they may then be uncomfortable when someone is standing on that side of them.

NOTE

A little tidbit: In a study carried out by the Canadian Mounted Police, it was shown that when burglars exited a building in a hurry or a panic (afraid to be caught), they almost always turned to the right. By noticing this, the police were able to narrow the area of a search with good results. It is also for this reason that, for instance, if a 7-11 has double doors, the one to the right might remain locked.

Vocal Characteristics

The following are characteristics of voice that provide meaning to what someone says, above and beyond the words themselves.

- Tonality
- Tempo
- Timbre
- Volume
- Rate of speaking
- Rhythm
- Pitch
- Clarity (enunciation)
- Accents (on syllables)
- Non-words (such as uh, um, ah)

Mannerisms That Reveal That Someone Is Thinking

Sometimes when people are thinking deeply, it is revealed in something they do or how they behave, such as:

- Resting head in hand(s)
- Touching nose or mouth
- Clasping hands (restricting natural movement)
- Staring in a fixed manner, as if seeing something in the distance (or seeing nothing)

Other Ways to Show Character Emotions/States

Sometimes you want to indicate a character's emotional state without necessarily spelling it out to the player. In addition to the nonverbal cues from the previous section, there are ways to use scenes, settings, and other elements to let the player know what is going on with the character. As an example, if you want to show that someone is not doing too well, you might show him with messed-up hair, unshaven, and with stained and sloppy clothing. Or his house/apartment is clearly neglected, with stuff all over the place, dishes piled up in the sink, and so on. To show that someone is very sad, have him sitting in a slumped posture, surrounded by used tissues. To show that someone is nervous, have him fidgeting or being overly busy while you are observing him. And so forth. This section suggests a few other ways to show a character's emotional state, focusing on a few of the main emotional states.

Anger

The obvious way to handle anger is to have someone act out dramatically—to yell, to hit things, to fight, to rage. But although these are appropriate responses in some cases, there are more interesting ways to show that someone is angry.

- Easily becoming impatient or frustrated with minor things
- Walking away
- Becoming very quiet
- Giving very short answers
- Reddening of face, widening of eyes, tightening of lips
- Slamming a door just a little too hard
- Chopping food (or wood) with too much vehemence
- Hands gripping or wringing
- Suddenly being agreeable to everything or saying "you're right" over and over again
- Giving up easily in an argument or when doing something challenging
- Eating too fast
- Doing something physical with great intensity, such as running or shadow boxing

Fear

Classic responses to fear involve running away, cringing, shaking and stuttering, and so on. But fear can be more subtle, too.

- Using bravado to mask fear.
- Showing subtle hesitancy.
- Showing a sudden interest in something else.
- Raising objections or suggesting flaws in the plan—attempting to change the plan.
- Volunteering someone else.
- Volunteering to do something that's not dangerous. ("I'll wait here and guard the women and children.")
- Making an excuse to get angry and leave.

Sadness

When you see someone who is sad, how do they look? How do they act? Here are some of the signs you might notice from someone who is feeling sad.

- Lacking enthusiasm.
- Having sluggish actions.
- Body language (slumped posture, heavy eyes).
- Having slow, monotonic speech.
- Sitting surrounded by clippings, pictures, or some other nostalgic items.
- Having a lot of used tissues and a nearly empty bottle of booze in their apartment.
- Doing a bad job of dressing or grooming.
- Wearing darker colors or more subdued clothing than usual.
- Having red circles around their eyes, as if they might have been crying.
- Masking sadness with anger, lashing out at things and people around them. This is a secondary emotion, and the sadness lies beneath it.

Happiness

These also apply mostly to people in love.

Happy people exhibit certain behaviors. Here are a few ways you might depict someone who is happy.

- Dancing around the room
- Having an extra spring in the step
- Putting flowers everywhere
- Having a glow about the face and smiling a lot
- Chuckling to oneself from time to time
- Being especially friendly
- Chattering about almost anything
- Giving gifts to others or even to themselves
- Being very enthusiastic
- Having flowing movements and erect (but not stiff) posture
- Singing, humming, or whistling happy tunes
- Telling a lot of jokes and/or making good-natured wisecracks

Anxiety/Nervousness

When people are nervous or anxious, what do they do? Here are a few ways you might be able to show an anxious character.

- Fidgeting
- Getting obsessed over small details
- Lacking concentration and focus and being easily distracted
- Doing some mindless action, such as drumming fingers or tapping a foot, smoking incessantly, eating or pacing the floor
- Buttoning a shirt wrong
- Having movements that are more jerky and stiff than usual
- Having problems with simple tasks, such as operating a can opener, threading a needle, or mixing a potion
- Checking out occasionally, as if one's mind is somewhere else
- Having unsteady hands and poor eye/hand coordination
- Looking around, darting eyes, as if expecting something that isn't there—yet

Hiding Something

When someone is hiding something, how can you tell? Here are a few ways you might depict a character who is keeping secrets.

- Having shifty, intentional avoidance of eye contact during conversation
- Being evasive
- Attempting to divert attention from whatever one is hiding
- Using uneven speech patterns, especially if you are close to what he is hiding
- Displaying artificial friendliness or enthusiasm
- Being abnormally watchful (as if one is afraid of being discovered at any moment)
- Displaying signs of anxiety/nervousness
- Being reactive to attempts to find the truth, displaying angry or self-righteous behaviors
- Being highly defensive
- Vehemently protesting if accused; over-explaining and/or attempting to rationalize
- Changing story in mid-stream—lack of consistency
- Trying especially hard to convince you of something that obscures the truth
- Using gestures and head movements to seem convincing—the person will escalate the behavior the more suspicious you seem or the closer to the truth you get

Apathy

- Who cares?

Physical Changes

Does the character change physically during the course of the story? If so, how? Here's a list of basic ways a character might be physically altered during the course of a story.

- Age (older, probably, but possibly younger)
- Gender
- Injury/mutilated
- Amputated limb(s)
- Healthier or less healthy
- Pregnant
- Diseased or cured
- Scarred
- Piercings and other cosmetic body mods
- Morph into something else
- Hair (style, length, or color)
- Apparel (anything the character wears)
- Skin color
- Eye color
- Breast size/shape
- Facial reconstruction (new face or new facial features, such as nose, chin, ears, etc.)
- Taller or shorter
- Heavier or lighter
- Larger or smaller
- Stronger or weaker in appearance
- More or less handsome/beautiful
- Death (see Chapter 32, "Ways to Die")
- Reincarnation
- Whole new body
- Discorporate (no body)

Facial Expressions

Facial expressions tell us a lot about people—whether they are happy or sad, interested or bored, nervous or calm, and so on. In addition to the information offered in the previous section on NLP principles, this section looks at more ways we might use facial expression to depict our characters more effectively. This is one of many ways to communicate information to the player. In multiplayer games, someday we may use facial expressions the way we currently use emotes, but with even better results.

Six Basic Emotions

Some people have reduced basic human emotions to the following six. Certainly, these sum up much of our human interaction.

- Anger
- Fear
- Happiness
- Sadness
- Surprise
- Disgust

Ways to Greet Someone

How do you greet someone? A lot can be implied by the way in which someone meets and greets others. Here's a short list to get you started.

- Glad
- Mad
- Sad
- Surprised
- Afraid
- Wary
- Reserved
- Shy

- Disdainful
- Friendly
- Over-the-top phony friendliness
- Welcoming
- Loving/adoring
- Embarrassed

Ways to Indicate Agreement or Disagreement

In fact, though Americans assume that nodding the head up and down indicates agreement and shaking the head from side to side indicates disagreement, this isn't universally true in all cultures. However, since it is so common in the Western world, it's probably best to accept that these conventions are the best ones to use for the Americas and Europe.

More on Facial Expressions

The following list is simply to give you some ideas for different situations, the responses to which might produce specific and interesting facial expressions:

- **Intensity.** Eyes tightening, as if you are looking closer at something clearly important. You are serious, with a slight frown.
- **Spotting an Enemy.** What sorts of reactions might you have?
  - You are focusing on them.
  - You recognize them but are not taking them too seriously.
  - You recognize them suddenly and are concerned, scared, or shocked.
  - You are not very impressed by them.
- **Taking a Painful Hit.** Somewhere on the body. (Getting punched or kicked.) Pain can be low, moderate, or high, with appropriate facial expression.
- **Delivering a Blow.** Punching or kicking someone—varying intensity based on effort.
- **Fright.** A range from slightly nervous to outright panicked.
- **Laughter.** Range from a chuckle to a long belly laugh.
- **Meaningful Smiles**
  - Cunning. You know the trap is set.
  - Happy. They fell into your trap.
  - Pleasantly Surprised. They have not noticed your trap.
  - Come-on. You and I are going to hook up tonight.
  - Sly. Nice to meet you; I know all about you, and you know nothing about me.
  - Big/Huge. I'm so happy/relieved/fulfilled to see you.
- **Forced Expressions.** Trying to hide real emotions/responses.
- **Sadness.** Ranges from moderately disappointed to tragically melancholy.
- **Shock.** Ranges from dazed, dizzy, frozen, to shell-shocked, and so on. Varies with events and causes of the shock, such as the difference between seeing a major accident, seeing your family killed, or being in an accident yourself, and so on.
- **Amazement.** Jaw dropped, eyes wide—the look of utter surprise at what you are witnessing. Imagine seeing a whale fall out of the sky and hit the ground 30 yards in front of you.
- **Ultimate Effort.** Putting everything you have into it. The last-ditch, all-or-nothing look of grim determination, concentration, and physical exertion.
- **Nervous.** Approaching a situation that makes the character nervous, such as meeting someone important for the first time, going to court, meeting a love interest, on the way to prison, and so on.
- **Aggression.** Displaying aggressive or hostile emotions in the face—scowling, squinty eyes, clenched teeth, and jutting jaw.

- **Issuing a Challenge.** Taunting or challenging an enemy. Faces may vary with the attitude of the character—could be disdainful, casual, bored, insulting, angry, and so on.
- **Ooops!** The look you get when you goof up—ranging from a minor gaff to a really big blunder.
- **Repose.** The look of the character at rest or in a peaceful moment.
- **Concentration.** For instance, listening to someone tell you directions versus reading some complicated instructions on how to disarm a time bomb with less than a minute to go.
- **Flirtatious.** Winks and smiles, tilts of head, and so on.
- **Asleep.** Ranges from peaceful repose, to restless tossing and turning, to a range of potentially comical snoring behaviors.
- **Irritation.** Eyes or nose irritated by noxious gasses or smells, ears irritated by painful or annoying sounds.
- **Dry Mouth.** Expressions and actions of someone whose lips, tongue, and/or mouth are very dry. How might that person react when spotting a soda, a water fountain, or an oasis in the desert?
- **Sneezes.** A range of ways that people build up to and consummate a sneeze.
- **Fixing Jaw.** After being hit there.
- **Choking.** From noxious fumes, from being in a chokehold or strangulation device, or from having been hit in the throat, and so on.
- **Huffing and Puffing.** Out of breath from exertion.
- **Coughing.** Various kinds of coughing, from a light clearing of the throat to horrifying, hacking-up-blood, emphysema wracking, gasping fits.
- **Curiosity.** Ranges from mild to extreme to obsessive.
- **Chewing and Swallowing.** Might be indicative of someone chewing gum, betel nuts, or whatever.
- **Whistling and Humming.** Often a nervous habit. People who whistle or hum around others may be unaware of their effect on people or may not really care. They may use whistling or humming as a way to split their focus while working.
- **Confusion.** Someone who looks around and is obviously uncomfortable or doesn't understand what is going on.
- **Sick.** They look drawn and pasty-faced, tired. They may or may not look sad. In fact, someone can look sickly but not unhappy.
- **Blank Stare.** Just looks as if without seeing.
- **Urgency.** Eyes wide, mouth open, an anticipatory look as if about to speak.
- **Getting Someone's Attention.** Staring fixedly at someone, maybe mouthing words. Presumably, they want to get that person's attention but haven't yet done anything about it.
- **Silent Words.** Mouthing words to a song or play, or simply sub-vocal self-dialog.
- **Crying.** Obvious expressions—puffy eyes, tears running down the face, red-faced, maybe runny nose.
- **Kissing.** Pursed lips, soft or wide and expectant eyes.
- **Licking Lips.** This could be anything from anticipating something yummy to Heath Ledger as the Joker. Take your pick or choose something else—perhaps they have a dry mouth, indicating that they are nervous or dehydrated, or the weather has chapped their lips.
- **Lovestruck.** Soft doe eyes, pursed mouth or mouth slightly open, thickened lips—can look almost sad.
- **Overcome with Emotion.** Fear, love, grief, pain, and so on.

Ways to Customize Avatars

These days, especially with games that allow players to create their own avatars, there are many ways to customize a character. So, this section deals with what options you might consider for physically determining the look of a digital character.

Body

The first aspect of an avatar's appearance is the body. In the old days, we only had two kinds of bodies—male and female. Now, with improved 3D technology, we can have variations on bodies for both sexes.

- Height (ranging from miniscule to gigantic—and all points in between)
- Body type
  - Heavy
  - Thin
  - Muscular
  - Athletic
  - Flabby
  - Rotund
  - Medium
  - Endomorphic, mesomorphic, ectomorphic
  - Erect
  - Bowed
  - Aged
  - Non-human (various)
  - Deformed (various)
- Features
  - Android features
  - Tattoos
  - Appliances (such as sci-fi gadgets surgically added to the body)
  - Piercings
  - Unusual skin (scales?)
  - Glow or sparks, etc.

Face/Head

After the body, more modern avatar customization programs allow us to modify the features of the face, beginning with head shape.

- Size (ranging from tiny to huge)
- Shape
  - Round
  - Square
  - Thin
  - Wide
  - Distorted
- Hair
  - Color (range)
  - Length (range and style)
  - Texture (range)
- Beard
  - None
  - Full
  - Partial
  - Goatee
  - Full with no mustache
  - Neatly trimmed
  - Wild
  - Five o'clock shadow
  - Three-day beard
  - Scraggly partial
  - Mustache
    - Handlebar
    - Normal
    - Hitler
    - Shaggy
    - Trimmed
- Forehead
  - Broad
  - Pronounced
  - Narrow
  - High
  - Low
  - Receded
  - Hairlines (widow's peak, high, balding, low, straight, etc.)

- Eyes
  - Color
    - Blue
    - Brown
    - Green
    - Yellow
    - Copper
    - Hazel
    - Aquamarine
    - Black
    - Purple
    - Orange
    - Red
    - Filmy (blind)
    - All black
  - Shape
  - Close-set
  - Wide-set
  - Color
  - Round
  - Oblong
  - Asian
  - Alien
  - Cat's eyes
  - Pupil variations
  - Open wide
  - Sleepy
  - Crossed
  - Wall-eyed
  - Range: long to short lashes
  - Range: thick to sparse lashes
  - Patched
  - Missing (one or more)
  - One or more than two
- Eyebrows
  - Full
  - Thin
  - Arched
  - Extend upward
  - Extend downward
  - Color
  - Unibrow
  - Wide-set
  - Narrow-set
  - Close over eyes
  - High over eyes
  - Bushy
  - Painted
  - Point down in middle
  - Slanted up and out
  - Slanted down and out
- Nose
  - Long
  - Hooked
  - Pointed
  - Large nostrils
  - Short
  - Button
  - Ski nose
  - Straight
  - Curved
  - Broken
  - Thin/narrow
  - Thick/wide
  - Red/inflamed (drunk's nose)
  - Crooked
  - Animal snouts (dog, pig, monkey, etc.)
- Cheeks/cheekbones
  - High
  - Low
  - Pronounced
  - Subtle
  - Wide
  - Narrow
  - Dimples
  - Beard
  - Five o'clock shadow
  - Made up
- Ears
  - High on head
  - Middle of head
  - Low on head
  - Large
  - Small
  - Range of large to small lobes
  - Pointy
  - Rounded
  - Range of rotation relative to skull (from sticking out to tight to head)
  - Animal styles (cat, dog, cow, reptile, etc.)

- Mouth
  - Full lips
  - Narrow lips
  - Wide mouth
  - Narrow mouth
  - Rosebud mouth (rounded)
  - Corner tilt range—down to up
  - Protruding/receding lower lip (range)
  - Protruding/receding upper lip (range)
- Teeth
  - Not shown
  - Perfect, even, and white
  - Perfect, even, and not white
  - Color—range from white to yellow or various shades of brown, green, or black
  - Uneven
  - Broken
  - Missing
  - Fangs
  - Buck teeth
  - Overall size—range from tiny to large
  - Range—how much is shown when character smiles
- Chin/jaw
  - Range: protruding to receding
  - Thick
  - Thin
  - Pointy
  - Round
  - Dimpled
  - Jutting
  - Wide
  - Narrow
  - Range: raised to lowered (head position overall)

Neck

Necks can vary to some degree. This list is simply a series of ranged qualities that necks might have.

- Range: long to short
- Range: thick to thin
- Range of angle: forward to back
- Range of age: smooth to wrinkled (see below)

Age Indicators

In a more sophisticated avatar customization program, we might be able to determine the age of a character—at least an adult character. Most games so far only let us create young-looking characters, though sometimes we can add white hair to them—but that doesn't really make them look old. Here are a few ways to indicate age in avatars.

See also the "Physical Changes" section earlier in this chapter.

- Age lines at corners of eyes
- Frown lines in forehead
- Smile lines in cheeks and forehead
- Hollow cheeks
- Sagging eyes and lids
- Sagging jowls
- Wrinkles in neck

Makeup

Adding makeup options can allow players to express more creativity in the way their characters (specifically female at this point) look. This list simply suggests some characteristic ranges. A full list of options would be huge!

- Range from none to subtle to garish
- For eyes, cheeks, face, lashes, eyebrows
  - Range of colors
  - Range of styles
  - Range of intensity

Jewelry

Jewelry can enhance someone's look, but it can also be a clue to or indication of the person's personality. In some cases, it can be an object of importance in the game as well.

- Earrings
- Nose rings
- Finger rings
- Toe rings
- Other piercings
- Bracelets
- Necklaces
- Pendants
- Pins
- Cufflinks
- Tie tacks
- Medals and awards
- Badges of rank

Tattoos

Tattoos are common today; they are basically an art form that allows considerable self-expression on the ultimate canvas—our own body. Just as the range of real tattoos is almost without limit, so are the possibilities for using tattoos in games. However, just as tattoos often have specific cultural or personal meaning to those who wear them, so, too, can they be used as interesting plot points, clues, or personality indicators in games.

- Range: anything goes
- Location: anything goes

Glasses

Glasses can alter the look of a character, and many games allow them as an option. Of course, glasses can be the prescription kind, but they can also be functional, ranging from goggles to high-tech eye gear. The possibilities are nearly endless, which is why we've only suggested the range of options.

- Range of eyeglasses
- Monocle
- Pince-nez

Hats and Head Gear

Hats and head gear are common in games, and they are excellent ways to personalize a character. The choice of hat can provide color and style, depending on the game context. Head gear can also be functional, as protection (helmets) or even as high-tech futuristic apparatuses of various kinds. The choices are up to you.

Here's a list that ranges from simple hats to helmets.

- Bowler
- Stetson
- Ten-gallon
- Baseball cap
- Sombrero
- Bucket hat
- Slouch hat
- Fedora
- Top hat
- Bandana
- Panama
- Tyrolean
- Beret
- Akubra
- Straw hat
- Veiled (old-style woman's hat)
- Captain's hat
- Tricorne
- Deerstalker
- Pith helmet

- Cossack hat
- Turban
- Birdcage hat
- Beanie
- Golf cap
- Yarmulke
- Aviator's leather helmet
- WWI German helmet
- WWI Doughboy helmet
- WWII helmets
- Breathing helmet
- Motorcycle helmet
- Bicycle helmet
- Football helmet
- Goalie's helmet
- Deep-sea diving helmet
- Miner's helmet
- Climber's helmet
- Chador
- Wimple
- Veil
- Hood
- Keffiyeh
- Brimmed cap
- Gas mask
- Visor
- Burqa
- Balaclava
- Noh mask
- Wedding veil
- Mitre
- Stocking cap
- Do-rag
- Crown
- Tiara
- Wigs and toupees
- Fez
- Galero
- Zucchetto
- Hardhat
- Fireman's helmet
- Judge's wig (England and other countries)
- Welding mask
- Headdresses (various)
- Rain hats (various)
- Sun hats (various)
- Diving hood

Clothing

If the clothing makes the man or woman, it certainly helps your basic avatar differentiate from all others. The more clothing options, the better. People love to dress up dolls and things, and avatars are the ultimate walking, talking action figures. It's a great opportunity to give players self-expression, and the more options, the better.

- Hats/hoods/helmets (and other head apparel, such as bandanas, headbands, etc.)
- Glasses/goggles
- Shirts/blouses
- Vests
- Jacket/coat/sweater/sweatshirt
- Gloves (various kinds)
- Belts
- Pants/skirts/dresses
- Shoes (and socks)
- Cloaks
- Capes
- Mufflers/scarves
- Ties
- Masks
- Arm and wrist bands
- Lingerie
- Other leg apparel (greaves, ankle bands, etc.)

Accessories and Tools

The things that your characters can carry, wear, or use can present opportunities for personalization and for gameplay. This very short list should help get you started. See also the "Individual Objects Carried by Specific NPCs" section in Chapter 19, "Objects and Locations."

These vary, depending on game and character types.

- Watches
- Holsters
- Utility belts
- Earphones
- Communicators (including cell phones)
- Weapons (various, depending on appropriate technology and game fiction)
- Badges and rank indicators
- Wallets and purses

Animations

Dressing up your avatar is fun, but what can it do? If it is your player character, it should be able to do a lot of things. Here are some of the common animation cycles that any well-made avatar should consider for its repertoire.

- Walk
- Run
- Jump
- Roll
- Kneel
- Sit
- Squat
- Crawl
- Lie down
- Idle state
- Fight/wield weapons/cast spells, etc.
- Die
- Take damage
- Converse/interact
- Specific tasks (varied and situational)
- Facial expressions
- Actions
  - Laugh
  - Cry
  - Point at something
  - Beckon
  - Ready weapon or put weapon away
  - Dance
  - Celebrate
  - Signal no (wave hands dismissively, shake head, etc.)
  - Signal yes (nod and smile)
  - Pick something up or put something down
  - Push a button
  - Type
  - Talk on phone

Human Universals

This list contains some of the elements common to all human beings. When you are creating characters and scenes, you can assume that your characters (if human or more or less human) will share these common traits and behaviors. But in what ways do they share them? For instance, maybe all people have beliefs, including false beliefs, but what specific false beliefs does your character have? What supernatural beliefs, childhood fears, and so on? And if your character is not human, what then? Which of these universal traits does the alien character lack, and which ones does it share?

When I look at this list with a particular character in mind, I ask myself, "How does this character express this common trait?" For instance, if I'm looking at aesthetics—what is the character's aesthetic? If I look at humor/joking, I ask how this character's sense of humor is manifest.

So, although it is not necessary to go through this whole list for each character, you may find it informative in completing your understanding of some qualities that human beings share and how specifically these qualities take form to make your character unique. In other words, by looking at what all people share, you can also look at how they differ in the way they express those common qualities.

NOTE

The following list was adapted from Donald Brown's Human Universals *(McGraw-Hill, 1991) and is used with permission of the author.*

- Abstraction in speech and thought
- Actions under self-control distinguished from those not under control
- Adjusting to the environment
- Admiring generosity
- Aesthetics
- Affection expressed and felt
- Age grades
- Age statuses
- Age terms
- Alternate naming of things and places (metonymy)
- Ambivalence
- Anthropomorphization
- Anticipation
- Antonyms
- Attachment
- Attempts to control weather
- Baby talk
- Banishment
- Belief in supernatural/religion
- Beliefs about death
- Beliefs about disease
- Beliefs about fortune and misfortune
- Beliefs, false
- Binary cognitive distinctions
- Biological mother and social mother normally the same person
- Black (color term)
- Body adornment
- Childbirth customs
- Childcare
- Childhood fear of loud noises
- Childhood fear of strangers
- Childhood fears
- Choice making (choosing alternatives)
- Classification
- Classification of
  - Age
  - Behavioral propensities
  - Body parts
  - Colors
  - Fauna
  - Flora
  - Inner states
  - Kin
  - Sex
  - Space
  - Tools
  - Weather conditions
- Coalitions
- Collective identities
- Concept of fairness or equity
- Concept of individual person
- Concept of precedence
- Conflict
  - Handling through consultation
  - Methods of handling
  - Mediation of
- Conjectural reasoning
- Connection between sickness and death
- Containers
- Continua (ordering as cognitive pattern)
- Contrasting marked and nonmarked sememes (meaningful elements in language)
- Cooking
- Cooperation
- Cooperative labor
- Copulation normally conducted in privacy
- Corporate (perpetual) statuses
- Coyness display
- Critical learning periods
- Crying
- Cultural variability
- Culture
- Culture/nature distinction
- Customary greetings
- Daily routines
- Dance
- Death rituals
- Decision making
- Decision making, collective
- Decorative art
- Different personality manifestations based on gender and age
- Differential valuations
- Directions, giving of
- Disapproval of stinginess
- Discernment of truth and falsehood
- Discrepancies between speech, thought, and action
- Dispersed groups
- Distinctions of normal versus abnormal
- Distinguishing right and wrong
- Distinguishing self from other

- Diurnality
- Divination
- Division of labor
- Division of labor by age
- Division of labor by sex
- Dominance/submission
- Dream interpretation
- Dreams
- Economic inequalities
- Economic inequalities, consciousness of
- Emotions
- Empathy
- Envy
- Ethnocentrism
- Etiquette
- Exchanges of labor, goods, services, and anything with value
- Explanation
- Facial communication
- Facial expressions of anger, contempt, disgust, fear, happiness, surprise, agreement, disagreement
- Facial masks (hiding behind)
- Facial recognition
- Family/household units
- Favoritism toward "us" more than "them"
- Fear of or wariness around snakes
- Fears (including fear of death)
- Feasting
- Females do more direct childcare
- Figurative speech
- Fire
- Folklore
- Food preferences
- Food sharing
- Future predictions
- Gender-differentiated terminology
- Gestalt or unification of senses
- Gift giving
- Gossip
- Government
- Grammar
- Group living
- Habituation
- Hairstyles
- Healing the sick
- Hope
- Hospitality
- Humor/joking
- Hygienic care
- Imagery
- Individuality of personalities and roles
- Inequalities based on prestige
- Inheritance rules
- Institutions
- Insults
- Interest in the living world
- Interpolation
- Interpreting behavior
- Judging others
- Kinships, closer ties to more distant based on blood connections
- Language
- Language for complex and abstract ideas
- Language used as manipulation or to misinform
- Language, prestige from proficient use of
- Language, redundant words
- Laws and rules
- Leaders
- Lever
- Logical considerations such as and, equivalence, general versus specific, not, opposites, parts and wholes, and so on
- Magic, especially for increasing or sustaining life and to win/gain love
- Making comparisons
- Male domination of public and political processes
- Males, more violence based on coalitions, more aggressive, more prone to lethal violence and theft; more travel on average than females
- Marriage
- Materialism
- Mealtimes
- Meaningful gestures
- Measuring
- Medicine
- Melody/music/rhythm
- Memory
- Men older than women in relationships
- Mental maps
- Metaphor
- Mood- or consciousness-altering techniques and/or substances
- Moral distinctions: good and bad

- Moral sentiments
- Mother generally with companion during child-rearing years
- Mourning
- Music (for children and adults), vocal and instrumental
- Music as art
- Music for dancing
- Music for religious activity
- Music, children's
- Mutually contradictory proverbs and sayings
- Myths
- Naming things
- Narrative
- Non-family groups
- Nouns
- Numbers and counting
- Numbers one and two
- Oedipus complex
- Oligarchy (de facto)
- One word can have more than one meaning (polysemy)
- Onomatopoeia
- Overestimating objectivity of thought
- Pain
- Past/present/future
- Personal names
- Personal preferences
- Phonemes
- Planning
- Play (for fun and for perfection of skills)
- Poetry/rhetoric (including some universal poetic and narrative structures)
- Positions/roles distinguished from individuals (such as king or tax collector)
- Possessiveness
- Practice to improve skills
- Preference for sweets
- Pride
- Private inner life
- Prohibitions against certain kinds of violence
- Prohibitions against murder
- Prohibitions against rape
- Promises
- Pronouns
- Proper names
- Property
- Proverbs and sayings
- Psychological defense mechanisms
- Rape
- Redress of wrongs
- Resistance to dominance or abuse
- Responsibility
- Revenge, retaliation
- Right-handedness as population norm
- Risk-taking
- Rites of passage
- Rituals
- Sanctions
- Self as subject and object
- Self-control
- Self-image, awareness of, manipulation of, need to see as positive
- Semantics
- Sexual attraction, attractiveness, jealousy, modesty, regulation or limitations, as a primary interest
- Shame
- Shelter
- Social manipulation
- Social structure
- Socialization
- Socialization expected from senior kin
- Spears
- Special cognition differences between genders
- Special speech for special occasions
- Status based on gender
- Statuses and roles
- Statuses from achievement or conveyed upon
- Subjectivity of meaning
- Succession
- Symbolic speech
- Symbolism
- Synonyms
- Taboos on foods, sex, killing, words/ expressions, etc.
- Taboos on incest
- Taking turns
- Taxonomy
- Territoriality
- Thumb sucking
- Tickling

- Time, concepts and cyclic nature, divided into units
- Toilet training
- Tools
  - Creating
  - Dependency on
  - Patterns of gender or cultural use
  - Used to cut or pound or make other tools
- Toys
- Trade/barter/exchange
- Treating patterns and relationships as things
- Triangular awareness (being able to distinguish relationships between self and two other people)
- Tying
- Us and them
- Verbs
- Visiting
- Weaning
- Weapons
- Word for hand
- Words for father and mother
- World view

13 Character Roles and Jobs

This chapter deals with the roles and jobs your player characters and NPCs can have, including roles and jobs you can have in multiplayer games. Roles are archetypes—ways that characters operate in the world, such as being a villain or a wise person. Jobs are what they do, such as being a blacksmith or an assassin.

Although this content might fit well within Chapter 12, "Character Design," it is an integral aspect of game design, so I included it here. However, for more options in character design, I recommend checking out Chapter 12. And for a more story-oriented look at character roles, see the specific section "Functional Character Roles" in Chapter 12.

In this chapter:

- NPC Roles
- NPC Jobs
- Evil Jobs
- Participatory Player Jobs
- Character Species/Type
- Character Race/Ethnicity
- Player Roles in Multiplayer Games
- Military Ranks and Divisions

NPC Roles

NPCs are non-player characters, and they populate most games. Even the ghosts in *Pac-Man* were NPCs, because your enemies in most games are also NPCs. Only in multiplayer games is anyone in the game other than you a player character. In one-on-one fighting games, the stock characters can be NPCs when you play against the machine or player characters when you fight against a human opponent.

Character roles have nothing to do with their skills, training, or professions, but with their relationship to the player's character and the story as a whole. These are basic roles such as hero, villain, father, mother, and so on. Of course, not all roles are suitable for all types of games, so some of these roles would only appear in RPGs, for instance. Units in strategy games, even vehicle and weapon units, can also be considered NPCs, although they aren't technically characters.

Note that some roles also could be jobs—such as being a guard, who might be a gatekeeper who bars the way or a law enforcer. However, such examples are included here because they can be seen both ways. For instance, a guard is a specific role in many games, even though it may also be the profession of that NPC. The same holds true for shopkeepers and a few other specific jobs that are also roles.

Character Roles

Listed in alphabetical order:

- Accomplice.
- Alien (extraterrestrial). (Actually, aliens may play any number of specific roles, but in some contexts, their being an alien is a role in itself.)
- Animal—ambient.
- Animal enemy.
- Animal friend/ally/pet (yours or someone else's).
- Annoying character.
- Aunt.
- Average Joe.
- Bank teller.
- Bastard.
- Beggar.
- Boss.
- Brother.
- Buddy.
- Bum.
- Cannon fodder.
- Captive.
- Casualty/sacrifice.
- Celebrity (movie/TV star).
- Character consumed by revenge.
- Child (son/daughter or other role).
- Comic relief.
- Cousin.
- Cowboy/cowgirl.
- Damsel in distress.
- Demon.
- Drug addict.
- Drug dealer.
- Explorer.
- False role (meaning the character appears to be someone—friend, enemy, etc.—but isn't what he seems).
- Farmer.
- Fast-food worker.
- Father.
- Filler character.
- Fireman.
- Fool.
- Fortune-teller.
- Freak.
- Friend.
- Funny NPC or sidekick.
- Gatekeeper (someone who bars the way).
- Geek.
- Grandfather.
- Grandmother.
- Greedy character (represents greedy people in general).
- Hacker.
- Heir (in line for some inheritance or position).
- Henchman/henchwoman/minion/grunt.
- Hermit.
- Hero.
- Hit man
- Hostage.
- Information giver.
- In-law relation.
- Inventor/wise man/magician/guide/oracle.
- Jogger.
- Law enforcer.
- Mailperson.
- Marine.
- Military characters (soldiers/cavalry/minor officers/major officers/ultimate leader).
- Mischievous kid.
- Mother.
- Mysterious silent person.
- Ninja.
- Non-interactive NPC. (Someone just there for atmosphere, but who has no active role in the game. This status can change as the game progresses, so an NPC may start as non-interactive but become interactive as certain plot elements are completed.)
- Office worker.
- Oracle or someone with information.
- Phony.
- Pilot.
- Pimp.

- Pirate.
- Player's party member.
- Policeman.
- Politician.
- Prostitute.
- Psycho.
- Retail worker.
- Romantic interest.
- Royalty/privileged class.
- Ruler.
- Sage.
- Savior.
- Seductress.
- Servant/slave (yours or someone else's).
- Shopkeeper.
- Shy guy.
- Sidekick.
- Sister.
- Slacker.
- Some who needs protection.
- Spirit from the dead.
- Standard party roles:
    - Buff mage
    - Crowd controller (party member who can control the enemy, such as by putting them to sleep, mezzing them, rooting them, etc.)
    - Damage mage
    - Healer
    - Puller
    - Ranged attacker (often an archer type)
    - Scout/thief/infiltrator/spy
    - Tank
- Sacrificial lamb.
- Step-relation.
- Student.
- Sub-boss.
- Teacher/trainer/guide.
- Terrorist.
- Thief.
- Townsperson.
- Tradesperson (someone who buys/sells/barters).
- Tyrant.
- Uncle.
- Unwitting accomplice.
- Usurper/pretender to some position.
- Victim.
- Village drunk.
- Villain.
- Wanderer.
- Wife/husband.

NPC Jobs

In the previous section, we looked at the various roles that NPCs can play in a game. In this section, we'll look at the kinds of jobs NPCs might fill in a game. The key to this is that the job should be something interesting that makes the scene look more real. For instance, in a large office, people at computer terminals and on the phone would be realistic, plus people hanging around the copier or the coffee dispenser. On the street, a window cleaner or construction worker would be interesting, and a homeless person (in this sense, a job) might add some sense of realistic atmosphere. Whenever possible, these jobs should be active jobs where the NPCs can be shown doing something. People in an office might be moving around, delivering papers, discussing plans, working on a white board (which could have real data on it—jokes, clues, mathematical formulae, whatever…).

These jobs could also be their defining role in the game. For instance, the court magician's job is to work magic, but this is also his role in the game. In a simplistic sense, a party member (ally) or an enemy can have a job/role that is pretty much the same. For instance, a guard is generally just that—a guard. And that is both his role and his job. Also note that the player's character could have one or more of these jobs.

These jobs can be further categorized by the type of environment you may find yourself creating. For instance, consider the lists in the following subsections.

General Environments

This list is a partial look at the jobs you might find in a game in various settings. These are general environments because they aren't very specific. For instance, an army base is a specific environment, and you would expect to see soldiers of various kinds there. But in towns, cities, countryside settings, and the like, here are some of the jobs NPCs might have. In some cases, they aren't "jobs" in the sense that someone is paying the NPC, but they are jobs in the sense that they have defining activities. For instance, a bicyclist is not necessarily a professional rider (though he could be a bicycle messenger or something), but in the sense that this is his activity, it makes it a job in the game sense. His job is to ride the bicycle through your scene.

- Acrobat
- Actor
- Agent: FBI/CIA/NSA/KGB/Matrix, etc.
- Alchemist
- Apprentice (or assistant...to any trade skill)
- Archer
- Armorer
- Arrowsmith
- Artist
- Assassin
- Barber
- Beggar
- Bicyclist
- Blacksmith
- Boat captain
- Boat crew
- Bodyguard
- Boyers (bow makers)
- Brewer
- Bus driver
- Businessman with briefcase
- Champion (knight stand-in during trial by combat)
- Chandler
- Clockmaker/watchmaker
- Clown on unicycle
- Conductor
- Cooper
- Cop
- Cordwainer or cobbler (shoemaker or shoe repairer)
- Cowherd
- Crazy person/raving lunatic
- Criminals (various types, footpads, robbers, kidnappers, swindlers, poachers, etc.)
- Cutler
- Dancer
- Detective
- Doctor/healer
- Dyer
- Engineer
- Entrepreneur (owner of tavern, shop, brothel, inn, or other business venture)
- Farmer
- Fireman
- Fisherman
- Fishmonger/fishwife
- Fletcher
- Fool
- Fortune-teller
- Gang member and/or leader
- Gardener
- Glassblower
- Glover (glove maker)
- Governor (prefect)
- Graffiti artist
- Groom (stable hand)
- Guard
- Gypsy
- Herald
- Janitor, street sweeper
- Jester
- Jeweler (including goldsmith)
- Juggler
- Logger
- Magic user (sorcerer, necromancer, elemental magician, etc.)
- Maid or chambermaid
- Marshall
- Master criminal
- Mayor
- Mercenary
- Merchant
- Messenger or delivery person
- Midwife

- Miller
- Minstrel
- Monk
- Oracle
- Pawnbroker
- Penitent
- Picketer/protestor
- Pilgrim
- Pilot
- Pirate
- Policeman (also constable, sheriff, etc.)
- Politician (various types)
- Priest/nun
- Private investigator/detective
- Prostitute
- Pushcart vendor
- Reporter
- Robber
- Ruler/leader
- Scholar
- Scooter
- Scribe
- Seneschal
- Shepherd
- Skateboarder
- Slave
- Sniper
- Soothsayer
- Spinner
- Spy
- Squire
- Stable master
- Steward
- Storyteller
- Street performer (mime, musician, dancer, juggler, etc.)
- Street person (miscellaneous)
- Streetwalker
- Swineherd
- Tailor
- Talking head/news anchor
- Tax collector
- Taxi driver
- Teacher
- Thief
- Tinker
- Traveler
- Traveling merchant
- Vintner
- Weaver
- Wet nurse
- Window washer

Jobs of Nobility

People of royalty often make an appearance in games, so here's a short list of the various noble ranks. Of course, they would be surrounded by servants, advisors, and other non-royals, but this list is reserved for those of noble blood.

- King
- Queen
- Prince
- Princess
- Duke
- Grand Duke
- Duchess
- Grand Duchess
- Earl
- Marquis
- Marquise
- Count
- Countess
- Viscount
- Baron
- Baroness
- Baronet
- Baronetess
- Knight
- Dame
- Lord
- Lady

Ecclesiastical Jobs

The clergy has its specific positions, and here's a partial list.

- Pope
- Cardinal
- Archbishop
- Bishop
- Abbott
- Abbess
- Prelate
- Monk
- Nun
- Priest
- Deacon
- Rabbi
- Muezzin
- Shaman
- Saint
- Friar
- Choirboy
- Altar boy
- Organist (musician)
- Pastor
- Assistant pastor
- Nursery worker
- Doorman/greeter
- Sunday School teacher
- Usher
- Van driver

Military

There's no way we could fit all the various military ranks into this book and have room for much more, but here are a few general ideas. If you are doing a military game, you will want to do more research on the specific period and military division you are depicting.

(See also the "Military Ranks and Divisions" section later in this chapter.)

- Soldier (any rank)
- Pilot
- Navigator
- Bombardier
- Gunner
- Sniper
- Driver (tanks and other vehicles)
- Boat captain
- Boat crew
- Cook
- Master sergeant
- Officer (captain, lieutenant, colonel, general, admiral, etc.)
- Demolitions expert

Shops

What do we find in shops and stores? Here are a few examples to get you started.

- Cashier and salesperson
- Store detective
- Other shoppers, particularly strongly characterized ones
- Shoplifter
- Busybody
- Guy on the prowl
- Children running amok
- Grunt laborer (stock boy, janitor, mail clerk, etc.)
- Fix-it guy (repairing something)
- The boss or owner (or manager)
- Customer

Ships

Sometimes games are set on ships, and people on ships have very specific jobs.

(See also the "Military Ranks and Divisions" section later in this chapter.)

- Captain
- Navigator
- Crewmember (various)
- Passenger (various)
- Stowaway
- Medic
- Engineer
- Entertainer (possibly)
- Mess crew
- Various gunners and weapons experts, if appropriate
- Pirate
- The quintessential parrot

Spaceships

Spaceships are a type of ship, but generally futuristic. We've grown accustomed to some of the jobs we would expect to see on spaceships thanks to movies and TV. Here are a few ideas.

(See also the "Military Ranks and Divisions" section later in this chapter.)

- Captain
- Navigator
- Crewmember (various)
- Passenger
- Alien
- Medic
- Engineer
- Science officer
- Guard
- EV (extra-vehicular) worker
- Stowaway

Small Village

Small villages seem to crop up often in games, especially in Role-Playing and adventure games. Who might you encounter in these small towns and villages?

- Mayor
- Stable master
- Blacksmith
- Farmer
- Store owner
- Important businessman (local boss)
- Prostitute
- Village idiot
- Priest/clergy/nun (appropriate to setting)
- Old wise man
- Witch
- Child at play
- Loiterer
- Thief
- Cultist
- Scientist/inventor

Laboratories

Laboratories are always fun, but who do we find there?

- Scientist
- Administrator
- Secretary
- Janitor
- Experimental subject
- VIP visitor
- Sentient experimental subject
- Lab animal
- Student or understudy

Sports

If you were putting together a game with a sports setting, who would you want to include in that game? Here are a few ideas to get you started.

- Athlete
- Owner
- Manager
- Fan
- Umpire
- Reporter/commentator
- Ticket taker
- Janitor
- Equipment handler
- Concession worker
- Accountant
- Sports therapist
- Medical personnel
- Water boy
- Fan
- Field care specialist

Wilderness

Far from civilization, we still find people with specific jobs, such as:

- Logger
- Hunter
- Trapper
- Farmer
- Artisan
- Crazy recluse
- Witch, warlock, druid, etc.
- Explorer
- Native person
- Someone who is lost
- Firefighter
- Activist
- Herbalist/wild crafter
- Cultist
- Hiker or recreationalist
- Kayaker or rafter
- Mushroom hunter

Malls

It's a fact of modern life that malls have their own denizens—both those who work there and those whose "job" it is to shop and hang out.

- Shopkeeper (various kinds)
- Guard
- Teenager
- Shopper
- Janitor
- Office person
- Strange person
- Lost person
- Person carrying bags and such
- Pickpocket
- Loiterer
- Gangsta
- Child or baby
- Window shopper

Castles

Traditionally, castles housed a wide assortment of people with a very wide assortment of jobs. They were like mini-cities, and this list will get you started thinking about who would be in *your* castle.

- Guard
- Warrior
- King/queen/ruler/royalty
- Serf/peasant
- Slave
- Jester
- Juggler
- Dancer
- Performer of any kind
- Visiting nobility
- Blacksmith
- Livery keeper
- Bowman
- Armorer and weapon maker
- Jeweler
- Scullery worker
- Stable master
- Various officials
- Vagrant

See also "Castle Architecture and People" in Chapter 33, "Historical and Cultural Weapons."

Bars and Pool Halls

Nightlife also requires people in various jobs. Who else might you find in bars and pool halls?

- Bartender
- Bouncer
- Dancer (professional or patron)
- Bar girl
- Waiter/waitress
- Drunk
- Ordinary patron
- Hooker
- Card player
- Card shark
- Pool hustler
- Girlfriend hanging around
- Musician or other entertainer, according to setting
- Patron (various kinds, depending on setting)

Part IV

Restaurants

Restaurants have specialized workers. Here are a few. Can you think of more?

- Cook/chef (various kinds, depending on setting)
- Waiter/waitress
- Patron (depending on setting)
- Busboy
- Host/hostess
- Dishwasher
- Sommelier
- Bartender (depending on whether there is a bar)
- Cocktail waitress/waiter
- Manager
- Cashier

Banks

If you were going to make a bank scene, who would be working there?

- Guard
- Teller
- Loan officers
- Manager
- Clerks
- Computer technician
- Customer
- Bank robber
- Armored car driver
- Undercover security

Offices

If you create a game that uses office settings, who would you find there?

- Typist
- Receptionist
- Secretary
- Manager
- Mail person
- Janitor
- Upper manager
- Bosses (president, VPs, CEO, CFO, COO, etc.)
- IT administrator
- Intern
- Client or visitor
- Security
- Gofer
- Specialty worker (depends on type of office)

Movie Set

Another specialized setting, movies employ a wide variety of people. Here are a few suggestions to get you started.

- Actor or actress
- Extra
- Boom operator
- Director
- Assistant director
- Camera operator
- Director of photography
- Set construction
- Stunt person
- Special effects person
- Makeup
- Hair
- Costume
- Continuity
- Lighting
- Grip or other support worker

Evil Jobs

Some villains have no visible means of support or seem to be independently wealthy, but it's interesting to think about the jobs that best fit the bad guys. They are usually jobs that involve the acquisition of a lot of money, the wielding of power, or both.

Note that the player's character could have any of these jobs, too, if the player is an anti-hero or the story calls for a player in a sketchy profession.

- Pharmaceuticals (legal or illegal)
- Drug dealer
- Arms manufacture and/or distribution
- Money laundering
- Evil banker
- Evil stockbroker
- Politician
- Emperor/king/dictator (or other totalitarian leader)
- Advisor to the leader
- Smuggler
- Spy/mole
- Barbarian
- Alien
- Brain in a bottle
- Evil magician/sorcerer
- Serial killer (can seem to be quite an ordinary character)
- Spawn of Satan
- Mastermind who works at a video store, fast-food chain, convenience store, etc.
- Evil janitor
- Bartender
- Mad scientist
- Bad cop
- Mayor
- Evil toymaker
- Clown
- TV repairman
- Fast-food server

- Company mascot
- Evil animator
- Evil professor
- Pimp/madam/prostitute/escort
- Exterminator
- Zookeeper
- Balloon salesman
- Army general/Navy admiral, etc.
- High school principal
- Mortician
- Evil schoolgirl
- Corporate executive
- Hacker

PARTICIPATORY PLAYER JOBS

In some games, particularly RPGs and MMOGs, players can pick specific jobs or skills and actually practice them in the game. For instance, in some games a player could be a weapon maker and specialize in making weapons as a part of the gameplay. Other player characters might be traders, buying low and selling high, or even cooks, alchemists, and engineers. Here's a list of some of the trade skills you might be able to provide to players.

- Armorer (possibly specialized)
- Weapon crafter (possibly specialized)
- Engineer
- Scientist
- Cook
- Alchemist
- Enchanter
- Trader/shopkeeper
- Tailor
- Hunter/tracker/explorer/scout
- Miner
- Herbalist
- Builder
- Private detective
- Spy
- Police officer
- Politician
- Dog catcher
- Sniper
- Assassin
- Pilot for hire
- Bounty hunter
- Farmer
- Animal wrangler/tamer
- Carnival or circus worker or act
- Prostitute/pimp/gigolo
- Drug dealer
- Dancer
- Musician
- Doctor/healer
- Clown
- Preacher
- Mayor (or other politician)
- Taxi driver
- Boat captain
- Filmmaker
- Photographer
- Reporter
- Military job (any)
- Ruler of any nation
- Chairman of the board (or other company official)
- Speculator
- Thief
- Stock trader
- Delivery boy
- God (it's a job)
- Caretaker
- Vet
- Pet sitter
- Dog walker
- Priest
- Nun/monk
- Repairman

Character Species/Type

Although these aren't technically roles or jobs, the species of a character can have a considerable effect on how we see it and on what atmosphere it creates in the game. For instance, an avian banker would be somewhat more interesting than the standard human model.

Earthly Origin

- Human
- Humanoid
- Insectoid
- Reptilian
- Aquatic
- Amphibious
- Avian
- Vampiric
- Demonic
- Fungal
- Gaseous
- Viral
- Amorphous
- Prehistoric
- Futuristic
- Robotic
- Ape
- Rock/siliconoid
- Arborial

Alien (Extraterrestrial)

- Humanoid
- Insectoid
- Reptilian
- Aquatic
- Amphibious
- Avian
- Vampiric
- Non-corporeal
- Gaseous
- Fungal
- Viral
- Robotic
- Android

Spirit

- Nature Spirits
  - Earth
  - Air
  - Water
  - Fire
  - Spirit (ether, etc.)
- Evil
- Good
- Spirit of ambiguity
- Spirit of justice

Fantasy

- Elvish
- Dwarven
- Ogre
- Troll
- Barbarian
- Halfling
- Undead
- Gnome
- Orc
- Centaur
- Minotaur
- Cyclops

- Demon
- Angel
- God
- Fairy
- Nymph
- Siren
- Cerberus
- Leviathan
- Dryad
- Satyr
- Griffon
- Manticore
- Gargoyle
- Chimera
- Dragon
- Imp
- Naga
- Ent

Character Race/Ethnicity

- Generic human
- Caucasian
- Black
- Latin
- Asian
  - Chinese
  - Japanese
  - Korean
  - Thai
  - Malaysian
  - Singaporean
  - Tibetan/Nepalese
- Jewish
- WASP (White Anglo-Saxon Protestant)
- Scandinavian
- Irish
- Scottish
- French
- German
- Italian
- Spanish
- Portuguese
- South American (various)
- Brazilian
- Mexican
- Australian
- New Zealander
- Filipino
- African
- North African
- Gypsy
- Inuit
- Native American
- Indian
- Middle Eastern
- Arabic
- European (generally)
- Mongolian
- Polynesian
- Basque
- Aborigine
- Pygmy
- Zulu
- Masai
- Nomad
- Faerie
- Elvish
- Dwarvish
- Orcish
- Goblin
- Troll
- Giant/titan
- Hobbit
- Gnomish
- Centaur
- Entish (tree creature)
- God or demi-god
- Mer-person (mermaid/merman)
- Monster type (varies)
- Sentient plant creature
- Insectoid
- Avian
- Reptilian
- Sentient mineral creature
- Discorporate entity
- Shape-shifter
- Alien (other planetary—varies)

Player Roles in Multiplayer Games

In multiplayer games, the players themselves often fill roles and perform jobs that NPCs perform in single-player games, in addition to roles and jobs that may or may not be filled by NPCs. Basically, players can fulfill any of the job functions listed in the "Participatory Player Jobs" section of this chapter. However, they may fill specific roles within multiplayer games, sometimes the same and sometimes different from typical NPC roles.

- Player killer
- Ally
- Betrayer
- Guildmate
- Ad hoc teammate
- Buyer/seller
- Scout
- Tank
- Buff mage
- Damage mage
- Range attacker
- Crowd controller
- Healer
- Spy
- Thief/burglar/stealther
- Mentor/advisor
- Helper and benefactor
- Enemy
- Rival
- Romantic interest
- Friend
- Leader
- Follower
- Manager
- Virtual family role
- Observer/spectator

Military Ranks and Divisions

Earlier in this chapter, we listed some military jobs. Here's a listing of military ranks and divisions. This list can be useful not only when creating a strictly accurate military game, but even in fantasy games where you want to create a believable military organization.

Army, Air Force, Marines

- General of the Army (5-star)
- Marshal (Europe)
- General (4-star)
- Lieutenant General (3-star)
- Major General (2-star)
- Brigadier General (1-star)
- Colonel
- Lieutenant Colonel
- Major
- Captain
- First Lieutenant
- Second Lieutenant
- Chief Warrant Officer (W-4)
- Chief Warrant Officer (W-3)
- Chief Warrant Officer (W-2)
- Warrant Officer (W-1)
- Sergeant Major
- First Sergeant
- Chief Master Sergeant
- Master Sergeant
- Sergeant First Class
- Specialist 1–7
- Gunnery Sergeant
- Technical Sergeant
- Staff Sergeant
- Sergeant
- Corporal
- Lance Corporal
- Private First Class (PFC)
- Airman First Class
- Private
- Airman
- Recruit
- Cadet

Navy and Coast Guard

- Fleet Admiral
- Admiral
- Vice Admiral
- Rear Admiral
- Commodore
- Captain
- Commander
- Lieutenant Commander
- Lieutenant
- Lieutenant Junior Grade
- Ensign
- Chief Warrant Officer (W-4)
- Chief Warrant Officer (W-3)
- Chief Warrant Officer (W-2)
- Master Chief Petty Officer
- Senior Chief Petty Officer
- Chief Petty Officer
- Petty Officer 1st Class
- Petty Officer 2nd Class
- Petty Officer 3rd Class
- Seaman
- Seaman Apprentice
- Seaman Recruit
- Midshipman

Army Sizes

- Field Army (2–5 corps)
- Corps (2–5 divisions)
- Division (3 brigades: 10,000–18,000 soldiers)
- Brigade (3 or more battalions: 3,000–5,000 soldiers)
- Battalion (3–5 companies: 500–900 soldiers)
- Company (3–4 platoons 100–200 soldiers)
- Platoons (3–4 squads: 16–40 soldiers)
- Squad (4–10 soldiers)

Additional Unit Types

Here are some of the other unit types, besides the main ones mentioned a moment ago.

ACR: Armored Cavalry Regiment

- Armored cavalry squadrons (ACS)
  - Armored cavalry troops
  - A tank company
  - A self-propelled artillery battery
- Aviation squadron
  - Air cavalry/reconnaissance troops
  - Attack helicopter troops
  - An assault helicopter troop
- Support squadron
- Combat support companies and batteries

ACR(L): Armored Cavalry Regiment (Light)

- Armored cavalry squadrons
- An aviation squadron (minus attack helicopter troops)
- A support squadron
- Separate combat support companies and batteries

Separate Brigade

- A brigade headquarters and headquarters company for command and control
- Limited combat support assets to include military police, chemical and air defense elements
- Armored and mechanized infantry battalions
- An armored cavalry troop
- An engineer battalion
- A military intelligence company
- A support battalion of several support units and direct link to corps support
- A field artillery battalion

Corps Aviation Brigade

- Attack regiment with three AH-64 helicopter attack battalions
- An aviation group
  - Assault battalion
  - Command aviation battalion
  - Combat support aviation battalion
  - Medium helicopter battalion
  - Light utility helicopter battalion
  - Air traffic services battalion
- Main roles:
  - Air assault
  - Air movement
  - Target acquisition
  - Reconnaissance and security
  - Air traffic services
  - Enhanced command control
  - Communications
  - Forward arming and refueling point operations
  - Command and staff support
  - Limited casualty evacuation
  - Command search and rescue
  - Downed aircraft recovery
  - Rear area reconnaissance and surveillance
  - Aerial mine delivery

Corps Artillery

- Field artillery cannon battalions
- Guided missile brigades
- Multiple-rocket battalions
- Target acquisition units with artillery-locating radars
- Main roles:
  - Add depth to battle
  - Support rear operations
  - Influence battle at critical times

Military Intelligence Brigade (MPs)

- Brigade headquarters
- Operations battalions
- Tactical exploitation battalions
- Aerial exploitation battalions
- Main roles:
  - Support of troops through acquisition and analysis of data:
    - Communications interception
    - Enemy prisoner interrogation
    - Imagery exploitation
    - Weather forecasts
    - Links with theater and national sensors
  - Assist G3 with electronic warfare, operations security, and deception planning

Air Defense Artillery Brigade

- Protects forces from aerial attack
- Protects against missile attack
- Provides surveillance at all altitudes

Engineer Brigade

- Combat engineer battalions
- Engineer battalions (combat heavy)
- Separate engineer companies (combat support equipment, assault float bridge, topographic, tactical bridge companies)
- Provides support for:
  - Mobility
  - Counter-mobility
  - Survivability
  - Topographic engineering
  - General engineering

Signal Brigade

- Provides voice and data communications within and between corps command and control facilities, and in some situations provides links with host nations, the UN, allied forces, and government and non-government agencies.

Chemical Brigade

- Commands, controls, and coordinates combat support operations of attached chemical units.
- Provides command and administrative and logistic support to attached chemical battalions.
- Brigade commander recommends nuclear, biological, and chemical mission priorities to the corps commander.

- Provides smoke generator; nuclear, biological, and chemical reconnaissance; and nuclear, biological, and chemical decontamination support (other than patient decontamination).

Military Police Brigade

- Roles:
  - Battlefield circulation control
  - Area security
  - Enemy prisoner of war and civilian internee operations
  - Law-and-order support to the corps
  - Including reconnaissance and surveillance for supply routes and other key areas in the corps rear
  - Can act as a response and tactical combat force to augment base and mission requirements
  - Maintains liaison with host nation civil and military police and may provide civil-military operations support

Special Forces Group

- Primary operations:
  - Foreign Internal Defense (FID) and coalition warfare/support (working with developing nations by working with host country military and police forces to improve their technical skills and understanding of human rights issues and to help with humanitarian and civic action projects).
  - Unconventional warfare
  - Special reconnaissance
  - Direct action
  - Counterterrorism
- Special qualities and training:
  - Maturity
  - Military skills
  - Language skills
  - Cultural awareness
  - Operations and intelligence
  - Communications
  - Medical aid
  - Engineering
  - Weapons
  - Operations, training, and teaching

Ranger Regiment

- Special operations and light infantry operations. Focus on deep penetration raids or interdiction operations against targets of strategic or operational significance. Generally requires intact seizure of a facility and/or limited collateral damage, including:
  - Command, control, communications, and intelligence centers at front and army level
  - Nuclear, biological, and chemical weapons storage sites and delivery means
  - Key logistic centers
  - Air defense and air traffic control integrating centers and air defense weapon sites

- Radio and television stations, microwave terminals, satellite receiving stations, telephone lines and exchanges
- Key power generation and distribution facilities, lines, transformers, and grid monitoring centers
- Airfield and critical transportation nodes
- Key choke points (such as bridges, tunnels, locks, dams, and mountain passes or routes in restrictive terrain) on vital locations
- Rescue and evacuation missions
- Tactical reconnaissance

Special Operations Aviation Regiment

- "Night Stalkers" night-flying special operations force

Psychological Operations Tactical Support Battalion (PSYOP)

- A specific division of the military dealing with psychological health of soldiers as well as psychological warfare.

Civil Affairs Brigade

- Composed of various experts, such as lawyers, engineers, doctors, police, firemen, computer experts, farmers, and bankers, among others. Civil Affairs works with civil authorities and populations to mitigate the impact of military operations at different times during, before, or after conflict.

Corps Support Command (COSCOM)

- Principal logistics organization providing supply, field services, transportation (mode operations and movement control), maintenance, and combat health support to divisions and non-division corps units. Functional control centers:
  - Material management center
  - Movement control center
  - Medical brigade
  - Transportation group (if three or more functional transportation battalions are assigned)
  - Corps support groups

Medical Brigade

- Controls all corps medical units not organic to divisions, separate maneuver brigades, and cavalry regiments, as well as:
  - Controls and provides staff supervision for medical groups, a medical logistic battalion, dental, combat stress control, preventative medicine, and veterinary units.
  - Tasks organizations to meet medical workload demands.
  - Advises senior commander on medical aspects of combat operations and operations other than war.

- Provides for medical regulation of patient movement between medical treatment facilities within the corps and coordination for patient movement out of the corps.
- Provides consultative services and technical advice in preventative medicine (environmental health, medical entomology, radiological health, and sanitary engineering), nursing, dental, veterinary medicine, and psychiatry.
- Provides control and supervision of Class VII supply and resupply movement.

Personnel Group

- Performs the following tasks:
  - Database management of personnel accounting and strength reporting
  - Casualty operations management
  - Personnel information management
  - Identification documents
  - Personnel evaluations
  - Promotions and reductions
  - Officer procurement
  - Soldier actions

Finance Group (Some Positions)

- Commander, finance support unit, finance group, or theater finance command
- Accountants (officer-level and enlisted)
- Bookkeepers (officer-level and enlisted)
- Managers/officers
- File clerks
- Disbursing officer

Transportation Group (Some Positions)

- Watercraft or vehicle project/product manager
- Installation transportation officer
- Movement control agency/center unit commander
- Passenger/freight/personal property movements officer
- Director of inland traffic Military Traffic Management Command (MTMC)
- Director of personal property
- Traffic engineer
- Watercraft unit commander/officer
- Terminal service/transfer unit commander/officer
- Director of international traffic
- Terminal operations/documentation officer
- Terminal or port commander
- Marine maintenance officer
- Rail transport plans officer
- Rail transport staff officer
- Rail equipment maintenance officer

- Motor transport plans officer
- Motor transport staff officer
- Driver
- Mechanic
- Route manager
- Shop manager
- Parts clerk

Quartermaster Group

- Logistical specialist
- Petroleum supply specialist
- Food service specialist
- Mortuary affairs specialist
- Parachute rigger
- Shower/laundry and clothing repair specialist
- Water treatment specialist
- Unit supply specialist

During Military Occupation

- Property accounting technician
- Supply systems technician
- Airdrop systems technician
- Food service technician
- Petroleum technician

In Areas of Concentration (AOCs)

- Quartermaster, general
- Aerial delivery and material
- Petroleum and water

Explosive Ordinance Group

- Capabilities include:
  - Identifying and rendering safe foreign and U.S. military munitions (chemical, conventional, and nuclear)
  - Disposing of munitions encountered and rendering safe terrorist-improvised explosive devices (IED) (such as pipe bombs, booby traps, etc.)
  - Responding to WMD incidents
  - Conducting training in military munitions and IED to LEAs
  - Providing support to the U.S. Secret Service (USSS) and DOS

Psychological Operations Group (Psyop)

- Psyop's mission is to cause dissention among the enemy's ranks while at the same time convincing the local population to support friendly forces. In addition, the unit provides continuous analysis of attitudes and the behavior of enemy forces to field commanders.

Design Challenge

1. Examine several games, paying particular attention to roles, professions, and racial traits.
   a. Do any of these games allow for a player profession or trade skill?
   b. How does the choice of professions affect your enjoyment of a game?
   c. Can you think of more imaginative ways to use NPC roles and jobs?
2. Imagine you are creating an NPC.
   a. Pick an environment.
   b. Pick from various racial options.
   c. Pick a role.
   d. Pick a job.
3. For the player character:
   a. Pick from racial options.
   b. Pick a role.
   c. Pick a job.
   d. Pick a story/story world.

14 Enemies

Without enemies, most games would leave the heroes with nothing at all to do. One of the traps designers fall into is making enemies without much thought—taking a cookie-cutter approach. In this chapter, I explore some ways to create more interesting enemies and some ways to deal with them. But I'll start out by looking at the kinds of enemies you might find in games.

- Types of Enemies
- More on Bosses
- Enemy Fighting Styles
- Boss Battles
- Ways to Make More Interesting Enemies
- Ways to Encounter Enemies
- Ways to Avoid Enemies
- How to Make You Hate Them

Types of Enemies

Enemies seem to fall into several (more or less) consistent categories:

- **Sword Candy.** Not even up to the level of a mindless drone, these are simply weak, mindless creatures designed only for the purpose of dying whenever the hero attacks them—usually in one hit. They are grass to be mowed. They are swarms of gnats to be swatted aside…usually there are lots of them.
- **Generic Enemies.** In some games, many of the enemies you encounter are just mindless drones, only slightly more dangerous than sword candy. Usually there are a lot of them, and usually they can be defeated quickly, in just a few good strokes. They don't all come in the same flavors, however. Some may be melee types, some spell casters, some ranged fighters.... In any case, these are the lowest of the low in the enemy pantheon (other than the sword candy enemies, and they hardly count) and are often tossed at the hero like rice at a wedding. Sword candy and generic enemies are often used to make the player feel more powerful, let him gain experience or general loot easily, and give him a sensation of being powerful—at least until the real bosses show up.
- **Minions.** Minions can arguably be described as any of the followers of the boss or the syndicate, or whatever the main big enemy is, meaning that there can be a wide range of minion types—grunt minions, specialized minions, lieutenant minions, and so on. Their obvious affiliation with that group, gang, or boss distinguishes them somewhat from generic types of enemies. The lowest level of minions are the grunt types—the basic foot soldiers of the game who are generally on a par with, or slightly more interesting than, the generic enemies described a moment ago. They are generally low-level enemies associated with a specific boss or group. They are still pretty much cannon fodder—used to hone your skills, gain you experience, or charge up your character, depending on the type of game.

- **Specialists.** Some enemies have special abilities. These can still be minions or even generic enemies, but they are somewhat distinguished by their specialized abilities. For instance, they might be snipers, magic users who specialize in hypnotizing heroes, thieves who steal your items, shape-shifters, or ninja assassins. In any case, the specialist enemy is generally more dangerous, often harder to fight, and certainly more interesting than either the generic enemy or the minions.
- **Mini-Bosses.** Far more difficult than the average minion, the mini-boss is generally placed to provide additional challenge to the player. Early in a game, you'll probably begin to encounter characters who serve this purpose. They are often the first real test of a character and are tougher, meaner, and more dangerous than most other characters. (Mini-bosses in some games are associated with the end boss [see below], and fill the role of lieutenants in the end boss' organization. In other cases, the mini-bosses are unrelated to the end boss and simply serve as special challenges. They may also serve as gate-keepers to test the player's readiness to advance, but at points not quite as significant as those guarded by bosses.)
- **Bosses.** Bosses are really sub-bosses in that they generally appear at key points in a game chapter, mission, or level. They aren't the big cheese (the end boss), but they are tough and generally have a variety of dangerous attacks, with only certain weaknesses. They may have some similarities to the end boss, but, while never as dangerous or complex to defeat, they should provide a good test of the player's skills.
- **The End Boss.** The ultimate test of the character, and generally the culmination of many games, is the so-called *boss battle*, in which the hero fights the ultimate bad guy. Bosses (and, to a lesser degree, sub-bosses) may have a variety of ways to attack the heroes. They may have devastating melee attacks, a variety of magic attacks, the ability to call minions or resurrect the dead, or just about any power, ability, or cheap trick a designer can think of. In addition, they often have very few weaknesses, so that damaging them requires precise aim or precise timing, or the employment of a specific device, weapon, or technique. In old-style games, there was often a loophole, such as a simple maneuver that was always effective or a safe spot where the boss's attacks always missed.

  Bosses sometimes start out fairly ordinary-looking, but somewhere in the battle—even after they appear to have been defeated—they morph into something even worse. This is a common trick for making boss battles seem longer and more difficult. I've seen a boss morph three or four times, appearing to have been defeated between each time. Also, some bosses may be segmented, so that you have to defeat different parts of them, either in sequence or simply one at a time.

All of the aforementioned enemy types can also be categorized as I did in Chapter 12, "Character Design," in the "Villains" and "Minions" sections.

Villains

- The Great Tyrant
- The Conqueror
- The Patriarch/Matriarch
- The Smooth Villain
- The Mad/Evil Genius
- The Sociopath
- The Professional Killer/Assassin
- The Demon
- The Defector
- The Unscrupulous Bastard/Nasty Bitch
- The False Ally
- The Avenger
- The Rival/Personal Enemy
- The Fanatic
- The Complete Lunatic
- The Unseen
- The Meek
- Giant Monsters

Minions

- The Number 2
- The Lieutenant
- The Random Grunt
- The Red Shirt
- The Guard
- The Jailer
- The Muscle
- The Sadist
- The Lab Minion
- The Sneak
- The Crazy Joker
- The Family Member
- The Worshiping Fan
- The Mole
- The Elite Guard
- The Hired Hand

More on Bosses

Bosses in games often tend to be more like comic book villains than the more complex characters from literature or even good films. They tend to be simplistic, driven by a single drive for power, greed, or revenge, and are rarely shown in any detail during the course of the game. They are almost always power-mad megalomaniacs. However, villains can also be subtle and complex. They can have a good side, for instance, or conflicts. They might be certifiably crazy, but also have certain redeeming traits. For instance, Saddam Hussein was a brutal dictator, but apparently he also wrote quite a few romantic novels...whatever passed for romantic to him, anyway.

The point is that the main enemy in a game can be a powerful archetype that is never given much personality—just a lot of dangerous abilities. Or it can be developed by borrowing from cinematic and literary techniques. Here are a few ways you can further develop a main enemy:

- **Flashbacks.** Include flashbacks to events of the past that show the boss, perhaps before he was completely driven to take over the world or before he came to hate the hero. Think of how Gollum is developed in *The Lord of the Rings*, so that he goes from being just a monstrous creature to a tragic figure, who is nevertheless still evil and unredeemable—even though often he promises to "be good" to the "nasssty Hobbitses." Flashbacks are presented most often these days in FMV (*full-motion video*), though sometimes the player is actually taken to an earlier time to play through past events.
- **Interludes.** You can include scenes that show what the enemy is doing while the hero is happily slashing his way across the landscape. Basically, you can use these interlude scenes both to further the depth of the main villain and to create foreshadowing and tension in the plot of the game. It's all the more interesting if you know what the enemy is up to and can anticipate it, but you can't do anything about it until the time comes. Or, perhaps in a more interesting game, you have some choices to make based on what you know from that scene, so there is some opportunity for strategy. Another type of interlude is one you might think of as the "plot thickener," in which you observe a scene that totally changes your perception of the situation, forcing you to reconsider your imminent course of action.
- **Character Encounters.** Have the hero encounter the main boss several times during the game, each time learning more about him. These scenes can be dramatic, action-oriented, and revealing. Another type of character encounter might involve actually having the main villain as an ally at some point in the game. This could be because he really is on your side at some point or because he is messing with you. In any case, that experience with the enemy can deepen your experience of him and make the game more powerful. In some examples of character encounters, you may cross paths with the villain but be able to do nothing but observe. This sort of encounter can serve to deepen your feelings of righteousness or anger toward the bad guys, since you may see them do

heinous acts, and, being powerless, your frustration and desire to punish them will grow. By the time you finally get to whack them, it's all the more satisfying.

- **Switching Sides.** Similar to the previous example, the enemy may start out as a friend and become the enemy during the game, due to some event that sends him against your side. Or, the enemy may even simply change allegiances, switch to an enemy side (or fall under the control of an evil power), then take over that group and become its leader—hence, your ultimate foe. In an interesting twist, the reason your former ally became evil might be something you can relate to—it might even seem, from a particular point of view, justified. That doesn't mean you can let him get away with it, but just that you can understand the enemy's feelings and responses to the story's events. Of course, it could be the hero who switches sides, as the player determines that the "other side" is the one he prefers to support.
- **Third-Party Stories.** You can learn more about the main boss by getting stories from various NPCs you meet, books you find, scenes you witness, or conversations you overhear. They can also come by listening to recordings or talking with a team member who once knew the villain.
- **Foreshadowing.** This could be in the form of a change in the background music, distant villainous laughter, or some other indication that things are about to get violent. Sometimes you will get a cut scene that shows what is happening in real time, but at a different location—for example, the villain is about to cut the throat of someone the hero loves or push the plunger on the dynamite that will bring down the citadel of the good king. That kind of imminent danger increases the urgency of the situation, but simultaneously tells you that you're getting close—because, of course, you are going to save the day. Aren't you?

Enemy Fighting Styles

There are only a few ways that enemies will fight you. Some are quite common, while some are less often used:

- **Basic Melee.** Hands and feet; simple weapons, such as swords, knives/daggers, clubs, etc.
- **Standoff Melee.** Longer-reach weapons, such as spears, pole arms, and pikes.
- **Ranged Weapons:** Guns, bows, throwing weapons.
- **Big Ranged Weapons.** Catapults, mangonels, cannons, and other artillery.
- **Spells (and Magical Ranged Weapons).** Includes a wide variety of types of casting, including direct damage, damage over time (such as poison), controls (such as putting you to sleep), debuffs (such as lowering your defense or offense), and so on. Enemies who cast spells may also heal themselves or their allies as well as cast enhancement buffs on themselves and their allies. In essence, spell-casting enemies can cast any type of spell. (See also "Magic Abilities" in Chapter 15, "Character Abilities.")
- **Stealth.** Less common is an enemy who can use stealth to take you by surprise, and even escape by disappearing from view.
- **Bull Rush.** Enemies who rush at you to attack.
- **Leapers.** Enemies who jump in to attack you and may keep leaping about, making them difficult targets.
- **Airborne.** Enemies who attack from the air.
- **Mechs.** Enemies who attack from vehicles or mechanical suits.
- **Summoners.** A magic class that summons other creatures to attack you.
- **Hammer Blows.** Some enemies have exceptionally strong attacks that can do massive damage if you get in the way.

- **Berserker.** Some enemies can enter into a berserk phase where they do tons of damage and are hard to bring down.
- **Exploders.** Some enemies will detonate when you attack or defeat them, possibly causing massive damage to you if you are too close at the time. Although generally exploder-type enemies won't take you from full health to zero, if you are already somewhat damaged this can be fatal, and in a large battle, the extra damage from the exploders can also be fatal. Obviously, killing exploders from a distance is preferable, but some exploder enemies are also like homing missiles, in that they will run directly at you and try to get close enough to explode on death.
- **Phasing.** Some enemies can phase in and out of tangible form. When they are intangible, they can't be damaged.
- **Control and Debuffs.** Some enemies can immobilize you, slow you down, put you to sleep, strip you of your offensive or defensive abilities, and otherwise mess you up.
- **Return the Favor.** Some enemies actually return the damage you do to them or hurt you upon contact. Examples are enemies who have "damage shields" that actually reflect back some of the damage you inflict on them or enemies with some sort of natural protection (such as fire, acid, or cold) that can damage you when you attack them.
- **Passive Damage.** Like the previous example, some enemies may have a field around them that can do damage or otherwise affect you when you get too close. In contrast to the "Return the Favor" example, this field can affect you regardless of whether you attack.
- **Indirect Damage.** Using the surroundings to their advantage, the enemies cause it to attack you or cause you to hurt yourself by accident. It could be a cannon-like weapon, rolling boulders, forcing you off edges, maneuvering you so you get damaged, or getting you to trigger traps.

Boss Battles

Here are some of the typical elements of boss battles, which occur either at significant points in the story or, most specifically, at the end of the game. Key questions to ask are:

- How do you attack?
- How do you defend?
- How does the boss attack?
- How does the boss defend?
- What does the boss care about?
- Does the boss display any patterns of attack and defense?
- Does the boss have any weaknesses or vulnerabilities?
- Does the boss have minions? If so, can you ignore them and concentrate on the boss, or do you need to defeat them first? Or, even if you don't need to defeat them first, perhaps it's strategically a good idea because they can do too much damage to you and they are easier to kill. Or, perhaps they are healing the boss or otherwise making the boss stronger or better defended. The same may hold true for items, weapons, and other structures that assist the boss in various ways. For instance, guns may protect the boss, but so might magical wards that increase the boss's defenses.
- Are there conditions you must meet or tasks you must accomplish before you can defeat or even harm the boss?
- Does the boss have different phases, forms, or parts that must be dealt with in some order?

Boss Battle Examples

- **Shoot 'Em Up.** Keep firing (and maybe dodging counterattacks) until you win and he loses.
- **You Da Man.** Somehow being strong enough (even temporarily) or having access to enough enhancements and/or healing and recharging to stand up to the boss and duke it out.
- **Patterns.** Many bosses follow a preset pattern of attacks and defenses, and all you need to do is figure out the pattern and the moments at which to attack or defend. If you can execute your counter-pattern properly, you can't lose. Of course, the boss might change the pattern at some point.
- **Patterns within Patterns.** The simple pattern boss is one type, but others might have patterns within patterns, so that you can get lulled into a repetitive, high-frequency pattern, only to be blindsided by an attack that occurs less frequently or even randomly.
- **Find the Weakness.** The boss is probably nearly invulnerable, but there is a weakness—or there may be several that become vulnerable at different times in the battle.
- **Is It Safe?** Good places to hide from wave attacks or when a boss is on a rampage. These safe spots may shift or may be moving.
- **Keep Moving.** Sometimes there are safe spots, but they are moving. Other times, moving is simply a good strategy to prevent the boss from getting a good shot at you.
- **Stillness Is Death.** Even more difficult than the previous example, some bosses will hit you almost immediately if you stop moving. You must carry out the battle on the move, attacking whenever the opportunity presents itself. This is especially interesting when there's a very slight delay in the boss's attack—just long enough for you to stop, aim, and deliver a shot or blow, but no longer. If you fail to move quickly enough, BAM! You get hammered. Of course, as a game designer, you get to choose how much delay there is. Technically, the boss could attack at the speed of the computer that runs the game, but then no human being could beat it, so some delay it necessary.
- **Periodic Waves.** This boss sends waves of either minions or direct attacks at the player.
- **Delegation.** This boss primarily (or totally) has others fight for him. This may be as part of a wave, or it may be that the boss himself is weak except for his ability to control, summon, or inspire other creatures to fight for him.
- **Destruction of Property.** In some cases, the way to defeat a boss is to destroy the area around it. For instance, you can't kill the boss directly, but if you take out all four columns holding up the building, the resulting crash-boom does the job.
- **Berzerker.** This boss is a mad destroyer, hard to avoid because he is so aggro, random, and, generally, fast moving.
- **Tradeoff.** Some bosses can attack in a multitude of ways, but each attack has its associated weakness or vulnerability. You must learn not only to avoid his attack, but to exploit the opening when it's presented.
- **The Lure.** In some cases, the player character must expose himself to danger in order to lure the boss into the open. From then on, the battle can take any of the forms listed here.
- **Retreat and Regroup.** Sometimes the boss will appear to be defeated (or close to it) and will run, but beware. Some bosses only use this as a diversion to a) draw you into a more dangerous location, and/or b) recharge and renew the attack. They may also have a secret weapon or a devastating ability that they are just waiting to spring on you as you rush in for the kill.
- **Don't Feed the Boss.** Against some bosses, certain attacks not only don't work, but they can actually increase the boss's power. For instance, using fire against a fire monster might actually make it stronger. In such cases, there is always an alternative power or a way to redirect the attack so that it damages the enemy instead of feeding it.

- **Freedom Fighters.** You enlist an ad hoc army by freeing the boss's prisoners or releasing them from the boss's mental hold, for example. Once freed, these people will fight on your side, giving you an edge against the boss.
- **The Element of Surprise.** If you can somehow get off the first attack, you might do sufficient damage to the boss to shorten the battle and give you the edge.
- **Critical Systems.** Perhaps you can destroy the source of the boss's power or his life support, leaving him more vulnerable.
- **Multitasking.** In many boss battles, you are simultaneously trying to destroy the boss and avoid being destroyed by his powerful attacks while also fighting/dodging attacks from other sources. Sometimes it is other minions, while in other cases it can be natural or technological dangers. For instance, you might have to avoid boiling lava pools and flying fireballs while fighting a boss inside a volcano, or you might have to avoid numerous automated machine-gun nests around the boss's lair while you maneuver in your fight against the boss.
- **Charge Up.** In some battles, either you or the boss will buy time to charge up a significant weapon or attack. If you are doing the charging, the chances are you're also dodging the boss's attacks and trying not to get hit, since getting hit often causes the charge-up procedure to restart.
- **Hit Him Where It Hurts.** In some cases, attacking what the boss most values can give you an edge. You might distract the boss or weaken him in some way, or you might simply make him angry and cause him to make mistakes. This assumes that there's something the boss thinks is worth protecting.
- **Clues**
  - **Sound Clues.** Sometimes a specific sound will signal the boss's location or an imminent attack or phase change.
  - **Visual Clues.** Very commonly, there will be a visual indication of a boss's imminent attack or moments of vulnerability. This can take the form of specific patterns of movement or something as simple as a glow or visual effect that occurs just before or during the moment in question.
- **Sense Deprivation.** Some bosses can affect the player's senses, such as sight or sound. Generally, this is not a total blackout or lack of hearing, but a distortion of those senses to make it harder (but not impossible) to conduct the battle.
- **Timers**
  - **The Timed Attack.** This boss's pattern is very precise, such that you can time each aspect of it and know that, for instance, every 30 seconds the boss will unleash a powerful nuke that flattens everything within a specific radius. The best bet is to plan on being outside that radius when the attack comes.
  - **The Countdown.** This boss must be killed within a specific amount of time, or you lose (or have to reset). Often there is a countdown timer displayed on the screen to show you how long you have remaining.
  - **Survival Test.** In this case, the boss will die or be defeated in some other way if you can only survive for a specific period of time or until that other event transpires.
- **Morphology.** Some bosses can change into different forms. Some, like the mythical phoenix, can rise from their own ashes (so to speak) to be even more powerful than ever. Others simply have the ability to take different forms during a battle, each form having its own strengths and weaknesses. Countering these forms may involve simple logic—attack the fire creature with ice, for instance, and vice versa—or it may be more obscure, and you might have to use trial and error, spells, or prior knowledge to figure out what your most effective attacks will be against the boss' different forms.
- **Mental Powers.** The boss may have a variety of special powers, such as telekinesis, where the boss has the ability to control the physical world with his mind and uses the objects in the environment

to attack you. As another example, pyrokinesis would allow the boss to control fire. Just think X-Men, and you'll have a good list of mental powers in no time.

- **Faker.** This boss pretends to be defeated, but he's only fooling. You relax, and he strikes again.
- **The Small(er) World.** You and the boss are fighting in an area that is getting smaller in some way—the walls could be closing in, a platform could be falling apart at the edges, a force field could be failing and the safe zone shrinking, a fire could be raging around you and closing in, and so on.
- **Natural Hazards.** Where you are fighting has its own hazards, such as boiling hot steam vents or falling rocks, and so on.
- **Outside Forces.** You find yourself confronted with forces or creatures who are not associated with the boss, such as wild animals or the police, and you have to deal with them as well as the boss.
- **Teamwork.** Some bosses cannot be defeated by one character alone, and you must rely on other players or NPC characters to fulfill necessary roles in vanquishing the boss.
- **The Secret Boss.** This boss is hidden or hiding, and you must find him or even fight numerous enemies in search of him. Perhaps he has made himself appear like one of his minions, and only by attacking him can you get him to reveal his true identity. Or you might have to try other means, such as a detection device or an action that causes it to appear, and so on.
- **Charge Up Minions.** Sometimes the boss has generous numbers of minions who will drop useful charge-up items, weapons, or anything that can help you in your battle against the boss. Mowing down a few minions is often necessary to get that next healing flask, ammunition pack, or temporary power.
- **Healing/Buff Minions or Items.** Some bosses have minions or items that either heal them or in some way enhance their power(s). Taking out the minions/items is often advisable to make the boss more vulnerable.
- **Preliminary Minions or Items.** Sometimes a boss is invulnerable until you take out certain minions or items. In such cases, you have no choice but to deal with the minions or items first—but the boss may be able to attack you while you're doing so!
- **Bombardier.** The boss (or minions) tosses or drops devices on you—generally not to help you out. However, in some cases, you may be able to take their weapons and reflect, catch, toss, or otherwise redirect them against the boss. So, for instance, suppose you have an umbrella as an item in your inventory. The minion tosses a bomb at you, but you use the umbrella to bounce the bomb at the boss, where it does some damage. Keep this up, and you'll have him down lickety-split. But don't get hit.
- **Boss in the Round.** The boss battle takes place all around a boss who sits in the center of the battlefield.
- **Boss-in-a-Boss.** As you defeat a boss, another form is revealed—generally worse and almost always different from the last. A boss can go through several incarnations in a single battle, usually culminating with something so visually stunning and scary-looking that you really feel a great sense of accomplishment and relief when you've defeated him.
- **Modular Bosses**
  - **Attacking Parts.** Some bosses can break up into various smaller parts, each of which attacks or in some way participates in the attempt to dismantle you.
  - **Slow Destruction.** You slowly destroy the boss's weapons, armor, or other parts, such as tentacles, hands and arms, legs, and so on.
- **Bull Rush Boss.** This boss thinks he is a rhinoceros (or perhaps he is one) and charges quickly at the enemies, who would be best advised to get out of the way.
- **Leapin' Lizards.** This boss likes a jump attack, and, like the bull rush boss, it's a good idea to time the attack and be somewhere else when he lands.
- **Chaser.** This boss is chasing you, and you have to reach a specific goal before he kills you.

- **Racer.** This boss is actually trying to reach the same goal you are. Whoever gets there first wins.
- **Runner.** This boss is running from you, essentially playing hide-and-seek. He may be setting traps for you along the way, too.
- **Weak Point.** This boss is invulnerable unless a certain part of him is attacked.

Ways to Make More Interesting Enemies

As I said before, it's possible to create enemies without really giving them much thought. After all, they have one purpose—to attack the good guys whenever they see them, right? And sometimes that's good enough. But what if you could create enemies that were more interesting, challenging, and rewarding to the player? Here are a few ideas:

- Give each enemy type at least one special quality or ability in addition to its basic attack.
- Give some enemies the ability to adjust to the player's style of fighting, particularly if the player uses the same patterns over and over again. This will require that the player make counter adjustments and will add a challenge to the encounters.
- Make enemies better at seeking advantages in a fight by moving to a better attack position, finding cover, acquiring items in the environment to use as weapons, and so on.
- Give the enemies some ability to tell where the threats are—not just the sources of damage, but other threats, such as characters who can heal or who can cast control spells or debuffs.
- Give enemies better group strategies so that they take advantage of their various strengths, but also so that they respond to the player's changes in tactics.
- Put in something surprising—something that doesn't happen often. For instance, have a grunt enemy occasionally take something from the environment and use it as a weapon. This should be rare enough to take the player by surprise when it happens.
- In groups with leaders and minions, have the group fight better with the leader than without, so that if the player can kill the leader first, the minions will become less effective.
- Provide the enemies with funny or colorful dialog, even if it is just a variety of things they say when they attack, during a battle, or when they are defeated—or even when you are defeated.
- Give them the ability to surrender or try to cut a deal. This often works well in games where you have minions of your own, thus increasing your troops.
- Give some enemies the ability to change sides. What do you do, as a player, if an enemy starts fighting for you? Do you trust him?
- Give them the ability to set traps—physical or situational—for the player.

Ways to Encounter Enemies

The setup is like this: The hero is walking into a situation where the enemy awaits. Or perhaps the hero is setting a trap. Or the enemy is setting a trap. In any case, how do we, as designers, create the situations and encounters that make the game interesting and fun? What are some of the ways the player and the enemies collide? Here are a few suggestions. Can you think of more?

- **Sitting Duck.** The enemy gets caught out in the open.
- **Sitting Duck 2.** You are in a vulnerable position that can get you killed if the enemy spots you. You need to get to a better position quietly before engaging the enemy.
- **Toast.** You are instant toast if you get spotted. This is even worse than the previous example.

- **Bad Position.** The enemy has some cover but it kind of sucks, such as hiding behind breakable glass or cardboard boxes.
- **Really Bad Position.** The enemy hides behind very dangerous cover—for instance, behind a gas tank/collapsible bridge/fish tank.
- **Weak and Cornered.** A wimpy enemy is stuck in a corner or dead end and will have to go through you to get away.
- **Stuck.** The enemy has gotten stuck—for instance, a strap caught on a nail.
- **Trapped.** You have trapped the enemy. (See Chapter 26, "Traps and Counter Traps.")
- **Trapped 2.** Of course, you may be the one who's trapped when your enemy comes across you. Bummer.
- **Frozen/Paralyzed/Immobilized.** You may come across an enemy who is somehow restrained or unable to attack when you first encounter him. You may not even realize he is an enemy. For instance, the enemy may be a statue that later comes to life, an innocent-looking creature that turns out to be a ravenous beast, or a demon currently held by magical wards (that will later fail, you can be sure).
- **Frozen/Paralyzed/Immobilized 2.** Of course, you might be the one in the compromising position. Better hope the enemy doesn't recognize you or that you have a way out of the situation.
- **Good Position.** The enemy has good cover, and you'll have to blast away his cover, get into another position, smoke him out, or use high explosives.
- **Great Position.** The enemy has great cover, and you will probably need to use a special weapon, guile, or some other means to get to him. If all else fails, you can either lure out the enemy or try to infiltrate his position.
- **Up/Down.** The enemy is at a different elevation, which may give one of you an advantage or disadvantage.
- **Side Vulnerability.** The enemy can be flushed out by moving and shooting at angles.
- **Group Tactic #1.** Shoot the closest enemy first, then the rest.
- **Group Tactic #2.** Shoot the farthest enemy first because he might be stronger, could run for help, or might cause some other problem.
- **Group Tactic #3.** Take out any stragglers, guards, or lookouts before you take on the main force.
- **Group Tactic #4.** Take out the weakest enemies first so they can't hamper you when you go after the stronger ones.
- **Group Tactic #5.** Ignore the weak enemies and concentrate on the strongest ones.
- **Group Tactic #6.** Take out a specific kind of enemy, such as the magic users, the healers, or the ones that can do the most damage.
- **Ambush.** The enemies have an ambush ready—when you walk into an area to challenge one, more appear behind and/or around you.
- **Enemy #1.** Shoot the *most important* enemy first. The most important enemy may be the strongest, the most dangerous, the leader, or the one whose death means the most to your mission (and who might get away if you don't get him early).
- **The Big Weapon.** Shoot the enemy with the biggest weapon first (on the premise that big weapons do more damage).
- **Position Control.** Shoot the enemy in the best position to reach cover first.
- **Fancy Dress.** Take out the enemy who has the fanciest costume.
- **The Lure.** Bait the enemy (use something to draw his attention), then shoot him when he goes over to investigate.
- **Turn the Tables.** The enemy is waiting to ambush you, but you know exactly where he is. (Time to surprise him!)
- **Surprise!** You catch an enemy by surprise—for instance, you sneak up from behind, catch him in the bathroom, or plug him through a window when he doesn't know you're there.

- **Cat and Mouse.** An enemy is stalking you—just playing and taunting you, but not risking his life. (For example, a bullet hits the wall beside you, then silence. Or an object falls over, but there is nobody there.)
- **Cat and Mouse Turnabout.** You are chasing a very dangerous enemy, but now you don't know where he is. The cat has become the mouse, and you are now the hunted.
- **Cat and Mouse Advantage.** You play cat and mouse with the enemy, luring him into traps and other dangers or simply into vulnerable positions from which you can attack.
- **Unseen.** You haven't seen the enemy yet, but you have an indication that he's coming. Perhaps someone says something or you hear a sound or ominous music or see his blip on the radar.
- **Accidental Meeting.** The enemy blunders into you, and he is completely unprepared to fight.
- **Accidental Meeting 2.** You blunder into the enemy and are completely unprepared to fight.
- **Intentional Meeting.** You've set up a meeting with the enemy. Perhaps it ends up in violence, perhaps not. It starts out with talk, negotiations, revelations, threats. How it ends is up to you—and them.
- **Otherwise Engaged.** Your enemy is fighting someone else—perhaps another of your enemies, some random heroic type, or even an innocent victim. There are no rules. Frag him while he is otherwise occupied.
- **Turned Tail.** The enemy runs for his life. You must chase him down to catch him.
- **Preservation.** You must not kill this enemy for some reason. For instance, killing him will cause someone else's death, cause you to lose information you need from him, or get you into some bigger trouble.
- **Disabling.** You don't want to kill this enemy, but you had better disable him.
- **The Perfect Shot.** You really need to take this enemy down in one shot (head shot), or things will get a lot worse. It may be that he will reach cover, that his counterattack will be deadly, or that he has a power he can activate that makes him invulnerable if you fail to take him out.
- **Kill Them All.** Kill everyone in an area before they signal help or trigger an alarm. This will be a combo of explosions, disabling fight moves, and disabling shots.
- **Special Enemy.** You must kill a specific enemy within a group of others—for instance, you must take out the guy with the radio.
- **I Have Seen the Enemy, and I'm It.** Sometimes you must fight your own doppelganger. It may be a shape-shifter taking your attributes, it could be you from another dimension, or it could be a battle with your inner self as represented on the outside…something like that.
- **The Spirits Within or Without.** Sometimes the enemy is not corporal, and you have to find a way to fight it without using physical force.
- **Look Out Below.** Sometimes the enemy is able to fly or hover, presenting special challenges unless you can fly and/or hover, too.
- **Subterfuge.** Disguise yourself so they don't realize you are an enemy. You may be able to infiltrate the enemy's organization and do great harm to them before you must reveal yourself.
- **3D Battle.** You will need to use all the angles, moving three-dimensionally, to pick off the enemies.
- **Mass Destruction.** Don't worry about the individual enemies; just destroy the whole room with whatever WMDs you have.
- **Shoot On Through.** You can shoot the enemy through whatever they are hiding behind, such as a door, wall, or bed sheet.
- **Shoot the Cover.** Whittle away at the enemy's cover. For instance, if he is behind a solid oak table, keep shooting until you blast a hole in it. If he is hiding behind a sculpture, blast it to bits until he is exposed.
- **Control the Environment.** You can cause the environment to change; for instance, turn off the lights or control the electric fences or door-locking mechanisms.

- **Control the Environment 2.** The enemy can cause the environment to change; for instance, turn off the lights or control the electric fences or door-locking mechanisms.
- **Control the Environment 3.** A third party can cause the environment to change; for instance, a worker could turn on very noisy machines.
- **Invisibility.** You become invisible by any means—magic, potions, flash-bangs, turning off the lights and using infrared, and so on.
- **Invisibility 2.** The enemies become invisible.
- **Ingenuity.** You need to choose the right weapon, tool, or even object for the job, such as a screwdriver to open the doors to a control panel, which will let you get around and behind the enemy.
- **Screw-Up.** The enemy makes a fatal mistake—for instance, a corrupt beat cop shoots a SWAT member, or a mobster betrays the big boss.
- **The Enemy Within.** Someone who you thought was a friend turns out to be an enemy. At the moment of realization, you find yourself in a battle.
- **Battle Among Friends.** Sometimes you have to fight an ally in order to accomplish some goal. This is rarely to the death.
- **Frame-Up.** Perhaps you can place the blame on an enemy and cause his own allies to turn on him.
- **Be Afraid.** This enemy is extremely deadly. You will need to stock up on everything to face him, or possibly find a way to defeat him without direct confrontation, with a secret weapon, or with the "Perfect Shot" (as described earlier in this list).
- **Not That Way!** The enemy runs away—that's good—but toward something you don't want him to reach, such as a gun or the switch to the nuclear detonation device—that's bad. Or maybe toward an even worse enemy or a whole squad of other enemies—also bad.
- **The Slow Advance.** The enemy is advancing slowly using good cover (riot shields, vehicles, and so on). The player must shoot the hell out of his cover, create a barrier (such as a wall of flame), flank the enemy, land a shot to a specific vulnerable point, and so on.
- **The Unstoppable Force.** The enemy is rapidly advancing. It's an unstoppable force. For instance, a charging rhino, a jet airplane, a speed-enhanced villain, a cattle stampede, and so on.
- **Light Games.** You and/or the enemy can only see where the light is shining. Everything else is in darkness.
- **Protection.** The enemy is trying to get to someone or something you're protecting.
- **Ultra Ambush.** The enemy or enemies are hiding practically in your pocket and suddenly jump out at you, resulting in hand-to-hand battle. (Note: This must be cool and believable, and not seem like a cheap shot that could not have possibly been avoided.)
- **Surrounded.** Multiple enemies appear from all sides instantly, as if coordinated by some larger intelligence. (For example, they can enter through doors, stairs, or ladders or even drop in from ropes.)
- **Tracker.** You can trail the enemy. Perhaps he is unaware of you and it's actually to your advantage to follow him unobserved. He might lead you to some clue or essential location, or he might be walking into a trap…or you might be!
- **Sniper.** The enemy is only within sniping range, and any other approach is too dangerous and exposed. You need some long-distance attack to take him out, or something bad will happen.
- **Gun-Fu.** You can charge into a crowd of enemies, guns blazing (or weapons flashing), and take them out with superior combinations, techniques, and reflexes.
- **No Safety.** The enemies can kick in doors, attacking you in a room in which you thought you were alone or stuck. They can shoot locks or break windows to get into the room with you, even if you thought you lost them.
- **Quiet Please.** Move slowly and quietly, or the enemy will become alerted to you. (He is listening.)
- **Upwind Only.** The enemy can smell you.

- **Choose the Moment.** The enemy is exposed only during a brief cycle of time. (For example, shooting from a moving car at a truck full of enemies, firing through the spaced gaps in the freeway wall, or shooting someone through slowly rotating fan blades.)
- **Flushed Out.** The enemy has done something clever that will soon flush you out into the open, where he will be waiting. (For example, he might fire tear gas into your room or set it on fire and wait outside.)
- **Patrols.** The enemy is patrolling and will find you no matter where you hide. Either find another place to hide or figure out his patrol pattern and move to avoid discovery.
- **A Great Spot.** This is a great spot to ambush a patrolling guard, target or assassination, squadron of enemy soldiers, or other enemy you need to take out.
- **Follow the Trail.** The enemy has fled. Follow his trail of blood or other telltale signs.
- **Chase Technique.** If you are being chased, try to create obstacles in the enemy's path or destroy the path as you pass (such as blowing up a bridge or blocking the path with an avalanche).
- **Shoot and Run.** Sometimes you can't win in a straight firefight, but you can run and shoot, picking your spots to fire and then getting out of his range or sights until you're ready to take another potshot.
- **Diversion.** You must distract the enemy, giving your partner a chance to kill him somehow. Or the other way around—your partner does the diversion while you do the killing.
- **Remote Control.** Use some remote mechanism to defeat your enemy, such as a heavy steel door closing on him.
- **Lost in the Crowd.** Your enemies can sometimes blend into a crowd and escape you. However, you may have occasion to do the same.

Ways to Avoid Enemies

Fighting is fun, and prevailing is even more so. However, there are times when discretion is the better part of gameplay, and avoiding the enemy is better than direct confrontation. How do we get past, around, over, or under the enemy? Here are a few ideas. Keep thinking…

- Fly over them
- Sneak, staying in shadows or behind cover
- Become invisible
- Teleport past them
- Alter time—freeze it or jump to the past or future
- Stay out of their range of detection
- Create a diversion
- Disable them temporarily and run
- Run really fast
- Get somewhere they can't reach
- Go underground
- Duck into a building
- Hide in a crowd
- Disguise yourself
- Hypnotize them
- Send something toward them that scares them and makes them run away
- Play dead
- Significantly change your appearance
- Have accomplices distract them
- Choose another route or path

How to Make You Hate Them

It's usually not too hard to hate enemies. After all, they generally want to kill you and/or destroy what you are protecting. That is what enemies do—nothing exceptional about it. But what about the enemies who really get to you—the ones you just have to take out? How do you create enemies who get your blood boiling and fuel your determination to defeat them? Here are a few examples:

- Have them hurt or kidnap someone important to you.
- Even better, have them hurt someone weak and innocent.
- Even better, have them murder a whole village.
- Or, have them do something nasty to your (player) character, especially something underhanded that you can't prevent.
- Have them do something really low, such as slapping around a woman or being cruel to kids.
- Have them do something disgusting, such as killing puppies and eating them raw.
- Have them gloat and be truly obnoxious about their victories and the suffering/destruction they cause.
- Have them get away with terrible crimes and somehow appear to be innocent when you know they are guilty as hell.
- Have them say really obnoxious or stupid things.
- Have them wear really ugly and stupid costumes.
- Have them be untouchable—meaning that ordinary law and order can't get to them—such as a corrupt judge who uses the legal system to protect him.
- Have them violate the player's sense of fairness, ethics, morals, or other strong values.
- Have them pretend to be the player's friend and betray him. The longer and more trusting the involvement with the player and the more serious the betrayal, the better.
- Have them steal something valuable to the player.
- Have them always be one step ahead of the player.
- Script it so that they defeat the player in some contest or fight, enough to motivate the player to avenge the loss. Make it personal!
- Even better, have them be strong enough to perhaps defeat the player's character once or twice in a fair fight. There's no motivation greater than revenge on the enemy who ganked you—particularly the boss or significant characters. Make it really personal...they must die!
- Have them use guerrilla tactics on the player or allies. This gets worse when the mobs get in your way.
- Have them betray you, preferably at a key moment in the story or just before a major battle.
- Have them run away just when you think you have them where you want them, stealing victory and just making you want to thrash them even harder next time—and you know there will be a next time!
- Have them simply not shut up about their diabolical plans.
- Have them frustrate the player by seeming to be able to survive all his best tricks and abilities. It helps if they taunt the player a bit or even feign defeat to get the player's hopes up before revealing that the player hasn't beaten them—not yet, anyway.

Design Challenge

1. As always, consider the games you have played and the kinds of enemies they have in them.
   a. What made the enemies in good games interesting?
   b. How much variety was there, not only in the visuals and character design, but in the enemies' behaviors and abilities?
   c. In how many different ways did you encounter the enemies?
   d. What kinds of bosses did you encounter? Refer to the "Villains" section earlier in this chapter, as well as to the section on basic prototypes, "More on bosses."
   e. How could your character avoid bosses, if necessary?
   f. In what ways, if any, did the designers of these games motivate you or cause you to hate the enemies you faced?
2. For your own projects, consider how you will design enemy characters.
   a. What types of enemies will you create? (Refer to the "Types of Enemies" and "Villains" sections earlier in this chapter.)
   b. Consider the fighting styles of each of the enemies you plan to include in your game. With the list in the "Enemy Fighting Styles" section earlier in this chapter, there's no reason to limit yourself to the mundane! And then there's a lot of additional information in Chapter 15, "Character Abilities."
   c. What kinds of bosses will you include? Again, refer to the sections in this chapter and the "Villains" section in Chapter 12, "Character Design."
   d. What abilities/powers will each of the sub-bosses and the main boss have? How will they affect the player's battles with them? Check out Chapter 15, "Character Abilities" and other areas of this book.
   e. Consider how to make your enemies more interesting by referring to the "Ways to Make More Interesting Enemies" and "How to Make You Hate Them" sections earlier in this chapter.
   f. Set up interesting situations. Use the "Ways to Encounter Enemies" section earlier in this chapter and Chapter 11, "Scenarios," for some ideas.
   g. Can you come up with some interesting and novel ways for the player to avoid enemies when necessary?
   h. Finally, deepen your players' responses to the enemies to enrich the experience of defeating them. It's a given that the enemies hate your character, but how do you motivate the player and the player's character? Not that these are necessarily always the same–the player and the player's character could have very different motivations. You could have, for instance, a nonviolent Buddhist monk as the main character, but the player could still hate the enemies and want to blow them away. The challenge would be to find a way to use the nonviolent character to accomplish the player's goals!
3. Finally, create some boss characters using the resources in this chapter and Chapter 12, "Character Design" (and anywhere else you can think of).
   a. What if these bosses all got together? What do you think would happen?
   b. What if you turned one of these bosses into your hero character?

15 Character Abilities

In Chapter 12, "Character Design," we dealt with how to create a character and looked at character traits and, to some degree, the behavioral side of characters. This chapter is all about the abilities that characters can have. Included in this chapter are:

- Range of Human Abilities
- Superhero Abilities List
- Useful Superhero Jobs/Knowledge
- Statistical Abilities
- Fighting Abilities
- Magic Abilities
- Known Superhero List

Introduction

Every person has abilities. Some are natural, such as our five senses and abilities granted to us by our skeletal and muscular systems. Some may be learned or developed during the course of our lifetime. At any rate, we have a lot of natural abilities. But games often deal with larger-than-life characters, and these characters may have a range of abilities that far exceeds what we consider normal.

In this chapter, we'll look at what we might consider "normal" human abilities, followed by a look at the kinds of abilities superheroes (and other fantasy characters) might have.

Also, because games are created with computer programs and mathematical formulae, I included some of the abilities that are often used in determining how a computer character performs in its world, including how the outcomes of attacks and defenses are figured. I call these *statistical abilities* because they are often used as the visible or behind-the-scenes statistics that help define a character.

Also in this chapter is a section on fighting abilities, with a focus on hand-to-hand fighting and nifty ways to disable or kill an opponent. Following that is a section on magic spells, and, as an added bonus, a list of every superhero I could come up with.

Range of Human Abilities

This section deals with basic human abilities—not superpowers, but those abilities that are inherent in the human experience. Some of the examples may extend past the provable, but can still be arguably "normal" capabilities. In all cases, these abilities occur in a range from one individual to the next, such that some people are blessed with (or develop through training) much more heightened abilities, while others may have very minimal abilities. For instance, someone may have very poor eyesight but excellent intelligence, hearing, or even strength. Some people may, for clinical reasons, lack some of these abilities, but they are exceptions to the general rule.

- Sight (range)
- Hearing (range)
- Taste (range)
- Smell (range)
- Touch (sensitivity of; range)
- Physical strength
- Speed (movement)
- Speed/quickness (actions)
- Reflexes/reaction time
- Agility
- Flexibility
- Power
- Coordination
- Balance
- Jumping
- Mechanical aptitude
- Physical manipulation of objects
- Eye-hand coordination
- Reach
- Perception of details
- Adaptability
- Lung capacity (and breath control)
- Ingestion (ability to ingest food and liquid and convert it into energy and tissue)
- Rest and sleep (ability to recover energy and clarity from resting and/or sleeping)
- Mental focus
- Deductive reasoning
- Inductive reasoning
- Recognizing patterns and shapes
- Reproducing patterns and shapes (in its ultimate evolution—art)
- Mathematical abilities
- Spatial/geometrical abilities
- Imagination (ability to visualize something that does not physically exist or is not physically present)
- Psychic senses (possibly including precognition, seeing auras and other so-called invisible energies, healing others through energy, telekinesis, mind control, clairvoyance)
- Facial expressions (using them in different ways to communicate)
- Body language (using the body to communicate)
- Pantomime
- Short-, medium-, and long-term memory
- Common sense
- Wisdom
- Morals and ethics (or lack thereof)
- Intelligence (various forms)
- Empathy
- Sympathy
- Emotional control
- Charisma
- Sex appeal
- Language aptitude
- Communication abilities (not only the ability to communicate basic meaning, but also the ability to calm people, to hypnotize them, to manipulate or convince them, etc.)
- Rapport with people or animals (or aliens)
- Logic
- Developed skills (the ability to take a learned skill and get very good at it)
- Sense of humor
- Being funny
- Musical ability
- Voice/singing
- Voice control (communication and manipulation)
- Reading
- Writing

Superhero Abilities List

Superheroes, being super, either have normal abilities at superhuman levels or they have abilities that are simply not available to normal people. In any case, these types of abilities often occur in games, and you may want to provide one or more of your game characters with some of these abilities.

Ways Superheroes Obtain Abilities

- Technology
- Intensive training (possibly under the guidance of a master)
- Freak accident
- Animal attack
- Magic
- Mutation
- Medicine/science
- Heredity
- Being an alien (which is one case of heredity)

List of Superhero Abilities

- Super strength
- Invincibility
- Super speed
- Super agility
- Flying
- Hovering/levitating
- Body armor
- Direct links with computers
- Super jumping
- Super digging
- Super throwing
- X-ray vision
- Rays
  - Heat
  - Cold
  - Electricity
  - Poison
  - Antimatter
  - Energy
  - X-ray
  - Plasma
  - Mystery
- Stealth/invisibility/cloaking
- Super willpower
- Telepathy
- Telekinesis
- Telepathic attacks/mental control
- Levitation
- Magic pathways (the hero can create special paths that nobody else can use)
- Trouble-seeker (always is forced to go where there is trouble, whether willingly or not)
- Super swimming
- Underwater breathing
- No need to breathe
- Heightened senses
  - Animal origin
  - Technology origin
  - Freak accident
  - Magical
  - Mutation
- Control of elements
  - Fire
  - Water
  - Ice
  - Air/wind
  - Metal
  - Earth
  - Electricity
  - Gravity
  - Radioactivity
  - Nature (plants, insects, birds, etc.)
  - Magnetism
  - Sound
  - Light
- Control of sound
- Control of time
- Control of animals
- Control of plants
- Control of people
- Chemical attacks
  - Poison
  - Hallucinogenic
  - Paralyzing
  - Light
  - Bioluminescence
  - Burning
  - Disintegrating
- Walk on water

Part IV

- Hand size
- Body splitting
  - Astral projection
  - Being in more than one place at the same time
- Possession (ability to possess the bodies of other characters)
- Flight
- Teleportation/tele-reformation
- Dimensional travel
- Astral travel
- Time travel
- Chameleon/shape-shifter/mimic (ability to mimic other creatures and/or objects)
- Life support
- Rate of aging slowed
- Whirlwind
- Lung adaptability
- Pheromones
- Self-regeneration
- Self-sustaining (doesn't need food or water)
- Stealth
- Suspended animation
- Vocal mimicry
- Physical mimicry
- Steal someone's abilities
- Remove someone's abilities
- Cancel out any powers
- Death touch
- Mind control
- Jekyll and Hyde character
- Laser cut across room with finger
- Man/machine/cyborg/android
- Martial arts mastery
- Genius
  - Technological
  - Mechanical
  - Robotics
  - Tactical/strategic
  - Information
  - Deductive
- Marksman
- Languages
- Acrobatics
- Climbing
- Master of disguise
- Escape artist
- Digestive adaptation
- Astral form
- Carrier wave (can become pure energy and travel through energy waves)
- Super climbing
- Mental or energy blast
- Ensnarement
  - Telekinesis
  - Ionic containment beam
  - Force field
  - Electromagnetic attractor
  - Freeze
  - Hypnosis/sleep
  - Burn/fire
  - Earth imprisonment
  - Blinding/stunning
  - Controlling
  - Slow movements
  - Slip and fall
  - Confuse
- Master thief
- Danger sense
- Super hearing
- Super sense of smell
- Super sensitivity of skin
- Super vision
  - Infrared
  - Ultraviolet
  - 360-degree vision
  - Telescopic
  - X-ray
  - Microscopic
  - Thermal
  - Truth sight (see through any disguise)
  - Danger (sees danger ahead)
  - Clairvoyance (sees the future)
  - Remote viewing (sees events in other places)

Useful Superhero Jobs/Knowledge

- Demolition/blasting
- Criminology
- Scientist
- Law enforcement
- Archeology
- Statistics (quotes odds)
- Local knowledge guru
- Linguistics
- Mythology
- Climbing
- Asian martial arts and culture
- Acrobatics
- Marksmanship
- Biochemistry
- Biology
- Observation
- Tracking
- Survival
- Sleight of hand
- Escape artistry
- The occult
- Mental control
- Computers
- Electronics
- Mechanics
- Performing (singing, dancing, playing instruments)
- Equestrian skills
- Gambling
- Piloting
- Medicine
- Art
- Driving

Statistical Abilities

Regardless of whether they are visible to the player, certain types of abilities are often tracked statistically for various characters and used in algorithms that determine the character's effectiveness in a number of situations. There are certainly hundreds of systems for assigning statistical abilities to characters in games. Some use very specific modifiers to achieve very specific character responses in very specific situations. Most, however, use simple statistical values to affect the character's general effectiveness in a variety of situations.

In many games, the statistics operate like simple sliders. Push it to one end, and the character will be impossible to defeat. The other extreme results in a worthless pushover. One common use of these sliders has to do with the range of the character's senses, particularly sight and hearing. By adjusting such aspects as the distance the character can see or the width of his cone of vision, you can affect how soon he might become aware of the player. If his vision is highly limited compared to that of the player character, then the player will always have some advantage—not the least of which is the choice of whether or not to approach.

Hearing, too, can be part of the basic statistical model. Here, the character might be able to detect approaching danger based on a hearing acuity slider. And, suppose one character does become aware of an enemy. In some games, all the nearby allies also become aware at the same time. This isn't realistic. But suppose the first character yells something. Then, based on the other characters' hearing, and accounting for distance and the ambient noise, you might have a realistic detection system. So, if you sneak up on an enemy standing near a noisy machine, even if he detects you and yells out, chances are the noise will, at least partly, cancel out his alert and few, if any, friends will come to help him. Strategy…

Other games make the stats visible, and they are part of the player's direct experience. This is never more obvious than in traditional Role-Playing Games, where basic statistics are used to determine the character's class or type as well as how effective the character is at various tasks within the game. This is true of both the player's character and many of the NPCs.

The following sections contain some examples of common abilities that are statistically tracked in Role-Playing Games and a few ways they might be used.

Strength (STR)

- How much damage characters can cause with a blow or weapon.
- How much they can carry (based on weight).
- What weapons they can carry (based on a statistical level requirement).
- What armor they can wear (based on a statistical level requirement).
- The ability to move or lift heavy objects.
- Sometimes STR can be used in calculations involving stamina or endurance. STR could also be used to help determine how much damage characters will sustain and how much they can endure, but it isn't generally used that way.

Dexterity (DEX)

- Used in calculations to determine a character's defensive abilities—particularly the ability to dodge blows or take less damage.
- Used in calculations that affect the overall agility of the character, which can affect defense, but also the likelihood that the character will connect when he or she attacks.
- Can be used to help determine whether a character can effectively use certain weapons and/or armor, and can be used to scale the effectiveness of the character or as an absolute requirement level.
- May also be used as part of a calculation of the overall speed of a character's movements.
- In some systems, dexterity is used to determine the likelihood of delivering a critical blow.
- Can be used to determine non-combat skill levels of any kind.

Constitution (CON), Stamina (STM) or Endurance (END), Vitality (VIT)

- How much endurance characters have—which affects how active they can be over extended periods.
- Sometimes used in the calculation of a character's overall health or "hit points."
- Often used in calculations of the energy it takes to perform certain actions, particularly attacks and defenses, but sometimes also running and/or jumping.

Intelligence (INT), Will (WIL)

- Most often used to determine a character's ability to use magic effectively, particularly martial magic (though some systems use it for any kind of magic ability, such as healing magic). May be used as an absolute cap on skills (only cast Greater Fire when Intelligence is above 15, for instance) or as a modifier for the relative effectiveness of a spell.
- In some systems, Intelligence can also affect a character's defense.
- Resistance to enemy magic.
- The ability to use certain objects or as a modifier to the object's effectiveness. Though I haven't seen it used this way, Intelligence could be used to determine whether a character receives certain clues in a game, or perhaps whether he can read or decipher a message, and so on.

Speed (SPD), Quickness (QUI)

- Slightly less common, speed can be used to determine how fast a character moves—both in the travel sense and in the speed of the character's actions. Quickness is also sometimes used in similar ways.
- May determine who gets his attack off first or the frequency of his attacks.
- May be used as a defensive modifier, so that a faster or quicker character has greater ability to avoid attack.

Wisdom (WIS), Piety (PIE)

- Wisdom is usually used to determine ability with healing and natural styles of magic.
- Piety is sometimes used in a similar way, especially with clerical characters.

Charisma (CHA), Personality (PER)

- Charisma is often used as a statistic to determine how a character affects another character, such as the price he gets when shopping or whether people will follow him or help him in need.
- Charisma and Personality statistics may also be used to determine a character's ability to persuade another or to influence, fool, hypnotize, or manipulate him.

Luck

- Luck is one of those statistics you can use as a way to give a character subtle, even mysterious advantages. It is used to determine intangible elements in characters, such as:
  - Modifying their chances to avoid blows or to avoid critical blows.
  - Modifying their chances of success when attacking or their chances to strike a critical blow.
  - How often they will successfully open a locked chest.
  - How well they will avoid damage from a trap, etc.
  - The quality or quantity of rewards, loot; the likelihood of finding something exceptional, etc.
  - How they will resist enemy spells.

Mana, Spell Points

- Mana is one of the common terms to describe the kind of energy needed to cast magic spells. Often, Mana is increased by increasing the Intelligence statistic, just as Health (or hit points) is increased by the Constitution (and sometimes Strength) stats.

Experience (EXP or XP)

- Experience is generally used to determine the "level" of a character based on certain milestones or plateau values. Attaining another level generally results in an increase in some or all of the character's base statistical abilities. Although experience is almost always visible to the player in Role-Playing Games, it can be accumulated and interpreted invisibly as well. Players gain experience (and sometimes, though rarely, they lose it) as a consequence of the actions they take in a game, such as defeating enemies, completing quests, discovering clues and significant milestones in the game, and so on. In general, the greater the accomplishment, the greater the experience points gained.

Other Statistical Abilities

The statistical qualities in the previous list are pretty common, and for the most part, they serve the role-playing gamer quite well. However, there are other abilities that could be used, though they tend to be less common. In fact, the possible abilities that could be tracked are practically infinite. For instance, you could track throwing ability, or perhaps with an electronic entity you could track battery power, charge capacity, or something. A plant entity might have a chlorophyll statistic, which would be the basis of its energy and power.

The following sections discuss a few statistical abilities that can be used easily in games. For the others, simply base them on the type of characters you're creating and what you need to track or use to determine their success rate at specific actions and tasks in the game.

Sight

- This could be used to determine characters' range of vision—the distance they can see, the width of their vision cone, and/or their ability to see in the dark. This can affect the player's character in very direct ways, but it could also alter the effectiveness of an NPC.

Hearing

- This statistical ability could be used to determine how well a player character can hear distant sounds and how soon he gets a sound cue. It also could be used to help determine the effectiveness of an NPC character in reacting to upcoming events and could affect the transmission of oral information and warnings from one character to another.

Detection

- This could be used to help determine the effectiveness of rogue-type characters in spotting and disarming traps of various kinds.
- It could also be used for player characters to determine how visible subtle features of an area might be. For instance, high detection might allow a player to spot hidden walls or other hidden features more easily than if detection was low.
- It can be used to determine how well a character (player or otherwise) is able to detect nearby enemies and the effective range of detection.
- It can also be used to determine how much of a map a player character can perceive from a given location.

Focus

- This might be used to determine the availability of specific mental energies or the effectiveness of certain mental attacks or skills.
- It might be used as a modifier of the effectiveness of other skills or abilities.
- It also might be used as a meter that is expended as the player uses certain abilities and recharged as the player uses other abilities.

Leadership

- This is used more specifically in getting other characters to respond to your orders. Higher Leadership might allow you to command more characters, or it might make the ones you command more effective.
- It might provide special skills associated with Leadership.
- If Leadership is high, it also might provide extra experience for tasks created.

Stealth

- This can be used to move around in a game unseen and undetected.
- Different levels of a Stealth statistic might determine the effectiveness of skills based on this statistic.
- Likewise, different levels of the Stealth statistic might confer other stealth-based skills.
- This can be used as a modifier on certain types of attacks that are carried out while undetected by the enemy. These attacks typically result in higher damage, although the character becomes visible when attacking.

Fighting Abilities

In the majority of games, characters have some ability to fight, whether it is hand to hand (mano a mano) or with various types of weapons and/or magic. See Chapter 33, "Historical and Cultural Weapons," and Chapter 34, "Standard Modern Weaponry and Armor," for lots of historical, ethnic, and/or modern weapon choices. For magic, see the following section in this chapter, "Magic Abilities."

Besides direct physical or magical confrontation, there are other more subtle forms of fighting abilities, such as getting others to fight for you (leadership, manipulation, and so on) or psychological warfare (making your enemies fear you or confusing or misleading them).

This section is about direct *mano-a-mano* fighting. Fists, feet, elbows, skulls—it's the sweet art (or science) of hand-to-hand combat. The goal is to give you a glimpse of some of the elements of fighting to help you develop better and, in some cases, more realistic fighting styles and methods in games.

> ***A Personal Note:*** *This is one of my pet peeves, and since it's my book, I decided to include it. It has to do with how characters react to damage and lethal attacks. I've noticed a trend lately to use the "rag doll" mode of whatever physics engine to control when a body collapses. The trouble is that these rag-doll effects aren't at all realistic. The bones are tied together with virtual strings, and there's no friction in the joints when the body collapses. I'd like to see more attention paid to the way people take damage and die in games. After all, if you're going to kill a thousand enemies in a game—not an unrealistic number for many of today's games—they shouldn't all react to damage in exactly the same way. I'd like to see more attention paid to the reactions of different people to attacks that stun, disorient, do severe damage, or kill. I've seen interesting approaches in movies, too, such as the super slow-mo of* The Matrix: Revolutions, *where you saw every drop of water on Neo's fist and the ripples of flesh as it hit Smith's face, or a sort of "bone-cam" view in Jet Li's* Romeo Must Die, *where you got to see a sort of X-ray of the body as it received the punch, complete with the bone fracturing. These are just ideas, but perhaps they suggest different ways to approach how we depict the severity and impact of damage and how characters react. Thank you…*

Fighting and Games

When you are considering how to depict fighting in games, it's important not only to be aware of the various kinds of fighting techniques available to your characters, but also to consider the variables involved. For instance, how strong is the attack? Attacks may vary between lighter, faster kicks and punches and harder, slower techniques. Here's a list of variables to take into consideration:

- **Speed.** How fast are the attacks (on both sides)? Are faster attacks also weaker ones?
- **Strength/Power.** Do you vary the strength of attacks, providing lighter blows and stronger ones? Is there a correlation between speed and power?
- **Target.** Do you specifically target parts of an opponent's body, or do you simply target the opponent in general?
- **Angles.** Do you take into account the angles of attack and the relative vulnerabilities of your fighters? Do they move to improve their chances by using angles?
- **Movement.** How much does foot movement play into your characters' fights? What about upper-body movement or even mid-body flexibility?
- **Timing.** Do you manage the timing of attacks and counterattacks, or do you use a modified turn-based system in which each character gets an attack or block each turn (perhaps with speed of attack variations based on character statistics)?
- **Grappling.** Does your combat system allow for grappling, or is it all ranged melee (kicks, punches, blocks, throws)? If so, how far do you go in modeling grappling techniques?
- **Multiple Enemies.** Is there any modification of a character's effectiveness when fighting against multiple enemies? In some systems, certain magical abilities might actually increase a character's abilities when surrounded, but in most real-world situations, a fighter must have even more than usual special abilities to fight multiple attackers or subdue multiple opponents. Of course, this also varies with the relative skills of the opponents. A highly trained martial artist can take out a roomful of barroom brawlers in very short order, but with equal skills, the results aren't as certain.
- **Weapons.** Do your characters use weapons or have access to them? Do they have methods of fighting empty-handed against opponents with weapons?
- **Intention.** This is not just the intention of the character—does he want to kill, maim, incapacitate, subdue—but also the intention you have as a designer. Do you want a flashy fight or a quick finish? What kind of battle do you want? How long? How complex or challenging? What's the purpose of this combat in the larger scheme of the game?
- **Using the Vision.** Do you use tunnel vision or wide angle?

NOTE

According to the Apache fighting strategy, an enemy killed in battle takes out one enemy, but an enemy maimed in battle takes one or possibly two enemies out of the battle because he needs someone to care for him or take him back to his camp. Therefore, it is often more effective to maim than to kill. Could you use this in a battle game?

- **Elements.** Take weather into consideration. What is the position of the sun? Is it in the enemy's eyes? Which way is the wind blowing? Could you toss dust or blinding powder in the enemy's eyes? Or would it be blown back in your own face? Is it raining? If so, which way is it being blown? At night, is it cloudy or clear? Is the moon full?
- **Terrain.** Can you take terrain into account? Most natural places are uneven. In a forest, there are branches, foxholes, roots, and uneven ground. Even in cities there are sidewalks and curbs. Tripping over a curb or hitting your head on one when falling can be fatal. And what is the footing like? Is there sand, gravel, or dirt? Are you on slippery metal, wet river rocks, or an icy frozen surface? Are you up to your knees in water? Your waist? Underwater? How much can you use terrain to affect battle strategies and outcomes?

Worldwide Martial Arts Systems

Some of the systems of martial arts worldwide include:

- Kung Fu (many styles)
- Karate—many styles, including:
  - Kyokushinkai
  - Shotokan
  - Goju-Ryu
  - Shorin-Ryu
  - Kenpo
- Jujitsu
  - Japanese
  - Brazilian
  - Gracie system
- Kendo
- Sumo
- Tae Kwon Do
- Muay Thai (Thai boxing)
- Judo
- Escrima
- Tai Chi Chuan (different forms)
- Ninjutsu (Ninja training)
- Jeet Kune Do
- Lan Shou
- Bagua
- Hsing Yi
- Wing Chun
- Boxing (Western style)
- Hapkido
- Pencak Silat (Indonesian style)
- Street fighting
- Kuk Sool Won (modern Korean fighting style)
- Capoeira
- Aikido
- Russian Sambo
- Arnis
- Fencing
- Wrestling (Greco-Roman or others)
- Savate
- Haganah
- Krav Maga
- Taebo
- Testa (African "big knuckle" head fighting)
- Kapu Kuialua (Hawaiian "bone-breaking" style)
- Modern pragmatic hybrid martial arts, such as those inspired by the Ultimate Fighting Championships (UFC):
  - Ruas Vale Tudo
  - Shootfighting
  - Moo Yea Do
  - Pitfighting
  - Trapfighting
  - Tung Kung Kalan
  - Jo Son Do
  - ASAX
  - SAFTA

Weapons of the Body

Besides simple fists and simple kicks, fighters often use:

- The edge of the hand in a knifelike attack.
- Extended fingers in a flicking or penetrating attack.
- Fingers folded at the second knuckle.
- The fist with knuckles extended (various styles).
- The second knuckle of the second finger protruding from the fist.
- The thumbs in a gouging motion—particularly into the eyes and soft spots between the ribs or behind the ears. If the opponent is wearing armor, it would do no good to punch the armor, but if you could get a thumb strike in between the armor pieces, you could deliver a deadly or disabling blow.
- The palm or heel of the hand.
- The forearm.
- The elbow.
- The shoulder.

- The hip.
- The head (particularly used in African "big knuckle" fighting).
- The ball of the foot.
- The side of the foot.
- The heel of the foot.
- The top of the foot.
- The knees.
- The teeth.
- The whole body.
- The voice. Kai—spirit yelling—can easily startle someone enough to cause them to freeze or even fall over.

Basic Techniques

At its most basic, fighting is simply a means of stopping your opponent from doing you harm and/or doing harm to your opponent. Preventative fighting involves simply doing whatever is necessary to stop an opponent and prevent them from harming you or someone else. But some fighting is meant to incapacitate or destroy the opponent.

Although anything goes in unstructured fights, there are some common basic techniques used the world over, including:

- Punching
- Chopping
- Flicking
- Kicking
- Blocking
- Dodging and ducking
- Feinting
- Tripping
- Throwing
- Holding
- Joint locking
- Breaking
- Shocking
- Crushing
- Slapping/smacking
- Hammering
- Grappling
- Head butting
- Gouging
- Biting
- Spitting
- Yelling
- Body blocking and checking

Clearly, many of these basic techniques have numerous variations. For instance, punching alone can include jabs, straight punches, roundhouse punches or hooks, body punches, groin punches, and even punches to the tops of the feet. Punches can be done with a closed fist, with the palm heel, with different knuckles extended, and so on. Kicks, also, have many variations. In fact, almost every basic technique can be executed in a variety of ways, and perhaps it is far oversimplified to include a list as basic as this. However, a complete study of every type of technique is certainly beyond the scope of this book, since each martial art in the world has many different ways to approach the art of fighting.

Hands/Wrists/Fingers

Among the primary weapons of any fighter are the hands, wrists, and fingers. Hands are used to punch, poke, grab, slap, and chop, among other things. They affect their target by impact, compression, opening wounds, harming sensitive areas, bending joints, tearing muscle and ligament, and even attacking pressure points and damaging internal organs. The following lists describe some of the techniques of the hands, wrists, and fingers.

Punches

- Straight
- Jab
- Hook
- Uppercut
- Groin
- Body
- Downward attack
- One-inch punch (Bruce Lee's specialty)
- Cross
- Speed punch
- Whirlwind attack
- Simultaneous block/punch combo
- Backfist
- Spinning punch
- Crushing blow
- Open hand (slap)

Specific Technique Variations

- Hand positions
  - Pronating
  - Palm heel
  - Claw
  - Fist with knuckles protruding
  - Straight fist
  - Open hand with folded middle knuckles (kikaken)
  - Open hand
  - Knife edge/ridge hand
  - Cupping hands
- Finger variations
  - Thumb strikes
  - Thumb knuckle (koppoken)
  - Flicking
  - Poking
  - Pinching
  - Grabbing
  - Pressure-point attacks (see also the "Fatality Systems" section later in this chapter)
- Wrist (ox-bow)
  - Wrists can be used to attack when the hand is folded down and the wrist bone is used to strike or block.
- Grabs
  - Hair/clothing
  - Weapons
  - Limbs and joints
  - Fingers
  - Groin and other delicate parts
  - Muscle
  - Ears

Shoulders

The shoulder is used in many styles and circumstances, such as:

- Strike
- Leverage (arm bars and throws, etc.)
- Destroy enemy balance

Elbows

Elbows can be used to strike at the head, ribs, abdomen, back, or any other exposed part of the body. They can be used as part of a series of attacks—for instance, following a body check or following the block of an incoming punch. Elbows can often be used when the opponent is expecting an attack from the fist instead or as a counter to an attempted hold or poorly executed joint lock. Elbow attacks can be directed upward or downward, sideways or straight in, using the elbow in almost any possible position. One popular elbow attack is the pile driver, bringing the elbow down hard on someone's head, neck, or back.

FEET

Any part of the feet can be used to attack, including the shin (see below).

- Top of foot
- Bottom of foot
- Heel
- Toes
- Sides of foot
- Shin bone

Kicks

- Short range
  - Inverted heel stomp (take out the leg low)
  - Stomp kick
  - Sweep
  - Groin kick (top of foot)
  - Low hook kick
  - Check kick with top of foot at ankle joint
- Medium range
  - Heel kick
  - Toe kick (medium)
  - Front kick (ball of foot)
  - Low roundhouse
  - Crescent kick (inside or outside)
  - Axe kick
  - Ridge kick (knife edge side of foot)
  - Sweep (medium, including spinning sweep)
  - Butterfly kick (alternating sides)
  - Brush kick (knocks opponent off balance)
- Long range
  - Toe kick (toes folded or straight)
  - Side kick
  - Roundhouse (top of foot or ball of foot)
  - Jumping kick
  - Flying side kick
  - Flying roundhouse
  - Spinning kick
  - Jumping/spinning kick
  - Jumping/spinning/flying kick
- Traps
  - Stepping on foot to pin it down
  - Hooking the foot or leg
  - Grappling holds and leg locks

Stepping

- Controlling the line of attack
- Stepping in or out (closing or making distance)
- Running up an opponent's body
- Stepping into an attack (punch or body attack)
- Stepping to hook or trip an opponent
- Cartwheels and tumbling

Running

- Getting away
- Running toward as an element of surprise or aggression
- Running up walls, trees, etc.
- Running for repositioning and advantage
- Running to lure enemies into a trap

Knees

Knees are good for striking and for leverage, and they are vulnerable places to attack.

- Pin
- Attack leg
- Attack feet
- Attack head/face
- Attack knee
- Attack back
- Hook ankle with ankle and compress with knee

Shins

The shin is a hard bone often used to block, but also as the striking surface for kicks.

- Low kicks using shins
- Blocking low kicks

Hips

Like shoulders, hips are often used to move an opponent or put him off balance, or as a leverage point for throws.

- Leverage for throws and positioning advantage
- Blocks to throw off enemy balance
- Blows from the hip

Body

The whole body is not only a weapon, but in many forms of martial arts, the central point from which all attacks emerge. Of course, there are many uses for the human body. Here are just a few.

- Full charge
- Use dead body as a weapon or shield
- Roll into someone to take out their legs (back, front, side, etc.)
- Spinning for position and to facilitate spinning attacks
- Round-off attack

Head

The head is hard but vulnerable. However, properly used, it can be both a devastating weapon and a prime target.

- Head butts (different types)
- Leverage for arm bars, etc.
- Head whips
- Teeth (biting)
- Thinking (using your head)
- Hair (whipping a braid)
- Bald heads wiping sweat and throwing it at your opponent's eyes
- Blowing (using breath to startle or attack eyes)
- Yelling, using the voice, calling for help, etc.
- Spirit yelling (trained martial technique)

Blocks

There are many ways to block an attack. Blocks can be static, sweeping, moving sharply, attacking or even giving ground, or avoiding contact all together. Some blocks involve subtle shifts of position, and other blocks can be used to cause significant damage or even death to the opponent. Some blocking techniques are used to divert or control the opponent's incoming weapons. Other techniques are designed to stop an incoming attack dead. Commonly, blocking techniques involve:

- Hand
    - Grabbing
    - Smacking
    - Twisting and locking
    - Attacking with a punch (simultaneous block and attack)
    - Pressure points
    - One hand/foot blocks, while the other attacks at the same time
        - The attack also blocks at the same time, with one hand or foot.
        - Simultaneous step and attack, avoids opponent's attack and repositions and attacks, all at the same time.
- Wrists (front or back)
- Arm
    - Warding
    - Sweeping
    - Redirecting
    - Locking
    - Attacking
- Elbows
- Legs
- Knees
- Shins
- Shoulders
- Hips
- Body check
- Head
- Blocking with kia (using voice to stop attacker)
- Movement
    - Moving inside
    - Shifting center
    - Ducking
    - Weaving
    - Moving outside
    - Jumping over a leg sweep
    - Dropping below an attack
    - Rolling
    - Spinning
    - Jumping (in eight directions)
    - Misdirecting (changing their focus), then attacking or running

Joint Locks and Breaks

In addition to punches and kicks, there are many ways to control and incapacitate an enemy, such as using joint locks and breaking bones. Joint locks involve manipulating a person's joints in such a way as to cause them extreme pain, forcing them to submit to whatever pressure you put on them. A simple joint lock on the wrist, for instance, can bring an opponent to the floor in microseconds. Taken to extremes, joint locks can be used to tear and permanently damage ligaments or even break bones.

There are certainly dozens of specific joint locks and bone-breaking techniques, and it is beyond the scope of this book to present even a moderately complete list of them. In any case, a simple list would do very little good, since these are complex techniques that require timing, sensitivity, and specific sequences of subtle whole-body movements. Also, every joint lock has some kind of counter. In an interesting fight, a master martial artist can easily reverse a joint lock on the unwary opponent, who then becomes the victim of a lock or hold.

Joint locks can be deceptively simple and effective. Some of the areas particularly vulnerable are:

- Fingers
- Wrists
- Elbows
- Shoulders
- Neck
- Ankles and knees (in grappling on the floor)

Holds

Holds are used to subdue an opponent, but they can be intended for different results. For instance, some holds are simply ways to restrain someone without really doing much damage. Other holds are intended to cut off the blood supply to a particular area, resulting in loss of function in that area (a limb, for instance) or unconsciousness and/or death if the area deprived of blood supply is the brain. The sort of hold used to prevent a victim from breathing is known as a *choke hold.*

With the growing popularity of mixed martial arts as a sport, many different holds have become popular, often deriving from judo and Brazilian Jiu-Jitsu. Names of the holds are often interesting and colorful, such as the kimora, the guillotine choke, or the rear naked choke.

Throws

There are dozens of ways to throw an opponent, and like locks and holds, they involve various complex approaches. Some are simple trips and hooks, while others involve sophisticated body positioning and various hand and foot motions. Each particular throw is best used in specific circumstances. Several throws use the hip for leverage, while others, such as the popular tomoe nage, pull the opponent down and over by going all the way to the floor.

A full list of throws would involve specific details in order to be useful and is not really necessary. If you want to use throws in your games, some research, particularly into judo, jujitsu, and Aikido techniques can be highly rewarding.

Bluffing and Intimidation

Many martial arts techniques include yells and loud noises to intimidate would-be opponents. These, along with very martial-looking stances, can be used to bluff opponents, causing them to hesitate while you run like hell. Another kind of bluff is to call out to imaginary friends nearby. If the attacker believes you have allies, he or she may hesitate or back off. Anything that gains you a few split seconds of advantage is worthwhile in a fight, and whether you follow the bluff or intimidation tactic with an attack or you cut out of the scene, this can be useful.

Cheating and Dirty Tricks

Real fighting isn't clean and orderly. It's dog eat dog, kill or be killed. So in real fights, there are no rules—there's only survival, taking out the enemy, and avoiding damage. Therefore, there's really no such thing as cheating in fights, unless there are rules, such as in an organized match. Where there are rules, there are always ways to break them. But where there are no rules, then anything you can do can spell the difference between victory and defeat. This is especially true when you are confronted with a stronger or more skilled enemy, but it's safe to say that in the real world you should never underestimate anyone.

Some ways to gain advantage that are not necessarily on the approved list are:

- Throwing or kicking dirt or powder into the eyes.
- Spitting.
- Biting.
- Gouging.
- Scraping.
- Pinching.
- Sucker punching (hit opponents when they still think the talking phase is in effect).
- Blowing (breath attack).
- Blowing with weapons (needles, stones, steel balls, etc.).
- Head butting.
- Stomping on the tops of feet hard.
- Using anything you can as a weapon.
- Using hair and clothing.
- Attacking particularly painful areas.
- Running and leading the opponent into a trap.
- Humiliating opponents (by giving noogies or wedgies, spitting, blowing raspberries, slapping, or pantsing them).
- If you have some busted teeth in your mouth, spitting them at the enemy.
- Tickling, possibly breaking their focus and stance and giving openings, such as fewer flexed muscles.
- Saying something really funny. This sounds strange, but it's really hard to fight when you're laughing.

Perhaps my favorite dirty trick is when some martial artist is all revved up and ready to attack, showing all sorts of postures and moves as intimidation, and someone calmly pulls out a gun and shoots him. I've also heard stories of people about to test each other in sophisticated martial arts contests, when one of them simply runs over and decks the other, punching as hard as he can. This works because the opponent expected some kind of preliminary squaring-off or feeling-out process. There are no rules. Survival is the only option....

Attack Approaches

In designing any fighting situation, of course there are different ways for the characters to approach the battle.

- They can sneak up and surprise the victim.
- They can set a trap, perhaps lying in wait, or initiate an attack, then retreat to lure the enemy into the trap.
- They can run in screaming and take the enemy by surprise that way.
- They can attack with ranged weapons, staying at a safe distance.
- They can issue a formal challenge—especially for one-on-one battles.
- They can enter the battle deliberately, sizing up the opponent and then engaging.
- They can be in disguise as a passerby (the little old lady) and pull a knife out of the flowers they are carrying in their hand or use a blade concealed in a cane or umbrella, and so on.
- They might pretend to be dead or wounded and execute a sneak attack on an unwary enemy.

- They might be hiding somewhere above the enemy and attack from above or jump down and execute an attack from the air.
- They might be on a horse or other creature.
- They might be in a vehicle—anything from a chariot to a tank.
- They might find an enemy already engaged in battle with an ally and simply attack that enemy when he isn't looking.
- They might convince someone else to attack for them.

Human-to-Human Vulnerabilities and Attacks

Although warriors and highly disciplined fighters can harden their bodies to resist damage and to deliver fantastic amounts of power, there are some areas where the human body is more vulnerable than others. In untrained people, these areas are more numerous and more vulnerable. However, even the most highly trained martial artist cannot protect his or her eyes from damage (other than by wearing some kind of protective gear or using superior blocking or avoidance techniques).

Unless a character has a weapon or can use an object from the environment, attacks will occur with the body. The most common attack will be a simple punch or kick. However, in hand-to-hand combat, there are many types of attacks, including various punches and kicks, locks, throws, and holds. Some attacks are very effective, but not very dramatic looking. For instance, if someone has you in a headlock, a sharp poke with the thumb in the floating rib area will very likely get the person to back off in response to an unconscious withdrawal reflex (similar to when you unconsciously remove a hand that has been placed on a hot stove). A quick flick of the fingers to the eyes—nothing very hard—can do incredible damage and possibly stop a fight right there, if properly delivered.

The easiest types of hand-to-hand combat to model in games involve definitive punches and kicks, with some simple holds and throws. The complexities of grappling, joint locking, and more sophisticated techniques and counters are difficult at best.

This section deals with various aspects of hand-to-hand fighting, including the main weapons of the body, the main types of attacks, and the main vulnerabilities in the human body, including those areas said to be vulnerable to so-called fatality or death blows—the knowledge of which is contained in the Chinese art of Dim Mak and the Japanese Atemi system. See also the "Fatality Systems" section later in this chapter.

This list contains many of the most vulnerable areas of the body, and how they might be attacked. Caveats:

- Improperly executed attacks can sometimes result in more damage to the attacker than to the intended victim.
- For maximum effectiveness, many attacks should hit the intended target at a 90-degree angle, particularly if the intention is to break a bone.

Head

Any blow to the head is dangerous and can cause brain damage, unconsciousness, or death. However, the results of blows to the head are not reliable. In some cases, it will just make the victim angrier. However, focused and specific blows to parts of the head, such as the eyes, ears, septum, and base of the skull, can be more effective.

Eyes

Eyes are particularly vulnerable to scrapes, flicking motions, and gouges. Attacks of these kinds can cause temporary disorientation and blindness or permanent blindness. There is a saying, "A grain of sand in the enemy's eye can hide a mountain." So eyes are also vulnerable to foreign matter thrown or blown into them.

Neck

The neck is a very vulnerable area with several preferred points of attack:

- The third vertebra at the back—midway between the shoulders and the base of the skull—a forceful, focused blow can cause pain, numbness, and possibly paralysis.
- The side of the neck just above the collarbone is especially vulnerable because of the presence of the jugular vein and the carotid artery. Severe blows to this area can cause the victim to be stunned temporarily or even die.
- Hitting the muscles at the base of the neck with sufficient force and focus can result in pain, muscle spasms, loss of mobility of the arm on that side, numbness, and injury to the neck muscles.
- The throat is very vulnerable, particularly in the hollow at the base, just above the chest bone. A forceful attack to this area can cause serious injury to the trachea and, some say, even death. Some people also target the Adam's apple/larynx, which can cause the airway to collapse and the victim to die unless treated immediately.

Nose

Striking the bridge of the nose can cause tearing in the eyes, pain, disorientation, and broken bones. There are some people who claim that an upward strike to the nose can drive the nose bone into the brain. This is probably not easily accomplished for a number of reasons, but, given that it is technically feasible, it remains a favorite fantasy move.

Septum

A well-focused blow to the septum can cause an extreme amount of pain due to the cluster of nerves there, as well as bleeding and disorientation.

Ears

Solid slaps or claps to the ears can damage or break the eardrum, resulting in pain, bleeding, loss of balance, and possible permanent loss of hearing. A well-aimed blow to the vulnerable area under the ear can result in unconsciousness. Also, it only takes 10 pounds of pressure to pull someone's ear off.

Temple

Striking the temple can cause a helluva headache, but also disorientation and even unconsciousness. Some sources claim that a well-directed blow to the temple can damage arteries that are vulnerable in that area, and even cause instant death.

Front Teeth

Every school kid knows that getting bashed in the teeth hurts, but losing a few teeth generally won't stop a determined attacker.

Side of the Jaw

A well-placed blow to the side of the jaw can cause painful dislocation or fractures of the jawbones.

Joints (Generally)

All joints are necessarily vulnerable to twisting, tearing, compression, hyperextension, and focused blows, especially those that hit the joint against its normal motion—such as a hard kick to the front or especially to the side of the knee. A damaged joint can result in total loss of the effective limb, so if a shoulder or elbow is severely damaged, that arm is no longer a threat. Likewise, taking out a knee makes the opponent one-legged.

Collarbone/Clavicle

The collarbone is relatively delicate and can be hit hard enough to cause a fracture, resulting in severely impaired use of the arms, though this is less likely to be effective when the opponent is much larger than the attacker.

Sternum/Chest

Blows to the chest have to be very powerful to do much damage, but they can cause broken bones and other types of damage. There is one effect, however, that can kill instantly. It is called *commotio cordis*, and it occurs when the chest is struck at a particular moment in the heart's cycle. This results in wild spasms of the heart and nearly instant death. There are many documented instances of this, and the blow does not have to be particularly hard. This may be the basis for certain historical and mythical "death blow" techniques; however, there is no way to determine the heart rhythm, so this is not a particularly useful effect to include in a game. The player would not understand the result or why it worked at all. For more, see the upcoming "Fatality Systems" section.

Back

A sharp blow to the upper back—midway between the shoulder blades—can cause pain, loss of balance, and even injury to the spinal column. A blow to the third lumbar vertebra, located approximately opposite the solar plexus, can cause paralysis.

Kidneys

Blows and kicks to the kidneys can be extremely damaging, and even relatively light blows can cause extreme pain. Severe blows can cause permanent injury to the kidneys and possibly death.

Floating Ribs

Blows to the floating ribs can be painful. In addition, it is theoretically possible to dislocate the floating ribs and cause them to puncture a kidney or lung, depending on the force and direction of the blow. Some systems also claim that proper attacks to the floating ribs can result in a death blow.

Abdomen/Solar Plexus

The solar plexus is highly vulnerable, particularly in untrained individuals. Strong blows to that area can cause temporary incapacitation—having the wind knocked out of you, and even unconsciousness. Some systems claim that a proper blow to the abdomen can cause instant death.

It may also be possible to break the zyphoid process—the little bone at the bottom of the chest—by hitting the solar plexus hard. In addition to being very painful, breaking this bone could cause damage to other internal organs.

Pelvic Area

Solid attacks to the area above the pubic bone but below the bellybutton can cause pain and possible injury to the bladder or other organs.

Groin

Solid blows to the groin area can cause extreme pain in both men and women. In particular, a strike to the unguarded testicles can be a devastating attack. Some sources, however, state that a solid blow, which can cause shock in the victim, may also leave the victim capable of attacking back long enough to do severe damage to the attacker. An alternative attack would consist of a quick, flicking attack, causing extreme pain but not the associated delayed reaction of shock. It also should be noted that some highly trained martial artists, such as some of the Shaolin monks, can condition their groin area to be invulnerable to normal attacks. Among other things, this involves training to be able to draw the testicles up into the body, thus protecting them from direct attack.

Coccyx/Tailbone

Highly focused, accurate, and powerful blows to the tailbone can result in a variety of nasty effects, ranging from extreme pain to the severing of the bone itself, which will likely result in spinal cord damage. In any case, a well-placed blow to that area is likely to cause some severe consequences.

Radius Bone

Striking this forearm bone can cause numbness in the hand and possible fractures.

Inner Thigh

Hard strikes to the inner thigh can cause the muscles to cramp or the lower leg to go numb. If you are held in a headlock or similar position, a hard pinch to the flesh of the inner thigh can be surprising and painful and may cause an attacker to loosen his hold or lose focus.

Knees

Well-aimed strikes to the knee can cause dislocation, pain, and incapacitation of the leg. Strikes can occur to the front, sides, or back of the knee, each of which can cause severe damage, depending on conditions. It is particularly easy to dislocate the kneecap (patella), which will incapacitate just about anyone, and it is also possible to break the kneecap, which will result in permanent injury.

Shins

Hitting the shins—or, even better, scraping the edge of a shoe or boot down someone's shins—causes extreme pain, though no permanent injury.

Foot

Feet have a lot of small bones, and a good stomp on the top of the feet is guaranteed to be painful to most people. A strong blow to the instep is possibly even more effective, though more difficult to deliver effectively.

The Achilles tendon is also vulnerable to proper strikes, but ordinary attacks may not have much effect.

Other Vulnerable Areas

- **Wrists.** Vulnerable to jamming, twisting, dislocation, and breakage.
- **Elbows.** Elbows are strong, but can be broken if the right force is applied in the right direction.
- **Hamstrings.** Although they are quite strong, very powerful blows to the hamstrings can cause damage and at least temporary weakness in the legs. This is probably best accomplished with a weapon or at least a strong and well-directed kick, however.
- **Muscles.** Some martial arts systems actually strengthen the hands so much that they can literally grab muscles and rip them loose. This is a little-known technique, and some martial arts moves, which seem to make little sense to the uninformed, are actually designed to do that.
- **Balance Points.** There are places on the body where you can instantly cause someone to lose their balance. One particular point is at the top-front of the head, to either side. A gentle shove will force a person to fall over.
- **Ankles.** Ankles tend to be strong, but under some circumstances, they can be sprained or dislocated.
- **Hair.** Hair can be used to control a victim.
- **Clothing.** As with hair, grabbing loose clothing can allow you to control someone or even strangle or temporarily blind them.
- **Accumulation Effects.** Repeated blows, even to less vulnerable areas, can cause a gradual sapping of strength or other weakening or cumulative damage. Professional boxers often are content to keep hitting their opponent's arms, and of course the abdomen, in the theory that it will weaken the opponent and ultimately cause his guard to fall, leaving him open to more devastating blows. So there is an accumulation effect that is really not modeled in games so far.

In addition, certain "fatality" attacks rely on sequential stimulation of specific points on the body, causing an accumulation overload to the system, which can result in unconsciousness or death. (See also the following "Fatality Systems" section.)

Fatality Systems

Martial arts lore is full of stories of seemingly supernatural methods of attack that can result in instant or delayed death. The Chinese system of Dim Mak and the Japanese Atemi system use the acupuncture points as targets and claim to be able to incapacitate an opponent with attacks to certain points.

Although these systems base their knowledge and descriptions on the concept of energy systems (chi or ki) and various energy attacks, there is also a Western scientific explanation for much of it, and it turns out that some of these attacks are quite real.

To understand fully how these attacks function, it is necessary to understand a good deal about human neurology and the neurological concepts of convergence, summation, facilitation, and aberrant reference, in addition to having a working knowledge of various major nerves and how they connect to the spinal cord.

In very simple terms:

- *Convergence* refers to a neurological connection between the external nerves of the body and the sympathetic nerves that connect to the internal organs, which occurs at the dorsal nerve roots along the spine. Pain occurring in one of the external nerve points can be perceived by the brain as coming from the internal organ itself. This, in part, explains how working with specific points on the outside of the body can stimulate or suppress internal organ functions—the principles used in death-blow systems as well as various healing arts.

- *Summation* occurs as a result of simultaneous attacks on convergent nerves. In other words, attacking more than one nerve point, where each enters the spinal cord at the same location, can increase the effect on the targeted organ.
- *Facilitation* occurs when sequential attacks are performed on convergent nerve points. Again, in simple terms, each attack further "potentiates" or stimulates the pain response associated with the targeted organ, so that it is more sensitive. In some cases, using facilitation through sequential attacks can result in an organ point becoming so sensitive that a light touch could result in unconsciousness or worse.
- *Aberrant reference* refers to a quality of the nervous system to find the middle point where pain is being experienced simultaneously in points on opposite sides of the body. This is more easily understood if you understand the way the nervous system and, in particular, the spinal entry zones work, but the idea is that the body finds the middle point between two simultaneous sources of pain. In sophisticated Dim Mak attacks, two seemingly unrelated attacks can cause stimulation of a specific organ because it is associated in the spine with the middle point between the sources of attack. This is used to further sensitize and weaken the opponent and in some cases can have a devastating effect immediately.

Again, these explanations are excessively simplified, and this is fairly complex material. There are other important concepts as well, but even oversimplified as it is, this information can help to explain how and why the Dim Mak attacks can and do work. Furthermore, it turns out that the acupuncture points also correspond to specific nerves that, due to their connections to the spinal cord, can directly or indirectly affect various internal organs. This is the key to the system—the target points, if you will.

Some death-blow attacks can damage an organ directly. Most, however, cause a stimulation of pain that ultimately affects the operation of one or more specific organs, such as the heart, lungs, or digestive system. As such, properly applied techniques can cause unconsciousness, cardiac arrest, and ultimately death.

The practical application of these death blows is far from simple and requires not only a lot of knowledge, but intense training. But conceptually, from a game design standpoint, they can be understood and possibly applied in a simplistic combat system. It should be noted, however, that an accurate application of these techniques would be difficult, because most require either simultaneous attacks to more than one point or sequential attacks to "setup" points with subsequent attacks to relevant "follow-up" points.

One interesting possibility here is to create preset moves and combos with reasonably accurate graphics to make the attacks look authentic. These could be modeled as either specific "moves" or specific combos that have devastating effects. In the real world, these are quite advanced techniques and not easy to implement effectively. In games, they might also be used as highly advanced abilities given as a reward for an advanced character, or even given to specific types of enemies who can incapacitate or kill opponents with precision, skill, and minimal effort. Stealth classes might especially benefit from these sorts of techniques.

Although there are charts that contain "formulas" for Dim Mak and Atemi attacks, these are beyond the scope of this book. Anyone who would like to conduct a more thorough investigation of this subject should look for books on Dim Mak and Atemi. For the scientific viewpoint, try *Death Touch: The Science Behind the Legend of Dim-Mak* (Paladin Press, 2001) by Michael Kelly, D.O.

Magic Abilities

The real world has its share of magic, and martial artists can do amazing feats, many of which seem like magic. However, in games, we can have anything we want, and magic has become a staple of the game designer. Of course, this means that many conventions have evolved. The lists in this section can help you both by suggesting some ideas, but also by challenging you to go beyond the simple form of these examples and to expand, extend, or reformulate the concepts into modes and methods of your own. Create your own magic. That's what it's all about.

Ways to Deliver Magic

How is magic actually directed to its target? How does it achieve its effect? Here are some ways to deliver magic. Can you think of more?

- Bolt
- Wave
- Spin
- Aura/field
- Internal attack
- External effect (such as an explosion)
- Cloud
- Weather/storm
- Emotion-based
- Psychic (mind direct)
- Proxy (such as voodoo doll—also known as puppeting objects or creatures)
- Curse (through object or directly)
- Through items carried or worn
- Through projectiles, magically enhanced or created through magic (magic arrows, magically enchanted items)
- Enchantment
- Incantation

Tools of Magic

Magic has both traditional and fanciful artifacts—items that are often associated with its practice. Here are some of the tools you might find among magicians.

- Words (incantation)
- Gestures
- Wands
- Staves
- Daggers, swords, and other ritual weapons
- Scrolls
- Jewelry (rings, amulets, etc.)
- Runes, dice, coins, etc.
- Crystal ball
- Dancing and movement
- Herbs, potions, tinctures, etc.
- Blood
- Animals (dead or alive)
- Bones and innards
- Noisemakers (rattles, drums, etc.)
- Music and song
- Purification practices (sleep deprivation, fasting, meditation, solitude, etc.)
- Rites and rituals
- Fire and smoke/incense
- Sacred objects
- Offerings and sacrifices
- Masks and costumes
- Familiars
- Drugs
- Magical spaces, such as the pentagram
- Visualization and imagination
- Tarot
- Minerals (iron, mercury, salt, etc.)
- Candles and wax in general
- Cauldrons

Color Coding

There are some conventions often used for magic. This isn't to say you can't change them, but it's good to have them for reference. Note that there are some variations, and some colors can be commonly found associated with more than one type of element.

Element	Color
Fire	Red, Orange, Gold
Earth	Brown or Green
Air/Wind	White, Gray, Violet, Sky Blue, or Yellow
Water/Ice	Blue
Electrical	Yellow or White
Crushing/Gravity	Gray/Brown, Black
Black/Dark	Black
Healing	Green
Psychic	Purple
Mental	Blue
Nature	Green

Direct Magical Attacks

This list contains examples of magic that attacks a target directly.

- Elemental
  - Fire
  - Earth
    - Crushing/gravity
    - Earthquake
  - Air
  - Water/ice
  - Electrical
- Psychic
  - Emotional base (hate, love)
  - Physical manipulation
  - Mental manipulation or control
  - Music and/or song
  - Projectiles
  - Magnetic (against metal enemies or using metal objects to attack)
  - Drains
  - Abrasion
  - Choking
  - Sonic
  - Shrinking
  - Explosive
  - Death touch/black magic
  - Hate magic
- Damage over time (DOT) spells
  - Pain
  - Poison
  - Curse
  - Fire (burning)
  - Ice (freezing)
  - Music and/or song
  - Choking
  - Bleeding
  - Acid

Area of Effect (AOE) Spells

Note that some area of effect (AOE) spells can be beneficial, such as many spells found in the upcoming "Buffs and Debuffs" section. Other AOEs can be control-type spells, such as those found in the "Controlling: Taking the Enemy Temporarily Out of Action" section. And, of course, many AOE spells are direct damage spells:

- Nuke
- Other explosive
- Fire/heat
- Ice/cold
- Earthquake
- Electrical
- Psychic
- Gravity
- Clouds
- Storms
- Light
- Projectiles
- Sonic
- Music and/or song

Trap Spells (Damage Type)

These are basic spells that leave a trap for unwary enemies. These traps often do damage to the enemy, either as damage over time (DOT) or instant damage, although they may also do no damage, but affect enemies through various types of immobilization and/or reduction of abilities (such as speed). They are the equivalent of landmines, but they can take many magical forms and can deliver any kind of damage (see the "Direct Magical Attacks" section) or other effects (see, for instance, the next section, "Controlling: Taking the Enemy Temporarily Out of Action").

Controlling: Taking the Enemy Temporarily Out of Action

There are many ways to incapacitate or temporarily render an opponent ineffective or harmless. These types of magic can be used in a variety of game settings, and in MMOGs, they are often used by characters who specialize in crowd control.

- Sleep/unconsciousness
- Immobilize
- Blind
- Stun
- Slow
- Silence
- Mesmerize
- Mind control/charm (turning an enemy against its own side)
- Fear (tries to run away)
- Panic (like fear or confusion , may continue to attack randomly or run)
- Disorient and confuse
- Remove magic abilities or enhancements to the character (buffs)
- Barrier
- Wind (whirlwinds or blocking winds)
- Ice (slippery or freezing in place)
- Burn (immobilizes while doing damage)
- Shock (electrical immobilization)
- Telekinesis (lift them from the ground and hold them there)
- Physical traps (various kinds)
- Interrupt (spell or attack)
- Music and/or song
- Transform (into something harmless—generally temporary)
- Shrink
- Reveal (reveals stealth or invisible enemies)
- Turn undead

Transformations and Summons

Some magic is effective in changing the form of the caster, an ally, or an enemy. Other types of magic summon creatures or items to help win the battle or achieve specific ends. This list is necessarily short. Can you extend it with more examples?

- Turn an enemy into something else (a pig, a rat, a piece of limburger cheese, etc.).
- Cause an enemy to fight for you.
- Resurrect a dead character as a zombie.
- Transform yourself or another ally (taking another form).
- Transform items.
- Shape-shift.
- Summon a creature to help you fight. This can be an animal, a godlike creature, elemental, and so on.
- Summon an item, such as a magic sword.
- Change the battlefield itself in some way.
- Control or change the weather.

Buffs and Debuffs

Some spells simply increase the abilities of allies (buffs) or decrease the abilities and stats of enemies (debuffs). In some cases, a spell may do damage and also cause some debuff to an enemy at the same time—for instance, doing some cold damage while also slowing the enemy's movements. Various buffs and debuffs can include:

- Strength
- Health (hit points)—enhance or drain from enemies
- Endurance—enhance or drain from enemies
- Spell points (mana)—enhance or drain from enemies
- Invisibility/visibility
- Defense
- Accuracy
- Speed (movement or attack)
- Sight
- Invisibility/stealth
- Flight
- Resistances (to specific types of attacks, such as cold or fire, etc.)
- Cause/resist disease
- Size (make bigger or smaller)
- Berserk (high damage for a short time with some negative side effects)
- Meditate (enhance energy for spells or fighting)
- Damage shield (a magical shield that returns damage to the attacker)
- Energy shield (causes some positive effect on the character when it is hit, such as transferring health or energy to the user of the shield)
- Nullification shield (can block or nullify a certain amount of damage or certain types of attacks)
- Protection (can apply to characters or things)
- Enhancement (as in making crops grow better)
- Charms for self-protection, success in love, good fortune, etc.
- Curses (may affect specific enemy abilities or just their overall fortunes/luck)
- Protect property or crops
- Damage/weaken property or crops

Healing/Self-Repair

There are many types of magic that benefit the character by healing, restoration, or resurrection.

- Basic health healing for self, an individual, a group, or within a defined area
- Resurrection
- Regeneration of health and/or stamina or mana, etc.
- Love magic
- Create potions
- Use potions
- Music and/or song

Other Magic

Still other magic abilities may include:

- Divination (remote viewing or seeing the future)
- Clairvoyance
- Telekinesis
- Astral travel

Travel

Travel in games is covered in Chapter 18, "Travel," but this section is specifically devoted to magical means of travel.

- Teleportation (self, other, or group)
- Speed burst or enhancement
- Flight
- Jump enhancement
- Magical vehicle
- Mount (animal, monster, mythical creature)
- Swim (on top of the water or underwater)

Known Superhero List

You can expect game companies to license many of these characters over time, unless you do it first. That's why we are offering this list. You can research them, too, and use them for inspiration.

- Ant Man
- Aquaman
- The Atom
- Batgirl
- Batman (and Robin)
- Batwoman
- The Bionic Woman
- Black Adam
- Black Canary
- The Black Knight
- Black Panther
- Black Widow
- Blade
- Buffy the Vampire Slayer
- Captain America
- Captain Atom
- Captain Marvel
- Changeling
- Colossal Boy
- Crusader Rabbit
- Cyclops
- Daredevil
- The Demon
- Dick Tracy
- Doctor Fate
- Doctor Mid-Nite
- Doctor Who
- Fantastic Four
  - Mister Fantastic (Reed Richards)
  - Human Torch (Johnny Storm)
  - Invisible Woman (Susan Storm)
  - The Thing (Ben Grimm)
- The Flash
- Ghost Rider
- Green Arrow
- Green Hornet

- Green Lantern
- Hank Pym
- Hawkeye
- Hawkgirl
- Hawkman
- Hawkwoman
- Hellblazer (John Constantine)
- Hercules
- Hourman
- The (Incredible) Hulk
- The Human Torch
- The Huntress
- Invisible Woman (Susan Storm)
- Iron Fist
- Iron Man
- Jakeem "J.J." Thunder
- Jean Grey
- Johnny Thunder
- Justice League of America
  - The Flash
  - Green Lantern
  - Hawkman
  - Sandman
  - Doctor Fate
  - Hourman
  - The Atom
  - Johnny Thunder
  - The Red Tornado
  - Superman
  - Batman
  - Doctor Mid-Nite
  - Starman
  - Wonder Woman
  - Mister Terrific
  - Wildcat
  - Black Canary
  - Robin
  - The Star-Spangled Kid
  - Power Girl
  - The Huntress
  - Sand
  - Nuklon (Atom Smasher)
  - Jakeem "J.J." Thunder
  - Black Adam
  - The Spectre
- Marvel Girl
- Mary Marvel (Captain Marvel)
- Mighty Mouse
- Mister Fantastic
- Mister Terrific
- Ms. Marvel
- Nuklon (Atom Smasher)
- Plastic Man
- Power Girl
- Power Man (Luke Cage)
- Professor X
- The Punisher
- Quicksilver
- The Red Tornado
- Robin
- Samson
- Sandman
- Sandy the Golden Boy (Sand)
- Scarlet Witch
- Silver Surfer
- Spider-Girl
- Spider-Man
- Starman
- Storm
- Streaky the Super Cat
- Superboy
- Supergirl
- Superman
- Superwoman
- The Avengers
  - Iron Man
  - The (Incredible) Hulk
  - Ant Man
  - The Wasp
  - Scarlet Witch
  - Quicksilver
  - Hawkeye
  - Hercules
  - The Black Knight
  - Black Widow
- The Star-Spangled Kid
- The Thing
- The Tick
- TMNT
- The Wasp
- Wildcat
- Wolverine
- Wonder Woman
- X-Men (various versions)

16 Speech

Speech in games can make a big difference to the feel of authenticity and the sense of immersion the player has. Poorly written or unconvincing speech weakens a game, and as we strive to make better and better games, we can't ignore the importance of good writing overall, and realistic scripting in particular.

This chapter covers a lot of ways to create more believable speech, including:

- ➤ Dialog Input
- ➤ Phonetic Alphabets
- ➤ Military Time
- ➤ Nicknames
- ➤ Slang
- ➤ Buzzwords
- ➤ Speech Patterns
- ➤ Interactive Conversation
- ➤ Common Hand and Body Expressions
- ➤ SWAT Communications
- ➤ Police and Military Codes
- ➤ Foreign Languages and Foreign Dialogue
- ➤ Colorful Language: Scatological Terminology and Other Dirty Words

Dialog Input

Dialog works very well in some games and not at all in others. It tends to slow down the action and become repetitive, and, if not very well written, it can be boring or annoying. Some players have the patience to enjoy well-written dialog, however, while others do not.

At the same time, some developers feel the need to write 100 lines of dialog to make a single point, or they choose to explain something that could have been inferred. "Wow, something crashed outside." Okay, I'm being mean, but if you find yourself writing what's called *ABABABABAB* dialog, where A says something, B says something, and it's becoming like a game of endless verbal tennis, consider it a warning sign. For one thing, real conversations don't actually work that way. For another, players generally aren't interested in that kind of back and forth in a game unless it's a) informative, b) funny, or c) interesting (at least).

While dialog has its drawbacks in games, it also has some benefits. Good dialog can bring characters to life and help establish the uniqueness of their identities. It can also allow the player to explore his character's personality (as distinct from the player's own) within the context of the game. For instance, whereas the player may be very timid in real life, the game character could be assertive or a "hard case." Or, the player might tend to be a bit overbearing (that's why he's playing this game alone), but the in-game character persona could be very sensitive, with lots of friends. In many cases, the in-game character is a fantasy projection of the player, so giving players plenty of dialog options allows more nuance and more complex identities to emerge. It allows them to wear that fantasy costume and mask even more.

Dialog is also a good way to impart information, but again, only if it is worth reading or listening to (assuming there are voices in the game). Here are a few tips for writing dialog in games:

- **Don't Cut Corners!** If you really don't have time to put effort into the dialog, don't. Bad writing—and worse, bad acting—can make a game seem amateurish and embarrassing. Good writing and acting can make it seem polished and far more immersive. Do it right or don't do it. And, if you can't commit the resources to the best writing and acting, then "cheat." Think of *The Sims* characters making vocal-like sounds, because babble is better than bad dialog—at least it can convey emotion, and the player can imagine it's very interesting. I'm not saying *The Sims* would've had bad dialog; I'm saying it's a good example of how you can have non-speaking characters that still convey meaning through the sounds they make (along with some other clues).
- **Worth It.** It takes time to sit through a dialog scene, so the dialog itself should be entertaining and sometimes surprising (don't say everything—leave some mystery), should reveal relationships, and certainly should be believable. Moreover, the result of the dialog scene should be rewarding. The player should come away with new information or new tasks or clues—something that furthers the experience of playing the game. There can be purely cosmetic, humorous, or personal dialog scenes, but they should be used with restraint. "Still haven't quit?" That simple question is a good example of using dialog to establish the existing relationship between one character and another as one of them reaches for a cigarette. It's short and simple, but it tells you that the two have history.
- **Unique Characters.** One secret to creating dialog in games is to consider each NPC character and the player's character to be unique. You can get more information about creating unique characters in Chapter 12, "Character Design," but whenever you are writing dialog for characters, consider who they are, what motivates them, what they are distracted by (for example, are they worried about something?), where they live, what their life is like generally, and what specific mannerisms or quirks they might have that can differentiate them from every other character in the game.
- **Simplicity.** Generally, you want to keep it simple and to the point, with only a little digression or verbosity where it's necessary to establish character. There can be exceptions. For instance, in a game where dialog is used as a major part of the character's exploration of self or others, you can explore more complex interactions where the interaction itself is an adventure, but you want to be sure that the kind of game you're creating attracts an audience with the patience and interest in such scenes. More drawn-out dialogs are probably more important in rare adventure or RPG games and games that are based on properties in which the writing, dialog, or personalities are important. For instance, we might want to hear more from Harry or Dumbledore if we are major *Harry Potter* fans. In contrast, putting involved dialog in a game where players are expecting a lot of non-stop action is not recommended.
- **Variety and Exploration.** Make a player's options in choice-oriented dialog scenes meaningful, but offer some variation by which the player can explore different paths to discover different kinds of information.
- **The Way Out.** Always offer the player a way out. Don't leave them embroiled in a long, seemingly never-ending conversation. There should always be an "I gotta go" type of option.
- **Logical Consistency.** Avoid contradicting your own story or characters. Make sure that your characters are consistent and not contradicting themselves or others—unless that is intentional because they are lying or misinformed as part of the story. There's nothing worse than getting a quest from a character that said to go right at the fork when you were supposed to go left, to enter 111213 instead of 112233 as the combination, or to talk to the Ragged Peasant in Felorin Township instead of the Peasant's Relative in Falstadt Village. You get the point, and even subtle inconsistency will get spotted quickly (thanks to the Internet generation).

- **Don't Forget Humor.** There's really nothing quite like a good laugh in the middle of a game that seems to take itself seriously. If you can find a way to make someone chuckle or laugh out loud, by all means use it. For more information about how to make things funny, see the section "Creating Comedy" in Chapter 19, "Storytelling Techniques." A good example is people signing a funny song in the game *Black and White*. Humor is generally very difficult to write, so it comes with a warning too, but we do have a section on adding humor in this book for those who dare to go there.
- **Don't Be Afraid to Innovate.** Test out different ways to handle dialog. For instance:
  - Offer emoticons for the mood in which the instruction will be delivered (angry, sad, forgiving, mischievous, and so on). When you click that icon, it offers the dialog. (This is good if you're stuck with text and have no facial animations to work with.)
  - The NPC can respond at any time. Make it more fluid, so it feels more like a live conversation. Real people interrupt each other, so why not in games? Ever heard an NPC say, "Back to the point I was going to make earlier...?"
  - Explore an artificial-intelligence environment in which characters respond to what your character says with a variety of possible responses, including becoming more receptive, becoming angry, cutting off all communication, giving you everything you asked for, and so on. Allow the player in this dialog to say anything, and have a parser engine that can interpret words and meanings. This is not an easy task. The best example I've seen so far is *Façade* (www.interactivestory.net).

Where is the future of this stuff going? Writers will tell you they can never be replaced, and they are correct. But with speech cognition (code that understands what you say into your microphone), speech generation (where the code responds with a voice), and voice font technology (where voices have proper intonation), you can see where the writers will be able to interact with the players like never before. How can you be the one to make this happen first? I'd start by looking for people who are publishing white papers in this space. It's complicated, but it's exciting to see where that could go.

Phonetic Alphabets

Military

- A: Alpha
- B: Bravo
- C: Charlie
- D: Delta
- E: Echo
- F: Foxtrot
- G: Golf
- H: Hotel
- I: India
- J: Juliet
- K: Kilo
- L: Lima
- M: Mike
- N: November
- O: Oscar
- P: Papa
- Q: Québec
- R: Romeo
- S: Sierra
- T: Tango
- U: Uniform
- V: Victor
- W: Whiskey
- X: X-ray
- Y: Yankee
- Z: Zulu

Civilian

- A: Adam
- B: Boy
- C: Charles
- D: David
- E: Edward
- F: Frank
- G: George
- H: Henry
- I: Ida
- J: John
- K: King
- L: Lincoln
- M: Mary
- N: Nora
- O: Ocean
- P: Paul
- Q: Queen
- R: Robert
- S: Sam
- T: Tom
- U: Union
- V: Victor
- W: William
- X: X-ray
- Y: Young
- Z: Zebra

WWI Phonetic

- A: Ack
- B: Beer
- C: Charlie
- D: Don
- E: Edward
- F: Freddie
- G: Gee
- H: Harry
- I: Ink
- J: Johnnie
- K: King
- L: London
- M: Emma
- N: Nuts
- O: Oranges
- P: Pip
- Q: Queen
- R: Robert
- S: Esses
- T: Toc
- U: Uncle
- V: Vic
- W: William
- X: X-ray
- Y: Yorker
- Z: Zebra

MILITARY TIME

Military time is used not only by police and military personnel, but often by firefighters, hospitals, and paramedics, among others.

Basically, military time can be converted using the following table:

Regular Time	Military Time	Regular Time	Military Time	Regular Time	Military Time
Midnight	0000	8:00 a.m.	0800	4:00 p.m.	1600
1:00 a.m.	0100	9:00 a.m.	0900	5:00 p.m.	1700
2:00 a.m.	0200	10:00 a.m.	1000	6:00 p.m.	1800
3:00 a.m.	0300	11:00 a.m.	1100	7:00 p.m.	1900
4:00 a.m.	0400	Noon	1200	8:00 p.m.	2000
5:00 a.m.	0500	1:00 p.m.	1300	9:00 p.m.	2100
6:00 a.m.	0600	2:00 p.m	1400	10:00 p.m.	2200
7:00 a.m.	0700	3:00 p.m.	1500	11:00 p.m.	2300

Basically, the way to pronounce military time is in hours. So if it were 6:23 p.m., it would be 1823 hours ("eighteen twenty-three hours" or simply "eighteen twenty-three"). The early hours are pronounced with zeros—for instance, 12:18 a.m. would be "zero zero eighteen hours" or "zero zero one eight" or "oh oh eighteen." 1:00 a.m. would be "zero one hundred hours" or, more commonly, "oh one hundred hours." 8:00 p.m. is 2000 hours, spoken as "twenty hundred hours."

Nicknames

Nicknames are helpful in making characters more colorful and personal. Nicknames often say something about a person that their given name does not. For instance, nicknames like Slim and Killer are more interesting and suggestive than Bill and Fred. If someone is called by a diminutive name, such as Joey instead of Joe or Joseph, or Katie instead of Kate or Katherine, what does that say about them? What about Big Jim, Stinky, Tricky Dick, or any of a wide variety of nicknames?

Nicknames can tell a story or indicate something specific about a character. They also sound more interesting and can even help give more personality to a character who tends to give other people nicknames—for instance, the boss character who never refers to people by their names, but calls them Numbnuts or says things like, "Hey you there, the bozo in the T-shirt...."

Although it is possible to list some of the more common nicknames, many nicknames are given to people based on specific circumstances. If Michael Jordan was known as Air Jordan, it was because of specific characteristics of his performance as a player, but Air wouldn't necessarily be a common nickname. It could still be used, however.

Some nicknames are plays on words, such as those who call George W. Bush by the nickname Shrub. Others employ someone's initials, such as JFK or LBJ. In giving nicknames to characters, be creative. You can make up new nicknames or you can use nicknames that are authentic to a specific ethnic group, time period, or geographical region. For instance, the name Bubba is not uncommon in some quarters, but would be out of place, for instance, in Manhattan.

Speaking of places, they can have nicknames, too. For instance, Chicago is the Windy City, and New York is the Big Apple.

Remember also, while some nicknames are more or less permanent replacements for someone's given name, others can be off-the-cuff temporary monikers. For instance, some tough guy might say, "Get over here, nerd-o" to a weaker kid. Nerd-o isn't a permanent nickname (hopefully), but it is a nickname of sorts anyway.

Given the assortment of names people can call each other, there's a nearly infinite range of possibilities. This list is intentionally short and contains a few fairly common nicknames. It's up to you to discover or invent others. In fact, you can always make up your own buzzwords and slang, especially if you are creating a completely fictional location or setting.

Sample Nicknames

- Babe
- Big Red
- Bomber
- Bruiser
- Bubba
- Doc/Doctor
- Doofus
- Dutchess
- Dweeb
- Easy
- Fats
- Fatso
- Fatty
- Killer
- Mom
- Monkey Boy
- Mother
- Nerd
- Poison
- Princess

- Professor
- Puddn'head
- Punky
- Queen/Queenie
- Red
- Slim
- Spanky
- Speedy
- Sugar
- Sugar Lips
- Sweet Cheeks
- Sweetness
- The Brain
- The Doctor
- The King
- The Man

Slang

Using appropriate slang not only adds to the realistic quality of characters' speech, but it also makes them far more colorful. The choice of slang expressions and other types of jargon used can further identify a character's cultural, social, or ethnic origins.

Of course, the pitfalls of using slang and other words specific to a culture, geographical area, or specific group is that you may use it incorrectly, which will turn players off. It's best to know the culture you're writing about or to have someone who does if you are going to use slang, jargon, or group-specific buzzwords.

Also, don't lay it on too thick. You don't want some bozo to spew a load of slang every time he opens his yap. I mean, some whack job might actually go over the top and motormouth nothing but lingo. You want summa this? Huh?

At any rate, slang should be used selectively and should be appropriate to the situation. Probably the best way to create colorful speakers is to listen to colorful speakers from the appropriate group or region. Or hire someone who uses that slang. Or at least watch some good movies from the appropriate era.

Keep in mind that slang reflects common usage and is constantly changing. You can easily characterize a has-been hippie by having him say "far out" and "groovy" a lot. But no self-respecting street person would say that now. Every decade or so brings a whole new slang lexicon, and in today's culture, new words and phrases are introduced practically daily—or so it seems. You need to do research to be authentic, unless you are writing your own "native" slang.

To further this point, slang in the '20s was quite different from slang in the '40s, the '70s, the '80s, the '90s, and today. British slang is commonly used in movies and sometimes in games, but British slang varies from one region to another. Even parts of London have different slang. Then there's Australian slang, which is colorful and has been popularized in recent years. There's Jewish/Yiddish slang (which is commonly heard in movies and read in books), slang from the South, and slang from other various parts of the country, such as Maine or the Midwest or Boston. There are foreign words that become part of our vocabulary, such as *gringo*, which is Spanish for a foreigner or *haole*, which is Hawaiian for pretty much the same thing.

The lines also begin to blur between different types of ethnic, regional, and generational slang as well as various buzzwords that ultimately become common usage. One easy example is the use of the term "cop" to refer to police. This is pervasive to the point of being a part of general language. Another term, "pushing the envelope," originated with pilots pushing their planes to maximum performance, but now the term is often used to indicate any situation or action that takes things to the extreme.

Because this is such a vast subject and because it is changing so rapidly, I can't really give you the kind of one-stop reference I'd like to, listing all the words and phrases you might need and saving you the trouble of finding them. That would take a book in itself. However, this book will have an associated website (davidperry.ning.com) that will contain links to other resources and various tools to help you in this and other areas of game development and design.

Finally, there's nothing wrong with making up some terms of your own, particularly if they can help further identify a character. Someone who consistently uses a term of his own devising can become associated with that term. For instance (and this is typically odd), some guy might call everybody he meets Mitchell. As in, "Hey Mitchell, whaddup?" It's his own pet name for everyone, and it says something about who he is and how he thinks of people. Never mind that Mitchell makes no sense...or does it?

In futuristic stories, it's common to make up new types of slang and terminology. William Gibson's *Neuromancer* comes to mind, and somewhat later, *The Matrix*. These stories take place in a society and an era that hasn't yet come to pass, so you can be most creative with slang and terminology.

I have included a few terms as samples from different types of slang:

- '20s slang
- '30s/'40s detective slang
- '60s/'70s slang
- '80s slang
- '90s slang
- Surfer slang
- Skateboarder slang
- British slang
- Cockney rhyming slang
- Australian slang
- Yiddish terms
- Rasta slang
- Modern (circa 2005) slang
- Cops and criminals slang

'20s Slang

The Roaring Twenties produced a lot of slang terms, many of which are still in use today—for example, "baby" to denote someone's sweetheart or "dead soldier" to refer to an empty beer bottle. Other terms are typically '20s, such as "bee's knees" or "jeepers creepers." Occasionally, you might come across a familiar term, only to see its meaning is quite different today. For instance, "bimbo" in the '20s meant a tough guy, while today it means a ditzy woman...go figure. Anyway, here's a peek into the language of the times:

- Ab-so-lute-ly (spoken as separate, distinct syllables; means "I definitely agree.")
- All wet (as in "You're all wet," meaning you're wrong)
- And how! (You bet...I agree)
- Applesauce (nonsense)
- Attaboy/Attagirl (good job, well done)
- Baby (sweetheart)
- Baby grand (a big guy)
- Balled up (confused; "I'm all balled up, baby.")
- Baloney (untrue or nonsense, as in "That's a load of baloney.")
- Beat it (go away, scram, get lost)
- Beat your gums (to chatter away)
- Beef (a complaint, or, as a verb, to complain)
- Bee's knees (the best, really great)
- Beeswax (used as a synonym for "business" in the phrase, "That's none of your beeswax.")
- Bent (drunk; also blotto, tanked, stewed, shot, polluted, plastered, pie-eyed, oiled, juiced, jiggered, fried, crocked, canned, zozzled, and so on)
- Big cheese (someone very important)
- Bimbo (a tough guy)
- Bird (term to refer to a man or woman: "He (She) was a tough old bird"; also tended to refer to someone odd: "a strange bird")
- Blow (a wild party, also "to leave")
- Bluenose (a prude)
- Bohunk (a derogatory term applied to immigrants from Eastern Europe)
- Bootleg (illegal liquor, also to bootleg was to make, sell, or transport illegal booze)
- Breezer (a convertible)
- Bubs (breasts)
- Bull (could mean either a policeman or nonsense, as in "That's bull.")

Part IV

- Bullsh*t (idle conversation or something not true)
- Bump off (kill someone)
- Bum's rush (forcible removal of someone from a location)
- Bunk (nonsense)
- Bus (an old car)
- Bushwa (a euphemism for "bullsh*t")
- Cake-eater (a ladies' man)
- Caper (a criminal act or robbery)
- Carry a torch (to have unrequited love for someone)
- Cash (a kiss)
- Cash or check (a question indicating whether to kiss now or later)
- Cat's meow (sort of like the bee's knees, something great; also "cat's pajamas" and "cat's whiskers")
- Chassis (a female body, as in, "She's got a great chassis on her.")
- Cheaters (eyeglasses)
- Chewing gum (making no sense, doubletalk)
- Chopper (the Thompson submachine gun)
- Chunk of lead (an unattractive female)
- Ciggy (cigarette)
- Clam (a dollar)
- Copasetic (it's good)
- Crasher (an uninvited guest, as in a party crasher)
- Crush (infatuation)
- Daddy (refers to a young woman's boyfriend/lover, particularly if he's rich)
- Daddy-o (hipster/jazz era way to address someone)
- Dame (a woman)
- Dead soldier (empty beer bottle)
- Deb (debutante)
- Dick (private investigator)
- Dinge (derogatory term for a black person)
- Dogs (feet)
- Doll (an attractive woman)
- Dolled up (fancy, dressed up)
- Don't take any wooden nickels (don't get fooled, watch yourself)
- Don't/Doesn't know from nothing (clueless, has no information)
- Dope (drugs, especially cocaine or opium)
- Double-cross (to cheat or betray someone)
- Dough (money)
- Drugstore cowboy (someone who hangs
- around in public trying to pick up women)
- Dry up (shut up)
- Ducky (just great)
- Earful (enough)
- Edge (have a buzz on)
- Egg (a guy, as in, "He's a good egg.")
- Ethel (effeminate male)
- Fag (a cigarette, also a homosexual)
- Fall guy (someone who takes the rap, a scapegoat)
- Fella (a guy)
- Fire extinguisher (chaperone)
- Fish (a college freshman, also someone doing a first prison term)
- Flapper (a woman of the '20s typified by short hair and flouncy short skirts)
- Flat tire (someone who's boring)
- Flick (movie)
- Flour lover (a woman who wears excessive face powder)
- Flyboy (a pilot)
- For crying out loud! (You gotta be kidding!)
- Four-flusher (a moocher who pretends to be wealthy, a fake)
- Frame (to set someone up to take the blame, to take the fall, etc.)
- Futz (a more polite replacement for f*ck)
- Gaga (nuts)
- Gams (legs)
- Gatecrasher (same as crasher)
- Gay (happy)
- Getup (a person's outfit, what they're wearing)
- Giggle water (alcohol)
- Gigolo (a dancing partner)
- Gimp (a cripple)
- Gin mill (a cheap bar or speakeasy, also someone who sold hard liquor)
- Glad rags (fancy clothes for partying and going out)
- Gold-digger (a woman who goes after men for their money)
- The goods (the facts of a situation or the stuff needed for a specific situation)
- Goof (a dopey person or a flapper's boyfriend)
- Goofy (infatuated)
- Grummy (depressed)

- Grungy (envious)
- Gyp (to cheat)
- Hair of the dog (a drink of alcohol, particularly after a night of drinking when hung over; the full expression is "hair of the dog that bit you")
- Half under (very drunk)
- Handcuff (an engagement ring)
- Hard-boiled (tough)
- Harp (an Irishman)
- Hayburner (a losing horse or a car that guzzles gas)
- Heavy sugar (a good quantity of money)
- Heebie-jeebies (the shakes, the creeps)
- High hat (a snob)
- Hip to the jive (with it)
- Hit on all sixes (to do something really well—reference to six-cylinder cars; could also be "hit on all fours," in reference to common four-cylinder engines)
- Holding the bag (to take the blame or to be cheated out of a share)
- Hooch (alcohol)
- Hood (criminal/hoodlum)
- Hooey (crap, as in "a load of hooey")
- Hoofer (a dancer)
- Hop (drugs, such as opium or marijuana; also a teen dance party)
- Hope chest (a cigarette package)
- Hopped up (drugged)
- Hotsy-totsy (that's cool, neat-o)
- I have to go see a man about a dog (a common expression meaning "I have to go now" or "I'm going to buy booze.")
- In a lather (worked up, angry)
- Insured (engaged)
- Iron (a motorcycle)
- Iron your shoelaces (to go to the bathroom)
- Ish kabibble (Yiddish expression for "I should care?" or "So what?" Popularized in the '20s, also the name of a trumpet player in the Kay Kyser orchestra)
- Jack (money)
- Jake (really good, as in "That's Jake with me.")
- Jalopy (a car—often a rundown one)
- Jane (generic term for a female)
- Java (coffee)
- Jeepers creepers (Yikes! Might have been a euphemistic way of saying, "Jesus Christ!")
- Jerk soda (from the action of pulling the handle on the soda machine; origin of the term "soda jerk")
- Jitney (a car used as a private bus or taxi; because the fare was usually five cents, it was also known as a "nickel")
- Joe (coffee; also might refer to a guy: "a regular Joe")
- Joe Brooks (a snappy dresser)
- John (toilet)
- Joint (a place or establishment)
- Juice joint (a bar, speakeasy)
- Kale (money)
- Keen (cool/good, interested)
- Killjoy (not the life of the party)
- Kisser (mouth)
- Knock up (to get someone pregnant; also "knocked up," meaning to be pregnant)
- Lay off (cool it, stop it)
- Let George do it (a common phrase used to avoid work)
- Level (to be straight or honest with, as in, "I gotta level wit ya, Frankie. I took the dough." Also, "on the level" and "on the up and up.")
- Limey (someone of British origins)
- Line (an untrue story or excuse, also insincere flattery)
- Live wire (an energetic or intense person)
- Lollapalooza (a real whopper, a humdinger)
- Lollygagger (someone who hangs around watching but doing nothing, also a guy who likes to make out)
- Lounge lizard (a ladies' man)
- Lousy (bad)
- Main drag (the main street in town)
- Make out (to engage in various sexual activities with someone)
- Malarkey (bull, lies)
- Manacle (wedding ring)
- Mazuma (money)
- Milquetoast (a timid or wimpy, unassertive person)
- Mind your potatoes (mind your own business, also "mind your Ps and Qs")
- Moll (a gangster's girlfriend)

Part IV

- Mooch (to leave)
- Moonshine (homemade whiskey)
- Mop (handkerchief)
- Munitions (face powder)
- Neck (to kiss with passion)
- Nifty (good, great)
- Nitwit (idiot)
- Noodle juice (tea)
- Nookie (sex)
- Off one's nuts (crazy)
- Oh yeah! (a retort meaning "No way" or "I don't think so")
- Old boy (often a way that a man would address another man, particularly in society circles)
- On a toot (on a drinking binge)
- On the lam (running from the cops)
- Orchid (an expensive item)
- Owl (someone up late, as in "night owl")
- Palooka (an average [or worse] boxer, also someone who is a social outsider)
- Panic (something extraordinary, as in "That show was a real panic.")
- Panther sweat (whiskey)
- Pet (advanced making out)
- Petting pantry (movie theater)
- Petting party (a make-out party of one couple or more)
- Piffle (nonsense)
- Piker (a cheapskate or a coward)
- Pill (a jerk or obnoxious character, also a teacher)
- Pinch (to arrest, to be pinched was to be arrested)
- Pinko (a liberal)
- Pipe down (shut up)
- Pos-i-lute-ly (spoken in distinct syllables, means "absolutely")
- Putting on the Ritz (doing it up, high class)
- Quiff (a cheap whore or a slut)
- Ragamuffin (a dirty person, often a kid)
- Rain pitchforks (heavy rain)
- Razz (to goof on or make fun of)
- Real McCoy (the real deal, the genuine article)
- Regular (a normal sort, as in a regular Joe)
- Rub (a student dance party)
- Rube (a country bumpkin, also "Rueben")
- Rubes (money/dollars)
- Rummy (a drunk)
- Sap (sucker, fool)
- Says you (a response to someone who expresses doubt or disbelief)
- Scram (to make a fast exit, to leave)
- Scratch (money)
- Screaming meemies (like the heebie jeebies)
- Screw (get out of here, get lost)
- Screwy (nuts)
- Sheba (a girlfriend)
- Sheik (a boyfriend)
- Shiv (a knife)
- Simolean (a dollar)
- Sinker (doughnut)
- Sitting pretty (in a good situation)
- Skirt (a female, particularly an attractive one)
- Smarty (a nice-looking flapper)
- Smoke-eater (someone who smokes)
- Smudger (someone who dances very close)
- So's your old man (a common retort, basically an insult)
- Speakeasy (a bar, but because of Prohibition, an illegal establishment)
- Spiffy (fancy)
- Spill (to talk, as in "spill the beans")
- Spoon (to make out or to romance someone)
- Static (meaningless discourse or a conflict of opinions)
- Stilts (legs)
- Stuck on (infatuated with)
- Sugar daddy (an older guy who provides material comforts and gifts to a younger woman in exchange for sex)
- Swanky (classy)
- Swell (really fine, also someone high class)
- Take someone for a ride (basically, to take someone out and murder him or her in a deserted place)
- Talkie (a sound movie)
- Tasty (good stuff)
- Teenager (Actually not commonly used in the '20s; came into more general use in the '30s. The term previously was "young adults.")
- Tell it to Sweeney (I don't believe what you're saying)
- Tight (nice-looking)

- Tin Pan Alley (the New York district known for its music industry)
- Tomato (a well-endowed or very attractive female)
- Torpedo (a hit man or thug for hire)
- Unreal (extraordinary)
- Upchuck (vomit)
- Vamp (a seductress; to vamp was to seduce)
- Voot (money)
- Wet blanket (a bore, also "killjoy")

'30s/'40s (Detective) Slang

Throughout the '30s and '40s detective novels and movies were popular, and a whole raft of slang developed. A lot of '30s and '40s slang carried over from the rich era of the '20s, but some of it was wholly a part of its own era. Here's a sample:

- Alderman (a pot belly)
- Ameche (a telephone)
- Ankle (a woman [as a noun] or to walk [as a verb])
- Babe (a woman)
- Baby (a way of referring to a person: man or woman)
- Bangtail (racehorse)
- Barber (talk)
- Be on the nut (broke)
- Bean-shooter (gun)
- Beezer (nose)
- Behind the eight-ball (in a fix, in difficulty, in a tight spot)
- Bent cars (stolen cars)
- Berries (dollars)
- Big house (jail)
- The big one (death)
- The big sleep (death)
- Bim (a woman)
- Bindle (a folded piece of paper containing heroin, also the bundle carried by a vagrant)
- Bindle punk, bindle stiff (vagrants and itinerant workers, bums, criminals, and so on—people who carry a bindle)
- Bing (crazy; term for solitary confinement in the "big house")
- Bird (man)
- Bit (prison sentence)
- Blip off (kill)
- Blow (leave)
- Blow one down (kill someone)
- Blower (telephone)
- Boiler (car)
- Boob (a dope)
- Boozehound (someone who drinks excessively—today we'd call that person an alcoholic)
- Bop (to kill)
- Box (common term for a safe, also a bar)
- Box job (cracking a safe)
- Brace (to grab or shake someone)
- Bracelets (handcuffs)
- Break it up (stop what you're doing)
- Breeze (to go)
- Breeze off (get lost)
- Broad (a woman)
- The Broderick (a good beating)
- Bruno (a tough guy)
- Bucket (car)
- Bulge (an advantage)
- Bull (cops and guards)
- Bump gums (idle chatter)
- Bump/bump off (kill)
- Bum's rush (forcible ejection)
- Bunco (fraud)
- Bunk (as a verb, to leave or to sleep; as a noun, something false)
- Bunny (someone being stupid)
- Burn powder (fire a gun)
- Bus (car)
- Button (the face, nose, jaw, as in, "He popped me right on the button.")
- Button man (hit man)
- Buttons (police)
- Butts (cigarettes)
- Buzz (to come to someone's door, to "give a buzz")
- Buzzer (policeman's badge)
- C ($100, also "C-note" or "century")

- Cabbage (money)
- Caboose (jail)
- Call copper (snitch, inform)
- Can (jail, car)
- Can house (brothel)
- Can opener (a low-class safecracker)
- Canary (woman singer)
- Century ($100, also "C" or "C-note")
- Cheaters (sunglasses)
- Cheese it (trouble's here, hide the goods, stop what you're doing or scram)
- Chew (eat)
- Chicago lightning (gunfire)
- Chicago overcoat (coffin)
- Chick (woman)
- Chilled off (killed)
- Chin (conversation; to chin is to talk)
- Chin music (a smack on the jaw)
- Chinese angle (an unusual way of looking at something, a twist or trick)
- Chinese squeeze (stealing profits off the top)
- Chippy (a loose woman)
- Chisel (to cheat)
- Chiv, chive (a knife)
- Chopper squad (guys with machine guns)
- Clammed (not talking, also "clammed up")
- Clip joint (generally a term referring to a place that cheats its customers in some way—for instance, by watering the booze or by fixing gambling tables)
- Clipped (shot)
- Close your head (shut up)
- Clout (shoplifter)
- Clubhouse (police station)
- Coffee-and-doughnut (cheap, crappy)
- Con (a swindle, from "confidence game")
- Conk (head)
- Cool (to knock out)
- Cooler (jail)
- Cop (a policeman or private dick; to take or win something)
- Copped (apprehended by the coppers)
- Copper (policeman; also refers to time off for good behavior)
- Corn (bourbon, from corn liquor)
- Crab (figure out)
- Crate (car)
- Croak (to kill, to die)
- Croaker (doctor)
- Crushed out (escaped)
- Cush (money)
- Cut down (shot)
- Daisy (effeminate male)
- Dame (woman)
- Dance (to be hanged)
- Dangle (get out, get lost)
- Darb (superior)
- Daylight (as in put a hole in someone)
- Deck (cigarette pack)
- Dib (share)
- Dick (a cop—a private dick was a private detective)
- Dingus (generic word for just about anything)
- Dip (pickpocket)
- Dip the bill (take a drink)
- Dish (a pretty woman)
- Dive (a cheap establishment, such as a bar, restaurant, or hotel/flophouse)
- Dizzy (infatuated, as in "He's dizzy over that dame.")
- Do the dance (to be hanged)
- Dogs (feet)
- Doll, dolly (woman)
- Dope (drugs; information; or, as a verb, to have figured something out: "I had it all doped out.")
- Dope fiend (drug addict)
- Dope peddler (drug dealer)
- Dough (money)
- Drift (get out, scram)
- Drill (shoot)
- Drink out of the same bottle (friends)
- Drop a dime (rat someone out, make a phone call to inform on someone)
- Droppers (hit men)
- Drum (a speakeasy)
- Dry-gulch (to ambush and knock someone out)
- Duck soup (easy)
- Dummerer (a beggar who pretends to be deaf and dumb)
- Dump (a place—possibly a rundown place, but any place can be a dump)
- Dust (nothing; to leave—also "dust out")
- Dutch (to be in trouble)
- Dutch act (to commit suicide)

- Eel juice (alcohol)
- Egg (a guy)
- Elbow (a cop or an arrest)
- Electric cure (electrocution)
- Elephant ears (police)
- Fade (scram, get out)
- Fin (a $5 bill)
- Finger (to point someone out, to accuse or identify them)
- Flat (broke, or "for sure," as in, "I tell you flat, I didn't do it.")
- Flattie (flatfoot, cop)
- Flimflam (a swindle)
- Flippers (hands)
- Flogger (overcoat)
- Flop (to go to sleep, to fail)
- Flophouse (a cheap hotel)
- Fog (to shoot)
- Frail (woman)
- Frau (wife)
- From nothing (not knowing, as in, "He don't know from nothing.")
- Fry (to be electrocuted)
- Gams (a woman's legs)
- Gashouse (rough)
- A half (50 cents)
- Gasper (cigarette)
- Gat (gun)
- Gate (the door; to leave, as in, "Show him the gate.")
- Gee (man)
- Geetus (money)
- Getaway sticks (legs)
- Giggle juice (liquor)
- Gin mill (bar)
- Girlie (woman)
- Glad rags (dress-up clothes)
- Glom (to steal or to take a gander at)
- Go climb up your thumb (get outta here)
- Gonif (Yiddish word for thief)
- Goofy (crazy)
- Goog (black eye)
- Goon (thug)
- Goose (man)
- Grab air (put up your hands)
- Graft (stealing from profits or any type of con)
- Grand ($1,000)
- Greasers (generic term for various hoods and punks)
- Grift (a con, confidence game, swindle)
- Grifter (con man)
- Grilled (interrogated)
- Gum (screw up, as in "gum up the works"; also opium)
- Gum-shoe (a detective)
- Gun for (to be going after with intent to kill—or at least do something bad to)
- Guns (hoods and pickpockets)
- Gunsel (various meanings: a gunman, a brat, an informer, a male sodomist)
- Hack (taxi)
- Hammer and saws (from the Cockney rhyming slang [see the upcoming "Cockney Rhyming Slang" section]—laws or, by extension, the police)
- Hard (tough)
- Hash house (a low-class restaurant)
- Hatchetmen (hired goons)
- Head doctors (psychiatrists)
- Heap (car)
- Heat (a gun, also heater)
- Heeled (packing, carrying a gun)
- Highbinders (corrupt politicians)
- Hinky (suspicious)
- Hitting on all eight (everything going smoothly; see '20s slang "Hitting on all sixes")
- Hitting the pipe (smoking opium)
- Hock shop (pawnshop)
- Hogs (engines)
- Hombre (a man)
- Hooch (liquor)
- Hood (hoodlum)
- Hooker (a drink of a strong alcoholic beverage)
- Hoosegow (jail)
- Hop (drugs, a short term for bellhop)
- Hop-head (a drug addict, heroin especially)
- Horn (telephone)
- Hot (stolen)
- House dick (hotel detective, also "house peeper")
- Hype (shortchange artist)
- Ice (diamonds)
- In stir (in jail)
- Jack (money)
- Jake (okay)
- Jam (trouble, as in "in a jam")

- Jane (a woman)
- Java (coffee)
- Jaw (to talk)
- Joe (coffee)
- Johns (police)
- Joint (a place)
- Joss house (a Chinese temple)
- Jug (jail)
- Juice (interest on a loan from a loan shark)
- Jujus (marijuana cigarettes)
- The jump (a hanging)
- Junkie (a drug addict)
- Kale (money)
- Keister, keyster (1. a suitcase; 2. a safe or strongbox; 3. someone's butt)
- Kick (a complaint)
- Kick off (to die)
- Kicking the gong around (smoking opium)
- Kiss (to punch)
- Kisser (mouth)
- Kitten (a woman)
- Knock off (to kill)
- Knockover (a heist, a job)
- Large ($1,000, as in "His share of the take was fifteen large," meaning $15,000.)
- The law (cops)
- Lead poisoning (to be shot)
- Lettuce (money [bills])
- Lid (a hat)
- Lip (a lawyer, particularly one who defends criminals)
- Lit (to be drunk)
- Looker (an attractive woman)
- Look-out (the guy who keeps watch during a heist, the outside man)
- Lousy with (having an abundance)
- Lug (1. a bullet; 2. someone's ear; 3. a man, as in "Come 'ere ya big lug.")
- Made (to be recognized)
- Map (face)
- Mark (a potential victim, a sucker)
- Mazuma (money)
- Meat wagon (ambulance)
- Mesca (marijuana)
- Mickey Finn (1. a drink that has been drugged to knock someone unconscious; 2. as a verb, to go, to leave)
- Mill (typewriter)
- Mitt (hand)
- Mob (a gang—in those days, it didn't necessarily refer to the Mafia)
- Moll (a gangster's girlfriend)
- Moniker (someone's name)
- Mouthpiece (a lawyer)
- Mud-pipe (an opium pipe)
- Mug (a face)
- Muggles (marijuana)
- Mugs (can refer to men, as in "They was a buncha dumb mugs.")
- Mush (face)
- Nailed (arrested)
- Nevada gas (cyanide)
- Newshawk (a reporter)
- Newsie (a newspaper seller)
- Nicked (stole/stolen)
- Nippers (handcuffs)
- Nix on (to say no, as in "Nix on that, fella.")
- Noodle (head)
- Nose-candy (one reference to heroin)
- Number (can refer to a man or woman, as in "That's the number you want over there" or "She's a hot number.")
- Off the track (someone who is nuts, especially violently crazy)
- On the lam (to be running from the cops)
- Op (short for "operative"—a detective, especially a private one)
- Pack (to carry, particularly a gun)
- Palooka (a man, generally referring to someone not too bright; also, a mediocre boxer)
- Pan (face)
- Paste (to punch)
- Patsy (someone who is being set up, also a fool, similar to a mark)
- Paw (a hand)
- Peeper (a detective)
- Pen (the penitentiary)
- Pigeon (a snitch, a stool-pigeon)
- Pill (can be either a bullet or a cigarette)
- Pinch (either a noun or a verb referring to an arrest)
- Pipes (basically, someone's voice, especially a singer: "She has great pipes.")
- Plant (a person inside the scene; to bury)
- Plug (to shoot)

- Poke (to hit; also a bankroll or cache of money)
- Pooped (killed)
- Pop (to kill)
- Pro skirt (a prostitute)
- Pug (a boxer)
- Pump (hear)
- Pump metal (to shoot a gun)
- Punk (a hoodlum; also refers to someone in jail who "gets punked," meaning to be taken advantage of sexually)
- Puss (someone's face)
- Put down (to drink)
- Put the screws on (to interrogate or get tough with someone)
- Queer (1. something counterfeit or false; 2. sexually abnormal; 3. to screw something up, as in "You shouldn'ta come in just now. You really queered the deal.")
- Rags (clothes)
- Rap (1. a criminal charge; 2. information, "the rap"; 3. a hit, as in a "rap on the knuckles")
- Rappers (phonies, setups)
- Rat (to inform)
- Rate (having value)
- Rats and mice (dice, meaning craps)
- Rattler (a train)
- Reefers (joints, marijuana cigarettes)
- Ringers (fakes, like rappers)
- Rod (a gun)
- Roscoe (a gun)
- Roundheel (1. an easy woman; 2. a glass-jawed fighter)
- Rube (a simpleton or potential mark, a country bumpkin)
- Rub-out (a rub-out is a killing; to rub someone out is to kill them)
- The rumble (news)
- Sap (1. a blackjack; 2. a dope: "He's a real sap.")
- Savvy (smarts)
- Savvy? ("Do you understand?")
- Sawbuck (a $10 bill; a $20 bill was called a "double sawbuck")
- Schnozzle/schnozz (nose)
- Scram/scram out (to leave)
- Scratch (money)
- Screw (1. to leave, so that if you said "screw" to someone, you meant, "Get out of here"; 2. a prison guard)
- Send over (send to jail)
- Shamus (a private detective)
- Sharper (a con artist or swindler)
- Shells (bullets)
- Shine (bootlegged liquor)
- Shiv (a knife)
- Shylock (a loan shark)
- Shyster (a lawyer)
- Sing (to confess)
- Sister (a woman, as in, "Listen sister, I'm not taking the fall for you or any skirt.")
- Skate around (what an easy woman does)
- Skip out (to leave without paying your bill, or someone who does so)
- Skirt (a woman)
- Sleuth (a detective)
- Slug (1. a bullet; 2. to hit or knock someone unconscious)
- Smoked (drunk)
- Snatch (to kidnap)
- Snitch (to inform or someone who informs)
- Snooper (a detective)
- Snort (a drink, used as a snort of gin or whiskey, etc.)
- Snow-bird (a cocaine addict)
- Snowed/snowed up (to be drugged, probably on heroin or cocaine)
- Sock (punch)
- Soup (nitroglycerine)
- Soup job (to use nitroglycerine to crack open a safe)
- Spill (to talk, to give information)
- Spinach (money)
- Square (honest; to be "on the square" meant to tell the truth, like a straight shooter)
- Squirt metal (to shoot)
- Step off (to be hanged)
- Sticks of tea (marijuana cigarettes)
- Stiff (a corpse)
- Sting (what a con game was all about)
- Stoolie (a stool-pigeon)
- Stool-pigeon (an informer, also pigeon)
- Stringin' (short for "stringing someone along," meaning feeding them a line)
- Sucker (a potential mark)

- Sugar (money)
- Swing (to hang)
- Tail (to follow, to shadow someone; can be noun: "You have a tail" meant "someone is following you.")
- Take a powder (to leave)
- Take the air (to leave)
- Take the fall for (to take the rap for or to take the punishment for someone else)
- Tea (marijuana)
- The third degree (interrogation)
- Three-spot (a jail term of three years)
- Throw lead (shoot)
- Ticket (a private investigator's license)
- Tighten the screws (to increase the pressure on someone)
- Tin (a badge)
- Tip a few (have a few drinks)
- Tip your mitt (reveal something, same as "tip your hand")
- Tomato (a pretty woman)
- Torcher (a torch singer)
- Torpedoes (hired gunmen)
- Trap (mouth)
- Trigger man (a gunman)
- Trouble boys (a term for gangsters)
- Twist (a woman)
- Two bits (25 cents, a quarter)
- Under glass (incarcerated)
- Weak sister (someone easy to dominate, a pushover)
- Wear iron (to pack a heater, to carry a gun)
- Wheats (pancakes)
- White (1. gin; 2. all right)
- Wire (used to refer to information, as in, "I got the wire on the latest caper.")
- Wise (refers to knowing; to "be wise" is to be in the know, to "put you wise" is to inform you)
- Wooden kimono (a coffin)
- Yap (mouth)
- Yard ($100)
- Yegg (a mediocre safecracker)
- Zotzed (killed)

'60s/'70s Slang

There's an amazing amount of slang and many expressions that are associated with the '60s and '70s. Here's a sample:

- A gas (a lot of fun)
- A trip (as in, "He's a real trip.")
- Ape/Apesh*t (crazy, wild, pissed off)
- Bad (good)
- Badass (someone tough)
- Bag (to steal)
- Ball (have sex)
- Bogart (to hog something, generally a joint)
- Boogie (to get going)
- Book (to "book" was to leave somewhere, also "bug out" or "blow this popstand")
- Bookin' (moving fast)
- Boss (cool)
- Bread (money)
- Brew (beer)
- Brodie (to skid a car 180 degrees)
- Bummer (a drag)
- Burn rubber (to accelerate so fast your tires spin)
- Candyass (something really lame or someone wimpy)
- Cat (a guy, as in "a cool cat")
- Chick (a female)
- Cool (good, still often used)
- Copasetic (everything's all right)
- Dope (drugs, most often marijuana)
- Fag hag (a woman/girl who likes to spend time with homosexual men)
- Foxy (attractive, generally referring to a female)
- Fuzz/the Heat/the Man (cops)
- Groovy (good)
- Heavy (not a precise term, could mean very serious or very intense or very pushy, as in, "Hey man, don't heavy out on me.")
- Hip (to be cool)
- Jive turkey (a jerk)
- Keep on truckin' (carry on)

- Let it all hang out (get loose)
- Old man/old lady (someone's partner)
- Outta sight (really great)
- Pad (home, as in, "Come over to my pad tonight.")
- Psychedelic (something really amazing)
- The rabbit died (a way to describe that someone is pregnant)
- Right on! (totally righteous, total agreement)
- Righteous (really good, as in, "This is some righteous hash, man.")
- Straight (the establishment, not hip)
- Streak (to run naked in public)

'80s Slang

Almost every decade we invent new words and phrases. Following the cultural expansions of the '70s, the '80s offered a few new expressions, many of which have remained in our language today, while others pretty much date the speaker.

- As if (response to something you don't agree with)
- Bad (good)
- Brody (a policeman)
- Chill (to take it easy; also, "chill out" or "take a chill pill," meaning "relax")
- Cool beans (cool, awesome)
- Crib (someone's home)
- Def (really cool and hip)
- Dope (like def—very hip)
- Dude/dudette (carryover from previous eras: a cool guy or girl, also a greeting, as in "Dude!")
- Dufus (dork)
- Duh (like saying, "That's so obvious.")
- Dweeb (a very uncool character)
- Fly (hip and cool)
- Fresh (something original or really cool)
- Gag me with a spoon (valley-girl talk for "disgusting")
- Geek (sort of like a dweeb)
- Heinous (something not good, not really as bad as the literal meaning of the word)
- Homeboy/homey (a friend, one could say, "Hey homey, howzit?")
- Hood (neighborhood)
- Kickin' (something fun and exciting)
- Killer (really cool)
- Like (a modifier, sometimes a replacement for other verbs, in common use among some groups: "He was like, 'I'm serious, dude,' and I was like, 'No way,' and he was like all over me, and I was like outta there.")
- Major (something significant or very cool)
- Nerd (kinda like a dweeb and a geek, but often refers to someone who is into computers or something dorky)
- No way ("You're kidding" or "Absolutely not")
- Oh my god (OMG: common expression started with val-speak as originated in Southern California among so-called "valley girls," who were popularized in Frank Zappa's song, "Valley Girl" and in movies such as *Clueless* and *Wayne's World.*)
- Psyche (fooled you)
- Slang that carried over from other eras (stoked, rad, preppie, poser)
- Solid (for sure, as in, "You going tonight?" "Solid, man.")
- Stellar (really good)
- To the max (extreme)
- Tubular (older skate term for really cool)
- Way (opposite of "no way," meaning "for sure")
- Way cool (very cool)
- Whatever (a way of responding to something someone says without really responding: "Whatever, dude.")
- Wicked (really cool)
- Word (agreement)
- Yo ("Hey")
- Yuppie (Young Urban Professional: what hippies became)

'90s Slang

Gradually, '80s slang evolved into '90s slang. People are so creative!

- 'Sup (what's up)
- All (used similarly to "like" in the '80s, as in, "He was all, 'Give me something, honey,' and I was all, 'No way,' and he was all mean and stupid, and I was all freaked out.")
- Atari (a description in some circles of a bad DJ)
- Back in the day (former times)
- Bama (a redneck, short for Alabama)
- Blazed (refers to smoking weed)
- Bling bling (nice jewelry)
- The bomb (the best)
- Bone out (to leave, to go)
- Brutal (bad)
- Buggin' (tripping out)
- Carried over from other slang, but still used in the '90s (dope, dude, duh, chill, chill out, crib, fly, freaked out, fresh, oh my god, old school, pig, piggy, po po, whatever!, wicked)
- Chapped (annoyed)
- Chica (girl)
- Chick flick (a movie guys think women would like, generally missing good car crashes, gratuitous violence, frontal nudity, and so on—lots of drama and good dialogue and tear-jerking moments, though)
- Damn skippy (exactly)
- Dank (awesome)
- Dawg (friend)
- Dead presidents (paper money)
- Deal (to deal with, to cope with what happens)
- Don't go there ("Let's change the subject.")
- Ecstasy (MDMA, a designer drug, also known as E and X)
- Fine (nice, good-looking, word, yo)
- Gank (to steal)
- Get a room (said to people engaging in PDAs—no, not personal data accessories, but public displays of affection)
- Getting jiggy (dancing or putting the moves on someone; also "I'm jiggy with that," meaning "I'm down with it," meaning "It's all right with me.")
- Going postal (going crazy, getting violent)
- Hella (very)
- Hottie (a nice-looking guy or gal, depending on the observer)
- Jack (nothing, as in, "I got jack"; or to steal, as in, "He jacked a car last night.")
- Jack someone up (to beat them up)
- Junk (a universal descriptor that can refer to just about anything: "That's total junk," "What was all that junk going on last night?" and so on)
- Like (used the same way as "like" in the '80s)
- Mad (extremely)
- My bad (my mistake)
- Not! (often used just after saying something you don't mean, as in "I really dig Brussels sprouts…not!")
- Peace out (goodbye)
- Phat (very hip or very enticing)
- Props (respect, as in, "You gotta give the guy his props.")
- Rolling (being high on Ecstasy)
- Salty (angry)
- Score! (an expression relating to success at something—can relate to success with the opposite sex, but not necessarily)
- Shady (unfair, disreputable)
- Sweet (nice, cool)
- Talk to the hand (I'm not interested)
- Throw down (to fight)
- Tight (the best)
- Too much information (TMI, similar to, "Let's not go there.")
- Trippin' (getting too obsessed with something)
- Tweak (can refer to drugs, such as crystal meth, or to using drugs—also "tweakin'")
- Whacked (crazy or screwed up)
- What up? (What's going on?)

- Wig out (go nuts, also "wiggin'")
- Yada yada yada (a way to make a long story short by skipping the details)
- You go, girl (good for you)

Surfer Slang

I've included surfer slang because a lot of expressions from the surfer culture were ultimately included in common slang throughout the '70s, '80s, '90s, and, to some degree (especially among Baby Boomers) today.

- Amped (excited, stoked)
- Awesome (common expression for something really cool)
- Baggies (swim trunks that were oversized and baggy, as opposed to the trim Speedos often worn by non-surfers—baggies became common and were used by people all over the world, but started with surfers)
- Beach bunny (a girl who likes to hang out on the beach and watch the surfers, or any girl on the beach)
- The Big Kahuna (from the Hawaiian word, came to mean someone of importance)
- Bitchin' (very cool, primo)
- Bodacious (beautiful or impressive, as in, "She's a bodacious dudette.")
- Bogus (wrong)
- Boss (great)
- Bro/Bra (short for "brother," but a common way to refer to someone)
- Bummer (a downer)
- Ding (a hole or dent in a surfboard, became a common term for any little scratch or dent in something that is [generally] in good shape)
- Dork (dumbass)
- Dude (a guy, a girl might be a dudette)
- Dweeb (a fool or someone acting like an idiot)
- Excellent (used as a comment by itself)
- Fer sure (a way of expressing agreement)
- Geek (someone just not with it)
- Gnarly (can mean dangerous or difficult, or it can mean cool or bitchin'; also hairy)
- Hot dogging (showing off)
- Max out (to take something up to or past its limits)
- Mondo (big)
- Off the wall (strange or odd in a good way)
- Outrageous (like excellent, an expression of how good something is)
- Poser (a wannabe)
- Primo (the best)
- Rad/radical (another way of saying something is really good or cool)
- Selling Buicks (vomiting)
- Shred (to do something really well—one could be a "shredder")
- Stoked (really happy or content)
- Wipe out (to fall off your board, to go over the falls)
- Woodie (a wooden-sided station wagon)

Skateboarder Slang

A lot of skateboard slang has to do with descriptions of tricks. I won't go into all that. If you're really interested in getting all the skateboard tricks, a little research on the Internet will get you what you need. Here's a small sample of skateboard slang to whet your appetite.

- Bomb a hill (to skateboard down a big hill)
- Burly (a trick with risk of injury is burly, and someone who likes these tricks can also be called burly)
- Bust (to skate well; to "bust a trick" is to do it well)
- Carve (making a big, fast turn)
- Catch (stop the board from rotating by getting your feet on it while in the air)
- Darkside (the bottom of a skateboard—the board is "darkside" if it is upside down)
- Focus (to break a board in half)
- Gnarly (really good, sick)

- Grind (any trick where the hangers of the trucks grind along the end of a surface)
- Grommet (little kids who skate)
- Hipper (a bad bruise on the hip)
- Line (a series of tricks performed one after the other or a planned skate course)
- Ollie (a basic aspect of skateboard tricks that involves smacking the back of the board down with the back foot while the front foot raises the front of the board into the air)
- Pig/FiveO/Po Po (derogatory terms for police)
- Poser (someone who pretends to be a skateboarder or who pretends to be anything they are not)
- Pro ho (a female who likes to hang out with pro skaters)
- Ripper (a really good, consistent skater)
- Sketch/sketchy (an unsmooth trick or a person or situation that is not quite right)
- Spot (somewhere you can skate)
- Wallie (getting all four trucks in contact with a wall)

British Slang

The British have developed their own unique form of slang, which is often heard in British movies and read in books by British authors. It tends to be colorful, imaginative, and sometimes rhyming.

- Advert (advertisement)
- Aerial (antenna)
- Afterthought (youngest child)
- As near as damnit (very close)
- Auntie Beeb (BBC)
- Barmy (crazy)
- Barney (a tiff, squabble)
- Bird (girl)
- Bloke (fellow)
- Blower (telephone)
- Bluebottle (policeman)
- Bobbie (policeman)
- Bonnet (the hood of a car)
- Bottle (courage)
- Brekkies (breakfast)
- Broads (playing cards)
- Bungalow Bill (a dimwit)
- Bunk off (skip school)
- Busker (street musician)
- Cabbage (money)
- Cack-handed (left-handed)
- Chemist (pharmacist)
- Chokey (prison)
- Click (kilometer)
- Clobber (personal items)
- Collywobbles (nervous stomach)
- Cor! (God!)
- Cousins (Americans)
- Crisps (potato chips)
- Cuppa (cup of tea)
- Dab hand (aficionado)
- Daft (stupid or foolish)
- Demister (defroster)
- Dial (face)
- Dodgy gear (stolen items)
- Dropped (arrested)
- Elmer (an American tourist)
- Fag (cigarette)
- Fancy (to like or take a liking to, to imagine)
- Fiddle (swindle)
- Flaps (ears)
- Get stuffed (go to hell)
- Give over (stop, cease)
- Go spare (get angry)
- Gobsmacked (astonished)
- Graft (hard work, also a grafter is a hard worker)
- Grammar (textbook)
- Grotty (ugly)
- Hoover (to clean/vacuum)
- Indicators (turn signals)
- Jacket potato (baked potato)
- Jakes (men's toilet)
- Jubbly (money)
- Knackered (tired)
- Larder (pantry)
- Lift (elevator)
- Loo (toilet)
- Macintosh (raincoat)
- Mauley (fist)
- Mum (mother)

- Nap hand (a sure thing)
- Noel (coward)
- Nosh (food, snacks)
- Noughts and crosses (tic-tac-toe)
- Nuppence (no money)
- Nutter (a crazy person)
- Oofy (rich)
- Owt (anything)
- Park a custard (vomit)
- Pasty (a filled pastry, rhymes with "nasty")
- Pissed (drunk)
- Pit (bed)
- Post (mail)
- Prezzie (present)
- Queue (a line, as in waiting in line)
- Quid (British pound)
- Ramp (swindle)
- Rhino (money)
- Scroat (a despicable person)
- Scrotty (dirty)
- Scrummy (delicious)
- Shag (to have sex)
- Spanner (wrench)
- Sparkers (unconscious)
- Tea (evening meal)
- Torch (flashlight)
- Tots (shot of booze)
- Trainspotter (a nerd)
- Unmentionables (underwear)
- Vest (undershirt)
- Vet (to inspect)
- Wedge (sandwich)
- Wonky (off kilter)
- Zizz (a nap)

Cockney Rhyming Slang

Cockney rhyming slang is famous throughout the English-speaking world for its humor and imaginative use of rhyming words to refer to other items. It also once served as a sort of code that allowed the people of ill repute in London's East End to communicate with each other without being understood by outsiders, though it is not clear where it originally came from. The slang itself became best known due to the efforts of law enforcement officials, who published manuals to teach their officers how to understand the language used by the criminals of the area.

- Adam and Eve (believe)
- Airs and graces (faces)
- Alligator (later)
- Almond rocks (socks)
- Apples and pears (stairs)
- Aris (arse)
- Aristotle (bottle)
- Army and Navy (gravy)
- Arnold Palmer (farmer)
- Babbling brook (crook)
- Bacon and eggs (legs)
- Baked potato (see you later)
- Bangers and mash (cash or slash) (urinate)
- Biscuit and cheese (knees)
- Bottle and stopper (copper) (police)
- Bottle of beer (ear)
- Bottle of sauce (horse)
- Bottle of scotch (watch)
- Bottle of water (daughter)
- Bread and honey (money)
- Bricks and mortar (daughter)
- Bright and breezy (easy)
- Brown bread (dead)
- Bubble and squeak (someone of Greek origin) (derogatory)—may have other meanings, such as beak (which somehow stands for magistrate); also a dish made with mashed potatoes, cabbage (typically), and various leftovers
- Bucket and pail (jail)
- Hammer and saws (laws) (police)
- Near and far (car)

Australian Slang

English-speaking people all over the world have created their own regional expressions, and the Aussies were as colorful and imaginative as any. Australian slang was not well known outside of Australia until the *Crocodile Dundee* movies, which introduced the world to some of their best-known sayings.

- Ankle biter (a kid)
- Apples (all right, as in, "He'll be apples.")
- Barbie (barbeque)
- Beaut/beauty (fantastic)
- Bities (biting insects)
- Blue (fight: "They had a blue at the watering hole the other night.")
- Bush (the wild outdoors, the Outback)
- Bush oyster (nasal mucus)
- Bush telly (campfire)
- Bushranger (outlaw, highwayman)
- Cactus (nonfunctional)
- Chunder (vomit, also "liquid laugh")
- Cobber (friend)
- Coldie (a beer)
- Corker (something excellent)
- Cut lunch (sandwiches)
- Dead horse (tomato sauce)
- Digger (soldier)
- Dipstick (loser)
- Docket (bill, receipt)
- G'day (hello)
- Good onya (good for you, well done)
- Gutful of piss (drunk)
- Knock (to criticize, also a knocker is someone who criticizes)
- Lob/lob in (to visit, drop in for a visit)
- Mate (friend)
- Matilda (a bed roll)
- Mystery bag (sausage)
- No worries (no problem)
- Nuddy, in the (naked)
- Piss (beer)
- Porky (a lie, from "pork pie")
- Quid (making a living)
- Rage (party, also "rage on" is to party on)
- Rotten (drunk)
- Schooner (a large glass of beer)
- Seppo (an American)
- Sheila (a woman)
- Spit the dummy (get angry)
- Stoked (pleased)
- Swagman (hobo)
- Tucker (food)
- Veg out (relax in front of the TV)
- Walkabout (traditional walk through the Outback done as a rite of passage by the Aborigines)
- Whacker (idiot)
- Woop Woop (any small, unimportant town—generic term)
- Yabber (talk a lot)

Yiddish Terms

A lot of Yiddish words have become common expressions in the English language, although not all speakers know the literal meanings of the words.

- Bupkis/bopkis (nothing or of very little value)
- Chutzpah (nerve, guts)
- Cockamamie (ridiculous)
- Farklempt (choked up)
- Futz (to fiddle around, fuss, procrastinate)
- Ganif (thief)
- Gelt (money)
- Glitch (minor malfunction)
- Goyem (non-Jews)
- Klezmer (a musician)
- Klutz (someone who is clumsy)
- Kvetch (to complain or to be a complainer)
- Mazel tov (congratulations)
- Megila (a long, drawn-out story)
- Mensch (a good man)
- Meshuggenah (crazy)
- Mish mash (disorganized, a mess)
- Mishegas (a crazy situation, a mess)
- Nebish (nerd)
- Nosh (snack)
- Nudge (a pest, pronounced *nuj* more or less)

- Oy/oy vey (exclamation, generally disapproving)
- Schiksa (non-Jewish woman)
- Schlemiel (screw-up, dope, fool)
- Schlepping (carrying something heavy, doing a lot of walking and carrying)
- Schlimazel (someone who's unlucky)
- Schmaltz (chicken fat, also overly sentimental)
- Schmatta (a rag—often refers to "this old dress?")
-
- Schmootz (dirt)
- Schmooze (to mingle, make small talk)
- Schnapps (booze)
- Shlump (a slob)
- Shmendrik (a stupid person)
- Shpiel (or Spiel) (a long speech, a sales job)
- Shpilkes (nervousness)
- Shtick (a routine or repetitive behavior)
- Shtup (have sex)
- Yente (busybody, gossip)

Rasta Slang

English has taken on distinctly local flavors in various parts of the world, and none more colorful than the slang that developed in Jamaica and the Caribbean, particularly among the Rastafarians. This slang became better known to the rest of the world through the reggae music of Bob Marley, Jimmy Cliff, and others, as well as in movies such as *The Harder They Come.*

- Babylon (the establishment)
- Bad (good)
- Bald-head (someone who works for Babylon, no dreads)
- Beast (policeman)
- Black up (smoke weed)
- Bucky (homemade gun)
- Clot (means "cloth" but common in nasty expressions, such as bumbo clot, meaning butt cloth or toilet paper)
- Craven (greedy)
- Darkers (sunglasses)
- Dogheart (a cold, cruel person)
- Dreadlocks (traditional hairstyle, never combed or cut)
- Fas' (to be rude or meddling)
- Ganja (marijuana)
- Gorgon (really cool dreadlocks)
- Haile Selassie (revered Ethiopian leader considered to be the Lion of Judah and personification of the Almighty)
- I & I (we, us)
- I-man (me, mine)
- I-rey (a greeting, or can mean excellent)
- Irie (greeting, or as an adjective, powerful/pleasing)
- Jah (god)
- Ku ya (look here)
- Leggo beas' (out of control, as in "let go, beast")
- Manners (discipline or punishment, for instance, "The town was under heavy manners" means they have a curfew or there is martial law)

Modern (2005 or So) Street Slang

Slang continues to evolve, and there's no way to keep up with modern terminology. Here are some reasonably contemporary expressions, but new words and phrases seem to enter our language almost daily, so no list of contemporary slang will ever be completely up to date. The best sources of information are songs, stories, and websites devoted to youth culture and to different ethnic group interests.

- All that (to have good qualities)
- Banging (doing gang-related things)
- Barrio/varrio (the neighborhood)
- Base head (someone addicted to cocaine)
- Bo/bud (marijuana)
- Bone out (to leave)
- Boo ya (totally fine, dope)
- Booty (bad or not good, bottom, can mean stolen goods)
- Breakdown (shotgun)
- Bucket (old car)
- Buster (a young person who wants to be a gang member)
- Cap (to shoot at)
- Chingasos (fighting)
- Chota (police)
- Click up (to get along well with a homeboy)
- Cluck (someone who smokes cocaine)
- Cop a 'tude (have an attitude)
- Crunked (high)
- Cuzin (friend)
- Dis (to disrespect someone)
- Drockers (great sound system)
- Drop a dime (to rat someone out)
- Flag (a handkerchief in gang colors)
- Flying colors (wearing gang colors)
- Gat (gun)
- Generation Alpha (people born after 1999)
- Generation X (people born between 1980 and 1989)
- Generation Z (people born between 1990 and 1999)
- Glazing (sleeping at school or work with eyes open)
- Green (money)
- Ho (whore or sleazy woman)
- Hook up (to connect, mostly to have some kind of sexual encounter)
- I hear that/I heard that (I agree)
- Jawn (all purpose noun, can refer to just about anything)
- Jet (leave)
- Kickin' it (just relaxing)
- Laters (see you later)
- Lit up (shot at)
- Loc (locos)
- Mad dog (a hard stare)
- Metrosexual (an urban male who spends a lot on appearance but isn't homosexual)
- Murk (hurt, kill, murder)
- No diggity (for sure)
- O.G. (original gangster, may refer to someone who has killed someone)
- On hit (good, excellent)
- Peace'n (not looking for trouble)
- Peeps (people)
- Phat (way good)
- Popo (police)
- Posse (group of friends)
- Shorti (girlfriend)
- Simon (yes)
- Slinging rock (selling cocaine)
- Soda (cocaine)
- Strapped (carrying a gun)
- To be down with (to be in agreement with)
- Whadup or whadup dawg (just saying hi)

Cops and Criminals Slang

This is a compilation of slang from several eras that's specific to cops, criminals, and parolees. You'll find modern terms, as well as terms that were in use back in the '20s, '30s, and '40s. Many of these terms are appropriate to modern usage, even those that seem older.

- Ad seg (administrative segregation—parolee)
- AFIS (Automated Fingerprint Identification System)
- Alphas (someone with prior contact with the police or a prior record)
- APS (national Automated Property System database)
- Assist (to call for backup)
- At large (someone who is wanted or a suspect or parolee who is not accounted for)
- Auto burg (a locked auto break-in)
- Backup (to call for help at a specific location/event, or a noun referring to someone there to assist)

- Bad guy (a crime suspect, a serious criminal)
- Bag man (guy who collects bribes or picks up protection money)
- Bail (1. a security deposit or bond to guarantee someone's appearance in court; 2. to leave)
- Bars (lieutenant's insignia, also a promotion to lieutenant)
- Beat cop (a policeman who patrols a particular area, his "beat")
- Beater (an old beat-up car)
- Beef (a crime)
- Blow (cocaine)
- Blow away (to kill someone, particularly with a gun)
- Bogey (a cop)
- BOLO (cop term standing for "be on the lookout")
- Book (1. processing a criminal into the system; 2. to go or leave hurriedly)
- Box (polygraph, lie detector)
- Box lab (a small-scale clandestine drug laboratory)
- Brass (the higher officers in the police department)
- Bucket (jail)
- Bullet (generally references a one-year prison term, in addition to its normal meaning as ammunition)
- Burg (short for burglary)
- Burgin' (a crime spree of burglaries)
- Bus (cop term for an ambulance)
- Bust (1. to arrest or raid a location; also, as a noun, an arrest or raid; 2. to reduce someone's rank; 3. to break or smash up something; 4. to hit someone, as in "bust them in the chops")
- Buzz (a badge, or to display a badge)
- C/O (correctional officer)
- Can (jail/prison)
- Case (1. a crime investigation and report; 2. a nut case)
- Case number (the number assigned to a case when it comes through dispatch)
- Cash in (to die)
- Centerpunch (to broadside, as in a traffic accident)
- Check-by (a police call for minor assistance)
- Chip/chippy (1. girlfriend or mistress of a cop; 2. "Chips" is also a nickname for the California Highway Patrol; 3. infrequent use of narcotics)
- Choir practice (a police party or social gathering)
- Chop shop (where stolen cars are disassembled for parts to be sold)
- Cite (issue a ticket)
- Cite out (release from jail on a signed promise to appear, no bail required)
- Citizen (someone not in the police force)
- Civilian (someone not in the police force)
- Clan lab (place where methamphetamine or other drugs are made)
- CLETS (data interchange switcher for state data files, outside information)
- Clink (prison)
- Clobber (1. to hit someone; 2. to severely criticize; 3. to thoroughly defeat)
- Clock (1. to hit someone, usually a serious assault; 2. to notice something)
- Clout (stealing from an unlocked vehicle)
- Code (meal break, from Code-7)
- Code-1 (no particular hurry, whenever convenient)
- Code-2 (some urgency, get moving)
- Code-3 (all-out emergency, lights and sirens)
- Code-33 (emergency situation, emergency radio traffic only)
- Code-4 (under control, no further assistance necessary)
- Code-5 (stakeout)
- Code-6 (on foot, walking patrol)
- Code-7 (meal break)
- Cold (old, past event)
- Cold paper (report on an old crime)
- Cold turkey (1. quitting drug addiction without help; 2. someone with a cold personality; 3. procedural methods)
- Come across (to comply with an order or request)
- Comes back (information from a remote source)
- Complainant (someone who has called the police into the situation or who is pressing charges)
- Complaint (the formal criminal charge)

- Conk (1. the head; 2. a blow to the head)
- Conked out (1. to stop functioning; 2. to fall asleep or pass out; 3. to die)
- Cook (1. make methamphetamine; 2. to prepare drugs for shooting up)
- Cooker (someone who makes methamphetamine)
- Cool (1. good; 2. it's okay, as in "It's cool with me"; 3. "It's worth a cool 10 Gs.")
- Cool it (1. chill; 2. stop what you're doing)
- Cop (1. to steal; 2. to get something or to win something; 3. to take something illicit, as in "cop a feel"; 4. the police, the Man)
- Cop a plea (to enter a guilty plea to a lesser charge)
- Cop out (to avoid doing something expected of you)
- Cop the plate (to take down a license plate number)
- Copper (police)
- CORI (Criminal Offender Record Information)
- Cough up (to give something demanded of you, willingly or not)
- Cover (assisting another officer)
- Cover unit (an officer on roving assignment to assist)
- Crank (methamphetamine)
- Cranked (stoned on methamphetamine)
- Crash (a motor vehicle accident)
- Creating (short for "creating a disturbance")
- Crook (a criminal or suspected criminal)
- Cross (short for "cross street")
- CSI (crime scene investigator)
- D.L. (driver's license)
- Deal (1. to buy and sell illegal drugs; 2. to cope with a situation)
- Deck (a package of narcotics)
- Dee wee (police term for a DWI [Driving While Intoxicated])
- Detail (an assignment or service call)
- Deuce (a drunk driver)
- Dime (10, $10 worth of narcotics (also "dime bag"), 10 years in jail)
- Dirty (guilty)
- Do (1. to kill someone, also "do in"; 2. to take drugs; 3. to cheat someone, as in "do them out of their cash")
- DOB (date of birth)
- Dog call (a police term for a boring and unserious assignment)
- Dope (illegal narcotics)
- Dopin' (participation in use/sales and manufacture of illegal drugs)
- Dorm (housing unit)
- Double-deuce gat (.22 caliber pistol)
- Down for (guilty of or responsible for)
- Down paper (reports that need to be prepared)
- Drive-by (to go somewhere for observation)
- Drop (to take acid)
- Drop a dime/dime (1. make a call; 2. to inform on someone—a term used since the '20s when a pay phone call cost a dime)
- Druggie (drug addict or anyone who uses drugs)
- DT (street slang for a detective)
- DUI/DWI (driving under the influence or driving while intoxicated)
- Duke in (to introduce or vouch for someone within criminal circles)
- DV (domestic violence)
- E (Ecstasy)
- Feebie (FBI agent)
- Felon (someone convicted of a felony)
- Felony (a serious crime that carries a prison sentence if the felon is found guilty)
- FI (field interview)
- Finger (1. to identify or point out; 2. to inform on)
- Fink (a snitch)
- Fixit ticket (a citation for mechanical problems, no fine imposed if fixed within a specified time)
- Flash (1. to remember something suddenly; 2. to expose yourself in public, also "flasher"); 3. something ostentatious; 4. the rush associated with a drug hit)
- Flatfoot (a cop, particularly a beat cop)
- Floater (a corpse found floating in water)
- FST (field sobriety test)

- FTA (failure to appear at a court hearing)
- FTP (failure to pay a court-imposed fine)
- Fuzz (police)
- G.P. (general population in prison)
- Gaff (1. a trick used to rig a game, or as a verb, to rig a game; 2. abuse; 3. to swindle someone)
- Gangbanger (a gang member)
- Garnish (extorted money, especially by a jailer from a new prisoner)
- Gat (a gun, generally a pistol)
- Gated out (released from prison)
- Go by complaint (charging a crime by affidavit without prior arrest)
- GOA (gone on arrival)
- Going down (something happening, as in "It's going down at 3.")
- Good for it (they did it, or at least they could have done it)
- Goon (1. someone hired to threaten and/or harm enemies or victims; 2. an idiot)
- Guff (1. bull; 2. back talk)
- Gyp (to cheat or swindle)
- Hall (juvie, the juvenile hall)
- Hard-ass (someone who follows the rules to the letter)
- Heat (firearm, police, problems, adverse attention)
- Heavy (a mobster)
- Hit (information match found; i.e., warrant is outstanding)
- Ho (a prostitute)
- Hook (1. a tow truck; 2. the driver of a tow truck; 3. an auto wrecker; 4. as a verb, to arrest or to tow a car)
- Hook up (To arrest, or more specifically, to handcuff)
- Hooked up with (involved with, as in a relationship)
- Hooker (a street prostitute)
- Hoopty (a dilapidated old car)
- Hoosegow (jail)
- Hootch (1. liquor, particularly low-grade or bootlegged; 2. marijuana)
- Joint (1. a place, generally low-class; 2. a marijuana cigarette; 3. prison)
- Hot (1. freshly stolen or anything stolen; 2. someone wanted by the cops; 3. descriptive of ability, as in, "He's really hot with videogames"; 4. sexy or otherwise impressive, as in a "hot chick" or a "hot sportscar"; 5. being lucky, as in "a hot streak"; 6. something current, opposite of "cold")
- Hot prowl (burglary of an occupied dwelling)
- Hustle/hustled (1. to acquire or peddle something, as in, "He hustled stolen car parts all over the city"; 2. to put pressure on someone to buy or do something; 3. to play a con game by pretending to be a beginner at something, as in hustling pool; 4. to get something illegally; 5. as a noun, a con or swindle)
- Hustler (1. a street prostitute; 2. someone who hustles others)
- IA (Internal Affairs)
- Ice (1. diamonds; 2. methamphetamine; 3. to kill someone; 4. a scalper's profit over list price on a ticket to an event; 5. to clinch or ensure victory)
- IFO (in front of)
- III (someone who has a record from another state)
- Impound (taking and storing a car for various reasons, also the place the car is taken)
- In custody (under arrest, under control)
- In progress (happening now)
- Incident (refers to a police action that does not require a formal report)
- Infraction (a minor violation punishable by fines only)
- Ink (tattoo)
- Intel (information/intelligence)
- Invoke (short for "invoke the 5th Amendment" or exercise one's right to remain silent)
- Issue (the original crime of a prisoner or parolee)
- J (refers to kids under 18—juveniles)
- Jam (to get out, split, scram, blow this popstand)
- Jam up (annoy, anger, harass)

Part IV

- Juice (political power/influence)
- Junk (drugs, typically heroin [archaic])
- K&A (knock and announce)
- Kite (a note or letter, parolee or prisoner)
- Knock and announce (process for serving a search warrant)
- Knock and talk (go to talk to someone without a warrant)
- Lawyer up (to request or to be represented by an attorney)
- Legit (legitimate)
- Lifer (1. a career military individual; 2. someone serving a life sentence)
- Light 'em up (turn on emergency lights and siren)
- Line-up (daily meeting at beginning of day for the patrol team)
- Lo (legal owner)
- Loaded (stoned on drugs)
- Loo (police slang for "lieutenant")
- Loot (money or what is gained in a heist)
- LT (lieutenant)
- Magazine/mag (where the ammunition goes in a gun)
- Mahaska (a concealed firearm)
- Make the bucket (get arrested)
- Mark (a potential victim of a swindle, robbery, etc.)
- Masher (a man who forces himself on women)
- MDS (Mobile Data System; the patrol vehicle video screen)
- MDT (Mobile Data Terminal; the patrol vehicle video screen)
- Mechanical (traffic citation for equipment violation)
- Mickey Finn (a drink drugged with knockout drops)
- Miranda (legal statement informing a suspect of his/her right to remain silent)
- Misdemeanor (a crime less serious than a felony with lower punishments)
- Mitt (hand/fist)
- Monkey (1. someone who is made a fool of; 2. a term for drug addiction)
- Mover (traffic citation for a hazardous violation)
- Mug (1. a victim; 2. make faces at, taunt, harass)
- Mug shot (the picture taken when someone is arrested)
- MUPS (Missing Persons database)
- Nail (1. to stop or capture; 2. to catch or find someone out; 3. to take down someone or something; 4. to do something really well)
- Narc (narcotics officer)
- NCF (No Complaint Filed)
- NCIC (National Crime Information Center, group of national crime databases)
- Nick (steal)
- Nickel (5—$5 worth of narcotics, 5 years in jail)
- No sweat (no problem)
- Off the hook (to be released from blame or charges)
- Off/offed (1. go away; 2. to kill or be killed)
- On ice (1. certainty of success; 2. in reserve; 3. out of circulation; 4. in a bad situation, as in "on thin ice")
- On the box (taking a lie-detector test)
- On-view (witnessed)
- OZ (ounce of narcotics, usually heroin)
- P.C. (protective custody)
- Packin' (carrying a firearm)
- Palooka (originally a mediocre fighter, now a big dumb guy)
- Paper (1. report and investigation; 2. search warrant)
- Parkers (citations for parking violations)
- PAS (Preliminary Alcohol Screening device, pronounced "pazz")
- Pat down (a quick search for weapons)
- Patsy (a victim of cheating or ridicule)
- PC (Probable Cause)
- Perimeter (exterior positions at a crime scene)
- Perp (the person who did it, or at least a suspect—the perpetrator)
- PERS (state Personnel Retirement System)
- Photo lineup (a grouping of six photos, one of which is the suspect, used for witnesses to identify)
- Pig (a cop)
- Plastic (credit card or ATM)
- PO (Probation or Parole Officer)
- Points (a way of assessing the risks involved with a prison inmate when released)

- Poke (to hit someone)
- Pokey (jail/prison)
- Pop (arrest)
- Po-po (police officer)
- Precursors (chemicals used in the manufacture of illegal drugs, especially methamphetamine)
- Prelim (preliminary examination)
- Priors (previous arrests)
- Prison (area of confinement for criminals)
- Prisoner (someone in custody or an inmate)
- Probation search (searching the home or car of someone on probation)
- Program (how a prisoner does his/her time)
- Pruno (homemade prison alcohol)
- PX (1. same as prelim; 2. polygraph examination)
- QOA (quiet on arrival)
- Rabbit (police term for a fleeing suspect)
- Railroad tracks (insignia of captain, promotion to captain)
- Rap (1. a criminal charge; 2. a reprimand or bad mark, such as, "He has a bad rap"; 3. beat the rap—to get away with)
- Rap sheet (official police or FBI record of criminal arrests and dispositions)
- Rat (1. a prior criminal record [priors]; 2. a snitch or any basic louse)
- Red-P (red phosphorus, a chemical in making methamphetamine)
- Reg (generally refers to the status of a vehicle registration)
- Reg out (expired vehicle registration)
- Respond (to go to the scene)
- Responsible (a crime suspect)
- Ride (a vehicle)
- Rig (the paraphernalia involved in shooting drugs)
- Ripoff (a thief or a theft, also "rip off"—a verb meaning to steal)
- RO (registered owner, usually of a motor vehicle)
- Rock (1. crack cocaine; 2. a big jewel, usually a diamond)
- Roll (to confess to a crime and/or to cooperate with the police)
- Roll up (to arrest someone)
- Roscoe (firearm)
- RP (reporting party—whoever called the cops)
- Run (check for warrants or the status of a vehicle, as in "run the plates")
- Run in (to arrest)
- Run out (obtain data on a person or vehicle)
- Sales (drug sales)
- Sap/saphead (a dope, also a club)
- Sarge (sergeant)
- Scag (heroin)
- Score (1. to complete a robbery; 2. to buy illegal drugs; 3. to have success with someone of the opposite sex)
- Scratch (to issue a traffic citation)
- Screw (1. a prison guard; 2. to have sex)
- Scum/scumbag (someone you definitely don't like or respect)
- Search clause (a condition of probation that allows the person to be searched at any time)
- Sector (a geographical division of a city)
- Sergeant (someone who supervises police officers or detectives)
- Shank (a prison-made knife)
- Shiv (a knife or other cutting weapon)
- Shop (police use this term to refer to their patrol car)
- SHU (security housing unit—parolee term for prison)
- Skate (1. to evade being caught or being charged with a crime; 2. to evade work)
- Slam/slammer (jail)
- Sleeved (tattooed arms)
- Sling (indiscriminate sales or processing of narcotics)
- Slug (bullet)
- Smack (heroin)
- Snatch (a kidnapping or to kidnap)
- Snitch (1. to inform on someone; 2. to steal; 3. an informer; 4. a thief)
- Social (social security number)
- Speed (methamphetamine)
- Speedball (a mix of cocaine with heroin or an amphetamine that's taken by injection)
- Spike (a hypodermic needle)
- Spun (messed up by use of narcotics)
- Stick-up (robbery)
- Stiff (1. a corpse; 2. someone who's drunk; 3. as a verb, to cheat or refuse to pay what's owed)

Part IV

- Stooge (an informer, a stool pigeon)
- Stoolie (another word for stool pigeon)
- Stop (a vehicle pullover or pedestrian encounter)
- Streetwalker (a street prostitute)
- Strike (1. conviction of a crime [referring to the three-strikes law]; 2. stripes [sergeant's insignia])
- Stub (a traffic citation)
- Sucker (1. an easy mark, someone to take advantage of; 2. a generic reference to people and things, as in "He's a real dumb sucker," or "Pass me that sucker over there.")
- Super court (superior court)
- Sus (suspect)
- Sustained (refers to a personnel complaint upheld by Internal Affairs)
- SVS (state Stolen Vehicle System)
- Sweat (to interrogate or to get information from someone under duress)
- Sweat bullets (excessive sweating, generally as a result of anxiety, fear, or worry)
- Sweat out (to wait or to endure something)
- Tacs (prison term for tattoos)
- Tag (1. to hit or assault or run into; 2. to draw graffiti on something)
- Tagger (serious graffiti artist)
- Take (arrest)
- Take paper (make an official report)
- Take the rap (to take the punishment or blame for someone else)
- Talking smack (insulting, threatening, harassing, verbally abusing)
- Tank (jail, particularly the community cell you're brought to when first arrested)
- Tat (tattoo, prison or jail tattoos in particular)
- T-bone (to broadside, as in a traffic accident)
- Tier (levels in a parolee housing unit)
- Tipped up (gang-related)
- Tool (someone who does someone else's dirty work)
- Topped out (off parole)
- Tough (1. too bad; 2. great; 3. durable)
- Tough it out (to get through something difficult)
- Tracks (marks caused by damage to veins from injecting narcotics)
- Trey-eight gat (.38 caliber revolver)
- Trick (1. what a prostitute does with a john; 2. a theft)
- TRO (Temporary Restraining Order)
- Troll (1. to patrol; 2. as a noun, a patrol)
- Turf (1. a territory controlled by a certain person or gang; 2. someone's specific area of influence, expertise, or control)
- Turfed (killed)
- Unit (a police vehicle)
- Valid (meaning someone's driver's license is not expired or suspended)
- Verbal (1. confirmation of facts by voice; 2. verbal warning instead of a traffic citation)
- Visual (able to see, under observation)
- Walk (to skate, to be released without a charge)
- Warner (same as "verbal")
- Warrant (an arrest order issued by the courts)
- Waste (to kill someone)
- Weed (marijuana)
- Weirdo (someone strange or dangerously strange)
- Went down (happened)
- Whack (to kill someone)
- Whacked out (seriously stoned)
- Wobbler (a crime that can be charged as a felony or a misdemeanor)
- X-unit (portable radio carried by officer)
- Yard (the outdoor recreation area of a prison)
- Yolked (muscular)

Buzzwords

I distinguish buzzwords from slang because I think of buzzwords as those terms used in specific circumstances and/or by specific groups. For instance, in airports you are asked to report to the "white courtesy telephone" and to move down the "concourse." In a court of law, you might hear a lawyer say, "I object," and the judge say, "Sustained." Or the judge may require the attorneys to "approach the bench." In normal life, you might refer to the automated teller machine as the ATM.

I've listed some specific groups and locations/circumstances in which there occurs specific terminology, with a few examples under each category. Hopefully, this will inspire you to explore more sources and find more examples for any type of group you will be depicting in your games.

Keep in mind that some terminology changes, particularly with the increase in political correctness and the growing use of euphemisms to describe uncomfortable subjects. The use of PC terms depends largely on the timeframe and the culture of those speaking, as well as the intimacy of those conversing. People do tend to be less politically correct with people they are close to than with strangers or professional contacts.

Note that you can always make up your own buzzwords and slang, especially if you are creating a completely fictional location or setting.

Medical Terminology

Like other groups with unique vocabulary, the medical profession has created a lot of terms and expressions, some of which are simply useful while others seem to serve as a proprietary code among those in the know. I've divided this section into two lists. The first is that of the old-time historical terms, in case you're dealing with doctors from the 19th century or something like that. The next list is more contemporary, in case you're dealing with doctors or hospitals of the 20th or 21st century. Beyond that, you're on your own. Neither of these lists is complete, but they can give you a taste of medical slang.

Historical Terms

Modern medicine has a rich and complex language that has developed and changed over the last 50 years, but if you're basing a game in an earlier time period, you might find it adds realism to refer to some more antiquated terms, as long as the player won't be overly confused by them. Here are just a few terms from historical medical terminology:

- Ague (malarial fever)
- Apoplexy (paralysis due to stroke)
- Bad blood (syphilis)
- Black fever (acute infection with high temperature, dark-red skin lesions, and high mortality rate)
- Black Plague or Black Death (bubonic plague)
- Black vomit (vomiting old black blood due to ulcers or yellow fever)
- Bloody flux (bloody stools)
- Bright's disease (chronic inflammatory disease of the kidneys)
- Bronze John (yellow fever)
- Camp fever (typhus, a.k.a. camp diarrhea)
- Canine madness (rabies, hydrophobia)
- Chilblain (swelling of extremities caused by exposure to cold)
- Congestion (any collection of fluid in an organ, such as the lungs)
- Consumption (tuberculosis)
- Delirium tremens (hallucinations due to alcoholism)
- Dock fever (yellow fever)
- Dropsy (edema [swelling] often caused by kidney or heart disease)
- Enteric fever (typhoid fever)
- Flux (an excessive flow or discharge of fluid like hemorrhage or diarrhea)

- French pox (syphilis)
- Grippe/grip (influenza-like symptoms)
- Horrors (delirium tremens)
- Jail fever (typhus)
- Lumbago (back pain)
- Miasma (poisonous vapors thought to infect the air)
- Milk fever (caused by contaminated milk)
- Nervous prostration (extreme exhaustion from an inability to control physical and mental activities)
- Plague (an acute, febrile, highly infectious disease with a high fatality rate)
- Putrid fever (diphtheria)
- Rickets (disease of skeletal system)
- Rose cold (hay fever or nasal symptoms of an allergy)
- Scarlet fever (a disease characterized by a red rash)
- Screws (rheumatism)
- Scrivener's palsy (writer's cramp)
- Shakes (delirium tremens)
- St. Vitus's dance (condition characterized by involuntary jerking motions)
- Viper's dance (St. Vitus's dance)
- Winter fever (pneumonia)
- Yellow jacket (yellow fever)

Medical Modern

The world of modern medicine is loaded with terms. Some are the kinds of expressions you see on TV shows and movies with doctors and hospitals in them. Others are a bit more private and not really known by the general public. Although these latter expressions are not as useful in creating realistic scripts, they could still be considered, depending on the context or if you have a way for players to understand their meaning. I've included a few choice ones as examples. There are many, many more.

- "Calling Doctor Blue" (meaning roughly, "I don't understand this case. Can someone else come and try to figure it out?")
- Benny (a patient on benefits)
- Blade (surgeon)
- Blood suckers/leeches (lab techs who take blood)
- Bordeaux (blood-stained urine)
- Coffin dodger (elderly patient, particularly one who has survived against expectations)
- DSTO (veterinary expression meaning "dog smarter than owner")
- Freud squad (psychiatrists)
- Gassers (anesthetists)
- GPO (good for parts only)
- Meat hooks (surgical instruments)
- Rose cottage (mortuary)
- STAT (abbreviation of the Latin *statim*, meaning immediately)
- TMB (too many birthdays)
- Treat 'n street (emergency-room term for patients treated and released)

Military Terms

Here are a few choice excerpts from the extensive slang and jargon used by various military personnel. These are sample lists, greatly reduced in length, just to give you a sample of some of the colorful terms you could use in games.

Pilots

- Angels (refers to 1,000 feet in altitude—10,000 feet would be "angels ten")
- Angle of attack or A.O.A. (the wing angle relative to the forward flight path of the plane)
- Angles (refers to the relative position of a plane in a dogfight, with a zero angle being directly behind the enemy)
- Augured in (crashed)

- Bag (1. as a verb, to collect or acquire; 2. as a noun, a flight suit or anti-exposure suit)
- Bandit (an enemy plane)
- Basement (the hangar deck of an aircraft carrier)
- Bat turn (a tight turn)
- Big chicken dinner (bad conduct discharge)
- Bingo (minimum fuel required for safe return to base)
- Birds (aircraft)
- Blower (afterburner)
- Blue water ops (aircraft carrier operations that take place beyond the reach of land bases)
- Bogey (unidentified, potentially hostile aircraft)
- Bohica (bend over, here it comes again)
- Bought the farm (died)
- Bravo Zulu (great job)
- Burner (afterburner)
- CAG (Commander Air Group)
- Cat shot (an airplane launch from an aircraft carrier by means of catapult)
- Check six (checking the rear for danger)
- Cherubs (altitudes under 1,000 feet—cherubs five means 500 feet)
- Envelope (the maximum performance of an aircraft, as in "pushing the envelope")
- Fox One, Two, etc. (radio call that refers to firing of air-to-air missiles—Fox One is a Sparrow, Fox Two refers to a Sidewinder, and Fox Three refers to a Phoenix missile)
- G/Gs (forces equal to equivalent gravity—3 Gs is three times the pressure of normal gravity)
- Go juice (fuel)
- Goo (bad weather that causes extreme visibility problems)
- Head on a swivel (keeping constant watch for enemies in all directions, also known as "doing the Linda Blair")
- HUD (heads-up display)
- INS (inertial navigation system)
- Jink (threat evasion by using a violent maneuver)
- Judy (radio call indicating that an enemy is in sight and you are about to intercept)
- Lights out (radar off)
- Lost the bubble (got confused)
- LSO (landing signal officer)
- Mother (boat from which an aircraft is deployed or from which it launched)
- Music (electronic countermeasures designed to deceive enemy radar)
- No joy (failed to make visual sighting)
- Padlocked (having a bogey locked in sights)
- Passing gas (what a refueling plane does)
- Pinging on (paying close attention to)
- Plumber (an unskilled pilot)
- Pole (control stick)
- Pucker factor (an informal measurement of how scary something is)
- Punch out (eject)
- Roof (flight deck of the aircraft carrier)
- SAM (surface-to-air missile)
- SAR (search and rescue)
- Sortie (a single-aircraft mission)
- State (in radio communication, refers to the amount of fuel [in hours/minutes] you have before you run out and fall [splash]—the interchange would be "Say your state," answered by, "Four plus three five to splash," or 4 hours 35 minutes)
- Tank (refuel)
- Texaco (aerial tanker)
- Throttle back (slow down or go easy)
- Tilly (mobile crane on a carrier flight deck that picks up and moves disabled aircraft)
- Trick or treat (if the aircraft does not successfully land on the current pass, it will need refueling)
- Washout (failing to make it through flight school)
- Waveoff (signal from LSO telling a pilot not to land)
- Whiskey Charlie (means who cares?)
- Zero-Dark-Thirty (refers to the time after midnight and before dawn)

Nautical

- 99 (precedes a radio call describing a group of aircraft sighted)
- Abaft (aft of any point in the ship—for instance, the bridge is abaft the bow)
- Acey deucy (a term for backgammon)
- Angles and dangles (submarine term referring to steep ascent or descent used to perform rapid turns)
- Avast (meaning, "Stop what you're doing.")
- Aweigh (term meaning that the anchor is no longer in contact with the sea bottom—the term for raising the anchor is "weigh")
- Balls or four balls (midnight)
- Belay (to secure, to stop, or to disregard, depending on context)
- Bilge rat (someone who works in the engineering decks)
- Binnacle (the pedestal upon which the compass is mounted)
- Binnacle list (the list of those who are sick or injured in sick bay)
- Biologics (sounds of sea life picked up on sonar)
- Bird farm (aircraft carrier)
- Birds free (permission to fire missiles)
- Birds tight (no permission to fire missiles)
- Blue water (deep water)
- Bone dome (also "hardhat" or "brain bucket"—a flight helmet)
- Boomer (missile submarine)
- Boondoggle (travel more for fun than function)
- Boot (a rookie or new recruit)
- Brown water (shallow water)
- Bug juice (typical beverage aboard ships, color similar to Kool-Aid, consisting largely of ascorbic acid and used to clean and strip various parts of a ship)
- Bulkhead (wall)
- Bulldog (a harpoon cruise missile)
- Buster (maximum speed of an aircraft attainable without afterburners)
- Careen (to lay a ship on its side in shallow water, usually for maintenance on the hull)
- Check valve (someone who helps themselves but not others)
- Class alpha fire (a fire that leaves ashes)
- Class bravo fire (a fire with flaming liquids)
- Class charlie fire (an electrical fire)
- Class delta fire (special situation fires, such as burning metal or possibly a deep-fat fryer on fire)
- Coffee pot (a nuclear reactor, also a teakettle)
- Coffin (bed, also "rack")
- Commodore (former term for a one-star admiral)
- Condition 1 (general quarters: battle stations alert)
- Condition 2 (a general quarters alert sometimes used on larger ships)
- Condition 3 (wartime readiness condition where about half the ship's weapons are in a ready and manned state)
- Condition 4 (peacetime readiness)
- Condition 5 (peacetime, in port status)
- Conn (can refer to responsibility for steering and engine orders, as in "I have the conn"—also can refer to the conning tower of a submarine or any general area from which conn orders are given)
- Crash and dash (touch-and-go landing)
- Crash and smash crew (crash and rescue personnel)
- Dead head (the resistance built into a magnetic compass that prevents it from swinging too much)
- Deep six (a call meaning that water is six fathoms deep, but more commonly used to mean throwing something overboard)
- Deflection (adjustment of guns to the left or right—on aircraft, this refers to the angle or lead needed to hit an opposing aircraft)
- Deuce (Browning .50 caliber machine gun)
- DIW (dead in the water)
- Dog watch (short watch periods, generally about two hours)
- ESW (electronic submarine warfare)
- Fart sack (sleeping bag)
- Field day (to scrub or clean the ship)

- Fish eyes (tapioca pudding)
- Flat top (a carrier)
- Floor (a horizontal surface on a ship that does not run the whole length of the ship, as opposed to the deck, which does)
- Flotsam (floating wreckage from a sunken ship)
- Foul deck (flight deck that is unsafe for landing)
- Ganked (stolen)
- Gash (garbage or anything unwanted)
- GLOC (loss of consciousness due to excessive Gs, pronounced "gee-lock")
- Grand slam (radio call for the successful destruction of an air contact)
- Green water (water coming aboard from a swell or wave)
- Grunt (a marine)
- H and I (military mission designed to harass and interdict enemy forces and supply routes)
- Hangar queen (an aircraft that never seems to be in flyable condition)
- Hash marks (stripes on the sleeve of a uniform that signify years of service)
- Hatch (an opening in the deck and its closure)
- Head (toilet)
- Heave the lead (to throw a lead weight overboard to take depth soundings)
- Heave to (to turn into the wind and stop—specific to sailing ships)
- Hook (anchor or the tail hook on a plane used to arrest motion on carrier landings)
- Hot runner (someone who does consistently well)
- Indirect fire (gunnery where the fall of a shot cannot be observed from the firing location and requires someone to report results)
- Influence mine (a mine that doesn't require physical contact to detonate—generally a magnetic or acoustic mine)
- Jetsam (objects thrown over the side of a ship, generally to lighten it—jetsam does not float, whereas flotsam does)
- Joe (coffee, as in "a cup of joe")
- Joker (critically low fuel state)
- Judy (a radio call that indicates that a fighter has contact with an enemy [bogey or bandit] and is ready for intercept)
- Knock it off (a call to stop an aerial engagement for any reason)
- Knot (a measurement of speed that equals one nautical mile per hour)
- Lifer (career military personnel)
- Line (1. rope; 2. the Equator)
- Splice the main brace (1. historically, to repair the main mast supports—a difficult job traditionally rewarded by a shot of rum; 2. Modern usage means to have a drink, presumably after a hard day's work)

General Military

- Beans and bullets (any supplies)
- Blue falcon (someone who doesn't help another soldier)
- Blue-on-blue contact (an incident involving friendly fire)
- Bubblehead (anyone serving on a submarine or in the submarine service)
- Fruit salad (cluster of medals on a soldier's dress uniform)
- Goat rope (an activity directed by a higher authority that's considered to be useless or futile)
- Goldbrick/goldbricker (a soldier who pretends to be sick to avoid duty, a military slacker)
- Grunt (basically, a foot soldier—originally thought to mean "government reject, unfit for normal training")
- Gun (artillery piece—rifles and pistols are referred to as "small arms" and "sidearms" or just called "weapons")
- Hit the silk (to bail out of a plane using a parachute)
- Jet jockey (pilot)

Part IV

- Leatherneck (a marine, from the high leather collar used in original formal uniforms)
- Lima Charlie (loud and clear)
- Puddle pirate (a term for someone in the U.S. Coast Guard)
- Rock (a very stupid soldier, based on "dumber than a box of rocks")
- Rock and roll (fully automatic setting on a weapon)
- Scrambled eggs (decorations on an officer's dress uniform cap)
- Sparks or Sparky (someone who runs radios and electronic devices)
- Spook (a spy)
- Squid/swabbie (a sailor from the U.S. Navy)
- Tango Mike (stands for "thank you much")
- The old man (unit commander)

Some Political Terms

- Abrogation
- Absolutism
- Academic freedom
- Accord
- Accountability
- Acid test
- Activism
- Adjudication
- Adversary system
- Aegis
- Affidavit
- Affirmative action
- Agenda
- Agitprop
- Aide-de-camp
- Alien
- Allegiance
- Alliance
- Ambassador
- Amendment
- Amnesty
- Anarchy
- Annexation
- Bill
- Constituency
- Czar
- Filibuster
- Graft
- Lobby/lobbyist
- Paper trail
- Pork
- Promise
- Special interest
- Stump
- Take it under advisement
- The First Amendment
- Treaty
- Under the table
- Voters

Crime Terminology

- **Aggravated Assault.** An unlawful attack with the intention to inflict physical damage, generally with a weapon capable of causing death or severe bodily harm.
- **Arson.** Intentional or malicious setting of fire or attempt to burn any property, such as buildings, vehicles or personal property. Such an act is considered arson, whether or not there is an intent to defraud.
- **Bias Motivated.** Defines cases in which a person's rights according to state law or the U.S. Constitution have been infringed due to bias of race, color, religion, ancestry, national origin, disability, gender, or sexual orientation, or simply the perception of one or more of these traits. This includes acting as an agent of the law, threatening force or causing injury, damaging or defacing personal property in order to intimidate, and so on.

- **Bomb, Actual.** Refers to any violation of laws governing possession and use, providing to others, and manufacture of explosives and explosive devices.
- **Bomb, Threat.** Refers to falsely reporting a bomb or explosive devise in a public or private location.
- **Burglary.** Unlawfully entering a place with the intention of committing a felony or theft, including an attempted forcible entry.
- **Disturbing the Peace.** Refers to public fighting or threatening to fight, loud behavior or noisemaking, ot the use of offensive language that would reasonably be expected to cause a violent response.
- **Driving Under the Influence.** Driving or operating a vehicle while intoxicated or under the influence of narcotics.
- **FBI Crime Index Offenses.** Also known as the *Crime Index*, this refers to a list of seven crimes that are used to gauge the fluctuations of criminal behavior. The crimes tracked are murder and manslaughter (other than negligent manslaughter), forcible rape, robbery, aggravated assault, burglary, larceny-theft, motor vehicle theft, and arson.
- **Felony.** A felony is a serious crime for which the punishment is imprisonment in a state institution or even death.
- **Forgery/NSF.** Refers to the act of signing another person's signature without authority. It also refers to creating false documents. NSF refers to making or offering as payment a check for which there are insufficient funds.
- **Infraction.** Refers to a crime or other offense for which the punishment is a fine or other, non-incarceration penalty.
- **Larceny-Theft.** Refers to the attempt or act of taking someone else's possessions, including carrying, leading, or riding away of such property. Does not include embezzlement, fraud, forgery, or NSF.
- **Miscellaneous Offenses.** Any violation, other than traffic violations, of state or local laws that is not otherwise listed in a crime report.
- **Misdemeanor.** Refers to a crime that would be punishable by a fine or by imprisonment in a county jail, or both. In some cases, a felony crime can be treated as a misdemeanor.
- **Motor Vehicle Theft.** Stealing or attempting to steal a motor vehicle.
- **Narcotics.** Refers to violations of local and state laws regarding the sale, use, growing, manufacturing, and unlawful possession of narcotics.
- **Property Crime.** Refers to any burglary from a building, larceny-theft, motor vehicle theft, or arson.
- **Public Drunkenness.** Refers to violations that stem from drunkenness or other intoxication, excluding DUI (driving under the influence).
- **Rape.** Forced, attempted forced, or threatened forced sexual acts against an individual without consent, including cases where the victim is not capable of giving consent due to mental conditions, developmental or physical disability, intoxication, or unconsciousness. Rape can also be the result of intentionally fraudulent representation or trickery.
- **Robbery.** Refers to any instance where something is taken from the "care, custody, or control" of another person by force or by threat, or by any action that causes the victim fear.
- **Sex Offenses: Nonviolent.** Refers to violations that do not involve rape or physical contact, such as indecent exposure, solicitation, loitering that is considered to be for the act of engaging in "lewd conduct," and so forth.
- **Sex Offenses: Violent.** Refers to sexually related violations other than rape, that include physical contact. These include child molestation (without rape), sexual battery, statutory rape, and so forth.
- **Simple Assault.** Refers to weaponless attacks or attempted attacks in which no serious injury resulted.
- **Stolen Property.** Stolen property violations refer to the buying, receiving, or possession of stolen property, or any attempt to do so.
- **Trespass.** Refers to unlawful acts on public or private property, such as being present without permission or refusal to leave when asked to do so.

- **Uniform Crime Reports/UCR.** Reports gathered from law enforcement agencies around the country and provided via a federal reporting system.
- **Vandalism.** Refers to damage caused to public or private real or personal property as a result of willful or malicious acts and without the permission of the owners or custodians of the property.
- **Vehicle Code-All Other.** Refers to any violation of the vehicle code, excluding driving under the influence or hit and run.
- **Vehicle Code-Hit and Run.** Refers to a driver's failure to stop at the scene of an accident in which they were involved, and to notify the property owner and the police.
- **Violent Crime.** Refers to crimes such as willful homicide, forcible rape, robbery, and aggravated assault.
- **Weapons.** Refers to any violation or attempted violation of laws governing the carrying, using, possession, furnishing by sale or gift, and manufacturing deadly weapons.
- **Willful Homicide.** Refers to the act of intentionally killing another human being, which includes manslaughter (non-negligent) and murder.

Cavers/Climbers

Cavers, rock climbers, and tree climbers all have adopted their own sets of expressions. With the increased popularity of extreme sports, especially rock climbing, these terms can come in handy.

- Air rappel (an accidental fall down a pit)
- Australian descent (tree climber's term for rappelling upside down)
- Baby hog (a not-so-long coil of rope to be carried through a cave)
- Bang (explosives)
- Biner (carabiner, a locking device used to secure ropes and other equipment)
- Birth canal (narrow passage)
- Bomb-proof (1. suitable natural rig point; 2. very secure, unlikely to move when subjected to great force)
- Bottomed or bottomed out (reaching the lowest point of a vertical cave)
- Brain bucket (helmet)
- Carbide pig/piglet (a piece of knotted car inner-tube used for carrying carbide in caves)
- Cell (1. any electric light; 2. a battery pack)
- Chest compressor (a crawl that cannot be negotiated by a caver without exhaling)
- Cratering (falling off a climb to the ground)
- Death march (a very grueling caving trip)
- Dufus (an inept caver)
- Ear dip (a low, wet passage that causes one's ear to get wet while crawling through)
- Enduro-caver (a caver who goes on frequent death marches or grunt trips)
- Entrance fever (when a caver is anxious to get out of a cave)
- Flat rock (knocking someone unconscious with a rock, usually by causing rocks to fall on him when he is below you)
- Gnar or knar (a gnarly, narrow passage that has popcorn and/or other features that catch on packs or clothing)
- Goosh (boiled, condensed milk)
- Gorp (granola, oats, raisins, and peanuts, commonly known as "good old raisins and peanuts," a popular caver food)
- Grots (any well-used caving clothing)
- Grunt (a rugged, challenging caving trip)

- Hardware (carabiners, pitons, ascenders, or any of the metallic paraphernalia used in vertical caving)
- Headache (climber's call when something is falling from above)
- Hog (a long coil of rope to be carried through a cave)
- Hydrothermia (hypothermia from cold water)
- Jack (to decide not to start a trip or not to continue a trip)
- Janglies (assorted SRT hardware)
- Krab (carabiner)
- Minion (anyone conned into being a model or holding a flashgun on a photographic trip)
- Mundane (a non-caver)
- Nerd gate (an obstacle that prevents most climbers from accessing the rest of the cave)
- Pig (anything that is tough to carry through a difficult cave)
- Pitch (a section of a rock face that differs in angle from the sections above and below it)
- Pot-holing (exploring predominantly vertical caves)
- Rock solvent (explosives)
- Rout (exit the cave)
- Safety loop (a length of rope connecting the top ascender to the sit harness)
- Scoop (1. to discover an unexplored cave; 2. to explore a cave someone told you about before they were able to explore it)
- Sherpa/sherp (carrying a load through a cave for someone else, sometimes as a supply run for a cave group that comes later)
- Short-roped (when a pitch is rigged with a rope that's too short)
- Speleobopper (1. flashlight caver; 2. teenager in a cave; 3. someone who only participates in spot caving)
- Spelunk (the sound a caver makes when he hits the bottom of a pit)
- Spelunker (someone who explores caves, generally as a hobby)
- Sporting (1. an extremely wet cave trip; 2. gym climbing or climbs that emphasizes short, difficult climbs with bolted protection)
- Squeeze (a really tight spot)
- SRT (1. single-rope technique (tree climbing); 2. solid rubber trussing)
- Stink (carbide)
- Stinkies (carbide lamps)
- Stout (a caver with exceptional strength and endurance)
- Suckin' spiders (trying to breathe where there's not much air)
- Tight spot (a squeeze)
- Winker (a fray in a caving rope when a core is exposed)

Speech Patterns

What people say and the words they use are only part of the message they are delivering. How they say it is also very important. Many factors go into the way people speak, including:

- Volume.
- Tone of voice, including:
  - Pitch
  - Timbre
  - Breathiness
- Speed of delivery.
- Rhythm.
- Musicality.

- Specific word choices and constructions based on local dialects and technical trade terminology. These are also often based on what in neuro-linguistic programming are called *representational systems.* People who are not speaking in their native tongue may also construct sentences in unfamiliar ways, perhaps echoing the constructions of their native language.

And, along with all these subtleties are the nonverbal messages.

VOLUME

Clearly, the volume of someone's speech can indicate something about him. Some people naturally speak loudly, and others speak very quietly. A bombastic fellow might be very loud most of the time, even when he's whispering conspiratorially, while a bookish cleric might speak very quietly.

Volume can also indicate the level of passion, excitement, or anger in a character. People often raise their voices when angry or when they are particularly fired up about something.

TONE OF VOICE

Tone of voice is a complex aspect of communication that involves pitch and timbre, among other qualities. A person's tone can indicate a wide variety of emotional content, including sweetness, harmoniousness, aggression, sarcasm, manipulation, questions, dominance, submissiveness, compassion, disdain, and so on. Everyone intuitively understands this on some level, though describing it in print is difficult. However, when creating characters in games, a great deal of information can be presented through tone of voice, and you can use a character's tone to stimulate emotional responses in the player.

For instance, a low-pitched voice can be sinister, soothing, threatening, or even commanding, depending on other qualities. A high-pitched voice can be nonthreatening (as is usually the case in greeting someone new, courting a love interest, or talking to children), or it can be an indication of excitement and even anger. Again, other specific qualities help determine which meaning to give a specific voice, and other factors must be taken into account, including loudness, breathiness, harshness, speed of delivery, rhythm, and more.

SPEED OF DELIVERY

Some people naturally speak quickly, while others may speak much more slowly. This can be cultural. For instance, Cubans speak Spanish faster than people from Spain or many other Spanish-speaking countries. People from New York speak faster overall than people from the South or from Hawaii. A person's natural speaking speed can be due to other factors, too, including how those people process information. However, in addition to people's natural tendencies, people do speak faster when they are excited or emotionally charged. They may tend to speak more slowly when confused or unsure. However, there are no absolutes. Some people run off at the mouth when nervous. Others stammer and have a hard time getting anything to come out.

RHYTHM

A person's overall speaking speed is only one part of the story. People also tend to have natural rhythms, which can change based on emotional states. Some people speak very smoothly, their words flowing with a definite meter, as in poetry. Others speak in choppy segments, with uneven gaps in their words, perhaps speaking very quickly and then stopping abruptly and speaking quickly again after a short pause. Some people's statements tend either to accelerate or to decelerate as they speak. They may trail off or even end abruptly without completing a thought, following with a whole new thought that may or may not be completed.

Musicality

I made up this category to describe the quality of speaking that includes rhythm, tone, speed, and other factors to achieve a more or less flowing quality. For instance, many religious leaders create a sort of singsong musicality to their delivery. Other people speak with a flow that can be entrancing and even hypnotic. People from different ethnic origins may have a cadence that's unique to their language. But most people's conversations are not particularly musical. Using the idea of a sort of internal meter to someone's voice can distinguish him from others, though it should be subtle unless he is specifically intoning something, such as if he is a priest, rabbi, or muezzin.

Word Choice and Construction

The words and constructions people use in speech vary for many reasons, both personal and cultural. This section looks at some of the ways you can differentiate speakers in your games. I'll start by listing some of the causes of individual speech patterns and then follow with some more specific ideas. People's speech patterns may vary because:

- **They are foreign speakers.** They aren't speaking their native language, and everything must be translated.
- **They use local dialects and expressions.** They are speaking in a local dialect, which has unique expressions that are especially meaningful within their local culture. (See the slang lists earlier in this chapter, for instance.)
- **They use trade terms.** They are using words specific to their trade, profession, or technical expertise. For instance, politicians might use specific phrases that nobody else would use; likewise, plumbers, nuclear physicists, car mechanics, clergy, or thieves may do the same.
- **They are educated speakers.** Sometimes highly educated people will speak differently than people who have had little formal education. This doesn't mean that the content of what they say is necessarily better or smarter, but it is often expressed in different language and construction.
- **They are intoxicated, emotional, or stressed.** People speak differently when they are intoxicated or drugged, in great pain or very frightened, or breathless or bone tired.
- **They speak with condescension, reverence, or inferiority.** People speak differently when they feel superior (condescension), when they feel reverence, or when they feel inferior.
- **They speak formally versus informally.** People speak differently among people they know well than they do around strangers or people they have just met. This is intensified if there is the potential or perception of danger involved. Many people are guarded around others at first. Why? What is it that they fear? Knowing what they fear to reveal can tell you something about who they are.

In addition to these ways that people's speech may vary, there are some very specific language patterns that can further distinguish and characterize people or help determine their current emotional state. Some constructions can even help show something about how they interact with the world. The more you study these language patterns, the more you can see how a specific individual may order his life based on which patterns he tends to use.

Representational Systems

We experience the world through our senses—for instance, by seeing, hearing, feeling, smelling, and tasting. We remember our experiences most often in terms of pictures, sounds, and feelings, and we often express ourselves in words and phrases that echo the way we perceive our experiences. So some people seem to see the world most in pictures, while others seem more auditory- or feeling-based (kinesthetic). These three systems—visual, auditory, and kinesthetic—form the basis for much theory on how people think, remember, and express themselves.

Although this is a cursory introduction to the subject, in very crude terms, people can be differentiated through the kind of language they use. In conjunction with the information in Chapter 12, "Character Design," you can, with further study and some hard work, create characters who model some of the subtleties of real people.

For instance, people who are using a predominantly visual representational system may have different posture and mannerisms, and they may use expressions such as, "I see what you mean" or, "I get the picture. I really painted myself into a corner and didn't see the forest for the trees."

People using a predominantly auditory system might say, "I hear you. You're coming through loud and clear." Or they might say, "I like the sound of that. It really resonates with me, and I'd like to hear a lot more about it."

People who are using a predominantly kinesthetic system might say something like, "I have a gut feeling about that. It just doesn't feel right. In fact, that whole subject gets me all churned up inside, and I just want to find a comfortable place with it all."

There is another kind of representational system, which the NLP (neuro-linguistic programming) people call *auditory digital.* It is about the kind of inner talk we have with ourselves, and it tends to be very unemotional—digital in the sense of on or off, ones and zeros. This kind of language would be something like, "I don't perceive this problem at all. I am skilled at using facts and analyzing data, and this is not computing correctly. It's simply not logical." Mr. Spock from *Star Trek* was, to some extent, this kind of speaker.

The following lists are samples (albeit incomplete) of the many words that fit into each representational system. They might give you some ideas about how to create speech for characters who uniquely represent those systems. Remember, however, that the best communication happens when people match systems. So if one person is speaking primarily in visual language and the other answers primarily in kinesthetic terms, they aren't going to do quite as well at communicating as they would if they matched. This might also be true of characters speaking to players. If the player happens to be primarily auditory, for instance, then a character expressing in visual terms may not reach the player as well as one speaking in auditory terminology. Some of the best speech writing makes sure to include all three systems, therefore increasing the chances of connecting with everyone in the audience.

Also note that all people use all systems some of the time, but most people have one (sometimes more than one) that predominates over the others. Thus, someone who is predominantly visual may still use auditory, kinesthetic, or auditory digital expressions. If you pay attention to how people speak, however, you may discover that some people have recognizable speech patterns and tendencies toward one representational system over the others.

Visual Words

- Appear/disappear
- Attractive
- Blurry
- Clear
- Clear cut
- Eye to eye
- Foresee
- Imagine
- In light of
- Mind's eye
- Observe
- Peer
- Perspective
- Preview
- Reflect
- Reveal
- See
- See to it
- Shortsighted
- Tunnel vision
- Under your nose
- Visualize
- Vivid

Auditory Words

- Attuned
- Blabbermouth
- Clear as a bell/loud and clear
- Complain
- Explain
- Hear
- Hold your tongue
- I'm all ears
- Loud
- Make music
- Manner of speaking
- Melodious
- Outspoken
- Quiet
- Shout
- Sing
- Sound/sounds
- Talk
- Tell
- Translate
- Unheard of

Kinesthetic Words

- All washed up
- Angle
- Bend
- Break
- Comfortable
- Concrete
- Feel
- Get a hold of/get a handle on
- Grab
- Hard
- Hug
- Keep your shirt on
- Know-how
- Pain in the neck
- Pressure
- Push/pull
- Slipped my mind
- Smooth operator
- Soft
- Solid
- Start from scratch
- Stiff upper lip
- Thick
- Touch
- Warm
- Weigh

Nonspecific Words (Auditory Digital)

- Change
- Conceive
- Consider
- Decide
- Describe in detail
- Distinct
- Doesn't add up
- Doesn't compute
- Experience
- Factor in
- Feel that
- Figure it out
- Get an account of
- Hash it out
- Insensitive
- Know
- Learn
- Make sense of
- Motivate
- Pay attention to
- Perceive
- Process
- Question
- Sense
- The bottom line
- Think
- Understand
- Without a doubt
- Word for word

Speech Distortions

Each of the following examples occurs commonly in normal communication. For it to be a character-identifying element, it would need to be exaggerated. The character would have to use one or more of these language patterns frequently enough for the player to identify that character with its most common patterns of speech, although that identification is likely to be unconscious.

The first five examples are known in neuro-linguistic programming terminology as *distortions.*

Nominalization

Nominalization is the tendency to turn a verb into a noun. It is very common. For instance, when someone refers to a *relationship* as a noun, they are nominalizing a process. There are two standard tests for nominalization. One is by asking, "Can it be put in a wheelbarrow?" Can you put a relationship in a wheelbarrow? No, because it is a process, not a thing. The other test is to say, "An ongoing ________." If the word can fit adequately in that phrase, it is, again, a process. For instance, an ongoing *relationship* or an ongoing *illness.* At any rate, because the tendency toward nominalization is very pervasive, it isn't as uniquely descriptive as some other language patterns, but it is something you can be aware of when writing character speech.

Mind Reading

Mind reading is attributing some knowledge of what someone else is thinking/feeling, such as, "I know she feels terrible about this" or, "Raymond hates me." Again, this is fairly common, but in some people can be a habit of thought and conversation.

Cause-Effect

Cause-effect statements are those that indicate something external caused an internal response, such as, "You make me mad" or "If you were nicer to me, I'd feel much better" or "You left that roller skate in the driveway and made me slip and fall." In essence, cause-effect statements place the responsibility or blame for the speaker's experience and response on something outside of him. In contrast, people who speak in more accountable terms might say, "When you raise your voice, I feel nervous." Note the distinction—not, "it makes me feel nervous," but "I feel nervous." Again, people who tend to use cause-effect language are common, but in someone who does it a lot, it could be recognized as a trait.

Making Connections

Similar to cause-effect, *making connections* is a language pattern (really a thought pattern, as these all are) of making part of a situation or behavior equal with its whole internal meaning. For instance, "You looked away when I entered the room. You must be angry with me." Or, "Sally knew the answer to my question. That must mean she's very smart." Or, "The magician helped me kill the dragon, so he must be a good magician, and I can trust him."

Presuppositions

Presuppositions are the assumptions people make but don't actually state when they say something. "You can have a better life" presupposes that the person's life is not good enough. "Why aren't you working harder?" presupposes that they aren't working hard enough or working as hard as they can. "You're going to learn so much today" presupposes that they will learn something, but perhaps they won't.

The next seven examples are known in NLP as *generalizations.*

Universal Quantifiers

Universal quantifiers are universal generalizations, such as "All politicians are lying scumbags," or "Nobody's perfect," or "Everyone knows how to fix a tire."

Modal Operators

This somewhat technical-sounding term refers to certain kinds of words that people use in speaking: words such as "should/should not," "can/can't," "want/need," "will/will not," and "possible/impossible." These words say a lot about a person's belief systems and way of dealing with the world, and even though they may seem very subtle, there's a very distinct difference between someone who says, "I should do that," and someone who says, "I want to do that" or someone who says "I can do that." These words can be further categorized as opportunity words—obligation versus empowerment words.

Lost Performatives

Lost performatives are statements that eliminate the speaker from the statement. For instance, statements such as, "It's not a good idea to go out in the rain" or "Everybody should go to church." These statements generally express some value judgment without the person making that judgment really being identified, which makes the statement seem more like a statement of fact than of opinion. Often people who think they know best will use lost performatives, making pronouncements for other people to accept and follow.

Simple Deletions

Simple deletions involve statements that leave out information about a person, thing, or event. An example is saying, "I don't know." What does the person not know? Another example is "I am in pain." What is causing the pain? Where does it hurt? There is information left out of the statement.

Comparative Deletions

Comparative deletions use words such as better, best, worse, richer, poorer, smarter—all sorts of comparative terms—while deleting some significant information related to the comparison. For instance, "He's much better off" or, "That is the best spell you can buy."

Unspecified Nouns and Verbs

Unspecified nouns and verbs refers to statements in which someone is referenced but not identified, such as, "They took my money." Who took the money? Other examples include, "Nobody loves me," "This sucks," and so on.

It also refers to situations in which the verb of the sentence indicates some action, but there isn't much information about the action. For instance, "Roger hurt me" doesn't describe how Roger hurt the person or where, what he did to hurt him, or even why he hurt him. Other examples include, "If you only knew," "I'm going shopping," "I'll be back," "Make my day," and so on.

Interactive Conversation

Historically, conversations in games have been pretty lame or, at best, simplistic. Attempts have been made to create a more interactive approach that allows the player to have meaningful discourse with non-player characters. Most existing methods have been less than exciting, but research and development on intelligent systems is underway. In the meantime, here are a few of the ways people have attempted to create interactivity in conversations:

- Premade questions/answers
- Premade branching questions/answers
- Context-sensitive responses
- Basic sentence formation
- Menu "speech" systems
- Topical (limited) preset sentences you can blurt out, such as "Drop the weapon," or simple basic commands, such as "Retreat"
- Artificial intelligence

Common Hand and Body Expressions

Here are some communications that can be expressed easily, some in a variety of ways, by using hand and body expressions. Some involve simple gestures, while others are closer to pantomime. Some are common to almost everyone, while others tend to be used mostly by specific groups of people, whether professional or cultural. When you read this list, I'm sure you'll imagine the way you could express each of these communications nonverbally.

- American Sign Language
- Angry fist
- Big greeting (arms open wide)
- Boredom or frustration (hands in pockets with appropriate posture)
- Boxing stance
- Bring to an end (slicing a hand across the throat)
- Come (curling fingers or moving hand back toward you)
- Crazy (circling finger at ear)
- Cutting motion
- Disbelief (hands in the air with the appropriate facial expression)
- D'oh!
- Downcast (head down)
- Drumming fingers
- Earth to…
- Encompassing all (arms wide)
- Enumerating (counting fingers or pointing at palm)
- Fingers counting down
- Gang symbols
- Gen X/valley girl hand signals
  - Loser
  - Whatever
- Go away
- Here
- High-five
- Huh? (cupping hand to ear)
- I don't want to see this (covering eyes)
- I love you
- Impatience
- Italian salutes
- Karate stance
- Me
- Mock shooting of a gun (pistol, rifle, or machinegun)
- No/no way (head and/or hands)
- Obscene gestures
- Over here!
- Peace
- Pick a hand
- Praying/pleading gesture
- Right on/thumbs up
- Shaka
- Slapping thigh
- Stop (holding up a hand)
- Stretching motion
- Tapping foot
- There
- Think
- Thinking (scratching head)
- Thumbs up/thumbs down (approval/disapproval)
- Victory
- Wave (various kinds)
- Woot!
- Yes (head)
- You

SWAT Communications

SWAT teams have developed their own system of code and hand signals to handle the kinds of high-pressure situations they deal with as part of their jobs. You might find them useful, not only in dealing with games that use SWAT teams, but as inspiration for coded communications and hand gestures in other contexts.

10 Series

- 10-4: OK (acknowledgment)
- 10-10: What is your location?
- 10-15: In position
- 10-16: Arrived at scene
- 10-17: Completed last assignment
- 10-18: Request for relief
- 10-19: Report to this station
- 10-97: In service
- 10-98: Out of service
- 10-99: Stop transmitting

Hand Signals

Check the Internet for good images of these hand and body signals. One good source is at www.airsoftgent.be/dbase/hands.htm.

- 360-degree formation (rally)
- Ammo
- Around
- Automatic weapon
- Automobile
- Column formation
- Come
- Cover me
- Disregard
- Dog
- Door
- Down
- Enter
- Female
- File formation
- Gas
- Go
- Hear/listen
- Hostage
- Hurry
- Line formation
- Male
- Me
- Message received
- No
- Number addition
- Numbers indication
- Pistol
- Rifle
- See/watch
- Shotgun
- Silence
- Sniper
- Stop
- Suspect
- There
- Unable to understand
- Wedge formation
- Window
- Yes
- You

Police and Military Codes

Whenever we design games that involve cops and robbers or military scenarios, the specific codes can be used to provide authenticity. They also serve as indicators of the kinds of situations you might encounter. Perhaps simply by reading these code lists, you can imagine new situations to add to your games.

Military Police Codes

Following are some common codes used by the military police:

- 10-2: Ambulance urgently needed
- 10-3: Motor vehicle accident
- 10-4: Wrecker requested
- 10-5: Ambulance requested
- 10-6: Send civilian police
- 10-7: Pick up prisoner
- 10-8: Subject in custody
- 10-9: Send police van
- 10-10: Escort/transport
- 10-11: In service
- 10-12: Out of service
- 10-13: Repeat last message
- 10-14: Your location?
- 10-15: Go to...
- 10-16: Report by landline
- 10-17: Return to headquarters
- 10-18: Assignment completed
- 10-19: Contact/call...
- 10-20: Relay to...
- 10-21: Time check
- 10-22: Fire
- 10-23: Disturbance
- 10-24: Suspicious person
- 10-25: Stolen/abandoned vehicle
- 10-26: Serious accident
- 10-27: Radio check
- 10-28: Loud and clear
- 10-29: Signal weak
- 10-30: Request assistance (non-emergency)
- 10-31: Request investigator
- 10-32: Request M.P. duty officer
- 10-33: Stand by
- 10-34: Cancel last message
- 10-35: Meal
- 10-36: Any messages?
- 10-38: Relief/change
- 10-39: Check vehicle/building
- 10-40: Acknowledge
- 10-50: Change frequency

Common Police Codes

The following sections cover some common codes used by police, sheriff, highway patrol, or other law enforcement agencies in the U.S.

NOTE

Note that police codes may vary between departments and are subject to change; codes are added as needed.

Abbreviations

- AC (aircraft crash)
- ADW (assault with a deadly weapon)
- AID (accident investigation detail)
- BO (out of order)
- BT (bomb threat—"Bravo Tango")
- CP (complaining party)
- CPD (city/county property damaged)
- CRT (information computer)
- DB (dead body)
- DMV (vehicle registration)
- DOA (dead on arrival)
- ETA (estimated time of arrival)
- GOA (gone on arrival)
- GTA (grand theft, auto)
- HBD (has been drinking)
- J (juvenile)
- NCIC (National Crime Information Center)
- PC (person complaining or penal code)
- PR (person reporting)
- QT (secrecy of location required)
- UTL (unable to locate)
- VIN (Vehicle Identification Number)
- W (female)

Basic Numeric Codes

- Code 1: Answer on radio
- Code 2: Proceed immediately without siren
- Code 3: Proceed with siren and red lights
- Code 4: No further assistance necessary
- Code 4A: No further assistance is necessary, but suspect is not in custody
- Code 5: Uniformed officers stay away
- Code 6: Out of car to investigate
- Code 6A: Out of car to investigate, assistance may be needed
- Code 6C: Suspect is wanted and may be dangerous
- Code 7: Out for lunch
- Code 8: Fire alarm
- Code 9: Jail break
- Code 10: Request clear frequency
- Code 12: False alarm
- Code 13: Major disaster activation
- Code 14: Resume normal operations
- Code 20: Notify news media to respond
- Code 30: Burglar alarm ringing
- Code 33: Emergency! All units stand by
- Code 99: Emergency!
- Code 100: In position to intercept

Specific Numeric Codes

- 187: Homicide
- 207: Kidnapping
- 207A: Kidnapping attempt
- 211: Armed robbery
- 217: Assault with intent to murder
- 220: Attempted rape
- 240: Assault
- 242: Battery
- 245: Assault with a deadly weapon
- 261: Rape
- 261A: Attempted rape
- 288: Lewd conduct
- 311 or 314: Indecent exposure
- 390: Drunk
- 390D: Drunk unconscious
- 415: Disturbance
- 415C: Disturbance, children involved
- 415E: Disturbance, loud music or party
- 415F: Disturbance, family
- 415G: Disturbance, gang
- 417: Person with a gun
- 459: Burglary
- 459A: Burglar alarm ringing
- 470: Forgery
- 480: Hit and run (felony)
- 481: Hit and run (misdemeanor)
- 484: Petty theft
- 484PS: Purse snatch
- 487: Grand theft
- 488: Petty theft
- 502: Drunk driving
- 503: Auto theft
- 504: Tampering with a vehicle
- 505: Reckless driving
- 507: Public nuisance
- 586: Illegal parking
- 586E: Vehicle blocking driveway
- 594: Malicious mischief
- 595: Runaway car
- 647: Lewd conduct
- 901: Ambulance call/accident, injuries unknown
- 901H: Ambulance call: dead body
- 901K: Ambulance has been dispatched
- 901L: Ambulance call: narcotics overdose
- 901N: Ambulance requested
- 901S: Ambulance call: shooting
- 901T: Ambulance call: traffic accident
- 901Y: Request ambulance if needed
- 902: Accident
- 902H: En route to hospital
- 902M: Medical aid requested
- 902T: Traffic accident: non-injury
- 903: Aircraft crash
- 903L: Low-flying aircraft
- 904A: Fire alarm
- 904B: Brush fire or boat fire
- 904C: Car fire
- 904F: Forest fire
- 904G: Grass fire

- 904I: Illegal burning
- 904S: Structure fire
- 905B: Animal bite
- 905N: Noisy animal
- 905S: Stray animal
- 905V: Vicious animal
- 906K: Rescue dispatched
- 906N: Rescue requested
- 907: Minor disturbance
- 907A: Loud radio or TV
- 907B: Ball game in street
- 907K: Paramedics dispatched
- 907N: Paramedics requested
- 907Y: Are paramedics needed?
- 908: Begging
- 909: Traffic congestion
- 909B: Road blockade
- 909F: Flares needed
- 909T: Traffic hazard
- 910: Can you handle?
- 911: Advise party
- 911B: Contact informant/contact officer
- 912: Are we clear?
- 913: You are clear
- 914: Request detectives
- 914A: Attempted suicide
- 914C: Request coroner
- 914D: Request doctor
- 914F: Request fire department
- 914H: Heart attack
- 914N: Concerned party notified
- 914S: Suicide
- 915: Dumping rubbish
- 916: Holding suspect
- 917A: Abandoned vehicle
- 917P: Hold vehicle for fingerprints
- 918A: Escaped mental patient
- 918V: Violent mental patient
- 919: Keep the peace
- 920: Missing adult
- 920A: Found adult/missing adult
- 920C: Missing child
- 920F: Found child
- 920J: Missing juvenile
- 921: Prowler
- 921P: Peeping Tom
- 922: Illegal peddling
- 924: Station detail
- 925: Suspicious person
- 926: Request tow truck
- 926A: Tow truck dispatched
- 927: Investigate unknown trouble
- 927A: Person pulled from telephone
- 927D: Investigate possible dead body
- 928: Found property
- 929: Investigate person down
- 930: See man regarding a complaint
- 931: See woman regarding a complaint
- 932: Woman or child abuse or open door
- 933: Open window
- 949: Gasoline spill
- 950: Burning permit
- 951: Request fire investigator
- 952: Report conditions
- 953: Check smoke report
- 954: Arrived at scene
- 955: Fire under control
- 956: Available for assignment
- 957: Fire under control
- 960X: Car stop, dangerous suspects
- 961: Take a report or car stop
- 962: Subject is armed and dangerous
- 966: Sniper
- 967: Outlaw motorcyclists
- 975: Can your suspect hear your radio?
- 981: Frequency is clear or need radiological
- 982: Bomb threat or are we being received?
- 983: Explosion
- 995: Labor trouble
- 996: Explosion
- 996A: Unexploded bomb
- 998: Officer involved in shooting
- 999: Officer needs help: urgent!

"10" Codes

- 10-0: Use caution
- 10-1: Poor reception
- 10-2: Good reception
- 10-3: Stop transmitting, change channels
- 10-4: Message received, affirmative, okay
- 10-5: Relay this information to ______
- 10-6: Busy
- 10-7: Out of service
- 10-8: In service
- 10-9: Please repeat your message
- 10-10: Fight in progress, out of service, negative, transmission completed, welfare check
- 10-11: Animal problem, talking too fast, en route
- 10-12: Stand by, visitors present, disregard, call in reports, at scene, check revocation
- 10-13: Advise weather/road conditions, civilians present and listening, call-in resume
- 10-14: Suspicious person or prowler, convoy or escort
- 10-15: Civil disturbance, prisoner/suspect in custody
- 10-16: Domestic disturbance, make pickup at ______
- 10-17: Meet complainant, pick up papers at _______, urgent business
- 10-18: Urgent, complete assignment ASAP, drunk, anything for us?
- 10-19: Return to station
- 10-20: Specify location/my location is ______
- 10-21: Please telephone _______
- 10-22: Disregard, report to _____, send blood technician
- 10-23: Arrived at location/on scene, stand by on this frequency, status check, en route to call, sex offense
- 10-24: Assignment completed, trouble at station, unit not available, direct traffic
- 10-25: Report to ______, please contact ______, come in for traffic, officer needs help, do you have contact with person?
- 10-26: Detaining suspect (implying "please expedite"), check auto registration, ETA, disregard last info, phone residence
- 10-27: Driver's license request, vehicle registration request, I am moving to channel ______, any answer
- 10-28: Vehicle registration request, driver's license request, identify your station, missing person
- 10-29: Arrests/warrants request, time is up for contact
- 10-30: Unauthorized use of radio, danger/caution, special check at ______, juvenile
- 10-31: Crime in progress, domestic disturbance, check for local warrants, suspicious person
- 10-32: Person with gun, fight in progress, radio check, check NCIC, DWI test
- 10-33: Emergency, all units stand by, officer needs help, disturbance at ______, fire
- 10-34: Riot, frequency open (cancels 10-33), help needed, trouble at jail, correct time, meet officer
- 10-35: Major crime alert, confidential information, suspicious person
- 10-36: Correct time of day?
- 10-37: Suspicious vehicle, identify yourself, wrecker needed at ______, shoplifter, time of day?
- 10-38: Stopping suspicious vehicle, ambulance needed, station report satisfactory, phone communications, vandalism
- 10-39: Run with lights and siren, your message was delivered, false alarm, premises were occupied, contact officer, disturbance
- 10-40: Run silent (no lights and siren), false alarm, no activity, premises appear secure, please tune to channel ______, expedite, advise if available, suspicious person, dead animal, mental patient, lunch

- 10-41: Begin duty, radio test, intoxicated person, debris in street, neighbor trouble
- 10-42: End duty, traffic accident at ______, malicious mischief, request dispatch times
- 10-43: Information, traffic jam at ______, request criminal history, pick up passenger, armed robbery, rescue call
- 10-44: Permission to leave patrol, I have a message for you, transmission received, rape, traffic accident (no injury)
- 10-45: Animal carcass, pick up officer, fueling vehicle, all units in range please report, coffee break, traffic accident (injury)
- 10-46: Motorist assist, lunch break, fuel break, wrecker
- 10-47: Emergency road repair, call home, missing person, drunk driver, blood run
- 10-48: Traffic control, request criminal history, runaway juvenile, use caution
- 10-49: Traffic light out, en route to assignment, bathroom break, any traffic, serving warrant
- 10-50: Accident, no messages, break channel, auto accident with property damage
- 10-51: Wrecker needed, auto accident with injuries, phone message
- 10-52: Ambulance needed, fatal auto accident, message for assignment, alarm
- 10-53: Road blocked, silent alarm
- 10-54: Animals on highway, silent pursuit, car stop
- 10-55: Intoxicated driver or DWI, security check, ambulance call
- 10-56: Intoxicated pedestrian, warrant indicated, arrived at scene
- 10-57: Hit-and-run accident, narcotics, officer at pistol range
- 10-58: Direct traffic, wrecker, DOA, teleprinter message
- 10-59: Escort or convoy, out of car checking violation, ambulance, bomb threat
- 10-60: Squad in vicinity, traffic stop, coffee break, assist motorist,what is next message number?
- 10-61: Personnel in vicinity, stand by for CW traffic, clear of traffic stop, weather conditions?, lunch break
- 10-62: Reply to message, unable to copy—use phone, check for rising water, logged on/off
- 10-63: Prepare to copy, make written copy, net directed to ___, need barricades
- 10-64: Local message, message for delivery, net clear—resume normal traffic, field investigator
- 10-65: Net message assignment, kidnapping
- 10-66: Net message cancellation, bathroom break
- 10-67: Clear for net message, prepare to copy, person calling for help, all units comply
- 10-68: Dispatch message, repeat dispatch, switch channels
- 10-69: Sniper, message received, any calls holding for me?
- 10-70: Fire alarm, fire, fire follow-up, prowler, net message, chemical spill
- 10-71: Advise nature of fire, gun involved, proceed with transmission, officer needs assistance, fire inspector
- 10-72: Fire progress report, shooting, check safety of officer, follow-up rescue, radar assignment, street blocked
- 10-73: Smoke report, advise current status, speed trap at ______, notify coroner, arson investigation
- 10-74: Negative, tactical plan
- 10-75: In contact with ______, you are causing interference, drunk driver, miscellaneous out code
- 10-76: En route, traffic accident, send SWAT team
- 10-77: ETA _____, negative contact, accident with injury
- 10-78: Need assistance, major accident with injury, request wrecker
- 10-79: Notify coroner, bomb threat, hit and run
- 10-80: Pursuit in progress, bomb has exploded, tower lights out, on assignment, demonstration
- 10-81: Breathalyzer request, stop for interrogation, reserve hotel room, officer _____ will be at your station, at vehicle maintenance, civil disturbance/riot

- 10-82: Reserve lodging, stop for interrogation/arrest, traffic signal out, cover assistance
- 10-83: Work/school crossing detail, call station, units stop transmitting, at radio shop, officer in trouble
- 10-84: Advise ETA, checking officer status, my telephone number is ______, follow-up, broken utility main
- 10-85: Arrival delay due to ______, prepare to copy info, my address is ______, loose livestock
- 10-86: Officer on duty, utility line down
- 10-87: Pickup or prisoner transfer, pick up payroll check, dead body
- 10-88: Advise telephone, station call, special assignment, true alarm
- 10-89: Bomb threat, send radio repair, officer at academy
- 10-90: Bank alarm, radio repair to be at station, officer at headquarters, false alarm
- 10-91: Pick up prisoner/suspect, talk closer to the mic, prepare your inspection, vehicle fuel, bank holdup alarm
- 10-92: Parking violation, your signal is weak, officer at court
- 10-93: Blockage, please check my frequency
- 10-94: Drag racing, give me a long count
- 10-95: Prisoner/suspect in custody, transmit dead carrier for five seconds
- 10-96: Detain prisoner/suspect, psych patient
- 10-97: Test signal, arrived at scene, possible wanted person in vehicle, known offender, officer at court
- 10-98: Prison/jail break, criminal history indicated, officer at juvenile court, assignment complete
- 10-99: Warrants/stolen indicated, officer needs assistance/held hostage, mission complete, bathroom break
- 10-100: Bathroom break, dead body
- 10-200: Police needed

DEA Radio Codes

- 10-1: Unable to copy
- 10-2: Message received
- 10-4: Relay my message
- 10-6: Stand by
- 10-7: Out of service
- 10-8: In service
- 10-9: Please repeat message
- 10-10: Prisoner present at...
- 10-13: Agent needs assistance
- 10-15: Residence
- 10-16: Change frequency
- 10-19: Return to...
- 10-20: Location
- 10-21: Call by landline
- 10-22: Disregard
- 10-25: Respond to...
- 10-28: Registration check
- 10-30: Subscriber information
- 10-33: Emergency traffic
- 10-99: Emergency: agent needs assistance
- 10-100: Radio silence

EMS Codes

- AB3: Abdominal complaint/vomiting with signs of shock
- AS1: Reserved for victims of gunshot wounds, cuttings, or rapes
- AS3: Assault victim
- BE3: Behavioral problem with a stated medical need to respond along with police
- BK3: Non-traumatic back injury in patient over 40, or unable to move for unknown reason
- BL3: Bleeding and unable to control

- BR1: Breathing problems with signs of shock or unable to talk or turning blue
- BR3: Breathing problem with no other symptoms
- BU1: Burn victim with over 18% of body covered, regardless of area
- BU3: Burn victim up to 18% burns on non-vital areas (i.e., legs/arms) or sunburn, etc.
- CH1: Chest pains with two or more of assorted symptoms
- CH3: Chest pains with only one other symptom (such as chest pains and nausea)
- DI1: Person going into diabetic coma, noted behavioral change leaning to violence
- DI3: Diabetic problem not yet unconscious or severely affected
- DR1: Drowning with victim unconscious and difficulty or not breathing
- DR3: Person not drowned but was under water and has been brought back
- EL1: Severe shock by electrical device with other symptoms
- EL3: Electrical shock
- EY1: Same as above but object is penetrating
- EY3: Foreign object in eye (mace counts here) which is non-penetrating
- FA1: Fall more than 20 feet with no known traumatic injuries (if obvious or stated injuries, this becomes a trauma)
- FA3: Person fell, still down, unknown status
- HC1: Same as above but also unconscious
- HC3: Heat or cold problems
- HE3: The worst headache the patient has ever had
- IN3: Inhalation incident (such as in mixing of ammonia and bleach or that sort of thing)
- MN9: Man down, usually used for detox wagon
- OD1: Overdose and unconscious
- OD3: Overdose
- SK3: Sick person meeting triage criteria for Code-3 response from ALS ambulance, usually only showing signs of shock and unable to fit any other code
- ST3: Stroke
- TA1: Same as above but additionally violent mechanism (if caller calls and says head-on accident or pedestrian, motorcycle, or bicycle involved, this code is used—also with a pin-in or rollover)
- TA3: Injury accident
- TA9: Multi-vehicle accident, fire only to check
- TR1: Traumatic injury to critical area or to possibly critical area with other symptoms
- TR3: Traumatic, injury to possible non-critical area
- UK3: Unknown medical problem, as in "I don't know what is wrong; someone just told me to call."
- UN1: Unconscious, not breathing, or having difficulties
- UN3: Unable to rouse, but no other problems

Common Radio Protocols

- **All after.** Part of the message to which I refer is all of that which follows...
- **All before.** Part of the message to which I refer is all of that which precedes...
- **Authenticate.** Station called is to reply to the challenge that follows.
- **Authentication is.** Transmission authentication of this message is...
- **Break.** I now separate the text from other parts of the message.
- **Correct.** What you have transmitted is correct.
- **Correction.** There is an error in this transmission. Transmission will continue with the last word correctly transmitted.

- **Disregard this transmission.** This transmission is in error; disregard it.
- **Do not answer.** Stations called are not to answer with a receipt for this message, or otherwise to transmit in connection with this message. When this expression is used, the transmission will end with *out.*
- **Go ahead.** Transmit.
- **Groups.** This message contains the number of five-letter code groups indicated by the numeral following.
- **I read back.** The following is my response to your instructions to read back.
- **I say again.** I am repeating transmission or part indicated.
- **I spell.** I shall spell the next word phonetically.
- **I verify.** The following message (or portion) has been verified at your request and is repeated. Used only as a reply to *verify.*
- **Message.** A message that requires recording is about to be transmitted. Not used on nets primarily used for conveying messages; intended for use on tactical nets.
- **More to follow.** Transmitting station has additional traffic for the receiving station.
- **Out.** This is the end of my transmission to you, and no answer is required or expected.
- **Over.** This is the end of my transmission to you, and a response is necessary.
- **Radio check.** What is my signal strength and readability?
- **Read back.** Repeat this transmission to me exactly as received.
- **Relay to.** Transmit this message to all addresses or to the address designations immediately following.
- **Roger.** Have received your last message satisfactorily, loud and clear.
- **Say again.** Repeat all of your last transmission. Followed by identification data; means repeat [portion indicated].
- **Silence lifted.** Resume normal transmissions. Silence can only be lifted by the station imposing it or by higher authority. When an authentication system is in force, the transmission imposing and lifting silence is to be authenticated.
- **Silence.** Cease transmission on this net immediately. If repeated three or more times, silence will be maintained until lifted.
- **Speak slower.** You are transmitting too fast—slow down.
- **This is.** This transmission is from the station whose designator immediately follows.
- **Time.** That which immediately follows is the time or date-time group of the message.
- **Unknown station.** The identity of the station with whom I am trying to establish communications is unknown.
- **Verify.** Verify entire message (or portion indicated) with the originator and retransmit correct version. Used only at the discretion of the addressee of the questioned message.
- **Wait, out.** I must pause longer than a few seconds.
- **Wait.** I must pause for a few seconds.
- **Wilco.** Have received your last message, understand it, and will comply; to be used only by the addressee of a message. Since the meaning of *roger* is included in that of *wilco,* the two expressions are never used together.
- **Word after.** I refer to the word of the message that follows...
- **Word before.** I refer to the word of the message that precedes...
- **Words twice.** Communication is difficult; transmit each phrase or code group twice. Used as an order, request, or information.
- **Wrong.** Your transmission was incorrect. The correct version is...

Foreign Languages and Foreign Dialogue

The use of foreign language words and phrases is of limited usefulness. However, since some terms, such *joie de vivre* and *coup de grace*, are part of our language, they are acceptable. However, if you are using non-English-speaking characters in a game, it's a good idea to know something of the language they speak and have an expert on hand to be sure you appropriately use their expressions. Another option is to actually have their dialogue in their native language (by hiring native speakers) and use subtitles. Although this is not so common, it was used beautifully in Jordan Mechner's *The Last Express* and created a far more realistic atmosphere than would have been the case if all the characters had spoken English, or even if they had spoken with appropriate French, German, and Turkish accents.

Design Challenge

1. How well have games made use of speech, language patterns, slang, and specific expressions? Look at popular games and listen to the dialogue. Does it ring true? Do the actors convey an authentic character?
2. Write some dialogue using slang and buzzwords appropriate to the characters you plan to use in your games. If you want a challenge, write some dialogue in each type of slang or with a variety of specific groups and their buzzwords.
3. Listen to the dialogue in good movies and study the inflections of the actors.
4. Go places where people hang out and listen to how they speak. If you can, go to different areas and listen to diverse groups of people. Note what they say and how they say it. Extra credit: Watch the body language of different groups of people. There's a lot more to what they're communicating than just the words they use!
5. Look at the section on speech patterns and play with different types of speech patterns in your dialogue. For instance, if you change the cadence and musicality of the speech, how does that change the character? Or, if you use some of the NLP distortions, such as nominalization, mind reading, and so on, how can you further distinguish characters by these specific forms of communication?

Colorful Language: Scatological Terminology and Other Dirty Words

Although colorful and "dirty" language is often looked down upon in polite society, the truth is that almost everyone uses these expressions. In some sectors of society they are among the most common words and are used to punctuate just about every sentence. To create realistic characters in certain types of games, it's useful at least to know what these words are and how to use them in a sentence. This is not to say that you should or must use them, but you should consider where they are appropriate and then decide who your audience is and what kind of rating you want your game to have.

Note that it is possible to include colorful language that isn't too off-color, but using euphemistic language can often seem inauthentic and will put people off if it is used in the wrong place. For instance, in some cultures using *darn* instead of *damn* would be completely wrong. But in some cultures it would be completely right. The trick is to know the language of the people and culture you are modeling and use it appropriately. But if you choose not to use the real language because it is too disturbing or it will destroy your game's ratings, then by all means do not use soft euphemistic language in its place!

Speaking of euphemisms, they are used often, and the variety is staggering. Some are used quite often, while others are obscure. The nice thing about such terminology is that you can make it up. Slang and euphemistic expressions lend themselves well to experimentation and invention, so feel free to come up with your own. As long as the context is clear, most people will grok what you mean and get jiggy with it.

We have compiled some lists of euphemisms and also words that are often banned from various games and websites. However, rather than print them here, we will provide them on our associated website, davidperry.ning.com.

Part V Worlds

17 Game Worlds

Are you tired of playing games with "Iceworld" or "Fireworld"? Why do developers keep reaching for the same environments? What other kinds of worlds are there? As a mental exercise, pick a story you love—say, *The Godfather*—then imagine it in one of the worlds discussed in this chapter. Fantasy, for example—how could you change the story if you were released from the rules that a realistic world requires? The movie *The Matrix* did that with the story of the Messiah, for example.

In this chapter:

- What Is a World?
- Types of Worlds
- Perception of Freedom
- Ways to Make a World Feel Alive and Real
- Randomness
- Cause and Effect
- Continuity
- NPCs
- Animation and Effects
- Lighting
- What Is Reality? (Common Reality Distortions)
- Dangerous Places
- Places to Get Lost In
- Environmental Effects on Locations
- Good Places to Attack or Defend
- Moving or Transient Locations
- Weather Types and Phenomena
- Location Surfaces
- Location Sizes
- Money and Commerce
- Politics
- Creating Your World

What Is a World?

What constitutes a world? In game terms, it is the entire environment in which players have their experiences.

- **The Terrain.** The terrain of a world can be anything. It can be as vast as space or as contained as a single building, or even a single room. Wherever the game takes place, that is the game world. It can be mountainous, flat, a water world, a volcanic inferno, or any combination you can imagine. It can be under the ground, above the ground, in space, or a combination of each. It may consist of dozens of separate and distinct areas, or it may be more or less homogeneous throughout.

- **The Rules.** Determining the rules that govern a world is one of the most important jobs, because the rules will determine behavior and gameplay. For instance, most worlds assume a more or less earth-like environment—breathable air, gravity, basic cause-and-effect physics, and so on. However, worlds don't have to have the same rules. To create a unique game experience, one place to start is with the rules. Obviously, many fantasy games use earthlike rules, but add a component of magic that is outside our modern world view. Can you take that concept further? What about a world where the logic and rules of cartoons prevail, but everything else is normal? So, you might be able to manifest a gigantic hammer out of nowhere to hit someone, and he would flatten like a pancake. Maybe the only rule in that world would be that it be funny. The hammer would be there, and you would have to do something funny with it. Or maybe the rule change would affect only one aspect of what we know as reality. For instance, imagine that you created a world where all the water was caustic and would destroy anything that touched it. How would that suggest different stories and different puzzles, challenges, and experiences? What would happen if the planetary poles suddenly shifted, and north was south and vice versa?
- **The Sentient and Non-Sentient Creatures.** Who and what populate your world? What purpose or role do they play in the game? Many games use some imagination in creating visually distinct enemies, but spend little time considering NPC characters that might be different from the usual shopkeepers, guards, warriors, and general populace. How could you create some different characters? Likewise, what non-sentient creatures inhabit your world? What do they look like? How do they interact with each other, with the other races, and with the player's character? What function, if any, do they serve in the game?
- **The Flora.** Are there plants? If so, what are they? Do they serve any function in the game, other than decoration? Are they sentient? Are they usable for food or materials? Are some of them dangerous? How do you deal with them in the game? Do they change with the seasons or with night and day? Do they grow as the game progresses? Are they made of something other than normal plant matter, such as crystals or stone?
- **Political and Environmental Systems.** The world you create in a game is more than just the set you create and the flora and fauna you add to it. The world is also the interconnected elements—the way the various elements interact in the world. This can include the ecology of the world—what eats what and what factors limit overpopulation, for instance. And who controls the world? What kinds of governments (if any) exist? Who is feuding or at war with whom? Who rules? Who rebels? Who allies? Who is trustworthy? Who is not?

  Creating the elements of the situation involves an understanding of the overall relationships of every important element of the game. It helps to know the past—what led up to the current situation. It also helps to understand how different characters and groups feel about each other character/group. If you think of your game world as a system, you can see what affects the system and how. What stabilizes the system? What destabilizes it? Finally, add the player's character. How does the player's character change or affect the system? What is the player character's *role* in this world?
- **Value Systems.** In addition to the various political systems, there are systems of values. What is money? What do people use for trade or commerce? What are the belief systems and moral/ethical values that govern the world you are creating? Are there some universally held beliefs among the entities of your game? Are they in some ways different from those held by modern people? What views do the entities of your game have on:

- Family relationships
- Love
- Sexuality
- Power
- Money and ownership
- Trust and respect
- Honesty and integrity
- Conflict
- Violence
- Life and death
- Fairness
- Medicine
- Magic
- Technology
- Outsiders
- Humor (what kind, if any?)

What other values might the residents of your world have?

Before creating a game, consider whether you have made absolute assumptions about these and other value systems. How might a game be more interesting if some of these views were different from modern norms? Certainly if a game is set in the past or the future, beliefs might be different. When you are creating a world, you should be aware of what values are common, what values are regional or unique to a specific ideological group in your world, and what values your main characters have. Also consider whether the player's character starts out with some specific value system or ideology. Might those values change during the course of the game, based on the player's decisions and actions?

- **Culture.** Are there some very specific cultural behaviors among the inhabitants of the worlds you are creating? For instance, are there actions an ordinary person from the United States might take that would be considered insulting or scandalous in your world? Are there simple gestures that might have unexpected meaning? To what extent do you want to create a unique culture with unique expectations and behavior? How does the culture reflect the value systems of the group? Sometimes cultures can be designed from the history of a single group of people, such as merchants who started a trading post that over time became a city. What other groups could become the foundation for an entire culture?

Types of Worlds

The world you create can have a broad definition or identity. For instance, it could be the planet Earth, or it could be some other planet. Your game could take place in a world so unlike ours that it would hardly be recognizable, or so close as to be indistinguishable, but with certain key differences. Here are a few suggestions for types of worlds you might create, but they are suggestions only. You might come up with worlds totally different from any on this list. As long as you can make it fun, it works.

- **Fantasy.** Creating a fantasy world is pretty much unlimited. If you can think of it, you can do it. In a fantasy world, you can modify the rules as you see fit—nothing needs to be as it is in a normal world. This includes elements such as gravity, light, shadows, and the size of things (a 40-foot mouse!). Inanimate things can become alive (such as tombstones); animals can talk; plants can be mobile and have emotions (aggressive or sympathetic trees!); perceptions can be altered; abilities can be altered. Basically, every element you think of, you can twist and adjust its behavior. So don't just add in a unicorn and think you're making a fantasy game.
- **Perspective Worlds.** This is a variant of a fantasy world, but where the player's perspective is changed in some significant way. Think of worlds where you are very small or very large, or where your way of perceiving the world is unique (for example, you see into the infrared or you can visualize through hearing).

- **Our World.** The world we know is both fascinating and full of opportunities. It's fun to explore the places we all know or have heard of. It might be even more fun to explore places we aren't allowed to go—such as Area 51, inside the space shuttle, or inside a nuclear reactor. Or, perhaps exploring other cultures and locations that we ordinarily wouldn't experience.
- **Futuristic.** It's our world (or one somewhat like it), but with new inventions, new ideas, new places, extrapolations of today's trends, worlds that result from our actions today, variants of places we already know. Like New York, but with 500 more skyscrapers or a world dominated by sentient reptiles (who could survive radiation better than mammals). Futuristic science fiction has been written for more than a hundred years. There are plenty of potential future worlds to choose from. Take one from literature or create one of your own.
- **Sci-Fi.** Science fiction worlds contrast with fantasy worlds in that the rules are based around science and scientific principles. However, a sci-fi world can use just about any backdrop and can be futuristic, past-focused, or even a variant on our own world. Sci-fi worlds often include space travel or other planetary systems, but they can also take place on a single world or even in a single city. The rules of sci-fi worlds generally follow our accepted concepts of physics, with a bit of imagination thrown in. For instance, in a sci-fi world, it is perfectly acceptable to have faster-than-light travel, nanotechnology, unlimited energy from cold fusion, teleportation devices, and any number of cool technologies that we wish we had now but don't.
- **Past or Historical or Period.** History is a vast playground for stories and for adventures. You can create historically accurate experiences or something that approximates history and uses some recognizable period as its backdrop. For instance, you could (more or less accurately) re-create the Peloponnesian War, or you could simply place a made-up hero in Ancient Greece and involve him in some made-up story, but with all the backdrop, culture, and politics of the times. Games have been set in the samurai culture of medieval Japan and the warlord world of ancient China. What other fascinating historical or modern settings would make interesting games?
- **Mythological and Supernatural.** Human history is full of myths and stories of supernatural events. Like true historical subjects, myths and stories are perfect for game development, particularly if they have stood the test of time and still exist as part of our modern mythos. Some myths and supernatural subjects have been used, often in bits and pieces. For instance, there are tons of vampire games. But there are a lot of stories and myths that have never been turned into games, so there's a reasonably wide-open field of opportunity if you're looking for a world to inhabit.
- **Exploration of Worlds.** You might create a game that explores different worlds—such as a science fiction game in which you explore many worlds, each unique. Oh wait. That's been done many times. That's *Star Trek*. That's also *Spore*. But seriously, because the potential variety of worlds is practically infinite, games that explore different worlds can each have unique qualities. Perhaps your game is about conquest, in which you must subdue world after world. Or it's a game of collecting items—an intergalactic scavenger hunt. Or it's about commerce and manufacturing. Or it's a game of social exploration, perhaps seeking a clue to a great mystery or even chasing an elusive enemy who flits from one world to the next.
- **Fictional Works.** A lot of games can be (and have been) based on famous books/movies/TV shows. You can adhere strictly to the type of world of the original source or just use the basic elements or inspiration gained from the original story. Think of *Lord of the Rings*, which has influenced a lot of games, or James Bond or *Harry Potter*. But perhaps you can gain inspiration from mythology or Polynesian cultures or your favorite science fiction author. You can choose to be inspired or re-create the property faithfully by licensing it or using one that is in the public domain.

Design Challenge

1. Can you combine different worlds? How?
    a. Explore combining different types of worlds with different features.
    b. Explore combining elements of your favorite books, TV shows, or movies and creating a world that is unlike any of them.
2. Can you come up with a functional world that you've never seen before? Would it make the setting for a great game?

Point of View

Part of your world's design includes how you visualize it. Check out Chapter 5, "Game POV and Game Genres," and think about the world perspective you will give the player and the style of presentation. Is it going to be cartoon-like, super-realistic, or even presented in some *avant-garde* artistic style? Is it first-person view, some form of third-person, or some combination of POVs?

Perception of Freedom

Games are necessarily limited, although cyberspace is potentially without limits. However, in all games there are resource restrictions and content restrictions. Still, it is often preferable for the player to think he is in control and that the world is very open-ended. The key to creating a sense of freedom in games, however, does not necessarily mean making the game bigger. A larger game environment can certainly seem freer, but only if it is well designed.

This section has three subsections:

- Basics of Creating Freedom
- Principles of Player Freedom
- What Restricts the Player?

Basics of Creating Freedom

Some of the key elements in enhancing the sense of freedom are:

- **Choice.** Choice is arguably the biggest factor in enhancing the sense of freedom. The more options players have (within limits), and the more choices they can make when exploring those options, the freer they will feel. Another example of choice comes when the player can interact with the environment so that there is a lot to do, even within a limited space.

  It's important to note that simply offering a lot of choices and options does not necessarily make a game feel freer. The choices and options should enhance the gameplay, not add complexity for complexity's sake. In addition, choices must be meaningful. The choices the player makes must each have a different effect on the game or situation—or at least the player's responses. If all choices essentially lead to the same result, then they aren't really choices. For instance, if all weapons do exactly the same damage and are equally effective in all situations, then the choice of using one weapon rather than another is not really a choice. However, if weapons have different looks, and players prefer, say, carrying a giant club over carrying a jewel-encrusted sword, then the choice they make is meaningful to them, which is what counts. However, even more significant is the difference between an assault rifle and a flamethrower, or a standard shrapnel grenade versus a flash bang. Or imagine the player has

Part V

two roads to take. If each leads to the same location and nothing really different happens on either, then the choice is not particularly meaningful unless the scenery is particularly appealing. But if one road leads to specific encounters or to new routes that the other road does not, then the choice is quite meaningful in game terms.

- **Nonlinear Design.** As a corollary to choice (really, a subset), consider nonlinearity. Linear games are games in which the plot or game action tends to move along a single line, forcing the player to experience a series of game scenarios that are predetermined and only reachable if the player can get past previous obstacles. There's nothing wrong with this approach—it works remarkably well in some games, particularly in action games that seem to propel you forward—but if a sense of freedom is desirable in a game, then choice is far preferable, and nonlinear game design is a key element. Imagine *GTA III* if you could only drive from one mission location to the next and only do what the missions required. Nonlinear design often goes hand in hand with emergent stories, as opposed to predetermined stories. Emergent stories emerge from the player's interaction with the environment and other characters and, as such, contribute to the magic of the game. Whether an emergent story feels freer than a predetermined story may depend on the game itself and how things unfold, but it is true that many games that feature emergent story elements also have more open-ended structures, thereby being freer from the player's perspective.
- **Size.** A larger world or a bigger story or mission structure can make a game seem more open and, if combined with other factors, freer. Certainly it's likely that players would feel a greater sense of freedom if they played a game set in an entire city than they would if the whole game were set in a single room, and possibly more sense of freedom if the game were set in a landscape with open spaces and several cities over one that is confined only to one city. Of course, good game design can affect the situation, so these are generalities, and the result depends largely on other design factors—choice being among the most critical. A well-designed game set in a single house could seem freer than a poorly designed game set in an entire city.

  Another way to look at size is through the level or amount of detail present in your world. The more detail you include, the more options you may offer the player, and the larger the set of choices they will have. For instance, in many games, you walk down a street, and the buildings to either side of you cannot be entered. They are mere façades. What if every door leads somewhere? Does that make a better game or just give the player a lot more to explore? The question is, in this case, does size matter? More is not always better. So if you have doors that lead somewhere, that "somewhere" should provide enjoyment, good gameplay, and some kind of payoff. If not, then there's just a lot of empty space to explore.

  I'm not suggesting that you shouldn't increase the detail of your games. Quite the opposite—I encourage you to do so, but to make sure the player is having a meaningful experience interacting with all that added detail. If you do that, you not only have a functionally larger game, but a more compelling one that offers more experiences to the player.
- **Unpredictability.** Unpredictable events make a game feel more real and more alive and can enhance the idea of freedom by changing a player's focus from a one-pointed goal to flexible responses to unexpected situations. A one-pointed focus can feel restrictive, so keeping the player's mind flexible will also keep it freer. One caveat: Randomness and unpredictability can enliven your game, but too much of it can become frustrating. Remember that, to some extent, predictability is at the core of a lot of game design. Players want to be surprised, but they also want to feel empowered. In a world where nothing makes sense, they will not have the necessary control over their environment to feel empowered and effective. The basic structure of your world has to make sense to players, and they need to understand how they can operate in that world. Once you have established that foundation, you can offer random and unpredictable elements to keep players on their toes.

Principles of Player Freedom

What is freedom? In the political sense it is the ability to make fundamental choices about how you live your life. In games, freedom is also largely about choice, but since the game designer determines the rules of the game world, it is also the designer who defines the limits or extent of freedom the player has. In order for a game to be fun, there have to be some restrictions—rules that govern outcomes and allowable actions, for instance—but there also should be opportunities, and in the game sense, freedom is about opportunities. Here are some of the kinds of freedoms that work well in games. Can you think of some others?

- **Freedom of Movement.** Nothing gives the perception of freedom as instantly as allowing players to choose their own directions and giving them either a choice of paths or a pathless, open environment. Let the player explore the available world without too many obvious restrictions. It's good to create some obstacles and to hold out areas that can be explored as the game progresses (see also Chapter 25, "Barriers, Obstacles, and Detectors"), but letting players wander and explore, take alternate routes, and determine their own strategies, destinations, and directions enhances the perception of freedom, even if the plot or game structure is ultimately directing them in a particular direction.
- **Exploration.** Games in which there is a lot of exploration tend to feel more wide open. There's nothing like exploring an area and then discovering a whole new region or some really interesting new location—or even an extensive underground tunnel/maze/cave that provides further opportunities for exploration. And having incremental rewards (see also Chapter 23, "Goals," and Chapter 24, "Rewards, Bonuses, and Penalties") helps keep the exploration fresh.
- **Experimentation.** A game that encourages creativity and allows for experimentation engages players and makes them forget the limits imposed within the game. Experimentation goes well with games that also encourage open-endedness and the elements of freedom. Give players plenty to work with and different ways to approach situations or to combine elements.
- **Interactive Objects.** Make as many objects in the environment as interactive as possible. The more alive the world seems, the more there is to explore, and therefore the less restrictive and limited the world feels. However, to the extent that you can, make the interactions with objects in the environment as meaningful as possible. For instance, if you let the player get a soda from a machine, that soda should do something, such as give the player a little health or provide him with a temporary ability or boost to existing abilities. Or the soda might be used to trade with another character for a useful item. The more meaningful the result of interaction, in general, the better. The thing you need to keep in mind, though, is that meaningful doesn't always mean useful to the system. Some interactive objects can have comedic value, surprising the player, such as the soda spraying all over the place. These things are not meaningful to the actual gameplay, but they do add value to the game.
- **Player-Created Content.** Allowing players to create anything from unique avatars to useful items such as weapons, armor, and power-ups, to whole new levels or even completely independent modules can significantly increase the novelty and variety offered in a game or game system. Of course, in games played in the real world, there's often considerable opportunity for flexibility and variety among players. In computer and video games, however, this sort of flexibility often has to be designed carefully to achieve desirable options and individual expression without unbalancing or otherwise becoming detrimental to the overall game experience. Although this may be important in single-player games, it is of even greater significance in multiplayer games.
- **Recycling.** It's very politically correct to recycle, and game designers do it all the time. The idea is to allow a player to pass through an area or zone and experience a lot of gameplay there, but design it so that there is more that can be done once the player has gained in abilities or new plot/story elements reveal more about the area and make it interesting to revisit. The reward of being able to

Part V

complete tasks or actions that were previously impossible also enhances the feeling of being in control, and, especially if players are allowed to rediscover the area on their own, the perception of freedom as well. This concept also works with NPCs where, when players return to a city or settlement, they can find new interactions with the NPCs, rather than the same old stale ones.

- **The Plots Thicken.** Create more than one plotline, and let the player choose among various clues leading to different situations. (See also Chapter 9, "Storytelling Techniques.")
- **Optional Activities.** Create as many optional quests, missions, tasks, and activities as you can. These can be as simple as discovering false walls or hidden doors, which lead to new areas to explore, or as complex as offering whole optional quests or even professions for players to engage in. Interactive objects, experimentation, and exploration come together to make the world seem more believable by showing the official plot isn't the only thing going on.
- **Many Missions.** Another way to enhance the concept of freedom is to create a lot of missions in a mission-based game. If you can randomly generate many of the missions, you further enhance the sense of openness to the game, particularly if a player can choose from among several mission paths, so the game does not appear to be linear. Creating multiple reward paths and bonus goals further enhances the sense of choice and therefore the sense of freedom.
- **Open-Endedness.** The idea of a game that has no beginning and no end but is an ongoing experience can provide a great sense of freedom. Good examples are sim games, which are not games with specific predetermined goals. Players create their own goals, which can change from one time to the next. Some level-based action games can go on forever, simply getting harder as they go, until they become too hard for human reflexes to cope with. Such games certainly challenge players to achieve greater and greater success and, in a minor way, enhance a sense of freedom in that there is no end in sight. After all, you know you can always do a little better next time. Massive Multiplayer Games and games with exceptional levels of choice, such as *Grand Theft Auto III* and its sequels, also seem endless and full of options for how to play.
- **The Elements of Freedom.** Many games, MMORPGs in particular, create the elements of interaction without necessarily creating the story or the specifics of the players' activities. By setting the necessary elements of a game before the player, you can encourage individual expression and a wide variety of game experiences, including emergent stories and meaningful social interaction. This is similar to open-endedness in that the game and the momentary goal-setting within the game are pretty much up to the player and are not necessarily predetermined. God games (such as Peter Molyneux's *Populace* or *Black & White*) work this way too, by suggesting an outcome but allowing players to determine any number of ways to get that outcome, using the elements that come with their godlike nature.
- **New Openings.** Periodically during a game, you should expand the scope of the game. This is common in RPGs, where the world at the beginning is generally very small but continues to expand as the plot unfolds. Often, about mid-game, the player gains the ability to travel everywhere, even the places that had previously been closed. The world seems very large by comparison. This can also occur in strategy games, especially with the development of new technologies that allow access to areas previously out of reach. In story-based shooters, whole new story elements can be introduced at key points in the plot, which could significantly open up the game experience, even going as far as to switch sides completely, as in *Halo.*
- **Freedom in Complexity.** In some games, such as Turn-Based and Real-Time Strategy games, you may begin with a very small amount of information and a very small circle of influence. However, as the game progresses, you will find yourself managing a much greater amount of information, directing dozens of units and ranging over a very wide territory. The way such games build up and add on enhances the idea of freedom and expansion, and they rarely feel restrictive. If all that information

were presented to you from the beginning, the game would seem confusing and impossible to manage. A good example of this is any game from Sid Meier's *Civilization* series.

- **Random Generation.** One way to keep a game open and free is to create random elements, such as events, scenes, objects, quests and missions, and even territories. Such randomness creates a different rhythm and pace to the game, keeps it fresh and unpredictable, and makes the game seem more open.
- **The Great Big Map.** Some games create a sense of freedom by having a massive map or by randomly generating new locations. For instance, many games set in outer space can randomly generate planets with almost no limits, making them seem unlimited. It may also be possible to randomly generate NPCs with whom the player can interact. Other games simply create a world on a very large scale and allow players to explore freely, perhaps with some restrictions to control pacing and story development.
- **The Effect of Time.** Time pressure—urgency—can have a narrowing effect on players. Partly, this is because the very nature of racing against a deadline or countdown timer restricts the range of options a player has. In contrast, when there is no real urgency or time pressure, players have the luxury to experiment and try everything. However, that is not to say that time pressure should be avoided. The trick in establishing a sense of freedom is to allow players to explore at leisure and to use time pressure in specific circumstances to change the pace and urgency of the game on occasion. Also, many games impose an artificial sense of time pressure, making it seem urgent when it really isn't. Experienced players generally will recognize this kind of false urgency and take their time exploring and checking out all their options before proceeding. However, an inexperienced player may think the false time pressure is real and hurry through parts of the game that were better played at leisure. If a player takes a false time pressure seriously, the result will be a reduced perception of freedom, but possibly a good learning experience.

  Additionally, time can be used to affect the player's experience in other ways, such as changing the time of day or the seasons of the year. Various gameplay-related elements may depend on time or the effects of time passing. Maybe you can't reach a cave that is on the other side of a lake until the lake freezes in winter. Or maybe you can't catch the werewolf until the full moon. For more on the effects of time in games, see Chapter 29, "Time Limits and Time Manipulation."
- **Use All Dimensions.** To further enhance the sense of freedom, allow players to experience three-dimensional thrills. Let them swim and dive to the bottom. Let them fly. Let them go underground and explore dark, dank places or fiery caverns...whatever. But let them move. In some games, it's even useful to let them move through time—the fourth dimension. Or outer space. Or even inner space (the dimension of the mind). Different-sized frames/scales could include cellular, microscopic, small, large, planetary, or galactic.
- **Puzzles.** By puzzles, I don't necessarily mean literal puzzles, like crosswords or Rubik's Cubes. I mean that situations players find themselves in should engage their minds. While engaged and focused, time passes very differently from when things are ho-hum and same old, same old. Mental (and physical) challenges can make even a small environment seem much bigger, simply by the additional energy and time it takes to interact with them. Therefore, instead of having a room in a game where you add a few enemies and call it done, consider creating a situation in that room—a situation that the player must figure out in order to advance. This makes that room more than just something the player has passed through. It becomes an experience. Which would seem bigger—a game with 10 rooms, each of which was pretty much the same and had limited options, or a game with 10 rooms, each of which was a new challenge to master and possibly full of different activities, options, or opportunities? The answer is obvious. But even in a very large game, you can add significantly by considering the makeup and nature of challenges in every aspect of the game and in every location. (See also Chapter 27, "Puzzles.")

- **Open Spaces and Safe Zones.** As a corollary to the preceding paragraph, however, players also need relief from stress. In some high-intensity games, every step the player takes is contested. However, in many games varying the pace is preferable, and having the player go through a sequence of heavy challenges to be followed by some exploration with minimal challenge or a chance to rest in a town or do something less focused can enhance the openness of the experience. This can be especially true in games with large maps. Some parts of the map might be especially dangerous, but others can be quite tame, with perhaps a few interesting views, items to locate, or something new to discover. Sometimes just the feeling of running across a vast landscape can provide a feeling of freedom.
- **Deep Immersion.** Some games give you the impression of freedom because, although they are not gigantic in size or scope, they have you so immersed in the action that they just seem bigger. *Doom* was a great example of a game that wasn't all that large, really, but that seemed big because every moment was intense. You didn't think about size in traditional terms, but about how deeply you were embedded in the experience when it was happening.

What Restricts the Player?

While many elements of a game can contribute to the sense of freedom, other elements can be restrictive. In this section, I'm not talking about traps, barriers, and obstacles put into the game to restrict motion or freedom intentionally. Those are covered in Chapter 25, "Barriers, Obstacles, and Detectors," and Chapter 26, "Traps and Counter Traps." This list is about ways that people may inadvertently restrict the sense of freedom in a game.

- **Time Pressure.** This tends to constrict a sense of freedom, though it can be used effectively, especially if balanced with less time-sensitive experiences. In large map games, time pressure can be used to encourage players to explore further (especially timid or less aggressive players). By giving them a mission or quest that requires them to go to a new area within a specifically allotted amount of time, time pressure becomes an asset that broadens freedom. (See also Chapter 28, "Controlling Pacing," and Chapter 29, "Time Limits and Time Manipulation.")
- **Small Game without Big Gameplay.** Having a small map or small area doesn't necessarily restrict the impression of freedom for a player, but in a game with a small space, there has to be a lot to do. (Of course, this doesn't refer to arcade games such as *Tetris* or *Missile Command*, where the size of the game space is not relevant but the ongoing challenge is.)
- **Lack of Choices.** This is the most basic of restrictions. If the player is forced into very narrow options, the experience of freedom is necessarily limited. For instance, having a shooter in which there is only one gun and no power-ups would be pretty restrictive—and possibly boring. Having an RTS with only one technology path or with only one type of warrior would be boring and restrictive. Giving players at least some options and choices certainly creates better games in almost every case, but it also enhances the perception of freedom.
- **Too Many Choices.** Obviously, the corollary to having a lack of choices is that too many choices, particularly meaningless complexity, is actually restrictive as well. Just having a hundred different unit options doesn't make a game necessarily better. It might be that the ideal number is five…or twenty. So, players need to have choices and options, but the choices and options you offer them must be meaningful to the game and to the players' goals. (See Chapter 23, "Goals," and Chapter 24, "Rewards, Bonuses, and Penalties.")
- **Non-Interactive Environments.** You can have lots of rooms with lots of objects in them, but if you can't interact with any of them, they are window dressing. I'm not saying that a good game has to make every object and NPC interactive to the player, but to the extent that you increase interactivity in the environments you make, you increase the perception of freedom by virtue of additional player

choices. Still, interaction with the environment, to be really useful, should be meaningful. You can chop down trees. So what? But what if you can use the lumber or clear a road, or what if cutting too many trees changes the local ecology and displaces wild beasts or causes the climate to change? What if you can cut down trees to block your enemy's supply lines or even to drop them on top of your enemies? In each case, cutting trees has meaning to the player and is worth doing. Cutting trees where there is no effect whatsoever is ultimately boring, and in my world, boring is restrictive. (Also, see the upcoming "Interactivity with the Environment" section.)

- **Too Much Information.** Players often get a lot of information at different points in a game, but if the game is well designed, they are ready to use and absorb that information. But if too much information is given to players when they aren't prepared to deal with it all, they can retreat into confusion, and overly confused players are restricted in their sense of connection to the game. Some confusion is desirable. Players should be mystified at times and curious. So it's just a matter of not overloading a player or presenting too much at once.
- **Too Little Information.** On the other hand, when there is just not enough information to work with, players can feel restricted by not knowing what to do or even what the options are. There's a range between too much and too little information; players want to have stuff to figure out, but not be totally in the dark—at least not usually. Sometimes leaving players floundering can be okay, but not when there's too much of it. And, if you are going to leave players completely in the dark about something, it's sometimes helpful to make it obvious that they *aren't supposed to know that yet.* There are many ways to inform players that they aren't going to get their questions answered—yet—through interactions with NPCs or sometimes simply by the way you unfold events, where the mysterious aspects of the world are obvious, and it's clear enough that the answers will come in time.
- **Too Few Options/Skills/Weapons/Etc.** This is obvious and similar to the Lack of Choices item, but it is more specific to the system, where lack of choices refers more to the story or player decisions during the game. Having one gun, one or two skills or abilities, and limited options for enjoying the game is restrictive, although having one or two weapons and a lot of ways to use them is not. Imagine *Tomb Raider* without the ability to climb up to high places or without the ability to jump. You might still enjoy the game, but it wouldn't be the *Tomb Raider* we know.
- **Meaningless Interactivity.** Despite the previous item, some activity does nothing to enhance a game or to enhance the perception of freedom. For instance, it doesn't do much for a player if he can go up to a soda vending machine and have it pop out some pop if you can't get something from the pop itself—such as quenching thirst or perhaps reviving health or even a special buzz that makes you move faster for a short time. Just having a can come out of the machine isn't really meaningful interactivity and ultimately does little after the first time a player does it and finds out it is useless. In this case, where there's a reward or purpose, it's meaningful. Otherwise, it's not.

  This same principle applies to interaction with NPCs. For instance, just because you can interact with every NPC in a game, that doesn't mean it's good. If most of the interactions lead to meaningless dialog that has nothing to do with the gameplay, then it's mostly a waste of the player's time. That doesn't mean the relevance of an interaction has to be obvious. It could be subtle or obscure, but it should ultimately have some meaning. (Refer to the Too Much Information and Too Little Information items earlier in this list.)
- **Linear Fixed Missions.** Although many games successfully work with fairly fixed structures of missions and/or levels, these types of games often do not feel as free and unrestricted as games in which players have more choices of what they do. (See the next item on the list.) However, even with fixed mission structures, a well-designed game can feel free if the gameplay within the mission allows for experimentation, choice, and variety.
- **Fixed Paths.** Like fixed missions, putting your characters on a rail or steering them to only one path, even when others seem to be available, is restrictive and lessens the perception of freedom. Some

games have beautiful artwork that suggests a larger world around the player, but they cannot visit any of the landscape they see. They can only stay on a very restricted path, perhaps with occasional intersections and forks. Seeing a larger landscape and being unable to enter it feels restrictive.

- **Repetitive NPCs.** NPCs who continually say the same thing hurt the sense of immersion and illusion that makes a game seem real. It's a cliché that NPCs rarely change their tune unless they are part of a mission/quest or about to tell you about one. However, games where there is variety and a bit of the unexpected seem more real and, as a consequence, more free. It's a minor point, and less important than some others, but more interesting NPCs can create a more interesting world environment, and it probably would only require a good writing team a few days to come up with plenty of variations, jokes, and interesting comments from NPCs. With a little more work, the NPCs could actually make relevant statements based on the player's own experience in the game to that point.
- **Repetitive Mission Types.** This is pretty self-explanatory. Variety is the spice of life and gaming, and having a bunch of cloned-off missions that all feel the same is stifling to a game and ultimately, in an indirect way, to the sense of being free. Conversely, having missions that are different and surprising, offering different experiences and challenges, makes a game seem bigger, broader, deeper, and freer. There are advantages to having some predictability or consistency within a game, however. And there are games that seem to thrive on repetitive mission types. So this isn't a fixed rule, but an invitation to make games more interesting by adding more variety to the way missions, tasks, and quests are designed.
- **Lack of Mental Challenge.** If a game doesn't challenge the mind, it ultimately gets boring and feels restrictive. How often have you played a game that seemed fun at first, but never got beyond its original premise? You found yourself doing the same things over and over by rote and ultimately asking yourself, "Why am I still playing this?" Chances are those aren't the games you finish.
- **Repetitive and Awkward Interfaces.** Having done the same thing over and over again in an inefficient manner can be very irritating. Many games require repetitive actions—in fact, most games do. But when the repetitive action is annoyingly awkward to do, especially when the immediate reward is minimal, it is tiring and restrictive from the point of view of wanting to continue playing.
- **Too Much Character Maintenance.** In some games, it's fun to have to feed your character, rest when they get tired, repair equipment, clean up after them, and so on. It works in some games, but too much of it can be stifling and can detract from the main fun of the game (unless that is the fun). In a game of exploration and/or action, too much character maintenance may limit your range of exploration, the speed at which you can experience the action, and other aspects of the game. What? I have to stop and feed this guy again? I have to repair that sword? I just did that five minutes ago. (It was probably an hour ago, but that's the nature of subjective time-shifting in games.) Balance plays a large part in this, however, since character maintenance is often intentional and a part of the game, but you need to find the line where it becomes too much.
- **Sore Feet.** Too much meaningless travel from this place to that place, with little purpose or little reward, is not fun. Travel from place to place can be very rewarding and fun and can further the game in many ways, but the fourth or fifth time you've done the same long trek to deliver a message, it will seem dull and annoying. This is restrictive. If you have to make me travel, give it some variety and a decent amount of reward. Or give me a shortcut after the first or second time I've already made the journey—a teleportation device, fast conveyance, or something. On the other hand, depending on the game, you may need to be careful that you don't make travel too easy or convenient, particularly if world exploration and chance encounters form a large part of the gameplay. As always, balance is key.
- **Bad Acting/Dialog/Plot.** Yes, a game will seem more restrictive if you aren't engaged. If a story sucks or the acting is totally lame, the game won't feel as open and engaging, the rooms will seem to shrink in on you, and you'll just want to get out. If you're deeply immersed in the world, you feel expanded somehow, but if you're barely tolerating it, you may be looking for something else to do

instead of playing this game. Well, at least that's what happens to me. Of course, where the acting is intentionally bad, as in a parody of bad acting, that can be amusing if it's not overdone.

Note that each of the examples in this section depends on subjective evaluations. None of them is absolute, and each game requires its own balance of elements. For that reason, I encourage you to consider each of these items as suggestions or warning signs, but not as absolute truisms. (See also Chapter 21, "Experiential Design"—the sections on what is fun or not fun.)

Design Challenge

1. Take a few games you have played—some you liked a lot and some you didn't like all that much. Analyze how those games enhanced or restricted your sense of freedom. Use this chapter as a reference, but also see whether you can detect any methods not mentioned here.
2. Think of ways to enhance a player's sense of freedom in the following types of games:
    a. Role-Playing
    b. First-Person Shooter
    c. Real-Time Strategy
    d. Arcade action
    e. War/battle
    f. Massive Multiplayer
3. Take a game concept of your own and find at least five ways that you can enhance the player's perception of freedom in its implementation.
4. Consider how restricting the freedom of players can be useful. How would you define the limits of freedom versus restriction, and what games that you've played have had the best balance? Are there differences in how you see freedom versus restriction based on the game genre? Do you expect different types of freedom and restriction in First-Person Shooters, Real-Time Strategy games, Role-Playing Games, and Massive Multiplayer games? Can you define the differences and consider why they are different? Think about the player's motivation in each genre, as well as the types of activities they engage in.
5. Learning to identify restrictive elements can improve your games, so take a look at the "What Restricts the Player?" list and try to find examples of these restrictive elements in games you like and in games you didn't like—and in your own games. Were there some examples that you thought were restrictive, but that turned out to be fun anyway? Were there examples that you thought were fine, but on second thought felt restrictive after all?

Ways to Make a World Feel Alive and Real

Every game involves a world of its own, and immersive 3D games in particular provide environments that are diverse and full of opportunities to create a sense of reality and the unpredictability of a living world. In this section I look at some of the ways you can bring life and a greater sense of involvement to your worlds.

Interactivity with the Environment

Creating an environment that is interactive and responsive to the player's actions is one of the best ways to create a living world. While every game creates a world, not every game world takes full advantage of its many opportunities for player interaction. The more players can interact with the elements of the game world, and the more the game world itself responds to the player's actions, the more vibrant and real that world will seem...and the more satisfying the player's experience will be. Most games allow players to interact with doors and other common and necessary objects. However, to create the most realism in the game, you can go much further.

One caveat is to avoid interactivity that is simply frustrating. For instance, suppose you make a world in which every container, cabinet, or appliance can be opened, but you never put anything interesting inside these containers. What's the point of the interactivity? Be sure there's a reward for curiosity, exploration, and experimentation. How you reward players is up to you. You can do it in predictable ways—you open a desk drawer and find a clue, some money, or a gun—or in unpredictable ways—you open a desk drawer, and a jack-in-the-box springs out, or you find a girly magazine, a note from your girlfriend, or your most recent email (from the real world). The opportunities are pretty much endless.

Again and again in this book you'll encounter this idea. Interactivity is what it's all about. I've said it repeatedly. This chapter is all about the way to make a game as interactive as possible. There's plenty of room for expansion, however. This is just a guidepost for you to come up with your own ideas.

The General Environment

Players should be able to have an effect on the world around them. That means what they do should change the world. For example:

- You walk out into traffic, and the cars stop or swerve, perhaps causing a traffic jam or an accident. The cars might even hit you and show damage (not to mention the damage you suffer).
- You walk around town brandishing a weapon. People back away and try to avoid you, or they attack you.
- You are walking around with something interesting in your hand, and people respond to you because of it. For instance, you are carrying a balloon, and a kid comes up and asks whether he can have it. (What do you do, and what is the result of your decision?) Or you just completed a quest and obtained a fantastic jewel-encrusted amulet that gives you added health or something—and some people notice it and offer compliments or try to buy it, and some people want to steal it.
- You shoot a wall, and parts of the wall crack and fall away. When you come back later, the wall is still damaged, or perhaps someone is repairing it.
- You feed a barking dog one day, and the next time you pass by, it doesn't bark at you, but wags its tail expectantly.
- Elevators might work and allow you to punch your floor, hold the doors open, hit the emergency button, and so on. Think of gameplay reasons to control the elevator directly.
- You can pick flowers off bushes. Of course, there's the issue of what you do with those flowers, but there are lots of ways flowers can be useful—as gifts, as food or medicine, as decorations, as a way to jazz up your image, or as a way to cheer someone up or brighten an environment. There is also the possibility of getting in trouble for picking the flowers. Perhaps you are trespassing, and now you have to deal with the angry owner of the property—and the flowers. Any of these ideas could have impact in a game, depending on the premise and situations.
- You can open almost anything—a box, a drawer, a cabinet, a refrigerator or freezer, a cookie jar, and so on. But why do you open it? What's the reward?
- You pull a book from the bookshelf, and it opens a hidden doorway (or some other variant on that theme). Or maybe it has a loose sheet of paper in it with a clue, or some money or jewels hidden in a cavity carved into the middle, or it contains special magical incantations or a recipe for Aunt Martha's Pot Roast Pudding.

- When you pass near an NPC, he makes a comment—particularly a personalized comment—that acknowledges your presence. This is particularly effective in contested areas of a game. For example, you enter a town, or a section of a town, that's under siege. As you pass through the entrance to the area, the guards make a comment like, "Help has arrived. <*Your name*> is here. I've heard tell she's among the best and the bravest of our warriors." It doesn't matter that the player might be a relative beginner; hearing such a message from an NPC tends to give even the most jaded of players a little thrill. In MMOs this is even more effective because all players within the vicinity hear the message.

Vehicles

Vehicles have often been depicted in simplistic terms, except in vehicle simulators. There's nothing wrong with using vehicles as basic transportation, or, in arcade games, as simple objects that speed up, slow down, turn, crash, and little more. However, in making a game seem more alive, vehicles can be designed to enhance the experience in a variety of ways.

- The gauges work properly.
- You can turn your head and see what is going on to the side.
- You have a rear view (mirror, camera, etc.) that allows you to see behind the vehicle.
- The controls are logical and all functional.
- The vehicle moves realistically (for what it is) and with applied physics.
- You can use the radio or insert music CDs and have the game music change to whatever you have chosen.
- The vehicle has a GPS guidance system or equivalent.
- The vehicle talks to you.
- You can open the glove compartment and perhaps find interesting items inside.
- Likewise, you never know what might be hiding in the trunk.
- Windows are breakable.
- Damage is noticeable and increases over time if you are not careful with the vehicle.
- Vehicles are responsive to damage, so if you blow out one of your tires, the car handles differently.
- There are realistic passenger limits.
- Other people in the vehicle can use things, such as mounted weapons or power windows.

Other Machines

Other machines include the bizarre, the fantastic, and the mundane. For instance:

- You can open a cash register and find money.
- Telephones work unless you smash them up. Who can you call? Who will answer?
- Refrigerators, microwaves, and other kitchen appliances function.
- You find a blender in the kitchen and some fruit on the counter. You get some ice from the freezer and make yourself a smoothie. When you drink it, you feel better. Maybe different blends of ingredients affect you differently.
- Televisions, radios, and stereos function when you click on them. So do remote controls. Different programming is available, and perhaps some of it contains clues or is relevant to the game's plot, such as a news bulletin stating that you are wanted by the police.
- Data devices, such as computers, PDAs, and so on, should function and should access something.
- Vending machines should do something, even if it isn't useful. (Useful is by far preferred, however.)
- ATMs might be a way to get money.

- If something has buttons, levers, or knobs, they should do something when pressed, pulled, yanked, or twisted.
- Perhaps you can come up with a clever way to use a paper shredder, a stapler, or a paint sprayer?
- You find a mysterious alien device that's either an all-day sucker or a universal translator.
- Exposed live wires can cause shock or be used to electrocute an enemy or to power something.

Buildings

Often in games, buildings are nothing more than containers with walls and entrances/exits. However, buildings are full of opportunities for interaction:

- Windows can be opened, closed (locked or not), or broken.
- Lights turn on and off (unless you shoot out the bulbs or turn off the breakers).
- Bookshelves can contain readable books (and clues).
- What the player does should have an effect. For instance, if the player drops something, it stays where it was dropped. If he moves furniture, it stays where it was moved to.
- If the player shoots something—for instance, puts a bullet hole in a wall—it remains there. Maybe the police find the bullet and trace it to your gun.
- Vacant buildings can have people squatting in them. You can interact with them.
- Random buildings might contain useful items.
- Preferably, the interior of a building would match the exterior. For instance, if a building is several stories high, as seen from the outside, it should have several stories on the inside. It can be more interesting (though not required) if accessing the higher stories involves some kind of challenge or puzzle.

Caveat: If a building is empty and never has a purpose in the game, then having it be open and accessible is not so desirable. It simply wastes the player's time and leads to disappointment. If there's a place to explore, make it worthwhile, even if it cannot be explored until later in the game.

Shops

Many games feature shops, which are more often than not treated essentially as vending machines, even if there is the fiction of a shopkeeper. There is no haggling over price; rarely a concept of economy, where items might fluctuate in value based on supply and demand; and so forth. Here are a few ideas for making shops more interesting—but only if doing so would enhance the enjoyment of your game.

- Shops should have items on display. If possible, they should be items you can interact with.
- Shopkeepers will bargain, but they try to get the best price. Some might even refuse to bargain with the player if they are as low as they can go, the player doesn't have the authority to bargain, or the player has made an enemy out of the shopkeeper.
- If you keep selling the same thing, unless its value is established as a firm quantity, it will ultimately become less valuable.
- Some items are subject to fluctuations in price. For instance, food items might be more expensive in winter. Metal weapons and armor might fluctuate with availability of raw metal. You discover an iron deposit while exploring, and metal goods get cheaper. Iron deposits are exhausted, and metal objects gain in value and price. Gems and jewelry might change in value. For instance, suppose you found an emerald mine and brought in and sold a bunch of emeralds. Perhaps jewelry that uses emeralds (possibly for some magical purpose) would become cheaper. Or you found a great source of iron ore, and you go into business with the local blacksmith, also getting better prices from him for his products and services. And so forth...

- You can steal from shops, but don't get caught!
- You kill a shopkeeper, and the store is closed and boarded up the next time you come to shop there. Maybe you see a funeral procession driving by with mourners lamenting that the poor soul was killed by <*your name*>—but only if you left clues or someone saw you do it. Otherwise, how would they know it was you?
- If you're a good regular customer, the shopkeeper remembers you—he might even offer a special deal, a discount, a "buy 10 items, get one free card," or a bonus item.
- If you do something to upset or offend the shopkeeper, you'll have a hard time getting good deals or trading at all!
- Items you sell remain in the shopkeeper's inventory for a while. (However, they might get sold to someone else!)
- You might sell some unique item to a shop, only to find it on one of your enemies later. The enemy bought it and tried to use it against you.

Natural World

You can consider the natural world as simple window dressing—nice artwork and scenery—or you can consider it a living system that responds to the actions of the NPCs and the player. Here are some ideas for making the world seem more alive in your games. I'm sure you can think of many more.

- If you cut down a tree, it leaves a stump and a fallen log. Unless your game covers hundreds of years or someone uses the log for lumber, the stump and log should remain. Over time, animals move in and use it as a home. Termites eat it and fungus grows on it. If your game covers sufficient time, the natural features of the world would change.
- If you plant something, it should grow as time passes (unless conditions are so unfavorable that it dies).
- Some trees lose their leaves in winter. Others do not.
- Wind blows and varies in intensity and direction. Sometimes it gusts through the environment. Some places it's more or less constant. It blows more intensely during a storm.
- The world is dynamic—seasons change, day and night and dusk and dawn happen, moons rise and fall and go through phases, things grow, die, and decay, and so on. City streets get dirty; street cleaners come once a week and eliminate the trash. Planes fly overhead at intervals—more frequently (and lower) in the vicinity of an airport. Weather happens. When it rains, puddles are formed and dry up over time. When it snows, the snow may stick for a while, or it may build up and make routes difficult or impassable.
- You hunt predators, and consequently there are fewer of them. Moreover, there are more prey animals, which could become a problem. Or, you hunt the prey animals, causing the predators to be more desperate for food and therefore more aggressive over a wider territory.
- Creatures respond to you realistically. Some respond with fear; others with aggressiveness or even curiosity. It may be possible to alter a creature's response, perhaps by feeding it or helping it against an enemy. In some games, it's possible to tame creatures and make them your pets and companions.
- Creatures have a range of hearing, smell, and sight. It may be possible to sneak up on them or pass by unnoticed if you can judge the wind direction and other factors—and avoid stepping on a twig in the forest.

NPCs

NPCs often do very little to enhance the sense of realism in a game. They are like movable icons, sometimes representing a simple concept. There's nothing wrong with that—many of the early Role-Playing Games treated NPCs as simple scenery, with an occasional NPC who was an information giver. However, in recent years NPCs have begun to seem more alive and more like individuals with specific personalities and their own stories. Here are a few ways you might enhance the player's experience by enhancing the NPCs. You'll come up with more if you think about it.

- You steal something or do something mean, and the people around you notice and act differently. Conversely, you might do something kind or generous, and NPCs might notice that and act differently toward you.
- NPCs should always be true to their nature, which means that they will attempt to fulfill their purpose, whatever it is. So, NPC interactions should be consistent with who they are and what role they are playing. (See also Chapter 13, "Character Roles and Jobs.")
- You attack an NPC, who reacts with a realistic response—attacking back or cowering and possibly running away. It shouts at you, "What do you think you're doing?" It threatens, pleads, or complains. In the majority of games, if you attack an NPC who is not flagged to be attackable, then they are a) invulnerable, and b) completely unaffected in any way. Their body doesn't move. They don't say or do anything. Although this is pretty much a game cliché by now, it's far more interesting if your victim did or said something to indicate that attacking them wasn't cool, even if they don't fight back. One notable exception can be seen in the games *Morrowind* and *Oblivion*, in which you can kill pretty much anyone if you are strong enough, and they all tend to react to being attacked.
- You walk up to an NPC on the street and initiate conversation. The NPC reacts like anyone would. Some will talk to you. Some will tell you to buzz off. Some will look at you like you have a big gaping hole in your face.
- NPCs react to the players actions. For instance, if you are being chased by the police, some NPCs might try to stop you, and others will dive for cover. In a high-speed pursuit, people will pull over to let the police go by. Or you steal an ambulance, and people get out of your way when you turn on the lights and siren.

Random Objects and Effects

In addition to the predictable and expected items you'll find in any game, the world can also be populated by random items and effects.

- You shoot the tire of a car, and it loses control or begins to swerve.
- You open a mailbox and find mail in it.
- Parking meters are counting down time. People are coming and feeding the meters, and meter cops are giving tickets if they don't. You can put a quarter in the meter and stop the cop.
- The locals are having a parade. You can join it.
- A couple is having an argument. You step in and help them calm down. Maybe it works and something good comes of it. Maybe you end up in a fight.
- A drunk starts getting belligerent. You step in and help him sober up.
- You're exploring a house and find a coffeemaker with coffee in it. You pour yourself a cup and drink it. Maybe you feel a little energized.
- You can climb to the top of an electrical tower and make a zip line out of the high-tension wires.
- Some random passerby drops a wallet full of cash. You can keep the cash or return it. If you return it, the NPC accuses you of theft and starts calling for the cops. Or the NPC turns out to be a very

important person and offers you a job or a mission. Or he turns out to be very wealthy and offers you a big reward for your honesty. Or another NPC witnesses your act of honesty and offers you some kind of reward. You get the picture. It all started with your decision about whether to return the wallet or keep the money.

Using Physics

From the amount of skid in the tires of a fast-moving vehicle rounding a corner on asphalt or gravel to the impact of a bullet hitting a person's body or the effect of a thousand-pound safe landing on someone's head, physics plays an increasing role in game design. But the use of physics in the world model is only part of how it applies to games. Physics can also be used to imply gameplay. For instance, the physical property of displacement, meaning essentially that matter takes up space and cannot coexist in the same space with other matter, can be used to create a puzzle involving raising the level of a quantity of liquid by dropping items into it to make it rise. Less commonly, imagine that principle applied to teleportation. What would happen if someone were teleported into solid matter? For that matter, what happens to the air molecules that exist where someone is teleported?

Physics also comes into play, for instance, in a puzzle that involves expanding or shrinking a metallic object (which would use heat or cold, respectively). These are just a couple of examples showing how understanding basic properties of physics with regard to the real world can lead to some game design opportunities. Can you think of more?

To begin with, it's good to be versed in Newton's famous laws:

1. Every object in a state of uniform motion tends to remain in that state of motion unless an external force is applied to it.
2. The relationship between an object's mass *m*, its acceleration *a*, and the applied force *F* is $F = ma$.
3. For every action there is an equal and opposite reaction.

Newton also developed a law of universal gravitation, which, according to Wikipedia goes something like this:

> Every point mass attracts every other point mass by a force pointing along the line intersecting both points. The force is proportional to the product of the two masses and inversely proportional to the square of the distance between the point masses:
>
> $F = G\frac{m_1 m_2}{r^2}$, where
>
> - F is the magnitude of the gravitational force between the two point masses,
> - G is the gravitational constant,
> - m_1 is the mass of the first point mass,
> - m_2 is the mass of the second point mass,
> - r is the distance between the two point masses.
>
> Newtons' gravitation formula can be simplified to $F=mg$.

Other useful calculations include Galileo's research on falling bodies, which helped to describe how fast something falling from a height will accelerate. To make the calculation lot simpler, however, you can find gravity calculators such as the one at www.gravitycalc.com, where you can even apply the calculations to other planets in our solar system and see, for instance, how far a body would fall in five seconds on Earth as compared to Jupiter (122.5 meters versus 323.5 meters).

Armed with a bit of basic physics knowledge, you can design puzzles and situations based on any number of other physical properties. Of course, in a world of your own creation, you can alter known physics or even invent your own. Turn Newton on his head and see what happens.

Many of the physical properties in the following list are properties we all take for granted, such as the fact that various materials burn or melt, or the hardness of steel or the resilience of rubber. We live with gravity every day of our lives. But keeping in mind these properties, how can they be used within game situations to make interesting puzzles and challenges for players?

The more accurate and consistent the physics of a world are, the more realistic it will seem. It doesn't have to be the physics we are used to here on Earth, however. It just has to be consistent for the world you are creating. So, in a world where magic works, there might be some different physical properties. In a world with lower gravity, the physics would be the same, but many of the applications of those physics would be different. It is possible to create worlds where the physics are completely alien, but if they are applied consistently players will become accustomed to the rules of the world and will come to see them as realistic—for that world, at least. However, in games based in Earth reality, the proper application of physics is even more important, since that is what we know best. This is very noticeable in simulation games but can apply to every type of game, from arcade platform to FPS. The more realistically you attempt to render a world environment, the more important the application of proper physics is.

The following lists are meant to inspire you to think about the properties of matter and the physical universe. In some cases, the lists contain merely elements for you to explore more deeply—suggestions as to how you can design better games by being curious and researching how things work. As always in this book, the idea is to inspire you to create better, more innovative and original games. Knowing how physics works is just one area that can help you do that.

Basic Physical Properties

What are the basic physical qualities of matter in our universe? Here is a fundamental list:

- Mass, density, and weight
- Hardness
- Brittleness
- Shear and splitting
- Flexibility
- Malleability
- Ductility (metals)
- Resilience
- Moldability (shape memory)
- Luminance
- Friction quotient
- Transparence/opaqueness
- Color
- Reflectiveness (including albedo)
- Absorbency
- Magnetic properties
- Oxidation
- Conductivity (heat/electrical)
- Freezing temperature
- Melting temperature
- Kindling temperature
- Boiling temperature (turns to gas)
- Wind resistance
- Inertia
- Acceleration
- Balance point
- Abrasiveness
- Tensile strength

Temperature

Understanding the effects of temperature on objects and materials can be useful in designing puzzles and situations in games, and also in developing realistic special effects. Here are a few temperature-related variables:

- Heat (effects of)
  - **Melting Temperature.** You face a barrier that can't be moved or destroyed, but with heat, you can melt it to remove it.
  - **Boiling Temperature.** You heat a substance until it boils and use the gas to power a machine, to locate an invisible enemy or item, or to poison them.
  - **Kindling Temperature (Flammability).** Use a heat source—a mirror focusing the sun or a laser or a flame spell, for instance—to cause something to catch fire. Perhaps it's a dangerous creature about to attack you or an evil book of magic that can only be destroyed by fire.
  - **Heat Conductivity and Insulation.** You have a frozen demon embryo, and you have to take it through a hall of flame to the waiting exorcists. You must find something that will insulate it and keep it frozen. You are trapped in an ice chamber, but there is a source of heat through a wall. You force your sword through the wall to conduct heat from the source into your chamber, melting the ice wall.
  - **Effect on Gasses.** You apply heat to a container of gaseous material, causing it to explode.
  - **Effect on Metals.** You use a torch to cut through a metal wall and escape a prison, or you use heat to weaken the bars of a prison so you can spread them open and get through.
  - **Effect on Liquids.** Use hot liquid (such as a hot bowl of soup) as a weapon. Boil a liquid to create pressure to blow something up.
  - **Effect on Solids.** Use heat on a solid surface to reveal a hidden message embedded in the surface. (See the Melting Temperature entry above.) Use heat on a stone to cause it to crack. Perhaps it reveals a secret item inside. Freeze a contained liquid to break the container without losing a lot of the liquid.
  - **Effect on Organic Material.** Heat generally cooks organic material, killing it if alive, killing germs and viruses, and making it palatable for eating. The possibilities are virtually endless.
- Cold (effects of)
  - **Freezing Temperature.** Lure a lizard alien into a cold place where it freezes at a higher temperature than warm-blooded humans.
  - **Heat/Cold Conductivity and Insulation.** Build an igloo to stay alive in the frozen north.
  - **Effect on Gasses.** A dangerous gas has been released. Bring down the temperature of the area to cause the gas to condense and liquefy.
  - **Effect on Metals.** Use extreme cold to make a metal object brittle, then break it.
  - **Effect on Liquids.** Use a source of cold to cause a liquid to freeze solid so you can contain or transport it or use it as a weapon. Freeze a liquid so you can walk on it.
  - **Effect on Solids.** Pour water on a stone and then freeze it, causing it to crack. Freeze a metal to make it brittle so you can break through it.
  - **Effect on Organic Material.** Use cold to keep someone from dying of a fever. Use cold armor to protect someone from extreme heat. Freeze someone in their tracks.

Mass versus Volume

More fun with physics. How do mass and volume affect matter, and how could you use these principles in your games?

- Gravity
    - Drop something to break it, to hurt someone below, to break something else, etc.
    - Use gravity to roll a grenade or bomb down a hill at an enemy.
    - Cause an avalanche.
- Buoyancy
    - Float empty containers on water and use them to cross to the other side.
    - Figure out how much a particular boat can hold, and possibly how many boats or trips you'll need to transport some cargo.
    - Use buoyancy to design something that can float on water, perhaps getting you or your cargo across some water.
- Displacement
    - Throw objects into a body of water to cause the water level to rise and overflow, possibly putting out a fire or allowing you to drink.
    - Use displacement of objects to measure a particular amount of water.
- Pressure (internal or external)
    - Jam an air hose into the mouth of an enemy and make him explode.
    - Use hydraulic systems to increase the amount of force applied.
    - Jettison someone out a torpedo tube and let the water pressure crush them.
    - Switch out liquids for a hydraulic system to make it more effective.

Motion

Physical motion is as common as it gets. Just about everything moves in a game set in a realistic world.

- Newton's laws. (We use these in all physics.)
- Friction (causes heat, slows down moving objects, can wear away surfaces).
- Centrifugal and centripetal forces (create pressure and tendency to move inward or outward).
- Lift (as in airfoils—basically upward or downward pressure from moving gasses over a surface).

Electromagnetic

Understanding electrical and magnetic effects can lead to new game elements and options. Here are a few areas related to electromagnetism that you might want to understand. Once you get a sense of how these things work, you can use them to good effect in some of your games.

- What are amps, volts, watts, and ohms?
- Magnetism (attraction and repulsion, electricity induction with motion).
- Electrical conductivity, resistance, and insulation (levels of conductivity).
- Mechanical switching of electricity.
- Electromagnets and electric generators.

Waves

What waveforms exist in our world? Delve deeper, and you might find ways to use the principles of wave propagation in your games.

- Frequency and intensity
- Electromagnetic: UV, visible, heat, radio

- Sound propagation
- Reflection, refraction, and diffraction (going around corners)
- Superposition (the property behind a sonic boom)
- Harmonics

Potential and Kinetic Energy

What is the difference between potential and kinetic energy? How can you use that in games? Here are a couple of areas to consider:

- Motion (springs, collisions)
- Thermodynamics (heating, cooling, and state of matter changes)

Randomness

Living worlds are unpredictable, so adding elements of the unexpected can help a world seem more real and alive. Random elements can be incorporated into the gameplay as part of the critical path or as side tasks, or they can be non-interactive, meaning that they are just effects, such as sounds and visuals, meant to add more variety to the world's environment. For example:

- **Accidents.** Things happen in the world that are both unpredictable and accidental. People stumble when they walk or slip on a banana peel. Trees (or parts of them) fall in the forest. Cars have fender-benders or bone-crunching impacts. Birds poop on people, windshields, and just about anything. Having low-probability accidents can add to the aliveness of the world.
- **Breakdowns.** Things sometimes break, fall, or shift positions from a sudden gust of wind. Things wear out and stop working. All kinds of random events can happen when things break down. Breakdowns can function as part of the plot by providing new and unexpected challenges for players, or they can simply occur as events without direct relation to gameplay. Having breakdowns function within a game can cause sudden shifts in the player's focus. This can be frustrating at times; for instance, if the player is rushing to complete a task, and the vehicle or weapon (or whatever) he depends on stops functioning. If there is a rewarding side task in getting it fixed, the player may forgive you. But, just as in real life, players will often be frustrated by having unexpected obstacles thrown in their path toward success.
- **People.** People often do random and mysterious things. Having random NPCs do something completely out of the ordinary could provide at least some amusement for players. Animals (and robots and computers and gods) can be used in the same way.
- **Rewards.** Certainly many reward systems in games have an element of randomness. For instance, if a game world typically has many chests or secrets that offer special rewards, it is common to create somewhat random outcomes each time a player searches one of these items—unless it is part of a very specific situation or quest, in which case its contents probably never change and always remain in context for the current quest, task, or situation. But random rewards function much like lotteries: Even if most of the rewards are ordinary and many are essentially useless, the possibility of something really great appearing keeps up the anticipation. But of course that great reward has to happen with sufficient frequency to allow the player to maintain the sense of anticipation—looking forward to each opportunity to gather a reward in the hopes of gaining something remarkable.

Cause and Effect

Consider the actions and events that occur in the game. Does each action produce recognizable consequences? One form of cause and effect is very simple and direct. For instance, if you hit a vase with a baseball bat, the vase will probably break if you hit it hard enough. Or, it might simply fall off its pedestal and roll around on the floor. If you shoot a window, it might shatter, or the bullet might simply make a small hole in the glass with some cracking around it. If the glass is bulletproof, what happens to the bullet? If you water a plant every day, it will likely grow, unless it is a cactus and you cause its roots to rot. What the player does (and what NPCs do) should cause direct effects consistent with the game's world.

Continuity

A world feels more real if there is some consistency and follow-through in the game design. One way to achieve this kind of realism is to create a self-consistent world in which events have consequences, and consequences are consistent as you play. If the player has shot someone and gets away, that person should remember the player shot him and act differently toward him in the future—perhaps with anger, aggression, or fear. If the player breaks something in the environment or takes something, it should remain broken or taken. In movies it would be part of what is called *continuity*. The world should be consistent and true to its rules. Of course, if objects naturally repair themselves in the world you are creating, then they should do so. But in most worlds, broken things stay broken unless someone comes to fix them.

Many games are guilty of continuity errors, and players are often quite forgiving of them. For instance, the NPC who keeps telling you the same information over and over or who doesn't remember that you already completed a quest is annoying (see also the following "NPCs" section) is common enough to be overlooked by many players. However, it is much more satisfying if that NPC offers appropriate responses based on previous encounters and actions.

Another common mistake is not to coordinate events throughout the world and the plot of the game. If actions should have an effect on people and events outside the immediate surroundings of the player, then they should do so. In many games, such continuity is handled well, but not always. Continuity leads to a consistent world that allows players to become more immersed, and immersion is one of the keys to keeping players happy and involved in a game.

While all of the above is true, there are times when designers cheat, and making allowances for small continuity lapses can be a way of allowing players to do things that would otherwise not be possible—such as killing the same creature again and again for experience and loot. So, while continuity in games and stories is preferable, sometimes you can get away with small deviations from the rule, but with the caveats that it needs to enhance the game, and it needs to be intentional. In other words, "I did it on purpose. It's a feature, not a bug."

NPCs

Most worlds are populated by non-player characters (NPCs), and they can either enhance or detract from the illusion of reality in several ways:

- **Dialog.** Through dialog, NPCs can add to the story and display a wide range of personalities. The more varied and interesting (and well acted, if there's voice involved) the dialog, the more real and alive the game will seem.

- **Scenes.** Through scenes, NPCs can also add to the aliveness of the world. Enacting comic, serious, or even tragic scenes can add to the energy, story depth, and sense of reality of a game world.
- **Idle States.** NPCs are most often found standing around, waiting for the player to interact with them. However, by giving them realistic tasks, using repetitive animation and pathing, they can appear to be engaged in real work or play and can therefore add to the sense of a living world. This is especially effective if they occasionally do something unexpected but consistent with their character type. Notice that most people will inherently attempt to find the easiest way to do something. Have your NPCs be aware of their environment enough to make their decisions realistic and believable. Or at least have them do interesting things that real people do, such as picking lint off their clothing, pulling out a handkerchief and sneezing/coughing, or even picking their nose and scratching their butt (but looking around afterward to see whether anyone was watching).

  Another idle state element that could use some thought is character breathing. In many games, NPCs and player characters breathe as if they had been running for miles. In fact, they may have been engaged in battle or travel, which would make such breathing patterns realistic. But, gradually, if they stand around, their breathing should slow and become more relaxed. Creating realistic breathing animations is an element that could subtly but noticeably change the realism factor in a game.
- **Realistic Motion.** In addition to making more interesting animations for NPCs, make their motions seem natural. People don't act and move in a series of steps, such as walk, walk, stop, stand taller, stick out arm, open door. In fact, if you observe 10 people going to a door to open it, each of them may do so differently. Observe how people do things and model that.
- **Realistic Responses.** In addition to the idle state of NPCs, giving them realistic responses to situations also enhances the realism of a game. For instance, if a pedestrian begins to cross a street and sees a car coming, he steps back to the curb and waits (or dives for cover if the car is speeding toward him like two tons of doom). Or if a snake happens to slither near a loitering NPC, he might back away or even attack the snake. Maybe he starts talking to the snake, which is a clue that he is crazy, has Dr. Doolittle–like abilities, or maybe is in league with some cult that talks to snakes. Or maybe the snake isn't really a snake after all.
- **Character Depth.** Another way to add realism to a game is to create believable emotion and response in NPCs. There are several ways to accomplish this, including using dialog and scenes. In addition, since most communication is conveyed through the voice and the body, paying attention to such things as realistic voices and good acting, varied body language, and realistic expression changes can dramatically change the realism and believability of characters in a game. Suggestion: Study the actors from silent movies, such as Charlie Chaplin, Harold Lloyd, and Buster Keaton. They knew how to use body language to convey a story. See also Chapter 12, "Character Design," specifically the "Mental/Emotional Signals: The Other 93%" section.

Animation and Effects

In the early days of 3D games, the environments were mostly static and simple. With the limited tools and processing power available to designers in those days, it was all that could be expected. But today, the tools are robust, the processors far superior, and any world that does not have some animation and special effects is missing the mark.

Animation effects can be small additions to an environment, such as a flag waving in the wind (but be sure it waves realistically with ambient wind, if you want to do it right). Or the effect can be dramatic, such as a view of the Northern Lights from the top of a mountain. For easy realism, think of things that move in your environment, such as a clock's second hand ticking, bushes and trees swaying in the breeze, or someone in the environment stopping to cough or sneeze (with appropriate sounds). In addition, consider effects such as dust kicked up by someone walking by, steam or fog whirling around a character's body in complex patterns, patterns where rain has made the ground wet or where something has blocked the rain and the ground is dry, little random dust devils, waves of varying size and intensity crashing on a shoreline, birds and other animals going about their business in the world and responding to other creatures, and so on.

Consider varying these animations so that every so often an event takes place that is unusual (and not often repeated). For instance, you witness a deadly predator attack an unsuspecting creature, or a sudden gust of wind whistles through the trees, or a flash rainstorm comes and goes suddenly. Such random events suggest to players that the world they are in is dynamic and perhaps more complex than it really is.

LIGHTING

The lighting of a world can dramatically affect how the world impacts players. Much of what we know about dramatic lighting comes from years of experience in photography, stage, and cinema. With proper lighting you can affect mood, expectations, the amount of information revealed, and much more. Here are some of the main ways that you can use lighting effects to add to the realism and aliveness of games:

- **Shadows.** One of the most basic elements of our world is the shadows things cast. These can be as dramatic as your shadow cast in strong sunlight or as subtle as the slight darkening on the side of an object that is further from the ambient light source. Having shadows change realistically with changes in location and orientation to light is one way to enhance the sense of immersion in games. Shadows also provide places for characters to lurk—yours and others.
- **Shading.** It's easy enough to create stark, cartoon-like games, but when creating realistic worlds it helps to create more variation in the shading of the objects and people in those worlds. Use the shading and art style to make a statement about the game and to establish a style.
- **Reflection.** Like shadows, reflections are pretty common in the real world (in fact, everything we "see" is in some ways a reflection of light off an object), and reflectivity is easy enough to create with today's physics engines. Use reflections in various ways, such as to create a sense of realism and depth in scenes or as part of the gameplay. For instance, a player might use a mirror to spot the enemy or even to bounce a laser beam at that enemy! Or a movement behind the player might be noticed in the reflection off a shiny vase, alerting the player to imminent danger.
- **Transparency.** Not everything in life is completely opaque. Some examples of objects with various levels of transparency are glass, gemstones, some clothing (such as diaphanous gowns and lingerie), skin, water, and even air.
- **Changes.** Another way to add to the aliveness of a game is to have the light change in various ways. For instance, the light will change with the passage of time and the position of the sun or moon. It will change when clouds pass overhead or when the sun comes out from behind the clouds. It will also change as the player moves to various locations. It might also change suddenly when someone turns on a bright light in an otherwise dark place. Change is the natural state of things, so having changes of lighting will enhance realism.
- **Dramatic Lighting.** Another way to add to a game's aliveness is to pay special attention to how scenes and environments are lit. There are many techniques for establishing dramatic lighting, such as lighting a subject from the back (backlighting) or washing a scene with color, spot lighting, or using atmospheric effects to create contrasts. Using lighting effects with discretion and imagination can add a great deal to a game's atmosphere. For instance, the lighting in a forest might be muted and made up of dappled sunlight and shadow. In contrast, the lighting in a deep cave would be dark

and probably illuminated by specific spot sources, such as lamps, flashlights, or flickering torches. Each would create a different environment. Or, a modern scientific laboratory would probably have harsh fluorescent lighting that casts minimal shadows, so that everything is bright and more or less uniformly lit. For games within specific genres, a good place to find inspiration is from movies in similar genres. Movie lighting is often an art in itself, and the same techniques can be achieved, sometimes more easily, by using digital tools.

- **Sudden Darkness.** Plunging a player suddenly into a dark world can be disconcerting and effective under some circumstances. At any rate, it will get the player's attention and provide new challenges as he attempts to make sense of the situation, anticipate danger, and seek a solution or a way out of the darkness.
- **Surreal Lighting.** Sometimes lighting can be made so strange and surreal, with odd colors in odd configurations, that the whole effect is like a hallucination. If the goal is to make the player's character seem drugged or otherwise messed up, this technique might work.
- **Flashbacks and Dream Sequences.** Often, when a game takes the player back to previous events in the form of flashbacks or when the player is inside a dream state, the colors and lighting may be changed as a way of constantly reminding the player that he is in a different reality from that of the main game. This is often done by color changes, such as going to black and white or sepia tones, surreal lighting (as above), muted color values, or a penumbra effect around the scene. Such scenes can be interactive or not.

Dynamic Response Systems

Another highly effective method of creating realism in games is to create what I call *dynamic response systems*, meaning systems that respond directly to the player's actions. There are many possible examples, one of the most common of which is dynamically responsive music, but there are other types of response systems that can be created as well:

- **Music.** Music can be dynamically triggered to vary with changes in the player's circumstances. Although this kind of musical change does not necessarily create more realism (after all, who in the real world has music following them around all the time?), it does have a noticeable effect on a player's immersion and response to the game, and we are all familiar with how music in movies sets the mood and conveys information. So, having music change dynamically can create a more alive world and a deeper response. For instance, during ordinary exploration, the music might be light and melodic, but entering a dark cave might change the music to something darker, and entering combat might change it to something heroic and dramatic—which also reminds you that you are fighting or about to fight. (For more information about music and sound in games, see Chapter 20, "Music and Sound.")
- **Situational Response.** Another way to enliven a game would be to create realistic responses by NPCs to the player. For instance, if the player walks around with a drawn weapon, people and other creatures might shy away and draw back. If the player were carrying a very valuable object, some of the NPCs might be curious, while others might be more inclined to attack the player. Or people might respond to players based on what they were wearing. For instance, an armored knight might provoke a different response than a minstrel carrying an instrument or a provocatively dressed woman. Someone dressed extravagantly might attract more pickpockets and muggers than someone plainly dressed, but he might get more attention at a store. If he were wearing a concealed weapon instead of an obvious one, he might seem even more vulnerable to thieves. In the proper disguise, players might be able to walk among enemies without attracting attention, but they might be attacked by their allies.

- **Special Environments.** Sometimes your players will end up in very specific areas and associated situations, such as a haunted house, a dungeon, or a deep, dark forest. Think of these environments as systems and develop the area with the entire experience in mind. This would include music and sound effects, but it might also include the kinds of creatures that appear and how often, the likelihood of being attacked (which might increase if the player is there a long time or if he does something noisy, such as knock over a statue or kick a rock), the lighting and how it might change, the passage of time and how it affects the environment and the player's experience, the buildup of danger as the player explores, and so on. Think about what the player can do in this environment and create a system that responds to the player's actions (or non-actions).
- **Environmental Responses.** If you do too much hunting or fishing, the game or fish will be reduced. The predators will be hungrier, and the basic ecology of an area will become unbalanced. Likewise, if you cut down forests, you can change weather patterns and animal survival and behavior. Several games have modeled the cause/effect nature of environmental forces, but it is one of those dynamic response systems that can have a profound effect over time on gameplay and player strategies. Whether these effects are desirable in a game depends on what kinds of gameplay and limitations you want to provide the player with.
- **Enemy Responses.** Consider if an enemy thinks a situation is under control. He will be less alert and possibly won't field as many soldiers or operatives to counter resistance. But suppose you (the player) start killing their people or destroying their installations. Then what? In a realistic situation, the enemy will respond. He will be more alert and on guard. He might put more troops and guards on duty. He might change orders from "don't shoot" to "shoot to kill." Basically, if you do something in the world, the world should respond appropriately.

Sounds

Sounds can have a very powerful effect on a player's game experience. There are two kinds of sound to consider: ambient sound and sounds directly associated with the action of the player or other characters. Ambient sounds can sometimes be loud and constant, such as the sounds of a NASCAR racetrack—cars zooming closer and farther away, crowds cheering or exclaiming, random bits of conversation in the crowd, various air horns, whistles, vendors, the occasional fender-crunching smashup, and so on. Other times, the sounds can be sparse and used for dramatic effect, such as the sound of a faucet dripping at the scene of a mass murder or a hollow rumble that permeates a cavern. The sounds should reflect the reality of the scene. For instance, having a jackhammer operator within 20 feet of the player and the player not hearing the sound of the jackhammer would seem wrong, wouldn't it? Unless the player was in some ultra sound dampening field... But having a card game in progress nearby and hearing the banter from the table, the slap of cards, and the occasional sound of shuffling would make the atmosphere seem realistic.

In contrast, sounds caused by player and NPC actions, such as shooting a gun or a bow or hitting someone with a fist, walking along a path, flying through the air, or blowing up a balloon—all these sounds should, obviously, correspond to the action being taken. Consider the sounds of the player character's footsteps on different types of terrain, or perhaps a cape whipping in the wind. All this may seem pretty obvious, but think about sounds that you haven't heard in a game. Are there any sounds you would hear in the real world that you haven't heard used appropriately in games? (For more information about sounds in games, check out Chapter 20, "Music and Sound.")

Terrain Variation

One of the easiest ways to save on art assets is to tile an environment, using repetitive art pieces to assemble the world. This is fine, but it can lead to a dullness or sameness about the look of an area.

Creating a lot of variation in the terrain makes the world seem more realistic and interesting. It also requires more work, but the result will be a far more interesting game that may keep the player's attention much longer. (Of course, the gameplay is the most important element, and all the terrain in the world won't make up for poor game design.) Almost exclusively today, games are built using sophisticated 3D modeling tools, and the environments are highly original and detailed. Here are some elements to consider:

- **Views and Scenes.** One way to add some amount of realism and aliveness to games is to create very cool views and scenes. Generally, these are nothing more than eye candy, but they do make a world more fun. In addition, views and scenes can be used to offer the player some clues about the landscape and might even be used to allow the player to see some landmark or discover some clue.
- **Variable Terrain.** Most games today offer landscapes that have hills and valleys, rivers, lakes, forests and meadows, and other variations on terrain. (A fabulous example is *Oblivion*, which offers a lot of terrain variations as well as interactive elements throughout.) Letting the player experience these terrains—and even better, incorporating them into the gameplay—makes for a more interesting world to explore.
- **Things That Move.** Yes, there might be things that move and change in the landscape. A tree might fall across the path when the player approaches, or rocks might fall from a cliff. I've already mentioned such things as branches moving, the effects of wind on water, grass, or shrubs, and other environmental effects.
- **Things That Are Movable.** Sometimes elements of the landscape should be movable or changeable by the player. Perhaps the player can shoot down a bird from a tree, or even chop down the tree, or roll a boulder onto the path below—which could be used as a trap against an unwary enemy.

TIME

In our daily lives, we observe events in terms of the passage of time. In games, quite often time is ignored. However, time can be used in many ways to add to the aliveness and realism of a game.

- **Day and Night.** Having day and night (and twilight, sunrise, sunset, and so on) can add elements of realism and immersion to a game and can add all kinds of opportunities for design variations based on the time of day. In addition, events can be scheduled according to exact game times, further adding to the game's depth.
- **The Economies of Time.** Time can be used as a commodity, making it something to be preserved or used sparingly, especially in games where every action takes some time, and there is a time limit imposed on events.

  In a simple way, just having clocks in the world reflect real time or applicable game time adds to the realism of the environment.
- **Time Limits.** In some games, having timers on events can add to the game's aliveness. For instance, in a game with a slow pace, having a high-pressure timed event can add energy and intensity to the player's experience. (See also Chapter 28, "Controlling Pacing," and Chapter 29, "Time Limits and Time Manipulation.")
- **Deadlines.** As in the great movie *High Noon*, time can be used to create tension and anticipation of an upcoming event that inexorably comes closer and closer in time as the game progresses, and whose impending effect on the player or the world looms over the game. In terms of reality, this kind of situation can create very real emotional responses and anxiety in players, especially if they have invested a lot of time and energy into their characters.

- **Games with Time.** Time can be used as an element of exploration when time travel is possible. It can open up all kinds of gameplay options and make a game world come alive in a very different way—by being mutable and changeable and by exploring the paradoxes of time manipulation.
- **Events That Show Time Passing.** Time can seem endlessly flat in some games, especially because the player is so absorbed in specific gameplay that there is no real sense that anything changes. In fact, sometimes reminders of time passing are more annoying than interesting. For instance, if the game models day and night and the only difference is that it is harder to see at night, then it's probably more of an annoyance than a cool feature of the game. However, if something changes at night—for instance, there are more interesting enemies who don't appear during the day, or the player's character gains (or loses) abilities at night—it becomes more integrated in gameplay. Other events that can signal the passage of time would be:
    - Changes in day and night.
    - Changes in seasons.
    - Church bells or clock chimes signaling the time.
    - Clouds passing overhead and changing the lighting.
    - Characters getting hungry periodically and needing to eat.
    - Fuel running out in a vehicle.
    - Fresh food beginning to spoil and rot.
    - Plants growing, flowering, producing seeds, and dying. Or simply dropping leaves and growing new ones as time passes.
    - People growing visibly older as the game progresses.

For more on time, see Chapter 28, "Controlling Pacing," and Chapter 29, "Time Limits and Time Manipulation.")

Nature (Weather and Events)

Mother Nature is one of the most unpredictable forces in any world, and, along with obvious weather effects such as wind, rain, snow, and fog, think of other natural occurrences that might enhance your world. One great way to use such effects is to implement them very infrequently. In fact, it should be possible for players to play through a game and never encounter all such effects. Many designers make the mistake of thinking that every effect they have created should be seen every time the game is played. But it can actually be a good conversation starter if some cool effects happen very infrequently. So, use the bigger natural events with great restraint, and they'll serve a greater purpose than if they become predictable or so frequent as to seem ordinary. For instance:

- Sudden, short-duration gusts of wind could be used periodically.
- Earthquake tremors, spaced a few minutes apart, followed by a big one could be used very sparingly.
- Lightning storms that start in the distance, with delayed thunder, and move unpredictably—possibly closer and possibly farther away—could be used with discretion.
- Snow falls and changes the landscape slowly. Or it falls, but it does not fall heavily enough to stick. By varying the intensity of a snowfall, you can create interesting effects, such as turning a green landscape white, using footprints in the snow as clues or as a way for enemies to track your player characters, and so on.
- Hail could actually damage your characters—and their enemies, if it became really intense and the hailstones were large enough. This could be varied, and very, very rarely could they become big enough to hurt. (Getting under cover and leaving your enemies outside would be an advantage.)
- A volcanic eruption could create some unexpected obstacles and challenges.

- Very rarely, perhaps add other natural disasters, such as tornadoes and hurricanes, floods and tsunamis, meteor hits, and so on. How would the characters deal with such events? Could they be used to vary gameplay or further immerse the player?

Nature (Flora)

Plants can add a lot to games, often providing:

- Decoration of a scene with color, form, character, and movement
- Barriers to movement
- Resources (such as food or wood for building) or props (such as a bouquet of flowers to give to someone)
- Refuge
- Danger
- Delineation of a path (or hiding one)
- Perspective as they grow and change with the passage of time
- Habitat for other creatures
- Something to climb
- Growth over time and/or change with the time of day or the seasons

Or does your game have man-eating plants or plants that walk?

Nature (Fauna)

The animal world can add a lot to the realism and aliveness of a game. For instance, it can provide:

- Endless enemies to fight
- Allies, friends, and pets
- Food and/or resources—for the player, for NPCs, or for each other
- Objects of quests
- Ambience (sounds, sights, animations)
- Clues, such as birds flying off when someone approaches
- Random events
- A hint of things to come, such as seeing a big tiger in the distance walking around, but when it's not a danger yet

Nature (Environmental Effects)

As mentioned earlier, another way to create realism in games—especially strategy, simulation, and Role-Playing Games (but not limited to them)—is to include the environmental impact of player actions. For instance, if people hunt the deer in the woods, not only will there be fewer deer, but the predators that normally would feed on the deer will now range farther to find food, and encounters with them will increase. Logging the forests causes weather changes as well as different patterns of animal movement. Creating industrial developments causes air and water pollution with a variety of effects on people and property, including increased disease, lower overall energy, and erosion of buildings due to acid rain.

Law and Order

In most worlds, there are places where there is no law other than survival of the fittest and whatever people take with them. However, in many environments, especially cities and other human (sentient) population centers, there is generally some kind of law and order. Creating police and guards who enforce those laws and keep the order can add to the depth and realism of an environment. Taking it even further, you could create an entire court system and jail structure, making breaking the law an interesting experience in itself. Although this would be a distraction in most games, it could certainly add to the realism of a game world, and it might become part of an interesting sub-story or even lead to new quests or missions.

Sex Appeal

The opposite sex (whatever applies) is generally an attention suck, so why not use some sort of sexual content to spice up a world? This does not need to be lewd or overly obvious, either. Simply having some slightly provocative outfits on NPCs or perhaps the occasional encounter with a pretty woman/handsome (intriguing) man... I wonder why more game designers haven't thought of it (/snark). There is a wide range of possibilities—some passive and environmental and some highly interactive.

- Attractive people randomly occurring in the environment
- Love interests—NPCs who might become romantically involved with the player's character
- Seductive NPCs
- Appealing or sexy player outfits
- Sexy main character (Lara Croft)
- Streetwalkers
- Strip bars
- Nude or sex scenes
- Photo models as part of the game
- Sexy people battling it out (*Dead or Alive*, for instance)

Subtleties and Details

In addition to all the other ways that games can be made alive and real, there is the all-important attention to details—for instance, placing signs and billboards in city environments (and making them interesting). There are many types of details that can be included in game worlds, such as:

- **Wear and Failure.** This is making things look used by giving them marks, dents, scratches, and other signs of wear. Streets should have potholes and patches, especially in the less affluent parts of town or in the country. This could also include items that sometimes give out and stop working, just like real things do.
- **Effect Details.** A car peels out on the street. It should leave skid marks. Sometime later, perhaps in the wee hours of the morning, a street cleaner comes out and scrubs the rubber off the road. But he probably doesn't do a perfect job.
- **For the Birds.** Birds fly to roost in trees at twilight and start singing again at dawn. Maybe they leave little piles around below their roosting spots.
- **People Walk Uniquely.** This may be faster or slower, even or choppy, limping, leaning forward or back, purposeful or just ambling along, and so on.
- **Ambient Sounds/Noises.** Are the sounds in different scenes realistic? Do they add to the sense of being there? For instance, on a farm, would you hear cows mooing and chickens clucking? In a city, would you hear sirens, the occasional car wreck, police whistles, boom boxes blasting from passing cars, horns honking, people having arguments? There are lots of ways to create a realistic ambience.

Construction and Player-Created Content

In most media, such as books, movies, fine arts, and so forth, the creativity is left almost entirely to the artists or to the people who produced the work in question. However, in games it is possible to give players the building blocks of creativity—the raw materials from which they can construct or create something in the course of playing the game. Some games, such as *SimCity*, are all about this creation experience, almost to the exclusion of other kinds of play. But almost any game can offer the player an opportunity to construct, combine, or create something from diverse elements found within the game environment, or even from more sophisticated extra-game tools. Even in the various strategic or tactical choices they make in playing the game, players are exercising a creativity that is less possible in other sorts of media. (This not to argue that appreciation of art and literature is entirely uncreative, but it is in a different and somewhat less direct way.)

Building and construction can be rewarding in games, and it can also be quite functional. In fact, there are two basic reasons to build—for aesthetics or for utility. It is possible to have both, of course—a very pleasing structure that performs a useful function, for instance.

But when I talk about construction in games, I'm not speaking only about physical structures, but about anything you can create from parts or diverse elements or from dedicated toolsets. For instance, in some games you can build armies, which are made up of structural elements. In other games, you may be able to take component parts and create magic spells or potions from them. This is also a kind of construction. In still other games, you can create whole new items or even levels or standalone modules using tools provided by the developers of the game.

Thinking in wider terms, then, what kinds of things can you create in games?

- Complete playable levels, such as racetracks in racing-type games
- Weapons and explosives (from soap-carved pistols to weapons of mass destruction)
- Armor (wearable)
- Protective barriers
- Fires
- Chemical compounds
- Homemade bombs
- Homes (from hovels to mansions)
- Furniture
- Castles
- Lakes, rivers, aqueducts, etc.
- Dams
- Cities
- Monuments
- Roads
- Walls
- Military bases
- Armies, police forces, vigilante groups
- Businesses
- Political organizations
- Bridges
- Vehicles (from skateboards to rocket ships to space stations)
- Creatures of all kinds
- Custom characters
- Robots
- Electronic devices
- Other machines of all kinds (anything you can imagine)
- Planets
- Research facilities
- Gardens
- Forests
- Hybrid animals
- Clones
- Genetically engineered plants, animals, and sentient beings
- Changes in land (flattened mountains, cleared fields or forests, etc.)
- Tunnels and dungeons
- Spells, runes, potions
- Clothing
- User-created game levels
- User-created game modules

Now how about some items that might not ordinarily be used much in games? How could you use the following items in a game? Could you construct something interesting with these items?

- Musical instruments
- Jewelry
- Pots and baskets
- Chopsticks
- Silly Putty or Play-Doh or modeler's clay
- Paintbrushes
- Sheets of paper
- Garbage bags
- Duct tape
- String or twine
- Rope
- An alarm clock
- Speakers
- Microphones
- Ceramic tiles
- A place setting
- A turkey carcass
- A water glass
- A can of soda
- A box of baking soda
- A pop or liquor bottle
- Fizzy water
- A pet frog, snake, cricket, or monkey
- Ordinary items from a medicine cabinet or bathroom
- A TV set
- A radio
- A pickle
- Sports equipment, such as golf clubs, baseball bats, balls and mitts, hockey puck, etc.
- Cleaning tools and products
- Garden tools and products
- Items found in a wood shop, car garage, or metal shop
- Pocket change
- A hair comb
- A bottle of shampoo
- A key or set of keys
- A handkerchief or bandana
- A banana
- A 50-gallon drum

Design Challenge

1. Pick several games, both games you like and games that you didn't like, and look at how they made the worlds real and alive—or not.
   a. If they did so, how? List the ways that the games succeeded in bringing life and interactivity to your experience.
   b. Did they make clever use of physics, nature, economies, and so on?
   c. Were you able to construct or create something? How did that add to or detract from your experience?
2. Design a scenario (or use one you are already working on) and:
   a. Pick a basic game setting…period of history, specific location, and some characters who would be present.
   b. Now add elements to this scenario that would make it more real and alive, choosing from the following methods (where applicable):
      - Interactivity with environment
      - Physics
      - Randomness
      - Cause and effect
      - Continuity
      - NPC dialog, scenes, idle states, and specific character actions
      - Animation and effects
      - Dynamic response systems
      - Sound effects
      - Terrain variation
      - Views and scenes
      - Time effects
      - Nature
      - Commerce and money
      - Law and order
      - Sex appeal
      - Other subtleties and details
      - Construction

What Is Reality? (Common Reality Distortions)

Some of what happens in games makes little or no sense. We have gotten used to games that allow the player to run into a wall and get stuck on the run cycle, bumping continually into the same wall until we do something about it. But, used to it or not, it does detract from the sense of immersion and believability of the game when that happens. A note of caution: Just because something is realistic, that doesn't necessarily make it fun. So, when reading the information in this list, consider whether a particular solution would be fun in *your* game. For instance, in some games, having to open every door by clicking on the doorknob would be a genuine pain in the butt and not fun in the least. However, it might work admirably in other games. Here, then, are a few of the common situations we encounter in games that often have not been addressed:

- Walking/running into walls.
- Walking/running into low-hanging obstacles.
- Walking through something, such as a dead body or another character.
- Graphics problems of various kinds, such as where you see odd spots or seams in the landscape or where a character's coat pokes through his cape or his sword shows incorrectly through his overcoat.
- Awkward animations, such as where characters move in strange and illogical ways during dialogs, especially during close-ups when they are supposed to be acting normally, and they look like people with motor dysfunctions.
- Bodies disappearing after a few seconds.
- Missing incremental damage—in many games, one hit kills.
- Healing. In most games characters heal unrealistically, more or less by magic. Unless healing is based upon magic spells or futuristic technology, the rate at which characters recover their "hit points" is almost always detached from the way people really heal from injuries.
- Things we carry. In many games, the player can carry six large weapons, a whole pile of healing items, numerous trophies of his adventures, and enough gold to sink a couple of battleships. Some games attempt to put weight or space limits on characters, but in reality, to make it fun you have to allow some latitude for most games. A few, however, have restricted characters to what they could realistically carry—but they are the exceptions, not the norm.
- Fall damage. Often characters can jump from great heights without taking any damage or taking only a sort of token damage. This is convenient to gameplay but not realistic. There would be a lot of sprained ankles and broken legs in cyberspace if we played by the rules of the real world.
- Endless ammo. Yes, it's so much fun to shoot something that we always make sure there's enough ammunition available, one way or another, and generally it's not a very realistic method.
- Non-interactive environment. Often an environment is full of interesting graphical representations of objects, but most of them can't be used. For instance, in a game with a locked door, there might be a perfectly useful crowbar in the nearby tool shed, but you can't use it to pry open the door because you can't even pick it up. Also, with the same door, suppose you are carrying an axe as a weapon. Most games won't let you bash your way through the door. The axe is only for fighting enemies and can't cut down trees or bash anything else. In the case of the door, for instance, you have to find a particular key because that is the puzzle the designers have set for you.
- Weapons. There are a number of reality distortions with weapons in games. First of all, many weapons are quite deadly and would kill just about anyone in one or two solid blows. But in many cases, you (the hero) or certain enemies can take blow after blow, and not only don't you die, but you actually continue to function at full capacity. You don't even get weakened or incapacitated by, say, a blow to the leg or arm or a bleeding wound.

- Weapons also can't be used for anything but fighting. As in the previous example, the axe you carry as a weapon is almost never used to bash in a door or to chop wood—even if the game presents such necessities. Likewise, your rifle, pistol, or shotgun can't shoot through a locked door or do anything useful other than kill enemies.
- Eating and drinking. Most games don't require you to eat, drink, use the bathroom, or sleep on any regular schedule. Frankly, most that do get tedious because of it, so there's probably a good reason that cyber-people don't have to indulge in the bodily functions as regularly as the rest of us, if at all. Interestingly, some games require (or allow) characters to eat, but none I can think of have the option for them to poop or pee or even fart (other than *Boogerman*, which did include farting, and *The Sims*, of course).
- Pathing. In general, the paths you can take in a game are very specific, and if you reach an impassible location, that's it. It could be a hedgerow, a steep mountainside, or even something that seems arbitrarily impassable. In contrast, certain identifiable areas are passable. Some can be climbed, but not others. Some can be passed through, but not others. The conventions of these "passability" issues are pretty established, but they don't always conform to what would seem to be reality. This is at its worst when you are confined to a specific path and, even though the way off the path seems entirely open, you simply can't go there.
- Respawning. We have to populate our games with enemies, so we often have them simply appear out of nowhere, especially if their predecessors have met an untimely end at the player's hands. As convenient as this respawning of enemies is, it is often contradictory to anything resembling the world we all live in.
- Self-repair. A lot of things that get damaged or altered in a game will somehow magically restore themselves if you leave the area and then return.
- Disappearing bodies. Yes, it would probably be pretty inconvenient if everything you killed just laid there, dead and taking up space. It's much neater and cleaner if they conveniently dematerialize without explanation. Nice and tidy. No muss, no fuss.
- Clean and sanitary death. Likewise, most things are killed in an unrealistically clean way. In some games enemies blow up in gruesome detail, but in most—especially if they want to avoid a restrictive ESRB rating—the damage you do, even fatal damage, rarely shows on the bodies of your victims. Somehow, you whittled down their hit points, but their bodies and faces show no negative effects. They just run out of hit points, drop to the floor, and ultimately disappear. Note to self: Life (death) is not really like that.

Dangerous Places

Danger is often an important aspect of a game. It creates challenge, opportunity, and tension. But how does a place become dangerous? In fact, there's always a dangerous version of just about anywhere; however, your intent must be to make the area dangerous from the very start. So you are a lawyer in New York…not so interesting. So you are a lawyer lost in New York, you just passed a twisted sort of soup kitchen that has been feeding rich people to the homeless, and you happened to witness something you shouldn't have seen…that's another matter altogether. This is one way that the element of danger will add interest to even mundane locations. For instance, a post office that is a secret shipment area for weapons and body parts is much more interesting and dangerous than a post office that just ships items people have purchased on eBay...unless they are secret weapons and body parts....

Some areas are inherently dangerous for obvious reasons. I've included a short list of such places. But the real art is in how you make something dangerous. Sure, it's easy to see that a jungle is dangerous because it has the usual wild animals, deadly insects, unfriendly tribes, man-eating plants, and so on. That's the usual fare. But how could a jungle be dangerous in unexpected ways? Perhaps there's something in the jungle that's so mean and bad that even the usual dangers are afraid of it—something new and frightening. Or, perhaps the danger is from poachers or heavy-equipment operators and their bosses, who are involved in clear cutting the land. Or a drug cartel's base. Or there is an undiscovered alien base deep in the jungle, and you unwittingly get too close to it. Or maybe the danger is embodied in a beautiful, seductive, feral female creature who may or may not be all she appears.

For each area, think not only of the most obvious ideas, but also about different ways to *make them dangerous.* And, for sure, think about places that are not usually dangerous and how you could add elements of danger to them.

- City streets
- Small towns
- Jungles and wild forests
- Hiking trails
- Oceans (on, in, and under)
- Volcanoes
- Mountains
- Rapids and waterfalls in rivers
- Deserts
- Caves and tunnels
- In the air
- In space
- In airless places (moons, asteroids, etc.)
- In vehicles—airplanes, submarines, hot-air balloons, blimps, etc.
- Enemy territory
- The corporate world
- In a bathroom
- A bar
- A pool hall
- A political protest march in Washington
- A blind date in the big city
- A suburban back yard
- Politics (not a place, per se, but a minefield of sorts)
- Freeways
- War zones
- Occupied territories
- The Wild West (or similar periods/places)
- Alien (otherworldly) terrain
- Swamps and bayous
- Subways, alleys, and other urban settings
- London during the Black Plague
- South and Central America (in the time of the Conquistadores)

Places to Get Lost In

As games like those in the *Grand Theft Auto* series have shown, it's fun to play around in cities, which are familiar to us all and yet can be places where we can cut loose and experience adventures of various kinds. If the city feels too small, too repetitive, or not real, then the illusion fails. So places to get lost in, to explore, are very important. The experience can also be like peeling an onion, offering layer after layer of new experiences. Such well-designed areas have room for surprises, but also feel comfortable or sufficiently familiar to make exploration interesting. Cities, airports, castles, prisons and dungeons, factories—these are just a few places to consider, but remember, you can also make the *über* version of something. For example, you could create the factory that makes 95 percent of the illegal guns in the world, the lab that makes 95 percent of the illegal drugs in the world, the genetic testing hospital somewhere in South Africa where all other labs send their samples, and so on. Just thinking this way—making the location BIG; I mean the really *massive* version of it—gives you plenty to work with when creating interesting places to explore. Here are some other places you can get lost in and explore:

- In the dark
- In the fog
- In forests and jungles
- In the mountains
- In the desert
- In space (solar systems, galaxies, planets and moons, etc.)
- In a maze
- In cities
- In buildings (factories, hotels, mall complexes, etc.)
- In and around prisons
- In castles
- In tunnels and caves
- Inside a body (in the bloodstream)
- On freeways and/or country roads

Environmental Effects on Locations

An easy way to add some variety and drama to an area is to use environmental effects. All of a sudden, the same location takes on different aspects. Something safe could become dangerous. Something ordinary could suddenly become beautiful or dramatic. A quiet moment could suddenly explode into action.

- Darkness
- Blinding light
- Shifting light
- Fog
- Black light
- Night/day/twilight
- Distracting movement
- Earthquake
- Avalanche
- Quicksand
- Color changes
- Tone changes
- Weather effects (see the "Weather Types and Phenomena" section)

Good Places to Attack or Defend

These are the places you would want to have as your base—or, what actually works better is to give the good location to your enemy and challenge the player to overcome greater obstacles. Generally, the high ground is best, whether it be in ground battle or in air combat. However, there could be exceptions to this rule. Other places are obvious, such as castles/fortresses, a gun-laden warship, an underground bunker, and so on. Standing on the turrets of a castle shooting at the hordes approaching, or being on the outside thinking, "How the heck can I get in there?" Some examples include:

- Castle/fortress
- Any high ground or high position
- Nest
- Narrow pass (where the enemy can only attack in small numbers)
- River fjord or bridge
- Ditch
- Valley
- Mountain pass (from above)
- Where you have cover and the enemy does not
- From vehicles against infantry
- From space
- Bunker
- Mobile fortress (tank or something like it)
- Dreadnaught-class ship or spaceship
- Security buildings—both small-scale, such as outside a marina, and large, such as the Pentagon or FBI headquarters

Moving or Transient Locations

These are the places where you have split attention because you are trying to focus on the location you are in, but that location is moving somewhere else. That can leave you worrying about your current situation, worrying about the control of the movement you are undergoing, and worrying about the arrival at destinations you are heading for. Good moving locations are things such as:

- Trains
- Planes
- Boats
- Surfboards/sailboards/jet skis
- Spaceships
- Planets on a collision course
- Cars
- Conveyor belts
- Skis and other snow vehicles
- Escalators and conveyor belts

Weather Types and Phenomena

Games used to include very few weather effects because weather is pretty complex to program. Now, however, many games add basic weather, such as rain and snow. That said, times are changing, and programmers are welcoming challenges, so to keep the creative juices flowing, here's a list of weather ideas and other phenomena, including some more interesting suggestions. Some can directly affect the player or the environment. Others are primarily for visual and atmospheric effect. But, if you think about it, you might be able to find some clever ways to use these effects and phenomena to add new elements to your games:

- White squall (a line of thunderstorms)
- Rain
- Sleet
- Snow
- Blizzard
- Breeze
- High wind
- Hot-dry wind (like the Santa Ana)
- Tornado
- Hurricane
- Monsoon
- Hail (of any size)
- Thunderstorm
- Lightning
- Heat wave
- Drought
- Shooting stars
- Meteor storms
- Rainbows
- Moonbows
- Dew
- Humidity (high or low)
- Sunset
- Fog
- Mist
- Jet streams
- Frost
- Ice
- Black ice
- Icicles
- Acid rain
- Acid snow
- Sandstorm
- Dust storm
- Eclipse
- Solar storm
- Coriolis effect
- Currents
- Ball-lighting
- Aurora borealis
- El Niño/La Niña (or something like it)

Location Surfaces

Where do you set the action? What is the terrain like? Some of the most basic places include grass, forest, jungle, sand, rock, water, mud, concrete, asphalt, metal, carpet, snow, ice, lava, and so on. However, these are just basic choices and will often lack personality or interest if not combined with other elements. So the game design goal is to think about how these can be modified to make more interesting or unusual terrains for gameplay. You can begin by blending the accessible surfaces with permanent places that add dimension to the terrain, such as hills, mountains, escarpments, plateaus, volcanoes, craters, and valleys. Also consider various qualities your terrain may have, such as temporary, forgotten, crumbling, rotting, sparse, lush, destroyed, abandoned, scorched, frozen, burning, icy, and so on. Thinking in these terms, you might end up with a scorched jungle crater or a rusting metal roadway.

Mix and Match Locations

Use the following chart to pick a location surface and put various modifications on that surface, choosing from the options in the columns to the right of the basic surface.

Basic Surface	Additional Surfaces	Modifications
Grass	Mountain	Temporary
Dirt	Hill	Forgotten
Rock	Escarpment	Rotting
Sand	Plateau	Rusting
Forest	Volcano	Sparse
Jungle	Crater	Lush
Water	Valley	Slippery/Slick
Mud	Chasm	Destroyed
Snow	Rift	Crumbling
Ice	Path	Scorched
Lava	Road	Frozen
Wood	Fence/Wall	Burning
Carpeted	Bouldered	Icy
Asphalt	Cliff	Defaced
Concrete	Cave/Tunnel	Mossy
Metal	-	Cold
-	-	Hot
-	-	Pulsating
-	-	Exploding

Location Sizes

Every location can be large or small. It's a matter of scale. And it may be useful to consider the scale of some of the natural and manmade locations you might use.

Here are a few more examples:

- Meadow – field – plains
- Marsh – swamp – bayou

- Campsite – settlement – village – town – city – metropolis – county – country – continent – hemisphere – planet – solar system – galaxy – universe
- Copse – forest – sea of trees
- Hillock – hill – mountain (small) – mountain (large) – Everest
- Hills – mountains – mountain range
- Spring – ditch – creek – river – lake – ocean
- Island – archipelago
- Room – building – complex – block – city – county – state/province – country – continent – hemisphere – world – solar system – galaxy – universe

Money and Commerce

The use of money and commerce in games can create an expansion of the game concept and a sense of familiar reality. It can be a big part of the game—in fact, the central focus of it—or it can be a minor aspect, but the use of money and value exchanges generally does add to the sense of aliveness and realism of a game world. Using the basic principles of supply and demand can further add realism, so that if something is scarce and useful, it is worth more than something that is plentiful, even if it is also useful. More ways to use commerce and money include the following:

- Have merchants who buy and sell.
- Create a true supply-and-demand economy.
- Have banks.
- Allow players to take out loans. What are the consequences for not paying them back? Who lends the money? Banks? Mobsters? Angel investors? Scammers?
- Allow investments (with varying degrees of risk and return). Consider how complex the investment model will be.
- Allow players to create and run their own businesses, own rental property, provide services to other players or to NPCs, and so on.
- Allow players to find items and/or resources in the environment that are valuable.
- Allow in-game auctions.
- Allow connections between game money and value and real-world money and value (as in environments such as *Project Entropia* and *Second Life*).
- Have a game in which the government manipulates the value of money and/or the interest rates.
- Allow gambling and wagering. Who controls it? Is it organized and institutionalized or randomly encountered?

Some other considerations:

- **What sets value in your game?** What is the standard of trade? In games set in our world, of course, paper money is the basic unit of trade and buying power. In many games, it's gold or some artificial item of value. In any game that has a commerce component, some standard of measure must be considered.
- **Why is it valuable?** Most games do no more than follow the conventional method of making something useful only for commerce and nothing else. But why is it valuable? Paper money was originally redeemable for gold or silver. Today, it has no intrinsic value, but people agree to honor it as if it did. The same holds true for credit cards and other exchange methods where no actual money changes hands. But consider that something may be of value in the world because it has specific uses. Consider that gold and silver, two of the most common units of value in human history, also

had very specific qualities that made them ideal for working into jewelry. They were malleable, heavy, and shiny. Does the unit of value in your world have any intrinsic qualities? Can it be used in other ways within the game, in addition to its value in commerce?

- **Does your unit of trade conform to real-world physics?** Many games allow players to carry insane amounts of gold, a very heavy metal, without any weight penalty. Consider whether this is important and whether creating a unit of trade that is realistic in the world you create is desirable.
- **Trade and Travel.** In our world, each country creates its own money, and in order to trade with other countries, you must find some way to convert currency or use something of universally accepted value, such as gold or diamonds. Games generally assume one money standard throughout. What would happen if you couldn't spend all that hard-earned cash so easily when you travel to other places?
- **Business.** Most games have no business component, or they have a very simple shop interface for purchasing items. A few games are focused mostly on business as a simulation. However, very few games feature anything more complex than the simple store concept. But business can be a source of money and power, of risk and reward. And even in games with other types of main focus, putting in a business component can add variety and new options and challenges.

Here are a few ideas for adding business to your games (many of which could be fronts for other agencies—good or evil):

- A small shop on the side
- A pawn shop
- An Internet café and/or game parlor
- Halliburton or Blackwater (whatever they mean to you)
- A global enterprise
- A manufacturing company
- A distribution company (could be a front for some other activity)
- A mob-based racket
- A saloon or bar
- Investments in businesses or stock markets
- A plot focused around rival businesses, global business, or a world controlled by large corporations
- A string of rental properties
- A multinational conglomerate
- A shipping, trucking, or parcel service
- An import company

Politics

How do you handle the political climate of your game? Does politics enter into it at all? And how does the player influence or interact with the political situation? Since much of politics involves winning the favor of others, balancing opposing interests, and manipulating power, what are the ways that players can be involved in a political world? Or is the player at the mercy of politics? Even though politics may not be integral to a game, it's often helpful to know who's in charge, what they want, what they'll do to get it, and how they enforce their rules/laws.

Types of Political Structures

In your world, what kind of society or societies exist? The politics of a world or community affect the kind of experience the player will have. Consider the way your world might be different if it were set in any of the following types of political systems. What gameplay or high-concept inspirations could you get by changing the political structure of your society?

- Anarchy
- Monarchy
- Oligarchy
- Plutocracy
- Republic
- Democracy
- Totalitarian/Dictatorial
- Fascist
- Theocracy
- Kleptocracy
- Tribal

Ways Political Worlds Can Be

Along with the large-scale labels—democracy, monarchy, plutocracy, and so forth—there is a general sense of the atmosphere of the world. Is it friendly? Terrifying? Dangerous? Open? Here are some ideas for how your world could *feel*:

- Easy and free
- Lenient
- Benevolent
- Disinterested
- Strict
- Meddling
- Harsh
- Brutal
- Suspicious
- Fearful
- Apathetic
- In turmoil
- Unstable
- Dangerous

Things the Player Can Do to Gain Favor or Influence (in a Political Setting)

Not all games deal much with politics, but if you create a world in which there is a local or macro-level political structure, you might also consider ways that the player can manipulate or gain advantage within that system. For instance:

- Bribe someone
- Contribute to someone's cause
- Build something
- Save someone
- Find something valuable
- Bring special power or skill to the situation
- Spy (obtain information)
- Manipulate through sex
- Double-cross
- Blackmail
- Hold hostages
- Swear allegiance
- Threaten
- Run for office
- Work for the rulers
- Help the rebels
- Fight the rebels
- Marry into an influential family or marry for political ties

Creating Your World

What worlds will you create? Can you make original worlds? Can you take what has been done and reshape it, as they did in *The Matrix*, or will you be content with worlds that have been used again and again? If you use the worlds we know well, how will you make them feel alive and provide the player with the most compelling experience? There are plenty of ideas in this book to help you create great games in any world. Have at it.

18 Travel

In this chapter we'll look at the functions and methods of travel we use in games, including a section on police pursuit methods. This chapter contains the following sections:

- The Functions of Travel in Games
- Methods of Travel
- Travel Dos and Don'ts
- Types of Vehicles
- Driving and NPCs
- Rules/Methods of Police Pursuit
- Secret Routes
- Ways to Display Maps
- What to Display on a Map

The Functions of Travel in Games

Travel functions in games pretty much the way it functions in real life—to get from one place to another—even if the "places" in question are entirely virtual. But what do we mean by "travel"? Not all games involve travel. Puzzle games, such as *Tetris*, don't. Single-screen arcade games, such as *Space Invaders*, didn't involve travel either, unless you count the many light years the aliens had to travel to get to you. A lot of sports games don't involve travel, although some, such as racing games, do. But since sometime in the 1980s, the majority of games have involved moving from one place to another. The reasons are pretty obvious, but I thought it might be useful to make a list of them. (Go figure…)

Why do we include travel in games?

- To provide a chance to explore and to introduce new opportunities, scenery, characters, and so on.
- To create zones of varying difficulty.
- To provide variety in the game.
- To provide additional challenges.
- To give the player a chance to accomplish tasks involving different locations and people in different places.
- When you're traveling, there's more potential for surprises…for the unexpected to happen.
- To increase the impression of the size of the game world.
- Sometimes the game is all about travel.
- Because travel is adventure, and adventure is fun.
- Because adventure is discovery, and discovery is fun.

Methods of Travel

Okay, we have travel in games. How do we travel?

- A screen at a time—an exit in one screen leads to another full screen
- Walking/running
- Riding/flying
  - Horses
  - Elephants
  - Ostriches
  - Donkeys
  - Mules
  - Ponies
  - Eagles
  - Dragons
  - Magic carpets
  - Carts and wagons
  - Cars
  - Trucks
  - Motorcycles
  - Tanks and ATVs
  - Rickshaws
  - Palanquins
  - Skateboards
  - Scooters
  - Skis
  - Snowboards
  - Windsurfers
  - Paddleboards
  - Boats (sail or motor)
  - Hang gliders
  - Gliders
  - Ultra-light planes
  - Airplanes (as a pilot or passenger—all kinds)
- Being carried
- Teleporting
- Via links (like teleportation, but not called that—simply click on something, such as a door or an icon, and you move to another location)
- Zoning—when you move to a zone barrier, and the program loads a new map (especially common in MMOs)
- Astral—your mind/spirit moves, but your body stays where it is
- Possession—you take over the body of another being and travel in it
- As a prisoner of some enemy
- In time—you go forward or backward in time
- Accidentally—you stumble into something that takes you for a ride, or you fall down a mountain or into a river, and so on

Travel Dos and Don'ts

Do:

- Provide a reward for travel—make it worth the player's while.
- Provide players with options to explore.
- Unless you're making a very restrictive type of game (such as a "rail game"), allow for freedom of movement.
- Allow options for quickly moving to places that have already been explored.

Don't:

- Require excessive travel for no reason or reward.
- Make people travel slowly over long distances just to make the game seem longer.
- Make players retrace their steps for trivial events or tasks.

TYPES OF VEHICLES

There are certainly crazy numbers of vehicle types, ranging from various mechanical devices, to animal mounts, to a character's innate abilities (the character is the vehicle). This includes cars, trucks, boats, planes, spaceships, horses, camels and a host of other real and mythical creatures, feet, wings/flying, and so on. Within some of these categories there is even further variety. For instance, think of all the kinds of planes, trains, ships, and automobiles you can. The category is pretty much wide open. Here are a few to whet your appetite. How many more can you think of?

- Palanquins
- Rickshaws
- Bicycles (tricycles, unicycles, etc.)
- Motorcycles
- Sedans
- Station wagons
- SUVs
- Sports cars
- Hybrid cars
- Electrical cars
- Hover cars and hovercrafts
- Vans
- Hotrods
- Racecars
- Armored cars
- Limousines
- Pickup trucks
- Small trucks
- Large trucks
- Semis
- Tanks and ATVs
- Trains (various kinds)
- Rafts
- Paddleboards
- Canoes
- Swamp buggies
- Ocean liners
- Swift boats
- Battleships
- Carriers
- Schooners
- Frigates
- Outriggers
- Windsurfers
- Submarines
- Speedboats
- Small sailboats
- Racing boats
- Skis
- Snowboards
- Small planes
- Jet fighters
- Refueling planes
- Cargo planes
- Passenger planes (various sizes)
- Stunt planes
- Vintage planes (WWI, WWII, etc.)
- Gliders
- Parasails
- Hang gliders
- Ultra-lights
- Spaceships (all kinds)
- Teleportation units
- Horses
- Donkeys/mules
- Ostriches
- Elephants
- Camels
- Dogs (sleds)
- Dragons
- Tigers and lions (mostly mythical)
- Whales
- Astral projection

Driving and NPCs

What happens when there are vehicles on the roads? What do NPCs do under different circumstances? Although it's not a big part of the game, to add to realism, consider how your non-player characters might respond when dealing with traffic and other common elements of street travel. It's a small bit of extra coding, but it could have a big effect on the player's sense of being in a "real" place.

- Civilians aimlessly drive around the city heading to an ever-changing destination (generating traffic).
- They avoid breaking the rules of the road; however, they will avoid debris or people in the road, and so on.
- They will happily sit in traffic.
- They would not consider driving on the pavement even if the entire road was blocked. (They would turn around and find an alternate route.)
- Civilians often fill all lanes with traffic, forcing you to slow and wait for an opportunity to pass and overtake them (or forcing you to go around them by heading into oncoming traffic).
- They tend to pile up at red lights.
- They also tend to pile up in certain zoned areas (such as the city center or at toll booths).
- Civilians, especially taxi drivers, can become extremely hostile when irritated by other drivers or you! (Expect to hear foul language, or expect them to speed right up beside you, waving their fists/flashing their high beams/giving you the finger/shouting/honking their horns to share with you what they think of your driving style.)
- Civilians tend to follow the speed limits or maybe go just slightly over.
- Taxis know the clever shortcuts.
- Civilians swerve at the sight and sound of gunfire. (This makes them unpredictable—they might just slam on the brakes, or they might pull over.)
- Civilians will avoid officers. On hearing gunfire or sirens, they pull to the side of the road. Sometimes they will just stop when they think the officers are trying to stop them.
- Pedestrians standing in the road cannot be run over. They will always dive and scoot out of the way. (This is to avoid leaving their bodies in the streets.)
- Pedestrians hearing gunfire will duck and hide behind objects between them and the source of the gunfire. (Expect to see pedestrians peering over the edge of parked cars or from behind telegraph poles as you whiz by, guns blazing.)

Rules/Methods of Police Pursuit

This section looks at different descriptions of what a patrol car would do when involved in a routine traffic stop or a car chase. I've included a few different approaches, including some directly from the files of different police departments.

- Patrol
  - They are looking for trouble and listening to police radio.
  - Sometimes they will use the external flashlight connected beside the driver's wing mirror to help scan for problems. (It's controlled by a small handle inside the car.)
- Routine stops and chases
  1. If they know the description of the car you're driving, or you are dragging a fender, or they spot something "wrong" like that, then you catch their attention.
  2. They pull out and follow you for a short while.
  3. They determine whether you need to be stopped...a short delay.

4. They turn on their flashing head lamps—left bulb, then right bulb, repeating.
5. Then they turn on the top steady lamp—not flashing, just a constant blue and red light (orange if seen from the rear).
6. Then they flick their siren on, then instantly off again. This generates a loud/low garbled, burping horn sound.
7. If you do not pull over:
   a. They start to chase you.
   b. Then they turn on the flashing lights (bright red/white/blue flashing lights). Then they turn on the wailing police siren.
   c. Then they radio other cars regarding your constantly updated location.
   d. Then they try to get up close to get your plates and see who is in the car.
   e. Then they use the megaphone to demand that you pull over (or they pull up beside you and urgently point to the curb).
   f. If you still ignore them or speed up, generally they will just keep up, hoping to tap the rear end of your car when you take a corner.
   g. If you fire shots at them, then they will drop back, returning fire, and their aggression level will spike.
   h. If you stop, they will try to park their car across your nose or tail to box you in (a police-car sandwich).
   i. If they cannot stop you:
      i. They will set up blockades on upcoming streets.
      ii. They will attempt to use spike strips thrown by officers at the side of the road.
      iii. They will try to get you to turn onto a dead-end street.
      iv. If you continue not to comply, they will call in a helicopter to track your progress and coordinate better blockages.

Typical Police Pursuit Rules (Based on City of Detroit)

- Activate the oscillating roof light and flashers.
  - Direct by visual or audible signal for car to stop.
  - Activate the headlights and siren.
  - Officers shall not initiate a pursuit unless all emergency equipment is functional (Detroit, 1993, III-15-15.2).
- Determination
  - Nature of the violation
  - Time of day
  - Weather conditions
  - Geographic location
  - Population density
  - Familiarity with the area
  - Police vehicle capability
  - Speed required to maintain the pursuit
  - Proximity to school areas during school hours

- Pursuit
  - Once the decision to commit to the pursuit is made, the zone dispatcher needs to be notified and given the following:
    - Reason for the pursuit
    - Location and direction
    - Description of the vehicle, including license number, if known
    - Description of the occupants (Detroit, 1993, III-15-15.3)
  - Upon completing that task, the zone dispatcher will then:
    - Determine the primary and secondary units.
    - Assign a patrol supervisor to monitor the pursuit.
    - Advise members to buckle seatbelts.
    - Advise to activate emergency equipment.
    - Alert aviation.
    - Check the license plate of the suspect vehicle.
    - Alert neighboring communities if necessary.
    - Coordinate the pursuit (Detroit, 1993, III-15-15.3).
  - The monitoring supervisor shall consider the following:
    - Location.
    - Traffic density.
    - Weather and road conditions.
    - Driver's training and experience.
    - Length and speed of the pursuit.
    - The possibility of capture at a later date.
    - Make a determination to continue or discontinue the pursuit (Detroit, 1993, III-15-15.6).

Methods of Police Pursuit

The methods of pursuing fleeing vehicles are always evolving, and modern technology is offering new methods that, in some cases, can eliminate the old-fashioned car chase. From a game design standpoint, this may not always be desirable, but consider how your fictional forces can use some of these innovations—in police work or elsewhere in your game. (Note that these are real developments and innovations, not made up.)

- **Spikes.** Spikes are often used to stop vehicles by deflating tires, and many innovations have been applied to this simple technology, such as remotely controlled spikes that can be deployed or withdrawn as needed, spikes that stay in the tires of the car that runs over them, and even exploding spikes that can prevent fugitives from continuing to drive on the wheel rims. Spike systems currently in use allow the slow leakage of air from the tires, ultimately forcing the vehicle to a controlled stop.
- **Auto Arrestor System.** This deploys a short electromagnetic burst that disables the electronic components of the pursued vehicle. It works with modern vehicles and causes damage to electronic ignition parts.
- **The Road Patriot.** This is a guided rocket-powered missile that can be mounted on a scout car and launched from a distance of seven car lengths. It pursues the vehicle at 20 MPH faster than the vehicle is moving and emits a crippling electromagnetic pulse when within range, forcing the vehicle to a stop.
- **The Road Sentry.** This is similar to the Road Patriot, but it is built into the concrete of the roadway in key areas and is able to be activated when a pursued car passes over it.

- **Fleeing Vehicle Tagging System.** This fires a polymer projectile that attaches to the pursued vehicle and allows that vehicle to be tracked by radio signals.
- **Speedbump.** This is a net technology that consists of a vinyl net capable of stopping a speeding car. It is useful at checkpoints and roadblocks.
- **Netting.** Netting can also be used to stop escaping small craft on water. The nets can be dropped ahead of escaping craft by helicopters, preventing them from taking evasive maneuvers.
- **Air Nets and Harpoons.** Nonlethal methods for use against aircraft have been difficult to deploy, as most attacks that affect the airworthiness of a plane or the pilot's ability to control it are likely to be lethal. Still various air nets have been tested, as well as air-to-air harpoons with parachutes or other devices that could adversely affect the enemy plane.
- **Silver Shroud.** One way to disable a vehicle is to cover it entirely, obscuring vision and/or mobility. This has been developed in a system called Silver Shroud, which can fire a very thin polymer film coated with aluminum P4. This film is 0.0005 inches thick and can cover an area of 1,960 square feet. When used against tanks, the film also entangles the turret if the crew attempts to move it.
- **Superacids.** Destroy tires chemically using superacids millions to billions of times more potent than fluoric acid—injected in tires by use of caltrops or other means.
- **Caltrops.** For simple tire deflation, a caltrop with a hollow tube to defeat self-sealing tires is sufficient.
- **Catalytic Depolymerization.** Another way to attack tires is catalytic depolymerization, which causes the tire to degrade very quickly and requires very little of the applied substance.
- **Motor Mayhem.** Engines can be attacked directly by a number of chemical means, such as by using agents to clog air filters—spray devices that deploy thin, long-chain polymer films. Bypass methods are ineffective in that the polymers will destroy the engine if allowed to bypass the filter.
- **It's a Grind.** Another method of attacking the engine is to use small abrasive material, such as extremely strong ceramic or Carborundum particles, causing highly increased friction and wear and destroying engines over a few days' time.
- **Metal Fireballs.** You can use metal fireballs to ignite metals. For instance, cerium oxide produces very fine ceramic dust, small enough to penetrate air filters and enter the engine.
- **Engine Combustion.** Affecting engine combustion is also possible—either by damping it so the engine dies or by supercharging it. Acetylene gas can cause an engine to race so hard that it blows the pistons out and destroys it.
- **Pyrophoric Particles.** Another way to destroy an engine is to introduce pyrophoric particles, such as cesium, which burn intensely and generate enough heat to destroy the engine.
- **Viscosification Agents.** Also, viscosification agents can thicken fuels and cause them to clog the fuel passages and cripple the engine.
- **Traction.** Modern technology has created some "superlubricant" substances, such as Teflon and potassium soaps, which can be used to severely inhibit movement through an area. Modern use might include crushable packets (known as *slick 'ems*) distributed over an area, which would release a superlubricant when run over by enemy vehicles, making movement very difficult. The opposite, of course, are *stick 'ems*, which can make an area sticky and hard to pass. New technology is being worked on to allow some materials to change composition based on certain conditions, such as temperature, pressure, or electromagnetic signals. These "smart" materials could resolve cleanup problems with some of the chemical weapons in development and could lead to other clever uses.
- **Optics.** Some materials can almost instantly cause the crazing of optical surfaces, rendering them unusable or at least severely impaired. Many methods have been considered for "blinding" tanks, which have limited capabilities for viewing the outside, but they might work against fleeing automobiles, as well—for instance, paint bullets, chemical etching agents, and adhesive foams.

More Ideas for Police Interactions

The following ideas are based specifically on game design concepts, not necessarily on real-life police work. However, they can be useful ways to control the action in a game and may or may not apply to the real world.

- Officers avoid harming civilians if at all possible. Put civilians in front of them, and they'll be forced to not shoot and to work around the civilians.
- Officers fear for their lives. They can get aggressive but will always hold back slightly.
- Officers avoid gunfire like the plague. Watch them swerve and hang back when you shoot at their cars.
- Police enjoy spinning out an assailant's car by hitting the car's rear left or right side as they take a corner (the pit maneuver).
- Over the course of the chase, officers will gradually surround your car and slow to a halt when they have you trapped.
- Police carry pistols and shotguns. They only use these weapons when they get clear shots with no civilians in harm's way.
- Given a clear shot at a tire, an officer in the passenger seat will hang out the window to take the shot.
- The police driver does not shoot while driving.
- The police shooter will not shoot to kill unless you're considered a deadly threat.
- Officers will use a loudspeaker to try to get you to comply before using deadly force.
- Police are always communicating. If one spots you, they will all know your position. You have a limited time after an officer spots you to take him out or destroy his car before he calls out your location over the radio.
- Police will attempt to set up an impromptu roadblock. These roadblocks consist of two or three police vehicles askew in a line.
- Major roadblocks involve three or more police vehicles, wooden barricades, or spike traps. SWAT teams and agents will participate in roadblocks as well.
- When you run a roadblock, the police at the roadblock will give chase. The only exception is if they are trying to trap you in a confined area.
- Police helicopters are armed and store weapons. As long as one chases you, the police will coordinate good roadblocks in your path.
- Police also have 4-wheel-drive SUV police trucks, so they can still give a good chase if you are in a 4×4.
- If an officer driver is killed, the car will either go out of control or roll to a stop.

Secret Routes

One of the more enjoyable ways to travel is by means of secret routes, assuming the game designers have supplied any. Secret routes are often shortcuts that allow players to get from one place to another far more quickly and safely (sometimes) than the ordinary routes. In order for them to be "secret" routes, they have to be somewhat hidden or obscure. Some examples are:

- Secret doors and/or false walls leading to hidden passageways or tunnels or to secret areas.
- Hidden mountain passes.
- Underground passages.
- Teleportation locations.
- Flight, if it's something unusual for the character.
- Passages that can only be entered by some special means, such as a small passage that can only be passed by small characters—or by larger characters who have found a way to become smaller.

- Secret ways that are guarded by a gatekeeper. You must appease or defeat the gatekeeper in order to use them.
- Puzzle routes that require you to perform some sequence of actions or otherwise that are only revealed or made accessible by solving a puzzle.
- Obscure magical routes, such as entering a picture in a book and finding yourself in a new place.
- Hitching a ride on some passing creature or other means of conveyance.

Ways to Display Maps

Maps are extremely useful in many games to help players figure out where they are and where they're going. How do you display the map? The following list contains many of the most commonly used methods. Can you think of some novel ways to incorporate maps into your game?

- Transparent over screen.
- Solid image—modal.
- Radar readout.
- Mini-map.
- Scrollable.
- Zoomable.
- Resizable.
- Annotatable.
- Fog of war.
- The map is the playfield.

What to Display on a Map

What you choose to display on a map will depend largely on what kind of game you are creating and what information is significant to the player in that game. For instance, in some games it's desirable to display the locations of nearby enemies. In other games, that would defeat the surprise and be completely inappropriate. In MMOs, it's often useful to be able to locate friends and teammates. However, in single-player games, this isn't so much an issue. Also, the question of fog of war arises. With fog of war implemented, then you display only what the player has explored, regardless of what kind of data you have decided to include on maps.

Some things you might display on a map include:

- Topographical features (mountains, rivers, lakes, lava, quicksand, and so on)
- Cities and towns
- Caves, dungeons, and so on
- Enemies
- Friends and allies
- Troops and units (yours and/or your opponent's/enemy's)
- Team members/guild members
- Key locations
- Quest goals and milestones
- Paths, walls, barriers, and so on
- Items (sometimes)
- Traps (maybe)
- Icons

Design Challenge

1. Look at a number of popular games and examine what methods of travel were offered. How were they implemented?
2. How will you handle travel in your games? Can you think of some original ways to get characters from one place to another?
3. Imagine you were creating a game in which the characters had to move through a map, but they couldn't walk or run. How might you solve their travel needs?

19 Objects and Locations

In game terms, an object is generally a collection of graphics and associated code that represents a piece of the overall game system. It has attributes that give it uniqueness and possibly behaviors within the game context. In addition, it may have relationships with various other objects, characters, and other aspects of the system. Object qualities, relationships, and functions may change as contexts change. For instance, an object might be charged or depleted, full or empty, intact or destroyed, broken or fixed, and so on. In each of these cases, certain qualities of the object have changed, and their perceived value, utility, and function in the game have also changed. Some objects have the special quality of being interactive with characters in the game. Others do not.

Objects can be representations of familiar items, such as bottles and a haunch of meat or a gun or a bowler hat. But in games, because these objects are simply art and code, they can be anything imaginable, so they don't have to conform at all to our conventional concepts of reality. For instance, something that appears to be a machinegun might simply be used to spread flowers, or it might be some kind of speaker system—it could even "shoot" musical notes, themselves objects in the game. We can make anything we want in our virtual worlds. Sometimes, however, we have to make things conform more or less accurately to physics, history, and what we think of as reality.

A problem many games have is that they take place in the "real world." Sometimes you simply have no choice—for example, if you are making a game based on a TV show or movie. So, for example, you might end up having to make a "fun" level from a boring office building or a car chase on a freeway (yawn). So you start thinking about these familiar locations, what you could find there, and what you can use (as a designer) to create interesting gameplay. It's like reinventing the wheel (so to speak) each time, because anyone else who has made a driving section on freeways has had to do the same work.

The real purpose of this chapter is to help you see what objects might be relevant to gameplay without you having to spend a lot of time considering your locations. However, what I really hope is that you'll also consider new and different ways to use these objects. Simply by looking down these lists and thinking, "How can I use that in my game?" you may come up with some novel applications. And by looking at the first section, "Some Qualities an Object Can Have," you may find ways to make even seemingly ordinary objects far less ordinary.

This chapter contains information to help you populate your worlds with interesting objects. For more information about the interactivity of environments, see Chapter 17, "Game Worlds," and for some ideas on how to use objects in games, see Chapter 27, "Puzzles," Chapter 25, "Barriers, Obstacles, and Detectors," Chapter 26, "Traps and Counter Traps," Chapter 33, "Historical and Cultural Weapons," and Chapter 34, "Standard Modern Weaponry and Armor."

In this chapter:

- Some Qualities an Object Can Have
- Other Qualities of Objects in Games
- Relevance to the Game
- Objects by Locations

- ➤ Tools of Magic
- ➤ Good Places to Hide Objects
- ➤ Objects with Cultural Meaning
- ➤ List of Machines
- ➤ The Many Uses of Ordinary Items
- ➤ Individual Objects Carried by Specific NPCs
- ➤ Things You Can Also Love

Some Qualities an Object Can Have

All objects have qualities that describe them and, as it is in the real world, these qualities affect the meaning and value we give them. For instance, diamonds in the real world are prized for their high refractive index, their transparency, their hardness, their relative rarity, and the quality that allows us to shape them in pleasing forms. So diamonds, which we tend to think of as having an intrinsic value, actually have many values—as jewelry, as an investment, as a target for theft, as a symbol of marriage in a ring, as a "girl's best friend," and so on.

Similarly, objects in games may have different qualities and different values, based on the game and the player's needs and expectations. Some of the qualities and values of objects in games may coincide directly with their qualities and values in the real world, but in specific cases, a game object has special meaning. A wolf's hide in the real world has some value, perhaps to make a coat or to use as a trophy of some sort. In a game, collecting 10 wolf hides may be necessary to satisfy the conditions of a quest or mission, or they might even be used as an alchemical ingredient. So objects in games can be evaluated based on their value to the player and their utility within the world, based on the context in which they are introduced. As another example, diamonds in games can be all of the things they are in the real world. They could also have magical qualities, or they might be the object of a quest, a key component to a fantasy machine, or something to use to bribe someone. In many games an ordinary healing potion or medical kit is useful but not highly valued (except when you really need one). On the other hand, a similar object that is very rare and that makes you invulnerable for a couple of minutes might be valued far more than the relatively common healing item.

Pretty much anything in a game is an object, though in this chapter we primarily refer to items that are found in various settings and locations. NPCs are also objects, as are creatures, weapons, armor, and so forth. Even a spell, which has no visible representation but is simply something learned by the player or a skill he uses, is an object in that it has utility and can affect the game environment when its qualities are exploited. It can be owned or possessed, but it is represented by some programming code and maybe an icon or entry in a "spell book" or something. It may also have a visible effect, but there is not necessarily an object called *Fire Spell* or *Healing Level One.* Still, these spells and acquired skills have some qualities, like many (if not all) objects in a game environment.

Every object has qualities associated with it. Not all objects have all qualities, but there is considerable range in describing objects, and that's good news because it means you can be incredibly creative when designing and conceiving of objects for your games. Even though the list of qualities an object can have is practically infinite, that vastness of potential can open great vistas of opportunity. So, I hope you'll use the following lists to inspire and spark ideas for new items. For instance, we generally think of a nuclear blast as something huge and devastating. What about the world's smallest nuclear explosion? As always, use these lists as suggestions, and by all means come up with your own entries and examples.

Size

These are ranges:

- Sub-Atomic – Microscopic – Tiny – Small – Large – Huge – Massive – Moon-Sized – Planet – Dwarf Star – Red Giant – Solar System – Galaxy – Universe – Infinity
- Narrow – Wide – A Barn – An Aircraft Hangar – The Great Wall of China
- Miniscule – Short – Tall – Gigantic
- Molecular Width – Thin – Average – Thick – Thicker – Thickest

Shape

- Round/spherical
- Elliptical
- Square/cubical
- Rectangular
- Pyramidal/triangular
- Regular
- Irregular
- Random
- Cone-shaped
- Star-shaped
- Spiky
- Curved
- Fractal

Material Qualities

- Flexible
- Stiff
- Hard
- Soft
- Malleable
- Retains shape when deformed or impacted
- Brittle
- Shrinkable
- Expandable
- Luminescent
- Transparent
- Translucent
- Opaque
- Semi-transparent
- Shiny
- Dull
- Albedo—low to high
- Gaseous
- Liquid
- Solid
- Frozen
- Absorbs/does not absorb liquids
- Floats on water
- Reactive
- Radioactive
- Explosive
- Produces heat
- Produces cold
- Produces gasses
- Caustic
- Rough
- Smooth
- Visible
- Invisible
- Dangerous
- Deadly
- Sticky
- Slippery
- Magical
- Ordinary
- Deteriorating
- Indestructible
- Electrical conductor
- Electrical semiconductor
- Electrical insulator
- Is magnetic/magnetized
- Is attracted to magnets
- Can/cannot be magnetized

Material Types

- Stone
- Wood
- Earth/dirt
- Metal
- Liquid
- Ionized
- Gas
- Pottery/clay/ceramic
- Crystalline (gemstone)
- Acid
- Futuristic/alien
- Living cellular
- Etheric

Color

- The whole spectrum
- Solid
- Partial/mixed
- Swirling
- Changing
- Adaptive
- Lack of (invisible)
- Level of opacity

Mass/Weight

- Heavy
- Light
- Average
- Dense
- Black hole
- Diffused
- Variable

Movement

- In motion
- Still/motionless
- Erratic
- Moving inwardly, still outwardly
- Circular
- Revolving/spinning
- Orbiting
- Fast
- Slow
- Very fast
- Very slow
- Falling
- Flying
- Rising
- Jumping
- Aiming
- Searching/scanning
- Periodic (like a pendulum or alarm sweep)
- Exploding
- Imploding
- Pulsating
- Vibrating
- Shaking

Temperature

- Hot
- Cold
- Freezing
- Melting
- Stable
- Unstable
- Radiating
- Absorbing
- Absolute zero
- Inferno
- Burning
- Glowing
- Molten
- Steaming/boiling
- Within normal range (whatever that is)

Value

- Important
- Unimportant
- Insignificant
- Crucial/critical
- Coveted
- Priceless
- Ignored
- Undiscovered
- Reviled
- Feared
- Misunderstood

Aesthetics

- Beautiful
- Ugly
- Repulsive
- Entrancing
- Odd
- Mysterious
- Sexy
- Boring
- Beguiling
- Perfect
- Imperfect
- Ruined
- Damaged
- Irresistible
- Exquisite
- Horrifying
- Disgusting

Age

- Old
- New/young
- Recent
- Ancient
- Indeterminate
- From the future

Condition

- Perfect
- Imperfect
- Good
- Bad
- Damaged
- Defaced/vandalized
- Ruined
- Rusted/corroded
- Scratched
- Scraped
- Dented
- Bent

- Twisted
- Cracked
- Crushed
- Broken
- Scarred
- Stained
- Smeared
- Smudged
- Erased
- Splintered
- Patched
- Fused
- Open
- Closed
- Locked
- Unlocked
- Cursed
- Full
- Empty
- Half-full
- Half-empty
- Unused
- Partially used
- Used up
- Worn
- Shabby
- New
- Aged/old

Other Qualities of Objects in Games

- Lost
- Found
- Boring
- Interesting
- Necessary
- Useful
- Useless
- Coveted/priceless
- Worthless
- Has some value
- Mysterious
- Ordinary
- Extraordinary
- Super
- Rare
- Good
- Evil
- Safe
- Dangerous
- Radioactive
- Funny
- Absurd
- Scary
- Out of place
- Intentional
- Magical
- Activated
- Inactive or deactivated
- Limited uses
- Combinable with other objects
- Mutable (can change form)
- Consumes resources on use
- Requires specific ability, skill level, and/or other object to use
- Imbued with special abilities/powers
- Can be created/constructed
- Is sentient/intelligent
- Can talk
- Can operate autonomously
- Form and function differ (doesn't look like what it is)
- Can/cannot be given, traded, or lost
- Can/cannot be used as a weapon
- Can/cannot be thrown
- Can/cannot be dropped
- Can/cannot be broken
- Can/cannot be repaired
- Can/cannot be destroyed
- Solid
- Hollow
- In machines:
  - Is electrical
  - Internal combustion power
  - Steam power
  - Manual power
  - Moving parts
  - No moving parts
  - Requires external energy source
  - Can convert its own energy
- Interactive

- Non-interactive
- Can be lifted, carried, dragged, pushed, or rolled
- Can be used to hide or as cover against attacks
- Can be worn by a player
- Can hold/contain other objects
- Can be eaten or drunk
- If eaten or drunk, is poisonous, intoxicating, hallucinogenic, healing, or damaging; or tastes really good or really bad; or makes you bigger or smaller; or has some other specific effect (stronger, faster, smarter, etc.)
- Nullifies or enhances magic
- Improves or harms health
- Recharges abilities
- Contains information in the form of text or other sorts of clues
- Functions as a key
- Acts as a vendor (sells or supplies other objects to players)
- Acts as a catalyst or necessary tool for some player-enabled creative process (such as an alchemist's table, which is necessary to make potions using alchemy skills, or a forge for making weapons and armor)
- Allows players to save/load a game
- Relevant to the game

Relevance to the Game

The last item in the previous list referred to relevance, which is a contextual quality. The relevance of an object may change as the game progresses, but it is a quality that matters to the player and to the designer. An object in the environment may seem innocuous until story elements reveal its importance or function. From a gameplay perspective, an object can be useless for much of the game but suddenly become very useful. Think of the burnable bushes in the original *Legend of Zelda*. They weren't meaningful until you gained the power to burn them and reveal hidden secrets by doing so.

Some objects are useful throughout the game—a vending machine that dispenses sodas that replenish your energy, for instance. In contrast, a vending machine that does not dispense anything or that dispenses items without any use whatsoever is merely a prop and, in the context of this discussion, is irrelevant.

In some games, books reveal clues and important information, and in that context they are relevant. In other games, books are merely cosmetic, and they have no impact on the plot or gameplay. They may contain nice stories, and if the player enjoys reading those stories, then they achieve some relevance for entertainment value; however, in the more serious context of the game design, they are essentially irrelevant.

Here's a very short list of items that could be relevant to the player for different reasons.

- **Terrain Objects.** Generally, objects in game terrains have little purpose, but the more interactive the environment, the better. Think about ways that ordinary objects can achieve meaning/relevance to the player. For instance, telephone poles are destructible, they can be used as obstacles, you can knock them down to block a passage or to land on enemies, or you can climb them or read notices posted on them.
- **Telephones.** Call a contact, receive a call, destroy or disconnect the phone to cut off communications, or use the phone to make calls to gather information or to determine whether someone you're after is home. Throw a phone, plant a bug in one, hide a clue inside, examine a cell phone address book for clues, and so on.

- **Traffic Signs.** Remove one to cause a traffic accident or to misdirect someone, deface one by shooting it and leaving bullet holes, collect one for your house, find a message taped on the back of one, use one as a shield, and so on.
- **Storm Drains.** Clog one up to cause a flood, unclog one to clear up a flood, hide items inside, have monsters appear from them, and so on.
- **Murals and Other Wall Art.** Use gang signs as clues, allow players to spray paint graffiti, notice the artist's style and seek them out as part of a storyline, use them to display clues about the world the player is in, and so on.
- **A Shopping Cart.** Use it to carry items, as a weapon, to help move a wounded comrade to safety, to cause a traffic accident, as a diversion, as an obstacle to impede pursuit, and so on.
- **Drainpipes on Buildings.** Use them to climb or to destroy. Repair them to solve a problem, rip one from the wall and use it as a weapon, or rip one from the wall and use it as the barrel of a makeshift cannon or giant blowgun (for a giant, presumably). Use it as a design element when creating your own house, hide objects inside, use it as a portal for enemy creatures, and so on.
- **Spatula.** Make eggs, put one on heat and then use it as a burning weapon, removing something stuck to a surface, use it as an emergency paddle on a small boat, sharpen it into a weapon, use it as the key to a special lock, and so on.
- **Fork.** Use it for eating (of course), but also for poking, stabbing, completing a circuit, grabbing something just out of reach, as a makeshift lock pick (by bending the tines), as a source of metal, and so on.
- **Paperweight.** Use it as a gift for someone special or hide a clue in it. Perhaps real people have been imprisoned in it.... Throw it at an enemy or to break a window. Perhaps gazing into it hypnotizes the gazer, and so on.
- **Broom.** Use to clean up (of course), use the handle as a makeshift staff, use the bristles to light a fire, use it to move something just out of reach, sharpen the handle into a spear, make a set of nunchucks, and so on.
- **Zip Ties and Duct Tape.** If you can't think of dozens of things to do with zip ties and duct tape, you're not thinking.
- **Deck of Cards.** Hide clues, tell fortunes, gamble or make important wagers with enemies, throw them to distract someone, do magic tricks, pass the time playing Solitaire, use them to give people paper cuts, and so on.

Design Challenge

1. Look at how different games use the objects in their environments.
   - Make notes of all the interesting ways objects are used.
   - Make notes of all the objects that could have been used and how you would have used them.
2. Look at your own game designs. Are there ways to make them more interesting by making the objects in your game more relevant? How does that change your design philosophy, your story, or your action sequences?

Objects by Locations

The following lists can give you a good start when you're planning an art list and designing game environments. This is by no means the whole enchilada. But as a handy-dandy starting point, the objects listed in the following locations can give you a quick start and save you time trying to visualize what to put in your game spaces. More than that, think about how to use these objects interactively. Most of them can be used to do something—as weapons or lock picks, for instance. With creativity, you can make almost any of the objects in these locations useful or at least interactive.

Street and Vehicle Objects

The following lists include items you might find on streets and freeways and on vehicles.

Basic Freeway Elements

So what objects make and are on a freeway? It's not a short list when you really scratch your head and think about it, but if you are making a driving game that takes place in or around a city, here are some of the things you will want to consider.

- Straight road (wide or narrow)
- Curve left (wide or narrow)
- Curve right (wide or narrow)
- Hill down (gentle or quite steep)
- Hill up (gentle or quite steep)
- Wide bridge (for cars/trains/etc.)
- Narrow bridge (for bikes/pedestrians/etc.)
- Bridges over water
- Toll bridges
- Telephone and electrical poles
- Light poles
- Lit area (various kinds of lamps)
- Construction areas (holes/cones/repairs/special vehicles)
- Detour or redirection
- Accident areas (flares on road/trashed vehicles/damaged property)
- Jackknifed big rigs
- Breakdown areas (vehicle on jack/tow truck, etc.)
- Emergency phones
- Traffic (slow or moving)
- Speeders and reckless drivers
- Big trucks and semis
- Lane separators, opposite directions (road lines [see below]/mud/concrete/railing/fence/vision-blocked fence/earth or grass median)
- Lane separators, same direction (road lines [see below])
- Road lines (solid white, double solid white, solid yellow, double solid yellow, dashed, dashed with reflectors and bumps, worn out and barely visible)
- Police crossings (plastic poles or dirt paths)
- Trash (shredded tires, hubcaps, papers, small rock debris, bottles, ashtray dumps, road kill)
- Birds (crows, ravens, vultures, seagulls, chickens, wild turkeys, hawks, etc.) eating trash and road kill or just crossing the roadway
- Animals (cats and dogs, cows and horses, deer, squirrels, rabbits, skunks, raccoons, opossum, coyotes, bears, alligators, mice, snakes, lizards, frogs and toads, etc.)
- Dead animals
- Flat terrain
- Hilly terrain
- Mountainous terrain

- River valleys
- Deserts
- Forests
- Jungles
- Things that fell from cars and trucks (old bicycles, furniture, pet carriers, crates of chickens, a coffin, a huge pile of garlic, somebody's grandma strapped to a chair, a bag full of stolen money—the stranger the better)
- High raised freeway—straight
- High raised freeway—banked left
- High raised freeway—banked right
- Overpasses
- Off-ramps (including crossing roads to return on-ramp)
- On-ramps
- Metered on-ramps
- Pedestrian overpasses
- Lane merging (such as from four lanes to three lanes)
- Lane addition (such as from three lanes to four lanes)
- Hard shoulder (British term for the lane that you are not allowed to drive on but you can use if your car breaks down)
- Dead men's fingers (British term for the area with the white chevrons painted on the exits that you are not supposed to drive on)
- Snowy or icy passes
- The yellow barrels (for impacts before concrete dividers)
- Police blockages (using cars/fences/etc.)
- "Rumble" painted lines on the sides of the road
- Reflectors or "cat's eyes" on the lane markings
- Traffic lamps (used on on-ramps during rush hour)
- Freeway signs/sign bridges (often surrounded by barbed wire)
- Billboards
- Graffiti
- Major construction (all the complex wooden lattice supports, tarps, containers, portable toilets, piles of sand, etc.)
- Stalled cars
- Hitchhikers and other pedestrians (guy walking with a gas can, derelict, hiker)
- Police cruisers and motorcycles (stalking or just driving)
- Airplanes and helicopters in the air
- Electrical and phone wires and poles
- Lakes and large rivers
- Farms (in the country)
- Railroad or municipal commuter trains paralleling the highway for a time
- UFOs (especially in desolate stretches)
- Indications of previous accidents (skid marks/broken glass and other debris/spilled paint/burnt-out cars/marks/oil marks, etc.)
- Toxic spills
- Expansion seams (usually on bridges or raised freeways)
- Heavy, rusty metal cover plates (covering construction holes in the road)
- Drains and gratings (storm and rain drainage)
- Rocks/boulders

- Potholes, cracks, and ruts
- Crack-repair tar (making those squiggly lines over the road surface)
- Traffic cameras (mounted on poles and bridges)
- Lamp poles (various kinds, single head, multi-head, leaning)
- Construction lamps/flashing lights/flashing arrows
- Carpool lane
- Islands/sound barriers/high cement walls/trees
- Murals on support walls
- Tunnels
- Middle of lanes darker due to dripping oil from cars
- Gas stations
- Restaurants
- Rest areas
- Truck stops
- Weigh stations
- Toll booths
- Turnouts
- Water on road (risk of hydroplaning)
- Ice on road (risk of skidding)
- "Brakes-out" exit (run-off) in mountainous area
- Multilevel road (meaning one lane is higher than the other, with a small slope down to the lower one)

City Streets Objects

Many of the same objects and features found on freeways can also be found on city streets. However, city streets will also have many additional features. In fact, given the immense variety of possible objects found in, on, and around city streets, no list could possibly be complete. Here are some ideas, however:

- Straight (wide or narrow)
- Curve left (wide or narrow)
- Curve right (wide or narrow)
- Hill down (gentle or quite steep)
- Hill up (gentle or quite steep)
- Corner intersection
- Blind-corner intersection
- Major intersection
- T intersection
- Railroad or mass transit crossing
- Bus lane
- Bus stop
- Subway entrance/exit
- One-way streets
- Freeway on-ramps and off-ramps
- Street signs
- Advertising signs
- Shops of all kinds
- Office buildings
- Malls
- Mini-malls
- Street vendors
- Street performers
- Bicyclists
- People going to and from work
- Homeless people
- Loiterers
- Animals (varies with size of city—can be dogs, cats, pigeons, etc.)
- Wide bridge (for cars, trains, etc.)
- Drawbridges
- Multi-deck roadways
- Raised rail lines
- Narrow bridge (for bikes, pedestrians, etc.)
- Lit area (various kinds of lamps)
- Construction areas (holes/cones/repairs/special vehicles)
- Accident areas (flares on road/trashed vehicles/damaged property)
- Traffic cameras (mounted on poles and bridges)

- Traffic lights
- Stop signs
- Yield signs
- One-way signs
- Other street signs (no parking, no entry, bus routes, etc.)
- Other cars and trucks—driving or parked
- Lamp poles (various kinds, single head, multi-head, leaning)
- Drains and grates (storm and rain drainage)
- Busses and rail systems, such as cable cars and raised rail
- Bus stops, with or without benches, covered or not
- Subway stations
- Narrow alleys
- Mirrors (in European cities to see around corners in areas with especially narrow streets)
- Cobblestone streets
- Brick streets
- Trolley tracks in streets
- Sidewalks
- Pedestrian crosswalks
- Potholes and ruts
- Manhole covers
- Drainage grates
- Detours and construction
- Blocked streets
- Traffic jams and gridlock
- Pedestrians (all kinds)
- Trash (including bottles, twisted metal)
- Trashcans (large and small)
- Gutters
- Multi-lane streets (major arteries)
- Lane narrowing or merging
- Bus-only lanes
- Parked cars, trucks, and busses
- Delivery vans and trucks
- Parades, picketing, and protest marches
- Colorful characters
- Newspaper kiosks and vending machines
- Storefronts (including liquor stores, gun shops, pharmacies, groceries, restaurants/delis/cafés, etc.)
- Churches and meeting halls
- Parking lots (simple or elaborate multi-story, above ground or underground, etc.)
- Landmarks (such as city halls, opera buildings, museums, convention centers, large hotels, etc.)
- Billboards and other signs
- Graffiti
- Construction sites (steel beams; wooden planks; tools such as riveters, nail guns, saws, hammers, screwdrivers, etc.)
- Vacant lots
- Vacant houses/apartments
- Prostitutes
- Transients, homeless people, beggars, crazy people
- Hotels/motels
- Crack/meth houses
- Gang members
- Neighborhoods (predominantly ethnic)
- Neighborhoods (wealthy or poor)
- Garage sales and street sales
- Flea markets/swap meets
- Docks
- Warehouses and factories
- Electrical and phone wires
- Power stations
- Bicycles and scooters
- Valet parking
- Gas stations
- Fast-food drive-throughs
- Bank drive-throughs

Roadside Objects

This includes things that can block, things that can hurt, things that can distract, things that can damage, and things that can be used as weapons.

- Orange/reflective white traffic cone (light, no damage to car)
- Orange/white painted wooden sign (A-shaped/striped)
- Orange plastic pole cones (used as medians to separate traffic)
- Portable wooden barricade (for instant roadblocks)
- Portable construction barricade ("Road Construction Ahead")
- Crashed or abandoned vehicles
- A shopping cart
- Kids playing in the street
- Sidewalk sales
- Barricades (various kinds, including wooden barriers, cars, armed soldiers or police, etc.)
- Toll booths (the hut style with window)
- Wooden barricades (for toll booths, the arm that lowers down)
- Flashing stoplights (for train tracks and streets)
- Metal pole barricades (for train tracks, with big stop signs)
- Train tracks (makes cars jiggle)
- Curbs (different colors—concrete/white/red/yellow/green/blue)
- Drainpipes on buildings (can clip off a wing mirror)
- Sidewalk end ramp (where pedestrians cross)
- Speed bump—long (long, shallow one)
- Speed bump—short (D-shaped bump)
- Cat's eyes (small reflectors on road)
- Orange bump (bump the size of half a grapefruit for traffic-lane definition)
- Pothole (dip in road)
- Cement road separator (curved—used to separate traffic)
- Metal barrier (used to stop you driving off the edge of an embankment)
- Plastic barrels (used where lanes split on the freeway)
- Pillars (separating traffic in tunnels)
- Statue (can be destroyed)
- Fountain (large and flat, can be crossed)
- Flagpole (on sides of buildings)
- Signposts
  - Stop
  - Bus stop
  - Yield
  - Speed limit
  - One-way
  - No parking
  - No entry
  - No exit
  - Freeway exit
  - Train crossing
  - Hotel
  - Loading zone
  - Freeway markers
- Mailboxes (sidewalk style)
- Trashcans (old "Oscar the Grouch" style)
- Trashcans (the permanent city type, with a logo)
- Trashcans (the wire mesh type)
- Dumpsters (alleyway)
- Bus shelter (made of glass—explodes when you hit it)
- Black plastic bags of trash (alleyway)
- Cardboard boxes of trash (alleyway)
- Crates of empty bottles (alleyway)
- Phone booths
- Patio furniture (for the front of a café, chairs/table/umbrella)
- Trash (paper/leaves that get thrown up into the air as you pass)
- Trash (broken glass or metal that can damage tires)
- Large puddles that might kill an engine or at least slow you down and splash a lot
- Trees (small)
- Trees (large)
- Burning police flares (around old accidents)
- Bushes (3 feet)
- Bushes (6 feet)
- Manhole cover
- Park bench (for grassy areas)
- Parked bicycles (leaning on their kickstands)
- Parked motorcycles
- Badly parked cars sticking out into the roadway
- Construction materials that have fallen off a truck, such as 2×4s or piles of sheetrock, tools, nails, etc.

- Fruit vendor stand
- Hot-dog stand (the cart style on a street corner—spews hot dogs when hit)
- Magazine vendor stand (throws papers if you hit it)
- Boxes on the street that sell newspapers (throw papers if you hit them)
- Electrical wiring box (throws sparks in air if you hit it)
- Downed electrical or telephone wire
- Fire hydrant (gushes water into the air when struck)
- Parked cars (by the side of the street)
- Traffic lights (need light bulbs)
- Walk/Don't Walk lights (for crossings)
- Gates (metal bars)
- Sand piles
- Picket fences (around the homes)
- Chain-link fences (wire mesh—noisy when hit)
- Lamp posts (the L-shaped overhanging version)
- Lamp posts (the decorative version—breaks off—sparks come from base)
- Telephone poles (very difficult to break!)
- Parking meters (throw coins if struck hard...they do a nice lopsided spin)
- One-way spikes on exits
- Nails and screws on the roadway—can flatten tires
- Caltrops

Vehicle Objects

- Wheels
- Tires
- Hubcaps
- Hood
- Trunk (British: boot)
- Engine (multiple components)
- Battery
- Front fender
- Rear fender
- Doors
- Door handle
- Hatchback
- Side van doors
- Truck bed (various sizes)
- Pickup-truck canopy cover
- Front-door windows
- Rear-door windows
- Rearview window
- Front windshield
- Side mirrors
- Rearview mirror
- Rearview mirror ornaments
- Headlights
- Tail/brake lights
- Backup lights
- Interior lights
- License-plate lights
- Side panels
- Exhaust pipe/system
- License plate
- License-plate holders
- Steering wheel
- Roof
- Gas pedal
- Brake pedal
- Clutch (if applicable)
- Gearshift(s)
- Glove box
- Center storage compartment
- Front and rear seats
- Emergency-brake lever or pedal
- Radio/stereo/CD player/hand's-free cell phone system/DVD player
- Cup holders
- Aerial/antenna
- Pedals
- Seatbelts
- Airbags
- Front grille
- Suspension
- Manual gearshift
- Automatic gear stick
- Key
- Dashboard
- Cab lights
- Radio/CD player
- Dashboard knobs
- Dashboard ornaments
- High beam
- Spare tire

- Windshield wipers
- Axles
- Hazard lights
- Bumpers (front and rear)
- Trailer hitch (front or rear)
- Jack
- Lug wrench
- Spare fuses

Road Surfaces

- City streets (tarmac/asphalt/cobbled/brick/concrete)
- Underground/tunnels/etc.
- Tarmac (airport taxiways or open-surface parking lots)
- Weather-related (ice, snow, standing water, etc.)
- Metal (as on metal bridges)
- Grassy areas (parks, etc.)
- Paved pedestrian areas
- Freeways
- Off-road/countryside terrain
- Country roads
- Aqueducts
- Parking structures
- Racetrack

Household Objects

This includes bedrooms, kitchens, bathrooms, attics, basements, garages—if you can't find something interesting to do with this lot, keep thinking....

- Ice pick
- Knife (various kinds)
- Cleaver
- Spatula
- Fork
- Pantry
- Meat locker
- Wine cellar
- Trapdoor
- Plates and glassware
- Pans hanging from ceiling
- Blender
- Toaster
- Toaster oven
- Microwave
- Glass bowl
- Ceramic bowl
- Steel bowl
- Cooking pots—tiny to huge
- Grater
- Hot plate or hot griddle
- Sink full of water
- Coffeemaker
- Espresso maker (with milk steamer)
- Foreman Grill
- Seal-a-Meal
- Garlic press
- Plastic and Ziploc bags
- Stool (wood, metal, or plastic)
- Burner cover (from stove)
- Refrigerator
- Stove/oven
- Dishwasher
- Sink sprayer
- Sponges
- Steel wool
- Cleansers (soaps and abrasives)
- Dishware (plates, cups, glasses, bowls, etc.)
- Silverware (spoons, forks, knives, etc.)
- Huge spoons, forks, and knives
- Anything cast iron
- Egg timer
- Ashtray (various shapes and sizes)
- Fireplace tools (pokers, shovels, bellows, etc.)
- Lamps (floor and table)
- Ceiling fans
- Heaters (portable/electric)
- Wall sockets
- Breaker boxes
- Exposed electrical wiring
- Vacuum cleaner
- Mop

- Broom
- Duster
- Washer
- Dryer
- Detergents
- Bleach
- Glass cleaner
- Floor cleaners and waxes
- Furniture polishes and waxes
- Other household chemicals
- Guns (on walls or in cases)
- Trophies (on walls)
- Collectible objects (could be stamps, coins, dolls, plates, Hummels, weapons, musical instruments, baseball cards, *Magic: The Gathering* cards, etc.)
- Swords and other weapons used ornamentally
- Paintings and photographs
- Decorative vases and bowls of flowers or fruit
- Picture-hanging wire
- Electrical cords
- Bar
- Liquor bottles
- Marks on walls (could be bloodstains, dark or light sections marking where something used to be, bullet holes, etc.)
- Rugs (various shapes and sizes)
- Chairs (various kinds)
- Tables (various kinds)
- Beds
- Blankets and sheets
- Pillows
- Dressers
- Cabinets (various kinds)
- Bed tables
- Clothes hanging in closets (or laying on the floor)
- TVs
- VCRs/CD players/DVD players
- Camcorders
- Stereos
- Radios
- Telephones
- Game consoles
- Computers
- Domestic robots
- Musical instruments (piano, guitar, banjo, flute, drum, etc.)
- Pool table (plus balls, triangle, and cue sticks)
- Ping-pong table
- Floor safe
- Wall safe (probably hidden)
- Mirrors of all kinds
- Hairdryer
- Bathtub or sink full of water
- Toilet
- Toilet paper and dispenser
- Shower
- Showerhead
- Shower door (glass)
- Pharmaceuticals in medicine cabinet
- Towels
- Plumber's helper/plunger
- Toilet brush
- Jewelry
- Watches
- Iron
- Ironing board
- Washer
- Dryer
- Tissue
- Pens and pencils
- Clocks (all kinds)
- Books and bookshelves
- Chandelier
- Stairs
- Banister
- Balcony
- Paperweight
- Letter opener
- Jewelry box
- Hunting knife
- Machete
- Hand tools (hammer, screwdriver, wrench, crowbar, saw, etc.)
- Power tools (saw, router, nail gun, chainsaw, weed whacker, drill [and bits], etc.)
- Garden hand tools (picks, shovels, forks, etc.)
- Ladders
- Lawnmower
- Pesticide
- Pesticide sprayer
- Fertilizers
- Other garden chemicals
- Posthole digger
- Paints

- Hose
- Pool cleaner
- Swimming pool (various kinds and sizes)
- Diving board
- Children's toys (such as old rocking horse, skates, skateboards, etc.)
- Sports equipment (including bats, clubs, balls, etc.)
- Filing cabinet
- Candlesticks
- Fire extinguishers
- Home security system
- Doghouse
- Other pet paraphernalia (food dishes, leashes, cat litter boxes, etc.)

Typical Bathroom Objects

- Toilet
- Sinks
- Towels (various sizes)
- Trash receptacle
- Stalls (public)
- Urinals (public)
- Bidets (Europe)
- Showers
- Bathtubs
- Steam showers
- Jacuzzis
- Body towels
- Face towels
- Shampoo
- Soap (bar or dispenser)
- Shower cap
- Toothbrush (manual or electric)
- Brush/comb
- Toilet brush
- Razors (electric, safety, straight)
- Mouthwash
- Medicine cabinet
- Cabinets and drawers
- Cleansers
- Toilet paper and dispenser
- Lights and light switches
- Decorative pictures, wallpaper, etc.
- Anti-mildew sprays
- Disinfectants

Typical Kitchen Objects

- Foods
  - Canned goods
  - Boxed goods
  - Fresh fruits and vegetables
  - Dry goods
  - Frozen foods
  - Brand names
- Sinks
- Sink sprayer
- Dishwashers
- Soap
- Cleansers
- Bleach
- Sponges
- Scrubbers (plastic or metal)
- Steel wool
- Brushes (various kinds)
- Pots and pans
- Potholders
- Dishrags
- Paper towels
- Broom
- Whisk broom
- Mop
- Knives (food preparation)
- Cutlery/silverware
- Measuring cups
- Measuring spoons
- Napkins
- Placemats
- Tablecloths
- Spatulas
- Whisks
- Tongs
- Chopsticks
- Ice pick

Part V

- Baster
- Cleaver
- Corkscrew/can opener
- Oven
- Burners
- Hood (fan)
- Microwave
- Cuisinart/blender
- Stove
- Oven
- Refrigerator
- Freezer
- Toaster
- Toaster oven
- Mixer (hand or electric)
- Coffeemaker
- Coffee grinder (hand or electric)
- Disposal in sink
- Trash compactor

Other Typical Objects

This list contains objects that are commonly (but not always) found in typical locations.

- Telephones (land line, switchboard, pay phone, cell phone, etc.)
- Clocks
- Computers and monitors
- Printers
- Fax machines
- Portable devices, such as iPods or handheld game systems
- Broom
- Mop
- Vacuum cleaner
- Desks
- Chairs
- Sofas/couches
- Televisions
- VCRs and DVD players
- Ladder
- Pens, pencils, and markers
- Art on walls
- Lamps (floor, desk, and ceiling)
- Books and bookshelves
- Fire extinguishers (especially in public places)
- Water heater
- Ceiling fan
- Space heater
- Floor or desk fan
- Books
- Bookshelves
- Pad of paper
- Loose paper
- Piles of paper
- Clothing (various kinds, including shoes and boots)
- Doors (interior and exterior)
- Windows (interior and exterior)
- Mirrors
- Wine and liquor bottles
- Potted plants (real or fake)
- Cut flowers
- Vending machines
- Cigarette packages
- Beer cans
- Guns
- Ashtrays

Common Signs

These are common signs other than street and freeway signs.

- Just about any business sign
- Restroom
- Men's
- Women's
- Exit
- Emergency Exit
- Gas (advertising)
- Gas (pricing)
- Please Remove Shoes
- Menu specials (in restaurants)
- Menu (on wall of deli)
- Billboards and advertising (various places—on streets and highways, in and on busses, etc.)
- Do Not Litter

- Neon advertising signs
- Open/Closed
- Vacancy/No Vacancy
- Subway signs
- No Smoking
- Out of Business
- Sale!
- Slippery When Wet

Office Objects

These include reception, conference rooms, working areas, cubicle areas, storage areas, eating areas, elevators, and so on.

- Doors and windows (various kinds)
- Video surveillance equipment
- Telephones
- Receptionist station
- Computer equipment (various)
- Documents
- Vending machines
- Coffee machines
- Water dispenser
- Arcade games and pinball machines
- Elevators
- Stairs
- Emergency exits
- Bathrooms and bathroom objects
- Mirrors
- Art on the walls
- Rugs
- Various chairs, couches, etc.
- Floor protectors
- Conference-room objects
- Tables
- AV equipment
- Safes
- File cabinets
- Closets
- Books and bookshelves
- Cubicles
- Kitchens (from minimal to complete)
- Dining area
- Utility rooms (including furnace, electronics and networks, mail room, maintenance equipment and tools, etc.)
- Executive offices
- Desks
- Keys
- Letter openers
- Pencils and pens
- Paper
- Tissue
- Chairs that roll (or not)
- Signs
- Bulletin boards
- White boards
- Fire extinguishers
- Gym (see the following section for objects)
- Vending machines
- Scanners
- Copiers
- Fax machines
- Security systems and alarm

Gym/Health-Club Objects

- Barbells and weights
- Treadmills
- Punching bags
- Gloves
- Showers
- Lockers
- Locks
- Medicine balls
- Various exercise machines
  - Stationary bikes
  - Treadmills
  - Rowing machines
  - Weight machines (various)
- Benches
- Boxing ring
- Martial-arts mats

- Lights
- Towels
- Clipboards
- Pens and pencils
- Food and drink
- Vending machines
- Telephones
- Bathrooms and bathroom objects
- Shop (for anything from snacks and water to clothing and equipment)
- Receptionist station

Hospital and Medical Objects

- Doors (normal and automatic)
- Gurneys
- Telephones
- Switchboard
- Nurse stations
- Clipboards
- Pens and pencils
- Chairs and couches
- Wheelchairs
- Crutches
- Canes
- Beds (powered and not)
- Blankets and sheets
- Pillows
- Hampers
- Cabinets (locked and not)
- Chairs and stools
- Skeletons
- Cadavers
- Organs in bottles
- Blood
- Charts showing systems of the body
- Gift and flower shop
- Restrooms (public and private)
- TVs
- Medical equipment
  - Scalpels
  - Stethoscopes
  - Syringes
  - Ear scopes
  - Thermometers (various kinds)
  - Rubber tie-offs
  - Surgical thread and needles
  - Surgical staples
  - IV drip equipment (needles, tubes, bags of solutions, stands)
  - Cotton swabs
  - Bandages (all kinds)
  - Plaster (for casts)
  - Splints, slings, patches, etc.
  - Blood-pressure cuff/reader
  - Tongue depressors
  - Biological waste containers
  - Biological material transportation containers
  - Bone saws
  - Anesthesia tanks and equipment
  - Ophthalmoscopes
  - Reflex hammers
  - Tuning forks
  - Small flashlights
  - Ultrasound units
  - MRI facilities
  - X-ray equipment
  - X-ray films hanging on light walls
  - Defibrillators
  - EKG equipment
  - Examination tables (powered and not)
  - Fetal Dopplers and monitors
  - Microscopes
  - Narcotic cabinets
  - Medicines (all kinds)
  - Speculum
  - Scales
  - Surgical gowns and masks
  - Doctor and nurse uniforms
  - Patient gowns
  - Prosthetics of various kinds
  - Dialysis equipment
  - Iron lung

Dental Office Objects

- Chairs (ordinary)
- Chairs (dentist's)
- Chairs (patient's—usually a single adjustable unit with drill, lights, x-ray, etc.)
- X-ray unit
- X-ray films hanging on light walls or on light tables
- Drill assembly
- Drill attachments
- Cabinets and storage
- Picks and other hand tools
- Disinfectant/contamination control systems
- Mobile equipment and storage cart
- Control panels
- Cuspidor
- Syringes
- Tanks of nitrous oxide (laughing gas)
- Facemask for anesthetic
- Novocain and other drugs
- Various kinds of filling materials, from metal to ceramic or acrylic
- Uniforms/facemasks/head protection/ eye protection
- Lead bib
- Defibrillators (apparently)
- Toothbrushes
- Dental floss
- Stereo equipment and speakers
- Headphones
- Magazines
- Low tables
- Receptionist station
- Artwork of questionable taste on walls

Police Station Objects

This includes the front desk, cells, examination rooms, and so on.

- Cells
- Holding cells/examination rooms/line-up
- One-way mirrors
- Front desk
- Telephones
- Evidence room (with evidence)
- Evidence (drugs, weapons, documents, computers, etc.)
- Desks
- Computers
- Cots
- Eating area
- Locker room
- Lockers
- Bathrooms
- Gun safes
- Guns—handguns, rifles, riot guns, etc.
- Ammunition (various kinds)
- Tear-gas canisters and ammo
- Gas masks
- Pepper spray
- Knives (various)
- Road spikes, etc.
- Police utility belts/holsters
- Batons/clubs
- Shoulder holsters
- Handcuffs
- Stun guns
- Face shields
- Body shields
- Body armor
- Crowbars and pry bars
- Jaws of life
- Battering rams
- Zip ties
- Shackles
- Handheld radios
- Badges
- Uniforms
- Police radios
- Police vehicles
  - Police cruisers
  - Unmarked cars
  - Helicopters
  - Paddy wagons
  - Police trucks
  - Horses (for mounted patrols)
  - 4×4s and snowmobiles where needed

Part V

- Police dogs
- Bulletproof vests/personal armor
- Benches and chairs
- Loudspeakers/megaphones
- Signs
- Keys
- Buzzers
- Fire extinguishers
- Polygraph
- Riot gear
- Nonlethal weapons (stun guns, rubber bullets, etc.)
- Rope
- Barricade tape
- Sun and safety glasses
- Climbing and rappelling gear
- Skis (where needed)

Fire Station Objects

- Fire bell
- Fire pole
- Desks
- Chairs
- Beds
- Fire trucks
- Ladders
- Axes
- Deck of cards
- Hoses
- Uniforms
- Fire-protection suits
- Gas masks
- Lockers
- TV
- Telephones
- Radio equipment
- Bells
- Fire extinguishers

School/College/University Objects

This includes administrative offices, student lounges and commissaries, classrooms, maintenance storage, and so on.

- Books (plenty of them)
- Chalk and blackboards
- White boards
- Pens, pencils, markers, paints
- Chairs (various)
- Lecture halls
- Podiums
- Open areas with grass and/or trees and shrubs
- Telephones
- Computers
- Bells
- Public-address system
- Kitchens and eating areas
- Restaurants (various kinds and sizes)
- Books
- Shelves
- Campus bookstore
- Student social centers
- Gardens (possibly)
- Restrooms
- Playing fields/stadiums
- Dark alleyways
- Dorms
- Lots of windows
- Fire extinguishers
- Lockers
- File cabinets
- Vending machines
- Bicycles
- Skateboards
- Audio/visual equipment
- Laser pointers
- Sports equipment
- Auditoriums and theaters
- Parking lots
- Calculators
- Clocks
- Maps and globes

- Anatomy props (skeletons, charts, etc.)
- Biology props
  - Preserved animals for dissection
  - Dissection tools
  - Animals in cages
- Chemistry props
  - Chemicals (all kinds)
  - Bunsen burners
  - Various flasks, retorts, condensers, Petri dishes, etc.
  - Specialized tools
  - Emergency eye wash
  - Posters of the periodic table
- Physics props
  - Stopwatches
  - Marking paper
  - Graph paper
  - Plumb bob/pendulum

Sewer Objects

Sewers are essentially mazes of tubes that contain water and sewage. In games and sometimes in movies, sewers are depicted as tunnels that people can enter and pass through. In these sorts of sewers, one might find just about anything. Conditions can be quite funky, too. When designing gameplay within a sewer, you can work with the variety of objects that could appear there, as well as a topology that is full of possibilities. Imagine the sewer is very modern or very old. Or that it is in terrible disrepair. Imagine where it goes and what kinds of buildings it passes under. Banks? Office buildings? Homes and warehouses?

- Ladders
- Walkways
- Stairways
- Manholes and covers
- Dark tunnels
- Rats
- Alligators
- Fish (various kinds)
- Spiders
- Mutant creatures
- Weird vegetation
- Luminescent vegetation
- Secret areas
- Mysterious stains on walls
- Cave-ins
- Crevasses, nooks, and crannies
- Walkways and bridges
- Bats and sticks
- Old crates
- Bones/skeletons (animal and/or human)
- Objects (such as tools, maps, food wrappers, cameras, etc.) left behind by other explorers or adventurers (or workers)
- Mysterious messages carved or painted (in blood?) on the walls
- Buried treasure
- Jewelry
- Algae
- Sewage
- Discarded furniture set up as living arrangements (abandoned or inhabited)
- Rails
- Lights
- Pipes
- Apparitions
- Control panels
- Cables
- Gates and locked gates
- Graves

Library Objects

- Books and bookshelves
- Tables
- Signs
- Microfilm, microfilm viewers
- Magazines
- Study stations
- Computers
- Telephone
- Tables/desks
- Chairs
- Book carts
- Front desk
- Librarian
- Fire extinguishers
- Card catalogs
- Audio books
- Scanners
- Copiers
- Maps and globes

Shop/Market/Miscellaneous Store Objects

- Shopping cart
- Cans
- Boxes
- Bottles
- Cash registers
- Scanners
- Freezers
- Food
- Kitchen utensils
- Cookware
- Mop bucket
- Mop
- Broom
- Heat lamps
- Shelving units
- Cleaning solutions
- Security mirrors
- Security cameras
- Meat lockers
- Meat hooks
- Saws
- Knives
- Display cases
- Overhead lighting
- Signs
- Large windows
- PA system
- Fruit bins
- Bathrooms
- Fire extinguishers
- Telephones

Research/Tech Facility Objects

- Bunsen burners
- Glass tubing
- Computers
- Testing equipment
- Strange and mysterious devices
- Chemicals (liquid, powdered, blocks, etc.)
- Remote sensors
- Video equipment and surveillance equipment
- Security systems
- Alarm systems
- Dials and levers
- Button arrays
- Glass enclosures
- Robotic hands and other robotic equipment
- Crackling electricity
- Warning signs
- Radiation counters
- Fire (and chemical) extinguishers
- Secret documents and formulae
- Telephones and intercoms
- Cleaning facilities, from sinks to eye-washing stations
- Tesla coils
- Cages
- Monkeys
- Mutants
- Rats
- Pools
- Cranes

Weapons Facility Objects

- Weapon parts
- Electronic parts
- Computers
- Blueprints
- Shelving units
- Decontamination stations
- Giant biped machine(s)
- Firearms
- Protective suits
- Machine tools
- Lockers
- Benches
- Chairs
- Tables
- Missiles
- Control panels
- Cranes
- Assembly units and machinery
- Plans
- Explosive, corrosive, and/ or radioactive material
- Other chemicals

Military Base Objects

- Walkie-talkies
- Radio equipment
- Hand weapons (all kinds)
- Jeeps
- ATVs
- Tanks
- Planes
- Beds and bunks
- Missiles
- Bombs
- Ammunition
- Grenades
- Uniforms
- Batons/clubs
- Body armor, shields, helmets

Airport Objects

- Planes
- Shops and restaurants
- Chairs and tables
- Phones
- Gates
- Security scanners (luggage/walkthrough/ handheld)
- Alarms
- Security guards
- Uniforms and badges
- Stun guns
- Guns
- Handcuffs
- Bomb disposal equipment
- Bomb/chemical detection equipment
- Sniffer dogs
- Ticket counters
- Lines of people
- Luggage
- Baggage claim areas
- Baggage carousels
- Busses and cars (outside)
- Signs and ads
- Arrival/departure displays
- Pedestrian slideways
- Escalators and elevators
- Loudspeakers and PA system
- Shuttle busses
- Electric carts
- Hand carts
- Ear protectors
- Hangars
- Airplane parts
- Tools
- Luggage trains
- Plane haulers
- Fuel trucks
- Fuel tanks and storage

- Flight crews (with uniforms)
- Huge windows
- Air traffic control tower (and equipment)
- Communications systems
- Radar and radar towers
- Runways

Factory Objects

- Conveyor belts
- Big machines (drill presses, stampers and flatteners, large welders, molding machines, mixing machines, etc.)
- Vats
- Control panels, valves, and switches
- Catwalks
- Tools (hammers, drills, etc., plus arc welders, riveters, hydraulic lifts, etc.)
- Stockyards and inventory storage
- Cleanup equipment
- Fire extinguishers (various kinds)
- Emergency medical supplies
- Pipes carrying steam, liquids, etc.
- Chemical storage
- Smokestacks
- Parking lots
- Fences
- Locked doors
- Clipboards and paper/pens, etc.
- Computers
- Telephones
- PA system
- Alarm systems
- Clocks
- Time clock
- Locker rooms
- Elevators
- Stairs
- Hand trucks
- Trucks
- Forklifts
- Trash
- Broken or incomplete assemblies
- Gloves, goggles, aprons, and other protective clothing
- Loading doors and docks
- Security system and alarms
- Offices
- Restrooms

Warehouse Objects

- Storage bins and shelves
- Hand trucks
- Forklifts
- Offices
- Loading doors and docks
- Security system and alarms
- PA system
- Trucks
- Merchandise (various kinds)
- Locks and locked doors/cabinets/sections
- Gated areas
- Dirt, dust, and trash

Medieval Village Objects

A lot of games are set in fantasy worlds that are similar to medieval worlds. Along with the requisite castles, there are inevitably smaller villages, and sometimes larger cities, that feature various types of buildings typical of olden times. These locations may be historically based, but often they are simply set in fantasy worlds, even on other planets. Yet the medieval styles (or those of other periods and ethnicities) form a useful and well understood framework upon which to construct the game

- Store(s)
- Blacksmith (weapons/armor)
- Church
- Stables
- Inn/tavern/bar
- NPC homes
- Watchtowers
- Wise NPC
- Gardens
- Schoolhouse
- Tanners
- Carpenter's shop
- Charcoal maker

Castle Objects

Along with medieval villages, castles often make an appearance in games, both historical and fantasy. Castle architecture has varied a great deal over time and from one culture to another. This list is only a suggestion of some of the bits and pieces you might use to create a castle in your game.

- Wooden washtubs
- Fireplaces
- Ladders
- Stairs—spiral stairs in a castle were oriented to climb clockwise, which caused enemies to expose more of their body as they ascended in order to use their swords (which were carried in the right hand)
- Canopies and tents
- Screens
- Stone basins (built in)
- Water pipes and holding tanks (sometimes)
- Taps and spouts (sometimes)
- Horses and harnesses
- Hauberks
- Suits of mail
- Bows and crossbows
- Cables
- Cords
- Coal
- Arrows
- Bolts
- Iron
- Lead
- Swords
- Daggers
- Axes and poleaxes
- Maces
- Shields
- Helmets
- Tapestries
- Pottery
- Straw
- Sleeping cloaks
- Blankets (heavy, fur, feathered)
- Beds
- Chamber pots
- Candles
- Chairs
- Couches
- Wimple (woman's headpiece)
- Woolen stockings
- Leather purses
- Prayer beads
- Hair pins
- Leather shoes
- Food preparation utensils (spoons [bone, pewter, horn, silver, bronze], [no forks], flesh hook, knife, bowls, etc.)
- Iron pots (for foods and other uses)
- Typical tools
  - Auger (drilling holes in wood)
  - Axe (felling small trees or cutting firewood)
  - Adaze (cutting slivers from the surface of the wood)
  - Basket (holding stone while it was hoisted at a building site)
  - Billhook (pruning)
  - Cloth shears (cutting cloth)
  - Crowbar (for manhandling the heavy stones at a quarry and placing stones in their final resting places)
  - Dividers (for measuring)
  - Hammer (to butt stone and drive wooden pegs)
  - Handsaw (to make small wood cuts and more delicate woodworking)

- Hold on/tongs (holding metal as it was being hammered)
- Mallet (used in conjunction with a chisel to carve wood or stone; the mason or carpenter would strike the chisel with the mallet)
- Mason chisel (used by the masons, along with the mallet, to carve decorative designs into the stones and for cutting and dressing stone)
- Nippers (cutting through wire)
- Pitchfork (thrusting into sheaves, bundles of hay, so that they could be pitched into a cart)
- Sharp blade (cutting through leather)
- Shearing shears (cutting fleece from sheep)
- Sickle (cutting crops)
- Snip (cutting sheets of metal)
- Trowel (laying and smoothing mixed mortar on stone or brick)
- Wood chisel (shaping and cutting designs into the wood, or splitting wood)
- Brooms
- Dying vats
- Musical instruments (various)

Medieval Foods

Ironically, nobles would eat the richest foods, while the peasants ate simpler, but in some ways healthier, fare. Although many diseases ravished whole populations in ancient times, nobles were susceptible to certain ailments that peasants did not suffer from, due to differences in diet. Of course, if you were starving, it mattered little if the food was rich or plain. The foods on the following list were primarily eaten by the noble classes.

- Cheese
- Beans
- Oats
- Malt and barley for beer
- Wine (lots of it)
- Bread
- Venison
- Beef (from bulls, cows, calves, and oxen)
- Lamb
- Pork
- Herring
- Rice
- Figs
- Nuts
- Onions
- Garlic
- Peas
- Beans
- Raisins
- Jellies
- Tarts
- Custards
- Spices (typically buckwheat, ginger, coriander, cinnamon, cloves, cumin, aniseed, licorice, pepper...but not salt, which was a status symbol and was served at the table in a boat-shaped container called a *saltcellar*, which was placed in front of the lord of the castle)
- Wafers
- Cooked apples
- Cooked pears
- Seville oranges
- Dates
- Prunes
- Pigeons (especially in winter, since they could be bred)
- Starlings
- Vultures
- Gulls
- Herons
- Storks
- Cormorants
- Swans

- Cranes
- Peacocks
- Capons
- Chickens
- Geese
- Ducks
- Dogfish
- Porpoises
- Seals
- Whale
- Haddock
- Cod
- Salmon
- Sardines
- Lamprey
- Dolphins
- Tunnies
- Eels
- Mullet
- Sole
- Shad
- Flounder
- Plaice
- Ray
- Mackerel
- Trout
- Crab
- Crayfish
- Oysters
- Commoners' foods (turnips and salads, dark breads, porridges, some fish, cheese curds, beer, ale, mead)

Provisions List

This would be for feeding a garrison of approximately 1,300.

- 112 1/2 quarters of corn
- 10 1/2 quarters wheat malt
- 112 1/2 quarters beans
- 7 bushels of mixed beans and barley
- 2 tons of pilcorn
- 9 1/2 quarters of oatmeal
- 78 carcasses of salted meat
- 81 oxhides
- 40 mutton carcasses
- 72 hams
- 1,856 stockfish
- Wine, honey, and vinegar
- Sweets
- Salt
- Water
- Cookware
- Utensils

Theater Objects

Most of the items on this list would be found only in stage theaters. Some would only be found in movie theaters.

- Seats with aisles
- Balcony seats
- Snack bar
- Sticky floors
- Rugs
- Projection booth (in movie theater)
- Spotlights and area lights
- Colored gels
- Light bar (where lights are mounted)
- Curtains
- Sound system
- Stage area
- Sound and lighting control panels
- Curtain controls
- Counterweights (on curtains and scene backdrops in older theaters)
- Ladders
- Dressing rooms
- Set materials (flats, furniture, props, etc.)
- Orchestra pit
- Trapdoors
- Lower level
- Green room
- Microphones

- Electrical cords
- Rope, string, twine, wire
- Fog machine
- Gaffer's tape
- Paint, buckets, and brushes/rollers
- Hand tools
- Storage closets or rooms
- Janitorial supplies
- Janitorial closet
- Reception area
- Podium
- Long poles (for reaching items high up)
- Projectors (movie theaters)
- Film canisters (movie theaters)
- Lighted Exit signs
- Chandelier (common in older theaters and fancy ones)
- Trash receptacles
- Ticket office/booth
- Manager's office
- Restrooms
- Telephones
- Computers
- Alarm system
- Stairs

TV Studio Objects

- Cameras (handheld, on rollers and dollies, on cranes)
- Director's booth
- Monitors and control panel
- Outside sound system
- Internal (director's) sound system
- Lights and light bars
- Spotlights
- TV sets
- Chairs
- Reception area
- Green room
- Dressing rooms
- Audience area
- Lit signs (Exit, Applause, etc.)
- Editing decks
- Video tapes (1", 3/4", etc.)

Amusement Park Objects

- Ticket booths
- Rides
- Lines
- Shuttles and tour trolleys
- Snack bars and restaurants
- Vending machines
- Souvenir shops
- Mascots (people in suits)
- Parades
- Carnies
- Skill games
- Luck games
- Penny arcade
- Trash containers
- Random trash
- Plainclothes security guards
- Security guards
- Maintenance people
- Balloons
- Cotton candy
- Toys and prizes
- Stuffed animals
- Popcorn
- Litter
- Funhouse
- Crazy mirrors

Objects on a Train

- Seats
- Restrooms
- Bar
- Restaurant/dining car
- Sleeping lofts
- Pull cords
- Signs
- Doors between cars
- Private compartments
- Magazines
- Engine room
- Coal car (on steam trains)
- Furnace (on steam trains)
- Controls and dials
- Caboose
- Car linkages
- Wheels
- Ladders (on sides of cars)
- Whistle

Objects on a Cruise Liner

- Staterooms
- Restrooms
- Decks (various)
- Deck chairs
- Other chairs
- Games (shuffleboard, darts, etc.)
- Pools
- Dining hall
- Kitchen (galley)
- Restaurants
- Bars
- Card rooms
- Meeting and conference rooms
- Business center
- Casino
- Arcade
- Wheelhouse
- Engine room
- Crews' quarters
- Sundries and souvenir shop
- Gym/spa
- Control room
- Theaters/dance clubs
- Infirmary
- Storage areas

Objects inside a Mine

- Tools (picks/shovels/drills/buckets/etc.)
- Rocks and boulders
- Support beams and struts
- Mine carts
- Tracks
- Stalagmites and stalactites
- Helmets
- Broken tools
- Gemstones and mineral deposits
- Lamps and lanterns
- Elevators/mine shafts
- Maintenance supplies
- Laundry
- Smokestacks
- Communication system

Objects inside a Museum

- Ticket office
- Ticket takers
- Souvenir shops
- Statues
- Paintings and drawings
- Carvings
- Furniture
- Mummies

- Documents
- Lighting (various)
- Alcoves
- Display cases
- Maps
- Electronic talking guides
- Signs and descriptions
- Doors (ordinary)
- Doors (security)
- Maintenance area
- Storage areas
- Repair facilities
- Offices
- Weapons
- Models and tableaux
- Chairs and benches

Open-Air Market Objects

- Stalls
- Fruit (all kinds)
- Meats (all kinds)
- Whole carcasses
- Fish
- Flowers
- Souvenirs
- Art
- Cafés
- Bakeries
- Candy sellers
- Carvings
- Jewelry
- Tools
- Utensils
- Dogs and cats
- Entertainers (on the fringes or on small stages)

Spacecraft Objects

- Heat tiles
- Navigation equipment
- Power controls (including steering)
- Airlocks and hatches
- Acceleration chairs
- Hibernation equipment
- Computers
- Complex and mysterious controls
- Spacesuits
- Space food
- View windows or technology
- Bunks
- Holodeck
- Eating area
- Food preparation
- Sick bay
- Medicines and first-aid kits
- Audio equipment and loudspeakers
- Dilithium crystals
- Engineering section
- Engine rooms

Futuristic Objects

- Matter synthesizer
- Teleporter
- Holodeck
- Laser guns
- Energy beams
- Force fields
- Nanotech devices
- Med kits
- Antigravity
- Telepathy
- Super-intelligent computers
- Star maps
- Flying cars
- Instant communicators (voice/picture/etc.)
- Ubiquitous surveillance (or is that in the future?)
- Energy transmitter
- Solar furnace/engine
- Ether engine
- Time/space machine

Tools of Magic

- Words (incantation)
- Gestures
- Wands
- Staves
- Spell books
- Daggers, swords, and other ritual weapons
- Scrolls
- Jewelry (rings, amulets, talismans, etc.)
- Runes, dice, coins, etc.
- Crystal ball
- Dancing and movement
- Herbs, potions, powders, tinctures, etc.
- Mortar and pestle
- Blood
- Animals (dead or alive)
- Bones and innards
- Noisemakers (rattles, drums, etc.)
- Music and song
- Purification practices (sleep deprivation, fasting, meditation, solitude, etc.)
- Rites and rituals
- Fire and smoke/incense
- Sacred objects
- Offerings and sacrifices
- Masks and costumes
- Familiars
- Drugs
- Magical spaces and signs, such as the pentagram
- Visualization and imagination
- Tarot
- Minerals (iron, mercury, salt, etc.)
- Candles and wax in general
- Cauldrons
- Alchemical devices (various)
- Stage-magic items (hoops, disappearing boxes, doves, top hats, etc.)

Good Places to Hide Objects

Good places to hide objects might be, for example, in a lake, in a river, in a volcano, in space—usually places that are either dangerous to go to find the object or that will destroy the object automatically.

- In a tree.
- In a river or lake.
- In a cave.
- Under leaves in the forest.
- In a volcano.
- In a beehive (or very near it).
- Halfway down a cliff.
- On an isolated mesa.
- In plain sight, but disguised as something else. For instance, take a powerful scepter, stand it on its end, and put a lampshade on it.
- Encased in some outer covering that disguises its nature.
- Amid a pile of garbage or trash.
- At the top of a mountain.
- Behind a false wall or secret door.
- In a fireplace (with a fire burning).
- In the trap of a sink.
- Behind the toilet or in the tank.
- Inside someone's body.
- In a vat of acid.
- In the gas tank of a vehicle.
- In a dog kennel.
- In the lion's den (literally or figuratively).
- In a snake pit.
- In an insane asylum.
- On a bomb triggered to go off.
- In a pool full of crocodiles.

Objects with Cultural Meaning

"A rose by any other name would smell as sweet," they say. To Sigmund Freud, "a cigar is just a cigar." However, objects do obtain special meaning based on our emotional responses to them or special meanings we give to them. In essence, they become symbols. For instance, a wedding ring, if not worn on the proper finger, might be just a nice gold ring. However, when worn specifically on the third finger of the right or left hand (depending on the culture), it signifies the marriage bond. The following list is just a starting point—a suggestion of objects that achieve certain emotional and/or cultural meaning beyond even their physical attributes or their direct uses. As always, we encourage you to come up with more examples of your own and to consider how using these common symbols in your games can be useful.

- Flowers (in general)
- Roses
- Rings of various kinds
- Horse's head
- "Dear John" letter
- Pink slip
- Lady's garter
- Chador
- Tattoos
- Colors (as in gang uniform)
- Uniforms of all types
- Tie-dye
- Formal suit
- Pipe (such as corncob, calabash, etc.)
- Badge
- Cowboy hat
- Top hat
- Hearts
- Daisies
- Forget-me-nots
- Pomegranates
- Lilies
- Oak trees
- Ribbons (of support for causes)
- Flowers in hair (can mean different things in different cultures)
- Cameo
- Friendship bracelet
- Costumes
- Hair pin
- Heirlooms
- Regales
- Family crests
- Flags
- Musical instruments
- Animals

List of Machines

There are so many machines in this world—and we can even invent more of them. This list is necessarily truncated, but perhaps will serve to get you thinking about machines you can use in your games. Can you make them interactive? Part of a mission? Can you take the purpose of a machine and invent something else to serve the same purpose? Can you invent a machine that combines the qualities of several others? Machines can be fun, so have at it!

- Teleporter
- Typewriter
- Car
- Plane
- Bus
- Glider
- Computer
- PDA
- Recording device
- Videotape recorder
- DVD player/recorder
- Game console
- Holographic display
- Diagnostic/healing device
- Hot-air balloon
- Bicycle
- Sled

- Robot
- Popcorn machine
- Candy vendor
- Pop vendor
- Force-field generator
- Time machine
- Toaster
- Microwave oven
- Telephones (all kinds)
- Chair lift
- Trolley
- Tractor
- Rototiller
- Lawnmower
- Post-hole digger
- Backhoe
- Dump truck
- Forklift
- Computers (all kinds)
- X-ray machine
- Dental drill
- Cash register
- Universal healing machine

The Many Uses of Ordinary Items

This section is designed to give you some ideas about how you can place ordinary objects in your game environments and have them be used by players in a variety of possible ways. I've included just a few examples to whet your appetite. How many more uses can you think of for the ordinary objects we encounter all the time?

- **Ladder.** Used as a ladder, scaffold, bridge, firewood, weapon, or shield.
- **Bottle.** A weapon (thrown as a club or broken and jagged), container, flute, for juggling, or a glass.
- **Rope.** A weapon, restraint, noose, whip, something to raise or lower with, leash.
- **Keys.** To unlock things, weapon, open package, to make electrical contact, to make a jingling noise.
- **Water Glass.** A container for liquid or dry material, a weapon (thrown or broken and jagged), to amplify sound through a wall, to stand on to be a little taller.
- **Cardboard Box.** Use to mail something, to hide something, as part of a temporary shelter, as garden mulch, in a fire or furnace, as impromptu clothing, to make a sign, to sit on (instead of the ground), to clean up a mess.
- **Sheet of Paper.** For writing on, to stuff into a hole (someone's mouth, a gaping wound, a hole in a wall, etc.), to inflict paper cuts, to make papier-mâché, to make a temporary hat, to burn it, to use as stuffing in a box, to wrap something in it.

Part V

Ordinary Things That Can Be Weapons

Some things were not designed to be weapons, but in the right circumstances, they can become deadly. How many things in your daily life could be lethal? Here are a few suggestions to get you started.

- Chopsticks
- Keys
- Rope, wire, string, towels
- Chairs and stools
- Ladders
- Water glass
- Bottle
- Poker
- Golf club
- Baseball bat
- Cricket bat
- Fishing net
- Drumstick
- Clarinet, trumpet, flute
- Shakuhachi (bamboo flute)
- Ceramic tiles (for throwing)
- Saw blades
- Hand saw
- Electric saw or chainsaw
- Hammer

- Screwdriver
- Nail gun
- Stapler
- Measuring tape
- Fork
- BBQ fork
- Fan (hand or electric)
- Iron
- Cane
- Walking stick
- Scarf
- Heavy flashlight
- Lamp
- Electrical cord
- Water in sink, bathtub, or toilet
- Any hard surface
- Candlesticks
- Fireplace poker
- Ice pick
- Sledgehammer
- Pick
- Shovel
- Broom
- Statue

Accessory Objects

These include bracelets, rings, shoes, and so on.

- Ring
- Bracelet/wristband
- Tie
- Scarf
- Necklace
- Brooch
- Belt
- Cape
- Diadem
- Tiara
- Crown
- Hat
- Glasses/goggles
- Shoes
- Wings
- Horns
- Tails
- Gloves
- Watches
- Collar
- Anklet
- Earrings
- Medal/badge
- Piercings (other than earrings)

Individual Objects Carried by Specific NPCs

What do the characters in your game carry around with them? Many NPCs have nothing but cosmetic clothing and, in some cases, objects they carry or wear. For instance, a policeman NPC might wear a hat or helmet and carry a gun and a billy club. A businessman might carry a briefcase. But then, going beyond the obvious cosmetic elements, think about what your NPCs might actually have on them. For instance, suppose your character kills one. What would you find if you looted the body? Would it be useful in your game? Or, perhaps you need something to complete a quest. Who might have the item you need? Clearly, each NPC type would be likely to carry or have access to different items. In some cases, this level of depth is unnecessary, but when you delve deeper, you often come up with ideas you would not have considered before. So, as you think about NPCs and what they might be carrying, consider also how you might expand your game based on what you have come up with.

Policeman

- Gun
- Handcuffs
- Badge
- Baton/billy club
- Radio
- Shotgun/riot gun
- Sniper rifle
- Ammunition (various)
- Tear-gas canister
- Shoulder holster
- Keys
- Flak jacket/bulletproof vest
- Gasmask
- Shield

Fireman

- Axe
- Flameproof suit
- Boots
- Radio/communicator
- Hose
- Extinguisher
- Smoke hood
- Gasmask
- First-aid kit
- Fireman's hat
- Gloves (flameproof/heatproof)
- Deck of cards

Businessman/Lawyer/Accountant

- Pad of paper
- Pens and pencils
- Money/wallet
- Important documents
- Briefcase
- Cell phone

Soldier

- Handgun
- Rifle
- Submachine gun
- Grenades
- Ammunition
- Flak jacket
- First-aid kit

Things You Can Also Love

Where you can create empathy for characters and deepen a player's experience, you can also put objects in the game to which the player can form some kind of attachment. Perhaps love is too strong a word. The psychological term is *cathect*, but that's not too important.

- A special weapon, such as a customized sword.
- An object given to you by someone important.
- An object that took a great deal of effort to obtain, particularly if it's also very useful in some way.
- A cute and cuddly object.
- Anything that helps save or preserve your life. This could be armor or something basic like that, or it could be a magic ring or amulet, or even a robot sidekick (like R2-D2).
- A very familiar object, such as a very comfortable old sweater—the equivalent of that in a game. This is something that has been with you a long time, that you have relied on or gotten considerable use out of. Even if it is no longer the best item you could have, your attachment to it remains.

Design Challenge

The goal of this chapter was to look at objects from different points of view and to offer some resources to help you manage objects in the games you create. But lists of objects are only useful up to a point. It's how you use them that will be most interesting.

1. Look at how objects are used in different games. Look specifically at which objects in specific environments are interactive and which are simply static images.
   a. Why did the designers make the choices they did?
   b. If the objects in each scene were more interactive, what gameplay opportunities would be presented?
   c. What objects common to other types of locations could you use in nontraditional places and ways?
2. Think about the qualities of objects. What qualities can you use to add to gameplay? What happens if you exaggerate or minimize some normal quality of an object?
3. How can you give meaning to objects in a game?
4. How can you find ways to provide multiple uses for objects—especially unusual uses?
5. Create some scenes for a game and use this chapter to put objects into them. Now refer to some of the other chapters, such as Chapter 11, "Scenarios," Chapter 17, "Game Worlds," Chapter 21, "Experiential Design," Chapter 25, "Barriers, Obstacles, and Detectors," Chapter 26, "Traps and Counter Traps," Chapter 27, "Puzzles," and Chapter 32, "Ways to Die." Look for ways to use those objects in puzzles, traps, scenarios, and so on.

20 Music and Sound

When you think of a game, you certainly think of the visuals, which over the years have become more and more eye-popping. But how often do you think about how the sounds and the music of the game have affected your experience?

This chapter contains information on how music and sound can affect the game experience, including:

- Music
  - Early Game Music
  - Modern Game Music
  - The Core of the Score
  - Functional versus Decorative Music
  - Ways to Score
  - Intros, Endings, and Interstitials/Cut Scenes
  - Incidental Music
  - Orchestrations and Arrangements
  - Ways to Affect the Player's Experience
- Sounds
  - Ambient Sounds
  - Sounds as Clues
  - Sound and Location
  - Effects and Feedback

Music

Games have had music almost from the beginning, and today the music we hear in games is often as compelling as the music we hear in movies. It is rich, complex, and relevant to the situation. In games, music even provides clues that help us know what is going on, themes associated with situations or characters, and great atmospherics.

In the beginning, however, the music of games had none of the depth and meaning that it does today.

Early Game Music

The first game to make sound an integral part of the experience was *Pong*. The characteristically electronic sound of the "ball" hitting the "paddle" brings instant recognition to all those who played *Pong* and its many variants in the 1970s. Likewise, the music and sound effects of games such as *Space Invaders*, *Pac-Man*, and, later, series games, such as *Mario* and *Legend of Zelda*, provided music that is specifically associated with that game. All you need to do is listen to a few notes of any of these game themes, and you instantly remember the game and the experience you had with it.

This kind of imprinting and association was particularly effective when games used a repetitive eight-bar loop over the entire game, with maybe a few special sequences for entering a level, dying, and completing a level. But overall, you heard the same piece of music over and over again for however long you played the game.

Modern Game Music

Today, the situation is more complex. The eight-bar loops and simple "pong" sounds are gone, and the music and sounds used in games now fill different and more sophisticated roles.

There is a lot that can be learned from the movie industry and how it uses music. Film composers know a lot about how music can affect a scene, alter a viewer's emotional reaction, convey information, or intensify a scene. But there is a difference between game music and movie music. In the movies, you sit in a dark room, a captive, passive audience, and you are immersed in the film's world for two or maybe three hours. In a game, you may play for 10 hours or 50. In the case of persistent-world games, you may play hundreds or thousands of hours in that world.

Game producers are asking for variety, and scoring music for games can require hours' worth of music—a far, far cry from the simple *Pac-Man* theme. But that's only part of the challenge. In addition to the need for variety—new themes for new levels, each area having its own music, special music for special situations, and so on—there are the issues of musical tastes. Many players today prefer to turn off the music in the game, put in their own CD or set the music in some online player, and listen to what they like. In this case, the hours of composed music for a game go to waste.

There are ways to encourage people to listen to the game's music and sounds. For instance, you can make the music and sound truly part of the interactive experience—meaning that the information they convey is not just window dressing, but is an integral part of the game experience. The player receives useful information that makes the gameplay experience better in some way.

For the rest of this section, we'll look at some of the ways that music is used in games, and I'll offer some information about how to approach each of these specific types of uses.

The Core of the Score

One way to look at almost any music is to imagine it as a combination of pace, intensity, and mood or style. These qualities are often intuitive to the composer, and it can be revealing to look at how these elements combine in different types of music.

For instance, in the following sections, I've listed a few of the possible types of music you might include in a game setting. Music that accompanies a peaceful moment would most likely be low pace, low intensity, and low in mood/style. In contrast, music designed to accompany battle or a chase or race scene would probably be high in all three qualities. Music that indicates tension or the threat of danger might be low pace, high intensity, and moderate in mood.

You can visualize this in terms of an X, Y, Z graph, where:

X = Pace
Y = Intensity
Z = Mood, such as military, pastoral, heroic, romantic—style of music

Functional versus Decorative Music

One of the key distinctions in game music is between music that is more or less decorative—meaning that it is just there to be enjoyed and to put some kind of background on the game—and music that is more functional, meaning that it connects more directly with the action or that it conveys some specific type of information to the player.

Background Music

What I call *background music* is music that is generally unrelated to the action, but simply there to entertain and provide a musical accompaniment to the player. This music does not respond to changes in the action. Early eight-bar background loops were typical of the background music of games in the '80s and early '90s. Some games still use background music that has the general effect the designers want—whether it be heart-pounding action, eerie surrealism, or a pastoral and quiet mood (which is not too common in games).

A good example is an action, platform, or racing game that has a rhythmic, stirring bit of music for the background. It's common to create a different theme for different levels or, perhaps in the case of a racing game, for different races, tracks, or routes. The difference between background music and situational music in this case is that the background music stays the same regardless of the player's situation on that level or in that race.

Often, using simpler background music, a composer can still create a recognizable theme or melody that will become associated with the game in the player's mind. The more a game is played, and the more often a player hears a particular theme, the more likely it is to imprint. However, it is also possible to use recognizable themes with situational music as well.

Situational Music

I contrast background music and situational music by one simple test: Does the music reflect what is actually happening in the game and does it change with changes in the gameplay? Movies almost always use situational music (though there are some exceptions). In movies, the music changes as the story unfolds. Sad moments are generally accompanied by sad music, heroic moments by heroic music, and so on. Anyone who has watched a few movies is already aware of these musical associations, whether consciously or not.

In this section, I'll look at some types of music that can be related directly to the events of the game.

Related to Action

Music often relates directly to what the player is doing or to the situation around the player. Some of these are binary pairs—such as combat or non-combat, running or walking, and so on. Here are some of the places that the music can function seamlessly with the action of the game:

- **Peace (Non-Combat).** The player's character is not fighting or in the fighting mode.
- **Combat.** The player's character is fighting or in the fighting mode.
- **Danger.** There is something dangerous nearby. Danger music acts like a sixth sense for the player—an early warning system, if you like.
- **No Danger.** Apparently, there's nothing to worry about. How reliable do you want this to be?
- **Fast-Moving Thrills.** This music is used for chases, fast cars and vehicles, extreme sports, and the like—from snowboarding to bungee jumping to tearing down the middle of the road on a motorcycle, and so forth.
- **Running/Sprinting.** You might play this music to enhance the sense of speed when the player is running. If there are different modes for running and sprinting, you might even have a change in the music when the sprint mode is activated.
- **Walking.** This music might be distinguished from the running music to indicate a more sedate pace.
- **Specific Areas, Levels, Missions, Vehicles.** This music is used for particular places or player POVs. For instance, there could be different music for each town you visit or each level you play. There could be special music just for caves or dungeons, and similarly, there could be music for plains, mountains, floating cities, and outer space. Vehicles, too, can have their own music, so that you

might get something different in an old Buick than you would in a brand-new Ferrari and something still more different if you were driving a tank or flying a plane. In *Grand Theft Auto*, you not only have a sort of background music, but you can choose different radio stations when you drive a vehicle. This is brilliant because it allows the player to choose the kind of music he'd prefer to listen to—within the limits imposed by the designers of the game, of course. The possibilities are pretty much endless and depend mostly on the type of game and the type of scenes you are developing, in addition to your budget (of course) and the kind of effect you want the music to have.

- **Music for Spells and Magic.** This music would be used for specific types of spells or magical conditions—especially, but not in any way limited to, music-based magic.

Emotional Effects

Can you make a scene bigger or smaller? Can you directly convey sadness, tragedy, wild elation, or outright terror through music and sound? You bet.

Besides its direct connection to functional game elements, music in games can emulate movie music and affect the emotional or psychological aspect of the player's experience. See also Chapter 30, "Ways to Communicate with the Player."

Point of View

To begin with, it helps to consider the music the way a film composer would. The first question to ask is whose point of view does the music represent? Does it represent:

1. What's on the screen?
2. The character's point of view?
3. The audience's (in this case, the player's) point of view?

Let's take a romantic scene and look at how this works. In one case, the characters are flirting, and there's some real connection happening. Things are going well. This is number 2, the character's point of view, and the music could reflect this by being romantic.

But then, imagine that the guy is a dork, the girl thinks he's a loser, and he's doing all kinds of things to impress her that backfire. Here, from the audience's point of view, it's probably pretty funny, so some comedic music might work. This would be number 3.

Now imagine that this courtship scene is taking place, but there's an axe murderer hiding in the closet. The audience knows it, but the characters don't. This is number 1, what's on the screen, and the music would likely reflect the tension and impending danger of the scene.

These are some simple examples, but really, the choice of music can be more varied. The axe murderer could be lurking in the background, but the music stays romantic. What effect would that have? Or the music could stay comedic. Again, the effect is different. These sorts of choices are generally made by directors and/or composers to achieve the particular effect and convey a particular message to the audience, but it is clear that different combinations of events and music produce different audience (player) responses.

Ways to Score

Again, borrowing from the movies, there are basically two main ways to score a film (though there is at least one less-common third way). The two main approaches are:

- Character themes
- Completely contextual

Character Themes

Star Wars is a perfect example of the first approach. Each main character—Luke, Darth, Leia, Han—has a theme. The themes are woven through the movie, varied in ways to fit the action, mingled with the ostinato (a sort of under-theme) in various ways to achieve all sorts of emotional connections to the action.

To take a closer look at this, suppose you have the hero and villain in an epic struggle—I think of Luke and Darth. You play the theme of the enemy with perhaps the under-theme of the hero, and you give the impression that the enemy is going to win. Shifting the intensity of these themes and mixing them in different ways will convey different information to the audience/player.

In an interactive sense, this thematic approach could actually be tied to the situation and to how successful the player is at any given moment in a battle.

Primary character themes fall into a few main categories:

- Good guy (hero).
- Bad guy (villain).
- Ingénue (romantic interest, female lead).
- Comedic.
- Strong characters. (Characters who are very strong, but not necessarily the hero or villain, might get a theme—for instance, a dragon that is essentially a force of nature in itself, but is neither good nor bad.)
- Sides (such as good guy/bad guy, but for whole group perspectives—Empire/Rebels, Fellowship/Mordor, and so on).

Using character themes in this way helps identify the action, especially when cutting back and forth, and creates a musical aura around the character. As one composer says, it's a ballet of thematic material created as the editor cuts back and forth.

Contextual

The second approach is a purely contextual one, in which the music follows the events of the story without regard to specific character themes. This is a very common way to score a film, and it can work very well in a game. In a happy moment, the music reflects the happiness. In a sad moment, it reflects the sadness, and so on. Of course, as I discussed before, there is a wide range of options possible within this approach, and the music does not necessarily have to be in a one-to-one connection with the events.

The first approach actually borrows from the second approach in that character themes can be modified, such that in a sad moment, for instance, Luke Skywalker's theme music can seem sadder by changing the pace and the instrumentation, perhaps even altering the key from major to minor, and so on. In any case, character theme music can also be contextual.

A less common method of scoring a film is similar to the work of John Barry (who scored *Out of Africa* and *Somewhere in Time*, among others). This could be called the "Arc" approach, in which the score establishes an overall feeling that does not change with the action, but simply establishes a single mood and continues it, possibly with minor exceptions, throughout the film. This is also an option for games, particularly those that do not seem to require a more complex thematic or contextual approach.

Intros, Endings, and Interstitials/Cut Scenes

Many games today have elaborate noninteractive scenes that must be scored as well. These scenes serve specific purposes to introduce, show important information, provide the player with special rewards, and establish certain dramatic flow from the beginning, key middle points, and the ending. Consequently, the music should fit the intent of the scene. In this way, it is likely to be very much like composing for movies, and the information in the previous sections should be useful.

For instance, a lot of games use big, heroic music to introduce the game. Some use dark, moody music. How much information can you convey simply with the way you handle the opening?

Incidental Music

Surprisingly, the music composer is also responsible for an odd array of music that seems almost too inconsequential to be noticed, but it is just the kind of music that can help immerse a player in the world's fantasy. Examples of this type of incidental music are:

- Hold music when the player is on the phone.
- Background TV playing something—could be soap operas, cartoons, a chase scene, or some schmaltzy drama.
- Elevator music or the music in a department store or mall.
- "Live" musicians on the street or in a pub or bar.
- Car radios.

Orchestrations and Arrangements

The object of this book is to encourage creativity and give you some resources from which to draw. The concept of how to orchestrate the music for a game is a very subjective topic, and one that will depend entirely on the tastes and intentions of the game's designers, producers, and composers.

In other media, such as movies and TV, there are two meaningful ways to describe orchestrations:

- Classical
- Contemporary

The classical approach is familiar to all moviegoers—the large orchestra that seems bigger than life. It creates a sense of magic and can color a score with any emotion—heroic, romantic, funny, quirky, eerie, frightening, pastoral, exciting, mysterious, and so on. It can range dynamically from pianissimo to double forte (very soft to very loud) in the same piece. However effective and common it is, though, it does carry with it a traditional, dated quality.

In contrast, the contemporary sound—which can be dated more or less from the '80s on—relies on urban music, techno, electronics, and contemporary styles. It is somewhat more difficult to establish the entire range and spectrum of emotion and imagery with modern instrumentations, but it isn't impossible. Lacking a couple of hundred years of classical history and composition and lacking the first 70 to 80 years of film composing, contemporary scores must work harder to convey some of the more complex emotional associations. However, it does very well with many common themes, such as danger, heroism, action, and excitement. And it does convey an immediate sense of its era.

This strength of being recognizable from a specific era is also a potential drawback, because contemporary music can quickly become dated and even quaint or passé. Anything that's recognizably contemporary has probably about a five-year window of freshness, after which it becomes dated.

Many composers approach the situation by using a hybrid of classical and contemporary, giving them access to the best of both worlds and the most versatility.

Some music is outside these categories, such as jazz and most ethnic/exotic music, including African, Middle Eastern, Indian, oompah, bar mitzvah/wedding music, big band or period music (such as Gregorian chant), and other music associated with a particular geography, ethnic group, or period in history.

Ways to Affect the Player's Experience

Given that you have decided on the point of view to use in any given situation and the other parameters of your score, what are some other ways to affect the player's experience? How much control do you have?

Part of the effect of music is cultural, so we recognize certain kinds of music as being sexy (soft jazz, saxophones, and so on) or romantic (swelling strings, perhaps), but these represent a cultural language developed, in some cases, over several hundred years. If the listener was born in the Congo or the Middle East, without exposure to the music of Western culture, he or she might have a different response.

Even within our cultural setting, people might have different responses to recognizable types of music. If you take an electric guitar with big vibrato and wah wah, you may instantly think of the '60s and its associated music, but whether you respond with nostalgia or you think it's funny and silly depends on your perspective. Another example is the accordion, which is a pretty cool instrument, but has been associated over the years with some decidedly staid and unhip music. For that reason, people generally hear accordions and have a negative reaction.

The "color" of music is established by a number of different factors, including melodic and harmonic choices, as well as instrumentation. It is pretty clichéd to use brass in 4th and 5th intervals for heroic music—the Roman trumpeters announcing Caesar, for instance. But in jazz, the brass is orchestrated in block voicing (where the harmony instruments always move in the same direction as the lead). And you would get a very different effect using flutes, woodwinds, or strings. Again, if you want it to, this can get very technical, but much of it is so ingrained in our minds that we know it when we hear it, and composers don't generally sit around analyzing what they are doing. It is a language they have become fluent with.

Besides instrumentation, there are a lot of other buttons you can push, including how you use tempo, pace, meter, melody, and harmony. For instance, watch (and listen to) the Batman movie, *The Dark Knight*, and notice the driving force of the underlying music, which continually seems to build throughout the movie. The rhythmic theme is repeated again and again, with different melodies and effects over it. It moves to the background to create an underlying, increasing tension and to the foreground to create immediacy and drama. Like the *Jaws* theme, it's simple and effective.

For trained musicians, there is a lot of information about the types of scales, modes, harmonies/chords, and melodic sequences that can reliably change a listener's experience and mood. For instance, chords such as suspended and diminished chords tend to lend a sort of undefined quality to the music, while the dominant 7th begs for resolution.

Also, music can almost immediately tell us something about a character or theme. For instance, if you show someone walking down the street and you play in the background the steady "boom boom" rhythm of a rap song, the audience/player instantly has an impression of that character.

The job of the composer for movies, TV, or games is to push the listener's buttons by first knowing what those buttons are, and then using them effectively.

Types of effective music include:

- Romantic
- Military/pageantry
- Victory
- Defeat
- Creepy/scary/tension
- Suspense/tension
- Dark/moody
- Big/huge
- Small/intimate
- Action (such as fast-moving sports or chase scenes)
- Dramatic moment
- Sad
- Jubilant
- Determined
- Heroic
- Indeterminate (what's happening, anyway?)
- Funky (being hip/with it/bad/fly, or whatever is current)
- Pacey (responding to elements of timing in the story and events)
- Comic/silly

Sounds

Sounds and sound effects are used extensively in games, and while a lot of attention is paid to the latest graphics innovations, today's games would be stale and somewhat empty without the many sound effects that enhance the player's experience. In some of the same ways as movies and in some unique ways, sounds and sound effects are an integral part of a game design.

This section deals with some of the ways sounds are used in games, along with a few specific examples of each type of use.

Ambient Sounds

Ambient sounds are used to set the scene and the environment. These are the sounds and noises that are characteristic to a location. For instance, a cave might have a certain low hum inside and echoes from various small events—bat wings, small stones falling, the splash of a fish in a subterranean river, and so on. In contrast, an office building might have a slight buzz from the fluorescent lamps and the whir of computers, the background ringing of telephones, and so on. A jungle might have the call of a peacock or a monkey's chatter in the distance. Here are a few types of ambient sounds:

- Crickets
- Machine whir/hum
- Distant roar of ocean or babble of brook
- Gunfire in distance
- Heavy machinery
- Traffic sounds
- Aircraft sounds (ambient)
- Footfalls (different surfaces)
- Room sounds (ambient, variable with acoustics of room or location)
- Electrical discharge of force field or something like it
- Voices (ambient)

Sounds as Clues

Sounds are often used as clues for the player. In this, they are unique to interactive entertainment. The sound clues can be very artificial and obvious, such as a special beep issued by an item the player needs to find. However, they can be far more subtle—distant voices that get closer as you approach, warning you of possible danger ahead; the soft padding of an animal or the splash of a frog jumping into a pond, calling your attention to a half-hidden path. Designers generally don't waste their time putting in animations or specific sounds without meaning. There are always ambient sounds and animations that are used frequently enough to become meaningless in terms of information, but those one-of-a-kind events almost always point to something useful or important. Here are some of the kinds of sounds that can be used as clues:

- Voices
- Beep or ticking of a clock—or is it a time bomb?
- Rustle of leaves to indicate the presence of enemy or animal in forest
- Sounds of breathing or other natural sounds to locate people or creatures
- Sound of footsteps (player's) to indicate some change in the ground or floor
- Whistle or whine of an incoming shell
- Gunfire to tell you you're being shot at
- Cocking of a gun as a warning
- Breathing sounds to indicate whether the player's character is getting winded/tired
- Cracking sound as something breaks

Sound and Location

Sound has become far more sophisticated as games have evolved, and now it's entirely possible to give players a sense of realism and a better sense of location by creating sound that more or less realistically depicts the distance of the player's character from the source of the sound. This can be used as a clue, or it can simply enhance the enjoyment of the game by making it seem more alive. The ultimate of this experience is to use surround sound technology to put the player in the middle of a real environment. Distance and surround effects can be used with any type of sound effect. In essence, the closer a sound, the louder it will be. The farther the player's character gets from the sound source, the lower the volume. Of course, the player character's presence alone might cause the sound to change, to become quieter, silent, or louder.

Effects and Feedback

There are many unique, event-specific sound effects used in games. These are sounds associated with specific game events, such as the contact of a fist with someone's face, a shovel digging in dirt, or the casting of a magic spell, and so on. They can also be any sound that is specifically associated with any event. These sounds bring the world to life and tie the actions of the player and other characters to sounds that provide more feedback to the player and a sense of continuity and realism.

Feedback is an important aspect of these event-driven sounds. It often provides an auditory method of checking that you have done something—for instance, a fizzled spell will sound different from a successful one. A missed punch will sound different from one that connects. In many circumstances, where a player's attention is focused on many things at once, these sound distinctions can sometimes be the most important ways of knowing what has happened and what is happening.

- A telephone rings.
- Someone gets hit.
- Any type of spell is cast. (The sound will vary.)
- There is a knock on the door.
- The door opens.
- Someone walks across the room or along a path. Is it wood, stone, masonry, gravel, leaves, or something else?
- The elevator rings the floors and dings when it reaches a selected floor.
- Someone lights a match.
- A rock is thrown into a pond.
- Your character (or another) screams in pain or grunts.

Design Challenge

1. Spend some time listening to the music and sounds in your favorite movies. How do they use sound to influence you? How do the ambient sounds affect the scene? Make a list of what you discover.
2. Play some games you are already familiar with and do the previous exercise. Then answer these questions:
   a. Does the game genre affect how the designers used music and sounds?
   b. Which types of games used situational music?
   c. Which games used sounds as clues, and how did they do so?
3. Think of five different scenes you might find in a game—preferably in your own games—and make a list of every sound that could occur in those scenes.
   a. How would ambient sounds help or detract from your scenes?
4. Think of a game you want to make. What kinds of music would you want and why? Make a list.
   a. Would you go with situational music? Why or why not?
   b. Would you go with character themes? Why or why not?
   c. What would be the effect of having no music at all?
5. Make a list of ways your favorite games used music.
6. Make a list of the ways your favorite games used sounds.
7. Can you think of an innovative way to use sound? Create a game concept that uses sound in a novel way—not just as a novelty, but as an integral part of a game you would like to play.

Part VI Experience Design

Section A The Elements of Experience

21 Experiential Design

When you set out to design a game, there are a lot of questions you can ask and answer. Of course, you need to know what genre you want to use. You want to know who your players are and what they like to do in a game. You also need to know what the game experience will be like...but do you?

It always surprises me that someone can work for hours, weeks, and even months on a game concept and not be able to describe the gameplay to me. I ask them, "Can you describe in detail what the player will be doing when playing your game?" They can give me general concepts: They are riding a horse through fields and avoiding arrows. They can fly planes and shoot down dragons. They can make a lot of money in the stock market. But they can't tell me exactly *what the player does.*

This chapter is all about what I like to think of as "high-speed game design." I call it *experiential design*, and it can function as your own personal proof of concept. Instead of spending hours writing charts of monsters or drawing maps, take some time to describe, in detail, everything the player sees, hears, thinks, and does.

To help you think about your experiential designs, this chapter also offers a number of lists of activities that are common in games. How many of them will you use? Are there some you haven't thought of that would fit perfectly into your game idea?

We also offer a section on what we've found to be fun—and not fun—in playing games. As always, we encourage you to add to or amend the list to reflect your personal experiences in playing games.

In this chapter:

- Experiential Design Activities
- Things to Do in Games
- What Can We Learn from Sports Games?
- Defining Fun

Experiential Design Activities

Try the following five activities before reading this chapter, then try again, using the sections of this chapter for reference. See whether you come up with new ideas that you hadn't considered the first time through.

1. Sit down and describe in detail everything you experience during the first 10 or 20 minutes of a game you like.
2. Choose some of your favorite missions or quests from a game you like and describe everything you saw, everything you heard, every challenge you faced, every thought you had while playing, and every action you took. Break it down and understand that it is the sum of these sights, sounds, mental exercises, and actions that creates the fun.

3. Now do the first two activities with a game you're designing. You may need to do this in your imagination, so think of it as a game design visualization exercise. If you can't think of what the player would be seeing, hearing, thinking, and doing while playing your game, then you haven't fully developed your concept yet. Once you have done these exercises, however, I bet you'll be much clearer when you return to the drawing board to sketch out your design.
4. Take one or more games you like and ask yourself the following questions:
   a. What did I do while playing this game? Make a list of every action you took. Notice which ones are repetitive and common and which are uncommon. Which were the most interesting?
   b. What do I remember best?
   c. What did I do too often?
   d. What did I not do often enough?
   e. Was there anything missing? If so, what was it, and how would it have improved your experience?
   f. What made this game fun? List all the things about the game that felt like fun to you.
5. Do the previous exercise with a game you're designing. Ask all the same questions and imagine what the answers would be.

Game Activities

When starting this book, I was challenged by Chris Hecker to make a list of *all* the things you could do in a game. (He laughed as he said it.) Initially, it seems like an impossible task, as there are millions of things you could do in games. That's true, but if you step back and change your perspective, certain activities tend to be common in many games. The following list mentions the ones that jump to mind.

As a game designer, one of the interesting challenges, however, is to consider how you might be able use some of these actions in games where you might not expect to find them. For instance, what about building or constructing something in a First-Person Shooter? Sound boring? Perhaps you could block off a tunnel entrance to stop an attack. You could construct a barricade (using a pile of physical objects, such as tables, chairs, and so on) with a bomb hidden in it. Then when the enemies are trying to climb over it and are tearing it apart on the other side, you detonate. Or better still, you could make others build it for you at gunpoint. This would be an unusual activity for a First-Person Shooter, but it could probably be made fun. The point is the idea comes from reading the list of game activities and thinking about how to apply them in unusual ways.

So look over this list and consider how you might combine these activities in new and different ways.

Basic Game Activities

1. Prepare for a battle (such as constructing fortification, putting on armor, casting protective spells, and so on).
2. Hold or protect a position (perhaps to protect something or someone).
3. Fight through enemies (who are trying to stop you from getting somewhere).
4. Fight enemies (who are there to kill or capture you).
5. Allow capture. (You give in and allow capture or maybe even allow your own death, but why? That's the challenge.)
6. Head to a goal (which can be an unconventional path to somewhere).
7. Offer a sacrifice (where you must deliver or sacrifice someone or something).
8. Retreat or flee. (You need to get yourself or everyone out safely.)

9. Remote control something (such as a vehicle or another entity, using radio waves or even your mind).
10. Ride in or on something (such as a horse, car, airplane, or ship).
11. Explore (such as searching for something or for a way out).
12. Find out information (for example, by conversing with other players or other characters).
13. Expose information (such as finding hidden or encrypted messages).
14. Collect items (can be currency, weapons, property, and so on).
15. Equip with items (such as clothing/armor, food, and weapons).
16. Buy, sell, auction, or trade. (You can sell anything—places, people, objects, and so on.)
17. Gamble and bet (games of chance, for money, items, or maybe a life).
18. Race (formal races or just getting to somewhere before something happens).
19. Form parties and/or alliances (have relationships, get followers, form a gang, form a cult, etc.).
20. Betray an ally.
21. Build or construct something (can be a structure, a place, an item, a weapon, soldier, and so on).
22. Grow or nurture something (such as a plant, an animal, or a desire to be free).
23. Cook or brew something (such as a magic potion, food, or a poisonous drink).
24. Eat/drink. (What effect does it have?)
25. Destroy or heavily damage something (such as throwing a monkey wrench into the works, arson, and so on).
26. Sabotage something. (Poison horses so troops can't leave, take clips from guns, and so on.)
27. Gain levels, skills, and character attributes. (These are ways to show your character is bigger, better, and badder!)
28. Save or load a game state.
29. Use/learn/develop magic or technology (can be from magicians, books, scriptures, scientists, by accident, and so on).
30. Solve puzzles/mysteries. (Experimentation will be required to find the complex solutions.)
31. Complete specific tasks/quests (very specific tasks, such as "take this object and keep the enemy from obtaining it").
32. Kill or terminate someone (such as killing the head of the organization or executing someone in a sequence chain so that the sequence fails—for example, taking out the delivery boy so the package doesn't arrive on time).
33. Rescue someone (such as rescuing the princess or someone who is captured, unable to move, or simply trapped).
34. Escape (get out of the prison, get off the planet, find the exit, etc.).
35. Escort and protect (for example, make sure the old man, the valuable jewels, or the antidote makes it).
36. Steal or borrow something. (Be a thief or find a way to take something without being caught.)
37. Be the villain. (It's your chance to step into the villain's shoes.)
38. Deliver something (such as an important letter or a declaration of war).
39. Document or photograph something. (Sell the photo, use it for blackmail or to prove a court case, become a famous photographer, and so on.)
40. Activate or use a specific object (for example, pull the lever, inject the virus, insert the disc, break the glass, trigger the alarm, and so on).
41. Hunt someone/something/some animal. (It might also be hunting you!)
42. Repair something (such as taking your sword to the blacksmith, fixing the broken spaceship so you can get home, repairing the life support before you all die, and so on).
43. Upgrade something (for example, make new bullets for your gun or strap two guns together).
44. Close a path (for example, build a barricade, cause an accident to block the path, and so on).

45. Open or clear a path (such as hacking through the jungle with a machete or a flame thrower).
46. Discover some information (such as being a fly on the wall or a spy).
47. Be invisible. (Get somewhere without being detected or seen.)
48. Have a romantic encounter (for example, flirt with the girl, leave a love letter, or be seen with the wrong girl at the wrong time).
49. Possession. (Take over the bodies of other characters, pretend to be them, or force them to take pain for you, such as beating out the fire or killing themselves, etc.)
50. Use torture (for example, torture enemies to get them to talk, or put people into their own traps).
51. Be tortured (undergo torture as part of the game).
52. Distract. (Create a distraction or cause something interesting to happen to trigger people to go and look.)
53. Use prediction (cause the player to try to predict the future).
54. Blend in (such as by pretending to be someone you are not, moving with a crowd, and so on).
55. Play sports. (Compete in a skilled event.)
56. Chase (to try to catch something or someone).
57. Use education (to learn something mental, such as a tactic, method, or even just interesting facts or gossip).
58. Lie or misrepresent (to cause people to believe something to your advantage, or to fake out the enemy, such as using the Trojan horse).
59. Rules (follow, bend, or break the rules).
60. Practice (hone your skills, such as target practice and so on).
61. Move things (either physically or by telekinesis).
62. Rest or pause. (Stop to sleep or watch something, such as a vista or a movie on a screen that you pass by, and so on.)
63. Win a prize or award (for meeting certain goals or conditions).
64. Use pets and creatures (for training and managing).
65. Do charity (such as bringing food into a hungry town, taking from the rich for the poor, and so on).
66. Use hero-worship (helping or saving others, becoming their hero, and then they root for you).
67. Practice security and safety. (Become the security force that others rely on.)
68. Politics. (Win the favor of others by policy; engage in a political campaign or try to influence politicians to achieve goals within the game.)
69. Be a dictator. (Force others to do things under the threat of punishment or death.)
70. Be a director or a leader.
71. Use humor. (Entertain others in the world.)
72. Make music. (Play an instrument.)
73. Sing (such as a magical chant or an entertaining song).

More Game Activities

Of course, the previous list is not everything you can do in a game, and it's doubtful that I can come up with all possible options. However, here's another list, just to get you started. The idea is not to read these lists to learn what you *can* do, but to challenge yourself to do something in your games that *nobody* has done. Sure, you can get some inspiration from these lists. "Oh, I forgot that I can do that!" But even more, you can use them as a challenge. In any case, enjoy, and let us know if you can think of something to add.

Movements and Positions

See also Chapter 15, "Character Abilities."

- Run
- Walk
- Brisk walk
- Jump
- Roll
- Strafe
- Swim
- Dive
- Float
- Flip
- Spin
- Crouch
- Kneel
- Go prone
- Hang
- Crawl
- Somersault/flip
- Fly
- Hover
- Glide
- Skate
- Climb
- Teleport
- Operate a vehicle

Attacks

- Use a weapon
  - Guns
  - Melee weapons
- Use magic
- Use your body
  - Punch
  - Kick
  - Block
  - Throw
  - Hold
  - Choke
- Use your mind
  - Control someone using your mind
  - Figure something out (solve a puzzle)
  - See the future
  - Use telekinesis
- Charge up an attack or defense
  - Duel or challenge someone
  - Use the environment
  - Set something on fire
  - Make something explode
  - Drop something
  - Throw something
  - Use a random item as a weapon

State of Being

- Turn into a zombie
- Return to life
- Confused
- Asleep, stunned, or unconscious
- Afraid
- Angry
- Live/survive
- Dead
- Doing nothing

Socialize

- Persuade someone
- Seduce
- Bribe
- Intimidate
- Threaten
- Argue
- Criticize
- Chat using voice or text
- Teach someone a skill
- Compliment
- Taunt
- Make an expression (point a finger, make a face)

- Use body language to convey some meaning
  - Puff up and act threatening
  - Show flirtation through body and expression
  - Cower to show fear
  - Lower head to show subservience
- Engage in activities with people
  - Go to the bar with a group of people
  - Go dungeon crawling with a group of people
  - Plan or strategize with people
  - Party with people

Resource Management

- Collect resources
- Spend or utilize resources
- Grow and tend to resources (as in farming)
- Sell or buy resources
- Recombine resources
- Store resources
- Drop or destroy
- Salvage material from resources
- Deconstruct

Objects

- Move an object
- Spin an object
- Break an object
- Place an object
- Push or pull an object
- Use an object as a stepping stone
- Make it disappear
- Duplicate an object
- Throw an object
- Punch or stomp an object
- Paint or dye an object
- Make an object
- Plant an object
- Eat an object
- Steal an object
- Buy or sell an object
- Deconstruct an object
- Combine objects
- Transform objects
- Shape objects
- Carve objects
- Open and close an object

Doors

- Open a door
- Close a door
- Lock a door
- Unlock a door
  - Pick a lock
  - Use a key, pass card, biometric information, etc.
  - Break it down or break the lock
- Destroy a door
- Remove a door from its hinges
- Knock on a door
- Carve your initials (or a magic sign) on the door
- Set fire to it
- Use acid or a blowtorch or laser on it
- Blow it up
- Punch or kick it

Vehicles

- Fly a plane or glider
- Parachute out of a plane
- Drive a car or truck
- Drive a tank
- Steer a boat
- Hover with a hovercraft
- Fly a rocket or a UFO to space
- Drill underground
- Submarine underwater

Economics

- Buy
- Sell
- Trade
- Steal
- Illegally obtain stock information
- Find money
- Open a shop
- Launder money
- Create different types of economies (token economy)
- Donate
- Collect
- Haggle or beg
- Cheat someone out of money (con artist, scam)
- Tip an economic scale
- Destroy an economy
- Get a job
- Hire or fire somebody
- Quit or go on strike
- Manage a welfare system
- Get rich, poor, or somewhere in between

Menu System

- Change game options
  - Difficulty
  - Sounds and effects volume and toggles
  - Brightness
  - Graphics (details, resolution)
  - Color
  - Gore level
  - Key assignments
  - Cheat codes
  - Miscellaneous game-specific options

Create a Character

See also the "Ways to Customize Avatars" section in Chapter 12, "Character Design."

- Race or type
- Body type/size
- Face and hair
- Skin color
- Gender
- Clothes
- Class or job
- Starting stats
- Starting skills
- Starting equipment (sometimes)
- Starting location (sometimes)

Manage Inventory

- Drop
- Move
- Combine
- Trade
- Buy/sell
- Rearrange/order
- Use

User Interface

- HUD (Heads-Up Display)
  - Manipulate health bar
  - Manipulate skill or mana bar
  - Adjust the map or mini-map
  - Use targeting reticules
  - Change quick slots for items, weapons, spells
  - Change chat windows
  - Move and resize information display elements
- Input device
  - Push a button
  - Click a mouse
  - Twist a dial
  - Move a stick
  - Press a key
  - Shout in a microphone
  - Dance on a dance pad
  - Use steering wheels
  - Use foot pedals
  - Beat on drums
  - Shake maracas
  - Touch screen/pad
  - Use stylus

Strategize

- Command teammates
- Cheat
- Make enemies
- Negotiate with enemies
- Make a strategic movement or position
- Manage time and resources
- Call a target
- Delay a battle
- Choose your players, characters, items, weapons
- Bluff
- Buff/debuff
- Surprise attack
- Trap
- Get advice
- Blackmail
- Change equipment
- Play dead
- Disguise yourself

Quests/Missions: Using This Book to Create Content

Quests are one of the common structures used in games to give players activities and short- to medium-range goals. Quests are especially common in RPGs and MMOs. In other games, such as military games and shooters, they are often called *missions*, but they amount to the same thing.

Quests can come in many shapes and sizes, so to speak. Some are extremely simple, such as, "Go kill that dude." Others can involve multiple steps and even many sub-quests. At any rate, this book is full of information that could be useful in designing quests and missions for your games. So, let's pretend we are creating a quest and see how this book could be useful.

Creating a Quest/Mission

Quests and missions are always based on the context of the game and/or story. However, one thing is always true: Quests and missions are obtained somehow during gameplay. They involve actions that the player must take, challenges he or she must meet, and goals that must be accomplished for the quest/mission to be considered successful. In addition, quests and missions generally have some kind of explicit—or at least implicit—reward for success. Sometimes they also have penalties for failure.

So, what does the player do in a quest? Let's look at each aspect of a quest or mission and see how to use this book to help make them more interesting.

The Source

The source of a quest is the method by which the player gets the task in the first place. Sometimes quests are given by NPCs. Other times, they may be obtained by reading a text or solving puzzles that lead to a quest. Sometimes quests are given as qualification tests, and successful completion of the task or quest is required to prove your fitness, worthiness, integrity, or skills to the quest giver. Other types of quests are integral to the overall game plot, such as a quest to go find proof that a certain minister is corrupt as part of a larger political storyline.

Some are simple: Go kill so-and-so, and I'll give you 50 bucks. Some are slightly more complex:

- Simple Premise: Go find a cure for the disease that's turning the townspeople into zombies.
- But…
    1. You'll have to first find the stable boy in Amarzuna who knows where the White Witch Dunbar lives.
    2. Then get Dunbar to give you the formula.
    3. But she won't give it to you unless you do her a favor and bring her five unicorn horns, three giant toad warts, a dozen dragon scales, and a Coke.
    4. To get the Coke, you'll have to travel to a different dimension where Cokes are sold, earn some money to buy it (or steal one), and then get back to your original dimension with it intact.
    5. Once you have done all this, she'll tell you that, sadly, the only way to create this formula is to obtain the rare Imperial Magnolia blossom that only blooms once a century on a certain hill near the capital.
    6. And it turns out that the hill in question is being flattened to make new high rises for the corrupt minister's 100 concubines, so now you have to hightail it over to the capital and prevent the Imperial Magnolia from being cut down.
    7. Harvest the magic blossom.
    8. Return to Dunbar.
    9. Wait for her to create the potion and then take it back to where you started to save the village.
    10. Oh, and didn't I mention that there are some really bad guys trying to stop you from succeeding?
    11. And along the way, you'll have to confront the evil minister, who is really an emissary from the underworld intent on enslaving all the good people.
    12. And he's almost invincible.
    13. And perhaps you'll have to find some very rare weapon to do away with him, or the whole thing will fail utterly.

Good luck!

Military missions and FPS missions are sometimes given by NPCs, but sometimes they are simply part of the interface—a mission offered by a level structure or some sort of built-in mission dispenser.

A great many quests and missions start with someone giving you the task; however, you can somehow stumble onto the goal by other means. For instance, you figure out a riddle that tells you the most beautiful woman who ever lived, or the most precious jewel, or the secret to eternal life—whatever—can be obtained if you can reach the Holy Crag of Bemonstous—or something like that—but a) you don't know where the Holy Crag is; b) once you ultimately *do* find out how to get there, you have to get there; c) getting to the top is pretty damn dangerous; and d) once you get there, you have no idea how to obtain the thingy that you were after, or if you do get it, you don't know how to use it. There's probably someone, somewhere, who can tell you what you need to know, but their advice will come at a price. And so on... Anyway, although many quests and missions are obtained from NPCs of one kind or another, some can be found in the environment. A great source of inspiration for such environmental options might be found in Chapter 30, "Ways to Communicate with the Player." Ideas for NPC quest givers might be found in Chapter 12, "Character Design."

The Goals

All quests and missions inherently have goals that the player must accomplish. These can be simple, single goals, or an ultimate goal that entails many steps (as in the aforementioned example).

At any rate, goals come in many shapes and sizes, and I've done some work to describe them in Chapter 23, "Goals." However, both Chapter 27, "Puzzles," and Chapter 11, "Scenarios," have useful information for creating more interesting goals for your quests and missions. Still, good tried-and-true ideas, such as "kill everyone in the enemy base" or "get Shorty" are always valid.

The Challenges

Mission and quest challenges appear in all kinds of ways:

- Some challenges are physical, such as crossing a great chasm, fighting your way into the enemy's stronghold, or defeating a very powerful boss enemy in single combat.
- Others are situational, such as realizing that the only way you can complete the quest is to stop the hill that has the magical Imperial Magnolia tree from being razed.
- Still others are mental, such as figuring out what the riddle the old man told you really means or finding a way to get the pharaoh's tomb to open and how to avoid the many deadly traps it contains.
- Sentient obstacles can also be quite challenging. Often this involves NPC characters who you can't fight, but who hold the key to your success and won't easily be convinced to assist you or who actively oppose you. Sentient obstacles can be human, humanoid, robotic or computer, or any kind of sentient creature. These kinds of challenges can have elements of a situational challenge and something of a mental challenge, and could turn into a physical challenge as well. But the agency of the challenge in this case is a sentient being who impedes your progress and threatens your ultimate success.

Clearly, you must offer the player some obstacles to overcome, whether they are physical, situational, mental, or sentient. Especially helpful for reference would be Chapter 27, "Puzzles," Chapter 11, "Scenarios," Chapter 25, "Barriers, Obstacles, and Detectors," Chapter 26, "Traps and Counter Traps" Chapter 32, "Ways to Die," and Chapter 14, "Enemies," though many other chapters also contain useful resources. (See the list at the end of the next section.)

The Rewards and Penalties

Most quests and missions offer some sort of reward. Some offer quite substantial rewards, while others are content to present the successful player with something dinky and virtually useless. But the ultimate reward is a job well done, right? Anyway, rewards do vary, but there is almost always some positive gain on the part of the successful player—if nothing else, the opportunity to keep playing forward in the game.

Of course, Chapter 24, "Rewards and Penalties," is the ideal resource for both rewards and penalties as they relate to games, missions, quests, and all that.

And speaking of penalties, not all quests and missions offer specific penalties, though often there is the real possibility that your player will die, with any unfortunate effects that accompany player death. However, some quests and missions also reward failure with some kind of penalty, and for some ideas about that, see Chapter 24, "Rewards, Bonuses, and Penalties."

In all, creating quests, missions, and tasks is a common activity in game design, and this book is full of resources that can offer inspiration and help you create interesting and well thought-out elements for your games. So, to find ideas and inspiration, look at the following chapters in addition to this one:

- Chapter 11, "Scenarios"
- Chapter 22, "Game Conventions and Clichés"
- Chapter 23, "Goals"
- Chapter 24, "Rewards, Bonuses, and Penalties"
- Chapter 25, "Barriers, Obstacles, and Detectors"
- Chapter 26, "Traps and Counter Traps"
- Chapter 27, "Puzzles"
- Chapter 28, "Controlling Pacing"
- Chapter 29, "Time Limits and Time Manipulation"
- Chapter 30, "Ways to Communicate with the Player"
- Chapter 31, "Common Game Design Problems"
- Chapter 32, "Ways to Die"

These chapters contain many of the basic elements you will want to consider when creating quests. Sure, it's a lot, but to make interesting quests you want to consider all the possibilities, such as how to trap someone, what kinds of puzzles might work, what kinds of scenarios might be appropriate, interesting ways to kill the player, and so on.

Other chapters also contain useful information, such as:

- Chapter 17, "Game Worlds," for some ideas on the settings you might use, and specifically the "Ways to Make a World Feel Alive and Real" section in that chapter for ways to make even more interesting quests and missions.
- Chapter 9, "Storytelling Techniques," for some more ideas on story options.
- Chapter 12, "Character Design," if you want to have more characters appear within the quest/mission, and specifically the "Creating Comedy" section in Chapter 9 to put your characters into some humorous situations or the "Making Things Scary" section (also in Chapter 9) to, well, make things scary.
- Chapter 15, "Character Abilities," if you want to think about special abilities for your characters or to look at some general options for what characters can do.
- Chapter 14, "Enemies," if you want to include some different enemy types and different battles in your quests/missions.
- Chapter 19, "Objects and Locations," to consider what kinds of objects to use for different locations you are considering.
- Chapter 33, "Historical and Cultural Weapons," and Chapter 34, "Standard Modern Weaponry and Armor," if you want to consider some interesting weapons and/or armor as part of the quest/mission.
- Chapter 18, "Travel," if traveling is part of the quest/mission.
- Chapter 16, "Speech," particularly if conversation is part of your quest/mission.
- Chapter 20, "Music and Sound," for some ideas on how to use music and sound effectively within a quest/mission.

Interesting...that's most of the book! Perhaps that's because quests are microcosms of the game—little sequences of goals, challenges, and rewards. In essence, any of the material in the chapters listed above can be useful when you are designing a game or a quest/mission within a game. Of course, it all depends on the nature of the quest or mission you want to design. Some may not have other characters in them, or enemies, or weapons. Others might not require any special abilities for the characters, or traps, or even the possibility of the player's death. But in constructing a good quest, any of these chapters can come in handy for inspiration and direction.

More Quest Examples

Among the most common types of games where you'll encounter quests are RPGs and MMOs. These quests are actually useful in other types of games as well, but they happen to be more commonly used in RPGs and MMOs. In the next section, "Things to Do in Games," see the NPC quest examples.

Design Challenge

1. Imagine you are on a team, making a First-Person Shooter. (Heck, there are tons of designers doing this, and it's not easy to be original with so much competition!) Your job is to come up with something fresh. So you sit down to a blank piece of paper. Time to come up with the key goals of the level you are about to make. Most First-Person Shooters leave you with the goal of getting to the exit, killing everyone on the way! That's cool, but you want to add some extra spice to your level. There are many lists in this book to help, but let's start with the lists in this chapter, and for extra inspiration, you can also refer to Chapter 11, "Scenarios." Let your mind wander. What could you add to your level (from the ideas in this chapter and elsewhere) that you haven't seen before?
2. Say you came back with "steal something" and "activate an object" and "hold or protect a position." How could you make that fun? Well, suppose you steal an amazing new bomb from the enemy research labs. Actually, it's the one they have been threatening you with! You take it back to their headquarters (with your scientist following you), then you place it and he starts arming it. You need to protect him and the bomb while he completes his sequence, then you need to get at least 700 meters from the blast. There are changing paths and surprise attacks as you try to get the range meter onscreen to 700m before the clock hits zero. Suddenly, you are doing three things at once. Then BOOM—you made it.
3. So it's your turn now.
4. Once you've done that, then what about trying it for another genre—for example, try to design an arcade game concept from the list.

The list is only supplied to help you brainstorm. So don't hold back—mix it up, shake it up, flip them to the opposite meanings.... You should find some nice combos. For more on brainstorming, see Chapter 2, "Brainstorming and Research."

THINGS TO DO IN GAMES

This section contains ideas about different types of games. It is not by any means everything you could possibly do in these types of games, but it gives you a good start at some of the options and possibilities at your disposal when you create games. The real reason for this section is to look at different genres and hopefully inspire you to:

- Find new and different things to do in each of these types of games.
- Go beyond these lists.
- Find ways to combine elements of various genres in order to create original and creative game ideas and implementations.

Things You Can Do in FPSs

First-Person Shooters are characterized by the point of view of the player and the kinds of activities that they typically include. The earliest FPS games were essentially mob hunts and very simple death matches. But FPS games have become more and more sophisticated, and many—at least in their single-player modes—have complex stories and options. In the multiplayer world, the stories are mostly individual experiences generated within the action.

Things you can do in either single player or multiplayer FPS games include the items in the following lists.

Single or Multiplayer

- Ambush someone
- Attack/kill/shoot another character
- Attack/kill/shoot something
- Be stealthy
- Call for support (airstrike/backup)
- Carry out missions
- Carry someone
- Carry things
- Change clothing
- Change form
- Check stats
- Climb up buildings and other places
- Complete an objective
  - Protect the base/hold the fort
  - Capture the enemy base/capture the flag
  - Control an area of the map
  - Kill everyone
  - Destroy some specific thing or person
- Control NPC allies
- Craft/build an item
- Demolish objects
- Destroy part of the level
- Die
- Drag or push things
- Drive vehicles
- Duel wield (guns or close-combat weapons)
- Enchant objects/weapons
- Escort someone
- Fail objective
- Find secret areas and routes
- Find something that has been lost
- Find weapons/ammo/armor caches
- Find/buy new items
- Fly
- Get night-sight equipment to see in the dark
- Get the power-ups first
- Give orders
- Grab someone
- Hack a computer
- Have allies
- Heal
- Hide and pick people off (sniper)
- Hover
- Infect someone
- Inject someone with something
- Interact with environment (objects)
- Interact with NPCs
- Jump
- Kamikaze (or just take a suicide pill)
- Light a match/fire for vision at night
- Load the game
- Look around
- Look at a map
- Make a force field
- Move/hide bodies
- Open chests, safes, and other containers
- Operate high-tech devices
- Operate machinery
- Order NPCs (friendlies)
- Parachute
- Pause game
- Perform acrobatics
- Pick a lock
- Pick up or drop an item
- Plant bugs or traps
- Play dead
- Read signs and messages
- Receive promotions
- Reload
- Repair objects
- Rescue people
- Restart the game
- Ride vehicle (animal) as driver/gunner/passenger

- Run shooting into a crowd (gun-fu)
- Run/jump/crouch/lie prone/roll, etc.
- Salute
- Save the game
- Set up a trap
- Sleep
- Sneak past the enemy
- Snipe
- Solve mysteries
- Solve puzzles (all kinds—see also Chapter 27, "Puzzles")
- Steal items from players/NPCs
- Summon a demon
- Swim
- Switch weapons on the fly
- Tag (graffiti)
- Take damage/wound
- Take orders
- Take pictures
- Teleport
- Threaten someone
- Throw things
- Upgrade weapons and armor/protection
- Use a computer terminal
- Use a variety of weapons ranging from melee to guns to just about anything you can think of
- Use emoticons or other special communication commands
- Use grenades (damage, smoke, flash-bang)
- Use magical spells/special skills
- Use mind control
- Use object (flashlight)
- Use protection, such as armor or shields, force fields, etc.
- Use telekinesis
- Watch a cut scene

Multiplayer

This list contains things you can do (or in some cases, things that happen to you) in a multiplayer First-Person Shooter.

- Attack/kill/shoot another player
- Be part of a team with other player characters
- Change roles (support/attack/defense)
- Change teams
- Chat/talk with other players
- Check the scoreboard
- Humiliate other teams
- Set up a strategy
- Taunt

Things You Can Do in RTSs

Real-Time Strategy (RTS) games are all about high pressure, resource management, and, of course, strategy, and they require the ability to split one's attention between simultaneous tasks and situations. Of course, there is generally plenty of combat and the ultimate quest to dominate the map.

- Create buildings
- Upgrade buildings
- Destroy buildings
- Create or destroy troops
- Upgrade troops
- Create or destroy workers/peasants
- Create or destroy specialists
- Create or destroy mobile vehicle units
- Find and obtain resources/wealth, including:
  - Gold
  - Lumber
  - Food
  - Stone
  - Radioactive fuels
  - Minerals (other than gold)
  - Fossil fuels
  - Animals for breeding/eating/work

- Assign tasks to individual NPCs
- Create selectable groups
- Assign tasks to groups
- Explore research paths (technology, magic, and so on)
- Explore the map
- Travel on land, over water, under water, in the air, in space, in alternate realities
- Defend your turf
- Set traps and defenses
- Create new settlements
- Spy on the enemy
- Sabotage the enemy
- Attack the enemy
- Destroy an enemy
- Make allies
- Help allies
- Call for help (from allies)
- Break alliances
- Destroy enemy buildings and defenses
- Destroy an enemy settlement
- Gather an army
- Complete special quests
- Make hero characters
- Change allegiance/alignment
- Cheat
- Purchase/trade for special items
- Include weather effects
- Include environmental impacts to resource gathering
- Include a political model
- Include a financial model
- Sell items to others
- Buy items from NPCs and allies
- Build roads/rails, etc.
- Carry out tactics
  - Rush!
  - Barricade and wait
  - Ambush
  - Split and flank enemy
  - Wedge
  - Hit and run
- Strategize (by yourself or with teammates)
- Cancel actions
- Build up your resources
- Exchange resources
- Talk to people (teammates)
- Heckle other players
- Surrender
- Force units to suicide (may be necessary for victory)
- Set group/unit stance
- Make formations
- Set waypoints
- Patrol
- Pay tribute or demand obedience from your units
- Level up your hero
- Backstab your teammates
- Slaughter critters
- Lay a trap
- Spy on opponents
- Activate unit abilities
- Pause the game to build a complex queue of moves or strategies
- Equip units; have a single unit type able to equip many different types of weapons
- Change your people's government (for a game that uses a political device)
- Build epic-scale buildings and units (or something that would be really cool to have—for example, the Great Wall of China)
- Create your own maps/scenarios
- Influence your units' morality (possibility for a supernatural force, devil's influence, angelic harmony, and so on)
- Heal/repair units/buildings
- Grow farms to feed your people
- Convert the opponent's units
- Capture buildings
- Pollute the world (changes the environment of the game)
- Play in a nontraditional setting
- Terraform (take a lifeless world or region and make it earthlike)
- Play multiple scales in the same environment (fight as ants, then dogs, then humans, then gods!)
- Attack ground
- Play a strategy game first that sets up your RTS game
- Use naval bombardment
- Use aerial bombardment
- Start a pandemic
- Buy and sell items/units/resources on a black market

- Progress a story
- Introduce a new storyline
- Retreat
- Garrison units (in a building)
- Transport (teleport) units
- Take control of a unit and go to an FPS
- Stealth your units
- Sabotage your opponent's research/buildings
- Form alliances
- Build an inter-player network of spies
- Disable enemy units
- Capture enemy units as POWs
- Query units and buildings for their status
- Sell units to make up resources
- Recycle units and buildings (similar to selling units)
- Liberate POWs/cities/buildings, etc.
- Hunt/fish
- Escort units
- Breed super soldiers
- Use genetic engineering
- Control territory—the territory may give a certain benefit to the player
- Temporarily enhance your units' abilities
- Queue production
- Use psychic powers to possess opponents (control the other player, not just his units)
- Fortify buildings

Things You Can Do in RPGs

Role-Playing Games (RPGs) probably allow the greatest diversity of possible tasks and activities of any game genre. Think of this list as just a beginning, because you can probably do just about anything you can think up in an RPG.

- Walk
- Run
- Jump
- Fight
- Heal self and others
- Get diseases and curses
- Heal diseases and remove curses
- Drink and get drunk
- Bribe people
- Accept bribes
- Give orders
- Take orders
- Own property
- Own and run businesses
- Control henchmen, slaves, or other characters
- Lie or tell the truth
- Send and receive messages
- Send and receive items
- Save and load the game
- Die
- Die and resurrect yourself or be resurrected
- Resurrect others
- Use weapons
- Wear armor
- Wear items (rings, amulets, etc.)
- Wear clothing
- Pick up items
- Drop and/or destroy items
- Alter items
- Sell items
- Buy items
- Use magic (usually)
- Search and find
- Find secret items, places, and characters
- Disguise yourself
- Converse with NPCs
- Improve statistics
- Learn new skills/spells
- Level up
- Create a party
- Join/leave a party
- Befriend people and creatures
- Make enemies
- Tame creatures
- Hunt for food
- Gather resources
- Obtain and complete quests (many)
- Create a reputation with others in the world
- Rescue people
- Recover lost or stolen items
- Upgrade equipment
- Be poisoned or diseased

- Be cursed
- Be enhanced by magic or by other means (such as potions, enchanted items, and so on)
- Physically change (grow bigger/smaller, transform into something else, change appearance, and so on)
- Hide
- Sneak
- Steal
- Spy
- Cheat
- Gamble
- Do good deeds
- Do bad deeds
- Escort people, things, caravans, and so on
- Trade items or money
- Manage inventory
- Set fire to something—torch a house, village, city, wagon, etc.
- Set fire to some character or creature
- Craft (create or combine) items
- Be betrayed
- Betray someone
- Fall in love
- Get married
- Have children
- Grow old
- Grow younger
- Go back and forth in time
- Ride in vehicles of various kinds
- Ride on beasts of various kinds
- Farm
- Log
- Mine
- Gather herbs
- Practice alchemy and other arcane arts
- Look cool
- Look scroungy bad
- Use banks (to store money and items)
- Keep a log
- Teleport
- Do just about anything you can do in a game

NPC Quest Examples

One of the most common things you do in RPG games is to carry out quests generated by NPCs and other sources. (See also "Quests/Missions: Using This Book to Create Content" earlier in this chapter.) Here are some kinds of tasks you can carry out in RPG quests, mostly given by NPCs. Keep in mind that these tasks can often be done serially as part of a single quest, or even simultaneously:

- Find certain recipe item(s) and bring them back
- Find certain recipe items(s) and combine them to create something else
- Just locate the enemy position (don't engage) and report back
- Follow someone—a group or thing
- Protect someone—a group or thing
- Lead someone—a group or thing
- Hide someone—a group or thing
- Place a bet/wager
- Pay for something
- Deliver something (an item, a message, information, a person or creature, and so on)
- Steal something from someone (such as a horse)
- Threaten someone (just verbally)
- Hurt someone physically (don't kill them)
- Terminate someone (who must die)
- Terminate someone with no mercy as an example to others ("Bring me the head of...")
- Terminate everyone at a location
- Lie to someone
- Activate something
- Move/relocate something
- Go and worship something or deliver a prayer or sacrifice
- Break something (to stop it from working)
- Witness something or obtain specific information
- Distract someone
- Catch/capture something
- Collect a group of people at these locations, then do something with them or to them, or have them do something
- See whether something is true/false and report back
- See whether someone is still alive (or find the corpse[s]) and report back

Part VI

- Collect a number of a certain item and deliver them to a place or NPC
- Report to a person who is on your side and wants to help you
- Infiltrate an enemy base and pretend to be on their side
- Disable enemy defenses
- Impersonate someone (such as the king or an important scientist)
- Get to a location before someone else does or before something happens (race)
- Get a message translated (when it's in some alien or foreign language)
- Obtain a special power or an object that activates a special power
- Convert an enemy into an ally

Things to Do in Arcade/Action Games

Arcade games and games that are primarily about action have their own clichés and common activities. Of course, the challenge is to add new ideas and new opportunities to the genre, so use this list as a starting point and see whether you can map out some uncharted action territory.

- Run
- Jump
- Climb
- Fall
- Slide
- Go extra fast
- Go extra slow
- Collect items
- Gain temporary powers, abilities, or enhancements
- Explore
- Take alternate routes
- Find secret places
- Discover special techniques or strategies
- Find Easter eggs
- Cheat
- Defeat enemies
- Be defeated
- Gain extra lives
- Buy items
- Help others
- Fight bosses
- Get new weapons
- Get new abilities
- Get new armor or protection
- Use magic
- Control enemies
- Be frozen or petrified
- Fly
- Glide
- Swim
- Sail
- Skate
- Crawl
- Crouch
- Hop
- Perform acrobatic moves
- Use combo moves and special moves
- Manipulate objects in the environment
- Enter doors and other openings
- Get trapped
- Escape traps
- Complete levels
- Get scores, including high scores
- Fire projectile weapons
- Solve puzzles nonviolently
- Move items
- Destroy or change elements of the environment
- Become invulnerable
- Change size or shape
- Dance
- Taunt enemies
- Be funny or silly

What Can We Learn from Sports Games?

Thousands of years before there were video games, people played sports of all kinds, ranging from simple feats of athleticism to complex team games, such as the ancient Mayan game similar to today's basketball, but using the heads of defeated enemies instead of a ball.

Because sports are some of the oldest games around, along with some practically prehistoric board games, I thought it might be good to look at how sports games work and apply their principles to other types of games.

The goal here is simply to take a look at what we are preprogrammed to expect from our various sports-related experiences and use those concepts when brainstorming new ideas, new challenges, or even new sports. (Harry Potter's Quidditch was a good example. See also the upcoming "Sports Lists" section.)

Basic Sports Principles

You would want your idea to require at least some of these.

- **Quick Reflexes/Reactions/Speed.** Used in most sports, but also in many other games, such as FPS, arcade, martial arts, and so on.
- **Power/Strength/Stamina/Endurance.** Like speed and reflexes, power, strength, and endurance are all common to sports and, not coincidentally, are among the primary statistics given to characters in Role-Playing Games. There are exceptions, of course. A few sports are more about finesse and accuracy than power and endurance (darts or fencing with an epée, for instance). But most sports require some combination of power, strength, endurance, finesse, and accuracy.
- **Aggression/Prowess/Intimidation.** Because sports are competitive, a certain level of aggression often figures into the play. Likewise, intimidation can affect the outcomes of many sports encounters. How can you use these elements in non-sports games? Imagine ways in which character aggression or intimidation can play a part in other types of games and help determine an outcome as they might do in a sporting contest.
- **Timing/Precision (Accuracy).** Most sports involve timing or precision, or both. This is obviously true of many sports and non-sports games as well. Using well-timed button presses and accurate cursor positioning is a common element of many games.
- **Finesse.** Games—even power games—often involve a degree of finesse. A Michael Jordan or Julius Irving drive to the hoop involved speed and power, but their ability to finesse—to fake out defenders and do a gentle finger roll into the basket—helped to set them apart from ordinary players. The "touch" of a great quarterback or wide receiver in football is often the extra factor separating the good players from the great ones. Creating finesse in games requires that you create more subtle controls. For instance, in a martial arts battle, using brute force rarely is the best method against a worthy opponent. But using subtle combinations of blocks, feints, side moves, nerve locks, and effective combos could allow even a slightly weaker competitor to defeat his opponent. That's finesse. As another example, the quarterback has to drop a pass in to a receiver in tight coverage. By slightly adjusting the strength of the throw or the angle, he can place it where the receiver can get it, but not the defenders. In golf, just the right amount of "English" can spell the difference between a great shot and a double bogey. Likewise in pool...finesse.
- **Aim/Targeting/Allowing for External Forces.** Aim is critical to many sports, ranging from hockey to golf, and from football to darts. It is particularly important in basketball and soccer. It is one of the most primal abilities we have and could arguably be the reason why we have sports at all. The thrill we get out of a well-aimed throw or kick is something shared by nearly all people. I don't think we need to go into examples of aiming, but keep in mind that external factors can add subtle variations to the process of aiming and can add to the challenge and interest in games. (For an example of how to

adjust to external forces, see the "The Sniper's Lexicon" section of Chapter 34, "Standard Modern Weaponry and Armor.") Think how you might adjust the aiming and targeting aspects of a game to allow for external forces. For instance, imagine trying to aim a bow or gun from the deck of a boat in choppy seas.

- **Psychological Aspects of Sports.** There are psychological aspects to sports that somewhat transcend the sport itself. Among these aspects are the personalities of the players, their reputations, and the dynamics and reputations within and between teams. These elements add to the emotional appeal of games and also to the intensity level of play, both for participants and for spectators.
  - **Personalities.** Clearly, personalities can become dominant in various sports, such as professional wrestling. The personality of an athlete can be enhanced by his or her performance (such as Michael Jordan) and/or by his or her non-sports-related actions, such as Joe Namath during his heyday, or Mike Tyson or Kobe Bryant. Strong personalities, either by performance standards or by unusual actions and traits, make for more interesting sports, and the same principles can be (and are) applied to non-sports games.
  - **Reputations.** In any game that has a past history, the reputation of the characters can play a role. Consider the Oakland Raiders of the 1970s or someone like Mohammad Ali or Mike Tyson (both of whom also had very striking personalities). Reputation is established by history and functions in other game genres probably even more than in sports, but it is clear that it is one of the psychological aspects of sports.
  - **Inter- and Intra-Team Dynamics.** Rivalries and alliances happen all the time in life, and they occur often in sports. Among teams, there are often certain special rivalries—such as the Red Sox and the Yankees or every San Francisco sports team against every Los Angeles sports team. These rivalries add to the intensity of contests and up the stakes. (See the following bullet point.) Within a team, rivalries and alliances can affect how the team plays and can be part of a good team sports game design. For instance, it was well known that Joe Montana had a great affinity with Jerry Rice. They clicked. On the other hand, many stories exist of players who simply didn't fit in their current team dynamics. Mostly, if they played football, they ended up happy with the Oakland Raiders.
  - **Pressure/Stakes.** Anything that increases the importance of winning or losing increases the stakes and the pressure of the situation. This can range from needing the money to pay for your grandmother's operation to emotional issues, such as hoping the underdog wins (think Seabiscuit). In rivalries, the stakes are always higher. Grudge matches. Good versus evil. In sports, all these pressures exist at one time or another. Making a good game, it's always important to understand the stakes involved—both for the characters in the game and for the player.
  - **Goals/Meaning.** The goals of all sports games are similar. First is winning; second is winning well. The saying "winning is everything" is mostly true in sports, but the idea of sportsmanship also applies. In most sports, there is an underlying meaning to success, and it means superior performance according to the rules of the sport. For some, cheating to win is okay. In fact, it's sometimes more fun to cheat than to play fair. It's therefore interesting to notice that, though the primary goal—to win—doesn't change, the meaning behind the goal may differ from one player to another. There are gentlemanly sports, and there are rough-and-tumble sports. There are even sports—such as professional wrestling—in which cheating and getting away with it again and again heightens the emotional involvement of the spectators (and, presumably, the athletes), thereby raising the intensity and the stakes.
- **Rapid Analysis of the Current Situation.** In many sports, rapid assessment of a situation is a critical factor. These sports, such as boxing, baseball, basketball, football, hockey, soccer, tennis, and so on, all involve rapid events. However, some sports are far more leisurely, such as golf, darts, or pool. This

is a factor that involves action sports, and, as such, it also involves action games, which cover a wide range, from arcade and platform games to First-Person Shooters and even Real-Time Strategy games.

- **Judging Progress in Real Time.** Any sports contest is a temporal event—meaning that it evolves as the contest continues over time. Athletes, managers, and even spectators are always assessing the current situation. Is the boxer tiring? Is the team losing momentum? Is that basketball player beginning a hot streak? The same is true of many games. For instance, in an RTS game, which has a lot of similarities to sports games, you are constantly assessing your readiness and overall progress against that of your enemies. In a First-Person Shooter, you are assessing the relative strength and health of your player character against the circumstances that lie ahead. You are often determining which weapon or tactics to use for any given situation, just as a basketball player might decide to drive to the basket or pull up and shoot a jump shot, or a baseball hitter might decide whether to swing for the fences, bunt, or play it safe. Even in RPGs you must be aware of your current status within the overall game, often making specific choices about how you develop your character in order to be prepared for what's coming and adjusting as you encounter new situations.
- **Control/Focus.** The ability to control a situation and focus on a problem is also common to many sports. In boxing, it's necessary to control the ring, and clearly focus is a big factor. The same is true in other games. In both baseball and football, there are times between the action, but the managers and players are attempting to control the situation by their alignment of players. (See the following Strategies/Tactics/Pre-Planning bullet point.)
- **Strategies/Tactics/Pre-Planning.** Almost all sports involve some aspect of strategy, tactics, and/or pre-planning. Even a platform diver carefully plans the order of his or her dives. Teams prepare for their opponents before meeting them on the field and then continually adjust their approaches to the game to respond to the situation. In a long-distance race, runners often use the tactic of "drafting" on other runners, who eventually tire out faster, at which point the good runners take the lead and finish the race. There are endless examples. What can you learn from this? One interesting way to look at this subject is in reference to how a sports event unfolds and what the participants do. Imagine that the sport was actually a story or other type of event. How could the strategies, tactics, and even the pre-planning be applied to a different type of story or event? Imagine an adventure game or a team shooter game paralleling a really competitive game of football or hockey. How might that affect your design?
- **Offense versus Defense.** This is a version of the situational awareness and strategic/tactical elements of games—the role and timing of offensive versus defensive approaches. Sometimes the roles of offense and defense are predetermined, such as in games like football and baseball. The change from one to the other can be precisely governed, or it can be quite sudden, such as in games of hockey, basketball, and soccer. In martial arts, both offense and defense are practically simultaneous, with very quick switches from one "posture" to another—and sometimes your offense is your defense and vice versa (a particular tenet of Wing Chun, for instance). There are some obvious ways in which offense and defense come into play in other games, too. However, it might be possible to consider such factors in less obvious games, such as simulations or Role-Playing Games. Consider offense and defense as elements of other types of games.
- **Managing Risk/Danger/Resources.** Many games are physically risky. Others lack physical risk, but all games involve some risk—if only the risk of losing and suffering disappointment. At different times within a sports contest, the athlete must determine how far to go, how hard to try, how fast to run or drive—in essence, how much to risk at any given time. Do you try for a haymaker knock-out punch, risking a counterattack by your opponent? Do you put the pedal to the metal to go just a little faster than is safe in order to gain an advantage in a road race? If you're a diver, a gymnast, or a figure skater, do you try for the hardest (and riskiest) tricks you have, hoping to blow away the competition if you "hit" them, or do you go for a steady routine that you likely won't screw up? The

element of risk versus reward is inherent in many sports challenges and can be equally important in the context of other games. Clearly, an all-out assault on your enemy encampment in a war game or a Real-Time Strategy game is a risky, all-or-nothing tactic. Sometimes that's the one you'll choose. Other times, you will be more methodical and patient. How else can the sports metaphor of risk versus reward be applied to non-sports games?

- **Survival (Last Man Standing/Surviving Rounds).** Survival is part of winning, and in a survival setting the stakes are obviously quite high. For instance, it really doesn't matter that much if you fall behind in a game like football or baseball. The chance to come back always exists. But if you're in the seventh game of a seven-game playoff series or the semifinals leading to the Super Bowl, failure means the end of the season and the loss of the opportunity to gain the ultimate prize. Or in boxing, for instance, which is scored round by round, you can fall too far behind to have any chance of winning other than by knockout. And, of course, the risk in boxing is of a sudden ending of the game when one boxer or the other gets knocked senseless. In a sport where it's the "last man standing" who wins—which could refer not only to extreme martial arts contests, but also to long marathon-like races, such as the Tour de France or any endurance contest—the stakes are very high because any falter or mistake can cost the whole enchilada. In non-sports games, creating the same sort of stakes can be very powerful. Look at Frodo in *The Lord of the Rings*. In some ways, the efforts of all the others were unimportant if he failed. He truly had to be the last hobbit standing, at least figuratively.
- **Collecting.** Although not a direct aspect of sports, there is a phenomenon of fandom that revels in collecting autographs, player cards, and other paraphernalia associated with sports. Obviously, collecting is big in games as well, such as *Pokemon*.
- **Scoring.** Scoring affects us emotionally and gives us a situational reality against which to check our progress in a game. Keeping score can also be seen as a part of many types of games, even if the score is not always used in the same way as it is in sports. Sometimes the final score is all that counts—the high score. But in many games, a comparison of numeric data gives you situational awareness—an idea of where you stand. How much ammunition do you have? How many troops? How many guns? How much health does your character still have, or how many healing or med kits? Where does your group compare to other groups within a competitive game world? There are many games that use scores directly, but other games, which don't ostensibly use scores, also use numeric or other data to help you measure your progress. Games in which characters achieve levels are another example of this. How else is scoring or something like it used in games? Can you think of untried ways to use the scoring idea in games?
- **External Influences.** In sports, there are people who can affect the outcome who are not athletes or direct participants in the sport's action—for example, a coach calling the shots. These people may range from on-field coaches to recruitment people, accountants, and team owners. Trainers, wives, cutmen, and various other support people can affect outcomes. The news media can affect players' performances. Police can bust players for various reasons. Managers can leave or die—same with family members. Viruses can make an athlete sick and degrade his or her performance. In looking at how external influences can affect the outcome of sports events, it's clear that the same (or similar) effects can affect games from the story/character level to the plot and even the design level. How can you create games in which outside influences affect the action? The characters? The player? What kinds of outside influences and effects work in different types of games?

Sports Lists

What kinds of sports are there? Here are some lists to jog your memory.

Team Sports

- Football
- Baseball (softball, etc.)
- Basketball
- Soccer
- Rugby (Australian rules)
- Ice hockey
- Field hockey
- Street hockey
- Unicycle hockey
- Tennis (doubles)
- Badminton (doubles)
- Juggling (passing)
- Roller derby
- Cricket
- Rowing (sculling)
- Dodgeball
- Tug of war
- Relay racing (running/swimming, etc.)
- Synchronized swimming
- Paintball (war games)
- Sailing
- Wrestling (tag team)
- Bobsled racing
- Volleyball
- Netball
- Handball
- Curling
- Rounders
- Figure skating (pairs)

These lists are also useful if you are making a "sporty" character. It's cool to see the character doing something a bit different (such as depth record breath-hold diving).

Individual Sports

These sports rely most heavily on one person or on one-on-one competition.

- One-on-one versions of any *team* sport (tug of war/basketball, etc.)
- Acrobatics (flying)
- Archery (bow/crossbow, etc.)
- Track and field (sprinting/hurdles/javelin/discus/pole vaulting/shotput/long jump/high jump, etc.)
- BMX (racing/tricks/stunts, etc.)
- Boat racing (sailing/powerboats, etc.)
- Bodybuilding
- Bowling
- Boxing
- Bullfighting
- Canoeing/kayaking
- Climbing
- Diving (board/depth record, etc.)
- Dog racing
- Figure skating (individual)
- Fencing (Bushido, etc.)
- Fishing
- Gymnastics (beam/vault/uneven bars/floor/trampoline/horizontal bar/parallel bars/rings/pommel horse, etc.)
- Highland games (caber tossing, etc.)
- Hunting (fox/drag/game, etc.)
- Jetskiing
- Kite surfing
- Martial arts (karate/judo/jujitsu/taekwondo, etc.)
- Mountain biking
- Parachuting (sky-surfing/paragliding)
- Rodeo (horse/bull riding, etc.)
- Roller-skating
- Shooting (pistols/rifles/target/skeet, etc.)
- Skateboarding
- Skiing (downhill, slalom, stunts, etc.)
- Snowboarding (half pipe, downhill, slalom, stunts, etc.)
- Surfing/boogie boarding/body boarding, etc.
- Swimming (various strokes/ocean/pool, etc.)
- Waterskiing/wakeboarding/bare-footing/jumping, etc.
- Weightlifting
- Windsurfing
- Wrestling

Racing

- Some track events
- Skiing (show)
- Horse racing (equestrian/camels/elephants, etc.)
- Motorbike racing (motocross, etc.)
- Car racing (drag/formula one/NASCAR/rally/remote control, etc.)
- Kart racing
- Marathon/endurance running (Iron Man/triathlon/pentathlon)
- Swim races

Social Sports

- Croquet
- Billiards (snooker/pool, etc.)
- Boulle
- Darts
- Polo
- Shuffleboard
- Table tennis

Illegal or Dangerous Sports

- Dog fighting
- Cockfighting
- Street racing
- Sword fighting
- Fight clubs
- Stick fighting
- Backyard wrestling
- Knife throwing

Incorporating Sports Ideas into Non-Sports Games

It's not always easy to break into the sports-game arena. The big licenses are tied up in deals and are very expensive. But that doesn't mean you can't use sports in games. There are a few ways to do so:

- Invent a new sport or modify one in intriguing ways. (Speedball comes to mind, as well as Harry Potter's Quidditch.)
- Use principles of sports in your story or character development.
- Create a game in which you include sports-based mini-games.
- Have a game in which the world of sports is the backdrop.
- Create a game based on some real or fictitious sports personality.
- Use a sports-like action in your character, such as an arcade character who can swing a big bat to launch enemies or a shooter game where the hero can catch incoming grenades like fastballs and throw them back accurately at the enemy.

Design Challenge

Perhaps the most useful aspect of this chapter is to look at the main activities you might include in specific types of games—not so much to see every activity possible, but more to lay out the types of activities you could choose from when you design a game of any genre. For instance, suppose you were designing a Real-Time Strategy game. You might find some interesting ideas in the sections on FPSs, action games, or RPGs. Use these lists as opportunities for brainstorming, not as fixed and set concepts.

1. Examine games you have played and compare them to these lists. How many of the possible activities did they include? Did they include activities not present on these lists?
2. For your own designs, compare the list of possible activities with the activities you have included.
   a. Can you add any or subtract any without adverse effect?
   b. Could you include activities from other genres to make the game more interesting or original?
3. Create design concepts that use elements of:
   a. FPS and RPG
   b. FPS and RTS
   c. RTS and RPG
   d. RTS and action
   e. RPG and action

Defining Fun

It's often called the *fun factor*, and there's nothing more fundamental to games. A game can have cool graphics, the most kick-ass engine to drive it, and a marketing budget in the umpteen figures, but all that means nothing if it isn't fun.

So that brings up the question, "What is fun?"

Many researchers, game designers, and other curious people have written articles and books on the subject of fun. In the introduction to this book, we explored some of the reasons why we play games, and these reasons tie more or less directly to the theory of what makes something fun. But this chapter is devoted less to the theory of fun than to the things we know are fun from our direct experiences in games.

Certainly fun is something developers generally just hope their games will somehow end up being. Sometimes they strike gold and actually create a *new* way to have fun. If you do that, email me so we can add it to future editions of this book! For now, here's our desk reference of the fun things we have been able to do in the games of the past. (They make excellent brainstorming tools when trying to introduce fun new gameplay.)

We've divided this section into two parts:

- What is fun
- What is not fun

Obviously, it's good to know what works, but equally important, you need to know what to avoid.

Play Styles

Before we explore what we think is fun or not fun in games, let's look at how people play. Not everyone approaches their games in the same way or expects to get the same experience. Have you ever considered how different people play? Here are some of the styles your players might adopt in your games. How do you provide fun, entertainment, challenge, and reward for people who approach the game differently?

- Violent
- Nonviolent
- Calm
- Powerful
- Meek
- Domineering
- Feeble
- Aware
- Blind
- Risk-taking
- Safe
- Stealthy
- Showoff/flamboyant
- Fast
- Slow
- Patient
- Restless/always moving
- Thrifty
- Spendthrift
- Funny
- Creepy
- Ingenious
- Dumb
- Respectful
- By the book
- Sneaky
- Trustworthy
- Honorable
- Unpredictable/chaotic
- Focused/methodical/orderly
- Multitasking
- Action-oriented
- Counter/reaction-oriented
- Tactics-oriented
- Strategy-oriented
- Reflex-oriented
- Preparation-oriented
- Misinformed/tricked
- Builder
- Destroyer
- Protector
- Hunter
- Healer
- Diplomat
- Mentor
- Co-op/collaborative
- Competitive/antagonistic

What Is Fun

Now for the fun. What do you think is fun? Did I include it in this list?

Interaction

- **Shooting Something.** Anything. As long as there's some effect or response, shooting things is fun. This is a broad category, and it includes a wide variety of situations and game genres. The simple fact is that shooting something that reacts is generally fun. How it reacts can boost the level of fun. (For example, shooting a guy in the butt with rock salt versus just shooting a guy.) So consider the response of the person shot or the response of others seeing the shot happen to inject more fun. And don't forget the environment. If you shoot a wall, it's a lot more fun if you leave bullet holes—and even more fun if you break off chunks of concrete that go flying. Vases or windows—in fact, anything that shatters—are fun to shoot, too.
- **Destroying or Breaking Something.** You can do this with a bomb, bullet, hammer, bazooka, large rock, airplane, car, big stick, sticky goo, C4 explosive, or anything that does the job. Commonly, the more overdone it is, the more fun it becomes. So instead of using a crowbar to open the door, you tear off the entire roof. Incorporating surprise by not using the obvious route generally boosts the fun factor.
- **Playing with a Pet.** This is fun when the animal plays back with you. This includes teaching a pet and watching it learn.

Challenge

- **Winning a Battle.** This can be one on one, a huge war, or even prevailing in a multiplayer team battle. Having others witness and respond to the events of the battle generally can improve the fun factor.
- **Hunting and Gathering.** This is a fundamental part of gameplay, and it takes many forms. In many games you spend a lot of time doing essentially two things: seeking out and fighting enemies and seeking out and gathering resources. Resources can be power-up items, items you can sell, items you can use directly, mysterious items, and even situational locations, such as a fountain that heals all your wounds or makes you permanently or temporarily stronger or faster, and so on.
- **Learning Something New.** Games generally involve some learning, and the mastery of new skills is challenging and fun. In particular, gaining new abilities and then being able to use them and finding out that they are really effective—that's fun. You learn a new sword combo or a new magic spell or you obtain a new weapon, and you can't wait to go out and test it. The fun comes when you see that it is more effective than what you had before. The fun also comes with the satisfaction of having earned these new skills or increases in power based on your own efforts. (Raph Koster, in his book *A Theory of Fun for Game Design*, states it simply: "Learning is a drug.")
- **Defeating Real People.** Beating a real-life player in a contest is somehow much more satisfying than simply defeating NPCs.
- **Problem Solving.** Having to think your way out of a situation and then actually overcoming the challenge is fun.
- **Escape to Freedom.** Freeing yourself from a trap is also fun.
- **Challenging Others.** Choosing to enter a competition against another, such as a fight, is fun.
- **Gambling.** Taking a risk that worked out and improved your position is naturally fun.

Community

- **Joining Forces.** For example, teaming up with others, or being teamed up, and questing together. The added strength of the group can greatly increase the speed of your progress. As long as you get to feel relative weakness alone and strength when your team is going all-out, then as the team forms and as it grows, the feeling of fun will be enhanced by the contrast.
- **Making Friends.** This can be online or in person, but finding another person you really enjoy being with, hanging out with, or who entertains you can be very rewarding. Giving friends the chance to hang out, communicate easily, or do some things together can help grow the friendship and actually improve the perceived memory of having fun. To a lesser degree, even making friends with an artificial personality in a game (a humanoid, an animal, or even an alien NPC, for instance) can provide some social reward, though less satisfying than friendship with a real-live person.
- **Meeting Someone Interesting.** This is either a live gamer or an NPC who you meet. However, they tend to be a bit outrageous. They do crazy, funny, risky, or surprising stuff. They are generally not clichéd, but they are also not just weird. You know they are fun when you want to stick around to see what they do next or how they will respond to a situation that you know is soon to occur.
- **Bragging Rights.** Even in intra-office games, having the chance to gloat when you beat someone adds to the fun. Of course, you have to bear the humiliation if you lose—but there's always next time!
- **Playing with Friends.** Playing with real people, either competitively or cooperatively, is fun.
- **Competition Ranking.** Realizing you are rated high when compared to competitors, like knowing you are in the lead, is fun.

Emotion

- **Looks Stunning.** Seeing something that is absolutely breathtaking.
- **Totally Captivated.** Being completely immersed and captivated in an interesting new world and realizing you don't want to leave.
- **Complete Surprise.** Experiencing the unexpected and being caught off guard.
- **The Winner.** Winning the competition and being the best.
- **Comedy.** Finding yourself laughing.
- **Thrill.** Pushing you to your limit, being tested to the max and surviving—or better still, thriving.
- **You Sexy Thing.** Being seen as a sex object. Getting attention from the opposite sex.
- **The Finishing Line.** Overcoming exhaustion and making it to your goal.
- **Predictability.** Making predictions, and slightly to your own surprise, you are actually correct.
- **Love.** Realizing you truly care about someone or something.
- **Collector.** Building a collection of rare or valuable things, then finding a missing part of the collection.
- **Power.** Feeling safe/strong/unbeatable.
- **Discovery.** Finding something really cool, totally by surprise.
- **Found It.** Finding something that you have been searching for.
- **Lost and Found.** You had it, then you lost it, then you find it again.
- **Completion.** Knowing you have overcome a major challenge and can now get on with your life.
- **Skill.** Being able to tell that you have clearly improved at something.
- **A Surprise Glimpse.** Seeing something you were not supposed to have seen, such as seeing what the butler was putting in the pudding or getting a glimpse of the mysterious masked femme fatal without her mask.
- **Getting Away With It.** You did something that you know you shouldn't have gotten away with, but you did.
- **It's Magic.** Seeing something absolutely impossible.
- **Backing a Winner.** Seeing someone or a team you care about conquering or winning a challenge.
- **A Clumsy Accident.** Seeing someone look like they just did something painful (but not serious) by accident, such as banging their head.
- **Imitation.** When something or someone tries to imitate you or someone you know.
- **Nostalgia.** Finding, seeing, or experiencing something that is a warm memory from the past.
- **Child's Eyes.** Seeing the world through a child's eyes, seeing how they overreact to things, such as a gift.
- **Yummy Food.** Finding your favorite food or experiencing a new food that you love.
- **Music to my Ears.** Hearing music you really like and get into.
- **Scary Moment.** Being scared and then realizing that you are okay.
- **Absent Friend.** Finally seeing someone you've not seen for a long time and who you missed.
- **Award Winning.** Winning an award or being celebrated for some reason.

Expression

- **Customizing Your Character.** It's more fun when, instead of playing a preset character, you can inject your own personality into the choice. Better still, gamers don't sit down with the same mood every time they play, so allow them to change up how they look; they will have more fun if they are able to experiment and see the responses each persona gets from others. (For more on character customization, see "Ways to Customize Avatars" in Chapter 12, "Character Design.")

- **Swapping Race or Gender.** This is a variation of customizing your character. It's possible in games to appear to be a different race or gender. The fun is seeing how people react to you; you can also make fun of their stereotyping of you.
- **Looking Cool.** This does not mean customizing your character (I already covered that); it's when your character handles a situation well. For example, when a character causes a massive explosion or scores a touchdown, the way the character acts reflects the feeling we *know* the gamer is experiencing right then. If you can get the synergy between the character onscreen reflecting the gamer's real-time feelings, then you will be creating more fun for the gamer.
- **Fantastic Moves and Combos.** This is when your character (under your control) performs better, cooler, more impressive moves than you even knew you could do. Meaning that (for a moment) you feel smarter and cooler than you really are. The game makes you believe you have skills you don't really have. Better still, the reaction of the game to those mad skills you appear to have enhances the effect. The result is that the gamer feels he is having fun then, and he'll be addicted to trying to get that feeling again. (It's up to the designer to make sure it's not too long before the gamer will be getting that feeling again.)
- **Customizing the Game.** The concept here is that you get to adjust the rules. Very commonly people do this by cheating in games. Meaning you just got the bag of endless grenades. The result is a short period of fun when they realize they've been able to invoke a desired change and maybe improve their situation, even if only temporarily. Sometimes the controls are simple modifications of the rules that are in play right then. So for example, if the battle is to capture three buildings, you could "easily" adjust that to five if you're feeling like the battles are too short. Allowing the tweaks often quells discontent and keeps the fun alive. The best example of this is the common game option that lets you flip the Y axis when controlling a flying vehicle (because some people feel up should be up, and some feel that up should be down).
- **Creating Your Own Levels/Missions.** This is commonly too technically challenging to attract most gamers. There are some games that let you lay out simple rooms; some offer development tools to make your own levels, but it's clear that if that feature is enabled, it can become addictive (or add to the replay value) when a gamer is motivated to modify the game levels. The challenge for the designer is to give that ability in an uncomplicated way. Remember that "the level" does not just have to be the physical level—it can also be the rules of the level. So for example, perhaps the player can adjust gravity. The ability to fling bodies 100 feet instead of 10 feet is the kind of thing players will find fun, and they will be driven to experiment more.
- **Creating (Generally).** Making or building something that you or others care about.
- **Entertaining Yourself.** When you have enough tools or a playground to entertain yourself, it's fun.

Exploration

- Of places
- Of relationships
- Of systems
- Of obstacles
- Of behaviors
- Of items and properties
- Of magic or alchemy
- Of mysteries

More of What Is Fun

- Having powerful weapons/abilities.
- Explosions (especially when you cause them).

- Amassing a fortune in gold (or whatever passes for money in the game) or in goods.
- Stealing a fortune in gold or goods.
- Having the best of everything.
- Obtaining a cool object (weapon, power-up, armor, widget, etc.).
- Finding the last item on a list of items you needed.
- Building something useful or cool.
- Discovering a secret.
- Discovering Easter eggs.
- Winning in games of chance or skill.
- Winning a prize.
- Unlocking a secret area or character.
- Escaping the police or any enemy.
- Successfully sneaking through or past a dangerous situation (being stealthy).
- Spotting a trap before you walk into it—avoiding it or disarming it.
- Making an enemy fight for you by using guile, magic, possession, or some other control method.
- Looking forward to an interesting outcome to an ongoing situation (anticipation).
- Exploration.
- Jumping and climbing—also swinging, dropping, gliding, flying, spinning.
- Successfully completing a really hard jump or sequence.
- Getting to the top of something.
- Getting to the bottom of something.
- Seeing a spectacular view or a dramatic event—especially something blowing up!
- Sex is fun, but not very acceptable in games. Still, it appears in places. Look at *Lara Croft*, for one—or, more recently, *God of War*. In the case of the old *Leisure Suit Larry* games, it was the flirtation and seduction that was fun, although treated in a humorous way. Flirtation in *The Sims* and *The Sims Online* was also an integral part of those games, although not done with such a slapstick or mocking approach.
- Finding more than one way to do something.
- Finding/earning/making money (or the game equivalent).
- Having lots of money and buying the coolest stuff.
- Clearing an area.
- Completing a quest.
- Completing a level.
- Completing a level/round perfectly.
- Getting increased stats or abilities.
- Being invincible (or nearly so).
- Defeating a boss.
- Watching a really cool cut-scene movie, especially if it is a reward for having completed a task or level.
- Solving a puzzle or mystery.
- Getting the high score.
- Beating your previous high score.
- Just about anything you do well in a sports game, such as:
  - Getting a hit
  - Hitting a homerun
  - Getting a double play
  - Getting the third out

  - Completing a long pass
  - Getting a first down
  - Intercepting a pass for a touchdown
  - Getting a touchdown
  - Making the extra point
  - Getting a goal
  - Getting a hole in one, birdie, eagle, double eagle…
  - Taking the lead in a race
  - Winning a game, match, or race
  - And so on...
- Successfully pulling off your most special moves/spells/abilities/combos.
- Mastering a challenging sequence or area.
- Flying a plane.
- Driving a car.
- Operating a boat.
- Performing stunts.
- Moving really fast.
- Riding a horse (camel, elephant, dragon, ornery mule, etc.).
- Dying spectacularly.
- Balanced responsibilities.
- Personalizing something in the game—making it your own.
- Being challenged.
- Being antisocial.
- Being social.
- Saving the princess (the world, the day).
- Developing a plan that works!
- Solving a puzzle.
- Getting a joke (for example, if you remember the culture reference the joke is about).
- Coming up with a clever/obscure scheme to solve a problem and finding the game lets you do it.

What Is Not Fun

After years of playing games, we all know what we *don't* like. Here are a few ideas of what we like to avoid in our games.

- Walking/running endlessly and repeatedly to accomplish some unimportant task(s)—"no sore feet in cyberspace." If you have to travel by foot or other slow means across endless tracts, it had better be worth it!
- Repeating the same action or task too many times, especially without any significant reward.
- Doing a lot of work without any reward.
- Unbalanced responsibilities.
- Games where money is really hard to get at first, then becomes meaningless later on.
- Getting stuck because of a bug.
- Getting stuck because the game is too obscure.
- Finding out that some item you once had was critical to completing some aspect of the game—but you threw it away or sold it, and there is no alternative but to go back to a saved game you made 20 hours ago.

- Stupid, unimaginative NPC dialog that's always the same. For instance, having NPCs give you the same clue after you already accomplished the task.
- Solving a puzzle under fire.
- (Bad) cut scenes that can't be skipped.
- Having to read the manual to get into the game.
- Playing a buggy game.
- Not being able to save the game when you really want to.
- Having to sit through the same cut scenes you've already seen, especially because you died and have to repeat a sequence.
- Having to sit through any lengthy scene without the ability to skip it.
- Having to sit through the credits and intro screens every time you boot up a game.
- Having to constantly feed or water your character. In most games, this is more trouble than it's worth, although it is integral to some games.
- Playing a game that's always predictable.
- Having your path randomly blocked by wandering NPCs or other characters.
- Trying to read dialog or player communications in over-the-head bubbles that block each other out.
- Having a game be too hard to complete.
- Losing.
- Having really cool moves or combos, but never being able to get them to work.
- Joining a multiplayer game where everyone else is super advanced, and getting murdered over and over again without much hope of catching up.
- Discovering that a game that seemed really cool is really a one-trick pony and doesn't keep delivering fresh experiences after the beginning.
- Games with horrible dialog delivered by even more horrible actors.
- Games that are bad imitations of good games.
- Games where the controls don't make sense and/or are not customizable.
- Games that rely almost entirely on flashy graphics and technology but have no content or gameplay value.
- Random deaths, as I call them, make the gamer feel like a loser. They should be blaming themselves for their gameplay mistakes, not the designer for illogical situations that lead to the character's death.
- Blind jumps suck. Often found in platform action-style games… One of the most common kinds of bad level design is when the player is left jumping into open space, hoping there is a floor down there somewhere to catch him. It also happens in third-person games when the camera can't properly capture you and the enemies who are about to shoot your head off at the same time. On occasion this can be cool, but it should be done consciously and made a part of the gameplay, such as at the end of the original *Prince of Persia*, where it was a one-time event.
- Seeing evidence that the game is cheating. Designers often cheat to tune the player's experience, but such little tweaks should never be apparent to the player. Any time the player can tell that the designers are cheating, it's like revealing the man behind the curtain. Not good.

Design Challenge

1. Look at the games you have played and enjoyed. How many of the "fun" examples from this chapter do you find in those games? How many of the "not fun" examples do they have?
2. Now look at one or more games you didn't like so much. How many of the "fun" and "not fun" elements did they contain?
3. What's the difference between the games in the first step and the games in the second step? Is it possible to have "fun" elements and still not be fun overall? Is it possible to have "not fun" elements and still be fun overall?
4. Look at your own game designs and compare them to the "fun" and "not fun" lists. Could they be improved by adding fun elements and eliminating or changing those that are not fun?

22 Game Conventions and Clichés

In the previous chapter, "Experiential Design," I offered a lot of examples of things we do in different types of games. This is one way to look at the variety of possible activities we all enjoy in the games we play. In this chapter, I'm again going to look at the things we do in various games, but this time with an eye toward the conventions and clichés that games have developed over the years.

In this chapter we'll look at:

- Clichés
- Enemy Clichés
- Weapons
- Objects and the Environment
- NPC Clichés
- Martial Arts Clichés
- RPG Clichés
- FPS Clichés
- Action Adventure (Platformer) Clichés
- RTS Clichés
- Fighting Game Clichés
- Racing Game Clichés
- Simulation Game Clichés
- Puzzle Game Clichés
- MMO Clichés

So yes, we do have game clichés. Like all entertainment media, games have developed some clichés—situations and actions that are recognizable or that lead to predictable results and other predictable stereotypes. Some clichés are borrowed from literature and movies, while others have evolved out of the specific environment of game playing. Although clichés are useful because they allow players to operate within a familiar environment and they allow game designers to assume certain elements of a game and predict some of the responses of the players, they can also be an opportunity to throw some surprises into the mix. (See also the "Misdirection: Ways to Mislead the Player" section in Chapter 30, "Ways to Communicate with the Player.")

Remember also that people have often messed with clichés, creating anti-clichés or reverse clichés, and in doing so have often created new clichés. For instance, the cliché of the big powerful enemy has been messed with many times, where it ends up that the ultimate evildoer is some mousy little innocuous-looking guy instead of the obvious bruiser you would normally suspect. But this reverse cliché has been done enough to be a cliché in its own right.

Of course, new clichés spring up every so often, particularly when a game with some unique or recognizable elements becomes very popular. For instance, in the wake of the popularity of the

Dynasty Warriors series from Koei, a lot of games are beginning to feature battles with hordes of mostly weak enemies, each with a health bar floating above him. You mow these enemies down with a mighty sweep of your weapon, occasionally running into various kinds of tougher enemies who provide some amount of challenge. If a game looks too much like *Dynasty Warriors* (or functions pretty much the same way), it begins to look like a cliché in the making.

Clichés often develop from the logical needs of a particular kind of game. Structurally, a First-Person Shooter is quite different from a Real-Time Strategy game, and designers use the kinds of game elements that work in those types of games. The hordes of weaker enemies typical of the *Dynasty Warriors* games represent a design decision that has been echoed in other games. Is it a cliché or a convention? Without those enemies, the games in this style would be something completely different. Because some game structures and decisions are logical or key elements of a particular game style, they get used a lot. In the end, they become clichés precisely because we have grown to expect them, though in some cases you could also call them game conventions.

I want to note that there is a fine line between a cliché and a convention. Some of the examples I offer in the following sections might be considered conventional approaches to specific in-game situations and structures. As such, you could argue that they are not really clichés. Take it as you like it. I've included them, and I encourage you to decide for yourself whether they are clichés. However, one reason I have for looking at them as clichés instead of conventions is to inspire you to think about them instead of taking them for granted. If they are conventions, I think we are all too likely to accept them as givens within a game we create. If we consider them as clichés, perhaps we will be more likely to explore alternatives and look for novel approaches to the same situations and structures.

General Clichés

Some clichés have transcended genres and occur in a wide variety of games. This list is just a taste of what we see all the time in games. Perhaps you take these things for granted. What else do you commonly see in games that has become a cliché?

- In most games, there are specialized textures used as functional indicators. For instance, certain types of walls are climbable, others are breakable, but the majority are impenetrable. Color is often used, as well, to indicate function or to single out an object or creature for one reason or another. The use of textures to indicate function is common enough to be considered a cliché.
- Alien spacecraft and other installations generally feature a lot of flashy lights and weird displays that have no obvious function.
- Equipment and monitors, especially computers found in games, generally display meaningless information and are not interactive, and often the displays have no relevance at all to the game or its fiction. Moreover, you can shoot these faux machines without any result or noticeable effect. If they are functional somewhere, they are also invulnerable.
- Wounds can be healed by a truly odd assortment of items, such as candy bars, sodas, and mysterious med-paks that can reverse nearly mortal conditions in the blink of an eye.
- In a lot of online games, colors are used as a guide to the relative danger level of a creature. Although this method of enemy identification originated in the popular MMORPG *EverQuest*, it is now sufficiently common to be considered a cliché.
- It's always good to place something explosive near a group of bad guys so you can shoot it and wipe them out *en masse*.
- Characters never need to do laundry. Even after slogging through the swamps, crawling through caves, and fighting hordes of enemies, their costumes are in perfect condition and are never soiled or ripped. Moreover, they never need to take a bath or use the toilet (except in *The Sims*), and they

can move immediately from an intense battle to the king's court without anybody turning up their nose or suggesting they use some deodorant or at least some cologne.

- If there is a "good" monarch or ruler, his advisor or second in command is frequently in league with evil forces and is hatching a plot to take over. Inevitably, you arrive just as the plot is reaching fruition.
- If a ruler is evil, his second in command is likely even worse.
- Armor made for female characters always manages to reveal lots of strategically located skin and to accentuate their breasts by being somewhat exaggerated and formfitting.
- No matter how many wounds characters get, they never end up with any scars as a result. Apparently, in-game healing techniques are far superior to what we currently have in the real world.

Enemy Clichés

Most games are full of enemies of one kind or another (see Chapter 14, "Enemies"), and we've grown used to how we encounter them. Here are a few of the clichés related to enemies. Where did they come from? What other enemy-related clichés do you notice in the games you play? Are there ways to shake things up, to avoid the clichés and come up with original treatments?

- Villains are obvious: Most games depict the enemy as being obviously bad. If the villains are human, then they are generally dark, shifty-eyed, and unpleasant-looking. Or they are big, nasty brutes who look like they chew glass instead of gum. If the enemies are alien, they generally look gross, reptilian, like giant insects, or just nasty, like the human villains. If the enemies are animals, then they generally look fierce and feral, rarely cuddly or docile. Even enemy robots tend to look cold, menacing, and heartless, whereas friendly robots tend to look cute, harmless, or may even closely resemble innocuous humans.
- Ordinary enemies are weak and easy to kill.
- Ordinary enemies have a very limited repertoire of attacks—generally one type of attack per minion.
- Magic casters, healer types, and archers are almost always weak to direct physical attacks.
- Boss enemies are very strong, can attack in a variety of unique ways, and are very hard to kill.
- Boss enemies are found specifically at milestone points, such as the ends of missions, ends of quests, at story/plot points, and at the end of the game. They don't just appear randomly in a game.
- Whenever a monster is big enough and powerful enough to level a city by itself, it is also stupid, brutal, violent, and bestial. It is invulnerable to weapons until a) an accumulation of attacks wears it down, b) just the "right" weapon is discovered, c) it can be lured into some deathtrap, d) it can be driven back where it came from, or e) it falls in love with a human woman, which is its downfall.
- Bigger enemies are stronger.
- Enemies at higher levels have more hit points, drop better items and more gold, give more experience points (if applicable), and have higher offense and defense. (Makes sense, of course.)
- Enemies don't learn or adapt. They perform the same tactics and actions over and over again, regardless of the fact that you continually beat them with the same attacks or strategies. (Although this is a common cliché, some games are creating more adaptive enemies.)
- If a character was really good and somehow falls under the influence of some evil power, he will always return to "good" status eventually, once the evil effect has worn off or the hero has done something to snap him out of it.
- On the other hand, if a "good" character is somehow converted to the evil side, he suddenly increases in power and deadliness a hundredfold.

- Enemies don't seem to react when one of their group is dropped by a high-powered sniper shot. They just stand around as if nothing happened.
- Enemy bosses always like to stop to explain the brilliance of their plans and the hopelessness of the player's cause. This is pretty much true in almost every fictional genre, not just in games. This also, inevitably, allows the hero of the story to defeat them, because if the boss were smart and simply plugged the hero when he had him helpless, the story would be over and the boss would win. But what fun would that be?
- Enemies always have only one weapon but a seemingly unending supply of ammo, whereas in many games you get multiple weapons but (except for your generic weapon) limited ammo.
- If an enemy catches sight of you or you trigger an alarm, he will forget about you if you can stay hidden long enough. Then he'll go about his normal business as if he never saw you or heard an alarm.
- Unless you are in some stealth mode, any enemy that sees you instantly recognizes you as an intruder, no matter how you are dressed or how many minions are around. In most cases enemies will start shooting without any warning or attempt to ascertain whether you are in fact an enemy or just a pizza delivery boy. (In rare exceptions, you can wear a very specific disguise and fool at least the underlings, though not necessarily the higher-ups.)
- Every enemy you manage to kill with a particular type of attack dies exactly the same way as all the others.
- Most criminal or enemy organizations are building a secret weapon of immense power.

Weapons

Weapons, too, have their clichés. Here are a few. Can you think of more?

- Bigger weapons are more powerful.
- There are several clichés related to firing weapons:
  - **Target and Shoot.** Some weapon-firing systems only require the player to select the target. They will then hit the target every time they fire (or they will hit according to some algorithm based on certain of the player character's skill statistics). In some games, the next target is automatically selected after the original one dies.
  - **Target Reticule.** In some games, the player must move a target cursor over the target before firing, and success will depend on how well the player aims the cursor.
  - **Just Shoot.** In some games, you just shoot in the direction you are facing. If there is an enemy in the line of fire, it's likely you'll hit it.
  - **Auto-Target.** Like Just Shoot, you simply fire in a direction or use an attack, but in this case, a nearby enemy is automatically targeted when you use your attack.
  - **Lead and Fire.** In some games, particularly air combat games, you must lead a target that is moving across your position (as opposed to toward or away) to hit it, accounting for their movement and the speed of the bullets you are firing. This isn't really a cliché, but a proper use of physics. I included it here to contrast with other common methods.
- Borrowed from arcade games, to reload a weapon you must move the cursor to the bottom of the screen and press an action button.
- Players should always start with weak weapons, even if their enemies have bazookas, flamethrowers, and assault rifles. The player should start with a pistol or some kind of knife.
- For some reason, your weapons can't hit your allies or neutral NPCs, and you can't be hit by friendly fire, either. This is true in a majority of games—with a few notable exceptions.

Objects and the Environment

Things have their own clichés. Items you find in the game world often conform to rules that we have all grown to accept. Here are a few; perhaps you can think of more.

- The good bonus items are generally hidden in hard-to-reach places and obscure locations. Ordinary ones are nearly as common as grass in the park.
- The smaller a bonus item is, the less powerful/useful/effective it is. For instance, if it is a mana recharge, the small ones recharge less than the big ones.
- If something can be pushed or pulled in the environment, you will almost always have to stack it on something, use it to gain access to something higher up, place it on a pressure plate, or use it to create a configuration. (See the "Configurations" section in Chapter 27, "Puzzles.") Games rarely put movable (pushable, pullable) objects in the environment unless they are going to be used.
- Some objects in the environment allow interaction; some can be destroyed. But rarely is an interactive object also destructible. This partially varies with the relative importance of the interactive object. It would truly suck to be able to destroy the only object that could allow you to escape the prison, disable the enemy superweapon, or open the vault containing the best weapon in the game. Also, destructible objects often do not allow partial damage. Often, it's all or nothing.
- In some games, particularly arcade games, certain objects are "destroyable," and they sometimes contain power-ups. But these objects are easily identified by various consistent appearance clues, such as color, shape, or type of object. All other objects in the environment successfully resist even the most determined attempts to mar their perfection.
- Walls that can be destroyed have special cracks or other distinct textures in them. Likewise, secret passages are generally discernible by walls with special markings. And walls that can be climbed must have a different texture from ordinary walls, which cannot be climbed.
- Likewise, certain objects can be opened or "searched" while other objects—even identical ones next to the special ones—reveal nothing and cannot be opened or searched. For instance, in an office building, it's possible that there are a dozen desks, each with five drawers, but only one drawer in one particular desk can be opened. Or, in a warehouse, there might be 50 crates, but only certain ones can be broken, possibly to reveal some kind of item.
- Similar to the previous cliché, some environments can contain a lot of doors, but most of them won't open.
- Light bulbs cannot be shot out.
- Tinting a scene with red lighting always makes it seem more dangerous. Green lighting can make it seem poisonous or in some way sickly. Other environmental colors are less common.
- Inventory in games is what your character is carrying around. Several common methods have been devised to allow player access to this information:
  - **Grid Space.** One of the most common inventory methods is to use images to represent different inventory items and fit them into a limited space delineated by a grid. Items will take up anywhere from one to six grid spaces (or more), and a character can only carry what will fit within the grid.
  - **Weight.** Another common method of limiting inventory is to allow characters to carry only so much weight before they become encumbered and either lose effectiveness and speed or become completely immobilized. The amount a character can carry is often determined by his "strength" statistic, which can sometimes be temporarily altered by use of magic spells or power-up items.
  - **Items.** Still another common way to handle inventory is to allow players to carry only so many items, regardless of weight or space used. This can also be combined with the weight method so that characters can carry either a total number of items or a maximum weight, whichever fills first. In some inventory systems, items can stack to a maximum number (such

Part VI

as 5, 10, 100, or 500). In other inventory systems, you can carry only a certain number of some items, but more of another type of item. A simple example is that you can carry perhaps only one kind of gun, but five different types of ammunition, each type in quantities that may vary. For instance, you might be able to carry only one rocket, 10 armor piercing shells, but 100 ordinary slugs.

- **Increasing Capacity.** There are several main ways that inventories can be extended:
  - Stacking items
  - Bags within the inventory (sub-inventories)
  - Strength enhancement or weight reduction

NPC Clichés

The people we meet and with whom we interact have their own clichés. We've come to expect certain behaviors and qualities in our NPCs. Perhaps this list will help you consider new ways to deal with NPCs.

- In many games NPCs simply say the same things over and over again. They never change, no matter how circumstances have changed. (In rare cases, where, say, the town has been burned to the ground since the last time you visited, they may have a new repetitive statement, but it will be just as repetitive as the first one.)
- NPCs will do the same things over and over again. They don't really respond to their environment, and even when it appears that they are doing something constructive, they never really are.
- Children cannot be killed or even injured, but they can succumb to various conditions or diseases that must be cured.
- When a player character jumps, he often makes a grunting sound.
- Often, when an NPC says, "Hurry. You must save the princess [kill the evil sorcerer, disarm the bomb, etc.]...," there is really no time pressure at all. When there is real time pressure, there is generally a time clock or countdown to enable the player to track the remaining time. (See also Chapter 29, "Time Limits and Time Manipulation.")
- There are several methods of identifying significant NPCs:
  - The NPC says something without being addressed or specifically addresses the player character.
  - The NPC has an identifying icon or color or other characteristic.
  - The NPC has a distinct appearance.
  - The NPC shows up as an icon on the map.
  - The NPC has a big arrow (or some variant) floating above his head.
- There are several ways to identify enemy versus neutral versus friendly NPCs:
  - Whether they are targetable
  - Color cons (such as the weaker ones have green markers, stronger have blue and yellow, dangerous have red or purple—or some variant of this scheme)
  - By appearance
- Important NPCs are almost always completely invulnerable and don't even seem to notice when you unload a full clip at them or clonk them on the head with a blunt object.
- Dwarves in games always have long, shaggy beards and heavy eyebrows, and they carry axes.
- Aliens and robots all talk funny, no matter how ultra-sophisticated their technology is.
- Aliens always want to destroy the Earth or at least enslave the human population. They never want to run for Congress or open an alien fast-food chain.

- Unless they are water creatures already, NPCs almost never swim, so you can always escape by diving into the water (assuming that the game hasn't made it instant death to touch the water). This has changed in more recent games. Somehow, the guild of NPCs has been giving them swimming lessons.

Martial Arts Clichés

Fighting in games is common, of course, but in creating games where we fight, designers have also created clichés. Here's a taste, but you can probably come up with even more.

- Female characters are faster but do less damage.
- Bigger characters are slower but hit harder (in general).
- Female characters are always attractive.
- Female characters generally wear tight or sexy outfits—often short skirts.
- Male characters are often absurdly buffed and muscular.
- Characters that use magical attacks as a main aspect of their fighting style are generally weaker in direct, brute-force hand-to-hand combat.
- Attacks that require a big buildup generally do more damage when they hit. They are often less reliable or accurate, however. They also generally require more energy, if energy (stamina/endurance/mana) is part of the game.
- A well-timed (and properly positioned) block will stop almost any type of attack.

RPG Clichés

Many common RPG clichés are found in movies and literature, and in games that use various RPG-like story elements.

- The main character is usually a kid. The kid's parents are usually dead or are killed at the beginning of the story. The kid was raised by an aunt and uncle, grandparent, or some other "guardian" (who often knows the kid's destiny). Usually there is only one guardian figure, though occasionally there can be two. (Both Luke Skywalker and Harry Potter fit this model as well.)
- Even if the main character is a soldier in the king's army, he's still a kid.
- The heroes of most RPGs are male, though some games allow choice of gender.
- Most characters have only a single name, and often a good character has a first name only, and an enemy character will only have a last name. Furthermore, characters with names are generally important in some way. Other characters have no names, but are simply called by generic titles, such as "peasant" or the ultra-simplistic "man" or "woman."
- The hero usually lives in some small village, which is often destroyed at the beginning of the game or sometime in the first act.
- The plot usually involves something that will ultimately destroy the world.
- The world in question is almost always some fantasy world that features lots of monsters who are invariably aggressive and whose combat combines traditional hand weapons with various kinds of magic. Some modern and futuristic exceptions do exist.
- Most fantasy RPGs owe a great amount of their material to *D&D*, which, in turn, owes a lot to Tolkien.

- RPGs make thorough and repeated use of "the elements," such as fire, ice, air, earth, water, ether, spirit, and so on. Various territories within the game often reflect these elements, as do various schools of magic or objects with special properties.
- The world "map" always fits into a perfect square or rectangle.
- Although your character's movement can easily be arrested by a small fence, a rock, or even a different-colored tile, he will at certain points in the game be able to make death-defying leaps from one moving platform to another.
- Any damsel in distress is invariably beautiful (or cute, as the case may be) unless the game is somehow looking for comic relief. The hero is always ready to defend any female, no matter how little he knows about her—this is predominantly true of male heroes.
- Either guard NPCs are impossibly strong and unbeatable or they are excessively ordinary and weak.
- Party members will invariably include some combination of:
  - An old wizard or mage
  - A spunky girl
  - A runaway princess
  - A tough-talking female warrior or a rogue
  - A mysterious but adorable girl with locked powers who is the last of her kind anywhere and who has a tragic story
  - A guy with a tragic past
  - Someone who will turn out to be a spy or will betray the hero
  - A "cute" character who is more annoying than helpful
  - A surface-tough character who is really a sweetheart underneath
- Some typical villains (see also "Types of Enemies" in Chapter 14, "Enemies") include:
  - The doppelganger who has been masquerading as the king, thus explaining why the king has been somewhat brain dead or unable to deal with what is going on
  - The right-hand man/woman of the boss (who is either very dangerous or quite incompetent)
  - Someone who "died" in the first act but really didn't die and turns out to be either the major villain or a henchman of the villains
  - Mad scientists (the madder the better)
  - Suave noble types who are arrogant and disdainful of the hero and his party
  - The honorable enemy who was really under a spell and ultimately atones for his wrongs by dying heroically or joins you against the boss who had enslaved him—or both
  - The complete nutcase who is so off the wall that he's almost impossible to kill
  - The nasty witch who is really calling the shots (though she might have masqueraded as a beautiful but mysterious woman through much of the game)
- Typical NPCs (see also "NPC Jobs" in Chapter 13, "Character Roles and Jobs") include:
  - Shopkeepers (sometimes general, sometimes specialized)
  - Blacksmiths/armorers
  - Stable keepers
  - Children playing games (who almost never have anything useful to say, but will waste your time anyway if you try to talk to them)
  - The mayor
  - The wise man or woman of the village
  - The priest, the king (and sometimes the queen)
  - The tinkerer or mad but friendly scientist
  - The scheming advisor or second in command
  - Star-crossed lovers (whom you can help reunite)

- Somebody who has lost a dog or a relative
- The fearsome-looking monster who is really just a pathetic creature in need of your help
- The occasional talking dog/cat/parrot
- A loiterer who is unfriendly but occasionally knows something useful
- The adventurer who might like to join your party (for various reasons, including gold, excitement, or some personal quest)
- "Filler" characters who play no real role in the game except to make a village or city look populated
- Farmers
- Fishermen
- Ladies of the evening
- Nobles (various varieties)
- Guards (of course)

- Typical locations include:
  - The medieval castle
  - The desert city
  - The snow/mountain city
  - The industrial evil city or factory
  - The floating magical city
  - The futuristic alien environment (perhaps on another planet)
  - The future (ours)
  - The "sin" city
  - A mining town or outpost
  - Seaports
  - A thief's den
  - Caves, caverns, and mazes
  - Basements
  - Someplace that was once great and is now destroyed
  - Some little innocent village that was destroyed
  - Jungles
  - Islands (with one person living on them)
  - Forest villages
  - The village inhabited by some strange race of sentient creatures
  - The village that's at peace on the surface, but is really controlled by some evil force
  - A village or outpost of a specific group, such as mages and sorcerers, martial monks, or a priestly sect
- When NPCs tell you about something or someone, it's almost always a clue to what you should do. Whenever NPCs tell you not to do something or that it's dangerous to go someplace, you definitely need to do it or go there.
- When you encounter an NPC who is a potential party member, they are a) fighting an impossible group of enemies and kicking their asses, b) fighting an impossible group of enemies and getting their asses kicked (meaning you have to rescue them), or c) standing around in a bar. In any case, if they are super-powerful, they become a lot more ordinary when they join your party. If they were being overwhelmed, they will turn out to be far more useful than you expected—some of the time, anyway. On the other hand (and in part depending on your play style), they might turn out to be simply this side of worthless.

- You can take anything you can get your hands on. In essence, though you are supposed to represent the good side of things, you can steal at will (even when the person you're stealing from is standing right there), with rare exceptions.
- People don't seem too concerned that you walk around their towns and even inside their houses carrying nasty weapons in your hands.
- If you need something to solve a puzzle, whatever you need is probably close by, with the exception of specific heirloom or magical items obtained from special NPCs, such as amulets and rings that will open a magically sealed door. Other necessary items are almost always easy to obtain nearby.
- A great Evil Entity, which has been sealed behind magical wards, is going to be freed to wreak havoc on the world unless you, the hero, can prevent it by gathering the five directional talismans or some similar thing to stop the Evil Entity's escape. In the end, you'll usually fail right at the end (or be victim to some treachery) and have to fight the Evil Entity and drive it back where it came from. There's probably a story that gets relayed over the course of the game to explain how the Evil Entity got behind the wards in the first place, and you may have to have the ancient hero's talisman/sword/ring/amulet/etc. to defeat the Evil Entity.

  Often, the Evil Entity either was defeated before by your father or was responsible for your father's death. Your father was a hero, of course, and you are carrying on the family tradition.
- Villains often have the uncanny ability to materialize and dematerialize at will, but only when it suits the plot. Their teleportation abilities are inconsistent and only apply when the designers want you to have an encounter with the villain without having any opportunity to fight, or, if there is a fight, without having an opportunity to win.
- The main villain will often have some minions or henchmen who reappear throughout the game and are expected to deal with you instead of the boss, who at that point in the game could easily defeat you blindfolded and with both hands tied behind his back. But he always leaves things to his incompetent minions, who never actually die, but only succeed at anything they do if it's necessary to the plot. Every time you fight them, you defeat them, but they escape to harass you again later in the game.
- Even when villains claim to want peace and a solution appears to be offered that would disarm a dangerous situation, it's never true. Even if the one you're dealing with tries to cut a deal, there's always a shadowy overlord monster who will stab him in the back and return to the festivities of taking over or destroying the world. In other words, peace is never an option until the last boss is defeated or the fat lady sings.
- Villains must always gloat, brag, or tell their stories, allowing the hero time to figure out how to defeat them. If the villain simply did what was smart—kill the hero and brag later—he would always win. (This is not just a game cliché, but seems to exist in literature and movies, too.)
- Villains have basically the following options at the end of the game: 1) die, 2) join the good guys, 3) be imprisoned behind powerful magical wards, 4) escape into space or some alternate dimension (making them available for sequels), or 5) be sentenced to a lifetime of community service.
- If you can attack it, you probably should. Usually you can't attack neutral or friendly NPCs, and rarely is it a bad idea to attack anything that allows you to attack it. This essentially means that when you are out in the wild, you should probably kill everything you see, in addition to hacking up the countryside looking for hidden items.
- Many spells, skills, and scrolls that will work on ordinary enemies will not work on bosses. Moreover, they are essentially useless against ordinary enemies simply because it's often much easier to slash them with a weapon than to resort to unnecessary magic.
- On the other hand, many spells that you can't seem to land on a boss work just fine when the boss uses them on you.

- Politically speaking, empires are evil and kingdoms are good. Democracies and republics are rarely seen in games unless they are historically based.
- Defeating a boss or disabling the ultimate world-destroying machine seems to trigger the complete collapse of the area you're in, which is dramatic and may provide an opportunity for you to have to run for your life, though often the threat is fake and there's no way it will collapse completely until you have gotten out safely. Or will it?
- If the hero is ever put in jail, there is always a convenient way to escape—by talking with another inmate who has an escape plan, by stealing the guard's keys, because you helped someone earlier in the game and they come to help you, or because you find a loose brick in the cell that reveals a lever that opens the cell door, and so on.
- Anything you buy from a shop instantly loses about 90 percent of its value. On the other hand, when you sell something, you either never see it again or it enters the shop's inventory at an inflated price—just about like real life.
- All merchants in the game—no matter that they are from different countries—accept and trade with the same currency and often buy and sell the exact same merchandise.
- As a corollary to the previous example, merchants in cities that you reach later in the game will have better, more advanced, and much more expensive merchandise. This is okay, because you will be fighting more difficult monsters who drop better items and more money. One way to look at this is that shops farther away from the starting village or city will always have better goods for sale, even if they are in a high mountain village populated by exactly five people and the starting city was a huge international seaport.
- Even when your fame is legendary throughout the land and everybody knows you are the sole hope remaining to save the world, shopkeepers will charge full price for everything and will never, ever give you anything free, even if it might spell the difference between the world's ultimate survival and utter defeat.
- No matter how serious a wound is, you can always regain full health by using healing potions or healers or by getting a night's sleep. You never have any scars afterward, either.
- No matter how virulent a plague or how devastating a catastrophe, the hero is never affected at all, unless the designers decided to make a special quest out of it. However, sometimes party members may be lost, only to be found again later.
- Characters can jump or fall from incredible heights and take only minor wounds, if any.
- You can save a game and reload it as often as you like. The game never notices when you try to beat a boss character and fail 30 times, reloading the same saved game each time to try again.
- There is generally minimal correspondence between the size of building from the outside and the space depicted inside.
- Monsters always get tougher as you progress through the game. Often, designers use the same graphic model but simply give it higher stats and maybe a different color, armor, and/or weapons.
- No matter how arduous it was for you to get from Town A to Town B, certain NPCs you previously met in Town A, including frail old wizards, will already be there when you arrive, if they are necessary to the plot.
- Terms and creatures from various kinds of mythologies are combined at random, not necessarily in their original forms. Often only the names of mythological creatures, powers, weapons, gods, and other concepts are kept.
- Main characters (usually player characters, but not always) who don't remember their past histories will usually learn who they are and what they did (or what was done to them) through flashbacks that occur at key moments in the storyline, by meeting specific NPCs, or by completing certain quests. These "memories" will take place as dream sequences or other typical flashback movies, but in some

cases you will actually have to play through the past events as the younger version of the hero through some sort of fantasy time travel.

- Technology is generally reserved for the bad guys while good guys use traditional weapons (swords, bows, axes, and so on) and "white" magic. Bad guys also use "black" magic.
- On the other hand, there are only so many ways to damage, kill, or destroy someone, so magical spells and technological weapons often do essentially the same things. You could have a freeze spell or a freeze ray, a flamethrower or a spout of fire spell, and so on. You can shoot bullets or fire magical missiles that do physical damage, and so on. (See also Chapter 32, "Ways to Die.")
- Class types have clichéd armor/weapon choices. For instance, warriors will have a variety of weapons but almost always a sword, rangers and scouts use bows, cleric types use maces or staves, magic users pretty much exclusively use staves (maybe a dagger), and stealth characters use daggers and possibly throw weapons, such as shirokens. This is highly influenced by standard *Dungeons & Dragons* character descriptions.
- If a world has gods, they are either evil and powerful or good but nerfed. Often they are the Guardians of the World who have had some special artifact(s) stolen, and you have to save the day by returning whatever gave them their power.
- Any ancient ruins of long-forgotten civilizations provide clues that they were, in fact, far more advanced than the current one and often more advanced than the designers of the game.
- With rare exceptions, weapons and armor never wear out, break, or even require any maintenance.
- Legends, predictions, and prophecies are always true.
- In game sequels (such as most of the *Final Fantasy* series), the main character is always back at the beginning with almost no skills or weapons.
- The bad guys are united into something like an empire.
- Quite often, the main character is actually (but unknowingly) doing the work of the villains and only discovers that fact late in the game.
- There is a hierarchy of metals that is always used for currency and also for weapon and armor value. The hierarchy goes something like this (from least to most): copper, iron, silver, gold, platinum, diamond, mythril. There are some exceptions, such as brass, steel, or adamantine. But generally, something made of copper is less effective than something made of gold or silver, and, somehow, weapons and armor can be made of diamond.
- When you finally beat the ultimate villain and win the game, you will often be rewarded with weapons, armor, and items beyond compare. You really could have used them earlier, but by the time you get them, they are entirely useless because there's nothing left to fight. And don't even think that you will still have them in the sequel. You always start with "trainer" weapons in the sequel, and there's no hint of your former accomplishments or loot.

FPS Clichés

The First-Person Shooter genre leapt into prominence in the 1990s and has become one of the most popular types of games. Of course, there are FPS clichés, some of which date back to the beginnings of the genre, with *Wolfenstein 3D* and *Doom*. As it is with other genres, some clichés simply reflect logical design decisions, but there's always room for innovation. What other FPS clichés can you think of? Are there different ways to handle the situation?

- Walking causes an exaggerated bobbing effect.
- An ominous voice describes the action.
- You almost always use some sort of gun.

- There's a single melee mode (such as your fists).
- There is the same set of game modes.
- Walking over items picks them up.
- Ammunition for weaker weapons is far more plentiful than ammunition for kickass weapons of incredible destructive power.
- You can't see your feet.
- There is a minimal storyline.
- You should kill everything.
- Enemies are not defensive.
- Enemies can't figure out how to use teleporters, while players do it all the time.
- Enemies rarely use available cover, often charging into a situation without regard to tactics or self-preservation.
- Shooting someone in the head means instant death. Other types of hits result in various levels of health damage, but rarely instant death.
- Shields/armor can be worn down, and once worn down, the wearer (you or the enemy) is vulnerable.
- You have weightless inventory.
- Be sure to include suspension bridges over acid pools, preferably green and bubbling.
- Enemies have a single weapon, while you have many.
- Enemies never carry anything but weapons and ammo, and possibly the odd med kit—certainly never anything interesting, like a photo of their kids at home or their girlfriend, unless they are a "special" enemy who carries a key or ID card that you need to get to another section of the game.
- Specific enemy types can be relied upon to each carry the same weapon. So, for instance, if one type of soldier carries a shotgun, all soldiers like him generally carry a shotgun, but other types may carry an energy slicer, and all of that type will carry an energy slicer.
- Some enemies, depending on the game, have a ranged weapon and a different weapon or type of attack at melee range.
- Somehow you can carry an improbable arsenal (both weapons and ammunition) and switch between weapons instantly.
- There is instant healing.
- Female characters have overly endowed, jiggle-prone, ultra-mobile breasts.
- Baddies disappear into nothing/the ground.
- There are highly explosive barrels/crates.
- There is bad voice acting.
- There are stereotypical representations of race/class/ethnicity.
- Meat is over-consumed to heal oneself.
- Meat always heals for more than vegetables or tofu do.
- The game is set in a WWII locale or situation.
- There is mass-market licensing of Hollywood films.
- Weapons generally range from a knife or pistol to a BFG, with various sniper rifles, shotguns, machineguns or assault weapons, and grenades. There can be a staggering array of available weapons, but mostly they are variants of basic types. (There is usually something bizarre, such as a chainsaw, a two-handed meat cleaver, or something that will cause a lot of bloodletting effects.)
- Accumulation of knowledge is often the primary story motivation from the player's perspective, although the storylines, such as they are, may vary.
- There are lots of explosions.
- There are squirting blood effects (less spraying blood).
- There are RPG mechanics in non-RPG games.
- Dialog is canned.

- Environments are minimally interactive.
- There are invisible walls.
- There are badly built terrains/levels.
- You will be killing dragons.
- Killing can solve a problem.
- There is killing, killing, killing...and more killing.
- There are collecting/hunt-and-gather missions.
- There are gopher missions.
- You can break the game universe to tell the player how to play.
- There are crazy blonde spiky-hair power-ups.
- The hero is pretty much always a badass.

Action Adventure (Platformer) Clichés

The platform action game is one of the oldest game genres, and there have been multitudes of variants on the theme. Naturally, there have been some tried-and-true design decisions over the years, and many of them have become clichés of the genre.

- Millions of items to collect.
- Plenty of low-level NPC enemies to fight.
- Your character is very acrobatic.
- There are many animals as main characters.
- Oddball storylines.
- Jumping.
- Climbing.
- Moving platforms.
- Levels.
- Bosses.
- Keeping score.
- Minimal story.
- Special power-up and pick-up items.

RTS Clichés

Real-Time Strategy games absolutely require certain elements, such as resources and units, so many of the clichés of the genre are simply among the basic requirements of the game. Still, it's entirely possible that you could do something different in an RTS. What do you think?

- Three-quarter perspective.
- A main "town hall"–style building.
- Tech-tree upgrades.
- Two or three layers of combat (land/air/sea).
- Fog of war.
- Infantry can take out a building.
- Buildings create units.
- Units are of a generic style.
- There are a few key hero or heroine characters.
- Resources and resource management.
- You play as some sort of god that can communicate with any of your units instantaneously.
- Resource gatherers are very weak.
- Units do not develop or change after they are formed (though exceptions exist).

Fighting Game Clichés

Fighting games have been around for decades. They came into prominence with the *Street Fighter II* series and with *Mortal Kombat*, but they have evolved considerably since then. Still, some of the early games already contained elements that would be destined for clichédom. Let's look at a few, and feel free to add your own observations.

- Fighters wield all sorts of magic.
- There are very similar controls across games.
- Button mashing is a valid strategy.
- Fast and weak versus slow and strong.
- Jumping very high.
- There is a life bar.
- Players fight at the same capacity until they are actually defeated. They do not weaken in ability, despite being bashed repeatedly by the opponent's attacks.
- There is a special ability bar.
- Corner bashing.
- Jumping off invisible walls.
- Fighters take a lot of damage.
- Falling off the arena.
- Fighters only know one style of fighting.
- Formulaic fighter types.
- Small fighters are weak and fast, especially females.
- Larger fighters are generally slower and stronger.

Racing Game Clichés

Racing is racing, right? Well, racing games have their own conventions and clichés. Can you think of any others? How would you break stereotypes and create a racing game that was different from all the others?

- You start off with a horrible car.
- Cars don't take damage (in arcade-type racing games, anyway).
- Instant respawn after crashing.
- You run out of time, not fuel.
- You always do laps.
- Rubber-band AI.
- Your only goal is to finish first and progress.
- Upgrade parts and buy new cars.
- You can't do anything else but race.
- You can't leave your car.
- Your car never breaks down.
- Going off track or getting spun around slows you down considerably.
- Cars vary in predictable ways—handling, top speed, acceleration, and sometimes durability.

Simulation Game Clichés

Simulations are often different from most games in that they don't necessarily have fixed goals or storylines. They don't generally have levels, acts, or quests, though they may have specific tasks with goals, depending on how they are created. In many cases, the goals of a simulation are set by the players, based on what interests them. Here are a few simulation clichés. What others can you think of?

- Authenticity.
- No end game.
- Realism is important.
- Often nonviolent (unless you let the buffalo out of its enclosure in Zoo Tycoon).
- Attention needed to detail (micromanagement).
- Lots of "tools" and items to work with.
- Control of the environment.
- You can set your own goals.
- Ways to cheat.
- Ways to destroy your own creations.

Puzzle Game Clichés

Puzzle games, such as *Breakout*, *Tetris*, and *Bejeweled*, are among the most frequently played games in the world. Here are a few of the clichés that have developed with puzzle games.

- Falling blocks.
- Good but repetitive music.
- Moving objects around to complete puzzle.
- *Tetris*-based. Yes, *Tetris* is practically a cliché in itself.
- Clearing things—making objects disappear.
- Changing things—making objects change shape, color, or position.
- Combos.
- Color or shape matching.
- Line up items using shape or color—three or four in a row.
- Specials—such as special icons that can give you advantages or that can mess up your play.
- Modes of play—such as unlimited, timed, clear the stage, and so on.

MMO Clichés

Massive Multiplayer Games have accumulated a great many clichés and conventions over the years. Here are just a few to whet your appetite. What other MMO clichés can you think of?

- Item collecting.
- Spawn camping.
- Player interaction.
- Forming parties.
- Slow skill progression.
- Economies.
- Item level restrictions.
- Formulaic questing.
- Class- or skill-based players.
- Instant dungeons.
- Level cap increases.
- New content—expand or die.
- Guilds and parties.
- Factions.
- Mounts at higher levels.
- Better gear at higher levels.
- Inventory management.
- Player housing.
- PvP zones and servers.
- Griefers.
- Exploits.
- Raids.
- Crafting.
- Trading (P2P and auction).
- Always a pure fighter, pure mage (at least one type), pure cleric.
- Almost always pure ranged (archer type), pure rogue or stealth character, and various hybrid characters, such as paladins, rangers, and wardens.

Design Challenge

This chapter just hints at the many clichés that have developed over the years in games. Why did we include it here? Because knowing what is common, expected, anticipated, and known in games is a good place to start. It's a good place from which to expand and innovate.

1. Go through the lists in this chapter and think about the clichés that were left out. Try to expand the lists and consider where these clichés came from.
2. Look at the clichés in this chapter, at your own list, or at the games you play, and ask yourself, "What problem does this cliché solve?"
3. If you know what problem a cliché solves, what purpose it serves, then ask yourself, "How could I serve that purpose or solve that problem in a different way?"
4. Create a scenario for a game that, as completely as possible, avoids using clichés. How hard was that to do? Will it still be fun to play?

Section

B Goals and Rewards

23 Goals

So what retains a player's interest in a game? In online games, part of that interest could be the social aspect of the game, but in all games there are goals—something to strive for, a reason to succeed—even if you made up your own goals. Game players are often treated like the proverbial donkey chasing the carrot on the stick. And game designers are always coming up with new carrots and retreading old ones. This chapter deals with three types of goals: long-term goals, intermediate goals, and moment-to-moment goals.

In this chapter:

- Introduction to Goals
- Player-Created Goals
- Multiple Goals
- Long-Term Goals
- Intermediate Goals
- Moment-to-Moment Goals (Feedback Systems)

Introduction to Goals

The three types of goals (long-term, intermediate, and moment-to-moment) form a hierarchy of the player's experience and direction in the game. At the top of the hierarchy are the long-term goals, which provide the overall framework for the player's experience. Below that in the hierarchy are the intermediate goals. You might think of them as short-term goals, but that could be misleading. Intermediate goals are of variable length and are started and (hopefully) completed during the course of pursuing the game's long-term goals. Intermediate goals are often optional and, as such, can offer considerable variety and choice to players. In some cases, however, intermediate goals must be completed to move forward through the game. So an intermediate goal could consist of a five-minute side quest, or it could involve hours of complex tasks to perform. These goals could also be called *middle* goals, because they complete their cycle at various points in the middle of the game.

Moment-to-moment goals are based on decisions the player makes, which in turn are based on immediate feedback from the game. For instance, if you get hit by a mighty blow and your health meter plunges toward the brain-dead marker, it's time to do something. An example of a moment-to-moment goal in this case would be to a) run, b) use a healing item, c) go into a defensive mode, d) seek help quickly, e) hide, and so on. In other words, based on the immediate situation, you must do something. It's a "now" sort of thing.

Player-Created Goals

Some games have no specified goals. Games such as *SimCity* allow players to explore a toolset and environment without imposing specific win/lose conditions. And games such as *Grand Theft Auto*, although they do have a story arc and specific mission-based goal structures, also encourage a lot of creative free play.

But common among all games of this sort is that the player creates his or her own goals internally. And these player-created goals can be of any type—short- medium-, or long-range. For instance, in *GTA*, a player might have the long-range goal of collecting every cool car and stashing them all in garages. There's no great benefit to be obtained in the game by doing that, but it's cool to the player. Likewise, they might have a medium-range goal of collecting a certain sum of money in a certain period of time. Moment-to-moment goals often come into play—for instance, when you are being chased by the cops and looking for a place to hide until they stop looking for you. Similar player-created goals exist in *SimCity* and other games without explicit goals.

While you are considering goals in your own designs, there are other chapters and sections of this book that you may find relevant, such as Chapter 11, "Scenarios," Chapter 9, "Storytelling Techniques," and the "How a Character Grows...Character Arcs" section in Chapter 12, "Character Design."

Multiple Goals

Clearly, players will almost always be engaged in assessing multiple goals. There will always be long-term goals, ranging from "save the world" to "get the highest score" or "come in first." And players will also have to be aware of the moment-to-moment goals at all times. But it is also possible that, with these goals firmly in mind, players could find themselves tracking and managing multiple intermediate goals as well. In fact, in some games the number of simultaneous tasks and goals can add up quickly, until you are actually tracking dozens of separate goals at the same time. As an example, in some Role-Playing Games you might be:

- Seeking a specific enemy, location, or item.
- Finding your way through a maze, zone, or map.
- Seeking people to join you in the current quest(s).
- Gaining experience or skill points, trying to reach a certain milestone.
- Collecting a needed amount of resources (such as metals, money, skins, herbs, recipe items, potions, and so on).
- Collecting "rare" items (such as armor set pieces, items from other quests, "special" drops from fallen enemies, magical items, jewels, treasure, and so on).
- Seeking specific types of enemy creatures to fill a kill quota or to exterminate them because they are a nuisance or danger.
- Seeking information associated with other quests on your quest log, providing the next step to completion of a quest line.
- Looking for characters who can give you new quests, tasks, advice, or information.
- Looking for hidden entrances, new areas, new access, and so on.
- Monitoring and managing half a dozen (or more) moment-to-moment goals.
- Collecting survival items (such as food, water, heat [wood], health, magic, and so on).
- Collecting travel items (such as gas, bags, suitable clothing, and so on).
- Controlling an area (either protecting it or dominating it).

Even in a simple puzzle game, such as *Tetris* or *Bejeweled*, you may be simultaneously:

- Assessing the current overall state of the game.
- Determining what to do with the current move.
- Planning one or more future moves.
- Attempting to implement an extended strategy.
- Attempting to prolong the game (avoiding end-game conditions).
- Attempting to maximize the score on each move.
- Responding to changing conditions with moment-to-moment goals.
- Attempting to get the highest score possible.

Long-Term Goals

This section looks at the larger goals found in games. These are the big-picture goals that, when met fully, will end up winning you the game. These are goals such as "free the people," "save the planet," "end the war," or "take him dead or alive." Basically, the purpose of these goals is to help you make short-term decisions and take actions that are likely to help you win the game—in other words, achieve the long-range goal. Note that these goals may be well established from the beginning of the game, or they may be revealed more slowly as the plot unfolds. Admittedly, some games have no fixed and final goal. Many sim games, such as *SimCity*, have no fixed goal, and, of course, persistent-world online games have no ultimate goal that would end the game.

In some cases, the ultimate outcome of the game is determined to a greater or lesser extent by the decisions you, as the player, make. A good example is *Fable*, in which you can choose a good or an evil path or one somewhere in between. The ultimate outcome of the game varies somewhat based on these choices. However, these are exceptions, and most games do have long-term goals that are the culmination of the game experience. Note that some games can have more than one long-term goal, all or some of which can be met simultaneously, or they may have different long-term goals, such as in the case of *Civilization*, which can be won in a variety of ways (depending on the version you're playing)—by conquest, by diplomacy, by culture, or by technology.

Here are some examples of long-term goals. When designing a game, will you have one long-term goal, as in the original *Mario Bros.* games, where you had to save the princess (and beat Bowser to do it)? Or will you have multiple long-range goals. You might have multiple paths to the end with different results, such as in *Civilization*, where you can win by military domination, by colonizing space, or even by being elected to lead the United Nations. Looking at this list of long-term goals, how can you use them in your own games? Can you combine them in unusual ways or find goals not mentioned on this list?

- Save the princess (and variations thereof)
- Free the people
- Cure the people (or some people)
- Save the town/city/map/zone/planet/world
- Dominate the building/town/city/map/zone/planet /world
- End the war/win the war
- Defeat the enemy/nemesis...the big boss or ultimate monster, etc.
- Avert the disaster (an asteroid is on a collision course with Earth, the plague is spreading, the zombies are loose, etc.)
- Get the highest score
- Variant on highest score: End up with the most money/property (*Monopoly*/poker, etc.)
- Achieve social status and reputation
- Last the longest (last man standing)
- Be the fastest/win the race(s)/win the test(s)
- Save the gods
- Solve the mystery
- Discover your identity
- Achieve a position/ultimate identity in the world (king, hero, archmage, etc.)
- Attain mastery (max skills)

- Reach the highest level of character development
- Get to the last/highest level of the game
- Unlock the end game secrets/prizes
- Reach the final destination
- Collect everything
- Rate at 100% (tracked by achievements)
- Save your own life or escape
- Escape the town/city/map/zone/planet/world
- Free yourself from prison (physically or mentally)
- Complete the story
- Have history go the way it's supposed to (time-travel paradox)
- Solve a mystery
- Raise and/or train a "pet" creature or a sentient being
- Destroy the thing that could have destroyed the world

Design Challenge

1. Consider each of these long-term goals and think of all the ways you could set them in games.
2. It sometimes seems that the list of game-winning plots is pretty limited, although there can be many variations on high-score types of plots. For instance, selling the most pizzas in a game about pizza parlors would constitute a high-score goal. Think about other kinds of high-score goals and how to implement them in games.
3. Can you think of some alternative long-range goals?
4. Think of games in which the player can strive to attain more than one long-range goal at the end of the game.
5. Think of games in which you might have a choice of long-range goals.
6. Think of variations on multiple long-range goals—different combinations of long-range goals that could be simultaneously reached or that could form choices in an interesting game concept.
7. Think about games that have no explicit goals. What kinds of long-range goals could a player have in a game that doesn't spell out an end-game strategy?

Intermediate Goals

Intermediate goals are often steps along the path to achieving the long-term goals mentioned in the previous section. However, intermediate goals can also occur independently of the major game storyline. For instance, you might engage in a side quest or leave the main game path in order to explore a secondary opportunity—perhaps to get more experience or to obtain information or a useful item or weapon.

Completing some intermediate goals, while often enabling other goals to be completed, can also eliminate goals from the game. An example would be in a game where you can complete a level by defeating a boss, but if you defeat him too soon you may lose out on some other opportunities that exist elsewhere on the level. By choosing to defeat the boss without fully exploring every option, you effectively complete one goal but make others impossible to complete. In clever game design, achieving some intermediate goals, such as killing an enemy who happens to be a security expert, might prevent you from accomplishing future goals, such as using that enemy to help you break into a secure location.

In any case, intermediate goals can still be relatively simple—such as finding a place to rest and recuperate or locating and talking to a particular character—or they can involve multiple steps, such as performing a diplomatic mission to resolve a feud between two kingdoms in order to gain the support of their rulers.

In essence, if you look at Chapter 21, "Experiential Design," you will see many of the activities that can be the objects of intermediate goals. In addition, any long-term goal can also be an intermediate goal. For instance, in some games saving the princess might be the ultimate goal of the game, but in others saving the princess might be only one step along the way to saving the world. However, not all intermediate goals make good long-term goals. Finding a horse to ride across the prairie would not be a very good long-term goal, but it could be a completely valid intermediate goal.

Intermediate goals also function as what some people call *supporting goals*—that is, goals that can make other goals easier to accomplish or goals that are necessary for completing other intermediate goals. Thus, you might want to defeat a specific enemy, but it will be difficult with your current equipment. One supporting goal would be to obtain better weapons and armor so that you will be in a position to defeat that enemy. Defeating the enemy in question may, however, only be a stepping stone along the path of the game—itself an intermediate goal.

Some examples of intermediate goals include:

- Travel to a specific location.
- Travel to explore territory.
- Find someone or something.
- Find a safe location.
- Clear an area to make a safe location.
- Resolve a conflict.
- Repair or alter something important.
- Grow or nurture something.
- Train or breed a pet or creature.
- Poison or kill a pet or creature.
- Find a pet or creature.
- Clear a path.
- Block a path.
- Defend a position.
- Pummel a position.
- Defeat an enemy or group.
- Build a structure.
- Destroy a structure.
- Create something.
- Collect something.
- Rescue someone or something.
- Escort or protect someone/something.
- Plant something (supplies, food, weapons, evidence).
- Escape.
- Survive (almost always a prerequisite short- and long-term goal).
- Get healed/cured/uncursed.
- Obtain specific information.
- Kill/terminate/destroy.
- Deliver/return something.
- Complete a task for someone or act on their behalf.
- Solve a puzzle or mystery, or at least get the next clue.
- Prove yourself/demonstrate something.
- Qualify for something.
- Enter/compete in a race or tournament.
- Find where the danger lies.
- Scope out an area.
- Win at something.
- Earn enough money or valuables for some purpose.
- Gain a level.
- Gain a skill or ability, a better weapon, more experience, etc.
- Charge up a character (get strong enough for future encounters, maybe speed recovery).
- Increase standing or notoriety in the game/world/town/group.
- Intercept an enemy force/convoy.
- Redirect something.
- Capture a position.
- Reveal a secret.
- Complete a level.
- Collect specific items, possibly in a specific order.
- Combine specific items, possibly in a specific order (recipe).
- Strengthen something.
- Weaken something.
- Prepare a trap.
- Booby-trap something.
- Perform surveillance.
- Guard something.
- Mislead others.

- Complete a quest/mission.
- Make it to the next save point.
- Sell/trade items.
- Read documents to acquire information.
- Destroy/burn/deface important information.
- Rearrange your equipment (for better stats).
- Complete training (collect the set of achievements).
- Take a picture/video-record something.
- Make or block the transmission.
- Disable/enable/detonate something (maybe a bomb, maybe a nuclear attack).
- Use an item in a certain way.
- Open or unlock a door/remove a barrier/ use some kind of elevator system.
- Break through to the other side.
- Capture and hold a position.
- Find or enhance a strategic position or location.
- Maintain the health and progress of a virtual pet or a sentient being.

Intermediate goals can actually be combined in various ways. For instance, you might have to complete a race, then kill someone at the end or deliver a message. You might have to kill a group of enemies and also obtain an artifact of importance. In fact, all complex, multistep intermediate goals will involve several sub-goals, and players will have to determine how to accomplish each sub-goal in order to complete the overall task.

Design Challenge

1. In looking at the list of possible intermediate goals, think about different ways they might combine to create scenarios that haven't been used over and over again.
2. Create a scenario that involves a single intermediate goal with many steps.
3. With different long-term goals in mind, think of some intermediate goals that would move the player closer to the end. Think of some goals that would be worthwhile but would not further the story, plot, or attainment of the ultimate goal(s) of the game.
4. What are some other intermediate goals you can think of to challenge players?
5. What intermediate goals could also be long-term goals?

Moment-to-Moment Goals (Feedback Systems)

In contrast to long-term and intermediate goals, moment-to-moment goals serve the purpose of providing feedback and reinforcement to players involved in reaching their other goals. Without the information provided by the moment-to-moment feedback systems, players would have no way of knowing whether they were making progress toward short- and long-term goals, or even if they were surviving or in danger of immediate extinction!

So, where an intermediate goal might be to escort someone to safety, one of the feedback systems players would need is a way of telling whether the person they are escorting is still following them, if he is in danger, and if his health is low or he is otherwise in trouble. This kind of information can change from moment to moment, and players must be aware of any significant changes in the person's status. Likewise, players have to monitor their own health, their position along the path to safety, possibly the condition of their weapons or spell-casting energy, and so on.

The goal of a designer is to be sure that feedback systems exist and to be aware of how many systems the individual player will have to be tracking at any point in the game. Sometimes it is the very intensity of information to track that can affect the sense of involvement and challenge in a game. Varying the amount of feedback at different parts of the game can also affect the pacing of the game, varying between times of slower activity and times of frenetic action. (See also Chapter 28, "Controlling Pacing.")

By calling this section "Moment-to-Moment Goals," I imply that the goal of staying alive, for instance, is connected with the feedback systems of monitoring health as well as assessing the current threat level and situation. Although the goal is to stay alive and maintain health, the feedback systems are used to accomplish this goal.

Feedback Systems and Situational Awareness

- Check health.
- Check weapons and attack options.
  - Check ammo.
  - Check available weapon types.
  - Check weapon condition (in some games).
- Check defensive options.
- Check the condition of someone you're protecting.
- Check the enemy/enemies.
  - How many are there?
  - Which are the most dangerous?
  - Which are the easiest to kill/disable/defeat?
  - What is the condition of each enemy—particularly any bosses?
  - Who is getting ready to attack?
  - Who is vulnerable right now?
  - How effective are your attacks, particularly on bosses?
- Check the map or landmarks to determine location and direction.
- Seek locations that provide safety, resource acquisition, and/or strategic advantage.
- Check instruments (vehicle).
- Search surroundings (for items, enemies, traps, cover, etc.).
- Check hunger or thirst, if applicable.
- Check energy.
- Check weight carried or inventory space, if applicable.
- Check money/score/resources.
- Check condition of equipment.
- Check other stats.
- Check morale.
- Check for allies.
- Check objectives.
- Check time (remaining).
- Check available skills.
- Check frag count.
- Check penalties for dying (MMORPG).
- Check condition of sidekick, pet, or other dependent creatures.

Other Moment-to-Moment Goals

Whereas the previous examples of feedback systems and situational awareness are examples of information you need to track while playing, other moment-to-moment goals are actions you take as a direct result of the information you receive from these feedback systems, such as:

- Heal from injuries.
- Regain energy/stamina/mana/ammunition or any expendable resource you need to survive and continue.
- Find certain items that can prolong gameplay, such as extra lives or health items—particularly when you are low on either lives or health and the game could end if you don't find these things.
- Rest.
- Seek cover (in battle).
- Find the next enemy.
- Find the enemy doing the most damage.
- Find the most important enemy.
- Find any group of enemies that a) can be attacked or b) poses a significant threat.
- Change strategies if your attack and/or defense strategies aren't working.

Part VI

- Retreat if failure is imminent.
- Determine the best attack strategy, including choice of weapons, attack position, patterns of attack and defense, and so on.
- Determine whether an item is useful, better than what you have, or required (for a quest, for instance).
- Determine whether you can afford something from a vendor.
- Reload/switch/drop/pick up/fire weapon.
- Perform a skill.
- Cast a spell.
  - Perform a ritual.
  - Summon a creature.
  - Cast a buff/debuff.
- Repair item/structure/vehicle.

Design Challenge

1. Think about different parts of a game, such as battles of different kinds, exploring a map, flying a plane or driving a car, buying/selling/trading, and so on. Name the feedback systems the player must track during those sequences.
2. Being aware of feedback systems is important to understanding the player's experience. Now, think of sequences in games that are familiar to you and add another feedback system to that sequence—one that normally would not be associated with it. Does adding another feedback system present possibilities for different designs?
3. Make a chart of feedback systems and actions they lead to. For instance, what actions might you take if your health bar was low, and under which circumstances? What actions would you take if you saw a dangerous enemy heading your way? What actions would you take just before battle, and which feedback systems would help you decide on those actions?

24 Rewards, Bonuses, and Penalties

People play games because they are fun, and there's nothing more fun than getting rewarded in some way for your efforts. In games, it's necessary to reward players frequently and in different ways. This chapter will cover the main types of rewards:

- Known and Unknown Rewards
- Indirect Rewards
- Shared Rewards
- Incremental Rewards
- Milestone Rewards
- End-of-Game Rewards
- Bonus Goals and Rewards
- Penalties

Known and Unknown Rewards

One parameter of rewards is whether they are known or unknown. For instance, in many games, you may recognize that an object is a *pick-up* or *power-up*, but you won't know what the item it contains is until you actually acquire it. In other cases, each specific item you see in the environment is clearly identifiable, such that a health potion, for instance, always looks like a health potion.

In another example, the completion of certain quests or major events in a game can often result in significant rewards. In some games, these significant rewards are exactly known. For instance, you kill the Black Knight and receive his magical sword. This will be consistent from one game to another and may even have been told to you before the quest began. This is an example of a known reward. If the reward is of great value, then the motivation to complete the tasks leading to it will be high.

In contrast, some major quests and events result in randomized rewards, as do some containers, such as chests in games. In this case, the possibility always exists to receive something of exceptional value, even from unexceptional containers or battles. In major events, the expectation is that something of great value will be acquired, but it is not known what it is. This adds to the anticipation of the reward, but it can also result in disappointment and/or frustration if the expected reward is not particularly useful or valuable to the specific player.

Randomization has its upside and its downside. Of course, in games with save/load states, players can replay a situation in order to get the best reward, but this is a sort of way to get around the randomization system or use it outside of the original game design intention. It's good to anticipate this sort of approach, however, because many players will use it in order to gain something they really want.

Indirect Rewards

In some games, a reward will consist of points or other accumulated credit toward something else. For instance, in some Role-Playing Games, players can receive skill points. These points are a reward in themselves, but specifically in their later application toward improving the player's skills. In this way money rewards and experience rewards are indirect, because their actual value is for something that will be redeemed or experienced later.

In contrast, many items are usable directly in the game, with rewards such as leveling up (with accompanying increases in abilities and stats) or achieving a high score–giving move in a score-based game such as *Tetris* (removing several rows at once) or *Bejeweled* (getting a series of high-scoring cascades). Both of the two previous examples also extend gameplay time, a direct reward in addition to the increased score.

Shared Rewards

In multiplayer games and even in some single-player RPGs, the rewards of various activities are shared among members of the group engaged in the activity that produces the reward. This is particularly true in the case of battle rewards, such as items, money, and experience, and rewards given at the completion of various quests or tasks. The nature of the rewards is still the same, but the disposition of the rewards may vary, depending on the system used by the game or chosen by the players themselves. Rewards can be equal, based on contribution to the event, based on the players' relative levels, or distributed on a "most needed" basis...or even on a group-decision basis, such as rolling dice to determine who gets specific reward items.

There is also the possibility of involuntary sharing—in other words, enemies may be able to steal items or money, and even allies may be able to betray the player.

Incremental Rewards

Incremental rewards are generally small in nature, but frequent. There may also be a random chance of something really good appearing, which increases the anticipation of finding the incremental items. In multiplayer games or games in which you have NPC sidekicks, these rewards can sometimes be traded or given to other players and NPCs. Here are some examples of incremental rewards:

- **Power-Ups.** Among the most frequent and useful incremental rewards are items that you can pick up in the environment, either randomly or after ordinary events, such as defeating a normal, non-boss enemy or opening a container. Power-ups can be:
  - Health potions/med packs (anything that increases or regains health/stamina, etc.)
  - Ammunition to reload your weapon
  - Mana potions for spell-casters
  - New weapons or armor
  - Money (gold or whatever is valuable and tradable)
  - Appearance of or accessibility to containers with items inside, such as chests, secret rooms, desk drawers, and so forth
  - Special items needed for special rewards (or just to complete a level), such as power dots that can increase your score on a level in an arcade game or bags of gold that must all be obtained
  - Items that temporarily (or sometimes permanently) increase your stats (such as a strength/stamina/intelligence/dexterity enhancer or a force shield)
  - Items that give you new skills or abilities

- **Sanctuaries.** Safe locations, including save points, can often seem like a reward in a particularly challenging game and can be placed strategically to seem like a reward (or at least a relief) to the players.
- **Random Items.** These are usually items that aren't directly usable by your character or party, but that can be used to trade for goods or money.
- **Scavenger-Hunt Scenarios.** You might have to find x number of something to turn it in for a reward, or you might have to find various parts of a single item. Finding such items can constitute an incremental reward, especially when the items turn up occasionally while you are out doing other tasks or when the hunting itself is fun.
- **Mystery Items.** As a corollary to the random item, there are mystery objects that can intrigue a player and may turn out to have value or use later in the game, but when they are first located they simply exist as a puzzle to be solved. This includes items that are unidentified, meaning that you don't know what they are until someone identifies them. These are common in Role-Playing Games.
- **Side-Quest Items or Actions.** Sometimes items are part of an unknown quest, and, like mystery items, their purpose is unknown. The difference is that when a player obtains one of these items, he is informed of its value as a quest item. For instance, in a scavenger-hunt scenario, the player may pick up a blue gelatin cube and be informed by the game "1 of 10 blue gelatin cubes collected." This tells the player that blue gelatin cubes have some value and that, in order to fulfill the parameters of the unknown quest, he will have to obtain 10 of them. This differs from a straight scavenger-hunt scenario in that the quest is not given specifically and is only known by the reinforcement message the player receives when obtaining one of the quest objects.

  Instead of a scavenger hunt, the side quest may involve specific actions. For instance, it might involve rescuing trapped miners (when the more specific quest is to get to the bottom of the mine and obtain some special object, kill some boss, etc.). But for every miner the player rescues, he gets a message such as, "3 of 20 miners saved." This kind of side quest has two rewards. The first is simply finding something that gives you credit toward a larger goal, even an unknown one. The second is achieving the goal itself and obtaining the rewards—which might be experience points, money, a special weapon, the opening of a new area or opportunity, a new skill, and so on. Rewards from quests and tasks are often shared among team/group members in multiplayer games.
- **Battles.** In many games, every opportunity for a battle is also an opportunity to score experience and possibly gain items, money, or status—not to mention the fun of the fight itself. In this way, even a battle can be seen as an incremental reward, and tuning the frequency and severity of battles is a big part of perfecting a game's pace and intensity. Rewards such as experience, money, and items are often shared among members of a team or group in multiplayer games.
- **Leveling.** Especially in Role-Playing Games, the ability to increase your character's stats periodically by reaching a level is an example of an incremental reward, even though it is also a milestone achievement. However, it happens so frequently in Role-Playing Games that I consider it to be an incremental reward more than a milestone reward. This kind of incremental leveling can also apply to weapons or other items that can grow in power as they are used or as you obtain special items to empower them. In contrast, the achievement of a new skill, spell, or ability could be considered a milestone achievement. (See the following section, "Milestone Rewards.")
- **Fog of War.** In many games, the map of the territory you are exploring becomes revealed as you move through it. In a way, the ability to see more of your world is an incremental reward of exploration.
- **Running Scores.** In some games, you can see a tally of your score/experience/kills/acquisitions, and so on. As you play, the counter or meter keeps going up. This is another incremental reward that is increased every time you are successful in an ordinary task.
- **Scenes, Sounds, and Views.** One way to reward a player is to provide spectacular graphics or special sounds from time to time. This can be in the form of a dramatic cut-scene movie or in-game event,

or it can simply be reaching a location with a spectacular view of a mountain, valley, lava pit, or other dramatic imagery. It could also be an encouraging statement or a special sound or graphic associated with successful completion of tasks.

Milestone Rewards

Whereas incremental rewards are obtained during ordinary gameplay, milestone rewards are obtained when you complete something relatively significant. These rewards are often in the form of experience or money, as well as items of value, status enhancers (medals, badges, and so on), and even level or character status enhancements. In addition, milestone rewards are often shared among members of a group in multiplayer games, and items gained as a result of milestone rewards can often be traded, sold, or given away. Some milestone rewards are:

- The completion of a quest, chapter, or mission.
- The achievement of a level or promotion.
- The achievement of a new level of technology or research (particularly in Turn-Based or Real-Time Strategy games).
- The defeat of a boss character other than the final boss.
- The discovery of a character who is significant to the story (and who may be able to grant you some special item/ability/power, and so on).
- The discovery of (or access to) a new area/land/terrain/world.
- The achievement of sufficient skills or levels to enter new, more dangerous places. This is a very common method of controlling a game's flow and a player's progress, but it is also a reward in Massive Multiplayer Games.
- Increased character stats
- New abilities/powers/spells/weapons/vehicles, etc.
- Special unique, useful items
- Increased rank or titles
- Social status or reputation within a community
- Awards and decorations
- Important new information
- Opening of new areas or opportunities within the game, including new quests, new characters, and new terrains
- New characters for your party
- Cool cut scenes
- New clothes
- Collectibles (items that serve as trophies to commemorate accomplishments)
- Buildings or parts of buildings (such as the palace that was improved incrementally in *Civilization* games)

End-of-Game Rewards

The end of a game is a very specific milestone. Generally, the reward is found in the amount of challenge the endgame represents, the satisfaction of meeting that challenge, and the cool stuff or celebration you get for completing the game. In some games, the end-of-game reward is actually to unlock a whole new opportunity to play the game again—perhaps as a different character or with increased challenges and cool new stuff. In other cases, the ending is meant to give you a sense of great accomplishment. In relatively rare cases, completing a game allows you to save a character who will be able to start a sequel to the game (when it comes out) and transfer your saved character to that game. There are several ways, then, to create an end-of-game reward:

- **Big Boss Battle.** One of the standard ways to end a game is to lead the player throughout the game to a confrontation with something so dangerous, big, evil, and powerful that it seems inconceivable that a mere mortal could ever defeat it. Of course, by the time you reach this formidable enemy, you have gained powers, abilities, and perhaps the knowledge of its weakness and how to exploit it. To be truly satisfying, however, the battle should be epic and full of physical and/or mental challenges. (See also "Boss Battles" in Chapter 14, "Enemies.")

- **Alternate Endings.** Some games offer multiple endings, which vary with the accomplishments of the player. In most such cases, there are endings that are more desirable than others, and those endings require a higher level of performance or the accomplishment of specific tasks. In other cases, the endings are of equal value, but just depend on which path or decision branch a player took at certain points in the game.
- **Unlocking More.** Another way to end a game is to give successful players more gameplay. This is done either by unlocking new characters or new levels or by altering the game in some way and allowing players to re-experience it from a new perspective. This has been done in many games, among the best being the original NES *Legend of Zelda*, which let you play the entire game through a second time, but with everything somewhat different. If a game is really good, then you don't want it to end. This kind of ending allows players to get the satisfaction of completion and the added satisfaction of continuing the play.
- **The Celebration/After-Effect.** Usually, when you complete a game, you have accomplished some heroic task. You have saved the day for someone—possibly the whole world. At the end of the game, you may get a chance for some catharsis by meeting grateful NPCs who tell you how wonderful you are. The world, which was dark and gray under the evil force, is now bright and full of colorful flowers. The music swells with grand drama. You get to marry the princess...or something like that. This is the equivalent to the scene in *The Lord of the Rings* in which Frodo and the other Hobbits are honored for their heroism by all the men, elves, and dwarves, or the end of *Star Wars*, when Luke, Han, and Leia are honored.
- **The Personal Reward.** In some cases, the hero of an epic game is on a personal quest, with which the player comes to identify. This might be finding his home, solving the mystery of his past, or being freed from some lifelong curse. Such endings are less public, but, having been sought for the entire game, they are no less satisfying when they come.

Bonus Goals and Rewards

Something that is often considered an optional component of games is also something that can distinguish a great game from a good game. This is the element of bonus goals and rewards. What distinguishes a bonus goal or reward from any other type of reward offered within a game is the fact that it isn't at all necessary to the successful completion of the game. It is purely a sidetrack, an extra. Often, however, gaining a bonus goal or reward benefits the player and makes completing the game easier or more rewarding. So, in most cases, it is not without value. Still, it is not something you have to do, and it can often entail considerable challenge and the investment of time and effort beyond the completion of the main track of the game. And occasionally a bonus goal or reward is completely without utility in the game, and its sole value is the entertainment it provides. Some examples include:

- **Side Quests.** Often a game can offer a task or quest that has nothing to do with the main story, but which may offer some special reward, such as a useful item or ability. Or it may be that doing a good deed for one person will open some story element later in the game. Side quests are common in RPGs, adventure games, and story-based RTS games and, in a different form, may appear in FPS games as well.

- **Hard-to-Get Items.** One of the bonus goals often dangled before players is some desirable item or power-up that is in plain sight but not obviously reachable. It is certainly not necessary to get the item, and it will involve considerable effort—mentally and physically—to find your way to it, but diehard players can't resist the challenge. This type of reward is also mentioned in the section "The Obscure Object of Desire" puzzle example in Chapter 27, "Puzzles."
- **The Hidden.** Great games often have secret stashes, found behind false walls or hidden doors, up in high places out of sight, behind locked doors with no obvious key, under floors, inside ordinary items, and so on. Finding these hidden items is often not necessary to complete a level or pass through an area, but it is part of the fun to find everything. These are true Easter Eggs in that they serve the same purpose as Easter Eggs do for kids on Easter morning. Even if it isn't anything really valuable, the act of searching and finding is a reward in itself. And sometimes these hidden rewards are of truly great value....
- **The Obscure.** Some bonus goals and rewards are based on really obscure events, such as completing a level within a certain time period, killing a certain number of enemies, or achieving a specific score on a level. Some of them are very obscure, such as your score at the end of a level matching the last two digits of a randomly generated number, or exploiting some oddball behavior in the game that seems like a random glitch but ends up yielding a reward if you are persistent. Some rewards are even planned to occur at a very low percentage of times. In one very large game, I remember one single room where you could kill a certain creature. There was a 1-in-255 chance of a particular creature spawning and a 1-in-255 chance that when you killed it, it would drop a specific and obscure item that could be used in the making of a super weapon. Such obscurities are meant to capture the imaginations of very dedicated players, but they also make good conversation pieces, which is like free publicity for your game.
- **The Mini-Game.** Some games have smaller activities built into them. These activities may or may not have an application to the overall game. A good example is a gambling game that's a fun diversion but may also be a good way for a clever player to gain some extra cash to spend on good weapons and armor, and so on. Or there may be a game of breeding creatures that can be used in other parts of the game, but the breeding game itself is fun. There may be little arcade games placed somewhere within a larger adventure or Role-Playing (or even FPS) game. In some cases, the mini-game offers no real reward other than a small diversion. In other cases, the mini-game could lead directly or indirectly to a significant reward if the player can master it.
- **Unlocking Abilities/Characters/Levels/Areas/Endings.** Sometimes you can create a higher level of challenge for a player. If the player can complete that challenge, he gets extra rewards above and beyond the normal completion of the task, quest, or game itself. This can involve extra abilities, new characters, special levels, special or secret areas, and even alternate endings to the game.
- **Emergent Behavior and World Interaction.** In some games, there is considerable reward in just messing with the game's world. In games such as *SimCity*, *The Sims*, or *Grand Theft Auto III* (and its sequels), the worlds are so complex and offer such varied opportunities that players can simply experiment with different actions and outcomes, sometimes revealing special emergent behaviors that cause totally unplanned and unexpected results. This kind of free access to a complex world can lead to a host of new experiences, which in themselves are rewards. Sometimes they can lead to opportunities within the game that can directly benefit the character. Whether this takes the form of alternate tactics and strategies or of exploits (taking advantages of glitches in the game to essentially cheat) depends on the circumstances.

Design Challenge

1. Take some of your favorite games, preferably from different genres, and list all the types of incremental and milestone rewards they offer. Also note how they handle the end-of-game rewards.
2. List at least five ways to offer players incremental rewards. Can you come up with 10 ways?
3. Think of at least five types of bonus rewards.
4. Think of some nonstandard ways to offer incremental rewards. For instance, how could you offer arcade-style rewards in a First-Person Shooter or a Real-Time Strategy game?
5. Think of five strange items that could be used to represent a reward—for instance, a cash register for money or different-colored balloons for different types of rewards, such as health, money, powers, and so on.

Penalties

Generally speaking, for rewards to be meaningful, they have to exist in a context that also includes some element of risk. The risk involves some undesirable consequences that result from the player's actions or choices or from outside events. If the result of success is the attainment of a reward, failure leads to penalties.

There are different types of penalties involved in the risk/reward structures of games, such as:

- Loss of life
  - Dying while attempting to defeat an enemy.
  - Dying as a result of a failed jump.
  - Dying by drowning when your breath gives out.
  - For more ideas, see Chapter 32, "Ways to Die."
- Loss of health
  - Any action that causes the player to take unacceptable damage as a result of an attempt to reach a goal or claim a reward. Unacceptable is relative.
  - You take significant damage from a trapped chest or door.
  - You fight the boss's underlings but end up near death after the battle, severely reducing your chances to prevail against the boss. This can also occur from other situations, such as having to take a treacherous path to the boss, at the end of which you are depleted.
  - You have to cross a lava field or wade through a pit of acid (or equally inhospitable region) to attain a goal. This can be done, but it would be much easier with proper protection.
- Loss of skills
  - Sometimes the risk involved can lead to loss of experience, levels, or skill values. The situations that can cause this are very specific and, generally, rare in games.
  - On the other hand, every time you use specific skill points to upgrade a particular skill, you also pay an opportunity cost related to the ability to upgrade other skills with those same points.
- Loss of items and/or resources
  - You die and items are lost, even after you are resurrected.
  - Attaining a goal is difficult, and you have to use items to replenish lost stats.
  - Another player or character successfully steals items from you.

  - You fail in an attempt to combine items while crafting, and you lose the items you tried to combine.
  - You succeed in a crafting attempt, but the resources are used up.
  - In order to attain a reward, you must use up a specific item, such as a key, a stick of dynamite, or a magic scroll, which disappears after use.
- Loss of position (relative or physical)
  - You try a shortcut or otherwise attempt to gain an advantage in a race, but you hit a wall or otherwise fail, resulting in losing standing in the race.
  - You attempt to negotiate a tricky area, but you fall or otherwise slip off the path, which puts you in a position worse than you were before.
  - You attempt to teleport directly to a goal, but the spell goes awry, and you end up at the beginning of the maze you where you began.
- Loss of time
  - In a timed race, you try to take a shortcut, but you fail to negotiate it successfully and you lose time.
  - You try to get power-ups, but you go off course.
  - In a timed trial, you miss when attempting a spectacular feat or otherwise mess up, costing you precious time.
  - You try to get to a power item that will disappear after a short time, but you mistakenly run into an enemy that forces you to fight. Similarly, you fail to negotiate the distance from a switch you have activated and the door it opens.
  - You take the wrong route while escaping the lab, which is set to self-destruct in 30 seconds.

Section C Obstacles

25 Barriers, Obstacles, and Detectors

This chapter is about how a character's progress is impeded by barriers, obstacles, and detectors. It contains the following sections:

- Introduction to Barriers and Obstacles
- Barriers
- Obstacles
- Methods of Detection

Introduction to Barriers and Obstacles

I use the term *barrier* to describe something that prevents a character's movement or advancement—generally something physical that stands in the way or something on a game map that is impassable. However, there can be exceptions to that rule, such as a post-hypnotic command that prevents advancement or an illusory barrier of any kind. Barriers are used often to define an area and its entrances and exits. They can be permanent features of the game environment, or they can be transitory. Barriers can be affected by the player's actions or not, depending on their use.

Although it is a subtle distinction, I define obstacles differently from barriers. All barriers are obstacles, but some obstacles are not necessarily barriers—though they are, by their very definition, challenges. While barriers present challenges to movement, obstacles can impede any sort of progress, even where movement is not necessarily the primary purpose. Put another way, obstacles prevent you from doing what you want or intend to do. Although barriers often serve that purpose admirably, other obstacles might exist, such as legal, moral, or ethical considerations, people who try to prevent you from performing your tasks, or even something as simple as a traffic jam that slows you down.

Barriers

Barriers can often be an impediment to the player's progress—something to be overcome—but they also serve strategically to the advantage of players, depending on the situation. Thus, a castle wall is a problem to be overcome if you're attacking the castle, but it is a great help to the defenders.

Hindrance Barriers and Partial Barriers

Barriers won't always stop your progress all together. Some barriers will simply slow you down or otherwise make progress more difficult. I call these *hindrance barriers.* In essence, if a barrier doesn't absolutely stop you, it can:

- Slow you down
- Harm you or expose you to harm

- Make travel more difficult or dangerous
- Reduce or nullify abilities (such as magic or even sight)
- Some combination of the above

For instance, a poison gas field will poison the character, but it's possible that the character will still make it across. An oil slick or ice field might make the going more dangerous and more difficult to control, but you can still get across. Deep mud can slow you down, but it probably won't stop you. In some games hot lava is deadly, but in others it can be passed, though it often causes damage. A minefield is only dangerous if you trigger a mine, and a barbed-wire barrier is passable if you are careful, but it will slow you down considerably. An open area with no traps or other features can still be a barrier if it is protected by snipers or subjected to artillery fire. These types of barriers are more in the nature of impedances rather than absolute barriers.

Besides hindrance barriers, some barriers stop you, but only partially, so I call these *partial barriers.* For instance, you can see into a space and maybe even throw or shoot something into it, but you can't enter. A window is an example of a partial barrier, where you can see through it but you can't enter without breaking it. Likewise, bars (such as a prison cell) would be a partial barrier because you can see and hear through them and even reach your arms through them. Or consider a magnetic field that allows organic matter to pass but prevents any metal from getting through, or even those detectors that sound an alarm if a shoplifter attempts to leave with a package that hasn't been properly checked out.

This segues nicely into a specific type of barrier that is based on detectors. Detectors can be used to prevent passage, operate various devices, and otherwise make life difficult for players. Detectors are covered in a separate section ("Methods of Detection") later in this chapter.

Barrier Examples

Barriers can be fun. They always serve a purpose—to prevent the player character (and sometimes NPCs) from going from A to B, or at least to make it more difficult. They often serve to alter the player's route, but sometimes they serve as challenges to overcome. At any rate, games that involve physical movement in a space always have some kinds of barriers, whether it is simply walls to contain the action or something more elaborate.

- Openings—doors, gates, windows, turnstiles, portholes, air locks, etc. Any way to enter or exit a location that can be latched, blocked, or locked.
- Natural barriers:
  - Mountains
  - Steep canyons, rifts, crevasses, cliffs
  - Rivers and canals
  - Oceans
  - Lakes
  - Swamps
  - Forests
  - Thickets and briars
  - Fallen trees
  - Quicksand
  - Boulders
  - Cave-ins, landslides, and avalanches
  - Storms
  - Snow and ice
  - Thin ice
  - Sticky mud
  - Rapids and waterfalls (especially for boats)
  - Shallow water, sandbars, reefs, ice for boats
  - Animals (packs of wolves, army ants, etc.)
  - Fire
  - Fallen buildings (rubble) and/or crashed or wrecked cars/trucks, etc.
- Fences:
  - Barbed wire
  - Electrified
  - Tall
  - Spiked
  - Chain link
  - Wooden
  - Picket
  - Bamboo

- Walls:
  - Brick
  - Concrete
  - Wooden
  - Stone
  - Metal
  - Barbed-wire, glass- or razor-topped
- Mazes:
  - Tunnels and underground
  - Hedge mazes
  - Inside buildings
  - Surreal environments
- Traps:
  - Spikes
  - Explosives
  - Trapdoors
  - Teleporters
  - Electrified or other damaging barrier
  - Projectile trap, auto-firing (crossbow, shotgun, giant spear, poisoned darts, etc.)
- Enemies (bad guys, aliens, killer robots, etc.) blocking a path.
- Enemies of a higher level than the player can yet handle. This is a way of controlling pacing and player advancement in many games, particularly Massive Multiplayer and Role-Playing Games, where zones and areas are populated with increasingly difficult enemies, and the player can gain access to those areas only when he is strong enough to deal with the threats they contain.
- A herd of large or dangerous animals (such as cows, elephants, or wildebeest).
- Other dangerous creatures, such as piranhas, stinging jellyfish, or a flock of mad crows.
- Black hole or warp field.
- Meteor cloud.
- Gas or poison cloud (or vacuum).
- Toxic waste (radioactive, industrial, etc.).
- Force fields.
- Pile of bodies (or just one body blocking an opening).
- Invisible disorientation beam (such as certain sonic beams that can cause a variety of disorientation [and physical] effects).
- Police barrier.
- A car crash or overturned bus or truck.
- A minefield.
- Spikes in the road, caltrops, etc.
- Artillery fire or a line of tanks.
- Hidden entrances/exits or hidden mechanisms to open/close.
- A giant airbag.
- Slippery conditions (natural or manmade).
- Lack of food or water. (For instance, a desert where someone will die of thirst if they try to cross. Also, an area without the ability to feed an advancing army is a barrier to that army.)

Passing Barriers

Barriers can be defeated by various means. In this section, I'll provide a few examples of common types of barriers and how to get past, through, or around them.

A mountain range could be defeated by:

- Flying (airplane, hot-air balloon, hitching a ride on a large bird, etc.)
- Secret pass (over or under)
- Teleportation
- Going all the way around
- Changing the molecules in your body so you can walk through solid matter
- Blasting a tunnel
- Getting really big and stepping over it
- Getting really big and crushing it
- Nothing—may not be passable (used as a border on a landscape)

A high wall could be defeated by:

- A ladder
- A ramp
- A pile of boxes/barrels
- Someone to help you climb
- A rope and grapple
- A subtle hand/foothold (rock-climbing metaphor)
- A trampoline
- Springy shoes or a high-jump ability
- Stilts
- A sledgehammer
- Explosives
- A friendly rhinoceros
- A secret door
- A bazooka
- Going around
- Tunneling under
- Tentacles that lift you over the wall

A locked door could be defeated by:

- A key
- Lock picks
- A battering ram (or strong shoulder/kick/axe, etc.)
- Explosives
- A helpful NPC who can unlock it
- Magic (an open-door spell, for instance, or a teleportation spell)
- Transformation, such as turning into a mist and drifting under the door or through the keyhole or becoming able to pass through matter
- Getting someone inside to unlock it
- Traveling to the future or past when it wasn't locked
- Burning it
- Ramming through it

A force field or other trap could be defeated by:

- Turning off its source of power
- Coming up with a suit or item that nullifies it

NOTE

There are lots more ways to defeat a force field. To avoid repetition, I suggest you check out the "Methods of Detection" section later in this chapter.

A pile of stuff (boxes, barrels, rolls of wire, old dolls, and so on) could be defeated by:

- Burning it
- Breaking it
- Restacking it
- Scattering it
- Getting something to eat it
- Using acid
- Using weapons and/or explosives
- Driving something through it
- Using magic spells
- Getting an off-duty garbage man to take it away
- Blowing it up

A police roadblock could be defeated by:

- Ramming it and driving through
- Going in disguise
- Going around it
- Becoming invisible
- Infiltrating it (as a policeman)
- Flying over it
- Tunneling under it
- Finding another path
- Blowing it up
- Causing a diversion—such as a nearby fire—and sneaking past
- Taking a hostage

A chasm or rift could be defeated by:

- Flying over it
- Building a bridge across it
- Using magic (many options, ranging from teleportation, to super jumping ability, to flying, to conjuring a creature to carry you)
- Climbing down and back up
- Finding a secret path
- Jumping it in a vehicle
- Hitching a ride on a passing bird
- Hang-gliding over
- Using a rope and grappling hook to make a tightrope and crossing on it
- Relying on an earthquake that closes the rift
- Nothing—it may not be passable

A massive storm could be defeated by:

- All-weather gear
- Weather magic to counteract it
- Flying over it
- Going underground or underwater
- Waiting for it to pass
- Changing the environmental or enemy-made cause of the storm
- Conjuring a storm elemental to control it
- Teleportation
- Passing through and hoping for the best

An enemy group or army could be defeated by:

- Another group or army
- Superior weaponry
- Divine intervention
- Magical attacks
- Illusion
- Distraction
- Infiltration or disguise
- Going around it
- Sneaking through it (stealth)
- Capturing the leader and holding him hostage
- Capturing a messenger and sending in false orders (to move, to let you pass, etc.)
- Sheer tenacity
- Waiting for the enemy or army to move on

A group of dangerous animals or a herd of large creatures could be defeated by:

- Distracting them with something else they will attack
- Spooking them so they run
- Sneaking among them (disguising your scent, perhaps, or being invisible)
- Going around
- Morphing and becoming one of them
- Luring their natural enemies among them
- Destroying them somehow
- Waiting for them to leave
- Feeding them
- Charming them
- Taming and riding them

Keeping Contained within a Map

Games generally impose limits on a player—how high can you jump or how fast can you run, for instance. Games also generally impose limits on a player's movement within the game environment, but if the limits are believable, they enhance the sense of reality of the game. There are several ways to create limits to travel and movement:

- **Natural Barriers.** Natural barriers are often displayed on maps with recognizable textures or tiles (on tile-based maps). Players learn very quickly that these areas cannot be crossed.
  - Water (large body—surrounding an island or at the edge of a continent).
  - Water (flowing—impassable rivers, for instance).
  - Mountains.

    - Creatures (such as sharks or piranhas in the water or killer bees on land, etc.).
    - Dense forests.
    - Deserts.
    - Chasms and cliffs.
    - Landslides, large boulders, etc. (You may be able to pass these later when you find the dynamite or learn some useful new ability or spell.)
- **Manmade Barriers.** Note that some of these are not absolute barriers, but may be impassable at certain stages of the game.
    - Bridges (broken, guarded, or raised).
    - Military zones. (Shot on sight?)
    - Guards (won't let you pass).
    - Force fields.
    - Landmines.
    - Barricades.
    - Auto-turrets (will shoot you).
- **Indoor Barriers:**
    - Locked doors/barred windows, etc.
    - Walls.
    - Gates that cannot be opened.
    - Guards (human, animal, or other).
    - Detectors.
    - Traps.
    - Secret passages. (The entrance is hidden.)
    - Treacherous paths—jumps, narrow pathways, high places, moving platforms, toxic conditions, etc.
    - Configuration and sequence puzzles. (See the "Configurations" section in Chapter 27, "Puzzles.")
    - Psychological pressure/threats.
    - Illusions. (The character is somehow made delusional.)
    - Intolerable sounds.
    - Force fields.
    - Cells (as in jail/prison).
    - Walls.
    - Collapsed areas.
- **Game Mechanics.** Although there are many believable and realistic ways to limit movement, there are some that are simply convenient but not part of the realism of the game, such as:
    - You reach a place where the game asks, "Do you wish to quit the level?"
    - You receive a message saying, "You can't go there."
    - You try to move forward but hit an invisible and unexplained barrier, even though you may be able to see a landscape stretching into the distance.
    - Teleporting the character to the same area or an undesirable area.

Obstacles

While barriers are always obstacles that prevent movement, this section looks at some other ways your progress can be impeded.

- **Obstructionist NPCs.** Someone who won't let you proceed or give you what you need until you meet certain conditions.
- **Phobias.** Fear of snakes, height, outdoors, confinement, and so on. See also "Phun with Phobias" in Chapter 12, "Character Design."
- **Post-Hypnotic.** A command preventing a character from advancing.
- **Law.** This applies to a character who can't or won't do anything illegal.
- **Morals or Ethics.** This applies to characters who can't or won't violate certain value systems.
- **Ignorance.** You have a lack of necessary information.
- **Size.** You're too big or too small to accomplish a specific task.
- **Missing Equipment.** You lack some necessary items, such as a key to unlock a door or chest.
- **Missing Skills.** You lack the necessary skill—such as lock-picking when faced with that locked door or chest for which you lack the key.
- **Other Players.** Competitive or even cooperative players can act as obstacles either intentionally or unintentionally.
- **Distractions.** You are tracking too many simultaneous events, or some emergency requires your attention.
- **Physical Restraint.** Something holds you physically and prevents you from moving or advancing.
- **Threats.** You are prevented from acting because of threats to yourself or others.
- **Blackmail.** Blackmail is a specific kind of threat, which may involve harming others or revealing secret information about you that you don't want known. Someone can use blackmail not only to extort something of value from you, but also to control your actions, which makes it an obstacle to your progress.
- **Physical or Mental Incompetence.** It's always an obstacle when your own body can't do what is necessary or your mind cannot deal with the issues at hand. If you are too weak to move a large stone, it's an obstacle. If you are Hercules, perhaps it's not. If you don't have the mental powers to decipher a code, it's an obstacle. If you're some kind of brainiac, it may be nothing more than a momentary annoyance.
- **Devotion.** You cannot proceed if someone would be left behind.

Methods of Detection

Many obstacles, barriers, and traps rely on detecting the player's movements and activities. Methods may vary, from high-tech invisible laser beams to a simple string with cans tied to it to make noise if someone walks through the string—and just about anything between these two extremes. In this section, I'll present a few ways to detect someone, with some suggestions for how to get past them. This is just a partial list, so there's plenty of room to innovate and come up with your own detection methods.

Breaking a light beam can be defeated by:

- Timing the sweep of the beam
- Crawling under or gliding over the beam
- Fooling the beam with a special non-reflective suit or other cloaking system
- Moving really slowly
- Using acrobatics to get around the beam

Part VI

Movement sensing can be defeated by:

- Moving very slowly
- Crawling under or gliding over the sensor's area
- Wearing a suit that cancels out the movement sensor
- Teleporting or using astral (non-physical) travel

Sound sensing can be defeated by:

- Moving very quietly
- Crawling under or gliding over the sensor's area
- Wearing sound-canceling clothing
- Creating a sound-canceling device to fool the sensor

Infrared (heat) sensing can be defeated by:

- Freezing yourself
- Wearing a cold suit
- Transforming into a reptile

Radar can be defeated by:

- Avoiding the radar
- Wearing stealth gear
- Fooling the radar with false signals
- Jamming the radar

A guard seeing you can be defeated by:

- Keeping to the shadows
- Wearing a disguise
- Disabling the guard
- Being invisible
- Creating a diversion to distract the guard
- Tricking the guard (preferably without setting off alarms)
- Distracting the guard
- Killing the guard

A remote camera can be defeated by:

- Staying in the shadows
- Timing the sweep of the camera
- Destroying the camera
- Patching in a fake image to display a false image on the monitors
- Staying out of the camera's range

Conduction changes in an object as you touch it can be defeated by:

- Wearing gloves
- Using a nonconductive device to manipulate the object
- Using telekinesis

Change of weight on a platform can be defeated by:

- Replacing the object quickly with something of equal weight
- Jamming the platform to prevent it from moving
- Freezing the platform

Shadows being detected over the item can be defeated by:

- Moving so that your shadow doesn't hit the item
- Shining a light to compensate for the shadow
- Using an implement that doesn't cast a shadow

A little switch under the item popping up can be defeated by:

- Sliding something under the item to keep the switch from popping up
- Freezing the switch to prevent it from moving

For all electronic devices you can also do the following:

- Break/destroy the item.
- Using EMP (*Electro-Magnetic Pulse*) to disable the detector.
- Hack the detector to use it to your advantage.
- Take out the power grid.

Design Challenge

Each game, each project, and each situation is different. However, how often do you simply come up with the most obvious solution when you need to limit the player's freedom of movement or erect a barrier of some sort? This design challenge has several parts:

1. Think of barriers you have created or barriers you've seen in other games and come up with at least three other types of barriers that could have been used in those situations.
2. Think of at least one type of barrier or detector not listed in this chapter. Even if you can't think of one, the exercise will stimulate your creativity. Now design a way to use this barrier in a game situation, or, if you didn't come up with anything new, consider whether you could create more interesting barriers now, based on what you have seen here.
3. For each of the following environments, come up with at least three types of barriers or detectors, and how they would function in the game:
   - A city street
   - A freeway
   - An office building
   - A mountain pass
   - A river or lake
   - A prison or jail
   - A mental institution
   - An enemy stronghold
   - A tunnel or cave
   - An outer-space adventure
   - A military engagement
   - An individual's race against time (on foot? in a land vehicle? in an aircraft?)
4. In your own designs, what kinds of barriers will you use? Try discarding your first thought and coming up with something else. Does that change the game and give you some new ideas? Keep substituting different ways to control the player's freedom or movement. Think of some unique methods.
5. Think of the kinds of detectors you've encountered in the games you have played. List them and then list the ways you got around them.
6. Can you think of any other types of detectors, or possibly some unique ways to use them?
7. Write down some specific applications of some of the detectors. What would the scene be exactly? Where would you use detectors and what would they do? How would your player's character get around them?

26 Traps and Counter Traps

The art and craft of traps is very important in games, and traps occur frequently. Both player characters and non-player characters may be trapped at times, and you, as the player, may also set traps within a game. When you stop to analyze the way traps work in games, you may see several ways in which characters become trapped.

In this chapter:

General Solutions

While trapping someone (the player or another character) is one of the primary design problems you may encounter in creating a game, ways to escape or counter the trap are just as necessary, especially for the player character, who must ultimately be able to escape. However, it is also important to understand how NPCs may be able to overcome player-set traps to keep things interesting.

For that reason, I've included some specific ways to escape each of the types of traps listed in this chapter, but first, here's a short list of surefire escapes:

- **Don't Do It!** The primary method of countering a trap—and the most reliable of all—is not to get trapped in the first place. For help with that, see The Good Boy Scout entry.
- **The Good Boy Scout.** A Boy Scout is always prepared, and so should a good hero be. Prior planning, early detection, and avoidance or immunity measures are pretty reliable ways to escape a trap or, in many cases, to avoid it altogether.
- **The Cavalry Arrives.** Someone comes to your rescue and helps you escape
- **Spatial Realignment.** You teleport or phase-shift out of the trap (assuming you have or can obtain that power).
- **The Road Less Traveled.** You find a way out of the trap other than the obvious one—often involving barrier/obstacle-type traps.

- **Divine Intervention.** Something unforeseen and out of your or your enemies' control sets you free. Note that this is not something a player can rely upon, but it can be one way to alter the situation. Note also that this works equally for player characters and for NPCs that have been trapped.
- **Patience Is Its Own Reward.** Sometimes all you have to do is wait for the right time to escape. Circumstances can often realign themselves to allow you the perfect opportunity if you wait, watch, listen, and learn.
- **Manipulating the Captors.** One way or another, you may be able to manipulate those who hold you captive (assuming there is a sentient agency involved in the trap). There are various ways to manipulate others, and any of them is acceptable for escaping a trap, including converting them to your side, threatening them, tricking them, or even completely confusing them until they are vulnerable to your attack.
- **The Suicide Option.** The trap has no meaning if you're dead. Of course, you shouldn't really be dead, but you can fake it or perhaps have a power that allows you to resurrect later, after the trap has been sprung or your captors have given up.

The following sections contain some examples of several types of traps, along with a few ways to counter them.

Physical Containment

Physical containment involves restricting someone's movements by using physical barriers, the most obvious of which is a locked door. Although there are many specialized situations involving physical containment, there are a few solutions commonly used in many of these scenarios. For instance, in pretty much every containment scenario, finding another exit is a potential option.

Some basic physical containment examples include:

- You're confined in a jail or prison cell or a mental ward.
- You're locked in a room.
- The room isn't locked, but it's guarded by vicious henchmen or even more vicious animals.
- The room isn't locked, but there's a force field that prevents your escape.
- You're trapped in a tunnel or mine that has caved in.
- You're eaten or swallowed whole by something big, such as a whale or a giant space creature.
- You're alone on a ship or space vehicle and unable to control it or escape it.
- You're lost in the forest, and malevolent trees are closing the path so you can't find your way out.
- You're sent to an alternate dimension or parallel universe.
- The entrances are blocked. You can:
    - Clear the way; remove whatever is blocking the exit. This may be some quick and easy method, such as blasting it out of the way or simply dragging something aside, or it could be time consuming and complex, such as digging through a cave-in with a spoon.
    - Go over (or under) the blockage.
    - Find something to help you clear the blockage (such as a creature strong enough to move it or that can eat it).
    - Bribe or force someone to remove the blockage.
    - Find an alternate exit. (Note that this is one of the universal escapes and won't be repeated in each of the following examples.)
- Getting to the area requires jumping or falling, and you can't get back out. You can:
    - Get help from someone up top.
    - Plan ahead and secure a rope or other means of return before descending.

    - Use a piece of clothing to tie to an anchor or to give you additional traction or protection.
    - Change the nature of the area so you can return. (For instance, carve steps or remove the slippery surface with a blowtorch.)
    - Use a device or power to get back up.
    - Find another way out.
    - Send someone else.
- Walls or doors mysteriously disappeared or moved, making escape impossible.
    - Find the mechanism or trick to return the configuration of the room to its original setting.
    - Someone may be in charge of the mechanism. Try to trick him into letting you out.
    - Blast your way out.
    - Get help from an ally on the outside.
    - Use telekinetic powers to reconfigure the room.
    - Use other magic or supernatural powers, such as the ability to pass through solid objects, super strength, or the ability to pick up a cell phone and call for help.
- The door mechanism is broken or the key broke in the lock. You can:
    - Find some way to fix the mechanism or push the key out of the lock.
    - Remove the lock somehow.
    - Break in the door.
    - Find a way to turn the broken key, perhaps by attaching something to it or using grippers or telekinetic powers.
    - Use any of the other ways to escape a locked room (mentioned earlier).
- The way out is impassable (including, but not limited to, blocked entrances). You can:
    - Make it passable. For instance, if there is a cave-in, dig a tunnel; if there is a river of lava, drop a stone formation to make a bridge over it.
    - Protect yourself from whatever danger faces you and go through it.
    - Use specific magic to counter the obstacle.
    - See also "Barriers" and "Methods of Detection" in Chapter 25, "Barriers, Boundaries, Obstacles, and Detectors."
- The perimeter is electrified, or there is a force field you can't pass. You can:
    - Find the power to the grid and disable it.
    - Short out the power with a piece of metal, some jewelry, a counter force field, and so on.
    - Use something to neutralize the effect, such as insulating gloves, a suit that neutralizes the force field, an identification card that allows you to pass, and so on.
    - Get someone else to turn it off.
    - Throw things into the force field until it is overwhelmed and shorts out.
    - Find a way to get above or below it.
    - Use an insulator or other means to protect you from its effects.
    - Find an entrance/exit that is not protected.
- You had the keys but you lost them, or the keys are hidden somewhere. You can:
    - Find the keys or a duplicate set.
    - Find a way to open the door without keys (such as picking the lock).
    - Flash back to the time when you lost the keys and remember where they are (which may or may not help if they are no longer accessible).
    - Create a new key.
    - Destroy the door.
    - Look again.
    - Wish really hard that the keys are still in your pocket and then check for them again.

- Someone stole the keys.
  - Get the keys back if you can.
  - Find a duplicate set of keys.
  - Find a way to open the door without the keys.
  - Go another way.
- There is a code, password, or incantation needed to open the way out. You can:
  - Remember something someone said that was actually a clue to the code, password, or incantation.
  - Try different codes in an orderly sequence or try different passwords or incantations.
  - Think about your captor(s) and think about what they would use as a code, password, or incantation.
  - Observe when your captor(s) enter the code, password, or incantation—either before being imprisoned or during imprisonment.
  - Defeat the mechanism in some way so that you can bypass the password.
  - Destroy the mechanism and blast your way out.
  - Interrogate, manipulate, or trick a guard or someone who knows the password and get him to reveal it.
- The exit requires some form of ID (scan card, thumbprint, retinal scan, voice print). You can:
  - Steal an ID card from one of the guards or have one hidden on your person when you are captured.
  - Use the finger, eye, or voice of a guard or other authorized personnel—whether or not they are alive.
  - Make a duplicate.
  - Hack the system.
  - Blast your way through.
- The door is actually easy to open, but it requires some simple procedure, such as lifting while you turn the lock or hitting it a certain way to release the seal. You can:
  - Use trial and error.
  - Observe someone else opening the door.
  - Have someone tell you the secret.
- You must solve a riddle or other mental puzzle to open the way out. You can:
  - Look for or remember clues.
  - Use trial and error.
  - Drive yourself crazy to be able to match the crazy state of your captor(s).
  - Have someone tell you the answer—maybe under duress, as a result of a bribe, or because you did a favor for them.
- The way to get out requires a complex series of tasks or a simple task done repetitively. You can:
  - Figure out what needs to be done and do it.
  - Practice until you're good at it.
  - Review any clues you might have gotten that would reveal what to do.
  - Have someone tell you what you need to do.
  - Find a manual that explains the procedure.
  - Find someone who already knows how to execute the sequence and bribe, manipulate, cajole, or force him to do it, unless he is an ally, in which case he will do it willingly
  - Create an automated script that performs the act for you.

- You are injured or hurt in some way that reduces your physical ability to escape. You can:
  - Seek help.
  - Heal yourself or use some temporary stimulant to give you the ability to escape.
  - Do it anyway.
  - Pretend that you're even worse off than you are, so they'll leave you alone and you can escape.
  - Take a temporary drug to simulate death. They will remove you from the room.
  - Play dead. (Refer to the "General Solutions" section at the beginning of the chapter.)
- The room you are in was constructed with alien materials and/or techniques, and you don't understand how it works. You can:
  - Examine the environment carefully and seek clues or instructions.
  - Use trial and error.
  - Seek help.
  - Force one of the aliens to either teach you or operate the systems for you.
- The room (or something that controls it) is intelligent and adaptive and counters your every move. You can:
  - Make friends with it/get it to change sides.
  - Give it an impossible riddle so it becomes overwhelmed trying to solve it.
  - Challenge it to a contest you can win.
  - Think crazy thoughts, so the room goes mad.
  - Think "ethical thoughts"—they are new to the room, but the room feels them and spiritually grows, and thus releases you.
  - Think one thing and *do* another.
  - Sing or recite difficult poetry, which completely confuses the room due to its "illogical" nature, so you escape while it is pondering the meaning of your song or poetry.
  - Overwhelm the room with emotional discharge.
  - Distract the room in some way so that you can escape or take control of the room itself.
- You're in a containment bubble. You can:
  - Find a way to burst the bubble.
  - Absorb the bubble's material somehow.
  - Make the bubble move and move with it.
  - Neutralize the bubble.
  - Use a spell or some type of field that allows you to pass through the bubble's walls.
- You're in a labyrinth. You can:
  - Use trial and error to escape.
  - Dig or bash through the walls or under the floor to find another way out.
  - Find a way to destroy the maze.
  - Find the master of the maze.
  - Find another explorer with information about the maze.
  - Find a map.
  - Use markers to help you figure out where you've been (the old bread-crumb method).
- Fire
  - Put out the fire.
  - Find a way to protect yourself from the fire and smoke.
  - Find another way out.
  - Wait it out.

- You're stuck in goo or a sticky trap. You can:
  - Find a way to dissolve it.
  - Eat the goo.
  - Absorb it.
  - Freeze it.
  - Burn/melt/vaporize it.
  - Struggle until you have gotten free.
  - Kill it (if it is alive).
  - Electrocute it.
  - Explode it.
- You're trapped by a force field. You can:
  - Shut off the power to the field.
  - Overload the field.
  - Find a way to be immune or invisible to the shield.
  - Destroy the field itself.
  - Go over or under the field.
  - Find its weakness.
- You're trapped in a digital world (like in *TRON*). You can:
  - Find a way to rewire/rehack the software from inside.
  - Find a way to reset the world.
  - Find an exit to your reality.
  - Figure out why you're there and use that information to figure out how to escape.
  - Take control of the computer.
  - Hey, it's not so bad in here. Why leave?
- Ice
  - Melt it (using heat).
  - Break it.
  - Vaporize it.
  - Use salt, antifreeze, or some other chemical compound to melt it.
  - Hibernate.
  - Cut your way out.
  - Gnaw your way out.
  - Wait for warm weather.
  - Expand yourself so it shatters.
- Height (you are trapped in some high place where you would die if you jumped). You can:
  - Climb down.
  - Dig through the floor to find another way.
  - Use something to slow your fall so you can survive.
  - Jump to another place.
  - Hitch a ride with some passing creature that flies.
  - Fly away yourself, if you can.

Common Solutions to Locked Doors and Other Containment Scenarios

Some containment scenarios are quite common. How many times have you encountered a locked door in a game, knowing that you would have to (or at least *want* to) get to what is on the other side? Other barriers are also common in games, and here are a few ways to get past the most common ones.

- Find another way out.
- Wait for the exit to be opened by a third party.
- Wait for the exit to be opened by a timed lock.
- Smash or blow your way out.
- A third party smashes or blows you out.
- Get airlifted out.
- Fly out (by making/stealing/using a flying machine/plane or by some flying ability).
- Tunnel out. (Make or find a tunnel.)
- Take a vent or a pipe.
- Climb out (using a rope/ladder/fire escape/fence).
- Jump out. (This might require something to break your fall.)
- Hurt yourself to trigger a medic. (For example, get in a fight or dislocate your own joints.)
- Hurt someone else to trigger a medic.
- Trigger an alarm system or sprinkler system to call the guards or the fire department.
- Pick the lock or acquire a key or code to open it.
- Hack the electronic lock or the computer that controls the locking mechanisms.
- Cut your way out. (For example, use a torch through sheet metal.)
- Appear to have disappeared (so guards will open the door to look for you).
- Play dead (or find a way to make it look as if you have escaped) and attack when the guards come to investigate.
- Sneak out a message somehow to let your friends know to rescue you.
- Learn how the trap works and use it against your enemies.
- Appear to have changed sides.
- Insult or challenge the guard.
- Find another, possibly secret, entrance/exit.
- Review the clues. What you have already observed/gathered that may hold a solution?
- Use an opening that is not a door, such as a fireplace or a dumbwaiter.
- Call in a partner to get you out or a backup evac team.
- Bribe the guard.
- Force someone to help you.
- Take a hostage.
- Yell for help.
- Use a signal fire or flare.
- Build an escape vehicle.
- Find, within the trapped area, ingredients or materials you can use to create an escape (for example, materials to make a catapult, to make dynamite, to make acid, to make poisonous gas, and so on).
- Carefully explore the trapped zone and find a weakness in construction.
- Perform some sort of meditation that allows you to concentrate your strength and thus break out, though it takes considerable force.
- Learn (through records or a story) how someone else broke out and do that.
- Have someone on the outside find the trap's/building's architect and force him to divulge a weakness in the design that could allow for an escape—then get this message to the trapped person.
- Hypnotize a guard into letting you out.
- It turns out that those who sent you on this mission knew there was a chance of capture. Thus, unbeknownst to you, they've embedded a method of escape (for example, a little plastic explosive) in your clothing, hat, boots, and so on—and you discover it.
- Through conversation and persuasion, convert the guard to your side so that he lets you escape.
- You have unrealized or inactive super powers and suddenly realize you can use them to escape.

- You join an escape in progress with other prisoners.
- You convince a fellow prisoner to help you escape—perhaps one with special abilities that make escape possible.
- Flatten yourself and go under.

Containment by Threat

Containment by threat can be combined with physical containment, but generally the threat is enough to prevent your leaving. The threat is often about bodily injury to yourself or to some other important character(s). The threat may be active, in that it is something that will be carried out by one or more enemies, or it can be passive, in that it is simply the environment that poses the threat—such as an Arctic wilderness or an airless planet. There are some solutions to the containment by threat scenarios that are more or less common, while specific scenarios may have specific solutions as well.

Common Solutions to Containment by Threat

- Disable or remove the threat.
- Go for it in spite of the threat, using force if necessary.
- Turn the threat back on the enemy.
- Review the clues—what you have already observed/gathered may hold a solution.
- Threaten the enemies with something worse—something they believe you can carry out. For instance, you previously placed a bomb somewhere in their headquarters and only you can disable it, or, if you don't call someone within 15 minutes, all hell will break loose.
- Plead for leniency.
- Manipulate the enemy to turn them to your side or in some way get them to help you escape.

Containment by Threat Scenarios

- Your comrade is injured, and you must stay to defend him. Or your companion is too afraid to attempt an escape, and you don't want to leave him.
  - Leave anyway and come back for him.
  - Give him a pep talk and convince him to come along.
  - Find a way to heal the injured.
  - Find a way to remove the danger so even the scared and the injured can leave without fear.
  - The comrade dies and no longer needs protection.
  - The comrade turns out to be a traitor.
  - Force him, by whatever means you need, to come with you.
  - Convince him that he'll die anyway if he stays there.
  - Knock him out and take him with you.
- You are forced to wear an explosive collar or an item that prevents you from leaving the area. You can:
  - Find a way to remove the item, ideally placing it on one of the bad guys.
  - Disable the device.
  - Get someone to disable it for you—possibly by force or guile.
  - Shrink your head so you can escape.
  - Cause the device to expand for the same result.
  - Create a shield that protects you from the effect of the collar, then explode it or, if it is not explosive, just go for it!

- You are under surveillance, and if you try to escape, you will be shot. You can:
  - Find a way to fake what the camera sees, using a fake picture or recorded loop.
  - Do crazy things so the observers will become concerned and will come to check what you are doing.
  - Talk to the observers and win them over to your side.
  - Destroy (or block) the cameras.
  - Fake a heart attack or other collapse.
  - Find a way to protect yourself from attack, then go ahead and escape.
  - Find something in the environment that you can use as armor or other protection, then go for it.
- The area is surrounded by something dangerous—snipers, deadly lava, deadly creatures, and so on. You can:
  - Find a way to neutralize the threat.
  - Find a way to protect yourself while escaping.
  - Use a disguise or other method so that whatever is out there no longer sees you as a threat.
  - Be very stealthy.
  - Use any other means, such as digging, teleportation, flying, and so on.
  - Take out one part of the perimeter or neutralize it, then go through.
- If you try to move, something bad will happen. For instance, you are standing on the trigger to a landmine, and moving will detonate it. You can:
  - Find something to put in your place.
  - Get an enemy to come near and force or fool him into taking your place.
  - Run really fast before it explodes (doubtful).
  - Find a way to disable it or render it harmless.
  - Carefully slide an effective barrier of some sort between you and the threat. For instance, in the case of the landmine, find a way to take a thick steel plate and carefully slide it under you without releasing the trigger. This is another sort of doubtful tactic, but it would be nice if you could make it work.
- You are in a safe spot in a remote location, and you will likely die if you leave (from freezing, exposure, hunger, heat, drowning, lack of air [vacuum], and so on). You can:
  - Find or fashion something to protect you from the danger, then venture forth.
  - Call for help, if possible.
  - Wait for someone to show up to help you.
  - Start out and hope for the best.
- If you escape, it will trigger some terrible consequence to you or to someone else.
  - If it involves someone else, make sure you can rescue him or disable the threat to him, then go for it.
  - Perhaps you know that you can resurrect the other person, or someone can resurrect you, if you make it far enough.
  - Give up on the important person(s).
  - Anticipate this and have an alternate plan that protects the important person(s).
  - Disable the trigger mechanism.
- You're trapped and require rescue, but all your comrades believe you are already dead, so they won't come. You can:
  - Find a way to get a message to them. The subtler, the better.
  - Find your way out of the trap (by any methods mentioned earlier).

- Something in this room is required for your survival, and you can't take it with you. If you leave, you will be without it and you will die. You can:
  - Find a way to make it portable.
  - Find a replacement for it.
  - Find another way out that doesn't endanger you.
  - Mutate, transform, or evolve into a form that does not require whatever it is that keeps you there.
- A guard will kill you if you move. You can:
  - Possess the guard.
  - Wait it out—maybe he'll fall asleep or something.
  - Convince the guard to help you by force, guile, bribery, threats, or other means. Perhaps even the truth might do it sometimes.
  - Provide an alternate target.
  - Disable the guard.
- There is a threat to your personal property. You can:
  - Replace your property.
  - Reinforce your property.
  - Destroy your property before the threat does.
  - Hide your stuff.
  - Convince them that you don't care.
  - Threaten a worse reprisal.
- You can't leave because you're scared. You can:
  - Get over it/get therapy.
  - Get more scared of something else.
  - Think happy thoughts.
- There is a threat of physical (mental/sexual) harm/torture. You can:
  - Take drugs or use some mental conditioning to get through the torture.
  - Resist the torture.
  - Call their bluff—convince them that the threat does not frighten you.
  - Tell them what they want to know.
  - Lie to them.
  - Commit suicide (or appear to), only to resurrect yourself later.

RESTRAINT (PHYSICAL)

Physical restraint occurs when a character is tied up or mechanically restrained. It may also involve methods that prevent a character from moving, such as drugs. With physical restraint, the most common solutions are to:

- Untie the knots
- Cut the rope
- Pick the locks
- Use a blowtorch on the chains

Or, to regain whatever ability has been taken from you, you can:

- Take an antidote
- Remove a blindfold
- And so on...

However, these are not the only ways to counter physical restraint. Other ways depend on the type of restraint used and the situation itself.

Other Physical Restraint Scenarios

There is more than one way to trap someone, but certainly methods that physically restrain someone are among the most common.

- You are tied up or otherwise mechanically restrained (by handcuffs, clamps, chains, and so on). You can:
  - Talk to your captor(s) and somehow get them to release you.
  - Threaten them with something worse—something they believe you can carry out.
- Your ability to walk has been removed. You can:
  - Use your hands.
- You have been blinded (in various ways) to prevent you from escaping. You can:
  - Use your other senses.
- You have been paralyzed. You can:
  - Use your wits.
- You have been rendered unconscious by drugs, blows, or other means. You can:
  - Attack from a dream state.
  - Wait until you wake up.

Betrayal/Treachery

Another sort of trap is more situational and will result in one of the other types of traps as a result of the situation. This type of trap occurs when a character enters a situation involving other characters, thinking it will be safe, only to find out that it is a trap. It involves broken agreements and expectations and possibly betrayal by someone the character trusted. It can involve a confrontation with the betrayers or just the springing of a trap of any of the other types—in other words, the result of a betrayal or treacherous trap could be confinement (either physical or by threat), restraint, direct damage, or any of the other types of traps.

Common Solutions to Betrayal Traps

There are a few solutions common to pretty much every trap that is the result of betrayal or treachery. For instance:

- Be aware of the clues and avoid the trap.
- Be aware of the clues and come prepared to counter the trap.
- Investigate the situation before you enter the trap—find out who you can trust.
- Bring friends or have allies standing by.
- Have a trump card—something you can spring on your captors that will force them to do as you demand.

- Go in disguise.
- Betray or ambush the betrayers. Set your own trap.

Betrayal and Treacherous Traps

- You have been invited to a meeting by someone you trust, but it is a trap.
- You go to negotiate with your enemies, but they capture you instead.
- You are sent on an errand by someone you trust, and it turns out to be a trap.
- You have been told that if you leave, something horrible will happen to someone or something you care about.
  - Call their bluff.
  - Be sure that person/thing is safe.

NOTE *The following scenarios could also be considered mental traps, since they involve the manipulation of the character's beliefs and/or thoughts. These traps would be betrayals if the person(s) responsible were trusted in the first place.*

- You have been convinced by someone you trust that you must stay here for your own good—that you will be in danger if you leave or that you are insane and must stay where you are so as not to endanger others.
  - Leave anyway.
  - Find a way to prove to yourself that you are sane.
  - Necessity or danger forces you to try to escape.
  - You overhear someone talking and revealing the truth.
  - Find someone who tells you the truth.
  - Find some evidence that reveals the truth.
- False memories have been implanted into your brain, and you believe you are supposed to be here.
  - A device or mental implant "reminder" kicks in to remind you of who you are.
  - Necessity or danger forces you to try to escape.
  - Something someone says doesn't correspond to something someone else said, and the inconsistencies cause you to reason out the real situation.
  - Find evidence (such as old photos, diaries, newspaper clippings, and so on) that reveals the truth.
  - Find someone who tells you the truth.
  - Overhear someone talking and revealing the truth.
- You have been convinced that you have done something horrible and that you deserve to be imprisoned.
  - A comrade convinces you that you're wrong, or someone tells you the truth.
  - Necessity or danger forces you to try to escape.
  - The person you thought you hurt or killed is discovered (directly or indirectly) to be fine.
  - You learn that the person you hurt or killed was really an enemy.
  - You overhear someone talking and revealing the truth.
  - Find evidence (such as old photos, diaries, newspaper clippings, and so on) that reveals the truth.
  - You learn (somehow) that these feelings you have are exactly what they planned (in other words, you find records of the plan, or someone in the know voluntarily confesses or is forced to confess).

Mental Traps

Mental traps affect the mind and generally are illusory. They can involve direct hallucinations and manipulated illusions or even attitudes formed by observation or by what you learn from others. Some scenarios involve the intentional manipulation of your thoughts or even mind control techniques. Others may only involve distorted views of reality based on information, manufactured situations, or illusions. In any case, if the attitude or illusion prevents you from acting or moving, it is a trap.

- You see a way out, but it is a further trap or an illusion. You can:
  - Test it.
  - Throw or shoot into it to reveal the illusion.
  - Figure out the enemy's methods and realize that it isn't real.
  - Close your eyes and go by touch so the illusion can't affect you.
  - Remember clues that might reveal that this is fake.
- Someone is playing God with you and toying with you. You can:
  - Stop doing what amuses him.
  - Challenge him on moral grounds.
  - Show pity for the emptiness of his life, humiliate him, or cause him to question himself.
  - Pretend to go along with him and lull him into a false sense of security...then turn the tables.
- You are not where you think you are.
  - Find clues and small discrepancies that prove things aren't what they seem.
  - Close your eyes and feel the walls and objects.
  - Despite apparent danger, act on what you know is reality and ignore the falseness of your surroundings.
- You are drugged and can't function or find your way out. You can:
  - Fight off the effect of the drugs.
  - Keep acting drugged even after the effect wears off and then catch your captors off guard.
  - Drug your captors so they aren't any better off than you.
  - Find and use an antidote for the drug.
- You are hallucinating. You can:
  - Find a way to counter the hallucinatory agent.
  - Face the hallucinations in order to see through them and make sense of your situation.
  - Use superior mental discipline to overcome the hallucinations.
  - Find and use some substance or spell that will allow you to see reality.
- You are in a pleasant enough place—perhaps a small village or a mountain hideaway, an idyllic forest, or the wing of a castle. It is all too nice. In reality, you are a prisoner, but you don't know it yet. You can:
  - Find the flaws in the situation.
  - Remember your purpose.
  - Discover the evil being(s) that control the place.
  - Spy and overhear someone talking about you.
  - Try to leave.
- You learn that the last 10 people to try to escape were all killed, and you are afraid you will be number 11. You can:
  - Find out what killed them.
  - Accept the possibility of death and go for it.
  - Investigate further until you know how to get away safely.
  - Get an ally on the "inside."

- You and a comrade are both trapped, and only one can escape (that is, make it over the burning rope bridge before it breaks). You can:
  - Try anyway and suffer the consequences.
  - Let him go and find another way out.
  - Find some way of modifying your situation (for example, throwing away supplies to make yourself lighter) that permits both of you to get out.
- Your worst fear/phobia is right outside the door (fire, rats, snakes, and so on). You can:
  - Face your fears and overcome them, by force if necessary.
  - Find another way.
  - Have someone else deal with it for you.
- You designed the trap yourself and know it to be foolproof.
  - Boy, you're in trouble. What loophole did you leave?
  - Maybe someone else can help you.
  - Of course it's not foolproof. Nothing is perfect.
- You believe that the door leads to nothing—a void or an abyss. You can:
  - Test it by throwing something or tying a mouse to a string and letting it walk through.
  - Walk out anyway.
  - Find someone else to test it first.
- Reverse psychology: Inevitably, if you tell a player in some way that he "shouldn't go there…," he will. So, you make a door that's heavily padlocked, a really scary-looking hallway, or even a sign saying "Keep Out!" You know he will think there's something especially worthwhile beyond that point because so many games have exactly that kind of setup, but instead it's a trap, and he is stuck.
- It all seems too easy, so you suspect a further trap—something worse than what you are in now. You can:
  - Kidnap a guard or hold him at gunpoint and convince him to tell you of the trap.
  - Act as if you don't know it's a trap to make them believe you're a goner—but it turns out that's part of your trap for them.
  - Proceed with the utmost caution, looking all around (including above and below you).
- You face a metaphysical threat. (God will hate you, or the universe will end.) You can:
  - Convert theologies.
  - Make an offering to the deity.
  - Ignore the outcome.
- You face the threat of doing something personally immoral. You can:
  - Change your morals.
  - Do it for the greater good.
  - Find someone else to do it.
  - Convince yourself that it's okay.
  - Talk to God/the authority to absolve your sin.
  - Compromise with your threatener.
  - Find another way to accomplish what you must.
  - Pretend to go along with the plan, then find a way to double-cross the threatener before you do the immoral thing.

Removal

Sometimes a trap will physically remove you from the area you're in and send you somewhere else. It's possible that such a trap could also do physical harm. In fact, sometimes the main intent of the trap is to do physical harm, such as a trapdoor that drops you directly onto some long, sharp spikes or into a pool of acid or a pool full of sharks. In other cases, the main intent is to move you to another place. That place is probably also dangerous, but mainly, it is somewhere other than where you were. Traps that are focused primarily on direct damage should be among the ones listed next (in the "Injury/Direct Damage" section). Removal traps are primarily concerned with getting you away from where you are and leaving you somewhere else.

- A trap door drops you into a different area.
- A teleportation trap moves you somewhere else.
- The room you entered really was a vehicle, and it drives you somewhere else.
- You get in a cab, but the driver is working for the enemy and takes you somewhere far away from where you intended to be.
- Combined with a previous type of trap (betrayal and treachery), you are captured and sent on a boat, plane, train, or automobile to parts unknown.

Injury/Direct Damage

The other traps in this chapter cover situations in which someone is restrained, constrained, removed, or fooled, but one of the most common types of trap is simply there to cause damage directly to the unwary explorer. In some ways, this is the simplest type of trap, often designed to fire when triggered by some sensor. Traps may also be placed on doors, chests, and other items that you open, and, of course, opening triggers the trap. This is an example of the contact (making or breaking) type of sensor. Of course, direct damage traps can also be triggered manually, and some traps require no trigger—for instance, a pool of acid placed in your path or a guardian beast. For more information on different types of detectors used in traps, see Chapter 25, "Barriers, Boundaries, Obstacles, and Detectors."

Common Sensors

How do traps get sprung? Some of them require a sensor or some kind of detector that will cause the trap to be set in motion. Of course, not all the kinds of traps mentioned in this chapter fall into that category, but many do. So how do you spring such traps?

- Trip wire or other manual sensor
- Light/laser beam
- Pressure plate
- Motion/sound/heat
- Contact (making or breaking)
- Other technology—for instance, alien or magical
- A giant spider's web

See also "Methods of Detection" in Chapter 25, "Barriers, Boundaries, Obstacles, and Detectors."

Common Direct Damage Counters

How do you get around or past the sensors that are waiting to spring a trap on you?

- Avoid both the sensor (if there is one) and the trap by finding another way.
- Avoid the sensor.
- Fool the sensor.

- Disable the sensor.
- Destroy the sensor.
- Disable or destroy the actual trap.
- Find a way to be immune to the effects.
- Accept the damage and either heal afterward or simply ignore it.

Injury/Direct Damage Scenarios

This list contains examples of traps that are set off by some kind of sensor or trigger.

- Rigged weapon, such as a shotgun or dart set to go off if triggered.
- Triggering the trap releases a poison cloud.
- Hypodermic needle or other sharp object that injects a substance into the bloodstream.
- Bomb or other explosive device, such as a mine.
- Trapdoor that drops you and causes harm. This can simply be a long drop onto a hard surface, or it can be further enhanced by poisoned spikes, poisonous snakes or insects, pools of acid or pools full of sharks, a lion's den, and so on. This also applies to any removal-type trap (see the earlier "Removal" section) that causes direct damage to the character.
- A wild, dangerous animal placed in your path or sprung from a hidden location.
- Poisoned drink or food.
  - Countered by avoiding the trap or by immunity.
  - Countered by having a "taster."
- High doses of some invisible deadly medium, such as radioactivity or high concentrations of carbon monoxide, and so on.
  - This can be countered by foreknowledge or immunity to the deadly agent or by quickly leaving the affected area.

Herding and Control

This isn't precisely a trap, but it is a way to control enemy movement, and it can involve traps. In Chapter 30, "Ways to Communicate with the Player," I look at ways that game designers can control a player's movement or direction in a game. However, players, too, can use specific strategies and techniques to control the movements of their enemies. In some cases, the same techniques may be available to players that are available to designers.

- **Hit and Run.** One common way to control enemies is to lead them into traps. In some games, you can get their attention, then retreat to an advantageous position or to where your allies are hiding. The enemy will follow, and then you spring the trap.
- **Diversion.** In some cases, you want to prevent enemies from attacking a specific location or unit, so you can create diversions to cause them to go in another direction or attack a different location or unit.
- **Attraction.** In some cases, the enemy will be attracted to some commodity or item. Seeding a path with items that the enemy desires can give players control over their enemies' movements. A similar effect may be accomplished by the use of decoys, which play upon the natural aggressiveness of some enemies and force them to follow a path of the player's choosing.
- **Obstacles.** If the enemy AI is able to choose alternate routes or change directions based on what it encounters in the game space, then placing obstacles along paths can divert the enemy. Clever players might even be able to cause enemies to double back on themselves, go in circles, or walk into traps.

- **Removal Traps.** Set a trap that causes the enemy to be moved to a new location.
- **Espionage.** Enemy movement might be affected by supplying them with false information and causing them to head off in the wrong direction as a result.

Trap-Maker Questions

Questions to ask when creating a trap:

- Does it cause physical damage?
    - Lethal damage?
    - How does it cause damage?
    - What part of the body does it damage?
- Does it restrain the person or prevent him from moving or from escaping?
    - Using ropes, chains, zip ties, duct tape, straight jacket, and so on
    - Using a container of some sort, such as a metal box, cage, or coffin
    - Using some sophisticated technology, such as paralysis beams or a stasis field
- Does it incapacitate the victim?
    - With unconsciousness
    - With drugs
    - With blindness
    - With deafness
    - With fear
- Does it cause any environmental effects?
    - Loud noise
    - Bright light
    - Strong smells
    - Released poisons or other chemical agents
- How is it triggered?
    - Physical contact, such as pressure plate, trip wire, and so on
    - Remote sensors (infrared, motion, sound, and so on)
    - Proximity sensor
    - Manual operation
    - Timer
    - Other sensors
- Is the victim relocated in space or time?
    - Is he also damaged physically?
    - Is where he is relocated especially dangerous?
    - Is where he is relocated a hard-coded destination, random, or one of several fixed choices?
    - How far away is he sent, and how hard is it to get back?
- How can the victim escape, avoid, or counter the trap?
    - You have to see it first.
    - Take another route.
    - Go above, below, or around it.
    - Disarm it.
    - Use something else to trigger it, then go on by.
    - Reverse it so it traps the trapper.
- What does it look like?
    - Something ordinary and nonthreatening.
    - Like an obvious trap, but perhaps camouflaged under or behind something safe-looking.
    - It's invisible or nearly so.
    - It's a mechanism within another object—for instance, a magically trapped chest or door.
    - It's contained inside some safe object, such as a stick of dynamite disguised as a candle or a hand grenade inside a pineapple.
    - It's big or small, huge or tiny, or microscopic or the size of an elephant.

Part VI

Design Challenge

1. Think about games you have played. How have they used traps and counters? Are any types of traps very commonly used?
2. Take some of the types of traps in this chapter and consider original uses of them. For instance, suppose you put in a typical-looking "Save Spot." Normally, the player would go there to save a game in progress, but this one is a fake, and they become trapped.
3. Look at your own designs. Do you have traps for the player? For other characters? If so, what kinds? If not, can you add some interesting ones?
4. Take each of the different trap scenarios (or as many as you feel like doing) and:
    a. Think of specific examples where you could use that type of trap.
    b. Think of several ways a character could counter them.
    c. Think of ways to combine different types of traps—for instance, a trapdoor with a bomb or an animal barrier with a hypodermic needle.

27 Puzzles

Games and puzzles are often synonymous because puzzles are, in fact, games. They have rules, goals, and often special rewards. However, puzzles are also among the building blocks of good game design, and as such, they are worth exploring in various ways. This chapter contains various discussions of puzzles in games with the following sections:

- What Is a Puzzle?
- Dilemmas
- Puzzles in Games
- Puzzle-Based Games
- Codes and Cryptography
- A Puzzle Story
- Puzzle Maker

What Is a Puzzle?

A puzzle is, according to one definition, "a baffling problem that is said to have a correct solution." The key is that it is a problem and that there is a solution. Puzzles can be solved by deduction, by induction, or even by random chance. The solution exists and can be found if the necessary action is completed. Some puzzles can be solved by more than one method. For instance, a Rubik's Cube may have only one solution, but it can be arrived at by different sequences of movements.

It is useful to distinguish puzzles from challenges. Although puzzles represent challenges, some challenges are not puzzles. Some challenges, such as having to fight an enemy who blocks your way, are not really puzzles...unless the enemy has some secret that you must uncover in order to beat him. For instance, the mythological Medusa would turn you to stone, but Perseus used a mirror to turn the tables on her. That was a puzzle... The challenge of finding something to eat when you're hungry is not really a puzzle. You just have to find food and eat it. But the challenge of figuring out which plants are edible and which are poisonous could be a puzzle.

Dilemmas

Some puzzles are pretty straightforward. They have obvious and definite solutions, and from the player's point of view, the solution is all good. But some puzzles involve more complex decision-making, where not all the consequences of solving the puzzle are desirable. I've included a separate discussion of dilemmas in the "Dilemmas" section in Chapter 9, "Storytelling Techniques." The "Dilemmas" section could have been included in this chapter, but I thought it somewhat more relevant in the chapter on stories because it often involves interesting and challenging plot points, which are, at the same time, puzzles.

Puzzles in Games

Puzzles are among the building blocks used to create games. Although the most obvious use of puzzles occurs in puzzle games (of course), adventure games, and Role-Playing Games, in a broad sense puzzles can be thought of as situational challenges. As such, puzzles may occur in many genres of games. For instance, a mission in a First-Person Shooter may involve completing specific steps or destroying a particular installation. To do so, you might have to get past a guard tower or other obstacle, and the way this situation is set up could be thought of as a puzzle.

Putting Pieces Together

One type of puzzle is finding pieces to something and putting them together. This could be a device—a bomb, an airplane, a shrink ray, a magical suit of armor, for example—or it could be a potion that involves many ingredients, or a map torn in pieces and scattered. The end result could be useful in itself, or it could be a token that must be delivered to an NPC in order to complete some task.

Missing Persons, Creatures, or Things

Another puzzle could involve finding a missing person/creature/thing.

- Persons
  - They have wandered off and must be located.
  - They have been kidnapped or otherwise captured by the bad folks.
  - They are on a quest or task of their own, and you must find them to deliver a message or item or to join forces with them.
- Creatures can be key figures in a story, often because they hold the key to a mystery or are really more than they seem. Sometimes, however, creatures are simply beloved pets that have been lost. In this scenario, they are usually part of a minor quest, whereas when they are key elements, they are part of a larger quest or story. They can appear to be the latter while really being the former.
  - The creature has wandered off and must be located.
  - The creature has been stolen or otherwise captured by the bad folks.
  - The creature is actually a sentient being on a quest or task of its own, and you must find it to deliver a message or item or to join forces with it.
- Things are often the object of a quest or puzzle. Sometimes they are part of a side quest or a less important story element. Other times, they are crucial to the successful completion of the game.
  - The object is in pieces and must be reassembled. (Refer to the "Putting Pieces Together" section earlier in this chapter.)
  - The object is in the hands of the bad guys and must be recovered.
  - The object is nothing more than a rumor or a myth, but somehow you must find it.
  - The object is in plain sight, but you can't seem to obtain/move/activate it.
  - The object is an ordinary item that nobody knows is really the important item. You must discover the truth about it.

Hard Choices

Puzzles often involve making choices among several options without knowing what the result will be. (That's what saved games are for, right?) Anyway, there are lots of types of choices:

- **Eating the Blue Pill or the Red Pill.** As it was with Alice, sometimes you have to take a risk to accomplish a task. In Alice's case, the risk involved eating something whose effect was unknown.

This sort of choice involves physical (or possibly mental) risk and could come in the form of a choice of magic spells to cast, machines to fire up, or teleport pads to step onto.

- **What's Behind Door #3?** Also known as "The Lady and the Tiger," this sort of choice involves different paths. It could involve a set of doors to try or different roads, ladders, elevators, warp points, and so on. One or more choices might open to doom—or at least something unpleasant. At least one choice should be preferable; however, the preferable path may not be the safest. For instance, the safest or easiest path might lead to a location you need to reach, but the most dangerous path might provide you the opportunity to obtain a great item that you would miss if you made the other choice. In games, the path of least resistance is not always the best path.

NOTE

The Lady and the Tiger is from an old fable, the short version of which is that a young man falls in love with a princess, but he is taken prisoner by the king and given this choice: Open one of two doors. Behind one is the princess. Open that door, and you will be married to her and become the heir to the throne. Behind the other door is a vicious tiger. Open that door, and you will be eaten. Of course, this kind of choice is too simplistic for a game, because both doors lead, essentially, to completed outcomes—unless, that is, marrying the princess is just the beginning of the adventure, in which case it's still not all that great for a game because the player has no clues. Without clues it's a matter of blind luck, and it's always better to let players feel as if they have made a choice based on skill or knowledge. Pure luck certainly plays a part in many games, but a Lady and the Tiger–type puzzle would be better if the player could somehow figure out which door hid the princess or perhaps could find a way to overcome the tiger, thus proving his worth and gaining the princess anyway. In any case, I like the story, so I mention it here.

- **Freeing the Prisoners.** In its purest form, this hard choice involves choosing among imprisoned characters, at least one of which may be evil. The classic example of this was in the original *Myst*, when you had to figure out which of two imprisoned brothers was the mad one and which was the "good" one.
- **Who Do You Save?** As in Freeing the Prisoners, you must choose who you will help. The situation requires that you make a choice. You can't help everyone, and your choice will have repercussions within the game, immediately or at a future time. In this case, you may be saving people from a fire, from an advancing army, from an impending avalanche, or from a death sentence.
- **Sacrifice.** This involves giving up something: an item of value, money, or perhaps a power or ability to accomplish a worthy goal. It might even involve sacrificing your life or that of someone you care about.

Kill Tasks

This type of puzzle involves finding and killing a specific monster to complete a quest or to trigger an event. This is pretty standard fare for most games, but it can be made more interesting by putting some twists on it:

- The target of the kill task is invulnerable. The puzzle is to find its Achilles heel.
- The target is your friend.
- The target is really on the good side.
- The target can offer you something that can help you achieve your overall quest.
- The target is somehow tied into you or someone you care about in such a way that killing the target also kills that person or causes him or her to turn against you.
- The target is the sole support for a poor village (or something like that).

- The target has reformed and wishes to be able to do good in the world to make up for his former misdeeds.
- You need the target alive for some other task.

Getting It Right

This type of puzzle deals with figuring out what to say/offer/give to an NPC. This kind of puzzle often involves clues given by the NPC or by another NPC. Clues may also be found in the environment or in documents, such as books or letters located somewhere in the world. In essence, the puzzle involves several stages. If the NPC wants an item, there are three essential stages:

1. Determine what the NPC wants.
2. Obtain the item in question.
3. Give the item to the NPC.

If the puzzle involves saying something specific to the NPC, there are two or three stages:

1. Figure out what you need to say to the NPC to further the story.
2. If necessary, take certain actions to unlock the trigger for that statement (such as talking to another NPC or witnessing some event—or obtaining an item, as above).
3. Talk to the NPC and say the appropriate phrase or pass along the significant information.

Unusual Objects You Can Carry or Move

Often in a game, if you come across an object that you can pick up or something you can drag or push around, there's a puzzle associated with it. For instance, moveable objects can be used in a variety of ways:

- As a way to gain height, for instance to climb or jump over a wall or to reach a high location
- As a moveable barrier, for instance to block incoming enemies or as protection from attack
- As a way to open up an otherwise closed route
- As a part of a configuration puzzle—an element in a larger scheme, pattern, or device
- As a way to trigger a device, such as a pressure plate
- As a weight to use to balance something or to drop from a height on someone or something
- As a way to fill a hole or to raise the level of a body of water
- As a floating platform to cross water, lava, or other liquid
- As raw material for some other use—such as carving a statue out of a huge rock, leaving a message carved in stone, or breaking off parts of the mass for various uses

Objects you can carry with you may also have special uses in solving puzzles. For instance, if an object has no perceivable use, it may be part of a puzzle or other challenge. Unknown objects are used:

- As keys
- As magical ingredients
- As items that can be collected (often to complete quests)
- As parts of something that can be constructed or repaired
- As objects that can be combined with other objects to produce a variety of results
- As weapons (or ammunition) whose existence or use is yet unknown
- As lost objects of quests, which can be returned to their owners for rewards
- As charms or protections from harm, even if their use is not understood

Ordering Things

Sometimes a puzzle involves changing the environment in some way. This can involve moving items to new locations (see also the upcoming "Configurations" section) or possibly destroying some items or changing their state. For instance, you might have to stack some boxes in a certain way to gain access to a high place. Or, you may have to rotate a set of objects with different-colored faces so that they form a specific color pattern. Or you might have to destroy some items in an area to make a path or to make room for something. A very basic puzzle might require you to move some boxes or other items into a specific order—for instance, largest to smallest or heaviest to lightest, and so on.

Buttons and Switches

Buttons and switches are commonly used in games to activate machines, doors, and other items. They can be shaped in many ways, some obvious and some quite clever. For instance, for game purposes, a specific book in a bookshelf that operates a secret panel could be considered a switch.

Sometimes the button or switch is a single object that controls a single result. However, sometimes buttons and switches are used in combinations, and you must either manipulate them in a certain order or manipulate several of them sequentially. In multiplayer games, some buttons and switches must be activated simultaneously, requiring teamwork. Other times, the sequence or configuration of buttons and switches can cause different effects, such as moving a set of bridges into new configurations. For more on that sort of application, see the upcoming "Configurations" section.

You can use buttons and switches to:

- Open doors and gates
- Deactivate or activate barriers (see also Chapter 25, "Barriers, Obstacles, and Detectors")
- Release or trap a person or creature
- Lower and raise drawbridges
- Start and stop machines (see also Chapter 19, "Objects and Locations")
- Open or lock a container
- Activate or deactivate a bomb or other dangerous device
- Activate or deactivate a weapon
- Create musical sequences or specific sounds
- Control remote sensors
- Reveal a hidden message
- Operate communication or computer-like equipment

Keys

Another type of puzzle could be finding a key to open a door, chest, and so on. Keys can come in all shapes and sizes; they don't all have to be standard skeleton keys from gothic novels. In the broadest sense, a key is anything that allows a player to gain entry into an otherwise closed location or container. Keys are used all too often in games, without much variation. However, it is possible to create not-so-obvious keys—consider the following possibilities:

- A weapon
- A severed head (or hand), perhaps to use the fingerprint to gain access to a secure facility—or something more obscure and arcane…
- A person or creature
- A piece of fruit (before it spoils, hopefully)
- A ring, bracelet, talisman, tiara, or other jewelry
- A basketball (or other sports object)
- A special item of clothing
- Magic glasses (or anything magical)
- A tattoo

- Just about anything harvested from a defeated enemy
- A glass of wine
- A note
- A headline from the paper
- A sound byte
- A musical sequence
- A password or magical incantation

Configurations

Configuration puzzles involve moving objects or causing them to move into specific configurations. When the required configuration is successfully created, there is usually some immediate effect. Often there is a very obvious change in circumstances, but sometimes there is no visual or auditory clue that you have successfully created a required configuration. Examples are setting movable platforms in a configuration to form a bridge across a chasm or stacking boxes (or other objects) in just the right configuration to allow you access to a high place or a clear path through a landscape. Configuration puzzles can often involve more than one setup. For instance, when making a bridge across a chasm, you might have to change the configuration several times to cross at different points or to reach different places. Examples of configuration puzzles include:

- Movable bridges and ladders
- Movable objects used to make a path
- Movable objects used to access otherwise unreachable locations
- Configurations of lights and/or levers used to accomplish any of a variety of different tasks (see also "Buttons and Switches" earlier in this chapter)
- A configuration of movable objects that sets a trigger, such as unlocking a door or disarming a trap
- Rotating mirrors used to aim a laser beam (or opening and closing sluice gates to redirect a waterway and so on)
- A formation of people, creatures, or objects used to redirect the movement of other characters or to block their passage
- A configuration of movable objects that weights one or more pressure plates to trigger some event
- A configuration of movable objects that balances weight or that distributes weight in a specific way
- A configuration of movable objects that forms a picture or text image
- A configuration of components that creates a working machine or properly connects a machine to its source of power/information, and so on

Sequence of Tasks

Sequence-of-tasks puzzles involve a set of tasks that must all be accomplished to solve the puzzle. (In reality, all puzzles involve sequences of events, so this is distinguished by the tasks being strung together.) Most quests in games and many missions in mission-based games are actually large sequences of tasks puzzles. It doesn't matter what the tasks are—scavenger hunts, killing enemies, finding missing items/persons/creatures, and so on. The idea is simply that the player must accomplish several tasks. However, one variant of this is that the tasks must be accomplished in a specific order. Specifying the order can make this sort of puzzle more difficult, particularly if doing so is complicated in various ways. For instance, it may be that a set of tasks must be completed in a specific order, but it's very easy to inadvertently complete one of the tasks out of order, thereby screwing up the sequence. Another way to make this difficult is to require some prerequisite to completing a task, which in itself requires a task to be completed or an ability to be learned, and so on. (See also "Follow the Leader.")

Some examples include:

- You must obtain a specific item, find a specific location, object, or NPC, and use the object there to obtain another specific item, which you then take back to where you got the quest originally. This second item is then transmuted into something—say a weapon—which you can then use to go after a boss or destroy a significant enemy installation, and so forth.
- You meet someone who asks you to escort him home (or somewhere significant to him, anyway), and along the way you have to perform numerous tasks and solve numerous puzzles in order to complete the mission.

Follow the Leader

Follow-the-leader puzzles can have a couple of variations. One variant is a very simple sequence type of puzzle that involves repeating some action, as in Simon Says. This can be as simple as repeating a sequence of lights by pressing certain buttons or mimicking an NPC's simple movements. These are generally simple puzzle games, either testing your skill with a controller or your short-term memory, or both.

More sophisticated follow-the-leader puzzles might involve actually following an NPC through a minefield or other dangerous location. If you don't do exactly what the NPC does, you get blown up, fall off the edge, or step on the wrong stone/break the laser beam and cause the alarms to go off.

Timing Challenges

The challenges inherent in many types of puzzles can be enhanced by putting time pressure on players, meaning they have to solve and complete the puzzle—whatever it is—within a limited amount of time. For instance, you must disarm a bomb before its timer expires, or you must complete a specific challenge or test within a time limit. In another typical situation, you must push a button, pull a lever, or step on a pressure plate that opens a door, releases a lock, or disables a barrier, then you must race to that location before the door closes, the lock resets, or the barrier is put back into action. These sorts of puzzles can also occur with sequence tasks. (See "Sequences of Tasks.") In some cases, you can make it to the goal in time. In other cases, it's impossible. In the impossible cases, you must find a way to trigger the button or pressure plate in such a way that you can reach the goal. For instance:

- Place something heavy on the pressure plate.
- Freeze the button in the "on" position.
- Use a gun or a thrown item to push the button remotely.
- Get someone else to press the button or stand on the pressure plate, and so on.
- Use some sort of magical spell that lets you remotely affect the trigger mechanism.
- Use something that makes you go extra fast.
- Short-circuit the mechanism so that it remains on.
- Rewire the mechanism.
- Break through.
- Go another way.

Timing challenges can be arbitrary—the game simply assigns a time limit to the action—or they can be part of a narrative structure or story, in which case they make a certain logical sense within the game story/fiction.

The Obscure Object of Desire

You can see it (or hear it), and you know you want to get to it, but there is absolutely no way to get to it. Generally, these teasing puzzles are set to tantalize a player, and often the goal can only be reached at a later time. However, you will almost always try to get to it, and sometimes there is a way. The only solution for "wait until later" puzzles is patience and perseverance. This and the next type of puzzle ("You Can't Do That...Yet") are closely related. The purpose of this kind of puzzle is to provide a clear goal for the player to strive for, as well as implying that there are skills to be acquired that can make it possible.

Examples include:

- A chest on the far side of a chasm.
- An NPC who seems to be asleep and won't wake up.
- A strangely shining light high in the air.
- An inviting weapon behind a locked gate or up too high to reach.
- The sound of water somewhere nearby.
- An NPC joins your party, and you know he has an important clue, but he will not speak about it or is temporarily unable to speak, and you have no antidote.

You Can't Do That...Yet

Like the "Obscure Object of Desire" section, this category is all about delayed gratification and is specifically about abilities. You can see what you need to do, but you aren't strong enough, fast enough, smart enough, able to jump high enough, in possession of that magic or specific ability yet, and so on. What this tells you is that you'll be able to come back later.

Barriers

Barriers are anything that impedes your progress. Some barriers are created to redirect your movements. Others are made to be defeated, if you can find a way. Check out Chapter 25, "Barriers, Obstacles, and Detectors," and specifically the section "Methods of Detection," for more about barriers, obstacles, and detectors.

Thinking Outside the Box

Some puzzles involve a seemingly ordinary or obvious situation, but the real solution is something quite different from the ordinary. For instance, suppose you are locked in a room and can't find any way to open the door. You search the room and find nothing that seems useful. However, you do find some matches or a lighter, which you then use to set off the fire sprinklers, which in turn sets off an alarm, and someone comes to open the door. When they do, you escape. Or suppose you are guarded by some thugs, and you probably can't defeat them in a fight. But you engage them in a game of chance (poker, dice, and so on) and ultimately start winning. Finally, you bet all or nothing against your freedom. The key to this kind of puzzle is to create a situation that looks hopeless, but allow some unorthodox way of solving it.

Managing Chaos (Too Much Too Fast)

This is a classic sort of puzzle in which things happen very quickly—often at an accelerating pace—and you have to make difficult decisions in a split second. This is often a scenario used in arcade games, where the situation starts out slow and manageable and gradually speeds up until you can't keep up without having superhuman reflexes. The instant decisions you make more or less constitute solving a puzzle, and sometimes you can develop specific tactical approaches to the chaos, which are even more like a puzzle solution. However, calling these types of situations puzzles does stretch the definition somewhat.

Examples include:

- People are jumping out of a burning building, and you are carrying the net to catch them.
- You're trying to protect someone or something, and the bad guys keep appearing faster and faster. You have to decide which ones pose the most serious threat and take them out first.
- You're flying through an asteroid belt, and the small asteroids keep coming at you faster and faster as you attempt to avoid or blast them.
- You're trying to dig your way out of a cave-in, but the dirt keeps falling faster and faster as you dig. On top of that, you're running out of air.
- You're bailing out a leaky boat.
- You're playing *Missile Command.*

Moral Dilemmas

Sometimes one solution to a puzzle may involve doing something antisocial, morally or ethically wrong, or against the nature of your character in some way. But that seems to be the way to solve the puzzle. In such cases, there is often another way that is less morally repugnant. However, creating a situation that has moral overtones can make players think and challenge themselves to find other ways to complete a task.

In many games, if you are given the quest, say, to kill someone, and you decided to let them go for some reason, you would not get credit for the quest. It would fail. But in a more clever game, failure to complete the quest under such circumstances could result in new game opportunities and possibly even better results in the long run. For instance, if the person you allowed to escape later crosses your path, he will be grateful and do something really good for you—something he could never have done if you had killed him earlier. Of course, he might have continued his evil ways and caused more havoc and suffering because you let him go, and you'd have to deal with that. But most games don't allow for such gray areas and alternate actions. In most games, a quest must be completed, and if it isn't, it's simply a failure.

Think of ways your players might be able to make decisions about the outcome of a quest or other interaction, particularly one with moral or ethical choices, and think about how the game might be changed if they decided not to complete the quest as given. Whenever there is a moral dilemma or an ethical choice to be made, there should be an alternate path that occurs based on the choice the player makes. And any path should be full of opportunity and good gameplay. Rules of thumb: Failure is only a vehicle for more gameplay. Everything adds to gameplay.

Examples of moral dilemmas include:

- **Kill Them All.** To get a special magical or otherwise desirable item, you must destroy the villagers who have it. Maybe someone else's life depends on getting the item, and you have to make a choice between the person you're trying to save and the lives of the villagers. Possible alternatives: Do something good for the villagers, and they give you the item you want. Or use stealth and steal it without bloodshed. Or even find someone outside the village who is capable of convincing the villagers to give you the object.
- **Precious Pet.** Your path is blocked by a dog. If you try to pass by it, you will be viciously mauled. However, the dog is a little boy's pet. Killing the dog will break the boy's heart, but you can't allow it to maul you, either. Possible alternatives: Perhaps you can find some tasty treat for the dog and divert its attention while you get past it, or even make friends with it. Or, perhaps you can talk to the boy and promise him something if he calls the dog back. Or you might find a way to tranquilize the dog without hurting it. Or, there may even be another path you can take.
- **Family Ties.** You have been chasing a criminal or other evildoer, only to discover that the person you have been chasing is a family member (mother, father, sister, brother, wife, husband, and so on). Do you kill them or capture them and take them back to answer for their crimes? Possible alternatives:

You enlist them to help right the wrongs they have done so that they can be exonerated. Or, you let them go and justify it by your relationship to them, accepting the consequences of that action.

- **The Loved One.** You must do something for the good of many people, but to do that is to sacrifice someone who is important to you (even yourself). For instance, a wizard has been struck down. Only he can save the world. But the potion that will revive him is also the only potion that can revive your sweetheart. Only one of them can have it. Generally, this is not really much of a choice, since to give it to the sweetheart dooms the world, and who wants to live in a doomed world? Even so, it's an emotional decision to make. And what would happen if you did give it to the loved one instead of the wizard? Is that the end of the game, or does it open a whole new path of your character in a doomed world, trying to atone for having made the selfish choice? This option could lead to a much more interesting game. Not all failures are necessarily bad....
- **Endangered Species.** In order to save the world or accomplish some exceptionally worthwhile goal, you must sacrifice the last creature of a particular race of benevolent beings. Or something like that...
- **All You Have.** Sometimes you have very little of something precious—food, medicine, gold, magic fairy dust, and so on—and you are saving it for some lofty purpose. But then you come across someone in dire need. Do you use your remaining resources to help him, or do you let him suffer or die and go ahead with your original intention? And what consequences result from either action?
- **The Big Bomb.** If you use your ultimate weapon, it will kill massive numbers of people, but you think it will end a war or stop something worse from happening.
- **Slash and Burn.** Some situations involve destruction in the name of preservation—for instance, an army slashing and burning the fields to prevent a pursuing army from getting the food. Or perhaps poisoning a well or oasis in order to destroy a monster that has been terrorizing the area. Or burning part of a forest to stop a forest fire from spreading (called *back burning*). Can you make the hard choice? What happens if you don't?

Riddles

In some ways, all puzzles are riddles. However, riddle puzzles are generally given in the form of clues that are somewhat obscure and open to interpretation. The clues may be given all at once, by one NPC or by something written in a book, scroll, or parchment, or carved or painted on a wall, monolith, tomb, sarcophagus, and so on. The clues may also be obtained piece by piece as the player explores, and they will only make sense after enough of the riddle has been obtained. Sometimes the riddles describe a thing or place exactly. Other times they may only describe an idea, or they may actually be part of a larger riddle that must be pieced together. A good example of a famous riddle, which dates back at least to the ancient Greeks, is "What goes on four feet in the morning, two feet at noon, and three feet in the evening?" Interestingly, this same riddle can be expressed in far more poetic style, as in a translation from an ancient Greek named Athenaeus:

"A thing there is whose voice is one;
Whose feet are four and two and three.
So mutable a thing is none
That moves in earth or sky or sea.
When on most feet this thing doth go,
Its strength is weakest and its pace most slow."

In case you're curious, the answer to the riddle is Man!

Signs and Wonders

Sometimes there are signs in the environment that point to something. I sometimes think of these as *attractors*. These can be as simple as animal tracks or an animal sound indicating that there is something nearby. Or they can be complex and puzzling, such as unexplainable burn marks or crop circles. These signs can be natural occurrences (as in the case of the animal tracks) or they could be artificial—made by some intelligence with an intention. An example might be if a being of superior intelligence left mysterious images carved onto cliffs. The images might be suggesting a new technology or way of thinking, but would only become important when people were ready to understand them. Often in a game, there will be clues in the environment that can lead the player to new places or new discoveries. Most often, they are made pretty obvious, such as a special glow around an area or a sparkle or other eye-catching device. However, they can also be quite subtle, such as a slight difference in the texture of a wall or a completely obscure pattern of lights that seems to have no purpose.

- A mysterious light appears in the sky somewhere to the east.
- A bush moves slightly in the path ahead.
- You spot the tracks of an animal moving off in a particular direction.
- There's a deep, earth-rattling boom that seems to get louder as you approach in a certain direction. Or perhaps it's the sound of running water.
- As you walk along a certain path, you notice a mysterious design carved into the rocks or a strange totem staked into the ground at regular intervals.
- You hear an animal cry in the distance.
- Random NPCs walk by uttering the same mysterious phrase. You figure it's a clue.
- As you approach, a small animal scampers off through the bushes, revealing the entry to a hidden path.
- A cloud of flies (or vultures) is hovering over something in the near distance.
- You see a brief flash of light—could it be a reflection off a lost sword, a gem, or some other treasure? Or perhaps it's just a discarded bottle. But then, even an empty bottle can be useful sometimes.

Devices

When exploring any world, whether it is a swords and sorcery fantasy world, a modern police or military adventure, or a futuristic environment, devices often play a role. Devices can be quite complex or quite simple. For instance, a door is a device. So is a computer. But the devices that are most interesting from a game point of view are those that require some effort to understand or operate. Their purpose may be mysterious. Or, their purpose may be quite understandable, but the challenge is in getting them to work. Or they may be easy to operate, but what you have to do with them is challenging. For instance, a gun emplacement may be simple to operate, but aiming, firing, and taking out advancing enemies might be quite challenging. The device may be broken and in need of repairing. Or it may require some specific kind of input—a key, a sequence of button presses, or a special substance to fuel or power it.

Operating the device can be the most all-important thing in the game, or it can be something quite peripheral to the main quest. The general requirement for the device to be a useful part of the game is that it fulfills some key role in the game or it does something very useful or very fun. For instance, a slot machine placed in the middle of a battlefield makes no sense. But a slot machine in the right place, even if it does nothing to further the game, might be fun as a diversion. If a device is not operational, getting it to run successfully must be fun or directly rewarding, or both. Because devices are objects in the environment, you can also check out Chapter 19, "Objects and Locations."

Although there are too many examples of devices to mention, here are a few interesting ones. But think of how they can be used, not just for their primary function, but in other ways as well:

- Telephones that can actually call people or that do something else (as in *The Matrix*).
- Vehicles—all kinds of vehicles can be considered as devices that enhance gameplay. (See also Chapter 18, "Travel.")
- Clocks can be used simply to remind the player about the time, especially in games with time-pressure events. (See also Chapter 29, "Time Limits and Time Manipulation.") But also, imagine that the clock was actually the key to time travel or a way to unlock a secret door, by setting it to a particular time, or in fact it controlled a bomb that needed to be disarmed.
- Mystery devices can easily be inserted into games, and their uses could vary greatly. Some might be used to influence people, for instance, or to spy on them. Or they might be weapons of great power or controllers for the physical environment. A special device might be used to control an army of robots or to open/close cell doors in a prison. The possibilities are endless.
- Computers can be used in hundreds of ways. I imagine you can think of a few.
- Besides the more obvious devices, what could you do with an electric can-opener, a blender, or a microwave oven?
- Devices don't need to be realistic. What about a device that translates any language? Or a device that heals all wounds or resurrects the dead? These have been done already. But what about a device that can pack a house inside a pill-sized container?

Sudden Responsibilities

Sometimes a character is forced into a position of sudden responsibility or required to accomplish tasks for which he may feel he is not qualified. The stereotypical example is the kid who must save the world in many early Role-Playing Games. Armed with a wooden sword, he must go out and conquer the greatest menace the world has ever faced. The odds seem stacked against him, yet he prevails. Frodo's burden of the Ring is similar. The puzzle here is, how does the character accomplish his goals? The answer depends on whether this is a long-range puzzle or a short-term one. If the character suddenly has to put out a fire singlehandedly, it is short term. If it is Frodo's Ring quest, it is long term, and the solution is embedded in the entire story. Sudden responsibilities could be considered a scenario (see Chapter 11, "Scenarios") more than a puzzle, but what makes it a puzzle is when you have to figure out how to deal with the sudden responsibilities.

Examples include:

- You are suddenly given the care of a young child. You must escort the child safely to a location. Or perhaps you simply have to take the child with you, and you have no idea what to do with it.
- You are exploring a location when suddenly it catches fire. You know something important is there, so instead of fleeing, you try to put the fire out.
- You go to talk to an NPC, and he tells you that the town/world/some person is in danger and only you can prevent a catastrophe. Now it's up to you to figure out how to save the day.
- The pilot of a plane dies or goes unconscious. You'll have to fly the plane to safety, which means you'll have to figure out how to fly—or die. Parachutes? Not on this plane.
- You're suddenly appointed to be a U.S. Senator or you become the ruler of a country suddenly, in the midst of a crisis (of course).

Sudden Loss of Power

Sometimes a character becomes powerful by the attainment of special powers or the acquisition of powerful weapons and/or armor. As the game progresses, the character becomes dependent on this power, but if circumstances change, and the character suddenly loses the power of weapons or abilities, what then? This sort of puzzle requires the character to find a way to prevail when suddenly gimped and comparatively helpless. In some scenarios, the obvious solution will be to regain what has been lost. In others, it may require playing in the weakened state for some time, perhaps regaining powers and/or weapons over time.

Examples include:

- You are in contact with something or in an area that weakens you and removes certain abilities.
- Your weapons and/or armor have been stolen or destroyed.
- You are under a spell or curse that affects your abilities.
- You are suffering from amnesia.
- You have gone back in time to when you hadn't yet gained the abilities you've gotten used to.
- You've taken a solemn vow not to use your powers ever again.
- You are wearing a device that will kill you or incapacitate you if you use your powers.
- If you use your abilities or powers, someone important to you will be killed.

Whodunit

The whodunit model is basically to pose a mystery and then discover its cause and method, and sometimes, in order to do that, you have to consider suspects and motive. A mystery of this kind can conform to the ordinary murder mystery genre; however, the concept also works with just about any mystery, even if the cause of it isn't a person or being. A deserted village poses a mystery of its own, and it may not be the result of foul play or other intentional misdeed. It might, for instance, be that the villagers discovered a better location and simply packed up and moved. In many Role-Playing and adventure games, there are multiple mysteries to solve. Some are a large part of the ongoing plot, while others are merely side quests that pose a diversion and usually result in some incremental reward once solved.

Some examples include:

- Someone has disappeared, and you are asked to find him.
- Someone has died under mysterious circumstances, and you must figure out how he died (and who did it, if applicable).
- The crops are failing for no apparent reason.
- The sun has stopped shining. All is dark.
- All the children in the village have fallen into a deep sleep and cannot be awakened.
- The dogs are meowing, and the cats are barking.
- Something has disappeared (it doesn't matter what, as long as it is something that has been noticed).

Mental Puzzles

Some puzzles require a lot of concentration and mental effort, such as:

- Spotting the difference
- Fitting pieces together
- Arranging and ordering (configurations)
- Finding what's wrong
- Chinese puzzle boxes
- Sudoku
- Chess games (and similar mental games)
- Matching patterns

PUZZLE-BASED GAMES

For the most part, the specific puzzle types in the previous section were situational events that would most often be contained within a larger game context. However, many games are based on simple puzzle concepts, and their entire game structure depends on that puzzle. Games such as *Tetris*, *Bejeweled*, and other similar games have come to be known as puzzle games.

Puzzle games rely primarily on relating puzzle pieces spatially, basing alignment generally on shape, color, and various alignment options. Some puzzle games contain a significant element of time pressure, while others are meant to be brain teasers that can be played in a leisurely fashion. Some, such as *Bejeweled*, contain a non-timed mode and a couple of time-pressure modes that increase the challenge and create added tension.

People may argue over what defines a puzzle game. For instance, is *Tetris* a puzzle game or an arcade game? What about *Breakout* or *Qix*? Is there a difference between an arcade/action game and an arcade/puzzle game? Where do you draw the line? Does a requirement for manual dexterity determine the difference? For instance, is *Qix* more of a puzzle game than *Q*Bert*? Clearly *Shanghai* is a matching puzzle game, but what about a board game such as *Scrabble*?

Whatever the definition, it's clear that certain elements and options can be found in puzzle games. The following list includes many of the elements that are found in puzzle games, although not necessarily in each of them:

- Matching by color
- Matching by shape
- Aligning pieces
- Constructing or reconstructing an image
- Creating or recognizing patterns
- Moving pieces
- Rotating pieces
- Changing the shape or color of pieces
- Spotting differences
- Memorizing
  - Shapes
  - Order or position of objects
  - Picture details
  - Words and/or numbers
  - Sounds
- Trading positions
- Selecting pieces
- Time pressure
- Wordplay
  - Crossword puzzles
  - Linking letters to form words
  - Word recognition
  - Anagrams
  - Trivia and facts
- Eliminating pieces
- Follow the leader (Simon Says)
- Special scoring bonuses
  - Match more than three
  - Create additional matches
  - Finishing quickly
  - Special pieces (see below)
  - Special configurations
  - Longer-word formation
  - "Secret"-word formation
- Puzzle pieces with special abilities or meaning
  - Wildcard pieces
  - Extra score pieces
  - Extra turn pieces
  - Special ability pieces
  - Extra time pieces
- Capture of space (ownership and/or control)
- Filling or emptying of spaces
- Calculations (mathematical)
- Combos
- Planning and strategy
- Speed sessions
- No timer sessions
- Multiplayer puzzles (competition or cooperation)
- Finding differences/exceptions in an ordered system
- Generally short-duration gameplay instances
- Infinite replayability
- Scoring and high scores
- Sound and visual cues
- Often single-player, though they can be multiplayer

Codes and Cryptography

One type of puzzle that has its roots in ancient history is the use of ciphers of various kinds. I'm using the word "cipher" to define a secret system for conveying information. Historically, information has been hidden in many ways:

- In text containing transposed letters
- In text containing letters shifted according to a certain formula
- In text using certain words or phrases to represent important information (phrase substitution)
- In text that could only be read with a mechanical device encoded with the correct "key" or built to specific standards (code sticks, digital and analog machinery)
- In monographs or other complex designs
- In pictures, using representational images and colors to convey secret information and meaning
- Using color codes
- Using hand signals

In addition, game designers may create new languages, such as a symbolic language of an alien race or a language based on runes or other symbols. Although not technically a cipher, such "new" languages can be used in the same way—to make information available, but only to those who can decipher their meaning.

Of course, riddles are also a sort of code—a way of conveying information in an obscure form that must be deciphered.

Most language-based codes are easily cracked using techniques such as frequency analysis, which can make pretty good guesses about the meaning of the coded text based on the general frequency of letters in the language the text was originally written in. For instance, in English, the mnemonic ETAOIN SHRDLU lists the most commonly used letters in order of general frequency. Simply by doing a general count of the occurrence of letters in a coded text and applying the letter "E" for instance to the most common letter and "T" to the second most common, you have a good chance of discovering some of the letters. Of course, if the first try doesn't seem useful, you can continue to try other letters. Eventually, you will most likely solve the puzzle. There are also systems of analysis that take into account common letter combinations—bigrams and trigrams. For instance, in English the letter Q is very rarely seen without a following U.

Other types of codes require that you have a "key" to the solution—either a physical device that can be used to translate the message or the necessary information that describes the solution. For instance, some codes simply use meaningless phrases in place of the real information. For example, the famous Paul Revere phrase, "one if by land; two if by sea" was a code understood only to the American revolutionary leaders. A phrase such as "the day is dawning bright" might mean "attack at dawn," but it could just as easily mean "wait until night." Only someone who has a list of the phrase definitions would understand this code, although it can be cracked by obtaining the list or even by observation over time. Of course, most wartime codes were changed frequently and only specific information about the "keys" was distributed on a "need to know" basis.

Using code puzzles in games should be done with some restraint. Not everybody enjoys poring over a text message and trying to do a frequency analysis or spending an hour searching for meaning in a series of obscure images. However, coded documents and images can be fun and can add some mystery and intrigue to a game. The key is to make it clear to the player that a solution can be found, possibly somewhere in the environment or from a specific NPC. Another way to deal with codes is to drop hints and clues along the way so that the player slowly gains the knowledge required to solve the puzzle.

Codes might also be incorporated into the players' bag of tricks. For instance, players might be able to send coded messages to characters in a single-player game. The game might be designed to require that the player use a specific "key" to code messages and prevent enemies from intercepting them. Or, in a Massive Multiplayer Game, player guilds might use coded messages that could be intercepted by the enemy but would not be easy to translate or understand.

Modern cryptography is based primarily on mathematics, and it gets very complex very quickly. Although a game that really delves into the arcane world of modern cryptography might be interesting, it will probably be the case that game designers will use modern mathematical methods as sort of black boxes for use within their games, if they use such concepts at all. Going into a lot of detail about data encryption standards and other modern systems would be far too intellectual and complex for most game players. However, having such systems exist in a game world seems perfectly feasible. But if any players are going to attempt to encrypt and decrypt modern coded messages, they would employ sophisticated computer equipment available within the game environment to do so.

A Puzzle Story

Here's a brief story that uses and identifies many of these types of puzzles....

Alfred is a stable boy, an orphan who one day finds himself imprisoned in his very stables with most of the residents of his village. A band of brigands has taken over the village and is preparing to steal all it has of value, then set it on fire, including the stables with all the villagers inside.

Alfred must first figure out how to escape. He does so by Putting Pieces Together and fashioning a rope and hook from wire that he slips over the doorway and uses to lift the bar that holds them captive.

Next, he must find the Missing Person—the village elder or mage. But to do so, he must make a Hard Choice by leaving the rest of the villagers imprisoned. He must slip out and replace the bar across the door. If he does not do so, the enemy will surely discover that the villagers have escaped. When Alfred finds the village mage, he is being guarded by two minions, who Alfred must deal with. There are several options, ranging from disabling them or killing them to fooling them in some way.

Alfred has no way to kill them, so he has to figure out how to Get It Right.... What will get them out of the way? He might call a false alarm. He might walk in and pretend to be one of them, then tell them they are needed elsewhere. Or he might bring them some strong drink, let them get intoxicated, and then slip the mage out from under their drunken noses.

Once the mage has been freed, he tells Alfred that he cannot defeat this menace without a magical scepter (or something like that), which has been hidden in a cave near the village for many centuries, just for such an occasion. Of course, the mage cannot go himself, so Alfred must Retrieve the Item.

Alfred finds the cave without trouble, but it is guarded by a series of Barriers that open by means of Buttons and Switches operated in a certain order and by Keys found in special chests. Alfred finds some weapons and armor in the cave and uses them to fight the monsters that guard the doors. Various pictographic clues indicate the Order and Configuration of the final series of levers that open the alcove containing the scepter.

While he is exploring the caves, he sees, on a high ledge, a marvelous-looking chest. It must contain something of great value, but he can't get to it. This Obscure Object of Desire taunts him as he returns the way he came. In a sudden moment of Thinking Outside the Box, he tries using the scepter, and it allows him to float up to the chest. Within it is a jewel-encrusted sword—a magnificent weapon. Wielding the sword, he feels stronger, quicker, and healthier than he ever has before.

But as soon as he hefts the weapon, hordes of enemies pour from the very stone walls around him, and he is in a fight for his life. The enemies keep coming as he hacks his way, Managing the Chaos, to the entrance of the cave. Once he steps out, the attacks end, and he is free.

Alfred hurries back to the village to the mage's hideaway. When he gets there, he finds the mage has been killed. Although he is convinced that the brigands could never have defeated the mage so easily, he has no idea who might have done the deed. He suspects an inside job or someone very powerful. This begins a Whodunit sequence. But it also means that Alfred must shoulder the Sudden Responsibility for the village and find a way to wield the scepter.

Luckily for Alfred, the mage has left him a clue in the form of a Riddle:

"Three become one and one becomes many
When up is down and down is up.
Front to back is not to be seen.
The longer is stronger
And the shorter comes closer
And a turn at the top
Is the difference..."

The riddle, once translated, means that Alfred must find two allies for the scepter to create a magical army when it's held upside down; that the scepter can be lengthened or shortened, changing the effectiveness of a spell; pointing the scepter at oneself will cause invisibility; and, finally, that the top can be twisted to change the outcome of the spell. But this is all for Alfred to figure out, and the first thing he needs are two allies.

Alfred returns to the stables and sneaks back inside. He asks the Mayor for help, but the Mayor looks down on him because he's a stable boy, and he suspects Alfred of having killed the mage somehow and being in cahoots with the baddies. The Mayor's daughter, Miya, tells him privately that she believes in him and joins his party. They need to find one more person to join them, and nobody is volunteering.

Together, Alfred and Miya leave the village in search of someone who will believe them. Miya has heard of a wild boy who lives in the forest by himself. They decide he might join them, so they go in search of him (Missing Persons). The boy also becomes, in some ways, a Key to unlock the power of the scepter.

Miya says she has seen the boy down by a small pond, picking murkberries, so she suggests they get some murkberries on their way to the pond. At this point, the game turns into a Scavenger Hunt to find enough murkberries to tempt the boy. You are already involved in a Sequence of Tasks puzzle with the ultimate goal of getting rid of the brigands. However, now you are also on a Sequence of Tasks to activate the scepter and yet another to obtain the murkberries for the boy. Charted out it looks like this:

Goal: Defeat the Brigands and Free the Villagers

- Sequence of Tasks using puzzle types from this chapter:
    1. Escape
    2. Putting Pieces Together
    3. Get Help
    4. Find the Missing Person (village mage)
    5. Hard Choice (leave the rest of the village in captivity)
    6. Save the Mage
    7. Get It Right (free the mage)
    8. Obtain the Scepter
    9. Get Past the Barriers/Buttons and Switches/Keys
    10. Order and Configuration
    11. Obscure Object of Desire
    12. Thinking Outside the Box
    13. Manage the Chaos

14. Sudden Responsibilities: The Mage Is Dead
15. Whodunit
16. Activate the Scepter
17. Solve Riddle
18. Sequence of Tasks: Find Two Allies
19. Sequence of Tasks: Miya Joins
20. Missing Persons, Creatures, or Things: Find the Boy
21. Scavenger Hunt (get the murkberries)
22. Return to Village
23. Confront Leader
24. Solve Whodunit (who killed the mage)
25. Use the Scepter
26. Vanquish the enemy

So Miya and the hero find the wild boy, and he joins them after eating a substantial portion of murkberries. Returning to the village, Alfred confronts the leader of the brigands and warns him to leave or suffer the consequences. When the bad guys refuse to move, Alfred works the scepter, standing with Miya and the wild boy. A magical army appears and vanquishes the brigands. The village is free and safe again...but this is only the beginning of the story, of course. More significant adventures await Alfred and his friends....

Puzzle Maker

Note: Chapters that would be of significant help in creating puzzles are Chapter 9, "Storytelling Techniqes," Chapter 11, "Scenarios," Chapter 23, "Goals," Chapter 24, "Rewards, Bonuses, and Penalties," Chapter 25, "Barriers, Obstacles, and Detectors," and Chapter 26, "Traps and Counter Traps."

Puzzles are generally comprised of situations and solutions. In a game, a puzzle can be almost anything that challenges the player to think and seek a solution. So it can be a locked door or chest or a group of enemies up ahead. It can be an apparently uncrossable chasm or an obstinate NPC who won't give you/tell you what you need.

In most cases, you'll start with a situation, such as one of those just mentioned. However, the situation itself is less relevant than the specific goal you seek, whether it is information, someone's death, an important object, or simply to open a door.

Goals, however, can often entail multiple steps—multiple smaller puzzles. For instance, if your goal is to rescue a hostage, the steps you might have to take could include a) sneaking into the prison, b) defeating or getting past the guard, c) locating the hostage, d) unlocking the cell, and e) getting the hostage out safely (which might entail several more steps). Each of these steps is actually a separate puzzle. For instance, to sneak into the prison, you might bribe a guard, kill a guard, find a back door, climb a wall, or get yourself intentionally captured in disguise.

Each of the methods you might use is dependent on the situation, but some methods can be used in more than one puzzle. Bribing or killing a guard, for instance, might be useful in a variety of situations. Climbing or finding an alternate route, using a disguise...all of these are methods that might be useful in other situations.

So now we have specific goals that might pertain to more than one situation and specific methods that might pertain to the attainment of more than one goal. There is one more aspect of many puzzles, which is the kinds of objects, skills, or tools that are needed. For instance, in some puzzles you must trigger a device that opens a door, for instance, and then make it to the door before it closes again. Imagine how helpful a speed spell or item might be in this case, or someone to help you by triggering the door while you stand there ready to go through it. As another example, what you need might be as simple as obtaining a key to open a lock. The key is necessary, however, so it is an object that provides the means to complete the puzzle, although obtaining the key itself may involve one or more specific puzzle situations.

Essentially, we have goals, methods, and means (in the form of tools, skills, and objects). To use my Puzzle Maker, then, you can simply:

1. Identify a situation.
2. Pick an applicable goal.
3. Select one or more methods that can be used.
4. Select the tools, skills, and/or objects needed to accomplish the method(s).

Note that sometimes something that can be a goal can also be a method. For instance, in some situations, the goal is to kill someone, and you must find out what method will work—such as poisoning, shooting, trapping, or tricking. These would be methods. But suppose you needed to get into a guarded building. In that case, perhaps killing the guard is a method and also a goal, because killing the guard becomes a situation in its own right, so a method must be found to kill that guard. But killing the guard is still the method you are using to gain entry to the building. Confusing? Try a few examples, and you'll soon see that it's clear when something is a goal or a method, even if they sound the same.

Goals

Goals are what must be accomplished. Someone needs to die. A door needs to be opened. You must obtain certain information. For each situation you have created in your game, pick a goal. What does the player need to accomplish?

- Open something.
- Destroy something.
- Find/obtain an object.
- Kill something/someone.
- Repair and/or activate something.
- Assemble or invent something.
- Discover some information.
- Get somebody's cooperation.
- Escape from something.
- Get to a place.
- Beat the clock.
- Stay safe/alive/unharmed.
- Set a trap.
- Avoid a trap.
- Get somewhere before someone else does (race to the finish line).
- Make money (usually an intermediate goal leading to something you need the money for—weapons and armor, to buy a house, to pay back a debt, to pay a ransom, to pay for food, etc.).

Methods You Might Use

How will the player attain his or her goal? What methods might work in the situation you have created? For instance, to operate a sequence of levers to open a vault, players might use Trial and Error, or they might obtain information from an NPC who knows the answer, or even blow the thing up (the Destruction option).

In designing a puzzle, you might want to offer more than one method to accomplish any given goal. For instance, the previous example listed three possible solutions. You could think of more if you like. It's certainly more interesting if there are multiple ways to accomplish your goals.

In addition, some methods create new situations. For instance, if you want to obtain information about the proper sequence to use in the example with the levers, you create a new situation. Perhaps the information is located elsewhere in the environment you're in. So you might try Search and Explore. Or the information you need is known only to a specific NPC. So you might need to use Persuasion (after you locate the NPC). Using the Puzzle Maker can be recursive, and you can design puzzles within puzzles as well as puzzles with multiple solutions.

What methods might you choose as solutions (or partial solutions) to your puzzles? Some suggestions:

- Destruction
- Construction
- Repair or activate something
- Circumvention
- Sequence of actions
- Search and explore
- Sneak and steal
- Information
- Guess
- Risk
- Trial and error
- Aim something
- Balance something
- Reveal something
- Get help
- Flying
- Digging
- Swimming
- Jumping
- Climbing
- Camouflage
- Persuasion

Tools, Skills, and Objects

The environment and the skills and tools of the player often come into play when you are designing puzzles. Once you have a goal and one or more methods, then you might need to determine the means by which the method(s) will be carried out. Again, the player will employ objects from the environment or skills and tools they either have already or can gain. Once again, as with methods, if a tool or skill is not currently in the player's possession, then a recursive nested puzzle situation is probably created. The simplest example is the goal of opening a chest. The method is to unlock it, and what is needed is a key (object), an unlock spell (skill), or a lock-pick (tool).

I've included a few ideas below, but because the range of possible objects, skills, and tools is, if not limitless, at least very large, this list is necessarily little more than a suggestion. You can use Chapter 15, "Character Abilities," and Chapter 19, "Objects and Locations" for more ideas and examples of tools, skills, and objects.

- Keys
- Guns
- Cannons
- Moveable objects
- Stackable objects
- Objects that float or sink
- Throwable objects
- Levers
- Buttons
- Pressure plates
- Doors
- Locks
- Computers
- Bombs
- Telekinesis
- Super speed
- Money
- Riddles and other clues
- Alarms
- Traps (physical/magical)
- Detectors
- Puzzle pieces

- Other characters
- Herbs
- Potions
- Magical spells
- Trapdoors
- Locked doors
- Regular doors
- Hidden doors and passages

Output

In order to make sense of puzzles created this way, it helps to put them in some kind of organized form. Here's a suggestion, though you may want to develop your own style.

Note that in many cases the means used to accomplish the task may generate another situation, method, and means. You can include these new situations and solutions within this outline, but it will soon get very hard to read. Another possibility is to name the new situation. For instance, in the following example I will describe a generic encounter with a locked chest. Clearly, if you don't have certain items—for instance, a key—and you decide (or are forced) to use a key to open the chest, then you must have a key. If you don't have the necessary key, then you must obtain one, and this sets up a new situation. In this case, then, you might use a specific name for the item ("ChestKey1") and possibly a marker text, such as using italics for items or methods that can generate new situations/puzzles of their own, as in *ChestKey1*.

However, it may turn out that just about any object, tool, or skill, and many methods as well, can generate new situations. So you may simply want to keep those situations separate, but name each puzzle type uniquely so you can call them from within other puzzle descriptions. In the following example, we'll call the first puzzle "GenericChest" and the "find the key" puzzle, "GenericKey." There would mostly likely be a "GetLockpick" subtask and possibly others generated from this simple situation description.

GenericChest

Situation: The player has come across a chest. It seems to be locked.

Methods and Required Means: The first level is the method, and the second-level lists describe possible means to implement the method:

- Pick the lock
  - Lock-pick (GetLockpick)
  - Open-lock spell
- Use a key
  - Key (GenericKey)
- Break it
  - Use a hammer or fists or another type of weapon or tool
- Take it with you (not a common option, but could be implemented)
- Burn it
  - Use a fire spell
  - Use a blowtorch
  - Use a match

Design Challenge

1. Look at your favorite games and notice the puzzles you encounter when playing them. Many games have puzzles that you would not necessarily notice at first, but, in fact, many of the challenges you face are some kind of puzzle.
   a. Notice the roles of puzzles in these games and compare the puzzles you find to the puzzles in this chapter.
   b. Can you find some that aren't mentioned here?
2. Consider different types of games, such as First-Person and Third-Person Shooters and adventure games, Real-Time Strategy games, arcade games, fighting games, and so on.
   a. What kinds of puzzles can you use in each of these types of games?
   b. How and when would you use them?
   c. Are there any types of puzzles that you could not use in a specific type of game?
3. Take any of your own game designs and consider the role that puzzles would play in them.
   a. Do your puzzle ideas layer, such that you have puzzles within puzzles within puzzles?

Section D Time

28 Controlling Pacing

> Concentration is so intense that there is no attention left over to think about anything irrelevant, or to worry about problems. Self-consciousness disappears, and the sense of time becomes distorted. An activity that produces such experiences is so gratifying that people are willing to do it for its own sake, with little concern for what they will get out of it, even when it is difficult or dangerous.
> —Mihaly Csikszentmihalyi, *Flow: The Psychology of Optimal Experience* (Harper Perennial, 1991)

This chapter is all about the way we experience time and intensity in games, what we call the pace of the game. The chapter contains the following sections:

- Introduction to Pacing
- Interest Level and Goals
- Does Focus Equal Pacing?
- Activity Levels
- Emotional Impact
- Intensity
- Pacing by Genre
- Pacing of the Game Experience

See also Chapter 29, "Time Limits and Time Manipulation," for some related ideas.

Introduction to Pacing

Each game provides a unique experience. Some involve intense action, while others may have sequences of story development and exploration interspersed with action sequences. Some may have almost nothing that you would describe as "action." Some games keep you in suspense, then suddenly propel you into a demanding and frenetic situation. Others keep up a pretty constant pace, with brief moments between waves, levels, missions, and so on.

Games use different methods to achieve these effects and to control, to some extent, the experience of the player. One of these ways is to plan for different levels of intensity and pressure as the game is played. For instance, in a classic First-Person Shooter, you feel the pressure of the hunt and the hunted. You are sneaking around this very dangerous place, but for long periods, nothing may happen at all. Then, suddenly, you are in a furious battle with guns blazing. When it is over, assuming you are still alive, you go back to the hunter/hunted pace. If your health is low, you will be desperately seeking a medpak while avoiding new confrontations. The game has sections that are flat but full of tension and anticipation, followed by spikes of intense action. The intensity of the game almost never lets up, but the level of action peaks from time to time. It is almost entirely in the user's control, however. Picking a safe location, the player can be safe and even experience a total downturn in tension and activity for extended periods. Once he begins to explore again, the tension returns. This is just one example of effective pacing.

Pacing is important for various reasons. It can provide structure or unpredictability to a game, depending on how it's used. It also creates and maintains tension and anticipation, interest levels, and variations of focus and activity, which, combined, provide an enjoyable experience. With good design, a game need never become boring.

The pacing needs of games are not all the same because game players aren't all the same. For some people, the ideal pace is a game that is intense from start to finish, such as an online death match in an FPS game. Others may prefer a game such as a typical RPG, in which you explore at leisure, with little pressure, only occasionally encountering a very intense experience or a pressured situation. In the FPS example, it doesn't require much to keep players interested and focused. If they don't want to die and be humiliated, they are involved every second of the match. In the RPG example, the story drives players forward, or the promise of some reward for completing a quest or mission. Only on occasion does the intensity reach the same life-or-death intensity of the FPS, but the players look forward to it!

I once heard it described that humans like to guess things subliminally, meaning they get a "feeling" when the next action sequence or reward will be coming up. They are more than happy to wait until then, as long as they are right a reasonable amount of the time. (They actually don't want to be right all the time.) This anticipation and reward can quickly add to the addictiveness of the game. It's like waiting for the long brick in *Tetris*, which is the key to a *Tetris* match. You get a feel for when it's likely to show up, when it feels right...about now...when you really need it, and when it shows up just in time. That cycle of anticipation adds to the experience. In an MMO, it's revealed when people grind, when they repetitively kill the same monsters, trying to anticipate when they will get rewarded with a rare drop or a particular item they need.

In an RTS, the pressure can actually be constant. You are in a mad rush, developing technologies or units, exploring, seeking and stockpiling resources, mounting attacks against the enemy or fending them off, and so on. The pace could best be described as ramping up from already very busy to hectic. Contrast that with a Turn-Based Strategy game, such as *Civilization*, or board games, such as *Settlers of Catan*, in which there is ultimately a lot going on but the pace is leisurely, because you can think between turns. But even in a turn-based game, situations develop in which the intensity of your choices increases. Perhaps your units are being threatened or you are about to launch a major attack on the enemy—something you have been planning for a dozen moves. The intensity seems higher at that point. Is the pace also higher then? What compels you to play just one more turn?

Interest Level and Goals

As it is in literature, theater, and cinema, pacing in games is often provided in the story setup and/or the dialog as well as the action, and also in the emotional intensity of the scenes. It is your level of interest in what happens next that keeps you going.

Put another way, pacing is a measure of how compelling the entertainment is and how it may go through different stages of intensity. So another way of seeing pacing at work is thinking about how driven you are to move forward through the game or story. Looking at it this way, pacing could be related to goals. The more compelling (and important) your current goals are, the higher the pace. If this were graphed, then a good game or story would always have a pace line well above the zero coordinate, but it would spike to much higher levels periodically. Depending on the type of game, the duration of the intensity spikes would vary from very short to long. On some graphs, the spikes would be almost continuous. In others, they would be separated by very long periods of "baseline" interest.

Does Focus Equal Pacing?

Another way of looking at pacing is to think about focus. In a very tense situation, where there could be an enemy around every corner or where you are fighting for your life against essentially constant attacks, your focus must be very intense to survive and avoid a deadly mistake. However, during a typical dialog scene, you may be on the lookout for clues, but you can relax your focus somewhat. So one possible measure of the pace of a game is how much focus you require at any given point. This is not the only way to look at it, however. You might need a lot of focus to look for some tiny, rare, but important item. If you spent a lot of time searching for this item without having to battle any enemies, the game might feel somewhat dull, and despite the fact that you had to focus pretty hard to find the elusive object, the pace would seem slow. Still, in life-or-death situations, your focus has to be amplified, which is why it might be used to measure pace. How focused does a player have to be at any given time while playing the game? Think about games you've played and compare your level of focus at different stages of the game.

"Okay, so how do I use pacing in my game?" I hear you asking. I will point out a lot of different uses, but if you only take away one thing from this entire chapter, it should be that you must sit down and look at the spikes you will put this gamer through—the emotional highs and lows. Make sure there are a lot of both, and make sure that when the player thinks they've experienced a high, there's actually a much higher high coming! That's really the point. Okay, now let's continue....

Activity Levels

Another way to measure the pace from the player's point of view might be something we can call the *activity level.* Clearly, if you are battling 100 enemies or working on a fast-moving assembly line, you will be performing many actions very quickly. You may be punching buttons or keys at a furious rate. Activity levels are highest when action is highest, and when activity levels are high, so, generally, is a player's focus. So, activity level, as seen from the player's point of view, may be another guide to the pacing of the game.

Emotional Impact

In Chapter 30, "Ways to Communicate with the Player," there is a section called "Emotion." The emotional impact of a game also determines the level of immersion the player has. As with a good movie, emotions can shift, moving to all extremes—comedy to tragedy, for instance—and through all emotions in between. How do we experience times of elation versus times of deep sadness or mourning? How do we experience the rush of fear versus the glow of victory? By carefully crafting a game's emotional timeline, we can further affect the pace—the perception of the experience.

There are any number of ways to impact a player's emotional responses, including story-based techniques, specific gameplay elements, and ambient elements, such as music and sound effects, lighting effects, and even changes in graphical style. For instance, the mood in a crystal city probably is different from the mood in a dank sewer or a poorly lit alleyway.

In the "Emotion" section in Chapter 30, "Ways to Communicate with the Player," we go into some detail about how we evoke emotional responses in players. Likewise, in Chapter 9, "Storytelling Techniques," you can refer to sections on "Creating Comedy" and "Making Things Scary" for more ideas on emotion in games.

INTENSITY

Putting the pieces together, pacing could equal some magical combination of:

- **Interest Level/Goals.** This helps a game achieve a high baseline pace and keeps a player absorbed and involved.
- **Action/Activity Level.** This measures the current player's level of activity and the game's action component. Depending on the type of game, this kind of experience is used to increase the intensity and the pace.
- **Focus.** This measures how involved the player is at any given time in the game. Focus generally accompanies periods of intense action, but focus can also be high during times of less intense action.
- **Emotional Impact.** This is a measure of the emotional timeline of the game, showing as best we can the anticipated experience the player will have emotionally in response to the unfolding game adventure. In some games, this would be a non-factor; however, in others it can be very important. In games where there are deeper stories, significant events, tragedy, comedy, surprise, fear, and other strong emotions, this becomes all the more significant in determining the overall impression the player will have and the subjective assessment of the pace of the game.
- **Overall Intensity of Experience.** In essence, taking all other factors, how intense is the experience the player is having at any given time? As the overall intensity level peaks and fades, the pace changes. Again, there is no one ideal pace for any game, but some genres suggest more constant overall intensity, while others benefit from a more varied pace.

PACING BY GENRE

Although some elements of pacing are common to most games, each type of game may achieve pacing in different ways. One quick warning about loading screens: They can actually have a negative score on pacing, meaning they can hurt the experience (negative equals boredom!), so on good games, the loading screens often give you some info (such as a goal, some story update, a new move, key functionality, your latest stats) or something to at least distract you while you wait for loading to happen.

The following sections discuss some of the ways that pacing is controlled, listed by genre.

ACTION GAMES (PLATFORM, ARCADE, FPS)

Platform games are generally all about action, and players of platformers are generally looking for a pretty high-intensity experience. So in a platform action game, there's rarely a complete lull in the action. There may be occasional scenes, and there's the respite that is offered at the end of a level, when you may get some score information and a setup for the next level. But during each level, there will only occasionally be moments when you can stop all together, and some platform games don't allow you to stop even for a moment—because a clock is ticking, because a relentless enemy is chasing you, or because the environment is changing, such as platforms that fall if you stand on them too long or a room with walls that are closing in on you.

- **Constant Pressure.** There are several types of action, even in action games. There is the kind of game in which there's no time at all to stop, but you must play at full speed to complete the level, defeat the enemy, and/or avoid the enemies and obstacles. This kind of game has a constant high level of intensity. Good examples are *Space Invaders*, *Donkey Kong*, *Lode Runner*, and *Zaxxon*. First-Person Shooters in multiplayer mode tend to be like this as well, depending on what role you choose to play in the contest. Many arcade games ramp up the level of pressure over time. (See the upcoming Escalating Events and Shrinking Worlds bullet.) Classic examples are *Space Invaders* and *Missile Command*, which started with a certain amount of manageable pressure and, over time, became so difficult that more often than not, it was only a matter of time before you were defeated.

- **Enemies and Bosses.** Some action games feature a lot of incidental action followed by larger battles, perhaps culminating with a boss battle. In these games, there is generally a pretty high intensity throughout, with spikes of activity on occasion and a generally frenetic battle against some massive creature that takes a long time to defeat. During boss battles, the intensity of action and the intensity of focus generally increase and stay elevated for longer periods of time than they do with normal battles. In this way, the pace of the game peaks when you fight a boss. After defeating the boss, intensity drops, and you get an often well-deserved opportunity to rest, recover, and celebrate victory.
- **Action with Some Strategy.** Some action games also contain elements of strategy or moments of quiet. Such moments are generally provided in safe locations, where the player can prepare for the next sequence, power up or heal, or enter into a stealth sequence. The pacing of this kind of game is different from that of more pure action games in that it allows you to escape the intensity for moments, rest, and prepare for the next phase.
- **Sneaking and Fighting.** Many games these days control intensity by creating an atmosphere of danger in which the player must be stealthy and move carefully, picking the time and location for battle whenever possible. A full-on attack without care will often result in disaster. Examples include *Thief*, *Abe's Oddysee*, and the *Metal Gear Solid* series.
- **Sense of Urgency.** In most action games there is a sense of urgency, even if there is no clock ticking. There's often no real urgency, but it's implied in the structure or back story of the game. In any case, players approach these types of games expecting a high intensity curve. For more on this, see Chapter 29, "Time Limits and Time Manipulation."
- **Escalating Events and Shrinking Worlds.** Another way that pacing in action games can increase is to have the intensity of action increase due to changes in the situation. A classic example of this would be the famous conveyor-belt scene from the old *I Love Lucy* show, where the belt suddenly speeds up, and the previously routine repetitive task Lucy is supposed to perform becomes impossible, but she keeps trying. In games, this can be accomplished by rate increases, such as having the blocks fall faster in *Tetris*, or by shrinking the available space in which the player can operate, thereby increasing the intensity of concentration and action. This also happens in *Tetris* as the space fills up and there's less time to react to each falling block. However, these effects can also appear in games with 2D or 3D representational worlds, using the same methods.
- **Level Break.** Players of high-intensity action games get a break between levels. This is the time to save the game and get ready for more. Presumably, the game will get harder with each succeeding level. Of course, some games, such as *Space Invaders*, *Defender*, and *Missile Command*, give you mere moments to get ready for the next level, while other games may give you a short cut scene or a level summary screen where you can linger somewhat and choose when to begin the next round.
- **Other Changes.** When you introduce significant changes in a game, the pace certainly changes. For instance:
  - If the difficulty suddenly increases, the player must focus and work harder to succeed. Likewise, if the number of enemies suddenly increases or decreases, the player feels more or less challenged, respectively.
  - The story changes, introducing new plot elements, new challenges, or even major twists. You are suddenly using a different weapon or a different armor system. You become more or less powerful, or you must master a new type of attack/defense.
  - Camera viewpoints may change—for instance, changing point of view or which character's viewpoint you are using. Even this sort of change can affect how the game feels to play.

Changing, for instance, from a top-down view into a first-person view brings more immediacy to the game and changes the way it feels to navigate the game terrain.

- **No Safety.** This is simply when you take away the safe zones. For example, maybe they had a bunker but it's gone now. In the *Commando* arcade machine, if you stood still, someone would lob a grenade right at you. Having no safety really keeps you moving.

Battle Sims (Games That Involve Warlike Battle Simulations)

Battle simulation games also feature different types of pacing. This is often as a direct result of the type of battle simulation it is. For instance, a submarine game will generally have long periods of quiet—hunting for prey—followed by relatively brief experiences of attacking and then escaping any countermeasures—or moments of panic as the sub is discovered by anti-submarine ships or planes, and it's suddenly life or death. Military flight simulators (if at all realistic) will also have longer periods of flying around seeking the enemy or reaching the objective, followed by very intense battle sequences. Typical moments in battle simulations include those in the following two subsections.

In the Action

To many players, war simulations are at their best when the action is intense and constant, although many players also like games that alter the pace between strategy planning or stalking the enemy and flat-out action. At any rate, when you are immersed in the action, what are the elements of the game that can affect the pace of the experience?

- **Briefing and Preparation.** Many battle simulation games involve sequences of mission briefing and preparation. These sequences are low on the intensity scale but create a sense of realism and involvement, as well as a full understanding of what the mission entails.
- **Travel.** Once the mission is underway, there is generally a sequence of travel, as you move toward the objective. Travel sequences can be somewhat low on the intensity scale, but they are increased if there is a threat of danger along the way, and they spike if there is an unexpected battle en route. (Some of this stuff even works for deer hunting games.)
- **Reaching the Objective.** This is the crux of the matter. Once you reach the objective, the battle begins in earnest. This sequence raises the overall intensity level, and suddenly the pace speeds up.
- **Peak Battles.** Even during the main mission objective, the battle may ebb and flow, and there can be moments of calm within the storm. On occasion, however, players will find themselves in epic battles or in situations where they must fight especially hard to survive and achieve their goals. These are peak battles, and these are where the pace is at its most intense.
- **Ebb and Flow.** Pacing can be dramatically affected by changes in the situation; for instance, if the enemy is bringing reinforcements and you know that they will arrive in two hours (accelerated game time), or if you are planning an assault, but some of your own forces are delayed. Unexpected circumstances can also occur, such as the discovery that the intelligence info was wrong and the enemy wasn't where they were supposed to be, or they were stronger than anticipated, and so on. Or they may appear to be much weaker than expected, but lead you into a trap where you have to scramble in a high-intensity battle to survive (such as in the movie *The Last Samurai*).
- **Retreat.** At some point in a mission, you may have to retreat—regardless of whether the objective has been reached. Some mission-based games will end the mission once you have gained or lost the objective. In such games, there is no retreat. However, the retreat or withdrawal experience can remain intense, gradually decreasing in intensity.
- **Debrief.** This is a chance to assess the mission and set up the next. This is, once again, a low-intensity sequence.

- **All Action.** Although the various stages listed here are typical of simulation games, and they form a sort of arc of intensity, some simulation games dispense with the slower segments and place you right at the objective, where you will then engage in high-intensity action through most of the game. However, even in games that dispense with lengthy preparation and travel sequences, there can be pacing similar to the Sneaking and Fighting entry described in the "Action Games (Platform, Arcade, FPS)" section, where you must be wary and pick your battles carefully.

The General's Perspective

Some battle games actually place you in the role of the general, while the action takes place under your command. In such games, there is a different sort of urgency and pacing. In particular, ebb and flow (discussed a moment ago) play a significant role, as the battle may go through different stages, with advantage falling to either side at one time or another. All of the other aspects of battle simulations can occur in the General's Perspective, but the overall intensity may be slightly lower. On top of that, there is generally a strategic aspect to the game, perhaps assigning more specific importance to each battle or mission in the concept of an overall war plan. With such long-range goals, the intensity of each battle may be slightly less, though some battles are critical, and circumstances can either increase or reduce the amount of intensity experienced. For instance, if you know that losing a particular battle will make it impossible to win the war, then that battle takes on some added value, and its intensity is probably going to be maximal. However, if you know you've really won the war already and you're fighting a battle that, in reality, doesn't matter, then the intensity of the battle is likely to be lower.

RPGs and Adventures

RPGs and adventure games have very different pacing from more action-oriented games. They operate at a generally slower pace, with long periods of moderate intensity and occasional "mobs and bosses" types of encounters. They have a lot more times of exploration, dialog, and even shopping in which the pacing is downright leisurely. However, such games are not flat, and various methods are used to control pacing.

- **The Big Goal.** Long-range goal, low intensity. The achievement of the long-range goals of the game keep you moving through the game, so they add somewhat to the basic interest level.
- **Incremental Goals.** Short- to medium-range goals, including side quests—moderate to high intensity.
- **Surprise Encounters.** High intensity.
- **Timed Events.** Generally high intensity due to time pressure.
- **Anticipation.** Anticipation in the story can lead to an increased intensity, but the overall pace may still be slow.
- **Story and Emotion.** Story and emotional scenes can add to the player's investment in the outcome and therefore to the intensity of upcoming events, but the pace at this point is generally slow unless the scene is very active and intense, at which point it may be able to gain some of the pacing energy of a good movie or book. In terms of interactive pacing it may be slow, but in terms of story development it may create drama and new information, set up situations, or in some other way increase the game's pace.
- **Mobs and Bosses.** Large-scale fights and boss fights are always high intensity and increase the pace, in interactive terms.
- **Mini-Games.** Mini-games are generally (but not always) arcade-like sequences that are fast-paced and require focus, especially because they may use different rules and controls from the main game (meaning the player is less familiar with them and has to focus harder). However, in terms of game pace, they are also (usually) not related to furthering the story. So, while they may fit the definition of fast-paced content, the fact that they are essentially irrelevant at the same time slows the pace.

Some mini-games are not fast-paced at all. For instance, playing cards or chess (or chess-like games) as mini-games is definitely not fast-paced. Generally, mini-games are used as a break from the main game action. Exceptions exist. Some games use mini-games as part of the overall game design, and therefore they figure into the overall story pace of the game. And some mini-games really have an intensity of their own, so they could be considered a separate experience from the pace of the overall game—like playing a game as a vacation from a game.

- **Equipment or Ability Changes.** A game can feel quite different when your character is suddenly much stronger (or much weaker) or faster (or slower) than before. This can happen somewhat when achieving a new "level" and therefore new skills or better statistics. But most games attempt to moderate the amount of increase you get from one level to another. There can be what I call *plateau* levels—levels in which your character obtains some key ability or reaches a milestone that, in either case, alters the character's effectiveness significantly. Another way in which a character can suddenly seem stronger is by obtaining equipment that is much better than before and that might even have associated spells or abilities far beyond the character's current level. In any case, this sudden increase in ability, whatever the source, generally leads to excitement and anxiousness to go test the new skills. This is generally an especially rewarding part of any game, and therefore the pace seems to be faster.

  On the opposite side, a sudden loss of abilities or essential equipment can lead to an increased sense of danger and more focus and immersion. Though you can't plow through the enemy landscape as quickly as you did before, you must play smarter and more carefully. Caution can seem like a slower pace, but concentration and focus can turn a few minutes of play into hours....
- **Cut Scenes.** Generally, breaking to a cut scene slows the pace. The scene may be fascinating or simply necessary to complete plot elements. Occasionally, a cut scene is visually so far superior to the main game that it captures your attention. And don't you find yourself wishing the whole game looked like that? But overall, sitting through a cut scene—particularly one that isn't really interesting for some reason—slows the pace. You might sit through it because you're afraid you'll miss something important, but chances are you won't want to sit through it again if you play the game more than once. And if the game does not include a way to skip the cut scene once it has been viewed, then it is really a pace killer.

Strategy Games

The general arc of a strategy game begins at a relatively low but constant intensity at the beginning of the game, becoming more and more intense as the game progresses. Generally, once the game has developed, there are plateaus where the action once again levels off, interspersed with high-intensity encounters and sequences. As I mentioned earlier, there is a difference between RTS games and Turn-Based Strategy games, though turn-based games are less common these days than the RTS variety.

Generally, strategy games, especially Real-Time Strategy games, are races against one or more opponents. It is critical to manage all the resources, tech trees, and exploration and battle strategies simultaneously, so there is a constant urgency. However, that urgency increases as the game matures and reaches peak levels occasionally when battles erupt, particularly when battles are happening in more than one location simultaneously.

The stages of strategy games include:

- Buildup and early exploration
- Exploration and encounters
- Next level tech
- Major battles
- Cat and mouse
- Incremental gains or losses
- Domination or defeat

So what controls pacing in strategy games?

- Developing new technology
- Amount of resources
- Time
  - Build time
  - Amount of time needed to build into the tech tree
- Enemy actions (attacks, land grabs, technology milestones, and so on)
- Discovering new lands
- Conquering or losing territories or assets
- Story-driven events (where present)
- Timers
- Cinematics
- Mission briefings

MMOGs

Pacing in Massive Multiplayer Games online is often quite different from pacing in single-player games. Partly, this is because MMORPGs are combinations of games and social networks and offer players a lot of freedom of choice, meaning that they can hang around in towns and talk or role play, or they can engage in exploration and high-paced battles. Typically, one of the few ways that designers can control pacing in MMORPGs is through the staging of events in the world, and to some degree by introducing expansions. Using plots, quests, and special events, designers can change the nature of the persistent online world by changing the sense of urgency inherent in the game or by increasing the danger level through the introduction of new enemies or even invasions.

In essence, with MMOGs, the designer can only provide the structure and opportunity. Using this infrastructure, players create games that meet their own pace requirements. Typically, however, the level of action and intensity will still vary, much in the same way that the intensity varies in RPGs, with a lot of exploration and player maintenance tasks and occasional battles. The frequency of battles generally varies with the location of the player, how the game has been populated with action-oriented activities, and the specific individual players' goals. The use of *instances*, which are adventure spaces specifically spawned for a player or group, allows designers more control over the experience of a specific player or group and can allow for deep, intense, fast-paced, or any other kind of experience without the potential confusion of other players coming in to affect the experience.

Another important way in which MMOGs achieve pacing variation is through the interaction of players with other players. It is simply a different experience when you play alone in a world than when you play as part of a group. However, explaining how that differs is somewhat challenging. Playing with groups often entails long periods of waiting for one or more players to join or to complete personal tasks, times when someone has to go "afk" for some reason and you wait for him to return, little emergencies, people being lagged out or disconnected…in short, many obstacles to smooth play through the game. And of course there are simply those times when people like to chat and get to know each other.

On the other hand, when you are actually engaged in battles and exploration, being with a group is very intense, offers a lot more concentrated action, and often requires a lot more quick decision-making. Even within the group, however, the intensity of action may vary. The *puller*, who takes the risk of attracting the enemy's attention and "pulling" him to the group, has a fairly high-intensity role. The *tanks*, who engage the enemy in close-quarters combat and protect the rest of the group, are pretty thoroughly engaged. *Archers* and *magicians*, who typically stand back and attack from a distance, have the pressure of doing a lot of damage and in some cases controlling enemies through spells that weaken, freeze, or slow them down, but the role is sometimes less "in your face" than that of the tanks. Still, if the enemy breaks loose and comes after them, things get really intense—quickly. *Healers*, like range fighters, have low-intensity jobs in fights that are not very challenging, but they have their hands full keeping the tanks and other players alive if the enemy is strong. They know that if they fail to keep the attackers alive, they will go down fast. Since group play is a hallmark of MMOGs, it's safe to say that most, if not all, players experience a lot of group play and the variations of pace it offers.

Other challenges exist in MMOGs when it comes to controlling pacing. For instance, in some special areas, people "camp" to fight the best monsters or to open special chests. Instances solve some of these problems, meaning that MMOG developers can put such special content inside private experience spaces available only to a specific player or group at a time. Bottlenecks in MMOGs often cause irritation and frustration in players, and when they do, certainly the pacing of the game slows, although often there are social interactions that result from the waiting period.

Grinding is another problem for some MMOGs. When a player is simply fighting low-level enemies over and over in order to gain items needed for a quest or money or to gain experience to level up, the pace of the game rapidly devolves. There is almost no risk, and the repetitive nature of the battles can quickly become boring.

There are many ways to avoid the pace reduction of grinding. One is to increase the level of challenge and danger associated with the challenges the player is trying to meet. Another is to increase the likelihood of highly prized *drops*, or rewards that appear when the enemy is defeated. Various theories of MMOG game design can encourage or discourage grinding as a primary mode of play. Asian MMOGs are famous for relying on grinding, but most of the major MMOGs have some element of it.

Given all the various ways in which the pace of gameplay in MMOGs can vary, it is still true that individual players have control over the pacing of the game, by choosing where to be at any given time and what to do when they are there. This freedom and control, combined with the immense variety of activities available and the social interaction, make MMOGs unique and popular by allowing people to create their own pace.

Pacing of the Game Experience

In addition to the overall subjective pace of a game, there are several ways in which the actual structure of the game can be paced. These include the pacing of:

- Skills development
- Difficulty
- Item values
- Information acquisition and story development
- Tasks/missions/quests
- Taking turns
- Game rewards

Skills Development

One significant aspect of a player's experience is how the character develops. This is particularly true in Role-Playing Games, but many other games, such as First-Person Shooters, strategy games, and even action games often contain some elements of character development in the form of added skills/technologies or character statistics and character levels. From a design standpoint, these specific improvements in the player's character should occur at a reasonable pace. In Role-Playing Games, improvements are often quick at the beginning but may become somewhat less frequent later in the game. In some games, such as action and arcade titles, character improvement can be steady, or it can only occur at very specific points during gameplay, when the player has accomplished certain significant tasks, such as collecting all of a certain item or completing a significant number of areas or levels. In RTS games, the development of new technologies, factories, unit types, and so on is largely based on the player's choices, but the mechanisms for such development are available.

Sudden temporary changes in skills and abilities can also be acquired during gameplay in various types of games. The acquisition of a special item or spell may grant temporary boosts to the player's abilities. Conversely, a curse or unfortunate encounter might actually lessen the player's abilities temporarily. These changes can affect the player's gameplay, making the game more fun in the case of a boost and more challenging in the case of a debuff or other temporary skill decrease.

Difficulty

Pacing difficulty is one important way that a game can feel right or wrong. If a game starts out too difficult or too easy, it suffers from the start, but the pace at which difficulty is increased can also significantly affect the player's enjoyment, involvement, and ability to continue. Some games offer a certain amount of difficulty adjustment based on player competence, as measured by gameplay. However, most games assume a lower level of competence and attempt to increase difficulty and challenge (for the stronger players) without overwhelming the less-skilled players.

When developing games, you soon realize that a computer playing against you, controlling multiple enemies simultaneously, is pretty impossible to defeat. So as the code gets better, suddenly this stuff really comes together, and you find yourself dead every time you turn a corner. This is a good thing, because we can see everything really works, and we know that we will always have a really good challenge coming for the best players out there.

I remember once watching a guy play the old arcade game *Missile Command.* The machine just couldn't defeat him. That's not good. So what we commonly do is get the AI so that you don't stand a chance—as if you stepped onto a battlefield with eight Rambos—and then we scale their intelligence back from there. The negative description is "we dumb them down." It's true: We do, and we have to. But remember, as the designer you completely control that—how it works, how they interact, how they respond to a player that's learning quickly, and so on. Ever played a game where you work out that a certain move kills just about everyone better than every other move, so you end up doing it a thousand times? That's when *you*, the designer, need to be diving in with a response. (Sure, let them think they have this walnut cracked!) It's trivial to detect when they use the same gambit again and again, "This player is just a one-trick pony! Let's surprise them!" If you design it right, you *know* what they're doing, and you can offer them some challenges by changing things up in a logical manner—logical from the game's point of view, that is. Keep the game a challenge (and interesting) for everyone!

Since all players are different, and there needs to be some variety and even unpredictability in games, it is a challenge to find the perfect pace for increasing difficulty. Some ways to control the pace of difficulty include:

- Difficulty modes, such as Easy, Medium, Hard, and Impossible (chosen before the game starts).
- Heuristic dynamic difficulty adjustment, in which the game tracks the player's success rate and adjusts such elements as enemy strength, aggressiveness, frequency of encounters, or simply the size or strength of enemy groups.
- Level matching, in which the enemies that appear (that are created on the fly) in the game are matched by some preset standard to the player's current skill base and statistics, often as measured by the character's level.
- Geographical distribution, in which harder enemies are found in specific geographical "dangerous" areas of the game world, allowing the player to make certain decisions about when to increase the stakes. It's fun when those "dangerous" areas are the shortcut to where you're going!
- Handicaps, in which some players are given slight advantages over characters or other players who have obvious superiority for one reason or another. The first time I saw this in action was in a game called *Virtua Racing* from Sega, where the guy who's losing the driving race gets a little boost so he can catch up. By always boosting the guy at the back, it makes the whole race less of a simulation and actually more "arcady" and exciting. Their *Daytona* arcade machine also made really good use of handicaps.

- Fixed ramping, in which the game simply gets harder in a smoothly increasing difficulty curve managed by the game code. This can be implemented as a gentle and slow increase or as sudden and steep increases in difficulty, depending on the designer's choices. Steep increases generally are accompanied by increases in the player character's knowledge or skills, so that players are actually prepared for the jump in difficulty. Otherwise, a word of warning: This is the point when I end up switching off a lot of games, at least when the designers get this wrong. Meaning, you're doing great—you are flying through the game. Then a new enemy (or situation) shows up that requires you to do five things at once. After dying for the hundredth time, you start to think maybe it's not you, it's the designer's fault, and you shut off the game. So be careful about your expectations, and make sure the game is ready to respond to a player who might be getting frustrated. Being challenged is great. Being way too frustrated is like cancer in the game world.
- Stair-step increases allow players to reach certain plateaus of skill, where they can play for a while, then increase the difficulty at certain points in the game by an incremental amount. The difference here is that the difficulty increases in discrete steps instead of in a smooth curve.

  Spikes may occur in some games, where the difficulty may increase very slowly at the beginning of the game, but at some point it may spike and become far more difficult at the beginning of some new event or level or at the end of some "training" or introductory period.
- Allowing pauses and save/load cycles can also affect difficulty. Pauses can allow players time to consider their actions, while saved games obviously allow players to try different approaches to situations and, if they didn't work out, to try again or take a different direction. Pauses and saved games also affect the overall pacing of the game by allowing players to stop the action at will, and even effectively reverse time.

Item Values

Like skills and statistics, the quality of items used in a game is often carefully planned, and the introduction of new or improved items is often a part of the overall pacing of the game development. This is true in First-Person Shooters, where the introduction of new weapons is a reward for the player, but also a strategic element in the overall game arc. In other games, such as Role-Playing Games, the ability to acquire better weapons and armor goes right along with other pacing issues. The same is true in strategy games, games of conquest and exploration, and even action games, where power-ups may get stronger as the player increases in abilities, and new items may appear that weren't available earlier in the game. These days, because gamers have so many choices of games to play, sometimes it's a good idea to reward them earlier in the game so they get pretty invested in their progress. Doing so can make the experience a little more sticky, meaning a little more difficult to walk away from.

Information Acquisition and Story Development

For obvious reasons, the pace at which a story unfolds or players obtain relevant information is important to the overall enjoyment of the experience they will have. Not all games have stories, but most games feature elements of the game world that need to be discovered during the course of gameplay. The pace at which this discovery takes place and is experienced by the player often spells the difference between a game that feels "short" and a game that feels substantial. Of course, this is a subjective impression, but pacing game information revelations, new area discoveries, and story elements does affect the experience. For more on stories in games, see Chapter 9, "Storytelling Techniques," and Chapter 12, "Character Design."

Tasks/Missions/Quests

As part of a story-based game, players must accomplish tasks, ranging from minor, short-term challenges to complex, multi-stage quests. (See Chapter 23, "Goals," for more on this.) The subjective pace of a game can be affected by how these tasks and quests are structured. By constantly having a range of tasks to accomplish, players are pushed forward in the game and sucked into the experience, not wanting to quit because they can complete just one more of several overlapping goals (remember, it's their choice) before they stop playing. By having secondary quests that span long periods of game time, the player has what I would call *looming goals*. These are goals that are established at a certain point in the game but are not completed until much later. This is typical in some MMOs and in games such as *Dungeon Siege II*, where secondary quests can often remain incomplete for long periods of gameplay.

Taking Turns

An excellent example of turn-based pacing can be seen in *Sid Meier's Civilization* series. Though the game starts simply, and things seem to move quickly in the early stages, little by little it gets more complicated. Yet the level of intensity and absorption creates a sense of near urgency. No turn ends without you wanting to start again. The cycle repeats again and again, and hours can go by. Though the game may not seem fast-paced compared to an action FPS or an arcade game, its pace is driven by the focus and the promise of nearly constant rewards as you build new units, settle new cities, develop new technologies, and maneuver politically or militarily with your rival civilizations, all the while building roads, irrigating land, and exploring the undiscovered territories on the map. A game like *Civilization* could seem leisurely and relaxed, but somehow it doesn't.

Game Rewards

Games generally offer some kind of reward, whether it be a high score or a game ranking, a title or other recognition of achievement, or even more tangible rewards, such as weapons and useful items, new characters to play or to play against, new skills, and so on. Generally, there is some sort of reward that occurs when the game ends successfully, but there are also other types of rewards. Check Chapter 24, "Rewards, Bonuses, and Penalties," for more about rewards, but here it's worth noting that the pace at which rewards are earned and received by players is an important aspect of the game design. Working with immediate, short-term, and long-term rewards, designers can keep players hooked and involved from the start of the game to the finish—and often beyond in repeat plays. So it's certainly worth considering how often players are rewarded, the processes by which they are rewarded, and what kinds of rewards they are getting.

Not all rewards are equally valued, and mixing up the kinds and qualities of rewards that can be achieved is often a good idea. One of the best ways to make something more valued is to compare it to less valuable items. In games such as *Diablo II*, there are many ordinary rewards, but the extraordinary items dropped by various enemies stand out all the more because of the ordinary ones you take for granted. In games such as the *Mario Bros.* series, there are all kinds of rewards, some more tangible and some simply experiential. There's really never a dull moment, and there's always a lot to anticipate.

Design Challenge

1. Consider the games you have played recently, specifically what the pace felt like. In each game, rate the pace according to the following criteria:
   a. Overall, how did the game action speed feel in the first level or zone?
      - Insane?
      - Fast?
      - Medium-paced?
      - Slow?
      - Chart your impression of the action speed over time as a graph. How could it have been more fun?

   b. How was the pacing in the first level?
      - Steady/constant?
      - Varying?
      - How much did it vary?
      - How often?
      - Chart your impression of the pace as a graph. How could it have been better?

   c. How was the challenge in the first level?
      - Couldn't work out what to do?
      - Just right?
      - Chart your impression of the challenge over time as a graph. How could it have been better?

   d. What was the intensity (pressure level) like in the first level?
      - How constant was the intensity?
      - How often did it change?
      - What was the range of intensity within the game?
      - Chart the intensity level for a specific section of the game. (How much pressure did you feel?)

   e. If there were areas in the game that required intense focus, what did they feel like? How long did they last?

   f. How did the game represent the passage of time? Did it feel fast, slow, or moderate to you?

   g. Did the game create tense situations or situations that made you anxious? If so, what was the effect on the feeling of the game and the pacing in particular?

2. Think of your own game designs and chart the overall activity and intensity graph, as well as what *your* ideal pacing would be.

3. For your own designs, consider different ways to control the pacing to accomplish the kind of game experience you want players to have.

29 Time Limits and Time Manipulation

The previous chapter dealt with pacing in games. Pacing has a significant impact on the way we experience a game, and one way to play with pacing is to increase or decrease the amount of pressure the player feels. There are a number of ways to do that, which were explored in the pacing chapter.

This chapter is about time limits and time manipulation. Players need challenges to make a game rewarding, and, as we explored in the previous chapter, one way to increase the level of challenge in a game is to increase the pressure the player feels. Putting time limits on the activities of the game can increase the pressure, even if those time limits are imaginary. All such time pressure involves a race against time—a race to accomplish something before a certain amount of time passes or before a certain event occurs. This chapter lists some common time-pressure scenarios. Can you think of others? How could you combine more than one to make an interesting challenge?

In this chapter:

- Time Limits in Games
- Time Manipulation

Time Limits in Games

The following list presents specific types of time limits and pressures; however, for the most part they are simply suggestions of a kind of time limit. Use these items to add elements to your games in different ways. For instance, the Conveyor Belt example mentions assembly lines and games like *Tetris*, but it could also relate to the frequency of enemies you face in a battle or trees you have to dodge when running through the forest. So my advice is not to take these literally, but to consider how the item on the list might be used in your game.

- **The RTS Scenario.** In Real-Time Strategy games, time pressure is real, because, well… it's in real time! So the whole game is one big time pressure from start to finish. Within an RTS game, there are many tasks to perform and an increasing amount of pressure as enemy armies build up and ultimately begin attacking; you are exploring, mining, building, creating resources, defending against or attacking enemies, and so forth.
- **Cure the Disease.** Someone is going to die of a disease, curse, or poison if you don't get the antidote or cure. That someone could be you.
- **The Enemy Buildup.** The baddies are building an army or super weapon, and you must strike before they are done.
- **The Supernatural Ritual.** Someone is summoning a terrible supernatural monster or is about to transform into something supernatural, and you must stop them before they can complete the process.
- **The Time Bomb.** A time bomb is ticking somewhere. You have to find it and disarm it.

- **Shrinking World.** Somehow, the place you are in is shrinking. The walls may be caving in, the playfield may be getting smaller over time, or the part of the world that has not turned evil/corrupted may be getting smaller. Or you may be standing on a platform that is slowly falling apart.
- **Unstable Paths.** The path you are on can only hold you for a brief time before it deteriorates, falls, or breaks, at which point you are in big trouble unless you keep moving.
- **The Sky Is Falling.** A comet (or something large) is hurtling toward your world, and you must find a way to prevent it from hitting the planet and destroying all life. This can also work on a more localized scale. For instance, you have to escape an imminent landslide or a volcano that's about to blow.
- **Cave-In/Avalanche.** You must escape the tunnel that is about to cave in or the area where an avalanche is about to hit. Or, you may be trying to outrun the calamity.
- **The Burning Building.** You are in a building that is going to explode, is on fire, or otherwise endangers you. You have only a few minutes/seconds to escape.
- **Burning Building Rescue.** As in the previous example, you have only a few minutes to rescue someone and escape before the building blows up, the fire traps you, or something really bad happens.
- **The Storm Is Coming.** There's a killer storm on the way, and you must accomplish one or more tasks before it hits. Or you have to outrun the storm on your boat, plane, horse, skateboard, or jet ski....
- **Lockdown.** The building is going to lock you in unless you can get past its defenses before all the passages can be closed.
- **Getting There First.** You must get somewhere ahead of your adversaries, perhaps to deliver a message, to prevent something unpleasant from happening, or to hide an important person or object. This also applies to any race—foot, car, plane, boat, etc.
- **Falling.** You are falling to Earth and must find a way to survive before impact.
- **The Attack.** You are under attack, and your defenses are gradually being whittled away. You must find a way to win the day before your defenses are all gone. (Sounds like *Space Invaders...*)
- **Out of Gas.** You are in a vehicle that is running out of fuel, yet you must arrive somewhere on time.
- **Wagers.** You have made a bet and must complete a task in a certain time or before someone else in order to win the bet (*Around the World in 80 Days*).
- **The Test.** You are being tested and must complete a task within a time limit to pass the test.
- **Time Trials.** In some games, particularly racing games, you must qualify for bigger and better things by matching or exceeding a minimum time in a race, lap, or other aspect of the game. Alternatively, you must qualify by positioning within the top three, five, or whatever. If there are different heats in the qualifying event, then you must have one of the top qualifying times.
- **Conveyor Belt.** You have to accomplish some task, such as performing an action on an assembly line, but the line gets going faster and faster. Meanwhile, you have to complete a quota within a specific time period. This scenario can be used in a variety of situations, not just assembly lines. For instance, in *Space Invaders*, the speed of the invaders keeps increasing, amplifying the pressure as the game progresses. Other games that use this principle are *Diner Dash* and *Tetris*, but the principle can also be applied to different scenarios in more sophisticated games.
- **The Environment.** Something is poisoning or damaging the environment, and you must stop it before it's too late to restore things or before some significant event occurs—such as the death of a critical character, the destruction of specific location or item, or the complete destruction of the environment itself.
- **The Arbitrary Timer.** There's no real reason for it, but the game is on a timer, and you have to complete a level or mission before time runs out.
- **The Coronation.** The wrong guy is going to be crowned as king, elected to office, or anointed in some way—or married to the wrong person. You must find a way to prevent it from happening.

- **Courtroom Deadlines.** Someone is about to be found guilty of a crime he didn't commit, unless you can turn up the proof in time.
- **The Death Sentence.** Somebody is on Death Row or otherwise about to be executed, and you must prevent his execution somehow.
- **Traditional Melodrama.** Any variant on the old tied-to-the-railroad-tracks or strapped-to-the-moving-saw metaphor from the old movies.
- **Traditional Melodrama 2.** Someone (you or someone else) will be evicted and thrown out onto the street if you don't find a way to pay the rent in time.
- **Connect the Dots.** Something really bad is going to happen, but it will take some time as different aspects of the evil plan or natural disaster are completed. Meanwhile, you are trying to prevent it from happening, and periodically you learn that yet another element of the disaster has been completed. This scenario can be a real time pressure, but often it's scripted so that the parts fall into place as you complete aspects of the game, and it always comes down to you against the boss to determine success or failure.
- **Financial Ruin.** You race against the clock to prevent something that will trigger a devastating financial loss.
- **Arrivals and Departures.** You must get to the station (train, bus, airport, spaceport, etc.) in time to catch a ride or in time to meet someone who is arriving (or perhaps to prevent his assassination or abduction).
- **Message in a Bottle.** You are stranded on a deserted island. You just finished the last of several bottles of carrot juice that washed ashore with you, and you know you will soon starve to death if you don't get help. You manage to scribble a message on your PDA and stuff it into the carrot juice bottle, corking it with a stick you managed to carve with your Swiss Army knife. Once you toss the bottle into the ocean, however, you must now guide it from current to current to get it into the hands of someone who can send help before you die.
- **Exponential Expansion.** If you don't stop or contain it, it will grow exponentially until it is too big to stop. This could refer to a disease, an outbreak of fast-reproducing creatures (tribbles), or even a slime mold that keeps growing at a faster and faster rate. It could also refer to financial systems out of control, to your own body expanding, and so forth.
- **Find the Weakness.** Something is killing and destroying everything in its path and seems to be unstoppable. It has to have a weakness. Can you find it in time?
- **The Dying Informant.** Someone is going to die, and only that person can give you the information you need. Can you get to him in time?
- **Deadline.** The paper comes out in the morning. Can you file the story of a lifetime before the deadline? Or can you find evidence to refute the story that is about to run?
- **Perishable or Waning Resources.** You must obtain or deliver a resource that degrades over time. Eventually it will be useless—such as a living heart for a heart transplant or an unstable chemical needed to power the super weapon that will save the world.
- **Resource Races.** You must collect a necessary and limited resource before the enemy can get it. There's not enough for both of you, and the one who is most successful at gathering the resource stands the best chance of winning.
- **Waiting.** Your opportunity hasn't yet appeared, but you know there will be a chance to strike. You must wait until the perfect time, when all your resources and all the conditions favor your victory. Presumably there's a pressure to succeed, so this scenario has its own time pressure, but instead of an activity designed to accomplish the necessary goal, it's patience and correct timing that succeed.
- **Waiting 2.** In this situation, you have to wait for something to happen. You know when it will happen, but you can't do anything about it until that time. Part of the pressure is working around the situation until you can act. The other part of the pressure is the danger that you will miss the

opportunity—either by forgetting or by being impeded by something—when the time does arrive. This works best where time is really passing within the game world, as opposed to the false time in which events actually trigger the illusion of time passing.

- **Meetings in Time.** Similar to Waiting 2, some games feature specific quests, activities, or unique encounters that are time sensitive, so you must be at the right place at the right time in order for a particular interaction or encounter to take place.
- **Holding the Fort.** Your NPC teammates are protecting a position, and you have to hurry to complete your mission before they get toasted.
- **Schedule.** You must complete specific actions on a schedule in order to complete a mission or achieve a goal. This could be part of a quest or even a car rally.
- **Natural Aging.** You need to accomplish your goals before your character gets old and dies, as in *Pirates!*
- **The Flood.** The water level is rising, and you must find a way to stop it, reach high ground, divert it at your enemies, and preferably also protect your own installations.
- **Hit Man.** Either you're acting as a hit man and you must find your target before he gets away or accomplishes the goal you are supposed to prevent, or a hit man is after you, and you must either kill him first, neutralize him somehow, or get to safety before it's too late. This applies to any dangerous pursuit, not just hit men.
- **Help Wanted.** You are engaged in an offensive or defensive situation, and you must keep the situation under control until reinforcements arrive.
- **Before It's Too Late.** You have to acquire an item in a certain amount of time.
- **Renewable Resources.** Sometimes resources used within a game will automatically (or by some player interaction) renew themselves. For instance, in a strategy game, planting a crop is an option for producing food later. Or, after logging or hunting in a game, the trees and/or game might replenish over time, becoming an available resource again. But because in neither case is the resource available immediately, there is a time aspect to these elements of gameplay, especially if you are in dire need of these resources.
- **Transitory Rewards.** A power-up or other item appears during gameplay, but will disappear after a short time if you don't get to it.
- **Power-Up Timers.** Some power-up items will reappear only after a set amount of time has passed, making it important to use them only when needed or to understand the timing of their regeneration.
- **Power-Up Timers 2.** Some power-up items will disappear after a short time if they are not used. If you need them, you have to use them soon after acquiring them.
- **Transportation.** Often, getting from one place to another requires that you use a means of transportation that is time sensitive. This could be as basic as boarding a train or a boat that arrives and departs on a specific schedule. It might also be more complex, such as entering a magic portal that only activates when the moon is full or that appears and disappears on a regular schedule.
- **Slow Death.** You have an item that will slowly kill you, but you need this item to finish your mission.
- **The Worm.** A virus or worm is eating up the data in your computer systems. Can you stop it before it's too)(*$)((I)$#(....
  ....
  ....
  ....That was close. I think I caught it in time.

Design Challenge

1. Look at several games that use time limits and explore how they did them.
   a. Did any of them use a scenario that isn't mentioned here?
   b. Did any of them use a conventional scenario in a unique way?
   c. Were the time limits (if any) real or implied—meaning were events really timed, or were they triggered by your actions and results?
2. Examine your own game concepts. How would you use time limits? Would they be real timers or implied ones?
3. How would you impose time limits in the following types of games:
   a. Role-Playing
   b. First-Person Shooter/Third-Person Shooter
   c. Arcade
   d. Real-Time Strategy
   e. Turn-Based Games

Time Manipulation

In addition to creating pressure through time limits, you can also play with time in other ways, often having a considerable impact on the player's experience. When you manipulate time in a game, you may be altering the action, or you may be altering the story. In any case, you are introducing an element that takes the player's experience out of the ordinary and into the extraordinary. Here are a few examples of time manipulation in games. Can you think of some others? Can you think of a way to manipulate time that has never been done before in a game?

- **Time Travel.** Tried and true, sending someone forward or backward in time can provide new experiences and challenges. Imagine being a medieval knight thrust into a modern world with guns, grenades, and rocket launchers. Or, you are a Green Beret sent back into a time where magic is everywhere, and brute force is hopelessly outclassed.
- **Time Straddle.** This is where you are in more than one place at once. Maybe you are trying to get forces from the past, present, and future to meet up.
- **Flashbacks.** A specific kind of time travel, you are sent to a previous time, either as a dream or vision or in reality, such as in *Ocarina of Time*, where you have to understand the lessons of the past and possibly even change past events to change the future.
- **Flash Forward.** On rare occasions, you may have visions or experiences in your "future," which is, after all, relative. What is now and what is then? You can have fun with time.
- **Bullet Time.** The *Matrix* movies popularized the ability to slow time around you (but not your time) and see even speeding bullets as slowly moving projectiles, giving you time to dodge them with an enhanced time relativity. There are various ways to use bullet time, also. In some cases, it can be a condition that is long-lasting, perhaps for the duration of a battle. In other cases, it is a temporary power you can turn on or off judiciously, perhaps with time or energy limits on its use.
- **Speedster.** This is where you are faster than the perception of others. Daphne in the TV show *Heroes* is a good example. She can be anywhere in the world in a moment, due to her speedster abilities. To most external observers she just appears as a blur. So remember, time effects can be based on the perception of others, meaning she doesn't change or affect time itself, but it's very confusing to talk to her on the phone when she's 3,000 miles away and then have her standing next to you a few seconds

later. This opens the concept of playing with the safety that time normally brings. "The storm won't be here for three hours" assumes that an hour takes an hour.

- **Rewinding or Fast-Forwarding Time.** This is treating time as a recording. As in *Prince of Persia* or *Braid*, you can rewind and fast-forward through anything that's been previously recorded. This is something Time Police usually have access to, but then again, so do security CCTV cameras.
- **Time Stands Still.** The most frequent use of time in games is probably the Pause feature. By hitting Pause, players can stop time all together. In some games, that's all they can do. Time stops, the game stops, and that's it. The player can answer the phone, get a snack, have a nap—whatever—and restart the game at any time. In other cases, the player may be able to manipulate inventory, check quest information, or accomplish any number of other tasks while the Pause mode is on. Of course, some games have no Pause feature, or the Pause feature is disabled during certain phases of the game to stop cheating. Stopping time can also be used as part of a story or plot in a game. It could be caused by technology or magic. It might be in the player's control, or it might have happened by outside means. In any case, if time stands still for everyone except the player, then there are all kinds of opportunities to explore. Or, imagine that time stands still for all ordinary people, but for the player and some of his enemies (or allies) it does not stand still. What are the opportunities and challenges inherent in that scenario? Hiro has this power in the *Heroes* TV show; he can freeze time, go around the room changing things (such as taking guns out of people's hands), then unfreeze. This concept was handled well in the game *TimeShift* (this would be good homework!), when they experiment with all kinds of time-based combinations and tricks—for example, a box explodes, you freeze time, and there are bits of box in midair, so you can climb on them to get somewhere you couldn't normally reach, or you go to where the box exploded, reverse the explosion, and now you are suddenly hiding inside the box *before* it ever exploded.
- **Save and Load.** One very simple way to manipulate time—and reality—is to use the Save feature and reload a game at a previous point. Many games provide this opportunity, which can allow players to try different approaches to the same situation—in effect, replaying the events again and again—or, after experiencing a bad outcome, try again for a better one. This is commonly an opportunity to cheat (if you want to call it that), where players just keep reloading when things don't go the way they want.
- **Passage of Time.** In many games, time passes in a regular cycle. There may be periods of day and night. Days, weeks, months, and even years may pass during the game. Game designers have considerable latitude on how to affect the passage of time. A whole day/night cycle might take one hour in a game, or it might sync to real-world time. A week could pass in five minutes, or a year in 60 seconds. Players might be given the ability to speed up or slow down the passage of time or simply to "rest" for a specified period in order to accomplish certain time-related tasks without waiting.
- **Synchronizing Time.** This is usually where multiple people in different locations or situations need to do the same thing at exactly the same time. It can also allow for dependencies, such as bank robberies (people in different parts of the bank doing different jobs that are coordinated), or maybe a specific sequence of steps to achieve a goal (take down the power plant, then take down the phone company, then open the secure door, all three within seven seconds).
- **Appointments and Schedules.** In some games, specific tasks must be accomplished at exact times.
  - For instance, if a character you suspect of committing crimes always visits a specific crypt in the dead of night on New Year's Eve, you might have to be present to follow him at midnight in order to catch him or discover his secrets.
  - If you know that someone is always drinking at the local tavern between 10 p.m. and 1 a.m., you can be waiting.

  - The movie *Commando* used the trick of someone being on a flight and you can't communicate with them while it's airborne, so you just need to wait until it completes its entire journey before you know whether the person you want is really on the plane.
  - If a beautiful woman offers to meet you at a specific location at sundown, you don't want to miss the appointment. (The obvious game design is to make it really difficult to be there on time, perhaps by presenting other tasks that have to be done simultaneously—or at least within the same general timeframe.)
  - Or, if you know that the bank vault opens at 7 a.m. and closes at 5 p.m., and you want to get into it to rob it or to prevent a robbery, you can even play with how time changes (such as Daylight Savings happened), or it could be a public holiday and the bank is closed, totally messing up a big plan.
  - Using time in this way forces the player to be aware of very specific increments and moments. Such scheduling issues can also cause difficulties for a player. There are many opportunities to use appointments and schedules to influence the player's experience. How many can you think of?
- **Looking into the Mirror of Time.** Sometimes you meet yourself face to face. You have come from the future/past/another dimension, but it's you. You might be identical, older, younger, or even...different. But in any case, through some manipulation of time/space, there you are, occupying the same general time/space continuum as...you. Now it's up to you (the designer) to figure out how that happened and how to make it interesting, challenging, and fun.
- **History (Time Periods).** One of the most basic ways to manipulate time is to place events in a real historical framework, such as during the period of the Roman Empire or in Europe during World War I or II. The manipulation is only that the player is now placed in a specific true period, full of factual realities. History is not fantasy, though there is a lot of latitude for fictional stories within historical contexts, but even then, there are some specific elements of the game that are strongly suggested by history. Fighter pilots in 1942 did not have laser cannons. Roman soldiers did not use assault rifles or walkie-talkies. Obviously, when playing with history, it's going to really require some homework to make it feel right.
- **Time-Saving Perspectives.** While not true time manipulation, the ability to change perspectives in a game can sometimes seem like it. For instance, having the opportunity to jump out of your character's immediate environment and scan a real-time area map or see the overview of an ongoing situation may violate realism, but it comes in very handy. I call it *time manipulation* because imagine the time it would take to gather all that intel in the real world if you didn't have spy cameras and scouts everywhere. It's something to think about. How does a more omniscient view affect the game, and how do you use it to your advantage as part of your design?
- **Cryogenics.** This is used in the sleep chambers in the *Alien* movies, or when Han Solo is preserved in carbonite. Being able to suspend time for an individual(s) and revive them any length of time later creates an interesting form of time travel.
- **Immortality.** This is the classic *Highlander* immortality, where you can't die. You can be a thousand years old, and all the knowledge, history, and relationships can be fun story elements. (That said, it's tough—though not impossible—to design games where people can't die.) A modification of this concept is to preserve only the parts of you that matter, such as your memories or brain. Then you can become immortal (living through many time periods) as you travel from host body to host body.
- **Perception.** This is simply the idea that everything operates at different speeds, even in a single species. For example, a professional human baseball player or a professional boxer can react faster than a normal human. The perception part is that the professional can react in ways that most of us can't. It's like when you try to swat a fly; the fly wonders why that slow-moving newspaper is even bothering to try to hit it. It "perceives" faster than you can move. How can you use differences in perceptive abilities to achieve time manipulation?

Section E Communication

30 Ways to Communicate with the Player

We think of games as something people play, but to a designer, a game is also a way to interact with the player. We are thinking about what the player will do and what will happen as a consequence of his actions. We have some idea what we want the player to experience, so we create rules, puzzles, scenarios, environments, characters, and all the elements that make up a game, just so we can influence the player to engage in the game and to have fun.

Getting players to understand the game they are playing and to do the things we want them to do often involves giving them clues or in some way alerting them to what is going on in the game. This is what we think of as communication with the player. Not all games have exactly the same types of interactions, but most games, in one way or another, have ways to communicate information to the people playing them, and it is the designer who determines how to accomplish that communication.

This chapter, then, is dedicated to exploring the ways we let the player know what is going on in the game.

In this chapter:

- Introduction
- Clues and Information
- Rules
- Story Elements
- Foreshadowing
- Atmosphere
- Emotion
- Misdirection: Ways to Mislead the Player
- Influencing Player Movement

Part VI

Introduction

In any medium of entertainment, part of the job is to convey information in more than one way. Movies commonly use dialog and actors, visual elements (such as lighting, close-ups or panoramic shots, point-of-view shots, filters, and more), sounds, music, and action to communicate meaning, emotion, anticipation, and much more to the viewer. In games, there are also many ways to communicate with the player. In this chapter, I take a look at several ways to communicate with game players:

- **Clues and Information.** This is probably the biggest piece of the communications puzzle in games. It is always necessary to be sure that the player has enough information to continue with the game and to enjoy the experience.
- **Rules.** Rules are part of the information a player needs to play a game, but they are a specific type of information—the core framework that determines how a player interacts with the game.

- **Story Elements.** In addition to the clues and information needed to complete the gameplay aspect of a game, many games also rely on an unfolding story to enhance the more puzzle-oriented nature of gameplay or the more hack/slash elements. In any case, the story aspect of a game is not very different from stories in other media, such as literature and movies.
- **Foreshadowing.** Foreshadowing of coming events isn't used in all games, but in some games it is a key element in establishing curiosity and/or tension in the player, plus that great sense of "I knew it!" that occurs when the player has caught the subtle hints and figured something out. (Of course, this can also be used in misdirecting the player; see also "Misdirection: Ways to Mislead the Player" later in this chapter.)
- **Atmosphere.** For a game to be truly immersive, it needs to establish its own unique reality. This can be done in simple ways by the basic game mechanics. For instance, *Pac-Man* sucked players into its world with a simple maze, a few simple rules, and a catchy toon...er, tune. On the other hand, many games made in 3D today go to great lengths to create a compelling and realistic atmosphere through the use of sound, graphics, and interactivity within the environment.
- **Emotion.** Games can trigger all kinds of emotions, from excitement to fear and from frustration to sadness. Although games don't rely on emotion to the extent that movies and other media do, all games involve our emotions in one way or another, and some games are designed to provoke emotional responses (other than frustration).
- **Misdirection: Ways to Mislead the Player.** Yes, some communication from the designer (or other players or, indirectly, from the NPCs) to the player can be intentionally misleading. Why? And how?

CLUES AND INFORMATION

Games are full of information. Some of it is provided through dialog, while much of it is simply in the environment or even in the music that is being played. This section explores various ways that clues and information are conveyed in games.

GENERAL WAYS TO CONVEY CLUES AND INFORMATION

Clues and information are basic elements of any game. They take many forms, to be sure, but there is always something to let you know how you're doing, what you need to be doing, or, in some cases, what you have just done. This list contains a few ideas. What ways can you think of to communicate information or clues to the player?

- **Dialog.** Having someone say it (including the player character talking to himself or to someone else).
- **Chat.** Chatting with other players (in a multiplayer game).
- **Sound.** A change in music or a new sound effect can also alert the player.
- **Force Feedback.** Some controllers offer such feedback and can also be used to give the player clues or information.
- **Secondary Display.** Such as the Dreamcast's VMU, using the GBA with the GameCube, or the Nintendo DS with two screens.
- **Props.** Having the clue or information conveyed through something written (book, scroll, poster, carving, computer screen, tattoo on someone's body, and so on). Clues can also be conveyed by pictures, signs in the environment, recognizable features and textures, and any number of different types of objects. For instance, a safe set in a wall behind a picture is probably a clue that there's something valuable inside.

- **Action.** Information may be conveyed by showing some action—for instance, two people fighting. These actions can be part of the gameplay, or they could be displayed in the form of cut-scene movies. The action may or may not include dialog that further conveys information.
- **Experimentation and Consequences.** A lot of game information is learned by trying things and figuring out whether the result was desirable. Good games offer opportunities for players to experiment and discover the best way to operate in different circumstances. Some games provide additional clues when the player is obviously having trouble or going the wrong way. These clues can take any form, from direct feedback to the player to visual effects or even the appearance of some sort of "helper" being.
- **Heads-Up Display (HUD).** General onscreen information, including:
  - **Character Status.** One important type of information has to do with the player's current status. This could include health (HP), available energy (in the form of spell points, bullets, energy charge, and so on), current weapon, facing direction (compass), and much, much more.
  - **Enemy Status.** In some games, being able to convey specific information about an enemy is important, and there are various ways to do so.
  - **Maps or Radar.** Various means of knowing where you are and what is around you, particularly enemies, friends, group members, and significant landmarks or goal locations.
  - **Text Pop-Up.** Something to give you information about a change in game state.
  - **Visual Cues.** When a player takes damage, the screen flashes red. An arrow directs you to where your objectives are, an icon blinks on and off or gets a glow effect to call attention to it, the next piece in a puzzle is displayed before being dropped, a bush seems to rustle from an unseen wind to let you know that there's a secret path off to the right, and so on.
  - **Camera Sweeps.** Another sort of visual clue is sometimes given as the player enters a new area and the game camera sweeps around the new area, briefly revealing items, characters, and other specifics of the area. After the sweep, the camera returns to the normal player's view (usually first- or third-person), and the player can now explore the area. If he was paying good attention, he knows approximately how to get to the items and locations in the area or where enemies are lurking, thanks to the sweep.
- **Inventory.** A special case of game data is inventory—what is the character carrying, and what is equipped and what is not?
- **The Environment.** The entire setting can change from night to day or season to season, informing the player that something has happened. And of course the basic setting tells a lot. Is it a barren snowscape, an idyllic forest glade, a roaring volcanic inferno, a sleepy village, a village burnt to the ground, or a diseased-looking swamp? Is it windy and stormy, balmy and bright, nighttime, foggy or misty, hot and humid? (How would you depict hot and humid? Think about what would tell the player that the environment was hot and humid, such as sweating NPCs, buzzing flies and/or mosquitoes, people dressed in loose, thin clothing and carrying fans to cool themselves, and so on.)
- **Other Game Data.** Sometimes players need information that is always available, and there are lots of ways to create elements within a game that accomplish this. Common ways include journals, mission description pages, and maps of various kinds. Sometimes the data is presented in the form of an item consistent with the game universe (such as a journal), but other times it is simply a dialog box or screen that the player can access to get a status report, perhaps using a menu system or a special button. Another type of data is an indicator system, such as a marker over the head of a specific character or a marker on a map, or perhaps a specific shading, blinking, or coloring of an active versus an inactive character, item, location, and so on.

Specific Examples of Clues and Information

Just to keep things interesting, here are a few specific examples of clues and information we've seen in games. This list could be a lot longer, but we've left you some room to think and add your own ideas.

- The player's character turns and looks in the direction of items of interest. Although this is very common in third-person games today, I first saw it in LucasArts' *Grim Fandango.*
- Discover a letter on a desk.
- Read it in a newspaper, in a book, or on a slip of paper hidden in a book. Or find a note written on someone's hand (the person may be dead or alive) or on a scrap of paper found in the pocket of a coat.
- Hear it on radio/television, on a news report, as gossip, from a talking aardvark, psychically from your cat, or in a cartoon.
- Hear a clue as a general announcement over a loudspeaker.
- Get a clue while visiting a psychic (or having a psychic vision).
- See it in a dream.
- Get a clue by some remote sensor, such as a security camera.
- Get information out of a captive, prisoner, or other enemy (by whatever means necessary).
- Read it in a letter, telegram, email, or fax.
- Read it on a computer screen or a handheld digital gadget.
- Find out by telephone, walkie-talkie, or intercom.
- Learn something by listening in on a phone tap.
- Hear it using high-tech surveillance equipment, such as one of those laser microphones that bounces a laser off a window and, via the vibrations of the window, can allow you to hear the speech of the people inside. Or via an infrared night scope or using a bionic ear...
- Show an icon somewhere on the screen to represent the player's status (health, energy, other effects).
- Use visuals to indicate something significant, such as a locked door, an open window, or perhaps a suspicious torch on the wall. This can often occur during a camera sweep (as discussed in the previous section).
- Use visuals to show events that are happening elsewhere (or nearby) that affect the player's current situation, such as someone about to shut off the power to the building or someone placing a bomb in a nearby location. This might be observed from close by, through a window or skylight, or even on a remote viewing apparatus, such as a security monitor (as mentioned earlier).
- Use visuals or scenes to reveal something hidden, such as having a bird land on a mine and detonate it, revealing a minefield.
- Give the player multiple instructions and have them repeat them "aloud" when required.
- Use obscure but decipherable pictographs and glyphs to indicate functions of an unfamiliar machine or to mark different areas of a landscape, dungeon, building, and so on.
- Put in a sign, such as a street sign or road sign (or graffiti), that points the way or offers some useful description.
- Have an airplane write a message in the sky.
- Overhear a conversation or witness a scene.
- Hear a conversation or other sound clue through an open conduit, vent, window, or half-open doorway, and so on.
- Listen through a wall (perhaps with some amplifying aid—glass, stethoscope, snoop device, etc.).
- Plant bugs in an area and listen in.
- Overcome an enemy and find a clue among his belongings.
- Have the player's character talk to himself.
- Another character simply states the information or calls it out or tells it to someone else.
- Cut to someone else saying what the player needs to know.

- Cut to another scene that shows what's going on from a POV other than the player's.
- Give multiple instructions to the player at once, then have the player vocally recall them when required.
- Cut to someone reading important information from a document or screen, then zoom in to let us read the same thing.
- Reveal the best path. So if you want to tell the player there are landmines around, have a bird land on one or find the body of someone that triggered one. Keep the central path more worn.
- See something through a medium or psychic.
- Beat the message out of someone.
- Smash the player's way into an area, then have their vehicle/transport block your exit. Message to the player is "Play here!"
- Message is "in" some pill or drug, which the player takes.
- Use a street sign indicating an upcoming turn or a street name.
- Measurements of certain tunnels/structures/chambers are a message. Okay, this is a bit obscure, but perhaps with other clues, you might learn that a specific chamber in a cave was carved to specific dimensions, and if you pace them off, you'll discover a code or other clue. Or, perhaps you'll discover the exact placement of a mirror that will reflect the sunlight onto a specific spot to reveal a long-lost treasure, but only on the first sunrise of the Spring Equinox. Something like that.
- The message could be "coded" in the seemingly banal speech of an ally or messenger who "seems" to be saying nothing at all to the player. The player was given the coding system earlier or has been led to discover it.
- The player finds a seemingly unimportant object—a cereal box, a matchbook, a children's book—and the message is there, in a coded or unencoded form.
- A bad guy is given a truth serum and confesses information.
- A talking parrot has been trained to say the message to the player—or the player trains the parrot to deliver a message.
- The message is delivered by a domesticated animal—perhaps attached to the collar of a dog or via a homing pigeon.
- A crazy person comes up on the street and talks to the player, but is actually conveying a message in coded form. The player was given the coding system earlier or has been led to discover it.
- Just like "African talking drums," the coded message is embedded in sounds (the pattern of church bells, the drums of a jazz band) or sights (the spacing or color of lights on a distant hill). The player was given the coding system earlier or has been led to discover it.
- The player had a message "implanted" in him by various means, such as posthypnotic suggestion, and "remembers" (perhaps hearing the voice of the person who implanted it there) when a certain event occurs.
- The message is in a tattoo on the body of another player.
- The message is in the song of a cabaret singer the player hears. Or it's delivered by the paperboy, the bank teller, or someone the player has contact with. It can be in coded or unencoded form.
- The player does "remote viewing," leaves his body, and sees the information he needs to see.
- The message is in a crossword puzzle or some other seemingly innocuous puzzle recreation. Spell it out in a bowl of alphabet soup, on a Ouija board, in a game of *Scrabble*....
- Have a godlike entity who "speaks" to the player for reasons known only to it. (See also "Misdirection: Ways to Mislead the Player" later in this chapter.)
- Force the player into making a difficult choice, such as killing an innocent creature or person, and have the message be delivered as a consequence (within the corpse or from someone who mourns the creature or someone who is grateful it was killed).

- Have the message arrive in the mail (sent by someone else, the player in the past, a mysterious person, a friend, and so on). Or even more convoluted, have a key to a lockbox enclosed in the letter. Inside the lockbox, once the player finds it, is a clue.
- Hear voices nearby or someone calling for help.
- Show a cut-scene movie that conveys the information.
- Use attractors, such as a sight or sound that catches the attention and clues the player in that something is there. Anything graphic or audible that is unusual or out of place will generally inspire curiosity. For instance, have a rock move as the player approaches or a branch shaking on a tree or bush, a glint of light off a surface, a ripple in a pond, the sound of a splash or an explosion, or an eerie alien moaning that gets louder as you approach, and so on. Show something mysterious, such as blood leaking down a wall, moving shadows, a foot stepping into view, or something tumbling over. Players know from experience that programmers and designers will rarely put in unique animation effects for no reason.
- Another type of attractor is the pick-up object, which often is used to indicate that the player is going the right way. Also, the absence of pick-up objects can be an indication that a) this isn't a fruitful path or b) the player has already been here and collected the items normally found in this environment.
- Enemy units often serve as clues because they are most often present on the path the player is intended to use or near significant locations. Often, the presence of a higher-level type of enemy indicates that the player is close to an important location or resource.
- Play the sound of footsteps, a rock falling into water, an unusual bird call, or a wildcat growling, and so on. Use sounds to indicate the presence of something unusual or the occurrence of a significant event (such as leveling up, gaining an ability, picking up a magical item, and so on), and use volume or spatial positioning (with surround or 3D sound) to indicate location and distance from the player's position.
- Play the battle music whenever an enemy is nearby.
- Display a tickertape message on the screen.
- Put a locked door among many unlocked ones. This generally motivates the player to find a way to open it.
- Use unusual textures on objects such as walls, floors, ceilings, and terrain to indicate a special element, such as a false wall, a thin spot to break through, a climbable surface, and so on.
- Have an NPC in the party offer information at various times as you travel.
- Show alert graphics on a radar or inset map, such as a blinking light or starburst effect.
- Use color coding to indicate different types of enemies.
- Use color coding to indicate different types of objects (such as magical, unique, set pieces, and so on).
- Use consistent enemy body styles and variations to indicate the relative danger level of enemies.
- Use information screens when examining NPCs and objects in the environment to provide a variety of information to the player.
- Use overhead labels to indicate character and NPC names.
- Use thought bubbles.
- Leave a roll of film or camera around and have the player develop it.
- Show some person or creature hurrying off in some direction that you want the player to follow...like the White Rabbit from *Alice in Wonderland.*
- Hit the player over the head with something.
- Set traps along the important path. Traps often mean that something important is up ahead.
- Put more monsters/enemies along the most important path or around something of value.
- Put up barriers to help direct the player.
- If there is a puzzle that requires a specific object to solve it, put the object nearby or put something that would remind the player of the necessary object.

- Use character mannerisms to indicate something about the character—such as shifty eyes for someone untrustworthy or playing with a knife for someone dangerous.
- A dying character gives critical information as he confesses to his priest.
- Someone reveals important information while on truth serum (or some other drug that reduces his inhibitions—perhaps even alcohol).
- The message is hidden in some electronic storage medium, such as a DVD, CD, or cassette tape, or a non-electronic medium, such as microfilm or a nano storage medium.

Rules

Rules are the core element of how a game is played, and they include the various key and button combinations used in the game. However, in addition to keys and buttons, a game may have rules associated with the specific world it's set in. For instance, as in the rock/paper/scissors game, there are rules that govern the interactions of the three elements, with rock defeating scissors, scissors defeating paper, and paper defeating rock. The underlying rules of a game must be communicated to a player somehow, even if it is only by intuition and trial and error. The following list shows various ways in which the different types of rules for a game are conveyed to the player:

- Manuals
- In-game help
- Pop-up screens
- Training levels
- Trial and error (with reliable consequences to choices the player makes)
- In-game NPC guide
- Talking to other players (multiplayer games)
- In-game audio
- A scripted demonstration of how to do something (a ghost player or a cut scene)
- Iconic representations (such as an X over something in a store that a player can't use and therefore shouldn't purchase)

Story Elements

Progressing a story can be accomplished by using the basic elements of good plot development, such as:

- NPC dialog
- Quests or mission instructions
    - Given by objects (random mission generator)
    - GUI
    - From NPCs
    - Cut scenes or cinematics
    - Scripted in-game events (*Half-Life 2*)
    - General game action
    - Audio in music or in speech
    - Reading in-game items (scrolls, books, etc.) to advance the storyline
    - Visual highlighting
    - From the environment
    - Character arcs
    - Foreshadowing (see the "Foreshadowing" section below)

For more story-related elements, see also Chapter 5, "Game POV and Game Genres," Chapter 9, "Storytelling Techniques," and Chapter 12, "Character Design."

Foreshadowing

Another way that information is given to a player is through foreshadowing of coming events or dangers ahead. Foreshadowing is used in storytelling to make a subtle suggestion about something that is going to happen in the future, not generally something that is going to happen immediately. Foreshadowing sets ideas into the player's head so that later, as the plot unfolds, everything seems to make sense. For instance, seeing one enemy may be an indication of more enemies nearby, but it's a weak form of foreshadowing coming events. On the other hand, a black raven flying through a scene might foreshadow a death. Add on a dark background musical chord, and you have a sure message to the player that something sinister is going on. Examples of foreshadowing in games may be subtle or not so subtle:

- People often make innocent-sounding statements, but within them is something that foreshadows the future. For instance, an old farmer might say, "I reckon it's been a bit hot this past summer. Unseasonable, it is...." What he may be foreshadowing is that some evil dude is messing with the weather, a great cataclysm is about to happen, or it is the early signs of global warming.
- An NPC or item reveals a myth or prophecy (or part of one), then the details of the myth or prophecy begin to come true as the player explores the game.
- The game might show a glimpse of a mysterious person or event without explaining it. The image might be repeated a few times during the game.
- The main character might dream or have a vision of something prophetic.
- Cut scenes can be used to foreshadow what's coming up, though this can take the form of very obvious exposition or of subtle clues. The subtle method is more like foreshadowing than the obvious exposition. For instance, to show what someone else is doing elsewhere in the story is not foreshadowing. But to show a bank of clouds swirling and growing into a great storm front could be foreshadowing some wild weather in the player's future.
- In another context, a change in sound or music can foreshadow something about to happen. This is often done by creating a low, subsonic undertone when approaching a dangerous situation or place or by using high string sounds or other tension-inducing music. This is one of the most commonly used types of foreshadowing in films.
- Another type of foreshadowing is changing the perspective of the camera to be in the first person of a watcher, which is generally a sinister sort of effect but less useful in games.

Atmosphere

Atmosphere is what I call those touches of detail that make a game or a game's world real and absorbing. Creating atmosphere is another way both to communicate with a player and to immerse the player more fully into the experience—although as a communication method it is more subtle than the normal clues and information used to further the game and plot. Still, atmosphere can convey a lot of useful information to the player while making the surroundings seem more real and complete. Think how you might use these atmospheric effects.

NOTE

This section deals specifically with the ways that elements of a game provide clues and information to the player. For more information about some of the elements in this section, see also Chapter 17, "Game Worlds" and Chapter 20, "Music and Sound."

Sounds

Sounds in games are often used simply to create ambience, but they are just as often used as clues. For instance, just the change in volume as you get nearer or farther from a location is a clue. Sometimes you hear a voice in the distance, before you blunder into a scene that would get you into trouble. Or you hear the distant sound of a machine, which is a clue that you are getting close to your goal. You might have a talisman (as in *The Witcher*) that vibrates and creates a specific sound when enemies are nearby. In the following list, think how each of these items might be used as a clue to the player. What situations would you create to use them? (For more on sounds in games, see Chapter 20, "Music and Sound.")

- Birds singing
- Water running
- Water dripping
- Water splashing
- Water roaring
- Animals roaring
- Strange alien sound effects
- Low subsonic tones
- High, almost ultrasonic sounds
- Rumbling
- Creaking (as in doors with rusty hinges or twisting metal)
- Crashes in the distance or nearby
- Machinery running in the distance or nearby
- Wind whistling
- A person whistling
- Repetitive sounds, such as chopping wood or an animal calling
- Rhythmic sounds, such as a clanking machine, a helicopter's blades, dripping water, waves on the seashore, a repetitive and rhythmic bird call, and so on
- Sudden musical chords (without any regular music)
- Interactivity with the environment, making it come alive

Music

Music is often used to affect a player's emotions, to make the scene feel ominous or light-hearted, sad and gloomy, or romantic. Here are a few ideas for how to use music as a way of communicating with the player. For more on music in games, see Chapter 20, "Music and Sound."

- Signaling a shift from peace to battle mode
- Creepy music to enhance tension and anticipation
- Sad music to enhance emotional response
- Heroic music
- Crescendos, which can be used to heighten excitement or to surprise a player
- Themes that signal the entrance of a hero, heroine, or villain
- Exciting music to accompany a chase
- General background music used to set a basic theme within a game (such as in *Super Mario Bros.* or *Pac-Man*, for instance)

Light Effects

Like music, light effects can affect mood and help set a scene in various ways, such as:

- Dark and oppressive, as on a stormy day
- Even darker and more oppressive, as in a dungeon
- Mostly dark with only a little circle or cone of light, to enhance the sense of danger and vulnerability
- Bright and sunny, as in a meadow on a spring day
- Too bright, as in a desert

- Fiery glowing red, as in a lava pit or the den of a fire creature
- Sunset or sunrise to create a romantic or visually appealing atmosphere
- Underwater, murky—to set a feeling of danger
- Remarkable colors, out of the ordinary, to establish an alien atmosphere
- Bright colors to set a cheery atmosphere

See also Chapter 17, "Game Worlds"—specifically, the "Lighting" section.

Terrain Imagery

The features of a world also affect both the player's mood and, to some extent, the gameplay options appropriate to the scene. For instance, desolate regions may be more depressing overall, whereas lush jungles may seem intriguing and a little dangerous. A sleepy country village may seem peaceful and relatively safe, whereas an inner-city ghetto may be loaded with dangers. Flowers may soothe the mind, while a hospital full of sick people (or zombies) may evoke less soothing feelings. Ruins may spark the imagination—are there treasures to be found or mysteries to be solved? Examples of natural terrains include:

- Forests
  - Dark and menacing
  - Light and inviting
  - Dense
  - Sparse
  - Jungle
- Water
  - Rivers
  - Streams/creeks/babbling brooks
  - Lakes
  - Oceans
  - Ponds
  - Swamps
- Hills
  - Grassy
  - Forested
  - Rocky
  - Pathless or pathed
  - Special features, such a flat top, craters or caves, etc.
- Mountains (passable or impassable)
  - High and steep
  - Snowcapped
  - Pathed or pathless
  - Caves and crevasses
  - Loose stones
  - Danger of avalanche
  - Changeable weather and conditions
- Ice/snow fields
  - Glaring light
  - Thin ice
  - Moguls
  - Treacherous crevasses
  - Deep snow
  - Dangerous footing
- Meadows
- Deserts
  - Oases
  - Sandstorms
  - Dunes
  - Rock formations
  - Sagebrush and other dry shrubbery
- Underground
  - Mine
  - Lair
  - Cave-in (trapped)
  - Dripping and dank
  - Dry and hot
  - Lava
  - Dark
  - Well lit
  - Civilization/city
  - Warren (crowded)

City/Town/Village Imagery

Urban settings of various sizes affect a game in many ways, such as by providing opportunities for shopping, rest, and NPC interactions. Each type of town setting can appear in various different guises. Note that larger cities can also have specific regions, "hoods," or districts, such as financial districts, shopping areas, ghettos, wharves, and so on. In smaller towns, such as towns and villages, it is not as common for areas to be as distinctly defined.

- City character
  - Ancient (historical)
  - Fantasy
  - Rustic
  - Modern
  - Gothic
  - Futuristic
- City sizes
  - Way station
  - Small village
  - Small town
  - Big city
  - Metropolis

Views

Views are generally panoramic moments, often encountered suddenly and unexpectedly, that can be used as rewards, such as:

- A spectacular valley seen from the top of a mountain pass
- A mountain seen in the distance through a light haze, with the sun rising behind it
- An erupting volcano
- A green expanse of rolling hills dotted with wildflowers
- A deep chasm
- A colorful and dramatic underground chamber
- Lightning flashing over the landscape
- The view of a forest from the top of a tree
- A city at night as seen from the rooftops
- A huge gas planet suddenly coming into view as your ship (or planet) rotates to face it
- A dramatic waterfall
- A windswept desert landscape
- Coming over a rise and seeing a city spread out in a valley below
- Discovering a river delta and viewing it from above

Weather Effects

Weather effects are most often used cosmetically in games, meaning that when it rains or there's wind in the game, it doesn't really affect the player character's abilities or the plot. However, even if the player's character is seemingly unaffected, the atmosphere feels different, and in some cases visibility is affected. Of course, weather can be used as clues. An impending storm may signify the arrival of an evil force. A moving cloud might be hiding a UFO. A heavy wind might allow the player to fly a kite or even fly on the breezes, go sailing (or batten the hatches), throw something into the wind so that it lands in another place, and so forth. Look at weather effects as ways to bring a sense of realism and life to your games, but also as opportunities to create new kinds of interactions, puzzles, and special gameplay moments.

- Rain
- Storm clouds
- Heavy winds
- Light breezes
- Dust storms
- Twisters and hurricanes
- Bright sun
- Snow
- Sleet
- Hail
- A light mist to create a slightly mysterious atmosphere
- Thick fog, to set a very mysterious and dangerous atmosphere
- Burning sun
- Rainbows

Other Life Forms

Other living creatures can add a lot to the atmosphere of a game. For instance, walking through a forest and seeing little fawns and bunnies creates one sort of image. Seeing slithering creatures and strange beasts with sharp teeth would probably convey a different image. The range of creatures is limitless. Once you have exhausted the ones we know about, you can start making up your own.

Note that these creatures are often just part of the scenery, meaning that you can't interact with them directly. However, in other cases they also play direct roles in the game; for instance, as something to hunt, something to endanger the player, or something to provide collectible objects (such as skins, horns, or other parts used for trade or in the preparation of items in the game).

Dungeons

Dungeons are a very specific part of many games, especially first-person and third-person adventures, Role-Playing Games, and shooters. As such, they have their own lexicon of atmospheric imagery, such as:

- Dark tunnels
- Bright tunnels
- Rock-face walls
- Brick-face walls
- Walls with carvings
- Archways
- Smooth walls
- Uneven terrain (sometimes requiring climbing and jumping)
- Vault-like doors
- Dilapidated wooden doors
- Invisible or secret doors and entrances
- Ledges
- Caverns
  - Natural
  - Made by sentient beings (human or otherwise)
- Mysterious altars
- Dark pits
- Lava pits
- Water
  - Flowing
  - Pond/lake
  - Waterfall
  - Stagnant
  - Murky
  - Clear
  - Inhabited by creatures
  - Can be fished?
  - Player can swim?
- Slippery slides
- Traps
  - Falling rocks
  - Breaking foundations
  - Various manmade traps
  - Unstable cliffs
  - Dangerous creatures or plants
  - Flash floods
  - Flowing lava
  - Unstable handholds or footholds while climbing

See also Chapter 26, "Traps and Counter Traps."

Other Effects

Game designers have total control over the game world's reality, and there are quite a few less common ways to change the atmosphere and often the gameplay opportunities as well. After reading the most common ways, think of some new ones, such as:

- Psychedelic graphics in a scene
- Distortion of vision (perhaps the character is drunk or drugged)
- Going to black (a light went out or the character is temporarily blind)
- Having everything in black and white or other monochrome technique to indicate a dream sequence, memory sequence, or some other change in the character's perceptive state
- Changing size—making the character very small or very large
- Changing form—from a man to a cockroach, for instance
- Putting everything upside down or sideways
- Changing colors around to something unnatural and weird
- Deformation of any character or object in the world.
- Changing from realism to cartoon shading (Cel shading)

Physics

Game developers use the principles of physics all the time in today's games. The handling of a car, the friction of your tires, the rate at which something drops, how an object deforms when struck, the trajectory of an artillery shell—these are all calculated by using physics. However, you can also use physics more directly, as challenges to your players. Give them puzzles that require them to figure out physical laws, such as the displacement of water (which was used in *Half-Life 2*) or the refraction of light into different colors. Play with gravity. What if your characters started a journey on Earth but visited several planets, all of different sizes and masses? How would the changing force of gravity affect them and the way the game plays?

Give a little thought to different laws of physics, and you can probably come up with some interesting puzzles for your games.

Emotion

Emotional response in games is also covered in Chapter 9, "Storytelling Techniques." This section describes some other ways to use emotion to affect the player's experience.

Emotion is one aspect of a game that can make it unforgettable. If you can cause the player to feel some emotions while playing, whether it is fear, surprise, excitement, sadness, joy and laughter, or any other memorable feeling, you will have enhanced that player's experience. One way to cause or strengthen emotional responses is through the use of music and sound, which is listed under "Atmosphere" earlier in this chapter and dealt with in some detail in Chapter 20, "Music and Sound." Lighting effects can also affect emotions, as listed earlier in this chapter. But there are other ways to elicit emotions from players, including:

- **Moral Dilemmas.** Put the player in a position of making a tough choice.
- **Untimely Death.** Cause a beloved character and/or a protector to die (such as Gandalf in the Mines of Moria).
- **Hopeless.** Put the character in a seemingly hopeless situation. If he loses, he feels sad. If he wins, he feels elated.

- **Creepy.** Put the character in an increasingly dangerous or creepy situation to cause him to get nervous. Reinforce it with music and throw more challenges at him. The more tense and threatening the situation, the better—such as in *Resident Evil*, when enemies might spring at you at any time, and you are constantly anticipating their appearance.
- **Surprise!** Use surprise to scare or amuse the player. This can be combined with sounds/music and atmosphere to create a really unexpected event. The key to surprise is that it must be something quite unanticipated. If you repeat the same trick more than once, the surprise is lost.
- **Funny.** Use humor—carefully—to provide comic relief. (For more on humor, see "Creating Comedy" in Chapter 9, "Storytelling Techniques.")
- **Outrageous.** Let the bad guys get away with a lot of bad actions, causing the player to become angry and morally outraged. Let the bad actions be really bad.... Let the bad guys' final comeuppance take a long time to come up.
- **Losing Someone Good.** Have a really powerful, useful character decide to leave the party and either go his own way or even join the other side.
- **Betrayal.** Have someone who the player trusts betray him.
- **Tragedy.** Create tragic events, such as having a madman blocking a bridge. One of your party steps up and fights him. She dies, but then the madman realizes that he has killed his own daughter and collapses in remorse. (This is something that happened in the original *Phantasy Star* on the Sega Genesis—a memorable moment. Not only was this a surprising plot turn and somewhat tragic, but it also caused you to lose a really good party member on whom you had come to rely.)
- **Turn Things Around.** Cause the player's perceptions of reality to shift. For instance, have the player fighting a sinister race of creatures, then have it turn out that they are really righteous beings defending themselves against the real bad guys—who you thought were your friends! (This was done by Richard Garriott between *Ultimas V* and *VII* with the gargoyle race.)
- **A Glimpse of What's to Come.** Let the player see or suspect a trap or impending battle. Perhaps you give the player a glimpse of a rifle barrel peeking out from behind a barrier. Build the anticipation. (This is similar to foreshadowing.)
- **The Hunted.** Strip your main character of weapons, abilities, or other elements that make him effective, then turn the character into the bad guys' prey.
- **Sweetness.** Have someone (a potential love interest, perhaps) do something really nice.
- **Sex.** Create a really sexy character for the young boys (or girls...or anyone, for that matter) who play the game to get excited over.
- **Personalization.** Let players assign personal traits, such as names, looks, custom items, and so on to the characters. The more they invest in making the character their own, the more they'll identify with that character and react emotionally to the game situations. (For more on this, see Chapter 12, "Character Design.")
- **Challenge.** Make the game hard enough to be a challenge, but not so hard that most players can't find a way to succeed. There's nothing like mastering a good challenge to fill a player with pride and a satisfying sense of accomplishment.
- Other emotions to play with include:
  - Embarrassment
  - Accomplishment
  - Caution/wariness
  - Suspense (see also "Making Things Scary" in Chapter 9, "Storytelling Techniques")

MISDIRECTION: WAYS TO MISLEAD THE PLAYER

To ensure that games do not become stale and predictable, game designers must always work to provide fresh experiences for players. One way to do so is to borrow from mystery stories and fool the player in various ways—what we call *misdirection*. However, in interactive media, there are ways to mislead and misdirect that aren't available in linear media, such as books, plays, and movies. Some of the tricks you can play on players can be quite nasty and mean. It may be advisable when using some of these tricks to make sure the player knows you are messing with him and that it is consistent in some way with the overall game design and purpose. Humor is one good way to do this. If you can do something really tricky and strange to mislead the player, but the result is funny rather than tragic, the player will be more likely to forgive you. The other way is to be sure that what you have done enhances the gameplay and is somehow consistent with what players have a right to expect. For instance, using some very complex story-level misdirection would be perfectly acceptable in a game such as *Deus Ex*, but perhaps not so acceptable in *Doom 3*, where some other kind of misdirection might work better.

Here are several ways to mislead or misdirect the player in games:

- **Play with Clichés.** Games over the years have created their own clichés, such that players have become accustomed to certain cause-and-effect relationships. (See also Chaper 22, "Game Conventions and Cliches.") By recognizing clichés and anticipating a player's response, you can mislead the player into predictable actions, with unpredictable results.
- **Foreshadow Falsely.** Foreshadowing is used not only in some games, but throughout literature, theater, and movies. We have become accustomed to such techniques as playing ominous music as a hero approaches a dangerous situation or having seemingly innocent or offhand statements turn out to be far truer than they seemed at the time. However, using these same techniques, you can mislead the player into expecting some event that either never happens or that happens quite differently from what is expected. For instance, playing an ominous theme can create the expectation of danger, and the player will be in a highly anticipatory mode. But then having something harmless jump onto the screen, such as a frog or a rabbit, can keep the player wondering...or laughing. Having the seemingly wise old villager predict the coming of a monster, only to have it never come to pass, would also create a misleading sense of impending danger or doom since often in stories it is just such a bit player who provides the foreshadowing of the plot.
- **The Truth Changes Everything.** Let the player draw his own false conclusions about a situation, based on carefully laid clues and misleading but convincing evidence. Or downright lie to the player and have him get all worked up over some quest, task, or earthshaking event. Then, after the player has gone to considerable trouble to resolve the situation, have the whole story shift as he learns a significant bit of information he didn't have before. This can be a frustrating device, but it can also make a game far more interesting if the player can be convinced that the false assumption was justified and the new information clarifies the situation far better or makes the game even more interesting by presenting new challenges and rewards. But it is important that the player not feel his time was wasted. The effort of following the false goal should have had some beneficial results—more experience, better equipment, more money, new clues or contacts, a new party member, some secrets revealed or uncovered, and so on.
- **False Appearances.** Make something that looks innocent actually be dangerous. An old, toothless grandma could be a wicked shot with a derringer or even a tommy gun. An ordinary-looking chest of drawers could be the casing for a devastating bomb. A gerbil could be the wisest creature in the universe. It's unlikely, but anything is possible in a game. Another kind of false appearance is the false wall that opens to a secret passage or chamber, or another ordinary item or element of the environment that actually is something out of the ordinary.

Part VI

- **The Trusted Advisor.** Here's a really nasty one. Have someone—either an NPC or even a godlike disembodied voice—consistently give the player accurate and timely warnings about upcoming danger or useful advice on how to complete his quest, always seeming to be a far-seeing friend. Imagine Gandalf. Now, unbeknownst to the player, this person is actually a devious fiend who has systematically gained the player's trust in order to betray him at the most crucial moment. And even then, this "advisor" may be able to claim a simple error—an honest mistake—and keep the player's trust a little longer.
- **Bigger Isn't Always Better.** Most players expect that a bigger enemy is a stronger one or a bigger weapon is more powerful than a small one. Without giving a lot of explanation, simply make some enemies tiny and extremely dangerous. Make some small weapons that pack a wallop. Make a smaller gemstone that is worth far more than a more garish large one. Make a huge hammer do minimal damage. And so forth.
- **Play with Color.** There are many expectations with regard to color—for instance, red means stop, danger, fire. Blue means water, cool, soothing, and mana in many games. Green can mean healing, but it can also mean poison, nature, and so on. To mislead a player, use colors differently from the expected way. Make blue things hot and red things cool, for instance. But do so for some specific reason or effect. There should be a payoff or logical consistency within the game to justify such differences. Just deciding to create a game where blue means hot and red means cool makes no sense and is simply irritating. But, suppose the player must choose between two unknown alternatives, and it turns out that the colors represent something other than what the player expects. And suppose that there is a malevolent force that has presented this challenge to the player. Now it makes sense why the player's assumptions were wrong.
- **It Costs What?** Usually in games, if you have to pay more for something, it's better. Occasionally throw in some stealth item that is especially valuable but appears ordinary on the outside and does not command a very high price. If this is done randomly or occasionally, it could be used to fool players and have them testing every item to be sure they don't miss something good.
- **Distraction and Misdirection.** Like a good magician, you can create situations in which players' attention is drawn to something while you spring a trap from another direction. For instance, put a sign for them to read or some writing on a wall, then ambush them while they are reading it. Or put a gun in the middle of a room. Most players will go after the gun, but it could be a trap—even a bomb. The concept is to get the player to do something predictable and then punish him for it—or at least present an unexpected challenge or result. Other examples involve movement, which always draws a player's attention and can distract him from something more dangerous that doesn't move, such as a trapdoor. Or, have the sounds of battle coming from over a hill. The player goes to investigate and finds no battle, only a speaker. The enemy then descends on the player from behind. Some of these types of misdirection can also be used by players against other players, if the tools are available for them to do so.
- **Decoys.** Like distraction and misdirection, decoys can be used to make a player focus on something and not notice or understand what's really going on. This can be used by NPCs and directly by designers, or it can be used as a strategy by players against other players. For instance, sending a small force within sight of an enemy army might cause that army to change its direction—either preserving a location that is in danger or leading the army into a trap.
- **Use Repetition to Spring a Trap.** In many games players must perform highly repetitive acts, so they begin to follow patterns of behavior and action. Use the repetitive nature of gameplay to throw a curveball or change-up at some point in the game. A great example was *Prince of Persia* creator Jordan Mechner's first game, *Karateka.* In *Karateka,* you played a young adventurer out to save the princess. The game was linear, and you ran from room to room and fought against enemies of increasing strength. By the end of the game, running into the next screen, fighting, and running

again was completely ingrained behavior. When you reached the room where the princess was held captive, you naturally rushed up to save her, only to receive a sharp kick to the head that took you out in one blow! As a player, you were conditioned to certain actions and fell into Mechner's trap. But there was a defensible logic to it. If you walked politely up to the princess, you won and saved her. It was running toward her that rewarded you with the kick in the head. This makes the trap far better because it isn't entirely arbitrary. Some players might have been annoyed by having to go back to the beginning of the game, but I thought it was hilarious.

- **Cheap Tricks.** There are some nasty tricks you can play that mess with the player in various ways. For instance, you can put random teleporters in places—this is especially effective in mazes and dungeons. Likewise, you can put spinners that change the direction players are facing without their realizing it—which is especially effective if a) there is no compass to orient them, and b) the view in each direction is the same.
- **Doppelgangers.** Another way to mislead players is to present a character who is known to the player, but have it be that character's double or impersonator. Let the player figure out that he is no longer dealing with someone familiar, but with an enemy in disguise.
- **Time Pressures.** One all-too-common cliché in games is to urge the player to complete a task or set of tasks "before it's too late." The truth is, in many games this time pressure is entirely fictional. The player has all the time in the world to complete the tasks. It's a sequence of events that controls the situation—not time in a literal sense. However, this is something that can be misleading to players. Or, in a case where the player is aware of how this cliché is usually employed, you could really fool players by making the time pressure real for a change!
- **Change the Rules.** In some games, a particular event or moving to a particular area can cause basic rules to change—such as gravity, time, colors, and other generally accepted norms. Judicious use of such shifts of the laws of physics can temporarily fool players. This won't last long, however, because most players will quickly adapt to the changes. However, it's also possible to create a system that changes the environment seemingly randomly or based on a consistent but obscure system. It would be up to the player, then, to discover what triggers the change and how to advance in the game despite the changes—or to put a stop to them by disabling the mechanism that causes conditions to change.
- **Repeated Lies Become Truth.** Continually provide players with information that contradicts their senses. Keep telling them the wrong information until they believe it, even despite evidence to the contrary. You can do this by using any of the methods found earlier in this chapter.
- **The Soft Start.** In some games the beginning is very easy, but almost immediately it becomes more difficult. For instance, in one *Final Fantasy* game, you began as a fully armored, advanced character. It seemed too easy...and it was. Within a short time, you had lost all your armor, your position, and everything that made you special. You were then at the real start of the game. But, for just a while, you were as strong as you could hope. This kind of technique can really piss off players if the transition is too rough. It's not particularly popular to give bunny missions and easy gameplay, only to amplify the difficulty suddenly and without reasonable transitions. But it does fool people. Some games make the ordinary enemies and situations relatively easy but the bosses impossibly hard. Others do the opposite. Balance is important, but you can play with it sometimes to create variety.

Influencing Player Movement

This chapter deals with ways to communicate with the player, but what is the purpose of this communication? In essence, everything that a game designer does in a game is meant to affect the player's experience. Clues spark curiosity and provide a sense of empowerment or satisfaction when they are obtained. Other information may bring sense to a story, and even the subtle emotional effects make the game more enjoyable. Misdirection adds to the intrigue of a game and often supplies an element of surprise, which keeps a game fresh and unpredictable. Therefore, communication with the player is meaningful, often in more than one way.

Similarly, some sorts of communication with players are used to herd or control the player's movement and actions. It is, therefore, directive. This sort of directive action is sometimes used to lead a player toward some area of the game where important events or opportunities can be found. However, sometimes these examples are used to distract a player and cause him to stay on a path while possibly missing less obvious paths that lead to special rewards. This is often the case with Easter Eggs and side quests, where the "main" path is well marked and has many obvious enticements, while other paths are more obscure and easy to miss. In fact, the alternate paths may even be quite visible and substantial, but the player will often follow the more obviously lucrative or enticing path, ignoring the other. This is especially true in games where there are frequent enemy groups to fight, as players will tend to go from one group to the next, often passing obvious paths in the heat of battle, then forgetting that those paths existed.

- **Trail of Breadcrumbs.** There are several ways to implement this type of herding communication—for instance, by leaving power-ups and other objects along a specific path. Another way to accomplish this is to set enemy spawn points along a specific route, which will encourage the player to go in the direction of the next enemy, since one of the many game clichés is that the more enemies you encounter in an area, the more likely it is that you're headed toward something important or desirable. In addition, players often get caught up in battle and simply go from one enemy group to the next without pausing to notice other potential paths and features of their surroundings. In any case, the Trail of Breadcrumbs is a way to entice the player to go in a certain direction.
- **The Distant Attraction.** In a 3D world, you can place something off in the distance that is obviously unique and interesting. Players will want to investigate this feature of the landscape, so naturally they will head in that direction.
- **Hit and Run.** Having enemies attack and then run away is a typical way to lead someone into a trap, and it can work with players who decide to pursue the enemy when they run away. This might be to lead the player into a trap, or it might simply be a way to get them to follow a particular path.
- **Clues.** Sometimes the player will discover clues that lead in a certain direction. These clues can be traditional information, such as something they learned from an NPC or from a book or other typical method. Or they can be clues gained by observation, such as a discarded item, a broken branch, footsteps in a muddy track, a special mark on a wall or on a rock, and so on. In any case, discovering a clue tells the player he is on the right track (or at least on some interesting track), so he will continue in the same direction.
- **No Clues.** In circumstances where some clue or indication is expected, the lack of clues can cause uneasiness in a player, sometimes resulting in his turning back and retracing his steps. So even the lack of information can serve to control the player's movement in appropriate cases.
- **Enemy Difficulty.** Especially in Role-Playing Games, adventures, and persistent worlds, but also in some action games, the difficulty of a specific challenge can help control the player's movement. For instance, in many games the enemies get more difficult as you move farther from the game's starting point. This is a way to control the learning curve of the game and add difficulty in a logical and predictable way. It also serves to keep players within areas where they are competent and prevent them from exploring other areas until they are ready. One main purpose of this is to allow the player's game experience to continue to expand over time and keep the illusion of freedom while actually controlling and limiting the player's options. Another important purpose is to allow the game to expand over time, enhancing the player's feeling of expansion and reward. Seeing the whole game at once takes away from the sense of exploration and anticipation and the overall impression of the game's scope.

- **Skills.** Often in adventure, Role-Playing, and action games, skills (or the lack of skills) can help determine the player's direction or the paths available. For instance, in an action game, one path may lead to a cliff and a long jump across a chasm. Until the player has obtained the ability to jump long distances, this path will be impassable, so players will have to choose other paths. In a Role-Playing Game, it could be as simple as a situation where a door is too heavy to be opened until the player has gotten stronger (increased the STR stat).
- **Barriers and Obstacles.** (See Chapter 25, "Barriers, Obstacles, and Detectors.") Barriers and obstacles can also be used as elements of control to force a player along an easier or more accessible path. A lake of lava is a serious impediment to the player's progress, particularly when a perfectly inviting path leads elsewhere. Of course, discerning and persistent players may find a way across the lake, particularly if they have reason to believe it's passable or if they can tell there's something (a path, object, enemy, reward, door, and so on) on the other side, but the other route will seem immediately more attractive. In another example, a tunnel may be blocked by a landslide, and the only way to get through is to find some dynamite to clear the passage. Of course, the designers can control how and when that dynamite will become available to the player.
- **Redirection or Relocation Traps.** Another way to control a player's movement is to place traps that force a change of direction or location. Much like the game *Snakes and Ladders*, an unexpected event or trap can relocate a player's character and force him along a different path. This can be in the form of intentional traps or even natural events, such as the tornado that sent Dorothy to Oz.

Design Challenge

1. Take any of your favorite games and list every way that the designers have communicated with you as a player.
2. Where have you seen foreshadowing in games? How could you use in it your own game(s)?
3. Think of games where the designers have misdirected or misled you on purpose.
4. In each of the following locations, list at least five ways you could communicate with the player and what kind of information you would convey. Extra credit if you can come up with something not already listed in this book or if you can create an original combination of methods:
   - In a bar or nightclub
   - In a forest
   - On a boat
   - On a train
   - In an office building
   - In a prison or jail cell
   - On a battlefield
   - In a sewer or cavern
5. Take your own game ideas and use this chapter to come up with fresh and interesting ways to communicate with your players.

Part VI

Section F Common Problems

31 Common Game Design Problems

To be clear here, *problems* doesn't mean "bad game design" issues, it means "stuff that designers face every day," such as how to contain a player. I can't ignore this, because it's really very important. While most of the chapters in this book are focused on providing information and inspiration for a specific element of game design, this chapter is a look at some additional concepts and challenges. There's no focused theme to this chapter; rather, it's a collection of lists that represent typical challenges in game design. These lists are just the beginning, and we can imagine what Edition 100 of this book might look like—there might be a thousand of these problems fully laid out! As always, our goal is to give you some ideas and to save you reinventing the wheel. You've seen some of the solutions used in the past (and you are more than welcome to use them), but you can also use them as a springboard to come up with new solutions to these very common problems. And, because the subject matter in this chapter deals with many different aspects of game design, we offer cross-references to other chapters in the book that might prove helpful if you want to explore a specific list further.

In this chapter:

- Ways to Start a Game (see also Chapter 9, "Storytelling Techniques")
- How to Contain a Player (see also Chapter 25, "Barriers, Obstacles, and Detectors," and Chapter 26, "Traps and Counter Traps")
- How to Destroy a Planet
- Ways to Kill a Character (see also Chapter 32, "Ways to Die," Chapter 33, "Historical and Cultural Weapons," and Chapter 34, "Standard Modern Weaponry and Armor")
- Ways to Play with the Players' Emotions (see also sections of Chapter 30, "Ways to Communicate with the Player" and Chapter 17, "Game Worlds," Chapter 9, "Storytelling Techniques," and Chapter 20, "Music and Sound")
- Customizing/Personalizing the Game (see also Chapter 12, "Character Design")
- Ways to Make a Game Replayable
- Qualification Tests (see also Chapter 11, "Scenarios," and Chapter 29, "Time Limits and Time Manipulation")
- Things You Can Do with NPCs
- Ways to Protect a Character or Place (see also Chapter 25, "Barriers, Obstacles, and Detectors")
- The Various Mechanics of Mini-Games

Ways to Start a Game

Classes in creative writing always stress the importance of the first line of a book or story. Movie directors, likewise, must consider how to grab the viewer's attention at the beginning of their cinematic masterpiece. When video games first started, the player got into the game via a simple splash screen, followed by the game itself. Thankfully, there were some great artists who could create some very compelling loading screens, but they left it up to the user to go and read the manual if they really wanted to know what the heck was going on.

Today's games are far more sophisticated than those early arcade games of the 1970s and 1980s, and there are opportunities to grab players with innovative beginnings. Here's a list of some examples of ways to start a game:

- **The Establishing Shot.** This is generally the shot that gives you a clue about where this is all about to take place in space or time. Sometimes it's as simple as a camera slowly pushing in through the forest toward the log cabin, then going through the cabin window so we can see what's happening inside.
- **The "Old School" Logo Treatment.** Simple arcade games—puzzle games and basic platform games, for instance—still commonly follow the splash-screen-to-action sequence of the early games. There's no story, scene, or situation to establish. You see the logo treatment just dive into the game.
- **The Simple Goal Setup.** Some games establish the situation before the actual playing begins. Generally, this is done through a simple movie sequence, such as the beginning of the original *Mario Bros.* game, where the princess is kidnapped. The sequence cares more about revealing the goal—to save the princess—than just teaching you all about the characters, and at the same time it presents you with your ultimate enemy. (You know who you're looking for!) *Ghost 'n Goblins* did the same kind of thing.
- **The History Sequence.** In contrast to the Simple Goal Setup, this option presents the player with a complex movie to set up the game situation. Games such as *Diablo II* and the recent *Final Fantasy* games feature elaborate and impressive opening movies. Generally, these movies establish the events that lead up to the point where the player joins the story, though occasionally they may refer to events in the future—a portent of things to come—or to events far in the past that only become relevant after the player has spent some time in the game.
- **The Dialogue.** Like the History Sequence, this option is all about a cinematic scene, but it's more of a dialog between characters that establishes the plot for you. This is not the best of beginnings to an interactive story, but it can be done well with good cinematic effects and writing. For instance, it might be that two people are talking over the body of an unconscious (or seemingly unconscious) person. That person is your character, and they are talking about what they are going to do with you—or to you. When the action starts, you'll have to deal with these people, one way or another, based on what you learned from their conversation. Perhaps, during the conversation, the camera revealed clues—a sword on the wall, or a rope, or a telephone. When the action starts, you already have some idea what resources are available to you.
- **The Long Flyover.** The game begins with an aerial view of the world in which the events will take place. This method is commonly used when you are heading out somewhere pretty remote. Sometimes it's used to give you glances of interesting things along the way there, such as a big war being fought just one mountain away. In any case, you get a look at a vast world, but when the game actually begins, you are limited to exploring a small area. The vast world is a promise of things to come, but you have to earn access to new areas.
- **The Grounded Hero.** The game jumps directly into the action—probably a battle sequence. You are playing a character who, in many cases, kicks butt. You fight the battle and possibly have some scenes with NPCs that establish the situation. Eventually, this prelude ends, and through some plot

point, you are stripped of your butt-kicking ability and have to recover it. This can be a way to reveal the hero's past and ground him at the same time.

- **Tutorial.** Many games, particularly ones that have complex interfaces and controls, offer a training "act" to teach you how to play the game. This can be more of a "bunny hill" approach—a simple and easy level of the game—or it can be a guided tour, complete with tips and instructions. When done subtly, the player doesn't really think of it as a training session, but more of an easy level or mission. So the intro of the game is really just designed as some kind of training, such as maybe a doctor checking you out after wakening from a cryo-sleep—they want to check that your body is working, but it's all written to hide the tutorial.
- **Establish Who You Are.** Many games today allow you to customize your character before the game begins. You can choose facial features, hair, clothing, body type, and so on. (For more on customizing characters, see "Ways to Customize Avatars" in Chapter 12, "Character Design.") Some games offer you a series of questions, and how you answer those questions will determine some aspect of your character's personality or profession. For instance, some answers make you an assassin, while other answers would suggest a cleric or a basic soldier. This technique was used long ago in an early *Ultima* game, and more recently in BioWare's *Star Wars: Knights of the Old Republic.* This sort of preparation section is in some ways distinct from the actual game start, but for many people character customization can be a fun and interesting aspect of the game.
- **Action Central.** There's no prelude, no storyline. You're just thrown into a battle, and the game is on. This sort of beginning is very compelling; it can culminate in a scene that establishes the story, or it may not. The story may simply unfold over time, as you play through the game—*BioShock* is a good example.
- **Time to Get a Beer.** I *have* to add this because it has happened to us all. It's where the designer/writer decides we need to sit through 20 to 60 minutes of intro (no real gameplay yet), usually boring talking heads and filler story, and the most offensive ones don't even let you skip it. When you notice clichéd, boring actors waffling on about nothing interesting, I call that the "time to go get a beer" intro. I remember hearing that Joel Silver (the Hollywood producer) believes that you take the scene and chop off the start and the end, and you'd be amazed by how that improves things. Get to the point—and if you have no point, get to the gameplay! That's the message here.
- **Misleading Beginning.** Sometimes the opening scene, whether a cinematic or an interactive sequence, turns out to be nothing but an illusion or misdirection of some sort. It might be a dream sequence from which your character awakens, only to discover that everything is all right. It might be an event you took part in, but long ago or far away. It might even be something that happened to someone else, but you somehow were "inside" that person when it happened. There are always lots of fun ways to play with false beginnings.
- **A Disaster Unfolding.** The environment has a massive problem, or something has become or is about to become a really major problem, and you're about to be thrown into that problem. It's the tidal wave building intro, the earthquake intro, and so on. This is usually best if the world *after* the disaster event is much more interesting than the world before. *Fallout 3* and *Half-Life 2* are good examples.
- **Witness.** You just witnessed something—probably something bad, such as a robbery (or the planning of a robbery), a murder (or a serial killer preparing to act), or the plotting of some terrorist attack. Regardless, everyone in the story is oblivious except for you (the player). Maybe nobody will believe you.
- **Expect Something Different.** Someone (maybe the player) is just different from everyone else, commonly spiritual. He can do something magical or mysterious, and he needs to learn why and how to control it. We generally see what happened to him or maybe just a clue that you can expect this person to be different. The intro to *Spider-Man* is a good example.

- **Observing the Character.** Movies sometimes begin by "watching" a main character doing what he does in his ordinary life. It's a way of establishing that person for the viewer. In some cases, it shows how strange or unusual the person is, or how strange the situation is that he finds himself in. Maybe he just got injected with something that will kill him in 24 hours. In other cases, it shows how absolutely normal the main character is, which generally means he is going to become embroiled in unusual events. Perhaps you watch the character up to a certain point and then, suddenly, you are in control of that character and have to complete what he started.
- **The Chain of Events.** This is when one thing happens after another, and combined, the problem just gets worse and worse. Imagine an intro where there's some serious terrorist activity, then an attack is launched, our response system has been completely compromised and fails, then the president drops dead giving a speech, and so on. It's basically a chain of events so that you wonder when the chain will end. Just how bad can this situation get?!
- **Clueless and Lost.** Your character is simply...somewhere. There's no prelude, no establishing scene, no action. Maybe you just wake up somewhere—in a desert, on a city street, at the top of a cliff or the bottom of a well. You have no specific motivation other than "What the heck?" Because it's a game, you can imagine that some challenge is waiting for you just around the corner—but what corner? What threat? Anything can happen from here. Who put you there? Why? How? By whose order?
- **Found.** This is the opposite of the previous option—you've just been found naked in an alleyway, or found somewhere that's impossible to get to, for example. Now you (and others helping you) need to work out what the heck happened. Most likely this will involve a lot of flashbacks, or drugs, or hypnosis to piece the puzzle together.
- **Freefall.** You might literally be in the process of falling. For instance, suppose you start the game plummeting toward the ground from a high altitude, falling down a cliff, sinking to the bottom of the ocean, or getting sucked into the gravitational pull of a planet, and so on. You must figure out how to survive. You might have a lifesaving device, you might get saved by someone, or you might do something clever, but you are literally dropped right into a major problem.
- **Credits over Action.** There's no splash screen or other introduction. You launch the game and you're in it—then the credits appear over time. I think *Metal Gear Solid* was probably the first game franchise I saw do this. So you begin to explore the world, and from time to time (usually in quiet moments) a credit appears. Then, when something big happens, the title of the game appears on the screen, but to be clear, the game is *still* playing. It's very slick when done well.
- **Small to Large.** Strategy games, whether real-time or turn-based, generally start your character off in a very small world, with the fog of war hiding the bigger world outside your starting point. You are weak, with maybe only one unit or building. The goal of the game is to build your empire and defeat your enemies, and slowly but surely, you'll expand your knowledge of the world and build your infrastructures. This kind of growth also occurs, but in a different way, in Role-Playing Games, where your character is weak and must grow stronger, and is limited geographically and must explore a larger world. The gameplay is completely different between strategy games and Role-Playing Games, but the principle of small to large is often present in both, so the intro is going to place you somewhere that you know is surrounded by incredible danger.
- **Large to Small.** This is the *Honey, I Shrunk the Kids* kind of situation, where you are now entering a big, dangerous, oversized world, so the intro is really all about establishing the scale and helping you get comfortable with the idea.
- **Losing What Matters.** It's clear that something really matters to the player character, and he just lost it in the first few minutes of the game. This could be anything from people to possessions to beliefs. Something important is now gone, and this hero is going to get it back.
- **Something Important.** You've found something or someone very important; maybe you don't even know what for, but you know their protection is imperative. This is the classic *E.T.*-style situation.

- **A New Society.** Everything seems fine, but you'll soon learn that maybe it's not. People here have a very different take on what's acceptable. This is like the classic shipwrecked story, when you find that the indigenous people are not all that they seem. *King Kong* was a good example of this. Another classic version of this is when you flee somewhere bad and end up in a much more complicated, much worse situation. (Plenty of horror movies use this trick.) So the intro makes you think the biggest problem is behind you.
- **Everyone Knows But You.** This is when the designer wants you to wonder what the *heck* is going on. There's lots of discussion and lots of inside references, but because you're not on the inside, it creates a real mystery for you.
- **A New Phenomenon.** Take an accepted problem, such as a hurricane or a white squall, then add a twist, a new phenomenon that's never happened before. What happens when a thunderstorm meets a tornado during heavy hail? It's like airborne bullets. That's just an example, but it's going to be much cooler if you can come up with a combination of situations that creates a phenomenon that just changes everything.
- **A New Invention.** Something we have always considered impossible just became possible. It can also be that some new invention combined with something else gives really interesting results. The movie *The Fly* was kind of like that.
- **An Accident.** Something just happened. It could be a minor accident with big impact (such as Spider-Man getting bitten by a radioactive spider), or it could be just a small mistake that turns out much worse than it seemed in the intro. This is the old "leaving a vehicle unlocked" trick, when the vehicle turned out to have something incredibly dangerous in it (in the wrong hands).
- **Reincarnation.** You or someone returns from the dead.
- **Start at the End.** In literature and movies, a story may begin at the end and then retell the story. You show the main characters in a dire situation, then cut back to the beginning of the story to show how they got there. This idea can work in games as well. For instance, you might have the player's character facing a defining battle—a win-all or lose-all situation. But before the battle is fought, you cut back to an earlier time and let the player experience the events that led to the battle. There are any number of variations on this theme.

It's impossible to list all the introductions I've seen over the years, but the goal is to make you think about this very important part of the game so it draws in the player right away.

How to Contain a Player

This is a common problem in games where you are trying to give players an illusion that they are free in a city, but in reality, maps always have to have edges to them to stop the player from walking off into open space. Common solutions are making all streets loop back or having an accident blocking the main exit road. (See also Chapter 25, "Barriers, Obstacles, and Detectors," specifically the "Keeping Contained within a Map" section.)

- Rolled-over vehicle—the old oil-tanker trick to block a street.
- Military/police or parked vehicles block the way.
- Police (or enemy) barricades/rolled wire, barriers, and so forth.
- Construction in street. (Construction crew is working on it; street surface has been lifted.)
- Damaged street (like a bomb blew a massive hole in it) with no way through.
- Hazard blocking street. (Can be fire, toxic waste, exploding stuff, broken glass, and so on.)
- Demolition problem. (Area is unstable, bricks and glass are falling, a building is collapsing over that area.)

- Fast-flowing water. (You'll be swept away if you cross it.)
- Deep water. (You plunge into it and automatically resurface back at the edge/steps out, or you can only swim so far before you get a message that you will drown or you hit an invisible wall.)
- There is a wall you can't get past (electric or very strong, for instance).
- Animals attack in that zone.
- Area is slippery; you can slide back to where you came from or possibly off into a hazard, such as a waterfall, or over a cliff (with warnings).
- Offer the player the chance to quit the level if they go this way.
- Have warning signs clearly stating, "DESERTERS WILL BE SHOT!" You then terminate the player automatically if he continues past that point. The irony is that in many games, such a sign would be a challenge to the player—a possible clue to an area worth exploring—but in some cases it's literally true, and if the player tries to escape the boundaries of the area, he will be shot dead on the spot.
- Loop around (*Pac-Man* style).
- Have the bridge to or from an area begin to collapse.
- Area has landmines. (Note: People will think this one is a puzzle, so they need to be told that it's a no-go area.)
- Drawbridge is open/closed (like the Tower Bridge in London).
- Something living underground attacks up through the ground when you enter that space.
- It's a dead end, usually surrounded by buildings or steep terrain.
- It's a turnaround (homes/buildings are in a circle around the end) or a traffic circle.
- The road narrows to an alley, then it's blocked. (Easier to block.)
- There has been a catastrophe (such as a plane/helicopter crash, a building collapse, or an avalanche).
- There is something *very* slow-moving that blocks your path.
- A force field...when you walk into it, you bounce off.
- There is an invisible killer down there.
- There are major electric gates, and they are locked down. (Like driving around inside a prison campus.)
- The area has been pedestrian-ized, meaning there are metal bollards (sticking out of the ground) that block the street. (This is for when you are in a vehicle, trying to get out of an area.)
- Darkness. (This is good if the deadly stuff lives in the dark.)
- The level graphics fade out gradually as you leave the controlled space. (This isn't so interesting.)
- The player enters a dark tunnel, and after a short while, you cut to them walking back out.
- Protect the leader or key thing/person. (The mission fails if you wander away.)
- NPCs accuse you of deserting if you keep going. You may be killed or merely relocated to another place on the map, such as the brig, your house, and so on.
- Pursue an enemy. (You lose if he gets away, meaning if you bail.)
- Use fog, haze, or smog to fade out the level.
- Speech. Talk to yourself: "Hmm, this doesn't look very interesting." "There's nothing this way."
- There is an unavoidable, immovable force. (Running down to the subway, if you run down the tracks, a train will come and kill you.)
- An arrow comes on to show you to go the other way.
- Invisible wall (should be combined with other ideas).
- Fire wall/ice wall.
- Form of dead end. Ends with something like a locked gate, razor wire, high fences, and so on.
- Dead bodies. (Think of the movie *300*.)
- Some ethereal magic wall of energy.
- Toxic spill.

How to Destroy a Planet

There are many games that try to have us pay the "ultimate" price. So how could this be done to lead to some interesting gameplay? Things such as concentrated pods of nuclear explosions, sending an asteroid on a collision course, firing something into the sun so it flares and burns the earth up, and so on...

- Toxic spill.
- Trigger a chain reaction in the core.
- Cause a catastrophic explosion that clogs the atmosphere and blocks the sun for decades, killing life on the surface. (It doesn't destroy the planet, but it kills life.)
- Somehow guide an asteroid or comet to smash into the planet.
- Introduce an alien plague.
- Surround it with a network of weapon satellites.
- Teleport it somewhere else, such as into the sun.
- Convince more powerful aliens that this world is their enemy and get them to destroy it.
- Set off a massive blast concentrated in one area, causing the planet to become unstable in its orbit and fall apart from shifting forces of gravity.
- Use a powerful death ray (Death Star–style).
- Suck the life out of it.
- Peel the surface off like an orange.
- Split it in half or cut through it in slices.
- Push a moon or large asteroid out of orbit so it crashes into the planet.
- Unleash a swarm of nanobots that eat the entire planet.
- Manipulate rival superpowers until they launch a simultaneous nuclear attack, which ultimately drives the planet into nuclear winter, killing all surface life.
- Find the magical power node that is the source of the planet's life and destroy it.
- Vote in the wrong president.

Ways to Kill a Character

Far too many games just use guns, so how about a list of all the possible ways to die, and then you can invent some new weapons. Oh, we already have some helpful chapters: Chapter 2, "Brainstorming and Research," Chapter 32, "Ways to Die," Chapter 33, "Historical and Cultural Weapons," and Chapter 34, "Standard Modern Weaponry and Armor."

Ways to Play with the Players' Emotions

How can games trigger emotions such as surprise, fear, sadness, anger, frustration, shame, and humiliation? Players' emotions are always involved in game playing to some extent. The very act of attempting to meet the challenges of a game implies some emotion, although people respond with different levels of intensity to games. Still, games inherently inspire frustration and feelings of triumph. Often, they can even inspire anxiety and determination in players. However, these are emotional responses to the game itself. How can you, as a game developer, further affect the emotional responses of the player? How can you provide the player with different kinds of emotions?

Think of the kinds of emotions that are possible, such as fear, anger, love, gratitude, happiness, satisfaction, confusion, and so on. If you wanted to cause the player to experience any of these emotions, what would you do?

Places to look:

- "Emotion" in Chapter 30, "Ways to Communicate with the Player"
- Chapter 17, "Game Worlds," particularly in the section on "Ways to Make a World Feel Alive and Real"
- Chapter 9, "Storytelling Techniques"
- Chapter 20, "Music and Sound"

Some examples just to get you thinking about invoking various emotions:

- Create situations of anticipated danger. Maybe you can even hear it or get glimpses of the impending danger. Think of *Doom* or *Resident Evil.*
- Completely sell the player on an idea, then flip it. What they thought they knew was wrong, or possibly terribly wrong.
- Cause the player to dramatically lose abilities or items they think are important.
- Create very difficult situations. (Doing the right thing also might be the wrong thing.)
- Provide high-intensity action; give them the feeling of losing control or being right on the edge of their limits. (This is like when the Nitro button was added to driving games.)
- Get the player attached to an NPC in some way, then make that NPC die or leave the player. This works great in RPGs where you may have a really cool character in your party, but then, for reasons of his own, he leaves. (See Chapter 30, "Ways to Communicate with the Player," specifically "Misdirection: Ways to Mislead the Player.")
- Put really cool items in ordinary places to pleasantly surprise the player.
- Create funny scenes. (Think of *Monkey Island.*)
- Create scenes in which characters deal with real-life situations, such as the loss of a child, a gang-related shooting or punishment, or intimidation by thugs.
- Create scenes in which the player must make very difficult choices, such as saving the woman he loves or the man who could save the earth. Or he chooses to stay (and possibly die) in defense of his friend/brother/sister/wife/father/mother or leave to carry out his task of saving the world (or whatever his primary role/purpose is in the game).
- Have a really evil villain do a lot of really evil things where the player can watch but can't stop him (such as destroying things he's worked hard to get). Finally, give the player the opportunity to pound the villain into the dust. It feels so much better when the bad guy is really, really bad, and you are helpless to stop him—until that moment of retribution comes! This is fondly known as *payback time.*
- Create a situation with sexual tension in it. It doesn't have to be overt. Even implied sexuality usually produces some emotion. (Or you can add implied sex, like *God of War.*)
- Create situations in which the player has one chance—one shot to succeed—and build up the moment until he takes that shot...and succeeds or fails.
- Have a trusted character betray the player in some way.
- Create a game in which the player must rely on help from other people, but he never knows who to trust.

Customizing/Personalizing the Game

More and more, the idea of putting something individual and unique into a game is becoming essential in some genres, and it adds to player identification and enjoyment in any type of game. Players love choice—whether it's in how they outfit a character or how they name it, or even the facial features, skill sets, genders, and body types. They also like to make a mark on the world. In online games, players can become famous or infamous within their server communities and can even leave lasting marks in the history of their worlds. By providing design tools, many game developers are encouraging the ultimate customization—*mods*. Mods are whole new games made by players who use the engine and tools of a particular game, such as *Half-Life*. But mods are time-consuming and challenging to create—particularly good original mods—so it's important to seek easier ways for players to personalize their games.

A good example of personalization is *The Sims*, which basically allows players to create a person with various ever-changing skills and social connections, jobs, houses, clothing, and so on—all controlled and guided by the players themselves. Even more, players can create and submit objects that enter the world of *The Sims* for use by other players.

You can do more than let players choose different options, however. For instance, if the player can choose an individual character name, use that name when NPCs speak to them. And find ways to use it elsewhere in the game. For instance, suppose they get a letter or email within the game. Use the name they chose. Put their name (and likeness) on bus billboards or Wanted posters. I love it how when I make a band name in *Rock Band* by EA, it's built into everything (so that's a great reference for this). So, here are some ideas for giving players the ability to customize and personalize their games. (More ideas can be found in Chapter 12, "Character Design.")

- Their names.
- Their faces, including hair.
- Their bodies.
- Items to hold (weapons, etc.).
- Clothing.
- Let them change the look/colors/style/lighting/weather in the environment.
- Wearable accessories.
- Voices (their own or synthesized from a set of options—something I haven't seen done).
- Houses within the game.
- Use their photograph to make the model.
- Let them affect the environment—carve their initials in the bench, so to speak.
- Make their actions affect the world, including the actions of other NPCs.
- Give them titles and ranks based on attainment.
- Let them design their own weapons, clothing, jewelry, and so on. Give them the tools and let them go for it.
- Let them choose or invent their color, race, and/or "look."
- Personality elements—choosing different sorts of personality profiles at the beginning of the game.
- Have their character (or the world they are in or other characters) change as a direct result of the player's choices and actions in the game. For instance, in *Black & White*, the world itself changes. In *Fable*, the character's appearance changes based on the player's actions during the game.
- Players create their own creatures and objects, which can be used in other players' games (*The Sims*, *Spore*).
- Allow players to create their own words and somehow make them part of the game world's special language. (For example, an NPC might start to mimic the way you talk.)
- Allow players to create their own special abilities, perhaps by setting different options or by adding mods to their character.
- Give players the raw materials for creating items in the world, then let them experiment. If the system is dynamic enough, they might discover objects with surprising and unique characteristics.
- Let players reshape the world.
- Use unique reward systems so that players can obtain special prizes, items, or recognition within the game for unique accomplishments. Let them make an award that can be won by others.
- Let players give their characters specific quirks and mannerisms.

In Chapter 12, "Character Design," see also "Ways to Customize Avatars" as well as "Real People's Attributes," "Character Traits," and "Quirks.")

Ways to Make a Game Replayable

It's always nice to inspire players to come back and play a game more than once. If you can get them to play the game over and over again, all the better. Some games are structured so that you will keep coming back—particularly skill and arcade games, such as *Space Invaders*, *Missile Command*, *Pac-Man*, *Breakout*, *Tetris*, and so on, that you can't really win. These kinds of games all keep you coming back to get a higher score. But this section refers more specifically to games that a player can complete but will want to play again even after completing it.

Here are a few ideas:

- **Alternate Endings.** Have more than one ending, based on gameplay performance or on the player's decisions.
- **Unlock Characters.** Completing the game unlocks new characters that will provide new experiences during replay.
- **Unlock Features.** Completing the game unlocks new features of the game previously unavailable.
- **Unlock Abilities.** Completing the game unlocks new abilities for your character.
- **Multiple Character Types.** The game provides several distinct characters you can play, each of which will provide some unique aspects of the game experience. This is common in RPGs, car racing games (where the cars vary), and games like *Dynasty Warriors*, where you can play the same missions but with different warriors.
- **Same Map, New Gameplay.** You complete the game, but an option to replay it is presented. Everything starts the same, but subtle elements have changed, and you get to experience the game in a new way. The original *Legend of Zelda* did this beautifully.
- **Difficulty Levels.** Players who can complete a game in Easy or Normal mode might like to test themselves on Hard or even Insane modes of difficulty.
- **Specific Difficulty Level Rewards.** Some endings, features, unlocked elements, and so on are only available to players who complete the game on a Hard setting.
- **Emergent Content.** Many games are so open-ended that each time you play them, it is a different experience. Games such as *SimCity* or *Spore* (most of Will Wright's games) are like that.
- **Different Paths.** The game allows players to choose different approaches to the game, with very different results in the world and story. Games such as *Black & White* or *Fable* are good examples of this method, where your decisions and actions cause the world or the character to move toward good or evil and change actual aspects of the game.
- **Character Migration (Sequels or Online).** The game allows your character to move directly into a sequel, keeping stats, equipment, and so on. Or the game allows you to migrate a single-player character into an online version of the game.
- **Too Much Content.** The game is so rich in experiences and possible activities that nobody can experience everything in one game session. Often players will play through a game, but then they will see a walkthrough that mentions a lot of stuff they didn't see or do, and they'll want to play it again to see everything. The Different Paths option is another way of accomplishing this.
- **Just Too Fun.** It's so fun it's addicting, and you just have to play again…and again.… Sid Meier's games often had that quality. (*Tetris* on Gameboy and *Fieldrunners*, now on the iPhone, are the same. The trick is that players must blame themselves 100 percent for making the mistake that lost the game, so they will try again.)

- **Secrets and Codes.** Some secrets (*Easter Eggs*, as they are known) and/or interesting cheat codes become available after the game has been released a while. Others simply make the game fun in a different way. For instance, an infinite money cheat in *SimCity* changed the game from one of scarce resources to one of purely building and zoning decisions. It was fun either way, but not as hard when money was no object.
- **Deep Strategy.** The game has enough strategy and variation that no two games are exactly the same. Most good Real-Time Strategy games are like that. Even if you can win by one strategy, you may want to try again using a different approach. Or, if you lose using one approach, clearly you won't go down in defeat so easily next time, so you try again.
- **Contests.** Sometimes a real-world contest can inspire people to play a game over and over again, in order to win the prize.
- **Achievements.** Sometimes people want to collect all the achievements that a game offers, so they spend time replaying to try to find all the obscure ones.
- **Completion.** Some gamers are really hardcore. If you say "Congratulations, you completed the game! 62% Discovered!" there's a certain set of people who take that as a slap in the face. They will not stop until they get 100 percent, so they replay the game until they have found everything!
- **The "Experts."** Watch some videos on YouTube to see people play *DDR* (*Dance Dance Revolution*) fast. I don't mean fast—I mean *really* fast! Or check out *Guitar Hero* on Expert. If your game design exposes talent and lets them get rounds of applause for their "performance," you have another hook for replayability.
- **The Mentor.** This is when people replay to teach others, to mentor them to help them experience the game. The point is that it can be another complete level for them. First master the game, then teach the game. Check out GamerCoach.com to see what I mean.

Qualification Tests

(See also Chapter 11, "Scenarios," and Chapter 29, "Time Limits and Time Manipulation.") These are activities that test a player's abilities and readiness for some other aspect of the game—often in the form of a mini-game, tutorial, or side quest. It can also be a qualification for a race (such as NASCAR) or some sort of round-robin sports tournament. In some cases, the qualification test is a part of the game's storyline—for instance, an NPC demands that you face some trial before you can obtain his cooperation. When a qualification test is a part of the storyline, it often serves as a mini-game—something to provide variety, new challenges, a break from the general gameplay, and possibly a good test of the player's abilities. In such cases, there is generally a reasonably desirable reward if the player can pass the test. Another type of qualification test is really about the developers of the game giving players an opportunity to practice the skills they need—ways to challenge, test, and assess their abilities—before they continue. This can be done in the form of a tutorial with obvious guidance, as qualification rounds or missions that are required before the player can continue to the next aspect of the game, in the form of easy early levels and situations, or in the form of a practice area specifically designated for the purpose.

- **Qualification Races.** These can be in actual racing games but sometimes are used within RPGs as a test and a way to give the player more experience with the controls.
- **Qualification Rounds.** These are used primarily in various sports games to train the player and bring him up to the level of the actual game.
- **Guided Tutorials.** These teach and test the player's understanding and abilities.

- **Logic Puzzles.** These are sometimes used to require a player to solve certain puzzles before continuing the game. These puzzles often demonstrate a certain principle of the game—something the player will see more of in more complicated circumstances.
- **Bosses.** In some ways, mid-bosses are qualification tests. If you can't pass the mid-boss, you clearly aren't going to get far in the game as it increases in difficulty.
- **Obstacle Courses.** These are a great way to provide a variety of challenges and practice for players before they move into the real game. The *Tomb Raider* games included basic obstacle course trainers.
- **Special Challenges.** Designers almost always include certain especially challenging obstacles that the player will have to get past in order to continue. This is similar to the mid-boss, but it may only be a particularly nasty group of thugs or muggers or an especially monster-infested area that must be navigated. This is an aspect of tuning a game and can be mostly transparent to the player who has mastered the necessary skills, but difficult for players who are not sufficiently prepared. This also works well in Role-Playing Games where a section can be tuned to be too difficult for low-level players without creating any artificial barriers to prevent them from trying it.

Things You Can Do with NPCs

I often ask, "What would you do if someone stood in front of you and jumped up and down repeatedly? Would you just *stand there* and say, 'Welcome to town, Traveler,' or would you say, 'Why the heck are you jumping up and down?'" Artificial intelligence in games still has a long way to go, but in reality (no matter what your programmers tell you), it's not that hard to trap and detect a lot of the things that players can do and respond interestingly. You're the designer, so that just became your problem. For related information on this subject, see "Ways to Encounter Enemies" in Chapter 14, "Enemies."

Taking this concept further, consider the valid and meaningful range of responses that NPCs might have to various player actions. For instance, in some games if the player attacks an NPC, that NPC may fight back, may simply say something appropriate, may say something stupid, or may do nothing at all. The attacked NPC may take damage or even be killed, or it may not be affected at all (which is annoyingly common). Of course, in many games, attacking NPCs is never an option unless it is a specific enemy NPC.

Players enjoy getting a response from the environment, whether it is the physical world or the characters in it. There's obviously a limit to the number and variety of responses you might create for NPCs in a game, but players always enjoy seeing something they haven't seen before. So NPC responses could be far more varied than they are in most games. Here are a few suggestions of ways to interact with NPCs.

- Talk to them.
- Make them laugh.
- Use sign language.
- Play games with them.
- Dance with them.
- Bump into them or shove them out of the way (in *Assassin's Creed* style).
- Use different types of physical interactions, such as bowing, waving, or pointing, and get different responses to each gesture.
- Mock or taunt them.
- Give them a memory of what you did last time or even the time before.
- Give them a rumor mill, so they respond according to the rumor or news. (For example, they hear you're a killer, and they hide their children.)

- Provide the player with more varied types of conversation options, such as telling a joke, threatening, showing empathy or compassion, showing disdain, and so forth. (The response of the NPCs is key here.)
- Let them show respect, or in fact they could literally bow down in your presence.
- Reveal prior relationships, such as an NPC horse is really happy to see you.
- Use body language effectively to reveal more about the NPC. For instance, does he look uncomfortable or scared? Or does he look interested or even sexually attracted? Or maybe he looks bored, and you should try a different approach.
- Convince them to follow you (or force them to do so).
- Follow them and see where they go, who they meet, or what they do. (This can be a form of voyeurism on the go, so make it interesting, as we know the player is watching! It can also be used to reveal subplots and opportunities if the NPC leads you to something otherwise hidden or to a special character in the game who might give you information or new quests or missions.)
- Reveal their emotion for each other. So, for example, one NPC drops to his knees to help another NPC who's having a heart attack.
- Communicate with them by phone, mail, or email (or through coded messages).
- Give them gifts, feed them, bring them drinks, and be kind.
- Insult them intentionally.
- Flirt with them.
- Intimidate or scare them.

Ways to Protect a Character or Place

Protecting characters is a common design feature in many games, especially when you have to accompany an NPC through dangerous territory, and they are the target of enemy attacks. This is commonly called an *escort mission.* On the other hand, protecting a place, which is stationary, requires different tactics. Here are a few ideas. For related ideas, look at Chapter 25, "Barriers, Obstacles, and Detectors."

Escorting a Character

You have to help someone get from one place to another. She may or may not be able to defend herself, but in any case, she will die or be captured without your help. If you want a good example of a great escorting game, check out *Ico.* How do you protect her? Pretending that you're escorting Princess Slowpoke, here are a few ideas. Can you think of other ways?

- **Clear the Way.** In some cases, you can tell the princess to wait in a safe place while you scout ahead and remove any ambushes or enemies lurking on the path.
- **Brute Force.** If clearing the way ahead is not an option or not your preference, you can simply rely on your superior skills to destroy any enemy attack before the princess is severely damaged or abducted.
- **Use Subterfuge.** You can disguise the princess, use stealth methods (such as an invisibility spell), hide her somewhere, or even send out a decoy. This is usually not the most entertaining solution because it may prevent the enemy from attacking, which means you get to fight less, but in some game situations this might be the best solution to avoid disaster. It's far more interesting if this more stealthy approach is only one option, meaning that you can try the Brute Force approach, but if it doesn't work, you have another option (after a reloading the level, of course).
- **Find Allies.** Sure, you can do it alone, but why not get some allies to help protect the princess, or whoever it is you're protecting?

- **Bribes.** Maybe you can find a way to bribe the enemy or make a deal so that they will leave the princess alone. Of course, you always have to consider who you're dealing with. Can they be trusted?
- **Run for It!** If you move quickly and keep moving, maybe you'll make it to safety. The problem is that Princess Slowpoke (and most NPCs in an escort scenario) rarely can run as fast as you can, so you end up running back to protect her.
- **Find Another Route.** Perhaps there's a road less traveled somewhere, and the main focus of your enemy is on the main road. Take the one the enemy isn't watching, and you'll get through far more easily—unless there are unknown dangers on that road that are even worse! You might go by air, by water, underground, or through an alternate dimension.
- **Use Another Method.** Everybody expects you to ride horses or walk from Point A to Point B. What if you fly or find a place from which to teleport? Or what if you take a boat and go by water?
- **You Need Them!** You can easily make mechanics where the character(s) you are escorting can actually help you make progress in the level.

Protecting a Place

Places are stationary, and we've all seen pitched battles in the movies where the heroes are holed up in a building, in a mountain pass, or on a bunker on a hill—somewhere that has to be protected. Here are a few ideas for protecting a place.

- **Fortify.** If you have time to prepare, create fortifications, dig moats or rings of flammable substances to set on fire, put spikes or mines in the ground, and so forth. See also Chapter 25, "Barriers, Obstacles, and Detectors."
- **Location!** Find the best spots from which to ambush incoming enemies.
- **Take It to the Enemy.** Infiltrate the enemy and thin their ranks before they can attack.
- **Set Traps.** There are lots of traps you might set, depending on the terrain and the resources at hand. For more ideas, see Chapter 26, "Traps and Counter Traps."
- **Ambush.** Try to set an ambush for the enemy before they reach the location you are protecting.
- **Magic.** Using magic, you may be able to fortify, move, or even make your place invisible to the enemy. Magic, being magic, can do just about anything you want it to, but of course it's a cheap trick unless it's interesting and has some element of risk.
- **Reinforcements.** Find a way to get help. You might be able to protect an area for a while, but if the enemy has overwhelming force, then you have to find a way to get the proverbial cavalry to come to your rescue.
- **The Mad Rush.** With all your weapons at the ready, charge the enemy and try to wipe them out before they can breach your protection.
- **Guerilla Tactics.** Use stealth to take out the enemy as they besiege your position.
- **Kill the Leader.** Take out the leader, and you may sap the will of the rest of the attackers. Or, it may be that the leader is the only one who really wants to attack you, so if you can get rid of him, the place is secure.
- **Make a Defense Grid.** Create some kind of array that protects an area.

Stealthy Ways to Play

The element of stealth has grown in popularity in games, partially as a natural outgrowth of First- and Third-Person Shooters where a certain amount of stealth was useful. Now, however, stealth has become an art in itself in games and is often an important aspect of a game. (Stealth in this case means not being seen, not being heard, not being smelled, not showing up on radar, not being sensed by sensitive equipment, and so on.)

- Hide in shadows.
- Use natural cover to stay unseen.
- Use remote viewing to watch the action and time your moves.
- Use magic or technology to create some kind of invisibility.
- Use different types of movement options (sneak/tiptoe, peer around corners, crouch, lie prone, and so on).
- Use long-distance listening and viewing devices, such as parabolic microphones and binoculars/telescopes.
- Find ways to disable sensors, distract guards (sentient or non-sentient), and so on.
- Use magic or technology to escape notice of sensors and guards (sentient or non-sentient).
- Wear special clothing to keep quiet or unseen or to defeat technology.
- Go over, under, or around the danger.
- Use disguises.
- Shape-shift or control something else.
- Take possession of another being and use it to get where you need to go or accomplish tasks.

The Various Mechanics of Mini-Games

Sometimes you want to add activities to your game that can add to the fun but are not necessarily a part of the main story or even related to the main gameplay style. These mini-games have been successful additions to several games. What kinds of mini-games can you include? Can you combine different types of mini-games to make something new and unusual?

- Races
- Reaction timing
- Collecting items
- Aiming
- Obstacle course
- Breeding
- Matching items
- Moving and sorting items
- Logic puzzles
- Guessing games
- Battle tournaments
- Gambling
- Game of wits/trivia
- Series of trials
- Series of tasks

Balancing items

Design Challenge

1. For any of the situations described in this chapter, consider how your favorite games have solved them. What are the most common solutions?
2. Take the most common solutions and think of alternatives. Think about what effect a different solution would have, for instance, in blocking a street or customizing a character.
3. This chapter really is just a start. What other design problems do you face? Come to our www.gamedesignbook.org site and continue the discussion there.

32 Ways to Die

Yes, I know this is a gory subject, but many games are based on conflict and empowerment. That often leads to some form of battle. So I tested an idea on some developers: "Design a new, unique weapon that has never been seen before in games; you have three minutes." Many were stumped, so I let them read this chapter and did the test again. Suddenly the room was filled with ideas, many that we had truly never seen before. So that's why I present you this work, even though it's a bit gory!

Many video games default to simply "shooting" enemies, leaving creativity to what the projectile does in the air, how the gun fires, or what the bullet trail looks like, or the visual effect of the impact. Why is innovation in weapons so commonly neglected? I could get into the technical reasons, but the truth is there are many, many other (more interesting) ways to die, and those ways lead to more creative weapons, more creative enemies, and more creative battles. So read the following lists of ways to die, imagining a situation where these could happen in a game, or try to think of a weapon (or player ability) that could *cause* these to happen.

NOTE

Most of these methods, if done slowly and deliberately, can be a form of torture. For instance, in the end of Braveheart, *Mel Gibson is disemboweled while still alive. Most of these methods, if done partially, can leave a person injured and disfigured or incapacitated. There are ways almost all of these deaths can happen accidentally. In situations where the enemy (or player) has certain psychic and telekinetic powers, then death can happen through "invisible" means. For instance, Darth Vader can strangle someone just with a thought.*

In this chapter:

- Direct Causes of Death
- Indirect Causes of Death
- Torture Methods
- Other Useful Links

Direct Causes of Death

This section describes types of occurrences that can directly result in death. Note that some of these methods can also be indirect causes of death—for instance, through reduced capacity to defend yourself or to survive. Many of these categories, although they do lead to death, often involve another specific cause. For instance, being sat on by an elephant might be called death as a result of an animal attack, but it also would qualify as a crushing death or even suffocation/asphyxiation, depending on what actually caused you to die.

Animal Attack

This is a deadly attack by any animal-like creature.

- Attacked by killer bees (or other stinging insects).
- Eaten alive by army ants or by piranhas or sharks.
- Bitten by a deadly spider.
- Crushed by a bear or a boa constrictor or python.
- Savaged by wild dogs, wolves, coyotes, dingos, etc. Also by cats, lions, tigers, etc.
- Eaten by rats and mice.
- Nibbled to death by ducks (or other birds).
- Swallowed by a whale.
- Eaten or poisoned by fish or jellyfish.
- Eaten by vultures while still alive.

Boiling

This refers to immersion in heated fluids until the cells break down from the heat. In other words, being cooked to death.

- Tossed in boiling water or other boiling material.
- Boiled by cannibals.
- Microwaved to death.
- Suddenly immersed in some hot, clinging substance that severely burns you, such as tar, boiling oil, or possibly a vat of napalm.

Biological Weapons

This describes death as a result of an attack that uses a biological agent that attacks the system. (See also the "Modern Biological Weapons" section in Chapter 34, "Standard Modern Weaponry and Armor.")

Bleeding to Death

This is death as a result of blood loss. It can be fast or slow.

- Wound or injury, especially to a major artery unless other conditions prevent stoppage of blood flow.
- Something prevents the blood from congealing/clotting (such as hemophilia).
- Vampire or other blood-sucking creature, or suicidal thirst.
- Mechanical blood sucker.
- Failed medical procedure.
- Drained with a juice-box straw.

Burning (Immolation)

You catch fire and burn to death, due to any number of causes.

- You burn up in flames.
- You are chemically burned up.
- You spontaneously combust.
- You are burned by radiant heat, such as being in an oven or a superheated room.
- You douse yourself in a flammable material and it catches fire. This could be intentional or accidental.

Bursting

This is like explosion, but asymmetrical breaking apart from within. It's usually slower than explosion.

- Slow buildup of pressure within the body that eventually bursts it open.
- Breaking of an organ, such as the appendix.
- Aneurism causing a blood vessel to burst (also can happen with fast ascent and no decompression from deep under water when scuba diving).
- An alien creature has been spawned inside you and decides to take a shortcut out.

Capture and Slow Death

This refer to being kept alive and slowly killed by someone (or something) that has control of you or who simply wants you to die slowly.

- Aliens who suck your blood or energy.
- Mad doctors who harvest your organs over time.
- Sadistic villains who like to watch you die slowly.
- Kidnappers who have you imprisoned and don't care whether you live or die.
- Prison where you are neglected (such as the old medieval prisons).
- Buried up to your neck in the ground.
- Made into a dispensable slave—such as a slave on a galley, in a mine, in warfare, or on a plantation where your health is ignored
- Cannibals who slowly boil you to death in the traditional (if clichéd) big iron pot. Or, cannibals who keep you alive for a time and ultimately kill you for food.

Chemical Weapons

This describes death as a result of a chemical attack. The actual cause of death could be from a variety of effects, such as poisoning, disintegration, asphyxiation, and so on. (See also "Chemical Weapons" in Chapter 34, "Standard Modern Weaponry and Armor.)

Conversion/Transformation

This describes being changed into something else that is no longer your living self, such as a rock or a donut that gets eaten by the police officer who was trying to arrest you.

Critical Hit

This is getting hit in a location that causes instant death or that results in a mortal blow. This does not need to be especially high impact, as long as it hits a critical location, such as the carotid artery in the neck, the heart, or any other lethal location.

- Getting hit in the neck by a fast-moving racquetball, bursting the artery.
- Hit with force to the chest, causing the heart to stop.
- A hit driving the nose bone up into the brain.
- A lethal hit to any vital organ.
- A hit in a part of the body that paralyzes critical functions—for instance, prevents breathing so that death results from asphyxia.
- See also Chapter 15, "Character Abilities," in particular the "Human-to-Human Vulnerabilities and Attacks" and "Fatality Systems" sections.

Crushing Death

This refers to getting pushed by a heavy weight in any direction that is blocked or from several directions at once. It could be an excess of gravity, getting caught between two moving objects, or something or someone physically shrinking or constricting around you.

- Constricted by a snake.
- Crushed under a falling boulder.
- Squashed between two moving walls.
- Crushed under a huge pile of bodies.
- Run over by a bulldozer or other heavy machine.
- Trapped under an elevator.
- Crushed in a bear hug (by a bear, human, or any creature that can exert deadly force).
- Crushed under a huge statue that falls on you or under a giant tree that falls.
- Crushed between two slow-moving vehicles.
- Crushed by pressure deep under water.
- Crushed by the gravity of a huge planet or dwarf star.
- Crushed by some nasty gravity weapon.
- Crushed under a 16-ton weight (as in cartoons).
- Crushed in the wheel well of a 747 when the wheels retract.
- Crushed by an excessive gravitational field. (See also the upcoming sections "Gravity" and "G-Forces.")
- Trapped under a falling building, cave-in, avalanche, etc.
- Stepped on by an elephant or a brontosaurus.
- Stepped on by a giant.
- Trampled by drunk soccer hooligans.
- Crushed by a giant animated foot. (See *Monty Python.*)

Dehydration

This refers to dying from the loss of liquids in your system. It is generally slow, but not necessarily.

- Chemical imbalance.
- Severe intestinal disease/nausea.
- Excessive heat without liquid to regenerate.
- Lack of water over a period of time.
- Drinking saltwater.
- Something physically or chemically sucks the liquid out of you.

Deletion

This describes being eliminated as a data element in the world. (It could be caused by a computer virus, a random glitch, or intentional sabotage, for instance.)

Disappearance

Someone simply disappears, is never seen again, and is presumed dead. (The consequences are that the person is effectively, if not in every case literally, dead.)

- Abducted by aliens.
- Kidnapped and sold into slavery, ultimately killed.
- Fell into a black hole.
- Stepped into a different dimension.
- Traveling in time.
- Becoming invisible and unable to communicate or make your presence known.

Disease or Illness

You might contract a disease or illness that gradually kills you (including viruses, infections, parasites, and so on).

- Ebola or other
- Flu
- Flesh-eating bacteria
- Gangrene
- Leprosy
- Virus/plague
- Magical
- Mental
- Cancer
- Aneurysm
- Organ failure (heart, kidneys, etc.)

See also "Modern Biological Weapons" in Chapter 34, "Standard Modern Weaponry and Armor."

Disembowelment

This is the removal of the internal organs (by accident, design, or animal attack).

Drowning (in any Liquid)

This describes death as a result of inhaling liquid instead of air.

- Kayaking or boating accident.
- Falling unconscious into a puddle.
- Falling into a well and drowning after suffering from exhaustion.
- Falling (or being pushed) into water or into any liquid other than water and inhaling the liquid. The liquid might poison or kill you anyway, so your choice of death is drowning or poisoning (or disintegration if it is an acid or other caustic substance).
- Succumbing to drugs/alcohol and drowning as a consequence of falling unconscious in your soup or other liquid.
- Slipping in the bathtub and drowning while unconscious.
- Getting a cramp or injury while swimming, causing you to drown.
- Having a five-gallon jug of water strapped to your face so you can either die of suffocation or drown in the water.
- Being held underwater by enemies or by a contrivance created by enemies to prevent you from breathing.
- Falling into quicksand.

Elemental Causes/Natural Disasters

This refers to death as a result of weather and other natural events.

- Earthquakes
- Hurricanes
- Lightning
- Solar flares
- Floods
- Avalanches

Actual death is generally caused by something specific, such as:

- Freezing to death
- Burning up
- Being crushed
- Being impaled
- Being electrocuted
- Suffocating
- Drowning

Exhaustion

This refers to dying as a result of continual effort without enough rest.

- You are a prisoner working in the mines until you drop dead.
- You are trying to escape capture and ultimately drop from exhaustion. Either you die on the spot or your pursuers kill you. Either way, you're dead.
- You are kept awake for days until you finally succumb. (See also the "Sleep Deprivation" section later in this chapter.)

Execution/Assassination

This is death as a result of a formal (or informal) execution.

- Hanging.
- Gas chamber.
- Decapitation.
- Lethal injection or other poison method.
- Electrocution.
- A hit man.
- Organized crime.
- Government agents.
- Being drawn and quartered.
- Being dragged behind a horse/vehicle until you're dead.

Of course, the real form of death occurs as a result of the method used, but in terms of game design, the intention and agency of the death matters.

Explosion

This is a pulse of expanding energy or shrapnel that is generated inside or outside the body. Explosion can be slow!

- A bomb or other explosive (grenade, missile, mortar, or explosive recoilless rifle shell) going off inside or outside the body.
- Magically created explosions.
- Chemical reaction from something introduced into your system that causes an explosion (which could be a slow process or a sudden one).
- A missile hits the vehicle or building you are in.
- The gas stove has been on for hours, and you light a match (or any scenario involving gas, propane, and other combustibles prone to explosion).
- You're swimming, and someone throws a huge chunk of sodium metal into the pool.
- You're standing on a volcano when it blows.
- A vehicle you're in is hit by something that causes it to explode.
- A furnace explodes in the building you're in.
- A gun backfires.
- An armory burns and explodes.
- You're trying to make dynamite in your home laboratory, and BOOM!
- You hear a high-pitched sound so loud and high that it makes your head explode.
- You eat or drink so much that you explode or die of internal ruptures.

Freezing to Death

You die, directly or indirectly, of extreme cold.

- You are lost in the mountains and freeze to death.
- You are hit by a freeze ray, slowing your reflexes and allowing your enemies to kill you.
- You are quick-frozen, then cracked apart by a hammer.
- You are cryogenically frozen, but the machinery fails. (See also the "Mechanical Failure or Malfunction" section later in this chapter.)
- You get locked in a freezer.
- You are in outer space and you have air and a suit, but it doesn't protect you from the cold, and you freeze.
- You get caught in an avalanche and buried in snow and ice.
- You are sprayed with liquid oxygen or liquid nitrogen.
- Aliens suck the heat out of you to power their ship or to make cocktails.

Friendly Fire

You are shot/stabbed/poisoned/sabotaged/pushed off a cliff...accidentally (or not) by allied forces.

G-Forces

This describes pressure built up generally as the result of extreme acceleration or deceleration of the body, causing similar effects to that of spinning. Blood flow is interrupted and/or the body is torn apart.

- A supersonic vehicle spins out of control.
- A carnival ride goes berserk.
- Aliens kidnap you, and the G-forces of their ship accelerating kill you.
- An evil genius traps you in a contraption that spins you to death.

Gravity

This is death by being crushed under one's own weight due to very high gravitational effects.

- Pulled into the sun.
- Teleporting to a planet with 50 times earth's gravity.
- A gravitation ray.
- A magic spell.

Grinding Death

This is death as a result of outside abrasion.

- A wood chipper.
- Sandpaper.
- Pushed up against a rough spinning or running surface.
- Dragged behind a horse or vehicle along a rough surface.
- Sent through a giant meat grinder.
- Chewed up by a larger creature (giant, troll, etc.).

Part VI

Impact

This describes a high-speed collision caused by a fall, a moving object (vehicle, falling boulder, and so on), or from enemy weapons or fists.

- Deadfall trap.
- Parachute failure or jumping out of a plane without a parachute.
- Shot from a cannon. It's the landing you have to watch out for.

- Falling off a cliff or balcony on a high building or tower, etc.
- Falling down stairs or down an elevator shaft.
- Punched in a lethal area.
- Hit with a bat, baton, fireplace poker, tire jack, mallet, hammer, mace, gun butt, baby, etc.
- Smashed by a speeding car, truck, tank, plane, or boat.
- Hitting a wall after being thrown from a vehicle that stops suddenly.
- Crashing in any vehicle, including planes and helicopters, boats, and spacecraft.
- Being thrown against a solid surface by a giant creature.
- Whacked by a board on a construction site.
- Obliterated by a falling meteorite.

See also the "Projectile Death" section. (Some projectiles can kill by impact.)

Impalement

This is death as a result of something penetrating your body, such as a bed of spikes or some form of twisted metal.

- Jousting lance.
- Spear or pole arm (or any sharp stick).
- Knife/dagger/sword (especially a rapier or other thrusting/stabbing weapons).
- Rebar (after a fall).
- Broken glass.
- Ice pick.
- Arrow or other penetrating projectile.
- Sharp edges of twisted metal, such as an airplane fuselage after a crash.
- Falling into a pit trap with sharpened stakes at the bottom.
- Being placed in an Iron Maiden.

Imploding

This describes a sudden inward collapse of the body.

- Crushed by outside air pressure (or water pressure).
- Having a small black hole appear inside the body.

Internal Invader

Something is living inside you and either eating you alive or will burst out of you, resulting in your death.

- An alien has hatched inside you.
- You have some kind of super-mutant tapeworm inside you.
- You have been infected by an experimental disease that grows inside you.
- You have cancerous tumors that are growing and will ultimately kill you.

Laughing to Death

This is literally laughing at something so funny you can't stop. Likely causes of death would be asphyxiation or convulsion, or possibly damage to internal organs.

- You are given drugs that make everything seem so funny you can't stop laughing.
- Under extreme stress, you crack and laugh maniacally until you can't breathe anymore and you die.
- You suddenly realize that all of existence is absurd and begin laughing uncontrollably. In the end, you die.

LIFE FORCE REMOVED

Something sucks the life out of you.

- Magic or sci-fi.
- Extreme sadness, depression, or tragedy. (You lose the will to live.)
- Alien creature or machine.

LIQUEFACTION

The body's organs turn to liquid.

- Extreme sonic weapons.
- Magic.
- Disease.
- Corrosive agents.
- Bones liquefy—something causes your bones to lose their strength or to become liquid. The body can no longer support itself, and death soon follows.

MAGIC AND SUPERNATURAL CAUSES

Whatever is unexplained is magic. But in games, magic and supernatural events are pretty standard and are often used to kill. See also the "Magic Abilities" section of Chapter 15, "Character Abilities."

- Death as the result of magical spells and/or supernatural entities or events (including witches, vampires, zombies, etc.). Examples are endless and can include most other forms of death.
- Possession by another (demon, ghost spirit, etc.).

MECHANICAL FAILURE OR MALFUNCTION

Some machine that you depend upon fails.

- Vehicle malfunction, causing an accident.
- Transporter malfunction, causing the scrambling of your atoms.
- Life-support malfunction.
- Weapon malfunction.
- Lethal short circuit.
- Radiation leak.
- Robot(s) running amok.

MEDICAL FAILURE

Something fatal occurs during a medical procedure or as a direct result of medical intervention.

- Failed operation.
- Wrong medicine.
- Wrong operation. (You go in for a Botox treatment, and they try a heart transplant instead...and it fails.)
- You catch a deadly disease while in the hospital.
- You have an allergic reaction to a medicine.
- The docs killed you on purpose because you posed a threat to them or to someone who bribed or threatened them—making it an execution as well as a medical death.

MELTING OR VAPORIZATION

This is death by excessive heat or corrosive substance. In the case of heat, it must be very intense, otherwise normal burning will occur.

- Lava
- Acid
- Supernatural effects
- Magical substance
- Nuclear blast
- Falling into the sun

Metaphysical Revelation

This describes a contradiction between the physical and metaphysical realities, causing death.

- End of universe.
- Explained through logic that you cannot exist. (This might also fit into the "Fooled You!" list.)
- Death of your god.
- You become so spiritually advanced, you simply leave the body behind. In this sense, personality might remain intact, but the body is abandoned. (This is what some people call nirvana, *Samadhi*, or enlightenment.)

Mind Control

This describes being forced to kill yourself or to perform actions that ultimately result in death by an outside entity that controls your mind and will or otherwise manipulates or tricks you.

- Walk off a high place and die in the fall.
- Stab yourself with a sharp object.
- Walk in front of traffic or other moving vehicles.
- Walk into a dangerous setting—wild animals, gang territory, etc.
- Think you're eating and drinking, but you're not—die of thirst or starvation.
- Drink poison thinking it's something else.
- Self-programming to kill yourself on a special cue.

Molecular Breakdown

The molecules that make up the body lose cohesion, causing the bonds between them to break apart. Similar to being pulled apart, but on a much smaller scale.

Mutation

Something causes you to mutate, and the mutation is not viable within the current environment, resulting in death. Alternatively, death could occur from outside forces if the mutation caused you to be less able to defend yourself or perceive danger.

Mystery

You die, but the reason is a mystery…cause unknown.

Mythical Death Blows

Although there are real ways to kill someone more or less instantly using special martial arts techniques (see also "Fatality Systems" in Chapter 15, "Character Abilities"), martial arts lore is full of special, but presumably mythical, lethal blows with colorful names. Each causes death by the precise use of force to a critical location or by the application of supernatural energy to the blow.

- Buddha palm strike
- Five fingers of death

Natural Causes

This describes death as the natural result of circumstances.

- Dying of old age.
- Starving.
- Dying of thirst.
- Dying of exhaustion.

Nausea

Something causes uncontrollable nausea, ultimately leading to reduced ability to reason or defend oneself. It may lead to a direct death through convulsions or dehydration, or it could lead indirectly to death due to reduced capacity.

Overwhelmed

This describes death caused by attacks by numerous enemies or other forces too great to escape or defeat.

- Torn apart by army ants.
- Killer bees.
- *The Birds* (Hitchcock).
- Hordes of enemies (of any kind).
- Cattle stampede.
- Flash flood.
- Avalanche.
- Hurricane/tornado.

Pinching/Restriction

This describes pressure applied to specific areas of the body, restricting the flow of fluids in the body or ultimately breaking connections of nerves, sinews, veins, and/or arteries. This may be accidental or intentional.

Poison

This refers to the introduction into the body of a caustic or destructive agent. It generally causes damage over time, resulting in death if no treatment is applied.

- Bite from a poisonous reptile, insect, fish, etc.
- Poisoned weapon (such as a dart, arrow, or shuriken).
- Hypodermic needle.
- Poison gas.
- Magic spell.
- Ingested through food or drink.
- Inhaled through the atmosphere.
- Absorbed through the skin, eyes, or other orifices.
- Intentionally passed by contact with an enemy agent.
- Intentionally inserted into drinking-water sources or foods.
- Intentionally placed on some object a character will touch or use.
- Drug overdose.

Projectile Death

This describes getting hit by one (or many) energy beams, shockwaves, or fast-moving, sharp, hard, or heavy objects.

- Bullets of various kinds.
- Cannon balls.
- Missile warheads.
- Rocks.
- Shuriken.
- Throwing knife.

- Arrows and crossbow bolts.
- A stick of straw blown at high speed by hurricane winds.
- Spear.
- Laser beam.
- Plasma bullet.
- Dart (poison or not).
- Harpoon.
- Sonic waves or pulses.
- Getting hit on the head by a nuclear bomb that doesn't detonate, but kills you.
- Shrapnel from anything that explodes and projects damaging shards.
- Meteorite.
- A flying screw or bolt kicked out by a machine or vehicle.
- Household objects, such as irons, kitchen knives, sharp tiles, etc.
- Office objects, such as paperweights, letter openers, etc.
- Sports items, such as baseballs traveling 90 mph, hockey pucks, polo balls, golf balls, etc.

Radioactivity

This is death as a result of cell damage caused by exposure to radioactivity. Also, it could refer to slower death as a result of cancer or other disease resulting from prior radiation poisoning. (Radiation poisoning is situational—exposure to lethal doses can occur for a variety of reasons.)

- Nuclear blast radiation.
- Nuclear accident radiation.
- Exposure to radioactive material in a lab, reactor, or other facility.
- Terrorist dirty bombs.
- EV activity in space.
- Death as a result of radiation damage due to ozone layer depletion.
- Spending too much time in a tunnel or mine containing natural radioactive materials.
- Alien radiation ray.

Rapid Aging

Something causes the body to age rapidly. This could lead directly to death as the aging process continues, or it could lead to simply turning you into a very old person with reduced reflexes, brittle bones, and slow movements. In the old state, you would be easily killed by any number of other events or causes. Rapid aging can be a direct or indirect cause of death.

Scared to Death

This describes death as a result of something frightening.

- Being buried alive.
- A horrible monster.
- Psychological torture.
- Magically induced terror.
- Drug-induced terror.
- Any extreme phobia in which the fear is unconquerable.
- A sudden event that is so frightening your heart stops. [See also "Shock (Mental)."]
- A threat—for instance, someone pointing a gun at you and threatening to shoot.

Shock (Electrical)

This is the passage of a high electrical charge through the body, resulting in heart failure or in superheating the organs, basically cooking you to death.

- Lightning strike.
- Electrocution (accidental or intentional).
- Magical attack.
- Freak accident.
- A high-voltage wire falls and hits you.
- You handle a machine or device that short circuits, and you die.
- You try to fix a broken electrical device but end up electrocuting yourself.
- Shock from an electric eel or other electricity-producing creature. (May result in drowning instead of death by electrocution.)

Shock (Mental)

Something unexpected overwhelms you, causing some kind of system failure.

- Extreme reaction to a surprising event that causes heart failure. Or, a reaction that causes a secondary event that kills you, such as losing control of a car and crashing or running away from something scary and falling and breaking your neck (or running headlong into something even more dangerous).
- Overstimulation of your mind. The mind is overwhelmed by your senses.

Sleep Deprivation

This refers to dying as a result of lack of sleep.

- As a prisoner, you are prevented from sleeping until your body rebels and you die.
- You go crazy manic and can't sleep. Ultimately, you die.
- You are given (or take) drugs that prevent you from sleeping.
- You try an experimental formula that ends up giving you super powers, but preventing you from sleeping. Ultimately, you die. (See also the upcoming "Sleep" section for indirect causes of death induced by sleep.)

Sliced and Diced

This describes getting hit by one (or many) objects that are sharp or moving fast, or that are moving in opposite directions.

- Sucked into a jet engine.
- Sliced to bits by a sword or other bladed weapon.
- Sucked into the propeller of a plane, helicopter, or boat.
- Falling or being sucked into an industrial ventilation fan.
- Tossed into a giant blender.
- Sliced up by a power saw or meat cutter.
- Many, many paper cuts.
- Attacked by scalpels or razorblades.
- Falling or being thrown into sharp metal or glass.
- Falling or being thrown into a plate glass window, which slices you up as it breaks and falls.
- Dying by guillotine.
- Dying by pruning shears, kitchen knives, scissors, letter openers, and other household (or office) dangers.
- Cut apart by monofilament wire.

Spinning

This describes being whirled around and around until the centrifugal force of the spinning causes the blood to pool and stops the flow, ultimately causing death. The body may or may not be torn apart by the force. Some examples are similar to those for "G-Forces."

Spirit/Body Separation

Somehow your spirit becomes separated from your body, and the body is destroyed or made uninhabitable.

- A magic spell.
- Arcane ritual.
- Failed astral projection experiment.
- Alien intervention.
- Demonic possession or other supernatural cause.

Spirit Death

Somehow a character's spirit is trapped, captured, taken over, or destroyed by something more powerful. It's similar to "Spirit/Body Separation."

- Evil shamans contain your spirit, and the body dies.
- Some mighty spiritual force takes your spirit and crushes it.

Splitting

This describes tearing apart, generally from internal forces (as opposed to stretching, which can cause splitting from external forces).

- Slow buildup of pressure that doesn't burst, but splits the body open.
- The alien creature from the previous example splits you open in order to escape.
- Cut in half by a large axe. (External force splitting—also in "Sliced and Diced.")
- Sliced by a pendulum blade, as in Poe's "The Pit and the Pendulum." (See also "Sliced and Diced.")

Starvation

The body dies from lack of nutrients.

- Lack of food.
- Inability (possibly due to a disease) to digest food.
- Eating food with no nutritional content.
- Hypnotized or controlled in some way to think you are eating, but you're not.

Stretching

This describes being pulled apart by opposing forces.

- The rack.
- Being attached to two or more points, at least one of which is moving away from another (such as a wall and a moving truck).
- Being torn apart by having your limbs tied to horses.
- Being ripped in half by a giant creature of immense strength.

Suicide

Self-administered death, the real cause of which is dependent on the method used. (Note: In some cases, suicide may be assisted by someone else.)

- Death by excessive drug intake—intentional or unintentional, legal or not—alcohol, heroin, sleeping pills, etc.
- Shooting.
- Jumping.
- Hanging.
- Poisoning.
- Enlightenment—voluntarily leaving the body. (See also "Metaphysical Revelation.")

Suffocation/Asphyxiation/Strangulation

This describes restriction of the ability to breathe or the absence of breathable air.

- Hanging.
- Accidental strangulation, such as a scarf getting caught in a car door or a tie caught in a machine.
- In a vacuum (such as outer space).
- Buried alive (by enemy action, cave-in, or avalanche).
- Inability to breathe as a result of something that fills your lungs with fluid (which is similar to drowning) or that shuts down your lungs or the blood's ability to process oxygen. This could be caused by biological (disease) or chemical agents.
- Shot into outer space.
- Auto-asphyxiation.

Taste (Direct Death)

You try to eat something so horrifically bad that it kills you.

- Someone develops something that is so bad that the very taste of it short-circuits the brain, and you die.

The Bends

This refers to nitrogen narcosis, or the formation of bubbles of nitrogen in your brain, causing embolisms and death. It occurs generally as a result of a rapid reduction in external pressure, often caused by ascending from deep water too fast, but it could also (theoretically) happen in outer space pressure locks or from other more devious means. It is a relatively common problem among scuba divers.

Tickling

Someone (or something) tickles you mercilessly, causing you to die, probably from lack of breath, but possibly from overstimulation or some weird science phenomenon.

Time Travel or Dimensional Accident

You are traveling in time or between dimensions, and something goes wrong.

- You accidentally touch a version of yourself from a different time period.
- You accidentally remove an ancestor from the timeline, causing your birth to never happen.

Turned Inside Out

Somehow your insides become your outsides and vice versa. You die.

Turning into Bait

This refers to being smeared or affected in some way that attracts predators, such as blood in the water around sharks. This could be accidental or intentional. The ultimate cause of death would be from animal attack (or whatever takes the bait).

Vehicular Death

You're traveling in some kind of moving conveyance. How did you die?

- Death while battling in a vehicle, such as an airplane, boat, underwater vehicle, car, tank, or space vehicle.
- Accidental vehicular death, such as running your car into another car or into a mountain, or having a plane crash as the result of weather conditions or equipment malfunction.
- Death as a result of sabotage to a vehicle, such as tampering with the brakes or planting a bomb that detonates upon ignition (or the first time the car turns to the right, etc.).

NOTE

Death in a vehicle can come from any number of sources, including crushing.

Vibration

This is death as a result of extreme cyclical movement, shaking the body until the cells break down or the blood cannot circulate.

- You are shrunk down to a tiny size and tossed in a paint-can shaker.
- Your interstellar vehicle begins to shake in a cosmic storm, and the vibrations ultimately kill you.

Writer's Pun

This refers to death or ceasing to exist all together as a result of ironic, comical, or convenient intervention by a writer, director, storyteller, creator, and so on. This is a unique subset of "Fooled You!" deaths.

- The animator suffers a fatal heart attack and, being an animated character, you cease to exist.
- The writer turns you into a trite metaphor and explains you away.
- You become inconvenient to the story, and the director removes you.
- The story in which you exist is forgotten, and all written, printed, or electronic record of that story has been lost.

Fooled You!

Something makes the idea of death irrelevant, invalid, or unimportant.

- You are already dead. (You discover that you are already dead, ergo you can't be killed...but then, you're dead anyway.)
- You can't die…you're immortal.
- Death only leads to an afterlife, anyway.
- You were an illusion, so you couldn't really die.
- It was all a dream.

Indirect Causes of Death

Death can also occur as an indirect result of something that happens. For instance, while hallucinating, you might walk off a cliff, drive into a brick wall, or ingest something poisonous.

Altered Physical Laws

Some part of your world doesn't react in the normal manner, causing death (by falling, G-force, gravity, crushing, and so on).

Bad Luck

This is death as a result of misfortune. This might be the result of a curse or other outside force or just an unlucky occurrence.

- Could be the result of a curse or spell.
- Could be simple bad luck.
- Could be some supernatural creature or force affecting you.
- Could be the will of the gods.
- A roll of the dice.
- Your "luck" statistic is set very low or even in negative numbers.

Blinding

This is death as a result of being blinded. It is probably an indirect death caused by blundering into a situation that causes death due to the inability to see the danger. Any number of events could cause the blindness in the first place.

Causes of Blindness

- Congenital.
- An accident.
- A disease that attacks your eyes or that affects the visual centers of the brain.
- Someone intentionally blinds you.
- Temporary blindness due to a blow to the head.
- You stare into a bright light (such as the sun) for too long.
- Someone sets off a Flash Bang grenade, and you are temporarily blinded.
- You step out of a brightly lit room into the dark, moonless night, and you are blind until your eyes adjust.
- Someone turned out all the lights.
- Some magic or curse caused you to go blind.

Indirect Causes of Death Due to Blindness

- You walk off a cliff or fall down the stairs.
- You step into a deadly trap.
- You bash your head on a low ceiling while attempting to run from a pursuer.
- You step into an empty elevator shaft.

Boredom

You become so bored that you end your life by some means or simply lose the will to live.

Broken Heart

This is wasting away as a result of extreme sadness/depression caused by some loss.

- You lost the love of your life.
- You lost a child.
- Your life's work was destroyed.
- You are the victim of a gypsy curse.
- You have been made to believe that everyone you love has been destroyed (true or not).

Deafness

You become deaf and do not hear the thing that kills you.

Hallucination

This describes death as an indirect result of hallucinations. They could be intentionally administered, accidental, or self-induced.

- In a drugged state, you think you can fly.
- You see something that is there, but you see it as something nonthreatening. For instance, you walk in front of a bus thinking it is a loaf of bread. Or you see a deadly alien as your mother.
- You choke on your own vomit (very common).
- You try to drive, with unfortunate and fatal consequences.
- You walk off a cliff or fall down a few flights of stairs, and so on.

Insanity

This refers to being driven insane and dying as a result of diminished capacity to detect danger, inability to defend oneself, or directly by internal pressures ultimately popping the blood vessels in your brain.

- Someone successfully drives you crazy.
- Someone is using mind-control techniques on you.
- The events of your adventure simply overwhelm you and cause you to lose touch with reality.
- You took too many drugs or the wrong kinds of drugs.
- Your brain chemicals just decided to go weird on you.
- You passed through a cosmic cloud that left you deranged.
- You have a congenital condition that suddenly kicked in, and you went crazy as a result.

Loyalty Death

Through loyalty to some person, agency, government, or cause, you will do anything, including risk (and lose) your life.

- Committing ritual suicide (like seppuku).
- Suicide bombers (like kamikaze pilots or modern terrorist bombers).
- Following orders, you commit acts that are likely to get you killed.
- You "take the bullet" for someone else.
- You are someone's food taster.
- You take the rap for someone and are executed.

Neglect

This refers to death because someone (including yourself) didn't care enough to maintain your life.

- Another person neglects you until some other ailment kills you.
- You neglect an aspect of your well-being and die from it. For instance:
  - An infection grows until it poisons your blood.
  - You eat food that doesn't nourish you, and you slowly starve to death or contract a disease or condition that ultimately kills you.

Sleep

You sleep until you die (by starvation, old age, and so on).

- The Rip Van Winkle effect.
- You are drugged.
- You are in a coma.
- Magic or curse.
- Really extreme depression.
- You dream of death.

Smell

This is death as a result of some powerful scent. It is probably indirect death, such as being caused to gag and have difficulty breathing and then blundering into a deadly situation because of it.

- Dropped into a vat of raw sewage or excrement.
- Breathing a stinging agent that burns your sinuses.
- Blinded by pheromones into doing something unintentionally suicidal.
- Eating something that smells really tasty but is in reality highly toxic.
- Someone develops a toxin, virus, or other agent that attacks or does something to the brain when you smell it, causing death.
- Inability to smell a dangerous gas before lighting a match.

Stupidity (Darwin Awards)

You do something so dumb that you die, or you are so stupid that you cannot (or don't) defend yourself.

- You wonder what cyanide tastes like if it smells like almonds.
- You didn't know it was loaded.
- You challenge a kickboxer to a fight.
- You date the mob boss's daughter, then dump her.
- You try to juggle balls filled with nitroglycerin.
- Stop hitting yourself! (But you don't.)

Taste

You cannot taste, so you consume something hazardous, toxic, or poisons.

Touch

You've lost the physical ability to feel through the sense of touch.

- You cannot feel, so you disregard serious injury.
- You run into something that is dangerous and you don't realize it.

Torture Methods

Death can come from many sources, including accidents, complications from injuries or disease, and direct conflict between someone and an adversary. But, in addition to death by all the means already mentioned in this chapter, there is the issue of torture, which may or may not result in death. As such, torture is a category of its own.

Torture methods vary greatly and can include physical and mental means as well as the torture of denial or deprivation.

Physical Torture

NOTE

Picket: *An early English punishment was called the* picket, *in which the victim was hung by the waist from a high post with his bare heel resting on a blunt, pointed stake driven into the ground. This punishment was used up until the late 18th century.*

- Drawn and quartered
- Flayed alive
- Bamboo under the fingernails
- Beatings
- Whipping, flogging, flagellation
- Electrical shock (strategically placed)
- Disfiguration
- Amputations
- Elemental effects, such as heat, cold, immersion in water, etc.
- Suffocation and strangulation/garroting
- The rack
- The Iron Maiden
- Hamstringing
- Hanging
- Crucifixion
- Impaling
- Iron boot
- Oubliette

NOTE

Riding the Wooden Horse: *An 18th-century punishment in the English military that involved tying a man to a horse-like cart (with his hands and feet tied together) with a sharply angled wooden back (the head and tail were just decoration to complete the effect). This punishment was abandoned after it was decided that it did too much permanent injury.*

- Pillory/stocks
- Pulled apart by horses
- Pulley (pulled apart joints of arms and/or legs)
- Incessant water dripping on the head
- Chemical agents, such as pepper spray or pepper swabs on the eyes or genitals
- Branding and burning
- Scalding
- Boiling
- Blinding someone by destroying or plucking out their eyes
- Causing someone deafness by attacking the ears
- Non-lethally removing parts of the body, such as ears, nose, fingers, etc.
- Intentional infliction of disease
- Drugs administered to cause pain, fear, or compliance
- Whipping, caning, and other flagellation
- Rape and sexual abuse
- Dunking in water
- Disemboweling
- Breaking bones or cartilage
- Waterboarding

NOTE

Whirligig: *The whirligig was once used as a form of military punishment. It consisted of a barred cylindrical cage mounted so that it could be spun around. When the cage was spun around very fast, the victim would become extremely nauseated.*

Denial and Deprivation

Although denial and deprivation could be considered mental tortures, I've put them in a category of their own because of the specific nature of these methods. There is a difference between punishment and torture. For instance, if an inmate gets in trouble, taking away the TV set in his cell may not be torture, but depriving him of food and water would be.

- Solitary confinement
- Deprivation of light
- Deprivation of food and/or water
- Deprivation of the ability to move—such as the bamboo cages used to confine Vietnam POWs
- Deprivation of darkness—24-hour light
- Deprivation of diurnal rhythms—changing light/dark cycles irregularly to disrupt a person's equilibrium
- Deprivation of sleep
- Deprivation of privacy (can be torture for some)
- Deprivation of facilities (bathroom)
- Banishment
- Excommunication

Mental Torture

One main tool of mental torture is fear. Playing on people's fears and beliefs can cause a breakdown in a person's resistance. Another kind of mental torture is mental overload, as in the Chinese water torture, where repetitive sounds of stimulants (such as the perpetually dripping faucet) can cause ultimate insanity. Of course, some deprivation tortures are primarily mental, as discussed in "Denial and Deprivation" a moment ago.

- Any of the denial and deprivation methods
- Threats of violence
- Sexual threats
- Threats to harm or remove sexual organs
- Threats to blind or deafen someone
- Excessive and incessant interrogation
- Exposure to something they fear or revile, such as rats, snakes, feces, etc.
- Forced to eat food against moral, natural, or religious principles—such as a Muslim forced to eat pork or anyone forced to eat excrement
- Forcing drug dependency/addiction on someone, then presumably withholding the drug at will
- Exposure to endless propaganda
- Exposure to repetitive sounds, such as dripping water or excessively loud noises
- Defiling of holy objects
- Constant, irregular interruptions of a person's concentration, either by physical, visual, or auditory means
- Waterboarding
- Forcing a person to make an impossible choice (such as choosing a family member to die)
- Use of hallucinogenic drugs or other tactics to confuse a person's sense of reality

Other Useful Links

- Chapter 26, "Traps and Counter Traps"
- Chapter 25, "Barriers, Obstacles, and Detectors"
- Chapter 34, "Standard Modern Weaponry and Armor"

Part VII Weapons and Armor

33 Historical and Cultural Weapons

> Jaya, a daughter of primeval Daksha (one of the Rishis or sacred sages), became, according to a promise to Brahma, the creator, the mother of all weapons, including missiles. They are divided into four great classes. The Yantramukta (thrown by machines); the Panimukta (hand thrown); the Muktasandharita (thrown and drawn back); and the Mantramukta (thrown by spells and numbering six species), for the Mukta or thrown class of twelve species. This is opposed by the Amukta (unthrown) of twenty species, to the Muktamukta (either thrown or not) of ninety-eight varieties, and to the Bahuyuddha (weapons which the body provides for personal struggles). All are personified.
> —Sir Richard Francis Burton, *The Book of the Sword* (Dover Publications, 1987)

Weapons and armor are common in games. They come in all shapes and sizes, ranging from simple hand-to-hand weapons and cloth armor all the way to sophisticated, modern nanotech devices and electronically enhanced personal shield technologies. The range is staggering. There are literally thousands of weapons throughout all of history, and most cultures have had their own variations on the basic themes of clubs, swords, daggers, axes, spears, hammers, throwing stars, bows, and crossbows. In this chapter I haven't tried to list *every* weapon (many of them I can't even pronounce!), but I've tried to look at the basic variations on the themes and to discover for you a few of the more unusual specimens. Why? Because I hope you will find inspiration in this list—ways to make your games more interesting and your weapon choices more varied.

In this chapter:

- Weapons
- Armor
- Medieval Castles
- Siege Equipment

Weapons

Although not every game requires weapons, it's hard to imagine the game industry without a healthy dose of good armament. In this chapter and the one that follows, we've attempted to give you a reference to the many weapons of history, weapons of different cultures, and, in the next chapter, modern weaponry. Depending on the game you are developing, you can look for inspiration in the appropriate sections.

There are all sorts of weapons, and we've categorized the lists in this chapter by weapon types—for instance, swords, clubs, daggers, and so on. However, before we get to the specific weapon lists themselves, we thought it would be very useful to list the qualities of weapons in more general terms, and also the qualities of different types of weapons. Whereas the specific weapon lists may prove helpful as references and inspirations to the different ways that weapons have been designed throughout history and around the world, simply looking at the qualities of weapons can help you consider the design of unique weapons, perhaps weapons that never existed but that serve interesting purposes within your game. This is especially useful if you are not necessarily going for historical or real-world accuracy, but more for fun and effect.

Qualities of Weapons

This section breaks down the qualities of weapons into different categories. Whenever you want to get creative with weapons, this is a good place to start. Simply choose different qualities to design your own weapon, changing around the different qualities to achieve different effects. For instance, how would you use a pocket-sized blunt instrument or a skyscraper-sized sword? Who knows what outlandish concept will suggest to you something you never thought of before—or something that nobody else has thought of. All you have to do is make it fun.

Size

- Huge
- Large
- Medium
- Small
- Tiny
- Nano

Weight

- Feather
- Light
- Medium
- Heavy
- Ponderous

Length

- Mini
- Short
- Medium
- Long
- Very long
- Ridiculously long

Material

- Wood
- Stone
- Obsidian
- Fire
- Ice
- Copper
- Tin
- Bronze
- Iron
- Steel
- Titanium
- Plastic
- Ceramic
- Combination
- Crystal
- Diamond
- Ruby
- Emerald
- Sapphire
- Mythril
- Energy
- Dark star matter
- Alien or futuristic

Primary Type of Attack

- Stabbing/piercing
- Cudgeling/crushing
- Slashing
- Ensnaring
- Strangling
- Poisoning
- Disease
- Penetrating (such as bullets, arrows, and so on)
- Incapacitating
- Plasma
- Light energy
- Electrical
- Body compromising (for instance, nano agents shot into the body)

Type of Grip

- One hand at end
- Two hands at end
- Either one or two hands
- Gripped in the middle
- Two hands spread apart
- Strapped on
- Changing hands
- Whirling
- Strapped on body
- Not held or attached to body at all

Balance

- Front-heavy
- Back-heavy
- Perfectly balanced
- End-heavy/middle-light
- Middle-heavy/end-light
- Variable (configurable)

Symmetry

- Symmetrical
- Asymmetrical

Maneuverability

- Highly maneuverable
- Somewhat maneuverable
- Awkward
- Forget it

Reach and/or Range

- Kissing distance
- Arm's length
- Body length
- Medium distance
- Long distance
- Very far away
- Interstellar distances

Sharpness (Edge or Point)

- Blunt
- Sharp
- Razor
- Molecular
- Irrelevant

Sighting or Aiming

- Hand/eye
- Crude sights
- Magnification sights
- Laser sights
- Guided sights
- Intelligent auto-aim

Durability

- Fragile
- Somewhat breakable
- Can take some abuse
- Rock-solid
- Malleable/flexible
- Unbreakable/indestructible

Can Block?

- No
- Very well
- Somewhat
- With luck

Throwable?

- In a pinch
- Somewhat effective
- Preferred method of delivery
- Not a chance

Portability

- Fits in a pocket
- Carried openly
- Huge
- Dragged along
- A team of horses might move it
- Requires a semi-truck
- Requires a barge
- Requires a battleship
- Fixed in place

Can Be Hidden?

- Easily
- Preferred method
- With difficulty
- With elaborate preparations
- No way

Ornamentation

- Plain
- Fancy
- Ornate
- Bling

Noise Level

- SBD
- Moderate sound
- Loud
- Wakes the neighbors
- Deafening

Speed of Use

- Instantaneous
- Rapid
- Moderate
- Slow
- Glacial

Speed of Reuse

- Instant/automatic
- Rapid
- Moderate
- Slow
- Glacial
- One use is all you get

Needs Ammunition, Loading, or Special Care?

- Needs no ammunition
- Needs no loading
- Nothing special
- Needs ammunition
- Needs loading
  - Every once in a while
  - Every time it's used
- Requires special care

Hits Multiple Enemies?

- Yes
  - How many?
  - What range?
  - Diminishing returns?
  - How lethal?
- No

Number of People Needed to Operate

- 1
- 2
- 3 or more
- None

Lethal/Non-Lethal

- Lethal
- Non-lethal
- Sometimes lethal, sometimes not

Other Uses

- Poison (just about any hand or non-combustion projectile weapon can be used to deliver poison to the victim)
- Blade breaker
- Walking cane
- Musical instrument
- Stool
- Belt and/or belt buckle
- Tie up or entangle
- Use as a step
- Climbing grips (shuko/tekagi)
- Use scabbard as a:
  - Listening device
  - Megaphone
  - Snorkel tube
  - Blowgun
  - Probe (in darkness)
  - Shield or weapon deflector
  - Weapon
  - Step
- Use spear as vaulting device
- Use to deliver blinding powders
- Key
- Symbol (of authority or rank, for instance)
- Message (contained somehow in weapon)

Primary User(s)

- Law enforcement
- Military
- Spy
- Criminal/rogue
- Hunter
- Royalty
- Common people
- Housewife
- Anyone
- Specialist
- Alien

Hand Weapon Types

Blade (Slashing, Cutting)

- Straight
- Curved
- Broad
- Double-edge
- Single-edge
- Triangular
- Round
- Notched
- Wavy
- Gutters
- Reinforced
- Wide
- Narrow
- Double-ended (two blades with middle grip)
- Combo weapon
  - Hidden dagger
  - Hidden gun
- Grips and guards
  - Simple guard
  - Basket guard
  - Spiked/bladed guard
  - Single-grip
  - Double-grip
  - Separated grips for two hands
- Scabbard
  - Full scabbard
    - Soft material
    - Hard material
  - Partial scabbard
  - No scabbard
  - Multi-use
    - Hidden knife/dagger
    - Hidden gun
    - Blowgun
    - Ninja step
    - Use as weapon
- Usage
  - Thrusting
  - Slashing
  - Hacking/crushing
  - Twisting
  - Throwing
  - Combination

Axe

- Blades
  - Single blade
  - Double blade
  - Spear end
  - Double-ended (blades on both ends)
- Blade shape
  - Curved
  - Recurved
  - Straight
  - Points

- Combinations
  - Blade and hammer
  - Blade and spike
  - Blade and gun
- Throwable?
  - Primary use
  - Yes, but not primary use
  - With difficulty

Blunt Weapons (Bashing)

- Club
- Hammer
  - Spikes
  - Combo weapon
  - Armor shredding
  - Material for head
    - Wood
    - Metal
    - Modern materials
- Mace
  - Shape variants
    - Round
    - Ovoid
    - Cylindrical
    - Other
  - Spikes
- Flail
  - Single head
  - Multi-head
  - Long chain
  - Short chain
  - Simple hinge
  - Spikes (number, length, and location variants)
- Staff (see the upcoming "Staff" section of this list)
- Nunchuks
- Possible blunt weapon variants
  - Spikes
  - Blades
  - Electrical charge
  - Explosive tips
  - Double-ended
  - Flexible heads (other than flails)

Pointed (Thrusting)

- Thrusting swords
- Spears
- Pikes
- Hairpins (used in kunoichi—female ninja)
- Needles

Staff

- Length
- Weight
- Flexibility
- Diameter
- Contoured or straight
- Folding
- Grips?
- Ends
  - Blunt
  - Bladed
  - Reinforced
  - Hidden blade
  - Hidden gun
  - Hidden chain and weight
  - Secret compartments

Ranged

- Throwing
- Assisted (spear thrower, sling, etc.)
- Powered (bow, crossbow)
- Blow gun
- Water gun (used by ninja to shoot poisoned water at enemies from a distance of up to 60 feet)
- Siege engine (such as catapult, mangonel, trebuchet, etc.)
- Firearm
  - Pistol
  - Rifle
  - Scattergun (such as shotgun)
  - Cannon or artillery
  - Semi-automatic
  - Automatic
- Futuristic (such as laser/energy/gravity/mind control weapons)

Thrown Weapons

- Shurikens
- Stones
- Knives
- Axes
- Darts
- Bolo
- Caltrops (tetsu-bishi—favorite ninja weapon)

Chain, Linked, or Corded Weapons

- Whip
- Lasso
- Kyoketsu-shogi (ring and blade)
- Kusari-gama (ball and scythe)
- Nunchucks
- Flail (see blunt)

Fist Weapons

- Blunt
- Spiked
- Bladed
- Shuko/tegaki
- Metal claws (over fingers)

Combination Weapons

- Rifle or pistol and blade
- Hammer and spike
- Dual blades
- Axe head and point
- Hidden retractable blade
- Point + hammer + axe
- Staff with hidden blade
- Staff with concealed chain and opposite end weighted like a club (shinobi-zue)
- Staff with hidden missiles in one end
- Staff with hidden gun barrel
- Sword with hidden dagger
- Bow with blades
- Double-sided weapon (top and bottom)

Projectile Weapons

Size

- Huge
- Large
- Medium
- Small
- Tiny
- Nano

Weight

- Heavy
- Light
- Medium
- Featherweight
- Dense

Length

- Long
- Short
- Tiny
- Extra long
- Extra, extra long

Type

- Combustion/firearm
- Spring/tension
- Breath
- Thrown
- Other
  - Kicked
  - Whirled

Material

- Wood
- Stone
- Ice
- Copper
- Tin
- Bronze
- Iron
- Steel
- Titanium
- Crystal
- Diamond
- Ruby
- Emerald
- Sapphire
- Mythril
- Energy
- Dark star matter

Primary Type of Attack

- Impact
- Penetration/piercing
- Explosion
- Poison
- Entanglement/entrapment
- Crushing
- Heat
- Cold
- Implosion
- Nano agent delivery

Portability

- Easy
- Not bad
- With effort
- With difficulty
- Really cumbersome
- Needs a forklift
- Needs a semi-truck
- Needs a barge
- Needs a battleship

Type of Grip

- One-handed
- Two-handed
- No hands
- Feet
- Hands and feet
- Mouth
- Other

Balance

- Even in middle
- Front-heavy
- Back-heavy
- Middle-heavy, light ends
- Ends heavy, light middle

Symmetry

- Symmetrical
- Asymmetrical

Range

- Kissing distance
- Arm's length
- Body length
- Medium distance
- Long distance
- Way far away
- Interstellar distances

Sighting or Aiming

- Hand/eye
- Crude sights
- Magnification sights
- Laser sights
- Guided sights
- Intelligent auto-aim

Durability

- Fragile
- Somewhat breakable
- Can take some abuse
- Rock-solid
- Malleable/flexible
- Unbreakable/indestructible

Useful in Melee?

- Very useful
- Moderately useful
- Barely useful
- Last ditch
- Not really

Throwable?

- In a pinch
- Somewhat effective
- Preferred method of delivery
- Not a chance

Can Be Hidden?

- Easily
- Preferred method
- With difficulty
- With elaborate preparations
- No way

Noise Level

- SBD
- Moderate sound
- Loud
- Wakes the neighbors
- Deafening

Speed of Use

- Instantaneous
- Rapid
- Moderate
- Slow
- Glacial

Speed of Reuse

- Instant/automatic
- Rapid
- Moderate
- Slow
- Glacial
- One use is all you get

Needs Ammunition, Loading, or Special Care?

- Needs no ammunition
- Needs no loading
- Nothing special
- Needs ammunition
- Needs loading
  - Every once in a while
  - Every time it's used
- Requires special care

Hits Multiple Enemies?

- Yes
- No

Number of People Needed to Operate

- 1
- 2
- 3 or more
- None

Lethal/Non-Lethal?

- Lethal
- Non-Lethal
- Sometimes lethal, sometimes not

Clubs and Hammers

Clubs were the first actual weapons, aside from simple sticks and stones. They are also the true ancestors of just about every subsequent hand weapon, such as swords, axes, and even boomerangs. The principle of a club is to increase the amount of power that can be delivered by placing the weight of the attack farther from the hand, thereby increasing the strength of the blow that can be inflicted. The simplest clubs were nothing more than sticks, with no adornment or special modifications. The Irish shillelagh is a good example; it's a simple log cut from a blackthorn tree, heavy at one end and narrow enough to hold in the hand at the other. Another interesting example is the Japanese flute, the shakuhachi, which was traditionally cut from the root piece of a large bamboo and made a nifty club often used by spies who carried no other visible weapons.

Clubs can be made of one material, such as wood, ivory, bone, or stone. Later clubs have been made of metal and even modern-age materials. However, historically, clubs were also made of combined materials. For instance, the early Native American tomahawk was made by mounting a stone to a stick. Other clubs have had teeth, sharpened rocks, spikes and nails, wood, or bone attached to the shaft to increase the damage done. These additions could add weight and therefore power to the club, or could add cutting and slashing damage to the club's attack. In the days when armor was common, all-metal clubs called *maces* were popular—and far more effective than swords in combating armored opponents.

Maces featured heavy heads with blades or flanges and sometimes spikes. Still other clubs were developed with flexible heads, such as the morning star or flail in Europe and other weapons around the world. These featured spiked balls and heavy weights, and the added power of the swinging part made them formidable weapons in the right hands. Even the nunchuks, made famous by Bruce Lee, are essentially a flexible club. Today, the policeman's truncheon, or nightstick, is an example of a club that is still in daily use.

Ornamental clubs have often been used as symbols of authority, and, as such, have been used as ceremonial weapons. Scepters and even batons evolved from clubs.

- **Baggoro.** A large, very heavy one-handed club or wooden sword used in Queensland.
- **Barkur.** A one-handed heavy club split from the trunk of a small tree. From Queensland.
- **Bec de Corbin.** A war hammer with a pointed end, like a beak.
- **Brandestoc.** A war hammer with a long concealed blade in the handle.
- **Bulawa.** A Russian mace.
- **Chacing Staves.** Twelve-foot-long clubs shod in iron, used by robbers in 17th-century England.
- **Club Shields.** Where clubs are a common form of weapon, defense against them may evolve as well. Special shields from Africa are designed specifically to defend against clubs. One is called a *quayre* and consists of a carved stick about a yard long with a rounded cavity in the middle, with a handhold. The other is similar but has strings, like a bow, which are strung tight and are used to catch the club attack.
- **Dabus.** An Arabian mace studded with nails.
- **Fakir's Crutch.** A crutch used by Indian fakirs, who weren't allowed to have weapons. The crutch served as a very effective mace, however, and sometimes contained a concealed stiletto.
- **Fang.** A Chinese weapon with two 5-inch blades—one straight and one at right angles to it at the end.
- **Flagellum.** A three-thonged scourge used by Roman gladiators.
- **Flail.** A weapon consisting of a short handle and a hinged or hooked attachment. The striking part of the flail often had weights and/or spikes attached. Flails were used for centuries and came in all shapes and sizes. Some were more like hinged clubs, while others featured chains with spiked metal balls at the ends. The basic form of handle and hinged extension remains, regardless of the specifics.
- **Furibo.** A 4-foot Japanese club covered with iron. (One specific design for the furibo uses the scabbard of a sword as the club, and the club's handle doubles as the sword's hilt.)
- **Hercules Club.** A heavy club with nails driven into the heads, used in sieges of the 17th century.
- **Hoeroa.** A double-curved Maori club made from the jawbone of a sperm whale.
- **I-Wata-Jinga.** A Native American club made by wrapping a stone in rawhide and attaching it to a 2-foot handle.
- **Ja-Dagna.** A Native American curved ironwood club with a ball at the end, sometimes spiked.
- **Ja-Weti.** A four-sided Native American club.
- **Jit-te.** A type of weapon in Japan that took many forms, but the simplest form was a baton or short club with a square iron hook close to the hilt. Primarily a parrying weapon, some were enhanced with blades and somewhat more like swords than batons.
- **Kauah.** A stone club about 15 inches long and 2 inches in diameter, meant to be thrown up to 20 yards.
- **Konnung.** A round club about 2-1/2 to 3 feet long, straight and spiked on the ends. It was meant to be held in the middle and used for stabbing.
- **Kotiate.** A Maori "liver cutter" club shaped something like a violin and made from wood or whale bone.
- **Leonile.** A wooden club. The handle ends in a point, and the striking edge is shaped something like a boomerang, with a sharp curve and a rounded, but sharp, point.
- **Lisan.** A club from ancient Egypt of consistent diameter, with a slight curve at the end.

- **Macana.** An odd-shaped club shaped something like an hourglass with a smaller and a larger end. Some macanas have stones set in them at 90 degrees, making them a form of tomahawk. They are used as clubs and as throwing weapons.
- **Mace.** A club made entirely of metal with a heavy, flanged head. It was especially useful for bashing in armor, so it was used for hand-to-hand fighting from the 11th century through the 16th century in Europe. Versions of the mace were used elsewhere in the world, although they varied a great deal in shape and size, with some resembling curved iron bars, others resembling fireplace pokers, and still others with spikes, blades, and circular heads.
- **Makana**. An Aztec club set with sharp stones.
- **Merai.** A Maori war club that was made from jade.
- **Miolner.** The mythical hammer of the Norse god, Thor, which would return to his hand when thrown.
- **Morning Star (also Holy Water Sprinkle).** A club with an enlarged head of wood or iron studded with spikes. Often a blade or extra-large spike would extend from the top of the head.
- **Pacho.** A club used in the South Sea Islands, lined with shark teeth.
- **Pagaya.** A Brazilian club shaped like a paddle.
- **Patu.** A short club used by the Maori as their principal weapon. It was roughly 14 to 20 inches long and shaped like a heavy paddle with a rounded handle and a hole at the base. Patus were made of various materials, such as wood, basalt, the jawbone of a sperm whale, or jade. The edges of the patu were very sharp.

  There were various forms of the patu, with different names to indicate the type of material it was made from. For example, the patu onewa was of basalt, the patu paraoa was from the whale's jawbone, and the patu pounamou (also called a *mere*) was made from jade. The kotiate (liver cutter) was more violin-shaped and made from bone or wood. The wahaika was generally made from wood, varied greatly in shape, and had more ornate carvings than the others, which tended to be quite plain.
- **Periperiu or Miro.** A 5-foot club from Australia, no more than 3-1/2 inches wide. It is slightly flattened on one end and blunt, and narrower on the other end, with a concave section. It's often decorated in red and white.
- **Plombee.** A 14th-century leaden mace, or one that is weighted with lead.
- **Pogamoggan.** A Native American war club that has an elastic handle with a stone attached at the end.
- **Quadrille.** A mace with four flanges.
- **Quarter Staff.** A walking staff that doubled as a club for fighting and was wielded with two hands.
- **Rang Quan.** A fighting club used by women. It tapers through its 6-foot length, being heavier at the end than at the handle, and it is pointed at both ends.
- **Sapakana.** A wooden club from South America with a rounded handle and a broad, almost shovel-like head.
- **Shashpar or Shushbar.** An Indian mace with six flanges.
- **Suan-Tou-Fung.** A mace with a globe-shaped or polygonal head attached to a straight bar handle.
- **Tambara.** A club from Australia that widens from the handle, then tapers to a point with three or four prongs on the end. About 28 to 34 inches long.
- **Tanda.** An Australian club with a globe-shaped end.
- **Tebutje.** Light clubs studded with shark teeth, from the Gilbert Islands.
- **Tewha-Tewha.** A wooden club commonly used in New Zealand. One end is a sharp spike and the other is shaped roughly like a quarter of a disk, somewhere between 3 and 6 feet long.
- **Tiglun.** An Inuit club only 6 or 7 inches long, made of ivory. It was made for fighting and was held like a dagger.
- **U'U.** A large club used in the Marquesas. It could be more than 4 feet long and carried a heavy head, all carved out of hardwoods. The head was carved and could be more than 5 inches thick.

- **Waddy.** The generic name for a club in Australia.
- **Wahaika.** An often ornately carved wood or bone club of the Maori of New Zealand.
- **War Hammer.** Used most extensively in Europe to combat armor, the war hammer generally consisted of a hammer head with an opposing spike and was tipped with a sharp point. The hammer head often had claws to better grip the armor and smash through it. In some cases the back spike was more of a cutting edge similar to an axe head. War hammers came in all shapes and sizes but were basically the same (or similar) configurations.

Swords

Although it is one of the most effective and popular weapons, the sword is not truly defined. There is no complete definition of a sword that clearly distinguishes it from a knife, a dagger, an espadon, or a glaive. There is overlap between all these weapons, so that although you generally know a sword when you see one, no specific and precise definition is generally accepted. The three classes of swords are those for cutting only, those for thrusting only, and those for cutting and thrusting. The earliest swords were probably of the cutting/slashing variety, having evolved from clubs.

In its simplest form, a sword is a long blade with a handle. The earliest swords probably evolved from clubs and may have been wooden, with somewhat sharpened edges such as are still seen in some aboriginal cultures. A sword-like club is made in the Gilbert Islands. It is wood or bone and studded with sharp shark teeth. However, thrusting was found to be superior in many circumstances, as it could be more precise and required less effort. With the development of fencing styles, the thrusting sword became far deadlier in the hands of a skilled swordsman.

The main sections of a sword are:

- The hilt
  - Pommel
  - Grip
  - Gurad
- The blade
  - Tang
  - Edge
  - Blade back or back edge

A sword is divided into the blade and the hilt. The blade is actually comprised of the tang, which fits into the hilt, and the blade proper. Some divide the blade further into the following sections, beginning with the hilt: the strong (22 percent), the half strong (22 percent), the half weak (37 percent), and the weak (19 percent). The blade also consists of the edge, the point, the back, and the false edge (a sharpened section on the back near the point of an otherwise single-edged sword).

NOTE

Sword knot: *A loop of soft leather or cord that was attached to the hilt of a sword and could be looped around the hand a few times to prevent being disarmed. It also allowed the wielder to drop the sword and let it hang from the sword knot, if need be.*

NOTE

Sword breaker: *A heavy-toothed blade designed to catch the enemy's blade and break it. There have been several weapons whose sole (or at least secondary) purpose was to break a blade.*

Many types of swords have been made, with various shapes, sizes, weights, and cross-sections. If you look at the cross-sections of many swords, you will often see certain types of construction. Some are simply carved from one edge to another, while others may have a central groove with a ridge in the middle. Single-edged swords often have a heavy back, a ridge, and a chisel-like edge.

NOTE

***Asidevata:** A mythical sword of the Hindu gods Shiva, Vishnu, and finally Indra. It was "fifty thumbs long and four thumbs broad."*
—Sir Richard Francis Burton, The Book of the Sword *(Dover Publications, 1987)*

Not all swords are equally adapted for every situation. Cutting swords are often curved and have a single edge (and possibly a false edge), which helps enhance the effectiveness of the cut. They may be sharp on the concave side or the convex side, depending on how they are intended to be used. Thrusting swords, on the other hand, are generally straight, like the rapier. Swords used for both cutting and thrusting are not as effective as those used for a single type of attack, but they are more versatile and generally are straight or slightly curved.

Basic Types of Swords

- Single edge
- Double-edged
- Stabbing (rapier)
- Slashing (saber)
- Straight
- Curved (scimitar)
- Two-handed

Two-handed swords were popular in Europe. For instance, in Switzerland, the two-handed sword was used until the beginning of the 14th century. Two-handed swords were, of course, used in many other parts of the world and were certainly the favorite swords for executions among many cultures. They generally had extra-long hilts to allow both hands to grip the sword, but the types of blades varied widely. Some were broad and heavy, and some were narrow and much lighter. Some were single-edged, while others were double-edged. And so forth...

Examples

- **Back Sword.** A sword with a straight or very slightly curved single-edged blade.
- **Basket Hilts.**
- **Broad Sword.** A straight, wide single-edged sword, often with a basket hilt. A very common weapon both in the military and among commoners.
- **Cutlass.** A name given to a variety of back swords through history, often associated with nautical swords.
- **Japanese Blades.**
  - **Ken.** An ancient double-edged straight sword. The oldest type of Japanese sword; it predates the more modern swords associated with samurai.
  - **Jin Tachi.** 33 inches and greater.
  - **Katana and Tachi.** 24 to 30 inches.
  - **Chisa Katana.** 18 to 24 inches.
  - **Wakizashi.** 16 to 20 inches.
  - **Tanto and Aikuchi.** 11 to 16 inches.
  - **Yoroi Toshi.** 9 to 12 inches.
  - **Kawiken.** 3 to 6 inches.
- **Quillon.** The part between the hilt and the blade. The quillon was generally formed of one straight bar terminated in either straight projections or curved pieces. If the curve was toward the blade, it was said to be *recurved.* Sometimes one of the bars curved back to form the counterguard to protect the hand.
- **Saber.** A straight or very slightly curved single-edged sword.
- **Sword Hilts.**

NOTE

Kwanyu was a great 2nd-century Chinese general who was deified in 1594 as the god of war and is often depicted on Japanese swords.

NOTE

The vajra (known as the dorje *in Tibet and the* tokko *in Japan) is the ancient Sanskrit symbol of the thunderbolt. It is often found in India, Tibet, Nepal, and Bhutan among Hindus and Buddhists. It is interesting that it has migrated all the way to Japan and is sometimes found ornamenting Japanese swords, on the hilts or carved into the blades.*

NOTE

One of the greatest Japanese sword makers, held only second to the famous Masamune, Muramasa is often left out of lists of the greatest Japanese sword makers, in part because there was a superstition that his blades were bloodthirsty, and if they did not taste blood often enough, they would force the owner into bad luck and ultimately to suicide.

NOTE

Tamashigiri: *The practice of testing sword blades on the bodies of criminals in Japan. Some accounts say the testing was done on the criminals after they were executed, but some stories say they were tested on live subjects, sometimes several standing together to see how many bodies the sword could pass through in one stroke. The counterpart to this was called* tsujigiri, *which meant to kill in the street to test a new sword. Sounds like* Grand Theft Auto, *samurai style. The more humane test involved a bundle of tightly bound straw, called a* tsukura, *which was said to do a decent job of mimicking a body.*

NOTE

Tengu are mythical Japanese beings, either human-shaped with wings and long noses or bird-like with strong beaks. They are said to have broken the precepts of Buddha and are denied either heaven or hell. In addition, their ruler, the dai tengu, is sick three times a day. Tengu are often depicted on Japanese sword mountings.

Specific Swords

NOTE

Ama No Murakumo Tsurugi: *Mythical sword said to have been drawn from the tail of the eight-headed dragon by Susano-O no Mikoto. It was said that Yamato Dake mowed his way out of a field of burning grass using this sword, after which it was called* Kusunagi no Tsurugi *("grass-quelling sword").*

- **Ayda Katti.** National sword of Malabar, featuring a long, broad blade and carried unsheathed.
- **Badelaire.** Sixteenth-century saber with a broad falchion-shaped blade and a straight hilt.
- **Basilard.** A short sword carried by civilians in the 15th century. It had a straight, tapering blade with diamond section, a straight hilt, and no guard.
- **Bastard Sword (also Hand-and-a-Half Sword).** Primarily a one-handed sword, the grip was long enough to allow a few fingers of the other hand to grip it for added power. The bastard sword was long and straight and featured a plain cross-guard and a rounded pommel.
- **Broadsword.** A straight, wide, single-edged sword used extensively in 17th-century military, usually featuring a basket hilt and various types of guards, shells, and loops.
- **Chikuto.** A Japanese bamboo fencing sword.
- **Chisa Katana.** An intermediate Japanese sword, shorter than a katana.

- **Claymore (or claidheamh-mor or claidhmhichean-mhora).** Of Scottish origin—a long, heavy-bladed, two-handed sword with a straight grip.
- **Curtana.** Called the "sword of mercy," it is one of three ceremonial swords that are borne before the sovereigns of England at their coronation. It is broad and straight, without a point.
- **Daisho.** A set of long (katana) and short (wakizashi) swords, standard weaponry for the samurai and Japanese military.
- **Dao.** A utility sword from Assam, unusual because it is wider at the tip than at the base and also sharper toward the base. It is used not only as a weapon, but as the main tool for anything that needs to be cut or fashioned.
- **Dha.** The national sword of Burma—a slightly curved, single-edged blade with no guard. Dha come in all lengths and generally have a long, sharp point.
- **Dusack.** A cutlass formed from a single piece of iron with the blade on one end and a loop that forms the grip and a knuckle guard or weapon as well.
- **Eared Daggers.** Daggers used in Europe that had coin-shaped discs attached to the pommels that in some cases vaguely resembled ears. Also sometimes known as *estradiots* or *stradiots.*
- **Elephant Swords.** Blades attached to the tusks of an elephant (possibly also to the trunk).
- **Espadon or Spadone.** A sword midway between a regular and a two-handed sword.
- **Estoc.** Long, narrow sword made for thrusting with a straight, quadrangular blade. Originally carried without a scabbard, on horseback or on the belt, they later were fitted with scabbards.
- **Falchion.** A curved, wide-bladed sword with a single edge. The blade is widest near the point, and the point is formed by curves from both the front and the back.
- **Firangi.** Named after the word for *foreigner*, it was a 16th- and 17th-century Mahratta blade used for cutting and thrusting—a broadsword or rapier.
- **Flamberge.** At one time this term was applied to any sword, but ultimately it came to describe swords with undulating curves along the blade. By the end of the 16th century, it referred to a special, very slender form of rapier.
- **Flyssa.** A Moroccan single-edged blade, anywhere from 1 foot to 3 feet or more, with an unusual shape. The blade is wide at the hilt, and the back is straight. The edge curves inward for about the first third of the length, then widens again, finally curving inward to a long point.
- **Hammasti.** A double sword blade.
- **Hangar/Sidearm.** A short sword slung from a shoulder belt, often carried by infantry of the 18th century as a secondary weapon, along with a musket and a bayonet.
- **Herebra.** A Phoenician sword.
- **Jinto.** A Japanese war sword.
- **Kamashimo Zashi.** A short sword often given to Japanese boys, but also worn by men in court dress because it was short enough to be worn in a litter.
- **Kaskara.** A Middle Eastern straight-bladed, double-edged sword.
- **Kastane.** A short, curved blade with a single edge and a handle-like hilt—the national sword of Ceylon, probably of Dutch origin.
- **Katana.** A Japanese long sword.

NOTE

The Yamabushi were Japanese warrior monks who carried swords as well as a rosary and a conch-shell trumpet. They wore a polygonal hat instead of a helmet and were much feared until they were destroyed by Nobunaga in the 16th century.

- **Katzbalger.** A German double-edged sword of the 16th century.

- **Kenuki Gata Tachi.** An older Japanese sword, generally carried for ceremonial purposes. The hilt was perforated at each end in the form of a pair of tweezers.
- **Khanda.** A very typical Indian sword with a wide blade that gets wider toward the tip. It is blunt-tipped and double-edged. The pommel features a curved guard and a spike extending out from it. This spike was used for two-handed strokes and also to rest the hand when the sword was sheathed.
- **Khrobi/Khopesh.** A sickle-shaped, double-edged sword of ancient Egypt. This design influenced blades all around the world, including the Greek Kopis, the Spanish Facata, and even the Kukri of Nepal.
- **Kilij (Kilig).** A Turkish saber with a curved blade. The pommel also curved in the opposite direction from the blade and terminated in a rounded projection. The blade widens toward the tip, at which point the back edge is sharp as well as the front.
- **Kledyv.** An ancient Welsh sword.
- **Klewang.** A Malaysian single-edged sword that widens toward the end and then comes to a sharp point as the edge side angles sharply in toward the back.
- **Kora.** The national sword of Nepal, it is a wide, curved-blade, single-edged sword, curving sharply at the end while widening considerably. The end of the sword is generally flat across or with short, spiky extensions. The handle is cylindrical, with disk-shaped guards at the base and just above the grip.
- **Long Sword.** Double-edged (30 to 40 inches long), sharp-pointed weapon used in the Middle Ages in Europe, common during the Crusades. Could be used for slashing or thrusting and was strong enough to counter some of the weaker elements of armor.
- **Machera.** A long, straight Greek sword.
- **Mandau.** The Malaysian headhunter's sword—a jungle knife used for many purposes, including headhunting. The blade is concave on one side and convex on the other, meaning that it can effectively be used with crosswise cuts. However, it is known to achieve considerable power despite its light weight. The scabbard held a smaller knife with a long handle, used to, among other things, clean the heads after they had been chopped off.
- **Manople.** A Moorish "boarding" sword with a short blade and two very short, curved side blades extending from the base of the main blade. From the 14th and 15th centuries.
- **Mel Puttah Bemoh.** A two-handed Indian sword that has two guards separated by about a foot—one round and the other shaped like a broad figure eight. The entire sword is about 5 feet long, but the blade is less than 4 feet.
- **Mopla.** A wide-bladed Middle Eastern sword about a foot or so long, with a double-edged curved blade that was carried blade up with the handle held in the belt.
- **Nimcha.** A Middle Eastern saber with a squared knuckle guard and drooping quillons coming out the base of the handle. The nimcha was curved, although the amount of curve varied.
- **No-Dachi.** An extra-long sword worn over the shoulder so that the hilt projected above the shoulder. It was carried in addition to a normal sword, which was carried in the belt.
- **Odachi.** A Japanese long sword from the 14th century. It was 4 to 5 feet long and was carried over the shoulder, similar to the no-dachi.
- **Opi.** Not Andy Griffith's son, but a variety of klewang, or sword with a horn hilt and pommel decorated with human hair.
- **Pakayun.** A saber from Borneo with a forked pommel carved of wood.
- **Palache.** A 17th-century Polish saber—straight or sometimes slightly curved with a short pommel and downward-facing quillons.
- **Parang Bedak.** A heavy sword from Borneo with a single-edged blade, convex along the blade and becoming concave near the tip.

NOTE

Singat: *A group of left-handed warriors used to ambush enemies of the Dyak in Borneo. The word literally means* hornet.

- **Parang Ginah.** A Malay blade with a sickle shape.
- **Parang Jengok.** A Malaysian thief's blade, also know as a "peeping knife." It has a sharp tip extending at 90 degrees from the end of the blade and was used to strike backwards, over the shoulder, hitting the victim in the back of the head with the spiked tip.
- **Parang Latok.** A jungle knife or sword with an unusual design. The single-edged blade angles down from the handle, then straightens out for most of its length, widening toward the end. A similar sword, the parang pandit, has an iron hilt and adds a short cross-guard.
- **Parang Nabur.** A Malay sword with a short blade that curves near the point. Similar to a Middle Eastern sword, it widens along the curve and has a handle with a knuckle guard.
- **Pata.** A gauntlet sword that evolved from the katar. As more protection was added to the katar, it eventually evolved into the pata, which was a shielded glove with a long, sword-length, double-edged blade attached, sticking straight out. Possibly used on horseback in place of a lance. In Southern India, a version evolved that was more of a knife, with a shorter blade. In the southern version, the gauntlet was not fully enclosed, but was partially open and therefore closer to the katar. Blades also varied from double-edged knives to simple spikes.
- **Paternoster Blade.** A sword pierced with openings to serve as a rosary for the pious swordsman who wished to say his prayers, even in the dark.

NOTE

The Mysterious Circle was the basis of a 17th-century system of fencing. It was based on a circle whose radius was the length of a sword blade.

- **Pattisa.** From Southern India, a straight, double-edged sword that widens toward the end and sometimes terminates in a broad, curved tip and sometimes in a point. It is a very heavy blade, roughly 3 feet long.
- **Pillow Sword.** A name for a particular sword that was kept by the pillow in case of emergency. In England in the early 17th century, it referred to a specific straight-bladed sword. The same name also described a sword in Japan that was used for the same purpose.
- **Pira.** A Malaysian sword with a falchion-like blade.
- **Pulouar.** A curved blade from India with a hemispherical pommel (a variation of the talwar).
- **Ram-Dao.** A Nepalese sword used for cutting off heads of animals in sacrifice. It is a formidable weapon with a wide, single-edged blade that curves downward sharply toward the end, then recurves back again to a knobbed point sticking nearly straight up. The curve of the blade focuses the power, weight, and cutting edge in such a way as to be perfect for lopping off heads.
- **Rapier.** A thrusting sword with an elaborate guard that dates from the 16th century—originally in Spain and later throughout Europe. Early rapiers were double-edged and capable of cutting as well as thrusting, but the rapier excelled in thrusting and ultimately became adapted solely to that method of attack. Rapiers were often paired with daggers, and fighting was done with the dagger in the left hand. (See the Main Gauche entry in the "Daggers and Knives" section.) The guards for rapiers were often quite ornate and often involved a cup-like shield at the base of the blade and sometimes a knuckle guard as well. The parts of a rapier hilt are:
  - Knuckle-bow or knuckle-guard
  - Side-rings
  - Arms of the hilt (pas d'ane)
  - Quillons
  - Counterguard
  - Ricasso

At one point during the reign of Elizabeth I, rapiers got so long that they were considered a danger, and it was decreed that any rapier longer than a yard would be broken. Over time, the rapier became smaller, ultimately being called the *smallsword.* Smallswords were not only shorter, but they had less elaborate hilts and became a gentleman's formal weapon. The so-called *pillow sword* was essentially a smallsword. (See the Pillow Sword item earlier in this list.)

- **Rebated Sword.** No, not a sword with a manufacturer's rebate, but a sword with the point blunted for practice.
- **Rudis.** A Roman gladiator's wooden practice sword.
- **Sabre or Saber.** A slightly curved blade with a single edge, or sometimes with a partial back edge. It is mainly a cutting or slashing weapon, although it can be used for thrusting as well.
- **Saif.** An Arab saber with a somewhat wide blade and a distinctive pommel, sometimes with a tight curve, almost a hook. It is worn in a scabbard with rings that attach to the belt.
- **Sapara.** An ancient Assyrian sword with a distinctive curve to the blade. It shot straight out from the hilt, then curved downward to form a shallow sickle shape. It had no guard, simply a handle somewhat like a large knife handle.
- **Sapola.** A saber that had a split point and a finger guard, straight quillons, and a griffon pommel.
- **Schiavona.** A 16th-century Venetian broadsword with a broad, straight blade and a heavy basket hilt that covered the entire hand. This sword was copied in the 17th century and called a *claymore,* although it was not a true claymore.
- **Seax.** A curved sword of the Anglo-Saxons.
- **Seme.** A Masai sword with a simple rounded hilt and a tapering double-edged blade that widens toward the tip before coming to a sharp point. The blade features a heavy central rib, and the sword is generally about 20 inches long, but sometimes is much longer.
- **Shamshir.** A Persian saber—also known as a *scimitar.* A curved, single-edged sword suited for slashing and cutting. The handle is generally simple, with or without a knuckle guard.

NOTE

Assad ul Allah (1587–1628) was the greatest of the Persian sword makers.

- **Shashqa or Chacheka.** A Russian sword with a nearly straight or back-curved blade—used all through the Caucasus.
- **Shearing Sword.** A light, flexible, double-edged sword of the 16th and 17th centuries.
- **Shotel.** A double-edged sword of the Ethiopians, remarkable for the amount of curvature in the blade, which curves out from the handle and then back in a wide sweep, almost like a sickle. It had a simple hilt with minimal or no guard. The whole blade was about 30 inches in a straight line, but 40 inches around the curve. It was reputedly used to reach around behind an opponent's shield.
- **Sica.** A Roman short sword made to fit under the armpit—a favorite of assassins, called *Sicarii.*
- **Sime.** A sword from Eastern Africa that varied from tribe to tribe. Some examples were more than 4 feet long with blades several inches wide. Their hilts were guardless and plain.
- **Sondang.** A Malaysian broadsword.
- **Sosun Pattah.** A forward-curving sword with a single edge and double-edged (false-edged) point from India. The hilt is similar to the khanda, even to the spike coming out of the pommel.
- **Spadroon.** A sword that was lighter than the broadsword and was considered good for both cutting and thrusting—superior to the broadsword in the latter and inferior in the former.
- **Spatha or Spata.** A Roman broadsword used by cavalry.
- **Sultani.** A heavy sword with a slight curve from 18th-century India.
- **Surai.** A sword with a straight blade for about two-thirds of its length and curved for the remainder.
- **Tachi.** The earliest form of single-edged Japanese blade. Tachis are very similar to katanas; in fact, they differ only in very subtle ways, such as the signature of the maker is on the opposite side of the tang

and that they are worn hung from the belt by two slings and with the edge facing down, while the katana is thrust through the belt and carried with the edge upward.

- **Takouba.** A single-edged sword of the Tuareg people of the Sahara. The blade is straight and the sword has no guard, but it does have a typical cross-shape projecting below the pommel.
- **Talibon.** A sword used by Christian natives of the Philippines. It has a straight back, but the edge begins narrow, widens in a curve in the middle to create a sort of shallow belly, then tapers to a very long, sharp point.
- **Tegha.** An Indian sword with a broad, curved blade and a hilt like a talwar.
- **Tulwar/Talwar.** The basic saber found in India. It is the most common variety of sword, although those with a more pronounced curvature in the blade are often known by the Persian word *shamshir.* Tulwars vary greatly in size and form. The hilts generally have heavy quillons and disk pommels; some have finger guards, but not all.
- **Verdun.** A 16th-century dueling rapier, with a lozenge or square section.
- **Viking Sword.** A short sword meant to be used with a shield—double-edged with a thick, but narrow, guard.
- **Wakizashi.** A Japanese short sword.
- **Xiphos Gladius.** A short Roman sword from around the 2nd century.
- **Yataghan.** A slightly forward-curving sword originally of Turkish origin, but commonly used throughout Northern Africa. They had no guards and a distinctive pommel, which often spread out at the top, although others had knife-like handles. In India, yataghan blades were common, but with more typical Indian hilts.
- **Zafar Takieh.** A sword worn by the kings and princes of India, often highly ornate and worked with gold, jade, and jewels. The blades varied—sometimes wide and curved, and sometimes narrow and more like a stiletto. There were also two kinds of hilts, one with a full finger guard and a sort of angled "T" at the top, with short quillons at the base of the hilt. The second type was a simple crutch shape. Both were designed to be used as an armrest for the royalty who wore them.
- **Zu'l Fikar.** The "lord of cleaving" is the sword given by the archangel Gabriel to Mohammed, who subsequently gave it to his son-in-law, Ali bin Ali Talib.

NOTE

Factoids: The pommel, which is the knob on the handle of a sword or knife or the butt of a pistol, got its name from the French word for apple *because many early pommels resembled that fruit. In the 13th century, inferior French troops were called* satellites.

Daggers and Knives

> The most widely used knife is the Arab jambiya, which is used from the Atlantic across North Africa, in Turkey, Arabia, Armenia, Persia through India and as far east as Borneo. It is one of the best fighting knives ever made. The best purely thrusting knife is the Persian peshkabz (which is the same as the Afgan choora), either the straight or curved variety. The best slashing knife is the Gurka kukri, a bow of which can split a man to the waist. The Moro barong is also excellent, especially if back-edged, as it is then effective both for thrusting and cutting. The Japanese knives are among the best, largely because they are made of better steel and extraordinarily well ground.
>
> —George Cameron Stone, *A Glossary of the Construction, Decoration and Use of Arms and Armor in All Countries and in All Times* (Dover Publications, 1999)

Besides clubs, knives of various kinds are among the most primitive and most common weapons, dating back thousands of years before Christ. The first documented knives were made of sharp stone, such as flint, although antlers might also have been used for stabbing. Early knives may also have been made of bone, horns, and wood, as well as a variety of other types of stone. People quickly learned the importance of a grip, although the first stone knives probably had no hilt. But the grip very soon became a part of the knife's construction, and various approaches were tried, from simple wrappings of leather to elaborate constructions with guards and other refinements.

There have probably been more kinds of knives and daggers in the world than any other weapon, partly due to the fact that knives were also used as common, everyday tools. Looking at the list in this section, you can see just some of the many types of blades that have been used around the world. These represent an incredible variety of construction methods, shapes, and sizes.

Knives and daggers often have two sharp edges, although some have only one, with a reinforced back for strength. Some, like the famous Bowie knife, have a sharp edge and a strong back, with a false edge (double edge near the point). Some daggers have no edge, but only a sharp point; obviously, they are stabbing/piercing weapons only. Blades vary in many other ways. Some are narrow and sharp; some are wide and very heavy. Still others have simple or complex curves. In metal blades, various methods are used to strengthen the blade, such as creating ridges and/or grooves in the metal or forging the knife in a diamond cross-section.

Daggers have been worn in various ways, including hidden in sleeves and boots, in garters, behind the back, in the hair, in a hat, under clothing in the front of the body, and even in other weapons, such as swords, canes, whips, and even other knives. During the Middle Ages in Europe, when armor was common, knives were not used much for fighting, although they could be used once an opponent was disabled, if you could find a crack or seam in the armor through which to stick the knife. With the advent of guns, people began attaching knives to the ends of their weapons, which ultimately led to the modern bayonet. Daggers were sometimes used as a second weapon when fighting with swords, and specialized weapons, such as the main gauche, were developed specifically for that purpose. A variation of the dagger (or sword, depending on whom you talk to) is the katar, which is a blade held by a horizontal grip and used to punch forward. (See more about katars later in this section.) One other unusual variation of the dagger is the "sword-breaker"—a dagger with a hard, strong blade that has been deeply notched to form teeth that can catch an opponent's blade and control or break it.

NOTE

Jood-Dan: *In India, when a prince grew old, he could request that another prince meet him in battle so he could die fighting. He would bring only a few men, whereas the other prince could bring as many as he pleased. This was known as "the gift of battle."*

- **Aikuchi or Kusungobu.** A dagger without a guard, from Japan.
- **Arm Knife.** A 6-inch knife carried on the arm near the shoulder, held in place by a scabbard fastened by loops to the arm. Used by the Sudanese. A slightly larger version is used by the Tuaregs.
- **Bade Bade.** Malaysian knife with a curved blade.
- **Barong.** A large, wide-bladed knife up to 16 inches long from Mindanao and Borneo.
- **Baselard.** A dagger of medieval Europe that had essentially a cross-shaped pommel and guard, usually double-edged.
- **Batardeau.** A one-piece knife, often concealed in a pocket in the sheath of a sword.
- **Bayonet.** Basically a knife affixed to the end of the barrel of a rifle. Bayonets originated in the 16th or 17th century. Originally, they were used by musketeers as an added defense, essentially turning the gun into a pike when not firing. To protect against cavalry, early muskets and bayonets were made at least a total of 6 feet long in order to reach a man on horseback. Some armies deployed

musketeers in ranks, where those in front would hold their guns and bayonets as a hedge of defense while those behind reloaded and fired. After firing, the ranks would exchange places. Later bayonets were made shorter, when their use moved toward close-quarters attack and defense.

The early bayonets were fixed at the side of the barrel so as not to interfere with either aiming or reloading, as the early muskets were muzzle loaders. Bayonets were fitted to the gun in different ways. Some were permanently fixed in place and could be retracted or swung around when not needed. Others were fixed by various kinds of collars and slots. The "plug bayonet" actually fit directly into the barrel and could be removed to use as a knife. Other bayonets were essentially long knives or short swords, complete with hilts, and could be used effectively independent of the gun. Bayonets have even been attached to pistols and blunderbusses, with spring releases for quick deployment. Bayonets have been made in a variety of shapes, including simple spikes, sword and knife blades, machetes, trowels, saws, mine-probing tips, and even wire cutters. Modern bayonets are often most useful as utility knives.

- **Bhuj.** A single-edged knife, sometimes called an *elephant's knife* because it often had an elephant's head at the base of the blade. It often concealed a smaller knife in the handle.
- **Bidag.** A Scottish dirk.
- **Bodkin.** A small dagger.
- **Chilanum.** A double-curved, double-edged dagger from India.
- **Chopper.** A generic name for a variety of broad, heavy-bladed, cleaver-like weapons. Some were used to smash through armor.
- **Choora/Chura or Khyber Knife.** A long, straight blade, between 14 and 30 inches in length, that tapers from the base to a sharp point. Made strong, with a single sharp edge.
- **Cinquedea, Anelace.** A double-edged straight dagger, very wide at the hilt and tapering in straight lines to the point. Cinquedeas were worn horizontally at the back of the belt and could be drawn quickly with the left hand. They ranged considerably in length, some being long enough to qualify as swords.
- **Coutel, Cultel.** A 13th- and 14th-century knife.
- **Dirk.** A typical Scottish dagger, which features a heavy-backed, single-edged blade that generally tapers uniformly from base to tip. The pommels were generally conical and flat on top.
- **Dudgeon.** A dagger with a wooden hilt.
- **Golok.** A Malay jungle knife with a heavy, broad curved blade and a single edge, ranging from 6 inches to 2 feet in length. A very common weapon/tool.
- **Hamidashi.** A short Japanese dagger, up to a foot long but often shorter.
- **Hand-Seax.** An Anglo-Saxon dagger.
- **Hanger, Whinger, Whinyard.** Variously, a type of 17th- and 18th-century saber or a Scottish name for a dagger.
- **Jambiya.** A common sort of knife found in Arabic regions. A curved, double-edged blade, sometimes with a rib down the middle. Shapes and sizes vary greatly.
- **Jamdar Katari.** Knives from India featuring straight double-edged blades and doubled guards at the top and base of the pommel.
- **Kard.** A straight-bladed Persian knife used especially for piercing armor. It had a straight hilt and no guard, and the tip was often given extra reinforcement so that it could penetrate an opponent's armor.
- **Katar.** The katar originated in India. It is essentially a flat, broad, and pointed knife with a handle built so that it can be used as an extension of the fist. The basic katar is simply a point extending from the crossbar-like handle. However, katars differ in size (from only inches long to 3 feet long), ornamentation (from completely plain to highly decorated), and other features. For instance, some katars were made extra thick at the point to penetrate armor. Others were made to appear as one

blade, but to split into two or three blades when the handles were pressed together. Still other katars hid a smaller katar inside, so that they acted as a sheath for the smaller one. Most katars were straight bladed, but some were slightly curved, and others were like needles, in contrast to the more standard broad blade.

- **Ketchil.** A Malaysian knife.
- **Khanjar.** An Arabic word for dagger or knife, it is applied to a great number of different types of daggers found in different regions.
- **Khanjarli.** A distinctive knife with a double curve and a pommel, sometimes with a hand guard and always with an almost mushroom-shaped top.
- **Kidney Dagger.** A long, straight blade that originated in the 14th century and was used up until the 17th century. It had a rounded pommel with a guard (called a *kidney guard*) that resembled two small balls, hence the name "kidney" dagger.
- **Kindjal.** A double-edged dagger that generally had very straight, parallel sides that ultimately tapered to a long, sharp point. They had no guard and a straight pommel with a wider end section to help form a handle. Kindjals were also made large enough to be considered short swords. Another name for larger kindjals was *quaddara.*
- **Kira.** An Australian aboriginal stone knife made from quartzite.
- **Kogai.** A slim knife or "skewer" fitted into the pocket of some Japanese sword scabbards. Some were split so that they fit together as one unit or could be separated. It was not sharp, but it may have had a variety of uses, such as locking the scabbard of the samurai's long sword, doubling as chopsticks in the field, severing an artery to put a wounded comrade out of his misery, and so on. It was decorated with a crest that was unique to the samurai's family and was sometimes used to mark and identify a fallen soldier.
- **Korambi.** A knife from Sumatra with a sickle-shaped blade, about 4 to 6 inches long.
- **Koshigatana.** A very short dagger used in ancient Japan. It was small enough to be hidden in the folds of a kimono. It ultimately became the weapon used by women to commit jigai—the ceremonial severing of the neck arteries in ritual suicide. It was then known as *kwaiken* or *kwaito.*
- **Kozuka.** A Japanese knife that was often carried in the scabbard of a sword or dagger. It was customarily made by welding a piece of steel to a piece of iron. Samurai boys learned to throw the kozuka with great accuracy before they were allowed to wear swords. The main targets of the kozuka were the forehead, throat, and wrist.

NOTE

***Raksha:** A Malaysian demon with a large, ugly face and terrible teeth, frequently found decorating kris hilts. Also, the word* sarong *commonly refers to a form of wraparound skirt, but a sarong is also the scabbard for a Javanese kris.*

- **Kris.** The typical knife found throughout the Indonesian region. There are many forms of kris, ranging from 5 or 6 inches to 2 feet in length. The best-known versions have wavy blades, although many kris have straight blades. The only feature common to all versions of the kris is that the blade widens at the hilt and comes to a sharp point on one edge, which serves as a guard, and sometimes includes a notch used to catch an opponent's blade.

NOTE

In ancient Japanese culture, a kubibukuro was a "head bag"—in other words, a net bag with broad shoulder straps meant to carry an enemy's severed head. The kubikiri was a knife especially made for cutting off the enemy's head. The name means "head cutter." The kubi oki was a bucket made of white wood and a tall cover. Inside was a long, sharp hardwood spike. This was a necessary item of any samurai household, in case they needed to send the head of a member of the family who had committed hari-kiri to the governor for identification. The bucket, along with the head, was returned to the family afterward.

- **Kukri.** A Nepalese knife with a very heavy curved blade. The blade widens from just past the hilt and then comes to a point. Since the weight is predominantly toward the front of the blade, it can be wielded to achieve maximum power with minimum effort and can deliver an axe-like blow. The kukri scabbard also carried a pair of smaller knives of the same shape, although one was not sharp and was probably used for sharpening. One account tells of being able to use a kukri to split a man from head to chest in a single blow.
- **Kwaiken.** A Japanese woman's dagger, generally used for cutting the neck veins when committing suicide.
- **Main Gauche.** Literally, the "left hand"—a dagger of 17th-century Europe that was used in the left hand. It had a long, straight, double-edged blade and a guard for the hand that often matched the rapier with which it was matched.
- **Mandaya Knife.** A Philippine knife with a double-edged, leaf-shaped blade. It was distinctive in that it had a long tang that extended from the handle and was flanked by two horn-like projections.
- **Mattucashlass.** A Scottish dagger that was carried under the armpit.
- **Maushtika.** An ancient Indian stiletto.
- **Misericorde.** Known as the "dagger of mercy," this straight, narrow dagger was made to thrust through the gaps in a wounded enemy's armor to deliver the death blow, or *coup de grace.* It is said that simply seeing the uplifted dagger would be enough to cause a wounded enemy to surrender.
- **Nata.** A small Japanese knife, often called a *gardener's* or *hunter's knife.* It is single-bladed with a chisel-like end. The handles and scabbards often resemble those of military weapons, such as the wakazashi and the katana.
- **Pahua.** A large dagger, about 2 feet long, used in the ancient Hawaiian Islands (then known as the Sandwich Islands). It had a straight, double-edged blade, sometimes doubled with a handle in the middle. It was held to the wrist by a cord passed through a hole in the handle.
- **Paiscush.** A katar with a guard built to protect the back of the hand.
- **Panabas.** A long-handled jungle knife with a curved blade that widened toward the end and bent back near the handle. It was employed in executions, among other uses.
- **Parang.** A Malaysian chopper or jungle knife.
- **Parazonium.** A broad-bladed knife used by the ancient Greeks and Romans. It was about 12 to 16 inches long and made of bronze—and later, of iron.

NOTE

Hoplites were heavily armored infantry, the formation of the Greek phalanx.

- **Pesh-Kabz, Peshcubz, PeshQabz.** A type of Persian and North Indian dagger specifically designed to penetrate armor. It is heavy and narrows from the base to a very sharp tip, sometimes with a slight backward curve, but often with a very straight blade. The back of the straighter blades remains straight, while the blade edge narrows to the point.
- **Phurbu.** A knife of exorcism used by Tibetan priests in driving out evil spirits. The blade was very short, like a three-bladed arrowhead, and was attached to an ornate handle that included sculptures of gods, animals, vajras, and so forth. It was generally made of iron or sometimes brass or wood, or some combination of these materials.
- **Pichangatti.** A knife from India that was used more or less in the way we currently use pocket knives, though it looked formidable enough. It had a broad, heavy, single-edged blade about 7 inches long and looked somewhat like a chef's knife, but with a rounded tip ending in a point. The scabbard carried several items, including tweezers and nail and ear cleaners. It was essentially the early Indian Swiss Army knife....

- **Pichaw.** A knife of the Khiva that was presented to heroes and was formed from a straight, single-edged blade and a hilt formed from two pieces of ivory or jade. The pommel was a cylindrical cap ringed in jewels, and the scabbard was a cylinder decorated with metal.
- **Piha-Kaetta.** A Sinhalese knife with a thin blade (1/2 inch to 2 inches wide), about 5 to 8 inches long. They were traditionally decorated with panels of metal toward the hilt or with engravings. The scabbards often carried a stylus as well.
- **Pisau Raut.** A somewhat unusual knife used by the Malay to trim rattan. It had a 4-inch blade, but the handle was about a foot long. Though not considered a weapon, it was still an interesting design.
- **Poignard, Poniard.** A small thrusting dagger with a square or triangular section.
- **Pugio.** A straight, double-edged Roman dagger.
- **Qama (Khama).** The Georgian national weapon—a dagger approximately 15 inches long. Georgians were scandalized when their hereditary enemies, the Cossacks, also began using the qama.
- **Raven's Beak.** An Indian knife with a double-curved blade attached to a long handle.
- **Rondel.** A medieval European dagger with a disk-like pommel and generally a narrow blade.
- **Sabiet.** A curved knife from Sumatra, sharp on both sides, though only for half its length on the convex side.
- **Sabiet Mata Dora.** Two curved blades that are flat on one side and are hinged by a pin at the top. They can be rotated out and held in the middle to strike in either direction.
- **Savigron.** Inuit knife for carving ivory and bone.
- **Savik.** Inuit knife—the word literally means "iron."
- **Scramasax.** A dagger with a wide blade, grooved on both sides. I like the name.
- **Sekin.** A knife from Sumatra with a slightly curved-in single-edged blade and a projection, sort of a beak, at the base of the hilt.
- **Sgain Dubh.** A Scottish stocking dagger.
- **Stiletto.** A thin-bladed thrusting dagger.
- **Tanto.** A Japanese short blade with a guard, not more than 12 inches long. The blade and fittings were identical to the long swords, although some tantos had straight blades and others were curved like the swords. The tanto was carried at all times, even when swords were left behind, and so were often decorated suitably for ceremonial and formal occasions. Other short blades were sometimes called tanto, but the name refers to a specific type of weapon.
- **Telek.** A Tuareg knife with a straight, double-edged blade and a pommel shaped like a cross. It was worn in its scabbard flat against the left wrist and could be drawn with the right hand.
- **Tooroom.** A South Indian grooved dagger with a long, broad blade and a basket hilt.
- **To-Su.** A small poignard carried by Japanese nobles. It was carried for personal protection, and sometimes several were placed in the same scabbard.
- **Tuba Knife.** A strangely shaped knife in which the edge is straight, but the back has a curve. The handle is set at or near 90 degrees to the edge.
- **Turup.** A katar with a guard and a chain or a bar connecting the guard over the top.
- **Ulu.** A woman's knife among the Inuit, originally made from sharp stone with a handle, but later from bone, ivory, and, ultimately, iron.
- **Vinchu.** An Indian dagger, "the scorpion," that was worn without a sheath, concealed in the sleeve. Typically, they were about 6 inches long and sharp at the point, with no edge, but variations occurred so that some were as much as a foot long and with single or double edges.
- **Wedong.** A ceremonial knife worn in Java when in the court. It symbolized the willingness of the wearer to cut a path through the jungle for the king.
- **Whinyard.** A Scottish name for dagger.

- **Yoroi Toshi or Metazashi.** A Japanese dagger designed for cutting through armor, it was originally about 11 inches long, but later versions were shorter—about 9 inches. Originally, it was worn thrust through the back of the belt, but ultimately it was worn on the right side, hilt facing front and with the blade up. The second name, metazashi, means "right side wear."
- **Zirah Bouk.** A mail piercing knife—refers to any dagger with the point reinforced to penetrate armor.

Fist Weapons

These are weapons used to enhance the power and effectiveness of fighting with the fists. Arguably, the katar could be considered a fist weapon, but we have included it in the sword section.

Weapons to enhance fist-fighting date back at least to the ancient Roman days, where they probably used gauntlets and certainly the cestus. In modern times, there are many options, notably the ever-popular brass knuckles.

- **Apache Pistol.** The name given to a commercial weapon that combined a dagger, metal knuckles, and a small revolver all in one.
- **Armlets.** Rings worn on the wrists or upper arm and used for a variety of purposes, including to add weight to the arm to increase the power of blows and also to attack directly, generally at close quarters to the enemy's head. Some armlets are fitted with spikes and sharp edges. They are generally made of stone or metal.
- **Bagh Nakh (Tiger Claw).** Indian hand weapon with rings for the fingers and several claw-like metal spikes, designed to be concealed in the palm and used to rake and tear the flesh of the adversary.
- **Brass Knuckles (Knuckle-Dusters).** Considered to be the logical descendant of the Roman cestus, brass knuckles basically were used by criminals, although similar weapons—often studded with sharp points or spikes made from various substances—were common around the world. They were meant to add weight to blows struck with the fists and to do more damage by striking with a harder surface or with something that cut.
- **Cestus.** Heavy leather thongs that were often weighted with lead or iron and wound around the hands and arms of Roman boxers to add to the weight and power of their blows.
- **Gauntlet.** A metal glove, often with spiked knuckles, that fits over the entire hand—probably used during the Roman era and also in medieval times.
- **Hora.** A knuckle-duster from India, made of horn and shaped with triangular spikes.
- **Knuckle-Duster.** A lead ring held in the hand, popular during the Civil War.
- **Knuckle-Duster Dagger.** A World War I weapon that combined metal knuckles with a blade, sharpened on the back end to more easily slit the throat of an unwary sentry.

Throwing Weapons

The simplest weapon of all is probably a stone, which may have been held in the hand as a simple club but was certainly also thrown. From such humble beginnings, a variety of throwing weapons have evolved, including spears and javelins, disks, bolas, boomerangs and various sticks, hatchets, knives, clubs, and finally grenades. In addition to the missiles that are thrown, various devices have been created to enhance the power and distance of a thrown object, including slings, throwing sticks, and spear throwers. (I've included spears and spear throwers in a separate section, since many types of spears were made. Some were only for thrusting, and others were only for throwing, but some could be used either way.)

Of course, the simplest and most direct sort of thrown weapon was simply something dropped from above on an attacker. Large boulders, pots of boiling oil or water, and any number of other weapons were often dropped from the walls of a fortress upon besiegers. A *hourd* was a wooden gallery built outside the battlements that allowed defenders to see down to the foot of the walls of the fortification and to throw stones or other missiles onto the enemy.

- **Aclys.** A Roman dart weapon, or possibly a throwing stick or boomerang.
- **African Throwing Knives.** Unusual knives made only for throwing, with a handle and blades created at all angles and shapes. Most had multiple blades and were said to be very powerful even at 50 yards.
- **Assegai.** Portuguese word for South African spears used for throwing. Some versions used for stabbing.
- **Bolas.** An arrangement of cords and either two or three balls used for throwing to entangle the legs of prey or enemy.
- **Boomerang.** Contrary to popular opinion, most boomerangs are not made to return to the user. They are flat wood or bone (or even metal) blades that are thrown as an attack weapon. Boomerangs have been used since ancient Egyptian times. Returning boomerangs are specific to Australia but are not used as serious weapons.
  - **Kandri.** A type of Australian boomerang with a slight curve.
  - **Katari and Katariya.** Two forms of boomerang from India.
  - **Kulbeda.** An African boomerang made of iron.
  - **Kylie.** A boomerang from the western part of Australia.
  - **Singa.** A boomerang from India.
  - **Tundiwung.** A very curved Australian boomerang with a handle on one end.
  - **Watilikri.** An Australian boomerang in which one end terminates in a beak-like shape; also known as the *beaked boomerang.*
- **Chakram or War Quoit.** A sharpened ring of metal designed to be thrown. Used by the Sikhs; sometimes several were carried on top of a pointed turban called the *dastar bungga.*
- **Facon.** A Spanish knife meant for throwing—about 2 feet long.
- **Francisca.** A throwing ax used by the Franks who inhabited parts of modern France and Germany. It was so named after them by the Romans, against whom it was used.
- **Grenades.** Of all hand-thrown weapons used in combat, the grenade is the one still used in modern warfare. A grenade is basically a thrown explosive that does damage in two ways: from the blast itself and from the fragmentation effect. This is the most basic anti-personnel grenade, although other specialized versions also exist. Grenades are detonated in two basic ways—by use of a lit fuse or by impact.

  Although the impact variety has some advantages—no chance of being thrown back or rolling back down a hill and no way to avoid it once thrown—they are more dangerous to carry and store. Impact grenades are ignited either by a plunger hitting the ground or by a weight inside that is thrown forward when the grenade impacts the ground—both of which require the grenade to hit at a particular point—or by a series of detonators that allow the grenade to hit anywhere and explode. With the two former types, it was helpful to create something that was heavier on one end or was somehow guided by fins so that it was more likely to hit on the plunger or the end where the weight was located.

  Fused grenades have been the most common variety. The early versions had actual fuses that were lit by a match or by other fire source. The early soldiers who lit and threw grenades were called *grenadiers,* although that name ultimately came to describe a troop of particularly large soldiers. Modern fused grenades use more sophisticated methods, such as levers secured by pins or rotating sections of the grenade itself. Many grenades were improvised in the field; this was particularly true during World War I, where grenades were highly effective in the trenches. Specialized grenades include anti-tank grenades and smoke, incendiary, or gas grenades.

- **All-Way Impact Grenades.**
- **Anti-Tank Grenades.** Specialized grenades created with shaped charges and made so that they would impact the side of an armored vehicle at a 90-degree angle, allowing the shaped charge to penetrate the armor. This kind of grenade belongs with modern weaponry and is more appropriate to the subject of the following chapter, "Standard Modern Weaponry and Armor."
- **Fused Grenades.**
- **Gas, Smoke, and Incendiary Grenades.** Specialized grenades created to do damage by expelling gas, smoke, or heat instead of by impact and shrapnel.
- **Hane's Excelsior.** A Civil War grenade patented but little used, it was formed from a sphere dotted with percussion caps, which was fitted inside another hollow sphere and packed with explosive. Anywhere the grenade hit, it was sure to detonate at least one of the caps, thereby exploding the whole shebang.
- **Impact Grenades.** Grenades created so that they would detonate no matter how they landed when thrown.
- **Improvised Grenades.** Grenades made from available materials, such as planks of wood with explosives attached and wound in barbed wire, glass jars filled with explosives, a bundle of nails wrapped around a stick of explosive, and so on.
- **Rampart Grenade.** A large grenade that was tossed from ramparts down upon besieging troops, so named to distinguish it from the smaller hand grenades.

- **Hunga-Munga.** A heavy throwing knife with a hooked end. It looked a little like a number 3 with a handle.
- **Jaculum.** A Roman javelin.
- **Jarid (Djarid).** Short throwing spears used in the Orient—about 3 feet long and with a steel head about 7 inches long.
- **Kerrie or Knobkerry (also Rungu).** A throwing stick made from wood and, sometimes, from rhinoceros horn. One end of the stick terminated in a large knob.
- **Koveh.** A spear, also known as "the assegai of torture," with a barbed head in which some barbs pointed back toward the shaft and others pointed toward the tip, making it impossible to pull or push out without doing more damage.
- **Lime Pots.** Earthenware pots used to throw quicklime in the faces of the enemy.
- **Nageyari.** A Japanese javelin with a short shaft and a short, heavy head.
- **Pelta.** An ancient Greek javelin that had a leather strap attached to aid in throwing it.
- **Pheon.** A barbed javelin carried by the sergeant-at-arms of the English kings from the time of Richard I.
- **Pincha.** An African throwing knife.
- **Rabbit Stick.** A Native American throwing club, similar to a boomerang, with a carved handle at one end, ultimately terminating in a wide, flat blade with a curve like a boomerang. Rabbit sticks were generally varnished and painted.
- **Shuriken.** Early references describe the shuriken as a plain, one-piece throwing knife; however, it is known in more modern times as a throwing star, of which there are many shapes and styles.
- **Simbilan.** A thin wooden javelin, which could be thrown four at a time.
- **Slings and Sling Poles.**
  - **Fustibal.** A sling attached to a pole; used by the ancient Romans.
  - **Fondes.** Slings used by 14th-century Spaniards.
  - **Funda.** An Etruscan sling.
  - **Gudo or Orta.** A Tibetan sling.
  - **Zumbai.** A Japanese sling.

- **Spiculum.** A light javelin of the ancient Romans.
- **Tomahawk.** Used by Native Americans as both a club and a throwing weapon. Made with a stick and a stone attached or, later, with a hatchet blade in place of the stone.
- **Ulas.** A throwing club from Fiji. They are carved of wood and about 18 inches long. The heads were rounded or knobbed and could be as much as 6 inches in diameter.
- **Vericulum.** A light javelin of ancient Rome.

NOTE

The supernumerarii were lightly armed troops of ancient Rome.

Axes and Pole Arms (Including Pikes, Picks, and Forks)

This section looks at axes, which are bladed weapons that evolved from clubs, and pole arms—longer weapons with different sorts of structures to do damage in a variety of ways and in a variety of circumstances. Some pole arms were used primarily against cavalry, while others were used in large-scale melee combat. Pole arms include pikes, picks, forks, and other variants.

Axes

A logical development of the club was the ax—essentially the replacement of the club head with a blade set at right angles to the haft. Early axes were made of stone, but axes have been made with blades of wood, bone, and, most commonly, metal. Like the knife, an axe was a common tool for cutting wood and other everyday uses, and ordinary axes were often called upon for self-defense or for other fighting purposes. Historically, ax blades have varied considerably in size and shape as well as in the way they are attached to the haft. Some designs appear to have been useful for chopping wood as well as for self-defense. However, specialized axes were made specifically for warfare and were especially favored when fighting men in armor.

Some war axes were made specifically for throwing, while others varied in size and weight, including large pole axes that were wielded in two hands. Some axes had one blade, while others were double-bladed. Shapes varied as well—some axes had straight edges, while others had convex or concave edges. Some even had a nearly triangular shape, with the base at the haft and the point at the edge. Some were long and created with a shallow curve, and some axes even defied the convention of being set at right angles to the haft and were more like long knives extending out a long handle.

War axes often had a single blade with a hammer head or spike balanced opposite. Axes were often combined with concealed daggers and even with pistols. Some had special hooks possibly used to cut through the bridles of enemy cavalry.

Pole Arms

A pole arm is essentially the attachment of a weapon head to a long pole or shaft, although, arguably, the simplest pole arms were the European quarterstaff and its Eastern counterparts, which were formed from a simple length of shaped wood. Pole arms have been used throughout recorded history and in almost all cultures. The range of pole arms is great, but they generally fall into certain categories of use: thrusting, cutting, cutting and thrusting, and specialized weapons, such as the bec de corbin, catch pole, quarter staff, and scaling fork. They variously carried heads with blades, hammers, hooks, spear points, spikes, and forks—individually and sometimes in combinations. Though often carried by foot soldiers, the lance was a pole arm made for use on horseback. Lances are well known as jousting weapons from medieval Europe, but they were used by many other cultures, too, including the Native Americans.

Although sometimes used as an individual soldier's weapon, pole arms were also quite formidable weapons when used in large groups. The Greek hoplites carried long thrusting spears and attacked in a tight formation called a *phalanx*. In the 17th century, long pikes, up to 16 feet long, were used to form a spiky barrier against charging cavalry, giving the musketeers time to reload and fire.

Pole arms can be roughly divided into several categories, based on the types of heads they have mounted:

- Thrusting weapons (awl pike, boar spear, Bohemian earspoon, chauve souris, feather staff, fork, fourche a crochet, korseke, langue de boeuf, linstock, partisan, pike, pike-fork, spontoon, and runca)
- Cutting weapons (berdiche, fauchard, glaive, jedburg axe, lochaber axe, pole axe, scythe, and voulge)
- Thrusting and cutting weapons (bill brandestoc, couteau de breche, godenda, guisarme, halbard, half moon, hippe, Lucerne hammer, and scorpion)
- Cutting and smashing or piercing weapons (war hammer, beaked axe, pole-axe, masa kari, ono)
- Specialized weapons (bec de corbin, bridle cutter, catch pole, flail, holy water sprinkle, quarter staff, and scaling fork)

The war hammer was one of several weapons designed for use against armored opponents. It consisted of a pick with a hammer head opposite the blade. The hammer end could stun an opponent or even break bones, while the pick end was effective at piercing the opponent's armor. Some war hammers also had a spike or blade that projected from the haft of the weapon, further adding to its attack options. War hammers varied greatly in shape and size. In some, the pick element was elongated or shaped more like a spike. And in some, the hammer side was very small, while in others it was quite formidable.

The basic European pole arms include:

- Bill
- Glaive
- Halberd
- Military fork
- Partisan
- Pole ax
- Quarterstaff
- Spear (for thrusting)
- Trident
- War hammer

NOTE

Retiarii: *Roman gladiators who wielded the net and trident. Their adversaries were called scutors, and they wore armor and carried a sword and a shield.*

Specific examples of pole arms include:

- **Awl Pike (Ahlspiess).** A long-shafted weapon with a round or octagonal guard about midway, used in the 15th century.
- **Bardiche.** A Russian pole ax from the 16th century, used until the 18th century. It was similar to the lochaber ax and consisted of a large ax blade with a convex, curved edge, attached at two points to the haft and terminating in a sharp point.
- **Beaked Axe.** An ax with a hook or beak on the back end of the blade.
- **Bill.** One of the earliest weapons in Europe, adapted from farm equipment. A broad-bladed pole ax with a spike or extension extending out opposite a curved blade with a downward-facing cutting edge. Came in various sizes and shapes, often with hooks and other modifications. Very effective against both armored men and horses. Also known as *Brown Bill* or *Black Bill.*
- **Boar spear.** A broad, leaf-shaped head with a crosspiece at the base, originally to prevent boars from running up the shaft and attacking the wielder. Boar spears were later used in warfare.
- **Bohemian Earspoon.** A pike with a long, broad point with two triangular projections at the base.
- **Bridle Cutter.** A sharp hooked blade used to cut the bridles of horsemen.
- **Bullova.** Indian fighting ax.

- **Chauves Souris.** A pole arm that terminates in a long triangular blade flanked by two shorter triangular blades on either side—a kind of partizan.
- **Couteau de Breche.** A pole with a long, flat, single-edged blade at the end. The blade shapes varied. The simplest form of this weapon was made by attaching a sword to a pole.
- **Crowbill.** A weapon with a short, pointed, sometimes curved blade. It can be mounted at 90 degrees to the handle, like an ax, or in line with the handle.
- **Falx.** A 14th-century two-handed pole arm with a sickle-like iron blade attached to a handle about 3 feet long. (There was also a smaller, one-handed falx.) Some falx had simple blades, while others may have also featured a bill (also known as a *coulter*) that projected from the back of the blade.
- **Fang.** A Chinese weapon with two double-edged blades. The first comes straight out of the handle; the second blade extends at right angles from the base of the first.
- **Fauchard.** A 16th-century pole arm with a broad, curved, single-edged blade and ornamental prongs on the back of the blade.
- **Fourche a Crochet.** A hooked fork used as a weapon—the fork was used to catch the bridle of enemy cavalry.
- **Glaive (also Coule).** A broad-bladed pole arm with an edge that curves backward near the point. It was used in Europe during the 12th and 13th centuries, and later in China.
- **Guisarme.** A European weapon used from the 11th to the 15th centuries. It was similar to a bill, but often had a very slender, curving blade, where the bill generally had a broader blade. Like the bill, the guisarme also had a hook or spike projecting from the back edge of the blade, which then turned parallel with the back edge of the blade in the direction of the tip.
- **Halberd (also Halbard or Halbart).** A long pole weapon that featured an ax blade with another blade or spike opposite and a long spear point terminating the weapon. Halberds were used as early as the 13th century and were still used by the British army until the end of the 18th century.
- **Half Moon.** A pole weapon that featured a crescent blade that extended from the shaft.
- **Hani or Taiaha.** A mostly plain staff from New Zealand with a flattened end on which is carved a face with an oversized carved tongue sticking straight out and forming a sort of blade. A favorite Maori weapon, which was used for fighting and also for gesticulating when speaking.
- **Jedburg Axe or Jeddart Axe.** A Scottish pole arm about 9 feet long with a hook or cutting edge opposite the blade.
- **Kama Yari.** A Japanese pick with a curved blade and a sharp edge facing downward, mounted at right angles on a short haft.
- **Kharga.** A ceremonial ax found in India.
- **Korseke.** A 15th-century pole arm with three blades at the end. The middle blade was considerably longer than the two side blades.
- **Langue de Boeuf (Ox Tongue).** A 16th-century pole arm with a broad, straight, double-edged blade.
- **Linstock.** A pike that held matches in branching sections off the main blade—used for lighting cannons.
- **Lochaber Axe.** A favorite 16th-century Scottish ax that fit over the haft with two collar rings. The blade had a curve or wave at the upper end and often a recurve hook at the bottom of the blade. Some lochaber axes had sharp points, while others were rounded. Some also had hooks at the top of the shaft or built into the blade, which faced away from the edge.
- **Lohar.** A short-handled pick used in India, generally highly decorated along the haft.
- **Lucerne Hammer (Bec de Corbin).** A variant on the halberd with elements of a war hammer, built with a single sharp, beak-like spike at right angles to the haft with two short, heavy spikes opposite and terminating in a very long, sharp spike above.
- **Magari Yari.** A weapon with a long central blade and two much smaller side blades that extend at right angles and only point upward toward the end.

- **Masa-Kari.** A little-used Japanese battle ax with a short handle, a rounded blade, and a long spike on the opposite side.
- **Military Fork.** Adapted from the peasant's fork, military forks were improved and modified in a wide variety of ways. They always had some number of tines—two being common. They might also have had various sizes and shapes of tines and added blades. Some military forks resembled pikes, while others had ax-like additions. The configuration options seemed quite numerous, and creative solutions were often tried. The military fork was most common in the 14th century, although it remained a peasant weapon for hundreds of years.
- **Nifo Oti.** A Samoan bill hook whose name means, literally, "death tooth."
- **Ono.** That's what you'd say if you saw this coming at your head. It was a 6-foot-long Japanese pole ax with a very large ax head with a large scrolled hammer head or "peen" opposite. A simple sheath covered only the ax blade and tied to the shaft.
- **Partizan.** A pole arm with a single broad, straight blade that had very short, curved branches at its base. Partizan shapes and variations varied greatly, and the partizan was often used as a ceremonial weapon, elaborately decorated, or as the weapon of choice for guards of important people.
- **Parusa.** A legendary battle ax from Indian history.
- **Pike.** A pike consists of a long shaft tipped with a relatively short blade or spike. The blades tended to be leaf- or diamond-shaped, and the shaft was generally protected for 3 or 4 feet from the tip to prevent it from being cut off. Pikes were designed generally as a weapon against cavalry, and they were wielded by bracing the butt into the ground and holding against the charge of the horses. In later years, pikemen were used to protect the musketeers while they were reloading. In the early days, pikes were very long, especially those used by the Greek phalanx. They gradually became shorter, ultimately down to about 18 feet long in Europe during the Middle Ages.
- **Pole Axe.** An ax with a spike or hammer opposite the blade, with or without an end spike, mounted on a long pole handle.
- **Runka, Ranson.** A pole arm with a long, very sharp, pointed central blade with two smaller side blades extending near the haft. The lateral blades could be either straight or curved.
- **Sarissa (Sarisse).** A Greek pike used by foot soldiers. The shaft of the sarissa was 16 to 24 feet long.
- **Scaling Fork.** A war fork with a hook on it—used for scaling walls.
- **Shoka.** An African battle ax with a triangular blade attached to the thickest part of a thin wooden shaft with a short tang.
- **Silepe.** An ax with a wide, shallow blade attached to a handle by a long, flat tang.
- **Skein.** An Irish dagger, short and straight with a double edge.
- **Sparte.** A battle ax of the Angle-Saxons.
- **Spetum.** A 16th-century pole arm with a long, narrow blade and curved lateral arms.
- **Spontoon.** A half pike used by the British up until the end of the 18th century, similar to a small version of the partizan.
- **Sudis.** A 12th-century pike.
- **Taavish.** A stone ax with the end of the handle carved like a man's head and the long, stone, 8- to 10-inch blade representing the man's tongue.
- **Tabar.** A battle ax from India. Tabars varied considerably in size.
- **Tabar-I-Zin.** A large ax meant to be wielded with two hands. The name literally means "saddle ax," and it was reputedly used by the Afghani.
- **Taper Ax.** A common northern European ax with a blade that flares in a double curve (top and bottom) from the base out to a wide edge, which is also curved outward.
- **Taru.** A pike of the ancient Egyptians.
- **Toki Kakauroa.** A long-handled ax of the Maori with an iron head and a bone or wood shaft.

- **Tomahawk.** A Native American fighting ax, originally made with stone heads and later with iron. Some tomahawks had pipe bowls opposite the blade and hollow stems for smoking. They were used for striking and also for throwing.
- **Tongia.** A small Indonesian ax with a semicircular blade.
- **Toporok.** A Russian battle ax.
- **Trident.** Essentially a three-bladed spear or fork. Tridents were used by the ancient Roman gladiators, but they have also been used all over the world and during many periods of history.
- **Tsuko-bo.** A pole arm from Japan that was kept near the castle gate, in the guardhouse. It had a cross-shaped head with teeth in it.
- **Tuagh-Gatha.** A Scottish battle ax used by the ancient Highlanders.
- **Tungi.** An ax of the Southern Indian Khond sect.
- **Venmuroo.** A battle ax from Malabar with a crescent-shaped blade.
- **Voulge.** A pole arm with an ax-like head and a spike or point at the end of the blade, held to the shaft by two open rings—the ancestor of the halberd. Some had a spike or hook extending opposite the blade and attached by a separate ring mounted between the two rings of the main ax head.
- **Wagoner's Axe (or Doloire).** A 15th-century battle ax in which the blade is set out from the handle at 90 degrees, but rounded at the bottom and pointed at the top.
- **Zaghnal.** An Indian ax with one or two heavy curved blades, like the blades of knives sticking at right angles from the haft, or possibly at just under 90 degrees so that they angled slightly downward. The hafts were around 21 to 22 inches long, and the blades varied—some certainly up to 10 inches in length.

Picks, Pikes, and Forks

In its application as a weapon, a pick is a pointed blade set at right angles to a shaft. It may have evolved from picks used in agriculture, but generally, in war, the pick was on a shorter handle, and the blades varied quite a bit in shape and size. Some were sharpened along the edge, making them more like scythes. The pick was effective against mail and plate armor.

Pikes were a type of spear used by early infantry, specifically against charging cavalry. They featured a small leaf- or diamond-shaped head mounted on a very long shaft, which was protected by several feet of metal to prevent being cut off by enemy riders. Pikes were very long, and even after centuries of use during which they grew shorter and shorter, pikes of the 15th century were still 18 feet long. Typically, pikes were braced against the ground at an angle to intercept and impale incoming cavalry.

Military forks derived from the peasants' pitchforks but were modified for fighting. They were most common during the 14th century in Europe, although they were also used as far back as the Roman times. Military forks often had some of their tines flattened and sharpened into blades. Others were modified in a variety of ways, including axe-like heads at the base of the tines, hooks, and even pike-like central tines. Forks were made generally with two or three tines.

Spears and Lances

Spears are common throughout the world, in all cultures and times. The earliest spears were wooden, although stone or shell was often added for sharpness. By far the most common spears have been tipped with iron, however. Bone, horn, and ivory have also been used. Spears have been used as weapons, of course, but are also often used for ceremonial purposes, decoration, dancing, and even as currency in Africa. Some of the most elaborate spears have been made in the South Sea Islands. The heads for spears are usually sharp and pointed or leaf-shaped. However, some spears have doubled tips or even elaborately sculpted and complex heads, such as some of the ancient Javan spears. Spears were often carried and stored in scabbards, which generally covered only the sharp tip; however, the use of scabbards was not universal.

Although spears were often used for thrusting or for throwing by hand, many cultures developed ways to amplify the velocity and distance possible when throwing a spear by creating spear throwers. In ancient Greece, they used a strap, called the ankule, that was fastened to the middle of their javelins. Others have used straps as well, but unlike the Greek versions, they would slip off the spear after it was thrown. Another common spear thrower was made from a carved stick. The spear was laid onto the stick with the butt up against a stop of some kind. The spear was then balanced on the spear thrower and tossed. Using the stick as a sort of lever, the spear could be thrown farther and harder.

- **Amentum or Ankule.** A sling or loop of cord used to throw a spear. Used by the ancient Greeks and still used in parts of Africa.
- **Chimbane.** A spear with barbs going in both directions, so it could be neither withdrawn nor pushed through.
- **Fal-feg.** A spear with backward-facing barbs, about 5 feet long.
- **Futomata-yari.** A Japanese spear with a forked head.
- **Harpoon.** A shaft with a barbed head used for spearing fish.
- **Hooked Spear.** A variety of spear that had a hook beneath the blade. The hook was used to catch the enemy's armor and pull him forward or, in certain situations, cause him to fall off ramparts or bridges.
- **Ja-Mendehi.** Native American lance made of ash. They are 6 to 8 feet long with a shaft about an inch in diameter and a broad head.
- **Lance.** The lance was the horseman's spear and was used all over the world. The lances of Europe were large, averaging about 13 feet long. Their heads were generally leaf-shaped or sharp spikes. The guard, called a *vambrace*, was generally conical in shape, although the shapes varied a lot. Jousting lances were blunted and much larger, up to 5 inches in diameter. Lances in other parts of the world are lighter and shorter and did not use the vambrace. They ended in a ball shape for counterbalance, terminating in a spike that was used to set the lance in the ground when not in use.
- **Markek—Ainu Salmon Spear.** Interesting because it is made from a hook attached to an 8-foot pole. When the fish is hooked, a rope pulls the hook back, further fixing it into the fish and keeping it secured. It has interesting possibilities for a weapon.
- **Mkuki (Farara).** A spear from East Africa with a long, narrow blade at the end. The blade was made from soft iron—so soft it could be bent with the fingers—but polished to a very fine point. The Mkuki is used for stabbing and is about 6 feet in length. The shaft is made from a particular variety of wood used for its toughness, close grain, and lack of knots. It is straightened over hot ashes and then oiled or greased. The socket of the blade is covered with the skin taken from the tail of an animal. The butt is covered with metal for planting in the ground when not in use.
- **Nagamaki.** A Japanese spear similar to the naginata, with a long, nearly straight blade.
- **Nagegama.** A weapon with a short sickle blade set at right angles to the haft. It was forged of one piece of metal and used in defending fortresses. A chain, which was attached, was used to draw it back up.
- **Naginata.** A Japanese spear with a sword-like blade for the head. The blade curved back very near the point. It was often given to women for exercise and contingency, and so was called the *woman's spear.*
- **Paralyser.** A Malaysian spear that used two blades of unequal length. Both were barbed, and, if stabbed by the first, the victim could not withdraw the blade. However, he could not advance through the spear to attack his enemy because of the shorter blade, which he would have to run through as well. It was a very clever weapon.
- **Pill or Pell.** A peasant weapon—basically a sharpened stake used in the Norman armies.

- **Pillara.** A spear cut from a solid piece of wood with two parallel heads set close together. Each head had a single row of barbs. It was about 9 feet long and was mainly a thrusting weapon, although it could also be thrown with a spear thrower.
- **Pilum.** The main spear of the Roman legions.
- **Rummh.** A lance from the Middle East with a diamond-shaped head and a 15- to 18-foot-long shaft.
- **Saintie.** A long rod of iron with a handle and a loop guard in the middle, tipped with a spear point. It was primarily a parrying weapon and sometimes had a second spear point in the hand guard or a concealed dagger in the weapon's shaft. It was used in India, although a similar weapon was found in China.
- **Sang.** A lance used when fighting in the desert on camelback. It was often all iron or sometimes wood banded with metal.
- **Sang.** Another type of sang was a Singhalese spear also used in India, with a very heavy head formed from a curved, double-edged blade. These blades were highly ornate, as were the socket sections that joined it to the staff.
- **Sangu.** A spear from central India, made from steel and with a long triangular or sometimes quadrangular head.
- **Saunion.** A Samnite spear about 3-1/2 feet long with a 5-inch head.
- **Sei-Ryo-Ken.** Known as the *temple spear* or *kwanyu's spear*, it featured a broad blade extending out of a dragon's mouth.
- **Siligis.** Wooden javelins from Borneo—some were meant to be thrown, but the ones with more valuable iron blades were used for close fighting.
- **Sinan.** A Persian spear, the blade was long and tapered to a fine point from the socket to the tip.
- **Sinnock.** A simple light spear from the Mosquito Coast in Central America.
- **Tao.** A Maori hardwood spear about 8 feet long.
- **Tumbak.** A Javanese name for spear.
- **Tumpuling.** A Javanese spear with a barbed head—either one barb or two.
- **Wainian.** An Australian stone-headed spear. Either quartzite or flint was used for the head, which could be quite sharp, and the wood or cane shaft was as much as 10 feet long.
- **Zagaye.** A Venetian lance, 12 feet long with iron-tipped points at each end.

NOTE

Kirin: *A mythical beast made from the male (k'i) and female (lin). It had a deer's body with legs and hooves of a horse, a head like a horse or dragon, and a tail like an ox or lion. It had one horn on its head, yellow with a fleshy tip. It was said to walk so lightly that it left no footprints, even on newly fallen snow.*

Bows and Crossbows

For millennia, bows were the most powerful handheld missile weapon—until the development of guns. Cave paintings dating as far back as 10,000 B.C. depict people using bows. The principle of a bow is simple: It is the application of force to a spring and its sudden release. As the archer pulls back the string, the tension on the bow increases slowly. All the tension is then released at one time, launching the missile.

Bows were made in different shapes and sizes and from different materials. Bows range in size from toy bows only a few inches long to certain Japanese bows more than 8 feet in length. The famous English long bow was just a little longer than a man's height. In contrast, the yag, or Turkish bow, which is arguably the best bow made, was around 4 feet in length.

The basic bow has a simple curve, but bows have been made with combinations of curves and recurves for added strength and power. There are even some bows made in a triangular configuration, while others are asymmetrical—generally meaning that the arrow pass and grip were closer to the bottom of the bow than to the top. Later bows, sometimes called *compound bows*, use cams and pulleys to hold the bow at full draw without requiring the archer to exert maximum effort and to fire arrows 50-percent faster (or more). This "bow with compound interest" was the invention of Wilbur Allen and was patented in 1969.

The draw weight is the amount of pressure needed to draw the bow, and, as such, is a measure of the bow's power. The famed English longbow, a self bow, had an average draw of about 80 pounds. In contrast, a traditional self bow from Kenya has a draw weight of 130 pounds.

Most bows fire arrows, although some bows, called *pellet bows*, are used to fire stones and small clay balls, making them somewhere between a bow and a slingshot. Pellet bows have very rarely seen military service and are usually used to hunt small game.

Archers traditionally carried various extra items, including a case for the bow, a quiver for arrows, a bracer to protect the left forearm from string abrasion, and, in the case of many Asian cultures, a thumb ring, which was used to draw the bow. The so-called *archer's ring* was used mainly in the Middle East, India, and China. It was worn on the thumb and used to pull the bowstring, as opposed to the European method of using two or three fingers to pull the bow.

Quivers have been used in every culture to carry arrows. Most were boxes or bucket/bag types that held the arrow, leaving the tops sticking out to make it easy to remove one. In some Asian countries, the quiver only held the heads of the arrows and kept each one separate so as not to damage the feathers, making it very easy to find and draw another one.

Construction of Bows

Bows are made in different ways:

- From a single piece of wood (called *self bows*).
- From various pieces glued together (known as *laminated* or *built bows*).
- From wood or bone and reinforced with sinew (known as *backed bows*).
- From wood, horn, and sinew (known as *composite bows*)—these originated in Turkey. The Turks reportedly made the best composite bows, historically.

The parts of a bow are:

- Bowstring
- Upper limb
- Lower limb
- Nock
- Arrow pass
- Handle/grip
- Belly (the side facing the archer)
- Back (the side facing away from the archer)

NOTE

Factoid: Some Japanese bows can be more than 8 feet in length.

Factoid: In 16th-century England, a crossbow was known as a latch.

Factoid: An effigy of a bird used as a target for archers and crossbowmen was called a popinjay. *In annual contests, the winner at popinjay shooting was "king" for a year.*

Some Specific Bows

- **Daikyu.** A large Japanese war bow.
- **English Long Bow.** A bow about the height of the person firing it, made from a solid piece of yew or, if none was available, of elm or witch hazel. It was said to have remarkable range and accuracy. The traditional method of making the bow was to leave some of the sapwood on the back of the bow, with the heartwood in the curved belly portion. English law regulated the manufacture of long bows, which were used by the military from the 14th to the 18th centuries.
- **Gulail, Ghulel, Gulel.** An Indian bow specifically designed to fire pellets or missiles, such as balls of baked clay or stones.
- **Kaman.** A Japanese composite bow.
- **Mande.** A Native American bow about 3-1/2 feet long, using twisted elk or buffalo sinew for the string and to reinforce the back, which featured a double curve.
- **Pellet Bow or Stone Bow.** A bow designed to shoot clay balls, stones, bullets, and other similar ammunition. It was a bow in which a pocket was attached to the middle of the string. In Europe and China, they were used for hunting game, but in other parts of the world, they were used for fighting as well.
- **Uma Yumi.** A Japanese bow designed to be fired from horseback.
- **Yag.** A Turkish bow—some say the best bow in the world. Bows can be shot very great distances, but none farther than the yag. Record shots are more than 600 yards. In fact, there are markings carved on columns in Constantinople that apparently measure bow shots from 625 to 838 yards.

Arrows

Arrows are very effective missiles. They seem quite simple, but in reality it takes considerable care to create an effective arrow.

- They must fit the draw of the bow that will fire them—in both length and weight.
- They must have a certain amount of flexibility because upon firing an arrow flexes, and it must not flex too much or too little for an accurate shot.
- The head must be of the right type to fit the purpose of the shot.
- For maximum performance, the flights (feathers) must effectively stabilize the flight of the arrow with the least impedance.

Arrowheads

Arrowheads vary a great deal in shape, material used, size, and function. The earliest arrows probably had nothing more than a sharpened point, but stone arrowheads have been used since prehistoric times. Flint, obsidian, horn, bone, and even petrified wood—anything that could be shaped to a sharp point—were commonly used until the Metal Age, at which time bronze, then iron, then steel became the preferred materials.

Arrowheads have also been made in a variety of shapes, from simple spike-like affairs to broad leaf-like heads. The most basic shapes are the lozenge, leaf, triangular, barbed, swallowtail, and chisel shapes, although many other shapes have been made, including pronged (especially for spearing fish) and fishtail, for slicing through armor like a can opener.

Parts of an Arrow

- The head or pile—usually of metal, but sometimes of stone, bone, horn, or shell. Often barbed and sometimes poisoned. Some arrows have no separate head, but consist merely of the sharpened shaft, although these do not tend to be nearly as effective.
- The body, stele, or shaft. Made of light wood, reed, light metal, or fiberglass, generally with a slight taper.
- The nock or notch is used to fix the arrow to the string—sometimes a simple notch in the shaft. Other times, bone or plastic is used. Some nocks are shaped so that the opening is narrower at the outside, allowing riders on horseback to keep an arrow notched without it falling off the string.
- Flights or feathers are glued or tied to the shaft to steady the flight of the arrow. The number of feathers varies from none (for very short-flight arrows) to as many as five, but three feathers is a common configuration. Feathers can be set straight or spiraled along the shaft to affect flight.

Unusual Arrows

- **Broad Arrow.** An arrow with a broad, barbed tip; often used at sea to rip the sails and rigging of enemy ships in the 14th and 15th centuries.
- **Rankling Arrow.** An arrow with a loose, barbed head meant to stay in the wound when the arrow was drawn out.
- **Whistling Arrow.** An arrow that whistled in flight, due to a hollow head—probably of Chinese invention, but also used in Japan. They were probably used as a signal mechanism.

Crossbows

A crossbow is a bow that has been mounted on a stock and is generally fired by rotating the bow spring 90 degrees. Crossbows have been known since at least 500 B.C., when they were mentioned in Sun Tzu's *The Art of War.* At one time, crossbows were very powerful and very accurate, but their widespread use as military weapons ended in the mid 16th century. They remain, even today, a hunting weapon.

Parts of a Crossbow

- Butt
- Stock (tiller)
- Trigger
- Nut
- Groove
- Bowstring
- Bridle (bow iron)
- Bow
- Stirrup

There are three steps to firing a crossbow. The first is cocking it, known as *spanning.* Once the bow is under tension, the string is held by a release catch. Next, the ammunition, called a *bolt* or *quarrel,* is fitted into a groove in the stock and placed up against the string at the catch, or *nut.* Finally, the bow is aimed much like a rifle and fired by means of a trigger, which lowers the nut and allows the bow to release the stored tension.

Parts of a bolt or quarrel:

- Butt
- Feathers or flights
- Shaft
- Head

Because crossbows sometimes required great effort to span, various methods were devised throughout history. The simplest was to step into the stirrup and then pull back the string with the hands. Very common was the *belt* and *claw*, which consisted of a belt around the waist and a hooked claw to grab the string. The archer would straighten up and use the back muscles to pull up the string while holding the bow down with a foot in the stirrup. A variation of that was the *cord and pulley* system, which allowed for stronger bows to be drawn. Two other methods involved levers that attached to the crossbow mechanism—the *goat's foot* and the push levers.

As crossbows became even more powerful, it became increasingly difficult to span them. Mechanical devices, such as the *windlass* (essentially a winch) and the *cranquin* (a geared device using a handle to wind the gear and pull the string), became necessary.

In general, the loading and firing of a crossbow was more cumbersome and time consuming that that of a bow. However, crossbows could be more accurate and could shoot farther than, for instance, the famed English long bow. With practice and the right equipment, some crossbows could be fired quickly, although never as quickly as a bow. As with regular bows, some crossbows were made to fire small missiles, such as rocks and clay balls. These were not used in warfare, but for hunting small game.

Specific Crossbows

- **Arbalest.** Another general name for the European crossbow. These came in all sizes, ranging from light arbalests that could be used in the field and armed by pulling with the arms, to arbalests that required the use of the feet in a stirrup, all the way to complex and very powerful weapons that required the use of cranks or windlasses and tackles. The heavier crossbows, although far more powerful than even the long bow, were time consuming to load and therefore used generally when defending fortifications. The crossbowmen were protected by large tower shields, such as the pavis or mantlet, which were sometimes held by attendants and sometimes set into the ground in a permanent position to protect the crossbowmen.
- **Arbalete a Jalet.** A crossbow designed to fire pellets instead of bolts or quarrels. Used by both Europeans and Chinese.
- **Chu-Ko-Nu.** A Chinese repeating crossbow that could be quickly cocked and fired using a lever system. A box on top contained multiple bolts. Some could fire two bolts at once. This crossbow was used as late as 1895 in the Chinese-Japanese War.
- **Nayin.** An African crossbow made to shoot either iron-tipped bolts or light bamboo missiles tipped with poison.
- **O-Yumi.** Japanese crossbows, often up to 12 feet in length. Lighter versions were called *teppo-yumi.*
- **Stirrup Crossbow.** Larger crossbows required both hands to winch the string and cock it, so some weapons were fitted with a stirrup to steady it with the feet while it was armed.
- **Tarbil.** A Malayan pellet crossbow.
- **Thami.** A powerful Thai crossbow that varied in size, but could be as much as 5 feet across. The bolts were feathered with folded leaves and tipped with poison strong enough to drop even an elephant, rhinoceros, or tiger.
- **Thang.** A Chinese crossbow mounted on wheels.
- **Tscheu.** A Chinese crossbow mounted in a wall that could be as much as 12 feet across.

Combined Weapons

Weapon makers often combined different weapons into one. This was especially true after the introduction of guns, which were variously combined with swords, daggers and knives, axes, hammers, pikes, whips, and even brass knuckles. While many weapons employed guns with hand-to-hand weapons, other combination weapons simply put together more than one type of attack—for instance, a combination of a sword for longer-range fighting with a katar for close-in attacks. Or spearheads attached to Japanese yumi or to blowpipes in various jungle countries. How might the idea of combined weapons apply to games and tactical fighting?

Other Weapons

NOTE

Inspiration in battle comes where you find it. The Bedouin tribes of Northern Africa had something called the uttfa, *which was a bamboo enclosure covered in ostrich feathers and carried by a camel. Inside rode a woman whose job it was to sing during battle to encourage her side. The uttfa generally became the center of the battle, as the other side believed her capture would spell destruction for the other tribe, while, of course, the uttfa's tribe would do their utmost to protect her.*

- **Agny Astra.** Rocket or fire-tipped dart used in ancient India. Fired from a bamboo tube, it was used against cavalry.
- **Blowpipe or Blowgun.** Blowguns are typically a tube of wood, reed, or bamboo used to propel a dart using the breath. They are used most commonly in South America and Malaysia. The construction of a blowgun is lightweight so that it can be easily held near the *breech*, or blowing end. The dart is inserted in the breech and then a piece of wadding—generally either cotton or pith—is stuffed in after the dart. A sharp exhalation of the breath will propel the dart very far and very accurately. The tips of blowgun darts are often coated in very virulent poison, both for hunting and for warfare. Some South American blowpipes can be 8 to 10 feet long. Typically, a blowgun hunter will carry a small tube for extra darts and a gourd filled with wadding material. Some types of blowpipes, such as those from Borneo, also had spear points that could attach to the end of the weapon.
- **Balasan.** Sumatran blowpipe made from a short, single joint of bamboo.
- **Banduk Doraha.** An Indian combined gun—two guns, one concealed within the other. The outer gun is a flintlock, and the inner is a percussion mechanism.
- **Bomb Lance.** Used to kill whales, this explosive was shot from a gun. The head penetrated the whale and could be unscrewed to allow the loading of powder in the center shaft. The back end contained a trigger, which would be pulled out when the gun was fired and would fire when the lance entered the whale's body. The bomb lance was rarely used because the gun that fired it had a tremendous kick and often propelled the shooter overboard.
- **Budge Barrel.** A barrel that stored 40 to 60 pounds of gunpowder, with a leather bag nailed to one end. It was meant to keep the powder from firing accidentally.
- **Cadge.** Used to carry a number of hawks, it is a frame within which a man can walk, carrying it on his shoulders. The legs fold up for carrying and down when at rest. The name of the carrier was *cad*. Because he was generally good for nothing else, the word ultimately became slang.
- **Calthrop or Caltrap.** Metal spike used to hinder cavalry or to slow infantry, consisting of four spikes forged so that one would always face upward. Calthrops were scattered along the path of the advancing enemy and could be considered the ancestors of barbed wire.
- **Capucine.** A band of metal holding the barrel of a gun to the stock.
- **Carpentum.** Latin name for a Gaulish war chariot.
- **Catch-Pole.** A pole terminating in a fork or collapsible loop that catches a man by the neck and does not allow him to escape. It was originally used to pull riders off their horses.
- **Chariot.** Originally, chariots were used simply to bring warriors to battle, after which they fought on foot. However, Cyrus innovated a stronger chariot with scythes attached to the axle—some pointed outward and some pointed downward to prevent enemies from simply falling and letting the chariot pass over them. Such war chariots continued to be used for centuries after.

- **Curare.** Fast-acting poison of South American natives, often applied to arrows and darts.
- **Fakir's Horns.** Although Indian fakirs were not supposed to carry weapons, they were allowed to carry a set of deer horns. These horns, with the points set opposite each other, could be used as an effective weapon. Some went so far as to add steel tips and even a small round shield in the middle.
- **Falcastra or Falk.** A scythe attached to a pole.
- **Feather Staff.** A 17th-century officer's staff that concealed one long and two short blades, which could be positioned by a jerk of the staff.
- **Feu Volant.** Early version of gunpowder.
- **Fire Carriage.** A wheeled carriage with several mounted flintlock muskets attached. All the muskets were loaded at once by means of a set of ramrods fastened together and guided by a traveling brass plate.
- **Fukidake.** A 9-foot-long Japanese blowpipe. Later versions were 5 feet long. Slivers of bamboo fitted with features were used as ammunition.
- **Greek Fire.** Reported to be a fire that could not be extinguished by water. Probably a mixture of gunpowder that would not explode but would emit sparks for a considerable time. Also known as *wild fire.*
- **Gunsen.** A Japanese war fan using metal spines and used primarily to parry attacks.
- **Hachiwara.** "Helmet breaker"—essentially a strong spike with a lateral guard built into the blade, used for piercing as well as for blocking, and possibly breaking an opponent's sword.
- **Infernals.** Floating mines constructed in the bodies of boats.
- **Jinsen.** A folding war fan from Japan with iron ribs.
- **Kagi-Nawa.** A silk cord 10 feet long (sometimes longer) with a four-hooked grapnel at the end.
- **Kamcha.** A Turkish whip mounted on a handle, coming off from one side of the handle's top.
- **Kau Sin Ke.** A Chinese chain whip made up of bars linked together with a weight at the end. A simple modern equivalent of this is the bicycle chain, which is often used in gang fighting.
- **Kumade.** A Japanese weapon that consists of a two- or three-pronged grappling hook mounted on a handle, with a spike or pick blade opposite the prongs.
- **Kusari-Gama.** A chain with two weights attached, used both for attack and for defense against the sword. A second variation had only one weight and was often attached to a kama yari. This had a long reach, was said to be used from the walls of a besieged castle, and was often wielded by women.
- **Madu.** A very small one-handed shield with horns of the black buck extending laterally to either side. It was used both for thrusting and for parrying, and it was carried in the left hand by swordsmen. It was also carried by beggars and wild men.
- **Maori Adze.** A style of stone chisel or knife used variously as a general work utensil, a ceremonial item, or a weapon. Found among the Maori of New Zealand, but also in other parts of Oceania.
- **Metsubushi.** A small box used to blow pepper in the face of criminals—used by the Japanese police. There were lacquer or brass boxes with a wide-mouth hole on one side and a small pipe to blow through on the other. A screen prevented the pepper from coming back through the mouth hole, and a plug was used to keep the box closed when not in use. Apparently, pepper spray isn't new.
- **Narnal.** An Indian cannon small enough to be carried by one man.
- **Oliphant.** Notwithstanding Sam Gamgee's descriptions of giant beasts, the historical Oliphant was a war and hunting horn used in the 12th century. It was often made from ivory and generally shaped like an elephant's tusk.
- **Orgue (Organ).** A group of gun barrels mounted in a frame so that they could all be fired at once. During the 17th century, as many as 160 barrels were grouped together this way.
- **Panji.** Sharpened stakes used to protect a Malay village or to place in the path of a pursuing force. Often carried in special pockets of the war regalia. The Dyak version was called a *tukak.*
- **Parabas.** A trap consisting of a tree, mostly cut through and held up by rattan cables. When the enemy approached, the cables were cut, causing the tree to fall on them.

- **Patobong.** A covered pit filled with spikes—about 3 feet deep.
- **Pen Case.** Tibetan lamas did not carry weapons, but in ancient times were known to defend themselves with their pen cases, which were more impressive than they sound. For instance, they were made of heavy iron, were more than a foot long, and could easily double as a baton or club.
- **Poeot.** A blowpipe from Borneo, interesting because it sometimes had a spearhead attached to it.
- **Quadriga.** A Roman chariot pulled by four horses.
- **Ranjau, Sudas.** A Malayan defense consisting of 6-inch bamboo spikes driven into the ground, sometimes tipped with poison.
- **Scythes.** Scythes were a common peasant weapon, as they were common on farms but could be adapted to fighting. They were single-edged and often consisted only of a long shaft with a blade mounted at the end.
- **Shrapnel.** Invented in 1784, Lieutenant Henry Shrapnel invented a weapon called a *spherical case* that was designed to hit troops outside the range of ordinary case shot. It was a shell filled with bullets and scrap iron with just enough powder inside to explode it. It took many years to develop. It was formally adopted by the British military in 1803. In time, it gained both a time fuse and an impact fuse.
- **Sickles.** Curved-bladed slashing and slicing instruments with only the inside edge sharpened. Adapted as a weapon from a common agricultural tool.
- **Sode garami.** A Japanese weapon used mainly for catching criminals. It was a pole more than 6 feet long with two sets of barbed hooks at the end and three lines of small spikes extending back from the tip for about 20 inches.
- **Sopok.** A name used in Borneo for both spear and blowpipe. Blowpipes often had spearheads attached.
- **Sosun.** A straight sword from India. The hilt featured a cup pommel and a spike on the end.
- **Taksh-Andaz.** 14th-century Indian rockets.
- **Tau-Kien.** A Chinese weapon that had a sword-like hilt, but instead of a blade, it was made of heavy, square, iron bars.
- **Tulup.** A Javanese blowpipe made of a straight piece of wood or cane, about 5 feet long. A Tulupan is a Javanese blowpipe made from bamboo.

Chinese Weapons

This section contains a list of some unique Chinese weapons. Although the weapons listed here are considered to be legitimate weapons, to a Chinese martial artist, anything can be a weapon.

- **Bagua Weapons.** Several hand weapons are most associated with the internal martial art called *Bagua*. Examples are the Sun and Moon Blades, Deer Antler Knives, and Heaven and Earth Blades. All are wielded in pairs and held in the hands. They have various spikes and edges and can be used to block or trap an opponent's weapons, and also to slice and cut critical tendons and arteries. The Sun and Moon Blades also sometimes are called the *Crescent Moon* or *Mother and Son* by some Chinese practitioners.
- **Benches.** Small benches are sometimes used in martial arts forms. The best place to see this is in various earlier Jackie Chan movies.
- **Bo Staff.** Chinese martial artists have developed many staff forms with staffs of different lengths, depending on the requirements. The bo staff is one of the most common Chinese staffs.
- **Broad Sword.** The Chinese broad sword is a curved slashing weapon with one sharp edge. It can be a single weapon; however, it is often used in pairs as well. Attacks are often sweeping and rounded, with various blocking techniques incorporated as well.
- **Butterfly Knives.** Twin hand blades, similar to a katar, used primarily as a Wing Chun weapon.
- **Canes.** The Chinese have developed several cane forms, using the hooked end in various ways.

- **Darts.** Various kinds of throwing darts have been developed.
- **Double Axes.** Another typical hand weapon consisting of two small axes, one for each hand.
- **Fans.** The fan can be a deadly weapon in the right hands. Fans made with metal ribs, carefully sharpened, can be used to block attacks at close quarters and then slash an unsuspecting enemy in vital areas.
- **Forks.** The Chinese have various kinds of forked weapons.
- **Guan Do.** Named after a famous general (Gaun), the guan do is a large weapon mostly designed to be used on horseback by generals, although forms for its use on the ground have also been developed. It is said that General Guan's weapon weighed 200 pounds, and guan dos today often weigh as much as 70 pounds. The weapon consists of a pole with a spear point at the back and a curved blade at the front end. The blade also has various hooks and details. The guan do is also known as the *spring-autumn big sword.*
- **Hanwei Dadao.** A strong military sword.
- **Hooks.** Hooks are used to capture, control, and break enemy weapons. There are numerous ways to use hooks, including swinging them, hooking them together for extra reach, or catching and breaking blades.
- **Horse-Chopping Blade.** A long weapon with a handle about 3 feet in length and a blade about the same length. The blade consisted of a pair of crescent-shaped blades meant to cut a horse's legs and a broad, curved slashing blade at the end.
- **Melon Hammers.** Most often wielded in pairs, these cudgels are made with wooden shafts just under 3 feet long and round, hollow steel ends about 7 to 9 inches in diameter.
- **Monk's Cudgel.** In the movies you often see monks walking around with a long pole topped by a heavy round ball of metal. This is great for crushing the heads of the unfaithful.
- **Monk's Spade.** This was originally for chopping tree roots and digging. It was really derived from a garden spade, later modified into a weapon. Some also have a crescent-moon blade at the back of the pole, and some have a plain end.
- **Sectioned Chain Whips.** Chain whips are long sections of chain that are tipped generally with sharp, dart-like ends or heavy balls, though some have been made to swing fire elements. Chain whips are moved rapidly, sometimes wrapped around the wielder's body and then released explosively, covering a large distance very quickly. One form of chain whip, with heavy metal balls at the end, is called a *meteor*, presumably because of the speed with which it can be used to attack.
- **Spear.** Chinese spears today are often made of flexible waxwood. When using them, the martial artist can make them shake and vibrate in a large whip-like action, which can be very difficult to block or defend against. Spears were used often in city environments where crowd control was necessary, as a guard or soldier could quickly whip the spear from side to side or reverse direction to control crowds.
- **Straight Sword.** The Chinese straight sword is constructed for finesse attacks, with several cutting edges. It was not meant to "muscle" an enemy, but to surgically cut tendons and arteries in critical places, such as the wrists, shoulders, neck, legs, groin, and feet. Attacks are designed to go around, over, or under the enemy's weapons. The blocking part of the blade is toward the hilt.
- **Three-Section Staff.** Very similar to a Japanese nunchuck in some ways, the three-section staff contains three pieces of rounded wood linked together. There are many uses for the three-section staff, such as trapping, hitting with blunt force, whipping, tripping, and more. A versatile but rarely taught weapon.
- **Yao Dao.** Waist sword worn by police and guards of various kinds.

ARMOR

Armor has been used throughout human history, and it developed along similar lines in different cultures. The earliest armor consisted of animal skins, but people soon found ways to enhance the protective capabilities of the armor they fashioned, including curing and hardening the leather, adding harder items to the armor, and ultimately using metal.

NOTE

***Kurdaitcha Shoes:** Among Australian aborigines, it was believed that only accident or injury was a natural way to die. Any other way was considered to be witchcraft, and the family of the deceased would consult the witch doctor to determine who was responsible—generally someone they weren't on good terms with. Then, they would weave the kurdaitcha shoes out of human hair and emu feathers, which were said to make the wearer invulnerable while pursuing the one responsible. It was perhaps the most efficient armor ever made because both the wearer and the victim believed utterly in its effectiveness.*

QUALITIES OF ARMOR

Weight

- Cumbersome
- Awkwardly heavy
- Moderately heavy
- Light
- Second skin

Detrimental Effects

- Practically immobile
- Reduction in hearing/vision, etc.
- Reduced mobility
- Increased potential for fatigue

Enhancing Effects

- Strength boost
- Flight/hover ability
- Enhanced senses (hearing/sight, etc.)

Location on Body (What It Protects)

- Head
- Face
  - Eyes
  - Brow
  - Nose
  - Chin
  - Temples
  - Ears
- Neck
- Shoulders
- Arms
  - Upper arms
  - Elbows
  - Forearms
  - Wrists
- Hands
- Fingers
- Chest
- Back
- Belly
- Stomach
- Hips/groin
- Thighs
- Knees
- Shins
- Feet
- Mouth/lungs

Amount of Protection

- Complete
- Partial
- Little
- Next to none

Type of Protection

- Piercing/penetration
- Impact
- Bludgeoning
- Shock
- Energy
  - Electricity
  - Heat
  - Cold
  - Negative
  - Magical
- Pathogens
- Chemicals

Durability

- Indestructible
- Extreme
- Strong
- Moderate
- Weak
- Next to nothing

Permeability/Vulnerability To:

- Sharp points
- Sharp edges
- Blunt weapons
- Projectile weapons
  - Bullets
  - Arrows/Darts
  - Other
- Shrapnel
- Heat
- Cold
- Other energy sources
- Magic
- Airborne chemicals and/or pathogens

Typical Stages in the Development of Armor Prior to Firearms

- **Animal Skins.** Basic protection from the fur and leather obtained from animal skins. The crudest and most basic of protection, little more effective than clothing. In some cases, other parts of animals, such as bones, scales, and shells, could be used for added protection.
- **Early Ring and Scale Armor.** Skins with harder ring- or scale-like material attached to the outside (called *Jazerant armor*). Also, armor made from wood or bone lashed together by sinew, as used commonly among Native Americans and in Eastern Siberia.
- **Brigantine Armor.** Hard material riveted or quilted between layers of leather or cloth—used in Europe between the 10th and 16th centuries and also very common in India and China.
- **Ecrevisses.** Armor made from overlapping plates or splints.
- **Padded Armor.** Armor made from pads woven in several thicknesses and quilted together.
- **Plated Armor.** Small plates of metal attached to cloth or leather. Very heavy, as the plates had to be overlapped. Plated armor of this type was used by the ancient Greeks and Romans.
- **Splinted Armor.** Narrow plates (splints) of metal were riveted together or attached to a backing of cloth or leather. Splinted armor was designed to be flexible and yet provide the protection of metal plates.
- **Mail.** Interlocking links of metal.

- **Mail reinforced with plate.** Combined armor that had sections of mail with other sections of plate mail for strategic added protection without the extra weight or lack of mobility of full plate.
- **Full Plate/Gothic Armor.** Specific to Germany and the Holy Roman Empire of the 15th century. Highlighted by curves, ridges, and flutings, gothic plate armor fully encased the wearer in some of the most artistically pleasing of all full-plate armors, though not necessarily the most comfortable or maneuverable.

> Every detail was carefully studied, and any change that increased efficiency was worked out with painstaking care. It was for this purpose that the two sides were made quite unlike each other to adapt them to the different functions of the right, or sword, arm and those of the left, or bridle, arm. The breastplate was made in two or more pieces overlapping in a long point and connected by straps or sliding rivets, thus giving a certain amount of flexibility. The feet were covered by laminated solerets with long, pointed toes which could be removed when the wearer was on foot. The shoulder and elbow cops were very large in order to guard the openings at the joints, and the hands were covered by mitten gauntlets. The thickness of the plates was regulated for the strains they would have to bear; not only did the different pieces vary, but different parts of the same plate differed considerably in thickness.
>
> —George Cameron Stone, *A Glossary of the Construction, Decoration, and Use of Arms and Armor in All Countries and in All Times* (Jack Brussel, 1961)

Typical Armor Elements

NOTE

How armor was tested: In the early days, a crossbow bolt was fired at it from short range. Later, a musket was used. If the armor passed, it was stamped with the armorer's mark.

- **Ailette.** Shoulder guard.
- **Aventail.** Mail neck protection.
- **Baldric.** Collar or shoulder belt used to support a sword or other weapon. Also used as an ornament from the 14th century.
- **Bevor.** Mail or plate protection for the lower part of the face.
- **Bracer, Kote, Vambrace.** Various types of protection for the forearm.
- **Breastplate.** Metal protection for the torso, also known as a *cuirass.* A cuirass made from overlapping upper and lower plates was known as an *emboitment.*
- **Breaths.** Slits in a full helm that allowed breathing.
- **Coif.** Mail hood, often integral to a full mail coat.
- **Corselet.** Body armor.
- **Couter.** Plate protection for the elbows, hinged to upper and lower arm guards.
- **Cuisses, Suissards, Cuissarts, Cuishes, Guarde de Cuisses, Quisshes, Quysshews.** Defense for thighs and knees, originally of padded or boiled leather, but ultimately fashioned from hinged plate.
- **Culet.** A skirt of articulated plates attached to the back plate to guard the loins.
- **Fauld.** Mail protection for the groin, worn under plate.
- **Gambeson.** Padded undercoat.
- **Gauntlets.** Protection (and weapons) for the hands.
- **Gorget.** Plate protection for the neck.
- **Greaves.** Protection for the lower half of the legs, specifically the shins.
- **Hauberk.** Mail garment that covered the body and at least part of the legs and arms. Split at the waist for use on horseback. Common in the 10th to 13th centuries.

- **Helm/Helmet.** Among some modern jokers, it's called the *brain bucket.* Protection for the head. (See the upcoming "Helms" section for more details.)
- **Pauldron.** Plate shoulder protection.
- **Poleyn.** Plate protection for the knees.
- **Side Wing.** Armor that protected the sides of the knees.
- **Solerets or Sabotons.** Armor for the feet.
- **Tasset.** More plate armor to protect the thighs.
- **Ventail.** Hanging mail protection that could be lowered between battles and raised before fighting to protect the throat and jaw.

Helms

NOTE

In Japan, if you examine someone else's helmet, it is considered very rude to look on the inside of it.

- **Armet.** Closed helmet that conforms to the shape of the head and covers it completely. Popular in 15th-century Europe. It was an improvement on earlier helmets as it was lighter and completely covered the head, face, and neck. It was improved further by the addition of a gorget that brought the weight onto the shoulders instead of the neck. The armet opened by hinged cheek pieces, which were covered by a visor when worn.
- **Arming Cap.** Padded cloth helmet, often worn under a metal helm but sometimes worn by itself.
- **Barbute.** A helm used during the Renaissance that resembled an ancient Greek helmet.
- **Barrel Helm.**
- **Basinet.**
- **Buffe (Falling Beavor).** A faceplate worn with open helmets, strapped to the helmet or bolted on, particularly during jousts.
- **Burgonet.** An open helmet with a brim that projects over the eyes. It also sometimes featured upstanding combs (one or three), a panache (plume holder) at the base of the helmet, and/or earflaps.
- **Cabasset.** An open helmet with a point or small projection on the top, possibly meant to represent the stem of a pear. *Cabasset* means pear in Italian.
- **Capeline or Chappeline.** Iron or steel cap used in the 13th and 14th centuries.
- **Casque.** An open helmet—a *burgonet.* Often ornately decorated, but weak as armor.
- **Cassis.** Typical Roman helmet that fit the head closely and had heavy guards over the cheeks and a large crest.
- **Chapel de Fer.** Literally, "iron hat," a common helmet used from the 12th to the 15th century and modified as the "pikeman's pot" until the 17th century.
- **Death's Head Burgonet.** A very heavy rounded helmet, weighing as much as 20 pounds.
- **Great Helm.** A heavy full helm that somewhat resembled a bucket with eye slits, though they were often adorned with distinctive heraldic decorations.
- **Heaume.** Common in the 13th century, the heaume was a heavy helmet that rested on the head over a padded cap. The heaume completely enclosed the head and had a slit, called the *ocularium,* through which the wearer could see. Breathing holes were eventually added. Because the heaume rested on the head and was not fastened to the body, it could be knocked off during battle, and some soldiers chained them to the body armor to prevent that from happening.
- **Kabuto.** One of several types of traditional Japanese helmets.
- **Kawagasa.** A Japanese helmet with a ribbed top and a broad front brim that looked a little like a baseball cap. It was often made from lacquered leather.

- **Kulah Khud.** A traditional Persian and Indian bowl-shaped helmet that had a moveable nose guard, a spike on the top, and a mail curtain that extended down the neck and sides of the wearer. They generally also had one or more plume holders for decoration and identification markings.
- **Kulah Zirah.** A Persian and Indian helmet of mail or small plates connected by mail, with a curtain of mail covering the neck and sides of the head.
- **Lobster Tail Helmet.** So named because of the neck guard made from overlapping plates, like a lobster's tail.
- **Mask Visor.** A face covering that resembled a man, beast, or monster—common in the 16th century.
- **Menpo.** A Japanese faceplate. Actually, there are several types—essentially masks. Some covered the entire face, while others only covered the upper or lower parts. Some were elaborately sculpted to resemble a realistic or fanciful face. Others were plain.
- **Morian (Morion).** A distinctive helmet of the 16th century that featured a bowl-shaped headpiece with a curved brim forming peaks in the front and the back. A comb as much as 4 inches high covered the top. It was used by pikemen at first and later became popular with the men guarding royal personages. It is possibly best known as the style worn by the Spanish conquistadors.
- **Salade.** A helmet that covered the entire head. There were different versions of the salade. In Germany, it had a long tailpiece extending out the back and often a visor in front. French and English versions lacked the long tailpiece, while in Italy it was lighter and had a T-shaped projection to cover the face instead of a complete face cover. This version was often called a *barbute* or a *celata.*
- **Spider Helmet.** A 17th-century helmet with a hinged bar that could be lowered to protect the face or raised to cover the crown.
- **Sugar-Loaf Helm.** A helmet with a pointed top that replaced the flat-topped helmets of the 12th century.
- **Ventail.** Mail flap attached to the chest armor that could be raised to protect the jaw and throat or lowered when not in battle.
- **Visor.** The visor was first developed in the 12th century by combining the nose and ear flaps of the helmets of the day. At first it was fixed, but over time movable visors were developed.

Arm and Shoulder Protection

- **Bazu Band or Dastana.** Armband worn throughout the Turkish Empire, Persia, and India for centuries, covering the outside of the arm from the wrist to the elbow.
- **Bracer.** A covering for the left forearm made from leather, horn, wood, metal, ivory, or just about anything that would protect the arm from chaffing and bruising by a bowstring.
- **Espallieres.** Shoulder guards.
- **Kote.** Protection for the forearm.
- **Pauldron.** Plate protection for the shoulders.
- **Spandrel.** Ancient Roman shoulder guards.
- **Vambrace.** Armor for the forearm.

NOTE

In the Middle Ages, a man was said to be armed if he was wearing armor and unarmed if he was not. The carrying of weapons had no bearing on whether he was armed or unarmed.

Body Protection

NOTE

Pots and Mops was a kind of over-decorated armor (officially called pisan*).*

- **Breastplate.** A plate or set of plates covering the front of the body from the neck to just below the waist. One of the oldest pieces of armor.
- **Buff Coat.** A 17th-century leather coat made from buffalo skin and used as outer armor, generally with jack boots, a lobster-tailed helmet, and back and breast armor under it.
- **Corselet or Corslet.** Originally leather breast armor, but later the name was used with plate armor as well. The corselet was only for the body, but a full set of armor was known as a *corselet furnished* or *complete.* The corselet could protect against a pistol shot, but not the heavier impact from a musket.
- **Cuirass.** Originally leather body armor, the cuirass became a standard front and back armor for the body that was strong enough to protect even against a musket shot.
- **Ichcahuipilli.** Ancient Mexican body armor made from thick quilted cotton, and leg and head protection fashioned from wood and leather or material. It was decorated with feathers and/or gold.
- **Lorica Segmentata.** Typical Roman armor that protected the body by use of horizontal bands of metal and the shoulders by use of vertical segments. A metal-studded skirt offered some protection for the lower body.
- **Subligaculum.** An apron worn by gladiators in Roman times. These gladiators were armed with a shield and a three-pronged scourge. Their opponents were traditionally armed with a sword and shield, but otherwise naked.
- **Surcoat.** Like the hauberk, the surcoat was meant to be worn over armor and was split in front and back to be worn on horseback. It was used in the 13th and 14th centuries.
- **Tabard.** A 15th-century garment worn over armor, with short, open sleeves and displaying the insignias of the wearer on the front and back as well as on each sleeve. It is still considered ceremonial dress for the English heralds—or it was in the 1930s, anyway.
- **Trellice Coat.** A 12th-century armor, probably made from leather-reinforced straps and studs of metal.

Leg Protection

- **Chausses.** Close-fitting armor for the legs.
- **Chaussons.** Armor for the upper part of the legs.
- **Greaves.** Armor for the lower part of the legs and ankles.
- **Poleyn.** Plate protection for the knee, hinged to the thigh and shin pieces.
- **Taces (also Tassets).** Laminated protectors for the thighs.

Other Armor

NOTE

Another name for basic rank and file armor of the 15th and 16th centuries was jack. *Such armor consisted of a padded coat, sometimes with mail plates or horn sewn into it, or a canvas garment made with small holes reinforced with a buttonhole stitch.*

- **Arming Doublet.** A padded garment of heavy material worn under armor to protect against chafing and to cushion blows.
- **Arming Girdle.** The sword belt used with armor.
- **Arming Spurs.** Used when riding horses in armor.

- **Bandolier.** Originally a baldric or waist belt that carried wood or metal containers, each with a measured charge of powder for a pistol or rifle. It may also have carried a primer and/or a bullet pouch. Later bandoliers were used to carry bullets.
- **Bardings.** Armor for horses, which evolved along similar lines to human armor, ultimately becoming complex plate and mail coverings.
- **Bishop's Mantle.** a long cloak of mail worn over armor.
- **Brayette.** Basically a codpiece, meant to protect the private parts. In the 16th century it was required by English law for every man above a certain rank, even though its protective value was dubious.
- **Chanfron, ChampFront, etc.** Armor used for the head of a horse—generally a plate covering the front of the head, sometimes with side plates. Originally made of boiled leather, they were ultimately fashioned from steel.
- **Fendace.** Throat protection that preceded the gorget.
- **Flanchards.** Plate armor used to protect a horse's sides.
- **Fontal.** An armor plate that protected a horse's head. Generally distinguished from the chanfron in that it only covered the front of the head.
- **Gads or Gadlings.** Knobs and spikes attached to the backs and knuckles of gauntlets. Found typically in armor of the latter part of the 14th century.
- **Hamata.** Roman armor made of hooked chains—a crude form of chain mail.
- **Imbricate Armor.** Armor made from overlapping scales over leather or cloth.
- **Jack Boots.** Heavy boots used by horsemen from the 16th to the 18th century. The leather of these boots was "jacked," hence the name.
- **Kamr.** Often ornate Indian belts made to carry flasks, bullets, and a variety of other objects. Examples used a variety of materials, including wood, horn, ivory, paper, leather, cloth, and metal.
- **Locking Gauntlet.** A plate glove made with extra-long fingers that could be locked to the wrist plate, preventing the user from being disarmed.
- **Pourpoint.** A padded and decorated leather armor that fit closely on the body and was worn under armor, although it was sometimes also used as light armor if heavily padded.
- **Prick Spur.** A spur with a single point instead of a rowel (toothed wheel).
- **Saboton.** Foot armor that covered the top of the foot and was strapped on. These were also called *bear-paw* and *duck-billed* solerets.
- **Surcoat.** An outer tunic worn loosely over armor and generally decorated with the wearer's colors or other heraldry
- **Take Gusoku.** Japanese fencing armor.
- **Tatami Yoroi.** Folding armor used in Japan, which included body armor and a helmet (tatami kabuto) that could all fold for easy transportation.

NOTE

Native American moccasins varied greatly according the tribe who made them. Some were soft-soled while others were stiff. Perhaps the most interesting were stiff-soled moccasins made so that it was difficult to tell from the tracks which direction the wearer was going.

Shields

NOTE

El-Darakah: *The Arabic word for shield, from which our word target derives.*

Shields have been used since before recorded history. They have been made of almost any material, including wood, leather and skins, wicker, metal, cloth, turtle shells, and more. The earliest shields were circular or sometimes elliptical. Some were flat, and others were curved and nearly cylindrical. Other shields, called *heater shields*, were rectangular or three-sided, with a straight or slightly curved top tapering to a point at the bottom. A lot of other shapes were used.

Two similar types of shields were bucklers, which were held in the hand at arm's length, and targets, which were carried by passing the arm through two handles in the back. Some shields were made so that they could be used as either buckler or target, such as the Persian sipar. Shields range in size from very small—only a few inches—to very large—large enough to cover two archers. Throughout the world, shields have been made in many other shapes and sizes and fashioned from many different materials.

- **Adaga.** Moorish shield used in 15th-century Spain.
- **Buckler.** Generally refers to a small round shield used in the left hand when wielding a sword. The buckler generally had one or two handles with which it was gripped. A similar shield, known as a *target*, was held by slipping the arm through loops in the back.
- **Cetra.** A small round Roman shield about 3 feet in diameter, used by light infantry.
- **Chimal.** An Apache shield made from animal skins ornamented with features and small mirrors in the center.
- **Chimalli.** Mexican shields of two varieties: wooden and cane covered in hide. They were often decorated with paintings, inlaid gold, silver and copper, and shells and feathers. The wooden variety was so strong and durable that the Spanish conquistadors adopted them.
- **Dhal.** A round shield used in India and Persia, made from hide, metal, or sometimes shell. One report says that rhinoceros hide was the best. These were often highly ornate.
- **Hoplon.** A large round shield of ancient Greece.
- **Ishilunga.** A South African shield made from hide and wood, with two additional leather strips woven into the front. From 2 to 4 feet high with a width about two-thirds the height.
- **Kliau or Klau.** A Dyak shield made from a single piece of wood, 3 to 4 feet long and about 20 inches wide. The top and bottom end in a point, and the body of the shield curves slightly outward. Decoration varies from very plain to very ornate.
- **Lave.** A wood or basketwork shield from New Guinea. Some varieties are shaped like a solid figure 8.
- **Manteu d'Armes.** A fixed tournament shield of the 16th century that was used to catch the lance point and hopefully break the lance. It was worn on the shoulder of the plate armor, although an earlier form may have been made of thick wood and extended from the neck of the horse.
- **Mantlet.** A large shield that rested on the ground and was used to defend when attacking fortifications.
- **Nagphani Dhal.** A Nepalese cobra shield, called the *snake hood shield* and carved with a border of interlaced cobras.
- **Pavis or Pavoise.** A large 15th-century shield used to protect archers—large enough to cover two men, it rested on the ground and was supported by a prop or by an attendant, known as a *paviser*. A similar shield in Japan was called a *tate*, and its bearer was called a *tate-mochi*.
- **Perforated Shield.** Any shield with a hole or opening in it designed to allow the user to see through the shield while holding it. Another type had an opening to allow a lance to be rested in a notch.
- **Rondache.** A 17th-century round shield carried on the arm.
- **Rondelle a Poign.** A very small, round fencing buckler. (Rondelle was also the name of the round plates used to guard the openings in armor.)
- **Rotella.** A shield carried by attaching it with two straps around the arm.
- **Scutem/Scutum.** A large Roman shield, about 4 feet high and 2 feet wide, slightly curved. It was probably made of wood and covered in leather with some metal pieces.
- **Talvas.** Similar to the pavis, a large shield of the 14th century.

- **Tamarang or Turnmung.** Shields used when fighting with clubs in Australia. There are two kinds, both of heavy wood. One is narrow and tapering at the top and bottom with a slot for the hand in the middle on one edge. The other is wide, almost rectangular, and has a handle built into the middle of the back.
- **Tameng.** A Javan shield. Early ones were narrow and had curved sides and straight ends. Later ones were small and round and had spikes projecting from the middle.
- **Taming.** A round shield from Mindanao.
- **Tamua.** A round buffalo-hide shield with rattan woven around the edge.
- **Targe or Target.** A round (or rarely oval) shield with loops in the back. The arm was passed through one loop, and the hand grabbed the other. Targes were used as early as the 12th century and as late as the 19th. They were usually about 2 feet in diameter, although earlier ones were sometimes larger. Some targes also had a central spike up to 10 inches long that could be unscrewed and carried separately.
- **Tarian.** An early British shield of bronze. The name means "clasher" to describe the sounds of them coming together in battle. They were small and round and had a single handle in the back.
- **Totochimalli.** Shields of Mexico that were carried by the higher rank. Made of parallel strips of cane or wood and reinforced.
- **Utap.** A long, oval-shaped shield of the Dyak made of bark and reinforced with wood down the center and on the edges. The top is rounded, and the bottom comes to a point. It is roughly 2-1/2 to 3 feet long.

Stirrups

NOTE

Saddles were invented in Europe around 340 A.D. and went through many years of refinement. Stirrups were not used, however, until the middle of the 6th century, more than 200 years later.

Sources differ as to the exact history of stirrups, some saying they were first in China around 200 B.C. Accounts also vary when describing their introduction into Europe, but most agree they were introduced somewhere between 700 A.D. and 1000 A.D. Stirrups created a revolution in cavalry, allowing men on horseback to brace themselves when using weapons—both melee weapons, such as swords, maces, and lances, and bows for ranged combat. Once they were discovered, their use quickly spread. In their simplest form, they can be nothing more than a rope with a knot tied to it, which was placed between the toes. Many early cultures, including the Natives of America, had stirrups of some form.

Early European stirrups were often made of metal, although wood and leather have been used for various types of stirrups. Stirrups varied in size and weight. There were very ornate versions and very simple ones. Some stirrups, such as those of the Spanish conquistadors, had projections off the sides and bottom that were probably used as weapons against the native peoples they conquered.

NOTE

Spurs were first used as early as 700 B.C. The earliest spurs were known as prick spurs, *and they were simple spikes that attached to the rider's heel, but they continued to develop over the course of centuries passing. Some grew longer and sharper, until around 1100 A.D., when they became a bit too long and sharp and began to endanger the health of the horse. Meanwhile, another line of spurs developed with a small wheel on the end, called a* rowel. *The rowel was most often tipped with spikes of varying lengths and sharpness, while the wheels themselves ranged from barely visible to several inches in diameter. While spurs were practical in nature, as with all military armor and weapons, there were highly ornate versions of them as well.*

NOTE

Cataphractes: *Greek heavy cavalry who wore casques over half the face, neck, and ears; cuirasses of plate, iron, or horn scales; plus armor for the right arm and thighs. They also wore boots and spurs and wielded the lance, long sword, and sometimes the javelin.*

NOTE

Cherkajis: *Persian fighters and horsemen. The word means, literally, "wheelers about." The Cherkaji were the best fighters.*

Medieval Castles

Castles were, in some ways, an extension of the medieval society and of its warfare. Although not technically a weapon or armor, castles were fortifications and bases from which the military functioned, and in some ways they were a type of weapon and a type of armor, if you think of them as both offensive and defensive structures. At any rate, we decided to include a brief description of some elements of medieval castles in this chapter because of their logical ties to the weapons of medieval history.

Castle Architecture and People

Basic Areas

- **Bailey/Ward.** Enclosed open area inside the walls.
- **Butt.** The archery range.
- **Castle Halls.** Often placed along the castle walls and connecting different areas. Also in the keep or towers. Castle halls were also used for meals and entertainment, ceremonies, and legal issues. Apartments might be available over the halls for guests, or they might sleep in the halls.
- **Chapel/Church.**
- **Dais.** Raised platform for the high table located in the great hall.
- **Ditch/Moat.**
- **Drawbridge.**
- **Drum Tower.** Typically, a round tower built to connect different sections of the outer curtain wall.
- **Dungeons.** Generally towers used for keeping prisoners.
- **Garderobe.** A chamber room with a seat jutting from the wall. Chamber privies were often used for private reading.
- **Gatehouse.** Often multistoried with guard rooms, machinery to operate the portcullis, residential quarters, garrisons and weapon stores, and even prisons. Often had passages with murder holes and arrow slits and may have been guarded by a barbican.
- **Inner Curtain Wall.** Inner protective wall, possibly with additional protective towers.
- **Inner Gate.** A gate within one of the concentric curtain walls, leading into the center of the castle.
- **Inner Ward.** The innermost area of the castle.
- **Kitchen.**
  - **Pantry.** Where food was prepared.
  - **Buttery/Bottlery.**
  - **Ovens.** Often large enough to cook two or three oxen at the same time.
  - **Scullery.** For washing dishes over sinks.
- **Mew.** Housing for hawking and falconry.
- **Oubliette.** Dungeon cells that were only accessible from above. Some, such as the *bottle dungeon*, were shaped so that a prisoner could never lie down.

- **Outer Curtain Wall.** Outer wall, often ringed with towers from which defenders could rain down arrows and other attacks on enemies.
- **Outer Gate.** The outermost gate to the castle.
- **Privy/Latrine/Jake/Draught/Gong/Necessarium.**
- **Solar/Great Chamber.** Originally, the *solar* was any room above the first level or was one that faced south or was well lit. Later, it was traditionally located beyond the dais, a lord's private apartment; sometimes it was in the mural tower or the keep. In a keep, it was located on a protected side so it could have windows instead of arrow slits. In some cases, the solar was used by the lady of the castle and was called a *bower*.
- **Towers** (of various kinds).
- **Treasury.**
- **Undercroft.** A room used for storage.

Castle Defenses

- **Allure.** The walkway on top of the outer curtain.
- **Arrow Loops.** For firing arrows.
- **Barbican (Barmkin).** Narrow exterior passage at the castle entrance.
- **Bartizan.** Small turret or lookout projecting at an angle from a tower or wall.
- **Bastion.** Prominent projection designed to cover dead ground (blind spot) or provide crossfire.
- **Batter/Plinth/Spur.** Angled footing designed to counter undermining and to deflect battering rams and dropped missiles.
- **Battlements/Crenellations.** Walkway on the wall summit.
    - **Embrasure/Crenel.** Openings in the wall for firing (usually 2 to 3 feet wide), sometimes with wooden shutters.
    - **Merlons.** The solid parts of crenellated parapet between embrasures, usually about 3 to 7 feet high and 5 feet wide, sometimes with arrow slits.
- **Berm.** Level area between castle curtain wall and the ditch/moat.
- **Braie.** Exterior defense—generally an earthen rise that hinders the enemy's approach.
- **Cross Wall.** An interior or exterior dividing wall.
- **Curtain Wall.** Surrounds the bailey or castle buildings, often connected by towers and pierced by arrow slits—ranging from 6 to 20 feet thick.
- **Hoarding/Brattice.** A covered wooden gallery in front of the battlements, with holes in the floor to allow observation and attack on defenders. Ultimately, evolved into stone machicolations.
- **Keep/Great Tower/Donjon.** Last refuge—a self-sufficient square or rectangular (sometimes round) building within the castle, sometimes up to 80 feet high and with walls 17 feet thick.
- **Machicolations.** Openings in the floor of a projecting platform or parapet placed along a wall or above an archway. Used to drop items or shoot projectiles on enemies below.
- **Moat/Ditch.** Often dry, but sometimes filled with water from nearby sources and used as additional defenses. Sometimes stocked with edible eels and fish, sometimes trapped with sharpened sticks called *bungy sticks*. Ranging from 3 to 30 feet deep, generally 12 feet or more in width.
- **Murder Holes.** Openings in a floor through which defenders could fire missiles, drop stones and other objects, or pour liquids (most likely boiling water, as oil was too precious) on the enemy.
- **Parapet.** Embattled wall shielding the castle defenders on the wall walkways.
- **Pele Tower.** Strong, solo tower used as a refuge or lookout—not a true castle, but found scattered through England and Scotland. Also known as the *poorman's castle*, as ordinary people built pele towers to protect their goods and cattle. Made of stone or sometimes wood.

- **Portcullis.** A heavy, grilled door that could be raised by means of pulleys or dropped vertically to seal off an area. Generally constructed from oak plated with iron and metal spikes on the bottom edge. Later versions were incorporated with the drawbridge, such that when the portcullis was raised, the drawbridge was lowered, and vice versa.
- **Postern.** Water gate used to supply the castle if access to a waterway existed.
- **Roof.** Generally made from wood, but also from thatch, lead, flagstone, slate, and clay tiles.
- **Towers.** Castles often had a variety of towers, such as flanking towers, gatehouse towers, and mural towers. They were often built rounded, square, or D-shaped.
- **Wells and Well Houses.** Wells were dug anywhere from 11 feet to more than 400 feet deep.

Key People in a Castle

- **Almoners.** They made sure the poor received alms.
- **Armorers.**
- **Atilliator.** Maker of crossbows.
- **Bailiff.** In charge of peasant jobs and repairs.
- **Billers.** They made axes.
- **Blacksmiths.**
- **Brewers.**
- **Butler/Bottler.** In charge of keeping enough drink stored in the buttery; also in charge of brewers, tapsters, cellarers, dispensers, cupbearers (who were responsible for tasting drinks) and dapifers (who brought meat to the table).
- **Carder.** Brushed cloth while it was being manufactured.
- **Carpenter.**
- **Carters.** Carriers of wood and stone for castle construction.
- **Castellan.** Resident owner or custodian of the castle.
- **Chamberlain.** In charge of the great chamber/hall and the personal finances of the castellan.
- **Chambermaids.**
- **Chandler.** In charge of making candles.
- **Chaplain.**
- **Clerk.** Accountant.
- **Cobblers.**
- **Constable.** Governor or warden of the castle—sometimes an honor bestowed on a minor royalty, sometimes hereditary.
- **Cook.**
- **Coopers and Hoopers.** They made barrels.
- **Cottars.** Lowest peasants, often swineherds, prison guards, or people who did odd jobs.
- **Ditcher.** Dug moats, vaults, foundations, and mines.
- **Doctors.**
- **Dyer.** Someone who dyed cloth,
- **Ewerer.** Responsible for heating and bringing heated water to the nobles.
- **Falconer.** Responsible for falcons and hawks.
- **Fruiterers.**
- **Glaziers.** Someone who cut and shaped glass.
- **Gong Farmer.** People who emptied latrine pits.
- **Guards.**
- **Hayward.** Someone who tended hedges.
- **Herald.** Assistant to knights and expert on heraldry.

- **Keeper of the Wardrobe.** In charge of tailors and laundries.
- **Knight.** A professional soldier who earned the title through long training or through heroism in battle or in contests.
- **Ladies-in-Waiting.**
- **Laird.** Small landlord or minor baron.
- **Lord and Lady.**
- **Marshal.** In charge of the stables, including horses, carts, wagons, and containers. Staff included farriers, grooms, carters, smiths, and clerks. Oversaw transporting of goods.
- **Master Mason.** Responsible for design and oversight of building.
- **Men-at-Arms.**
- **Messengers.** Carried receipts, letters, and commodities.
- **Miners.** Skilled diggers used to undermine enemy castles.
- **Minstrels.** Employed in the castle to provide musical entertainment.
- **Porters/Door Wards.** In charge of doors and controlled who came and went.
- **Poulterers.**
- **Reeve.** Supervisor of work in the castle, making sure that people started and stopped work on time, that nothing was stolen, and so on.
- **Sapper.** An unskilled digger of mines and approach tunnels.
- **Shearmen.** Trimmers of cloth.
- **Shoemaker/Cordwainer.**
- **Slaughterers.**
- **Spencers.** They dispensed items.
- **Spinners/Weavers/Embroiderers.**
- **Spinster.** Originally a woman who spun yarn.
- **Squire.** Young man who was in training to be a knight—attained at age 14 until 21, when manhood was reached.
- **Steward/Seneschal.** In charge of everything in the lord's absence.
- **Watchmen.** Official in charge of security, assisted by lookouts.
- **Weaver.** Worked to clean and compact cloth, along with the walker and the fuller.
- **Woodworkers/Board-Hewers.** Worked in the forests making beams and joists.

> In the 14th century an army was arranged in three "battles," or divisions, the avant-guarde, bataille and arriere-garde, the arriere-garde thus constituting the modern reserve. Sometimes the three formed in line, the avant and arriere-gardes forming the wings but retaining their names.
> —George Cameron Stone, *A Glossary of the Construction, Decoration and Use of Arms and Armor in All Countries and in All Times Together with Some Closely Related Subjects* (Jack Brussel, 1961)

Other Medieval Jobs

- Bakers
- Brick and tile makers
- Butchers
- Clergy
- Farmers
- Fishmongers
- Glass makers
- Goldsmiths and silversmiths
- Grooms
- Herdsmen

Part VII

- Huntsmen
- Innkeepers
- Members of the monastic orders
- Millers
- Pages
- Painters
- Parish priests
- Plasterers
- Potters
- Road menders
- Sailors
- Shipwrights
- Slingers
- Soap makers
- Tanners
- Wood wards (for the forests)

NOTE

Hussiers D'Armes: *The king's guards in France from the 14th century on.*

Jousting

NOTE

Scharfrennen: *A tournament of mounted contestants using sharp lances with no barriers.*

NOTE

Destrier: *The war horse of the Middle Ages. It was always a stallion. A* roncin *was a warhorse lighter than a destrier, but heavier than a hackney.*

- **Arrest.** A lance rest—used originally to distribute the shock over the breastplate.
- **Coronal, Coronel, or Cornel.** Head of a lance with three projecting "claws," which would grab the opponent's armor.
- **Glancing Knob, Bossoir, Pezonera.** Used on the poitrel/peytral (horse's breastplate) to deflect a lance.
- **Grand Guard.** A special plate worn over regular armor that covered part of the face, the left shoulder, and sometimes extended down to the waist. A similar piece of armor was called the *volant piece.*
- **Quintain.** A quintain is a practicing dummy for jousting practice. The first ones were nothing more than a post or a shield attached to a post, but in time, the quintain gained the ability to strike back by having a sandbag attached to an arm so that, when a blow was struck, the pole would spin and hit the unwary in the head. Later versions were made to resemble a typical enemy with sword and shield, and the shield could bash those too slow to get out of the way. Versions were even made that splashed water on those too slow to get out of the way.
- **Vamplate.** The wide, rounded shield guard toward the butt of the lance.

NOTE

Pel or Post Quintain: *A heavy post 6 feet high that was used for practice with a sword, mace, or ax. It was used with heavier-than-usual arms and with the shield employed as well.*

Siege Equipment

Where there were castles and fortifications, there was a need for siege engines of various kinds, meant to break down walls, fling various projectiles and other damaging substances over the walls, or allow attackers to breach the walls or the gates. These ranged from catapults of various kinds to rams and towers.

NOTE

"Riding the city" was an expression meaning to send the cavalry into a besieged town to prevent the citizens from erecting barricades.

Early Artillery

Before gunpowder and the invention of cannons, artillery consisted of engines designed to throw or launch objects based on stored energy of various kinds. There were three sources of this energy—springs, torsion skeins, and counterweights.

- **Spring Power.** Possibly the earliest siege engines were large crossbows using wood or wood-and-sinew bow springs. The early Greek gastraphetes, predecessor to the ballista, was one example that can be dated back to 400 B.C. Other engines, also known as *springnals*, with single springs also probably existed, in which a missile was launched by bending back a vertical wood or composite spring and releasing it with a stone or other heavy object on it.
- **Torsion Power.** One of the most common methods of storing power was to take a rope of twisted fiber—hair or sinew worked well—and wind it tightly on axles. Some torsion engines, such as the catapult, featured a single horizontal axle assembly, and others, such as the later *ballistae*, featured paired vertical axles. In the case of the catapult, releasing the twisted skeins forces the arm forward. When the arm hits the forward barrier, the load is launched. With paired skeins, the operation is more like a bow, with the skeins acting in place of the bow-spring.
- **Counterweight Power.** Possibly the most powerful of the early siege weapons used a counterweight to fling their ammunition. The addition of a sling to the end of the arm added to the power of the shot. The classical counterweight-operated engine was the *trebuchet* (See the following section.)

Some Early Artillery Examples

- **Ballista.** An engine for launching darts or stone balls. Early ballistae were essentially huge crossbows and were cocked by various mechanisms, such as worm wheel and long screw. Ballistae could be fired when partially cocked, allowing for adjustments in range. Later ballistae used torsion engines and were designed either to fire large stones or, in another version, to fire large arrows. The largest ballistae could throw 5- or 6-pound arrows or even heavier stones up to 450 to 500 yards. Stones were often made from baked clay filled with pebbles, which would shatter on impact, preventing the enemy from reusing them.
- **Bricole.** A 14th-century mechanism for throwing heavy stones.
- **Catapult.** Used to throw heavy stones and other heavy projectiles. Early catapults could throw a 50- to 60-pound stone at least 400 to 500 yards, though ancient Greek writing suggests ranges of 700 to 800 yards. The catapult was a frame with a movable lever beam attached to a twisted skein of cord or sinew. The beam was drawn back, loaded, and fired. Attaching a sling to the end of the beam increased range by anywhere from 30 percent to 50 percent and also allowed more range control. Shortening the sling sent the missile higher and shorter. Lengthening the sling caused a longer, flatter shot.
- **Falarica.** Used for firing darts that had burning substances attached.
- **Majanik.** An Arabic engine for throwing stones, also called a *maghribiha.*
- **Mangona.** An engine that fired darts or large stones. The smaller form was called a *mangonel* in the 11th and 12th centuries.
- **Martinet.** A 14th-century machine for throwing large stones.
- **Matafunda.** A device for throwing large stones, possibly using a sling for extra distance.

- **Mate-Griffon.** A device for throwing stones or darts.
- **Mines.** Before gunpowder, mines had a different meaning in warfare. There were two kinds. One was a tunnel dug under fortifications to allow access to the interior of the fortress. The other consisted of a series of tunnels dug under the walls and supported by wooden beams and trusses. The wood was burned away at the end, with the intention of creating a cave-in that would cause the fortification's walls to fall in.
- **Mouton.** A catapult 40 feet long, 20 feet wide, and 20 feet high, used in the siege of Ghent in 1382.
- **Onager.** A type of catapult used for throwing stones and named after a mythical monster, Onagre, who was said to throw stones with its feet. (Another story says it was named after a mule because of the kick it gave when the arm hit the front padding.)
- **Perrier, Patrary, Paterara.** Names for machines intended to throw stones. General names, not specific to any one design. Perrier is also a name of an early form of howitzer. (See the upcoming "Explosive Artillery" section.)
- **Robinet.** A type of artillery used to throw stones or to fire large darts.
- **Rochettes.** Fire arrows fired from a ballista of the 14th century.
- **Scorpion.** The name *scorpion* was given to a number of different weapons throughout history. One use of the name described a siege engine like a giant crossbow that fired missiles. Another description was a Roman whip with weighted lashes. In India, there was a knife called the *bich'wha.* In Europe, a particular halbard with a sharp, narrow blade was called a scorpion.
- **Spingarda or Spingardella.** A large 14th-century crossbow on wheels.
- **Springald.** A 14th-century siege engine that threw stones or bolts.
- **Topi.** A cannon from Southern India.
- **Tormentum.** A siege engine that threw stones. The name came from the twisted skeins used to fire it.
- **Trebuchet (Trabautium).** One of the most common types of siege engines, designed for throwing large stones, although other objects were thrown, including barrels of Greek fire, dead animals, and even live humans. The trebuchet had a weight on the short side of a pivoting arm. The weights were slings with open bags or baskets that could be filled with rocks. On the other, longer section hung a sling in which the payload was placed. The weights were sometimes movable, allowing some adjustment in the trajectory of the missile, and sometimes there were two weights, one fixed and one moveable. The back end was winched down and fastened until ready to fire. It was then released manually.

Rams and Towers

- **Battering Ram.** One of the oldest siege engines, it consisted of a heavy beam with a metal-capped end, suspended from an overhead frame and operated by several men who were protected by a roof barrier. The metal end was often shaped in the form of a ram's head, hence the name. Other versions included what was called a *star drill,* which radiated into bladelike points that cut through walls and gates.
- **Belfry.** The original meaning of belfry was a movable tower used in sieges. At the bottom of the belfry was a ram, while bridges were lowered from the top to allow forces to storm the works. Towers could be moved into position using oxen and pulleys or using men housed inside the tower with crowbars to ratchet the wheels forward. Towers used in sieges could be as tall as 80 or 90 feet, depending on the walls they were intended to storm.
- **Cat, Cattus, Cat-House, Gattus, Rat.** A long, low, wooden gallery placed on rollers or wheels and moved up to the foot of a wall to be attacked. It had a very steep roof that was strapped with iron.

Sometimes it had a ram inside. Miners would attempt to dig through the wall. Some cats had openings for archers and were called *crenelated cats.*

- **Musculus.** A shelter for besiegers used in the 9th century.
- **Petard.** A petard was a kind of mortar designed to be attached to a gate that someone wanted to blow down. It was slightly narrower at the bottom than at the top and was nearly filled with gunpowder. The powder was packed in with several layers of material, waxed over, and sealed with a piece of wood, and the whole affair was mounted on a board that could be attached to the gate in question. A fuse was lit, and the petard exploded. In practice, it sometimes blew down the gate, but it often did more damage to those using it. Is this where the expression "hoist with his own petard" came from?
- **Pluteus.** A 9th-century movable shelter used in sieges.
- **Rebeaudiquin.** A cart with spikes sticking out of it that was used as a movable fortification in the 14th century. Later versions had a cannon attached as well. This was also the name given to a large-scale weapon similar to a crossbow, but with a bow as much as 8 feet in length.
- **Scaling Ladder.** A light ladder used in scaling walls of towns and fortresses.
- **Terebra.** A 9th-century beak with a spike, designed to bore through the walls of a fortress.
- **Tortoise.** A movable covering for besiegers, which often also had a ram shaped like a tortoise head.

Siege Barriers

- **Agger.** Mounds of earth raised by the Romans on which to mount projectile weapons and also to protect troops.
- **Bastion.** An earthwork with the exterior faced with masonry projecting from a fortification.
- **Battlements.** A wall with alternating openings (indentations) and solid sections at the top.
- **Fascines.** Brushwood bundled and tied to make a temporary fortification or to reinforce an earth barrier.
- **Gabion.** A 3- to 6-foot-high cylinder made of woven twigs and filled with dirt. Gabions were up to 3 feet in diameter and were used in making fortifications.
- **Merlon.** A stone pier that separated the openings of battlements during the Middle Ages. Merlons had openings for archers to shoot through, which could be closed by means of wooden shutters.
- **Moveable Towers.** Towers were often used in sieges and could be several stories high. They carried bridges that could be lowered to storm the walls and battering rams at the bottom to attack the walls and gates. They were made from wood and covered with green hides to protect them from being set on fire. They probably smelled pretty rank, although there is no remaining account of that. The Japanese version of a siege tower was called an *untei.*
- **Palisado.** A stake of 5 to 6 feet in length studded with sharp iron and buried in the ground to protect against cavalry charges. Also known as a *hog's bristle* or *sweyne feather.*
- **Sow.** An 11th-century movable framework of wood and hides used while men were undermining the walls of enemy fortresses.
- **Testudo.** A movable covering to protect besiegers.
- **Turas.** A fortification that could be made in the field by weaving the branches of trees like basketwork. It was used in the 16th century.

NOTE

Variously called Sweyen's Feathers, Swedish Feathers, Pig Features, *or* Foot Palidadoes, *these 4-1/2-foot spikes had forked heads and were carried by foot soldiers who planted them in the ground as a defense against cavalry. Some were made entirely of iron while others were made from wood with iron tips.*

Explosive Artillery

In 1242 A.D., when Roger Bacon wrote down the formula for gunpowder (sulphur, saltpeter, and charcoal in a ratio of 1:6:2), the trebuchet was still the most powerful siege engine in use. A little more than 50 years later, the cannon became a fixture on the battlefield and has remained there since, in one form or another. Along with handguns, explosive devices have proliferated in a wide variety of forms, including:

- Airborne cannons
- Anti-aircraft guns
- Anti-tank guns
- Bombs
- Field artillery
- Fixed cannons
- Grenades
- Howitzers and rail guns
- Incendiary weapons
- Machine guns
- Mines and demolition packs
- Missile launchers
- Missiles and rockets
- Mortars
- Mounted artillery
- Naval guns
- Nukes
- Tanks
- Torpedoes

Evolution of Cannons

It is well known that the Chinese have had explosive powders from as far back as the 3rd century B.C. It is also thought that they and the Japanese developed small hand cannons nearly that long ago. It wasn't until the 13th century, however, that gunpowder came to be known in Europe. European cannons appeared in the 14th century and were perfected over the next couple of hundred years. An example is the French cannon circa 1551, which was just under 10 feet long, weighed 5,300 pounds, and fired a 33.25-pound ball. It was drawn by a team of 21 horses. Other cannons were larger or smaller, heavier or lighter.

Cannons are also distinguished by their main use—for instance, field cannons that had to be somewhat portable, naval cannons mounted on ships, and fixed or garrison artillery, which was used in permanent emplacements and could be far larger and heavier than any other type of cannon. Although some garrison cannons were mounted in fixed positions, some were still mounted on carriages that could be moved from place to place. Many of these carriages were made of metal, being that they could be stronger and more durable than wooden carriages. Specialized carriages included one called a *depression carriage*, which could be raised and angled to fire down from a height, such as from fortification walls. A special wad had to be inserted so that the ammunition wouldn't roll out of the barrel when it was tilted into position.

The first cannons were made by welding iron bars, reinforced with iron hoops and covered with leather. By the 16th century, cannon barrels were made of cast bronze and, somewhat later, of cast brass and iron. It was cast-iron barrels that remained most common until the mid 19th century, at which time the larger-caliber barrels were reinforced at the breach and, once again, reinforced with wrought iron. The first cannons most likely fired only stones, but in time they were used to fire a variety of other projectiles—iron and lead balls as well as smaller projectiles, such as small stones, grapeshot, case shot, chain shot, bar shot, and so on. When the first explosive shells were used, they had fuses that were lit before the cannon was fired. This was dangerous, since sometimes they blew up before the cannon fired.

Like the handgun, early cannons were muzzle loaders. Breech-loading cannons did not become truly feasible until the middle of the 19th century. Loading and firing a muzzle loader could be hazardous, and a strict routine was established to prevent unfortunate accidents—on or off the battlefield.

The bore was first sponged out. This was necessary to clean the soot from the barrel and, even more importantly, to remove any sparks that might ignite the powder when the barrel was reloaded.

Before loading the barrel, one of the crew would place his thumb over the touchhole and then the powder and shot were rammed into the barrel. These were two separate steps early on, but they were ultimately combined into one operation.

The gunner directed the aiming of the gun by sighting along the barrel. When the aiming was done, the primer was added. The gun was fired, the shot was calibrated, and the procedure began again.

This procedure required several tools of the trade:

- A protector for the thumb that was placed on the touchhole, called a *thumbstall.*
- A quadrant to measure the angle of the shot.
- A ram—basically a long wooden pole with a plug on the end.
- A sponge on a pole.
- A device called a *worm* that would have a metal device on the end to remove items from the barrel and to hold cleaning rags.
- A scoop on a pole for loading loose gunpowder. This was not needed if the charge was previously premeasured and bagged.

Aiming Early Cannons

The first cannons had no special mechanisms for aiming, and blocks of wood wedged under the carriage generally sufficed. In time, cannons were fitted with rods in the middle of the barrel. These projections—called *trunnions*—were used to mount the barrel to the carriage or frame and allowed the barrel to be tilted relatively easily on the axes. This greatly improved and sped up aiming and became the basis upon which many aiming mechanisms were designed.

Table 33.1 contains a listing of various cannon types, their weights, and their bore diameters. If you want to be realistic using cannons in a game, you might find this information useful.

Table 33.1 Different Cannon Designations

	Weight in Pounds	Caliber in Inches
Syren	8100	
Cannon of 8	8,000	8
Cannon of 7	7,000	7
Aspicke	7,600	7-1/2
Demi-cannon	6,000	6-1/2
Culverin	4,500	5-1/2
Sparrow	4,600	
Pelican	2,550	4-3/4
Demi-culverin	2,500	4-1/2
Saker	1,500	3-1/2
Dragon	1,400	
Minion	1,200	3-1/4
Falcon	700	2-3/4
Falconet	500	2-1/4
Cannon-perrier	3,500	9–11
Demi-cannon drake	3,000	6-1/2
Culverin-drake	2,000	5-1/2
Demi culverin-drake	1,500	4-1/2
Saker drake	1,200	3-1/2

Part VII

Early Ammunition

The first cannons fired stones and, later, iron balls. Interestingly, a round ball or stone might hit the ground, bounce, and do a lot of damage. When firing against personnel or ground installations (such as other cannons), they were fired at a flat angle. Against fortifications, they were fired at a higher angle.

Case shot, also known as *canister shot*, was used against personnel and consisted of a group of metal balls contained in a tin canister, which would break open when the cannon was fired and spread out like a high-powered shotgun, doing maximum damage. Grapeshot worked in a similar way. Both of these types of ammunition were ultimately replaced by shrapnel.

Expanding types of ammunition, such as chain shot and bar shot, would begin to expand after firing. In the case of chain shot, it consisted of two or more metal balls and/or blades attached to each other by a length of chain. Bar shot consisted of weighted bars that were interlocked, with one slipping inside the other and expanding upon firing. These types of loads were primarily for naval use because they could destroy vital rigging in addition to causing other damage.

Exploding ammunition was generally a hollow, powder-filled ball of iron with a fuse, which was lit before the cannon was fired. The resulting blast had many uses, including busting up buildings or terrorizing ground troops, although the simple versions of this type of ammunition were later replaced by shrapnel for anti-personnel uses.

Early Naval Guns

Cannons and other firearms became pretty standard on warships and ships that desired protection. It took some time for the kinks to be worked out, however. At first, cannons were too heavy, too unreliable, and too weak to be effective, and old-fashioned, non-explosive artillery was preferred. In particular, the danger of fire was very real when working with cannons. However, in time, cannons improved, and systems for working them aboard ships improved.

The basic naval cannon design took form in the 17th century and remained more or less the same until the middle of the 19th century. It worked something like this: The gun was mounted on a carriage that could roll back and forth a short distance. Upon firing, the recoil would propel the cannon backward, and the cannon would be controlled by the *breeching rope*—a thick, sturdy rope that could handle the weight of the cannon. The cannon would then be reloaded and pulled forward using ropes and pulleys. Although many cannons were fired by lighting a charge in a touchhole, some later cannons were fitted with flintlock firing mechanisms.

Cannons were arrayed on special decks—sometimes several stories of cannons facing out the broadsides of warships. For more up-close and personal protection, swivel guns were often mounted on the rails of ships. These guns could be rotated in a 360-degree arc. They were rotated backward for reloading.

- **Amusette.** A gun mounted like a cannon but fired like a musket. Used by French horse artillery.
- **Canister or Case Shot.** Cannon shot made from a metal case that contained a number of balls of lead or iron, which are larger than grapeshot.
- **Carcas.** A bomb filled with combustible materials used to set fire to buildings
- **Culverin.** A name applied to small cannons—those with bores between 1.5 and 6 inches.
- **Falconet.** A small cannon with a 2-inch bore.
- **Feringiha.** A large Mongol cannon of the 16th century.
- **Fusees.** 11th century rockets used in sieges to set fires.
- **Gagnal.** An Indian cannon mounted on an elephant.
- **Grapeshot.** A case or frame filled with small cast-iron balls that could be fired as one unit from a cannon. Ultimately replaced by shrapnel.

- **Howitz or Hobitz.** A kind of mortar mounted on a carriage like a gun.
- **Howitzer.** The howitzer was invented in the 16th century. Its predecessors were the perrier and the bombard. One of the principles that distinguished howitzers from other cannons of the time was the use of a short barrel and a narrow powder chamber, which could fire a large shell using less powder and a lighter barrel. These advantages were balanced against the howitzer's shorter range and the slower flight of the ammunition. Howitzers were generally mounted on a moving carriage with pivots (trunnions) at the balance point.

NOTE

Factoid: Indian names for cannon included (translated) "mouth of flame," "mighty tube," and "crocodile's mouth."

- **Lantaka.** A Malaysian brass cannon, ranging in size from a few inches up to 7 feet long. Commonly used both on water and on land, these cannons have been so common that at times they were used as currency. For instance, fines were levied by a certain number or weight of these guns. Some lantakas were made with double bores in one casting.
- **Mons Meg.** A famous cannon made at Mons in Belgium. It weights 4 tons and has a 20-inch bore. It is said to have shot stone weighing 350 pounds.
- **Mortar.** The earliest mortars, various forms of which date back to the 15th century, were a kind of cannon with a very short barrel devised to fire at a very high angle. This was especially useful for firing into fortresses and castles, as well as over barriers and obstacles. Most cannons could only fire against the walls of fortresses, hoping to break them down, but mortars could inflict damage inside by firing at high trajectories that would fly over the walls but drop inside instead of flying over the whole fortress. Early mortars could be quite heavy and were, essentially, small cannon barrels mounted to fire upward. Modern mortars, rare survivors of the muzzle-loading era, are discussed in the following chapter.
- **Quarter Shot.** A type of cannonball that was used in the 17th century but was thought by some to be damaging to the cannon if used too often.
- **Partridge Mortar.** A normal mortar surrounded by 13 smaller mortars, which were attached along the circumference of the central one, which fired a traditional shell, while the outer ones fired grenades.
- **US 12-Pounder (the "Napoleon").** Based on a French design and named after Napoleon III, this smoothbore muzzle-loading field gun was used during the Civil War. It had a range of 2,000 yards. It also required a crew of (ideally) six gunners, six drivers, and eight horses.

Want more weapon and armor information? We're not finished yet. Check out Chapter 34, "Standard Modern Weaponry and Armor," which looks at the weapons and armor of modern times.

34 Standard Modern Weaponry and Armor

The previous chapter looked at weapons and armor from history and from different cultures. This chapter takes up where Chapter 33 left off—specifically with the rise of guns and the evolution of modern weapons and armor.

In this chapter:

- Guns
- Modern Explosives
- Modern Artillery
- Automatic Artillery and Machine guns
- Armored Fighting Vehicles (AFV)—a.k.a. Tanks
- Mines
- Aircraft
- Bombs
- Ships
- Depth Charges
- Torpedoes
- Biological and Chemical Weapons
- Nuclear Weapons
- Modern Armor
- Nonlethal Weapons
- Information Warfare
- Brainstorming Weapons and Armor

Guns

Note: Even though the history of guns dates as far back as the 13th century, in many ways the evolution of gunpowder weapons could be seen as the beginning of the modern era of weaponry, and certainly guns were a great equalizer in combat. I considered splitting the coverage of guns into historical (old) and modern, but where do I draw the line? Significant developments occurred in the evolution of guns, such as the move from black powders to smokeless powders, and the development of breech loading, cartridge bullets, and rifling, to name some key examples. At any rate, this section contains a good deal of information about guns through history, from the earliest to some of the most recent.

A Primer on Handheld Guns (Small Arms)

Gunpowder revolutionized warfare, and nothing symbolized the changes it brought about more dramatically than the invention of handguns—both the *longarm*, or two-handed, variety and, to a lesser extent, the one-handed variety, or *pistol.* Today, we take guns for granted and rarely think about all the elements that define and measure their workings. Here, then, are a few basic facts about guns, how they work, and how they have developed historically:

- **Combustion and Propulsion.** Guns all work on the same basic principle of combustion and propulsion. An explosion takes place within a tube that is closed at one end and open at the other. The expansion of the gas of the explosive at the closed end forces the bullet out the open end at high velocity. That's how all guns, cannons, and artillery work.
- **Loading Method.** There are two main methods of loading guns—from the muzzle (*muzzle loaders*) and from the breech (*breech loaders*). Early guns were almost all muzzle loaders. They required packing of powder, ball, and wadding into the muzzle of the gun, using a ramrod to stuff it all down. Modern weapons are almost all breech loaders. The technology of breech-loading weapons was difficult for preindustrial civilizations. The Industrial Revolution made it more feasible to create breech-loading guns. Further, the invention of the self-contained cartridge bullet made muzzle-loading guns essentially obsolete.
- **Barrels.** There are two kinds of gun barrels—smooth bore and rifled. A smooth bore fires a projectile without any stabilizing influence, resulting in a less accurate gun. Further, smooth-bore guns generally fire round balls or shot. In either case, there is more room between the bullet and the bore, meaning that the pressure, and therefore the muzzle velocity, is lower than with the improved rifled barrel. Rifling is the cutting of spiral grooves on the inside of the barrel, which cause the bullet to spin, creating a gyroscopic effect. The bullets fired from rifled barrels are generally elongated and heavier at the back, fitting the barrel very tightly. In flight, they would tend to tumble, being back-heavy, but the rifling causes them to spin, and the gyroscopic effect keeps them traveling straight. As a consequence, rifled barrels produce more pressure, more stabilized, accurate shots, and higher muzzle velocity. Rifling was known quite early in the development of guns, because the principle upon which it worked was the same principle used to stabilize arrows in flight, by fletching them with feathers that caused them to spin. However, it was expensive to create rifled barrels until the Industrial Revolution, so many of the early guns remained smooth bored. The art of rifling a barrel has evolved over the years, until now the grooves spiral tighter as they near the muzzle.

NOTE

Both longarms and pistols can have rifled barrels, but a pistol with a rifled barrel is still not called a rifle. A rifle is always a longarm with a rifled barrel.

NOTE

Obturation. *The technical term for the expansion of the shell in the barrel that seals it, preventing any back blow of gas through the breech.*

- **Bore and Caliber.** One way that guns are categorized is by the bore size and caliber of the ammunition. The bore size is essentially the inner diameter of the gun's barrel. The older way of describing it involved the number of perfectly spherical lead balls that would fit the bore and weigh one pound. Thus a 10 bore would mean that 10 lead balls, collectively weighing one pound, would fit the bore exactly. Caliber is a measurement of cartridge size, and it takes into account the bullet size (essentially the bore, measured in millimeters or inches) and sometimes the length of the shell casing (which is an indication of how much explosive is available to the bullet). Typical handgun sizes are 9mm (for metric types) or .22, .38, and .45 inches. A typical European caliber is 7.62×39mm (7.62 millimeter bullet and 39mm case). An additional important measurement is the weight of the bullet head, measured in grains.

- **Shot Frequency.** Guns can also be categorized by the number and frequency of shots they can fire.
    - Some guns fire a single shot each time the trigger is pulled, but must be reloaded after that shot. Typical muzzle loaders were of that type. However, a single-barreled shotgun and most derringers work the same way.
    - Some guns will fire a single shot each time they are fired, but they have more than one barrel that can each fire a single shot before reloading. A double-barreled shotgun (of the breakaway variety) is typical of this style of gun.
    - Repeaters are guns that have a magazine of some kind that stores ammunition and allows them to fire repeatedly with each press of the trigger without reloading each time. Some kind of mechanical operation is necessary to seat a new bullet, such as a sliding bolt, a lever or pump, or a ratchet or spring (in the case of revolvers or magazine-based guns).
    - A semi-automatic gun uses the recoil force or gas pressure of the previous shot to work the mechanism and arm the gun for another shot so that it can be fired repeatedly without any additional arming action.
    - Fully automatic weapons will fire in bursts when the trigger is pressed, as long as there is ammunition available and the gun doesn't malfunction.
- **Types of Guns.** There are seven basic types of handguns:
    - **Handgun or Pistol.** A gun designed to be used in one hand. (Pistols may have rifled barrels, but they are not called rifles. They are still pistols.)
    - **Musket.** A musket was a longarm, or two-handed smooth-bore weapon. Nearly all muskets were muzzle loaders, beginning with the early matchlock guns and extending through to the various other firing mechanisms that preceded modern guns.
    - **Carbine.** The carbine was a longarm with a short barrel. It had a typical two-handed stock, but the barrel was kept short, making it easy to wield on horseback. Consequently, it was a popular cavalry weapon.
    - **Shotgun.** A shotgun is a smooth-bore weapon designed to fire small pellets instead of single bullets, and it is generally used in hunting and in riot control but not often in organized warfare.
    - **Rifle.** A rifle is a longarm, like the musket and the carbine, but it has a rifled barrel of full length. There are many types of rifles with different designs and firing mechanisms.
    - **Submachine Gun.** A fully automatic weapon that can be held in two hands and fired. It is distinguished from other machine guns, which are too large to be carried and must be mounted.
    - **Assault Rifle.** Generally, a gun designed to operate in either semi- or fully automatic modes, designed around traditional rifle lines.
- **Bullet Types.** There are many types of bullets in use today. In earlier guns, bullets were round lead balls, but bullets for rifled barrels have moved to a more lozenge-like shape for better aerodynamics and stability. Here are some of the common bullet types for rifles and for pistols, not including modern plastic and rubber bullets used in crowd-control situations, followed by some more specialized modern bullets.
    - Pistols
        - **Full Metal Jacket.** The bullet has a lead core that is completely encased in a strong metal core. This is a reliable bullet with good penetration and stability.
        - **Jacketed Hollow Point.** Similar to the full metal jacket, except that the tip of the bullet is hollow, exposing the lead inside. The bullet expands, which results in maximum energy transfer upon impact. In contrast, a full metal jacket might completely penetrate the target but do less damage than the hollow point.
        - **Semi-Jacketed Hollow Point.** This one has a fully exposed lead tip and expands even more than the jacketed hollow point.

    - **Full Metal Case, Truncated Cone.** The lead core is enclosed in a light copper jacket in a cone shape with a flat or somewhat cupped point. This is a middle ground between the jacketed hollow point and the full metal jacket.
    - **Soft Point.** A jacketed bullet with a fully open lead point.
    - **Lead Wadcutter.** A bullet entirely of lead that cuts cleanly for target shooting.
    - **Lead Semi-Wadcutter.** A more pointed tip for target shooting accuracy and clean scoring.
    - **Round-Nosed Lead.** A lead bullet for pistol shooting.
  - Rifles
    - **Full Metal Jacket.** The bullet has a lead core that is completely encased in a strong metal core. It's not a good hunting bullet, but it is good for some military applications and for clean target shooting.
    - **Full Metal Jacket Boat Tail.** Essentially a full metal jacket bullet with a tapered tail that reduces drag and increases long-range velocity.
    - **Hollow-Point Boat Tail.** A hollow-point bullet with the boat-tail design.
    - **Soft Point.** A jacketed bullet with the lead tip exposed, resulting in a considerable expansion and greater damage overall.
  - Specialized modern bullets
    - **Rubber Bullets.** Cylindrical metal bullets coated with rubber—fired at relatively low velocity. Large size does a lot of damage to flesh without penetrating. Used in riot control.
    - **Needle Bullet.** A bullet that responds to body temperature and explodes just before it enters the body, sending tiny sliver-like fragments into the body. They are very hard to locate and even harder to remove, tending to disappear more deeply into the body, doing further harm.
    - **Micro Ammunition.** Very small bullets shot at high velocity. So small that victims may not always know they have been hit. They feel it when they attempt to move the part that has been penetrated. The shape of the bullet helps cause it to move deeper into the body, damaging capillaries and potentially causing hematoma.
    - **Electric Bullets.** Bullets that can deliver a crippling shock on impact, incapacitating a subject instantly. Current technology uses piezoelectric effects from ceramic crystals that translate the energy of firing and impact into a high electrical charge, similar to a Taser or stun gun, but at much greater distance.
- **Explosives Used in Guns.** The earliest guns were probably created in Europe in the 13th century, although gunpowder had been around in weaker forms for use in fireworks, rockets, and incendiary bombs. Gunpowder was known in China as early as the 9th century, and experts believe that it was first introduced to Europe via trade with the Arabs. Refining techniques allowed for a stronger type of powder, which, in turn, made guns feasible. The first guns used black powder, which was made from various proportions of charcoal, sulphur, and saltpeter. The first black powder was a coarse mixture called *serpentine*, but ultimately a process called *corning* was developed, which allowed the manufacture of gunpowder as grains of powder, and the grains themselves could be created in different sizes. This resulted in much more powerful explosives—so powerful, in fact, that it wasn't immediately used in cannons because the explosions would blow apart the cannons of the time. It became common practice to vary the grain size of powder, depending on the use it was to be put to. For instance, larger grain could achieve the same muzzle velocity as a smaller grain, but with much less pressure.

  Modern bullets no longer used black powder. In the late 19th century, new "smokeless" explosives were developed, mostly based on nitrocellulose (also known as *guncotton*) and nitroglycerine. Various methods of combining the basic elements of modern explosives have resulted in a wide array of explosives for use in guns and for other types of weapons and other non-weapon uses as well.

In terms of modern usage, the explosives used in modern guns are called low explosives, in that their autocombustion rates are suitable for propellant applications, as opposed to high explosives, which create far more powerful blasts and are used for the sheer power of their explosions rather than to propel something else. In any case, they are far more powerful, more reliable, and less likely to combust accidentally than black powder.

Every gun has, in addition to its explosive powder, a method of detonating that powder and starting the explosion that results in the bullet firing. In early guns, this was done by touching a "match," or burning wick, to a touch hole or flash pan that led into the chamber with the powder. This method was done by hand at first, then later by mechanisms called *matchlocks*. Then came a series of different mechanisms—all called *locks*—that modified the original matchlock principle. (See "The Early Evolution of Guns" section a bit later in this chapter.)

- Cartridge details
  - There are five main types of cartridge bases:
    - **Rimmed.** The base has a rim or extractor flange with a diameter greater than that of the case.
    - **Semi-Rimmed.** The rim is only slightly larger than the case.
    - **Rimless.** The rim is the same diameter as the case. This is the most common military cartridge type.
    - **Rebated.** The rim's diameter is smaller than that of the case. This is an uncommon design that includes a defined extractor groove between the rim and the case.
    - **Belted.** A special projection or flange that rings the cartridge above the rim, with an extractor groove between the two.
  - Although there have been other schemes, such as the Dreyse cartridge (see the upcoming "The Modern Shell" section), modern shells use one of two types of ignition—centerfire or rimfire. The former has the primer in a separate cup in the center of the shell, which is struck by a center firing pin. The latter works the same way, except that the primer is distributed along the outer rim of the shell's back, which is where the firing pin strikes it. Most modern cased cartridges are centerfire.
  - Cartridges may be straight-walled or bottlenecked. Straight-walled cartridges have sides that are nearly parallel, and the base is the same or only slightly wider than the bullet at the head. Bottlenecked cartridges, used for more high-power guns, have a wide base that narrows toward the bullet, similar to a bottleneck, allowing a cartridge with a higher powder capacity behind a smaller bullet, resulting in dramatic increases in velocity.

Cartridge Charts

When you're creating a realistic game, details sometimes matter. Most gamers won't care what kind of cartridge you pick up for your weapon. "Ammo" is all that counts, generally speaking. But just so you can say you were accurate, here's some reference material about cartridges to work with.

Pistol and Submachine Gun	Case	Bullet Diameter (in.)	Case Length (in.)	Shoulder Diameter (in.)	Bullet Weight (grs.)	Muzzle Velocity (fps)	Muzzle Energy (fpe)
5.7×28mm FN	C	.220	1.13	.309	31	2345	378
.22 Long Rifle	B	.223	.595	-	38	1280	138
.25 Automatic	D	.251	.62	-	50	810	73
5.45×18mm Soviet	C	.210	.700	NA	40	1035	95
.32 Automatic	H	.308	.68	-	71	905	129
7.62×25mm Russian Tokarev	C	.307	.97	.370	87	1390	365
.380 Automatic (9mm Short)	D	.356	.68	-	90	1000	200
9mm Ultra	D	.355	.72	-	123	1070	350
9mm Parabellum (9mm Luger)	D	.355	.754	-	124	1150	364
.38 Special	B	.357	1.16	-	158	900	284
.38 Super	H	.358	.90	-	125	1150	367
.357 SIG	C	.357	.865	.424	125	1350	505
.357 Magnum	B	.357	1.29	-	125	1450	583
.40 S&W	D	.400	.850	-	155	1205	500
10mm Automatic	D	.400	.992	-	180	1150	528
.400 Corbon	C	.400	NA	NA	135	1450	600
.44 Magnum	B	.429	1.29	-	240	1350	971
.44 Auto Mag	D	.429	1.298	-	240	1400	1045
.440 Corbon Magnum	J	.440	NA	-	240	1800	1727
.45 ACP	D	.452	.898	-	230	855	373
.45 Colt	B	.454	1.29	-	185	1100	497
.45 Winchester Magnum	D	.451	1.198	-	230	1550	1227
.454 Casull	B	.452	1.39	-	300	1500	1500
.475 Linebaugh	B	.475	1.5	-	370	1495	1840
.500 Linebaugh	B	.510	1.405	-	500	1200	1599
.50 Action Express	J	.500	1.285	-	300	1579	1568

Rifle and Carbine	Case	Bullet Diameter (in.)	Case Length (in.)	Shoulder Diameter (in.)	Bullet Weight (grs.)	Muzzle Velocity (fps)	Muzzle Energy (fps)
22 Long Rifle	B	.223	.595	-	38	1280	138
.22 Hornet	A	.223	1.40	.274	45	2690	723
5.45×39mm Soviet	C	.221	1.56	.387	54	2950	1045
.223 Remington (5.56 NATO)	C	.224	1.76	.349	55	3250	1290
5.7×28mm (SS190)	C	.227	1.13	.309	23	2790	400
.243 Winchester	C	.243	2.05	.454	100	2960	1945
.270 Weatherby Magnum	E	.277	2.55	.490	150	3245	3501
30-30 Winchester	A	.308	2.03	.402	150	2390	1902
7.62×39mm Soviet	C	.311	1.52	.344	122	2329	1470
.303 British	A	.311	2.21	.401	180	2460	2420
.308 Winchester (7.62 NATO)	C	.308	2.01	.454	150	2750	2520
.30-06 Springfield	C	.308	2.49	.441	172	2640	2660
7mm Remington Magnum	E	.284	2.50	.490	160	2950	3090
.300 Winchester Magnum	E	.308	2.60	.489	200	2825	3544
.338 Winchester Magnum	E	.338	2.49	.480	250	2660	3921
.338 Lapua Magnum	C	.338	2.72	.540	250	2950	4830
.340 Weatherby Magnum	E	.338	2.49	.495	250	2980	4931
.375 Holland & Holland	E	.375	2.85	.440	300	2530	4265
.416 Remington Magnum	E	.416	2.85	.487	350	2520	4935
.458 Winchester Magnum	F	.458	2.50	-	500	2040	4620
.50 Browning (BMG)	C	.510	3.90	.708	720	2810	12630
.585 Nyati	I	.585	2.79	.650	750	2235	8320
700 Nitro Express	B	.700	3.50	-	1000	2000	8900

Case types:

- [A] Rimmed, Bottlenecked
- [B] Rimmed, Straight
- [C] Rimless, Bottlenecked
- [D] Rimless, Straight
- [E] Belted, Bottlenecked
- [F] Belted, Straight
- [G] Semi-rimmed, Bottlenecked
- [H] Semi-rimmed, Straight
- [I] Rebated, Bottlenecked
- [J] Rebated, Straight
- [K] Rebated belted, Bottlenecked
- [L] Rebated belted, Straight

How a Bullet Travels

Bullets do not travel in perfectly flat trajectories. They are subject to gravity and air resistance. In the case of gravity, a bullet starts to fall as soon as it is fired. It will hit the ground in exactly the same amount of time as if you simply held it in your hand and dropped it. The velocity of the bullet determines how far it will travel before hitting the ground. When a gun is fired, the shooter will determine a target by a straight line of sight. To hit the same target, a bullet of lower velocity will have to travel in a greater arc. At long distances, the sight on the gun must be calibrated to allow for the slow rise and faster fall of the bullet. There is a term called the *danger space*, which is defined as the distance the bullet travels while it is within the height of a man from the ground. With slower-velocity guns, sometimes the shot could travel over the heads of people in order to arc to a specific point. Shots from higher-velocity guns travel on a more flat trajectory, thereby increasing the danger space.

When the bullet first leaves the muzzle of the gun, it is traveling at a very high rate, and its power is maximal. Over time, its speed and power diminish. However, modern guns have very long ranges and can remain deadly, if not accurate, over these distances. The ranges of bullets vary. In a vacuum, bullets would travel more than 20 times the distance they can travel in air, but even in air they can travel several miles. A common .22 caliber bullet travels nearly a mile. The .30-06 bullet, common in hunting rifles, has a range of about two miles, and other high-powered bullets can travel as much as 4 miles or more!

The Sniper's Lexicon

For a sniper firing at long range, there is a lot to take into account. Here are some of the elements a good sniper must consider:

- Accuracy diminishes approximately one inch for every 100 yards.
- Wind affects trajectory.
- The bullet falls in accordance with gravity, at the same rate as any object. In other words, a bullet dropped from the hand will hit the ground at the same time as a bullet fired from a gun, all things being equal.
- Cold air is denser than warm air and therefore creates more drag on the bullet. In hot air, the bullet will travel farther.
- Humidity can also affect a bullet. Humidity is often associated with hot air.

- Bullets leave a rifle barrel at speeds greater than the speed of sound, causing a small sonic boom. At ranges of 600 yards or less, the target will hear the sound of the bullet. At more than 600 yards, however, targets will hear nothing, and a sniper could shoot at them all day and they wouldn't necessarily know it—until they get hit, anyway.

THE EARLY EVOLUTION OF GUNS

Whenever we do historical games, we strive to be accurate and to depict, to varying degrees, what the situation was really like. This section takes a look at the evolution of guns, starting with the earliest explosive projectile weapons and detailing the various stages that led to the modern gun.

Before the Matchlock

The earliest guns, which date back as far as the 13th century, were simple tubes with powder and some projectile stuffed inside. The person using the gun would touch something hot—a burning wick or a red-hot piece of iron—to what was called the *touchhole*, which ignited the powder inside the barrel. The earliest guns were probably made of bronze or brass, though iron and steel quickly became the standard for gun barrels. They were essentially hand cannons and were very difficult to manage. Generally, they rested on something, though they could have been braced against the chest, with one hand free to ignite the powder. Their range was probably not more than 30 to 40 yards.

The touchhole was soon made obsolete by the invention of the *flash pan*, a sort of cup to hold a small amount of gunpowder that would more reliably ignite the powder in the barrel. The flash pan was a part of the ignition system of guns for centuries after its invention.

The Matchlock

The matchlock, the first firing mechanism for powder guns, was formed by an S-shaped device that rotated on the side of the gun. This device, called the *serpentine*, would hold a "match"—or, technically, a lighted wick—and, when the trigger was pressed, it swung down into the flash pan, (hopefully) igniting the priming and (hopefully) firing the gun. It was invented in the 16th century and remained in use in some parts of the world even into the 20th century. The first improvement was the addition of a cover that protected the powder in the flash pan but retracted automatically when the gun was fired, although on many matchlock guns, the flash pan was part of the barrel, and the cover had to be retracted by hand. The main weaknesses of this type of gun were that it took time to light the wick, so it was useless in case of a surprise attack, and it was difficult to keep the wick burning in wet weather. However, matchlocks were cheap and easy to produce, hence their long popularity.

Wheel Lock

The wheel lock mechanism was developed around the same time as the matchlock, but it was expensive and complex, so it never replaced the matchlock. It was, however, used by the rich and the elite. The principle of it is known to anyone who has used a cigarette lighter that uses a round metal wheel that spins across a flint. The wheel lock used a spring-set wheel and a piece of flint or pyrites. When the gun was fired, the flash pan cover retracted, and the hammer fell, pushing the flint against the metal wheel, which spun and showered sparks on the priming gunpowder. And it went boom!

One of the problems of the time involved gun barrels and cannons bursting when fired. Because the early muzzle loaders were simply packed with gunpowder, it was possible to pack them too much. The barrels themselves were none too strong, and even a quarter-full barrel might burst. A new technique developed in Germany in the mid-16th century finally produced strong, reliable steel barrels. The technique was called *damascene*, and it involved winding finger-width strips of steel together, welding and forging, then boring out the barrel. The result was a much stronger gun barrel that could be packed with powder without danger to the one firing the gun.

Snaphance (or Snaphaunce)

This precursor to the flintlock simplified the mechanism of the wheel lock to something affordable. It was far less complex, involving a hammer that held a piece of flint and a steel plate across which the falling hammer would scrape the flint. The resulting sparks would fall into the flash pan and ignite the priming powder.

Flintlock

The main difference between the snaphance and the flintlock was that the steel striking surface and the flash pan cover were made as one piece, making the gun more reliable and cheaper to manufacture. It operated the same way as the snaphance, however. The hammer would fall and strike the steel, which would fall backward, exposing the flash pan. The sparks would ignite the priming, and so it goes. The flintlock was used extensively from the early 1600s to the 19th century. (One variation of the flintlock is called the *miquelet*, and it differed only in the addition of an external spring on the hammer.) A good gunman with a flintlock could fire several shots a minute.

The Percussion Lock

The next great innovation in ignition systems was the percussion lock, which was introduced in the early 19th century—about 300 years after the flintlock. The percussion lock was the direct precursor to the modern shell. It worked by using a hammer that fell onto a copper cap, which was loaded with fulminate of mercury, a substance that explodes when struck. The explosion of the cap traveled down a tube into the packed gunpowder in the barrel, detonating the charge that fired the bullet. Versions of early percussion locks were used in both muzzle- and breech-loaders. Although there previously had been many attempts to make a practical multi-shot gun, it was the invention of the percussion lock that made early revolvers practical. The percussion lock was used with devastating effect during the American Civil War. (A variant on the percussion lock was the *pill lock*, which used a small pill-shaped ball of percussive material instead of the copper cap.)

Early Gun Accessories

The early muzzle loaders required a lot of accessory items—some to carry the powder, for instance, some to ram the load down the barrel, and various elements of the load. Here's a list of some of the common items that early musketeers had to carry with them.

- **Powderhorns.** Powderhorns were containers for gunpowder that were made from the horns of animals. This practice was found all over the world.
- **Powder Testers.** As early as 1578, people were creating methods for testing the strength of a gunpowder mixture. Most were highly inaccurate. However, in 1647, a method called the *mortar eprouvette* was developed, and some years later, the French government passed an ordinance that rejected any powder that did not pass the test of the eprouvette—to wit, that three ounces of powder would fire a 60-pound ball at least 320 feet from the testing mortar.
- **Primer or Priming Flask.** A container to hold the fine powder used to ignite the charge in a wheel lock or flintlock gun. This finer powder was added to the flash pan, which was called *priming the gun*.
- **Ramrod.** Used to pack the charge in muzzle-loading rifles and pistols. Ramrods were generally plain wood or metal rods with a slightly larger end. Ramrods were often carried in the sheath of the gun they were used with, although sometimes they were carried separately.

- **Spanner.** A wrench used to wind a wheel-lock gun—often highly ornamental. Some doubled as primers to carry powder.
- **Detonators (or Pill Locks).** Intermediate between the flint lock and the percussion guns, the detonator used percussion to fire, but instead of having the fulminate in a copper cap, it was in the form of a small pill, tube, or paper backing.
- **What a Muzzle Loader Required.** All the guns mentioned so far were muzzle loaders (although there were breech-loading percussion lock guns). Among the items a muzzle loader might need were:
  - The ramrod (which fit into a slot in the gun stock).
  - A powder flask from which to pour the powder into the barrel.
  - A bullet mold.
  - Lead balls.
  - Patches and rags. (Patches were often stored in a compartment in the butt of the gun.)
  - A brush for cleaning the pan.
  - An oil bottle.
  - A turn screw.
  - A spring clamp.
  - A punch for making patches.
  - A cleaning rod.

Early Multi-Shot Guns

Today, we think nothing of guns that shoot multiple times without reloading, but in the days of matchlocks, flintlocks, and so on, multi-shot guns were far less common. However, they did exist, and many attempts were made to create practical guns that could fire more than once without reloading. One way that was common was to create a gun with two barrels and two ignition systems (locks). The barrels would be either side by side or over and under. Another method was called the *tap action*, which involved a rotating flash pan that would ignite first one barrel, then, after re-cocking the hammer, the other. If it was fired first in the wrong position, both barrels would fire. Still other schemes tried to superimpose several loads in one barrel, and the lock mechanism would slide backward from one touchhole to the next, firing each load separately. The more familiar revolver-type multi-shot gun did not achieve popularity until the advent of the cartridge bullet. But some were made, and there are examples of matchlock, snaphance, flintlock, and percussion lock revolvers. Some used the "pepperbox" style, with many separate barrels that all rotated. Others were more like modern revolvers—a rotating chamber that held the charge and fired through a single barrel. One significant danger with early revolvers was the possibility of more than one chamber firing at once, causing potential injury to the shooter.

Breech Loaders

Breech-loading guns have existed for some time, and there have been some interesting examples. King Henry VIII of England had a breech-loading rifle. An odd type of pistol, called the *turn-off* pistol, was a flintlock that had a screw-off barrel. The charge and ball were inserted in the body of the gun, then the barrel was screwed back on. A famous version of this style was called the *Queen Anne cannon barreled pistol.* But it was ultimately the self-contained cartridge that really allowed the breech loader to take over. Once the cartridge bullet became the standard, breech loaders, too, replaced muzzle loaders almost entirely, except in some far-flung parts of the world. Breech loaders fired faster, achieved greater velocity and greater accuracy, and were more reliable than muzzle loaders. All modern guns are breech loaders and use cartridge shells for bullets.

The Modernization of Guns

In the previous section, we ended with breech loaders—guns that didn't have to be loaded by stuffing the load down the barrel. This was a significant innovation in the technology of firearms and was part of the evolution of guns to the modern era. The other significant innovation was the cartridge, or shell—a bullet that had the primer, the powder, and the projectile all in one. This was the beginning of the modern era.

The Modern Shell

Two factors led to the modern cartridge and revolutionized guns all together: the percussion lock and the technology to make inexpensive and effective breech loaders. The modern cartridge bullet contains the detonating chemical inside the shell with the propellant explosive. A shock from the firing pin or other similar mechanism is sufficient to detonate the percussion mixture and start the explosion in the shell, which results in the firing of the bullet at high velocity. The earliest detonators used fulminate of mercury, which is highly explosive when hit. This is the material used, in very small quantities, in the caps used in toy cap guns. More modern substances include DDNP (diazodinitrophenol), lead picrate, lead azide, and cyclonite.

There were several milestones in the development of the modern cartridge.

- One was the *Pauly pistol*, created by a Swiss man named Pauly. He created a gun with a swivel barrel, much like a break-open shotgun of today. He then devised a self-contained cartridge and a hammer with a striker to fire it. This was the first time that the bullet, priming, and powder were all combined into one unit.
- In 1835, the Lefaucheux case was developed. It was a paper tube with a brass base, much like shotgun shells were made later, and it used what came to be known as *pinfire* ignition. It was the first self-contained bullet to achieve wide use, though mostly with sportsmen.
- The Boxer cartridge was developed in the mid-1800s and was the first metal-cased cartridge that saw widespread use. Its developer, Colonel Boxer, also designed a center-fire primer of a type still used with bullets today.
- A weapon used in the Prussian army around 1848 combined a bolt action with a self-contained cartridge of unusual design, known as the *Dreyse cartridge.* It was entirely encased in paper, and the primer was up near the bullet. The firing needle would completely pierce the cartridge to reach the primer and ignite the powder. This was combined with an effective single-shot bolt-action rifle.

Modern Repeaters

In the modern, post–Industrial Revolution era, repeating guns have become pretty standard, although single-shot guns are still used in some circumstances. There are several types of repeating guns, however, and we'll look very briefly at the different types of repeating pistols and longarms, starting with pistols.

Repeating Pistols

Repeating pistols come in several forms:

- A few feature multiple barrels. In these, either the barrels themselves rotate or a striking pin rotates internally to fire each in turn.
- More common is the revolver, which features a rotating cylinder that holds the cartridges. Revolvers are reliable and economical, and they have changed little since the late 19th century. Although several different schemes for loading and removing spent cartridges have been used, revolvers otherwise are

quite similar, and some of the early ones from the 1870s are still in production today, such as the Colt Peacemaker, the "gun that won the West."

Arguably, the earliest semi-automatic pistols were like the Webley-Fosbery revolver of the 1890s, which used recoil from firing to push back the barrel and cylinder, re-cocking the hammer and rotating the cylinder simultaneously. Later semi-automatic pistols used similar technology, but with a spring-loaded magazine, usually inserted into the gun's handle, to feed cartridges into the breech. Once the first cartridge has been manually fed, by cocking the breechblock, every subsequent shot automatically ejects the spent cartridge and loads a new one until the magazine is emptied. Most semi-automatic pistols are based on designs from before World War I. There are two basic types of semi-automatic mechanisms—the blowback system and the locked breech system.

- The blowback mechanism uses a fixed barrel and breechblock, which is held in position only by the force of a recoil spring. When the gun is fired, the pressure first fires the bullet, which offers the least resistance to the sudden buildup of gases. The breechblock and barrel resist the pressure until the bullet has left the barrel, at which point they are thrown back. The spent cartridge is ejected, and a new one is loaded as the breechblock travels backward, then forward again, pushed by the recoil spring back into position. The gun is ready to fire again. Blowback mechanisms work with lower-powered ammunition. With higher-powered bullets, the pressure would open the breechblock too quickly, and the cartridge would rupture and fail to eject.
- With breechblock pistols, the barrel is locked to the breechblock by some mechanism. Upon firing, the barrel and breechblock are thrown backward until the locking mechanism is released, at which point the breechblock continues backward, ejecting the shell and reloading as it slides forward again and relocks. Two famous mechanisms are the German Luger and the Colt 1911.
    - The Luger uses a joint-like mechanism located behind the breechblock. When the gun is fired, this joint is locked in place, but when it recoils, the barrel and breechblock slide back a short distance in machined grooves, which push them downward, opening the locking joint and freeing the breechblock to continue its cycle while the barrel stops.
    - In the Colt 1911, which was originally designed in 1911, the barrel is locked by interlocking ribs to the slide mechanism and is attached to the lower part of the pistol by a short, flexible link. Upon firing, the barrel and slide recoil. The barrel slides down on the flexible link, freeing it from the interlocking ribs. The slide continues rearward, ejecting the cartridge and reloading the gun as it swings back forward and re-engages the barrel. This design was modified in 1923 as the Colt 1911 A1, which is still in production and use around the world.

Repeating Longarms

The idea of repeating muskets and rifles was not new, but they were difficult to implement with muzzle-loading, black-powder guns. The development of the self-contained cartridge made them much more feasible. Equally important was the development of new "smokeless" powders, which would not foul the barrel as much. In the early guns, the amount of residue left behind after firing made repeating longarm weapons impractical, if not outright dangerous to the firer—which, of course, did not stop people from making them. But the repeating rifle didn't come into its own until the mid to late 1800s, when the necessary technology was all in place.

Repeating rifles use several types of mechanisms to fire multiple shots. All use some kind of magazine. There are three popular styles—loading from the butt, loading from a tube under the barrel, and loading from a magazine clip attached below the breech. In each case, a spring pushes the bullets up into the breech each time the gun is cocked. There are several methods of cocking a repeating rifle:

- Bolt action, still used today in many guns. The bolt action is a simple mechanism in which the breech is locked by the bolt and is manually opened by rotating, then sliding the bolt open. In a single-shot gun, the cartridge is manually inserted into the breech each time the gun is fired. In a repeating rifle, the bullets are readied automatically, often from a clip magazine or sometimes from a tube magazine running under the barrel and loaded from the side. The shooter only needs to open the bolt and close it again to ready another shot. The spent cartridge will eject upon opening, and the new cartridge will take its place as the bolt is closed and locked again. Some bolt-action guns automatically cock the firing pin when closed. Others require a separate step of cocking the pin.
- To make loading quicker, special clips were designed that could hold several cartridges at a time. These could be loaded quickly by inserting the clip into the breech from the top and shoving the cartridges down into the magazine. The clip itself was then discarded.
- Lever action was popularized by the famous Winchester Model 1873 and is still in use today. Opening the lever also opens the breech, ejects the spent shell, and loads a new one, simultaneously cocking the firing mechanism.
- Pump or slide action is also still in use today, most commonly in pump-action shotguns. Pulling the slide and pushing it closed will open the breech, eject the spent shell, load a new one, and arm the firing mechanism, all in a simple motion.
- Self-loading and assault rifles use a modified blowback system to re-cock the firing mechanism and reload the weapon automatically. Self-loading rifles are distinguished from assault weapons in that they will fire only one shot at a time. Some can be modified to fire continuously, making them effectively assault rifles or submachine guns.
- The blowback mechanism used in self-loading rifles and assault weapons differs slightly from that used in semi-automatic pistols and true submachine guns. It uses a piston and a system to bleed gas out of the barrel upon firing, which drives the piston backward, opening the breech and ejecting the spent shell. A recoil spring then pushes the mechanism back, reloading the weapon.

Submachine Guns

Submachine guns are fully automatic weapons small enough to be carried and fired by hand. They use low, pistol-caliber ammunition, minimizing recoil so that they can be fired from the shoulder or from the hip. For further portability, many submachine guns have retractable stocks so that they can be used in different situations.

Submachine guns use a blowback system similar to that used in semi-automatic pistols. When they are fired, the breech stays closed due to its own weight and the power of the recoil spring. By the time the breech does swing open, the pressure in the bore has reduced. The spent cartridge is ejected, and a new one is fed in as the recoil spring pushes the breech closed again. Ammunition is fed into the submachine gun using box or drum magazines. Theoretical rates of fire for early machine guns (from WWI and WWII) ranged from about 400 rounds per minute (rpm) to as high as 900 rpm; however, this did not account for changing magazines and re-cocking the mechanism. More modern submachine guns can fire up to a theoretical 1,200 rpm. Possibly the most infamous submachine gun was the Thompson Model 1928, used in WWII, but, more importantly, the gun used by gangsters during Prohibition and commonly depicted in the movies.

Grenade Guns and Rifle Grenades

Surprisingly, there have been guns to fire grenades as far back as the 16th century. These guns may have used any of the older mechanisms—matchlocks, wheel locks, flintlocks, and so on. There are two methods used to fire grenades from small arms—large-bored grenade guns made specifically to fire grenades and regular guns adapted to fire grenades. This section only talks about handheld guns used to fire grenades. Fixed grenade launchers will be covered under the “Modern Artillery” section.

Firing grenades from regular guns is done in three main ways:

- The cup discharger is an adapter fitted to the end of rifle. A regular grenade fits into the cup, and a blank charge is fired in the gun, which launches the grenade. There are variations of this method that allow a bulleted cartridge to be used, in which case the bullet may bypass the grenade or even fire through a center tube. Flare pistols operate similarly, although technically they are not grenade launchers.
- The rod grenade is one attached to a steel rod. The rod fits into the muzzle of the gun, which fires a blank charge to launch the grenade.
- The spigot grenade fits over the gun barrel and has stabilizing fins attached to it. Both blank cartridges and bulleted cartridges may be used with the spigot grenade. Because the fins help stabilize the flight of the grenade and keep it flying point first, this is a good way to fire anti-tank grenades.

Grenade firing techniques can be adapted to fire different types of projectiles, including anti-personnel grenades, anti-tank grenades, smoke grenades, and anti-riot gas grenades.

Air Guns

Most little boys had a BB or pellet gun at some point in their lives. These toy guns were examples of air-powered guns. However, air guns have been made at least since the 18th century, though they have rarely been used as serious weapons in war. Early air guns were rifle-shaped and stored compressed air in the stock or in an attached sphere. The reservoir was filled and compressed generally by means of a simple hand pump. This was long before the development of today's compact CO_2 cartridges. One of the few air guns to see combat was the Girandoni air rifle, which looked a bit like a flintlock from the outside, but was a repeating rifle from the late 18th century. It had a range of 130 yards, had a magazine of 20 13mm rounds, and was used by Austrian sharpshooters. Another common air gun was a 19th-century innovation—an air gun that was disguised as a walking cane, at one time a common weapon of self-defense.

Expressions from Guns

Many common expressions in the English language were derived from the use of guns. A few examples include:

- Lock, stock, and barrel.
- Flash in the pan.
- Keep your powder dry.
- In the line of fire.
- Quick on the draw.

Some of the Better-Known Gun Brands

Wondering what kinds of guns to use in your games? Here are a few of the best-known brands:

- Colt
- Smith & Wesson
- Browning
- Enfield
- Walther
- Ruger
- Remington
- Mauser
- Arisaka
- De Lisle
- Winchester
- Springfield
- Adams
- Heckler & Koch

Longarm and Rifle Examples

Here are some examples of longarms:

- **Arasaka Type 38 (Rifle and Carbine).** Standard Japanese rifle and carbine of WWII—named for the 38th year of the Meiji calendar, which was when this gun was introduced (1905).
- **Arquebus.** Matchlock (and later wheel lock) rifles dating back as far as the 14th century.
- **Blunderbuss.** A short gun or pistol with a bell muzzle. Typically used as personal protection against thieves and by guards, but not generally in war. They often had bayonets attached, sometimes on springs that would fold back unless needed.
- **Brown Bess.** The main British military musket used between around 1720 and 1840. Various versions of this musket were made.
- **Caliver.** A matchlock gun, larger than a musket and smaller than a carbine. A longer-barreled version was called a *Currier.*
- **Camel Gun.** A gun on a swivel carried by a camel.
- **Carbine.** A gun with a smaller bore than the musket, which ultimately became a horseman's gun because it was smaller and lighter. The earliest carbines were flintlocks.
- **Colt Lightning.** An 1885 slide-action repeating rifle.
- **Colt Model 1855.** A revolving musket using percussion-type ammunition; came in various lengths.
- **De Lisle Carbine.** A silenced bolt-action repeater designed for clandestine operations during WWII. It was based on the SMLE, but it used the same cartridge as the Thompson submachine gun.
- **Esclopette.** A wheel-lock pistol with a folding stock that could be carried in a holster like a pistol.
- **Henry Rifle.** An innovative 1860 lever-action repeating rifle created by B. Tyler Henry, who designed it as an improvement over Winchester's Volcanic repeating rifle—the immediate predecessor to the famed Winchester Model 1873. Used a .44-70 centerfire cartridge of Henry's design.
- **Jacob Rifle.** A double-barreled rifle used by the British Indian Army in the mid-1800s. It used a percussion lock and could fire pointed bullets or very small explosive shells. It was sighted up to 2,000 yards.
- **Jennings Rifle.** An 1849 improvement on the Volition Repeating Rifle (later in this list) that used external pill-lock percussion caps; another step toward the Winchester Model 1873 lever-action rifle.
- **Jezail.** A very long-barreled gun from Afghanistan with barrels as much as seven feet long with a one-inch bore. Very long range.
- **Kentucky Long Rifle.** Originally created by German craftsmen in Pennsylvania around 1725, it was the most accurate long-range rifle of its time. It is sometimes called the *Pennsylvania Long Rifle*, but its use in the frontier and its mention in an 1812 song, "The Hunters of Kentucky," gave it the more commonly used moniker, Kentucky Long Rifle. It was a .50-caliber weapon used during the American Revolution and was further distinguished by a downward curving stock and its 42- to 46-inch barrel. It went the way of all muzzle loaders once breech loaders and self-contained cartridges were developed.
- **Krag-Jorgensen.** A Norwegian bolt-action repeating rifle used in other countries (and the USA), created in 1888.
- **Lebel M1e 1886/93.** This French trendsetting bolt-action repeater was the first small-bore military weapon to use smokeless powder, and it set the standard for the world's armies.
- **Lee-Metford.** British Army repeating bolt-action rifle from 1888.
- **Mauser Gewehr 98.** Highly successful and much copied WWI era bolt-action repeater.
- **Mauser Kar 98k.** The standard German infantry rifle of WWII.
- **Mauser Model 71/84.** A German bolt-action repeating rifle from 1884.
- **Mosin-Nagant.** Soviet bolt-action repeater of WWII.
- **Mousqueton.** A flintlock with a smooth bore and a 4-foot barrel.

- **Musquet Arrow (Spright).** A wooden arrow that was actually fired from the musquet and was said to be able to penetrate objects that resisted bullets.
- **Musquet Fusil.** A gun used in the time when flintlocks were new. It contained both the flintlock mechanism and a matchlock.
- **Musquet Rest.** Originally just a forked stick used to rest the barrel of the musquet when firing, but ultimately modified by lengthening one fork and sharpening it to use as a defense against cavalry. Some, called *swine's feathers* (or *Swedish feathers*), had spring-loaded spikes concealed inside and were planted into the ground as protection.
- **Musquets or Muskets.** Evolved from cannons and were originally matchlock guns too heavy to be fired without a rest. It was typical to name cannons after birds, so the musket got its name from the sparrow hawk, the smallest of the hawks. Some muskets were as much as 4 feet long and had a 1-inch bore. As time passed, the term *musket* came to refer to any rifle carried by regular infantrymen.
- **No4 Mk1.** British bolt-action repeater of WWII, based on the SMLE.
- **No5 Mk1 (Jungle Carbine).** The No4 Mk1 in a light version for jungle fighting.
- **Percussion Cap.** Developed in the early 1800s, it uses a fulminating mixture (fulminate of mercury, plus other ingredients) to cause detonation of a shell upon impact.
- **Pun Lang Chan.** A Burmese swivel gun mounted on an elephant.
- **Punt Gun.** A large-bored English gun meant to be swivel-mounted on a boat and used to hunt water birds.
- **Remington Rolling-Block.** An 11mm single-shot gun used all over the world in the late 19th century.
- **Savage Model 77E.** A pump-action military shotgun used by Marines in Vietnam.
- **Sharps 1855 carbine.** A single-shot breech loader that used external percussion caps and linen cartridges.
- **Sher Bacha.** A heavy Persian "wall gun" with a pentagonal stock and a large back site.
- **Shutrnals.** Swivel guns mounted on camels in 18th-century India.
- **SMLE (Short Magazine Lee Enfield or Rifle No. 1).** Standard British bolt-action repeater from 1902 into the beginning of WWII.
- **Springfield Model 1873.** Single-shot breech-loading carbine used in 1876 by the U.S. Cavalry during the Battle of Little Bighorn; used .45-caliber metal cartridges.
- **Springfield Rifle (or U.S. Model 1903).** The principal rifle (bolt-action repeater) of the U.S. Army from the early 20th century until the beginning of WWII.
- **Toradar.** An Indian matchlock gun, some with a curved stock and others with slender straight stocks in a pentagonal section.
- **Tschinke.** A wheel-lock rifle with the butt set at a diagonal angle.
- **Volition Repeating Rifle.** Walter Hunt's 1849 precursor to the famous Winchester Model 1873, one of the first modern repeating rifles that used fixed (self-contained) ammunition. In the case of the Volition Repeating Rifle, the ammunition was Hunt's own patented "rocket ball" bullet, which was a hollow bullet packed with gunpowder, enclosed by a cap at the back.
- **Wall Guns.** Some guns were mounted in the walls of fortresses. These kinds of guns were used all over the world and were heavier and larger than the shoulder-mounted guns that were ordinarily carried.
- **Winchester Model 1873.** A lever-action repeating rifle, the successor to the Henry rifle, and the most famous lever-action repeater, emblematic of the Old West, along with the Colt Peacemaker. Like the Henry rifle, it used a .44-40 centerfire cartridge.
- **Zamburaq.** "Wasp," a camel-mounted swivel gun of old Persia.
- **Zarbuzan.** A light swivel gun or small cannon.

Self-Loading Rifles

- **Dragunov (SVD).** Soviet self-loading sniper rifle.
- **Frank Wesson Dagger-Pistol.** Two "over and under" barrels, rotated by hand, with a dagger blade extending out the front. Patented in 1868, it used .41-caliber rimfire ammunition.
- **Mondragon Modelo 1908.** An early self-loading rifle produced in Switzerland but used in Mexico.
- **Ljungmann Rifle.** A Swedish self-loading rifle often credited with innovating the gas-operation mechanism used in all subsequent self-loading rifles. Some sources say that the gas-operation mechanism was actually invented in 1900 by Monsieur Rossignol.
- **M1 Rifle and Carbine.** The M1 rifle (also known as the *Garand*, sometimes spelled *Garland*) was the first self-loading rifle to become standard issue in any army and was used throughout WWII and the Korean War.
- **M14 Rifle.** The predecessor to the M16, this was a self-loading rifle based on the M1 Garand used during WWII.
- **MAS 49.** A French self-loading rifle that came into use in 1949. MAS stands for NATO's *Military Agency for Standardization.*
- **Gewehr 43.** German WWII self-loading rifle.
- **Hakim.** An Egyptian copy of the self-loading Ljungmann rifle.
- **RSC Modele 1917.** French self-loading rifle used in WWI.
- **Siminov SKS.** A Soviet-designed self-loading carbine, designed at the same time and using the same ammunition as the Kalashnikov AK-47 assault rifle. The SKS was copied for use in the Chinese military and called the Type 56.

The Interesting and Convoluted History of the Winchesters

Historians date the history of Oliver Winchester's famous gun manufacturing company to an earlier inventor in the mid-1800s named Walter Hunt, who created a repeating rifle called the *Volition Repeating Rifle*, which used ammunition of his own invention. This was not a success, but the work was continued by Lewis Jennings, who built a magazine-fed lever-action rifle and marketed it for a few years. Jennings' work was picked up by Horace Smith and Daniel Wesson (Smith and Wesson), who created the Volcanic repeating lever-action pistol, followed by a similar Volcanic rifle. Their company name, Smith and Wesson, was changed to Volcanic Repeating Arms Company. One of the principal investors was Oliver F. Winchester. Both Smith and Wesson left the company, which was subsequently moved to New Haven, Connecticut, and renamed the New Haven Arms Co. The superintendent of this company, who was largely responsible for developing the lever action used in the Volcanic Repeating Rifle, was B. Tyler Henry, who also redesigned the rifle to use a .44-caliber rimfire cartridge of his own design. This became the Henry lever-action repeating rifle, a revolutionary step in the design of repeating rifles. Henry's ammunition continued to be produced from 1860 until 1934. In 1866, CEO Oliver Winchester changed the name of the company to Winchester Repeating Arms Co. In 1873, Winchester produced the ultimate lever-action rifle of the American West—the Winchester Model 1873, and the rest is history, so to speak. Although there is one last odd bit to add. Winchester's son, William, married Sarah Pardee, but he died in 1881 of tuberculosis. Sarah, who had lost her only child at nine days old, left New Haven and moved to the Santa Clara Valley in California, south of San Francisco, on the advice of a spiritualist who claimed to be in touch with William. The spiritualist told Mrs. Winchester that her family was cursed because of all the deaths caused by their guns. She was told that she was doomed unless she moved toward the setting sun and built a house. As long as she continued to build the house, she would not succumb to the curse. She did as she was told and began one of the most bizarre building projects ever, using her inheritance to continue work 24 hours a day for 38 years, until she finally died. The house is known today as the Winchester Mystery House.

Pistols

Pistols are guns made to be fired in one hand. They probably first appeared in the early 16th century, the first ones being matchlocks and wheel locks. Pistols have been fashioned in a variety of forms, styles, and sizes. The Japanese made tiny pistols as *netsuke* (small Japanese carvings that were used both as works of art and as fasteners), fully detailed, though no doubt useless as firearms. Some pistols were made with multiple barrels—as many as 24—but it's doubtful that they were very practical. Perhaps the most famous pistol was the Colt 45 (or Peacemaker)—"the gun that won the West." Pistols were also combined with just about anything else you could think of, including axes, spears, whips, maces, knives, swords, canes, and even belt buckles and stirrups. At one time or another, almost any weapon (and many non-weapons) have been combined with pistols. Here are a few examples, along with other examples of pistols from history:

- **Adams Revolver.** An 1872 five-shot revolver. Used .45-caliber cartridges.
- **Borchardt Pistol.** An 1893 precursor to the Luger—an early semi-automatic pistol.
- **"Broomhandle" Mauser.** An early semi-automatic pistol that had a detachable shoulder stock.
- **Browning High Power.** A semi-automatic pistol first produced in 1935. It had a magazine that carried 13 9mm cartridges.
- **Browning Modele 1900.** The first Browning pistol, semi-automatic, manufactured in Belgium by Fabrique Nationale.
- **Colt.** Colt was the maker of many important gun models, beginning in the 19th century. The post–Civil War saying went, "Abraham Lincoln may have freed all men, but Sam Colt made them equal." Some representative Colt guns, including pistols, rifles, machine guns, and assault rifles, include:
    - **Colt Patterson Model.** A five-shot revolver that used percussion ignition, made in 1836 in Patterson, NJ.
    - **Colt Walker Model.** A revolver used by the U.S. Army as early as 1847, using percussion caps. To load, the paper-wrapped cartridges were inserted from the front of the cylinder, and percussion caps were inserted from the back.
    - **Colt Model 1855.** See the "Longarm and Rifle Examples" section.
    - **Colt Model 1861 Navy Revolver.** A six-shot, .38-caliber revolver modified in 1870 to a side-gate breech loader.
    - **Colt Peacemaker.** Went into production in the 1870s and is still being made today. Known as "the gun that won the West." A six-shot revolver, side-gate design.
    - **Colt New Service M1917.** A six-shot, .45-caliber revolver with a swing-out cylinder. Used in both the U.S. and Britain (where it was a .455 caliber).
    - **Colt Police Positive Special.** Made from 1908 until the 1970s—a .38-caliber six-shot revolver that used a lengthened cylinder to house the .38 special cartridge, which is why it was called "special."
    - **"Snub-Nosed" 38 (Colt Detective Special).** A version of Colt's Police Positive Special revolver with a shortened barrel, designed for concealment and easy carrying, often in a holder under the armpit—a *shoulder holster*. Created in 1927.
    - **Colt Python.** A .357 Magnum revolver—six shot swing-out cylinder.
    - **Colt 1911 A1.** A semi-automatic .45-caliber pistol first produced in 1911 and modified in 1923; still in production.
    - **M1, M4, AR-15 (with ArmaLite), M16.** Colt manufactured these military weapons.

NOTE

In the latter 16th and early 17th centuries, a wheel-lock pistol was called a dag.

- **Demi-Hag.** A small kind of Hackbutt.
- **Deringer.** A very small pistol meant for concealment. Originally designed by Henry Deringer in Philadelphia, but often copied.

NOTE

Folding Trigger. *A folding trigger was used especially on pistols designed for the pocket. The folding trigger would disappear into the body of the pistol until the hammer was fully cocked, at which point it would swing out and be available to fire.*

- **Knife or Dagger Pistol.** It was not too uncommon to find a combination knife and pistol, where the barrel of the gun extended along the top of the blade. In Japan, some pistols were formed with hilts just like a knife, so that they could not be distinguished from knives when carried in a scabbard.
- **Hackbutt.** A 16th century gun that did not exceed 27 inches in length.
- **Harrison and Richardson 900.** A modern nine-shot revolver. The cylinder removes completely for reloading.
- **Heckler and Koch VP 70.** A semi-automatic pistol able to fire bursts of three shots with a shoulder stock. Uses an 18-shot magazine of 9mm cartridges.
- **Lancaster Pistol.** A four-barreled break-open pistol that was also made as a pistol shotgun.
- **Lefaucheux Revolver.** An early six-shot revolver made in 1845.
- **Luger Parabellum.** The prototypical semi-automatic German pistol of WWII, it was originally designed in 1898 by Georg Luger. The name was taken from the expression (in Latin) *Si vis Pacem, Para bellum.* ("If you want peace, prepare for war.") The locking mechanism was based on the earlier Borchardt pistol. The model P-08 was the standard military model of WWII. Many models of the Luger were created, including one with a shoulder stock, but all used the same blowback mechanism.
- **Man-Stopper.** A British six-shot revolver of the 1870s that used a .577-caliber cartridge. The cylinder was completely removed for reloading.
- **Marston Pistol.** A repeating pistol with three barrels that had to be turned by hand.
- **Modele 1892.** A French six-shot revolver with double action, used in both WWI and WWII.
- **Modello 89B.** An Italian six-shot revolver used from 1889 until 1920.
- **Nagant Model 1895G.** Seven-shot revolver used in WWI and WWII.
- **Niao-Chiang.** A matchlock gun from China that was remarkable in that it had a pistol stock and was fired like a pistol, but with both hands, yet it could be from three to seven feet long!
- **Pepper Box.** An early form of revolver made around the middle of the 19th century. Generally, when the trigger was pulled, the hammer was raised and the barrels revolved. In some the hammer was above, and in some it was below. Pepper Boxes varied in size and in the number of barrels. Some were a single action, and others were double action, meaning that the hammer was cocked by hand, and the trigger fired and rotated the barrels.
- **Petronel.** An ungainly 16th-century gun, midway between the earliest pistols and the Arquebus. It was short but of a large caliber, and it had a highly curved stock meant to be rested against the chest when firing.
- **Remington Derringer.** An "over and under" gun originally made in the 1860s and still manufactured today. Uses .41-caliber rimfire cartridges.
- **Robbins and Lawrence Pepperbox.** An early revolver (1849) with five barrels and a rotating striker—the barrels remained stationary.
- **Shattuck Palm Pistol.** An unusual, self-cocking small pistol held with the four barrels sticking out through the fingers. It was patented in 1906 and used .22-caliber rimfire bullets.
- **Shuju.** A Japanese pistol
- **Smith and Wesson .44 Magnum Model 29.** Modern six-shot revolver. A very powerful pistol.

- **Smith & Wesson Bodyguard Airweight Model.** Modern small revolver with internal hammer; fires .38 special rounds.
- **Smith & Wesson Model 60 ("Chief's Special").** A modern five-shot small revolver suitable for police work and concealment.
- **Tamancha.** An Indian pistol.
- **Tercerole.** A pocket pistol.
- **Remington-Elliot Derringer.** Four-barreled 1860 pistol with a ring trigger that was used to rotate the striker.
- **Remington Model 1867.** Used by the U.S. Navy, it was a repeater using a rolling-block breech more common in rifles.
- **Remington Model 1874.** A .44-caliber, six-shot U.S. Army revolver.
- **Ruger Blackhawk.** A modern single-action six-shot revolver that uses .38 special or .357 Magnum rounds.
- **Sharps Derringer.** A four-barreled pistol in which the hammer rotates to fire each in turn.
- **Volcanic Repeating Pistol.** A lever-action pistol created by Horace Smith and Daniel Wesson, based on the work of Lewis Jennings and his Jennings Repeating Rifle. (See the "Longarm and Rifle Examples" section earlier in this chapter.) This was followed by a Volcanic rifle. Soon after, Smith & Wesson became the Volcanic Repeating Arms Company. One of the principal investors was Oliver F. Winchester. Smith and Wesson soon left the company and ultimately re-started Smith & Wesson.
- **Volley Gun.** A flintlock created in the late 18th century that fired seven barrels simultaneously. It was presented to the British Navy but was later abandoned because the recoil was so powerful that it smashed the shoulders of those who fired it. Only someone very big and very strong could fire it with impunity.
- **Walther P38.** A semi-automatic pistol used by the Germans during WWII and manufactured for years afterward. Eventually replaced by the Walther P88.
- **Walther PPK.** A semi-automatic pistol featured in James Bond books. The initials stand for *Polizei Pistole Kriminal.*
- **Webley-Fosbery Self-Cocking Revolver.** Made around 1890, this could be considered one of the first semi-automatic pistols in that it used recoil from the previous shot to cock and load the next shot. It differs from what are considered to be modern semi-automatic pistols in that it used a cylinder instead of a magazine, and a different type of recoil system.
- **Webley Mk VI Revolver.** British military six-shot revolver, single- or double-action, used from 1915 through WWII. Used a .455-caliber cartridge. A lower-caliber version based on this design was the Enfield No2 Mk1 Star, which used a .380-caliber cartridge.

Submachine Guns (SMGs) and Assault Rifles

Submachine guns are lightweight, fully automatic guns that fire pistol ammunition. They lack the long-range accuracy of rifles and the armor-piercing power of heavy machine guns, but they can deliver a lot of bullets quickly while remaining light and easy to carry. They are generally fired from the shoulder or the hip.

Assault rifles are *selective-fire* guns, meaning that they can be set for semi-automatic or full automatic fire. According to Wikipedia, an assault weapon must have a provision for firing from the shoulder, must be capable of selective fire, must use a cartridge that is somewhere between a pistol and a rifle in caliber, and must use detachable box magazines for cartridges.

Rate of fire (measured as rounds per minute [or rpm]) means the gun's theoretical uninterrupted firing rate. In reality, this does not include time taken to change magazines and re-cock the mechanism, nor does it take into account heat buildup or fouling in the barrel from continuous use.

- **ArmaLite.** Originally a division of Fairchild, ArmaLite produced a series of U.S.-made assault weapons, beginning with the AR-5 .22 Hornet Survival Rifle. They subsequently developed the AR-10 and AR-15 assault rifles, ultimately licensing the designs to Colt, who manufactured them. In 1961, ArmaLite became independent of Fairchild. ArmaLite had attempted to get the U.S. military to adopt the AR-15, but the M14 won the military bid. Later, with the AR-18, they once again lost the bid to the redesigned M16. In 1998, they created the AR-50, a heavy-caliber assault weapon.
- **Bergmann MP 18/1.** One of the first SMGs, used in 1918 by the German army in WWI. It used a 32-round "snail" drum magazine. Rate of fire/caliber: 400 rpm/9mm.

NOTE

***Bull Pup.** A design that places the grip and trigger of a rifle forward of the breech, allowing a longer barrel on a relatively shorter gun.*

- **CETME Model C.** Spanish assault rifle. Rate of fire of 550 to 650 rpm, and a 30-round magazine of 7.62mm cartridges.
- **FG42.** A fully automatic German paratrooper's weapon—one of the first to adopt a straight stock to reduce "climb" from fully automatic fire.
- **FN FAL (Fusil Automatique Leger).** Assault rifle that was adopted in countries all around the world, developed by Belgian Fabrique Nationale beginning in the late 1940s and culminating in 1956 with the adoption of the NATO-standard T65 cartridge as its ammunition. Several versions were created, including a paratrooper version with a folding skeleton stock and a short barrel. Some versions were semi-automatic only, but the rest were full assault weapons. It used a gas-operated mechanism with an adjustment regulator that could even be defeated entirely for use with rifle-launched grenades. Some models had a straight stock to reduce "climb" from fully automatic operation.
- **Galil ARM.** Israeli assault rifle developed after the Arab-Israeli war of 1967. Rate of fire of 650 rpm and a 35-round magazine of 5.56mm ammunition.
- **Gewehr 3 A3.** West German variant of the Spanish CETME (see above).
- **Ingram Model 11.** U.S.-made SMG specialized for undercover operations, with a stock that slides and folds in. Rate of fire of 1200 rpm with .38 ACP (Automatic Colt Pistol ammunition).
- **K-50M.** A North Vietnamese SMG with a telescopic scope—based on the Soviet PPSH 41. Rate of fire of 700 rpm. Caliber: 7.62mm.
- **Kalashnikov AK-47.** Soviet standard assault rifle, used all over the world in various versions. Rate of fire of 600 rpm and a 30-round magazine of 7.62mm ammunition. A version known as the AK-74 was developed for use with smaller-caliber ammunition. The AK-74 had some modifications, but was essentially still the AK-47.
- **M16.** Standard U.S. military assault weapon manufactured by Colt, first adopted in the 1960s. The original version was, in essence, the AR-15 with the addition of a manual device for resetting the mechanism in case of jams. Several versions of M16 have been created over the years, some considerably different from the original. It is still standard issue and is comparable to the Soviet AK-47, although it is believed to be less reliable in harsh battlefield conditions than the latter.
- **MP38 and MP40.** German SMGs used in WWII. The MP40, also known as the Schmeisser, was the first SMG to use a folding stock. Rate of fire/caliber: 500 rpm/9mm.
- **MP44.** Also known as the Sturmgewehr 44 (StG44); often considered the original model for the modern assault rifle. Sturmgewehr translates to "storm rifle," which ultimately became "assault rifle"

in English. The StG44 saw limited use in WWII. Rate of fire of 500 rpm and a 30-round magazine of 7.92mm ammunition.

- **PPSH 41.** A Soviet SMG from WWII that used a drum magazine. Rate of fire/caliber: 900 rpm/7.62mm.
- **Sten Mk2.** British SMG from WWII that could be mounted with a silencer. Rate of fire of 550 rpm (450 with silencer) with .45 ACP (Automatic Colt Pistol ammunition).
- **Thompson Model 1928.** First designed by General John T. Thompson in 1920, this was the famous "Tommy gun" of the Prohibition era. It was also used during WWII, although the first government agency to purchase them was the U.S. Post Office. It was used by the FBI and the military until 1974, when it was declared obsolete. It could hold a 20-, 30-, or 50-round magazine, or a drum magazine of 60 or 100 rounds. Rate of fire/caliber: 700 rpm/.45in.
- **US M3.** Known as the *grease gun* for its resemblance to that tool, it used a telescopic stock. Rate of fire of 450 rpm .45 ACP (Automatic Colt Pistol ammunition).
- **Uzi.** Israeli compact SMG made in various versions. Rate of fire/caliber: 600 rpm/9mm.
- **F2000 Integrated Weapon System.** Gas-operated 5.56mm LMG with computerized fire control/sight and optional grenade launcher or nonlethal attachments for BBs or tear gas. Fully ambidextrous, with a front ejection system for spent casings.
- **FN P90 Personal Defense Weapon.** A submachine gun with a blowback mechanism that fires a 5.7mm cartridge and weighs only five pounds unloaded. It has a 50-round detachable magazine (translucent) and rate of about 900 rpm. It also has an unusual shape and molded plastic stock.
- **Walther MPL.** Common SMG used for border guards and police in Germany.
- **CornerShot.** A modern gun system that uses a color video camera attached to a gun, allowing the shooter to fire from around a corner without risking exposure.

World War II Guns from American Companies

Not all guns were produced during the war. Some models are shown with alternate names (in parentheses).

Table 34.1 Major Gun Manufacturers

Winchester Repeating Arms			
M1 Garand rifle	M1/2 carbine	M1917 riot gun (M97 shotgun)	M1917 riot gun (M12 shotgun)
	M1918 BAR		
Winchester Repeating Arms			
M1917 Browning machine gun	M11 shotgun	M31 shotgun	M1903 Springfield rifle
M1911 pistol			
Colt's Patent Firearms Manufacturing Company			
M1911 pistol (Model O)	M1908 pistol (Model M)	M1903 pistol (Model M)	M1908 pistol (Model N)

(continued)

Colt's Patent Firearms Manufacturing Company (continued)

Service Model Ace pistol (Model O)	Woodsman Match Target pistol (Model S)	Commando revolver	
M1917 Browning machine gun	M1919 Browning machine gun	M2 Browning heavy machine gun	
M1917 revolver	M1921 (and 21/8)	Thompson SMG	M1918 BAR

Smith & Wesson

British Pistol No. 2 (K-200 or S&W .38-200)	M1940 Light Rifle Mark 2	Victory Model revolver (M&P)	M1917 revolver

Harrington & Richardson

M999 Sportsman revolver	Defender revolver	M35 Premier revolver
Reising 50/55 SMG	Reising 60 carbine	M65 Military rifle

Marlin

M42 United Defense SMG	M1918 BAR	M1917 Browning machine gun

Savage - Stevens

M1 Thompson SMG	M1928 Thompson SMG	M620 Stevens shotgun	M2 Browning heavy machine gun
M1917 Browning machine gun	British Rifle No. 4 (Lee-Enfield)	M720 shotgun	

Auto-Ordnance

M1928 Thompson SMG

Ithaca Gun Company

M1911 pistol	M3 SMG	M37 shotgun

High Standard

USA Model H-D pistol	Model H-D MS suppressed pistol	Model B-US pistol
M1917 Browning machine gun	M2 Browning heavy machine gun	

Buffalo Arms

M2 Browning heavy machine gun

Government Arsenals

Rock Island Arsenal

M1917 Browning machine gun	M1903 Springfield rifle	

Springfield Armory

M1 Garand Rifle	M1903 Springfield rifle	M1911 pistol

Private Companies Not Usually Associated with Firearms

International Business Machines

M1918 BAR	M1 carbine	

Frigidaire

M2 Browning heavy machine gun

Brown-Lipe-Chapin

M2 Browning heavy machine gun

Kelsey Hayes Wheel Co.

M2 Browning heavy machine gun

General Motors

M1917 Browning machine gun	M2 Browning heavy machine gun	FP-45 Liberator pistol
M1 2/3 carbine	M2 Hyde SMG	M3 SMG

Companies Set Up Just to Make WWII Weapons

New England Small Arms

M1918 BAR

Cranston Arms (Universal Windings)

M1941 Johnson rifle	M1941/44 Johnson machine guns	

Modern Explosives

Explosives are present or at least implied in a lot of games. Most games don't deal with them in great detail. It's enough to know that you can blow up something with a gun, a bomb, or some other device. But suppose you wanted a game in which you had access to the materials of explosives and could, in a rough way, combine them to create mayhem and destruction in your virtual environment.

Explosions can be caused by a variety of circumstances, most often by materials called explosives, although some explosions can be caused by the buildup of pressure involving non-explosive materials, such as steam or even air.

What is an explosive? Simply put, it is a chemical or nuclear material that can be caused to undergo very rapid, self-propagating decomposition resulting in the formation of more stable material and the liberation of heat, or the development of a sudden pressure effect through the action of heat on produced or adjacent gases. In evaluating the effectiveness of an explosive, there are a number of factors to take into account, such as:

- Conditions under which it will explode (pressure, temperature, friction, shock, other agents, and so on).
- The velocity of its explosive reaction, also known as *brisance.* Measured "confined" velocities of modern high explosives range from about 4,000 to about 25,000 feet per second, although many conditions can affect those statistics.
- Temperatures produced.
- Relative stability under different conditions.

It all boils down to how much energy is produced and how fast. By nature, explosions involve a rapid release of energy. In general, the faster rate of propagation, the more powerful the explosive, and the more damage it can cause or the farther it can fire a projectile, and so on.

There are a lot of ways to make things explode. Dry ice and water in a sealed plastic or glass container will do it—but don't try it with glass unless you take appropriate safety precautions. You can get hurt.

That brings me to the warning in this chapter and the disclaimer: First, I'm not going to give you precise methods for making explosives. If you're really dedicated, you can find that sort of information, but I'm not going to be responsible for it. The only exception is the formula for making TNT, a high explosive that is so complicated to make that it should suffice to warn you that explosives are complex, especially modern ones. Second is the warning that, even if you have access to the materials mentioned in this chapter, I advise you not to mess around with them. If you really want to do some chemical experiments, work with an expert chemist and do it in laboratory conditions. Okay?

Anyway, since the actual methods of making most explosives are too complicated for any average game, they are also too complicated for this book. However, it wouldn't be too taxing on players to provide them with the ingredients for something explosive and, perhaps, a black box sort of device that will create the end result without being too particular as to the method. Having said that, I thought I'd provide you with some interesting information about explosives. If you're really curious how high explosives are made, check out the "Making TNT" sidebar later in this chapter. For a list of explosive terminology (no, not curses), check out the Glossary of Explosives later in this chapter.

The chemistry and science of explosives is, on one hand, relatively simple by comparison with some subjects, but it's still a lot more complex than, say, programming a VCR or a microwave oven. Although it might be quite interesting to go into considerable detail here, there's probably no way much of the very specific chemistry and science around explosives would be especially useful in games. If you can think of a way to use more specifics, I encourage you to do further research. For instance, did you know that modern explosives use ingredients classified as explosive bases, combustibles, oxygen carriers, antacids (Tums for explosives?), and absorbents?

Explosives are also categorized as high-order (HE) and low-order (LE) explosives. The main difference is that HE detonates, meaning that they produce a shockwave that travels through the material at speeds in excess of the speed of sound. This causes a very fast reaction and release of energy. Low-order explosives, on the other hand, burn rapidly, but not like HE. In LE, the process is called *deflagration* instead of *detonation*, although in some specific circumstances, low-order explosives can be caused to detonate, often unexpectedly. Black powder is a typical low-order explosive.

Explosives are further categorized as primary (highly susceptible to detonation) and secondary (more likely to detonate as a result of a specific initiation, such as the detonation of a primary explosive and in some cases even a "booster" charge). In the modern world, materials such as lead azide and lead styphnate are common primary explosives, while secondary explosives these days can be categorized, more or less, into "melt/pour" nitroaromatics (like TNT) or plastic-bonded explosives, which use a crystalline explosive such as RDX in combination with various types of binder materials.

In addition to explosives, there are also pyrotechnic materials used in flares for signals or illumination, smoke generators, incendiary bombs, some fuses, and flash compounds. Pyrotechnic material generally combines an inorganic oxidizer with a metal powder, mixed in some kind of binder. For instance, one "recipe" for an illumination flare combines 38% sodium nitrate, 55% magnesium, and 6% binder. An infrared flare might use different materials, such as cesium nitrate, barium nitrate, or red phosphorous. Signal flares, which are designed to be small and fast-burning, may use different metals for different-colored flares.

In contrast to standard military "manufactured" devices, the terminology to describe what terrorists use is *improvised explosive devices* or IEDs.

Useful Definitions

It may help to understand the following terms used in conjunction with explosives:

- Brisance is the measure of how rapidly an explosive develops its maximum pressure. A brisant explosive is one in which the maximum pressure is attained so rapidly that the effect is to shatter any material in contact with it and all surrounding material.
- A hygroscopic material (literally *water seeking*) is one that readily absorbs water (usually from the atmosphere).
- A binary explosive is an explosive material composed of separate components, each of which is safe for storage and transportation and would not in itself be considered as an explosive.
- A high explosive is characterized by the extreme rapidity with which its decomposition occurs; this action is known as *detonation.* When initiated by a blow or shock, it decomposes almost instantaneously, either in a manner similar to an extremely rapid combustion or with rupture and rearrangement of the molecules themselves.

Specifics of Explosives

There are different types of explosives, with different characteristics and components. This section will help you get a handle on explosive basics.

Propellants

The explosive mixture that propels the bullet or other projectile is called the *propellant.* Here are some of the main types of propellants used in guns.

- Black powder is your basic gunpowder, and it is considered a *low explosive.* It can be ignited easily by heat, friction, or a spark, making it one of the more dangerous explosives to handle. The basic formula contains potassium nitrate or sodium nitrate, charcoal, and sulfur. Black powder is known as a hygroscopic substance, which means it attracts and absorbs water molecules. Consequently, it will degrade rapidly when exposed to moisture. Black powder is no longer used in military guns, but there are many gun enthusiasts who enjoy firing guns using black powder, and it is still found in various ammunition components.

- Smokeless powder is not generally seen as a powder, but is prepared in such a way as to produce flakes, strips, sheets, balls, cords, or perforated cylindrical grains of uniform size. Used exclusively for gun and rocket ammunition, smokeless powder is not completely smokeless; however, it produces far less smoke than earlier propellants, such as black powder. Common types of smokeless powder are guncotton, ballistite, and Cordite N.
  - Guncotton is a nitrocellulose explosive that is used primarily as a propellant, though it is also used in electric primers and other electrically initiated devices. It is made from cotton fibers that contain 13 percent or more of nitrogen. It is sometimes referred to by various names, such as *pyropowder*, *pyrocellulose*, or *nitrocellulose*. When confined, it can produce a high-explosive detonation.
  - Ballistite, a double-base powder, is actually a mixture of nitrocellulose and nitroglycerin that have been blended with a stabilizer, diphenylamine. Used primarily as a rocket propellant, ballistite's rate of burning can be controlled by altering the characteristics of the powder grain, the pre-ignition temperature, and the pressure during reaction. It is generally produced as a solid propellant shaped to fit the housings of various rocket motors. It produces a lot of smoke, flash, and gas upon burning. Solid propellant charges, like ballistite, fall into one of two categories —restricted burning and unrestricted burning.
    - Restricted-burning charges are so named because a part of the exposed surface of the charge is covered with an inhibitor, which allows the burning rate and duration to be controlled.
    - An unrestricted-burning charge uses no inhibitors, and all surfaces burn simultaneously, resulting in a large output of thrust over a shorter time period, depending on the type of grain used. The grain can affect the duration and short- versus long-term output of thrust.
  - One commonly used propellant in aircraft guns is Cordite N, which is made from a combination of nitroguanidine, nitrocellulose, and nitroglycerin. In contrast to ballistite, Cordite N burns cool and emits little smoke or flash. It also has a higher burning rate, resulting in a higher velocity of projectile.

Initiating Explosives

Initiating explosives are used to detonate high explosives, and won't burn under normal conditions. While their strength and brisance are not as great as that of high explosives, they can detonate with enough force to detonate the stronger high explosives.

- Mercury fulminate will detonate when exposed to heat, friction, spark, flames, or shock. It generally appears as white, gray, or slightly brownish crystals. It is used in blasting caps and detonators, where it is packed into containers at 3,000 psi, though it can be "dead pressed" at up to 30,000 psi, which requires it to be detonated by another detonating agent. It loses potency if stored for long periods of time above 100 degrees Fahrenheit, and it is usually stored under water (if there is no danger of freezing) or in an alcohol and water mixture. When the substance is dry, it is highly sensitive, and accidental detonations are common. It also reacts strongly when it comes into contact with metals, such as aluminum, magnesium, zinc, copper, brass, or bronze.
- Lead azide is an initiating explosive that is generally seen in the form of white or cream-colored crystals. Unlike mercury fulminate, lead azide does not decompose when stored in hot conditions.

Although it is sensitive to both flame and impact, it requires a layer of lead styphnate priming mixture to initiate a reaction from a firing pin or electrical charge. Extremely sensitive to a chemical reaction with either copper or bronze, particularly in the presence of moisture, where it can form copper azide, lead azide is generally packed into aluminum housings. In addition, when it is stored in water, to which it is practically insoluble, the water must be clean and free of contaminants with which the substance might react. It is used in various devices, including priming mixtures, major caliber base detonating fuzes, point detonating fuzes, and of auxiliary detonating fuzes.

- Lead styphnate, like lead azide, is found as an orange- to brown-colored crystalline substance that is stored in conditions similar to those of mercury fulminate. Although it is sensitive to ignition from heat or static discharge, it is not considered a reliable means of igniting secondary high explosives. When dry, however, it can discharge simply from static electricity generated by a human body. It is used as an ingredient in priming mixtures for small arms ammunition, although it is usually mixed with other materials and pressed into a metallic container.
- Tetracene is insoluble in water, alcohol, benzene, or most other substances, although it is soluble in strong hydrochloric acid. It is generally a colorless or slightly yellow substance that is only moderately hygroscopic. Like mercury fulminate, it can be "dead pressed," which reduces its sensitivity under higher pressures (and therefore higher material density), and will explode when exposed to flame, emitting a great deal of black smoke; however, its brisance increases when detonated by tetryl or mercury fulminate.
- DDNP (diazodinitrophenol) is a primary high explosive that appears commonly as a yellowish-brown powder. It is used in commercial blasting caps that are initiated by a black powder safety fuse. It is more stable than mercury fulminate but less stable than lead azide. Insoluble in water, it can be dissolved in other solvents, such as acetic acid, acetone, strong hydrochloric acid, and others. It can be neutralized if dissolved in cold sodium hydroxide or if placed in water at normal temperatures. Although it is not as sensitive to impact as mercury fulminate or lead azide, it more powerful than either. It is used primarily in conditions where high sensitivity to flame or heat is preferred.

Auxiliary Explosives

Auxiliary explosives fall in the midrange of sensitivity between initiating explosives and high explosives. They are commonly used as filler charges or bursting explosives.

- Tetrytol is a cast mixture consisting of approximately 75 percent tetryl and 25 percent TNT. It is used as a demolition explosive, a bursting charge in mines, a burster charge in chemical bombs, and also in artillery shells and shaped charges. The explosive power of tetrytol is generally about the same as that of TNT, and it is generally initiated using a blasting cap.
- PETN (pentaerythritol tetranitrate) is almost the equal of nitroglycerine and RDX, making it one of the most powerful military explosives, with a detonation velocity of 21,000 feet per second. It is sometimes used in detonation cord (primacord), where it can be handled in transport safely, as its natural sensitivity to shock or friction is reduced. It is also used in booster and bursting charges of small-caliber ammunition and in the upper charges of land mine and artillery shell detonators.
- Tetryl (Trinitrophenylmethylnitramine) is a fine yellow crystalline material with very high shattering power. It remains stable when stored and is used as a standard booster explosive in detonators, where it is compressed for greater stability and reduced reactivity and generally initiated by a priming charge of mercury fulminate or lead azide. Reactions can be obtained by exposure to flame, friction, shock, or sparks, and it will detonate if burned in large quantities.
- TNT (Trinitrotoluene) is produced by combining toluene, sulfuric acid, and nitric acid, and it is widely used in a variety of applications, including steel cutting, breaching concrete and other

demolition, and even underwater demolition. It is also used in other explosives, such as amatol, pentolite, tetrytol, torpex, tritonal, picratol, ednatol, and composition B. TNT is stable, stores well, and is insensitive to shock, making it a reliable explosive under many conditions, although it will react with alkalis to form unstable compounds that are far more sensitive to heat or impact than the pure TNT. Under some conditions, TNT may form an oily brown liquid that is flammable and dangerous, and should be cleaned up if discovered. It is alternately called Triton, Trotyl, Trilite, Trinol, and Tritolo. In addition to general demolition work, TNT can be used as a booster or as a bursting charge for high-explosive shells and bombs. It is commonly detonated by blasting cap or primacord. Military-grade dynamite detonates at a rate of 20,000 feet per second.

- Nitrostarch, which is composed of starch nitrate, barium nitrate, and sodium nitrate formed through a dangerous process involving sulfuric acid, nitric acid, and corn starch, is a brownish or orange-colored crystalline powder (though in its pure form, it is white). While less powerful than TNT, it is more sensitive to flame, friction, and impact. It was used in WWII as a filler in hand grenades, though it is also used as an explosive in the mining industry.

Bursting Explosives

While high explosives detonate at a very high rate, bursting explosives, also known as *disrupting explosives*, are designed to create maximum damage, and they are used as a filler explosive in many applications, incuding bombs, torpedoes, mines, warheads, and shells. Bursting explosives vary in terms of their sensitivity, brisance, rate of detonation, and so forth.

- Ammonium nitrate is a white crystalline substance that is highly water absorbent. It is generally packed in sealed metal containers. It will react with metals, such as copper and brass, so it must be kept away from copper-based metals. Ammonium nitrate is a common ingredient in fertilizers, which homegrown bomb makers use as a source of the material; however, the agricultural grade (FGAN) is a low-porosity form that is less likely to detonate. By comparison, the "technical" grade is more porous and more reactive. Its velocity of detonation is low, at 3,600 feet per second, and it is considered to be only 55 percent as powerful as TNT, so it is often combined with other materials, such as amatol. In liquid form it is known as UAN (*Urea Ammonium Nitrate*). Some military uses include daisy-cutter bombs and sometimes in solid rocket propellants. Ammonium nitrate has been used by terrorists and insurgents, including the IRA and in the Oklahoma City bombings, among other examples.
- Nitroglycerin is a thick yellow-brown liquid formed by treating glycerin with a nitrating mixture of nitric and sulfuric acids. Normally colorless, it tends to discolor after it is manufactured. It is extremely sensitive to shock and easily detonated. It freezes at 56°F, and one source (from WWII) claims it is less sensitive to shock when frozen, but more modern sources claim it is even more shock sensitive. In any case, it is extremely dangerous to manufacture and to handle, and many catastrophic explosions are linked to its history. At the time of its discovery and first applications, Alfred Nobel (of the Nobel Prize) created an explosive compound of nitroglycerin and gunpowder (called *Swedish Oil*), but when that was proven too unstable, he combined it with more inert ingredients, such as charcoal and diatomaceous earth, in the first applications of dynamite. Nobel is also credited with creating blasting gelatin and ballistite, the first double-base propellant, a precursor to the more modern cordite.

  Nitroglycerin also has a medical use as a vasodilator in the treatment of heart conditions. Apparently it is also being inserted (as glyceryl trinitrate [GTN]) into the tips of certain condoms to stimulate erections during intercourse, which inspires one to hope that they have made the substance less sensitive to exploding as a result of shock or pounding.

- Blasting gelatin (Gelignite) is a gelatinous explosive material first discovered by Alfred Nobel in 1875. It is stable under most conditions and cannot explode without a detonator. It is made from a collodion-cotton (nitrocellulose or guncotton) dissolved in nitroglycerine and mixed with wood pulp and either sodium or potassium nitrate. It is used for large-scale blasting operations and, unlike dynamite, will not deteriorate and leak out unstable liquid nitroglycerin when stored.
- Amatol is a whitish substance made by mixing ammonium nitrate and TNT in proportions ranging from 80:20 to 40:60. Invented early in the 20th century, it was used in the warheads of the German V-1 and V-2 rockets. In WWII, amatol was used as a main bursting charge in artillery shells and bombs. In the Vietnam War, the Bangalore Torpedo used an 80:20 mixture of amatol to TNT, which produces a characteristic white smoke. More even mixtures produce a darker smoke. Like ammonium nitrate, amatol should not be stored in contact with copper or brass.
- Ammonal is a mixture of ammonium nitrate, TNT, and flaked or powdered aluminum in a ratio of about 22:67:11. It is about 83% as effective as TNT and explodes with a bright flash. It was used as a filler in artillery shells during WWII.
- ANFO (*Ammonium Nirate Fuel Oil*) is used in blasting and was originally developed for use in mining. It combines ammonium nitrate explosive with about 6% fuel oil, in part to keep it dry.
- Tritonal is a silvery solid composed of 80% TNT and 20% atomized aluminum powder. It is often used as a filler in bombs and shells.
- Picric acid is a highly sensitive explosive substance that can be somewhat controlled by "wetting" or diluting with water. It is normally found as a solid or paste and is highly sensitive to shock, heat, and friction. Its tendency to form salts with various metals, which are themselves even more explosive and sensitive than the pure substance, make it very hazardous, and it should never be allowed to come in contact with metals or even concrete, with which it can form calcium picrate. In contact with lead, it can form the highly unstable and explosive substance lead picrate. Picric acid can produce explosions superior in power to TNT, making it a class A high explosive. Picric acid can be synthesized rather easily in laboratory conditions using concentrated sulfuric and nitric acids, phenol, ethanol, and distilled water. The result is a yellowish crystalline powder. It can be further distilled to an even more pure grade. It can also be created directly from benzene. Picric acid can also be used to create a more stable explosive called, alternately, *ammonium picrate, ammonium piconitrate, Explosive D*, or *carazoate*. This substance can be used in armor-piercing shells because it does not detonate easily and will not react with casing metals to create dangerous salts. (An even more reactive substance, styphnic acid, can be derived from the common priming compound, lead styphnate.)
- Dynamite was commonly used in excavation and other commercial or military blasting projects. However, there are different types of dynamite. Among commercial types used up until the 1950s, which all used nitroglycerin as the primary explosive, there were straight dynamite, ammonia dynamite, and gelatin dynamite, which ranged (based on the nitroglycerin content) from a velocity of detonation of 4,000 to 23,000 feet per second. Dynamite had a tendency to be unstable and to "leak" nitroglycerin when stored. It was used in a variety of ways; one interesting use of it was by safecrackers who would melt down the dynamite to extract the nitroglycerin.
- Military dynamite is not a true dynamite, but an explosive substance consisting of 75% RDX, 15% TNT, 5% SAE 10 motor oil, and 5% cornstarch, packaged in standard dynamite cartridges of colored wax paper marked by size: M1, M2, or M3. All military dynamite detonates at about 20,000 feet per second, which is equivalent in strength to 60% straight dynamite. Military dynamite is far safer to store and to transport than commercial dynamite because it contains no nitroglycerin and is therefore less sensitive to heat, shock, friction, or bullet impact. The explosive substance inside military dynamite is granular, yellow-white to tan in color, crumbles easily, and is slightly oily. It does not have the characteristic sweet odor of true nitroglycerin-based dynamite.

- Pentolite is a high explosive created by mixing equal proportions of PETN and TNT. In WWII it was used as a main bursting charge in grenades, small shells, and shaped charges. It can be melted and cast into a container.
- HMX (*High Melting Explosive*), also known as *Octogen* and by other names, explodes violently at temperatures at or above 534° F. It was present in the pre-atomic era but is used now exclusively to implode fissionable material in nuclear devices, as well as being a component in plastic-bonded explosives, rocket propellants, and as a high-explosive burster charge. HMX is highly toxic and will break down in water if exposed to sunlight, discharging toxic chemicals into ground water.
- RDX (Cyclotrimethylene trinitramine or Royal Demolition Explosive), is also known as *cyclonite* or *hexogen.* RDX is used primarily in combination with other explosives or combined with oils or waxes. This white crystalline solid demonstrates very high shattering power, but it is very stable and can be stored effectively and safely. Considered to be possibly the most powerful military high explosive, RDX is used in various combinations, known (unimaginatively) as Composition A, Composition B, Composition C, HBX, H-6, and Cyclotol. Can also be found in fireworks, demolition explosives, heating fuel for food rations, and sometimes as a rodent poison.

  Pure RDX is used in press-loaded projectiles. Cast loading is accomplished by blending RDX with a relatively low-melting-point substance. RDX is also used as a base charge in detonators and in blasting caps. The various compositions created with RDX are classified as follows:
  - Compositions in which RDX is melted with wax are called Composition A (see details below).
  - Compositions in which RDX is mixed with TNT are called Composition B (see details below).
  - Compositions in which RDX is blended with a non-explosive plasticizer are called Composition C (see details below).
- Composition A is available in five different forms: Composition A-1, A-2, A-3, A-4, and A-5. Each variant of Composition A is a granular explosive made up of a quantity of RDX with a plasticizing wax, and the less commonly used A-4 and A-5 versions include a desensitizing agent. Composition A is used in different applications, including in rockets and land mines.
- Composition B is formed from a mixture of 59 percent RDX with 40 percent TNT and 1 percent wax. Its shattering power and relative effectiveness is greater than that of TNT alone, and it has been used in various applications, including Army projectiles, rockets, landmines, torpedoes, and shaped charges.
- Composition C is made of a combination of RDX and various plastics. The best known version of Composition C is the plastic explosive C-4, which is composed of 91 percent RDX with about 9 percent plastic as a binder. It remains pliant at temperatures ranging from about 70 to 170 degrees Fahrenheit. It can be used underwater, molded to different shapes, and used in shaped charges, for cutting steel or timber, and for breaching concrete. C-4 is the most widely known of the Composition C variants, but C-3 is also used, and less commonly, C-1 and C-2.
- HBX-1 and HBX-3 are explosives made from a combination of RDX, TNT, powdered aluminum, and D-2 wax with calcium chloride. They are castable explosives sometimes used in missile warheads and underwater weaponry.
- H-6 is an explosive created by mixing RDX, TNT, powdered aluminum, and D-2 wax with calcium chloride added. It is a castable explosive that is often used as a bursting charge in bombs.
- Minol is an explosive created by mixing TNT, ammonium nitrate, and powdered aluminum, though one formulation used potassium nitrate along with the other ingredients. Developed in WWII, Minol is now considered obsolete and has been largely replaced by various PBX compositions.
- Explosive D (Ammonium picrate)—also known as *Dunnite* for its developer, Major Dunn, in 1906. This explosive was used primarily in the early 1900s, especially by the U.S. Navy during WWI. It was very insensitive to shock or friction and was used as a bursting charge in armor-piercing shells. Because Explosive D would not detonate on impact, it was detonated by a fuse after the shell casing had burst open.

- Plastic Bonded Explosives (PBX) are polymer-bonded explosive materials in which particles of explosive are set into a matrix of synthetic polymers (plastics). Polymer-bonded explosives have several potential advantages:
  - The rubbery material matrix of PBX explosives makes them very insensitive to accidental detonation due to impact or shock.
  - Various types of polymers that create a harder surface can allow PBX to be rigid and shaped to exact engineering standards, even when under severe stress.
  - In the PBX form, the explosive can be cast as a liquid at room temperature, making it far safer than casting the explosive without the plastic bonding.
  - Some examples of PBX materials:

Name Explosive	Ingredients Binder	Ingredients	Usage
EDC-37	HMX/NC 91%	Polyurethane rubber 9%	
LX-04-1	HMX 85%	Viton-A 15%	
LX-07-2	HMX 90%	Viton-A 10%	
LX-09-0	HMX 93%	BDNPA 4.6%; FEFO 2.4%	
LX-09-1	HMX 93.3%	BDNPA 4.4%; FEFO 2.3%	
LX-10-0	HMX 95%	Viton-A 5%	
LX-10-1	HMX 94.5%	Viton-A 5.5%	
LX-11-0	HMX 80%	Viton-A 20%	
LX-14-0	HMX 95.5%	Estane & 5702-Fl 4.5%	
LX-15	HNIS 95%	Kel-F 800 5%	
LX-16	PETN 96%	FPC461 6%	
LX-17-0	TATB 92.5%	Kel-F 800 7.5%	
PBX 9007	RDX 90%	Polystyrene 9.1%; DOP 0.5%; rosin 0.4%	
PBX 9010	RDX 90%	Kel-F 3700 10%	
PBX 9011	HMX 90%	Estane and 5703-Fl 10%	
PBX 9205	RDX 92%	Polystyrene 6%; DOP 2%	
PBX 9404	HMX 94%	NC 3%; CEF 3%	Nuclear Weapons
PBX 9407	RDX 94%	FPC461 6% PBX 9501	
PBX 9501	HMX 95%	Estane 2.5%; BDNPA-F 2.5%	Nuclear Weapons
PBX 9502	TATB 95%	Kel-F 800 5%	Nuclear Weapons
PBX 9503	TATB 80%; HMX 15%	Kel-F 800 5%	
PBX 9604	RDX 96%	Kel-F 800 4%	
PBXN-106	RDX	Polyurethane rubber	Naval Shells
PBXN-3	RDX 85% Nylon 15%	AIM9-X	Sidewinder Missile
PBXN-5	95% HMX 5%	Fluoroelastomer	Naval Shells
X-0242	HMX 92%	Polymer 8%	

TATP (triacetone triperoxide) is a peroxide-based explosive used extensively by terrorists. It is easy to manufacture at room temperature and explodes with a force 80% greater than TNT. It is highly unstable and dangerous to produce. Unlike most explosives, it is formed without a nitrogen base, making it very difficult to detect with ordinary detection equipment (see PET in the Glossary of Explosives). When it does detonate, each of its molecules breaks into four molecules of gas, but at the density of a solid. The resulting sudden expansion creates pressure 200 times greater than the surrounding air.

Incendiaries

- Thermite is a mixture of three parts iron oxide and two parts aluminum powder by volume that, when ignited, creates very high heat in a local area. It does not explode, but it is so hot that it can selectively melt or weld metal. Although it requires a high temperature to cause ignition, once started it will burn even in cold and windy weather. The result of the reaction is molten iron and aluminum oxide.
- Napalm is a liquid fuel that is gelled by the addition of soap powder or other ingredients and is considered an incendiary weapon. It can be initiated using direct application of flame or by delayed ignition systems. It was widely used in Vietnam to burn structures, to clear out forests, and on people.
- Gasoline is often mixed with different ingredients to create a gelatinous incendiary. Some combinations include:
  - Lauryl amine (55), toluene diisocyanate (27)
  - Coco amine (55), toluene diisocyanate (27)
  - Lauryl amine (57), hexamethylene diisocyanate (25)
  - Oleyl amine (59), hexamethylene diisocyanate (23)
  - t-Octyl amine (51), toluene diisocyanate (31)
  - Coco amine (51), naphthyl isocyanate (31)
  - Delta-aminobutylmethyldiethorxysilane (51), hexamethylene diisocyanate (31)
- Paraffin-sawdust mixture is used as an incendiary to burn buildings and can be ignited using a flame or delayed ignition system. It burns slowly at first, but within a few minutes can produce a strong effect. Beeswax can be substituted for paraffin wax.

Making TNT

You probably don't think it's easy to make explosives, and you probably already know it's very dangerous. In fact, many people have lost their lives by making small but critical mistakes when formulating explosives. I thought I'd provide you with a little insight into the making of what we think of as a "common" high explosive, from *The Chemistry of Powder & Explosives* (Angriff Press, 1972).

Preparation of Trinitrotoluene (Three Stages). A mixture of 294 grams of concentrated sulfuric acid (s. 1.84) and 147 grams of nitric acid (d. 1.42) is added slowly from a dropping funnel to 100 grams of toluene in a tall 600-cc. beaker, while the liquid is stirred vigorously with an electric stirrer and its temperature is maintained at 30° to 40° by running cold water in the vessel in which the beaker is standing. The addition of acid will require from an hour to an hour and a half. The stirring is then continued for half an hour longer without cooling; the mixture is allowed to stand over night in a separatory funnel; the lower layer of spent acid is drawn off; and the crude mononitrotoluene is weighed. One-half of it, corresponding to 50 grams of toluene, is taken for the dinitration.

The mononitrotoluene (MNT) is dissolved in 109 grams of concentrated sulfuric acid (d 1.84) while the mixture is cooled in running water. The solution in a tall beaker is warmed to 50°, and a mixed acid composed of 54.5 grams each of nitric acid (d. 1.50) and sulfuric acid (d 1.84) is added slowly drop by drop from a dropping funnel while the mixture is stirred mechanically. The heat generated by the reaction raises the temperature, and the rate of addition of the acid is regulated so that the temperature of the mixture lies always between 90° and 100°. The addition of the acid will require about 1 hour. After the acid has been added, the mixture is stirred for 2 hours longer at 90-100° to complete the nitration. Two layers separate on standing. The upper layer consists largely of dinitrotoluene (DNT), but probably contains a certain amount of TNT. The trinitration in the laboratory is conveniently carried out without separating the DNT from the spent acid.

While the dinitration mixture is stirred actively at a temperature of about 90°, 145 grams of fuming sulfuric acid (oleum containing 15 per cent free SO_3) is added slowly by pouring from a beaker. A mixed acid, composed of 72.5 grams each of nitric acid (d. 1.50) and 15 per cent oleum, is now added drop by drop with good agitation while the heat of the reaction maintains the temperature at 100-115°. After about three-quarters of the acid has been added, it will be found necessary to apply external heat to maintain the temperature. After all the acid has been added (during $1\,{}^{1}/_{2}$ to 2 hours), the heating and stirring are continued for 2 hours longer at 100-115°. After the material has stood over night, the upper TNT layer will be found to have solidified to a hard cake, and the lower layer of spent acid to be filled with crystals. The acid is filtered through a Büchner funnel (without filter paper), and the cake is broken up and washed with water on the same filter to remove excess acid. The spent acid contains considerable TNT in solution; this is precipitated by pouring the acid into a large volume of water, filtered off, rinsed with water, and added to the main batch. All the product is washed three or four times by agitating it vigorously with hot water under which it is melted. After the last washing, the TNT is granulated by allowing it to cool slowly under hot water while the stirring is continued. The product, filtered off and dried at ordinary temperature, is equal to a good commercial sample of crude TNT. It may be purified by dissolving in warm alcohol at 60° and allowing to cool slowly, or it may be purified by digesting with 5 times its weight of 5 per cent sodium hydrogen sulfite solution at 90° for half an hour with vigorous stirring, washing with hot water until the washings are colorless, and finally granulating as before. The product of this last treatment is equal to a good commercial sample of purified TNT.

Regulated Substances

Our lawmakers have determined that some substances are too dangerous to be used freely and without oversight, so they've created lists of substances that must be regulated. We found the list of regulated substances for the state of Colorado, which is probably typical of most states in the U.S.

NOTE

The purpose of the following lists of dangerous substances is to give you some idea of what's out there. If you are interested in populating your games with any of the substances listed in this chapter, be sure to look them up in a reliable source to understand what they do and how they can be used. We love good explosions and ways to do damage, so here are some items that might inspire you to do more and to do it with a full arsenal of options.

Regulated Substances and Devices (State of Colorado)

(I) "Explosive or incendiary device" means:

(A) Dynamite and all other forms of high explosives, including, but not limited to, water gel, slurry, military C-4 (plastic explosives), blasting agents to include nitro-carbon-nitrate, and ammonium nitrate and fuel oil mixtures, cast primers and boosters, R.D.X., P.E.T.N., electric and nonelectric blasting caps, exploding cords commonly called detonating cord or det-cord or primacord, picric acid explosives, T.N.T. and T.N.T. mixtures, and nitroglycerin and nitroglycerin mixtures;

(B) Any explosive bomb, grenade, missile, or similar device; and

(C) Any incendiary bomb or grenade, fire bomb, or similar device, including any device, except kerosene lamps, which consists of or includes a breakable container including a flammable liquid or compound and a wick composed of any material which, when ignited, is capable of igniting such flammable liquid or compound and can be carried or thrown by one individual acting alone.

(II) "Explosive or incendiary device" shall not include rifle, pistol, or shotgun ammunition, or the components for handloading rifle, pistol, or shotgun ammunition.

(b) (I) "Explosive or incendiary parts" means any substances or materials or combinations thereof which have been prepared or altered for use in the creation of an explosive or incendiary device. Such substances or materials may include, but shall not be limited to, any:

(A) Timing device, clock, or watch which has been altered in such a manner as to be used as the arming device in an explosive;

(B) Pipe, end caps, or metal tubing which has been prepared for a pipe bomb;

(C) Mechanical timers, mechanical triggers, chemical time delays, electronic time delays, or commercially made or improvised items which, when used singly or in combination, may be used in the construction of a timing delay mechanism, booby trap, or activating mechanism for any explosive or incendiary device.

(II) "Explosive or incendiary parts" shall not include rifle, pistol, or shotgun ammunition, or the components for handloading rifle, pistol, or shotgun ammunition, or any signaling device customarily used in operation of railroad equipment.

List of Military and Pyrotechnic Chemicals

Here's a handy-dandy list of military stuff that blows up.

- Acid, Picric (Trinitrophenol)
- Adhesives (ELBA Solution)
- Akardite II (Methyl Diphenylurea)
- Aluminum Oxide
- Aluminum Powder, Flake, Grained, and Atomized
- Aluminum Powder, Spherical
- Aluminum Stearate
- Aminoguadine Bicarbonate, Aminate
- Ammonium Dichromate
- Ammonium Nitrate
- Ammonium Oxalate
- Ammonium Oxalate
- Ammonium Perchlorate, Conditioned
- Ammonium Perchlorate, High Purity
- Ammonium Perchlorate, Solid Propellant
- Ammonium Perchlorate, Special
- Ammonium Perchlorate, Tech.
- Ammonium Picrate
- Antimony Powdered, Tech.
- Antimony Sulphide (Pigment)
- Antimony Sulphide
- Antimony Trioxide
- Asphaltum (Gilsonite)
- Barium Chromate
- Barium Nitrate
- Barium Oxalate
- Barium Peroxide
- Barium Stearate
- Boron Amorphous, Powder
- Boron Potassium Nitrate, Pellets
- Butyl Sebacate, Di Normal
- Butyl Stearate, Normal
- Calcium Carbonate
- Calcium Hydride Charges

- Calcium Oxalate
- Calcium Phosphate, Tribasic
- Calcium Resinate
- Calcium Silicide, Tech.
- Calcium Silicate
- Calcium Stearate
- Carbazole
- Carbon Activated
- Carbon Black
- Carbon Black
- Carbon, Technical (Carbon Black)
- Cellulose Acetate, Plasticized
- Cellulose, Cotton
- Composition, A-3 and A-4
- Composition, B
- Riot Control Agent, CS
- Riot Control Agent, CR
- Composition, Delay
- Copper Monobasic Salicylate
- Chemical Agent CS1
- Chemical Agent CS
- Cupric Oxide
- Curing Agents (Dimeryi-Di-Isocyanate Isophorane-Di-Isocyanate)
- Delay Element, M2
- Di-(2-Ethylhexyl) Adipate, Technical
- Dioctyl Adipate
- Di-N-Propyl Adipate
- Dinitrotoluene 2,4
- Di-(2-Ethyl Hexyl) Adipate
- Dye, Benzanthrone
- Dye 1,4-Diamino
- 1,3-Dihydroanthraquinone
- Dye, Disperse Red 9
- Dye Mix, Disperse Red 9 Dextrin
- Dye Mix, Green Smoke IV
- Dye Mix, Green Smoke VII (metric)
- Dye Mix, Violet
- Dye Mix, Yellow Smoke VI
- Dye, Solvent Green 3
- Dye, Solvent Yellow 33 (metric)
- Dye Vat Yellow 4
- Emulsion, Polyethylene
- Ether, Diethyl, Tech.
- Ethyl Alcohol
- Ethyl Cellulose, Plastic Molding/ Extrusion Material
- Ethyl Cellulose, Tape Inhibiting
- Ethyl Centralite (Carbamite)
- Ferric Chloride
- Ferric Oxide, Tech.
- Graphite Dry
- Guanidine Nitrate
- Hexachloroethane
- HMX
- HMX Resin, Explosive
- Hydroxyl Terminated Polybutadiene
- Iron Oxide Black, Tech.
- Iron Oxide, Ferric, Red Dry
- Lactose, Tech.
- Lead Azide RD-1333
- Lead Beta Resorcylate
- Lead Chromate
- Lead Dioxide, Tech.
- Lead 2-Ethyl Hexoate
- Lead Nitrate, Tech.
- Lead Salicylate
- Lead Stearate
- Lead Styphnate, Basic
- Lead Thiocyanate
- Magnesium Aluminum Alloy
- Magnesium Carbonate
- Magnesium Oxide, Tech.
- Magnesium Powder
- Magnesium Stearate
- Manganese Delay Composition
- Manganese Powder
- Manganese Dioxide, Tech.
- MAPO [Tris-1-(2-Methyl Azirdinyl) Phosphine Oxide]
- Methyl Centralite
- Methyl Chloride
- Methyl Diphenylurea [Akardite II]
- Molybedenum Disulphide, Tech., Lubrication Grade
- Molybedenum Trioxide
- Nitrocellulose
- Nitrodiphenylamine
- Nitroguanadine [Picrite]
- Oxamide
- Oxamide
- Pentaerythrite Tetranitrate (PETN)
- Phosphorous, Red Oiled Tech.
- Phosphorous, Red Stabilized
- Phosphorous, Red, Tech.
- Phosphorous, White

- Polyisobutylene
- Polyvinyl Chloride
- Potassium Chlorate
- Potassium Nitrate
- Potassium Perchlorate
- Potassium Picrate
- Potassium Sulphate
- Powders, Ignition, Gasless, A-1A
- Powders, Metal Atomized
- Propellant, Double-Base Sheet, Type N-5
- RDX
- Resorcinol
- Silica
- Silicon Powder
- Sodium Azide, Tech. (Metric)
- Sodium Bicarbonate
- Sodium Carbonate
- Sodium Chromate
- Sodium Fluorescien
- Sodium Hexametaphosphate
- Sodium Hydroxide
- Sodium Hypochlorite Solution
- Sodium Metasilicate, Tech.
- Sodium Nitrate
- Sodium Nitrate
- Sodium Nitrite, Tech
- Sodium Phosphate
- Sodium Sulphate
- Stearic Acid, Tech.
- Strontium Nitrate
- Strontium Oxalate
- Strontium Peroxide
- Sulphur
- Tetracene
- Tetranitrocarbazole
- Titanium Dioxide Dry
- Titanium, Technical Powder
- Tolylene, 2-4, Diisocyanate
- Triacetin (Glyceryl Triacetate)
- Trinitrotoluene (TNT)
- Triphenyl Bismuth
- Tris-1(2-Methyl Aziridinyl) Phosphine Oxide [MAPO]
- Tungsten Carbide
- Tungsten Delay Composition
- Tungsten Powder
- Tungsten Powder
- Varnish, Phenol-Formaldehyde, Clear and Aluminum Pigmented
- Vinyl Alcohol-Acetate Resin Solution [VAAR]
- Zinc Carbonate
- Zinc Dust
- Zinc Oxide, Tech.
- Zirconium, Granular and Powdered
- Zirconium Nickel Alloy
- Zirconium Hydride

U.S. List of Explosive Materials

Here's the official U.S. list of things that blow up. Now you don't just have to make things explode in your games, but you can actually choose the substance you like. Look them up and see what pretty colors or devastating effects they have, then let your players use them to create all kinds of realistic mayhem.

- Acid, Picric (Trinitrophenol)
- Adhesives (ELBA Solution)
- Akardite II (Methyl Diphenylurea)
- Aluminum Oxide
- Aluminum Powder, Flake, Grained and Atomized
- Aluminum Powder, Spherical
- Aluminum Stearate
- Aminoguadine Bicarbonate, Aminate
- Ammonium Dichromate
- Ammonium Nitrate
- Ammonium Oxalate
- Ammonium Oxalate
- Ammonium Perchlorate, Conditioned
- Ammonium Perchlorate, High Purity
- Ammonium Perchlorate, Solid Propellant
- Ammonium Perchlorate, Special
- Ammonium Perchlorate, Tech.
- Ammonium Picrate
- Antimony Powdered, Tech.
- Antimony Sulphide (Pigment)
- Antimony Sulphide
- Antimony Trioxide
- Asphaltum (Gilsonite)
- Barium Chromate
- Barium Nitrate

- Barium Oxalate
- Barium Peroxide
- Barium Stearate
- Boron Amorphous, Powder
- Boron Potassium Nitrate, Pellets
- Butyl Sebacate, Di Normal
- Butyl Stearate, Normal
- Calcium Carbonate
- Calcium Hydride Charges
- Calcium Oxalate
- Calcium Phosphate, Tribasic
- Calcium Resinate
- Calcium Silicide, Tech.
- Calcium Silicate
- Calcium Stearate
- Carbazole
- Carbon Activated
- Carbon Black
- Carbon Black
- Carbon, Technical (Carbon Black)
- Cellulose Acetate, Plasticized
- Cellulose, Cotton
- Composition, A-3 and A-4
- Composition, B
- Riot Control Agent, CS
- Riot Control Agent, CR
- Composition, Delay
- Copper Monobasic Salicylate
- Chemical Agent CS1
- Chemical Agent CS
- Cupric Oxide
- Curing Agents (Dimeryi-Di-Isocyanate Isophorane-Di-Isocyanate)
- Delay Element, M2
- Di-(2-Ethylhexyl) Adipate, Tech.
- Dioctyl Adipate
- Di-N-Propyl Adipate
- Dinitrotoluene 2,4
- Di-(2-Ethyl Hexyl) Adipate
- Dye, Benzanthrone
- Dye 1,4-Diamino
- 1,3-Dihydroanthraquinone
- Dye, Disperse Red 9
- Dye Mix, Disperse Red 9 Dextrin
- Dye Mix, Green Smoke IV
- Dye Mix, Green Smoke VIl (metric)
- Dye Mix, Violet
- Dye Mix, Yellow Smoke VI
- Dye, Solvent Green 3
- Dye, Solvent Yellow 33 (metric)
- Dye Vat Yellow 4
- Emulsion, Polyethylene
- Ether, Diethyl, Tech.
- Ethyl Alcohol
- Ethyl Cellulose, Plastic Molding/ Extrusion Material
- Ethyl Cellulose, Tape Inhibiting
- Ethyl Centralite (Carbamite)
- Ferric Chloride
- Ferric Oxide, Tech.
- Graphite Dry
- Guanidine Nitrate
- Hexachloroethane
- HMX
- HMX Resin, Explosive
- Hydroxyl Terminated Polybutadiene
- Iron Oxide Black, Tech.
- Iron Oxide, Ferric, Red Dry
- Lactose, Tech.
- Lead Azide RD-1333
- Lead Beta Resorcylate
- Lead Chromate
- Lead Dioxide, Tech.
- Lead 2-Ethyl Hexoate
- Lead Nitrate, Tech.
- Lead Salicylate
- Lead Stearate
- Lead Styphnate, Basic
- Lead Thiocyanate
- Magnesium Aluminum Alloy
- Magnesium Carbonate
- Magnesium Oxide, Tech.
- Magnesium Powder
- Magnesium Stearate
- Manganese Delay Composition
- Manganese Powder
- Manganese Dioxide, Tech.
- MAPO [Tris-1-(2-Methyl Azirdinyl) Phosphine Oxide]
- Methyl Centralite
- Methyl Chloride
- Methyl Diphenylurea [Akardite II]
- Molybedenum Disulphide, Tech., Lubrication Grade
- Molybedenum Trioxide
- Nitrocellulose

- Nitrodiphenylamine
- Nitroguanadine [Picrite]
- Oxamide
- Oxamide
- Pentaerythrite Tetranitrate (PETN)
- Phosphorous, Red Oiled Tech.
- Phosphorous, Red Stabilized
- Phosphorous, Red, Tech.
- Phosphorous, White
- Polyisobutylene
- Polyvinyl Chloride
- Potassium Chlorate
- Potassium Nitrate
- Potassium Perchlorate
- Potassium Picrate
- Potassium Sulphate
- Powders, Ignition, Gasless, A-1A
- Powders, Metal Atomized
- Propellant, Double-Base Sheet, Type N-5
- RDX
- Resorcinol
- Silica
- Silicon Powder
- Sodium Azide, Tech. (Metric)
- Sodium Bicarbonate
- Sodium Carbonate
- Sodium Chromate
- Sodium Fluorescien
- Sodium Hexametaphosphate
- Sodium Hydroxide
- Sodium Hypochlorite Solution
- Sodium Metasilicate, Tech.
- Sodium Nitrate
- Sodium Nitrate
- Sodium Nitrite, Tech.
- Sodium Phosphate
- Sodium Sulphate
- Stearic Acid, Tech.
- Strontium Nitrate
- Strontium Oxalate
- Strontium Peroxide
- Sulphur
- Tetracene
- Tetranitrocarbazole
- Titanium Dioxide Dry
- Titanium, Technical Powder
- Tolylene, 2-4, Diisocyanate
- Triacetin (Glyceryl Triacetate)
- Trinitrotoluene (TNT)
- Triphenyl Bismuth
- Tris-1(2-Methyl Aziridinyl) Phosphine Oxide [MAPO]
- Tungsten Carbide
- Tungsten Delay Composition
- Tungsten Powder
- Tungsten Powder
- Varnish, Phenol-Formaldehyde, Clear and Aluminum Pigmented
- Vinyl Alcohol-Acetate Resin Solution [VAAR]
- Zinc Carbonate
- Zinc Dust
- Zinc Oxide, Tech.
- Zirconium, Granular and Powdered
- Zirconium Nickel Alloy
- Zirconium Hydride

Glossary of Explosives

- **Blasting Agent.** An explosive material used for blasting. It should not be otherwise defined as an explosive and should not be easily detonated in an unconfined state.
- **Blasting Cap.** A metallic tube closed at one end, containing a charge of one or more detonating compounds and designed to initiate detonation.
- **Booster.** An explosive used to initiate detonation in a less sensitive explosive material—generally a high explosive—or for intensifying the explosion.
- **Brisance.** A way to measure the velocity and power of a shockwave produced in an explosion.
- **Bulk Mix.** Bulk, unpackaged quantity of explosive material.
- **Commercial Explosives.** Explosives used for commercial, rather than military, purposes.
- **Common Chemicals.** Chemicals used in a mixture that are necessary for it to be explosive or any material used as an oxidizer or as a fuel source.

- **Critical Mass.** In pyrotechnics, this refers to an approximation of the mass of a composition that will explode when unconfined. This can vary with factors such as air pressure, purity of the composition, and the source of ignition.
- **Deflagration.** The rapid burning of a flammable substance, which may or may not result in an explosion. Common with low explosives, such as black powder.
- **Detection Taggant.** A material such as DNMB (2,3-Dimethyl–2,3-dinitrobutane) or ICPM added to an explosive material that makes it easier to detect, such as additives to plastic explosives that make them easier to spot using available detection equipment. Some detection taggants also have identification abilities so that they can be used both before and after detonation for detection purposes. *See also* Identification Taggants.
- **Detonation.** An explosive reaction that consists of the propagation of a shockwave through the explosive accompanied by a chemical reaction that furnishes energy to sustain the shock propagation in a stable manner, with gaseous formation and pressure expansion following shortly thereafter.
- **Detonation Velocity.** The rate at which the detonation wave travels through a column of explosives.
- **Detonator.** A device used to initiate an explosion using a primary explosive. Detonators are either instantaneous or delay charges, including electric blasting caps of either type, blasting caps using fuses, detonating cord, shock tube, and other detonator types.
- **Detonator Cord.** A flexible cord that has a high explosive core and is used to initiate detonation of other explosives.
- **Electric Match.** An electrical device used to ignite a fuse or explosive using electrical current. In the pyrotechnic world, they are called *squibs.*
- **Emulsion.** A material composed of substances that, like oil and water, will not mix (immiscible). Explosive emulsions consist of oxidizers dissolved in water and surrounded by a fuel that will not mix with the water.
- **Explosive.** A chemical or nuclear a material that, when detonated by various means, such as heat, shock, electrical impulse, or chemical or nuclear reaction, rapidly expands in a self-propagating decomposition, the result of which is the production of heat, gasses, and possible shock waves as a result.
- **Explotracer Taggant.** A substance used to trace the source of an explosive after detonation. It uses special granules dyed with fluorescent pigments and specific rare earths for further specific identification. Similar tracers include Microtrace and HF6.
- **Federal Dealer.** Someone who wholesales or retails explosives legally.
- **Federal License.** A legal license to manufacture import, buy or sell, or transport explosive material, either within the country or internationally.
- **Filler.** The substance that forms the basis of an improvised explosive device, which is combined with some type of initiation system.
- **Fuel.** A material that reacts with oxygen either in the air or as produced by an oxidizer as part of an explosive reaction.
- **High Explosive (HE).** Explosive that can explode even when unconfined and generates a very high rate of reaction, high pressure, and a detonation wave (faster than sound).
- **Identification Taggants.** Markers added to explosive materials used to trace the exact source of the explosive after detonation, including the manufacturer, the date, and the shift at which it was produced.
- **Importer.** Anyone importing explosives into the United States for sale or distribution.
- **Isotag.** A way of tagging explosives by creating unique isotopes of some of the ingredients. These isotopes will have specific unique numbers of neutrons—more or fewer than normal—and the residue of an explosive can be analyzed by sophisticated equipment to determine the source of the explosive.
- **Licensee.** Someone licensed to manufacture, distribute, buy or sell, or import/export explosives.

- **Low Explosive (LE).** A material that does not detonate under most conditions but will burn or "deflagrate" when ignited.
- **Metric Ton.** A measurement sometimes applied to explosives—2,204.6 pounds or 1,000 kilograms.
- **Microsphere.** A tiny (37-840 microns) ball of solid glass used as a holder for chemical tags used in identifying explosives.
- **Microtaggant.** First developed by the 3M Company, used in identifying explosives with a color-coded polymer microchip. The chip consists of 10 layers, including a magnetic layer and one that is coded with fluorescent material.
- **Nitrogen.** One of the primary ingredients of most high explosives. Others include phosphorus and potassium.
- **Oxidizer.** A material that will readily yield oxygen or that produces other oxidizing materials in the combustion of organic matter or fuels. A common example is nitrate.
- **Permit.** Required for the purchase of explosives for use or transport.
- **PET (Peroxide Explosive Tester).** A device that can detect peroxide-based explosives (TATP) favored by terrorists.
- **PETN.** Pentaerythritol tetranitrate, used primarily in detonation cord with a detonation velocity of 21,000 feet per second, making it nearly as powerful as nitroglycerin or RDX. It is stable and safe for transportation when combined into detonation cord.
- **Photoflash Powder.** Explosive used to create a loud sound and bright flash when ignited. Often contains potassium perchlorate or antimony sulfide combined with powdered aluminum.
- **Precursor Chemicals.** A substance (element or chemical compound) that can be further refined through chemical reactions into an explosive compound.
- **Pyrotechnic.** Specifically, a substance that produces a bright light and possibly a loud sound when ignited.
- **Reworked Explosive.** Recyclable part of the explosives manufacturing process that is either residue or below standards.
- **Sensitivity.** The common description for the ease with which a material can be ignited or detonated.
- **Slurry.** *See* Water Gel.
- **Smokeless Powder.** Mostly gelatinized cellulose nitrate compounds that are used as propellants and produce relatively low smoke output.
- **Taggant.** A substance used to identify an explosive material, either before use or after detonation. Taggants are also called *markers* or *tracer elements.*
- **TATP.** A peroxide-based explosive used extensively by terrorists.
- **Ton.** A non-metric ton is 2,000 pounds or .907 metric tons.
- **Tracer Element.** An identifier for explosives. *See also* Taggant.
- **Water Gel.** Explosive materials containing substantial amounts of water and high proportions of ammonium nitrate, some of which is in water solution. May be a high explosive or a blasting agent depending on sensitizing materials used. May be loaded in bulk or tube-type cartridges.

Modern Artillery

The natural segue from the discussion of siege equipment and cannons at the end of Chapter 33 and a natural direction to take the discussion of modern weapons is the category of modern artillery. I'll begin by discussing the evolution of artillery from muzzle-loading cannons to modern breech-loading guns with advanced and sophisticated types of ammunition.

The Modernization of Artillery

Early cannons had a lot in common with early handguns. They were both primarily smoothbore muzzle loaders. In the mid-1800s, the changes that occurred in handguns were paralleled by identical changes in artillery. For instance, new ammunition was being developed that carried the powder charge in a bag attached to the projectile. Since cannons did not have firing pins, the firing of such early fixed ammunition was somewhat complex. First, the bag was pierced by an ice pick–like device inserted through the vent. Next, a priming device was inserted down the vent and attached to a lanyard. A pull on the lanyard ignited the primer in the device, which in turn lit the powder and fired the gun.

Another type of mid-19th century shell was made to explode, either in the air or upon impact. These explosive shells were still crude by comparison with later armaments, but they did do away with having to light a fuse before loading the cannon.

At the same time that rifled barrels were becoming standard on handguns, the same was rapidly becoming true with artillery. Rifled barrels could effectively increase the weight of the shells fired from the same caliber and the range of equivalent smoothbore guns. In addition, the stabilizing effect of the rifled barrel allowed for more reliable explosive shells with front-mounted percussion firing mechanisms that could just about be guaranteed to hit nose first. Two main types of early shells for rifled barrels included the *parrot*, which had a soft metal cup in the base that was forced into the grooves of the rifling, and the *studded* shell, which had projecting "studs" that matched the rifling.

Breech-Loading Artillery

As it was with handguns, there were breech-loading cannons as early as the 15th century, but with the technology of the day, it was far more practical to design and build muzzle loaders. That all changed in the middle of the 19th century. With the development of self-contained shells and the practical application of rifled barrels, breech-loading guns became both more feasible and significantly more desirable, in part because it was much harder develop ammunition for muzzle-loading rifled artillery (as seen with the parrot and studded shells). Breech loaders were generally advantageous anyway, in that they could be loaded more quickly and more easily than muzzle loaders and, with the increasing use of rifled barrels, they could achieve a tighter fit and therefore more power and distance, and they could fire a heavier shell. Increases in caliber also have added significantly to the weight of a shell. A 100-percent increase in the caliber with a proportionate increase in the length of the shell works out to about a 700-percent increase in weight.

One necessary challenge that had to be met was how to seal the breech from the terrific force of the explosion. Two main methods were developed:

- The Quick Firing (QF) method uses a brass casing that expands into the breech, much the way a rifle cartridge does, and prevents any gasses from escaping out the back.
- The De Bange system can fire without a cartridge case. It uses a piston-like assembly with a mushroom-shaped end. A soft *obturator ring* compresses and completely seals the barrel as the piston is driven back by the force of the blast.

Each of these breech-sealing methods uses a different style of shell:

- Fixed ammunition is essentially like a bullet but much larger. It is a self-contained unit with a brass cartridge case that carries the propellant charge, the primer, and a payload of whatever kind is being used.
- Semi-fixed ammunition still uses a brass cartridge, but it is separate from the shell to be fired. This has the advantage of allowing a different strength of charge to be used to adjust for trajectory and range, if required.

- Separate loading systems, used with the De Bange breech-lock systems, use a bag that contains the primer, charge, and a separate shell. Like the semi-fixed ammunition, this type allows adjustment of the charge to compensate for range and trajectory changes.

Modern Ammunition

This section contains information about artillery ammunition used since WWI. It also includes some newer missile technologies that are currently being used in what are traditionally artillery situations.

Modern artillery shells are used for several purposes and use different types of triggering systems, or *fuzes.* There are several types of fuzes, including:

- **Time.** The shell is fired and explodes according to a set timer.
- **Time and Impact.** The shell will explode according to a set timer, but also upon impact, whichever comes first.
- **Proximity.** The shell uses radio waves to detect when it is near its target and explodes at a set distance.
- **Instantaneous Impact.** The shell explodes immediately upon hitting the target.
- **Delayed Impact.** The shell explodes moments after hitting the target, allowing the maximum penetration before explosion.

NOTE

Shell caliber is measured by the width of the bore of the gun. Sometimes the length of the barrel is measured in terms of the weapon's caliber—so many calibers. For instance, an 8-inch caliber gun with an 80-inch barrel might be described as 8in of 10 calibers.

Modern artillery is used in anti-personnel, anti-structure, anti-armor, or anti-aircraft applications, and a variety of different types of shells are used, based on the application required:

- **Shrapnel.** Used early in WWI to deliver deadly fragments over a wide area, it operated off a time fuze.
- **High Explosive (HE).** Probably the most common type of shell, the HE explodes and scatters fragments of its casing, which generally do most of the damage. The fuzes on such weapons can be set to explode in the air, spreading maximum fragments; on hitting the target; in the ground, which minimizes fragmentation but can create a strong shockwave in the ground itself; or into underground or covered installations.
- **Armor-Piercing (AP).** The pure AP shell is not very common today, but it was once a standard type of shell made with an extra-strong case and a shaped nose designed to penetrate armor. It was especially useful against naval targets. Some had a small bursting charge while others had none at all.
- **Armor-Piercing, Discarding Sabot (APDS).** A variant of the AP shell that was smaller than the caliber of the gun. It was carried in a light alloy *sabot* that would drop off after the shell emerged from the muzzle. This sub-caliber shell would then be able to attain much higher velocity and penetrate more effectively against its target. Typical shells were made of tungsten for density and increased penetration. A variation of this type of shell uses fins for stabilization and is constructed very long and thin for maximum penetration. Once a shell gets more than approximately 10 times longer than its width, it becomes unstable in flight, even with the spin applied from a rifled barrel. With the addition of fins, this type of shell looks a lot like a large metal arrow. This type can also be made of tungsten, but the most effective models are made from depleted uranium, which is 70-percent denser than lead. In addition, depleted uranium melts and burns as it penetrates steel, making it sharper rather than duller, and when it hits air on the other side of the armor, it bursts into a white-hot fireball, showering particles of molten shrapnel.

NOTE

Shaped Charges. *One of the most significant technologies used in anti-tank weaponry of the past 50 years is the* shaped charge. *The way this works is to have a shell with a high explosive contained in the body with what is called a* distance tube *on the leading edge. When the distance tube hits the target, it ignites the high explosive, which then funnels all its energy in a narrow jet of hot gas, burning through the armor plate and forcing hot metal and gas, along with blinding light, into the interior of the tank in what are called* after-armor *effects, otherwise known as* spalling. *This can kill the crew or ignite their ammunition.*

NOTE

Spalling. *This term originally described the flaking of concrete or masonry, where outer layers of a structure may separate and parts break off. The military use of it, with regard to anti-tank warfare, means the breaking or flaking of interior metal from the armor, which is caused by the explosion against the surface of the tank by a HEAT, HESH, or HEP type of artillery shell or other similar weapon. The result is a lot of high-speed debris flying around in a small space. Bad for equipment, worse for occupants.*

- **High Explosive, Anti-Tank (HEAT, which stands for High Energy/Explosive Anti-Tank).** Developed during WWII, the shaped charge is devastating against conventionally armored tanks. It uses the principle of the shaped charge to blast through tank walls and kill the occupants, possibly igniting any unused ordnance. HEAT charges are made with long, thin nose probes that are used to ignite the charge at the optimal distance from the tank's armor and to funnel the force of the explosion into the tank's walls. Although HEAT shells are highly effective against conventional tank armor, they have been defeated by the development of new kinds of armor, such as reactive and composite armor. (See the "Modern Armor" section for more.)
- **High Explosive, Squash Head (HESH) or High Explosive, Plastic (HEP).** These are anti-tank shells developed after the HEAT shell. They feature a very thick case that usually contains a charge of plastic explosive. When the shell hits a tank, it flattens against the armor plate, then detonates. This causes a considerable compressive shock that reflects off the interface of air and metal inside the tank. The result is that it spalls a "scab" of metal off the inside and propels it into the tank's interior. This type of shell is defeated by *spaced armor*. It is also the most effective shell used for demolishing structures of brick or concrete.
- **MCLOS.** Manual Command to Line-of-Sight missiles are guided to the target by hand-operated guidance systems in which the operator must track both the target and the missile.
- **SACLOS.** Semiautomatic Command to Line-of-Sight missiles have automatic systems that correct the missile's flight to target. Two primary methods are used. With radio link and wire-guided SACLOS missiles, the instructions are relayed from a sighting device, which sends correction information to the missile. Radio linking can be jammed, however, and wire guidance is limited to the length of the wire. The second type of guidance system is called the *Beam-Riding SACLOS*. It uses a sighting device that emits a signal directing the missile, which has sensors either in the back, to receive signals from the sighting device, or in the nose, to receive signals reflected by the sighting device from the target. This system was used commonly in anti-aircraft roles and used radar to send the beam. Another method being employed now uses a laser directed by the operator onto the target. The missile has a sensor that can detect the laser's signature and guide the missile. Examples: Wire-guided MILAN; radio-guided ASM-N-2 Bat; laser beam riding Kornet.
- **Artillery-Delivered Mines.** Shells that will scatter landmines across a remote area. Instant minefield.
- **Chemical Shells.** These use a small explosive charge to disperse a chemical compound. The compounds used will vary, and most of them have been banned by treaties—which doesn't mean they don't exist and might not be used.

- **AGM-84D Harpoon.** U.S. air-to-surface turbojet missile weighs 1,145 pounds. Range is "over the horizon," uses sea-skimming cruise monitored by radar altimeter; active radar terminal homing.
- **AGM-86B/C.** U.S. air-launched cruise missiles powered by turbofan jets. Weighs 3,150 pounds. Approximate ranges: AGM-86B: 1,500-plus miles; AGM-86C: 600 nautical miles. Guidance systems: AGM-86B, Litton inertial navigation element with terrain contour-matching updates; AGM 86C, Litton INS element integrated with multi-channel onboard GPS.

Nonlethal Shells

Shells that are not designed for lethal purposes may still ignite unintentional fires, and, of course, anyone hit by the spent carrier would, in all likelihood, sustain serious injury or die.

- **Smoke.** Used to create a smokescreen, these usually use white phosphorus, although there are variants that carry and distribute smoke grenades.
- **Illumination.** Used to release a pyrotechnic flare, which may emit white, colored, or even infrared light. It is released at a planned altitude and slowly drifts to the ground on a heat-resistant parachute.
- **Carrier.** Used to distribute items from a container. Often, these shells carry and release propaganda leaflets, but other items may be distributed via these shells. For instance, the weapons that deliver smoke grenades as well as the landmines of the artillery-delivered mine shell could be considered carrier shells.

Rocket-Powered Ammunition

Many anti-tank and air-to-air weapons employ rocket-powered ammunition. Here are some of the main types in use. These are man-portable or vehicle-mounted systems. For other types of missiles, see the "Modern Rockets and Missiles" section.

- **Tow.** U.S. two-stage anti-tank missile that weighs 40 pounds and has a range of 3,280 yards, vehicle or tube fired. Uses SACLOS guidance system.
- **Harpon.** Two-stage French anti-tank missile that weighs 67 pounds and has a range of 3,280 yards, guide rail or vehicle launched. Uses SACLOS guidance system.
- **Mamba.** West German anti-tank missile that weighs 24.7 pounds and has a range of 2,188 yards. Uses MCLOS guidance system.
- **Cobra 2000.** West German anti-tank missile, single stage plus booster, that weighs 227 pounds and has a range of 2,188 yards. Uses MCLOS guidance system.
- **Snapper.** Soviet anti-tank missile that weighs 49 pounds and has a range of 2,950 yards, guide rail or vehicle launched. Uses MCLOS guidance system.
- **Milan.** French/West German two-stage anti-tank missile that weighs 14.66 pounds and has a range of 2,188 yards, tube fired. Uses SACLOS guidance system.
- **Swingfire.** British wire-guided anti-tank missile with a range of 4,376 yards, fired from container or vehicle. Uses MCLOS guidance system.
- **Sagger.** Soviet anti-tank missile that weighs 24.9 pounds and has a range of 3,280 yards, guide rail, vehicle or man-carried launchers. Uses MCLOS guidance system.
- **Sparviero.** Three-stage (launcher, booster, and sustainer) Italian anti-tank missile that weighs 36.4 pounds and has a range of 3,280 yards, fired from tripod or vehicle. Uses SACLOS guidance system. Uses MCLOS guidance system.
- **Hellfire.** U.S. anti-tank missile that weighs 94.79 pounds and had a range of 5,470 yards, fired from helicopters or other air platforms. Uses terminal laser guidance system.

- **Grail (SA-7).** Soviet anti-air missile that weighs 33 pounds and has a range of 6.2 miles. Uses infrared homing guidance.
- **Blowpipe.** British anti-air missile that weighs 28 pounds. Uses radio command and optical tracking.
- **RBS 70.** Swedish anti-air missile that weighs 44 pounds and has a range of 3 miles. Uses laser beam-riding guidance.
- **Stinger.** U.S. anti-air missile that weighs 34.5 pounds with a 1- to 8-km range. Uses passive infrared or ultraviolet homing guidance.
- **Phoenix (AIM-54A).** U.S. air-to-air missile that weighs 985 pounds with a range of 126.7 miles, inertial, semi-active, and active radar/terminal guided.
- **Aspide.** Italian air-to-air missile weighs 486 pounds with a range of 50 miles, semi-active radar.
- **Saab 372.** Swedish missile that weighs 242 pounds, with infrared homing.
- **R-40R/T (AA-6A/B Acrid).** Russian air-to-air missile that weighs 475 kg with a range of 30 km (R-40) or 50 km (R40TD and R-40RD), with command, inertial, and semi-active radar guidance (on R-40T).
- **Magic R.550.** French air-to-air missile that weighs 198 pounds with a range of 31 miles, with infrared homing.
- **Magic 2 R.550 Mk2.** French air-to-air missile that weighs 198 pounds with a range between 320 meters and 5400 meters, infrared.
- **SRAAM.** British air-to-air missile with a range of 5 miles, with infrared homing.
- **AIM-9L/M Sidewinder.** U.S. air-to-air missile that weighs 188 pounds with a range of about 6 miles, infrared homing.
- **AIM-120A AMRAAM (Advanced Medium Range Air-to-Air Missile).** U.S. air-to-air missile that weighs 335.2 pounds with a range of 20+ miles (one source says 45 miles), inertial midcourse correctable, plus active radar.
- **AIM-7F/M Sparrow.** U.S. air-to-air missile that weighs 503 pounds with a range of 58.8 miles, with inverse-monopulse semi-active radar.
- **Skyflash.** British air-to-air missile weighs 425 pounds with a range of 28 miles, with monopulse semi-active radar.
- **AIM-132 ASRAAM.** European air-to-air missile that weighs 220.5 pounds with a range from 300 meters to 15 km, with strapdown inertial plus imaging infrared.
- **MICA.** French air-to-air missile that weighs 242.5 pounds with a range of 31.1 miles, with a combination of inertial, active, and semi-active radar, plus infrared on final approach.
- **Mistral (ATAM).** French air-to-air missile that weighs 18 kg with a range of 5 km, infrared.
- **Matra.** French air-to-air missile weighs 551.1 pounds with a range of 21.75 miles, semi-active radar.
- **Python 3.** Israeli air-to-air missile that weighs 264.6 pounds with a range between .5 km to 15 km, infrared.
- **Python 4.** Israeli air-to-air missile that weighs 264.6 pounds with a range between .5 km to 15 km, infrared.
- **R-60 (AA-8 Aphid).** Russian air-to-air missile that weighs 65 kg with a range of between 3–10 km, infrared (all aspect).
- **R-33E (AA-9 Amos).** Russian air-to-air missile that weighs 490 kg with a range of 160 km, inertial with command updates and semi-active radar.
- **R-27R/T (Aa-10 Alamo A/B/C/D).** Russian air-to-air missile that weighs 253 kg (R-27R), 254 kg (R-27T), 350 kg (R-27RE), 343 kg (R-27TE) with a range of 80 km (R-27R), 70 km (R-27T), 130 km (R-27RE), 120 km (R-27TE), SARH (R-27R, R27E), all-aspect infrared (R-27T, R-27TE).
- **R-73 (AA-11 Archer).** Russian air-to-air missile weighs 105 kg (R-73M1), 115 kg (R-73M2) with a range of 20 km (r-73M1), 30 km (R73M2), all-aspect infrared.
- **R-77 (AA-12 Adder).** Russian air-to-air missile that weighs 175 kg with a range of 50, 90, and 150 km, with radio command with active radar at terminal phase (<20 km).

- **PL-7.** Chinese air-to-air missile that weighs 196.25 pounds with a range from .5 to 14.4 km, all-aspect infrared.
- **PL-10.** Chinese air-to-air missile with a range from .37 miles, with radar-guided semi-active terminal.
- **SRAM.** U.S. nuclear air-to-surface missile that weighs 2,204 pounds and has a range of 100 miles, with a programmed inertial guidance system.
- **AGM-88 HARM "Anti-Radiation" Missile.** U.S. air-to-surface missile that weighs 780.4 pounds and has a range of more than 30 miles, with a passive radiation guidance system. Specifically designed to attack enemy radar-equipped air defense systems.
- **Kormoran (AS.34).** German air-to-surface missile that weighs 1,323 pounds and has a range of 23 miles, with inertial guidance and active terminal radar.
- **RB O 4E.** Swedish air-to-surface missile that weighs 1,323 pounds and has a range of 20 miles, with active radar.
- **Maverick (AGM-65 various versions).** U.S. air-to-surface missile. Weights: AGM-65B/H, 462 pounds; AGM-65D, 485 pounds; AGM-65E, 777 pounds; AGM-65F, 804 pounds; AGM-65G, 670 pounds; AGM-65K, 793 pounds. Range is classified—some versions are 30 miles. Guidance systems: AGM-65B/H/K, electro-optical television; AGM-65D/F/G, imaging infrared; AGM-65E, laser guided.
- **Sea Skua.** British air-to-surface missile that weighs 496 pounds and has a range of 9.3+ miles, with semi-active radar.
- **AGM-130.** U.S. air-to-surface missile that weighs 2,917 pounds (range classified), with TV/imaging infrared seeker "man-in-the-loop," autonomous GPS/INS. (Cost per unit according to the U.S. Air Force is $450,000.)

Mobility

At the beginning of the modern era of artillery, many cannons and howitzers were still hauled by teams of horses, but mechanization changed all that. The carriages used by mobile cannons also varied. Early ones had a *trail* that was used to haul and stabilize the gun. However, the single trail got in the way of the breech when aiming the cannon, so two new styles were developed—the *box* trail and the *split* trail, which were shaped pretty much the way they are described. Because these guns created a lot of recoil, they were often fitted with spades that would dig into the ground to prevent the gun from moving backward when fired. However, ultimately, recoil was further reduced by the development of a hydraulic inhibitor or brake. It worked by forcing a quantity of oil through a narrow opening. At the same time, the force of recoil was used to compress an air chamber, which, after firing, would push the assembly back to the firing position. The first gun to use this technology was the French M1897 75mm Field Gun, known as the *Seventy Five.*

Size Matters

Modern artillery comes in a great variety of sizes. For instance, field guns had to be light enough to be mobile and easily moved to new positions. Even so, field guns got bigger and bigger. Ultimately, some field guns became self-propelled—close relatives to tanks. In contrast, there were siege guns, which required a stable installation from which to operate, and guns designed specifically for coastal defense and fortress installations.

Field Guns

Here are a few examples that demonstrate the range of guns that were mobile enough to be deployed in the field.

- **Pack Artillery.** Several small artillery units were designed to be transported by animals—particularly those units that would be used in mountains, jungles, and other terrain that was difficult to traverse with a heavy gun in tow. Some examples include:
  - **British 10-pounder Mountain Gun.** A 2.75-in caliber gun of the WWI era designed to be taken apart, with a barrel that would screw apart, gaining it the nickname *screwgun*. It had a range of 6,000 yards.
  - **Japanese 70mm Type 92 Infantry Gun.** A 2.75-in gun from the WWII era that could be taken apart and carried by men in the jungle. It fired a variety of shells, including HE, smoke, shrapnel, and armor-piercing.
  - **U.S. 75mm M1A1 Pack Howitzer.** A 2.95in-caliber gun with a range of 9,760 yards, used in WWII. Originally designed to be carried by pack mules, it was more commonly delivered to the battlefield by parachute or glider. It could fire fixed HEAT shells or semi-fixed HE shells.
  - **Italian 105/14 Model 56 105mm Howitzer.** Highly versatile field gun developed in the late 1950s that could be packed by 11 mules, aircraft, helicopters, parachutes, towing vehicles, or even, for short distances, by men. It could fire 4.13-in shells at a range of 11,564 yards—either fixed HEAT or semi-fixed HE shells.
- **15-Pounder BL Mk2.** British field gun of the late 19th and early 20th centuries. Fired a 3-in caliber shell up to 6,000 yards. It primarily was used for anti-personnel shrapnel shells.
- **French M1897 75mm Field Gun.** The first of the modern artillery to include a hydraulic recoil absorber.
- **British 13-Pounder QF Horse Artillery Gun.** A WWI-era field gun with a recoil system and QF breech sealing. It used 3-in caliber ammunition and had a range of 5,900 yards.
- **German 77mm QF.** WWI field gun that fired a 3.03-in caliber shell up to 9,200 yards and used a breech assembly called a *sliding wedge*.
- **British 6-in Howitzer.** A standard howitzer of WWI, said to have fired more than 22 million rounds from 1914 through 1918. It fired 6-in caliber ammunition up to a range of 9,500 yards.
- **French St. Chamond Tracked Mount.** A WWI self-propelled gun that was transported by a tractor that carried a generator to power the electric motors of both the tractor and the gun trailer.
- **British 25-Pounder, Mk2.** An elaborate WWII-era weapon that could serve as either a gun or a howitzer, based on the size of the charge. It was mounted on a circular platform, which allowed it to rotate quickly for aiming. It fired a 3.45-in caliber shell up to 13,400 yards.
- **German 10.5cm 1eFH18.** WWII-era German field howitzer that fired a 4.13-in caliber shell up to 11,670 yards. It fired HE, HEAT, smoke, incendiary, illuminating, and even propaganda carrier shells.
- **U.S. 155mm M2.** A WWII-era field gun, known as *Long Tom* for its long barrel. It shot a 6.1-in caliber shell up to 24,000 yards and could be loaded with HE, armor-piercing, and smoke shells. Shell weight: 95 pounds.
- **French 155mm MkF3.** A self-propelled howitzer of the modern era. It required an eight-man crew, who rode in a separate vehicle. It fired 6.1-in caliber shells up to 21,000 yards. It could travel up to 27 mph. Its shells weighed about 94 pounds.
- **U.S. 8-in Howitzer.** Two versions—M110 self-propelled (which weighs 58,000 pounds and can travel at up to 34 mph) and M115 towed. It fires 8in-caliber shells up to 18,370 yards and can use HE, HE spotting, rocket-assisted HE. and nuclear shells.
- **Soviet 76.2mm M1942.** A 3-in caliber field gun with a range of 13,290 yards that can use HE, HEAT, armor-piercing HE, and High Velocity Armor Piercing Tracer (HVAPT) shells.
- **U.S. 155mm M109.** A self-propelled medium howitzer with an enclosed turret, making it in essence a mini-tank. It can travel up to 34 mph and fires 6.1-in caliber shells with a range up to 15,970 yards. It can fire separate-loading HE, chemical, canister, and nuclear shells, weighing up to 95 pounds. One of the reasons for using the separate-loading ammunition is to allow two rounds to hit the

same target at the same time. This is done by using a light charge first, at a high, slow trajectory, then firing a heavy charge on a fast, flat trajectory. Both shells hit at the same time.

- **Field Howitzer 70.** A multinational design with a motor assist, it fires 6.1-in caliber shells with a range up to 26,250 yards. It can fire semi-fixed HE, illuminating, and rocket-assisted HE shells (which have additional range up to 32,800 yards). The shell weight of an HE shell is 96 pounds.

Modern Mortars

Early and modern mortars have some things in common: They are (primarily) muzzle-loading weapons designed to fire at a very steep angle. However, whereas early mortars were essentially cannons, modern mortars are really bomb or rocket launchers.

The modern mortar was invented in 1914 at the beginning of WWI as a trench warfare weapon—particularly adapted to take out the German machine-gun nests that were wreaking havoc on the British troops. The Stokes trench mortar, named after its inventor, was a simple 3-inch-diameter smooth-bore tube with a metal cap fitted to the base. This 51-inch barrel rested on a metal base plate, which prevented it from digging into the ground when fired, and was supported by a bipod assembly, which could be adjusted to change the angle of fire. The weapon was fired by dropping a mortar shell into the tube. A shotgun-like blank cap on the shell would hit the fixed firing pin and ignite the primer and then the primary propellant rings, which would launch the bomb. The whole assembly broke down into three parts and weighed 108 pounds altogether. The rounds weighed 11 pounds each.

The British made some use of the new mortar starting in 1915, but it was the Americans, when they entered the war, who fully adopted the weapon, as they were more committed to an aggressive war, and the highly portable Stokes weapon, known to the Americans as the *3-inch trench mortar, Mark I*, was used extensively.

The ammunition used in these first mortars was a high-explosive shell that would detonate on impact. The 11-pound 11-ounce shell carried about 2.25 pounds of an explosive called *Trojan* nitrostarch, although TNT was sometimes used. The shells were color-coded according to the amount of propellant charge they carried. The more propellant, the farther and the faster the shell would travel. Range adjustment was a combination of the amount of propellant used and the angle at which the firing tube was set. The shells had safety catches that would be released before they were fired.

Since WWI, the field mortar has undergone some changes. The post-WWI era Stokes-Brandt design featured some additional mechanisms for adjusting the angle of the barrel and some other improvements, but it was still essentially the same design. Today's mortars, such as the model PRB 424, include some that are disposable and have no bipod. They are simply set on the ground and a strap laid out. The person firing the mortar steps on the strap at a marked location, which sets the angle of fire indicated by that mark on the strap. Other modern uses of mortars include the *multi-spigot* design, which can fire an array of mortars simultaneously, with the ability to cover about 1.5 acres with lethal fragments.

Field mortars, such as the Stokes and PRB 424, are classified as *light* mortars. There are also medium and heavy mortars. The heavier the mortar, the more likely it will have to be conveyed to battle on some kind of vehicle or on a trailer of some sort. Mortars up to 240mm caliber exist.

The area in which mortar technology has advanced the most is in the ammunition. Whereas the first mortars were essentially high-explosive bombs, modern mortars can fire a variety of shells, with a variety of options. High-explosive bombs, for instance, can be set to detonate on impact, on a delayed fuze (resulting in deeper penetration of armor), or as an air-burst shell for anti-personnel use. Mortar shells can also be used as smoke bombs, emitting sudden dense clouds of white phosphorus or releasing a slower curtain of smoke over several minutes. Still other shells can be used to release flares high in the air, illuminating an area or sending signals. In theory, mortar shells can also be used to spread gas or other agents into a battlefield.

Modern mortar shells are generally fitted with fins for stability, although some are also fired from rifled barrels. Generally, mortars are muzzle loaders, but the larger ones—too large to be loaded from the muzzle—are breech loaders. Most mortars are fired by the impact of the shell dropping into the tube, but some have optional trigger systems as well.

Static and Rail Guns

Some of the biggest guns made were used in siege conditions during WWI. They were assembled in semi-permanent emplacements or mounted on rails, sometimes with special angled tracks or turntables to allow more aiming range. These guns were mammoth in size, and their shells were sometimes as tall as a man. The kind of bombardment they provided in WWI has since been replaced by aircraft, so most of these guns are relics of a past era.

- **German 42cm Siege Howitzer (Big Bertha).** A monster howitzer that fired shells weighing 205 pounds.
- **British 12-in Mk4 Siege Howitzer.** A 37-ton beast that used an additional 20 tons of ballast to fire 750-pound HE shells up to 14,000 yards.
- **French 40mm Modele 1916 Railroad Howitzer.** Transported on special rails, this howitzer could fire 15.75-in caliber shells up to 17,500 yards. The shells weighed in at a more than hefty 1,984 pounds!
- **Paris Gun.** A siege gun developed by the Germans to bombard Paris during WWI, it fired small-caliber ammunition, accelerated through an extra-long barrel to very high velocities. It was fired into the upper atmosphere, where it encountered reduced air resistance and was able to attain a range of nearly 75 miles. The barrel was so eroded after each shot that the ammunition had to be adjusted between shots, and the barrel, which started at 8.26-in caliber, had to be rebored to about 9.13 inches after 70 shots.

Defense Guns (Coastal and Fortress)

On average, the largest guns have been those in fixed emplacements, such as fortresses and coastal defenses. Pre-WWII guns were mounted using four types of mountings:

- **Casemate.** The gun is mounted in a chamber, theoretically bombproof, and fires from within it. Casemate mountings were used by the Germans on the beaches to defend against the allied D-Day invasion. Their effectiveness is demonstrated by the fact that many of them still exist, despite sustaining direct hits.
- **Barbette.** The gun is mounted on a swivel and fires over a parapet that is curved to match the arc of the gun's rotation.
- **Disappearing Mount.** The gun is loaded in a pit and only raised for firing.
- **Cupola.** The gun is mounted in a steel dome, the upper rim of which is flush with the ground. Cupola emplacements were used also for machine guns and other weaponry.

Automatic Artillery and Machine Guns

Fully automatic weapons, such as submachine guns and assault rifles, have already been mentioned in the handgun and small arms section. Here, we deal with larger-scale automatic weapons—both the full machine guns and automatic artillery, including automatic anti-tank and anti-aircraft guns.

The idea of a fully automatic weapon is just about as old as weapons themselves. Certainly, the idea of rapid fire goes back to the bow and, especially, to the crossbow, where various schemes have been used to fire arrows in rapid succession. In guns there were many difficulties, all of which were overcome in the mid to late 19th century.

- Muzzle loading did not lend itself to rapid-fire devices, although some were tried. Various attempts to make multi-barreled weapons did succeed to a point, but although they could fire a volley of many simultaneous shots or several in succession, some were inherently dangerous to the person firing, and all required a long reloading time, so that the rate of fire could not be sustained.
- Black powder created a lot of smoke, and rapid-fire devices would create thick clouds of smoke that could blind the person firing and cause breathing difficulties.

These problems were solved by the combination of breech loading, self-contained cartridge ammunition, and smokeless powders, along with advances in machining and manufacture that came along with the Industrial Revolution.

Early attempts included hand-cranked mechanisms, guns with multiple barrels, and so forth.

- The most successful multi-barreled gun before the modern era was the Gatling gun, which, in its most refined models, could fire up to 1,200 rounds per minute. (Ironically, similar technology is used in today's "Minigun," which can achieve rates of fire up to 10,000 rounds per minute.)
- One even older attempt, the Organ gun of 1670, resembled drawings by Leonardo Da Vinci.
- Another, called the *Puckle's gun*, from 1718, was like an oversized revolver mounted on a tripod.
- In 1860, two years before the original Gatling gun, the Agar "coffee mill" used steel tubes as cartridges and could fire around 100 to 120 rounds per minute.
- In 1870, a French gun, called the *Montigny Mitraillieuse*, combined 37 barrels in a large tube and was loaded by a special plate that held 37 cartridges. It could be fired in a volley or in single shots in rapid succession.
- The 1873 Nordenfelt was a Swedish design that was manufactured in several calibers and found use in various settings, including as a naval deck-mounted gun. It could fire up to 100 rounds per minute.

The first modern machine gun was the Maxim gun, patented in 1883. This water-cooled gun was a true machine gun that, once a round was loaded in the breech, would fire automatically until the trigger was released or it ran out of ammo. It fired .45-in caliber rounds, up to 600 per minute. The Maxim was adopted in 1890 by the British, the German, and the U.S. militaries; however, only Germany had armed their troops with significant numbers of these weapons at the outbreak of WWI. Combined with the use of barbed wire as a barrier, this gave the Germans an early advantage in the war. By the end of the war, machine guns were being used on tanks and airplanes and in a variety of other ways, such as covering small advancing groups of soldiers.

In WWII, the influence of machine guns was significant, especially those mounted on airplanes and tanks. However, they were prominent on the ground as well. In modern warfare, machine guns have been, to some degree, replaced by assault weapons and weapons kits—multipurpose weapons, such as the Stoner system, in which one weapon can make use of different parts to perform a variety of roles.

How Machine Guns Work

Because machine guns must fire very rapidly, they have some added design challenges when compared to guns that fire one or even a few shots at a time.

- They must load and reload very quickly and reliably.
- They must have a mechanism to feed them ammunition in quantity.
- They must have a way to keep the barrel from overheating.

Firing

There are several methods used for firing machine guns—recoil, blowback, C Gas, and chain.

- **Recoil.** Before firing, the breechblock and the barrel are locked together. Each is on a separate spring. When the gun is fired, both move backward from the recoil, but the barrel stops short while the breechblock continues, ejecting the spent shell. At the point where the breech is opened, the pressure in the barrel is back to normal. A new round is inserted, and the breech is pushed back into position by the spring, as is the barrel.
- **Blowback.** In this system, the gas pressure pushes back the breech, which is on a strong spring. The breech opens, but only after a short delay, which is caused by the pressure of the spring and the weight of the breech itself. In some cases, an additional device is added to be sure the breech doesn't open until the pressure is sufficiently reduced in the barrel. Once the breech opens, the cartridge is ejected and the new one is seated as the spring closes the breech again, simultaneously firing the next round.
- **C Gas.** The breech and barrel are locked together in the C Gas system. When the cartridge is fired, the gas pressure bleeds into a chamber running parallel to the barrel. This pressure pushes a piston in the chamber and drives back the breechblock. The gun is reloaded and a strong spring pushes the breechblock back again.
- **Chain guns.** These use a separate motor to open and close the breech and eject and reload cartridges. They are more reliable than recoil and gas types. In addition, they can vary the rate of fire simply by varying the speed of the motor, and in the case of a misfire, they will eject the unfired cartridge and continue, whereas other systems will jam in the case of a misfire. A common chain gun is the M242 Bushmaster.

There is a real danger of a cartridge exploding in a hot barrel when a machine gun stops firing. This is countered by using an *open breech*, in which a cartridge will not be loaded until the trigger is fired. This open breech system will work with any of the firing methods described above.

Feeding Ammunition

How is ammunition delivered to the breech?

- **Hopper.** A basic angled box that drops the ammunition into place using gravity.
- **Magazine.** A spring-loaded box or drum that forces the shells into place.
- **Strip.** Cartridges held together on a stiff clip of metal.
- **Belt.** Cartridges held together on strips of cloth or by metal clips.

Cooling Systems

Here are a couple ways to cool a weapon:

- Water-cooled systems run water around the barrel. When the water boils from the heat, the steam can be collected into a container and recycled.
- Air-cooled systems use heat-radiating fins or even the mass of the barrel. Some use the explosion of firing to force air over the barrel. Most air-cooled systems also work best with quick-change spare barrels to rotate in times of heavy firing.

Gun Designations

Machine guns are designated by their size and, to some extent, by their intended roles. The following are major designations used by British and American armies (light, medium, and heavy):

- **Light Machine Gun (LMG) or "Squad Automatic."** Able to be carried by a man and fired from a bipod on the ground or standing. Uses a two-man crew—one to fire and one to handle ammunition and spare barrels, and so on. Used for close support.
- **Medium Machine Gun (MMG).** Used for sustained firing from the rear, although often taken farther forward by the Americans. Fired from a tripod and served by a small crew.
- **Heavy Machine Gun or "Fifty" (HMG).** High-caliber (.50-in) weapons that can be used in ground support or as an anti-aircraft gun.

Specific Machine guns

There have been many machine guns created through history. Here are a few to get you started:

Browning Machine Guns

In 1917, John Browning introduced the M1917 .30-caliber machine gun, and in 1918, the Browning Automatic Rifle, which was, in essence, a machine gun, though it looked more like an ordinary rifle. In 1919, he introduced the Browning Model 1919A4, which had a more typical machine-gun appearance and was used by the U.S. Cavalry in a variety of ways. Versions of Browning's heavy .50-caliber machine gun have been used continuously since 1933, with the most famous version being variants of the M2 .50 Browning machine gun.

- **Lewis Gun.** An important LMG of the WWI era, designed in America but used primarily by the British. .303 caliber, 26 pounds, gas-operated, drum magazine, 550 rpm, air-cooled, using muzzle blast to recirculate air over internal cooling vanes in the aluminum barrel.
- **Madsen.** Danish makers of various LMG models.
- **Hotchkiss Mk1.** WWII-era LMG used by various Allied armies. .303 caliber, 27 pounds, gas-operated, strip or belt ammunition, 500 rpm, air-cooled.
- **BAR M1918 A2.** BAR stands for *Browning Automatic Rifle.* LMG or *squad automatic* used in WWII. .30-06 caliber, 19.4 pounds, gas-operated, magazine-fed, 500 rpm, air-cooled.
- **Maxim 08/15.** German LMG. 7.92mm, 39 pounds, recoil system, belt-fed, 450 rpm, water-cooled.
- **ZB/vz26.** Czechoslovakian LMG made in 1926 using 7.92mm and other caliber ammunition, 21 pounds, gas-operated, magazine-fed, 500 rpm, air-cooled.
- **Bren Mk1.** Based on the ZB/vz26, one of the most successful LMGs of the WWII era. .303 caliber, 22 pounds 5 ounces, gas-operated, magazine-fed, 500 rpm, air-cooled with spare barrel.
- **Degtyarev DPM.** Soviet postwar copy of an earlier LMG. 7.62mm caliber, 26 pounds 13 ounces, gas-operated, drum magazine, 520–580 rpm, air-cooled.
- **10 Type 56.** Chinese copy of the Degtyarev DPM, used in various countries. 7.62mm, 15 pounds 7 ounces, gas-operated, belt-fed, 700 rpm, air-cooled.
- **Johnson M41.** American LMG with use by some services. .30-06 caliber, 14 pounds 5 ounces, recoil-operated, magazine-fed, 300–900 rpm (adjustable), air-cooled.
- **Finnish KK62.** Postwar LMG. 7.62mm caliber, 18.3 pounds, gas-operated, belt-fed, 1,000–1,100 rpm, air-cooled.
- **Browning-Colt Model 1914.** Nicknamed the *potato digger* because of a spade-like swinging lever. Various calibers, 101 pounds, gas-operated, belt-fed, 400–500 rpm, air-cooled.
- **Hotchkiss Model 1914.** Used in both World Wars, fires 8mm cartridges, 88 pounds, gas-operated, strip-fed, 600 rpm, air-cooled.

- **Browning M2.** HMG made in 1918. .50 caliber, 109 pounds, recoil operation, belt-fed, 600 rpm, air- or water-cooled.
- **Maxim PM1910.** Russian model used in both World Wars. 7.62mm, 152.5 pounds, recoil-operated belt-fed 600 rpm, water-cooled.
- **Maxim '08.** German machine gun of WWI, highly effective. 7.92mm, 70.5 pounds, recoil-operated, belt-fed, 450 rpm, water-cooled.
- **Schwarzlose Model 07/12.** Austrian MMG used in both World Wars. 7.92mm, 44 pounds, blowback system, belt-fed, 400 rpm, water-cooled.
- **Fiat-Revelli Model 1914.** Italian weapon updated in 1935 and used through WWII. 6.5mm, 37 pounds, delayed blowback, clip system and belt feed, water-cooled, 500 rpm, later air-cooled.
- **Degtyarev DShK 1938.** Soviet HMG used as an anti-aircraft gun. 12.7mm, 78.5 pounds, gas-operated, belt-fed, 550 rpm, air-cooled.
- **Type 92 Japanese 1938.** Based on the Hotchkiss. 7.7mm, 122 pounds, gas-operated, strip-fed (with oil device), 450–500 rpm, air-cooled.
- **Browning M1917.** Water-cooled gun that was the basis for later designs. .30-06 caliber, 41 pounds, recoil-operated, belt-fed, 450–500 rpm, water-cooled.
- **Vickers Mk 1.** British gun used from 1912 until 1965. Various models were made. It recirculated steam to recycle the water for the cooling system. It could be fired by compass bearings up to 4,500 yards. Reliable standard gun. .303 caliber, 88.5 pounds, recoil-operated, belt-fed, 450–500 rpm, water-cooled.
- **MG34 – GPMG (General Purpose Machine Gun).** German design from 1934; could be used as an LMG or an MMG. Used in WWII. 7.92mm, 26 pounds 11 ounces, recoil-operated, belt-fed, 800–900 rpm, air-cooled.
- **Kalashikov PK.** Soviet GPMG from the 1960s. 7.62mm, 19.75 pounds, gas-operated, belt-fed, 650 rpm, air-cooled.
- **SIG MG10-3.** Swiss design from 1961, used in various countries. Quick-change barrel. 7.62mm, 20.3 pounds, delayed blowback system, belt-fed, 600 rpm, air-cooled.
- **Stoner 63A.** Modular gun system that can serve various roles, created in 1963. Interchangeable parts allow it to be used as an LMG and in other roles (rifle, carbine, MMG, fixed machine gun, automatic rifle, and a drum-fed "Commando" LMG). 5.56mm, 11 pounds 11 ounces, gas-operated, belt-fed, 700 rpm, air-cooled.
- **MG42.** German WWII design with a versatile add-on tripod that handles recoil and can easily be reset for anti-aircraft use. 7.92mm, 25.5 pounds, recoil-operated, belt-fed, up to 1500 rpm, air-cooled (tripod weighs 34 pounds 13 ounces).
- **US M60.** Developed in the '50s, American GPMG with design features similar to the German MG42 and FG42. 7.62mm, 23 pounds, gas-operated, belt-fed, 600 rpm, air-cooled (tripod 15 pounds).
- **L7 A1.** British GPMG based on the Belgian FN MAG. 7.62mm, 22.3 pounds, gas-operated, belt-fed, 750–1,000 rpm, air-cooled (tripod weighs almost 30 pounds).
- **M2HB-QCB Heavy Machine Gun.** Tripod-mounted; fires explosive incendiary, ball, tracer, armor-piercing, and incendiary rounds.
- **FN M3M.** Fires up to 1,100 rpm, .50 caliber.
- **M249 (Minimi) LMG.** Adopted into the U.S. military in the early 1980s, a versatile weapon, reliable and capable of firing between 750–950 rounds per minute. Weight, fully loaded with 200 rounds, is about 22 pounds. Gas-operated, 5.56mm caliber.
- **FN MAG 58 GPMG.** Air-cooled, gas-operated general-purpose machine gun (GPMG) with quick-change barrels, approximately 23.5 pounds and 49 inches in length. It can fire .50-caliber ammunition at variable rates from 650–1,100 rounds per minute.

MOUNTED GUNS

Machine guns are ideally suited for use on vehicles and have been mounted on various types of tanks, boats, automobiles, planes, and helicopters since WWI.

The early WWI tanks had up to four machine guns mounted on *sponsons* on the sides of the vehicle. Today, with modern long-range weaponry, there are generally only two machine guns mounted on tanks—one for spotting the shot before firing the big gun and one for normal defensive use.

On ships, machine guns are used on small patrol boats for defense and offense. On larger boats, they are generally used for anti-aircraft defense, often in arrays of multiple guns since weight isn't a consideration on a large ship.

On planes, machine guns have become less important than they once were. In WWI, they were mounted on biplanes, first to shoot over the propeller or backward from the back seat, and later to shoot through the propeller with special synchronizing gears. In WWII, fighters often had twin machine guns in the wings and/or guns that fired from the nose. Bombers, such as the B-17 Flying Fortress, had machine gun turrets placed everywhere they could—in the rear, the sides, the top, the bottom. They bristled with guns, and the crossfire from a formation of bombers could be withering. Today's jets use rockets more than machine guns, but they still generally carry arrays of machine guns in the wings or under the fuselage. Helicopters often are fitted with front-mounted guns for ground strafing, as well as side mounts.

Tank-Mounted Guns

Here are just a few guns that were commonly mounted on tanks. See the section on "Tanks" for more information, and look up each type of tank to find out what guns they carried.

- **Vickers .5-in MkV.** A WWII gun with a water-cooling system linked with the cooling system of the tank.
- **BESA MkIII.** A British version of a Czech gun, the Zb53, used throughout WWII. It was also used by the Germans after they took the BRNO factory.
- **L37 A1.** British modern machine gun, a variant on the Belgian FN MAG.
- **MG73.** A U.S. gun used on the M60 tank.

Aircraft-Mounted Guns

A few aircraft-mounted guns. Of course, there have been many, so this is just a small sampling of the older models.

- **CEC Minigun.** Developed in the 1960s, this electric-powered descendant of the Gatling gun fires 7.62mm or 5.56mm rounds up to 6,000 per minute. It can be mounted on a helicopter side mount, among other uses.
- **Parabellum Model 14.** WWI machine gun used by the Germans on their planes.
- **Lewis Mk2.** British and American planes used this in WWI.
- **Vickers Mk2.** Also used in WWI by the British and American planes.
- **Browning M2 .50-in.** Possibly the most commonly used aircraft-mounted machine gun of WWII.
- **Browning Mk2 .303-in.** The machine gun mounted on Spitfires and Hurricanes during the Battle of Britain, early in the war. It was also used in bomber turrets.

Handheld Recoilless Guns (Rocket Launchers)

All guns are true to Newton's third law, which states, "To every action there is an equal and opposite reaction." In most handguns, the reaction is absorbed by the shoulder or other parts of the body and is called *recoil*. However, there is a class of guns that allows the force of the recoil to escape without being contained within the firing tube, either by allowing the gas to escape out the back or, in some versions, by using a free counterweight to absorb the backpressure. These recoilless guns are used primarily as anti-tank weapons.

The bazooka was developed during World War II for use as an anti-tank weapon. In its original form, it was a smooth-bore tube that fired a 2.36-in caliber anti-tank rocket and weighed only 13 pounds. The rockets fired by bazookas could attain a velocity of 25,000 feet per second. By the Korean War, bazooka rockets were 3.5 caliber and could penetrate armor plates of 11 inches thick. Today there are many sophisticated versions of the basic design, including disposable versions, such as the Swedish Miniman and the West German Armbrust.

Traditionally, the early bazookas were operated by two-man teams—one to load and the other to aim and fire. Today, many bazookas are preloaded and disposable and may even use fiberglass or plastic tubes to launch the rockets.

The essential operation of a recoilless gun is very simple. Pressing the trigger causes a firing pin to ignite the rocket. Where there has been a great deal of innovation and variety is in the ammunition—the rockets themselves.

One of the most significant technologies used in anti-tank weaponry is the *shaped charge*. The way this works is to have a shell with a high explosive contained in the body with what is called a *distance tube* on the leading edge. When the distance tube hits the target, it ignites the high explosive, which then funnels all its energy in a narrow jet of hot gas, burning through the armor plate and forcing hot metal and gas, along with blinding light, into the interior of the tank in what are called *after-armor* effects, otherwise known as *spalling*. This can kill the crew or ignite their ammunition. Such types of ammunition are called *HEAT (High Energy/Explosive Anti-Tank)*, and they are one of the common forms of anti-tank weapons.

Some other interesting innovations have been developed for these guns. For instance, some have rifled barrels, which cause the shell to spin and be more stable, but the spin also reduces the penetration effect of the shell. To counter that, an outer ring is mounted on bearings. This ring is set into rotation by the rifling in the barrel, but the shaped charge does not rotate and is, therefore, able to deliver all its power to the target. This system is used in the Carl-Gustaf RCL.

Another type of shell, used in the French ACL-APX gun, uses a separate rocket motor inside. The shell is fired normally, but the rocket motor takes it to the target. It can reach its full range of 660 yards in 1.25 seconds.

The U.S. Army M136 AT4 recoilless rifle is the Army's primary light anti-tank weapon—successor to the M72-series LAW (*Light Anti-tank Weapon*) first developed in the 1960s. It is a disposable fiberglass tube that carries a fin-stabilized, free-flight 84mm HEAT rocket cartridge. It has a range of up to 250 meters and can penetrate up to 14 inches of armor. The whole unit weighs 15 pounds and can be operated by one person.

Parts of a handheld rocket launcher (Venturi):

- Venturi fastening strap
- Firing-pin assembly
- Fire-rod tube
- Shoulder pad
- Cocking lever
- Pistol grip

- Trigger
- Front grip
- Iron foresight
- Telescopic sight
- Face pad
- Venturi axis-pin

Anti-Tank Guns

Although the first anti-tank weapons were nothing more than high-velocity rifles, most anti-tank weapons since WWI have used some modified form of ammunition as tank armor, and protection has become increasingly tough and sophisticated. In fact, there has been a constant evolution of tank defenses and anti-tank weapons meant to defeat them.

One predominant feature of a functional anti-tank weapon is that it should be able fire quickly at a moving target, use a flat trajectory to get quickly to the target, and disable or destroy the target before it can fire back. Modern weapons use guided systems for greater accuracy, precision, and ease of firing.

One of the predominant anti-tank weapons, beginning in WWII, is the recoilless gun, which uses a hollow tube to launch a heavy shell that can do considerable damage. (See "Modern Ammunition" for more information about the shells that can be used.) Because they are relatively lightweight and there is little or no recoil, these weapons can be used in a variety of situations. One of the dangers, however, is the backblast, which can be dangerous to troops behind the gun for up to 100 yards and can be severely dangerous within 15 feet to the rear. It can injure, destroy hearing, and even kill troops in its blast area.

- **Tank Gewehr 1918.** The first specific anti-tank weapon was a single-shot Mauser bolt-action rifle mounted on a bipod. It shot a .52 shell with a steel core bullet that could penetrate the relatively weak armor of the time. Other similar anti-tank rifles were deployed during WWI.
- **37mm PAK36.** The Panzer Abwehr Kanone was Germany's anti-tank weapon at the beginning of WWII, and other countries had similar guns. It fired a 1.45-in shell that was very soon made inadequate by improvements in tank armor. However, its usefulness was extended by the development of new ammunition, such as fin-stabilized HEAT bombs fired from the muzzle.
- **British 6-Pounder.** This weapon was adopted early in WWII but was soon replaced by a 17-pounder gun. It remained on the battlefield, however, and found its way to third-world countries long after the war was over. It fired 2.24-in shells.
- **Soviet M1944 100mm.** A 3.93-in caliber gun from late in WWII that could fire armor-piercing shells as well as HE and HEAT ammunition.
- **10.5cm LG40.** A German recoilless gun from 1940, the Leicht Geshütz could be delivered by parachute. It fired a 4.13-in HE projectile that was loaded before the drop. The casing would blow out the rear on firing.
- **M20 Recoilless Rifle.** A U.S. weapon from 1945 that doubled as a field gun, in which role it could fire HE or smoke rounds. It fired HEAT shells against tanks and could be carried by troops in two loads. The total weight was 158 pounds, and the range of its 2.95-in shells was about 7,000 yards.
- **U.S. 3.5-in M20 "Super Bazooka."** A rocket launcher weighing only 12.1 pounds that can fire a HEAT shell at up to 1,100 yards, fired from the shoulder.
- **U.S. 66mm M72 A2.** Disposable single-shot rocket launcher with telescoping tube weighing only 3 pounds, including the built-in rocket ammunition.
- **U.S. M47 Dragon.** Fires a wire-guided system with optical tracking with line-of-sight missile guidance and infrared missile tracking. The firing tube is disposable after firing, but the guidance system is reusable for subsequent missiles. It weighs 32 pounds.

Anti-Aircraft (AA) Guns

The role of aircraft in war began in WWI and continued to be of critical importance as the decades of the 20th century continued. To protect against air attacks, various defenses were created. These began with ground emplacements as well as airborne interceptors of various types. Guns have played a role throughout, although they are increasingly giving way to missiles and rockets.

AA guns have fired a variety of types of ammunition, including shrapnel shells, high explosives, proximity fuzes, and impact fuzes. During WWII, many shells were set to detonate at the calculated height of the planes, though later in the war, detection fuzes were developed that could "sense" the target within explosive range. In the 1930s, mechanical "predictors" were developed that could be used to guide gunners to the proper elevation, direction, and fuze settings for their AA guns. Modern AA employs missiles with MCLOS and, more likely, SACLOS guidance systems and HEAT warheads.

Here are some traditional AA guns from WWI to the present day:

- **British 12-Pounder AA gun.** Used in WWI, this gun was positioned along the coastlines of Britain. It was positioned on a pedestal mounting, allowing it full range of motion to point in any direction. This is an important aspect of aerial defense guns.
- **Swedish Bofors.** Used all over the world since the 1930s as a main defense against low-flying aircraft. They have been adapted to many types of mountings, including naval, self-propelled, and static mounts, and modern ones are fitted with radar-assisted aiming. They mostly fire 40mm shells.
- **88mm Flak36.** The main German anti-aircraft gun of WWII—the Flug Abwehr Kanone was the basis for many anti-aircraft guns, with a range up to about 26,250 feet.
- **3.7-in AA gun.** The British AA gun in use during WWII and still in service until about 1950, this gun had a range of about 35,000 feet and was ultimately fitted with more modern shells and technologies.
- **French AMX DCA 30.** A modern type of AA mounted on an AMX-tracked chassis and firing twin 30mm automatic cannons with radar fire-control systems on a revolving turret.

Naval Guns

The latter half of the 19th century produced many changes in the technology of guns and cannons, and these changes occurred also in the development of guns on ships. Along with the changes in the ships themselves, the 20th century ushered in an era of big battleships that lasted until the dominance of aircraft reduced them to a supporting role in modern warfare.

But guns didn't get much bigger, on average, than those that were mounted on the big battleships, and special technologies had to be developed to support these massive guns.

The model ship of the early 20th century was the British HMS Dreadnought, which mounted 10 12-inch guns and a secondary complement of 24 "12-pounders." The guns were arrayed in armored turrets around the deck so that she could fire broadside with eight guns at a time, as well as firing forward or to the stern.

Naval guns differed from other artillery in that they were ignited using electricity. This system was first used in the 1870s and ultimately became standard for naval guns. Passing a current through the primer would fire the gun.

Starting in the Civil War, armored ships began to appear, and the technology and design of armor continued to improve. It was logical, therefore, that the same effort would go into defeating that armor, and much research was done on armor-piercing shells, which had to be hard enough to damage the armor but not so hard as to be brittle. They also had to contain explosives that would detonate reliably and would have to be able to hit the smooth armor of the enemy ships at an oblique angle without simply bouncing or glancing off the smooth metal. One of the solutions found was called the *capped shell*, which had a softer steel cap over the point, which aided in penetration at oblique angles. Some even had a harder penetrating point within the soft cap.

On the larger ships, the big guns were contained in turrets, which could be controlled using hydraulics. The whole turret would rotate, and the guns could also be elevated or lowered. The crew was safely housed inside the turrets, which were heavily armored. Smaller boats used pedestal mountings instead of turrets.

Firing the big guns was a coordinated effort on the battleships and involved teams of observers and range-finders high in the superstructure of the ship, plus more range-finders in each turret. The data from each of these sources was processed on a large fire-control table, and the guns would be set and fired centrally from the captain's bridge.

One problem the big battleships encountered was their vulnerability to small, fast torpedo boats. To counter this threat, quick-firing guns were added to the arsenal. These guns could be aimed and fired by one gunner and could fire several large rounds a minute. They were often placed between decks in the WWI era, but by WWII they were replaced by High Angle (HA) guns capable of dealing with airborne threats as well.

After WWI, one of the main AA weapons elements of the arsenal included versions of the Swedish Bofors gun, a 40mm automatic cannon that could put a lot of shells in the air around enemy aircraft. Bofors guns were often mounted in arrays on ships.

Modern AA weapons are automated and are not manned. They are fed from magazines of ammunition below decks, where they are also controlled. Their rate of fire and technology allow even a medium gun to put out as much weight in ammunition as the big guns of earlier times.

Armored Fighting Vehicles (AFV)—a.k.a. Tanks

Armored fighting vehicles (also known as *tanks*) are a pretty modern invention, but they have ancestors in the ancient siege rams and towers and other armored war machines. In the 15th century, Leonardo Da Vinci drew out plans for an armored vehicle powered by four men working hand cranks, and a steam-powered tank was proposed in 1862 called (with faulty spelling) the *Anihilator*, which was inspired by the Civil War ironclad, the Monitor. There is even a statement in the Bible mentioning "chariots of iron."

But modern tanks came into existence during WWI and were first deployed in battle on September 15, 1915. The first tank—the Mark I—had two configurations, one with two 57mm guns and four machine guns and one with five machine guns and no cannons. The top speed of the Mark I was 4 mph on caterpillar tracks, and it was a noisy and unreliable machine, dangerous to its crew, difficult to maneuver, and easily exploited. However, it was the beginning of a history of tank warfare that still exists today.

The Mark I was followed by several versions, the Mark V being the most successful. A light tank, the Whippet, was also used successfully—with a top speed of 8 mph. When the U.S. entered the war, they used the British Mark Vs and a French light tank, the T-17.

Early tanks had to carry bundles of wood, called *fascines*, to lay down over ditches and wide trenches. However, by the end of WWI, tanks had improved and were influential in the outcome of the war, so much so that tanks formed a significant part of the German blitzkrieg at the beginning of WWII.

The first American tank corps to be established after WWI (other than some failed experiments) was developed under General Douglas MacArthur in 1931 as a mechanized cavalry brigade. Because of regulations, the cavalry tanks had to be called Combat Cars, a moniker that failed to stand the test of time.

By 1940, with the stunning German victories in Poland and France, the U.S. beefed up its armor divisions, but most of the 500 machines available in 1940 were already obsolete.

Tank Guns and Mountings

The first tanks had guns mounted in boxes projecting from the sides of the tanks. Later tanks had big guns projecting from the front, but by far the most common and successful design is the tank turret, which sits on top of the tank and can rotate in a wide arc. Early in WWII, turret guns were given stabilizing systems, usually hydraulic, which would allow them to keep accurate aim even when traveling over uneven terrain.

The basic design of a tank's gun, circa WWII, was to have a seat for a loader and a seat for a gunner. The barrel terminated in a *muzzle brake*, which reduced the recoil effects of rapid firing. Various wheels were used to elevate and site the gun, which was loaded by a breech-lock mechanism. This general configuration was common in tanks of the WWII era and after.

In addition to the big central gun, tanks generally have machine guns of various kinds. These could be used for offense and defense, but were also used for spotting the shot. The "ranging" machine guns were mounted in parallel with the main gun and fired tracer bullets that would also emit a visible sign on impact. When the ranging bullets hit the target, the main gun was instantly fired, with a high probability of a hit. The more modern alternative to the ranging gun is to use lasers to site the shot.

Some different approaches have been taken in modern tank design. The Swiss S-Tank, which appeared in the 1970s, uses a self-loading breech mechanism with the gun mounted on the front of the tank. A special suspension system allows the whole tank to be tilted or turned for accurate aiming.

The Rarden 30mm cannon is a British automatic cannon used on light AFVs, which fires at a (relatively) slow rate of 90 rounds per minute. This gun can be mounted on light tanks, armored cars, and APCs (armored personnel carriers). Its emphasis is on accuracy.

Tanks have generally been designed with rifled barrels, but some use a smooth bore in conjunction with fin-stabilized HEAT shells, since the spin given to these shells by rifled barrels makes them less effective.

Tanks

The Little Willie Landship (UK: 1915) was the first tank.

Mark I (U.K.: 1916)

There were two versions of the Mark I, called the *male* and *female* versions. Statistics for the two versions are marked. This was the first tank to see action.

Armament: Male version: 2–6 pounder QF guns; 4–8mm Hotchkiss MG; Female version: 4–7.7mm Vickers MG and 1–8mm Hotchkiss MG

Armor: 6–12mm

Dimensions: Length – 32'6"; Width – Male 13'9", Female 14'4"; Height – 7'11" (or 8'.5")

Weight: Male – 62,720 pounds; Female – 60,480 pounds

Speed: 3.7 mph

Range: 22 miles

- Schneider Assault Tank (France: 1915)
- St. Chamond Assault Tank (France: 1916)
- Schneider Char d'Assault (France: 1916)
- Mark IV (U.K.: 1917)
- Mark A Whippet (U.K.: 1917)

- Leichte Kampfwagen (LK II) Cavalry Tank (Germany: c. 1917)
- Renault FT-17 Light Tank (France: 1917)
- Sturmpanzerwagen A7V (Germany: 1918)
- K-Wagen Heavy Tank (Germany—proposed, never completed; a 150-ton monstrosity meant to roll through enemy lines)
- Mark VIII "International" Tank (U.K./U.S.: 1918)
- Mark IX a.k.a. "The Pig" (U.K.: 1918; world's first APC)
- Medium Mark C Tank (U.K.: 1918)
- Holt Gas-Electric Tank (U.S.: 1918; first prototype American tank)
- Six Ton Tank M1917 (U.S.: 1918)
- Medium C Tank (U.K.: 1918)
- Char 2C Heavy Tank (France: 1918)
- T-26 Light Tank (Russia: 1920)
- Strv m/21 Tank (Sweden: 1920)
- KS (M-17) Light Tank (Russia: 1920)
- Mark I Medium Tank (U.K.: 1923)
- Fiat 2000 Heavy Tank (Italy: 1923)
- Fiat 3000 Light Tank (Italy: 1923)
- Char NC1 Light Tank (France: 1923)
- Vickers Mark II Medium Tank (U.K.: 1920s–1930s)
- KH50 Wheel and Track Tank (Czechoslovakia: 1925)
- T3 Christie Medium Tank (U.S.: 1928)
- Vickers Six Ton Tank (U.K.: 1928)
- Char Amphibie Schneider-Laurent (France: 1928)
- MS Series Tanks (various models) (Russia: 1928)
- Carro Veloce CV29/33 Tankette (Italy: 1929/1933)
- Carden-Loyd Tankette Mark VI (U.K.: 1929)
- T-24 Medium Tank (Russia: 1929)
- Christie M1931 Medium Tank/T3 Medium Tank/Combat Car T1 (U.S.: 1931; highly influential design improvements that inspired future tank makers)
- Mark II Light Tank (UK: 1931)
- Renault Char D1 Infantry Tank (France: 1931)
- Strv m/31 "Landsverk" Tank (Sweden: 1931)
- Landsverk L-30 Light Tank (Sweden: 1931)
- TK-3 Tankette (Poland: 1931)
- BT-1/BT-2 Light/Medium Tank (Russia: 1931)
- T-26 Light Infantry Tank (Russia: 1931)
- T27 Tankette (Russia: 1931; based on the Carden-Loyd Mark VI)
- CKD/Praga R1 Light Tank (Czechoslovakia: 1932)
- BT-5 Medium Tank (Russia: 1932)
- Renault AMR 33 VM Light Tank (France: 1933)
- T-28 Medium Tank (Russia: 1933)
- T-35 Heavy Tank (Russia: c. 1933)
- T-37 Light Amphibious Tank (Russia: 1933)
- CKD/Praga T-33 Tankette (Czechoslovakia: 1933)
- TK S Tankette (Poland: 1933)
- T-28 Medium Tank (Russia: 1933)
- T-35 Heavy Tank (Russia: 1933)

- T-37 Light Amphibious Tank (Russia: 1933)
- AMC 34 Light Tank (France: 1934)
- Type 89B Medium Tank (Japan: 1934)
- Type 94 Tankette (Japan: 1934)
- Mark IV Light Tank (UK: 1934)
- PzKpfw 1 Light Tank (Germany: 1934; originally intended to be a training tank, it was the main German tank of the early years of WWII)
- Strv L-60 Light Tank (Sweden: 1934)
- Strv L-100 Light Tank (Sweden: 1934)
- LT-34 Light Tank (Czechoslovakia: 1934)
- 7TP Light Tank (Poland: 1934)
- Mark V Light Tank (U.K.: 1935)
- LT-35 Medium Tank (Czechoslovakia: 1935)
- BT-7 Light Tank (Russia: 1935)
- Type 95 HA-GO Light Tank (Japan: 1935)
- Mark VI/VIB Light Tank (U.K.: 1936/1937)
- Vickers Commercial Light Tank ("Dutchman") (UK: 1936)
- 10TP Wheel and Track Fast Tank (Poland: 1937)
- BT-7 Fast Tank (Russia: 1930s)
- Hotchkiss H-35/H-39 (France: 1930s)
- Char B1 Heavy Tank (France: 1930s/early 1940s)
- Renault R-35 Light Tank (France: mid-1930s)
- Char SOMUA S-35 Medium Tank (France: 1930s)
- M1/M2 Combat Car/M1A1 Light Tank (U.S.: 1935)
- M2 Light Tank (U.S.: 1935)
- PzKpfw II Light Tank (Germany: 1935–1942)
- Auto Mitrailleuse Amphibie DP2 (France: 1935)
- Renault R-35 Light Tank (France: 1935)
- Hotchkiss H-35 Light Tank (France: 1935)
- Samua S-35 Medium Tank (France: 1935)
- Char B1-bis Heavy Tank (France: 1935)
- AMC 35 Light Tank (France: 1936)
- FCM-36 Infantry Tank (France: 1936)
- A9 Cruiser Tank Mark I (U.K.: 1936–1941)
- PzKpfw III Medium Tank (Germany: 1937; with the PzKpfw IV, one of the mainstays of the Panzer divisions)
- CDK/Praga TNH Light Tank (export) (Czechoslovakia: 1937)
- Type 97 TE-KE/KE-KE Tankette (Japan: 1937)
- Type 97 Chi-Ha Medium Tank (Japan: 1937)
- LT-38 (Czechoslovakia: 1938–1942)
- A11 Matilda I Infantry Tank (U.K.: 1938–1940)
- LT-38 Medium Tank (Czechoslovakia: 1938)
- Hotchkiss H-39 Light Tank (France: 1939)
- PzKpfw III Battle Tank (Germany: 1939–mid-1940s)
- A13 Cruiser Tank Mark IV (U.K.: 1938; various versions, including Mark V, A13 Mark III)
- A12 Matilda II Infantry Tank (a.k.a. "Matilda") (U.K.: 1939–1942)
- Valentine Infantry Tank Mark III (U.K.: 1939–1944)
- PzKpfw IV Medium Tank (Germany: 1939–1946, last used 1967)

- T-40 Light Amphibious Tank (Russia: 1939)
- KV-I Heavy Tank (Russia: 1939)
- M2 Medium Tank (U.S.: 1940; used only for training)
- Mark VI Cruiser Tank ("Crusader") (U.K.: 1940)
- Mark III Valentine (U.K.: 1940)
- A17 Tetrach Light Tank (U.K.: 1940)
- VK 1601 Reconnaissance Tank (Germany: 1940; little used)
- KV-1 Heavy Tank (Russia: 1940)
- Carro Armato L6/40 Light Tank (Italy: 1940)
- Carro Armato M13/40 Medium Tank (Italy: 1940)
- Carro Armato P26/40 Medium Tank (Italy: 1940)
- Strv m/39 Light Tank (Sweden: 1940)
- KV-II Heavy Tank (Russia: 1940)

T-34/76 Medium Tank "Prinadiezhit-Chetverkior" (Russia: 1940–mid-1950s)

This was considered among the finest tanks of WWII and was highly influential in stopping the German advance into Russia.

Armament (several upgrades during the T-34's life): 76mm main gun; 7.62mm DTM bow MG; 7.62 DTM coaxial MG

Crew: 4 or 5

Weight: 31 tons

Dimensions: Length – 6.09m; Width – 2.98m; Height – 2.57m

Armor: Overall 16–45mm (47mm hull front; 65mm turret front)

Speed: 40–65km/h

Range: 432km (road wheels) 368km (tracks)

M3 Light Tank (a.k.a. British Stuart Mark 1, "Honey") (U.S.: 1940–1943; featured gyroscopic gun stabilization)

Armament: One 37mm (1.46in) M6 gun; three 7.62mm (.3in) MG

Armor: 51mm (2in)

Crew: 4

Dimensions: Length – 4.54m (14'10"); Width – 2.22m (7'4"); Height – 2.3m (7.7')

Weight: 12,927 kg (12.7 tons)

Speed: 58km/h (36mph)

Range: 113km (70 miles)

- M3 Grant/Lee Medium Tank (U.S. 1941–1943) (Grant = British-designed turret/Lee = American-designed turret)
- A22 Churchill Infantry Tank (U.K.: 1941–1950s)
- A24 Mark VII Cruiser Tank ("Cavalier") (U.K.: 1941)
- Mark VIII Cruiser Tank ("Centaur") (U.K.: 1941 through WWII)
- Type 97 CHI-HA Medium Tank (Japan: 1941–1942)
- T-60 Light Tank (Russia: 1941–1942)
- Ram I/II Cruiser Tanks (Canada: 1941–1943)
- Strv m/40 Light Tank (Sweden: 1941)
- T-60 Light Tank (Russia: 1941)

M4 Sherman Medium Tank (U.S.: 1941–1945; remained in use in some places until the 1990s; British "Firefly"; 55,000 made in all variants)

Armament: One 75mm (2.95in) gun; one 12.7mm (.5in) MG; two 7.62mm (.3 in) MG

Armor: 62mm (2.44in)

Crew: 5

Dimensions: Length – 5.88m (19'4"); Width – 2.68m (8'7"); Height – 2.74m (8.99')

Weight: 75,705kg (74.5 tons)

Speed: 39km/h (24mph)

Range: 160km (100 miles)

- T-70 Light Tank (Russia: 1942–1944)
- M5 Light Tank (General Stuart) (U.S.: 1942; featured twin automatic-transmission Cadillac engines)
- PzKpfw V Panther Battle Tank (Germany: 1942–1944)
- Carro Armato M15/42 Medium Tank (Italy: 1942)
- Strv m/41 Light Tank (Italy: 1942)
- Strv m/42 Light Tank (Italy: 1942)
- M22 Locust Light Tank (U.S.: 1942–1944; air transportable)
- Sentinel Australian Cruiser (AC) Tank (Australia: 1942)
- Type 2 Ka-Mi Amphibious Tank (Japan: 1942)
- Type 3 Ka-Chi Amphibious Tank (Japan: 1942)
- Ram I/II Cruiser Tank (Canada: 1942)

PzKpfw VI Tiger I Heavy Battle Tank (Germany: 1942–1944)

Armament: One 88mm gun; two or three 7.92mm MGs

Armor: 100mm at maximum

Crew: 5

Dimensions: Length – 8.45m; Width – 3.56m; Height – 3m

Weight: 56 tons

Speed: Max 37km/h (23mph)

Range: 195km (121 miles)

- KV-85 Heavy Tank (Russia: 1943)
- IS-1 Heavy Tank (Russia: 1943)
- A27M Cromwell Cruiser Tank (U.K.: 1943)
- A38 Valiant Infantry Tank (U.K.: 1943–1945)
- A30 Challenger Cruiser Tank (U.K.: 1943)
- A25 Harry Hopkins Light Tank (U.K.: 1943)
- Turan I/II 40mm Tank (Hungary: 1943)
- Grizzly I Cruiser Tank (Canada: 1943)

M24 Chaffee Light Tank (U.S.: 1943–1954, some until the 1990s)

Armament: One 75mm gun; two .30in MG; one .50in MG (anti-aircraft mount)

Armor: 9mm (0.35in) to 25mm (0.98in)

Crew: 5

Dimensions: Length – 5.5 m (18 ft); Width – 2.95m (9.67ft); Height – 2.5m (8.1ft)

Weight: 18,370 kg (40,500 lb.)

Engine: Cadillac V8-cylinder 44T24 petrol-engines developing 110 hp each

- PzKpfw VIII Maus Super-Heavy Tank (Germany: mid-1940s; prototype only; 188-ton monstrosity—a pet project of Hitler)

M26 Pershing Heavy Tank (U.S.: 1944–early 1950s)

Armament: One 90mm gun; one 0.3" coaxial MG; one 0.3" hull-mounted MG; one 0.5" AA MG

Crew: 5

Engine: Ford GAF, V-8 gas, 500 hp

Speed: 30 mph

Range: 92 miles

Weight: 42 tons

- A34 Comet Cruiser Tank (U.K.: 1944)
- Char ARL-44 Heavy Tank (France: 1944)
- PzKpfw VI Tiger II Heavy Battle Tank "Konigstiger" or "Royal Tiger" (Germany: 1944)
- A39 Tortoise Heavy Tank (U.K.: 1944)
- IS-2 Stalin Heavy Tank ("Victory Tank") (Russia: 1944)
- Type 3 Medium Tank (Japan: 1944)

T-34/85 Medium Tank "Prinadiezhit-Chetverkior" (Russia: 1944)

The upgraded T-34 once again more than held its own against the newer German tanks.

Armament (several upgrades during the T-34's life): 85mm main gun; two 7.62mm MGs

Armor: 90mm

Crew: 5

Dimensions: Length – 8.15m; Width – 2.99m; Height – 2.74m

Weight: 31 tons

Speed: 55km/h

Range: 300km

- A34 Comet Cruiser Tank (U.K.: 1945)
- A41 Centurion Battle Tank (U.K.: 1945–1990s)
- T-45 Tank (Russia: 1945; short-lived upgrade of the T-34/85)
- IS-3 Heavy Tank (Russia: 1945)
- ARL-44 Heavy Tank (France: 1946)
- M46 Tank (U.S.: 1947; an improved M26 Pershing—some featured a flamethrower)
- AMX-13 Light Tank (France: 1948)

T-54 Main Battle Tanks (Russia: 1948–1970s; 65,000 produced, plus 7000 Chinese Type 59 Models)

Armament: 100mm main gun; two 7.62mm DT MGs; one 12.7mm DShK AA MG

Armor: Up to 203mm (8 inches)

Crew: 4

Dimensions: Length – 6.45m; Width – 3.27m; Height – 2.4m

Weight: 35.4 tons

Speed: 48km/h

Range: 400km

Note: The upgraded version, the T-55, was introduced in 1958 and produced in huge numbers, with several improvements and changes, but it was essentially an upgraded T-54.

- Char AMX-50 Main Battle Tank (France: 1951)
- M41 Walker Bulldog Light Tank (U.S.: 1951–present [around the world])
- PT-76 Light Amphibious Tank (Russia: 1952–late 1960s)
- M47 Medium Tank (U.S.: 1950–1953; many years of service around the world—precursor to the M48)
- M41 DK Light Tank (U.S. [Denmark]: 1951 through 1980s)

M48 Patton Medium Tank (U.S.: 1952–1959; upgraded versions still in use as of 2002)

Armament: Main gun 90mm rifled cannon, 64 rounds; 105mm/51 cal M68 rifled gun with 54 rounds [M48A5]; Tank Commander .50 cal M2 HB machine gun with 3,000 rounds; coaxial 7.62mm M73 machine gun with 10,000 rounds

Ammunition: HEAT (High Explosive Anti-Tank); HEP (High Explosive Plastic); Canister WP (White Phosphorus)

Beehive Armor: Homogeneous cast steel; Hull front 120mm; Hull side, front 76mm; Hull side, rear 51mm; Hull rear 44mm; Hull floor 25mm; Turret front 110mm; Turret side 76mm; Turret rear 50mm

Crew: 4 (driver, gunner, loader, TC)

Dimensions: Hull length – 21 ft, with gun forward 30 ft 6 in; Width – 11 ft 11 in; Height – 10ft 1 in

Ground Clearance: 16 in

Track Width: 28 in

Weights: Total 52 tons; Hull 20 tons; Turret 18 tons; Engine/transmission 6 tons; Engine cover 2 tons; Track 2 tons each; Basic load 2 tons

Performance: Range 258 miles/463 km; Top speed 40 mph/48 km/h

Fuel consumption: 1 g/mi road, 2 g/mi offroad

Fording: 1.2m Vertical Obstacle: 0.9m

Gap Crossing: 2.59m Powerplant

(continued)

Engine: Continental AVDS 1790 cu in 690 horsepower

Transmission: Alison CD-850

Used by Greece (714 M48A5), Iran, Israel (400 M48A5), Jordan, South Korea (950 M48A5K), Lebanon (90A1&A5), Morocco (224 M48A5), Norway (38 remaining A5s awaiting disposal), Pakistan (280 M48A5), Portugal (86 M48A5), Spain (164 M48A5E), Taiwan (309 M48A5, 158 M48H), Thailand (100 M48A5), Tunisia, and Turkey (578 M48A2C, 179 M48T-5, 1369 M48A5T1, 750 M48A5T2)

- AMX-13 Light Tank (France: 1952–early 1960s)
- FV214 Conqueror Heavy Tank (U.K.: 1955–1966)
- T-10 Heavy Tank (Russia: 1955–1966)
- M103 Heavy Tank (U.S.: 1957–1960s)
- Strv 74 Light Tank (Sweden: 1958)
- M60 Main Battle Tank (U.S.: 1959–1991)
- Char AMX-30 Main Battle Tank (France: 1960)
- M60 Series
  - M60A1 Main Battle Tank (U.S.: 1960)
  - M60A2 Main Battle Tank ("Starship") (U.S.: 1972–1978 approximately)
  - M60A3 Main Battle Tank (U.S.: 1978–1990s)
  - M60-2000 Main Battle Tank Upgrade Kit (U.S.: 2001)
- T-62 Main Battle Tank (Russia: 1961–1975)
- Pz61 Main Battle Tank (Switzerland: 1961)
- T-55 Main Battle Tank upgraded (Iraq: 1961)
- T-55 Main Battle Tank upgraded (Israel: 1961)
- Type 62 Light Tank (China: 1962; modified Type 59 [Russian T-54])
- Type 61 Main Battle Tank (Japan: 1961)
- Leopard 1 Main Battle Tank (Germany: 1963–1987, all models)
- FV4201 Chieftain Main Battle Tank (U.K.: 1963–present; used worldwide, including Middle East)
- Type 63 Light Tank (Amphibious) (China: 1963)
- Vickers Mark 1/Mark 3 "Vijayanta" Main Battle Tank (U.K. [India]: 1964)
- S-Tank (Stridsvagen 103) (Sweden: 1966)
- T-64 Main Battle Tank (Russia: 1967–end of service period unknown)
- Centurion Main Battle Tank Upgraded (Israel: 1967)
- AMX-30/AMX-30B2 Main Battle Tank (France: 1967? to ?)
- Main Battle Tank 70 (Germany/U.S.: 1967)
- M551 Sheridan Light Tank (U.S.: 1968–1978; some service through the 1990s)
- Magach Main Battle Tank (Israel: 1970; upgraded M60)
- Pz68 Main Battle Tank (Switzerland: 1971)
- OF-40 Main Battle Tank (Italy: 1972; limited production and distribution)
- FV101 Scorpion Light Tank/Recon Vehicle (U.K.: 1972–mid-1990s)
- T-72 Main Battle Tank (Russia: 1973–2000s?; the most widely deployed tank in the world)
- Type 69 Main Battle Tank (China: 1974–2000s)
- Type 74 Main Battle Tank (Japan: 1975)
- TAMSE TAM Medium Tank (Argentina: 1976)
- Merkava Main Battle Tank (Israel: 1977)
- Bernardini X1A2 Light Tank (Brazil: 1978; based on M3A1 Stuart)

- Leopard 2 Main Battle Tank (Germany: 1979–?)
- Merkava Main Battle Tank/Mark I-Mark IV (Israel: 1979–present)
- Type 74 Main Battle Tank (Japan: 1980–1989)
- T-80 Main Battle Tank (Russia: 1980; improved T-64)
- Type 69 Main Battle Tank (China: 1980; another variant on the T-54, used in Iran and Iraq)
- Vickers OMC Olifant Main Battle Tank (S. Africa: 1980; upgraded Centurion)

M1 Abrams (U.S.: 1980–present; models may vary slightly between M1, M1A1, and M1A2)

Armament: One 105 or 120mm M26 gun; two 7.62mm MG; one 12.7mm MG

Armor: Steel and depleted uranium

Dimensions: Length – approx. 32 feet; Width – 12.0 feet; Height – approx. 8 feet

Top Speed: 41.5–45 mph

Weight: 60–68 tons, depending on model

Armament: 105mm (120mm later models)

Crew: 4

Range: 275 miles

- Shir 1 (Khalid) Main Battle Tank (U.K. [Iran]: 1981)
- Challenger 1 Main Battle Tank (U.K.: 1982–1990)
- Char AMX-40 Main Battle Tank (France: 1982)
- TR-580 Main Battle Tank (Romania: 1982)
- Bernardini M41 Light Tank Upgraded (Brazil: 1983)
- M-84 Main Battle Tank (Yugoslavia: 1984)
- Type 79 Main Battle Tank (China: 1984)
- Vickers Mark 7 Main Battle Tank (U.K.: 1985)
- Tariq Main Battle Tank (Jordan: 1985; improved Centurion)
- M1985 (PT-85) Light Amphibious Tank: (N. Korea: 1985)
- ENGESA EE-T1 Osorio Main Battle Tank (Brazil: 1985)
- Vickers VFM Mark 5 Tank (U.K./U.S.: 1986)
- LeClerc Main Battle Tank (France: 1986)
- TR-85 Main Battle Tank (Romania: 1987)
- Arjun Main Battle Tank (India: 1987)
- Stingray I Light Tank (U.S.: 1988)
- Ariete Main Battle Tank (Italy: 1988)
- Type 80 Main Battle Tank (China: 1988)
- SM1 AMX-13 Light Tank (Singapore: 1988)
- TR-125 Main Battle Tank (Romania: 1989)
- Type 85-II/III Main Battle Tank (China: 1989)
- M48H Main Battle Tank (Modified M60 with M48 Turret) (Taiwan: 1990)
- LeClerc Main Battle Tank (France: 1991–present)
- MBT 2000 (Al Khalid) Main Battle Tank (Pakistan: 1991)
- Type 90 Main Battle Tank (Japan: 1991)

- M8 Armored Gun System (U.S.: 1992)
- Challenger 2 Main Battle Tank (U.K.: 1992–present)
- PT-91 Main Battle Tank (Poland: 1993)
- T-59 upgrade of T-54 (Pakistan: 1993)
- T-90 Main Battle Tank (Russian Federation: 1994–present [rumor has it that a new tank, the T-95, is to debut in 2010])
- TM-800 Main Battle Tank (Romania: 1994)
- Zulfiqar Main Battle Tank (Iran: 1994)
- C1 Ariete Main Battle Tank (Italy: 1995–2002)
- T-84 Main Battle Tank (Ukraine: 1995)
- Type 90-II (MBT-2000) Main Battle Tank (China: 1995)
- Stingray II (U.S.: 1996)
- T-71Z Main Battle Tank (Iran: 1996; based on the Russian T-72)
- ASCOD Light Tank (Austria/Spain: 1996)
- Hyundai K1 Main Battle Tank (South Korea: 1997–2010 [rumor has it that a new K2 model will become available in 2010])
- CV 90-120 Light Tank (Sweden: 1998)
- Type 98 Main Battle Tank (China: 1998)
- RH-ALAN Degman Main Battle Tank (Croatia: 1999)
- Sabra Main Battle Tank (Israel: 1999; upgrade of M60A3)
- Type 99 Light Tank (China: 1999)
- T-95 "Black Eagle" (Russia: ?; newest Russian tank shown briefly in 1997, appears not to have entered production yet, but rumored to be in trials as of 2004 and to be deployed by 2010)

Self-Propelled Guns

Self-propelled guns are any gun—artillery, anti-tank, or anti-aircraft—that is mounted on a base with wheels or tracks, and thereby mobile. Here are some of the self-propelled guns from history, beginning around 1936.

- S-3 Self-Propelled Gun (Czechoslovakia: 1936)
- Sturmgeschutz II Self-Propelled Assault Gun (Germany: 1937)
- PanzerJaeger 1 Tank Destroyer (Germany: 1940)
- 15cm sIG33 (Sf) Heavy Infantry Gun (Germany: 1940)
- Semovente L40 DA 47/32 Antitank Vehicle (Italy: 1940)
- Semovente M41 Self-Propelled Gun (Italy: 1941)
- M7 "Priest" Howitzer Motor Carriage (HMC) (U.S.: 1942)
- M8 HMC (U.S.: 1942; based on M5 light tank chassis)
- M10 Tank Destroyer (U.S.: 1942)
- Deacon Tank Destroyer (U.K.: 1942)
- Bishop Self-Propelled Door (U.K.: 1942)
- Nashorn Tank Destroyer (Germany: 1942)
- Elefant Heavy Tank Destroyer (Germany: 1942)
- Marder II (Germany: 1942)
- SU-76 Assault Gun (Russia: 1942)
- M18 "Hellcat" Tank Destroyer (U.S.: 1943; light, fast [50mph] and effective in WWII)
- M12 Self-Propelled Howitzer (U.S.: 1943)
- A30 Avenger Tank Destroyer (U.K.: 1943)

- Archer Tank Destroyer (U.K.: 1943)
- Marder III (Germany: 1943)
- Jagdpanther Tank Destroyer (Germany: 1943)
- Jagdpanzer Tank Destroyer (Germany: 1943)
- Sturmpanzer IV Brummbar (Germany: 1943)
- Wespe Self-Propelled Howitzer (Germany: 1943)
- Hummel Self-Propelled Howitzer (Germany: 1943)
- SU-152/ISU-152 Assault Gun (Russia: 1943)
- SU-84 Assault Gun (Russia: 1943)
- Sexton Self-Propelled Gun (Canada: 1943)
- M36 Tank Destroyer (U.S.: 1944)
- Jagdtiger Heavy Tank Destroyer (Germany: 1944)
- Hetzer Tank Destroyer (Germany: 1944)
- Sturmmorser Tiger (Germany: 1944)
- Pan m/43 Self-Propelled Gun (Sweden: 1944)
- SU-100 Assault Gun (Russia: 1944)
- ISU-122/SU-122 Assault Gun (Russia: 1944)
- M37 HMC (U.S.: 1945; light replacement for the M7)
- M40/M43 Self-Propelled Gun (U.S.: 1945; used primarily in the Korean War)
- G-13 TD Tank Destroyer (Switzerland: 1947)
- M44 Self-Propelled Howitzer (U.S.: 1950)
- Mk 61 105mm Self-Propelled Gun (France: 1950)
- ASU-57 Tank Destroyer (Russia: 1951)
- M53 Self-Propelled Howitzer (U.S.: 1952)
- M56 SPAT (Self-Propelled Anti-tank) Tank Destroyer (a.k.a. "Scorpion") (U.S.: 1953)
- Hornet Tank Destroyer (U.K.: 1953)
- Charioteer Tank Destroyer (U.K.: 1954)
- M50 "Ontos" Tank Destroyer (U.S.: 1955; featured 6 recoilless rifles; ontos = *thing* in Greek)
- M52 Self-Propelled Howitzer (U.S.: 1955)
- Jagdpanzer Kanone (Germany: 1959)
- Type 60 Twin 106mm Tank Destroyer (Japan: 1960)
- M107/M110 Self-Propelled Gun (U.S.: 1961/1963)
- BRDM-1 ATGW Tank Destroyer (Russia: 1961)
- M108 Self-Propelled Light Howitzer (U.S.: 1962)
- FV438 Tank Destroyer (U.K.: 1962)
- Mk F3 155mm Self-Propelled Gun (France: 1962)
- ASU-85 Tank Destroyer (Russia: 1962)
- M109 Self-Propelled Howitzer (U.S.: 1963; standard Western self-propelled gun—several versions)
- Jagdpanzer Rakete Jaguar Tank Destroyers (Germany: 1963)
- Abbot Self-Propelled Gun (105mm) (U.K.: 1964)
- BRDM-2 ATGW Tank Destroyer (Russia: 1965)
- Catapult 130mm Self-Propelled Gun (India: 1965)
- Bandkanone 155mm Self-Propelled Gun (Sweden: 1966)
- L33 155mm Self-Propelled Gun (Israel: 1967)
- Type 54I 122mm Self-Propelled Gun (China: 1967)
- MT-LB AT-6 ATGW Tank Destroyer (Russia: 1968)
- M50 155mm Self-Propelled Gun (Israel: 1969)
- 160mm Self-Propelled Mortar (Israel: 1969; on Sherman tank chassis)

- Ikv-91 Tank Destroyer (Sweden: 1970)
- 2S1 122mm Self-Propelled Howitzer (Russia: 1971)
- 2S3 152mm Self-Propelled Howitzer (Russia: 1971)
- 2S4 240mm Self-Propelled Mortar (Russia: 1971)
- Giat GCT 155mm Self-Propelled Gun (France: 1972)
- Type 74 105mm Self-Propelled Gun (Japan: 1974)
- Striker Tank Destroyer (U.K.: 1975)
- 2S7 203mm Self-Propelled Gun (Russia: 1975)
- Type 75 155mm Self-Propelled Howitzer (Japan: 1975)
- SP-70 155mm Self-Propelled Howitzer (Germany/U.K.: 1975)
- M901 Tank Destroyer (U.S.: 1976; conversion of M113 with TOW missile launcher armament)
- MOWAG Piranha TOW Tank Destroyer (Switzerland: 1976)
- Palmaria 155mm Self-Propelled Howitzer (Italy: 1977)
- Dana Self-Propelled Gun (Czechoslovakia: 1980)
- LIW G6 155mm Self-Propelled Howitzer (S. Africa: 1981)
- 2S5 152mm Self-Propelled Gun (Russia: 1982)
- Type 83 152mm Self Propelled Gun (China: 1983)
- Pvrbv 551 Tank Destroyer (Sweden: 1984)
- Kkv 102/103 Self-Propelled Gun (Sweden: 1984)
- 2S9 120mm Self-Propelled Mortar (Russia: 1984)
- PLZ45 155mm Self Propelled Gun (China: 1985)
- Type 85 122mm Self-Propelled Gun (China: 1985)
- Koksan 170mm Self-Propelled Gun (N. Korea: 1985)
- Vickers OMC/Kentron Ratel Tank Destroyer (S. Africa: 1985)
- M44T 155mm Self-Propelled Howitzer (Turkey: 1986)
- ENGESA EE-18 Sucuri Tank Destroyer (Brazil: 1987)
- 120mm Armored Mortar System (Multinational: 1987)
- Textron LAV Assault Gun (U.S.: 1988)
- Model 89 122mm Self-Propelled Gun (Romania: 1989)
- 2S23 120mm Self-Propelled Mortar (Russia: 1989)
- 2S19 MSTA 152mm Self-Propelled Howitzer (Russia: 1989)
- Type 89 122mm Self-Propelled Gun (China: 1989)
- Panzerhaubitze 2000 Self-Propelled Howitzer (Germany: 1990)
- PRAM-S 120mm Mortar System (Czechoslovakia: 1990)
- Slammer 155mm Self-Propelled Gun (Israel: 1990)
- XT-69 155mm Self-Propelled Gun (Taiwan: 1990)
- VAB Tank Destroyers (France: 1992)
- Zuzana Self-Propelled Gun (Czechoslovakia: 1992)
- AS90 Self-Propelled Gun (155mm) (U.K.: 1993)
- M109A6 Paladin (U.S.: 1994)
- LIW T6 155mm Artillery System (S. Africa: 1994)
- M52T 155mm Self-Propelled Howitzer (Turkey: 1995)
- BMY/ARE 122 Self-Propelled Howitzer (Egypt/U.S.: 1995)
- Thunder 122mm Self-Propelled Gun (Iran: 1996)
- 2S31 Vena 120mm Self-Propelled Mortar (Russia: 1997)
- Thunder 155mm Self-Propelled Gun (Iran: 1997)
- AMOS Advanced Mortar System (Finland/Sweden: 1997)
- NORINCO 203mm Self-Propelled Gun (China: 1998)

- 2S25 125mm Tank Destroyer (Russia: 1999)
- K9 Self-Propelled Gun (S. Korea: 1999)
- General Motors Defense LPT Assault Gun (Canada: 1999)
- Rascal 155mm Self-Propelled Gun (Israel: 2000)
- Type 99 155 Self-Propelled Howitzer (Japan: 2000)
- Giat Caesar 155mm Self-Propelled Gun (France: 2003)
- LOSAT (Line-of-Sight-Anti-Tank) based on M1114 HMMWV chassis (U.S.: 2004; KEM kinetic internally guided "hit to kill" missiles)
- Crusader Self-Propelled Gun (U.S.: future tech)

Armored Cars, Personnel Carriers, and Reconnaissance Vehicles

- Simms Motor War Car (U.K.: 1902)
- Charron-Giradot et Voigt Armored Car (France: 1902)
- Austro-Daimler Armored Car (Austria: 1904)
- Armstrong-Whitworth Armoured Car (U.K.: 1906)
- Ehrhardt BAK Armored Car (Germany: 1906)
- Talbot Armoured Car (U.K.: 1914)
- Delaunay-Belleville Armoured Car (U.K.: 1914)
- Rolls-Royce Armoured Cars (U.K.: 1915, 1920, 1924)
- Lancia Armoured Cars (U.K.: 1915)
- Seabrook Armoured Car (U.K.: 1915)
- Lanchester Armoured Car (U.K.: 1915)
- Renault Model 1915 Armored Car (France: 1915)
- Ehrhardt E-V/4 Armored Car (Germany: 1915)
- Lancia 1ZM Armored Car (Italy: 1915)
- Pierce-Arrow Armoured Truck (U.K.: 1916)
- Leyland Armoured Car (U.K.: 1916)
- Austin-Putilov Halftracked Armored Car (Russia: 1916)
- Austin Armoured Car (U.K.: 1918)
- Mernerva/SAVA/MORS Armored Cars (Belgium: 1918)
- Peerless Armoured Car (U.K.: 1919)
- Vickers-Armstrong Wheel-Cum-Track Vehicle (U.K.: 1926; Retractable tracks, could run on wheels or tracks)
- Vickers-Guy Indian Pattern Armoured Car (U.K.: 1927)
- Lanchester Mark I and Mark II Armoured Cars (U.K.: 1927)
- Vickers-Crossley Armoured Car (U.K.: 1928/1930)
- Ursus W29 Armored Car (Poland: 1929)
- BA-27 Armored Car (Russia: 1929)
- Crossley Mark I/II/III (U.K.: 1931; triple axle)
- Renault UE Supply Carrier (France: 1931)
- SdKfz 13 Light Armored Car (Germany: 1932)
- SdKfz 231/232 Armored Reconnaissance Vehicle (Germany: 1932)
- BA-10 Armored Car (Russia: 1932)
- Model 2592 Osaka Armored Car (Japan: 1932)
- Laffly-White Armored Car (France: 1933)
- Model 2593 Sumida Armored Car (Japan: 1933)

- Bren Gun Carrier (U.K.: 1934)
- Morris Armoured Car (U.K.: 1935; in service until 1943)
- Panhard et Levassor P 178 Armored Car (France: 1935)
- SdKfz 221 Light Reconnaissance Vehicle (Germany: 1935)
- Landsverk 180/181 Armored Car (Sweden: 1935)
- Alvis Straussler Armoured Car (U.K.: 1937)
- Chenilette Lorraine Type 37L (France: 1937; supply carrier)
- STZ Armored Tractor (Russia: 1937)
- Carden-Loyd Universal Carrier (U.K.: 1938; 35,000 built during WWII)
- Daimler Dingo Scout Car (U.K.: 1938)
- Guy Mark I/IA Armoured Car (U.K.: 1938)
- M3 Half-Track (U.S.: 1938)
- SdKfz 251 Armored Personnel Carrier (Germany: 1938); variant designations:
  - SdKfz 251: Personnel carrier
  - SdKfz 251/1: Rocket launcher carrier, “Stuka zum Fuss” or “Ground Stuka”
  - SdKfz 251/2: Mortar carrier
  - SdKfz 251/3: Radio vehicle
  - SdKfz 251/4: Ammunition transport
  - SdKfz 251/5: Combat engineer transport
  - SdKfz 251/6: Staff officer command vehicle
  - SdKfz 251/7: Combat engineer carrier, alternate version
  - SdKfz 251/8: Ambulance
  - SdKfz 251/9: Fire support vehicle for infantry with short-barreled 75mm gun
  - SdKfz 251/10: Anti-tank gun (37mm) platform
  - SdKfz 251/11: Field telephone switchboard unit
  - SdKfz 251/12: Instrument carrier for artillery units
  - SdKfz 251/13: Sound detection equipment for artillery units
  - SdKfz 251/14: Same as SdKfz 251/13
  - SdKfz 251/15: Flash-spotting equipment transport for artillery units
  - SdKfz 251/16: Flamethrower vehicle
  - SdKfz 251/17: Light air defense vehicle (20mm AA gun)
  - SdKfz 251/18: Artillery observation
  - SdKfz 251/19: Field telephone switchboard and enemy communications interception
  - SdKfz 251/20: Infrared detection system for tank support
  - SdKfz 251/21: Light air defense with triple mountings, either 15mm heavy machine guns or 20mm cannon
  - SdKfz 251/22: Anti-tank 75mm gun platform
- M3 Scout Car (U.S.: 1939)
- SdKfz 222 Light Reconnaissance Vehicle (Germany: 1939)
- SdKfz 250 Armored Personnel Carrier (Germany: 1939); variant designations:
  - SdKfz 250/1: Personnel carrier
  - SdKfz 250/2: Field telephone cable layer
  - SdKfz 250/3: Radio vehicle
  - SdKfz 250/4: Observation vehicle (replacing SdKfz 253)
  - SdKfz 250/5: Observation vehicle with different radio systems
  - SdKfz 250/6: Artillery ammunition transport
  - SdKfz 250/7: Mortar vehicle with 81.4mm mortar

    - SdKfz 250/8: From 1943, fire support with short 75mm gun
    - SdKfz 250/9: Light reconnaissance vehicle with 20mm cannon and later a coaxial machine gun
    - SdKfz 250/10: Fire support with 37mm anti-tank gun
    - SdKfz 250/11: Fire support with 28mm tapered-bore anti-tank gun
    - SdKfz 250/12: Artillery observation
- M39 Panzerwagen Armored Car (Netherlands: 1939)
- Marmon-Herrington Mk I/II/III Armored Car (S. Africa: 1939)
- Fordson Armoured Car (U.K.: 1940)
- Beaverette Mark II Reconnaissance Vehicle (U.K.: 1940)
- Humber Light Reconnaissance Vehicle (U.K.: 1940)
- Humber Special Ironside Saloon Mark I (U.K.: 1940; specialty armored car for royalty, cabinet ministers, etc.)
- LVT-1 (Landing Vehicle Tracked, a.k.a. "the Alligator") (U.S.: 1940)
- Autoblinda AB 40 Armored Car (Italy: 1940)
- Morris Light Reconnaissance Car (U.K.: 1941)
- Humber Scout Car (U.K.: 1941)
- BA-64 Armored Car (Russia: 1941)
- Marmon-Herrington Mk IV Armored Car (S. Africa: 1941)
- T17 Staghound Armored Car (U.S.: 1942)
- AEC Armoured Car (U.K.: 1942; many variations made, based on the AEC Matador gun tractor. AEC Basilisk Mark II was a version with flamethrower mounted. Another model was the AEC Anti-Aircraft Mark II, designed with a Crusader anti-aircraft turret and a pair of 20mm guns.)
- M20 Armored Car (U.S.: 1942; M8 with machine gun but no turret)
- Lynx Truck (Armored Truck) (Canada: 1942)
- Marmon-Herrington Mk VI Armored Car (S. Africa: 1942)
- M8 Armored Car (U.S.: 1943)
- SdKfz 234 Armored Car (Germany: 1943 and beyond; various versions—SdKfz 234/2 "Puma" was highly considered)
- LVT-2 (Landing Vehicle Tracked, a.k.a. "Water Buffalo" or "Buffalo") (U.S.: 1943)
- LVT-4 (U.S.: 1944)
- M39 Utility Vehicle (U.S.: 1944)
- Kangaroo Armoured Personnel Carrier (U.K.: 1944)
- AEC Command Post Vehicle (U.K.: 1944)
- Coventry Mark I/Mark II Armoured Cars (U.K.: 1945)
- OT-810 Armored Personnel Carrier (halftrack) (Czechoslovakia: 1948)
- Panhard EBR Reconnaissance Vehicle (France: 1950)
- AMX VC1 Infantry Combat Vehicle (France: 1950)
- BTR-40 Armored Personnel Carrier (Russia: 1950)
- BTR-152 Armored Personnel Carrier (Russia: 1950)
- M75 Armored Personnel Carrier (U.S.: 1952)
- M59 Personnel Carrier (U.S.: 1953)
- Ferret Mark 2/3 Scout Car (U.K.: 1953)
- Saracen Armoured Personnel Carrier (U.K.: 1953)
- SK 1 Armored Car (Germany: 1954)
- SKPF M/42 Armored Personnel Carrier (Sweden: 1954)
- Humber "Pig" FV1600 (U.K.: 1955)
- VP90 Light Combat Vehicle (France: 1955)

- HS-30 Armored Personnel Carrier (Germany: 1955)
- AT-P Armored Tractor (Russia: 1955)
- Hotchkiss Carriers (France [for Germany]: 1956)
- M1113 Armored Personnel Carrier (U.S.: 1956–present; 80,000 built and still in production)
- LVT-P5 (U.S.: 1956)
- BTR-50 Tracked Armored Personnel Carrier (Russia: 1957)
- MOWAG MR8-01 Armored Personnel Carriers (Switzerland: 1958)
- Saladin Armoured Car (U.K.: 1959)
- BRDM Scout Car (Russia: 1959)
- Panhard AML Light Armored Car (France: 1960)
- YP-104 Scout Car (Netherlands: 1960)
- Walid Armored Personnel Carrier (Egypt: 1960)
- Type 60 Armored Personnel Carrier (Japan: 1960)
- Marder 1 Infantry Combat Vehicle (Germany: 1961)
- Saurer 4K 4FA Armored Personnel Carrier (Austria: 1961)
- Pbv 301 Armored Personnel Carrier (Sweden: 1961)
- BTR-60 Armored Personnel Carrier (Russia: 1961)
- FV432 Armoured Personnel Carrier (U.K.: 1962)
- M577 Command Post Vehicle (U.S.: 1962)
- HWK 11 Armored Personnel Carrier (Germany: 1963)
- YP-408 Armored Personnel Carrier (Netherlands: 1963)
- BRDM-2 Scout Car (Soviet Union: 1963)
- Vickers OMC Eland Armored Cars (models 60 and 90) (S. Africa: 1963)
- MAC-1 Armored Car (U.S.: 1964)
- LAV-100 Commando (U.S.: 1964)
- OT-62 Armored Personnel Carrier (Czechoslovakia: 1964)
- OT-64 Armored Personnel Carrier (Czechoslovakia: 1964)
- OT-65/FUG Reconnaissance Vehicle (Hungary: 1964)
- Shorland Armored Patrol Car (U.K.: 1965)
- UR-416 Armored Personnel Carrier (Germany: 1965)
- SK105 Light Tank "Kurussier" (Austria: 1965)
- M-60P Armored Personnel Carrier (Yugoslavia: 1965)
- Shorland Tenix S55 Armored Personnel Carrier (Australia: 1965)
- Pbv 302 Armored Personnel Carrier (Sweden: 1966)
- Fox Armoured Car (U.K.: 1967)
- BMP-1 Infantry Combat Vehicle (Russia: 1967)
- United Defense Lynx Reconnaissance Vehicle (U.S.: 1968)
- AMX-10P Infantry Combat Vehicle (France: 1968)
- AMX-10P Marines (France: 1968)
- LUCHS (Lynx) Armored Reconnaissance Vehicle (Germany: 1968–2012[projected])
- MT-LB Armored Personnel Carrier (Russia: 1968)
- LAV-200 Armored Car (U.S.: 1969)
- Vixen Scout Car ("Fat Fox") (U.K.: 1970)
- GKN AT104 Armoured Personnel Carrier (U.K.: 1970)
- MOWAG Roland Armored Personnel Carrier (Switzerland: 1970)
- PSZH-IV Armored Personnel Carrier (Hungary: 1970)
- TAB-72 Armored Personnel Carrier (Romania: 1970)
- BMD-1 Airborne Combat Vehicle (Russia: 1970)

- Type 70 Armored Personnel Carrier (Japan: 1970)
- LAV-150 Armored Car (U.S.: 1971)
- Panhard M3 Armored Personnel Carrier (France: 1971)
- FN 4RM/62F AB Armored Car (Belgium: 1971)
- LVT-P7 (AAV7) (aka "Amtrak") (U.S.: 1972-)
- Timoney 4 × 4/6 × 6 Armored Personnel Carriers (Ireland: 1972)
- Iveco Type 6616 Armored Car (Italy: 1972)
- MT-LB Armored Personnel Carrier (Bulgaria: 1972)
- Armored Infantry Fighting Vehicle (U.S.: 1973; export only)
- Scorpion 76mm/90mm (U.K.: 1973)
- Scimitar 30mm/Sabre 30mm (U.K.: 1973)
- Renault VAB Armored Personnel Carrier (France: 1973; various versions)
- VTT-323/M1973 Armored Personnel Carrier (N. Korea: 1973; copy of Chinese YW 531)
- Bravia Chaimite Armored Personnel Carrier (Portugal: 1973)
- AMX-10RC Reconnaissance Vehicle (France: 1974)
- ENGESA EE-9 Cascavel Armored Car (Brazil: 1974)
- ENGESA EE-11 Urutu Armored Personnel Carrier (Brazil: 1974)
- Vickers OMC Ratel Infantry Fighting Vehicle (S. Africa: 1974)
- Saxon Armoured Personnel Carrier (U.K.: 1975)
- Panhard VCR 6×6 Armored Personnel Carrier (France: 1975; export version to the Middle East)
- M-980 Mechanized Infantry Combat Vehicle (Yugoslavia: 1975)
- Ramta Ram Reconnaissance Vehicle (Israel: 1975)
- MOWAG Piranha (6×6 or 8×8) Armored Personnel Carrrier (Switzerland: 1976)
- BTR-70 Armored Personnel Carrier (Russia: 1976)
- TAMSE VCTP Infantry Combat Vehicle (Argentina: 1976)
- Panhard ERC Sagaie Armored Car (France: 1977)
- Steyr 4K 7FA G 127 Armored Personnel Carrier (Austria: 1977)
- BDX Armored Personnel Carrier (Belgium: 1977)
- OF-24 Tifone Infantry Combat Vehicle (Switzerland: 1977)
- MOWAG Grenadier Armored Personnel Carrier (Switzerland: 1977)
- MOWAG Tornado Mechanized Infantry Fighting Vehicle (Switzerland: 1977)
- Bravia Commando Mk III Armored Personnel Carrier (1977)
- Spartan Armoured Personnel Carrier (U.K.: 1978)
- Sultan Command Post Vehicle (U.K.: 1978)
- Panhard VBL Scout Car (France: 1978)
- Condor Armored Personnel Carrier (Germany: 1978)
- TM-170 Armored Personnel Carrier (Germany: 1978)
- MOWAG Pirate Armored Personnel Carrier (Switzerland: 1978)
- MOWAG Puma Armored Personnel Carrier (Switzerland: 1978)
- AIFV Armored Infantry Fighting Vehicle (Taiwan: 1978)
- Buffel Armored Personnel Carrier (S. Africa: 1978)
- Transportpanzer 1 Armored Personnel Carrier (Germany: 1979)
- SIBMAS Armoured Personnel Carrier (Belgium: 1979)
- BMR-600 Armored Personnel Carrier (Spain: 1979)
- TABC-79 Armored Personnel Carrier (Romania: 1979)
- BMD-2 Airborne Combat Vehicle (Russia: 1979)
- ENGESA EE-3 Jararaca Scout Car (Brazil: 1979)
- General Motors Defense Grizzly APC (Canada: 1979)

- Vickers OMC Casspir Armored Personnel Carrier (S. Africa: 1979)
- ACMAT TPK 4.20 Armored Personnel Carrier (France: 1980)
- VEC Reconnaissance Vehicle (Spain: 1980)
- BTR-80 Armored Personnel Carrier (Russia: 1980)
- BMP-2 Infantry Combat Vehicle (Russia: 1980)
- Egyptian Infantry Fighting Vehicle (Egypt: 1980)
- Stormer Armoured Personnel Carrier (U.K.: 1981)
- Renault VBC 90 Armored Car (France: 1981)
- Bv 206S Armored Personnel Carrier (Sweden: 1981)
- Al-Faris Armored Car (Saudi Arabia: 1981)
- Armadillo Armored Personnel Carrier (Guatemala: 1981)
- Sisu XA Series Armored Personnel Carriers (Finland: 1982)
- Leonidas Armored Personnel Carrier (Greece: 1982)
- VCC-1 Armored Personnel Carrier (Italy: 1982)
- BTR-D Armored Personnel Carrier (Russia: 1982)
- Type 87 Reconnaissance Combat Vehicle (Japan: 1982)
- Type 82 Command and Communications Vehicle (Japan: 1982)
- Scout (U.S.: 1983)
- MLI-84 Infantry Fighting Vehicle (Romania: 1983)
- BOV Armored Personnel Carrier (Slovenia: 1983)
- Hotspur Hussar Armoured Personnel Carrier (U.K.: 1984)
- IVECO Type 6614 Armored Personnel Carrier (Italy: 1984)
- BMP-23 Infantry Combat Vehicle (Bulgaria: 1984)
- BVP-M-80A Mechanized Infantry Vehicle (Yugoslavia: 1984)
- Puma Heavy Armored Personnel Carrier (Israel: 1984; based on Centurion chassis)
- WZ 523 Armored Personnel Carrier (China: 1984)
- Vickers Valkyr Armoured Personnel Carrier (U.K.: 1985)
- Glover Webb Armoured Personnel Carrier (U.K.: 1985)
- Warrior Infantry Combat Vehicle (U.K.: 1985)
- LAV-600 (6 × 6) Armored Car (U.S.: 1985)
- BLR Armored Personnel Carrier (Spain: 1985)
- OT-90 Armored Personnel Carrier (Czechoslovakia: 1985)
- ML-VM Combat Vehicle (Romania: 1985)
- Fahd Armored Personnel Carrier (Egypt: 1985)
- Kader G 320 Armored Personnel Carrier (Egypt: 1985; Mercedes-Benz)
- WZ 551 Armored Personnel Carrier (China: 1985)
- Type 85 Armored Personnel Carrier (China: 1985)
- KIFV Armored Personnel Carrier (S. Korea: 1985)
- FAMAE Piranha Armored Personnel Carrier (Chile: 1985)
- Cardoen VTP-1 Orca Multi-Purpose Armored Vehicle (Chile: 1985)
- VAL Light Assault Vehicle (El Salvador: 1985)
- DN-IV Armored Personnel Carrier (Mexico: 1985)
- Vickers OMC Rinkhals Armored Ambulance (S. Africa: 1985)
- Bulldog Armored Personnel Carrier (S. Africa: 1985)
- Simba Armoured Personnel Carrier (U.K.: 1986)
- Glover Hornet Armoured Car (U.K.: 1986)
- CBHcp P4 Light Armorred Personnel Carrier (France: 1986)
- Panhard Buffalo Armored Personnel Carrier (France: 1986)

- Schutzenpanzer Armored Personnel Carrier (Switzerland: 1986)
- ENGESA EE-T4 Ogum Light Tracked Vehicle (Brazil: 1986)
- NVH-1 Mechanized Infantry Combat Vehicle (China/U.K.: 1986)
- Vickers OMC Rooikat Armored Car (S. Africa: 1986)
- Centauro VBC Armored Personnel Carrier (Italy: 1987)
- Sarath Infantry Combat Vehicle (India: 1987)
- Achzarit Infantry Armored Vehicle (Israel: 1987)
- Type 88 K1 Main Battle Tank (S. Korea: 1987)
- Vickers OMC RCV 9 Internal Security Vehicle (S. Africa: 1987)
- Glover Webb Tactica Armoured Personnel Carrier (U.K.: 1988)
- Ferret 80 Scout Car (U.K.: 1988)
- PUMA (4 x 4 or 6 x 6) Armored Personnel Carrier (Italy: 1988)
- VCC-80 Infantry Combat Vehicle (Italy: 1988)
- Bernardini AM-IV Armored Security Vehicle (Brazil: 1988)
- Moto Pecas Charrua Armored Personnel Carrier (Brazil: 1988)
- General Motors Defense Bison APC (Canada: 1988)
- Wiesel 1 Light Armored Weapon Carrier (Germany: 1989)
- BMD-3 Airborne Combat Vehicle (Russia: 1990)
- BMP-3 Infantry Combat Vehicle (Russia: 1990)
- Type 90 Armored Personnel Carrier (China: 1990)
- Type 89 Mechanized Infantry Combat Vehicle (Japan: 1990)
- TAMSE VCA 155mm Self-Propelled Gun (Argentina: 1990)
- ASCOD Infantry Combat Vehicle (Austria/Spain: 1990)
- Vickers OMC RG-12 Armored Personnel Carrier (S. Africa: 1990)
- Vickers OMC Okapi Armored Command Post Vehicle (S. Africa: 1990)
- NP Aerospace Armoured Personnel Carrier (U.K.: 1991)
- FNSS Infantry Fighting Vehicle (Turkey: 1991)
- Otokar Armored Personnel Carrier (Turkey: 1991)
- BRM-23 Reconnaissance Vehicle (Bulgaria: 1991)
- Vickers OMC Mamba Mk 2 APC (S. Africa: 1991)
- MAV-5 Armored Personnel Carrier (Italy: 1992)
- Fennek Scout Car (Netherlands: 1992)
- CV9040 Infantry Fighting Vehicle (Sweden: 1993)
- Alvis 4/8 Armoured Personnel Carrier (U.K.: 1993)
- M1114 Up-Armored HMMWV (U.S.: 1993; High Mobility Multi-Purpose Wheeled Vehicle—also known as *Hummer* and *Humvee*)
- RH-ALAN LOV Armored Personnel Carrier (Croatia: 1993)
- Vickers OMC RG-31 Charger APC (S. Africa: 1993)
- Wiesel 2 Light Armored Multi-Purpose Carrier (Germany: 1994)
- Pbv 401 (MT-LB) Armored Personnel Carrier (Sweden: 1994)
- MOWAG (10 x 10) Armored Combat Vehicle (Switzerland: 1994)
- Otokar Akrep (Scorpion) Scout Car (Turkey: 1994)
- Otokar Akrep (Scorpion) Armored Personnel Carrier (Turkey: 1994)
- ABI Armored Car (Romania: 1994)
- BTR-90 Armored Personnel Carrier (Russia: 1994)
- Gypsy Armored Personnel Carrier (India: 1994)
- Modified M1113 Armored Personnel Carrier (Israel: 1994)
- Danto Armored Personnel Carrier (Guatemala: 1994)

- Alvis Vehicles Reconnaissance Vehicle (U.K.: 1995)
- CV9030 Infantry Fighting Vehicle (Sweden: 1995)
- MOWAG Spy Armored Car (Switzerland: 1995)
- MOWAG Eagle Armored Car (Switzerland: 1995)
- BMP-30 Infantry Combat Vehicle (Bulgaria: 1995)
- Snezka Reconnaissance Vehicle (Czechoslovakia: 1995)
- MT-LB Tracked Vehicle (Poland: 1995)
- BRDM-3 Reconnaissance Vehicle (Russia: 1995)
- PRP-4 Reconnaissance Vehicle (Russia: 1995)
- Vodnik Multi-Purpose Vehicle (Russia: 1995)
- BTR-94 Armored Personnel Carrier (Ukraine: 1995)
- WZ 501 Infantry Combat Vehicle (China: 1995)
- M113 upgrade (Singapore: 1995)
- RN-94 Armored Personnel Carrier (Romania/Italy: 1995)
- Vickers OMC RG-32 Scout Armored Vehicle (S. Africa: 1995)
- Vickers OMC Kobra Armored Personnel Carrier (S. Africa: 1995)
- Scarab Scout Car (U.K.: 1996)
- Pandur 6×6 Armored Personnel Carrier (Austria: 1996; Pandur II in 6×6 and 8×8 versions are in development)
- Centauro Armored Car (Italy: 1996)
- Tatrapan Armored Personnel Carrier (Czechoslovakia: 1996)
- BWP 2000 Infantry Fighting Vehicle (Poland: 1996)
- Alligator Scout Car (Slovakia: 1996)
- DIO Armored Personel Carrier (Iran: 1996)
- Shorland (Tenix) S600 Armored Personnel Carrier (Australia: 1996)
- General Motors Defense LAV-25 Coyote Recce Vehicle (Canada: 1996)
- Stormer 30 Reconnaissance Vehicle (U.K.: 1997)
- Greys Panther Reconnaissance Vehicle (U.K.: 1997)
- ARIS Arisgator Armored Personnel Carrier (Italy: 1997; modified M113 APC)
- BvS 10 Armored Personnel Carrier (Sweden: 1997)
- Otokar Cobra Armored Personnel Carrier (Turkey: 1997)
- BTR-T Heavy Armored Personnel Carrier (Russia: 1997)
- Shorland Armored Patrol Car (Australia: 1997)
- Bionix Infantry Fighting Vehicle (Singapore: 1997)
- Kentaurus Armored Infantry Fighting Vehicle (Greece: 1998)
- Pbv 501 (BMP-1) Armored Personnel Carrier (Sweden: 1998)
- Al-Faris 8-400 Armored Car (Saudi Arabia: 1998)
- General Motors Defense LAV-III APC (Canada: 1998)
- Warrior 2000 Infantry Combat Vehicle (U.K.: 1999)
- Armored Duro Armored Personnel Carrier (Switzerland: 1999)
- MOWAG Piranha IV Armored Personnel Carrier (Switzerland: 1999)
- Otokar Cobra Reconnaissance Vehicle (Turkey: 1999)
- TAB-77 Armored Personnel Carrier (Romania: 1999)
- Boragh Armored Personnel Carrier (Iran: 1999)
- M35 Mine Protected Vehicle (Jordan: 1999)
- ADI Bushmaster Infantry Mobility Vehicle (Australia: 1999)
- YW 534 Armored Personnel Carrier (China: 1999)
- Type 96 Armored Personnel Carrier (Japan: 1999)

- M1117 Armored Security Vehicle (U.S.: 2000)
- Dingo 1 and Dingo 2 All-Protected Carrier Vehicle (Germany: 2000)
- 2T Reconnaissance Vehicle (Belarus: 2000)
- LAV-600 (U.S.: ?; ready for production but not yet built)
- Armored Modular Vehicle (Finland: 2000)
- Mohafiz Armored Personnel Carrier (Pakistan: 2000)
- All-Terrain Tracked Carrier (Singapore: 2000)
- Terrex AV81 Armored Infantry Fighting Vehicle (Singapore: 2001)
- ARTEC Multi-Role Armored Vehicle (Germany: 2001)
- GDLS RST-V Reconnaissance Vehicle (U.S.: 2003; hybrid gas/electric motor, in testing)

M2/M3 Bradley (U.S.: 1981; technically an armored infantry fighting vehicle)

Armament: One 25mm chain gun (Hughes Helicopter); one 7.62mm coaxial MG; one twin launcher for TOW anti-tank missiles

Engine: Cummins, 8cyl., water-cooled, turbo-charged, diesel, VTA-903T, 500 hp

Speed: 45 mph

Range: 300 miles

Crew: 3

Weight: 21 tons

Carries up to 7 infantry

- Textron Marine and Land Systems LAV-300 (Light Armored Vehicle) (U.S.: 1982)
- Dragoon/Dragoon 3 Security Vehicles (U.S.: 1982/1994)
- M4 Command and Control Vehicle (U.S.: 1998)
- BRDM-2 Scout Car (upgraded) (Poland: 2000)
- Satory Military Vehicles VBCI Infantry Combat Vehicle (France: anticipated for 2008)
- Mobile Tactical Vehicle Light (U.S.: 2002; upgraded M1113)
- Advanced Amphibious Assault Vehicle (U.S.: still in development)

Tank Glossary

What are all those parts on a tank? Who knew? Here's a mini-guide to the terminology.

- **AA.** Anti-Aircraft.
- **AAM.** Air-to-Air Missile.
- **AAMG.** Anti-Aircraft Machine Gun.
- **AAV.** Assault Amphibian Vehicle.
- **AAVC.** Assault Amphibian Vehicle Command.
- **AAVP.** Assault Amphibian Vehicle Personnel.
- **ACAV.** Armored Cavalry Assault Vehicle.
- **ACCV.** Armored Cavalry Cannon Vehicle.
- **ACE.** Armored Combat Earthmover.
- **ACP.** Armored Command Post.

- **Acquisition Range.** Different types of targets are categorized for varying ranges of accurate engagement, often using a *level of clarity* system. Levels of clarity are detection, classification, recognition, and identification, with identification being the most postitive level of clarity. The main categories of target are infantry, armored vehicles, or aircraft.
- **ACRV.** Armored Command and Reconnaissance Vehicle.
- **Active Armor.** *See* Explosive Reactive Armor (in the "Types of Modern Armor" section).
- **ACV.** Armored Combat Vehicle.
- **ADAMS.** Air Defense Advanced Mobile System.
- **ADATS.** Air Defense Anti-Tank System.
- **AFD.** Automatic Feeding Device (for feeding ammunition).
- **AFV.** Armored Fighting Vehicle.
- **AGL.** Automatic Grenade Launcher.
- **AGLS.** Automatic Gun-Laying System.
- **AIFV.** Airborne Infantry Fighting Vehicle (or Armored Infantry Fighting Vehicle).
- **AIV.** Armored Infantry Vehicle.
- **Anti-Tank.** Functional area and class of weapons characterized by destruction of tanks. In the modern context, used in this guide, the role has expanded to the larger one of anti-armor. Systems and munitions employed against light armored vehicles may be included within the category of anti-tank.
- **AOS.** Add-On Stabilization.
- **AP HE.** Armor-Piercing High Explosive (ammunition).
- **AP.** Antipersonnel/Armor Piercing.
- **APC.** Armored Personnel Carrier; it is used to carry soldiers to the close-combat zone.
- **APC.** Armored Piercing Capped—type of ammunition.
- **APC-T.** Armor-Piercing Capped Tracer (ammunition).
- **APDS.** Armor Piercing, Discarding Sabot.
- **APDS-T.** Armor Piercing, Discarding Sabot Tracer.
- **APE.** Armor-Piercing Explosive (ammunition).
- **APERS-T.** Antipersonnel Tracer (ammunition).
- **APFSDS.** Armor Piercing, Fin-Stabilized, Discarding Sabot.
- **API-T.** Armor-Piercing Incendiary Tracer (ammunition).
- **Appliqué Armor.** Armor added on.
- **APT.** Armor-Piercing Tracer (ammunition).
- **APU.** Auxiliary Power Unit; Auxiliary Propulsion Unit.
- **AR/AAV.** Armored Reconnaissance/Airborne Assault Vehicle.
- **Armor.** Tank armor varies considerably, but basic armor is steel plate, with the thickest plating in the front and the thinnest to the rear of the tank. (*See also* the "Types of Modern Armor" section.)
- **ARRV.** Armored Repair and Recovery Vehicle.
- **ARV.** Armored Recovery Vehicle.
- **ASM.** Air-to-Surface Missile.
- **AT.** Anti-Tank.
- **ATGL.** Anti-Tank Grenade Launcher.
- **ATGM.** Anti-Tank Guided Missile.
- **ATM.** Anti-Tank Mine.
- **AUV.** Armored Utility Vehicle.
- **Average Cross-Country (Speed).** Vehicle speed (km/hr) on unimproved terrain without a road.
- **B40.** Vietnam-era Soviet shaped anti-tank projectile ammunition.
- **Barbette.** An open gun mounting with protection on the sides and in front.
- **Basket.** The framework on a tank that holds and rotates the turret.

- **BAT.** Sonic and infrared anti-armor system; stands for Brilliant Anti-Armor Technology.
- **BATES.** Battlefield Artillery Target Engagement System (British).
- **BB.** Base bleed, a system used to reduce drag on long-range shells by feeding air through slots at the base of the shell.
- **Beam Riding.** Missile-guidance system using a laser or radar beam to guide the missile to the designated target
- **Beehive Round.** Vietnam-era cannon ammunition that fired 8,500 darts or flechettes, also called the *Green Can.*
- **Big Boy.** Vietnam-era radio code for a heavy tank.
- **BITE.** Built-In Test Equipment.
- **Black Can.** Vietnam-era ammunition round carrying 1,000 pellets.
- **Blitzkrieg.** Nazi Germany's version of "Shock and Awe," in which tank battalions would overwhelm enemy lines and penetrate to their objectives using power, numbers, and speed.
- **Bogie.** Wheel combination in track-laying systems—generally refers to a pair of wheels joined by a common axle.
- **Bore Evacuator.** Sleeve that fits around the barrel, used to remove fumes after firing so that they don't enter the crew compartment.
- **Bore.** The interior of a gun barrel.
- **Burst (Rate of Fire).** Artillery term: the greatest number of rounds that can be fired in one minute.
- **Bustle.** The part of the tank that overhangs the rear part of the turret.
- **Caliber/Cal.** Measurement of the internal diameter of the barrel; munition diameter (mm or inches), used to classify munition sizes; barrel length of a cannon (howitzer or gun), measured from the face of the breech recess to the muzzle. British calibre…
- **Canister.** Close-range direct-fire ammunition that dispenses a fan of flechettes forward.
- **CBSS.** Closed Breech Scavenging System; compressed air used to force remnants of ammunition out of the gun; used in M551 Sheridan and M60A2 tanks.
- **CC.** Cargo-Carrying (ammunition).
- **CCM.** Counter-Countermeasure.
- **CCTV.** Closed-Circuit TV.
- **CE.** Chemical energy: shaped-charge ammunition, such as HEAT and HESH (see below).
- **CEV.** Combat Engineer Vehicle.
- **CFV.** Cavalry Fighting Vehicle.
- **Char.** French word for tank—stands for *chariot.*
- **Chassis.** The lower section of the tank, which includes the engine, transmission, and suspension. The tracks are attached to the chassis.
- **Chobham Armor.** British-developed spaced armor with ceramic blocks set in resin between layers of conventional armor. (*See also* the "Types of Modern Armor" section.)
- **Christie Suspension.** Suspension system designed in the 1920s by J. Walter Christie, which allowed tanks to run on tracks or wheels. Although a U.S. design, it was more adopted in other countries, notably Russia.
- **CITV.** Commanders Independent Thermal Viewer.
- **CLGP.** Cannon-Launched Guided Projectile.
- **CM.** Countermeasure.
- **Coax.** Coaxial.
- **Coaxial.** Pair of machine guns mounted in the same turret or mantlet, aiming and firing together.
- **Combustible Cartridge Case.** A casing made of some combustible material so that it is completely consumed on firing, eliminating the need for cartridge ejection.

- **Composite Armor.** Armor composed of various layers of materials, which is designed to add protection against kinetic, shaped charges and plastic rounds.
- **Cradle.** The mount for the gun barrel.
- **Cruiser.** British designation for a tank that was meant for speed and independent operations—used in the 1930s and 1940s.
- **CRV.** Combat Reconnaissance Vehicle.
- **CTI.** Central Tire Inflation system—automatically inflates and regulates tire pressure.
- **Cupola.** Armored revolving dome on top of the tank—tank commander's station, often with independent controls and sighting apparatus.
- **CVR(T).** Combat Vehicle Reconnaissance (Tracked).
- **CVR(W).** Combat Vehicle Reconnaissance (Wheeled).
- **Cyclic (Rate of Fire).** Maximum rate of fire for an automatic weapon (in rd/min).
- **Decon.** Decontamination.
- **Depression.** The angle below the horizontal that a tank's gun can reach, which is limited by several factors of design.
- **DFCS.** Digital Fire Control System.
- **Direct Fire.** Line-of-sight firing.
- **Direct-Fire Range.** This describes the range at which a shot can be taken without adjusting for trajectory—in other words, it is the range of a bullet's trajectory that does not have to be aimed above the height of the intended target. In Russia, they call this the *point-blank range.*
- **Ditched.** Refers to situations where a tank tries to cross a trench that is too wide or when ground conditions prevent adequate traction for movement, such as very soft, waterlogged ground.
- **DP.** Dual Purpose.
- **DPICM.** Dual-Purpose Improved Conventional Munitions (ammunition).
- **DPICM-BB.** Dual-Purpose Improved Conventional Munitions, Base-Bleed (ammunition).
- **Drive Sprocket.** Transfers power from the transmission to the tracks.
- **DU.** Depleted Uranium.
- **DVO.** Direct-View Optics.
- **ECM.** Electronic Countermeasures.
- **EFP.** Explosively Formed Penetrator.
- **EGS.** External Gun System.
- **Elevation.** The angle above the horizontal that a tank's gun can point—all things being equal, the higher the angle, the greater the range.
- **EO.** Electro-Optic, Electro-Optical; referring to laser, visual, thermal, low-light, and infrared sights and targeting systems.
- **EOD.** Explosive Ordnance Disposal.
- **Episcope.** A fixed periscope.
- **ER.** Extended Range—referring to various techniques used to extend the effective firing range.
- **ERA.** Explosive Reactive Armor. *See also* the "Types of Modern Armor" section.
- **ERFB.** Extended Range Full-Bore (ammunition).
- **ERFB-BB.** Extended Range Full-Bore, Base-Bleed (ammunition).
- **ESRS.** Electro-Slag Refined Steel (specially purified steel used in tank guns).
- **Est.** Estimate.
- **ET.** Electronic Timing (ammunition fuze type).
- **FAAD.** Forward Area Air Defense.
- **FAASV.** Forward Area Ammunition Support Vehicle.

- **FAE.** Fuel-Air Explosive (ammunition). A technology used in aerial bombs and artillery shells to disperse the effect of the ammunition and cause intense heat and a high-pressure wave of longer duration along with an increased HE blast range.
- **FAV.** Fast Attack Vehicle.
- **FCS.** Fire Control System.
- **FEBA.** Forward Edge of Battle Area (newspeak for "front line").
- **FFAR.** Folding-Fin Aerial Rockets.
- **Fire Height.** Measurement of the height of the centerline of the main weapon when it is at 0 degrees elevation.
- **Flak.** WWII term for anti-aircraft guns and fire—based on German word, *flugabwehrkanonen* or *fliegerabwehrkanonen.*
- **Flechette.** Former Soviet artillery ammunition that dispenses *flechettes* (darts) forward over a wide area. Unlike canister rounds, these rounds use a time fuze, which permits close-in direct fire, long-range direct fire, and indirect fire.
- **FLIR.** Forward-Looking Infrared (thermal sensor).
- **FLOT.** Forward Line of Own Troops.
- **FO.** Fiber Optic.
- **FOO.** Forward Operation Officer.
- **Fording.** Describes the depth of water a vehicle can cross without flooding the engine. This can be described "with preparation" or "without preparation."
- **FOV.** Field of View.
- **Frag-HE.** Fragmentation-High Explosive (ammunition).
- **Fragmentation.** Describes the type of anti-personnel munitions designed to fragment on detonation, such as grenades, some mines and bombs, and so on.
- **FSU.** Former Soviet Union.
- **FV.** Fighting Vehicle.
- **G/VLLD.** Ground/Vehicle Laser Locator Designator.
- **Gen.** Generation. Equipment such as APS and (thermal and II) night sights are often categorized in terms of 1st, 2nd, or 3rd generation of development, with different capabilities for each.
- **Glacis Plate.** Front armor.
- **GLH-H.** Ground-Launched Hellfire-Heavy.
- **GMC.** Gun Motor Carriage—a WWII term for a self-propelled gun.
- **GP.** General Purpose.
- **GPMG.** General-Purpose Machine gun.
- **GPS.** Global Positioning System.
- **Gradient.** The degree of slope that a tank can climb.
- **Grenade.** Explosive device originally designed to be thrown, but now can be launched; often carried on tanks to fire smoke grenades.
- **Ground Contact Length.** The distance from center to center of a vehicle's front and rear road wheels.
- **Gun Truck.** Vietnam-era term for an armed and armored cargo truck.
- **Gunship.** An armed helicopter, often with guns, rockets, and guided missiles, used in a variety of ways, including tank destroying.
- **Hard Target.** A target that has some kind of protection against conventional small arms and fragmentation weaponry. Will require more sophisticated attack, such as armor-piercing, HEAT, or other penetrating munitions.
- **HB.** Heavy Barreled, referring to machine gun barrels that were made so as not to require water-cooling systems.

- **HE.** High Explosive. *See also* the "Modern Explosives" section.
- **HEAP.** High Explosive Anti-Personnel.
- **HEAT.** High-Explosive Anti-Tank (also referred to as *shaped-charge ammunition*).
- **HEAT-FS.** High-Explosive Anti-Tank, Fin-Stabilized (ammunition).
- **HEAT-MP.** High-Explosive Anti-Tank, Multi-Purpose.
- **Heavy.** A relative descriptor for tanks that tended to be larger than those designated as medium or light.
- **Hedgehogs.** Deployment of various combinations of armored vehicles, infantry, and artillery in defensible positions designed to slow enemy advance.
- **HEFI.** High-Explosive Fragmentation Incendiary (ammunition).
- **HE-Frag.** High Explosive-Fragmentation.
- **HEI.** High-Explosive Incendiary (ammunition).
- **HEP.** High-Explosive Plastic.
- **HEP-T.** High-Explosive Plastic-Tracer (ammunition).
- **HERA.** High-Explosive Rocket Assisted.
- **Herringbone Formation.** A formation used by armored units in which they turn their more heavily armored flanks in the direction of march, leaving freedom of movement and also forming a relatively protected zone within for units lacking armor.
- **HESH.** High-Explosive Squash Head (ammunition).
- **HIP.** Howitzer Improvement Program.
- **HMC.** Howitzer Motor Carriage, WWII term.
- **HMMWV.** High Mobility Multi-Purpose Wheeled Vehicle.
- **Hollow Charge/Shaped Charge.** Ammunition that focuses heat and energy in one direction on contact with target, designed to penetrate armor.
- **Howitzer.** Artillery with short barrel and high angle of elevation, originally designed for short range, but modern versions can fire at long range—generally an indirect fire weapon. *See also* Direct Fire and Indirect Fire.
- **HRV.** Heavy Recovery Vehicle.
- **HUD.** Heads-Up Display.
- **Hull.** Main body of the tank.
- **HVAP-T.** Hypervelocity, Armor-Piercing Tracer (ammunition).
- **HVSS.** Horizontal Volute Spring Suspension.
- **ICM.** Improved Conventional Munition.
- **Idler.** A wheel at the opposite end from the drive sprocket—not powered; used to adjust track tension.
- **IFCS.** Integrated Fire Control System.
- **IFF.** Identification Friend-or-Foe.
- **IFV.** Infantry Fighting Vehicle, a vehicle designed to carry troops and allow them to fight without dismounting, or to provide direct support if they are on foot.
- **II.** Image Intensification (night-sighting system).
- **ILS.** Instrument Landing System.
- **INA.** Information Not Available.
- **Indirect Fire.** Describes firing at a target that cannot be seen, for instance by arcing over an obstacle. Many early siege weapons were designed to arc over castle walls. Most modern artillery is designed for indirect fire, in contrast to tanks and self-propelled guns, which rely primarily on direct fire.
- **Infantry Tank.** British designation of slow, heavily armored tanks meant to move with and support infantry—in use during the 1930s and 1940s.
- **Infantry.** In reference to tanks, this refers primarily to armored vehicles used in support of infantry.
- **Internal Security.** Use of military or paramilitary forces in civil situations to keep order.

- **IR.** Infrared.
- **I-T.** Incendiary-Tracer (ammunition).
- **ITOW.** Improved TOW.
- **ITV.** Improved TOW Vehicle.
- **JGSDF.** Postwar Japanese army, the Japanese Ground Self-Defense Force.
- **JSDA.** Postwar Japanese defense ministry, Japanese Self-Defense Agency, changed to Japanese Defense Agency.
- **Kampfgruppe.** A designation for WWII German brigades, often put together of whatever units were available and named for their commanders.
- **KE.** Kinetic Energy: Ammunition, such as AP, APFSDS-T, and HVAP-T, that uses the momentum of impact to create a lethal effect.
- **K-Kill.** Catastrophic kill (simulation lethality data).
- **LADS.** Light Air Defense System.
- **LAFV.** Light Armored Fighting Vehicle.
- **LAPES.** Low Altitude Parachute Extraction, for dropping heavy equipment from the rear hatch of a cargo plane at very low elevation.
- **LARS.** Light Artillery Rocket System—German system.
- **LAV.** Light Armored Vehicle.
- **LAW.** Light Anti-Armor Weapon.
- **Light.** In pre-1940 terms, a smaller tank, relatively speaking.
- **LLAD.** Low-Level Air Defense.
- **LLTV/LLLTV.** Low-Light-Level Television.
- **LMG.** Light Machine gun.
- **LOAL.** Lock-On After Launch.
- **LOBL.** Lock-On Before Launch.
- **LOS.** Line of Sight.
- **LRF.** Laser Rangefinder (also Low Recoil Force).
- **LRV.** Light Recovery Vehicle.
- **LTD.** Laser Target Designator.
- **LVT(A).** Landing Vehicle Tracked (Armored).
- **LVT.** Landing Vehicle Tracked.
- **LVTC.** Landing Vehicle Tracked Command.
- **LVTE.** Landing Vehicle Tracked Engineer.
- **LVTH.** Landing Vehicle Tracked Howitzer.
- **LVTP(CMD).** Landing Vehicle Tracked Personnel (Command).
- **LVTP.** Landing Vehicle Tracked Personnel.
- **LVTR.** Landing Vehicle Tracked Recovery.
- **MAC.** Medium Armored Car.
- **Main Battle Tank (MBT).** Since the 1960s, this is the description of heavy tanks weighing 30 tons or more.
- **Mantlet.** Armor that protects against incoming fire in the gaps around the inner end of the barrel of the main gun.
- **Mast-Mounted Sight.** Extendable optical or video sight.
- **Max Effective Range.** Maximum range at which a weapon may be expected to achieve a high single-shot probability of hit (50 percent) and a required level of destruction against assigned targets. This figure may vary for each specific munition and by type of target (such as infantry, armored vehicles, or aircraft).
- **Max Off-Road (Speed).** Vehicle speed (km/hr) on dirt roads.

- **Max.** Maximum.
- **Maximum Aimed Range.** Maximum range of a weapon (based on firing system, mount, and sights) for a given round of ammunition, while aiming at a ground target or target set with sights in the direct-fire mode. The range is not based on single-shot hit probability on a point target, but rather on tactical guidance for firing multiple rounds if necessary to achieve a desired lethality effect. One writer referred to this as range with the direct laying sight. Even greater ranges were cited for salvo fire, wherein multiple weapons (for example, tank platoon) will fire a salvo against a point target.
- **MBA.** Main Battle Area.
- **MBT.** Main Battle Tank.
- **MCLOS.** Manual Command to Line of Sight.
- **MCV.** Mechanized Combat Vehicle.
- **Medium.** A midrange tank that was, relatively, heavier than a light tank and lighter than a heavy tank.
- **MEWS.** Mobile Electronic Warfare System.
- **MG.** Machine Gun.
- **MGMC.** Multiple Gun Motor Carriage—a self-propelled vehicle carrying multiple guns, often for anti-aircraft operations.
- **MICV.** Mechanized Infantry Combat Vehicle.
- **MILES.** Multiple Integrated Laser Engagement System.
- **Mk.** Mark—designates a major version of a military design.
- **MLRS.** Multiple Launch Rocket System.
- **MOPP.** Mission-Oriented Protective Posture—describes wearing mission-appropriate clothing.
- **MRBF.** Mean Rounds Before Failure—expected average life of a gun or gun barrel.
- **MRL.** Multiple Rocket Launcher.
- **MRS.** Muzzle Reference System, which can correct aim for degradation of the gun due to wear or sagging.
- **MTI.** Moving Target Indication.
- **Muzzle Brake.** A device mounted at the end of the main gun barrel, which redirects some of the gasses at the muzzle, reducing the recoil that must be absorbed by the turret.
- **Muzzle Velocity.** Speed of the projectile when it leaves the muzzle of the gun.
- **N/A.** Not applicable.
- **NBC.** Nuclear, Biological, and Chemical; often used to describe safety and protection features against those three threats.
- **Nd.** Neodymium; type of laser rangefinder.
- **NFI.** No Further Information.
- **Normal (Rate of Fire).** Artillery term: rate (in rd/min) for fires over a five-minute period.
- **NVG.** Night-Vision Goggle.
- **NVS.** Night-Vision System.
- **OP.** Observation Post.
- **OPTAR.** Optical Tracking, Acquisition, and Ranging.
- **Ordnance.** Military equipment.
- **PD.** Point-Detonating (ammunition fuze type).
- **Ph.** Probability of hit (simulation lethality data).
- **PIBD.** Point-Initiating Base-Detonating (ammunition fuze type).
- **Pintel.** Post attached to a firing point or vehicle, used to replace the base for a weapon mount.
- **Pk.** Probability of kill (simulation lethality data).
- **POL.** Petroleum, Oil, and Lubricants.

- **Pounder.** A British method of designating gun sizes, based on the weight of the shells, used up until about 1950.
- **PPI.** Plan Position Indicator.
- **Practical (Rate of Fire).** Maximum rate of fire for sustained aimed weapon fire against point targets. The rate includes reload time and reduced rate to avoid damage from overuse. Former Soviet writings also refer to this as the *technical rate of fire.*
- **Prime Mover.** A tracked or wheeled vehicle used for towing heavy equipment.
- **Protectoscope.** A periscope that protects against fragments or projectiles entering the viewer.
- **Quick Firing.** Refers to fixed ammunition in which the cartridge case and the projectile are joined. Some ammunition required separate loading of the projectile and the cartridge.
- **RAM-D.** Reliability, Availability, Maintainability, and Durability.
- **Range and Bearing Launch.** Firing indirectly on a target whose position, both distance and direction, are known.
- **Range Only Radar.** Radar that can determine the distance to a target, but possibly not altitude with airborne targets.
- **RAP.** Rocket Assisted Projectile.
- **Rate of Fire.** The number of rounds a gun can fire, generally per minute.
- **Rd.** Round.
- **RDF.** Ready Deployment Force.
- **Ready Rounds.** Ammunition that is ready for use in a weapon. It may be in an autoloader or in nearby caches.
- **Recoil Gear.** Mechanism that connects the gun to the cradle and absorbs the recoil, returning the gun to firing position by means of a *recuperator.*
- **Recon.** Reconnaissance.
- **Reconnaissance Vehicle.** Generally a lightly armored, highly mobile vehicle used to gather situational intelligence.
- **Return Roller.** Used to support the tracks and keep them away from the tops of the road wheels.
- **RF.** Radio Frequency.
- **RHA.** Rolled Homogeneous Armor, a standard measurement of the hardness of armor—used to evaluate the penetration ability of anti-tank weaponry.
- **RHAe.** RHA equivalent, a standard used for measuring penetrations against various types of armor.
- **Rifling.** Grooves set in a barrel to impart a rotation to the fired round, which improves both range and accuracy
- **RISE.** Reliability Improvement for Selected Equipment, a U.S. program for improving performance and reliability of various armored vehicles.
- **RMG.** Ranging Machine Gun—a machine gun that operates as a coaxial to the main gun in which the rounds fired have the same ballistic performance as that of the main gun.
- **Road Wheel.** A wheel at a position where it is in contact with the ground, through the tracks.
- **RP.** Rocket Propelled.
- **RPG.** Rocket-Propelled Grenade.
- **RPV.** Remote-Piloted Vehicle.
- **RTC.** British Royal Tank Corps.
- **Running Gear.** Consisting of the transmission, suspension, wheels, and tracks.
- **Sabot.** Refers to the outer *cladding* of an APDS round, literally means "wooden shoe" in French.
- **SACLOS.** Semiautomatic Command to Line-of-Sight.
- **SADARM.** Sense and Destroy Armor, a seeking artillery system using millimetric wave radar and infrared sensors to seek and destroy enemy targets.
- **SAM.** Surface-to-Air Missile.

- **SAW.** Squad Automatic Weapon, an alternate U.S. term for a light machine gun.
- **Semi-Active Laser Homing.** Refers to a missile system in which the missile follows a laser designator, which may be operated independently by another party.
- **Semi-Armor Piercing.** A round that has been partially hardened to give it some armor-piercing ability.
- **Semi-Automatic.** Refers to a gun that can fire, eject, and reload once with each pull/release of the trigger.
- **Separate-Loading Ammunition.** The propellant and the payload are loaded separately, generally with larger ammunition that must be single-loaded and that would be too heavy to handle if in one piece.
- **SFM.** Sensor Fuzed Munition.
- **Shoe.** An individual link of track.
- **Shorad.** Short-range air defense system.
- **SICPS.** Standard Integrated Command Post System.
- **Skirt.** Armor that hangs vertically from the track guard, protecting running gear, suspension, and the side of the hull, particularly from HEAT rounds.
- **Skirting Plate.** Same as skirt.
- **SLAP.** Saboted Light-Armor Penetrator.
- **SLEP.** Service Life Extension Program—program designed to increase the "lifespan" of weapons in various ways.
- **Sloped Armor.** Armor that is made at angles to cause deflection or imperfect impact of incoming rounds.
- **SMG.** Submachine Gun.
- **Smoke BB.** Smoke Base Bleed—a base bleed shell that emits smoke along its trajectory.
- **Smoke WP.** A shell that emits white phosphorus in flight—also known as *WP* or *Willie Pete*.
- **Smoothbore.** A cannon barrel without rifling, often used for finned projectiles that provide their own stabilization in flight.
- **Snorkel.** A pipe that provides air to the engines of submergible vehicles.
- **SOG.** Speed Over Ground.
- **SP.** Self-Propelled.
- **SPAAG.** Self-Propelled Anti-Aircraft Gun.
- **SPAAM.** Self-Propelled Anti-Aircraft Missile.
- **SPAT.** Self-Propelled Anti-Tank.
- **SPG.** Self-Propelled Gun.
- **SPH.** Self-Propelled Howitzer.
- **Sponson.** Early tank development featuring a gun that stuck out the side of the tank.
- **Spring.** Used to absorb vertical movement in the tracks on uneven ground and also to keep the tracks in contact with the ground.
- **Sprocket.** The power transfer toothed wheel sending power from the transmission to the tracks.
- **SSKP.** Single Shot Kill Probability.
- **Stadiametric.** In this guide, a method of range-finding using stadia line intervals in sights and target size within those lines to estimate target range.
- **Stowage.** Allows loading of ammunition within the weapon's firing rate—used for artillery shells, among other things.
- **Stowed Rounds.** Rounds available for use on a weapon, but stowed and requiring a delay greater than that for ready rounds. (They cannot be loaded within the weapon's stated rate of fire.)
- **Sub-Caliber.** Diameter smaller than the bore of the barrel, held in place by a sabot.

- **Submunition.** A smaller round or munition carried by a larger one—a bomb, artillery shell, or rocket.
- **Superstructure.** The upper hull assembly of a tank.
- **Support Roller.** A small wheel that guides the track as it runs back up, between the idler and the sprocket.
- **Sustained (Rate of Fire).** Artillery term: rate (in rd/min) for fires over the duration of an hour.
- **Tactical AA Range.** Maximum targeting range against aerial targets, a.k.a. *slant range.*
- **Tank Destroyer.** A WWII U.S. Army designation for a lightly armored tracked vehicle that carries a powerful gun, designed to ambush enemy armored units.
- **Tankette.** A very small (comparatively) tank meant for a two-man crew, c. 1920s.
- **TAR.** Target Acquisition Radar.
- **TAS.** Tracking Adjunct System, an anti-aircraft system for optical tracking using high-magnification TV imagery.
- **TEL.** Transporter Erector Launcher.
- **TELAR.** Transporter Erector Launcher and Radar.
- **TGP.** Terminally Guided Projectile, referring to the final phase of a projectile attack in which an unpowered, guided, and fin-stabilized projectile completes the attack
- **Thermal Imaging.** Using a heat and video display to sense and track targets.
- **Thermobaric.** HEI volumetric (blast effect) explosive technology similar to fuel-air explosive and used in shoulder-fired infantry weapons and ATGMs.
- **Time on Target.** Refers to a system of artillery in which separate weapons are fired to arrive at a target simultaneously.
- **TLAR.** Transporter-Launcher and Radar.
- **TOE.** Table of Organization and Equipment.
- **TOF.** Time of Flight (seconds).
- **Top Attack.** A missile using proximity sensors designed to detonate above a target, where the armor is thinner.
- **Torsilastic Suspension.** Rubber springs used on some U.S. LVTs. One advantage is that they are not corrosion-prone like metal springs.
- **Torsion Bar Suspension.** A system of independently sprung road wheels that allow greater travel and flexibility; common on modern vehicles, both military and civilian.
- **Torsion Tube Over Bar.** An even more flexible modification of the torsion-bar suspension.
- **TOW.** Tube-launched, Optically tracked, Wire-guided missile.
- **TP.** Target Practice.
- **Tracer.** A bullet or projectile with a phosphorescent base that glows as it's fired and displays a track to its target, which in turn can be used for aiming. Used in a variety of combat situations.
- **Traverse.** Defines the ability of a gun or turret to rotate from the centerline of the vehicle, up to a 360-degree traverse.
- **Tread.** The distance between the center lines of the tracks or wheels.
- **Trench.** Although tanks were originally developed to overcome wartime trench fortifications, the term came to describe the distance of the largest gap a tank can cross without being ditched. *See also* ditched.
- **TRV.** Tank Recovery Vehicle.
- **TTP.** Tactics, Techniques, and Procedures
- **TTR.** Target Tracking Radar.
- **TTS.** Tank Thermal Sight.
- **Turret Ring.** The mounting for the turret, which determines the size of gun that can be mounted.

- **Turret.** Revolving structure at the top of a tank that houses the main gun and often space for the commander or other crewmembers.
- **UI.** Unidentified.
- **Unditching Beam.** A heaving plank of wood carried by early tanks to give extra traction when a tank was ditched.
- **VADS.** Vulcan Air Defense System (an M113 APC with a six-barreled 20mm Gatling machine gun, designated the M163).
- **VDU.** Visual Display Unit.
- **VEESS.** Vehicle Engine Exhaust Smoke System.
- **Velocity.** A measurement of the speed of a projectile at any point in its flight.
- **Volute.** A suspension system used in the 1930s and 1940s.
- **Vs.** Versus.
- **W/.** With (followed by associated item).
- **WAM.** Wide Area Munitions—systems designed to spread "intelligent" submunitions over a wide area.
- **WP.** White Phosphorus (ammunition).
- **Zippo Track.** A Vietnam term for an M113 APC converted to carry a flamethrower, designated the M132A2.

Mines

Mines are used to protect perimeters and to cause damage to any enemy who attempts to enter that area. They are often hidden from view or have various methods of locating intruders and detonating. There are different types of mines—specifically, landmines and naval mines.

Landmines

Explosive landmines were probably first employed during the American Civil War, although they were called *land torpedoes* at the time. They consisted of various traps, tripwires, modified artillery shells, guns, and other equipment. However, these land torpedoes were not universally popular and were regarded as "infernal weapons."

During WWI, the Germans developed super-quick fuzed shells that would explode when tanks ran over them. However, it was in WWII that landmines came into more widespread use and began to fill the two main roles that they still fill—anti-personnel (AP) and anti-tank (AT).

Early mines were made of steel and were detectable using magnetic equipment or, in the case of anti-tank mines, which were set only to trigger by a weight of at least 250 pounds, using a bayonet or other long metal probe. During WWII, the Germans attempted to foil such methods by using mines made from pottery, glass, and Bakelite. The Soviets also tried using wooden mines. Today, many mines are made from modern plastics and ceramics, which are impossible to detect by the old means.

The goal of mine sweeping is often to clear one or more safe paths through the minefield, although in some cases it is to clear all the mines. Often the evidence of mine laying can be seen by the regular disturbance of the earth or even by the careless discarding of mine packaging or firing pins on the ground. Aerial reconnaissance can reveal the presence of mines, as can other kinds of intelligence, such as interrogating prisoners, finding minefield markers, and even finding enemy minefield maps.

While mine sweeping was once carried out entirely by hand, there are several more modern methods. Hand sweeping is still in use, and special "prodders" are used—non-ferrous rods that are stuck into the ground at a 45-degree angle. If the prodder hits something solid, the spot is marked or the area is investigated immediately using a grapple that will pull the mine out safely, even if it detonates. Some mines are intentionally buried at an angle so that the careless use of a prodder will actually detonate the mine.

Finding tripwires is very difficult, but it can be done using a thin piece of wire that will locate the tripwire without detonating the mine. A piece of straightened coat hanger can be used in such a role. Although modern mines use metal less and less, modern detectors can find even the smallest amounts of metal, although they are also prone to many false alarms.

Generally, in battlefield situations, speed is essential. There are several techniques in use, such as special mine-clearing tanks with heavy chains that flail the ground in front of them or rollers that extend out front. A specialized unit called the *Aardvark Joint Services Flail Unit (JSFU)* was used in clearing minefields in Kuwait after the Gulf War.

Some mines were designed to foil minesweeping methods by having double-impulse fuzes, which will explode upon second contact. These could be used in conjunction with an outer rim of single-impulse fuzes to lure minesweepers in and destroy them, or to destroy whichever vehicles are second in a line. To defeat these types of mines, tanks often simply use a front plow and push them out and off to the side.

The fastest way to clear a path through a minefield is to use explosives. Several systems have been developed, such as the British Royal Ordnance Great Viper, which uses eight rockets to carry a 230-meter hose filled with aluminized PE6/A1 explosives across the minefield. When it lands it detonates mines and clears a gap 183 meters long and 7.3 meters wide. It can be defeated by some double-impulse fuzes or blast-proofed mines, however. A tank with a mine plow is often used to further clear the path after this type of method has been employed. Similar systems are in use by the U.S. Army and Marines (M58A5 Mine Clearing Line Charge) and the Chinese Army, which uses a rocket system that will clear a lane 130 meters long and 12–22 meters wide. The American system will clear a path 13.7 meters wide and 100.6 meters long.

Other methods, such as the British Schermuly Rapid Anti-Personnel Minefield Breaching System Mark 2 (RAMBS-2) can be used on a smaller scale and carried by hand to be fired from a rifle with standard ammuntion. It deploys an explosive line 60 meters long and can clear AP mines to a width of about 0.6 meters. The Israeli POMINS II system can clear AP mines and barbed wire simultaneously.

Mines used to be laid by hand, often buried just beneath the surface. The German Tellermine 35 was typical of this type, and it could even be fitted with a special device that would cause it to explode if someone attempted to lift it out of the ground. Other mines included tilt rods, which stuck just above the surface and triggered the mine if pushed at any angle. Today, mines can be laid from the air, using cluster bombs or projected and scattered from ground vehicles.

Modern mines employ not only space-age materials, but digital technologies as well. They can use seismic or magnetic inputs and can often distinguish between different vehicle types and even explode when merely straddled by a vehicle. The Swedish Type FFV 028 is typical of this type. Other mines can be set off the route and triggered by tripwires or other means, such as the French GIAT MIACAHF1 and the Swedish FFV 016. Sensor-based mines, such as the British Hunting LAW80 and the French Manhurin Apilas, can be tripod-mounted and can destroy a tank with one shot of shaped charge.

Mines in modern warfare can be used to create barriers and to force vehicular or pedestrian traffic into specific "killing zones" where they will come under heavy fire—for instance, from anti-tank guided weapons. They can also be used tactically to surround enemy troops. And they can be used randomly to create havoc and the maximum in nuisance value.

There are essentially three types of anti-personnel mines—blast, directional shrapnel, and omni directional bounding shrapnel:

- Blast mines are small—as small as a tin of shoe polish. They pack enough explosive to blow a man's foot off, and they were used to maim, demoralize, and disrupt infantry advancement. Among the most widely employed of these mines are the Italian Tecnovar TS-50 and the Soviet PMN. The U.S. equivalent of the 1950s was the M14 anti-personnel mine.

- Directional shrapnel mines are exemplified by the US M1A1 Claymore, which blasts 700 ball bearings in a 60-degree arc at a height of close to 6 feet and over a distance of up to 150 yards.
- The bounding type of omnidirectional mines, such as the WWII German S.Mi.35 and S.Mi.44 (also known as Sprengmine 35 and 44), are triggered by tripwire or by direct pressure. When triggered, a propellant charge is fired, sending the mine about 3 feet above the ground, where it explodes and fires a container full of ball bearings in all directions, up to 150 feet. Anyone close to this blast will suffer multiple injuries, most likely fatal. Later versions of this type of mine are the Soviet OZM-4 and the Italian Valsella Valmara 69.

NOTE

Early anti-tank mines were designed to disrupt the mobility of tanks by severing the tracks or damaging wheels. This was called an M kill *or* mobility kill. *Today's mines, especially those using shaped charges, can destroy a tank and its personnel. Modern mines can be shaped quite differently from those of the WWII era. For instance, one modern British anti-tank mine, the L9 A1 Barmine is a small bar of plastic explosive meant to be "sown" by plow. It has a pressure plate—also made of plastic—that is narrower than the mine, ensuring that when a tank triggers it, there is plenty of explosive under the tracks.*

Naval Mines

Although the British Navy had used something called *floating petards* against the French Navy as early as 1627, the first known naval mine was developed in 1776 and used against the British during the American War of Independence. It was made from a keg filled with gunpowder that hung from a float. It wasn't effective and didn't destroy the British fleet as planned, but it was only the beginning. Even the famous steamboat inventor, Robert Fulton, designed mines between 1797 and 1812, but naval mines were not used effectively until the American Civil War, where the Confederates deployed mines (called *torpedoes*) successfully against the superior forces of the Federal Navy.

NOTE

The famous quote of Rear-Admiral David Farragut, "Damn the torpedoes, full speed ahead!" actually referred to a Confederate minefield during the Civil War at Mobile, Alabama.

In WWI, mines were even more effective, and American and British minelayers placed more than 72,000 mines in the North Sea to combat German submarines. All mines up to this time had been triggered by impact. However, in WWII, new "influence" mines were developed, which could respond to a variety of signals—acoustic, pressure change, and magnetic and physical contact. Such mines could be laid by ship, plane, or sub. More than 500,000 mines were laid by submarines alone during WWII. More than 1,300 Axis ships were destroyed and another 540 were damaged. More than 1,100 Allied vessels were destroyed. Mines were highly effective against the Japanese, crippling their shipping routes during WWII, whereas during the Korean War, the tables were turned as Korean mines disrupted the U.S. Navy's operations.

During the Vietnam War, Destructor mines were developed that used solid-state technologies fitted into general-purpose bombs, which could be activated by seismic or magnetic inputs.

Modern technologies even include mines that can detect and interpret optical shadows or electrical potential.

As an example of the effectiveness of naval mines, one WWI-vintage mine worth about $1,500 caused $96 million damage to the USS Samuel B. Rogers (FFG-58) in the Persian Gulf in 1988. Today, because mines are relatively simple technologically, there are many mine manufacturers and exporters, and mines are widely available.

Types of Naval Mines

There are several types of naval mines:

- **Bottom Mines.** Generally shallow-water mines with a negative buoyancy, so that they rest on the bottom, detonating when a ship passes over. They can be used in deep-water situations where submarines are the target. Bottom mines were used effectively to hinder landing craft during the invasion on D-Day.
- **Moored Mines.** In deep-water situations, a floating mine may be anchored to the sea bottom at a specific depth, depending on its intended target(s).
- **Drifting Mines.** Free-floating mines that stay at or near the surface. These types of mines were limited by the Hague Convention of 1907 and are not used by the U.S.
- **Attached Mines.** These are really bombs that are surreptitiously attached to the hull of an unsuspecting ship.

Specialized Mines

When we think of mines, we often think of floating explosives in water or hidden explosives that can destroy unwary soldiers on foot or in land vehicles. However, people have developed a variety of specialized mines with different capabilities, such as:

- Anti-sweep mines are small mines used to destroy mechanical minesweepers.
- Rocket mines, originally developed by the Russians, can fire a homing rocket—generally used by bottom mines to extend the range of destruction.
- Torpedo mines are simply torpedoes with triggering devices placed on the bottom. They can be defeated by other anti-torpedo measures, however, such as screens.
- Bouquet mines are arrays of floating mines attached to one anchor. They are designed so that if one mine is found by sweepers and detonated, another takes its place.
- Ascending mines may lurk beneath the surface, but they cut their moorings when they detect a target, floating up into range and detonating.
- Homing mines have small engines that let them move toward their target before detonation.
- Active mines are self-propelled mines that can be deployed, for instance in an enemy harbor, and move on their own.

Types of Damage

Mines do damage primarily by the force of a blast or by shrapnel, but those aren't the only ways that mines can be dangerous.

- Most mines cause some kind of direct damage from the high explosives used, creating holes in the hull and/or injuring crew members with shrapnel. This is most dangerous to enlisted personnel, who tend to sleep toward the bow of the ship, than to officers, who sleep elsewhere.
- The Bubble Jet Effect occurs when the mine's explosion causes a "hole" in the water, which collapses and then creates a pillar of water that can go more than a hundred meters into the air. This effect can cause severe damage to a ship's hull and can kill any crewmembers hit by the pillar. In some cases, it can even break a ship apart.
- The Shaking Effect occurs when a mine detonates some distance from the ship, causing a resonance that roughly shakes the ship and causes tremendous damage if the explosion is large enough. This is enough to shake engines off their mountings and cause numerous leaks that cannot be stopped.

A severely shaken ship often sinks. The most common injury to crewmembers is a broken femur close to the hip. Minesweeper personnel are taught to stand and walk with their knees slightly bent to compensate for the upward jolt from such an explosion—this is known as the *minesweeper walk*.

Laying Mines

Mines are dangerous, even to those who are placing them. Therefore, military geniuses have devised various ways to deploy them.

- Mines may be dropped from aircraft, which has many advantages, especially where access to a waterway is restricted or a minefield must be replenished after it has initially been laid.
- Traditional surface minelayers were the main method in the past, but aircraft and submarine operations have supplanted them for the most part. Surface laying is primarily slower than laying by aircraft and generally more dangerous due to exposure to enemy fire and even enemy mines.
- Submarine mine laying is highly effective. Although a single submarine can only carry a limited number of mines, it can place them very strategically and in complete secrecy. As an example of their effectiveness, WWII subs laid 576 mines, which resulted in 27 sunken ships and another 27 damaged, which means that they damaged or sunk a ship for every 10 mines they placed.
- Mines can be attached to ships by divers, small boats, or remote-controlled devices.
- Some reports speak of mines being attached to enemy craft using trained animals, such as dolphins or seals. More commonly known are the mine sweeping efforts that actually use dolphins to locate the mines.

Mine Examples

Here are some specific types of mines:

- **Spar Torpedoes.** These were early pre-mines (c. 1864) that were actually explosive bombs attached to poles and used to detonate against an enemy ship by prodding it against the hull.
- **Elia Mine.** A typical WWI moored mine that would be dropped off the stern of a minelayer. The cable and sinker mechanism would drop to the bottom, at which time the depth regulator, which hung below the sinker, would cause the cable mechanism to lock, and the mine would then sink to the predetermined depth.
- **Herz Horns.** A German technology for detonating mines was employed by both sides during WWI and WWII. It consisted of projecting lead tubes which, when crushed by contact, would release a bichromate solution or sulphuric acid, which, in either case, would create a simple electrical lead-acid battery cell, and the current would ignite the detonator.
- **Antenna Mine.** This used copper wire that was connected to a buoy above the mine. If a submarine's hull touched the copper wire, it would cause a slight current to run through the wire, due to the connection of dissimilar metals. This current was amplified and used to detonate the mine.
- **Parachute Mines.** In WWII the British would drop mines from planes. The mines would deploy a small parachute, which would detach when the mine entered the water, at which point the mine would drop to the bottom, and a hydrostatic device would arm it. These mines used magnetic sensors to detect the presence of ships above them.
- **U.S. MK23 Mod0.** A magnetic sensor mine that could be shot from the torpedo tube of a submarine.
- **Limpet Mines.** These attached mines used magnets or explosive nails to attach to the hull of a ship. They were deployed by divers or small boats and used delay fuzes.

- **Human Torpedo.** During WWII, the Italians and the British both employed torpedoes that were driven underwater by divers until close to the target, at which point the torpedo was detached, and the divers would escape before the torpedo would hit the enemy vessel.
- **Mine MK56.** A 2,000-pound mine delivered by aircraft, this is a moored mine that uses a *total field magnetometer* for target detection. When dropped from an airplane, it sinks to the bottom, at which time the case and anchor separate, and the case floats up to the preset depth. This mine is slated to be replaced by the Littoral Sea Mine.
- **MK60 CAPTOR.** A deep-water mine laid by aircraft that detects enemy subs and launches an MK46 Mod 4 torpedo.
- **MK62, MK63, MK64, and MK65 Quickstrike.** These mines are the state-of-the-art U.S. shallow-water mines, which come in 500- and 1,000-pound versions converted from general-purpose bombs, as well as a 2,000-pound stand-alone version. These use sophisticated programmable and modular technologies with highly sophisticated target identification and triggering devices.
- **MK67 SLMM.** A Submarine Launched Mobile Mine, developed from the MK37 torpedo, it was designed as a bottom mine for shallow-water targets. It can be delivered from long range by firing from the torpedo tubes of subs. A proposed replacement for the MK67 would convert MK48 torpedoes into dual-warhead mobile mines.
- **Littoral Sea Mine.** This has the ability to be triggered by remote control or by its own onboard Target Detecting System (TDS) and will be able to fire Mobile Homing Warheads (MHW).

NOTE

Littoral. *This means coastal.*

A Nuclear Mine

Blue Peacock was the codename of a British project in the 1950s (also sometimes called the *chicken-powered nuclear bomb*). The idea was to put some quantity of 10-kiloton nuclear mines in specific target locations around Germany, specifically in the Rhine and northern plains. They planned to detonate the mines using wires or an eight-day timer, but the mines would explode within 10 seconds if disturbed. Each mine weighed 7.2 tons. The project was developed at the Armament Research and Development Establishment at Fort Halstead in Kent in 1954.

The whole project was strange and flawed, and one particular element led to its odd nickname. The problem was that during the winter, the buried mines would not be expected to function correctly, and one of the more harebrained ideas (to mix metaphors) was to include live chickens, with feed and water, in the bomb casing to provide body warmth. Fortunately, the whole project was scrapped in 1958 due to the obvious risks of nuclear fallout and the political ramifications of the destruction it could cause.

Mine Countermeasures

Mines are dangerous and scary. They can do terrible harm to individuals and to machinery. They can destroy armored vehicles and sink ships. So it's no wonder that military technologists have devised ways to disable, avoid, or counter them. Here's a list of some common mine countermeasures:

- Degaussing can defeat magnetic sensors. A crude method involved running a wire around the hull of a ship and passing electrical current through it to nullify the ship's magnetic field. More modern methods use special degaussing stations that employ large coils to induce a canceling magnetic field in the hull. This solution has various problems, including the need to recalibrate all the ship's instruments afterward, the requirement that all metal parts remain in the same locations, and the need to repeat the process at least every six months because the ship will slowly regain its magnetic field.

- In an attempt to avoid detonating mines, ships are built with low signatures, to avoid deeper mines intended for large ships. Specialized ships, especially minesweepers, can be built of fiberglass or even wood to avoid magnetic sensors, and special low-noise engines are used to avoid acoustic sensors. Hulls are even designed to create minimal pressure to defeat pressure sensors. Slow-moving ships can use sonar to detect anything that might be a mine and take corrective action.
- Minesweepers often use a wire of hard steel to cut the moorings of mines, which could then be destroyed or collected.
- Paravanes are torpedo-shaped floats that can be pulled away from a ship that is towing them and can cut the wires of moored mines. They can be used in conjunction with a minesweeper or floated off the bow of a ship for added protection.
- Agate systems are anti-mine devices that come in several configurations, from towed to independently steered and unmanned drones. Agate stands for *Air Gun and Transducer Equipment*, and these systems can duplicate the acoustic signature of any ship using airguns, thereby causing acoustic mines to detonate safely. One self-steering version is known as the *Agate towfish.*
- Tidal lifts are inflatable bag systems used to capture mines and tow them to safe locations.
- Mine disposal charges are explosive devices that are deployed by remotely operated vehicles and destroy the mines by sympathetic detonation.
- Autonomous Unmanned Vehicles are used for surveying an area and detecting the presence of mines.
- New FAE (*Fuel Air Explosive*) bombs create a massive blastwave over a minefield and detonate the mines. (See the following "Bombs" section for more.)
- The U.S. Navy runs the Marine Mammal Program that trains and employs dolphins and/or sea lions to locate, detect, mark, and sometimes retrieve naval mines. These animals are also used to guard various sensitive coastal areas from various types of swimmer and diver attacks, according to the U.S. Navy website.

Aircraft

Although there were many precursors to manned flight, the first military aircraft was, ironically, the Wright Flyer, the plane that made history in 1903 by becoming the first machine-powered heavier-than-air plane to fly. The Wright brothers' Flyer (renamed Wright A) was in military service for two years before being retired to the Smithosonian Institute.

The first time modern aircraft were used in war occured during the Balkan war of 1912–1913, but it was in WWI that air combat first played any significant role and began nearly a century of development and increasing importance of air superiority. WWI saw the first air aces, such as Max Immelmann, Oswald Boelcke, Manfred Von Richthofen (the Red Baron), Georges Guynemer, Rene Fonck, Billy Bishop, and Eddie Rickenbacker, all flying in biplanes or triplanes.

One of the earliest roles of airplanes was reconnaissance, but they were quickly used as attack planes, for ground strafing and for crude bombing (which often involved the pilot or co-pilot manually throwing bombs and grenades from the open cockpit onto ground targets). In fact, the earliest bombers were balloons.

What followed was a further evolution of air combat, with dedicated air superiority fighters and bombers of various configurations. In some ways, the evolution of fighter air combat followed the ancient rules of chivalry, and it could be said, with some stretch of the imagination, that the plane had replaced the horse and the machinegun had replaced the lance, and that aerial dogfights were the equivalent of medieval jousting. At any rate, pilots did often tend to adopt a more chivalrous attitude toward their adversaries and, even into WWII, acted as if they were a class distinct from the foot soldiers and other ground- and sea-based combatants. This chivalry did not necessarily extend to the bomber, which was an indiscriminate killer and destroyer, nor did it extend into the modern era of jet fighters that can kill opponents without necessarily making visual contact at all.

At any rate, this list contains most of the aircraft used in combat for almost the last 100 years. It is a reasonably complete listing of all planes built in any numbers (excluding prototypes [for the most part] and one-offs), including, where possible, the name/designation of the aircraft, its type/role, its country of manufacture, and the year of first introduction. In some cases, I've added a few additional notes on points of interest.

Dirigibles

Technically, the term *dirigible*, which derives from the French word *dirigeable*, specifically refers to the idea that, unlike balloons, dirigibles are lighter-than-air craft that can be steered. It is widely believed that the Germans were the main users of dirigibles during WWI, but in fact the British, French, and Americans also used them. At that time, most were what are called *rigid* because they were built around a rigid skeleton. In contrast, non-rigid dirigibles are simply bags filled with a lighter-than-air gas, originally hydrogen and later helium. Non-rigid dirigibles are now known commonly as *blimps*.

- Entreprenant (France, 1794)—the first war balloon, used by Napoleon at the Battle of Fleurus
- Lebaudy Republique (France, 1908)
- ZR-1 USS Shenandoah (U.S., 1923)—dirigible

Zeppelins

- LZ-1 (1900)
- Deutschland (world's first commercial airship, 1910)
- Sachsen (1913)

NOTE

Zeppelin airships clocked 107,208 miles and carried 34,028 passengers and crew from 1910 to 1914.

At the beginning of WWI, Germany had 10 Zeppelin airships. By the end, they had built 67, of which only 16 survived. The first Zeppelin to function as a bomber was the LZ-38, which bombed London in May, 1915.

After the war, the Zeppelin company made a huge dirigible for the U.S., called the Los Angeles, which flew about 250 flights, including flights to Puerto Rico and Panama. Following that were two additional U.S. airships—the Akron and the Macon.

After the Treaty of Versailles period had passed, Germany built three giant rigid airships, called the LZ-127 Graf Zeppelin, LZ-129 Hindenburg, and LZ-130 Graf Zeppelin II. The Graf Zeppelin first flew in 1928 and made many trips, including circumnavigating the globe in 12 days with only three stops. In all, the Graf Zeppelin made 590 flights and crossed the oceans 144 times in 10 years, carrying more than 13,000 passengers.

The Hindenburg was built in 1936. It was 804 feet long, 135 feet maximum diameter, and contained 7 million cubic feet of hydrogen in 16 cells. It was powered by four diesel engines and could travel up to 82 mph carrying 70 passengers. It had a dining room, a library, a lounge, and observation windows. It carried out several successful flights and carried more than 1,300 passengers before it somehow ignited during a landing operation in 1937 over Lakehurst, New Jersey, killing 35 of the 97 people onboard and also killing the future of Zeppelins as commercial carriers.

The Graf Zeppelin II was built in 1938 but had no particular future and was scrapped in 1940.

Multi-Winged Planes

Early aircraft used multiple-wing structures for added lift. As engines became more powerful and airfoil technologies improved, almost all aircraft eventually moved to the monowing. This section details some of the multi-winged aircraft produced before the monowing came to dominate the field.

1909

- Wright A Recon (U.S.); Wright Bros.; first U.S. Army aircraft

NOTE

Ader Eole (France, 1890) claimed to have "flown" in hops under steam power from the ground on October 9, 1890. The wing structure was similar to a bat's.

1911

- Curtiss AH Triad Recon (U.S.); float biplane

1912

- B.E.2 Recon (Britain)
- Royal Aircraft Factory F.E.2 Pusher Fighter (Britain); one of the first aircraft to fly with a machine gun

1913

- Avro 504 Trainer (Britain)
- Sopwith Tabloid Recon/Bomber (Britain); first plane to complete a successful bombing mission of WWI
- Deperdussin Monococque (Belgium); personal aircraft of H. Crombez, who brought it with him to fight in WWI
- Maurice Farman MF.7 Pusher Biplane Recon (France); used by British (who called it *Shorthorn*) and Russian air forces, where it saw combat in 1917
- Dux 1 Pusher Biplane (Russia); the first armed Russian plane, with a nose-mounted machinegun

1914

- Aviatik B II Observation (Austria/Hungary)
- Lohner C I Recon Biplane (Austria)
- Aviatik B.I Recon (Germany)
- Kennedy Giant Heavy Bomber (Britain)

NOTE

The Bauer bomber (Germany, 1763) was probably the first bomber ever designed; the pilot flapped the wings and carried 45kg of bombs.

- Maurice Farman S.11 Recon/Bomber/Trainer (France)
- B.E.2 Recon (Britain)
- B.E.8 Bomber (Britain)

- Vickers FB.5 “Gun Bus” Pusher Biplane Fighter (Britain)
- Sopwith Gun Bus Fighter/Bomber (Britain)
- Martinsyde S.1 Obersvation Biplane (Britain)
- Sopwith Schneider Biplane Carrier or Float-Equipped Fighter (Britain); featured a gun angled upward for anti-aircraft defense
- Sopwith Tabloid Biplane Recon (Britain)
- Breguet 1914 Recon Biplane (France)
- Caudron G.III Recon Biplane (France)
- Henri Farman FH.20 Biplane Recon (France)
- Voisin 1 Biplane Fighter/Bomber (France); the first aircraft to shoot down another in mid-air combat; a series of Voison models followed, up to the Voison 10 in 1916; Voison aircraft were also the first genuine bombers created and were used to bomb Zeppelin plants in Germany in 1914
- A.E.G B I Recon Biplane (Germany)
- Albatros B I Recon Biplane (Germany)
- Albatros B II Recon Biplane (Germany); designed by E. Heinkel; Albatros C I variant added a stronger engine and an observer’s gun
- Aviatik B I Biplane Recon (Germany); observer might carry a rifle or pistol, or even a machinegun (which required leaving the cockpit to fire); otherwise unarmed
- Aviatik B II Biplane Recon (Germany)
- D.F.W. B I Recon (Germany)
- Gotha LD 5 Recon Biplane (Germany)
- Hansa-Brandenburg D Biplane (Germany)
- Hansa-Brandenburg W Biplane Recon Seaplane (Germany)
- Otto B Biplane Recon/Bomber (Germany)
- Rumpler B I Recon (Germany)

1915

- Paul Schmitt Seaplane (France)
- R.E. 7 Bomber (Britain)
- L.V.G C.II Recon (Germany)
- Nieuport 11 Fighter (France)
- Nieuport 12 Fighter/Recon (France)
- Vickers F.B.5 Fighter (Britain)
- Bristol Scout Fighter (Britain)
- Caudron G.4 Recon/Bomber (France)
- Airco D.H.1 Fighter/Recon (Britain)
- De Havilland/Airco D.H.2 Fighter (Britain); Fokker E.III killer
- Armstrong Whitworth F.K.3 Biplane Recon/Trainer (Britain)
- Royal Aircraft Factory R.E.7 Biplane Bomber/Recon (Britain)
- Bristol Scout Biplane Recon (Britain)
- Short 184 Biplane Torpedo Bomber (Britain); first aircraft to sink a ship with a torpedo, but otherwise unremarkable
- Short 320 Long-Range Biplane Torpedo Bomber on Floats (Britain)
- Short 827 Biplane Recon/Bomber (Britain)
- Breguet Bre.5 Pusher Biplane Fighter (France); also used as a night bomber
- Henri Farman F.40 Biplane Bomber/Recon (France)

- F.B.A.C. Biplane Flying Boat Recon (France)
- Caudron G.IV Biplane Bomber (France); 1350 built
- Ponneir M.1 Biplane Fighter (France)
- Nieuport 10 Sesquiwing Fighter (France)
- Nieuport 11 Bébé Biplane Fighter (France)
- Nieuport 12 Sesquiwing Fighter (France)
- SPAD SA.1 Biplane Fighter (France)
- SPAD SA.2 Biplane Fighter (France)
- Caudron R.4 Bomber/Recon (France)
- A.E.G. B II Recon (Germany); smaller, more maneuverable version of A.E.G. B I (A.E.G. C I was an armed version, and a smaller version of the C I was the C II)
- A.G.O. C II Biplane Bomber (Germany); long range and high speed and maneuverability
- Aviatik C I/II/III Biplane Recon (Germany)
- D.F.W. C I/II Biplane Recon (Germany); armed versions of B I
- Fokker B I/B II/B III Biplane Recon/Trainers (Germany)
- Fokker M.7 Biplane Recon (Germany)
- Friedrichschafen FF 29 Float Biplane Recon (Germany)
- Gotha Ursinus G I Biplane Bomber (Germany)
- Gotha WD 2 Float Biplane (Germany)
- Gotha WD 8/WD 9 Seaplanes (Biplane) (Germany)
- Hansa-Brandenburg FB Sesquiplane (Germany)
- Lloyd C II Biplane Recon/Trainer (Germany)
- L.V.G. C I Recon Biplane (Germany)
- L.V.G. C V Recon Biplane (Germany)
- N.F.W. B I Biplane Recon/Trainer (Germany)
- Rumpler C I Biplane Recon (Germany)
- Rumpler G I/G II/G III Biplane Bombers (Germany)
- Sablatnig SF 1 Biplane Recon Seaplane (Germany)
- Zeppelin-Staaken R VI Bomber (Germany)
- Caproni Ca.3 Biplane Bomber (Italy)
- Macchi L.1 Recon Biplane (Italy); copy of Austrian Lohner L40
- Anatra Anade Recon Biplane (Russia)
- Sikorsky Ilya Mourometz Biplane Bomber (Russia); the first four-engine bomber
- Grigorovich M-5/M-6/M-7/M-8 Biplane Flying Boat Recon (Russia); developed after four less successful versions (M-1 through M-4); approximately 300 built
- RBVZ S-XVI Biplane Fighter (Russia); Sikorsky built 21

1916

- Albatros D.I (Germany)
- Albatros D.II (Germany)
- Armstrong-Whitworth F.K.10 Fighter/Bomber/Recon (Britain); quadruplane (four wings); low production
- B.E.12 Fighter/Bomber (Britain)
- Curtis JN-4 "Jenny" Trainer (U.S.)
- Vickers F.B.12 Fighter (Britain)
- Dorand AR.1 Recon (France)

- F.E.2 Fighter/Bomber (Britain)
- Halberstadt D.II Fighter (Germany)
- Hansa-Brandenburg D.I Fighter (Austro-Hungarian Empire)
- Martinsyde G.100 "Elephant" Fighter/Bomber (Britain)
- Hanriot HD.1 Fighter (France)
- Handley Page 0/100 Heavy Bomber (Britain)
- Nieuport 16 Fighter (France)
- Nieuport 17 "Superbébé" Fighter (France)
- R.E.8 "Harry Tate" Recon/Bomber (Britain)
- Rumpler C.IV Recon (Germany)
- Sopwith 1½ Strutter Fighter (Britain)
- Sopwith Pup Fighter (Britain); popular fighter; first to land on a moving ship
- Sopwith Tripe (Triplane) Fighter (Britain)
- SPAD SA.4 Fighter (France); only 10 built for Russia
- SPAD S.VII Biplane Fighter (France); more than 3,500 built
- Spad S.XI Recon (France); more than 1,000 built
- Hansa-Brandenburg CC Flying Boat Biplane Fighter (Austria)
- Hansa-Brandenburg D I Biplane Fighter (Austria)
- Lloyd C II Recon Biplane (Austria)
- Avro 504 Biplane Trainer (Britain)
- B.E.12 Fighter (Britain)
- Vickers FB.9 "Streamline Vickers" Fighter/Trainer (Britain)
- Vickers FB.12 Pusher Biplane Fighter (Britain); few built
- Vickers FB.14 Recon/Fighter (Britain)
- Vickers FB.19 Tractor Biplane Fighter (Britain)
- Royal Aircraft Factory F.E.8 Pusher Biplane Fighter (Britain)
- Handley Page O/100 (H.P.11) Heavy Bomber (Britain); first British heavy bomber
- Handley Page O/400 (H.P.12) Heavy Night Bomber (Britain)
- Royal Aircraft Factory R.E.8 Recon (Britain); 4,077 built
- Dufaux Biplane Fighter (France); featured propeller mounted in center of fuselage
- Morane-Saulnier I Fighter (France)
- Short Bomber (Britain); replaced by Handley Page O/100 in 1917
- Sopwith 1½ Stutter Biplane Fighter (Britain)
- Sopwith Triplane Fighter (Britain); though largely unsuccessful, it did inspire the famous Fokker Dr.I triplane
- Nieuport 14 Biplane Bomber (France)
- Nieuport 17 Sesquiplane Fighter (France)
- A.E.G. C IV Biplane Recon (Germany); successful aircraft, with the C IVN used as a night bomber
- A.E.G. G IV Bomber (Germany)
- Albatros C III Recon Biplane (Germany)
- Albatros C V Recon Biplane (Germany); redesigned C III
- Albatros C VII Recon Biplane (Germany)
- Albatros D I/D II Biplane Fighter (Germany)
- Albatros W 4 Biplane Floatplane (Germany); developed from the D II
- Brandenburg D I Biplane Fighter (Germany)
- Brandenburg KDW Seaplane Fighter Biplane (Germany); based on D I
- D.F.W. C IV/C V Recon Biplanes (Germany); C V highly effective, could outmaneuver many enemy fighters and set world altitude record in 1919; more than 1,000 built

- D.F.W. R I/R II Bomber (Germany)
- Euler D I Fighter/Trainer (Germany)
- Fokker D I Biplane Fighter (Germany)
- Fokker D II/D III Biplane Fighter (Germany)
- Fokker D IV Biplane Fighter (Germany); improved D I
- Fokker D V Biplane Fighter/Trainer (Germany)
- Freidrichshafen FF 33 Biplane Recon/Fighter on Floats (Germany)
- Halberstadt D II Fighter (Germany)
- Halberstadt D V Fighter (Germany)
- Hansa-Brandenburg C I Recon (Germany)
- Hansa-Brandenburg Biplane Seaplane Fighter (Germany)
- Hansa-Brandenburg Biplane Torpedo Bomber Seaplane (Germany)
- L.F.G Roland C II Recon Biplane/Escort Fighter (Germany)
- L.F.G. Roland D I Biplane Fighter (Germany)
- Rumpler 6B 1/6B 2 Biplane Fighter (Germany)
- Rumpler C IV Long-Range Recon (Germany)
- Siemens-Schuckert D I Sesquiplane Fighter (Germany)
- Pfalz E IV/E V/E VI Biplane Fighters/Trainers (Germany)
- Ansaldo A.1 Balilla Biplane Fighter (Italy)
- Hanriot HD-1 Biplane Fighter (Italy); French design, but 831 built in Italy
- Macchi L.3 Flying Boat Fighter-Bomber (Italy)
- S.I.A S.P.2 Biplane Recon/Trainer (Italy); 400 built; based on French Farman biplanes
- Anatra DS Biplane Recon (Russia); improved version of the Anade
- Lebed XII Recon Biplane (Russia); 214 built
- Grigorovich M-9 Biplane Flying Boat Recon (Russia); developed from M-5, but with several improvements; about 500 built
- Grigorovich M-15 Biplane Recon (Russia); about 80 built
- Grigorovich M-16 Biplane Recon (Russia); operated on skis
- Sikorsky S-XVII Recon Biplane (Russia)
- Saveljev Quadruplane (Russia)
- Anatra VI (Voisin Iwanov) Biplane Version of French Voisin LAS (Russia); more than 150 built
- Gotha G II/G III/G IV/G V Biplane Bombers (Germany); the G IV and G V were the main German bombers of WWI
- Zeppelin Staaken R.VI (Germany)

1917

- Junkers J.I Observation (Germany)
- Heinrich Pursuit Fighter (U.S.)
- Nieuport 27 Biplane Fighter (France)
- Nieuport 28 Biplane Fighter (France); rejected by French and British; used by U.S.
- Airco D.H.4 (Britain); nicknamed the *Flying Coffin*
- Airco D.H.5 (Britain)
- Thomas-Morse S-4 Fighter Trainer (U.S.)
- Thomas-Morse S-5 Amphibious Fighter (U.S.)
- Aviatik D I Fighter (Austria-Hungary)
- Albatros D.III (Germany)

- Albatros D.V (Germany)
- Armstrong-Whitworth F.K.8 Recon Bomber (Britain)
- Aviatik D.I Fighter (Germany)
- Breguet 14 Bomber/Recon (France)
- Bristol F.2b Fighter/Bomber (Britain)
- Standard E-1 Fighter/Trainer (U.S.)
- Lanzius L I Biplane (U.S.)
- Pfalz D.III Fighter (Germany)
- Phönix D.I Fighter (Germany)
- S.E.5 Fighter (Britain)
- Sopwith Bulldog Biplane Fighter (Britain)
- Spad S.XII Biplane Fighter (France); mounted with an MG and cannon
- Spad S.XIII Biplane Fighter (France); 7,300 built
- Spad S.XIV Seaplane Fighter (Biplane) (France)
- Sturtevant B Fighter (U.S.)
- Curtiss H Flying Boat (U.S./Britain)
- Phoenix D I Fighter (Austria)
- Sopwith Baby Recon Float Biplane (Britain)
- Blackburn Triplane Fighter (Britain)
- Fairey Campania Recon (Britain); first aircraft design specifically for use on a carrier
- De Havilland D.H.4 Biplane Bomber (Britain)
- Airco D.H.5 Biplane Fighter (Britain)
- Airco D.H.6 Trainer/Recon (Britain)
- Armstrong Whitworth F.K.8 "Big Ack" Biplane Recon/Bomber (Britain)
- Fairey Hamble Baby Fighter (Britain)
- Fairey N.9 Biplane Seaplane Used for Recon (Britain)
- Royal Aircraft Factory S.E.5 Biplane Fighter (Britain); 5,205 built
- Beardmore W.B.II Biplane Fighter (Britain)
- Dorand AR.1 Recon (France)
- Breguet Br XIV Biplane Recon/Bomber (France); more than 8000 built
- Donnet-Denhaut DD.8 Biplane Flying Boat ASW (France)
- Hanriot HD.1 Fighter (France); 1,145 built
- Letord 4 Biplane Bomber (France)
- Nieuport 24/25/27 Biplane Fighters (France); developments of the Nieuport 17
- Nieuport 28 Biplane Fighter (France)
- Paul Schmitt 7 Biplane Bomber (France); obsolete when it enterered service; retired within months
- Salmson-Moineau S.M.1 Recon Biplane (France)
- A.E.G. J I/J II Ground Support Biplane (Germany)
- A.G.O. C IV Recon Biplane (Germany); few built
- Albatros C VIII Long-Range Recon Biplane (Germany); 400 built
- Albatros C X Recon Biplane (Germany); 300 built
- Albatros D III Sesquiplane Fighter (Germany); 446 built; Albatros fighters were superior from 1916 to 1917
- Albatros D V Biplane Fighter (Germany); approximately 1,612 built
- Albatros J I Attack Biplane (Germany); armored fuselage
- Albatros W 5 Biplane Torpedo Bomber Seaplane (Germany)
- Aviatik D III Biplane Fighter (Germany)
- Brandenburg CC Biplane Flying Boat Fighter (Germany)

- Brandenburg W 12 Biplane Recon Fighter Seaplane (Germany)
- Brandenburg W 18 Biplane Fighter (Germany); replacement for the Brandenburg CC
- Brandenburg W 19 Recon (Germany)
- Euler D II Fighter/Trainer (Germany)
- Fokker D VI Biplane Fighter (Germany)
- Fokker Dr I Triplane Fighter (Germany); only about 320 built, but made famous by the WWI German ace, Baron Manfred Von Richthofen (the Red Baron)
- Fokker V.8 Experimental Fighter with Five Wings (Germany); scrapped after the first flight
- Friedrichshafen FF 49 Biplane Recon/Fighter (Germany); several hundred built and used in WWI
- Friedrichshafen G III Biplane Bomber (Germany)
- Gotha WD 11 Biplane on Floats Torpedo Bomber (Germany)
- Halberstadt CL II/CL IV Attack (Germany); 900 built
- Hannover CL II Fighter/Attack (Germany); 639 built
- Junkers J I Attack Biplane (Germany)
- L.F.G. Roland D II Biplane Fighter (Germany)
- Pfalz D III Biplane Fighter (Germany); approximately 600 built
- Pfalz D IV Biplane Fighter (Germany)
- Rumpler 7D 4 Fighter (Germany)
- Rumpler C VII Recon (Germany); improved Rumpler IV
- Sablatnig N 1 Bomber (Germany)
- Sablatig SF 5 Biplane Recon Seaplane (Germany)
- Siemens-Schuckert D III Sesquiplane Fighter (Germany)
- Zeppelin CL II Biplane (Germany); all metal
- Zeppelin-Staaken R IV Four-Engine Biplane Bomber (Germany)
- Caproni Ca.4 Biplane Bomber (Italy)
- Caproni Ca.5 Biplane Bomber (Italy); 640 built
- Macchi M.8 Biplane Flying Boat Recon (Italy)
- Pomilio PC/PD Recon Biplanes (Italy); total production of both types: 545
- Pomilio PE Recon Biplane (Italy); 1,071 built
- Fiat R.2 Recon Biplane (Italy); 129 built
- S.I.A.I S.8 Biplane Recon/ASW Flying Boat (Italy)
- S.I.A 7/7B Recon Biplane (Italy)
- S.I.A S.P.3 Recon (Italy); 300 built despite being obsolete
- S.I.A S.P.4 Recon (Italy); twin-engined version of S.P.3; 146 built
- Yokosuka Yokosho Float Biplane (Japan); first Japanese-designed aircraft; 218 built
- Grigorovich M-11 Flying Boat Biplane Fighter (Russia); about 60 built; redesigned M-12 built only in small numbers
- RBV S-XX Biplane Fighter (Russia); Sikorsky built only five
- Hafeli DH-3 Biplane Recon/Trainer (Switzerland)
- Bristol F.2 "Bristol Fighter" or "Brisfit" (Britain); highly successful WWI fighter
- Sopwith F.1 Camel Biplane Fighter (Britain)

1918

- Orenco B Biplane Fighter (U.S.); never produced
- Pfalz D.XII Biplane Fighter (Germany); about 800 built even though the Fokker D VII was preferred
- Pomilio PE Recon (Italy); 1,071 built

- Salmson 2 Recon Biplane (France); more then 3,200 built, including 705 for the U.S.; used in bomber and attack roles as well
- Siemens-Schuckert D.IV Fighter (Germany)
- Sopwith 5F1 Dolphin Biplane Fighter (Britain); 1,532 built
- Phoenix 20.24 Fighter (Austria/Hungary)
- Sopwith T.F.2 Salamander Ground Attack (Britain); 419 built, but never saw action
- Caproni Ca.4 Series Heavy Bomber (Italy); tri-wing
- Curtiss HA HA Float Plane Fighter (U.S.)
- Fokker D.VII Fighter (Germany)
- Handley Page V/1500 (H.P.15) Heavy Bomber (Britain)
- Martinsyde F.4 Buzzard Biplane Fighter (Britain)
- Hannover CL.IIIa Recon (Germany)
- Phoenix C I Recon (Austria)
- Phoenix D I/D II/D III/ Biplane Fighters (Austria-Hungary)
- Ufag C I Recon (Austria)
- Sopwith Snipe Biplane Fighter (Britain); upgrade of the Sopwith Camel and easier to fly; 497 built in 1918; as many as 1,500 overall; premier RAF fighter post-WWI
- Sopwith T.1 Cuckoo Torpedo Bomber (Britain)
- De Havilland D.H.9A "Ninak" Bomber/Recon (Britain); post-war use in airlines until 1931
- De Havilland D.H.10 Amiens Biplane Bomber (Britain)
- Sopwith 5F1 Dolphin Biplane Fighter (Britain)
- Felixstowe Fury Triplane Flying Boat (Britain)
- Handley Page V/1500 Biplane Bomber (Britain)
- Blackburn Kangaroo Biplane Bomber (Britain); limited numbers used for sea patrol
- Port Victoria P.V.5a Biplane Seaplane Fighter (Britain)
- Sopwith T.F.2 Salamander Attack Biplane (Britain); never saw service
- Short Shirl Biplane Torpedo Bomber (Britain)
- Sopwith Snipe Biplane Fighter (Britain); replacement for the Camel
- Avro 531 Spider Biplane Fighter (Britain)
- Vickers Vimy Long-Range Biplane Bomber (Britain); famous for being the first aircraft to make a nonstop crossing of the Atlantic in 1919
- Farman F.50 Heavy Biplane Bomber (France)
- Hanriot HD.3 Biplane Fighter (France)
- Nieuport-Delage NiD-29 Biplane Fighter (France); large numbers built for France, Japan, Argentina, Belgium, Italy, Spain, and Sweden
- Caudron R.11 Biplane Bomber (France); not effective as a bomber, but successful as an escort craft
- Spad S.XX Fighter (France)
- Salmson 2 Biplane Recon (France); more than 3,200 built; 705 used in the U.S.
- S.E.A. 4 Biplane Fighter/Recon (France)
- A.E.G. G V Bomber (Germany); improved version of the G IV
- Albatros C XII Recon Biplane (Germany)
- Daimler L6 (D I) Biplane Fighter (Germany)
- Dornier Rs I Biplane Flying Boat (Germany); largest plane ever built as of 1918
- Fokker C I Biplane Recon (Germany); 250 built after WWI in the Netherlands
- Gotha G VIII Biplane Bomber (Germany)
- Halberstadt C V/C VIII High Altitude Recon (Germany)
- Hannover CL V Biplane Fighter (Germany)
- L.F.G. Roland D VI Fighter (Germany)

- Linke-Hoffmann R-II "Riesenflugzeug" (Giant Aircraft) Biplane Bomber (Germany); four engines linked to one nose propeller; reportedly the largest single airscrew aircraft ever built
- Pfalz D VIII Biplane Fighter (Germany)
- Pfalz D XII Biplane Fighter (Germany); about 800 built, but not as popular with pilots as the Fokker D VII
- Pfalz D XV Biplane Fighter (Germany)
- Rumpler D I Fighter (Germany)
- Schneider Biplane Fighter (Germany)
- Siemens-Schuckert D IV Fighter (Germany); considered superior to the Fokker D VII, but only 140 were built
- UFAG C I Recon (Germany)
- Idro-S.V.A. Float Plane Fighter Biplane (Italy); based on Ansaldo S.V.A.
- Macchi M.5 flying Boat Biplane Fighter (Italy); 344 built
- Macchi M.7 Flying Boat Biplane Fighter (Italy)
- Macchi M.9 Flying Boat Biplane Bomber (Italy)
- Macchi M.14 Biplane Fighter (Italy)
- Macchi M.15 Biplane Recon (Italy)
- S.I.A. 9B Light Bomber/Recon (Italy)
- Ansaldo S.V.A 3 Ridotto Fighter (Italy)
- Ansaldo S.V.A. 5 Bomber (Italy); approximately 2,000 of the S.V.A series were built
- Hei 2 Fighter (Japan); designation of a single Spad S.XX fighter in Japanese service
- TNCA Microplano Biplane Fighter (Mexico); only one built before the Civil War
- Fokker D VII Biplane Fighter (Germany); considered to be the best fighter of WWI

1919

- British Fairey III Recon Float Plane (Britain); enduring line of float planes
- Besson LB Patrol Triplane (France)
- Liore et Oliviere LeO 5 Attack Biplane (France)
- Mannesman Prototype Bomber (Germany); found after the war; a triplane bomber with 10 engines (!) estimated to have a range of 10,400 km and 80 hours of flight time; never completed
- Fiat B.R. Biplane Bomber (Italy)
- S.I.A.I S.16 Biplane Flying Boat Recon (Italy)
- Nakajima Type 5 Biplane Trainer (Japan); 118 built

1920

- Parnall Panther Carrier Recon Biplane (Britain); featured a hinged fuselage for storage on ships and flotation bags in the event of forced water landing/ditching
- Bleriot-Spad S.34 Biplane Trainer (France)
- Macchi M.18 Flying Boat Trainer/Transport/Recon (Italy)

1921

- Curtiss-Orenco D Fighter (U.S.); biplane
- Lewis-Vought VE-7 Bluebird Fighter Trainer (U.S.)

- Douglas DT Torpedo Bomber (U.S.); operated on floats
- Supermarine Seagull Amphibian Biplane Recon (Britain); Seagull V, named *Walrus*, was better known; not to be confused with 1948 monoplane by the same name
- Gloster Sparrowhawk Biplane Fighter (Britain)
- Fokker T.2 (F-IV) Torpedo Bomber (Netherlands); a few used by the U.S. Navy; famous for being the first aircraft to fly nonstop cross-country (Long Island to San Diego in 1923)

1922

- Curtis FC Fighter (U.S.); first USN fighter
- Thomas-Morse M.B.3 Biplane Fighter (U.S.)
- Curtiss TS Biplane Fighter (U.S.)
- Gloster Nighthawk Biplane Fighter (Britain)
- Breguet Br XIX Biplane Recon/Bomber (France); 3,280 built
- Caudron C.59 Biplane Trainer (France); 1,800 built
- Farman F.60 Goliath Transport (France)
- Caspar-Heinkel U-1 Float Biplane Recon (Germany)
- Ansaldo A 300 Multi-Role Biplane (Italy); used as recon, bomber, transport, and fighter
- Mitsubishi 2MR Recon Biplane (Japan)
- Hafeli DH-5 Recon Biplane (Switzerland)

1923

- Huff-Daland LB-1 Single-Engine Biplane Bomber (U.S.); limited production
- Fokker CO-4 Recon (Germany)
- Fairey Flycatcher Amphibious or Shipboard Fighter (Britain)
- Gloster Grebe Fighter (Britain)
- Aero A.18 Biplane Fighter (Czechoslovakia)
- F.B.A 17 (171) Biplane Flying Boat Trainer (France)
- Rohrbach Ro II Flying Boat (Germany)
- Gabardini G.8 Biplane Fighter (Italy)
- Macchi M.24 Biplane Recon/Bomber (Italy)
- Mitsubishi 1MF5 Biplane Fighter/Trainer (Japan)
- Yokosuka E1Y Biplane Recon (Japan); 320 built
- Fokker C.V Recon Biplane (Netherlands); German design; in use until 1954; Hungarian version called *Manfred Weiss WM 9 Budapest*, also WM 11, WM 14, and WM 16
- Fokker D.XI Fighter (Netherlands); used in various countries
- Grigorovich M-24 Biplane Flying Boat (Russia); 60 built; based on the M-9
- Dudakov-Konstantinov U-1 Biplane Trainer (Russia); based on British Avro 504k; produced until 1931
- Dudakov-Konstantinov MU-1 Float Biplane Trainer (Russia); based on U-1
- Polikarpov R-1 Recon Biplane (Russia); development of the British de Havilland DH-9; remained in production until 1931; another version, the R-2, used a different engine
- Rosamonde I Biplane Recon/Trainer (China); built with American consultants

1924

- Vickers Virginia Biplane Bomber (Britain); in service until 1941
- Aero A.11 Recon (Czechoslovakia)
- Aero A.24 Biplane Night Bomber (Czechoslovakia)
- Nieuport-Delage NiD-42 Biplane Fighter (France)
- Spad S.81 Biplane Fighter (France)
- Fokker D.XIII Sesquiplane Fighter (Germany); developed in Holland to avoid restrictions of the Treaty of Versailles; ostensibly for sale to Argentina, but really destined for the reborn Luftawaffe
- Rohrback Ro III Recon (Germany); carried mast and sails in case of emergencies
- Breda A 4 Biplane Trainer (Italy)
- Fiat B.R.1 Bomber (Italy); 150 built
- Mitsubishi B1M Torpedo Bomber (Japan); 450 built
- NVI FK.31 Parasol-Wing Fighter/Recon (Netherlands)

1925

- Martin M2O-1 Observation Biplane (U.S.)
- Douglas O-2 Observation (U.S.)
- Boeing PW-9 Biplane Fighter (U.S.)
- Curtis F6C Hawk Fighter (U.S.)
- Fairey Firefly Biplane Fighter (Britain); used mostly in Belgium; not to be confused with the 1946 Fairey Firefly
- Fairey Fox Biplane Bomber (Britain)
- Siddeley/Armstrong Whitworth Siskin III Biplane Fighter (Britain)
- Supermarine Southampton Biplane Flying Boat (Britain)
- Fairey Titania Biplane Flying Boat (Britain); four-engine biplane
- Hawker Woodcock Biplane Fighter (Britain); first RAF nightfighter
- Avia BH-21 Biplane Fighter (Czechoslovakia)
- Letov S-20 Fighter (Czechoslovakia
- Potez 25 Biplane Bomber/Multi-Role (France); 4,000 built
- Bleriot-Spad S.51 Biplane Fighter (France)
- Bleriot-Spad S.61 Biplane Fighter (France)
- Villiers II Shipboard Biplane Fighter (France)
- Parnall Peto Biplane Submarine-Based Recon (Britain); never put in production; an experimental craft designed to be stored on submarines and launched by a compressed-air catapult; had floats for water landings
- Heinkel HD 26 Float Biplane Recon/Fighter (Germany); intended to take off from the gun turret of a battleship; was never actually put in service, though two prototypes were built
- Fiat B.R.2/B.R.3 Light Bombers (Italy)
- Fiat CR.1 Biplane Fighter (Italy)
- Grigorovich MRL Biplane Flying Boat Recon (Russia); MR-2 based on this
- Tupolev R-3 Biplane Recon (Russia); 100 built
- M.F.9 Float Biplane Fighter (Norway); only 11 built

1926

- Boeing F2B Fighter (U.S.)
- Vought FU Fighter (U.S.)
- Curtiss P-1 Hawk Biplane Fighter (U.S.); basis for several other fighters and trainers; 115 built
- Blackburn Dart Biplane Torpedo Bomber (Britain)
- Handley-Page H.P.24 Hyderabad Bomber (Britain)
- Handley-Page H.P.33/H.P.36 Hinaidi (Britain); Hyderabad with radial engines
- Vickers 56 Victoria Biplane Transport (Britain)
- C.A.M.S. 37 Biplane Observation Flying Boat (France); still in service in 1940
- Farman F.150 Biplane Bomber/Recon/Torpedo Bomber (France)
- Liore et Olivier LeO 203 Heavy Biplane Bomber (France); LeO 206 (1933)
- Levasseur PL.5 Biplane Fighter (France)
- Levasseur PL.7 Torpedo Bomber (France)
- Villiers 10 Floatplane Fighter Sesquiplane (France)
- Albatross L 76 Aelus Recon/Trainer Biplane (Germany)
- Heinkel HD 17 Biplane Recon Floatplane (Germany)
- Caproni Ca.73 Sesquiplane Night Bomber (Italy)
- Savoia-Marchetti S.62 Biplane Flying Boat Bomber/Recon (Italy); some used in the USSR
- Bartel BM-2 Biplane Trainer (Poland); the first Polish training craft; one built
- Grigorovich I-2 Biplane Fighter (Russia)
- Grigorovich MUR-1 Flying Boat Biplane Trainer (Russia); based on M-5

1927

- Keystone B-1 Biplane Bomber (U.S.); only one built
- Eberhart FG Comanche Fighter (U.S.)
- Fairey IIIF Float Biplane Recon (Britain); the most successful of the Fairey III line that began in 1919
- Avia BH-26 Biplane Fighter (Czechoslovakia)
- Avia BH-33 Biplane Fighter (Czechoslovakia); standard Czech Fighter of 1930s
- C.A.M.S. 51 Biplane Flying Boat Bomber/Recon (France)
- Hanriot H.43 Trainer (France)
- Levy-Biche/Levasseur LB 2 Sesquiplane Fighter (France)
- Potez 29 Transport/Ambulance Biplane (France)
- Ansaldo A 120 Ady Recon (Italy)
- Fiat CR.20 Biplane Fighter (Italy)
- Romeo Ro.1 Biplane Recon (Italy); licence-built Dutch Fokker C.V
- Savoia-Marchetti S.59 Recon/Bomber Biplane Flying Boat (Italy)
- Kawasaki KDA 2 Recon Biplane (Japan); 707 built
- Fokker T.IV Floatplane Torpedo Bomber/Recon (Netherlands)
- Bartel BM-4 Biplane Trainer (Poland); 75 built
- Tupolev I-4 Sesquiplane Fighter (Russia); 369 built
- Boripatr 2 Biplane Bomber (Thailand)

1928

- Curtis F7C Sea Hawk Ship-Based Biplane Fighter (U.S.)
- Curtis F8C Fighter (U.S.); various versions, including dive-bomber versions known unofficially as *Helldivers*
- Boeing F3B Biplane Fighter (U.S.)
- Hawker Horsley Biplane Bomber/Torpedo Bomber (Britain)
- De Havilland D.H.60 Moth Biplane Liaison (Britain)
- Blackburn Ripon Recon/Carrier-Based Torpedo Bomber (Britain)
- Boulton-Paul Sidestrand Biplane Bomber (Britain); Mk. V known as *Overstrand*
- Westland Wapiti Biplane Bomber/Recon (Britain)
- Nieuport-Delage NiD-62 Fighter (France)
- Arado SSD.I Seaplane Version of SD.I (Germany)
- Heinkel HD 25 Biplane Recon Floatplane (Germany); made for Japan
- Heinkel HD 37 Biplane Fighter (Germany); used in the USSR as the I-7
- Yokosuka K2Y Trainer (Japan); based on British Avro 504
- Kawasaki Type 88 Model 2 Bomber (Japan); more than 400 built
- Bartel BM-5 Biplane Trainer (Poland); 60 built
- Heinkel I-7 Biplane Fighter (Russia); special Russian version of HD 37
- Polikarpov R-5 Recon/Bomber (Russia); 7,000 built; still in front lines in 1941
- Polkarpov Po-2 "Kukuruznik" Biplane Trainer/Night Attack (Russia); nicknamed *Nachthexen (Night Witches)* by the Germans in WWII; originally called the *U-2*; as many as 40,000 were built up until the 1950s; it flew night attack missions in WWII and Korea, flying meters above the ground and cutting engines to glide in for a bombing run; it gave a minimal radar signature and was difficult for more advanced fighters to shoot because of its low-altitude flight and speed below their stall speed; many pilots in WWII had more than 1,000 missions logged by the end of the war

1929

- Hawker Hart Biplane Bomber (Britain); more than 950 built; Hawker Hartbees version built for and in South Africa
- Letov S-16 Biplane Bomber (Czechoslovakia)
- Amiot 122 Biplane Escort Fighter (France)
- Levasseur PL.14 Biplane Torpedo Bomber/Recon (France)
- Levasseur PL.101 Biplane Carrier-Based Recon (France)
- Arado SD.II/SD.III Biplane Fighter (Germany)
- Heinkel He 55 Biplane Flying Boat Recon (Germany)
- Caproni Ca.100 Sesquiplane Trainer/Liaison (Italy); approx. 700 built
- Macchi M.41 Biplane Flying Boat Fighter (Italy)
- Fokker D.XVI Biplane Fighter (Netherlands); 21 built
- Polikarpov I-3 Biplane Fighter (Russia)

1930

- Boeing F4B Fighter (U.S.)
- Thomas-Morse O-19 Observation Biplane (U.S.)
- Fairey Gordon Recon/Bomber (Britain); similar to the Fairey III

- Handley Page Heyford Biplane Bomber (Britain); most important British bomber of the mid-1930s
- Breguet 270 Sesquiplane Recon (France)
- Arado Ar 64 Biplane Fighter (Germany); illegal fighter development between wars
- Heinkel He 59 Twin-Float Biplane Recon/Torpedo Bomber (Germany)
- Arado SSD I Float Biplane Fighter (Germany)
- Breda Ba.19 Biplane Trainer (Italy)
- Macchi M.71 Biplane Fighter (Italy); designed for shipboard use; catapult launched; dismantled for stowage
- Mitsubishi C1M Biplane Recon (Japan); unknown date; retired before WWII
- Shavrov Sh-2 Sesquiplane Amphibian Utility/Trainer (Russia); about 700 built; 16 ambulance versions (Sh-26) were also built

1931

- Waco CSO-A Fighter (U.S.)
- Boeing P-12 Biplane Fighter (U.S.)
- Caudron C.270 Luciole Biplane Liaison (France)
- Arado Ar 65 Biplane Fighter (Germany)
- Heinkel He 42 Recon/Trainer (Germany)
- Caproni Ca.113 Trainer/Utility (Italy); famous acrobatic plane; set altitude records of 14,433m and 15,650m; Ca.114 version built for Peru
- CANT 25 Biplane Flying Boat Trainer (Italy)
- Aichi E3A Recon Biplane (Seaplane) (Japan); based on Heinkel HD-56
- Nakajima E4N Float Biplane Recon (Japan)
- Yokosuka E6Y Biplane Recon (Japan); for use with submarines
- Grigorovich TSh-2 Attack Biplane (Russia); only 10 built
- VL Kotka Biplane Recon (Finland); seven built; served until 1944

1932

- Keystone B-6 Panther Bomber (U.S.)
- Hawker Osprey Fighter (Britain); based on the Hart Bomber
- De Havilland D.H.82 Tiger Moth Biplane Trainer (Britain); in use by the Royal Navy until the late 1960s
- De Havilland D.H.83 Fox Moth Biplane Transport (Britain); development of the Tiger Moth
- Avro 621 Tutor Biplane Trainer (Britain); 795 built
- Liore et Olivier Float Plane Biplane Bomber/Torpedo Bomber (France)
- Focke-Wulf Fw 44 Stieglitz Biplane Trainer/Liaison/Observation (Germany)
- Heinkel He 45 Biplane Recon/Bomber (Germany); 512 built
- Heinkel He 56 Biplane Recon (Germany); also the E3A in Japan
- Heinkel He 60/He 61/He 62 Recon Biplanes (Germany)
- Fiat CR.30 Biplane Fighter (Italy); 176 built
- Breda Ba.25 Biplane Trainer (Italy)
- Piaggio P.10 Biplane Recon Seaplane
- Nakajima A2N Biplane Fighter (Japan)
- Mitsubishi B2M Biplane Torpedo Bomber (Japan); 204 built
- Kawanishi E5K Float Biplane Recon (Japan)

- Yokosuka K4Y Float Biplane Trainer (Japan); 211 built
- Kawasaki KDA-5 Biplane Fighter (Japan); 380 built
- Fokker D.XVII Biplane Fighter (Netherlands); 12 built; seven saw action at the beginning of WWII

1933

- Curtiss F12C Fighter (U.S.)
- Berliner/Joyce OJ Amphibious Observation Biplane (U.S.)
- Stampe-Vertongen SV 4 Biplane Trainer (France)
- Arado Ar 66 Biplane Trainer/Liaison/Night Bomber (Germany); somewhere between 6,000 and 10,000 built
- Heinkel He 60 Recon Float Biplane (Germany)
- Heinkel He 72 Kadett Biplane Trainer (Germany)
- Fiat CR.32 Biplane Fighter (Italy); developed from the CR.30, but improved; 1,309 built; nearly 300 remained in service in 1940
- Yokosuka B3Y Biplane Torpedo Bomber (Japan)
- P.W.S.14 Biplane Trainer (Poland)
- P.W.S.16 Biplane Trainer (Poland)
- Polikarpov I-5 Biplane Fighter (Russia); 803 built
- Svenska Aero S.A.14 J 6 Jaktfalk Biplane Fighter (Sweden); in service until 1940

1934

- Grumman F3F Fighter (U.S.)
- Berliner-Joyce F3J Fighter (U.S.); biplane
- Curtiss BF2C Fighter/Bomber (U.S.)
- Curtiss C-30 Condor Transport (U.S.)
- Curtiss SOC Seagull Biplane Observation (U.S.)
- De Havilland D.H.89 Dominie Biplane Trainer (Britain); trainer version of the Dragon Rapide
- De Havilland D.H.89 Dragon Rapide Biplane Transport (Britain)
- Gloster Gauntlet Biplane Fighter (Britain); considered one of the best British biplane fighters
- Hawker Hardy Attack/Utility (Britain); built for Iraq
- Hawker Hind Biplane Bomber (Britain)
- Hawker Nimrod Biplane Fighter (Britain)
- Boulton-Paul Overstrand Bomber (Britain)
- Vickers Valentia Biplane Bomber/Transport (Britain)
- Vickers Vildebeest Biplane Bomber/Torpedo Bomber (Britain)
- Vickers Vincent Light Biplane Bomber (Britain)
- Aero A.100 Biplane Bomber (Czechoslovakia)
- Letov S.328 Biplane Bomber (Czechoslovakia)
- C.A.M.S 55 Biplane Flying Boat Recon (France)
- Heinkel HD 38 Biplane Fighter (Germany); used for training only
- Heinkel He 51 Biplane Fighter (Germany); used for ground attack mainly; 725 built, some with floats
- Yokosuka "Willow" K5Y Biplane Trainer (Japan); 5,570 built, some with floats and some with landing gear
- Nakajima Ki.4 Sesquiplane Recon (Japan); 516 built
- Polikarpov I-15 Biplane Fighter (Russia); 674 built
- VL Tuisku Biplane Trainer (Finland)

1935

- Curtiss R4C Condor Biplane Transport (U.S.)
- Avro 643 Cadet Biplane Trainer (Britain)
- De Havilland D.H.87 Hornet Moth Biplane Liaison (Britain)
- Blackburn B-6 Shark Biplane Recon/Torpedo Bomber (Britain)
- Short S.5, S.12 and S.19 Singapore Biplane Flying Boat Recon (Britain)
- Supermarine Walrus Recon (Britain); developed from the Supermarine Seagull; catapult launched
- Spad S.510 Biplane Fighter (France)
- Arado Ar 68 Biplane Fighter (Germany); last biplane fighter used by the Luftwaffe
- Bucker Bu 131 Jungmann Biplane Trainer (Germany)
- Bucker Bu 133 Jungmeister Biplane Trainer (Germany); highly aerobatic, many still flying
- Gotha Go 145 Biplane Attack/Trainer (Germany); 9,500 built
- Heinkel He 50 Biplane Dive Bomber (Germany); built to Japanese specs
- Henschel Hs 123 Biplane Attack/Dive Bomber (Germany); in service until 1944, by which time they had all been destroyed
- Caproni Ca.111 Biplane Recon (Italy)
- Imam Ro.37 Biplane Recon (Italy); more than 630 built
- Imam Ro.41 Biplane Fighter-Trainer (Italy); 437 built
- Yokosuka "Jean" B4Y Biplane Torpedo Bomber (Japan); 205 built; still in service on the carrier Hosho at the time of Pearl Harbor
- Nakajima "Dave" E8N Float Biplane Recon (Japan); 755 built
- Watanabe "Slim" E9W Biplane Recon (Japan); for use with submarines
- Kawasaki "Perry" Ki.10 Biplane Fighter (Japan); 588 built
- Tachikawa "Cedar" Ki.17 Biplane Trainer (Japan); 658 built
- P.W.S.18 Trainer (Poland); license-built Avro 621 Tutor
- Kocherigin DI-6 Biplane Fighter (Russia)
- Polikarpov R-Z attack (Russia); 1,031 built up until 1937
- S.E.T. VII Biplane Trainer (Romania); in service until 1944

1936

- Hawker Fury Biplane Fighter (Britain); popular pre-WWII fighter, not to be confused with the 1944 monoplane model
- Gloster Gladiator Biplane Fighter (Britain); last British biplane fighter
- Supermarine Stranrear Biplane Flying Boat Recon (Britain); originally called *Southampton Mk. V*
- Avia B.534/B.634 Biplane Fighter (Czechoslovakia)
- Arado Ar 95 Biplane Recon/Torpedo Bomber (Germany); mostly export; Spain used three until 1948
- Gotha Go 147 Recon (Germany)
- Heinkel He 114 Recon Sesquiplane (Germany)
- Caproni Ca.161 Experimental Biplane (Italy); set altitude record of 17,083m
- Imam Ro.43 Floatplane Recon Biplane (Italy)
- Nakajima A4N Biplane Fighter (Japan)
- Koolhoven FK.51 Biplane Trainer/Recon (Netherlands); 112 built
- P.W.S.26 Trainer/Dive Bomber (Poland); based on the P.W.S.16
- LKOD KOD-1 Biplane Trainer/Liaison (Latvia); license-built Estonian PON-1; also a slightly larger version, the KOD-2

- Fairey Swordfish "Stringbag" Biplane Torpedo Bomber (Britain); the most famous and successful biplane fighting aircraft of WWII, served throughout the war as a torpedo bomber, ASW, minelaying, ground attack, and trainer; 2,391 built
- Swordfish Mk.II

1937

- Grumman J2F Duck Amphibian Utility Biplane (U.S.); used throughout WWII
- Curtiss SBC Helldiver Biplane Dive Bomber (U.S.); last U.S.-built combat biplane, not to be confused with the Curtiss SB2C Helldiver monoplane used in WWII
- Hawker Hector Biplane Recon/Bomber (Britain)
- Saunders-Roe A.27 London Biplane Flying Boat (Britain)
- Fairey Seafox Biplane Float Plane Recon (Britain); launched from carriers by catapult; in service until 1943
- Dornier Do 17 Bomber (Germany); various versions
- Dornier Do 18 Recon (Germany)
- Caproni Ca.164 Sesquiplane Trainer (Italy)
- Aichi "Laura" E11A Biplane Flying Boat (Japan)
- Watanabe K6W Floatplane Trainer (Japan)
- Fokker S.IX Biplane Trainer (Netherlands)
- Fokker T.V Medium Bomber (Netherlands)
- Polikarpov I-152 Fighter (Russia); 2,408 built
- Liuchow Kwangsi 2 Biplane Trainer (China)
- I.A.R. 37 Biplane Recon (Romania)

1938

- Kawanishi "Alf" E7K Float Biplane Recon (Japan); 530 built
- Koolhoven FK.52 Biplane Recon/Fighter (Netherlands); obsolete and few built
- Borovkov-Florov I-207 Biplane Fighter (Russia); very small biplane
- Beriev KOR-1 Float Biplane Recon (Russia); catapult launched; also land version
- Manfred Weiss WM 21 Solyom Biplane Recon (Hungary); based on the WM 9/11/14 series, which in turn were based on the Fokker C.V

1939

- Westland Wallace Biplane (Britain)
- Fiat CR.42 Falco (Italy); possibly one of the best biplane fighters ever built, but obsolete by the time it was flown; 1,780 built between 1939 and 1943; one prototype reached speeds of 520 km/h
- Mitsubishi "Pete" F1M Recon Sea Biplane (Japan); 1,118 built; used in multiple roles during WWII
- Polikarpov I-153 Biplane Fighter (Russia); 3,437 built; in service until 1943
- I.A.R. 38 Recon (Romania)
- I.A.R. 39 Recon/Trainer (Romania); some in use into the late 1950s

1940

- Saiman 200 Biplane Trainer (Italy); used until 1947
- Fokker T.VIII W Float Plane Torpedo Bomber (Netherlands)
- Antonov KT Experimental Biplane (Russia); attempt to put biplane wings on a tank and fly it; to be towed by a heavy bomber; experimental only

1942

- Beech UC-43 Traveler "Staggerwing" Transport (U.S.)

1944

- Supermarine Sea Otter Biplane Amphibian Recon (Britain)

1947

- Antonov "Colt" An-2 Biplane Multi-Role STOL Transport (Russia); more than 18,000 built, including new versions, the An-2P in 1968 and An-3 more recently, as well as specialty versions (An-4, An-6); still in use

Unknown Date

- Mitsubish G1M Biplane Bomber (Japan); probably 1930s; obsolete before WWII
- Hiro G2H Monoplane Bomber (Japan); probably 1930s; obsolete before WWII
- Hiro H1H Biplane Flying Boat (Japan); probably 1930s; not in service during WWII
- Hiro H2H Biplane Flying Boat (Japan); probably 1930s; not in service during WWII
- Hiro H3H Biplane Flying Boat (Japan); probably 1930s; not in service during WWII
- Kawanishi H3K Biplane Flying Boat Recon (Japan); probably 1930s
- Hiro H4H Monoplane Flying Boat (Japan); probably 1930s; not in service during WWII
- Itoh Biplane Fighter (Japan)
- Yokosuka K1Y Floatplane Trainer (Japan)
- Kawasaki Ki.3 Biplane Light Bomber (Japan); early 1930s?; 244 built
- Fizir Triplane Trainer (1920s); among several built by Yugoslavian designer Rudolf Fizir

Monowinged Planes

1910

- Etrich A II Taube Recon (Austria/Germany); early monoplane design; used in WWI; wing design based on the Zanonia macrocarpa seed

1912

- Guidoni Torpedo Bomber Hydrofoil (Italy)

1913

- Morane-Saulnier L Fighter/Recon (France); more than 600 built
- Nieuport IV (France)
- Fokker M.1 "Spin" or "Spider" (Germany); Anthony Fokker's first aircraft; later used as a trainer; followed by several versions (2-4)
- Caproni Ca.18 Recon (Italy); designation (Ca.18) applied retroactively in the 1920s
- Macchi Parasol-Wing Recon (Italy)
- Sikorsky S-12 Observation (Russia)

1914

- Morane-Saulnier N "Bullet" Fighter (France); 1,210 built
- Morane-Saulneir P Recon (France)
- Blériot XI Recon (France)
- Morane-Saulnier P Recon (France)
- Fockker A I Trainer/Recon (Germany)
- Fokker M5 (Germany)

1915

- Morane-Saulnier AR Trainer (France); more than 400 built
- R.E.P N Recon (France)
- Fokker E I/II/III/IV Fighter (Germany); dominant for its time with synchronized MGs; best-known version was the E III
- Pfalz E I Fighter (Germany); partly based on the Morane-Saulnier H
- Pfalz E III Parasol-Wing Fighter (Germany)
- Siemens-Schuckert E I Fighter (Germany)

1916

- Junkers J 2 Fighter (Germany); the first all-metal monoplane fighter; only six built
- Mosca MB Fighter (Russia); Italian design

1917

- Bristol M.1c Fighter (Britain)
- Felixstowe F3/F5 Recon (Britain, 1917/1918)
- Morane-Saulnier N Recon/Fighter (France); first French Fighter
- Dornier Rs III Flying Boat (Germany)
- Thulin K Fighter (Sweden); most used by the Dutch Navy with fixed machine guns mounted

1918

- Loening M-8 Observation (U.S.)
- Martinsyde F.4 Buzzard Fighter (Britain)

- Fokker D.VIII Fighter (Germany)
- Junkers CL.I Ground Attack (Germany)
- Brandenburg W 29 Fighter (Germany)
- Brandenburg W 33 Fighter (Germany)
- Fokker D VIII (also Fokker E V) Fighter (Germany)
- Fokker V.37 Ground Attack Fighter (Germany)
- Junkers CL I Fighter-Bomber (Germany)
- Junkers D I Fighter (Germany); used to destroy observation balloons; highly dangerous
- Kondor E 3 Fighter (Germany); only about 10 were completed before the end of WWI

1919

- Armstrong-Whitworth Ara Fighter (Britain)
- Junkers F.13 Transport/Utility (Germany); some remained in service until 1943

1920

- Martin NBS-1 Bomber (U.S.)
- Gourdou-Leseurre GL-21 Fighter (France)
- Gourdon-Leseurre G-22 Fighter (France)

1921

- Fokker F.VI Parasol-Wing Fighter (Netherlands)

1922

- Dornier Do H Falke Fighter (Germany); early single-seat fighter; radical for its time, but never employed
- Dornier Do J Wal Flying Boat (Germany); produced in Italy because of the Treaty of Versailles
- Junkers H 21 Recon (Germany); 100 used in the USSR to suppress resistance to Stalin; built in the USSR
- Junkers Ju 20 Recon (Germany)

1923

- Vought UO Catapult-Launched Observation Craft (U.S.)
- Blackburn Blackburn Recon (Britain)
- Avia BH-9 Recon/Trainer (Czechoslovakia)
- Heinkel He 1/He 2/He 4/ Float Plane Recon (Germany); built for the Swedish Navy
- Caproni Ca.36 Recon (Italy)
- Piaggio P.8 Recon (Italy); designed for dismantling and stowing in a submarine hangar

1924

- Fairey Fawn Light Bomber (Britain)
- TNCA 3-E-130 Tololoche Fighter (Mexico); four built

1925

- Avro 555 Bison Recon (Britain)
- Hawker Danecock Fighter (Britain); only 15 built all together, 12 of them in Denmark as the Hawker Dankok
- Gloster Gamecock Fighter (Britain)
- Junkers K 30 Transport/Bomber (Germany); used in Spain and USSR
- Ansaldo AC 2 Parasol-Wing Fighter (Italy); based on French Dewoitine D.1
- Ansaldo AC 3 Parasol-Wing attack (Italy); in 1936 set altitude record of 11,861 meters
- Savoia-Marchetti S.55 Flying Boat Bomber/Transport (Italy)

1926

- Vought O2U Corsair Observation (U.S.)
- Martin T3M Torpedo Bomber (U.S.)
- Martin T4M Torpedo Bomber (U.S.)
- Morane-Saulnier MS.130 Trainer (France)
- Wibault Wib 7 Fighter (France)
- Dornier N Bomber (Germany); land version of the Wal; also built in Japan as the Ka.87
- Heinkel He 5 Float Plane Recon (Germany); improved version of He 4
- Junkers K 53 Fighter (Germany); for export
- Junkers W 34 Transport/Liaison (Germany); 1,991 built
- Polikarpov I-1 Fighter (Russia)
- Fokker F.VII Transport (Netherlands); a remarkably reliable aircraft; in 1926, an F-VII named the Josephine Ford flew Richard Byrd and Floyd Bennett over the North Pole, and in 1928 Amelia Earhart became the first woman to cross the Atlantic, while Charles Kingford-Smith was the first pilot to cross the Pacific Ocean in the same year, both also in Fokker F.VIIs

1927

- Spirit of St. Louis (U.S.); based on a Ryan M-2; one of the most famous planes ever built; specifically constructed for Charles Lindbergh's famous flight from New York to Paris in May 1927
- Armstrong Whitworth Atlas Recon (Britain)
- Loire-Gourdou-Leseurre LGL-32 Fighter (France)
- Heinkel He 8 Recon Float Plane (Germany); development of He 5 built for the Danish Navy
- Klemm L 25 Trainer (Germany)

1928

- Bleriot 127 Multi-Role (France)
- Morane-Saulnier MS.147 Trainer (France)

- Potez 32/33 Observation/Liaison (France)
- Junkers K 47 (Germany); built in Sweden and USSR; some sold to China
- Breda Ba.15 Trainer/Liaison (Italy)

1929

- Potez 36 Folding Wing Utility (France)
- Nakajima Recon Floatplane (Japan)
- Plage i LaÊkiewicz/Lublin R-X Parasol-Wing Recon/Liaison (Poland); included several derivatives over the next few years: R-XIV and R-XV (1930)
- Tupolev ANT-9 Transport (Russia)
- Tupolev TB-1 Bomber (Russia); 212 built; one made a flight from Moscow to New York
- Anbo V Trainer (Lithuania)

1930

- Bristol Bulldog Fighter (Britain)
- De Havilland D.H.80 Puss Moth liaison (Britain)
- Gordon-Leseurre GL-810 Observation Float Plane (France)
- Hanriot H.16 Trainer (France)
- S.I.A.I S.67 Flying Boat Fighter (Italy); only three built, but all three were in service until 1935
- Tupolev R-6 Recon Fighter (Russia); 435 built
- Tupolev TB-3 Bomber (Russia); four-engine version of TB-1; 818 built
- VL Viima Trainer/Liaison (Finland)

1931

- Dewoitine D.26 Trainer (France); one remained in use until 1970
- Dewoitine D.27 C.1 Fighter (France)
- Lockheed JO Utility (U.S., 1931 to 1955); first twin-engine plane to land on a carrier
- Latecoere Late 290 Seaplane Torpedo Bomber (France)
- Caudron C.270 Luciole Liaison (France)
- Nakajima Type 91 Fighter (Japan); 450 built
- P.W.S.10 Parasol-Wing Fighter (Poland)
- Plage i LaÊkiewicz /Lublin R-XIII Recon/Liaison (Poland); 220 built
- Tupolev ANT-14 Propaganda Plane (Russia); based on ANT-9

1932

- Martin BM Dive Bomber (U.S.); first U.S. Navy dive bomber
- Grumman FF Goblin Fighter (U.S.)
- Hawker Audax Observation/Fighter (Britain)
- Bloch MB.80 Ambulance (France)
- Morane-Saulnier MS.230 Advanced Trainer (France); more than 500 built
- Morane-Saulnier MS.315 Parasol-Wing Trainer (France)
- Nieuport-Delage NiD-121 Fighter (France)

- Caudron C.400 Phalene Utility Aircraft (France); in service until 1960
- Heinkel He 70 Blitz Recon (Germany)
- Junkers Ju 60 Transport/Liaison (Germany)
- Savoia-Marchetti S.66 Transport/SAR (Italy)
- Mitsubishi 2MR8 Recon (Japan)
- PZL P.7 Fighter (Poland)
- R.W.D.13 Liaison (Poland); folding wings
- Grokhovskii G-63 Glider (Russia); passengers lay prone inside the wing
- Grigorovich ShON Attack (Russia); counter-insurgency aircraft
- Anbo IV Recon/Trainer (Lithuania)

1933

- Northrop A-13 Fighter (U.S.)
- Curtiss F11C-2 Goshawk Fighter (U.S.)
- Stampe-Vertongen SV 4 (France)
- Hawker Demon Fighter (Britain)
- De Havilland D.H.84 Dragon Attack/Transport (Britain)
- Morane-Saulnier MS.224 Fighter (France)
- Heinkel He 46 Recon/Attack Parasol Wing Monoplane (Germany); 481 built; some in service until 1943
- Junkers Ju 52 "Auntie Ju" Transport (Germany) 4,835 built; Swiss Air Force used it from 1939 until 1981
- Mitsubishi Ki.1 Bomber (Japan); 118 built
- Mitsubishi Ki.2 Bomber (Japan); 61 built
- PZL P.11 Fighter (Poland); 250 built
- Tupolev ANT-25 Long-Range Experimental Bomber (Russia); flew over the pole from Moscow to San Jacinto, California
- Cheranovski BICh-11 Experimental Rocket Plane (Russia); never built, but was an early experiment in airplane design featuring a tailless fighter with twin rocket engines
- Tupolew I-14 Fighter (Russia)
- Grigorovich I-Z Fighter (Russia)
- Beriev MBR-2 Flying Boat Recon (Russia); about 1,400 built; used through the end of WWII
- Tupolev TB-4 Bomber (Russia); six-engine version of TB-3
- F+W C-3603 Recon/Attack (Switzerland)
- I.A.R. 14 Fighter/Trainer (Argentina)

1934

- Martin B-10B Bomber (U.S.)
- Grumman F2F Fighter (U.S.)
- Bloch 210 Bomber (France)
- Potez 39 Observation (France)
- Potez 54 Bomber/Recon (France)
- Curtiss A-12 Shrike Fighter (U.S.)
- Curtis A-18 Shrike Fighter (U.S.)
- Boeing P-26 "Peashooter" Fighter (U.S.)

- Blackburn B-5 Baffin Torpedo Bomber (Britain)
- Airspeed Envoy Transport (Britain); used as a bomber in South Africa
- Amiot 143M Bomber/Recon/Transport (France)
- Dewoitine D.510 Fighter (France)
- Farman F.220 Bomber (France)
- Caudron C.440 Transport (France); 1,702 built
- Morane-Saulnier MS.275 Parasol-Wing Fighter (France)
- Messerschmitt Bf 108 Taifun Trainer/Liaison (Germany)
- Dornier Do 15 Wal Flying Boat Recon (Germany)
- Breda Ba.27 Fighter (Italy); only 11 built for use in China
- Breda Ba.64 Attack (Italy)
- Caproni Ca.132 Bomber (Italy)
- Caproni-Bergamasca Ca.301 (also called *A.P.1*) Fighter/Attack (Italy)
- Savoia-Marchetti S.72 Bomber (Italy); six or more made for China; based on the S.71
- Savoia-Marchetti S.73 Transport (Italy)
- Savoia-Marchetti S.M.79 Sparviero Bomber/Torpedo Bomber (Italy); various versions made through 1944 (many for export to Brazil, Iraq, Romania, and Yugoslavia); 1,370 built
- Aichi "Susie" D1A Dive Bomber (Japan); based on the He 50; 590 built; production stopped in 1940
- Kawasaki Ki.5 Fighter (Japan); only four built
- R.W.D.8 Parasol-Wing Trainer (Poland)
- TsAGI A-7 Observation Autogiro (Russia); first autogiro to carry armament
- Tupolev ANT-20 Maksim Gorky Propaganda Plane (Russia); giant eight-engined plane; only one built—it was destroyed in a midair collision, but it carried 72 passengers and contained a bar, buffet, film processing lab, movie theater, laundry, pharmacy, and printing press; named after author Aleksei Maksimovich Peshkov, known as Maxim Gorky
- Grigorovich PI-1 Fighter (Russia)
- Rogozarski PVT Trainer (Yugoslavia)

1935

- Noorduyn C-64 Norseman Transport (U.S.)
- Kellet KG-1 Autogiro (U.S.)
- Curtiss P-36 Hawk Fighter (U.S.); 1,424 built in all versions
- Bristol Bombay Bomber/Transport (Britain)
- Avro 643 Cadet Trainer (Britain)
- Handley Page H.P.54 Harrow Bomber/Transport (Britain)
- Cierva Rota C.30/C.40 Autogiros (Britain, 1935/1938); used to calibrate top-secret radar installations during the Battle of Britain
- Renard R 31 Recon (Belgium)
- Caudron C.600 Aiglon Liaison (France); used throughout WWII
- Dewoitine D.500 Fighter (France)
- Morane-Saulnier MS.138 Trainer (France)
- Mureaux 110 (115) Bomber/Recon (France)
- Potez 58 Liaison/Observation (France)
- Potez 65 Troop Transport (France)
- Dornier Do 22 Recon/Torpedo Bomber (Germany)
- Focke-Wulf Fw 56 Stosser Trainer/Fighter (Germany); more than 900 built

- Junkers Ju 160 Transport (Germany)
- Klemm Kl 35 Trainer (Germany); used in various countries
- Breda Ba.65 Attack (Italy); based on Ba.64; 219 built
- Caproni Ca.133 STOL Bomber/Transport (Italy); 525 built
- Caproni Ca.135 Bomber (Italy); used largely in Hungary and Peru
- Nardi FN.305 Trainer/Liaison (Italy); 500 built
- Savoia-Marchetti S.M.81 Pipistrello Bomber/Transport (Italy); some continued as transports until 1951; 584 built
- Nakajima Ki.8 Fighter (Japan); only five built
- Tachikawa "Spruce" Ki.9 Trainer (Japan); 2,618 built
- L.W.S.3 Mewa Parasol-Wing Recon (Poland)
- Tupolev ANT-29 Fighter (Russia); when the gun system proved impractical, its designer (Kurchevski) was arrested and "disappeared"
- BOK-2 Research Craft (Russia)
- Bolchivitinov DB-A Bomber (Russia); limited production
- Polikarpov I-17 Fighter (Russia)
- Tupolev SB Bomber (Russia)

1936

- Northrop/Douglas A-17 Nomad Fighter (U.S.)
- S-43 Flying Boat (Sikorsky JRS) (U.S.)
- Douglas O-46 Observation (U.S.)
- Douglas TBD Devastator Torpedo Bomber (U.S.)
- Avro 652 Anson Trainer (Britain); called *Faithful Annie*, it was used until 1968; 11,022 built
- Aero A.304 Bomber/Recon (Czechoslovakia)
- Farman F.222 Bomber (France)
- Latecoere Late 298 Seaplane Torpedo Bomber/Recon (France)
- Loire 43 Fighter (France)
- Loire 130 Shipboard Flying Boat (France)
- Dornier Do 23 Bomber (Germany); based on Do 13
- Heinkel He 111 Bomber (Germany); various versions up through 1943; 7,300 built
- Heinkel He 112 Fighter (Germany); lost competitions to the Bf 109, but several versions were built and flown in other countries
- Henschel Hs 126 Parasol-Wing Recon (Germany); more than 600 built
- Junkers Ju 86 Bomber/Recon (Germany); not effective as a bomber, but untouchable at high altitudes in reconnaissance role
- Fiat B.R.20 Cicogna Bomber (Italy); 84 sold to Japan; fared poorly in WWII
- Caproni Ca-309 Ghibli Recon Bomber (Italy)
- Saiman 202 Liaison (Italy); used throughout and after WWII
- CANT Z.501 Gabbiano Recon (Italy); 454 built
- Mitsubishi "Nell" G3M Bomber (Japan); 1,048 built
- Mitsubishi "Babs" Ki.15 Bomber (Japan); 439 built
- Mitsubishi "Sally" Ki.21 Bomber (Japan); 2,064 built; first built in 1936 and upgraded during the war; retired in 1943 as obsolete
- Fokker D.XXI Fighter (Netherlands)
- PZL P.23 Karas Attack/Tactical Bomber (Poland)

- Polkarpov I-16 Fighter (Russia); 7,005 single-seat versions and 1,639 two-seat versions built
- Grigorovich IP-1 Fighter (Russia)
- Tupolev MDR-4 Flying Boat Recon (Russia)
- Yakovlev UT-1 Trainer (Russia); 1,241 built; used as attack aircraft in 1941

1937

- Douglas B-18 Bolo Bomber (U.S.)
- Vought SB2U Vindicator Dive Bomber (U.S.)
- Vought V-143 Fighter (U.S.)
- Fairey Battle Bomber (Britain); 2,419 built; obsolete in WWII and used primarily as a trainer
- Bristol Blenheim Bomber (Britain); 4,422 built
- Bristol Blenheim Mk.IF Nightfighter (Britain)
- Miles M.14 Magister Trainer (Britain); 1,393 built
- Vickers Wellesley Bomber (Britain)
- Vickers Wellington Bomber (Britain); main British bomber at the outbreak of WWII; various versions—11,461 built in all
- Noorduyn Norseman Transport (Canada); used extensively during WWII
- Loire 210 Fighter (France)
- Besson/ANF-Mureaux MB.411 Recon (France); used by the Free French during WWII
- Romano R.82 Trainer (France)
- DFS 230 Assault Glider (Germany); extensively used by German airborne units; had room for eight
- Siebel Fh 104 Hallore Liaison/Light Transport (Germany)
- Focke-Wulf Fw 58 Weihe Transport/Trainer (Germany); 1,987 built
- Caproni Ca.310 Libeccio Recon Bomber (Italy)
- CANT Z.506 Airone Torpedo Bomber/Recon Floatplane (Italy); 344 built
- Nakajima "Thora" Ki.34 Transport (Japan); 318 built
- PZL P.43 Karas Attack (Poland); developed from P.23
- R.W.D.14 Observation (Poland)
- Tupolev MTB-2 Four-Engine Flying Boat (Russia)
- Yakovlev UT-2 Trainer (Russia); 7,243 built; in service well past WWII
- Polikarpov VIT-1/VIT-2 Anti-Tank Attack (Russia)
- Ikarus IK-2 Fighter (Yugoslavia); only 12 built, but eight saw action against Germany in 1941
- Rogozarski SIM-X Trainer (Yugoslavia)
- Hawker Hurricane Fighter (Britain); Hurricane was the premier British fighter during the early stages of WWII until the Spitfire could be put up in sufficient numbers, with many Hurricanes defending during the Battle of Britain; noted for stability in flight and durability, even though it was inferior to enemy fighters in other ways; in all, 14,533 Hurricanes were built

1938

- Arado Ar 79 Liaison (Germany)
- Arado Ar 96 Trainer/Multi-Role (Germany); in production until 1948 (in Czechoslovakia); 11,546 built
- Boeing C-98 Transport (U.S., 1938)
- Brewster F2A (Buffalo) Fighter (U.S.)
- Grumman JRF/G-21A Goose Multi-Role Amphibious Flying Boat (U.S.)

- Westland Lysander Liaison (Britain); used to fly people out of occupied Europe during WWII; 1,652 built
- Blackburn B-24 Skua Dive Bomber (Britain); in service until 1941
- Bloch 131 Recon/Bomber (France)
- Bloch MB.150 Fighter (France)
- Bloch 200 Bomber (France)
- Morane-Saulnier MS.406 Fighter (France)
- Potez 63 Fighter/Recon (France); more than 1,250 built in various versions
- Fieseler Fi 156 Storch Liaison/Recon STOL Aircraft (Germany); 2,549 built; much copied in the USSR and Japan
- Heinkel He 100 Fighter (Germany); used surface evaporation cooling to reduce drag and set a new speed record; limited production
- Heinkel He 113 Fighter (Germany); never existed, but was used in propaganda, with pictures of the He 100
- Siebel Si 201 STOL Liaison (Germany)
- Breda Ba.88 Lince Fighter-Bomber (Italy); used in North Africa, but with disappointing results
- Nardi FN.310 Transport (Italy)
- Piaggio P.50 Bomber (Italy)
- Mitsubishi "Claude" A5M Fighter (Japan); 1,094 built
- Nakajima "Nate" Ki.27 Otsu Fighter (Japan); 3,387 built; possibly the most maneuverable monoplane fighter ever built
- Mitsubishi "Ann" Ki.30 Bomber (Japan); 704 built
- Kawasaki "Mary" Ki.32 Bomber (Japan); 854 built
- Tachikawa "Ida" Ki.36 Attack (Japan); 1,334 built; production ended in 1943
- Fokker G.I Fighter (Netherlands); used by the Dutch at the beginning of the war and by the Luftwaffe afterward; 62 built
- PZL P.37 Los Bomber (Poland)
- Tupolev ANT-20bis Transport (Russia); six-engined replacement for the ANT-20
- Nyeman R-10 Bomber (Russia); 490 built
- Rogozarski SIM-XIV-H Seaplane (Yugoslavia)
- Supermarine Spitfire Fighter (Britain)
- Messerschmitt Bf 109 Fighter (Germany); about 35,000 built; main Luftwaffe fighter in WWII; several versions made
- Junkers Ju 87 "Stuka" or "Sturzkampfflugzeug" Dive Bomber/Anti-Tank (Germany); more than 5,700 built; universally feared

1939

- Republic AT-12 Guardsman Trainer (U.S.)
- Vultee A-19 Fighter (U.S.)
- Boeing C-75 Stratoliner Transport (U.S.)
- Seversky P-35 Fighter (U.S.)
- Consolidated PBY Catalina Recon (U.S.); famous WWII flying boat
- Handley Page H.P52 Hampden "Flying Suitcase" Medium Bomber (Britain)
- Martin Maryland Bomber (Britain)
- Miles Master Trainer (Britain); 3,302 built
- Armstrong Whitworth Whitley Bomber (Britain); early night bomber; 2,900 built

- Breguet 690 Multi-Role (France)
- Caudron C.710 Cyclone Fighter (France)
- Dewoitine D.520 Fighter (France); best French fighter of WWII; some were flown by Germans, Bulgarians, Romanians…
- Farman F.223/224 Transport/Bomber (France)
- Koolhoven F.K.58 Fighter (Netherlands); 13 in French service in WWII
- Liore-et-Olivier H-246 Transport Flying Boat (France)
- Latecoere Late 611 Flying Boat Recon (France); only one was built, but it stayed in service until 1947
- Liore et Olivier LeO 450 Bomber (France); retired in 1957
- Liore-Nieuport LN 40 Dive Bomber (France)
- Arado Ar 196 Floatplane Recon (Germany); catapult launched
- Messerschmitt Bf 110 Fighter (Germany); used as intercepter, fighter-bomber and nightfighter; 6,100 built
- Bucker Bu 181 Bestmann Trainer, Utility (Germany)
- Dornier Do 215 Bomber/Night Fighter/Recon (Germany)
- Focke-Wulf Fw 200 Condor Recon/Transport (Germany); one of these was Hitler's personal transport, the Immelmann III
- Heinkel He 115 Torpedo Bomber/Recon (Germany); not a good torpedo bomber, but good in other roles; more than 500 built
- Caproni Ca.311 Recon Bomber (Italy)
- Caproni-Vizzola F.5 Fighter (Italy)
- Macchi M.C.200 Saetta Fighter (Italy); 1,153 built
- Savoia-Marchetti S.M.75 Transport (Italy)
- Savoia-Marchetti S.M.82 Marsupiale Transport (Italy)
- CANT Z.1007 Alcione Bomber (Italy); 564 built
- Nakajima "Kate" B5N Torpedo Bomber (Japan); 1,150 built
- Nakajima "Liz" G5N Shinzan Bomber (Japan); only six built
- Mitsubishi "Pine" K3M Trainer/Transport (Japan); 624 built
- Tachikawa "Ida" Trainer (Japan); 1,389 built
- Koolhoven F.K.58 Fighter (Netherlands); built for France; only 13 became operational
- Chertverikov "Mug" Che-2 Flying Boat Recon (Russia); called MDR-6 until 1941; several models
- Ilyushin DB-3 Bomber (Russia); 1,528 built
- Polykarpov I-180 Fighter (Russia)
- Bisnovat SK-1 Experimental Aircraft (Russia); research in high-speed aircraft
- Yakovlev Ya-22 Fighter/Recon (Russia)
- Anbo VIII Light Bomber/Attack (Lithuania); production stopped when USSR occupied Lithuania in 1940; the designer was later shot in Moscow
- VL Pyry Trainer (Finland)
- Junkers Ju 88 Fighter/Bomber/Recon/Dive Bomber/Nightfighter (Germany); versatile aircraft; 10,774 built (some sources say 15,000)

1940

- North American A-36 Apache Dive Bomber (U.S.); dive bomber version of P-51 Mustang; about 500 made; nicknamed *Invader*
- North American AT-6G Texan Trainer (U.S.)
- Beech AT-11 Kansan Trainer (U.S.)

- Vultee BT-13 Valiant Trainer (U.S.)
- Beech C-45 Expeditor (Various Versions) Transport (U.S., 1940s); more than 4,000 built
- Grumman F4F Wildcat Fighter (U.S.)
- Interstate L-6 Grasshopper Liaison/Observation (U.S.)
- Vought OS2U Kingfisher Amphibious Observation (U.S.); 1,519 built; used with USN, Royal Navy, and U.S. Coast Guard
- Fairchild PT-19 Cornell Trainer (U.S.); 4,845 built
- Lockheed PV Recon/Bomber (U.S.)
- Brewster SB2A Buccaneer Dive Bomber (U.S.)
- XSBA-1 Dive Bomber (U.S.)
- Curtiss SNC Falcon Trainer (U.S.)
- Fairey Albacore Torpedo Bomber (Britain)
- Blackburn B-26 Botha Recon/Bomber (Britain)
- Boulton Paul Defiant Fighter (Britain)
- Fairey Fulmar Fighter (Britain)
- Douglas Havoc Nightfighter (version of the U.S. A-20 Bomber) (Britain); some were outfitted with nose-mounted searchlights to illuminate targets for Hurricane fighters
- Bloch MB.152 Fighter (France); three were used by the British during the Battle of Britain
- Percival Proctor Recon/Trainer (Britain)
- Blackburn B-25 Roc Fighter/Trainer (Britain); designed as a fighter, but was a dismal failure; relegated to trainer role
- Short S.29 Stirling Bomber (Britain); first British four-engine heavy bomber, but replaced ultimately by Lancaster and Halifax; 2,375 built
- Fokker T-VIII W Float Plane/Torpedo Bomber (Netherlands); some used in Britain and Holland
- Westland Whirlwind Twin-Engined Fighter (Britain)
- Avia Av.135 Fighter (Czechoslovakia)
- Amiot 354 Bomber (France)
- Block 174 Recon/Bomber (France); used by Luftwaffe as trainers
- Liore et Olivier LeO H-43 Recon (France)
- NC.223 Bomber (Based on Farman F.222) (France)
- Blohm und Voss Bv 138 Flying Boat Recon (Germany)
- Focke-Wulf Fw 189 Uhu Recon/Trainer/Anti-Tank/Nightfighter (Germany); 864 built
- Heinkel He 280 Jet Fighter (Germany); the first jet fighter to fly, but abandoned in favor of the Me 262; only 9 were built
- Henschel Hs 293 Rocket-Powered Radio-Guided Missile (Germany); 2,300 fired; some later versions used wire-guided controls in case of radio jamming
- Junkers Ju 188 Bomber/Recon (Germany); based on Ju 88; 1,036 built
- Caproni Ca.313 Recon Bomber (Italy); 215 built
- Caproni Ca.314 Recon Bomber (Italy); improved Ca.313; 425 built; 1,000 ordered by the Luftwaffe (though obviously not all delivered)
- Fiat G.50 Freccia Fighter (Italy); 780 built
- Reggiane Re.2000 Falco I Fighter (Italy); used primarily in Sweden and Hungary
- Mitsubishi “Babs” C5M Recon (Japan)
- Aichi “Jake” E13A Recon Seaplane (Japan); 1,418 built
- Yokosuka “Cherry” H5Y Flying Boat (Japan)
- Kawanishi “Mavis” H6K Flying Boat Recon (Japan); 217 built
- Kawasaki “Lily” Ki.48 Bomber (Japan); most effective as a night bomber; 1,977 built
- Mitsubishi “Sonia” Ki.51 Attack (Japan); 2,388 built

- Koolhoven FK.56 Trainer/Recon (Netherlands); few were built because of the German invasion in May, 1940
- Antonov A-7 Transport Glider (Russia, 1940); 400 built; could carry six soldiers
- Archangelsky Ar-2 Bomber (Russia); 200 built
- Belyayev DB-LK Bomber (Russia)
- Lavochkin, Gorbunov and Goudkov LaGG-1 Fighter (Russia)
- Mikoyan-Gurevich MiG-1/MiG-3 Fighters (Russia); short career, but 3,422 built
- Petlyakov Pe-8 Four-Engine Bomber (Russia); only 81 built
- Arkhangelsky SBB Bomber (Russia); final version of SB
- Antonov Shs Liaison (Russia); version of the German Fieseler Fi-156 Storch
- Sukhoi Su-2 Bomber (Russia); more than 500 built until 1942; about 60 variants, called Su-4, were also built
- Saab B 5 Attack (Sweden); version of the Northrop A-17/Douglas 8A
- Commonwealth CA-1/CA-3 Wirraway Trainer/Attack (Australia); developed from the North American NA-33; various versions
- I.A.R 80 Fighter (Romania); 240 built
- Rogozarksi IK-3 Fighter (Yugoslavia); only 12 built, but six operational fighters downed 10 German aircraft
- Yakovlev Yak-1 Fighter (Russia); 8,721 built
- Mitsubishi "Zeke" A6M Reisen Fighter (Japan); the legendeary "Zero," a superior carrier-based fighter when it first appeared, but lightly built and increasingly fragile when faced with heavier and superior Allied fighter; 10,964 built
- Dornier Do 217 Bomber (Germany); 1,750 built in various versions, including several nightfighter variants
- Douglas SBD Dauntless Dive Bomber (U.S.)

1941

- Lockheed C-60 Lodestar Transport (U.S.); military version B-34 Ventura
- Cessna C-78 Bobcat Transport/Trainer (U.S.); 3,414 built
- Grumman J4F Widgeon Amphibious Utility (U.S.)
- Douglas A-20 Light Bomber/Nightfighter (U.S.); 7,385 built, 3,125 delivered to Russia
- Martin A-30 Baltimore Bomber (U.S.); 1,575 built; used in Britain only
- Douglas C-47 Skytrain Transport "Dakota" (U.S.)
- Douglas C-53 Skytrooper Transport (U.S.)
- Douglas C-54 Skymaster Transport (U.S.)
- Waco G-4 Assault Glider (U.S.); used at D-Day; could carry 15 troops or a jeep and its crew; 13,900 built
- Howard GH Nightingale Transport/Ambulance (U.S.)
- Taylorcraft L-2 Grasshopper Liaison Craft (U.S.)
- Piper L-4 Grasshopper Liaison/Observation (U.S.); 4,461 built; much used in WWII
- Stinson L-5 Sentinel Liaison/Observation (U.S.)
- Curtiss O-52 Owl Observation (U.S.)
- Bell P-39 Airacobra Fighter (U.S.); 9,558 built
- Curtiss P-40 Warhawk Fighter (U.S.); used by the legendary Flying Tigers
- Consolidated PB2Y Coronado Recon (U.S.)
- Armstrong Whitworth Albemarle (Britain)
- Martin Baltimore Bomber (Britain); British A-30, based on A-22; 1,575 built for the RAF

- Vought Chesapeake Dive Bomber/Trainer (Britain)
- Taylorcraft Auster Observation (Britain, approx. 1941); standard WWII observation and liaison craft; in use until 1964
- Hawker Typhoon Fighter Bomber (Britain)
- Arsenal-Delanne 10 Fighter (France); flown by Germany after the fall of France
- Arado Ar 231 Recon Float Plane (Germany); designed for storage on U-boats, it could be disassembled and stored in six minutes, but few were built
- Dornier Do 24 Recon (Germany)
- Messerschmitt Me 210 Fighter (Germany)
- Messerschmitt Me 321 Transport Glider (Germany); had to be towed by the five-engined He 111Z
- Fiat CR.25 Fighter/Recon (Italy)
- Nardi FN.316 Trainer (Italy)
- Fiat G.12 Transport (Italy); 104 built
- Macchi M.C.202 Folgore (Italy); 1,200 built
- Piaggio P.108 Bomber/Transport (Italy)
- Savoia-Marchetti S.M.84 Bomber/Torpedo Bomber (Italy); 309 built
- Mitsubishi "Mabel" or "Kate 61" B5M Torpedo Bomber (Japan)
- Aichi "Val" D3A Dive Bomber (Japan); 1,495 built; used as a fighter as well
- Yokosuka "Glenn" E14Y Recon (Japan); the only aircraft to drop bombs on the U.S. mainland—four firebombs in the Oregon forest, meant to cause a forest fire and damage wood production; years later, the pilot, Nobuo Fujita, visited Oregon and presented his family's 400-year-old ancestral samurai sword to the city of Brookings; sword is on display in the local library
- Mitsubishi "Betty" G4M Bomber (Japan); 2,446 built; late in the war it was used to carry MXY-7 Ohka suicide planes
- Kawanishi "Oak" K10W Trainer/Liaison (Japan); 176 built; version of the North American AT-6
- Kabaya Ka-1 Recon/ASW Autogiro (Japan); 240 built
- Nakajima "Oscar" Ki.43 HayabU.S. Fighter (Japan); various versions; 5,919 built
- Nakajima "Tojo" Ki.44 Shoki Fighter (Japan); 1,225 built
- Mitsubishi "Dinah" Ki.46 Recon (Japan); 1,742 built
- Tachikawa "Hickory" Ki.54 Trainer (Japan); 1,368 built
- Kawasaki "Thalia" Ki.56 Transport (Japan); 121 built; based on Lockheed 14
- KokU.S.i "Theresa" Ki.59 Transport/Liaison (Japan); 59 built
- KokU.S.i "Gander" or "Goose" Ku.8 Transport Glider (Japan)
- Showa/Nakajima "Tabby" L2D Transport (Japan); 485 built; based on Douglas DC-3
- Mitsubishi/Yokosuka "Tina" L3Y Transport (Japan)
- Gribovskii G-29 Assault Glider (Russia); approx. 100 built; took off on wheels and landed on a skid
- Beriev KOR-2 Recon (Russia)
- Lavochkin, Gorbunov and Goudkov LaGG-3 Fighter (Russia); 21 different versions; 6,258 built in all
- Iisunov "Cab" Li-2/Li-3 (Russia); version of C-47/DC-3 built by the Soviets; 2,800 built
- Petlyakov Pe-2 Bomber (Russia); 11,427 built
- Petlyakov Pe-3 Fighter/Nightfighter (Russia)
- Yakovlev Yak-2/Yak-4 Bombers (Russia); about 600 built
- Yermolayev Yer-2 Bomber (Russia); little-known bomber; about 320 built
- Saab B 17 Dive Bomber/Recon (S 17) (Sweden); in service until 1948
- I.A.R. 81 Fighter/Fighter-Bomber (Romania); different versions as fighter or fighter-bomber

1942

- Northrop A-35a Vengeance Dive Bomber (U.S.); 1,931 built
- Consolidated B-24 Liberator Bomber (U.S.); 19,256 built
- Grumman F6F Hellcat Fighter (U.S.); 12,275 built
- Curtiss P-60 Fighter (U.S.)
- Douglas P-70 Nightfighter (U.S.)
- Martin PBM Mariner Recon/ASW (U.S.)
- Curtiss SO3C Seamew Recon (U.S.)
- Curtiss SB2C Helldiver Dive Bomber (U.S.); versatile aircraft, though the first versions had problems; used successfully in WWII; more than 7,000 built
- Consolidated C-87 Liberator Transport (Disarmed B-24 Bomber) (U.S.)
- General Aircraft Hamilcar Glider (Britain); could transport a 7-ton tank and other heavy equipment; used in "Operation Overlord"
- Airspeed Horsa Assault Glider (Britain); used in WWII during invasions of Sicily, Normandy, and Germany; could carry troops or transport equipment; 3,655 were built
- Miles M-25 Martinet Target Tug (Britain); 1,793 built to tow targets
- Supermarine Seafire Carrier Fighter (Britain); in service until 1952
- Hawker Sea Hurricane "Hurricat" Fighter (Britain); early versions catapulted from special "CAM" ships and then ditched at sea after mission; later versions could take off and land from carriers
- Breguet Br 482 Bomber (France)
- Arado Ar 232 Transport "Taunsenfussler" (Centipede) (Germany); limited production
- Arado Ar 240 Nightfighter (Germany); limited production
- Gotha Go 242 Assault/Transport Glider (Germany); 1,528 built
- Gotha Go 244 Transport (Germany); version of Go 242 with an engine; quickly withdrawn
- Heinkel He 219 Uhu Nightfighter (Germany); the first production aircraft to feature ejection seats; only 219 built
- Henschel Hs 129 Ground Attack (Germany); heavily armored; 879 built
- Junkers Ju 252 Transport (Germany)
- Junkers Ju 290 Transport/Recon (Germany)
- Messerschmitt Me 323 Gigant Transport (Germany); Me 321 fitted with captured French engines
- Siebel Si 204 Liaison/Trainer (Germany); 1,500 built, mostly by SNCAC in occupied France
- Reggiane Re.2001 Ariete I Fighter (Italy)
- Reggiane Re.2002 Ariete II Fighter-Bomber (Italy)
- Fiat R.S.14 Recon/Bomber (Italy)
- Yokosuka "Judy" D4Y Suisei Dive Bomber (Japan); based on He 118; 2,157 built; also used in kamikaze attacks
- Kawanishi "Emily" H8K Recon (Japan); 167 built
- Aichi H9A Trainer (Japan)
- Nakajima "Irving" J1N Gekko Fighter (Japan); various versions; 479 built
- Kawasaki "Nick" Ki.45 Toryu Fighter (Japan); 1,701 built
- Nakajima "Helen" Ki.49 Donryu Bomber (Japan); 819 built
- Kawasaki "Topsy" Ki.57 Transport (Japan); 507 built
- KokU.S.i "Stella" Ki.76 Liaison/ASW (Japan)
- Tachikawa Ki.77 Experimental Long-Range Bomber (Japan); meant to fly from Tokyo to New York, but abandoned after the loss of one of two prototypes built; one made a flight from Tokyo to Berlin of 16,435 km

- Polikarpov BDP-2 Assault Glider (Russia); could carry 20 soldiers; took off with wheels and landed on skis
- Bereznyak-Isaev (Bolkhovitinov) BI Rocket Fighter (Russia); possibly the world's first rocket-engined fighter, but canceled after eight when handling problems were discovered
- Shcherbokov Shche-2 Transport (Russia); about 750 built
- Yakovlev Yak-7 Fighter-Bomber/Trainer (Russia); 6,399 built
- Yakovlev Yak-9 Long-Range Fighter (Russia); the ultimate of the Yak series; 14,579 built during WWII; total production through 1948 was 16,769
- Focke-Wulf Fw 190 Fighter (Germany); 20,001 built; one of the best fighters of WWII
- De Havilland Mosquito Fighter/Bomber/Recon (Britain); operated at night over Germany safely because no German nightfighter could catch it
- Grumman TBF Avenger Torpedo Bomber (U.S.)
- Lockheed P-38 Lightning Fighter (U.S.)
- Avro 683 Lancaster Bomber (Britain); the most important British bomber of WWII; flew 156,000 missions, many at night; 7,378 were built
- Ilyushin "Bark" Il-2 "Sturmovik" Attack (Russia); mainstay of Soviet ground attack; 36,163 built

1943

- Lockheed C-101 Transport (U.S.)
- Boeing B-17 Flying Fortress Bomber (U.S.)
- North American B-25 Mitchell Bomber (U.S.)
- Boeing B-29 Superfortress Bomber (U.S.); 3,895 built; dropped atomic bombs on Hiroshima and Nagasaki; the most expensive weapon of WWII, more expensive than the Manhattan Project, at a cost of around $3 billion
- Curtis C-46 Commando Transport (U.S.)
- Chance-Vought F4U Corsair Fighter (U.S.)
- General Motors FM Wildcat Fighter (U.S.)
- Vickers Warwick Search and Rescue (Britain); originally built as a bomber; 850 built
- Blohm und Voss Bv 222 Wiking Transport/Recon (Germany); six-engined flying boat
- Dornier Do 335 Pfeil Fighter (Germany); unusual design with front engine driving the nose propeller and a rear engine driving a rear propeller; only 28 were built before the end of WWII
- Messerschmitt Me 264 Prototype Long-Range Strategic Bomber (Germany); more important for propaganda purposes than reality, this long-range bomber was supposed to have carried 39,400 liters of fuel and 1800 kg of bombs with range to attack the U.S.
- Messerschmitt Me 410 Hornisse Fighter (Germany); 1,160 built
- Mistel Composite Unmanned Bomb (Germany); consisted of an unmanned Ju 88 packed with a 3,800-kg shaped charge and attached to another plane, a Bf 109 or Fw 190, to be released as a bomb; first tested in 1943; 250 were delivered, but with minimal success
- Focke-Wulf Ta 154 Nightfighter (Germany)
- Fiat G.55 Centauro Fighter (Italy); best of the Italian fighters
- Macchi M.C.205V Veltro Fighter (Italy)
- Reggiane Re.2005 Sagittario Fighter (Italy); only 43 built before Italy surrendered
- Imam Ro.57 Fighter (Italy)
- S.A.I 207 Fighter (Italy); 2,000 ordered, but only a dozen built; superceded by the S.403, which was never completed
- Savoia-Marchetti S.M.95 Transport (Italy)

- Kawanishi “Norm” E15K Shiun Recon (Japan)
- Mitsubishi “Jack” J2M Raiden Fighter (Japan); 480 built; high speed and climb
- Kyushu K11W Shiragiku Trainer/Utility/ASW (Japan); 789 built
- Kawasaki “Tony” Ki.61 Hien Low-to-Medium-Altitude Fighter (Japan); 3,078 built
- Kawanishi “Rex” N1K Kyofu Float Plane Fighter (Japan); approx. 90 built
- Kawanishi “George” N1K Shiden Fighter (Japan); land-based version of the Kyofu; 1,453 built
- Ilyushin “Bob” Il-4 Bomber (Russia); redesigned DB-3; approx. 6,800 built; 5,256 of the Il-4
- Lavochkin La-5N Fighter (Russia); 9,920 built
- Lavochkin La-7 Fighter (Russia); improved La-5N; 5,753 built
- Polikarpov MP Motorized BDP-2 Assault Glider (Russia)
- Tupolev “Bat” Tu-2 Bomber (Russia); 2,527 built; 1,100 before the end of WWII; some were used during the Korean War
- Yakovlev Yak-6 Transport/Liaison (Russia); around 1,000 built
- F.F.V.S. J 22 Fighter (Sweden); 200 built; in service until 1952
- Commonwealth CA-12/CA-13 Boomerang Fighter (Australia); about 250 built
- MAVAG Hejja II Fighter (Hungary); license-built version of the Italian Reggiane Re 2000
- Morko Moraani Fighter (Finland); converted Morane-Saulnier MS.406 and MS.410 fighters with new engines
- Yakovlev Yak-3 Interceptor Fighter (Russia); 4,848 built
- Republic P-47 Thunderbolt Fighter (U.S.)
- North American P-51 Mustang Fighter (U.S.)
- Curtiss 2B2C Helldiver Dive Bomber (U.S.)
- Bell P-63 Kingcobra Fighter (U.S.); 2,421 delivered to USSR out of 3,303 built; only country to use them in combat
- Fairey Barracuda Torpedo Bomber (Britain); 2,572 built
- Bristol Beaufighter Attack Fighter (Britain); 5,918 built
- Fairey Firefly Mk. I Fighter (Britain); Mk.5 version in 1947 was used as ASW aircraft and was in production until 1956
- Heinkel He 177 Greif Heavy Bomber (Germany); 1,094 built, but a dismal failure

1944

- Martin B-26 Marauder Bomber (U.S.); 5,266 built
- Douglas A-26B Invader Fighter (U.S.)
- Fairchild C-61 Forwarder Transport (U.S.)
- Lockheed C-121 L-749 Transport (U.S.)
- Grumman F7F Tigercat Fighter (U.S.)
- Bell P-59 Airacomet Fighter (U.S.); first U.S. jet, but not very successful
- Interstate TDR Remote-Controlled Attack Plane (U.S.)
- Hawker Fury Mk. I Fighter (Britain); not used in the RAF, but some bought by Iraq
- Handley Page H.P.57 Halifax Bomber (Britain); flew 75,532 missions during WWII
- De Havilland Hornet Fighter (Britain); very small fighter—smaller than the Mosquito; remained in service until 1955
- Miles M.38 Messenger Liaison (Britain)
- Hawker Tempest Fighter (Britain); 1,418 built

- Bachem Ba 349 Natter Rocket-Powered Fighter (Germany); unusual fighter that was designed to fire rockets into Bomber formations, then break apart—the pilot and engine were to be recovered by parachute; only 36 built, but it was designated as operational; probably never used
- Avia S 99 Fighter (Czechoslovakia, c.1944); Czech version of the German Bf 109; also the Avia S 199, famous only as the first fighter used in the Israeli air force
- Blohm und Voss Bv 40 Glider Interceptor (Germany); experimental head-on intercepter; never employed; seven prototypes built
- Blohm und Voss Bv 155 High-Altitude Fighter (Germany); development of the Me 155, but too late to be produced before the war ended
- Blohm und Voss Bv 246 Hagelkorn (Hailstorm) Radio-Guided Glide Bombs (Germany); approximately 1,100 built, but never used
- Fieseler Fi 103 Reichenberg Manned V-1 (Germany); concept of a manned V-1 flying bomb in which the pilot would aim the bomb, then bail out; 175 were built but never used
- Junkers Ju 287 Jet Bomber Experimental (Germany); one built, but development continued by the Soviets after the war
- Junkers Ju 352 Herkules Transport (Germany)
- Junkers Ju 388 Recon (Germany); also bomber and nightfighter variants
- Focke-Wulf Ta 152 Fighter (Germany)
- Nakajima "Jill" B6N Tenzan Torpedo Bomber (Japan); 1,268 built
- Aichi "Grace" B7A Ryusei Torpedo Bomber (Japan)
- Nakajima "Myrt" C6N Saiun Recon (Japan); after carriers were all sunk, it was converted into a nightfighter; 463 built
- Yokosuka D3Y Myojo Trainer (Japan); may also have been used as a kamikaze suicide plane
- Aichi "Paul" E16A Zuiun Recon/Dive Bomber Floatplane (Japan)
- Nakajima J5N Tenrai Fighter (Japan); only six built
- Mitsubishi "Peggy" Ki.67 Hiryu Bomber (Japan); 727 built
- Tachikawa "Patsy," "Pat" Ki.74 High-Speed, High-Altitude Recon Bomber (Japan); 16 built
- Mitsubishi Ki.83 Long-Range Fighter (Japan); a superior fighter, but only four prototypes were built before the war ended
- Nakajima "Frank" Ki.84 Hayate Fighter (Japan); 3,382 built
- Kawasaki Ki.100 Fighter (Japan); 396 built
- Kawasaki "Randy" Ki.102 Fighter (Japan); 238 built
- Mitsubishi Ki.109 Fighter (Japan); 22 built; poor performance in combat
- Yokosuka "Frances" P1Y Ginga/Kyokko Bomber/Nightfighter (Japan); 1,098 built; at the end of the war, many were sent on suicide missions
- Ilyushin Il-16 Ground Attack (Russia); low numbers; never entered service
- Yakovlev Yak-10 Liaison (Russia); only about 40 built
- Saab B 18 Bomber (Sweden); S 18 Recon version and T 18 Torpedo Bomber version as well
- DoFlug D-3802 Fighter (Switzerland)
- VL Myrsky Fighter (Finland)
- Arado Ar 234 Blitz Jet Bomber (Germany); first jet bomber; 274 built
- Gloster/Armstrong Whitworth Meteor Jet Fighter (Britain); first Allied jet fighter; 3,875 built; in service until 1961
- Messerschmitt Me 163 Komet Rocket-Powered Fighter (Germany); the first rocket-powered fighter
- Northrop P-61 Black Widow Nightfighter (U.S.)
- Budd RB Conestoga Transport (U.S.); all steel transport plane; few built
- Curtiss SC Seahawk Recon (U.S.)
- TBM Avenger Torpedo Bomber (U.S.)

- Consolidated-Vultee TBY Sea Wolf Torpedo Bomber (U.S.)
- Bristol Buckingham Bomber (Britain)
- Avro Lincoln Bomber (Britain)
- Short S-25 Sunderland Flying Boat (Britain); in service until 1959
- Avro 685 York Transport (Britain); transport based on Lancaster bomber
- Focke-Wulf 03-10225 Long-Range Bomber (Germany); never built, but designed to carry 3000 kg of bombs with a battery of 13 defensive guns; speed of 580 km/h and range of 9,050 km
- Nakajima "Rita" G8N Renzan Bomber (Japan); only four built
- Kyushu "Lorna" Q1W Tokai ASW (Japan); 153 built, but had little to no success against Allied submarines
- Mersserschmitt Me 262 Jet Fighter (Germany); one of Germany's secret weapons; the first operational jet fighter; too late to change the course of the war; 1,430 were completed; later built in small numbers in Czechoslovakia as the Avia S 92

1945

- Convair B-32 Dominator Bomber (U.S.)
- Boeing B-50 Superfortress Bomber (U.S.)
- Douglas C-74 Globemaster Transport (U.S.)
- Grumman F8F Bearcat Fighter (U.S.)
- McDonnell FH Phantom Fighter (U.S.)
- Ryan FR Fireball Fighter (U.S.)
- Douglas A-1 Skyraider Fighter (U.S.); many versions and many nicknames; in use until the late 1970s
- Northrop P-79 Flying Wing Rocket Fighter (U.S.); experimental only
- Lockheed P-80 Shooting Start Fighter (U.S.); first U.S. operational jet fighter; several versions created
- Blohm und Voss Ae.607 Jet Fighter (Germany); never built
- Arado Ar E.381 Parasite Miniature Fighter (Germany); rocket powered; never built
- Heinkel He 162 Salamander Jet Fighter (Germany); 275 built; 150 delivered; 800 in production at the end of the war
- Heinkel He 274 High-Altitude Bomber (Germany/France); designed in Germany, but completed and used in France until 1953
- Horten Ho IX (Ho 229) Jet Fighter-Bomber (Germany); flying-wing configuration; only three built; sometimes called the Go 229
- Henschel Hs 132 Jet Dive Bomber (Germany); a jet-engined dive bomber in which the pilot lay prone in the cockpit; ready for testing when the war ended
- Junkers Ju 488 Long-Range Bomber Prototype (Germany); reportedly assembled in occupied France and destroyed by French Resistance en route to Germany
- Messerschmitt P.1101 Variable Geometry Jet Fighter (Germany); first of its kind; never developed, though a prototype was built
- Heinkel Sk 274 Bomber (Germany); intended to be a long-range bomber designed for a one-way mission to New York; never built
- Focke-Wulf Ta 183 Jet Fighter Plan (Germany); though never built, it may have influenced the designs of post-war jet fighters, such as the MiG-15, the Saab J29, and the Pulqui II
- Mitsubishi "Sam" A7M Reppu Fighter (Japan); meant to replace the A6M, it suffered a series of misfortunes that lead to only 10 being built
- Yokosuka D5Y "Special Attack Plane" (Japan); probable kamikaze plane

- Yokosuka "Baka" MXY7 Ohka Suicide Manned Bomb (Japan); later versions included a jet engine; 852 built; only 80 used in combat
- Mitsubishi J8M Shusui Fighter (Japan); copy of the German Me 163 rocket interceptor; seven built; only one flew
- Nakajima Ki.87 High-Altitude Fighter (Japan); one built before the war ended
- Rikugun Ki.93 Fighter-Bomber (Japan); still in testing at the end of the war
- Kawasaki Ki.108 High-Altitude interceptor (Japan); intended to counter the B-29, which could fly higher than Japanese fighters; only four built before the end of the war
- Nakajima Ki.115 Tsurugi Kamikaze Plane (Japan); 105 built, but never used
- Nakajima Kikka Jet Fighter (Japan); smaller copy of the German Me 262; built but flown only twice
- Aichi M6A Seiran Attack (Japan); designed to be carried and launched from submarines; only 30 built
- Mikoyan-Gurevich I-250(N) Fighter (Russia); had a primitive jet booster, in service until 1950 as the MiG-13
- Ilyushin "Beast" Il-10 Attack (Russia); 14,966 built in the USSR and another 7,000 in Czechoslovkia
- Lovochkin La-126 Fighter (Russia)
- Mikoyan-Gurevich MiG-8 Research Aircraft (Russia)
- Saab J 21 Fighter (Sweden); not successful as a fighter, but converted to attack aircraft as A 21; about 300 built

1946

- Northrop B-35 Flying Wing Bomber (U.S.); only 15 built
- Bell X-1 Experimental Jet (U.S.); Chuck Yeager flew this plane to be the first to exceed the sound barrier
- De Havilland Canada DHC-1 Chipmunk Trainer (Britain); 1,292 built; retired in 1997
- De Havilland D.H.104 Devon Transport (Britain)
- Blackburn B-37 Firebrand Carrier Fighter/Torpedo Plane (Britain); bulky and largely unsuccessful
- D.H.108 Experimental Craft (Britain); first British plane to break the sound barrier
- De Havilland D.H.98 Sea Hornet Nightfighter (Britain); naval version of the Hornet
- De Havilland Vampire Fighter-Bomber (Britain); in service with Switzerland until the 1990s
- Vickers Viking Transport (Britain)
- Nord 1100 Ramier Liaison (France); version of the German Me 208
- Morane-Saulnier MS.470 Vanneau Trainer (France); several versions created (472, 474, 475) in succeeding years
- Ilyushin "Coach" Il-12 Transport (Russia); 663 built, though the number could be as high as 3,000
- Lavochkin La-9 (La-130) Fighter (Russia); development of the La-126; 1,895 built
- Sukhoi UTB-2 Trainer (Russia); derived from the Tu-2
- Yakovlev "Moose" Yak-11 Trainer (Russia); developed from the Yak-3 Fighter
- Yakovlev "Creek" Yak-12 Liaison (Russia); many built in USSR as well as Poland and China
- Yakovlev "Max" Yak-18 Trainer (Russia); more than 9,000 built; possibly as many as 3,500 still in service
- Nanchang CJ-5 Trainer (China); Chinese version of the Yak-18; first aircraft built by communist China; 379 built
- Pilatus P2 Trainer (Switzerland)

1947

- Convair C-99 Transport (U.S.); one built; in service 10 years
- Douglas C-118 Liftmaster Transport (U.S.)
- Fairchild C-119 "Flying Boxcar" Transport (U.S.)
- Lockheed P-2 Neptune ASW/Recon (U.S.)
- Handley Page Hastings Transport (Britain)
- Slingsby T.21 Sedbergh Trainer (Britain)
- Dassault MD 311 Flamant Liaison (France)
- Fiat G.46 Trainer (Italy)
- An-2/An-3/Y-5 Colt Biplane Transport (USSR/Poland/China); Polish version is the PZL LALA-1
- Ilyushin Il-22 Jet Bomber (Russia); first Soviet jet bomber, but the Il-28 was preferred
- Mikoyan-Gurevich "Fargo" MiG-9 Jet Fighter (Russia); 550 built
- Tupolev "Bull" Tu-4 Bomber (Russia); copy of the B-29 Superfortress; 420 built; some went to China for use as AEW aircraft
- Tupolev Tu-12 Jet Bomber (Russia); only about 50 built
- Tupolev "Bosun" Tu-14 Jet Bomber (Russia); only about 100 built
- Yakovlev "Feather" Yak-15 Fighter (Russia); about 280 built
- Yakovlev "Feather" or "Magnet" Yak-17 Fighter (Russia); about 430 built
- Saab 91 Safir Trainer (Sweden); widely used trainer throughout the world; in service with the Swedish air force until 1966

1948

- Martin AM Mauler Fighter (U.S.)
- Republic F-84 Thunderjet Fighter/Bomber (U.S.)
- North American F-86 Sabre Fighter (U.S.)
- North American FJ-1 Fury Fighter (U.S.)
- Martin P-5 Marlin ASW/Recon Flying Boat (U.S.); 284 built; used in Vietnam for coastal patrol
- North American P-82 Twin Mustang Nightfighter (U.S.)
- Lockheed T-33 Trainer (U.S.)
- De Havilland Canada DHC-2 Beaver Transport (Britain)
- Hawker Sea Fury Carrier Fighter-Bomber (based on 1944 Hawker Fury) (Britain)
- Fairey Primer Trainer (Britain)
- Supermarine Seagull Recon (Britain); not to be confused with 1921 biplane by the same name
- Hawker Sea Hawk Carrier-Based Jet Fighter-Bomber (Britain); about 537 built
- Vickers Valleta Transport (Britain)
- Piaggio P.136 SAR (Italy)
- LIM-1 Fighter (Poland); license-built MiG-15
- Ilyushin "Beagle" or "Mascot" Il-28 Jet Bomber (Russia); approximately 2,000 built; some reverse engineered in China; still in service
- Lavochkin La-11 Fighter (Russia); developed from La-9; 1,182 built
- Yakovlev "Mare" Yak-14 Transport Glider (Russia)
- Yakovlev Yak-16 Transport (Russia)
- Yakovlev "Flora" Yak-23 Fighter (Russia); mainly an export fighter, as the MiG-15 was more advanced
- Mikoyan-Gurevich "Fagot" MiG-15 Fighter (Russia); superior to any Western fighter when introduced in Korea; 18,000 built; the "Midget" was a trainer version

1949

- North American AJ Savage Bomber/Recon/Carrier Jet (U.S.)
- Martin B-61 Matator Unmanned Bomber (U.S.)
- McDonald F2H Banshee Fighter (U.S.)
- Grumman F9F-5 Panther Fighter (U.S.)
- Lockheed F-94 Nightfighter (U.S.)
- Bristol Brigand Attack (Britain)
- SCAN N 1400 Noroit Patrol/Rescue (France)
- Dassault MD-450 Ouragan Fighter (France)
- S.A.I. Ambrosini S.7 Trainer (Italy)
- Beriev "Madge" Be-6 Flying Boat Recon/ASW (Russia); in service through most of the 1960s
- Lavochkin "Fantail" La-15 Fighter (Russia); about 500 built; used until 1954 but less successful than the MiG-15
- Tsybin "Mist" Ts-25 Cargo Glider (Russia); exact date unknown
- CASA 201 Alcotan Transport (Spain)

1950

- Douglas A2D Skyshark Fighter (U.S.); cancelled because of the unreliability of the Allison T40 engine
- Grumman AF-2S Guardian ASW/Attack (U.S.)
- North American B-45 Tornado Bomber/Recon (U.S.); first U.S. Air Force jet bomber
- Douglas C-124 Globemaster II Transport (U.S.)
- Boeing F3D Skynight Nightfighter (U.S.)
- Consolidated Vultee L-13 Liaison/Observation (U.S.)
- Northrop C-125 Raider Transport (U.S.)
- Supermarine Attacker Fighter (Britain)
- English Electric Canberra Bomber (PR MK.9 Recon Version) (Britain); 974 built; some may still be in service
- Percival Provost Trainer (Britain)
- Nord 2501 Noratlas Transport (France)
- SIAI-Marchetti S.M.102 Transport (Italy)
- Fokker S.11 Instructor Trainer (Netherlands)
- Saab J 21R Fighter (Sweden); jet version of the Saab J 21

1951

- Boeing B-47 Stratojet Bomber (U.S.)
- Piper L-18 Utility (U.S.)
- De Havilland Canada U-1 Otter Transport (Canada)
- De Havilland D.H.112 Venom Fighter-Bomber/Nightfighter (Britain); standard ground attack plane of the RAF at the time; redesigned Sea Venom used as a naval aircraft
- Westland Wyvern Attack (Britain); used during the crisis in the Suez in 1956
- Morane-Saulnier MS.733 Alcyon Trainer (France)
- Breguet Br 761 Provence Transport (France)
- Breguet Br 960 Vultur Attack (France)
- Fiat G.59 Fighter/Trainer (Italy); 30 built for Syria

- Piaggio P.148 Trainer (Italy)
- Saab J 29 Tunnan (Barrel) Jet Fighter (Sweden); about 661 built
- 214-D Trainer/Transport (Yugoslavia)
- Soko J20 Kraguj Attack/Trainer (Yugoslavia); date approximate
- Ikarus S-49 Fighter (Yugoslavia)
- Valtion Lentokonetehdas VH Vihuri Trainer (Finland)

1952

- F9F-6 Cougar Fighter (U.S.)
- Republic F-84F Thunderstreak Fighter/Bomber (U.S.)
- Sikorsky HO5S Utility (U.S.)
- Karman HTK Trainer/Utility (U.S.)
- Grumman S-2 Tracker ASW (U.S.)
- De Havilland DH.114 Heron Transport (Britain)
- Supermarine Swift Recon/Fighter (Britain)
- Sud-Est SE 530 Mistral Fighter (France); French version of British Vampire
- Dassault Mystere IV Fighter (France)
- Fokker S-14 MachTrainer (Netherlands)
- CASA 202 Halcon Transport (Spain); larger and more modern CASA 201

1953

- Convair B-36 Bomber (U.S.)
- Boeing C-97 Stratofreighter Transport (U.S.)
- North American F-86D Sabre Fighter (U.S.)
- Northrop F-89 Scorpion Fighter (U.S.)
- Huntington Percival Pembroke Transport (Britain)
- Scottish Aviation Prestwick Pioneer STOL Transport (U.K.)
- Mikoyan-Gurevich I-350 Fighter (Russia); also the I-360, which became the prototype for the MiG-19
- Ilyushin "Crate" Il-14 Transport (Russia); somewhere between 1,000 and 3,500 built, depending on the source
- Saab A 32A Lansen Attack (Sweden)

1954

- Douglas A-3 Skywarrior Bomber (U.S.)
- Lockheed C-121 L-1049G Transport (U.S.)
- Convair C-131 Samaritan Transport (U.S.)
- Republic RF-84F Recon (U.S.)
- Corvair F-102 Delta Dagger Fighter (U.S.)
- North American FJ-2 Fury Fighter (U.S.)
- Grumman E-1 Tracer Carrier-Based AEW (U.S.)
- Cessna T-37 "Tweetie Bird," "Tweet," "Super Tweet," and "Dragonfly" Trainer/Attack (U.S.); 1,268 built (another 577 A-37 light attack aircraft developed from the T-37); retired in 2004
- Cessna C-126 Arctic Rescue (U.S.)

- Boulton Paul Balliol Trainer (Britain); first ever aircraft employing only turboprop power
- Hawker Hunter Fighter Bomber (Britain); highly successful and revered post-WWII jet fighter; 1,985 built; in service nearly 50 years
- Max Holste MH-1521 Broussard Liaison/Transport (France)
- Dassault MD 452 Mystere II Fighter (France)
- Dassault Mystere IVN Nightfighter (France)
- Sud-Ouest SO 4050 Vautour Attack/Fighter/Bomber (France, 1954/1956); various versions
- LIM-5 Fighter (Poland); license-built MiG-17
- Mikoyan-Gurevich "Fresco" MiG-17 Fighter (Russia); was used by at least 22 countries
- Tupolev "Badger" Tu-16 Bomber (Russia); used in a variety of roles; Chinese version designated H-6
- DINFIA IA 35 Huanquero Transport/Trainer/Recon (Argentina)

1955

- Boeing B-52 Stratofortress Bomber (U.S.)
- Martin B-57 Intruder Bomber (U.S.)
- Fairchild C-123 Provider Transport (U.S.)
- Grumman U-16 Albatross Utility (U.S.)
- Bell V-3 Experimental VTOL Adjustable Rotor/Propeller Craft (U.S.)
- Blackburn Beverley Transport (Britain)
- Avro 696 Shackleton Recon (Britain); maritime version of the Lincoln; last piston-engined RAF aircraft; AEW version in service until 1991
- Scottish Aviation Twin Pioneer STOL Transport (Britain)
- Vickers Valiant Nuclear Bomber (Britain)
- Avro Canada CF-100 Canuck Fighter (Canada); retired in 1981
- Potez 75 Pusher-Propeller attack (France)
- Antonov "Camp" An-8 Transport (Russia)
- Myasichew "Bison-A" M-4 Bomber (Russia); converted to tankers after the development of the ICBM
- Tupolev "Boot" Tu-91 Naval Attack Bomber (Russia)
- Tupolev "Bear" Tu-95 Bomber (Russia); various versions and roles; continued production past 1995; Tu-142 is an ASW version of Tu-95
- Yakovlev "Flashlight," "Mangrove," "Mandrake" Yak-25 Fighter/Recon (Russia); about 165 Yak-25RV recon were built and about 480 fighter versions; also about 180 Yak-27 "Mangrove" Recon planes were built
- Hispano HA-200 Seata Trainer (Spain); Egyptian version built as Al Kahira, designed by Willy Messerschmitt
- CASA 207 Aztor Transport (Spain)
- Hispano HA-200 Seata Trainer (Spain)

1956

- Douglas B-66 Destroyer ELINT (U.S.)
- Lockheed C-130 Hercules STOL Transport (U.S.); the standard of post-war transports; created in many versions, including C-130J, which entered service in 1995
- Boeing C-135 Tanker (U.S.)
- Douglas F4D Skyray Fighter (U.S.)

- North American F-100 Super Sabre Fighter (U.S.); the first supersonic fighter to be operational
- Cessna O-1 Bird Dog Liaison (U.S.); 3,400 built; in service for 20 years
- Gloster Javelin Fighter (Britain); in service until 1967
- Fairey Gannet ASW (Britain); in service until 1978
- Breguet Br 1050 Alize ASW (France)
- Dassault Super Mystere Assault (France)
- Dassault Etendard Fighters/Fighter-Bombers (France, 1956–1991); various versions
- Potez/Fouga/Aerospatiale CM.170 Magister Trainer (France); retired in 1997
- Dornier Do 27/28 Utility/Trainer/Transport (Germany); manufactured in Spain due to restrictions following WWII
- Beriev "Mallow" Be-10 Jet Flying Boat ASW (Russia)
- Myasichew "Bison-B" 3M Bomber (Russia); converted to tankers after the development of the ICBM
- Mikoyan-Gurevich "Farmer" MiG-19 Supersonic Fighter (Russia); approximately 2,000 built in the USSR and possibly twice as many in China
- Hispano HA-1112 Fighter (Spain); based on the German Bf 109G fighter
- Pilotus P-3 Trainer (Switzerland); in service until 1993
- Lockheed U-2 Recon (U.S. 1956)

1957

- McDonnell F3H Demon Fighter (U.S.)
- Grumman F11F Tiger Ship-Based Fighter (U.S.); used by Blue Angels
- McDonnell F-101 Voodoo Fighter (U.S.)
- Douglas C-133 Cargomaster Transport (U.S.)
- Piaggio P.149 Trainer (Italy)
- 213 Vihor Trainer (Yugoslavia)

1958

- Vought F-8 Crusader Fighter (U.S.)
- Northrop B-62 Snark Pilotless Bomber/Cruise Missile (U.S.)
- Lockheed F-104A Starfighter Fighter (U.S.); used for astronaut training; set altitude record of 36,273 meters
- Republic F-105 Thunderchief Fighter (U.S.)
- Supermarine 525 Scimitar Fighter-Bomber (Britain); small numbers produced; in service until 1969
- Canadair CL-28 Argus ASW/Recon (Canada)
- Aero 3 Trainer (Czechoslovakia); 3,568 built
- Nord 3400 Liaison/Recon (France)
- Morane-Saulnier MS.760 Paris Liaison (France)
- Fuji T-1 Trainer (Japan)
- Fokker F.27 Friendship Transport (Netherlands); commercial and military uses; also known as the Fairchild F-27 or FH-227
- Antonov "Clod" An-14 Pchelka Transport (Russia); approx. 300 built
- Saab A 32B Lansen Fighter (Sweden)
- Hispano HA-100 Triana Trainer (Spain)

1959

- Convair F-106 Delta Dart Fighter (U.S.)
- U-10 Super Courier Utility (U.S.)
- De Havilland Sea Venom Fighter (Britain); naval version of the Venom; also licensed to France as the Aquilon
- Aero "Maya" L-29 Delfin Trainer (Czechoslovakia); more than 2,000 delivered to USSR between 1963 and 1973
- Fiat G.91 Attack (Italy); 411 bought by Germany
- Fiat/Aeritalia G.91 Attack (Italy)
- TS-8 Bies Trainer (Poland)
- Mikoyan-Gurevich "Fishbed"/"Mongol" MiG-21 Fighter (USSR); various versions; more than 10,000 built in various versions worldwide; Chinese exports are called F-7
- Sukhoi "Fishpot" Su-9 Fighter (Russia); about 1,000 built
- Pilatus Porter and Turbo Porter PC-6 Utility (Switzerland); used in a variety of places, including in Vietnam, in a James Bond film, by numerous skidiver groups, etc.; many still in use

1960

- Lockheed F-104G Starfighter Fighter (U.S.)
- Grumman V-1 Mohawk Recon (U.S.)
- English Electric/BAC Lightning Fighter (Britain, 1960–1988); Mach 2+ twin-engined fighter
- Avro Vulcan V-Bomber (Britain)
- TS-11 Iskra Trainer (Poland)
- Antonov "Cub" An-12 Transport (Russia); larger than the C-130; about 900 were built
- Tupolev "Blinder" Tu-22 Supersonic Bomber (Russia); only about 250 built because of limited range; some exported to Libya and Iraq

1961

- Cessna O-2 Observation (U.S.)
- Northrop T-38 Talon Trainer (U.S.); supersonic trainer intended to stay in service until 2020
- Cessna U-17 Skywagon Utility (U.S.)
- Hawker Siddeley Argosy Transport (Britain)
- Handley Page Victor V-Bomber (Britain); Victor K Mk.2 tanker (1974); retired in 1993
- Antonov "Coke" An-24 Transport (Russia); used by 15 air forces worldwide; 1,465 built; reverse-engineered version in China is the Y-7
- Beriev "Mail" Be-12 Chaika Amphibious ASW/SAR (Russia)
- Soko G-2 Galeb Trainer (Yugoslavia)
- Soko J-1 Jastreb Attack (Yugoslavia); attack version of the Galeb; single seat
- HAL HF-24 Marut Jet Fighter (India); designed by Kurt Tank, formerly of Focke-Wulf

1962

- Folland Gnat Jet Fighter/Trainer (Britain)
- Tupolev "Cookpot" Tu-124 Transport (Russia)

- Yakovlev Yak-28 (Russia); several versions: "Brewer" bomber, "Firebar" interceptor, "Maestro" trainer, and "Brewer-D" recon, "Brewer-E" ECM
- Shenyang/Nanchang CJ-6 Trainer (China); designed and built in China; 1,796 or more built
- Pazmany PL-1 Chiensou Trainer (Taiwan, approx. 1962); American design

1963

- Northrop F-5 Freedom Fighter (U.S.); type F-5e (1973) limited use in U.S. forces, but used by 28 countries
- Mirage IVA Bomber (France); retired in 1996
- Mitsubishi MU-2 Airliner/SAR (Japan)
- IA 50 Guarani Trainer (Argentina)

1964

- North American A-5 Vigilante (U.S.)
- Grumman C-2 Greyhound Transport (U.S.)
- Lockheed C-141 Starlifter Transport (U.S.)
- Beagle Basset Utility (Britain)
- De Havilland Sea Vixen Fighter (Britain); in service until 1972
- NAMC YS-11 Tranport (Japan)
- Dassault Mirage III Fighter-Bomber (France)

1965

- Douglas A-26K Fighter (U.S.)
- Cessna T-41 Mescalero Trainer (U.S.); military version of the Cessna 172; 864 used by the U.S.A.F.; total production of all versions of the 172 (170, 172, 175, 182) was more than 60,000
- North American/Rockwell V-10 Bronco Recon (U.S.)
- Blackburn/Hawker Siddeley Buccaneer Attack (Britain)
- Dassault-Breguet Atlantique ASW (France); used by French, German, Dutch, and Italians
- Ilyushin Il-18 Transport (Russia)
- Sukhoi "Fitter"/ "Moujik" Su-7 Attack (Russia); began as a Mach 2 tactical fighter, but ultimately was used as a fighter-bomber
- Saab J 35 Draken Jet Fighter (Sweden); 606 built
- Saab MFI-9 Trainer (Sweden)
- Nanchang "Fantan" Q-5 Attack (China); development of the MiG-19, about 1,000 built

1966

- Short S.C.5 Belfast Transport (Britain)
- McDonnell Douglas A-4 Skyhawk Fighter (U.S.); 2,960 built; in service for 22 years
- Lockheed SR-71 Recon (U.S.); Mach 3+ delta-wing spy plane; fastest known aircraft to serve in any air force
- Tupolev "Fiddler" Tu-128P Fighter (Russia); about 200 built; possibly the largest fighter ever built; based on T-28 bomber; retired in 1990

- Saab 105 Jet Trainer (Sweden); several versions; still in use with upgraded Williams-Rolls Royce FJ44 engines
- Shenyang JJ-5 Jet Trainer (China); more than 1,000 built; created by combining the MiG-17 airframe with the MiG-15UTI cockpit; a trainer version was the JJ-6; recon version is JZ-6
- Neiva T-25 Universal Trainer (Brazil)

1967

- Cessna A-37B Dragonfly Jet Fighter/Trainer (U.S.)
- McDonnell F4 Phantom II Fighter (U.S.); more than 5,000 built; used in Vietnam and since
- North American T-28 Trainer (U.S.); so easy to fly that it wasn't a good enough challenge as a trainer; some modified for attack and COIN duties and redesignated as AT-28D
- Mirage 5 Attack (France); export version of Mirage III; Israel's Kfir Fighter is a copy of the Mirage 5; also sold to Abu Dahbi, Belgium, Columbia, Egypt, Gaboon, Libya, Pakistan, Peru, Venezuela, Zaire
- Aermacchi M.B.326 Jet Trainer/Attack (Italy); 761 built
- Sukhoi "Fishpot"/"Maiden" Su-11 (Russia); developed from Su-9
- Sukhoi "Flagon" Su-15 Fighter (Russia); about 1,500 built; famous for shooting down a Korean Airlines 747
- Kurnass "Heavy Hammer" (Israel); Israeli version of the F-4 Phantom II

1968

- LTV A-7 Corsair II Fighter (U.S.)
- BAC 167 Strikemaster Trainer/Attack (Britain)
- Lockheed/Aeritalia F-104 (Italy); improved version of the F-104 fighter
- Tupolev "Moss" Tu-126 AWACS (Russia)
- Hindustan HJT-16 Kiran Jet Trainer (India)

1969

- General Dynamics FB-111 Bomber (U.S.)
- Lockheed P-3 Orion ASW/Recon (U.S.)
- Hawker/BAe Harrier VTOL Ground Attack (Britain); many versions created and improved over the years
- Hunting/Percival/BAC Jet Provost Trainer (Britain)
- BAe Nimrod Recon/ASW (Britain)
- Canadair CL-215 Firefighting (Canada)
- MBB 223 Flamingo Trainer/Utility (Germany)
- Kawasaki-Lockheed P-2J Recon/ASW (Japan); version of the Lockheed P-2 Neptune
- Fokker F.28 Frienship (Netherlands); various models both commercial and military
- Antonov "Curl" An-26 (Russia); developed from An-24; about 1,000 built; used by more than 30 countries; built in China as the Y-7H
- Mikoyan-Gurevich "Flogger" MiG-23 Fighter (Russia); more than 5,800 built in various versions
- Sukhoi "Fitter" Su-17/Su-20/Su-22 Attack (Russia); various versions; export versions, Su-20 and Su-22, produced from 1973–1976
- CASA 223 Flamingo Trainer/Utility (Germany/Spain)

1970

- Beechcraft C-6 Transport (U.S.)
- Fairchild C-26Metro III Transport (U.S.)
- Aerospatiale N 262 Fregate Transport/Trainer (France)
- Dassault Mirage F1 Fighter (France)
- Aerfer-Aermacchi AM-3 Utility (Italy); used by the South African air force as the "Bosbok"
- SIAI-Marchetti S.m.1019 Observation/FAC (Italy)
- Shin Meiwa PS-1 Recon/ASW (Japan)
- Mikoyan-Gurevich "Foxbat" MiG-25 Mach-3 Long-Range Interceptor/Recon Plus Tactical Bomber Version (MiG-25RB "Foxbat-B") (Russia); about 1,200 built, mostly interceptors; production ended in 1983

1971

- Grumman A-6 Intruder Attack (U.S.)
- Lockheed C-5A/B Galaxy Transport (U.S., 1971/1982)
- General Dynamics F-111 Fighter (U.S.)
- Britten-Norman Defender Utility STOL (AEW/ELINT versions also) (Britain)
- Ilyushin "May" Il-38 Recon/ASW (Russia)
- Saab MFI-15 Safari Trainer (Sweden)
- F+W C-3605 Target Tug (Switzerland); modified from C-3603
- IAI Nesher Fighter (Israel); copy of the French Mirage 5 when France refused to deliver 50 Mirage 5s ordered and paid for; Israel managed to steal the plans for the engine and plane and built their own copy

1972

- Grumman E-2 Hawkeye AEW (U.S.)
- Aero L-39 Albatros Trainer (Czechoslovakia); 2,828 built
- SIAI-Marchetti SF.260 Trainer (Italy); more than 700 built
- Saab MFI-17 Supporter Trainer (Sweden)
- IAI 102 and 202 Arava Transport/EW (Israel)
- CASA C-212 Aviocar (Spain); used for maritime patrol, ASW (anti-submarine warfare), ECM (electronic counter measures), and ELINT (electronic intelligence)

1973

- Douglas C-9 Transport (U.S.); version of DC-9 airliner
- Boeing E-4 Command Center Aircraft (U.S.)
- McDonnell Douglas F-15 Eagle Fighter (U.S.)
- Beechcraft T-34 Mentor Trainer (U.S.)
- BAe/Scottish Aviation Beagle Bulldog Trainer (Britain)
- Sepecat Jaguar Ground Attack (Britain)
- Mikoyan-Gurevich "Flogger" MiG-27 (Russia); ground attack version of MiG-23
- PAC CT-4 AirTrainer (New Zealand)
- Embraer EMB-110 Bandeirante Transport (Brazil)

1974

- Northrop A-9 Fighter (U.S.)
- Grumman F-14 Tomcat Fighter (U.S.)
- Lockheed S-3 Viking ASW (U.S.)
- VFW 614 Jet Transport (Germany); only 19 built, most scrapped; three still in service in the Luftwaffe
- Antonov "Cock" An-22 Transport (Russia); about 100 built; at the time, the largest aircraft in the world, capable of transporting a main battle tank
- Antonov "Clank" An-30 Cartography Plane (Russia); based on An-24
- Ilyushin "Candid" Il-76 Transport (Russia); main Soviet transport, including Il-78 "Midas" tanker and A-50 "Mainstay" AWACS
- Sukhoi "Fencer" Su-24 Attack (Russia); variable geometry wings; also some versions for reconnaissance
- FMA IA 58 Pucara Attack (Argentina)
- GAF Nomad Transport (Australia)

1975

- Beech C-12 Huron Transport (U.S.)
- IAI F-21Kfir Fighter (Israel [used by U.S.])
- Westland Commando Transport (Britain)
- Fiat/Aeritalia G222 Transport (Italy)
- Piaggio P.166 Transport (Italy)
- Kawasaki C-1 STOL Transport (Japan)
- Shin Meiwa U.S.-1 SAR (Japan)
- Mitsubishi T-2 Fast Jet Trainer (Japan)
- Antonov "Cash" An-28 Transport (Russia); based on An-14
- Yakovlev "Forger" Yak-38 (Yak-36MP) VTOL Fighter-Bomber (Russia); about 231 built
- Pilatus PC-7 Turbo-Trainer (Switzerland)
- Atlas C4M Kudu Transport (South Africa)
- Valmet L-70 Vinka Trainer (Finland)

1976

- Fairchild A-10 Thunderbolt II Fighter (U.S.)
- General Dynamics/Lockheed F-16 Fighting Falcon Fighter (U.S.)
- BAE Hawk Jet Trainer (Britain)
- Tupolev "Backfire" Tu-022M Bomber (Russia); various versions up to 1985, at least; still in use past 2000; also known as the Tu-26
- Hindustan Ajeet Fighter (India); developed from the Folland Gnat
- T-CH-1 Chung Sing Trainer (China); developed from the North American T-28

1977

- Boeing E-3 Sentry AWACS (U.S.); based on the Boeing 707; several models built
- Beechcraft T-44 Trainer (U.S.)
- Dassault-Breguet/Dornier Alpha Jet Trainer/Strike Fighter (France/Germany)

- Mitsubishi F-1 Attack (Japan); combat version of the T-2 trainer
- Antonov "Cline" An-32 Transport (Russia); special version of An-26 for "high and hot" conditions
- Saab JA 37 Viggen STOL Jet Fighter (Sweden); multiple versions, including fighter-bomber, attack, tactical recon, sea surveillance, trainer, and pure fighter; attack version AJ 37
- Embraer EMB-111 Maritime Patrol (Brazil)
- Embraer EMB-121 Xingu Business Jet (Brazil)

1978

- Piper U-11 Utility (U.S.)
- Sepecat Jaguar Ground Attack (Britain); "international" export version of Sepecat Jaguar; Sepecat stands for "Societe Europeenne de Production de l'Avion d'Ecole de Combat et d'Appui Tactique" or, in English, "European Producion Company for Combat Training and Tactical Support Aircraft"
- Fuji KM-2 Trainer (Japan)
- Antonov "Coaler" An-72 STOL Transport (Russia); versions An-71 AEW and An-74 for polar operation
- Ilyushin "Coot-A" Il-20 ECM (Russia)
- Myasichev "Mystic" M-17 Balloon Interceptor (Russia); originally designed to hunt U.S. high-altitude reconnaissance balloons, but also used for recon missions as well as ecological survey and earth protection missions
- Sukhoi "Frogfoot" Su-25 Attack/Anti-Tank (Russia); counterpart to the U.S. A-10; used in Afghanistan; several versions
- FWA AS 202 Bravo Trainer (Switzerland)
- CASA C-101 Aviojet Trainer (Spain)
- Shenyang "Finback" J-8 Fighter (China); several versions have been built, including the J-8IIM version, with Russian radar and avionics, which made its first flight in 1990

1979

- Dassault-Breguet U-25 Guardian Utility (U.S.)
- BAE/Hawker Siddeley Andover (Britain)

1980

- McDonnell Douglass F-18a Hornet Fighter (U.S.)
- BAE Sea Harrier Harrier Jet (Britain); version of the Harrier used for small carriers
- Shanghai Y-10 Transport (China); only two prototypes built, but one was flown for years all over China and also to and from Tibet

1981

- General Dynamics EF-111A Electronic Warfare (U.S.)
- Lockheed F-117 Nighthawk Fighter (U.S.)
- Panavia Tornado IDS Multi-Role Fighter (Britain, Germany, Italy); could carry a vast array of weapons and used many methods to avoid detection; the most advanced NATO fighter made in Europe at the time; used in England, Germany, Italy, and Saudi Arabia; the Tornado multi-role

aircraft is operational in five different forms: Tornado GR 1 interdictor/strike aircraft for close air support; counter air attack, and defense suppression; GR 1A tactical reconnaissance aircraft; Tornado GR 1B long-range maritime attack aircraft; and Tornado F3 long-range air defense fighter. The GR 4 is a mid-life update of the GR 1. The Tornado entered service in 1980 and ceased production in 1998.

- Embraer EMB-312 Tucano Trainer (Brazil)

1982

- Schweizer G-7 Motorized Training Glider (U.S.)
- Northrop Tacit Blue Experimental Stealth Craft (U.S.); only one built, flown from 1982–1985
- Dassault-Breguet Atlantique 2 (ATL.2) ASW (France); upgraded from 1965 Atlantique
- Aerospatiale Epsilon Trainer (France)
- Pavania Tornado Attack (Germany, Britain, France, Italy)
- ENAER Pillan Trainer (Chile)
- Y-12 STOL Transport (China)

1983

- McDonnell Douglas V-8 Harrier Attack (U.S.)
- Dassault-Breguet Mirage 2000 Fighter (France)
- Mikoyan-Gurevich "Foxhound" MiG-31 (Russia); developed from MiG-25 with possible linking radar systems used to establish search patterns
- CASA-IPTN CN-235 Transport (Spain/Indonesia)
- IAI Kfir Fighter-Bomber/Fighter (Israel); Israeli version of the French Mirage
- Datwyler MD3 Trainer (Switzerland)
- Soko G-4 Super Galeb (Yugoslavia); completely new aircraft, not an extension of the Galeb

1984

- Cessna U-27 Caravan Utility (U.S.)
- Shorts 330 Transport (Britain); used by different air forces, the U.S.A.F. designates it the Shorts C-23 Sherpa
- Let L-410 Turbolet Light Transport (Czechoslovakia); able to operated from primitive airstrips
- Saab 340 Airliner (Sweden); also used as SAR and AEW
- AIDC AT-3 Tsu Chiang Trainer (Taiwan)
- Harbin SH-5 Flying Boat Patrol (China)

1985

- Rockwell B-1B Bomber (U.S., 1986); intended to replace the B-52, but cancelled in favor of the B-1B Lancer
- Rockwell B-1B Lancer (U.S.); can carry a staggering array of ordnance, totaling up to 75,000 pounds, including thermonuclear bombs
- Cessna T-47 Radar Trainer (U.S.)
- Grob G 115 Trainer/Airliner (Germany)
- Aermacchi M.B.339 Trainer/Attack (Italy)

- Fokker F60 Transport (Netherlands)
- Antonov "Condor" An-124 Ruslan Transport (Russia)
- Mikoyan-Gurevich "Fulcrum" MiG-29 Fighter (Russia); more than 2,000 built; called Baaz in India
- HAL HPT-32 Deepak Trainer (India)
- Embraer EMB-120 Brasilia (Brazil)
- Soko J-22/IAR 93B Orao Attack (Romania/Yugoslavia)
- Pilatus PC-9 Trainer (Switzerland)

1986

- Sukhoi "Flanker" Su-27 Attack (Russia)
- ENAER T-35T Aucan Trainer (Chile); turboprop development of the Pillan
- Voyager (U.S.); record-setting endurance airplane whose flight of more than 25,000 miles lasted just about exactly nine days, without refueling; Voyager carried 1,200 galllons of fuel; it weighed 9,750 lbs at takeoff and only 1,858 upon landing at the end of the flight

1987

- Schweizer G-8 Motorized Recon Glider (U.S.)
- Promavia Jet Squalus Trainer (Italy, Belgium)
- Shorts Tucano Trainer (Britain); version of the Brazilian Tucano turboprop trainer for the RAF, replaces the Jet Provost
- PZL 130 Turbo-Orlik Trainer (Poland)
- Sukhoi Su-33 Fighter (Russia); carrier version of Su-27
- Tupolev "Blackjack" Tu-160 Bomber (Russia); the largest combat aircraft ever built, similar to the B-1B, but much larger; capable of low-altitude penetration at transonic speeds or high altitude at Mach 1.9; can carry nuclear weapons with a range of at least 1,800 miles
- Atlas Cheetah Fighter-Bomber (South Africa); based on the Mirage III; many upgrades using Israeli technology; was due to be phased out and replaced in 2007 by Saab JAS-39 Gripens
- I.A.R. 99 Soim Trainer/Attack (Romania)

1988

- Northrop B-2 Spirit Stealth Bomber (U.S.)
- Northrop Grumman E-8 Recon (U.S.)
- Kawasaki T-4 Jet Trainer (Japan)
- Antonov "Cossack" An-225 Mriya Space Shuttle Transport (Russia); grounded due to the end of the Buran space shuttle project; the first aircraft to fly with a gross weight over 1,000,000 lbs
- Myiasichev M-17RM/M-55 High-Altitude Recon (Russia); twin-engine version of the M-17 "Mystic"
- Aeritalia-Embraer-Aermacchi AMX Light Attack (Italy/Brazil)
- IRGC Fajr (Iran)
- FMA IA 63 Pampa Jet Trainer (Argentina)

1989

- Boeing E-6 Mercury Communications (U.S.)
- McDonnell Douglas T-45 Goshawk (Britain)
- V-23 Skytrader STOL Utility (U.S.)
- Aerospatiale TB 31 Omega Trainer (France)
- Grob G 520 Strato 1 Surveillance (Germany)
- Siai Marchetti/Agusta S.211 Trainer (Italy)
- Yakovlev "Freestyle" Yak-41 VTOL Fighter (Russia); project began in 1975; meant to be the world's first supersonic VTOL fighter; it was never put into production due to budget constraints; the Yak-141, with added stealth technologies, is the continuation of the project, but that has not been put into production yet either
- Valmet L-90TP Redigo Trainer (Finland)

1991

- Slingsby T-3 Firefly Trainer (Britain)
- Slingsby T67 Firefly Trainer (Britain)

1992

- MANC/PAC K-8 Karakorum Trainer (China/Pakistan)

1993

- McDonnell Douglass C-17 Globemaster III Transport (U.S.)
- Rockwell/DASA Ranger 2000 Trainer (Germany)

1994

- PZL I-22 Iryda Trainer (Poland)
- Antonov An-70 Transport (Ukraine); replacement for the An-12; larger version An-170
- Sukhoi Su-34 Fighter-Bomber (Russia); ground attack version of Su-27, sometimes called Su-32FN
- Sukhoi Su-35 Fighter (Russia); improved Su-27
- AIDC Ching-Kuo Fighter (Taiwan)
- Pilatus P-12 Transport (Switzerland); "Eagle"version is being developed for surveillance
- IAI/Elta Phalcon 707 (Israel); Boeing 707 with Israeli Phalcon AWACS and AEW&C electronic systems

1995

- Schweizer U-38 Covert Surveillance (U.S.)
- Grob G 850 Strato 2 Surveillance (Germany); all composite construction; set many world records; G850C model could remain airborne for up to 50 hours at a stretch
- Shenyang J-11 Fighter (China); license-built Russian Su-27

1996

- Sukhoi Su-37 Multi-Role Combat Fighter (Russia); further improved Su-27
- Suchoi Su-39 Trainer (Russia)
- Yakovlev Yak-130 Trainer (Russia)
- Saab JAS 39 Gripen Multi-Role Fighter/Attack/Recon (Sweden)
- IAI Astra SPX Business Jet (Israel); some are used as ECW and transport
- Parastou Trainer (Iran); developed from the Beech Bonanza

1997–Present

- Aero L-159 Trainer/Attack (Czechoslovakia, 1997); rare jet fighter that can land on grass or non-reinforced runways
- Beriev Be-200 Amphibian Transport (Russia, 1997)
- CASA C-295 Transport (Spain); improved version of the CN-235
- Boeing/McDonnell Douglas F/A-18E/F Super Hornet Fighter (U.S., 2002)
- Mikoyan-Gurevich "Fulcrum" MiG-35 Fighter (Russia, first flight 2000); development of the MiG-29 with advanced features; has not entered service so far
- Boeing C-40 Transport (U.S., 2001)
- Mitsubishi F-2 Fighter (Japan, 2001)
- Antonov An-38 Transport (Russia, 2002); replacement for An-28
- Samsung KTX-2 Jet Trainer (Korea, 2005?)
- HAL LCA (Light Combat Aircraft) Supersonic Fighter (India, 2010?)
- J-10 "Jian-10" ("Fighter-10") changed to "Qian Shi-10" ("Attack 10") (China, approx. 2003)
- J-XX Stealth Fighter (China); reported to be in development
- R-3 Black Manta Stealth Recon (U.S.)
- Raytheon/Beech/Pilatus T-6 Texan II Trainer (U.S., 2001); replacing all T-37B Tweets by 2008 as primary trainer
- Fleetwing BQ-1/2/3 Radio-Controlled Bomb (U.S.)
- Tupolev Tu-330 Transport (Russia); quote from Tupolev's website: "According to Customer request the aircraft can be produced in following versions: refueler, ambulance a/c, hospital a/c, ecological monitoring a/c, a/c for hunting industry and fishery, icing survey, a/c for initial exploration under extraordinary conditions, fire fighting a/c, tanker to carry liquefied natural gas, repeater a/c, special administrative a/c (cabin+two motor cars) etc."
- Mikoyan-Gurevhich MiG-AT Advanced Trainer (Russia); not known whether this will enter production
- Azaraksh Fighter (Iran); supposedly a reverse-engineered F-5 fighter; much speculation
- JF-17 (FC-1/Super 7 Thunder Dragon) Multi-Role Fighter (China, 2007); entered the Pakistani Air Force in 2007
- Lockheed F-22 Raptor Stealth Fighter (U.S., operational 2005)
- PZL M-26 Iskierka Trainer (Poland, 2006)
- Mikoyan 1-42 Multi-Purpose Fighter (Russia, 2006?); reported to be superior to the F-22
- Dassault-Breguet Rafale Assault Fighter (France, c.2008–2012)
- V-22 Osprey Tilt Rotor Aircraft (U.S., 2005)

Helicopters and Gunships

- TsAGI 1-EA Helicopter (Russia, 1930); one built
- TsAGI 2-EA Autogiro (Russia, 1931); one built
- TsAGI 5-EA Helicopter (Russia, 1933); another experimental helicopter
- TsAGI A-4 Autogiro (Russia, 1934); 10 built
- Focke-Achelis Fa 61 Experimental Helicopter (Germany, 1937); probably the first workable helicopter; only two built
- Focke-Achelis Fa 269 Convertiplane (Germany, 1941); projected design for a vertical takeoff and landing craft where the rotors would swivel to act as propellers during flight
- Flettner FL 282 Kolibri Observation Helicopter (Germany, 1941); large orders were placed, but only 24 were completed
- Sikorksy R-4 Hoverfly Utility Helicopter (U.S., 1943); first U.S.A.F. helicopter
- Sikrosky R-5 Observation/Utility (U.S., 1943)
- Piasecki HRP-1/HRP-2 "Flying Banana" Helicopter (U.S., 1943/1948)
- Focke-Achelis Fa 223 Drache Helicopter (Germany, 1943); development impeded by Allied bombing
- Doblhoff WNF 342 Helicopter (Germany, 1943); first helicopter with tipjet drive using compressed air jets
- Sikorsky R-6 Utility (U.S., 1944)
- Hiller H-23 Raven Observation/Utility (U.S., 1946)
- Kamov Ka-8 Helicopter (Russia, 1947); used alcohol for fuel
- Westland Dragonfly (Britain, 1950); version of Sikorsky S-51
- Kamov "Hat" Ka-10 Helicopter (Russia, 1950)
- Piasecki HUP Retriever Utility Helicopter (U.S., 1950)
- Sikorsky H-19 Chikasaw Utility (U.S., 1951)
- Bristol 192 Belvedere Transport (Britain, 1951)
- Boeing-Vertol H-21 Work Horse Transport (U.S., 1952)
- Bell H-13 Observation (U.S., 1950s)
- Kellett-Hughes H-17 Transport (U.S., 1952)
- Kamov "Hen" Ka-15 Helicopter (Russia, 1952)
- Yakovlev "Horse" Yak-24 Helicopter (Russia, 1952); about 100 built
- Piasecki H-16 (U.S., 1953)
- Sikorsky HR2S SAR/Transport Helicpoter (U.S., 1953)
- Sikorsky H-34 Choctaw Utility (U.S., 1955)
- Sikorsky H-37 Mojave Transport (U.S., 1955)
- Bell HSL ASW Helicopter (U.S., 1955)
- Kamov "Hog" Ka-18 Helicopter (Russia, 1955)
- Kaman H-43 Huskie SAR (Search and Rescue) (U.S., 1958)
- Hiller H-12 Utility (U.S., 1950s); reordered in 1986
- Hughes H-55 Osage Trainer (U.S., 1961)
- H-50 Gyrodyne Unmanned Helicopter (U.S., 1962)
- Sikorsky H-52 SAR (U.S., 1962)
- Boeing-Vertol H-46 Sea Knight Transport (U.S., 1964)
- Sikorsky H-54 Tarhe Transport/Crane (U.S., 1964)
- Kamov "Hormone" Ka-25 ASW/SAR/Utility Helicopter (Russia, 1965); also Kamov "Helix-A, D" Ka-27 redesign in 1981
- Kamov "Helix-B" Ka-29/Ka-31 ASW/Attack Helicopter (Russia, 2003)

- Kamov "Helix-C" Ka-32 Utility Helicopter (Russia, 1981?); civil helicopter in several versions, including Ka32T (1993) with advanced avionics
- Kamov "Hokum A" Ka-50 Gunship (Russia, 1982); also Ka-40 export versions and Ka-52 "Alligator" two-seat version; also known as V-80 "Werewolf" or "Black Shark"
- Kamov Ka-60 Attack Helicopter (Russia, 1998); included in *Metal Gear Solid 2*
- Kamov Ka-226 "Hoodlum" Transport (Russia, 2000)
- Sikorksy H-3 Sea King ASW (U.S., 1966)
- Hughes OH-6 Cayuse Observation (U.S., 1966)
- Mi-1 "Hare" Liaison and Utility Helicopter (Russia, 1949)
- Mi-4 "Hound" Utility Helicopter (Russia, 1952); used also in the U.S. and Korea; about 3,500 built
- Mi-6 "Hook" Transport Helicopter (Russia, 1957); for several years the largest and fastest helicopter in the world (speed 300km/h)
- Mi-2 "Hoplite" Utility Helicopter (Russia, 1961); replacement for the Mi-1
- Mi-8 "Hip" Transport Helicopter (Russia, 1962); along with Mi-14 and Mi-1, the most commonly produced helicopter in the world
- Mi-10 "Harke" Crane Helicopter (Russia, 1964); based on Mi-6
- Mi-12 "Homer" Transport (Russia, 1969); the largest helicopter of its time; only two built
- Kamov "Hoodlum" Ka-26 Utility Helicopter (Russia, 1970)
- Mi-14 "Haze" Helicopter (Russia, 1978); based on Mi-8; has a float and is used in ASW, SAR, and mine sweeping
- Mi-22 "Hook-C" Airborne Command Post Helicopter (Russia, 1972); based on Mi-6
- Mi-26 "Halo" Muti-Role Helicopter (Russia, 1977); another largest in the world helicopter; empty weight 28,200 kg
- Mi-24 "Hind" Attack Helicopter (Russia, 1978); used in various countries; heavily armed and can carry up to eight troops
- Mi-17 Utility Helicopter (Russia, 1980); improved "hot and high" export version of the Mi-8
- Mi-28 "Havoc" Attack Helicopter (Russia, 1982); can fly sideways or backward at up to 100 km/h and forward at 300 km/h
- Mi-34 "Hermit" Light Helicopter (Russia, 1986)
- M-28N Night Attack Helicopter (Russia, 1996); night attack version of M-28
- Mi-38 Passenger Helicopter (Russia, 2007); carries 30 passengers
- Bristol 171 Sycamore Light Multi-Role Helicopter (Britain, 1951)
- Mi-4 Hound Jet Helicopter for ASW and Transport (Russia/China)

Mi-6 Hook

In 1957, this was the largest rotary-wing aircraft.

- Country of Origin: Russia
- Builder: Mil
- Role: Heavy Transport (65 equipped troops), vehicles
- Similar Aircraft: Mi-26 Halo, CH-3 Jolly Green Giant
- Rotor Diameter: 115 ft (35 m)
- Length: 109 ft (33.3 m)
- Armament: Machine gun
- Crew: Five
- Cost: User
- Countries: Algeria, CIS, Egypt, Iraq, Laos, Peru, Syria, Vietnam

- Mi-8 Hip Multi-Role Transport/Attack Helicopter (Russia, 1960)
- Agusta A 109 Multi-Purpose Helicopter (Italy, 1976)
- Mi-14 Haze (Russia)
- Mi-17 (Mi-8MT) Hip H Multi-Role Helicopter (Russia)
- Mi-24 Hind/Mi-25 Hind D/Mi-35 Hind E Assault Transport and Gunship (Russia)
- Agusta A 129 Mangusta Anti-Tank Helicopter (Italy, 1990)
- Mi-26 Halo Heavy Transport (Russia)
- Mi-28 Havoc Attack Helicopter (Russia, 1982)
- Ka-25 Hormone ASW Helicopter (Russia)
- Sud-Ouest SO 1220 (1221) Djinn Light Utility Helicopter (France, 1954)
- Ka-27 Helix A/Ka-29 Helix B/Ka-32 Helix (Russia); multi-use helicopters, including combat, transport, and assault (Helix B)
- Ka-50 Hokum/Ka-52 Hokum B/Black Shark/Werewolf Battle Helicopters (Russia); deployment uncertain due to budget constraints
- AS 565 Panther/SA 360 Dauphin 2/Z-9 (France)
- Hirundo A109 (Italy)
- Mangusta A129 Attack Helicopter
- Alouette 2 (France)
- Alouette III (France)
- SA 330 Puma/AS 532 Cougar (France)
- AS 532UL Cougar Mk I UL/Horizon (France)
- AS 550 Fenec (France)
- EC635 Light Utility Helicopter (LUH) (Germany)
- Merlin HM. 1/EH101 Merlin/EH101 Cormorant (European Helicopter Industries—Britain/Italy)
- Westland Wessex Transport (Britain, 1966); based on Sikorsky S-58
- Lynx (Britain, 1978)
- NH90 (NHIndustries—coalition of France, Germany, Italy, Netherlands, and Portugal, 2006)
- MBB Bo-105 Utility/Anti-Tank/ASW/Transport/SAR Helicopter (Germany, 1975–present)
- Bell H-1 Hueycobra Gunship (U.S., 1967); other versions included EH-1 (electronic warfare); UH-1 (utility); VH-1 (VIP Transport), and TH-1 (training)
- Hiller ROE Rotorcycle (U.S., 1959); experimental foldable one-man helicopter
- Boeing-Vertol H-47 Chinook Transport (U.S., 1962)
- Aerospatiale SA 315 Lama Utility Helicopter (France, 1969); set altitude record for helicopters (12,442 meters)
- Bell H-58 Kiowa Observation (U.S., 1969)
- Sikorsky H-60 Utility/Armed (U.S., 1980)
- Aerospatiale H-65 Dauphin SAR (U.S., 1982)
- Hughes H-64 Apache Attack Helicopter (U.S., 1986)
- Harman H-2 Seasprite ASW Helicopter (U.S., 1987)
- Boeing-Sikorsky RAH-66 Recon/Attack (U.S., 2005?)
- CSH-2 Rooivalk Attack Helicopter (South Africa, 1998)
- PAH-2 Tiger (Germany/France, 2002?)
- SA 341/SA 342 Gazelle (France, 1967)
- Super Frelon (France, 1962)
- Scout (1958), Wasp (1963) utility helicopters (Britain)

Bombs

Bombs are (usually) unpowered missiles dropped from above. They generally are made to fall headfirst, often with the stabilizing aid of fins. They employ various kinds of triggering devices and can carry a large quantity of explosives or other material. They often create damage by blast and by fragmentation effects, although incendiary bombs are also often used, and other types of modern bombs have been developed.

General Information and History

Various items have been dropped down upon enemies for centuries, including stones of all kinds, boiling oil and water, excrement, and...well, just about anything that could be heaved off the edge of a castle or fortress. However, today's bombs got their start with the invention of aircraft, and the earliest such weapons were simply held by hand and dropped out of the open cockpits of biplanes. Bombs were also dropped from balloons and the German Zeppelins.

Bombers were developed in WWI, however—planes whose sole purpose was to drop bombs on various targets. In addition to bombing from their infamous Zeppelins, the Germans developed the Gotha bomber and used it to attack English cities. The Russians, Italians, French, and British all developed bombers. The famous Russian bomber, the Ilya Mourometz, was the first four-engine airplane, and it entered the war in 1913, bombing over Germany and the Baltic states.

Compared to later wars, the bombs that fell during WWI were not very effective; however, they did cause widespread alarm and even panic when dropped directly over cities, such as during the air raids over London. Ultimately, those raids stopped when the maneuverable Sopwith Camel biplanes began shooting the German Gothas out of the sky too regularly.

WWI-vintage bombs generally had little or no penetrating power and simply exploded where they landed, lacking also timed fuzes. By WWII, bombs had grown considerably in size. Early WWII bombs weighed between 2,000 and 8,000 pounds. These high-explosive bombs (which the Brits called Cookies) were often combined with incendiary bombs. Dropped together over urban areas, they could cause great firestorms, such as the one in Dresden. Fragmentation bombs were also used, which could cause damage to property and personnel.

Special bombs were also developed, such as *skip bombs*, which would bounce and skip across water, used specifically as dam busters, and the great earthquake bombs—the 10,000 pound Tall Boy and the 22,000 pound Grand Slam, which were designed to penetrate the earth before detonating, effectively causing a localized earthquake and destroying underground targets. The Germans also developed a rocket-assisted armor-piercing bomb, the PC 100 RS. Toward the end of the war, the Germans reportedly had also developed a radio-guided bomb, which could be dropped at high altitude and guided by radio waves, sighting by a flare that lit up at the back of the bomb.

Of particular importance in the Pacific were the dive bombers, which dropped relatively smaller bombs from very low altitudes at the ends of a diving run. Both the Japanese and the Americans had success with dive bombers. The Japanese also were successful with torpedo bombers, which laid torpedoes down near their targets, then accelerated away. In the case of the Americans, who had terribly unreliable torpedoes, it was the dive bombers that helped them win the war in the Pacific by taking out the Japanese carriers.

Generally, there are several types of bombs, which can be divided into different categories:

- Explosive
  - General Purpose (GP)
  - Fragmentation
  - Demolition Using Blast
  - Anti Armor
  - Fuel Air Explosive

- Chemical
  - Gas
  - Smoke
  - Incendiary
- Pyrotechnic
  - Photoflash
  - Target Indicator
- Nuclear
  - Fissionable
  - Fusionable
- Biological
  - Inert Pathogenic Organisms
- Guided
  - Radio
  - Laser
  - Electro-Optical (TV)

The Importance of Timing

Bombs are most effective if they detonate at just the right moment, which varies with the situation and the intended target. At times, it's useful for the bomb to trigger immediately upon impact. In other cases, it's useful for the bomb to trigger some time after impact, and in still other cases, it's helpful to delay the bomb's arrival at the target for a short time. The first two cases are handled by fuzes of various kinds. The third case is dealt with by retarding the bomb's descent, using parachutes or retarding devices attached to the bomb that slow its descent—for instance, to allow the aircraft that dropped it time to get out of blast range.

Fuze Terminology

Various methods are used to detonate bombs, and they use a specific set of terms. Here are some of the basics:

- **Arming Time (Safe Separation Time [SST]).** The amount of time or the number of vane revolutions required for the firing train to be aligned or the bomb to be fully armed.
- **Delay.** Refers to any time the functioning time of a fuze is more than 0.0005 seconds.
- **External Evidence of Arming (EEA).** Some physical means by which a fuze's state (armed or safe) can be determined.
- **Functioning Time.** The time it takes to detonate after impact or a preset time.
- **Instantaneous.** Describes a fuze that activates in 0.0003 seconds or fewer.
- **Nondelay.** Describes a fuze that activates between 0.0003 seconds and 0.0005 seconds.
- **Proximity (VT).** Describes the action that causes a fuze to fire when an object of determined size or other characteristics is detected at a predetermined distance from the bomb.
- **Safe Air Travel (SAT).** Describes the distance that the bomb travels in an unarmed state from the releasing aircraft.

Most fuzes are either mechanical or electrical. Mechanical fuzes are similar in principle to the operation of a gun hammer and primer, but they usually entail several steps of ignition, such as priming charge and booster charge(s) before the main explosive is detonated. But in the case of a mechanical fuze, it is the mechanical force of the bomb hitting the target that initiates the sequence. They are armed usually by the rotation of the vanes in the tail after release, which cause the mechanisms inside the bomb to arm. Mechanical fuzes should be safe in storage and in transit and remain safe until they have fully cleared the delivery aircraft. They should only detonate in the intended manner, whether that be instantaneous or on some delay, and they should not detonate if accidentally released or jettisoned.

Modern electrical fuzes are similar to mechanical fuzes, but they are initiated differently. Generally, they receive a charge of electricity into onboard capacitors just before they are released from the aircraft.

Delay is created by various electrical circuitry, which controls the initiation of the firing sequence, and may contain timers or impact-sensitive switches. Whether they are mechanical or electric, fuzes are triggered in different ways. For instance:

- **Impact Fuze (Nose).** A simple mechanical fuze that triggers on impact.
- **Impact Fuze (Tail).** A simple mechanical fuze that triggers on impact.
- **Impact Fuze (Side).** A simple mechanical fuze that triggers on impact.
- **Mechanical Timer Fuze.** A timer, such as a clockwork device, that delays the triggering of the bomb for a set time.
- **Proximity Fuze.** A fuze that uses some sort of signal, such as radar or radio waves, to detect proximity to its target and initiate detonation.
- **All-Ways Fuze.** A fuze that will trigger no matter how the bomb impacts the target.
- **Hydrostatic Fuze.** A fuze that is triggered when immersed in water.

Many modern fuzes can be set for more than one possible triggering method.

Fins

Modern bombs are almost always fitted with some kind of stabilization method, generally in the form of fins attached to the back end of the bomb. Bombs are generally shaped to be aerodynamic, and the fin assemblies help them fall in a smooth arc to the target, nose first. Modern fin assemblies vary in shape and intended use. Some are fixed, such as the *conical* fin assembly, while others, such as the Snakeye, can be optionally opened to retard the fall of the bomb for some situations.

Modern Bombs

Military research is ongoing, and the search continues for more effective bombs in different configurations. This section discusses a few types of modern bombs.

Smart Bombs

Conventional bombs that simply drop from a plane without any steering mechanisms are often known as *dumb* bombs. In contrast, *smart* bombs can be guided, or in some cases can even guide themselves, to a target. They are like dumb bombs with the addition of sensor systems, control systems, and some sort of adjustable flight mechanism, usually adjustable fins. In essence, a smart bomb is a heavy glider that will fall with some control. It derives forward motion from the plane that drops it. Most smart bombs have proximity fuzes or impact fuzes.

The first smart bombs from WWII used radio waves. More modern smart bombs feature TV/infrared (IR) or laser guidance. With TV and IR, bombs can be controlled manually by an operator, usually in the bombing aircraft, using the visual signals sent by the bomb itself. Such bombs can also be locked onto a target through video surveillance and will guide themselves to the target automatically once they are dropped.

Laser-guided smart bombs use a sensor that can detect a specific frequency of laser light, which is shined on a target by a remote operator. The bomb will home in on the reflected laser light from the target. Just before dropping the bomb, it is programmed with a specific pulse pattern, which it seeks. It will not respond to a laser signature unless it has this specific pulse pattern.

The main drawback of these types of bombs is that they must maintain visual contact with the target. Smoke and clouds or other atmospheric conditions can disrupt their effectiveness.

Newer technology uses the JDAM, or *Joint Direct Attack Munitions* (GBU 31/32), to equip existing dumb bombs with sophisticated guidance systems, consisting of a tail kit that contains an inertial guidance system and a GPS receiver. Combined, these allow the bomb to "know" its position in space.

Before dropping the bomb, the aircraft's computer identifies the GPS location of the target and feeds that and the current position into the bomb's onboard GPS. The bomb can find its way to the target—accurate to within 40 feet, and generally more accurate than that—even in bad weather or through smoke and other visual barriers, since the GPS signals are not affected by such conditions. JDAM kits are also far more economical than other smart bomb options, costing only around $20,000 per tail kit, compared with $120,000 for a laser-guided bomb.

Cluster Bombs

Cluster bombs may be dropped from the air or launched from ground facilities. The main housing scatters smaller bombs (bomblets), which can have various uses, such as anti-personnel, physical infrastructure destruction, or even the delivery of chemical weapons or mines. Ninety-four nations have signed a treaty prohibiting the use of cluster bombs for the indiscriminate damage they do to noncombatants, even long after they have been dispersed. Here are some cluster bomb models:

- **MK20, CBU-99, CBU-100 Anti-Tank Bombs.** Air-launched freefall weapon used against armored vehicles. These bombs release 247 Mk 118 antitank bombs when dropped, weighing approximately 490 pounds. At the preset time, two shaped charges cut the bomb in half and release the bomblets, which spread in freefall trajectories. Mk 118 bombs will release a shaped charge warhead when they strike a hard surface, such as armor or concrete. If they hit a soft surface, such as earth or sandbags, they allow the bomb to penetrate, and an inertia-driven firing pin then detonates the "stab detonator" and fires off the warhead.
- **CBU-78/B and B/B GATOR.** Drops 60 mines from each unit. They can drop either the BLU-91/B, an armor-piercing warhead that uses a magnetometer sensor, or a BLU-92/B fragmentation mine with tripwire sensors.
- **Modern Fire Bombs.** Modern fire bombs (as distinguished from the incendiary bombs used during the two World Wars) are non-stabilized (lacking fins) bombs that are filled with fuel gel (the new terminology for what has been called NAPALM) and used against troops and various installations, or even on terrain to burn it away. The MK77 Mod 4 fire bomb used by the U.S. military weighs about 500 pounds and carries 75 gallons of fuel gel. Upon impact, the bomb will rupture and the fuzes will detonate, rupturing the igniters and setting fire to the mixture. The fuel gel is made to adhere to surfaces, causing maximum destructive effect.
- **BBU-55 Fuel Air Explosive (FAE) Bomb.** Dropped in clusters of three, these bombs create a cloud of ethylene oxide about 50 feet across by 8 feet high. When this cloud is detonated, it creates a blastwave approximately five times that of TNT. FAEs are often used to clear minefields.

Other Bombs

This list includes a few specific types of bombs to open your imagination and allow your destructive impulses further fuel.

- **Matra Durandal.** A penetration bomb that is dropped and retarded in descent until it reaches the proper angle, then rocket-boosted into its target for maximum penetration. It is used effectively to damage enemy runways and other targets.
- **HOBOS.** Electro-optical bombs, also known as HOBOS (*homing bomb systems*) use TV technology to guide them by means of movable fins. They can be locked onto a target before dropping or guided while falling by the crew, using pictures sent back from the TV unit in the bomb.
- **Paveway Bombs.** Paveway bombs are guided by laser. They are conventional bombs with special equipment added to allow them to home in on a laser beam and change course by means of movable

fin assemblies. The laser is generally beamed from a support aircraft, not the one dropping the bomb. There are different versions of the Paveway bombs, for different targets and purposes.

- **Bunker Busters.** Bunker busters are bombs intended to penetrate to targets that are far underground or are protected by thick concrete structures. Early bunker busters were the WWII-era Tall Boy and Grand Slam, but the need for new technology has resurfaced, so to speak, with the targets in the Middle East, which are often dug deep into the ground. The GBU-28 or BLU-113 is 19 feet long and 14.5 inches in diameter. It is fashioned from artillery barrels of hard steel and filled with nearly 650 pounds of tritonal explosive, which is a mixture of TNT and aluminum powder (about 20 percent). The aluminum powder improves the speed at which the explosive reaches its maximum pressure, which is called *brisance.* This bomb weighs 4,400 pounds. It is laser guided and uses adjustable front fins for steering and fixed, retractable back fins for stabilization. Because this bomb is very heavy and very strong, but very narrow by comparison, it can penetrate very deep—up to 100 feet into earth and 20 feet into concrete when dropped from a plane. Typically, bunker buster bombs have been fitted with delay timers that cause them to detonate after maximum penetration, but even more precise *hard target smart fuzes* (HTSF) are being employed that use an accelerometer to detect the exact perfect moment to detonate the bomb. A light (2,000-pound) version, the GBU-27/GBU-24 or BLU-109, is also being used. One material that is considered ideal for bunker buster bombs is depleted uranium (DU), which is 1.7 times heavier than lead and 2.4 times heavier than steel, almost five times harder than steel, and will burn with an extremely hot and intense flame when heated in an oxygen environment. However, the down side is that DU leaves radioactive material on the battlefield, and when it burns, the smoke can be very damaging to the human body. Another favored but politically problematical bunker buster is the tactical nuke, which can do tremendous damage but would inevitably leave a very large crater and spew radioactive fallout into the atmosphere.
- **E-Bombs.** No specific electromagnetic (EMP) weapons are officially in existence, but research into them has been going on for decades. The idea of an EMP weapon is that it would create a powerful electromagnetic pulse that would destroy just about anything that uses electricity or electronics without direct loss of life or other destruction of property. There are several types of proposed EMP weapons, varying from large-scale bombs to small and simple weapons that could disrupt equipment in a small area. A design was even published in Scientific American in 2001 that shows a small weapon made up of some wire coils and a charge of high explosive in a specialized casing. By passing a current through the coil and then detonating, the explosive would cause a moving short circuit through the coil, compressing the magnetic field and generating an intense electromagnetic burst. The idea behind EMP weapons is based on a 1925 theory by physicist Arthur Compton (known as the Compton Effect) that postulates that a large amount of electromagnetic energy can knock electrons loose from atoms of material with low atomic numbers, such as oxygen and nitrogen in the atmosphere. It is thought that this happened during early atmospheric tests of nuclear weapons in the '50s, where street lamps in Hawaii were blown out by blasts that were hundreds of miles away.
- **MOAB.** The Massive Ordnance Air Burst—one of the largest conventional bombs ever built. It weighs 21,000 pounds and measures 30 feet long and 40.5 inches in diameter. It is guided by satellite and is designed to detonate about 6 feet above the ground, causing it to disperse more of its enemy laterally, as opposed to a conventional impact bomb, which sends the bulk of its blast into the ground or into the air. This bomb replaces the Daisy Cutter, a Vietnam-era bomb that weighed 15,000 pounds and could create an instant helicopter landing site by clearing trees in a 500-foot diameter circle with one blast. The largest bomb ever created was the T-1, which weighed 43,600 pounds. Even though the MOAB is very large, its blast is miniscule when compared to a nuclear bomb.
- **GBU-15.** The U.S. Guided Bomb Unit is an unpowered glide weapon used to destroy enemy high-value targets and is dropped from F-15 aircraft. It weighs about 2,500 pounds and has a range of

between 5 and 15 nautical miles. Its guidance systems use television or imaging infrared seeker via man-in-the-loop link, autonomous GPS/INS. It costs in excess of $240,000 per unit.

- **JDAM (Joint Direct Attack Munitions) GBU 31/32.** A guided air-to-surface bomb using either a 2,000-pound BLU-109/MK 84 warhead or a 1,000-pound BLU-110/MK 83. They have a range up to 15 miles and use GPS/INS guidance systems. JDAMs were developed after the Desert Storm operation to provide munitions that could be used in low-visibility conditions. In addition, they can be launched from very high or very low altitudes and with a variety of versatile approaches by the launching aircraft.

Ships

I was about to begin a list of ships and offer a lot of information about them, but then I discovered that the work I was about to do was already being done. So, instead, I'm sending you to Wikipeda, specifically to en.wikipedia.org/wiki/Wikipedia:WikiProject_Ships. I think you'll find plenty of good information there.

Depth Charges

Depth charges were created as a direct response to the German U-boats of WWI. The first depth charge, the British "D" type Mk III, weighed 300 pounds and carried an explosive, usually TNT, which was triggered at a preset depth by an internal pressure-activated trigger device, called a *pistol.* It could go as deep as 300 feet and was rolled off racks at the stern of the boat. This was the standard method of dropping depth charges, but projecting systems were developed even during WWI, such as the K-gun, which could toss a charge 150 feet from the boat, could be launched to the sides as well as to the stern, and could be used to create patterns of explosions.

Depth charges had a small blast radius, but the effects of pressure waves could damage a submerged sub sufficiently to force it to the surface. Creating patterned explosions increased the likelihood of crippling a target submarine.

More improvements were added during WWII, including the use of a stronger explosive—Torpex—and casings that would sink faster, giving the sub less time to take evasive action. However improved they were, they weren't terribly effective because the submarines were made better as well, and could survive depth-charge damage unless the charge hit within five meters (15 feet) of the sub's hull—a matter of chance. In one documented case, German sub U-427 survived 678 depth-charge attacks.

More effective was the *hedgehog,* a device that fired an array of 24 bombs ahead of the launching ship. Guided by sonar, they only exploded on contact, but they were responsible for more "kills" than standard depth charges.

Modern anti-submarine weapons include the CAPTOR mines (see the "Mines" section earlier in this chapter), acoustic torpedoes, and ASROC, or anti-submarine rockets. Current research includes what are called *organic* anti-mine systems, including the ARCI sonar system, which is supposed to be 100-percent effective for SSNs to detect mines with sufficient time to avoid them, as well as the Airborne Mine Countermeasures (OAMCM) and the Airborne Laser Mine Detection System (ALMDS).

Torpedoes

Torpedoes were invented in the late 19th century. A torpedo is a self-propelled explosive device designed to operate in and under water. Torpedoes are often fired from submarines, although they were also fired from aircraft during WWII. One estimate contends that torpedoes have been responsible for 25 million tons of wreckage at the sea bottom since their invention by Robert Whitehead.

General Information and History

The term *torpedo* was derived from a species of fish that can deliver an electric shock. The word was applied to various devices used against shipping, some of which we would call mines today. Ultimately, the modern use of the word took hold and has remained. One early device that used the name was the so-called *Harvey torpedo*, which was an explosive device that was towed on a long cable behind another boat. As it swung out from the towing boat, it could be brought into contact with the enemy and detonated. But this design was subject to many hazards and limitations and was supplanted by Whitehead's torpedo.

One other "torpedo" of note was the so-called *spar torpedo*, which was an explosive charge at the end of a long pole, which was detonated by pushing it against an enemy ship by hand. The charge was ignited by a percussion cap. These weapons were actually used successfully during the American Civil War.

What is most amazing is that most of the core technologies and refinements that formed the basis of torpedoes used in WWII had already been developed and implemented by the turn of the century. Of course, there were further refinements, but the essentials of the torpedo were worked out long before they came into common use in warfare.

Early torpedoes used compressed-air engines, which underwent several phases of improvement—the most significant of which was the introduction of heated systems, which improved performance significantly. The heated air produced much more pressure and therefore more range and speed.

To maintain the torpedo's depth, Whitehead created a mechanism, which for years was referred to only as *The Secret.* It was a chamber sealed at atmospheric pressure containing a pendulum and a hydrostatic valve. Water pressure would cause movement of a moveable disk, which would cause changes in the equilibrium of the system and would translate to a system of levers that would control the horizontal rudders. The rudders would tilt up if the torpedo was too deep or down if it was too shallow. The system worked remarkably well, with a tolerance, even in its earliest form, of +/– 6 inches, and was adopted in all subsequent torpedoes, at least through the WWII era.

To further stabilize the torpedo's run, gyros were added, which would prevent the torpedo from wandering laterally. By oriented the gyro's axis in the direction of the torpedo's travel and attaching it to gimbals that could relay the pressure from the gyro when the course deviated, it was possible to fire air jets to either side, based on the pressure from the gyro, and correct the torpedo's course. This resulted in significant increases in accuracy. The addition of servo motors from the balance chamber assembly increased the ability of that mechanism to affect the movement of the horizontal rudders far more efficiently. All of these improvements were in place by WWI.

The contra-rotating propeller system, two propellers rotating in opposite directions on the same axis, was adopted for most torpedoes because it reduces the "swirl" effect of one propeller, recovering some efficiency, and it also further stabilizes the motivational force.

A parallel development with the compressed air torpedo was the electric torpedo. The first ones, built as early as 1873, had to remain wired to the ship or base that fired them. One version, built in 1889, could travel more than 2 miles carrying 400 pounds of explosives. The first self-contained electric torpedoes were developed around 1880 to 1890. The Germans perfected electric torpedoes around the end of WWI but really didn't put them into practice until WWII. Electric torpedoes had several advantages, not the least of which was that they left no "tracks," as the air compressed ones did—expelling exhaust air into the water, leaving a trail of bubbles. Electric torpedoes were also essentially silent, which became more and more important as time went on and sonar technology developed.

During WWII, the German G7e type came in three forms. The T2 torpedo had a range of 5,400 yards and a speed of 30 knots. The T3 and T3a had a range of 8,000 yards at 29 knots. The batteries in these weapons weighed 1,500 pounds, and the motor another 250. However, they were very successful and accounted for significant loss of Allied shipping during WWII. Based on research and analysis of captured G7e torpedoes, the U.S. created the Mk 18 electric torpedo, which was successfully used during the war.

A more modern U.S. torpedo is the Mk44, which is electric powered and can be fired from aircraft, ships, or subs or from the ASROC system.

Modern torpedoes usually use active or passive acoustic or wake-homing devices, allowing them to "find" their targets. Although it is well known that water transmits sound very well and over very long distances, it is also a very problematic medium for acoustic seeking devices. There is quite a bit of "noise" and distortion in water, based on various effects, such as reflection from the surface and/or the seabed, Doppler effects, and other effects. Modern acoustic sensors must attempt to filter out the noise in order to get true readings.

Many modern torpedoes actually use wire-guided systems, which allow direct two-way communications between the torpedo and its home ship. Among other things, this allows the operators to bypass torpedo countermeasures, such as bubble screens and distractive noisemakers. This type of system is used by both the U.S. Mk48 and the British Spearfish torpedo, although in either case if the wire breaks, the torpedo can perform on seeker mode alone. Both systems run the heavyweight torpedo (HWT) out near the target at high speed, which can interfere with the acoustic signal, carrying out the final phase of attack at lower speed, where the signal is not degraded by the water flow over the acoustic head.

Passive sensors are still useful against surface ships because they make a lot of noise, but today's submarines are very quiet, and active sensors are required.

Torpedoes with narrow depth-bands will often move in a helical search pattern, while those with more depth range may use a sinuous (snakelike) pattern.

Another type of system, used against surface ships, is called *wake homing*. The torpedo can sense the wake of a ship, and it crisscrosses the wake boundaries until it reaches the ship and makes contact. A somewhat more difficult but more efficient method is called *wake nibbling*, in which the torpedo can detect the wake and follow its boundary to the ship, instead of crisscrossing.

There are two main classifications of torpedoes—lightweight (LWT) and heavyweight (HWT).

Lightweight Torpedoes (LWT)

Modern torpedoes are extremely sophisticated, compared to their predecessors. An example is the U.S.-made Mk 46, which can be digitally programmed for a variety of behaviors. It can work on active or passive sensors and can use different search patterns, different depth settings (including a search ceiling set to prevent it from attacking its own ship), and a variety of other options. The redesigned version—the Mk 46 Mod 5—extends its capabilities significantly, including a sonar transducer, transmitter, and receiver, which allow it to detect submarines, even when their hulls are coated with Anechoic tiles. It has a search speed of around 30 knots and a range of 15 kilometers. It has improved sensor signal to noise and can reject false targets, and it can be programmed to recognize and attack the most vulnerable part of a ship—the control room. Another model, the M50 Barracuda, is claimed to be a dual-speed torpedo with even more improved sensing. Other LWTs include the British Stingray, the French Mu 90 Impact, the Swedish wire-guided Tap series (42, 43, 431/432, Tp43XO), and the Indian Shyena, which is named after a bird of prey known for its swift dive.

Excerpt from EuroTorp Website

U90 TORPEDO

The MU90 is a NATO-standard-calibre (323,7mm) fire-and-forget LWT of 304 kg and 2850mm length, designed to counter any type of nuclear or conventional submarine, acoustically coated, fast-evasive, deploying active or passive anti-torpedo effectors. The torpedo can be deployed from surface vessels, fixed/rotary wing aircraft or missile. Pre-arrangements to cope with submarine-launched SLAAM threats have been incorporated in the weapon as well as Hard-Kill (anti-torpedo torpedo), continental shelf mine and submarine launching capability. Designed and built with outstanding technologies, the weapon features any-task any-environment capability. It is presently in mass production for Denmark, France, Germany, Italy, Poland, and selected, as single source, by Australia and New Zealand.

HEAVYWEIGHT TORPEDOES (HWT)

Whereas lightweight torpedoes are primarily used for close-range attacks from aircraft, heavyweight torpedoes are used as a standoff weapon, generally from a submerged submarine. Though torpedoes are categorized by their diameter, the most common size for heavy torpedoes is 21 inches (533mm), although there are larger sizes, ranging up to 36 inches.

Some heavyweight torpedoes include the U.S. Mark 48, the German DM2A3 and DM2A4, as well as the WWII-era GE7 series, the Russian Type 53-65 torpedoes, and the famed Japanese torpedo from WWII, the Type 93 or "Long Lance," which was launched from surface ships, and its counterpart, the Type 95, which was launched from submarines. It was the most effective torpedo of WWII and far more reliable and destructive than any U.S. model of the time.

TORPEDO PROPULSION

Heavyweight torpedoes can run for distances of anywhere from 20 km to 100 km, depending on the model and the speed at which they move. Throughout the world, there are many versions of HWTs, including the British Spearfish Mod 1 and the U.S. Mk 48 ADCAP (stands for ADvanced CAPability), which can move at up to 65 knots with a range of around 20 to 30 km. The Soviet Union developed several HWTs, including a super HWT with enough power to sink a carrier (with a maximum range of 100 km!) and a rocket-powered torpedo rumored to be able to reach speeds of 200 knots or even 500 knots, depending on the source. According to one source, it uses an effect called a *super captivating bubble* to propel it forward through the water. Other Russian models include the DST-90, DST-92, and DST-96 gas-turbine torpedoes.

From the earliest compressed-air engines to the commonly used electric engines, torpedo development has resulted in new and better, faster, lighter, and more efficient engine designs. Using more modern fuels, such as High-Test Peroxide (HTP) and the nitrogen ester fuels, OTTO and OTTO II, many torpedoes are achieving far better performance. Some use a system called Sceps (*Stored Chemical Energy Power System*), which uses a block of lithium that interacts with sulphur fluoride to create heat and steam. Other systems use seawater batteries, and new electric systems are being developed, including the use of new brushless motors and Thrystor-controlled motors that offer an instant option of rotational speeds.

The standard propulsion method for LWTs is the pump-jet, while for HWTs it is new counter-rotating propellers with advanced materials and new configurations of blades, replacing the older two-propeller, four-blade configurations. Other improvements include advanced shape designs and even the introduction of new "animal skin" polymers that imitate the natural skins of marine creatures and create a boundary layer that prevents or delays the onset of turbulence and micro-cavitation.

Torpedo Countermeasures

Torpedoes remain one of the most deadly threats to seaborne vessels, and few countries can boast the necessary technology to counter the advances in torpedo development. The main requirement of any countermeasure system is the discovery of any torpedo threat with enough time to implement countermeasures. Most systems use passive sensors that listen for telltale signals, such as the specific sound of the torpedo's fast propellers or pump-jet operation and/or any emissions from active sensors on the torpedo itself.

There are three basic types of torpedoes, and each has its own countermeasures. (For more information on soft kill and hard kill, see the "Soft-Kill Options" and "Hard-Kill Options" sections.)

- **Straight Runners.** Generally HWTs with no homing sensors that follow a set short- or medium-range pattern and give off a high noise signature, making them relatively easy to avoid or destroy by hard-kill defenses.
- **Wake Homers.** These HWTs are counted by course/speed changes, the elimination of the wake, or by hard-kill defenses.
- **Acoustic Homing Torpedoes.** Either LWT or HWT, these are the most common type of torpedo in service today. They are very difficult to detect when in passive sensor mode, and they are often sophisticated enough to ignore false target information. They are also capable of re-attacking in case of a successful avoidance. Most HWTs of this type are also wire-guided and can gain additional effectiveness from their operators. Acoustic homing torpedo defense is of the soft-kill or hard-kill variety.

Submarine countermeasures are limited. LWTs are often launched from aircraft within 100 to 150 meters, at which point they use 3D active sonar to acquire the target, closing on the sub at high speed once acquired. If they lose the target, they have algorithms that can allow reacquisition. The submarine will counter by going at low speed and using only passive sensors, but will have only about a minute from splashdown to react. HWTs are generally launched from considerable distances and can close in silent, passive mode. They will switch to active sensors only on remote-controlled command (wire-guided), preset commands or upon target acquisition. HWTs can run at high speed and have long endurance in addition to a sophisticated and flexible array of passive, active, and even wake-homing sensor options. They have multi-frequency beams to use for target identification as well as multi-beam seekers for special discrimination. With the addition of the wire-guided control by operators, they are very hard to counter. Generally, any sub that does detect an incoming HWT will have little time to respond.

Submarines are limited in their evasive maneuvering, and most anti-torpedo systems rely on decoys and jammers. Some examples include:

- C-303/S (127mm diameter) and C-303 (76mm diameter) WASS models use decoys (target simulators) and jammers. The C-303/S adds a mobile target emulator that is based on the A200 mini-torpedo. They are launched by compressed air.
- The British Royal Navy uses the SSDE (Submerged Signal and Decoy Ejector) in three versions—the Mk56 (Swiftsure), Mk8 (Trafalgar), and Mk20 (Vanguard). These systems use reloadable tubes that fire Type 2066 and Type 2071 AMULET decoys.
- The U.S. system uses the Librascope 127mm diameter CSA Mk2 launchers to fire various type of torpedo and anti-sonar devices. ADC Mk2 is an older anti-torpedo decoy, while there is a more advanced version—the Mk3. Sea-Wolf class boats employ the WLY-1 system, which can launch 16 decoys. Then there is the MOSS (Mobile Submarine Simulator), a 254mm-diameter full-sized

torpedo that can generate an underwater signature very much like that of a sub. Originally used in 1976, it has been improved over the years and is standard on SSBN and SSN.
- Israel has developed a self-propelled decoy called the *SCUTTER*.
- The German navy has developed the TAU (Torpedo Abwehr Uboote) system, which is based on a combination of countermeasures, such as low signatures, evasive maneuvers, jammers, and decoys. The system will employ multiple small vehicles that can be preprogrammed to act as either jammers or decoys and can change on the fly.
- French anti-torpedo systems use target simulators called TOSC (towed source/target) and CALAS, which is a self-propelled torpedo-like target that can be used as a decoy.

Soft-Kill Options

The term *soft kill* refers to systems that defeat the torpedo's sensors and tracking ability or that provide escape for targeted craft. These use decoys and jammers primarily, though new "advisory" systems are currently deployed that gather data in the vicinity of the ship or sub, analyze that data, assess the threat level, and provide recommendations for evasive maneuvers or deployment of countermeasures.

- The main U.S. countermeasure is the AN/SLQ-25 NIXIE, which is a towed system that creates a false target effective against passive and wake-homing torpedoes. It includes a magnetic device that can cause the torpedo to detonate prematurely, and the Phase II version should include jammers and a towed torpedo alarm sensor. Similar systems are used by Russian ships.
- The British system is the Grasbey Type 182, which is a towed system using a noise generator and jammer.
- Two countermeasure solutions, MASKER and PRARIE, use various methods to create a gaseous curtain that absorbs and dampens the noise of the ship, both highly effective against passive sensors; however, they are very vulnerable to active sensor torpedoes, which can actually "see" the ships better when those systems are active.
- The French SALT system is a sophisticated combination of search module, threat evaluator, and countermeasure modules that can detect and evaluate a threat, then take automatic and coordinated countermeasures, including electro-acoustic decoys, stationary jammers, stationary and mobile target simulators, and, possibly, bubble decoys to work against wake homers.

Hard-Kill Options

Most current anti-torpedo defenses are soft-kill options. It is pretty much assumed that it will be difficult, at best, or nearly impossible to attack the firing ships, which these days can fire from very long range, although airborne torpedo launchers can be countered with anti-aircraft defenses. But the greatest danger comes from subs, which can launch torpedoes at long distances and remain out of harm's way.

Hard-kill options are definitely being explored, but there are many challenges to their successful implementation. For instance, when compared to the data received on an incoming Mach 3 missile, the effective rate of incoming data for a torpedo traveling at 40 knots is five times slower than that for the missile. This is based on some complex analysis and data manipulation, but one salient factor is that the propagation of radio-frequency data in air is 200,000 times faster than the propagation of acoustic data in water. And, as was mentioned before, water is a far less consistent environment in which to conduct any kind of detection methods, based on the variations of reflections from surface and floor, thermoclines, salinity gradients, and wake effects, to name a few. Also, hard-kill options would need to be designed so that they would not interfere with other systems or with each other, or endanger the ship that fired them or any friendly ships nearby.

Moreover, with many torpedo sensor systems being based on passive systems, the target ships, even if they can detect a threat, cannot easily determine the range information needed for effective hard-kill countermeasures. Research is happening in a number of directions, such as explosive charges towed behind the ship, launched and precisely placed charges distributed in the ship's wake, anti-torpedo torpedoes (ATT), Gatling guns with bullets capable of traveling several hundred yards underwater, underwater launched, supersonic projectiles, and non-explosive concepts. The U.S. Navy says they are working on such technologies as nanoelectronics and Micro-Electro-Mechanical Systems (MEMS) to create faster electronics and "advances in sensors for large area external acoustic and electromagnetic arrays." Anti-torpedo and anti-submarine technology is employing all the cutting-edge technology that the Western countries can bring to bear. It's changing year by year.

Layered Defenses

No one solution will entirely protect ships, given the sophistication of water- and airborne weapons. It is, therefore, essential to any effective defense strategy that it includes both passive and active, soft and hard kill, and even offensive and aggressive options. Putting these all together in a "layered" defense system seems the best alternative, with the highest likelihood of success, along with the employment of modern technologies.

Littoral Combat Ships

One of the most modern designs for seagoing vehicles is called the *Littoral Combat Ship* or *LCS*. These modern warships are highly maneuverable craft with an impressive array of modern weaponry, countermeasures, and onboard safety systems. They are being designed to be able to alter and simulate their own "signatures," to deploy a variety of hard- and soft-kill anti-torpedo and anti-missile defenses, and to maneuver quickly in threat environments. In addition to their sea-based capabilities, they will have hangars and flight decks to support helicopters and UAVs (Unmanned Aerial Vehicles).

A Very Brief History of Rockets

Rockets have been around a long time—much longer than other conventional firearms. In 400 B.C., a Greek named Archytas created a wooden bird that flew around using a steam-propelled rocket effect. Again, 300 years later, a Greek named Hero invented a steam-powered device called an *aeolipile.* Although not rockets, these simple devices still used the principles of propulsion that ultimately are the same principles used in rocket-powered engines. All are based on what, in the 17th century, Newton described as the Third Law of Motion.

Historically, the first to develop rockets were the Chinese. As early as the 10th century, the Chinese may have developed rocket-launched "fire" arrows shot from a handheld device that would launch multiple arrows. By the 13th century, the Chinese were using rocket weapons attached to sticks for stability—somewhat like the bottle rockets of today.

During the centuries that followed, many experiments in rocketry were carried out in Europe. As early as the 15th century, a Frenchman, Jean Froissart, began launching rockets from tubes, a precursor of the modern bazooka, and in Italy, Joanes de Fontana had designed a rocket-powered torpedo that would run on the surface and set enemy ships on fire. Although rockets as weapons fell out of favor in the 16th century, they were used as fireworks, and the first multistage rocket was developed by a German named Johann Schmidlap.

Also in the 16th and later in the 18th century, some people had developed rocket-powered spears, which were first fired from cannons, then driven farther by igniting rockets mounted behind the spearhead.

There is even one semi-legendary story of an early Chinese official named Wan-Hu designing a rocket chair powered by 47 fire arrows. The story has it that when all the rockets were lit simultaneously, there was a great roar and billows of smoke. When the smoke cleared, there was no sign of Wan-Hu or the chair.

In the 18th century, there was considerable experimentation with rockets, and they enjoyed a brief revival as weapons of war. Although they were inaccurate, they were generally launched by the thousands, and their cumulative effect was devastating. During the war of 1812, the British used Congreve rockets (designed by Colonel William Congreve) to assault Fort McHenry, which was the source of the line "the rockets' red glare" from the poem by Francis Scott Key that became "The Star-Spangled Banner."

In the 19th century, rockets were used occasionally, sometimes for practical and sometimes for odd purposes. As early as 1821, sailors used rocket-propelled harpoons to hunt whales, protecting themselves from the blast by use of a circular shield. On the odd side, an Italian named Claude Ruggieri was said to be rocketing small animals into space and recovering the payloads by parachute as early as 1806!

William Hale developed a principle for using small vanes to cause a rocket to spin, which had an effect similar to that of rifling on a bullet, making it more stable in flight and more accurate. This principle is still used, in some form or another, today. Soon, with advances in breech-loading artillery with rifled barrels, rockets once again became obsolete as weapons of war.

Russian Konstantin Tsiolkovsky published a paper postulating liquid-fueled rockets for space exploration in 1903 and is considered the father of modern astronautics. Another pioneer was American Robert Goddard, who developed the first working liquid-fueled rocket in 1926—a rocket that fired for only two and a half seconds and reached a speed of 60 mph and a modest altitude of 41 feet, coming to a landing in a cabbage patch 184 feet away. But this rocket, like the Wright brothers' first airplane flight, was the beginning of a new era. Goddard went on to further develop rocket systems, adding gyroscopes for stability, payload sections for instruments, parachutes for recovery, and more.

Another pioneer was Hermann Oberth, whose 1923 writings about rocket-powered space travel spawned rocket societies around the world and led directly to the development of the V-2 rocket (called the A-4 in Germany), one of the most feared weapons of WWII. Although the V-2 was developed and employed too late to change the outcome of the war, German scientists had already been developing rockets capable of spanning the Atlantic and attacking the U.S. Many of the German rocket scientists were brought to the U.S. after the war to continue research, including Wernher von Braun.

What followed was a time of experimentation, development, and competition, particularly between the U.S. and the Soviet Union, for the conquest of space. Along the way, rocket systems became more and more powerful, versatile, and deadly.

Types of Missiles (Strategic/Tactical)

In the context of war, missiles are used in two basic ways—as strategic weapons or as tactical weapons. The difference is generally in what is being targeted. Strategic weapons are used against population or industrial centers and specific installations, with the purpose of disrupting production, instilling fear, destroying supply lines, and so on. Tactical weapons are used within battle situations in a variety of ways, including as air or sea defenses, as anti-tank weapons, and as anti-personnel weapons, to name a few.

Propulsion Methods

All self-propelled devices use Newton's Third Law as the operating principle, which states that for every action there is an equal and opposite reaction. Of course, this law also applies to weapons that launch projectiles, and most are based on the explosive force of gasses from combustion of one kind or another. Propellers are used in some weapons, such as torpedoes, and the combustion of gasses or the use of gas pressure is secondary to the force that spins the propellers. Although the actual motion is caused by the pressure of the spinning blades against the water, Newton's Third Law still applies.

JET ENGINES

A jet engine essentially works by accelerating the air forced into it, combining it with a combustion medium or fuel and igniting the mixture to produce highly expanded gas pressure, which is expelled out the back of the engine. Rockets, on the other hand, used combustible fuels to create gasses at very high pressures, which are forced through a reduced opening of a precise shape to generate the most backward thrust while reducing turbulence. In reality, what is happening is that a great deal of mass is being propelled out in one direction, and the body that is generating that explosion then moves in the opposite direction. It's the same principle as that of a balloon being blown up and then released. What drives the balloon to fly around is not just pressure, it is the actual mass of the air molecules escaping at high velocity. In any case, the backward thrust is converted into forward motion in accordance with Newton's law.

There are three basic types of jet engine—the pulse jet, the ramjet, and the turbojet. A variant used on rockets is called the turbo-rocket:

- Pulse jets operate by forcing air into a valved compartment (though some designs have been created without valves), which is generally started by launching from a catapult or rocket booster of some kind. When the air pressure is sufficient, the valves open and the air is forced inside, where it is ignited with a fuel mixture. The resulting explosion closes the valves in front, and the gas pressure is forced to the rear, propelling the missile forward, which then causes the valves to reopen and allow more air to enter. After a few cycles, the hot gasses in the chamber will ignite the fuel/air mixture without a separate igniter. The only time this principle has been put into operation in a weapon was the German V1 rocket of WWII, which could reach speeds of up to 559 miles per hour and had a range of 150 miles. Eighty-five hundred V1 rockets were launched over London beginning in June of 1944. Among several drawbacks of pulse jets are inefficient fuel usage and high noise. The V1s were known as *buzz bombs* because of the noise they made. Pulse jets are used today in model airplanes, although research is being conducted on high-altitude, high-speed aircraft using pulse-detonation engines, or PDE.
- Ramjets are formed from a tube with an insert at the front that forces air entering the tube to slow down while building up pressure. They are the simplest form of jet engine and can be made smaller than any other type. Particularly handy for high-speed uses, they actually need a high startup speed or boosters. Within the diffuser section of the jet, the fuel is mixed with the air and ignited. A flameholder prevents the flame from being extinguished, and the gasses escape out the back nozzle. Ramjets require some boosters to get started, but once they have begun and forward motion creates the necessary air pressure, combustion and thrust are constant. Ramjets are used in long-distance, high-altitude missiles. At especially high speeds (aircraft speeds around Mach 5 or more), combustion in a standard ramjet will fail. To counter this problem, supersonic combusting ramjets, known as *scramjets*, have been developed with a wider inlet (typically, the entire underside of the craft), which reduces compression but keeps the air at supersonic speed. Scramjets require special fuels, but they can theoretically attain speeds above Mach 20.
- Turbojets use compressors to suck in and pressurize air. The fuel and air mixture is ignited, and the hot gasses pass over the turbine wheels, converting some of the energy into mechanical force to drive the compressor. As the exhaust gasses escape, afterburners inject additional fuel and ignite the mixture to further increase thrust. A variant called the *turbofan* or *fanjet* uses the first-stage compressor to blow air past the "core" of the engine. So-called *low-bypass* turbofans divert less of the air and are used on modern fighter jets. *High-bypass* engines are typical of those used on commercial jets. They are most efficient at speed ranges from 250 to 650 mph. Another advantage of these engines is that the bypassed air, which is cooler, can be mixed with the engine air. Since engine noise is related to the temperature of the engine gasses, this results in much quieter engines.

- Turbo-rockets are actually rocket engines that use a compressor system similar to that of jet engines to draw some of the air that can be used as an oxidizer into the engine. Because typical rockets must carry all their propellant fuels, using the turbo compressor can lighten the overall weight of the rocket, at least at low enough altitudes where the air is available.

SOLID-FUELED ROCKETS

Early rockets used solid fuels—gunpowder being the earliest form. In modern times, solid fuels have become more sophisticated, and rockets using solid fuels are designed for smooth burning at predetermined rates. These mixtures are called *grain*, which can be contained within a casing or case-bonded (bonded to the case itself) to reduce size and weight factors.

To control the thrust levels obtained by using solid fuels, different rocket designs and even different combinations of grain structures are used. Predictably, the larger the surface area of the burning propellant, the more thrust will be generated (and the faster the fuel will be burned), so rocket design can vary among several shapes:

- End-burning rockets burn the fuel only from the bottom, like a cigarette, providing constant, even thrust until the fuel is burned out.
- Multi-grain end-burning rockets may start out with a grain that gives an initially high level of thrust, followed by a grain that provides lower thrust once altitude or speed has been attained.
- Tubular configurations produce a progressively greater thrust. By burning from the middle of the tube outward, effectively, the area of burning propellant increases as the rocket continues to fire.
- A star-shape single grain system is an end burner that uses a fuel container flared at the bottom, providing maximum thrust, but as the fuel burns away, the container narrows, and thrust levels are reduced.

Different fuels can produce more or less thrust per unit, which is measured as *specific impulse*. Balancing the specific impulse of the fuel with the grain structure is important not only in determining the amount of thrust that will result, but also in controlling the overall pressure and heat that will be developed. If too much pressure is created inside the rocket, the result can be explosions, not liftoff. Some fuels used in modern rockets use ammonium nitrate mixed with various oxidizers, such as synthetic rubbers like polystyrenes, polysulfides, and polyurethanes. Homogeneous propellants, in which the oxidizer and the fuel are combined in one molecule, often use a double base (or combination of two propellants) of nitrocellulose and nitroglycerin.

Missiles such as the Poseidon C3, Minuteman Honest John, Nike Hercules, Polaris, Sergeant, and Vanguard are examples of solid-fuel weapons.

LIQUID-FUELED ROCKETS

Although there are many modern and advanced methods of propulsion, including improved solid-fuel engines, for sheer power, the liquid-fueled rocket is still the best choice. Many of our greatest achievements, including the 1969 moon landing, which required 8 million pounds of thrust to send the Saturn V rocket to its goal, was accomplished by using a liquid-fuel system.

In its simplest terms, a liquid-fueled engine is doing the same thing as a solid-fueled system. It is mixing a propellant with an oxidizer, with the difference being that the components are in liquid form instead of solid. However, this is the simple explanation.

In a liquid-fueled rocket, two separate tanks are generally filled just before firing the rocket. One contains the oxidant, and the other contains the propellant fuel. To control the flow rate, which is important to ensure an efficient firing of the engines and controllable thrust, one of two flow-control methods is used. In one, a pressurized inert gas, such as helium or nitrogen, is used to force the flow of liquid propellants under steady regulated pressure. The physics of this can be a little confusing, but basically, the pressure-regulated system can determine the rate of propellant flow and, therefore, the thrust delivery.

The second system uses a turbo pump to suck out the propellants and accelerate them into the combustion chamber, taking the place of the pressurized gas. To run the turbine of the pump, a second, but much smaller, rocket engine is added, which burns the same fuel as the main rocket engines, but its output is used solely to rotate the turbine of the pump. Two other turbines, connected along a single shaft to the original one, help pump the propellants into the combustion chamber. These turbines are sealed off from the main turbine and are connected by a series of gears to control the rate of flow for the propellants.

Liquid oxygen (LOX) is a common oxidizer used in rockets, although hydrogen peroxide and nitric acid are also used. Liquid fluorine can produce a higher thrust per unit than these other oxidizers, but it is highly corrosive and difficult to handle, so it is rarely used in modern rockets. Liquid fuels include liquid hydrogen, liquid ammonia, hydrazine, and kerosene.

Liquid versus Solid Fuels: Pros and Cons

When do you use solid fuels, and when do you use liquid fuels? Other than the fact that we all use liquid fuels in our gas-guzzler automobiles (unless you are going electric or fuel cell), in rocketry there are a few guidelines:

- Solid-fueled rockets are simple in design compared to liquid-fueled rockets.
- Solid-fueled rockets made with monopropellant fuels can be unstable and subject to shocks that can detonate the fuels. This is the reason for the development of double-base fuels that combine nitroglycerin with more stable nitrocellulose (a form of gunpowder).
- Liquid fuel must be kept at near Absolute Zero (–183 degrees Celsius in the case of liquid oxygen), making storage very difficult. Solid fuels are far easier to store, and rockets can be ready to go quickly.
- Solid-fueled rockets have the disadvantage that once they are ignited, they cannot be regulated or damped down. In contrast, liquid-fueled rocket fuel use and thrust can be varied after initial ignition.
- Liquid-fueled rockets are far more complex to build.
- Liquid-fueled rockets are also the most powerful, in terms of maximum thrust available.
- Liquid-fueled rockets, due to their increased complexity, are somewhat less reliable—causing many rockets to be rated for reliability. The Titan series are liquid-fueled rockets that were highly rated for reliability.

Nozzle Cooling

The nozzle of a rocket is, logically, a point of high stress, since all the power of the burning propellant gasses is concentrated through the narrow opening. There are many ways in which the nozzles of rockets are protected, including using heat-resistant materials, using a ring of cool-burning propellant to buffer the nozzle parts with a layer of cooler gas, and, in liquid-fueled rockets, using a liquid coolant injection system above the nozzle and a regenerative system that can circulate propellant gasses through the walls of the thrust chamber, both cooling the nozzle area and heating the propellant, which makes it burn more efficiently. With a regenerative system, the temperatures vary from 2700 degrees Celsius in the center of the nozzle to only 200 degrees at the inner wall, falling even further to only 60 degrees at the outer wall.

Rockets in World War II

The V2 rocket was a dramatic development late in the war and a precursor to modern rockets that traveled into space and those that can now carry nuclear warheads across continents. But other rockets were used in WWII by both sides. Rocket-launcher platforms were used to carry and fire multiple rockets. The British had several versions of a 2-inch anti-aircraft rocket array, which could fire up to 20 at a time and reach an altitude of 22,000 feet. The Germans had the Shwerer Wurfrahmen 40, a launcher mounted onto a converted halftrack that could fire six rockets, and the Nebelwerfer 41. The Soviets used Katyusha launchers, and the U.S. had their T34 Calliope launcher that could carry 60 4-inch rockets and mounted on top of a Sherman M4 tank.

WWII rockets had ranges from about 1,000 yards to more than 8,500 yards, with varying types of applications. Some were mounted on aircraft while others were used on ships and landing craft.

The first jet airplane to see actual service was the Me 262 German "secret weapon," which flew in 1944 using the Jumo 004 engine. It also was able to fire the Ruhrstahl A.G. X-4, a fin-stabilized air-to-air missile with a wire guidance system good for up to 3.7 miles. It used a bipropellant fuel. Another "secret" weapon that did not enter service was a manned rocket vehicle called the *Natter*, which was launched toward a target and could fire its solid fuel rockets for up to three minutes. At the end of its run, it would fire a bank of rockets mounted in the nose, at which point the pilot was to bail out and, along with the Natter itself, would parachute back to earth. The Natter was said to have a maximum speed of 620 mph, could reach altitudes up to 39,400 feet, and had a range of up to 12.4 miles.

Missile Subsystems

Missiles vary in complexity, but they all have at least a few systems in common—namely, a propulsion method and a payload or warhead, plus some kind of airframe to carry them. However, more sophisticated missiles also have guidance and control systems of various kinds. Some also have two or three stages, which are designed to work in different conditions—the first stage to achieve liftoff and propel the rocket through the dense air of lower altitudes, and later stages for thinner air, outer space, and/or final maneuvers, depending on the type of rocket or missile it is and its purpose.

In its simplest form, a missile's guidance system is a feedback loop that determines the missile's location, compares it to the programmed destination, and sends signals to the control systems to adjust as needed. This sequence is then repeated. However, that's the ultra-simple explanation. In early guided missiles, there were three main types of guidance systems—inertial, command, and active or passive homing. More modern systems employ Tercom (*terrain contour guidance*), GPS (*global positioning system*) and DSMAC (*digital scene matching area correlation*) as well.

Inertial Guidance Systems

Inertial guidance systems require complex and accurate calculations based on a wide variety of factors. The missile's flight can be adjusted during the period that the rockets are firing. When the engines shut down, the missile will be above the earth's atmosphere but still subject to gravitational force. In its basic form, the missile's payload is then subject only to gravitational force, and all maneuvers and calculations will have been made during the powered phase. However, both the multiple independently targeted reentry vehicle (MIRV) and the maneuverable reentry vehicle (MARV) are able to allow further adjustment after reentry.

The main sensors used in inertial guidance systems are accelerometers and gyroscopes.

- The accelerometer is basically a unit containing an object (mass) held against a spring that can be used to measure changes in acceleration and, therefore, velocity and position by computation. In an inertial guidance system, three accelerometers are arranged at 90 degrees to each other. In order to work, they must be kept horizontal with regard to the source of gravity.

- Gyroscopes are used to measure the missile's yaw, pitch, and rotation. Since the gyro will remain stable, any degree of change relative to the frame upon which it is mounted can be used to calculate the missile's movement, and the onboard computers can generate information to correct any deviations, which are sent to the control systems.

The sensor/computation/control sequence in an inertial guidance system flows something like this:

1. The missile is programmed with its flight plan at launch.
2. As it flies, information from the accelerometer measures lateral, vertical, and forward motion.
3. The gyroscopes measure roll, pitch, and yaw.
4. The computer uses the data from the sensors to calculate the missile's position and target destination and calculate instructions for the control systems.
5. Flight control systems are activated according to the computer's instructions, and corrections are made.
6. A follow-up unit relays information back to the main program, and the loop is repeated.

In calculating the missile's flight path, many factors must be taken into account, including the rotation of the earth, which, among other things, affects the overall amount of initial thrust of the rocket. If the rocket is launched traveling west to east, the earth's rotation will add to the rocket's initial thrust. Launching the other way decreases the initial thrust by the same amount. In addition, as the rocket flies, the earth is moving, so the second effect that must be compensated for is the actual shift of the target due to that movement. These factors are taken into account by the missile's programming.

The most advanced inertial guidance systems use solid-state ring gyros and can achieve far greater accuracy than their early counterparts.

Command and Homing Guidance Systems

In a command-guided missile, there is no guidance system onboard. Instead, guidance instructions are sent via wire or radar by remote stations that are tracking the missile and tracking the target at the same time. It works something like this:

1. The tracking system locks on the target.
2. The missile is launched.
3. The tracking system locates and begins monitoring the missile, often by watching the infrared radiation of its engines.
4. The tracking computer calculates any deviation of the missile's trajectory and sends correction information to the missile's control systems.
5. The control system makes corrections to the missile's path, keeping it on target.

There are various types of command guidance, including MCLOS *(manual command to line-of-sight)*, in which an operator actually controls a missile's flight manually, and SACLOS (*semi automatic command to line-of-sight*), in which a combination of manual and automatic systems control the missile.

Beam-riding systems use a radio or laser signal beamed from the missile or from an external source and pointed at the target, with sensors in the missile keeping it lined up with the beam. Beam-riding missiles can use SACLOS systems or be fully automatic.

Semi-active radar or laser homing systems use a radio or laser signal from a separate source to guide the missile. The signal does not necessarily have to be aimed at the target. In this kind of system, the missile itself is a passive sensor because it is not actually sending out any signals.

Modern Missile Sensor Systems

Guided missile technology is constantly evolving. Here are some of the ways that modern missiles can be guided.

- Tercom uses an onboard 3D database of the terrain it flies over and compares it with radar images it receives in flight. Technically, it uses a downward-pointing radio altimeter to measure 64-foot square areas of terrain and compare them against its 3D map. Tercom allows missiles to fly very close to the ground and make adjustments to match terrain shifts.
- GPS allows a missile to use the military's network of GPS satellites to locate its position with pinpoint accuracy.
- The DSMAC system is used when the missile is close to its target. This "terminal guidance system" uses an onboard camera and an "image correlator" to locate a target and can be used against moving targets, whereas most other methods of guidance are only reliable with stationary targets.
- Thermal imaging systems use infrared information as well as television images, in some cases, to detect, recognize, laser range, and automatically track targets in day, night, and low-visibility situations.
- Illumination sensors detect outgoing signals, such as radar, from a source and can be used to track the missile to that source.

Launching Systems

Basic rocket launching is accomplished by launching vertically from a platform, on ramps or rails at any angle, or through tube launchers, which can include handheld launchers of the bazooka model or blast-hardened missile silos, or any variant in between. Early rockets were most often fired from tubes or ramps. The German V2 was fired vertically from a platform in the way that modern-day space rockets are fired. Defense systems, such as the U.S. Minuteman and Nike missiles, are launched from tube silos. Missiles can also be launched from the ground, from the air, or from on or under the sea.

Modern Rockets and Missiles

This section contains a sampling of different types of rockets and missiles.

- **Gammon (SA-5).** Soviet air defense missile, semi-permanent platform. Weight: 22,045 pounds. Range: 155 miles (approximately). Guidance: Command plus active radar.
- **Nike Hercules.** U.S. air defense missile. Weight: 9,920 pounds. Range: 87 miles. Guidance: Command.
- **Bloodhound Mk2.** British long-range air defense missile with four rocket boosters and two sustaining ramjets. Range: 50 miles. Guidance: Semi-active radar.
- **Ganef (SA-4).** Soviet mobile air defense missile. Weight: 3,968 pounds. Range: 47+ miles. Guidance: Command.
- **Rapier.** British mobile air defense missile. Weight: 45 kg. Guidance: Command line-of-sight plus radar tracking.
- **Goa (SA-3, SA-N-4).** Soviet mobile air defense missile. Range: 18.5 miles. Guidance: Beam riding and semi-active radar.
- **Gecko (SA-8).** Soviet mobile air defense missile. Weight: 130 kg. Range: 10 miles. Guidance: Command.
- **Gainful (SA-6).** Soviet mobile air defense missile. Weight: 1,212 pounds. Range: 37 miles. Guidance: Command plus semi-active radar.
- **Crotale.** French mobile air defense missile. Weight: 176.4 pounds. Range: 6.25 miles. Guidance: Radio command.
- **Hawk.** U.S. mobile air defense missile. Weight: 265 pounds. Range: 22 miles. Guidance: Radar.

- **Patriot.** U.S. mobile air defense missile. Weight: 2,003 pounds. Range: 62 miles. Guidance: Command plus tracking via missile (TVM) homing.
- **Roland.** French/German mobile air defense missile. Weight: 1,396 pounds. Range: 3.9 miles. Guidance: Radio command.

Naval Surface-to-Air Missiles

- **Talos (RIM-8).** U.S. surface-to-air missile. Weight: 7,000 pounds. Range: 75.4 miles. Guidance: Beam riding plus semi-active radar.
- **Goa (SA-N-1).** Soviet surface-to-air missile. Range: 18.6 miles. Guidance: Beam riding plus semi-active radar.
- **Seawolf.** British surface-to-air missile. Weight: 309 pounds. Range: 328 yards to 4 miles. Guidance: Beam riding.
- **Terrier (RIM-2).** U.S. surface-to-air missile. Weight: 3,000 pounds. Range: 21.7 miles. Guidance: Beam riding plus semi-active radar.
- **Standard (SM-2 ER).** U.S. surface-to-air missile. Weight: 3,000 pounds. Range: 59.6 miles. Guidance: Command plus active radar.
- **Seacat.** British surface-to-air missile. Weight: 150 pounds. Range: 2.2 miles. Guidance: Radio command.

Surface-to-Surface Missiles

- **Gabriel.** Israeli surface-to-surface missile. Weight: 882/1,102 pounds. Range: 13.6/25.5 miles. Guidance: Inertial plus terminal.
- **Sea Killer Mk2.** Italian surface-to-surface missile. Weight: 661 pounds. Range: 12.4 miles. Guidance: Beam riding plus radio command.
- **Penguin.** Norwegian surface-to-surface missile. Weight: 727 pounds. Range: 12.4 miles. Guidance: Inertial plus infrared.
- **Exocet (MM40).** French surface-to-surface missile. Weight: 1,819 pounds. Range: 43.5 miles. Guidance: Inertial plus active radar.
- **Otomat.** Italian/French surface-to-surface missile. Weight: 1,697 pounds. Range: 124 miles. Guidance: Inertial plus active radar.
- **Harpoon (RGM-84A).** U.S. surface-to-surface missile. Weight: 1,400 pounds. Range: 68.3 miles. Guidance: Inertial plus active radar.

Surface-to-Subsurface Missiles

- **Subroc (UUM-44A).** U.S. surface-to-subsurface missile. Weight: 4,000 pounds. Range: 35 miles. Guidance: Inertial.
- **Asroc (RUR-SA).** U.S. surface-to-subsurface missile. Weight: 1,010 pounds. Range: 6.2 miles. Guidance: None until acoustic torpedo launched in water.
- **Ikara.** Australian/British surface-to-subsurface missile. Weight: 727 pounds. Range: 12.4 miles. Guidance: Inertial plus infrared.
- **Terne.** Norwegian surface-to-subsurface missile. Weight: 298 pounds. Range: 1.8 miles. Guidance: None.

Strategic and Tactical Nuclear Missiles

Strategic nuclear weapons are designed to be a threat and a deterrent, and they are capable of decimating large population centers. In contrast, a tactical nuclear weapon is designed for use in a battlefield situation and is a part of a limited nuclear strategy, as opposed to an all-out nuclear conflict.

- **IRBM.** Intermediate Range Ballistic Missile has a range of 1,719–3,437 miles.
- **ICBM.** Intercontinental Ballistic Missile is a long-range missile designed to achieve suborbital and partial orbital trajectories. Modern ICBMs often carry multiple independently targetable reentry vehicles (MIRVs), each of which can carry its own nuclear warhead. MIRVs are also used in anti-ballistic missile weapons (ABMs). ICBMs are launched from silos, submarines, or rail cars. ICBMs launched from submarines are also designated as SLMBs. They are classified as having a range above 3,500 miles.
- **Cruise Missiles.** Jet-powered unmanned aircraft designed to fly on low trajectories to avoid radar detection. They can carry conventional or nuclear warheads.

Some Specific Strategic and Tactical Nuclear Missiles

- **Atlas (SM-65, CGM-16).** First U.S. ICBM. Liquid-fueled three-stage system. Never used for combat, but part of the Mariner space probes and the Mercury manned spaceflights. Its unique design was known as a *1.5 stage* system because it did not drop all its engines and fuel tanks like most multistage rockets.
- **Atlas V.** First launched in 2002, the latest in a long series of Atlas missiles, dating back to 1957. Atlas missiles have been involved in various space launches as well as various military uses.
- **Titan I.** First U.S. true multistage ICBM. Used liquid fuels, although later Titan missiles used solid fuels. First launched in 1959.
- **Sandal (SS-4).** Soviet IRBM with a range of about 1,250 miles. First introduced in 1959. Capable of carrying a single 1-megaton bomb.
- **Scarp (SS-9).** Soviet ICBM with a range of about 7,450 miles. First introduced in 1969 and capable of carrying one 18-megaton bomb.
- **SS-6 SAPWOOD (R-7).** Soviet ICBM—the first ICBM, introduced in 1957. Modified versions put Sputnik 1 and Sputnik 2 in orbit. A redesigned version was introduced in 1959 and had a range of about 7,500 miles and could deliver nearly a 12,000-pound payload.
- **SS-18 Mod. 2.** Soviet ICBM with a range of about 7,500 miles. Introduced in 1977 and capable of carrying eight warheads of about 1 to 2 megatons.
- **SS-19.** Soviet ICBM with a range of about 6,210 miles. Introduced in 1975 and capable of carrying six warheads of about 200 kilotons.
- **SS-17.** Soviet ICBM with a range of about 6,220 miles. Introduced in 1975 and capable of carrying four warheads of about 200 kilotons.
- **SS-16.** Soviet ICBM with a range of about 5,900 miles. Introduced in 1977 and possibly capable of carrying three warheads of 300 kilotons.
- **SS-20.** Soviet IRBM with a range of about 3,540 miles. Introduced in 1976 and capable of carrying three 150-kiloton warheads.
- **Minuteman.** The first Minuteman missiles were introduced in 1960 and remained in use until 1997. The Minuteman I was the first ICBM to incorporate a solid rocket booster and a digital flight computer using a reprogrammable inertial guidance system. The storage disk in the Minuteman I had 4k of storage space on a rotating magnetic disk. Minuteman II introduced integrated circuits to the mix. Minuteman III was introduced in 1998 and is expected to remain active until 2005. (See the "LGM-30 Minuteman III" sidebar at the end of this section.)

- **MSBS M-20.** French SLBM with a range of 1,850 miles. Introduced in 1976 and capable of carrying a single 1-megaton warhead.
- **Tomahawk.** U.S. submarine-launched cruise missile with a range of more than 680 miles. First introduced in 1983 and capable of carrying one conventional 1,000-pound warhead or a 200-kiloton nuclear device. Guidance: Inertial plus TERCOM and DSMAC, plus Time of Arrival (TOA) systems.
- **ALCM (Air Launched Cruise Missile).** U.S. air-launched cruise missile. Operationally the same as the Tomahawk.
- **Polaris A-3/B-3.** U.S. submarine-launched cruise missile, first introduced (A-1) in 1960. The original version weighed 28,800 pounds and was 28.5 feet high and 54 feet in diameter, with a range of 1,150 miles. Later versions were even larger and heavier with ranges of more than 2,850 (A-3) and 2,300 (B-3) miles. The A-3 could be fitted with MIRVs. The A-3 was originally designed to counter Soviet anti-ballistic missile defenses, but ultimately evolved into the C-3 Poseidon missile.
- **Poseidon.** U.S. successor to the Polaris missile, later replaced by the Trident I in 1979. In its time, it was more advanced than its predecessors and could deploy up to 14 MIRV warheads.
- **Trident.** U.S. SLBM with a range of about 4,850 miles. Introduced in 1979 and capable of carrying seven 100-kiloton warheads. Guidance: Inertial. The Trident II was introduced in 1990 and could carry eight 475-kiloton warheads.
- **Pluton.** French tactical nuclear ballistic missile with a range of about 75 miles. Can carry 15- or 25-kiloton warheads. It is designed to be launched from an AMX-30 tank chassis. Guidance: Inertial.
- **Lance.** U.S. tactical nuclear missile designed to be launched from a self-propelled tracked chassis and to carry a warhead that can carry Terminally Guided Sub-Missiles (TGSMs)—each of which is released to home in on individual targets. Guidance: Inertial.
- **Pershing.** U.S. tactical nuclear missile. At one time the largest of the U.S. inventory, it was first introduced in 1962 with a warhead delivery of 400 kilotons and a maximum range of 460 miles. The Pershing II is launched from a trailer and uses sophisticated "radar area correlation" and other guidance. Instead of the overpowered 400-kiloton warhead of the original Pershing I, it carries a MARV capable of delivering five 50-kiloton warheads. Its range was increased to about 1,100 miles. As part of the Intermediate-Range Nuclear Forces Treaty of 1988, Pershing missiles were decommissioned and destroyed.
- **FROG (Free Rocket Over Ground) Series.** Soviet fin-stabilized unguided short-range tactical missiles. Dimensions of FROG 7: 29.7 feet in length, 5,952 pounds, 37-mile range. It can carry high explosive or nuclear warhead—no onboard guidance systems. Introduced in 1965. Ultimately replaced by the SS-21 (SCARAB) in 1981.
- **SS-21 SCARAB (9K79 Tochka).** Soviet replacement to the FROG 7 missiles with a maximum range of about 44 miles with a variety of optional warheads, including the 9N123F HE-frag warhead, a submunition warhead that carries bomblets or mines, or an AA60 tactical nuclear warhead. Inertial guidance systems, with more recent versions including GPS systems.
- **SCUD Series.** Soviet short-range tactical ballistic surface-to-surface missile system. Several versions have been developed: SCUD-A (SS-1b), SCUD-B (SS-1c), SCUD-C (SS-d), and SCUD-D (SS-1e). SCUD missiles differed from the FROG series in that they had moveable fins. Gyroscopes helped guide the missile, but only during the engine firing sequence, about 80 seconds, after which it coasted to the target unguided. The farther the missles flew, the more inaccurate they became. SCUD-C had a longer range and lower accuracy than the SCUD-B and was introduced in 1965. The final version, introduced in the 1980s, was SCUD-D, which had improved guidance systems and a wider choice of warheads. Its range was about 435 miles. The replacement for the SCUD series, which was introduced in 1999, is the SS-26.
- **Scaleboard.** First developed in 1960, Scaleboard missiles were designed to be used at the warfront, to be fired from pre-sited positions from a MAZ-543 chassis, the same as the SCUD-B. The MAZ-543

was then moved to another pre-sited position. The original SS-12 Scaleboard was improved with the SS-22 in 1979, which had greater accuracy at the same range (560 miles). These missiles were banned after the Intermediate-Range and Shorter-Range Nuclear Forces Treaty was signed at the end of 1987. The last of the SS-12 missiles were eliminated in July of 1989.

- **MIM-104 Patriot.** The original Patriot missile started development in the '60s and first became operational in 1984. It has gone through several upgrades, with advanced and improved guidance and jamming countermeasures added. The MIM-104 has evolved into the PAC-3 system, but it is confusing, as the ultimate PAC-3 missile will be an entirely new design based on the Lockheed Martin ERINT (Extended Range Interceptor), a smaller missile. (See Patriot Advanced Capability (PAC-3) in the "ABM Systems of the Future" section.) The MIM-104 Patriot missile weighs approximately 2,000 pounds, has an 80,000-foot ceiling, and has a range of about 43 miles.

LG-118A Peacekeeper Missile

General characteristics:

- Primary Function: Strategic deterrence
- Contractor: Boeing
- Power Plant: First three stages—solid propellant; fourth stage—storable liquid (by Thiokol, Aerojet, Hercules, and Rocketdyne)
- Warheads: 10
- Load: Avco MK21 re-entry vehicles
- Guidance System: Inertial; integration by Boeing North American, IMU by Northrop and Boeing North American
- Thrust: First stage, 500,000 pounds
- Length: 71 feet (21.8 meters)
- Weight: 195,000 pounds (87,750 kilograms), including re-entry vehicles
- Diameter: 7 feet, 8 inches (2.3 meters)
- Range: Greater than 6,000 miles (5,217 nautical miles)
- Speed: Approximately 15,000 miles per hour at burnout (Mach 20 at sea level)
- Date Deployed: December 1986
- Unit Cost: $70 million
- Inventory: Active force, 50; ANG, 0; Reserve, 0

LGM-30 Minuteman III

The "L" in LGM is the Department of Defense designation for silo-launched, "G" means surface attack, and "M" stands for guided missile.

General characteristics:

- Primary Function: Intercontinental ballistic missile
- Contractor: Boeing Co.
- Power Plant: Three solid-propellant rocket motors; first stage—Thiokol; second stage—Aerojet-General; third stage—United Technologies: Chemical Systems Division
- Length: 59.9 feet (18 meters)
- Weight: 79,432 pounds (32,158 kilograms)
- Diameter: 5.5 feet (1.67 meters)
- Range: 6,000-plus miles (5,218 nautical miles)

(continued)

- Speed: Approximately 15,000 mph (Mach 23 or 24,000 kph) at burnout
- Ceiling: 700 miles (1,120 kilometers)
- Thrust: First stage, 202,600 pounds
- Load: Re-entry vehicle: Lockheed Martin Missiles and Space MK 12 or MK 12A
- Guidance systems: Inertial system: Boeing North American; ground electronic/security system: Sylvania Electronics Systems and Boeing Co.
- Unit Cost: $7 million
- Date Deployed: June 1970; Production Cessation: December 1978
- Inventory: Active force, 500; Reserve, 0; ANG, 0

Anti-Ballistic Missile Systems

Under the Anti-Ballistic Missile (ABM) Treaty of 1972, both the U.S. and the Soviet Union agreed to deploy an ABM system only on one protected area. Back in the 1980s, Ronald Reagan promoted an anti-ballistic missile program called the Strategic Defense Initiative (SDI), more commonly known as "Star Wars." Like the movie after which it was named, it was largely fictional and came nowhere near operational.

SDI proposed a multiple systems approach, including directed energy and particle beam weapons fired from space, long-wavelength infrared weapons, reflected kinetic energy weapons and endo-atmospheric ABM interceptors as the last line of defense. No wonder it was called "Star Wars."

Meanwhile, the Soviets did deploy an ABM system to protect Moscow, using the Galosh missile, which has since been dismantled.

To date, no ABM system has worked. Patriot missiles used during the Gulf War to intercept SCUD missiles almost all missed their targets. However, when George W. Bush became President, in light of the 9/11 attacks (which ABM systems would not have been able to prevent) and perceived buildups of ballistic missiles in Korea and other countries, he pulled the U.S. out of the treaty and began a new ballistic defense program, intending to declare it operational in October 2004 (just before the 2004 election) with the deployment of 10 interceptor missiles at Fort Greely, Alaska. Most scientists agree that the current systems are not ready for deployment and will, in all likelihood, not work in any serious threat, although they may be designed primarily to intercept one or two nuclear missiles launched from North Korea. Given their positioning, they will not defend against any missile attacks from the Middle East.

In highly scripted tests where the target was known, its trajectory was known, and its launch time was known, only five of eight missiles were successful, and against very simple decoy missiles. More tests were originally planned but were scrapped. Total costs are between $8 to 10 billion per year, although total estimates are not available. Sources estimate anywhere between $100 billion and $1 trillion spent by the year 2030.

Among the proposed elements of the system are 1) early warning radar systems to detect any missile launches, 2) defense support satellites to track warheads in space and distinguish between live warheads and decoys, 3) X-band radar for further tracking, fire control support, and target discrimination, 4) interceptors (exoatmospheric kill vehicles [EKV]), 5) a command and control center, and 6) booster rockets capable of deploying the interceptors into space quickly enough to destroy the target missiles. Other systems currently in research are additional interceptors based at sea, in the air, and in space, a system to attack rockets shortly after they take off (called *boost phase defense*), and another system designed to attack just before a missile lands (called *terminal defense*)—which sounds a lot like a game of *Missile Command* at the arcades.

Although there is some system being deployed, and the previous administration wished to declare it operational, at the time of this writing most of the key components were years away from completing development, and even the systems that are currently in operation have been plagued with problems.

In addition, many experts agree that a ballistic missile attack is probably the least likely form of attack from a developing country, and we have no hope of deploying a system capable of defending against an all-out attack by a well-armed enemy, of which only Russia and China can be considered possible.

In historical precedent, the Safeguard missile defense system of the 1970s was deployed in North Dakota and very shortly dismantled when even its proponents realized it was useless.

An ABM Checklist

Suppose you were on QA for an ABM system. What would you need to test? Here's the checklist:

- Full-system operational tests
- Full-system operational tests scheduled
- Tested in bad weather
- Tested at night
- Tested three-stage booster in intercept test
- Tested without interceptor knowing in advance warhead's infrared and radar signature
- Tested against tumbling warhead
- Tested against realistic decoys and countermeasures
- Tested against complex decoys and countermeasures
- Tested against more than one warhead on one missile
- Tested against more than one incoming missile
- Tested without a GPS system on the target
- Tests overseen by contractors and managers
- Tests overseen by Pentagon's independent test office
- SBIRS high early-warning satellites
- SSTS space tracking and surveillance system
- Cobra Dane radar upgraded
- Cobra Dane radar included in integrated intercept test
- Ground-based X-band radar
- Sea-based X-band radar
- Protect Hawaii
- Fly-before-you-buy
- Declare the system operational

Arrow Interceptor Anti-Missile Missile

A joint development by Israel and the United States is the Arrow Interceptor Anti-Missile Missile. The Arrow is meant to intercept ABMs high in the stratosphere, or in some cases, in outer space. The first test of the Arrow missile was in July 2004, where it successfully intercepted and destroyed a SCUD missile. Further tests over the next few years were also successful.

The Arrow is a two-stage missile that uses a solid propellant booster with sustainer rocket motors. Its initial launch is what is called a *vertical hot launch*, with a secondary burn that takes the missile on a trajectory toward its target at a speed up to Mach 9 (2.5 km/second). When the second-stage sustainer motor is ignited, the first stage is jettisoned.

With advanced controls, the Arrow can be launched before the incoming missile's trajectory and target are known, and the missile guidance systems can continue to calculate the optimum interception position as more data is received. The "kill vehicle" part of the missile uses four aerodynamically controlled fins to allow low-altitude interception and carries the warhead, the fusing, and the terminal seeker.

The Rafael warhead uses high explosives and direct-blast fragmentation to destroy a target within a radius of 50 meters. Seeker capabilities include passive infrared and active radar. The missile can intercept at altitudes ranging from 10 kilometers up to 50 kilometers and has an intercept range of 90 kilometers.

ABM Systems of the Future

What's new in the world of anti-ballistic missiles? Here are a few of the more modern developments:

- Patriot Advanced Capability (PAC-3)—the latest "hit to kill" missile system expected to be used in modern and future anti-missile systems. It weighs 700 pounds, reaches a speed of Mach 5+, and has a range of 12 miles and a ceiling of 50,000 feet. Described as a "long-range, all-altitude, all-weather air defense system to counter ballistic missiles, cruise missiles, and advanced aircraft." Patriot missiles have been upgraded since they were first introduced. They all contain sophisticated guidance systems, including the TVM downlink that gives visual target acquisition (supplied from the missile's onboard sensors) and terminal course correction calculations via the Engagement Control Station. A proximity fuze detonates the fragmentation warhead, although the PAC-3 is designed to disable threats using the kinetic energy released by hitting the target head on.
- Along with the missile, a sophisticated tracking technology is employed. The AN/MPQ-53 phased array radar is a multifunctional component, carrying out search and detection, track and identification, guidance and tracking for the Patriot and electronic counter-countermeasures (ECCM). This radar array is mounted in a trailer and controlled via cable link by a digital control computer located in the Engagement Control Station. It can track up to 100 targets at a range of up to 100 km, providing guidance for up to nine missiles, and it can operate in manual, semi-automatic, or fully automatic mode. When the decision has been made to engage the target, the Engagement Control Station selects the Launch Station or Stations, and pre-launch data is transmitted to the selected missile. After launch, the Patriot missile is acquired by the radar. The command uplink and the TVM downlink allow the missile's flight to be monitored and provide missile guidance commands from the weapon control computer. As the missile approaches the target, the TVM guidance system is activated, and the missile is steered toward the target. A proximity fuse detonates the high-explosive warhead.
- The THAAD (Theatre High-Altitude Area Defense) missile is a transportable system designed to attack ballistic missile threats within a range of 200 km to be deployed and ready for action by sometime in 2009. It is designed to be a high-altitude interceptor working in conjunction with the Patriot PAC-3 (which intercepts at lower altitudes) to protect specific battlefield sites. The missile detaches a separate kinetic kill vehicle (KKV), which maneuvers via a liquid Divert and Attitude Control System (DACS), which uses a gimbal-mounted infrared seeker module (technically "an indium antimonide [InSb] staring focal-plane array operating in the mid infrared 3 to 5 micron wavelength band") in the nose section to guide final approach to the target. The THAAD is carried on an M1075 truck-mounted launcher and is controlled and deployed by ground-based radar systems. In addition, each THAAD battery will have two tactical operations centers (TOCs) equipped with HP-735 data processors. They will also have the ability to "hand over" targets to other systems and interface with other data information networks. They will use something called *Battle Management and Command, Control Computers and Intelligence* (BMC3I) units installed in hardened shelters or on High Mobility Multi-Wheeled Vehicles (HMMWVs). In addition, in this

acronym-happy project, their communications systems can use JTIDS, Mobile Subscriber Equipment, SINCGARS, and the Joint Tactical Terminal for voice and data communications and intelligence data transfer. Whatever that all means… (from www.army-technology.com/projects/thaad/.)

- MEADS (Medium Extended Air Defense System)—a joint German/Italian/U.S. development designed to replace Hawk and Patriot missile systems by 2014. It is designed to defend against next-generation tactical ballistic missiles, low- and high-altitude cruise missiles, remotely piloted vehicles, maneuvering fixed-wing aircraft, and rotary-wing aircraft. The first demonstration of this system's fire control radar, command center, launcher, and PAC-3 missile occurred in May 2004. The system will be designed around a multi-canister launcher that can be mounted on a wheeled vehicle. A 360-degree radar designed to work in highly stressed jamming environments will be part of the system. It is designed to be delivered to specific theaters of operation by C-130 and A400M aircraft and quickly deployed. The whole system is controlled through a communication network of distributed and netted architecture, allowing coordinated efforts across a wide area and with input from and interoperability with other air defense systems. They are using the Windows-like slogan, "plug and fight." Like the THAAD system, MEADS uses the Patriot Advanced Capability (PAC-3) hit-to-kill missile, which has a guidance system that is highly jam proof and multiple single-shot thrusters that allow very agile high-G maneuvers. Its guidance systems are inertial, with terminal phase guided by using a gimbaled forward-seeking active RF Ka-band millimeter wave seeker. It destroys targets by hitting with high kinetic energy, meaning it knocks the crap out of it, and has a "lethality enhancing" warhead for use against air-breathing targets. It is designed to use a variety of radar systems to provide 360-degree coverage.

Biological and Chemical Weapons

Though we think of hand weapons and guns primarily when we think of weapons, biological and chemical weapons have been around almost as long as there has been organized war—and maybe even longer. This section looks both at historical uses of biological and chemical weapons and modern developments.

Early Biological and Chemical Weapons

People often think that biological and chemical weapons are modern inventions that depend on technology and science to perfect. However, it turns out that the idea of such weapons goes back thousands of years, and that various kinds of biological and chemical warfare have been in use since very ancient times. Although various codes of conduct and popular opinion have often been against such types of warfare, as they are today, that didn't stop people from using them, especially in defensive situations or when in a weaker position relative to their foes. Of course, there have always been those who used whatever weapons they could find—those for whom winning was everything, and the means did not matter.

Some early uses of chemical and biological weapons, including stratagems:

- **Fire Arrows.** These were used throughout history. First mentioned in Western culture in the myth of Hercules, who uses arrows dipped in pitch to defeat the Hydra.
- **Poison.**
  - Poison was another chemical and biological method used in a variety of ways. The routine poisoning of weapons, according to legends, included heroes like Hercules, Odysseus, Achilles, and Paris.
  - Water sources, such as cisterns and wells, springs, rivers and streams, aqueducts, and so forth, were often poisoned to force an enemy to either die of thirst or die of poison.

- Poison arrows were used by people of many cultures, using various snake venoms and poisons derived from plants and from other animals. Again, the first mention is from the Hercules myth, as he dipped his arrows in the Hydra's poison. The consequences of this act were tragic for Hercules and those around him, indicating that the use of poisons was considered a bad idea by the ancient Greeks.
- Poison was often used to assassinate enemy leaders. Some kings routinely took a variety of real and magical antidotes against poison every day, hoping to gain immunity. One king was too successful. When cornered by his enemies, he tried to take poison that he always carried for emergencies, but he was immune. His death was less easy than he had hoped.
- Poison maidens were camp followers, prostitutes, and other femmes fatale who truly lived up to their names.

- **Disease.**
  - Disease figured fairly prominently in ancient warfare, and commanders were known to force their enemies to camp in swampy and marshy areas where diseases and noxious fumes were present. Although true germ theory wasn't known, observation was sufficient to know that fevers and gastrointestinal diseases would appear in troops camped in the wrong areas. In actuality, many soldiers died of malaria and dysentery, among other diseases.
  - Another use of disease was to send out diseased livestock or even diseased people into enemy areas with the intention of spreading plagues among them.
  - Disease could also be spread by clothing, and items were often sent into enemy areas, sometimes in the form of gifts or chests, which contained clothing exposed to disease carriers. Or, if sealed well, a diseased piece of cloth could retain its virulence for years. There are suspicions that the Greeks and Israelites both kept disease pathogens sealed up in temples for emergencies, and that some famous plagues may have been unleashed when temples were sacked and these sealed containers were opened.
  - Even more directly, disease was sometimes spread randomly by agents, such as in a documented case where saboteurs in ancient Rome were said to have pricked people randomly with infected needles.
  - Disease was often combined with poison. Some of the recipes used for poisoning weapons included bacteriological elements. For instance, several recipes would include snake venom, but would also include the rotted bodies of the dead serpents, complete with feces and bacteria of decomposition. This combination of poison and disease vectors was sure to result in death or, at least, very debilitating and unpleasant disease. The psychological effect of such deaths on others was as important as the specific impact of the poison on the individual victim.
- **Genetic Destruction.** Genetic destruction, which could be considered a form of biological warfare, was routinely used in ancient times. It was accomplished by killing all the male population, often including children, and then raping the women to further ensure the destruction of the genetic line of those conquered.
- **Food and Intoxicants in Traps.** This tactic preys on appetites (for example, the plot to give Castro exploding cigars).
- **Animals.**
  - Mice and rats may have been used to bring plague to enemies.
  - Today, the Pentagon is working on "remote-controlled" rats, which can be used for search-and-rescue operations, but also could be used to spread biological agents.
  - In addition, monkey brains can be wired up to control machines—making a sort of biocomputer system.

  - There is evidence that hornet nests may have been used in Neolithic times to hurl at enemies hiding in caves, making them possibly the first grenades of a sort. At other times, stinging and poisonous insects may have been used in similar ways.
  - Beehives and wasp/hornet nests were also dropped from the parapets of besieged castles and forts or released into the tunnels of enemies trying to dig under the walls. (Other critters, such as bears, could also be released in such tunnels.)
  - Some beetles in India and the Middle East can secrete a poison more toxic than cobra venom.
  - Bees have been used throughout history. It was a favorite tactic of Romans to hurl beehives by catapult at enemies, and the practice continued in Europe through the Middle Ages. Even in the Vietnam War, the Vietcong would use Asian honeybees against American soldiers.
  - The Pentagon was experimenting with developing a pheromone that simulates the bee's swarming behavior, which could be used to mark enemies to be attacked by bees.
  - Booby traps with tripwires were used in WWI to release bees.
  - The Japanese dropped ceramic pots full of noxious insects on the Chinese during WWII, a tactic also used as early as 199 A.D. The creatures used at that time may have been scorpions, some varieties of which were said to be deadly. Or they might have been *assassin bugs*, cone-nosed beetles that can fly and dig into exposed parts of a person's body, injecting a lethal poison.
  - A favorite of Central Asian torture, assassin bugs, of which there are many species, can detect human presence for many hundreds of yards.
  - Because assassin bugs make a sound that can be amplified, there were experiments for using them as human detection devices during the Vietnam War.
  - The Pentagon is also experimenting with bees to develop them as detectors for minute amounts of biochemical or explosive substances.
  - Hannibal used elephants.
  - He also stampeded cattle with torches burning on their horns at Romans in a narrow valley.
  - He also catapulted vases full of poisonous snakes on enemy ships during a naval engagement in which he was outnumbered. This was far from the last time serpents were tossed in among the enemy.
  - Alexander the Great tied bushes to sheep to make his army look even more formidable from a distance, and he tied torches to their horns so that the army looked much larger at night from a distance. The same sorts of tactics have been used with other common animals, such as pigs and cattle.
- In an earlier battle, the Persians fielded a wall of animals sacred to the Egyptians—cats, sheep, dogs, and ibexes—causing the Egyptians to hesitate in their attacks so they wouldn't harm these sacred creatures. This led to the Persians winning the battle and conquering Egypt.
- In addition, horses, donkeys, mules, camels, dogs, cats, birds, and elephants were used in various ways by armies—as pack animals, guard animals, mounts, messengers, and/or attackers.
- Dogs in war could even be fitted with coats of mail and spiked collars.
- Dogs were used in WWI and after. More than 10,000 dogs served the U.S. in WWII.
- Some species of animals can't tolerate each other. For instance, horses tend to shy away from camels if not acclimated to them. In at least one battle where an enemy cavalry had the clear advantage, camels were set in the front lines and so disrupted the enemy horses that they bolted and destroyed the formation, causing them to lose the battle they otherwise would have won.
- Also, where horses were unnerved by the sight and smell of elephants, the elephants were, themselves, unnerved by the squealing of pigs, and some successful defenses against war elephants were mounted by the use of pigs.

- In another instance, the pigs were covered with flammable pitch and other substances and set loose, flaming, on the elephants. Other instances of flaming animals include camels, cats, birds, dogs, and cattle-drawn carts.

NOTE

Modern research into the use of animals in warfare has centered on a veritable zoo, including dogs, skunks, rats, monkeys, seal lions, dolphins, and whales. For instance, sea lions were deployed in 2003 to pursue and capture enemy divers using leg clamps.

Ancient Toxic Substances

Throughout history, people have catalogued and used various toxic substances. Here's a list of just a few of the substances used by our ancestors to start you off. Of course, you can add to this list with all kinds of dangerous and deadly substances.

- Snake venom.
- Insects.
- Aconite, monkshood, wolfbane—starts as a stimulant, then paralyzes the nervous system, causing drooling and vomiting. Finally, the limbs go numb and death follows. Still used in India by elephant poachers—one of the most virulent plant poisons known. Used throughout history—even the Nazis extracted aconitine from it to make poisoned bullets.
- Hellebore—black (Christmas rose, helleborus orientalis) or white (Liliacea, veratrum). Symptoms for small doses include sneezing and blisters; symptoms for heavier doses include severe vomiting, diarrhea, muscle cramps, delirium, convulsions, asphyxia, and heart attack.
- Hyoscyamus niger, henbane—contains hyoscyamine and scopolamine, both narcotics. It has to be harvested without touching any part of the plant. It can cause violent seizures, psychosis, and death.
- Toad and frog venoms.
- Rabid dog saliva.
- Curare.
- Hemlock sap.
- Mandrake.
- Rhododendron honey.
- Yew. Berries have alkaloids. There's a story of conquered Spanish selling canteens made from yew to Romans, many of whom died from poison.
- Belladonna, deadly nightshade. Known as strychnos in Roman era—hence strychnine. Also known as dorycnion, or spear drug. Causes dizziness, raving agitation, coma, and death. Virulent for as long as 30 years once applied. Possible "berserker" drug taken by Gaelic warriors.
- Rhododendron sap—contains neurotoxins. Honey from bees fed on rhododendron flowers is poisonous and was used numerous times in history against the Romans and others.
- Lethal concoctions—Scythians, Indians.
- Intoxicants.
- Possibly the earliest recorded use of a substance that works, like nerve agents, by inhibiting cholinesterase (ChE) is by native tribesmen of western Africa, who used the Calabar bean as an ordeal poison in witchcraft trials.

CHEMICAL WEAPONS

This section deals with chemical weapons, both ancient and modern.

Fire and Weapons That Burn

Fire is arguably the most ancient of chemical weapons and is well documented back through recorded history, but it was probably used as soon as people learned to set and control fires. One of the famous burning weapons of antiquity was the Byzantine Greeks' burning mixture called *Greek fire,* made from naphtha and quicklime. It was thrown in pots (like early firebombs) and, like modern flamethrowers, it was even carried on ships and streamed from a nozzle known as a *siphon.* However, Greek fire, invented in the 7th century AD, was not even close to the earliest fire weapons.

- Fire arrows were used almost as soon as bows and arrows came into use and were the most common fire weapons of antiquity. However, fire was used in many ways, and ultimately chemicals were discovered to enhance its effects. One of the earliest modifications was probably the use of pitch from pine trees and the subsequent substances that could be derived from it, such as turpentine.
- A mysteriously burning garment figured prominently in the play *Medea,* written by Euripides around 431 B.C., and the first recorded use of a chemically enhanced fire was two years later, in 429, when Spartans used a pile of wood enhanced with pitch and sulphur (known also as *brimstone*) to attempt to burn away the walls of a wooden fortification. Historians of the time described the blaze as "greater than any fire produced by human agency." The Spartans either intentionally or inadvertently may have produced the first poison gas attack, since burning sulphur also produces toxic sulphur dioxide gas.
- The use of chemical enhancements to fire was quickly adopted.
  - Pitch, which would stick to people, siege engines, or wooden structures, was like an early form of napalm, although it wasn't a petroleum derivative. However, burning oils of various kinds were also used throughout the world.
  - The Romans developed an engine to fire large flaming, iron-tipped spears dipped in pitch and sulphur, called *falarica.*
  - Another method was to pack incendiary materials inside the shaft of a missile. One recipe from 390 A.D. included sulphur, resin, tar, and hemp soaked in oil.
  - Another weapon of a similar era used weak bows to fire hollow arrows filled with bitumen (a term used in the day for just about any petroleum product, such as asphalt, tar, naphtha, and natural gas). Such weapons had the added advantage that they would flare up if water was thrown on them, rather than be extinguished.
  - The Chinese had a similar weapon around 900 A.D. that used sulphur, charcoal, and "fire chemical" (probably saltpeter or nitrate salts), making it an early form of gunpowder. These chemicals were shot out of a bamboo tube like an early flamethrower, and later bits of sand, ceramic shards, and even metal shrapnel were added—even poisons, excrement, toxic plants, and arsenic.
- Fire was used in many other ways, as well.
  - Burning ships were sent into ports and into enemy fleets.
  - Red-hot sand and metal was rained down on besiegers.
  - There was even a heat ray developed by Archimedes using the polished concave shields of a group of soldiers arrayed in a parabolic shape to reflect the sun and ignite enemy ships at sea from a great distance. As odd and unlikely as it seems, this exploit has been re-created in modern times using 60 "soldiers" with polished shields.
- The modern flamethrower had its roots in antiquity as well. In fact, as early as 424 B.C., the Boeotians, allies of the Spartans, created a device that consisted of a metal-lined hollowed-out log with a cauldron of burning coals, sulphur, and pitch hanging from it. A tube ran into the hollowed log, and a large bellows was used to blow air through the device, causing a blast of air through the tube, projecting the chemically enhanced fire outward. Such early flame-throwing devices continued to appear through

history. One addition to the incendiary mixture was vinegar, which was found to cause some kinds of rock to disintegrate when applied at high temperatures. This was especially effective against limestone and marble, both of which were common materials in building stone fortifications.

- Smokes and gasses weren't ignored, and many times they were used against enemies, although an unfavorable wind might cause the attack to backfire.
  - Gas and smoke were particularly effective in tunnels, and they were used against enemies attempting to dig under fortifications during sieges.
  - One ancient Chinese toxic gas-producing formula included aconite, wolfbane, croton beans (which can cause blisters and pustules), arsenic, hemp (the hallucinogenic kind), blister beetles, sulphur, charcoal, and resin.
  - In ancient India, many toxic recipes were recorded, using a wide variety of ingredients, including the bodies of poisonous snakes, stinging insects, droppings of various creatures, toxic plants, and even hot peppers. They also used tree resins, turpentine, wax, and charcoal as burning agents.
  - Speaking of hot peppers, burning pepper seed fires were used in the Caribbean and in Brazil against the Spanish Conquistadors.
  - Various delivery systems were used, including complex devices powered by bellows to force gasses and smoke into confined spaces, or carts filled with lime powder that were used to engulf enemies in choking dust.
- One early discovery was that lime that has been roasted creates a calcium oxide, also known as *calx*. When water is added to this substance, it becomes slaked lime (calcium hydroxide). It also releases heat during this chemical action, and it was found that an incendiary mixture could be ignited simply by adding a drop of water to set off the reaction. Many clever uses of this principle were devised, including the formulation of a paste that could be painted on enemy siege engines at night so that, with the morning dew, they would burst into flame.
- The most destructive and dangerous ancient substances used for making war with fire were the petroleum derivatives, particularly naphtha, which was used extensively in the Middle East because it was quite plentiful in some regions. In fact, it is so prevalent in some areas that "eternal" flames have burnt in natural gas wells for centuries. One famous site at Baba Gurgur (northern Iraq) had burned continuously from 600 B.C. until 1927, when it was tapped for the first modern oil well in Iraq.

  Oil products weren't used only for war. They also were used for lamps and torches, pigments, cleaning and rituals, waterproofing, and so on since as early as 3000 B.C. But petroleum was never ignored in war, and many weapons were created to make use of it.
  - Flaming arrows.
  - Small pots full of flaming naphtha that could be slung at enemies.
  - Huge siege engines, such as the mangonel, which was designed to fire naphtha over cities. There were even troops, known as *naffatun*, formed to operate hundreds of mangonels and catapults with barrels full of naphtha to rain on their enemies.
- One of the qualities of weapons that used pitch and naphtha was that the fires could not be quenched with water and that the burning material would stick to structures, clothing and armor, and skin. These weapons were very difficult to defend against and caused horrible suffering and death. They were very much in the same vein as modern napalm, which is also made from naphtha and other ingredients.
- The ultimate weapon of its day, Greek fire was a mixture of naphtha with other ingredients that was used in naval warfare beginning around 673 A.D. The Byzantines already had been squirting petroleum incendiaries for more than a hundred years, but what made Greek fire so feared was its adaptation to naval warfare and the size of the siphons that spat out the fiery liquid, which would even burn on water. Greek fire was feared in its day much the way nuclear devices are

feared today, as its effect was horrible and absolute. In those days, there was no effective defense against it. Eventually, it was banned for use within Europe, and the exact formulas and mechanisms used were ultimately lost.

- The ancients explored the fire retardant and protective qualities of natural elements, such as alum (double sulphate of aluminum and potassium) and asbestos (also known in those days as *salamander skin*), and one warlord even made up asbestos suits for soldiers so they could set themselves on fire to panic the enemy. Since many fires used in warfare could not be extinguished with water, it was discovered that vinegar, in addition to its uses against stone fortifications, could be used to quench fires. Even today, people use vinegar-soaked handkerchiefs to protect against pepper sprays and tear gas.

Modern Materials that Burn

Common chemicals used in weapons that burn can be classified in several ways:

- Igniters include white phosphorus (which ignites spontaneously when in contact with air), zirconium, and depleted uranium. (The latter two produce very hot sparks.)
- Metal agents include magnesium and aluminum.
- Pyrotechnic mixtures include thermite, which is made up of powdered ferric oxide and powdered or granular aluminum, and thermate, which is thermite with added elements.
- Oil-based materials include napalm (a gel made from aluminum naphthenate and aluminum palmate) and Napalm-B (a liquid made from polystyrene thickener [50%], benzene [25%], and gasoline [25%]). Napalm-B burns hotter (1,562 degrees Fahrenheit) and two or three times longer than ordinary napalm.
- Mineral agents, such as white phosphate, which burns on exposure to air and can be even more deadly than napalm, in some cases burning down to the bone.

Modern Weapons That Burn

Using more modern technology, we've come up with a lot of ways to burn things and people. Here are some of them.

- Fire bombs
  - Early fire bombs
  - Molotov cocktails
  - Modern incendiary bombs
- Burning projectiles
  - Incendiary artillery
  - Incendiary bullets
  - Incendiary rockets
- Flamethrowers
- Nerve agents
- Blister agents
- Choking agents
- Blood gasses or systemic agents (hydrogen cyanide)
- Sensory irritants (such as pepper spray)
- Incapacitating agents (including psychotropic agents)
- Toxin agents

More Chemical Weapons

In addition to those chemical weapons that burn through fire and heat, there other types of chemical weapons, classified as lethal, wounding (possibly lethal), incapacitating, or indirect. Lethal agents include nerve, blood, choking, and toxin agents. Blister agents can be of the wounding variety or they can be lethal, while harassing agents (such as tear gas, for instance) as well as psychological ones are in the incapacitating area. Finally, indirect agents are those that affect the environment around the target, such as defoliants used to destroy an enemy's cover.

Chemical substances, then, can also be categorized as:

- Nerve agents
- Blister agents
- Choking agents
- Blood gasses or systemic agents (hydrogen cyanide)
- Sensory irritants (such as pepper spray)
- Incapacitating agents (including psychotropic agents)
- Toxin agents

Table 34.2 Overview of Chemical Agent Effects

	Nerve Agents	Mustard Agents	Organoarsine Blister Agents	Halogenated Oximes	Blood Agents	Choking Agents
Convulsions	X	-	-	-	X	-
Pinpoint Pupils	X	-	-	-	-	-
Sweating	X	-	-	-	-	-
Runny Nose	X	-	-	-	-	-
Drooling	X	-	-	-	-	-
Chest Pain	X	X	X	X	-	X
Wheezing	X	X	X	X	-	X
Frothy Sputum	X	X	X	X	-	X
Cyanosis	X	-	-	-	X	X
Bradycardia	X	-	-	-	X	-
Tachycardia	X	-	-	-	X	-
Rapid, Deep Breathing	-	-	-	-	X	-
Loss of Bowel and Bladder Control	X	-	-	-	X	-
Blister Formation	-	X	X	X	-	-
Immediate Pain	-	-	-	X	-	-

How Blister Agents Work

Sulphur mustards and nitrogen mustards (phosgene oxime [CX]) work in similar ways, except that nitrogen mustards work faster. They are both *bifunctional alkylating* agents, meaning that they actually do two things. First, through some biochemical reactions, they can bind to a wide variety of nucleic acids, proteins, and nucleotides, and they can create cross-links between the nucleotides of DNA and RNA, inhibiting the replication of these body-building blocks. Second, mustards can form links between molecules that, by a process called *alkylation*, can destroy large amounts of living tissue and cellular mutations.

These substances attack skin, eyes, lungs, and the gastrointestinal tract, and they can also cause damage to blood-generating organs. The symptoms don't show up until two to twenty-four hours have passed, but by the time symptoms do become apparent, the damage is done.

Mild exposure causes aching eyes and a lot of tearing, skin inflammation, irritation of the mucous membranes, coughing, sneezing, and hoarseness. Heavy exposure can cause blindness, nausea, severe breathing problems, vomiting, skin blisters, and diarrhea.

Another blister agent is lewisite (L), a dark, oily liquid that smells like geraniums and acts very quickly, producing more blistering effects than other blistering agents. It is also a systemic poison and can kill within 10 minutes if exposure is high. In addition to other, typical mustard symptoms, it can also cause low blood pressure, lung swelling, and bowel difficulties. There is deeper injury to the connective tissue and muscle, greater vascular damage, and more severe inflammatory reaction than is exhibited in mustard burns. In large, deep, arsenical vesicant burns, there may be considerable necrosis of tissue, gangrene, and slough. Lewisite is often combined with other chemical weapon substances for more extreme effects. An antidote for lewisite is Dimercaprol (British Anti-Lewisite [BAL]).

Phenyldichloroarsine (PD) is odorless and colorless and is most often in a liquid state. It is similar to other mustards, though somewhat less effective. However, it has characteristics that make it more effective against people wearing gas masks.

Ethyldichloroarsine (ED) is like other mustard agents, except that its effects are more immediate and it is less persistent than other mustards.

Wake Up and Smell the Poison

Distilled sulfur mustard is odorless, while a less-pure sample would have a faint garlic smell. The nerve agents sarin and VX are odorless; the choking agent phosgene smells like freshly mown hay, while hydrogen cyanide has an odor of bitter almonds.

How Nerve Gases Work

Most nerve gases are based on cholinesterase enzyme inhibitors made from organophosphorus compounds. Cholinesterase is part of the mechanism that allows muscles to contract and relax. When a nerve cell sends a message to another cell, it does so with the enzyme acetylcholine. Cholinesterase is used to clear the acetylcholine after the message has been sent. When the cholinesterase is inhibited, cell messages relating to muscle contraction are sabotaged, resulting in uncontrollable contraction of the muscles in the body and eventual death by suffocation, as the diaphragm remains contracted, making breathing impossible.

Nerve agents can enter the body through inhalation, through the skin, or even through ingestion, and the onset of symptoms varies with the type of exposure.

Low-dose symptoms include runny nose, pupil contraction, visual deterioration, headache, slurred speech, nausea, hallucinations, pronounced chest pains, and increased saliva. With higher doses, all the previous symptoms are intensified, plus coughing and breathing problems, followed by convulsions, coma, and death. At very high doses, convulsions can begin almost immediately, and death soon follows from suffocation. Symptoms may vary somewhat, depending on what agent the person has been exposed to.

It is possible to treat non-terminal cases with an injection of atropine combined with a reactivator, which helps protect against the excess acetylcholine and restores it to its normal function. This treatment is delivered by means of an *auto-injector* system.

There are five major nerve agents, which are categorized in two groups: the *G* agents and the *V* agents. The G agents are tabun, soman, sarin, and Cyclohexyl methylphosphonofluridate (GF). The V agent is typified by the agent known as VX.

G Agents

G agents tend to be volatile and non-persistent, but they can be combined with polymers to increase their persistence.

Tabun (GA)

Chemical Name	O-ethyl dimethylamidophosphorylcyanide
Molecular Formula	(CH3)2N-P(=O)(-CN)(-OC2H5)
Molecular Weight	162.1
Melting Point	–50°C
Boiling Point	247°C

Tabun (GA) is the easiest nerve agent to manufacture. It is almost completely odorless and colorless in its pure state. Symptoms, which can appear anywhere from seconds after exposure to 18 hours later, include:

- Runny nose
- Watery eyes
- Small, pinpoint pupils
- Eye pain
- Blurred vision
- Drooling and excessive sweating
- Cough
- Chest tightness
- Rapid breathing
- Diarrhea
- Increased urination
- Confusion
- Drowsiness
- Weakness
- Headache
- Nausea, vomiting, and/or abdominal pain
- Slow or fast heart rate
- Abnormally low or high blood pressure

Even a tiny drop of nerve agent on the skin can cause sweating and muscle twitching where the agent touched the skin. Exposure to a large dose of tabun by any route may result in these additional health effects:

- Loss of consciousness
- Convulsions
- Paralysis
- Respiratory failure possibly leading to death

Sarin (GB)

Chemical Name	isopropyl methylphosphonofluoridate
Molecular Formula	CH3-P(=O)(-F)(-OCH(CH33)2)
Molecular Weight	140.1
Melting Point	–56°C
Boiling Point	147°C
Binary Weapon Compound	methylphosphoryldifluoride (DF) + isopropanol

Sarin (GB) is treatable using the auto-injector. It is more soluble in water than other nerve agents. Symptoms can occur very rapidly and include difficulty breathing, miosis, blurred vision, headache, and nausea, leading to respiratory distress, convulsions, and eventually death.

Soman (GD)

Chemical Name	pinacolyl methylphosphonofluridate
Molecular Formula	CH3-P(=O)(-F)(-CH(CH3)C(CH3))3
Molecular Weight	182.2
Melting Point	–42°C
Boiling Point	167°C
Binary Weapon Compound	methylphosphoryldifluoride (DF) + pinacolyalcohol

Soman (GD) has a slight fruity smell and is mostly spread through inhalation and contact with skin. It is very difficult to treat. Although soman has a camphor or fruity odor, the odor may not be noticeable enough to give people sufficient warning against a toxic exposure. Low or moderate exposure by inhalation, ingestion, or skin absorption may cause some or all of the following symptoms within seconds to hours of exposure:

- Runny nose
- Watery eyes
- Small, pinpoint pupils
- Eye pain
- Blurred vision
- Drooling and excessive sweating
- Cough
- Chest tightness
- Rapid breathing
- Diarrhea
- Increased urination
- Confusion
- Drowsiness
- Weakness
- Headache
- Nausea, vomiting, and/or abdominal pain
- Slow or fast heart rate
- Abnormally low or high blood pressure

Even a tiny drop of nerve agent on the skin can cause sweating and muscle twitching where the agent touched the skin. Exposure to a large dose of soman by any route may result in these additional health effects:

- Loss of consciousness
- Convulsions
- Paralysis
- Respiratory failure possibly leading to death

Cyclohexyl Methylphosphonofluridate (GF)

Chemical Name	Cyclohexyl methylphosphonofluridate
Molecular Formula	CH3-P(=O)(-F)(cyklo-C6H11)
Molecular Weight	180.2
Melting Point	<–30°C
Boiling Point	92°C (At 10 mm Hg)

GF is transmitted through skin contact or inhalation.

V Agents

V agents are far more persistent than G agents and are also much more lethal. They generally enter the body by skin contact or inhalation.

VX

Chemical Name	O-ethyl S-diisopropylaminomethyl methlphosphonothiolate
Molecular Formula	CH3-P(=O)(-SCH2CH2N[CH(CH3)2]2)(-OC2H5)
Molecular Weight	267.4
Melting Point	–39°C
Boiling Point	300°C
Binary Weapon Compound	O-ethyl O-2-diisopropylaminoethyl methylphosphonite (QL)+ sulphur

VX is far more dangerous than any of the G agents, but it has the drawback of being highly flammable under certain conditions. Symptoms, which can occur within 30 minutes, include difficulty breathing, miosis, blurred vision, headache, and nausea, leading to respiratory distress, convulsions, and eventually death.

How Choking Agents Work

Choking agents are defined as "chemical agents which attack lung tissue, primarily causing pulmonary edema." Among them are:

- CG phosgene
- DP diphosgene
- Cl chlorine
- PS chloropicrin

Phosgene was first used in 1915 in WWI. It is a colorless, highly volatile liquid that has the odor of new mown hay. It is unstable in storage and must be kept refrigerated, and it combines with water to form hydrochloric acid and carbon dioxide. Its vapor density is 3.4 times that of air, so it will tend to settle over an area.

Heavy exposure to phosgene can prove fatal within 24 to 48 hours. If a victim survives, however, recovery is likely to be good. Symptoms include coughing, choking, tightness in the chest, nausea and sometimes vomiting, headache, and lachrymation. There is often a period after the first onset that is symptom free, but this is followed after a few hours by symptoms of pulmonary edema, including deep coughing, dyspnea, rapid shallow breathing, and cyanosis, with a possibility of nausea and vomiting. This will be followed by frothy sputum and shock symptoms, such as pale, clammy skin, low blood pressure, and rapid heartbeat. If a victim survives more than 48 hours, there's a good chance of a full recovery.

Except for several of its physical properties, everything else about diphosgene is the same as phosgene.

How Vomiting Agents Work

Vomiting agents are generally absorbed through inhalation, although exposure through ingestion, skin, or eye absorption can occur. Vomiting agents tend to be slower to take effect but longer acting than many riot-control substances. The first effect of a vomiting agent is in the form of irritation several minutes after exposure. By this time, however, it is too late to take precautions. What follows are a variety of symptoms, including headache, nausea, vomiting, diarrhea, abdominal cramps, and psychological shifts. The symptoms will persist for several hours, and death can occur in cases of extreme exposure.

How Blood Agents Work

Blood agents, such as cyanogens, are absorbed into the body through breathing, where they can cause lethal damage by their effect on the enzyme cytochrome-oxidase. Typical blood agents are hydrogen cyanide (AC) or hydrocyanic acid (HCN), cyanogen chloride (CK), and arsine (SA).

Hydrogen cyanide binds with enzymes that contain metals, such as the cytochrome oxidase enzyme, which is required for oxidation within the body's cells. With the inhibition of this enzyme, the cells cannot obtain necessary oxygen, and the body's systems shut down. The actual cause of death is suffocation.

Symptoms of exposure to hydrogen cyanide (AC) (depending on dose) include:

- "Metallic" taste
- Anxiety and/or confusion
- Headache
- Vertigo
- Hyperpnea followed by dyspnea
- Convulsions
- Cyanosis (may be absent; may be followed by a pink color in the skin)
- Respiratory arrest
- Bradycardia
- Cardiac arrest

While some texts describe a bright red coloration of the skin in cyanide poisoning, this appears to be only rarely observed in actual practice.

Onset is usually rapid. Effects on inhalation of lethal amounts may be observed within 15 seconds, with death occurring in less than 10 minutes.

NOTE

Strange Fact: *Approximately 82 percent of men can detect the presence of hydrogen cyanide by smell; however, 95 percent of women can detect it.*

With lesser exposure, the symptoms appear over time, beginning with restlessness and increased respiration, followed by giddiness, headache, heart palpitations, and trouble breathing. These are followed by vomiting, convulsions, respiratory failure, and coma. In nonlethal cases, some damage to the body is likely, especially in "oxygen-needy" areas. There are several substances that can help "clean" the cyanide ions out of the body, such as rhodanese enzyme combined with sulphur, cobalt compounds, or methaemoglobin (metHB). However, if a victim is fully conscious after five minutes and breathing normally, he probably does not need treatment, as his body has naturally gotten rid of the cyanide ions. Cyanogen halides, such as cyanogen chloride, ultimately form hydrogen cyanide through reactions in the body, so their symptoms and effects are almost the same except that they have added irritant effects, particularly to the eyes and mucous membranes, along with burning sensations in the throat and lungs. These added irritants can cause reactions similar to those of choking agents, with possible paralysis of the upper respiratory tract and the onset of dyspnea.

Arsine (arsenic trihydride) is another blood agent, said to have an odor similar to garlic. It is highly volatile, so much so that it can even explode on contact with air. In addition to symptoms similar to those of other blood agents, arsine can cause damage to the kidneys and liver. It is often combined with other agents, such as lewisite.

How Incapacitating Agents Work

Incapacitating agent is a military term used to denote an agent that temporarily and nonlethally impairs the performance of an enemy by targeting the central nervous system. The idea isn't new. (See the "Early Biological and Chemical Weapons" section earlier in this chapter.) As far back as 184 B.C., Hannibal's army used belladonna plants to induce disorientation in enemies. In 1672, the Bishop of Muenster used belladonna-containing grenades in his campaigns.

The modern military has experimented with a wide variety of methods to disorient people, including noise, microwaves, and photostimulation. In addition, they have tried many substances, such as stimulants (cocaine, amphetamines, nicotine), depressants (barbiturates, opiates, neuroleptics), and psychedelic agents (lysergic acid diethylamide [LSD] and phencyclidine [PHP]). None of these has proved as suitable as a group of incapacitating agents called *anticholinergics*, such as 3-quinulidinyle benzilate (BZ). Another similar substance that was said to be found in Iraq following the Gulf War is known as Agent 15.

The substances that are categorized as psychotomimetic agents are those that, when administered, cause conditions similar to psychotic disorders or symptoms emanating from the central nervous system. These effects cause an inability to make decisions and cause an incapacitation of the individual.

Examples of Psychotomimetic Agents

- **3-quinuclidinylbenzilate (BZ).** Part of the glycolic acid esters or glycolates, this group of psychotomimetics produces effects similar to those caused by atropine, causing distended pupils, short-distance vision deterioration, dry mouth, and heart palpitations. Another effect of glycolates, 3-quinuclidinylbenzilate in particular, is that it raises the body temperature and causes hallucinations and eventual coma. The effects can last for one to three weeks after the initial poisoning.
- **Phencyclidine.** Causes somewhat disturbed body awareness, vivid dreaming, and disorientation, as well as some anesthetic effect with low doses. High doses may result in death due to respiratory depression. Phencyclidine is widely used by drug addicts because of its low price and the fact that it is easy to produce.
- **LSD and Similar Substances.** Well-known as a recreational drug, LSD has little use as a weapon, partly because it is highly unstable; however, other LSD-like agents, chemically similar to a wide variety of amphetamines, could theoretically be used as chemical weapons, dispersed in an aerosol form.
- **Fentanyl.** Part of a group of medicines called *narcotic analgesics*, which are used to relieve pain. The transmucosal form of fentanyl is used to treat breakthrough cancer pain when the usual medicines used to control the persistent pain fail. Transmucosal fentanyl is only used in patients who are already taking narcotic analgesics. Fentanyl acts in the central nervous system (CNS) to relieve pain. Some of its side effects are also caused by actions in the CNS. An overdose can cause severe breathing problems or complete stoppage of breathing, unconsciousness, and death. Serious signs of an overdose include very slow breathing (fewer than eight breaths a minute) and extreme drowsiness in which a subject cannot even answer if addressed or cannot be awakened if asleep. Other signs may include cold, clammy skin; low blood pressure; pinpoint pupils; and slow heartbeat.

More chemical agents can be found in the "Nonlethal Weapons" section later in this chapter.

Anti-Personnel Agents Weaponized Since 1946

Since WWII, more chemical weapons have been developed as anti-personnel agents. This section looks at some of them. They can be categorized as disabling agents (such as tear gas), choking agents and lung irritants, vomiting agents, blood gasses, vesicants and blister agents, incapacitating agents, and nerve gasses.

Tear Gases and Other Disabling Chemicals

- CN (1-chloroacetophenone)
- Larmine, BBC or CA (a-bromophenylacetonitrile)
- CS (2-chlorobenzalmalononitrile)
- CR (dibenzoxazepine)
- OC (oleoresin capsicum)
- BZ (3-quinuclidinyl benzilate)
- Bromobenzylcyanide (CA)
- CNB - (CN in Benzene and Carbon Tetrachloride)
- CNC - (CN in Chloroform)
- CNS - (CN and Chloropicrin in Chloroform)

Choking Agents (Lung Irritants)

- Chloropicrin (PS)
- Chlorine (CL)
- Diphosgene (DP)
- Cyanide
- Nitrogen Oxide (NO)
- Perflurorisobutylene (PHIB)
- Phosgene (CG)
- Red Phosphorous (RP)
- Sulfur Trioxide-Chlorosulfonic Acid (FS)
- Teflon and Perflurorisobutylene (PHIB)
- Titanium Tetrachloride (FM)
- Zinc Oxide (HC)

Vomiting Agents

- Adamsite, or DM (10-chloro-5,10-dihydrophenarsazine)
- Diphenylchloroarsine (DA)
- Diphenylcyanoarsine (DC)

Blood Gases

- Hydrogen Cyanide (AC)
- Arsine (SA)
- Cyanogen Chloride (CK)
- Hydrogen Chloride

Vesicants (Blister Gases)

- Mustard Gas (bis(2-chloroethyl) sulphide)
- Lewisite (2-chlorovinyldichloroarsine)
- Agent T (bis(2-chloroethylthioethyl) ether)
- Nitrogen Mustard, HN-2 (tris(2-chloroethyl)amine)
- Distilled Mustard (HD)
- Lewisite (L)
- Phosgene Oxime (CX)
- Ethyldichloroarsine (ED)
- Lewisite 1 (L-1)
- Lewisite 1 (L-2)
- Lewisite 1 (L-3)
- Methyldichloroarsine (MD)
- Mustard/Lewisite (HL)
- Mustard/T
- Nitrogen Mustard (HN-1)
- Nitrogen Mustard (HN-3)
- Phenodichloroarsine (PD)
- Sesqui Mustard

Incapacitating Agents

- Agent 15
- BZ
- Canniboids
- Fentanyls
- LSD
- Phenothiazines

Nerve Gases

- Tabun, or GA (ethyl NN-dimethylphosphoramidocyanidate)
- Sarin, or GB (O-isopropyl methylphosphonofluoridate)
- Soman, or GD (O-1,2,2-trimethylpropyl methylphosphonofluoridate)
- Cyclosarin, or GF (O-cyclohexyl methylphosphonofluoridate)
- VX (O-ethyl S-2-diisopropylaminoethyl methylphosphonothiolate)
- Medemo (O-ethyl S-2-dimethylaminoethyl methylphosphonothiolate)
- VR (O-isobutyl S-2-diethylaminoethyl methylphosphonothiolate)
- GE
- VE
- VG
- V-Gas
- VM

Modern Biological Weapons

Modern biological dangers come in several forms. Primary threats come from:

- Bacteria, such as:
  - Anthrax
  - Brucellosis
  - Cholera
  - Pneumonic plague
  - Tularemia
  - Q fever
- Viruses, such as:
  - Smallpox
  - Venezuelan equine encephalitis (VEE)
  - Viral hemorrhagic fevers (VHF)
- Toxins, such as:
  - Botulinum (botulism)
  - Staph entero-b
  - Ricin
  - T-2 myotoxins

Categories of Biological Agents

These threats are further identified according to three categories.

Category A Diseases/Agents

The U.S. public health system and primary healthcare providers must be prepared to address various biological agents, including pathogens that are rarely seen in the United States. High-priority agents include organisms that pose a risk to national security because they:

- Can be easily disseminated or transmitted from person to person;
- Result in high mortality rates and have the potential for major public health impact;

- Might cause public panic and social disruption; and
- Require special action for public health preparedness.

Category B Diseases/Agents

Second-highest priority agents include those that

- are moderately easy to disseminate;
- result in moderate morbidity rates and low mortality rates; and
- require specific enhancements of CDC's diagnostic capacity and enhanced disease surveillance.

Category C Diseases/Agents

Third-highest priority agents include emerging pathogens that could be engineered for mass dissemination in the future because of

- availability;
- ease of production and dissemination; and
- potential for high morbidity and mortality rates and major health impact.

Known Biological Threats

The following are biological threats that have been categorized by government agencies.

Category A

- Anthrax (Bacillus anthracis)
- Botulism (Clostridium botulinum toxin)
- Plague (Yersinia pestis)
- Smallpox (Variola major)
- Tularemia (Francisella tularensis)
- Viral hemorrhagic fevers (Filoviruses [for example, Ebola, Marburg] and arenaviruses) [for example, Lassa, Machupo])

Category B

- Brucellosis (Brucella species)
- Epsilon toxin of Clostridium perfringens
- Food safety threats (for example, Salmonella species, Escherichia coli O157:H7, Shigella)
- Glanders (Burkholderia mallei)
- Melioidosis (Burkholderia pseudomallei)
- Psittacosis (Chlamydia psittaci)
- Q fever (Coxiella burnetii)
- Ricin toxin from Ricinus communis (castor beans)
- Staphylococcal enterotoxin B
- Typhus fever (Rickettsia prowazekii)
- Viral encephalitis (alphaviruses [for example, Venezuelan equine encephalitis, eastern equine encephalitis, western equine encephalitis])
- Water safety threats (for example, Vibrio cholerae, Cryptosporidium parvum)

Category C

- Emerging infectious diseases, such as Nipah virus and Hantavirus

Bacteria

- Bacillus anthracis (anthrax)
- Bartonella quintana (trench fever)
- Brucella species (brucellosis)
- Burkholderia mallei (glanders)
- Burkholderia pseudomallei (meliodosis)
- Franciscella tularensis (tularaemia)
- Salmonella typhi (typhoid fever)
- Shigella species (shigellosis)
- Vibrio
- cholerae (cholera)
- Yersinia pestis (plague)
- Coxiella burnetii (Q fever)
- Orientia tsutsugamushi (scrub typhus)
- Rickettsia prowazeki (typhus fever)
- Rickettsia rickettsii (Rocky Mountain spotted fever)
- Chlamydia psittaci (psittacosis)

Fungi

- Coccidiodes immitis (coccidioidomycosis)
- Histoplasma capsulata (histoplasmosis)

Viruses

- Hantaan/Korean haemorrhagic fever, etc.
- Sin Nombre
- Crimean-Congo haemorrhagic fever
- Rift Valley fever
- Ebola fever
- Marburg
- Lymphocytic
- Choriomeningitis
- Junin (Argentinian haemorrhagic fever)
- Machupo (Bolivian haemorrhagic fever)
- Lassa fever
- Tick-borne encephalitis/Russian spring-summer encephalitis
- Dengue
- Yellow fever
- Omsk haemorrhagic fever
- Japanese encephalitis
- Western equine encephalomyelitis
- Eastern equine encephalomyelitis
- Chikungunya
- O'nyong-nyong
- Venezuelan equine encephalomyelitis
- Variola major (smallpox)
- Monkey pox
- White pox (a variant of variola virus)
- Influenza
- Venezuelan equine encephalitis virus

Protozoa

- Naeglaeria fowleri (naegleriasis)
- Toxoplasma gondii (toxoplasmosis)
- Schistosoma species (bilharziasis)

Further Toxins

- Ricin
- Saxitoxin
- Clostridium botulinum toxin
- Staphylococcal enterotoxin
- Aflatoxin
- Bacteria and rickettsiae
- Bacillus anthracis
- Francisella tularensis
- Brucella suis
- Burkholderia mallei
- Burkholderia pseudomallei
- Yersinia pestis
- Rickettsia prowazeki
- Coxiella burnetii

In addition to known biological threats and agents, there have been many attempts to create more potent biological weapons or weapons that can target specific populations while leaving other groups untouched. With advances in genetic engineering, there is the potential for racially targeted viruses to be developed. In fact, some of the information needed can be found on the Internet, such as the DNA sequences for various viruses. New diseases are always appearing, often transmitted by mutated animal pathogens, such as AIDS and the various bird-flu variants coming out of China.

If animals can be considered biological weapons, then there are certainly possibilities, and governments have experimented with various populations of birds or rodents to be used as disease vectors. With innovations such as remote-controlled rats the possibilities grow. Even sea lions and dolphins have been trained for various martial roles. In history, many animals played roles in warfare, as pack animals, defenders, and attackers. Some were trained to fulfill their roles, while others, such as bees and hornets, were simply flung (so to speak) into the fray. Future uses of animals as agents of war may surpass all ancient and historical uses, particularly with advances in electronics and in genetic engineering.

Delivery Methods

Both chemical and biological weapons can be spread in various ways. In the historical section, you saw that very simple methods were used, including sending diseased people or livestock in among the enemy or even pricking random citizens with infected needles. Modern delivery methods would probably be different, but the intention is the same—to cause death and suffering to many people:

- Through the air—from planes or ground-based bombs or canisters, or even from cars or trucks spraying a toxic substance into the air
- Through water supplies
- Through the food supply
- Through drugs

Another type of bioterrorism threat could be carried out by infecting food supplies, such as the mad cow plagues (a version of foot-and-mouth disease). Viruses of this kind can mutate rapidly and cause disruption of food supplies. Other types of terrorist acts could be more direct, such as injection of poisons or other agents into packaged foods or pharmaceuticals.

Chemical Weapon Formulae

Interested in the chemical makeup of nasty chemical weapons? Here's some scientific gobbledygook for your enjoyment.

- O-Alkyl (<= C10 incl. cycloalkyl) alkyl (Me, Et, n-Pr oder i-Pr)-phosphonofluoridates
  - O-Isopropyl methylphosphonofluoridate (Sarin)
  - O-Pinacolyl methylphosphonofluoridate (Soman)

- O-Alkyl (<= C10 incl. cycloalkyl)-N,N-dialkyl (Me, Et, n-Pr oder i-Pr)-phosphoramidocyanidates
  - O-Ethyl N,N-dimethyl phosphoramido cyanidate (Tabun)
- O-Alkyl (H oder <= C10 incl. cycloalkyl)-S-2-dialkyl (Me, Et, n-Pr oder i-Pr)-aminoethyl alkyl (Me, Et, n-Pr oder i-Pr)-phosphonothiolates and corresponding alkylated or pronated salts
  - O-Ethyl-S-2-diisopropyl-aminoethyl methyl phosphonothiolate (VX)
  - Sulfur mustards:
    - 2-Chloroethylchloromethylsulfide
    - Bis(2-cloroethyl)-sulfide (mustard gas)
    - Bis(2-cloroethylthio)-methane
  - Sesquimustard: 1,2-Bis(2-chloroethylthio)ethane
  - 1,3-Bis(2-chloroethylthio)-n-propane
  - 1,4-Bis(2-chloroethylthio)-n-butane
  - 1,5-Bis(2-chloroethylthio)-n-pentane
  - Bis(2-chloroethylthiomethyl)ether
  - Bis(2-chloroethylthioethyl)ether (O-Mustard)
- Lewisites:
  - 2-Chlorovinyldichloroarsine (Lewisite 1)
  - Bis(2-chlorovinyl)-chloroarsine (Lewisite 2)
  - Tris(2-chlorovinyl)-arsine (Lewisite 3)
- Nitrogen mustards:
  - Bis(2-chlorothyl)-ethylamine (HN1)
  - Bis(2-chloroethyl)-methylamine (HN2)
  - Tris(2-chloroethyl)-amine (HN3)
- Saxitoxin
- Ricin
- Alkyl (Me, Et, n-Pr oder i-Pr)-phosphonyl-difluorides
  - Methylphosphonyl difluoride (DF)
- O-Alkyl(H oder <= C10 incl. cycloalkyl)-O-2-dialkyl(Me, Et, n-Pr oder i-Pr)-aminoethyl alkyl (Me, Et, n-Pr oder i-Pr) phosphonites and corresponding alkylated and pronated salts
  - O-Ethyl-0-2-diisopropylaminoethylmethyl-phosphonite (QL)
- O-Isopropyl methyl phosphonochloridate (Chlorosarin)
- O-Pinacolyl methylphosphonochloridate (Chlorosoman)

Nuclear Weapons

The world changed when we harnessed the power of the atom, and this section is devoted to an exploration of nuclear weapons. If you plan on using them in your games, why not get a handle on how they work?

Nuclear versus Conventional

A nuclear device works, like any explosive device, by the extremely rapid release of energy within a limited space. In the case of chemical (or conventional) explosives, the energy takes the form of rapidly expanding gasses caused by chemical combustion. In a nuclear device, the forces are more primal—the splitting of atomic particles and consequent release of subatomic particles and energy. However, weight for weight, the energy produced by nuclear explosives is millions of times greater than the energy produced by chemical explosions. In addition, nuclear explosions create heat, or thermal radiation, of tens of millions of degrees, whereas conventional explosives only generate temperatures of, at most, a few thousand degrees.

Here's a short list of the ways that nuclear explosions differ from conventional ones:

- Nuclear explosions can be many thousands (or millions) of times more powerful than the largest conventional detonations.
- For the release of a given amount of energy, the mass of a nuclear explosive would be much less than that of a conventional high explosive. Consequently, in the former case, there is a much smaller amount of material available in the weapon itself that is converted into the hot, compressed gases of an explosion. This results in somewhat different mechanisms for the initiation of the blast wave.
- The temperatures reached in a nuclear explosion are very much higher than in a conventional explosion, and a fairly large proportion of the energy in a nuclear explosion is emitted in the form of light and heat, generally referred to as *thermal radiation.* This is capable of causing skin burns and of starting fires at considerable distances. Close up, it simply incinerates everything.
- A nuclear explosion is accompanied by highly penetrating and harmful invisible rays, predominantly gamma rays, which are referred to as *initial nuclear radiation.*
- Finally, the substances remaining after a nuclear explosion are radioactive, emitting similar radiations over an extended period of time. This is known as the *residual nuclear radiation* or *residual radioactivity*, which takes the form of gamma rays and beta particles.

Why are they called *nuclear* weapons? Because the forces unleashed are the binding forces released by the rearrangement of the nuclei of atoms in either fission or fusion reactions—thus they are *nuclear* forces.

Fission

Fission devices work by splitting an atom of uranium or plutonium in two, which simultaneously releases two spare neutrons and about 32 picowatts of energy (32 millionths of a watt). These two free neutrons collide with other atoms, which split and release energy and neutrons. This quickly becomes a chain reaction, releasing vast quantities of energy in a very short time. One pound of U-235 can release 36 million watts of energy through this kind of chain reaction.

A modern fission atom bomb works by introducing a *neutron source* into a noncritical mass of U-235 or plutonium, simultaneously super-pressurizing the mass through the detonation of a high-explosive charge. (Fissionable plutonium-239 is created artificially from U-238 since very little plutonium exists naturally.) The sequence goes something like this:

1. The subcritical mass of U-235 or plutonium is surrounded in a tamper (neutron-reflecting) casing.
2. When the bomb is detonated, the neutron source is shot into position within the subcritical mass.
3. Simultaneously, the high explosive detonates, compressing the radioactive material, creating a supercritical mass.
4. It all goes bang.

The original "Little Boy" 20-kiloton atom bomb dropped on Hiroshima was a bit simpler in that it worked by using a high-explosive charge to drive a small segment of U-235 into a larger, subcritical mass section, thereby initiating critical mass and the resulting explosion.

The concentration of force in a fission bomb is immense and can be seen by comparing the force of a small amount of nuclear material to an equivalent force measured in TNT, which is how nuclear explosions are measured—1 kiloton of nuclear energy is equivalent to 1,000 tons of TNT. One pound of U-235 in a volume of one square inch can yield 9 kilotons of force if perfect fission were achieved. The equivalent TNT would occupy 210,000 square feet of volume. Twenty-two hundred pounds of U-235 with a volume of 2,000 square inches would yield 18 megatons. The equivalent volume of TNT would occupy 420,000,000 square feet.

Energy Released in a Fission Reaction

Complete fission of 0.057 kg (57 grams or 2 ounces) fissionable material results in:

- Fission of 1.45 × 1025 nuclei
- 1,012 calories
- 2.6 × 1025 million electron volts
- 4.48 × 1019 ergs (4.18 x 1012 joules)
- 1.16 × 106 kilowatt-hours
- 3.97 × 109 British thermal units

About Chain Reactions and Critical Mass

One condition necessary to a nuclear explosion is a chain reaction—a self-sustaining process that occurs when certain conditions are met. During the fission of an atom of U-233, U-235, or plutonium-239, two or three free neutrons are produced. Each of these neutrons is capable of interacting with another atom of the fissionable material and causing another fission reaction. However, under normal circumstances, most of these neutrons will escape the boundary of the fissionable material and will interact with other substances, such as air molecules or the molecules of their environment.

To achieve critical mass and a resultant chain reaction, it is necessary that enough of the free neutrons intersect and cause fission in the bomb's fissionable mass. If you look at two spheres of different sizes, it becomes clear that a greater mass provides more opportunities for collisions of this sort.

In a larger sphere, fewer of the neutrons escape the boundary of the fissionable material, and therefore there are more reactions, each of which releases two or three more free neutrons. The sphere with higher mass is more likely to achieve critical mass, whereas a smaller one is more likely to be sub-critical.

Another way to increase the rate of fission is to compress the matter. In a higher density, more interactions are likely, which is why, in a modern fission bomb, a high explosive is used at the point of fission to compress the mass in on itself and increase the severity and violence of the explosion by increasing the percentage of successful fission reactions within the fissionable mass.

By surrounding the fissionable material with a suitable neutron "reflector," also known as a tamper, the loss of neutrons by escape can be reduced, and the requirement for critical mass can thus be decreased. Moreover, elements of high density, which make good reflectors for neutrons of high energy, provide inertia, thereby delaying expansion of the exploding material. The action of the reflector is then like the familiar tamping in blasting operations. As a consequence of its neutron reflecting and inertial properties, the tamper permits the fissionable material in a nuclear weapon to be used more efficiently.

Because of the presence of stray neutrons in the atmosphere or the possibility of their being generated in various ways, a quantity of a suitable isotope of uranium (or plutonium) exceeding the critical mass would be likely to melt or possibly explode. It is necessary, therefore, that before detonation, a nuclear weapon should contain no piece of fissionable material that is as large as the critical mass for the given conditions. To produce an explosion, the material must then be made *supercritical*—in other words, larger than the critical mass—in a time so short as to preclude a sub-explosive change in the configuration, such as by melting. The introduction of neutrons from a suitable source can then initiate a chain reaction leading to an explosion.

Fission Byproducts

Because the fission reaction splits the atom of uranium or plutonium during a chain reaction, new elements are formed. The exact substances and proportions depend on many factors, including the intensity of the neutron collisions and the material that undergoes fission. However, at least 80 different fission fragments, all radioactive isotopes, are created. These, in turn, give off negatively charged beta particles and gamma rays, which cause them to alter composition even further during the process of radioactive decay. They will undergo approximately four stages of radioactivity before becoming stable, or nonradioactive. In all, there are more than 300 isotopes that result from a fission chain reaction. The radioactive byproducts have half-lives ranging from fractions of a second to around one million years. The overall rate of decay of the fissionable byproducts of an explosion falls rapidly within hours of the explosion. However, some always remains, and some of it has very long half-life and very damaging radiation.

In addition to the byproducts of the fission reactions, there is also some of the original material—uranium or plutonium—that does not get consumed in the reaction. Uranium emits alpha particles—heavier positively charged particles that are identical to helium nuclei. These particles cannot penetrate very far—in fact, they cannot even penetrate clothing or unbroken skin. Plutonium, however, can be very hazardous because its particles, if ingested or inhaled, can produce very bad effects in the body even in miniscule amounts.

Fusion

Fusion bombs, otherwise known as *hydrogen* or *thermonuclear* bombs, work not by splitting the atom but by recombining atomic particles—either two deuterium (also known as *heavy hydrogen*) atoms or one deuterium and one tritium atom. The nucleus of an ordinary hydrogen atom has one proton and no neutrons. Deuterium is hydrogen with one neutron in the nucleus, while tritium has two neutrons.

Where two deuterium atoms are involved, the fusion reaction results in a Helium-3 atom. With deuterium and tritium mixed, they combine into a Helium-4 atom. In any case, fusion explosions have some advantages over fission devices. Although the energy released from the fusion reaction is smaller than fission, the atoms are much smaller, resulting in three or four times the energy released from the same amount of mass, and six times as many neutrons. In addition, the materials are cheaper, more abundant, and not subject to the dangers of critical mass.

It is has been found that by using lithium deuteride (LiD), a compound of lithium and deuterium, the initial reaction produces a molecule of helium and a molecule of tritium, plus a free neutron and the release of energy. In addition, the tritium further interacts with the deuterium in a subsequent reaction, yielding even more energy as well as free neutrons that further react with the lithium. Because these free neutrons are at a very high energy level, they can bombard a "blanket" of U-238, which normally will not become critical, and cause it to undergo a fission chain reaction, adding even more energy to the bomb. In fact, in such "boosted" thermonuclear weapons, the energy obtained from fission constitutes a large percentage of the total energy yield.

A modern H-bomb uses a core of lithium deuteride surrounded by U-235 or plutonium. This layer is then surrounded by a layer of U-238, an inert form of uranium.

The sequence that initiates an H-bomb explosion goes something like this:

1. A fission reaction is set off (as set out previously).
2. The heat from the initial fission reaction causes the deuterium and tritium to undergo fusion. This is why it is called *thermonuclear.*
3. This causes the release of a great number of neutrons, which bombard the U-238 and cause it to undergo a fission reaction—a fission-fusion-fission process that releases massive amounts

of energy. The fusion of all the nuclei present in one pound of deuterium would release roughly 26 kilotons of energy. Combining the effects of the fusion reaction with the fission reaction of the U-238 thus compounds the power of the blast in a thermonuclear device.

Detonation Height

The height at which a nuclear device is exploded over the ground makes a considerable difference in its behavior and its effect on the target. Some sources identify five primary types of burst, although many variations and intermediate situations can arise in practice. The main types are:

- Air burst
- High-altitude burst
- Underwater burst
- Underground burst
- Surface burst

The Federation of American Scientists sums it up well at http://www.fas.org/nuke/intro/nuke/blast.htm:

> The magnitude of the blast effect is related to the height of the burst above ground level. For any given distance from the center of the explosion, there is an optimum burst height that will produce the greatest change in air pressure, called *overpressure*, and the greater the distance the greater the optimum burst height. As a result, a burst on the surface produces the greatest overpressure at very close ranges, but less overpressure than an air burst at somewhat longer ranges.
>
> When a nuclear weapon is detonated on or near Earth's surface, the blast digs out a large crater. Some of the material that used to be in the crater is deposited on the rim of the crater; the rest is carried up into the air and returns to Earth as radioactive fallout. An explosion that is farther above the Earth's surface than the radius of the fireball does not dig a crater and produces negligible immediate fallout. For the most part, a nuclear blast kills people by indirect means rather than by direct pressure.
>
> As the height of burst for an explosion of given yield is decreased, or as the yield of the explosion for a given height of burst is increased, Mach reflection commences nearer to ground zero and the overpressure near ground zero becomes larger. However, as the height of burst is decreased, the total area of coverage for blast effects is also markedly reduced. The choice of height of burst is largely dependent on the nature of the target. Relatively resistant targets require the concentrated blast of a low-altitude or surface burst, while sensitive targets may be damaged by the less severe blast wave from an explosion at a higher altitude. In the latter case a larger area and, therefore, a larger number of targets can be damaged.

Air Burst

An air burst is one that occurs no higher than 100,000 feet. It must have sufficient atmosphere in which to propagate through the air medium. A true air burst will result in a roughly spherical fireball that does not touch the earth's surface, but is propagated entirely in the air.

- A 1-megaton bomb would create a fireball approximately 1.1 miles in diameter at its maximum.
- Shock energy would be transmitted as an air blast, while thermal radiation from a 1-megaton bomb would travel long distances and could cause severe burns as far away as 12 miles on a clear day.
- Ordinary opaque materials, such as walls and clothing, would, however, provide protection at distances. Nearer such a blast—for instance, a mile away—a four-foot-thick concrete wall might provide protection from gamma rays and neutrons, but it would take a blast-resistant structure to survive the blast effect at that range.
- Thermal radiation goes through several phases. At first, due to extreme temperatures, a very short burst of X-rays is released, most of which are absorbed by the air around the blast and re-emitted as secondary thermal radiation—ultraviolet, visible, and infrared.
- The surface temperature of the fireball actually pulses, peaking, then dipping in a fraction of a second, peaking again and falling continuously afterward. During the first peak, most of the radiation is in the ultraviolet range. During the next pulse, which can last for several seconds, 99 percent of the thermal radiation energy is released. The temperatures are lower than the initial pulse, and most of the rays that reach the earth are in the visible and infrared spectrums. This is the most damaging to life and property.
- In addition to the thermal radiation, nuclear radiation in the form of neutrons and gamma rays is released in the explosion. When neutrons interact with fissionable materials in the bomb itself, more neutrons and gamma rays are released. Even when neutrons interact with molecules in the air, it results in more gamma rays being released. The rays released within approximately the first minute after the blast are considered the *initial nuclear radiation.* Gamma rays released after that point are high up in the nuclear cloud and should not reach the earth to be a factor.
- Intense electric and magnetic fields are produced, which can extend for several miles. These effects, known as *electromagnetic pulses (EMP)*, can damage unprotected electrical and electronic equipment, even at greater distances than the significant air blasts occur. This is especially true of low-yield weapons.

High-Altitude Burst

A high-altitude burst, one that takes place above 100,000 feet, has different characteristics from an air burst.

- With air density reduced at higher altitudes, less of the energy of a nuclear explosion is converted to blast and shock waves, and more is therefore available for thermal radiation.
- At lower air densities, the energy of the explosion travels farther than at lower altitudes. This effect is predominant at altitudes above 140,000 feet.
- Due to the way in which the radiation energy is propagated, a high-altitude burst of equal power may produce more initial radiation at ground level than a moderately high air burst.
- In addition, a high-altitude burst can cause electromagnetic pulse (EMP) effects over a wider area than a lower detonation, in part because of the ionization of the upper atmosphere.

Underwater or Underground Bursts

Underwater and underground bursts have similar characteristics.

- Most of the shock energy will appear in the ground or water. However, some may appear as an air blast, but less so the deeper the explosion in the earth or water.
- Much of the initial radiation and thermal radiation are absorbed into the ground or water and serve to heat them.

- Long-term effects, however, from the absorption of radiation in the water or ground can be more severe than they are with air bursts or high-altitude bursts.

The behavior of underwater bursts can be very complex and can vary further by the depth of the explosion. Deep-water explosions have complex patterns of behavior that are largely different from those of shallow bursts. Frankly, it is too complex to consider here, and I recommend that you look it up if you are interested.

For relatively shallow underground explosions, a sphere of extremely hot high-pressure gases, including vaporized weapon residues and rock, is formed. This is the equivalent of the fireball in an air or surface burst. The rapid expansion of the gas bubble initiates a ground shock wave that travels in all directions away from the burst point. When the upwardly directed shock (compression) wave reaches the earth's surface, it is reflected back as a rarefaction (or tension) wave. If the tension exceeds the tensile strength of the surface material, the upper layers of the ground will spall—that is, split off into more or less horizontal layers. Then, as a result of the momentum imparted by the incident shock wave, these layers move upward at a speed that may be about 150 (or more) feet per second. When it is reflected back from the surface, the rarefaction wave travels into the ground toward the expanding gas sphere (or cavity) produced by the explosion. If the detonation is not at too great a depth, this wave may reach the top of the cavity while it is still growing. The resistance of the ground to the upward growth of the cavity is thus decreased, and the cavity expands rapidly in the upward direction. The expanding gases and vapors can thus supply additional energy to the spalled layers, so that their upward motion is sustained for a time or even increased. This effect is referred to as *gas acceleration.*

The ground surface moving upward first assumes the shape of a dome. As the dome continues to increase in height, cracks form, through which the cavity gases vent to the atmosphere. The mound then disintegrates completely, and the rock fragments are thrown upward and outward. Subsequently, much of the ejected material collapses and falls back, partly into the newly formed crater and partly onto the surrounding "lip." The material that falls back immediately into the crater is called the *fallback*, whereas that descending on the lip is called the *ejecta*. The size of the remaining (or *apparent*) crater depends on the energy yield of the detonation and on the nature of the excavated medium. In general, for equivalent conditions, the volume of the crater is roughly proportional to the yield of the explosion.

What follows is called the *base surge*—a phenomenon also connected with shallow underwater explosions. It is caused by fallback as it descends to the ground again and carries air and fine dust particles downward with it. The dust-laden air upon reaching the ground moves outward as a result of its momentum and density, causing the base-surge phenomenon. The base surge of dirt particles moves outward from the center of the explosion and is subsequently carried downwind. Eventually, the particles settle out and produce radioactive contamination over a large area, the extent of which depends upon the depth of the burst, the nature of the soil, and the atmospheric conditions, as well as upon the energy yield of the explosion. A dry, sandy terrain would be particularly conducive to base-surge formation in an underground burst.

Throwout crater formation is apparently always accompanied by a base surge. If gas acceleration occurs, however, a cloud consisting of particles of various sizes and the hot gases escaping from the explosion cavity generally also forms and rises to a height of thousands of feet. This is usually referred to as the *main cloud*, to distinguish it from the base-surge cloud. The latter surrounds the base of the main cloud and spreads out initially to a greater distance.

Both the base surge and the main cloud are contaminated with radioactivity, and the particles present contribute to the fallout. The larger pieces are the first to reach the earth, so they are deposited near the location of the burst. But the smaller particles remain suspended in the air for some time and may be carried great distances by the wind before they eventually settle out.

Deep underground explosions have four general phases. First, the explosion energy is released in less than one-millionth of a second—that is, less than one microsecond. As a result, the pressure in the hot gas bubble formed will rise to several million atmospheres, and the temperature will reach about a million degrees within a few microseconds. In the second (hydrodynamic) stage, which generally is a few tenths of a second in duration, the high pressure of the hot gases initiates a strong shock wave, which breaks away and expands in all directions with a velocity equal to or greater than the speed of sound in the rock medium. During the hydrodynamic phase, the hot gases continue to expand, although more slowly than initially, and they form a cavity of substantial size. At the end of this phase, the cavity will have attained its maximum diameter, and its walls will be lined with molten rock. The shock wave will have reached a distance of some hundreds of feet ahead of the cavity, and it will have crushed or fractured much of the rock in the region it has traversed. The shock wave will continue to expand and decrease in strength, eventually becoming the *head* (or *leading*) wave of a train of seismic waves. During the third stage, the cavity will cool, and the molten rock material will collect and solidify at the bottom of the cavity.

Finally, the gas pressure in the cavity decreases to the point when it can no longer support the overburden. Then, in a matter of seconds to hours, the roof falls in, and this is followed by progressive collapse of the overlying rocks. A tall cylinder, commonly referred to as a *chimney*, filled with broken rock or rubble is thus formed. The end result of this chimney formation depends on whether the top of it reaches the surface, and a resultant crater forms (or not).

Surface Bursts

A surface burst is one that occurs at or slightly above the ground (or water). Detonations close to or at the ground behave similarly, although as altitude increases, there are some intermediate effects between the true air burst and the surface burst. With a surface burst, the fireball in its rapid initial growth touches the surface of the earth. Because of the intense heat, some of the rock, soil, and other material in the area is vaporized and taken into the fireball. Additional material is melted, either completely or on its surface, and the strong afterwinds cause large amounts of dirt, dust, and other particles to be sucked up as the fireball rises.

An important difference between a surface burst and an air burst is, consequently, that in the surface burst the radioactive cloud is much more heavily loaded with debris. This consists of particles ranging in size from the very small ones produced by condensation as the fireball cools to the much larger debris particles that have been raised by the afterwinds. The exact composition of the cloud will, of course, depend on the nature of the surface materials and the extent of their contact with the fireball. When the fireball touches the earth's surface, a crater is formed as a result of the vaporization of dirt and other material and the removal of soil and so on by the blast wave and winds accompanying the explosion. The size of the crater will vary with the height above the surface at which the weapon is exploded and with the character of the soil, as well as with the energy of the explosion. It is believed that for a 1-megaton weapon, there would be no appreciable crater formation unless detonation occurred at an altitude of 450 feet or less.

In a surface burst, large quantities of earth or water enter the fireball at an early stage and are fused or vaporized. When sufficient cooling has occurred, the fission products and other radioactive residues become incorporated with the earth particles as a result of the condensation of vaporized fission products into fused particles of earth, and so on. A small proportion of the solid particles formed upon further cooling are contaminated fairly uniformly throughout with the radioactive fission products and other weapon residues, but as a general rule the contamination is found mainly in a thin shell near the surface of the particles. In water droplets, the small fission product particles occur at discrete points within the drops. As the violent disturbance due to the explosion subsides, the contaminated particles and droplets gradually descend to earth. This phenomenon is referred to as *fallout*, and the same name is applied to the particles themselves when they reach the ground. It is the fallout, with its associated radioactivity that decays over a long period of time, that is the main source of the residual nuclear radiation.

Fallout from a small surface blast tends to remain localized, but fallout from larger bombs can create a mushroom cloud that reaches through the troposphere and into the stratosphere, in which case the radioactive particles are carried by the air currents and can have widespread and even global effects.

Density of Matter

It is apparent that the kinetic energy of the fission fragments, constituting some 85 percent of the total energy released, will distribute itself between thermal radiation, on the one hand, and shock and blast, on the other hand, in proportions determined largely by the nature of the ambient medium. The higher the density of the latter, the greater the extent of the coupling between it and the energy from the exploding nuclear weapon. Consequently, when a burst takes place in a medium of high density, such as water or earth, a larger percentage of the kinetic energy of the fission fragments is converted into shock and blast energy than is the case in a less dense medium, such as air. At very high altitudes, on the other hand, where the air pressure is extremely low, there is no true fireball, and the kinetic energy of the fission fragments is dissipated over a very large volume. In any event, the form and amount in which the thermal radiation is received at a distance from the explosion will depend on the nature of the intervening medium.

The Blast Wave

At a fraction of a second after a nuclear explosion, a high-pressure shock or blast wave develops and moves outward from the fireball. This *shock front* moves rapidly away from the fireball in the form of a moving wall of highly compressed air. For instance, after about 10 seconds, when the fireball of a 1-megaton nuclear weapon would attain its maximum size (5,700 feet across), the shock front would be about 3 miles farther ahead. At 50 seconds after the explosion, when the fireball is no longer visible, it would have traveled about 12 miles, moving at about 1,150 feet per second, which is slightly faster than the speed of sound at sea level.

When the blast wave strikes the surface of the earth, it is reflected back, like a sound wave producing an echo. This reflected blast wave, like the original (or direct) wave, is also capable of causing material damage. The direct wave and the reflected wave ultimately merge at a particular region on the surface, depending mainly on the height of the blast and the energy expended in the explosion. This merging phenomenon is called the *Mach effect.* The *overpressure*—that is, the pressure in excess of the normal atmospheric value—at the front of the Mach wave is generally about twice as great as that at the direct blast wave front.

For an air burst of a 1-megaton nuclear weapon at an altitude of 6,500 feet, the Mach effect will begin approximately 4.5 seconds after the explosion, in a rough circle at a radius of 1.3 miles from ground zero. The overpressure on the ground at the blast wave front at this time is about 20 pounds per square inch, so that the total air pressure is more than double the normal atmospheric pressure.

At first the height of the Mach front is small, but as the blast wave front continues to move outward, the height increases steadily. At the same time, however, the overpressure, like that in the original (or direct) wave, decreases correspondingly because of the continuous loss of energy and the ever-increasing area of the advancing front. For instance, in a 1-megaton blast, 40 seconds after the detonation the Mach front would be 10 miles from ground zero and the overpressure would have decreased to roughly 1 pound per square inch.

Strong transient winds are associated with the passage of the shock (and Mach) front. These blast winds are very much stronger than the ground wind (or afterwind) due to the updraft caused by the rising fireball, which occurs at a later time. The blast winds may have peak velocities of several hundred miles an hour fairly close to ground zero; even at more than six miles from the explosion of a 1-megaton nuclear weapon, the peak velocity will be greater than 70 miles per hour. These strong winds can contribute to the blast damage resulting from a nuclear explosion.

Effects of Nuclear Blasts

Nuclear explosions cause damage in several ways—from thermal radiation, from blast front pressure waves and high winds, and from nuclear radiation in the form of neutron bombardment and gamma rays, which can be lethal in sufficient doses. In addition, EMP effects can disrupt and even destroy electrically operated equipment.

At distances close to ground zero, the destruction is nearly total. Due to thermal radiation, metals will vaporize at ground zero and will melt a short distance away. People can sustain third-degree burns over a mile away. Blast effects are also total at ground zero, gradually reducing in severity. But even miles away, brick and wooden structures can sustain damage. Add to that the effect of overpressure winds, which, at ground zero for a 20-kiloton bomb, may attain velocities of nearly 700 miles per hour and pressures of 30 psi, gradually reducing over distance. With larger bombs, the effects are even more widely distributed.

Nuclear radiation is a significant danger, and living tissues absorb about 14 percent more radiation than air. And the initial gamma radiation of a nuclear blast can travel several thousand yards, penetrating even soil, water, lead, and concrete.

Table 34.3 Radiation Yields

Weapon	Radiation (1 mi)	2 mi	3 mi
10KT	90RAD	114mRAD	.342mRAD
20KT	180RAD	228mRAD	.684mRAD
50KT	500RAD	627mRAD	1.824mRAD
100KT	1140RAD	1.4RAD	4.2mRAD
200KT	2730RAD	3.4RAD	10.25mRAD
500KT	9120RAD	11.4RAD	34.2mRAD
1MT	19,150RAD	24RAD	71.8mRAD
10MT	456,000RAD	570RAD	1.7RAD

Table 34.4 Human Effects of Radiation

Dose (Whole Body) in RADs	Effects	Mortality	Convalescence
0–25	Negligible		
100	Nausea, sickness, changes in blood	Up to 7 days	
200	Blood cell damage, nausea, vomiting, diarrhea, hair loss, skin spots, fevers, hemorrhages, fatigue, possible heart failure	About 25% within 30–60 days	Up to 40 days
400	Increased levels of symptoms (above)	Up to 50% within 30–60 days	Weeks to months
600	Very severe symptoms (above) and faster onset	Up to 75% within 20–35 days	Months to years
800	All above symptoms plus rapid failures of circulatory system and parts of the nervous system	Up to 90% within days	Years
1000+	Symptoms very rapid and extreme	100% within hours	None

By looking at the two charts of radiation yield and the effects of radiation on the human body, it is easy to see how the larger the nuclear device, the more severe the effects at distances of one or two miles. In the case of a 10MT bomb, mortality would be 100 percent within a mile, and effects would be very severe, with approximately 50-percent mortality at two miles. This does not include the long-term effects of residual radiation.

How Nuclear Weapons Are Used

Delivery of nuclear weapons falls into two categories: strategic weapons, which are designed to destroy large targets, such as cities, and tactical weapons, generally of smaller yield, which are used to destroy specific targets—military, communications, and infrastructure.

During the heyday of the Cold War, in the 1950s and 1960s, nuclear weapons tended to be large, single-warhead bombs in the megaton range. Beginning in the 1970s, nuclear strategy changed, with the introduction of multiple re-entry vehicles, which can deliver more than one lower-yield bomb to several targets. MIRVs, or Multiple Independently-targeted Re-entry Vehicles, can carry several warheads and deliver them to separate targets. They can also carry decoys and are designed not only to attack multiple targets, but to overwhelm enemy defenses. MARVs, or Maneuverable Alternative-target Re-entry Vehicles, like MIRVs, can deploy several separate warheads. The difference is that with a MARV, the warheads each have independent rockets and onboard computers to guide them toward separate targets, allowing them to take evasive maneuvers to avoid ABM defenses, even targeting preselected alternative targets.

Currently, nuclear warheads are deployed from airplanes, artillery, or ground, sea, or air-launched ballistic or cruise missiles. Other nuclear devices include mines, torpedoes, and depth charges. In addition, man-carried devices, such as Special Atomic Demolition Munitions (SADM), were developed during the 1950s and 1960s. Various portable nuclear devices were a part of the U.S.

arsenal until 1989. The main device of this kind was the MK-54, which was fired by a mechanical timer and had a yield ranging from one ton to one kiloton. Another small nuclear weapon was called Davy Crocket, a small missile-launched nuclear warhead with a yield ranging from 10 to 250 tons. It was designed to be launched from either an M28 or an M29 recoilless rifle.

Who Has Nuclear Weapons?

There is no question that nuclear weapons exist in seven countries—the so-called *Nuclear Club.* These are the United States, Russia, France, Britain, India, Pakistan, and China. However, several other countries are considered to have or to be developing nuclear weapons capabilities, including Iran, Israel, and North Korea. Although there is no confirmation of it, many other nations have had or have announced intentions of developing nuclear weapons.

Many countries have extensive deposits of uranium, including Australia and Canada. The Netherlands, which does not have a nuclear weapons program, does, however, have something like two tons of reactor-grade plutonium stockpiled. Major political issues of modern times involve the spread and use of nuclear weapons, and the struggle to limit nuclear proliferation and to keep fissionable materials out of the hands of rogue states or terrorists.

Modern Armor

Armor has been used since early human history, and many examples of preindustrial armor were included in the "Armor" section in Chapter 33, "Historical and Cultural Weapons." However, as weapons have become more powerful, and mobile weapon platforms, such as tanks, ships, and planes, have become ever more sophisticated, armor has also evolved. Today, modern armor technology strives to keep up with the technology of weapons, although not always successfully.

Armor gives protection at a price. It adds weight and often encumbers mobility. Therefore, the strategic and most sensible application of armor balances protection against mobility and the effects of added weight. For instance, modern tanks place their heaviest armor at the front, with thinner armor on the sides and even thinner armor on the rear, top, and underneath, which reduces weight but creates vulnerabilities.

Types of Modern Armor

The main types of armor include:

- **Steel.** The basic type of armor in use for hundreds of years. Steel is used on modern tanks and ships and even on planes of various kinds. Some modern tanks, including the T-72 and M60, use cast steel turrets and hulls made in giant molds. Other tanks use welded plates of steel. However, steel is only effective relative to its thickness, and the thickness needed to protect against modern weapons, such as HEAT shells and KE (kinetic energy) warheads, would be prohibitively massive and impractical. Using sloping or rounded shapes can add to the effectiveness of steel plating, however. For instance, using 4-inch armor plate at an angle of 60 degrees can give it an armor effect similar to that of an 8-inch plate.
- **Explosive Reactive Armor (ERA).** Consists of boxes of explosive charge attached to the outside of a tank or Armored Fighting Vehicle (AFV); first deployed in the late 1970s by Israel and used in their M-60 and Centurion tanks in 1982. The reactive armor explosives detonate when they sense the impact of a HEAT-type missile, causing a counter explosion and disrupting the plasma jet of the HEAT warhead. Although this type of armor can produce five times the protection against HEAT warheads, it is not without drawbacks. First, once the reactive charges have blown, that area of the

vehicle is no longer protected by the ERA. Also, it is not effective against KE rounds, and, finally, modern warheads have been developed to counter reactive armor, such as the TOW missiles that defeat ERA by using dual warheads in tandem, one of which detonates a split second after the first, which effectively clears the ERA and leaves the vehicle vulnerable.

- **Spaced Armor.** Creates spaces within the armor plating that allow HEAT warheads to penetrate the first layer, but dissipate their plasma jet within the hollow spaces behind the first layer. This type of armor does not work against KE rounds.
- **Composite Armor.** Uses sandwiched layers of steel and other materials, such as ceramics, plastic honeycombs, and depleted uranium, to defeat modern warheads. The British-designed Chobham armor, used on M1 Abrams tanks as well as the German Leopard 2 and British Challenger, uses spaced armor with ceramic blocks set in resin between layers of conventional armor.
- **Anti-Spall Liners.** Not true armor, these are liners made of Kevlar or ballistic nylon that can help prevent spalling inside a vehicle that has been hit by a HEAT warhead.

Body Armor

Body armor reached its most elaborate levels during the Middle Ages with the European knights. However, even a full casing of steel over 100 percent of your body won't protect you from modern weapons and still leave you able to move. So, modern body armor is generally made lightweight and is designed to protect only the parts of the body subject to lethal attack—the head and torso.

Modern body armor—that is, armor that could protect against modern weapons—was explored throughout the 20th century. It came into relatively widespread military use with the flak jackets of WWII, which were bulky garments that used ballistic nylon to protect primarily against munitions fragments and not against high-velocity bullets. In the 1960s, new technologies were developed that used woven fibers to absorb and dissipate the impact of a bullet, causing it to spread out or "mushroom," and stop before penetration. The most well-known of such fibers is called by the trade name *Kevlar* and is five times stronger, by weight, than steel.

Other enhancements of modern body armor include cooling vests that work under the armor to keep soldiers from overheating. There are several versions of such cooling apparel on the market, some adapted from industrial cooling methods and others specifically for military use.

Hard Armor

Hard armor is used to protect against high-velocity weapons, such as high-powered rifles. It is generally made from thick ceramic or metal plates and is not substantially different in purpose than the armor suits of medieval knights. However, the modern materials are far more sophisticated, and they are hard enough to deflect bullets. The ceramics used in hard armor are called *alumina*, which is the same material that sapphires are made of. Other materials used include plastic plates of polyethylene.

Soft Armor

Essentially, soft bulletproof armor is a very sophisticated net of material that traps the incoming bullet. Such body armor consists of several layers—an outer layer of ordinary cloth with an inner layer of a woven webbing, such as Kevlar, sandwiched between layers of a plastic film. Other materials designed to compete with Kevlar are Vectran, which is said to be approximately twice as strong as Kevlar. Cutting-edge materials include BioSteel, which is made from spider silk created from genetically engineered goats. Yes, that's right—goats producing spider silk. Still another super-modern technology is called the *carbon nanotube*, which can make threads of exceptionally tiny diameter. Some people believe that carbon nanotubes can be used to create exceptionally strong and lightweight armor materials. A proprietary technology called *Spectra Shield* uses parallel threads of synthetic polyethylene fibers laminated on a tape of thermoplastic resin.

One danger of soft armor is the possibility of blunt trauma caused by the impact of the bullet, even if it doesn't penetrate the armor. The response to this problem is to design garments with tight weaves and multiple layers, plus a resin coating sandwiched between the layers of plastic film. The intention is to dissipate the force of the impact over the whole garment so that no strong force is applied to a single part of the body.

Classifications of Body Armor

Body armor is classified in seven categories, ranging from Category I (the lowest level of protection) to Category VII (the highest). Some body armor includes pockets that can carry special metal or ceramic plates for extra protection.

Body Armor of the Future

The military is exploring new types of body suits, known as BDUs (Battle Dress Uniforms) that can not only protect soldiers against projectile, chemical, and biological weapons, but can provide them with increased strength and endurance. These futuristic suits may make use of new technologies, such as BioSteel and multi-function exoskeletons, configurable camouflage systems, underwater "SmartSkin" that adjusts to underwater temperatures and a variety of sensors, temperature control systems, and health feedback monitors. One of the first suits to be demonstrated, which has only a few of these features, is called the *Objective Force Warrior System*, introduced by the U.S. Army in 2002 and scheduled for deployment somewhere between 2010 and 2012, although recent articles suggest that the program is having difficulties, so predictions of the technology going operational are prone to error. Going even farther into the future, military researchers are exploring the use of nanotechnology in the development of weaponry and advanced armor.

Nonlethal Weapons

Weapons that can produce control and compliance without lethal force are the objects of a certain branch of study. This section looks at some of the so-called nonlethal weapon solutions in use today.

Introduction to Modern Nonlethal Weapons

> Weapons that are explicitly designed and primarily employed so as to incapacitate personnel or materiel, while minimizing fatalities, permanent injury to personnel, and undesired damage to property and the environment. Unlike conventional lethal weapons that destroy their targets principally through blast, penetration, and fragmentation, nonlethal weapons employ means other than gross physical destruction to prevent the target from functioning. Nonlethal weapons are intended to have one, or both, of the following characteristics: a. they have relatively reversible effects on personnel or materiel, b. they affect objects differently within their area of influence.
> —Dept. of Defense, "Nonlethal Weapons: Terms and References"

One of the odd elements of modern life is that as we develop ever more devastatingly effective weapons, we are also attempting to create weapons that do not kill, but only incapacitate or prevent our enemies (whoever they are) from doing what they want to do. Nonlethal weapons use all kinds of technologies and methods, ranging from bright lights that temporarily dazzle an opponent to sticky foam that can engulf someone in an inescapable foam cocoon.

Nothing is 100-percent nonlethal. There is always some danger when applying force against another person. And being nonlethal doesn't necessarily mean it isn't damaging. For instance, there are laser weapons that can cause blindness. Admittedly, the victim is not dead, but the effect can be permanent and crippling.

The goals of those who develop nonlethal systems for deployment against human targets are to find ways to attack every weakness—smell, taste, hearing, feeling, sight, emotion, and motor functions. They are used for crowd control, to incapacitate individuals, to deny area access, and to clear facilities and areas. They are also used for area denial to vehicles on land, sea, and air as well as to disable or neutralize various vehicles, vessels, aircraft, and other equipment. They are also being designed to disable or neutralize facilities and systems and to deny the use of WMDs.

Energy-Based Nonlethal Weapons

Energy, in the form of light or electronic impulse, can be used as an effective weapon under the right circumstances and with effective application. Here are some examples:

- Eye-safe lasers are used to pinpoint targets, to dazzle enemies, and to discourage aggression by letting a target know that he is "in the sights." They can also be used to enhance night-vision devices, in sophisticated guidance systems and range finders, to warn suspected enemy planes, and possibly in other uses. Laser countermeasures often use a "notch filter" to filter out the particular frequency of the laser; however, these countermeasures can be foiled by using multi-frequency lasers or tunable lasers.
- High-energy lasers are also available, which can blind victims as well as burn holes in objects. A Chinese ZM-87 Portable Laser Disturber can blind someone at 3,000 meters!
- Battlefield Optical Munitions (BOM) are specialized weapons that can fire from existing weapon launchers, but operate completely differently. For instance, one system can emit blinding light to disrupt enemy optical sensors. This system uses existing grenade launchers, but instead of launching a projectile, they detonate a high-explosive charge within an atmosphere of a noble gas and reflect the excited gases into a dye rod, which in turn emits a dazzling laser light. This light can be released at different frequencies by using different types of dye rods. It can also be emitted in a cone of light that covers a greater area. Similarly, there is an omnidirectional light source known as an *isotropic radiator* that can be used to dazzle incoming anti-aircraft missile sensors. It is essentially a small bag filled with a high explosive in a noble gas. When exploded, the light emitted is brilliant enough to defeat optical sensor systems nearby.
- There are tasers that can temporarily incapacitate a person, either close up or from a short distance away (currently about 15 feet).
- There are mystery weapons, such as a reported system that would prevent guns within an area from firing (reportedly used by the Israelis during the famous raid on Entebbe, but subsequently repressed so that the developer of this mysterious system took the secret to his grave).
- Electromagnetic Pulse (EMP) weapons are designed to generate a high electromagnetic pulse that will disrupt or destroy sophisticated equipment, such as computers and other sensitive devices. It can be sent in through antennae or through various lines, such as telephone and power lines. If effective, it can knock out the electronic capabilities of an enemy. The EM pulse is a common side effect of nuclear blasts, but making practical and reliable EMP weapons is still in the development phase. Some success has been obtained using something called a *flux-compression generator*, which, in experimental conditions, has generated power in the tens of terawatts—the equivalent of the power output of 1,000 nuclear reactors in a single pulse.

- Ordinary light can be used to stun or temporarily blind a person. The natural reaction to very bright light, especially in dark conditions when the pupil is wide open, is to shut the eyes, and the effect can temporarily impair vision. Simple handheld lights can be made to output as much as 6 million candlepower, bright enough to read a newspaper a mile away. Other uses of light include strobing, which can disorient people, light grenades and flares used in a variety of ways, and even alternating light frequencies, which can cause disorientation and confusion by causing the brain to adjust quickly to the changes of frequency, say between red light (at the low end of the spectrum) and blue light (at the high end). It's no coincidence that police vehicles use strobing red and blue lights.

Physical Restraints

If you can restrain someone, you don't have to hurt or kill him. Here are some nonlethal restraint systems:

- Nets have many uses, including hidden nets of strong material that can impede men on foot and tangle them up. They can also be deployed from guns (the Netgun, which can fire a net up to 45 feet to capture a single person), larger net projectors for capturing multiple people, and even nets used to disable mines (using explosive *det-cord*) or to capture and destroy incoming missiles (also using det-cord).
- Nets are further enhanced by applying sticky substances, making escape more difficult, and by the addition of wires that can deliver debilitating shocks to anyone caught in the net. "Smart" technology would only deliver a shock if it sensed that the victim was struggling to escape.
- Another net technology (known as *Speedbump*) is a vinyl net capable of stopping a speeding car, useful at checkpoints and roadblocks.
- Netting can also be used to stop escaping small craft on water. The nets can be dropped ahead of escaping craft by helicopters, preventing them from taking evasive maneuvers.
- Barbed wire has been a standard element of the battlefield since WWI. Today, using portable dispensers developed during the Vietnam War, a 450-foot fence of wire can be deployed in about 8 seconds, fired from a canister only 3.6 inches in diameter and 12.25 inches long. Razor-sharp barbs can shred tires, entangle drive shafts, and prevent pedestrian entry to an area.
- Nonlethal methods for use against aircraft have been difficult to deploy, because most attacks that affect the airworthiness of a plane or the pilot's ability to control it are likely to be lethal. Still various air nets have been tested, as well as air-to-air harpoons with parachutes or other devices that could adversely affect the enemy plane.
- One way to disable a vehicle is to cover it entirely, obscuring vision and/or mobility. This has been developed in a system called *Silver Shroud*, which can fire a very thin polymer film coated with aluminum P4. This film is 0.0005 inches thick and can cover an area of 1,960 square feet. When used against tanks, the film also entangles the turret if the crew attempts to move it.
- Nonlethal mines are in development; rather than exploding and causing death or injury from blast and shrapnel, they would deploy nets. This technology would cut down on the problem of unintended casualties when noncombatants unexpectedly encounter mines.
- In an imitation of Spider-Man, the military has developed a binary system that deploys the chemicals hexamethylenediamine dissolved in CO2 with adipic acid in pressurized water. When these chemicals are combined under pressure, they form a thin, long-chain polymeric fiber that can be projected through nozzles for a variety of effects at distances up to 100 feet.
- Spikes are often used to stop vehicles by deflating tires, and many innovations have been applied to this simple technology, such as remotely controlled spikes that can be deployed or withdrawn as needed, spikes that stay in the tires of the car that runs over them, and even exploding spikes that can prevent fugitives from continuing to drive on the wheel rims.
- For restraining prisoners, air bags can be used to pin them into a seat.

Chemical Nonlethal Weapons

Modern chemical weapons can be horribly lethal, but not every use of chemistry leads to sickness or death. Here modern chemistry is used more to stop lawbreakers than to cause them harm.

- Anti-materiel targets
  - **Tires.** Use of superacids millions to billions of times more potent than fluoric acid—injected in tires by use of caltrops or other means. For simple deflation, a caltrop with a hollow tube to defeat self-sealing tires is sufficient. Another method is catalytic depolymerization, which causes the tire to degrade very quickly and requires very little of the applied substance.
  - **Engines.** Agents used to clog air filters applied from a spray device to deploy thin, long-chain polymer films. Bypass methods are ineffective in that the polymers will destroy the engine if allowed to bypass the filter. Another method: Small abrasive material, such as extremely strong ceramic or Carborundum particles, causing highly increased friction and wear and destroying engines over a few days' time. Application via metal fireballs—igniting metals such as cerium oxide produces very fine ceramic dust, small enough to penetrate air filters and enter the engine. Affecting engine combustion is also possible, either by damping it so the engine dies or by supercharging it. Acetylene gas can cause the engine to race so hard that it blows the pistons out and destroys it. Another way is to introduce pyrophoric particles, such as cesium, which burn intensely and generate enough heat to destroy the engine. Also, viscosification agents can thicken fuels and cause them to clog the fuel passages and cripple the engine.
  - **Traction.** Modern technology has created some "superlubricant" substances, such as Teflon and potassium soaps, which can be used to severely inhibit movement through an area. Such methods were used even in the French Resistance to make steep railroad tracks unusable by the German supply and troop trains. Modern use might include crushable packets (known as *slick 'ems*) distributed over an area, which would release a superlubricant when run over by enemy vehicles, making movement very difficult. The opposite, of course, are *stick 'ems*, which can make an area sticky and hard to pass. New technology is being worked on to allow some materials to change composition based on certain conditions, such as temperature, pressure, or electromagnetic signals. These "smart" materials could resolve cleanup problems with some of the chemical weapons in development and could lead to other clever uses.
  - **Optics.** Some materials can almost instantly cause the crazing of optical surfaces, rendering them unusable or at least severely impaired. Many methods have been considered for "blinding" tanks, which have limited capabilities for viewing the outside. Paint bullets, chemical etching agents, and adhesive foams are all possible methods.
  - **Fuels and Lubricants.** Various agents can affect the operation of fuels or lubricants, rendering machines inoperative.
  - **Tubing and Seals.** Corrosive agents can attack tubing and seals in motors, causing them to fail.
- Anti-personnel
  - **Water.** High-pressure water cannons can be used to control crowds. The addition of dyes—either visible or ultraviolet detectable—can also "tag" people for later identification.
  - **Riot-Control Gasses.** Tear gas and other agents (such as chloroacetophenone [CN], chlorodihydrophenarsazine [DM], O-chlorobenzylidene malononitrile [CS], pepper spray, or oleoresin of capsicum [OC] dibenz[b,f]1 : 4-oxazepine [CR]) can be sprayed, detonated, or mixed with water.
  - **Sticky Foam.** This can engulf a person or a weapon, rendering them inoperable, or create an instant denial-of-access barrier. It has a 50:1 expansion rate and is many times stickier than most common materials. Other foams, which are water based, can expand 1,000 times and

Part VII

create a soapsuds-like material that can quickly quell riots and impair coordinated resistance. They can also be used to disperse other riot-control materials, such as OC.
- **Malodorous Chemical Weapons.** Also known as *stink bombs*, these can make an area uninhabitable. Some of them have names that suggest the odors they release, such as putrecine and cadavercine.
- **Insect Pheromones.** These can be used to infest an area with nasty bugs, such as spiders, cockroaches, ants, and other unwelcome guests.
- **Pyrophoric Chemicals.** These can be spread around in the form of tars that will ignite when sealants are broken from pressure, such as stepping on them or driving over them. If used in a tar form, the agent will stick to people or objects and continue to burn.
- **Drugs.** Drugs such as barbiturates and other sleep- or drowsiness-inducing chemicals, as well as psychedelic agents, can be used to impair opposition. It is even proposed that the Soviets had developed an "ozone cannon," which could be directed to induce drowsiness on enemy forces.
- **Micro-Robot Delivery.** One futuristic chemical proposal suggests the delivery of chemical agents via micro-robots (millimeter-sized robots).

Low Kinetic Energy (KE) Weapons

Kinetic energy is the energy of a moving object intersecting with another object (moving or not). A baseball bat hitting the ball is using kinetic energy to send that ball out of the park. Low kinetic energy refers to objects that are using minimal physical force to have an effect, often to cause pain but not serious injury or death. Here is a list of some low kinetic energy nonlethal weapons:

- Bullets (baton rounds)
  - Original teakwood (knee-knockers).
  - Rubber bullets.
  - The ARWEN 37 fires five 2.7-ounce 4-inch plastic rounds up to 100 meters.
  - Israeli MA/RA 83 and MA/RA 88 are systems designed to attach to standard rifles, such as the M16, and fire rubber bullets; each bullet container holds 15 rubber cylinders weighing 15 to 17 grams.
  - Israel also has a system with plastic-wrapped rubber cylinders that separate after firing. Each rubber matrix is filled with steel particles. For crowd control, they have a heavier system that can fire up to 70 small balls and an even heavier vehicle-mounted system that can fire up to 1,400 balls in a determinable sequence.
  - Beanbag rounds are small canvas bags containing lead shot that distribute the impact and are nonlethal.
  - SPLLAT (Special Purpose Low Lethality Anti-Terrorist) shells can destroy door locks without penetrating the room using frangible metal/ceramic slugs that disintegrate, or a round without the ceramic binder. Another type of round delivers a terrific blast and brilliant sparklets but does no lethal damage.
  - The Baton Ball is a 40mm ball weighing 7 ounces and is shot from a blank cartridge. It can incapacitate a subject for more than an hour.
  - STINGBALL is one of several types of munitions that mix in irritants such as OC or CS with rubber and steel balls. There are many variations of this type of munition, including dyes, beanbag rounds with stinging agents added, and even 12-gauge rubber sabot projectiles.
  - A Ring Airfoil Grenade (RAG) uses a special launcher attached to an M16 rifle and fires ring projectiles that spin at 5,000 revolutions per minute, expanding as they spin and therefore distributing the impact.

- Foam baton rounds fire three 1.5-inch-long and 1.5-inch-diameter projectiles made from dense foam rubber. They are recommended to be fired at no more than 5 meters, and, in any case, lack accuracy past about 15 meters.

Acoustical Nonlethal Weapons

Acoustical weapons come in a variety of forms and are classified in three levels—infrasound (low spectrum), audible, and ultrasound (high frequency). Infrasound can penetrate buildings, cause structural weakness, and also inflict nausea and disorientation on people when delivered at high intensities. Audible sound can also be effective because it is very loud or because it evokes an emotional response—think of *Jaws* or *Psycho*.

- During WWII, work was done with low-frequency blasts intended to blow the wings off planes, especially Allied bombers. This is not considered feasible today.
- SuperPooper was the nickname given to a low-frequency weapon that causes involuntary release of bowels. It was rejected by the U.S. military as "undignified." (But a perfect *South Park* weapon?)
- Current research by SARA (Scientific Applications and Research Associates), based on German research, uses repetitive detonations to create intense toroidal vortices using mixed methane and oxygen. The device can emit pressure waves at greater than 130 dB, which is enough to incapacitate anyone. Because it is low-frequency sound, it cannot be blocked by protecting the ears or using other traditional defenses against sound. Another group uses propane and a series of tubes with holes cut in them, causing a phased-array system, which in turn cuts the size requirements of the device by an order of magnitude.
- Although focusing or directing low-frequency beams is difficult, SARA has developed multi-element RF antenna systems to focus and tune the acoustical waves in a variety of ways, including narrow or wide beams.
- Other SARA projects include:
  - Multi-Sensory Grenade—configurable sound, light, and odor.
  - Vortex Launcher—supersonic vortex of air hits targets at half the speed of sound and knocks them off balance (like having a bucket of ice water thrown into your chest).
  - Directional Sonic Firehose—focused acoustic energy directed at a specific target. Man-portable versions are in testing.
  - HPM Vehicle Stopper—high-power microwaves focused on a fleeing vehicle to disrupt electronics.
- HEW (High-Energy Whirls) weapons have been tested that send out invisible ring vortices of sound energy two feet in diameter and can travel more than 100 yards. These rings can hit targets very hard. In tests, the whirls were able to break off limbs from a pine tree several inches in diameter.
- Soviet research revealed that low-frequency sound could disrupt the ability to think, cause drowsiness and weakness, and, with prolonged exposure, could even put people to sleep on their feet. It could also change reaction times and impair peripheral vision and tracking ability. Various applications are suggested, including mounting sound generators for low frequency on tanks to keep away infantry or even civilians with Molotov cocktails.
- One technology, called *beam convergence*, uses two different frequencies that have unpleasant effects where they converge.
- Soviet tests approximated the rhythmic vibrations associated with earthquakes as a means for clearing an area, believing there is a natural reaction to such vibrations.

- Mythologically, the walls of Jericho were brought down by sound, and there have been eyewitness reports of Tibetan techniques for levitating objects using sound, involving perhaps 200 priests with trumpets and drums lifting 1.5-meter cubic stones 400 meters in the air.
- Acoustical weapons can be used against structures, to weaken concrete and metal. One system, placed near a railroad track, was able to weaken it invisibly. Though no damage was apparent to the eye, the next time a train ran over it, it would disintegrate.
- Pulsed Periodic Stimuli uses low-intensity acoustic energy to create disorientation in the human brain, based on electroneurophysiological research.
- It may be possible to link chemicals with acoustical weapons to increase effects of acoustical weapons, and vice versa.

NOTE

A baseball bat hitting a child in the chest at 80 mph is the threshold for death.

Other Concepts

Here are some additional nonlethal concepts, though we're not sure whether any of them are actually in use or just theoretical. For a game designer, however, it's just more fuel for the imagination.

- Microbes that eat roads and buildings (or just about anything else).
- Biocatalysts to break down plastics.
- Devices that can gradually corrode metals.
- Pain Beam (electromagnetic field that can heat the skin without burning, cause short-term memory loss, or even effect total disruption of bodily functions).
- Robotic devices equipped with nonlethal weapon systems and sensors that can be remote controlled or even autonomous.
- Paintball-firing robots, up to 1,500 rounds per minute.
- Use of nonlethal ultraviolet laser beams in two beams that cause an ionization of air and subsequent mild electric current that simulates the currents used to control skeletal muscles. In effect, it can cause people to twitch and lose control of their muscles. If improperly applied, it could cause sustained contractions (tentanization) and presumably death from suffocation or (possibly) even heart failure.
- Nonlethal delivery via mortar systems (in development).
- Nano devices—possibilities unlimited.

Information Warfare

The subject of information warfare is highly relevant to the modern and postmodern world. In the past, information warfare probably consisted of leaking false rumors or fabricating false information, which was common during WWII. Even older applications might be seen in the intense political machinations of almost every society in human history, from basic spying to infiltration to political manipulation by those in power. These types of activities fall into a broad definition of information warfare, but in modern terms, this also refers to various kinds of attacks on the information processing, storage, and pathways of various key networks and information systems.

- Attacks can take place by various means, including the introduction of viruses and worms to disrupt operations, destroy data, or even introduce false information.
- Cybercrime is a form of information warfare that involves stealing money, identities, access codes, and a variety of other individual and/or corporate assets.

- Cyberterrorism is a significant threat to modern life and could take the form of takeovers of key defense systems, disruption of economic information systems and travel systems (rails, air, and so on), or even tampering with weapon guidance systems, which might be created with hidden routines that could be activated to turn weapons against their own masters.
- Another type of information warfare, known in modern language as *perception management* but long known by the name *propaganda*, deals with how to win the war of opinions, sometimes using false or misleading information to cause people to act in opposition to their own values.
- Misinformation is also used to manipulate enemies into feeling vulnerable or overconfident or to place themselves in any of a number of self-defeating positions.
- Anything that deprives enemies of reliable information and leaves them uncertain and uninformed. In the Battle of Britain, when the British had very few fighter planes and trained pilots, they were able to win an information war against the Germans because they had an early form of radar that the Germans didn't know about. By always having planes intercept German raids, they gave the enemy the impression that their air force was well stocked and powerful, when it was really on its last legs. This is one of many examples where a superior technology that isn't known to the enemy can create an advantage in the information war.
- It is also desirable to attack an enemy in other areas, such as the public opinion of its own people and of the world around them. In fact, all aspects of the information war are intended to put the enemy in a very vulnerable situation while strengthening one's own situation and, ultimately, to impose your will on theirs.
- Even marketing and advertising could arguably be considered in the realm of information warfare's tenet of perception management, as they attempt to create demand for products and services where there is little or none naturally.

Today there are hacker sites that can sell you viruses, or even virus laboratories that allow you to create your own viruses. The potential in games could involve cyber-war either from the offensive or the defensive angle. It can be very technical, or it can be used as a plot element of a more conventional mystery or spy scenario. It could also be used to explore the world in the aftermath of a successful cyber attack that took out major systems of the modern world.

BRAINSTORMING WEAPONS AND ARMOR

Imagine you are brainstorming a weapon or some type of armor. You want to create something more or less from scratch. One way to approach the task is to model your idea on something you've seen before or something you can find by research. This is especially important if you are doing a real-world or historical simulation. But suppose you want to come up with something original. Instead of modeling on something you're familiar with, imagine creating a weapon from scratch by considering all the properties and features that go into it. With an understanding of basic properties, you can make adjustments and even create improbable (but cool) new weapons.

So first, imagine you are brainstorming all the qualities a weapon might have, and you come up with a list similar to the one at the beginning of Chapter 33, "Historical and Cultural Weapons." Ours is divided into two main types of lists—basic qualities and lists for some weapon types. Basic qualities are those like length, weight, size, and so forth that can be applied to most weapons. Not every weapon will have every quality, but most of these qualities can be applied to most weapons. Under weapon types, we list some specific data relating to traditional types of weapons, such as bladed, blunt, projectile, and so forth. Remember that the weapon-type sections assume the qualities listed in the "Qualities of Weapons" section (in Chapter 33) and only list specific options and variations associated with a specific type of weapon. Also remember that there are lots of specific examples of weapons in both Chapter 33 and in this chapter. Use them freely for inspiration.

There are essentially two ways to use these lists. You can begin with the basic qualities of the weapon, which lists qualities that could be applied to most weapons, then follow with the specific type—blade, polearm, axe, gun, missile, and so on—or you can begin with the type of weapon and then modify its qualities. Either way will work, though the results might be more diverse if you simply determine the qualities first and then the weapon type. You might surprise yourself. For instance, you might come up with something very tiny and dense, but not know whether it will be a blade, a gun, or something else. Suppose it's a club. How would you use a tiny club? Maybe it is enhanced somehow with a technology that makes it more effective. Maybe it's used to hammer people's toes. As you think about the weapon, imagine it taking shape and imagine how it would be used...and who would use it. Finally, once you have designed the basic weapon, move on to the next section and consider magical properties you might also assign to this weapon.

In Chapter 2, "Brainstorming and Research," we offered some specific examples of brainstorming weapons. This section is only to remind you that, having now come to the end of hundreds of pages of weapons and armor listed in two chapters, you have a lot of material with which to work. So get creative. That's what it's all about.

Epilogue
Last Words

It's a wrap!

So this is where Rusel and I stopped working on the first edition of this book. Now that you understand the structure, you can see that this book can never really be complete until we document every part of every game ever made! So for this first edition, we picked lots of interesting topics and designed it entirely as an inspirational reference book for you.

We've set up a website (www.gamedesignbook.org) so you can help us on the second edition, and hopefully together we can inspire new students and game designers all over the world.

We just hope that at some point, when going through the material, we helped trigger an idea that's completely original, that's yours, and that would be really cool in a professional video game.

As long as we achieved that, then mission accomplished, and now it's up to you to go and make that game experience happen.

I'm working on another site called www.gameinvestors.com to try to give great ideas a chance to get spotted by investors, publishers, and developers. So we might be able to help you again when you reach that milestone.

All the best,
David and Rusel

Index

E

G

J

T

X

Y

Z

COURSE TECHNOLOGY
CENGAGE Learning
Professional • Technical • Reference
THE BEGINNING SERIES
FROM COURSE TECHNOLOGY PTR
Essential introductory programming, game design, and character creation skills for the game developers of tomorrow.
BEGINNING GAME PROGRAMMING SECOND EDITION
BEGINNING DIRECTX 10 GAME PROGRAMMING
BEGINNING JAVA GAME PROGRAMMING SECOND EDITION
BEGINNING GAME PROGRAMMING WITH FLASH
Beginning Game Programming, Second Edition
1-59863-288-4 ■ $29.99
Beginning DirectX 10 Game Programming
1-59863-361-9 ■ $29.99
Beginning Java Game Programming, Second Edition
1-59863-476-3 ■ $29.99
Beginning Game Programming with Flash
1-59863-398-8 ■ $29.99
See our complete list of beginner through advanced game development titles
online at www.courseptr.com or call 1.800.354.9706

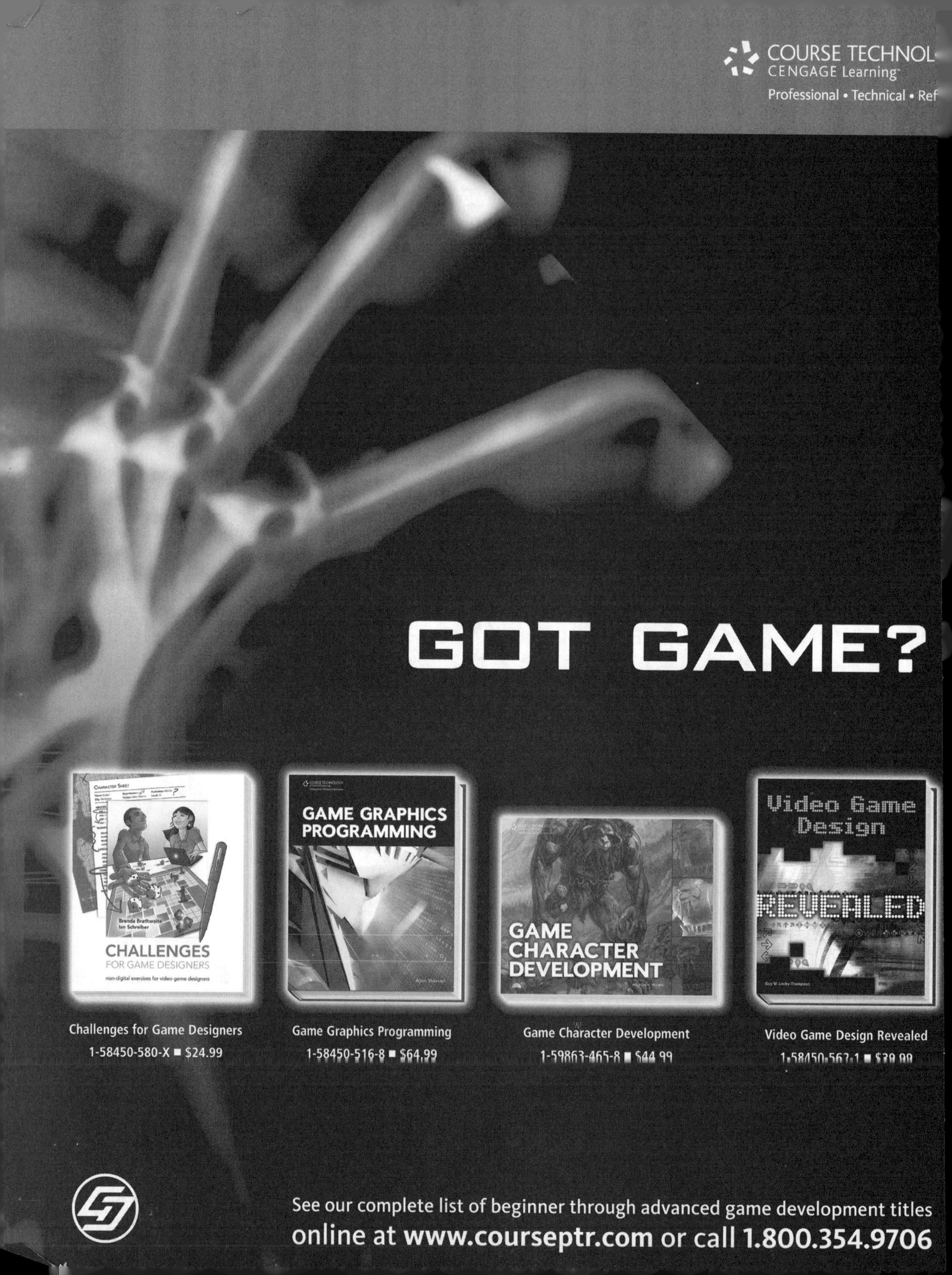
COURSE TECHNOL
CENGAGE Learning
Professional • Technical • Ref
GOT GAME?
CHALLENGES FOR GAME DESIGNERS
non-digital exercises for video game designers
Brenda Brathwaite
Ian Schreiber
GAME GRAPHICS PROGRAMMING
GAME CHARACTER DEVELOPMENT
Video Game Design REVEALED
Challenges for Game Designers
1-58450-580-X ■ $24.99
Game Graphics Programming
1-58450-516-8 ■ $64.99
Game Character Development
1-59863-465-8 ■ $44.99
Video Game Design Revealed
1-58450-567-1 ■ $39.99
See our complete list of beginner through advanced game development titles
online at www.courseptr.com or call 1.800.354.9706